T3-AKD-694

THE PAPERS OF

THOMAS JEFFERSON

RETIREMENT SERIES

THE PAPERS OF

Thomas Jefferson

RETIREMENT SERIES

Volume 10

1 May 1816 to 18 January 1817

J. JEFFERSON LOONEY, EDITOR

ROBERT F. HAGGARD, SENIOR ASSOCIATE EDITOR

JULIE L. LAUTENSCHLAGER, ASSOCIATE EDITOR

CHRISTINE STERNBERG PATRICK AND ELLEN C. HICKMAN,
ASSISTANT EDITORS

LISA A. FRANCAVILLA, MANAGING EDITOR

ANDREA R. GRAY AND PAULA VITERBO, EDITORIAL ASSISTANTS

CATHERINE COINER CRITTENDEN AND SUSAN SPENGLER,
SENIOR DIGITAL TECHNICIANS

PRINCETON AND OXFORD

PRINCETON UNIVERSITY PRESS

2013

Published by Princeton University Press, 41 William Street,
Princeton, New Jersey 08540
In the United Kingdom:
Princeton University Press, 6 Oxford Street,
Woodstock, Oxfordshire OX20 1TW

Library of Congress Cataloging-in-Publication Data

Jefferson, Thomas, 1743–1826
The papers of Thomas Jefferson. Retirement series / J. Jefferson Looney, editor ...
[et al.] p. cm.
Includes bibliographical references and index.
Contents: v. 1. 4 March to 15 November 1809—[etc.]—
v. 10. 1 May 1816 to 18 January 1817
ISBN 978-0-691-16047-4 (cloth: v. 10: alk. paper)
1. Jefferson, Thomas, 1743–1826—Archives. 2. Jefferson, Thomas, 1743–1826—
Correspondence. 3. Presidents—United States—Archives.
4. Presidents—United States—Correspondence. 5. United States—
Politics and government—1809–1817—Sources. 6. United States—Politics and
government—1817–1825—Sources. I. Looney, J. Jefferson.
II. Title. III. Title: Retirement series.
E302.J442 2004b
973.4'6'092—dc22 2004048327

This book has been composed in Monticello

Princeton University Press books are printed on
acid-free paper and meet the guidelines for permanence
and durability of the Committee on Production
Guidelines for Book Longevity of the
Council on Library Resources

Printed in the United States of America

DEDICATED TO THE MEMORY OF

ADOLPH S. OCHS

PUBLISHER OF THE NEW YORK TIMES

1896–1935

WHO BY THE EXAMPLE OF A RESPONSIBLE

PRESS ENLARGED AND FORTIFIED

THE JEFFERSONIAN CONCEPT

OF A FREE PRESS

ADVISORY COMMITTEE

THIS EDITION was made possible by a founding grant from The New York Times Company to Princeton University.

The Retirement Series is sponsored by the Thomas Jefferson Foundation, Inc., of Charlottesville, Virginia. It was created with a six-year founding grant from The Pew Charitable Trusts to the Foundation and to Princeton University, enabling the former to take over responsibility for the volumes associated with this period. Leading gifts from Richard Gilder, Mrs. Martin S. Davis, and Thomas A. Saunders III have assured the continuation of the Retirement Series. For these essential donations, and for other indispensable aid generously given by librarians, archivists, scholars, and collectors of manuscripts, the Editors record their sincere gratitude.

FOREWORD

THE 558 DOCUMENTS in this volume cover the period from 1 May 1816 to 18 January 1817. As heretofore, Thomas Jefferson followed current events closely. Although pleased by Napoleon's downfall, he was dissatisfied with the political settlement that brought peace to Europe after a generation of warfare. In the short term, Jefferson expected a political upheaval in Great Britain, continued uncertainty in France, and the expulsion of Spain from its colonies in the New World. In the United States, he hailed the Federalists' dwindling electoral prospects and welcomed the forthcoming presidential transition from James Madison to James Monroe. Jefferson also advised against the installation of an inscription commemorating the British destruction of the United States Capitol and recommended that John Trumbull be hired to execute historical paintings for the restored structure.

While contending in Virginia with an extraordinary drought and unseasonably cold weather, as well as torrential rainfall and widespread flooding, Jefferson contributed privately to the debate over amending the state constitution. In three letters to Samuel Kercheval and in notes he compiled on the same subject, he suggested a number of substantial alterations: an expanded male franchise, equal electoral districts, popular gubernatorial elections, the elimination of the Council of State, and the division of each county into wards, among others. In addition, Jefferson prepared a legal defense against the claims of the three youngest heirs of Bennett Henderson, who had decided not to confirm the sales of their Milton lands made during their minority; and he gave occasional legal advice, including an opinion on the possibility of committing perjury before a grand jury.

Jefferson grieved over the deaths of Philip Mazzei and Gouverneur Morris and complained about the burden posed by his extensive personal correspondence. He rejected requests that he sell Natural Bridge or forward advice about the internal governance of an agricultural and manufacturing society composed of expatriated Frenchmen. He also calculated the latitude of both Poplar Forest and Willis's Mountain; endeavored unsuccessfully to obtain a competent clockmaker for Charlottesville; exchanged the last of a long series of letters with Pierre Samuel Du Pont de Nemours on education and finance; and was appointed, along with Madison and Monroe, as a visitor of Central College. As usual, sojourners flocked to Monticello. Richard Rush, George Flower, and Josephus B. Stuart left brief accounts of their stays there, while the Baron de Montlezun and Francis Hall compiled lengthy, informative accounts of Jefferson's home, art collection, and thoughts on a wide range of subjects. The diversity in Jefferson's correspondence is also typified by Marcus Dyson's explanation of an underwater breathing apparatus, Eusebio Valli's intense discussion of the causes of yellow fever, and letters with John Adams about the functions of human grief, the earthly balance between pleasure and pain, and the hypothetical question of the willingness of the two men to live their lives over again.

Books remained central to Jefferson's life. He spent much time and energy attempting to replace many of the volumes he had sold to Congress a year earlier. Moreover, Jefferson persisted in his quest to bring both the unpublished papers arising from the Lewis and Clark Expedition and Destutt de Tracy's *Treatise on Political Economy* into print, and he provided Joseph Delaplaine with biographical information about himself and Peyton Randolph (ca. 1723–75) for *Delaplaine's Repository*. The artist Bass Otis executed Jefferson's life portrait, the first of his retirement, at Monticello for use in the latter publication, and shortly thereafter the sculptor Giuseppe Valaperta modeled a miniature likeness of him in wax. Jefferson also read and suggested revisions to drafts of Louis H. Girardin's history of Virginia and William Wirt's biography of Patrick Henry. Francis Adrian Van der Kemp and Jefferson exchanged a number of letters about the ex-president's syllabus on the life and teachings of Jesus, a manuscript that Van der Kemp arranged to have anonymously published in England and that inspired him to outline his own proposed book on the subject.

Religion, indeed, is an important theme in Jefferson's 1816 correspondence. After the ailing Charles Thomson circulated the mistaken idea that Jefferson had recently converted to Christianity, the former president was subjected to a new round of questions about his spiritual beliefs. He eventually asked Delaplaine to "say nothing of my religion. it is known to my god and myself alone. it's evidence before the world is to be sought in my life. if that has been honest and dutiful to society the religion which has regulated it cannot be a bad one."

ACKNOWLEDGMENTS

MANY INDIVIDUALS and institutions provided aid and encouragement during the preparation of this volume. Those who helped us to locate and acquire primary and secondary sources and answered our research questions include our colleagues at the Thomas Jefferson Foundation, especially Anna Berkes, Jack Robertson, and Endrina Tay of the Jefferson Library, and Elizabeth Chew of the curatorial department; Carolyn Holmes from Ash Lawn–Highland, James Monroe's home in Albemarle County; Brett Goodin at Australian National University in Canberra; Andrew Bourque of the American Antiquarian Society; Bibliothèque Nationale de France in Paris; Patricia M. Boulos and Mary Warnement from the Boston Athenæum; Cynthia Van Ness of the Buffalo History Museum; Lucas R. Clawson at the Hagley Museum and Library; Stephen G. Hague of Philadelphia; Jack Eckert of Harvard University's Francis A. Countway Library of Medicine; Olga Tsapina from the Huntington Library; Colleen Theisen of the University of Iowa; Katya A. Tilton at James D. Julia, Inc.; Katie Sambrook of King's College London; Emma Stern from the Laurel Hill Cemetery in Philadelphia; the library staff at the University of Leiden; the Library of Congress's Manuscripts and Serial and Government Publications divisions; Brent Tarter and his colleagues at the Library of Virginia; Gregory R. Krueger of the Lynchburg Museum; Alycia Rihacek from the Madison Township Historical Society in Matawan, New Jersey; Sylvie Clair and Evelyne Borghiero at the Archives Municipales de Marseille; Eben Dennis of the Maryland Historical Society; Sabina Beauchard, Anna J. Cook, and Tracy Potter from the Massachusetts Historical Society; Mystic Seaport: The Museum of America and the Sea; Adam Berenbak and David A. Langbart at the National Archives; Stephen J. Greenberg of the National Library of Medicine in Bethesda, Maryland; Fred Bassett and Christine Beauregard from the New York State Library; Jennifer Day and Lauren Riepl at the Oklahoma Historical Society; John Pollack of the University of Pennsylvania; Gabriel Swift from Princeton University; Agnes Colnot at the Université de Rennes; Jean Cannon of the University of Texas at Austin; Tilburg University in the Netherlands; Barbara L. Floyd and Kimberly H. Brownlee from the University of Toledo; John J. McCusker at Trinity University in San Antonio, Texas; Sean Benjamin of Tulane University; our friends at the University of Virginia's Alderman Library and the Albert and Shirley Small Special Collections Library; and Nancy F.

Lyon of Yale University. As always, we received advice, assistance, and encouragement from a large number of our fellow documentary editors, including Amanda Mathews of the Papers of John Adams; Ellen R. Cohn from the Papers of Benjamin Franklin; Martha J. King and Barbara B. Oberg at the Papers of Thomas Jefferson at Princeton University; Mary A. Hackett, Angela Kreider, and David B. Mattern of the Papers of James Madison; Heidi Stello from the Papers of James Monroe; and David R. Hoth at the Papers of George Washington. Genevieve Moene and Roland H. Simon transcribed and translated the French letters included in this volume; Coulter George helped us with passages in Greek; Christina Ball, Rosanna M. Giammanco Frongia, and Jonathan T. Hine provided aid with Italian; and John F. Miller assisted us with Latin quotations. Kevin B. Jones helped us to understand Jefferson's calculations. The maps of Jefferson's Virginia and Albemarle County were created by Rick Britton. The other illustrations that appear in this volume were assembled with the assistance of Lita Garcia, Olga Tsapina, and David S. Zeidberg of the Huntington Library; Leah Stearns at the Thomas Jefferson Foundation; Bonnie B. Coles, Tomeka Jones, and Julie Miller from the Library of Congress; Mark Fagerburg and Audrey Johnson of the Library of Virginia; Anna Cook, Elaine Grublin, Nancy Heywood, and Laura Wulf at the Massachusetts Historical Society; Robert Delap from the New-York Historical Society; and Janet Bloom and J. Kevin Graffagnino at the University of Michigan's Clements Library. We thankfully acknowledge the efforts of the able staff at Princeton University Press, including Dimitri Karetnikov and Jan Lilly, and our production editor and special friend, Linny Schenck. While we are relieved that Stephen Perkins of IDM USA will continue to assist us in digital matters, he and his colleagues will no longer be doing the bulk of the typesetting work, which is now in the capable hands of Bob Bartleson and his colleagues at IPS. We take this opportunity to extend our appreciation to Michele Newkirk, who for eight of our volumes provided marvelous expertise in laying out the pages and dealing with formidable formatting challenges while insuring a good aesthetic outcome. This work is seldom acknowledged but absolutely essential to a successful scholarly edition.

EDITORIAL METHOD AND APPARATUS

1. RENDERING THE TEXT

From its inception *The Papers of Thomas Jefferson* has insisted on high standards of accuracy in rendering text, but modifications in textual policy and editorial apparatus have been implemented as different approaches have become accepted in the field or as a more faithful rendering has become technically feasible. Prior discussions of textual policy appeared in Vols. 1:xxix–xxxiv, 22:vii–xi, 24:vii–viii, and 30:xiii–xiv of the First Series.

The textual method of the Retirement Series will adhere to the more literal approach adopted in Volume 30 of the parent edition. Original spelling, capitalization, and punctuation are retained as written. Such idiosyncrasies as Jefferson's failure to capitalize the beginnings of most of his sentences and abbreviations like "mr" are preserved, as are his preference for "it's" to "its" and his characteristic spellings of "knolege," "paiment," and "recieve." Modern usage is adopted in cases where intent is impossible to determine, an issue that arises most often in the context of capitalization. Some so-called slips of the pen are corrected, but the original reading is recorded in a subjoined textual note. Jefferson and others sometimes signaled a change in thought within a paragraph with extra horizontal space, and this is rendered by a three-em space. Blanks left for words and not subsequently filled by the authors are represented by a space approximating the length of the blank. Gaps, doubtful readings of illegible or damaged text, and wording supplied from other versions or by editorial conjecture are explained in the source note or in numbered textual notes. Foreign-language documents, the vast majority of which are in French during the retirement period, are transcribed in full as faithfully as possible and followed by a full translation.

Two modifications from past practice bring this series still closer to the original manuscripts. Underscored text is presented as such rather than being converted to italics. Superscripts are also preserved rather than being lowered to the baseline. In most cases of superscripting, the punctuation that is below or next to the superscripted letters is dropped, since it is virtually impossible to determine what is a period or dash as opposed to a flourish under, over, or adjacent to superscripted letters.

Limits to the more literal method are still recognized, however, and readability and consistency with past volumes are prime considerations. In keeping with the basic design implemented in the first volume of the Papers, salutations and signatures continue to display in large and small capitals rather than upper- and lowercase letters. Expansion marks over abbreviations are silently omitted. With very rare exceptions, deleted text and information on which words were added during the process of composition is not displayed within the document transcription. Based on the Editors' judgment of their significance, such emendations are either described in numbered textual notes or ignored. Datelines for letters are consistently printed at the head of the text, with a comment in the descriptive note when they have been moved. Address information, endorsements, and dockets are quoted or described in the source note rather than reproduced in the document proper.

2. *TEXTUAL DEVICES*

The following devices are employed throughout the work to clarify the presentation of the text.

[...] Text missing and not conjecturable. The size of gaps longer than a word or two is estimated in annotation.

[ ] Number or part of number missing or illegible.

[roman] Conjectural reading for missing or illegible matter. A question mark follows when the reading is doubtful.

[*italic*] Editorial comment inserted in the text.

<*italic*> Matter deleted in the manuscript but restored in our text.

3. *DESCRIPTIVE SYMBOLS*

The following symbols are employed throughout the work to describe the various kinds of manuscript originals. When a series of versions is included, the first to be recorded is the version used for the printed text.

Dft draft (usually a composition or rough draft; multiple drafts, when identifiable as such, are designated "2d Dft," etc.)

Dupl duplicate

MS manuscript (arbitrarily applied to most documents other than letters)

PoC	polygraph copy
PrC	press copy
RC	recipient's copy
SC	stylograph copy

All manuscripts of the above types are assumed to be in the hand of the author of the document to which the descriptive symbol pertains. If not, that fact is stated. On the other hand, the following types of manuscripts are assumed not to be in the hand of the author, and exceptions will be noted:

FC	file copy (applied to all contemporary copies retained by the author or his agents)
Tr	transcript (applied to all contemporary and later copies except file copies; period of transcription, unless clear by implication, will be given when known)

4. LOCATION SYMBOLS

The locations of documents printed in this edition from originals in private hands and from printed sources are recorded in self-explanatory form in the descriptive note following each document. The locations of documents printed or referenced from originals held by public and private institutions in the United States are recorded by means of the symbols used in the *MARC Code List for Organizations* (2000) maintained by the Library of Congress. The symbols DLC and MHi by themselves stand for the collections of Jefferson Papers proper in these repositories. When texts are drawn from other collections held by these two institutions, the names of those collections are added. Location symbols for documents held by institutions outside the United States are given in a subjoined list. The lists of symbols are limited to the institutions represented by documents printed or referred to in this volume.

CLjC	James S. Copley Library, La Jolla, California	
CLU-C	William Andrews Clark Memorial Library, University of California, Los Angeles	
CSmH	Huntington Library, San Marino, California	
	JF	Jefferson File
	JF-BA	Jefferson File, Bixby Acquisition
CtHi	Connecticut Historical Society, Hartford	
CtY	Yale University, New Haven, Connecticut	
DeGH	Hagley Museum and Library, Greenville, Delaware	

DLC — Library of Congress, Washington, D.C.
- TJ Papers — Thomas Jefferson Papers (this is assumed if not stated, but also given as indicated to furnish the precise location of an undated, misdated, or otherwise problematic document, thus "DLC: TJ Papers, 213:38071–2" represents volume 213, folios 38071 and 38072 as the collection was arranged at the time the first microfilm edition was made in 1944–45. Access to the microfilm edition of the collection as it was rearranged under the Library's Presidential Papers Program is provided by the *Index to the Thomas Jefferson Papers* [1976])

DNA — National Archives, Washington, D.C., with identifications of series (preceded by record group number) as follows:
- CD — Consular Dispatches
- CS — Census Schedules
- LAR — Letters of Application and Recommendation
- LRSW — Letters Received by the Secretary of War
- LSNO — Letters Sent to Naval Officers
- MLR — Miscellaneous Letters Received
- NPM — Naturalization Petitions to the United States Circuit and District Courts for Maryland
- PRWP — Post Revolutionary War Papers
- ROQG — Records of the Office of the Quartermaster General
- RUSAE — Register of United States Army Enlistments

DNAL — National Agricultural Library, Beltsville, Maryland
IaU — University of Iowa, Iowa City
ICHi — Chicago History Museum, Chicago, Illinois
ICN — Newberry Library, Chicago, Illinois
ICPRCU — Polish Roman Catholic Union of America, Chicago, Illinois
KyHi — Kentucky Historical Society, Frankfort
LN — New Orleans Public Library, New Orleans, Louisiana
LNT — Tulane University, New Orleans, Louisiana
MBAt — Boston Athenæum, Boston, Massachusetts

MBCo	Countway Library of Medicine, Boston, Massachusetts
MBPLi	Boston Public Library, Boston, Massachusetts
MdHi	Maryland Historical Society, Baltimore
MHi	Massachusetts Historical Society, Boston
MiU-C	Clements Library, University of Michigan, Ann Arbor
MoSHi	Missouri History Museum, Saint Louis
  TJC-BC	Thomas Jefferson Collection, text formerly in Bixby Collection
MoSW	Washington University, Saint Louis, Missouri
MWA	American Antiquarian Society, Worcester, Massachusetts
NBuHi	Buffalo History Museum, Buffalo, New York
NcU	University of North Carolina, Chapel Hill
  NPT	Southern Historical Collection, Nicholas Philip Trist Papers
NHi	New-York Historical Society, New York City
NjMoHP	Morristown National Historical Park, Morristown, New Jersey
NjP	Princeton University, Princeton, New Jersey
NN	New York Public Library, New York City
NNC	Columbia University, New York City
NNGL	Gilder Lehrman Collection, New York City
NNPM	Pierpont Morgan Library, New York City
NUt	Utica Public Library, Utica, New York
OkHi	Oklahoma Historical Society, Oklahoma City
OTU	University of Toledo, Toledo, Ohio
PHarH	Pennsylvania Historical and Museum Commission, Harrisburg
PHi	Historical Society of Pennsylvania, Philadelphia
PPAmP	American Philosophical Society, Philadelphia, Pennsylvania
PPAN	Academy of Natural Sciences, Philadelphia, Pennsylvania
PPL	Library Company of Philadelphia, Pennsylvania
PSC	Swarthmore College, Swarthmore, Pennsylvania
PWacD	David Library of the American Revolution, Washington Crossing, Pennsylvania
RHi	Rhode Island Historical Society, Providence
TxU	University of Texas, Austin
Vi	Library of Virginia, Richmond

ViCMRL — Thomas Jefferson Library, Thomas Jefferson Foundation, Inc., Charlottesville, Virginia
ViHi — Virginia Historical Society, Richmond
ViU — University of Virginia, Charlottesville
- JCC — Joseph C. Cabell Papers
- JHC — John Hartwell Cocke Papers
- TJP — Thomas Jefferson Papers
- TJP-CC — Thomas Jefferson Papers, text formerly in Carr-Cary Papers
- TJP-ER — Thomas Jefferson Papers, text formerly in Edgehill-Randolph Papers
- TJP-MJ — Thomas Jefferson Papers, text formerly in Moyer-Jefferson Papers
- TJP-PC — Thomas Jefferson Papers, text formerly in Philip B. Campbell Deposit

ViW — College of William and Mary, Williamsburg, Virginia
- TC-JP — Jefferson Papers, Tucker-Coleman Collection
- TJP — Thomas Jefferson Papers

The following symbols represent repositories located outside of the United States:

ItPiAFM — Archivio Filippo Mazzei, privately owned, Pisa, Italy
NO-OsNB — Nasjonalbiblioteket, Oslo, Norway
StEdNL — National Library of Scotland, Edinburgh

5. *OTHER ABBREVIATIONS AND SYMBOLS*

The following abbreviations and symbols are commonly employed in the annotation throughout the work.

Lb — Letterbook (used to indicate texts copied or assembled into bound volumes)

RG — Record Group (used in designating the location of documents in the Library of Virginia and the National Archives)

SJL — Jefferson's "Summary Journal of Letters" written and received for the period 11 Nov. 1783 to 25 June 1826 (in DLC: TJ Papers). This epistolary record, kept in Jefferson's hand, has been checked against the TJ Editorial Files. It is to be assumed that all outgoing letters are recorded in SJL unless there is a note to the contrary. When the date of receipt of an incoming letter is recorded in SJL, it is incorporated in the notes. Information and discrepancies revealed in SJL but not found in the letter itself are also noted. Missing letters recorded in SJL are accounted for in the notes to documents mentioning them, in related documents, or in an appendix

TJ Thomas Jefferson

TJ Editorial Files Photoduplicates and other editorial materials in the office of the Papers of Thomas Jefferson: Retirement Series, Jefferson Library, Thomas Jefferson Foundation, Charlottesville

d Penny or denier

f Florin or franc

£ Pound sterling or livre, depending on context (in doubtful cases, a clarifying note will be given)

s Shilling or sou (also expressed as /)

tt Livre Tournois

℔ Per (occasionally used for pro, pre)

„ Old-style guillemet (European quotation mark)

6. SHORT TITLES

The following list includes short titles of works cited frequently in this edition. Since it is impossible to anticipate all the works to be cited in abbreviated form, the list is revised from volume to volume.

Acts of Assembly *Acts of the General Assembly of Virginia* (cited by session; title varies over time)

ANB John A. Garraty and Mark C. Carnes, eds., *American National Biography*, 1999, 24 vols.

Annals *Annals of the Congress of the United States: The Debates and Proceedings in the Congress of the United States ... Compiled from Authentic Materials*, Washington, D.C., Gales & Seaton, 1834–56, 42 vols. (All editions are undependable and pagination varies from one printing to another. Citations given below are to the edition mounted on the American Memory website of the Library of Congress and give the date of the debate as well as page numbers.)

APS American Philosophical Society

ASP *American State Papers: Documents, Legislative and Executive, of the Congress of the United States*, 1832–61, 38 vols.

Axelson, *Virginia Postmasters* Edith F. Axelson, *Virginia Postmasters and Post Offices, 1789–1832*, 1991

Betts, *Farm Book* Edwin M. Betts, ed., *Thomas Jefferson's Farm Book*, 1953 (in two separately paginated sections; unless otherwise specified, references are to the second section)

Betts, *Garden Book* Edwin M. Betts, ed., *Thomas Jefferson's Garden Book, 1766–1824*, 1944

Biddle, *Lewis and Clark Expedition* Nicholas Biddle, *History of the Expedition under the command of Captains Lewis and Clark to the Sources of the Missouri, thence across the Rocky Mountains and down the River Columbia to the Pacific Ocean. Performed during the years 1804–5–6. By order of the Government of the United States*, Philadelphia, 1814, 2 vols.; Sowerby, no. 4168; Poor, *Jefferson's Library*, 7 (no. 370)

Biog. Dir. Cong. *Biographical Directory of the United States Congress, 1774–Present*, online resource, Office of the Clerk, United States House of Representatives

Biographie universelle *Biographie universelle, ancienne et moderne*, new ed., 1843–65, 45 vols.

Black's Law Dictionary Bryan A. Garner and others, eds., *Black's Law Dictionary*, 7th ed., 1999

Brigham, *American Newspapers* Clarence S. Brigham, *History and Bibliography of American Newspapers, 1690–1820*, 1947, 2 vols.

Bruce, *University* Philip Alexander Bruce, *History of the University of Virginia 1819–1919: The Lengthened Shadow of One Man*, 1920–22, 5 vols.

Burk, Jones, and Girardin, *History of Virginia* John Daly Burk, Skelton Jones, and Louis H. Girardin, *The History of Virginia, from its First Settlement to the Present Day*, Petersburg, 1804–16, 4 vols.; Sowerby, no. 464; Poor, *Jefferson's Library*, 4 (no. 127)

Bush, *Life Portraits* Alfred L. Bush, *The Life Portraits of Thomas Jefferson*, rev. ed., 1987

Callahan, *U.S. Navy* Edward W. Callahan, *List of Officers of the Navy of the United States and of the Marine Corps from 1775 to 1900*, 1901, repr. 1969

Chambers, *Poplar Forest* S. Allen Chambers, *Poplar Forest & Thomas Jefferson*, 1993

Clay, *Papers* James F. Hopkins and others, eds., *The Papers of Henry Clay*, 1959–92, 11 vols.

CVSP William P. Palmer and others, eds., *Calendar of Virginia State Papers … Preserved in the Capitol at Richmond*, 1875–93, 11 vols.

DAB Allen Johnson and Dumas Malone, eds., *Dictionary of American Biography*, 1928–36, 20 vols.

DBF *Dictionnaire de biographie française*, 1933– , 19 vols.

Delaplaine's Repository Joseph Delaplaine, *Delaplaine's Repository of the Lives and Portraits of Distinguished Americans*, Philadelphia, 1816–18, 2 vols.; Poor, *Jefferson's Library*, 4 (no. 139)

Destutt de Tracy, *Analyse Raisonnée* [Destutt de Tracy], *Analyse Raisonnée de l'Origine de Tous les Cultes, ou Religion Universelle*, Paris, 1804; Sowerby, no. 1296; Poor, *Jefferson's Library*, 9 (no. 470)

Destutt de Tracy, *Commentary and Review of Montesquieu's Spirit of Laws* Destutt de Tracy, *A Commentary and Review of Montesquieu's Spirit of Laws. prepared for press from the Original Manuscript, in the hands of the publisher. To which are annexed, Observations on the Thirty-First Book, by the late M. Condorcet: and Two Letters of Helvetius, on the merits of the same work*, Philadelphia, 1811; Sowerby, no. 2327; Poor, *Jefferson's Library*, 10 (no. 623)

Destutt de Tracy, *Treatise on Political Economy* Destutt de Tracy, *A Treatise on Political Economy; to which is prefixed a supplement to a preceding work on the understanding, or Elements of Ideology*, Georgetown, 1817; Poor, *Jefferson's Library*, 11 (no. 700)

DSB Charles C. Gillispie, ed., *Dictionary of Scientific Biography*, 1970–80, 16 vols.

DVB John T. Kneebone and others, eds., *Dictionary of Virginia Biography*, 1998– , 3 vols.

EG Dickinson W. Adams and Ruth W. Lester, eds., *Jefferson's Extracts from the Gospels*, 1983, *The Papers of Thomas Jefferson*, Second Series

Fairclough, *Horace: Satires, Epistles and Ars Poetica* H. Rushton Fairclough, trans., *Horace: Satires, Epistles and Ars Poetica*, Loeb Classical Library, 1926, repr. 2005

Fairclough, *Virgil* H. Rushton Fairclough, trans., *Virgil*, Loeb Classical Library, 1916–18, rev. by G. P. Goold, 1999–2000, repr. 2002–06, 2 vols.

Fielding, *Dictionary* Mantle Fielding, *Dictionary of American Painters, Sculptors and Engravers*, 1926, rev. ed. 1974

Ford Paul Leicester Ford, ed., *The Writings of Thomas Jefferson*, Letterpress Edition, 1892–99, 10 vols.

Groce and Wallace, *Dictionary of Artists* George C. Groce and David H. Wallace, *The New-York Historical Society's Dictionary of Artists in America 1564–1860*, 1957

Haggard, "Henderson Heirs" Robert F. Haggard, "Thomas Jefferson v. The Heirs of Bennett Henderson, 1795–1818: A Case Study in Caveat Emptor," *MACH* 63 (2005): 1–29

Harvard Catalogue *Harvard University Quinquennial Catalogue of the Officers and Graduates, 1636–1925*, 1925

HAW Henry A. Washington, ed., *The Writings of Thomas Jefferson*, 1853–54, 9 vols.

Heitman, *Continental Army* Francis B. Heitman, comp., *Historical Register of Officers of the Continental Army during the War of the Revolution, April, 1775, to December, 1783*, rev. ed., 1914

Heitman, *U.S. Army* Francis B. Heitman, comp., *Historical Register and Dictionary of the United States Army*, 1903, 2 vols.

Hening William Waller Hening, ed., *The Statutes at Large; being a Collection of all the Laws of Virginia*, Richmond, 1809–23, 13 vols.; Sowerby, no. 1863; Poor, *Jefferson's Library*, 10 (no. 573)

Hoefer, *Nouv. biog. générale* J. C. F. Hoefer, *Nouvelle biographie générale depuis les temps les plus reculés jusqu'a nos jours*, 1852–83, 46 vols.

Hortus Third Liberty Hyde Bailey, Ethel Zoe Bailey, and the staff of the Liberty Hyde Bailey Hortorium, Cornell University, *Hortus Third: A Concise Dictionary of Plants Cultivated in the United States and Canada*, 1976

Hosack, *Observations on Contagious Diseases* David Hosack, *Observations on the Laws Governing the Communication of Contagious Diseases, and the Means of Arresting Their Progress*, New York, 1815; Poor, *Jefferson's Library*, 7 (no. 304); TJ's copy in MiU-C

Jackson, *Papers* Sam B. Smith, Harold D. Moser, Daniel Feller, and others, eds., *The Papers of Andrew Jackson*, 1980– , 8 vols.

Jefferson Correspondence, Bixby Worthington C. Ford, ed., *Thomas Jefferson Correspondence Printed from the Originals in the Collections of William K. Bixby*, 1916

JEP *Journal of the Executive Proceedings of the Senate of the United States*

JHD *Journal of the House of Delegates of the Commonwealth of Virginia*

JHR *Journal of the House of Representatives of the United States*

JS *Journal of the Senate of the United States*

JSV *Journal of the Senate of Virginia*

Kercheval, *Jefferson's Letters* Samuel Kercheval, ed., *Mr. Jefferson's Letters on the Subject of Convention*, 1829

Kimball, *Jefferson, Architect* Fiske Kimball, *Thomas Jefferson, Architect*, 1916

L & B Andrew A. Lipscomb and Albert E. Bergh, eds., *The Writings of Thomas Jefferson*, Library Edition, 1903–04, 20 vols.

Latrobe, *Papers* John C. Van Horne and others, eds., *The Correspondence and Miscellaneous Papers of Benjamin Henry Latrobe*, 1984–88, 3 vols.

LCB Douglas L. Wilson, ed., *Jefferson's Literary Commonplace Book*, 1989, *The Papers of Thomas Jefferson*, Second Series

Leavitt, *Poplar Forest* Messrs. Leavitt, *Catalogue of a Private Library ... Also, The Remaining Portion of the Library of the Late Thomas Jefferson ... offered by his grandson, Francis Eppes, of Poplar Forest, Va.*, 1873

Leonard, *General Assembly* Cynthia Miller Leonard, comp., *The General Assembly of Virginia, July 30, 1619–January 11, 1978: A Bicentennial Register of Members*, 1978

List of Patents *A List of Patents granted by the United States from April 10, 1790, to December 31, 1836*, 1872

Longworth's New York Directory *Longworth's American Almanac, New-York Register, and City Directory*, New York, 1796–1842 (title varies; cited by year of publication)

MACH *Magazine of Albemarle County History*, 1940– (title varies; issued until 1951 as *Papers of the Albemarle County Historical Society*)

Madison, *Papers* William T. Hutchinson, Robert A. Rutland, John C. A. Stagg, and others, eds., *The Papers of James Madison*, 1962– , 35 vols.

Congress. Ser., 17 vols.
Pres. Ser., 7 vols.
Retirement Ser., 2 vols.
Sec. of State Ser., 9 vols.

Malone, *Jefferson* Dumas Malone, *Jefferson and his Time*, 1948–81, 6 vols.

Marshall, *Papers* Herbert A. Johnson, Charles T. Cullen, Charles F. Hobson, and others, eds., *The Papers of John Marshall*, 1974–2006, 12 vols.

Mazzei, *Writings* Margherita Marchione and others, eds., *Philip Mazzei: Selected Writings and Correspondence*, 1983, 3 vols.

MB James A. Bear Jr. and Lucia C. Stanton, eds., *Jefferson's Memorandum Books: Accounts, with Legal Records and Miscellany, 1767–1826*, 1997, *The Papers of Thomas Jefferson*, Second Series

Miller, *Treaties* Hunter Miller, ed., *Treaties and other International Acts of the United States of America*, 1931–48, 8 vols.

Notes, ed. Peden Thomas Jefferson, *Notes on the State of Virginia*, ed. William Peden, 1955

OCD Simon Hornblower and Antony Spawforth, eds., *The Oxford Classical Dictionary*, 2003

ODNB H. C. G. Matthew and Brian Harrison, eds., *Oxford Dictionary of National Biography*, 2004, 60 vols.

OED James A. H. Murray, J. A. Simpson, E. S. C. Weiner, and others, eds., *The Oxford English Dictionary*, 2d ed., 1989, 20 vols.

Papenfuse, *Maryland Public Officials* Edward C. Papenfuse and others, eds., *An Historical List of Public Officials of Maryland*, 1990– , 1 vol.

Peale, *Papers* Lillian B. Miller and others, eds., *The Selected Papers of Charles Willson Peale and His Family*, 1983– , 5 vols. in 6

PMHB *Pennsylvania Magazine of History and Biography*, 1877–

Poor, *Jefferson's Library* Nathaniel P. Poor, *Catalogue. President Jefferson's Library*, 1829

Princetonians James McLachlan and others, eds., *Princetonians: A Biographical Dictionary*, 1976–90, 5 vols.

PTJ Julian P. Boyd, Charles T. Cullen, John Catanzariti, Barbara B. Oberg, and others, eds., *The Papers of Thomas Jefferson*, 1950– , 39 vols.

PW Wilbur S. Howell, ed., *Jefferson's Parliamentary Writings*, 1988, *The Papers of Thomas Jefferson*, Second Series

Randall, *Life* Henry S. Randall, *The Life of Thomas Jefferson*, 1858, 3 vols.

Randolph, *Domestic Life* Sarah N. Randolph, *The Domestic Life of Thomas Jefferson, Compiled from Family Letters and Reminiscences by His Great-Granddaughter*, 1871

Shackelford, *Descendants* George Green Shackelford, ed., *Collected Papers ... of the Monticello Association of the Descendants of Thomas Jefferson*, 1965–84, 2 vols.

Sibley's Harvard Graduates John L. Sibley and others, eds., *Sibley's Harvard Graduates*, 1873– , 18 vols.

Sowerby E. Millicent Sowerby, comp., *Catalogue of the Library of Thomas Jefferson*, 1952–59, 5 vols.

Terr. Papers Clarence E. Carter and John Porter Bloom, eds., *The Territorial Papers of the United States*, 1934–75, 28 vols.

TJR Thomas Jefferson Randolph, ed., *Memoir, Correspondence, and Miscellanies, from the Papers of Thomas Jefferson*, 1829, 4 vols.

True, "Agricultural Society" Rodney H. True, "Minute Book of the Agricultural Society of Albemarle," *Annual Report of the American Historical Association for the Year 1918* (1921), 1: 261–349

U.S. Reports *Cases Argued and Decided in the Supreme Court of the United States*, 1790– (title varies; originally issued in distinct editions of separately numbered volumes with *U.S. Reports* volume numbers retroactively assigned; original volume numbers here given parenthetically)

U.S. Statutes at Large Richard Peters, ed., *The Public Statutes at Large of the United States ... 1789 to March 3, 1845*, 1845–67, 8 vols.

Va. Reports *Reports of Cases Argued and Adjudged in the Court of Appeals of Virginia*, 1798– (title varies; originally issued in distinct editions of separately numbered volumes with *Va. Reports* volume numbers retroactively assigned; original volume numbers here given parenthetically)

VMHB *Virginia Magazine of History and Biography*, 1893–

Washington, *Papers* W. W. Abbot and others, eds., *The Papers of George Washington*, 1983– , 58 vols.

Colonial Ser., 10 vols.
Confederation Ser., 6 vols.
Pres. Ser., 16 vols.
Retirement Ser., 4 vols.
Rev. War Ser., 22 vols.

William and Mary Provisional List *A Provisional List of Alumni, Grammar School Students, Members of the Faculty, and Members of the Board of Visitors of the College of William and Mary in Virginia. From 1693 to 1888*, 1941

Wirt, *Patrick Henry* William Wirt, *Sketches of the Life and Character of Patrick Henry*, Philadelphia, 1817; Poor, *Jefferson's Library*, 4 (no. 131)

WMQ *William and Mary Quarterly*, 1892–

Woods, *Albemarle* Edgar Woods, *Albemarle County in Virginia*, 1901, repr. 1991

CONTENTS

1816

CONTENTS

1817

MAPS

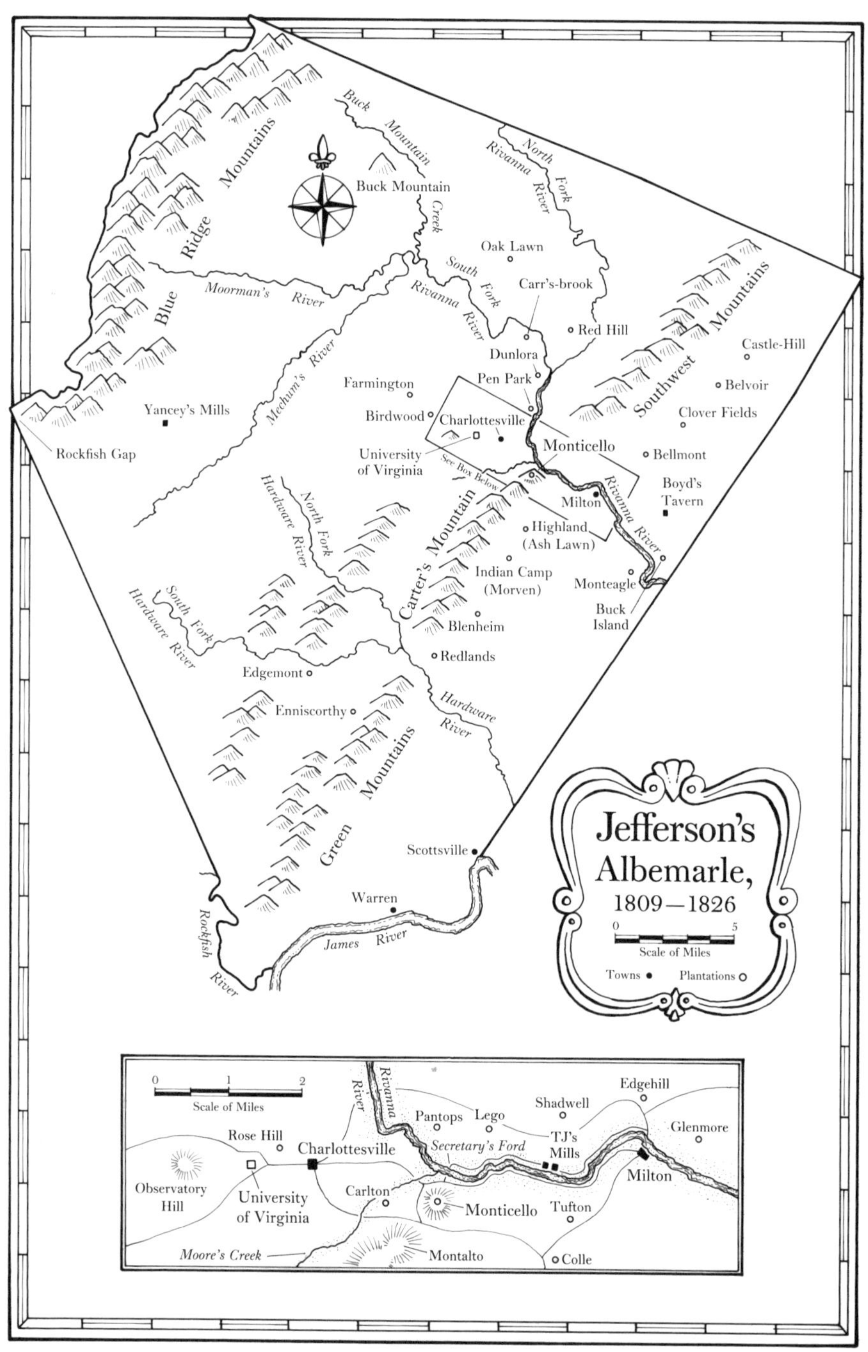

Jefferson's Albemarle, 1809–1826
0 5
Scale of Miles
Towns
Plantations
Buck Mountain Creek
Buck Mountain
Blue Ridge Mountains
Moorman's River
Mechum's River
North Fork Rivanna River
South Fork Rivanna River
Oak Lawn
Carr's-brook
Red Hill
Dunlora
Pen Park
Farmington
Birdwood
Charlottesville
University of Virginia
See Box Below
Monticello
Milton
Southwest Mountains
Castle-Hill
Belvoir
Clover Fields
Bellmont
Boyd's Tavern
Rivanna River
Yancey's Mills
Rockfish Gap
Hardware River
North Fork
South Fork
Carter's Mountain
Highland (Ash Lawn)
Indian Camp (Morven)
Monteagle
Buck Island
Blenheim
Redlands
Edgemont
Enniscorthy
Green Mountains
Scottsville
Warren
James River
Rockfish River
0 1 2
Scale of Miles
Rivanna River
Rose Hill
Pantops
Lego
Shadwell
Edgehill
Glenmore
Secretary's Ford
TJ's Mills
Milton
Observatory Hill
University of Virginia
Carlton
Monticello
Tufton
Moore's Creek
Montalto
Colle

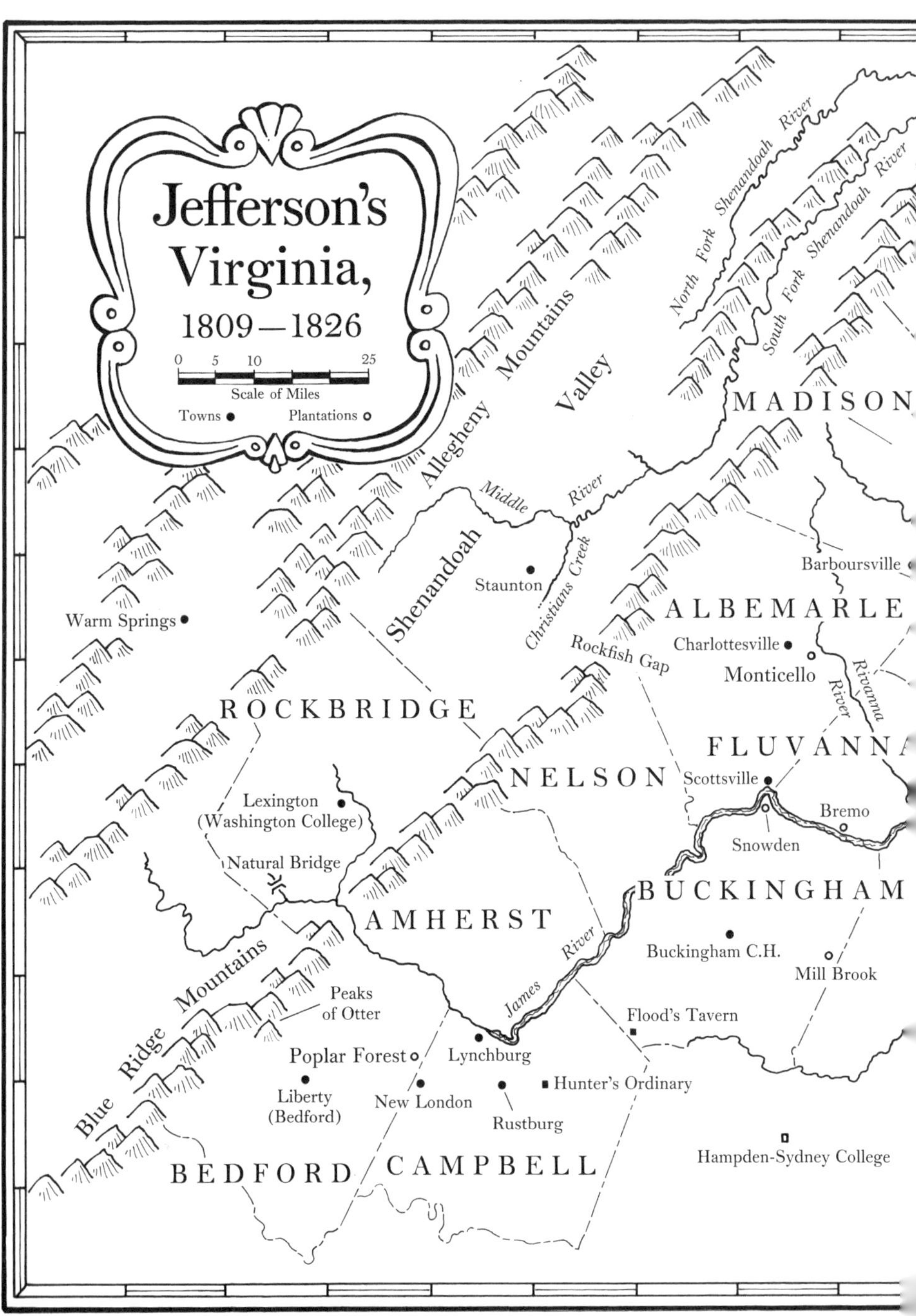

Jefferson's Virginia, 1809–1826
0 5 10 25
Scale of Miles
Towns
Plantations
Allegheny Mountains
Valley
North Fork Shenandoah River
South Fork Shenandoah River
MADISON
Middle River
Shenandoah
Staunton
Christians Creek
Barboursville
ALBEMARLE
Charlottesville
Monticello
Rivanna River
Rockfish Gap
Warm Springs
ROCKBRIDGE
FLUVANNA
NELSON
Scottsville
Bremo
Snowden
Lexington (Washington College)
Natural Bridge
BUCKINGHAM
AMHERST
James River
Buckingham C.H.
Mill Brook
Blue Ridge Mountains
Peaks of Otter
Flood's Tavern
Poplar Forest
Lynchburg
Liberty (Bedford)
New London
Hunter's Ordinary
Rustburg
Hampden-Sydney College
BEDFORD
CAMPBELL

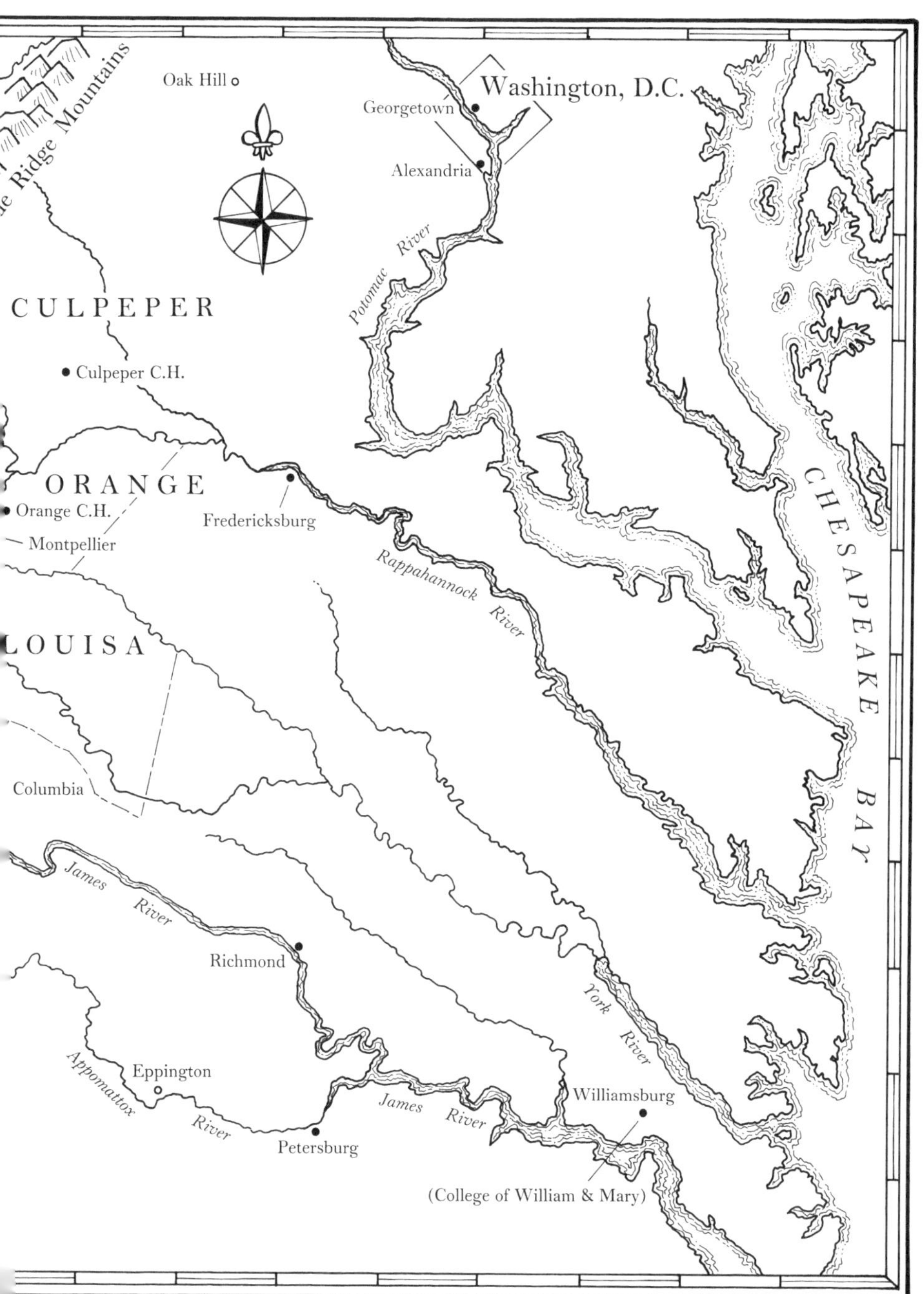

Blue Ridge Mountains
Oak Hill
Washington, D.C.
Georgetown
Alexandria
Potomac River
CULPEPER
Culpeper C.H.
ORANGE
Orange C.H.
Montpellier
Fredericksburg
Rappahannock River
LOUISA
Columbia
James River
Richmond
Appomattox River
Eppington
Petersburg
James River
Williamsburg
(College of William & Mary)
York River
CHESAPEAKE BAY

ILLUSTRATIONS

Following page 240

JOSEPH DELAPLAINE BY JOHN WESLEY JARVIS

John Wesley Jarvis (ca. 1781–1840), engraver and portrait painter, was born in England and immigrated to the United States as a child in the mid-1780s. After learning his craft in Philadelphia as an apprentice to the artist Edward Savage, he began work about 1800 as an engraver in New York City. Jarvis soon branched out into portraiture, and during the decades that followed he took likenesses in both his adopted hometown and in cities as far afield as Baltimore, Charleston, South Carolina, and New Orleans. He established his professional reputation between 1815 and 1817 with a series of full-length portraits of military leaders of the War of 1812. Over the course of his long career, Jarvis produced an estimated 750 to 1,000 paintings, a body of work that was marred on occasion by the haste with which he worked. His 1819 oil-on-canvas depiction of the Philadelphia publisher Joseph Delaplaine, which measures thirty-three by twenty-six inches, is, however, a strong example of his work (*ANB*; *DAB*; *National Portrait Gallery Smithsonian Institution Permanent Collection Illustrated Checklist* [1987], 77).

Courtesy of the National Portrait Gallery, Smithsonian Institution.

THOMAS JEFFERSON BY BASS OTIS

Joseph Delaplaine commissioned Bass Otis to execute a portrait of Jefferson as the source for an engraving to be printed in *Delaplaine's Repository*. Delaplaine and Otis arrived at Monticello during the first week of June 1816. Although William Thornton later criticized the finished product, stating to Jefferson that "Never was such injustice done to you, except by Sign Painters, and Gen[l] Kosciusko," the Pennsylvania Academy of the Fine Arts exhibited the original thirty-by-twenty-five-inch oil-on-canvas composition in 1818. The painting was thereafter returned to Otis, who used it to create several other portraits of the ex-president (Bush, *Life Portraits*, 64–7; Delaplaine to TJ, 11, 27 May 1816; Caspar Wistar to TJ, 28 May 1816; William Thornton to TJ, 20 July 1816; *Seventh Annual Exhibition of the Pennsylvania Academy of the Fine Arts* [Philadelphia, 1818], 10).

Courtesy of the Thomas Jefferson Foundation, Inc.

ENGRAVING OF THOMAS JEFFERSON BY JAMES OR JOHN NEAGLE

Joseph Delaplaine employed one of the Neagles in the autumn of 1816 to produce an engraving of Jefferson based on Bass Otis's recently completed life portrait. Although the obvious differences between Otis's and Neagle's handiwork have inspired some doubt whether the latter was actually derived from the former, they are more likely the result of liberties taken by the engraver to bring the piece into line with the other illustrations in *Delaplaine's Repository*. Neagle's rendition was published along with Jefferson's biography in the first volume of that work and reprinted numerous times during the first half of the nineteenth century, both in the United States and abroad.

Indeed, according to one scholar the image produced by Neagle was, partly because of its use by an American insurance company, "the most widely distributed image of Jefferson in retirement" (Bush, *Life Portraits*, 65–7; Groce and Wallace, *Dictionary of Artists*, 466; *Delaplaine's Repository*, 1:124).

Courtesy of Robert F. Haggard.

BOOK DEDICATION BY LOUIS H. GIRARDIN

This printed dedication to Jefferson, one of many in his lifetime, is from the fourth and final volume of *The History of Virginia; commenced by John Burk, and continued by Skelton Jones and Louis Hue Girardin* (Petersburg, 1816; Sowerby, no. 464; Poor, *Jefferson's Library*, 4 [no. 127]). Although Girardin revealed in the preface that he had "enjoyed the incalculable benefit of a free access to Mr. Jefferson's Library," which "proved of infinite service to my undertaking," the retired statesman's contribution extended far beyond the provision of books and other source material. Jefferson carefully reviewed the manuscript prior to publication, suggested numerous additions and alterations and, in so doing, defended his actions during the American Revolution against those, like Henry Lee, who had criticized his wartime record. He specifically dealt with his authorship of a 1778 bill of attainder against Josiah Philips and his inability as governor of Virginia to counteract effectively Benedict Arnold's raid on the state in 1780–81 (Burk, Jones, and Girardin, *History of Virginia*, 4:iv, vi, 305–6, and appendix, xi–xiii, xv; Malone, *Jefferson*, 6:218–24; letters from TJ to Girardin between 3 Dec. 1814 and 12 May 1815).

Courtesy of the Library of Virginia.

GREENHOUSE AT MONTICELLO

Jefferson's 240-square-foot greenhouse, which was sometimes referred to as the South or Southeast Piazza, was completed toward the end of his presidency. Connected to his private suite of rooms by a French door, it boasted five floor-to-ceiling, double-sashed, glazed windows to let in light and warmth during daylight hours. With the windows fully opened the chamber became an open-air porch. To regulate the temperature when they were closed, Jefferson had each window outfitted with louvered shutters. Although he apparently never used the greenhouse for serious gardening, it proved useful in sprouting seeds and as a place where delicate specimens could grow and develop until they were ready to be moved outside. This, indeed, was probably Jefferson's original intention, for he wrote in 1808 that he only intended it for oranges, *Mimosa farnesiana* (needle bush), and "a very few things of that kind." The space may have been a workshop as much as a conservatory, because the former president seems to have kept his workbench and tools there (William L. Beiswanger, *Monticello in Measured Drawings* [1998; new ed. 2011], 32; Stein, *Worlds*, 51–2, 99, 102–3; Jack McLaughlin, *Jefferson and Monticello: The Biography of a Builder* [1988; repr. 1990], 321, 324; Peter J. Hatch, *The Gardens of Thomas Jefferson's Monticello* [1992], 20; TJ to William Hamilton, 1 Mar. 1808 [DLC]; TJ to Bernard McMahon, 8 Apr. 1811).

Courtesy of the Thomas Jefferson Foundation, Inc.

ILLUSTRATIONS

SPHERICAL SUNDIAL

Jefferson received a model of the so-called "Corn Cob Capital" from the architect Benjamin Henry Latrobe in 1809. Latrobe then indicated that the addition of "a short frustum raising it about 4 feet from the Ground" would allow it to "serve for a Dial stand." Seven years later Jefferson informed Latrobe that he had placed the capital on a pedestal and surmounted it with a spherical sundial. This timepiece, which was manufactured out of locust wood, had a diameter of 10½ inches and was tilted in accordance with Monticello's latitude. Horizontal lines encircled the globe at the Tropic of Cancer, Equator, and Tropic of Capricorn. Vertical lines stretching from tropic to tropic gave the hours of the day, while progressively shorter lines represented intervals of thirty, fifteen, and five minutes. Jefferson remarked proudly in 1817 that "my dial captivates every body foreign as well as home-bred, as a handsome object & accurate measurer of time." Although the original capital and sundial are not known to have survived, in 2001 the Thomas Jefferson Foundation installed a replica at the far corner of the North Terrace, near the spot where the original stood during Jefferson's lifetime (William L. Beiswanger, "Jefferson's Spherical Sundial," Monticello Research Report, Nov. 2001 [ViCMRL]; Latrobe to TJ, 28 Aug. 1809; TJ to Latrobe, 27 Aug. 1816, 12 June 1817; John E. Semmes, *John H. B. Latrobe and His Times, 1803–1891* [1917], 250–1).

Courtesy of the Thomas Jefferson Foundation, Inc.

PORTABLE THERMOMETER

Although Jefferson may have acquired his prized pocket thermometer during a visit to England in 1786, it more likely arrived at Monticello in the summer of 1816 as a gift from James Madison's stepson, John Payne Todd. Manufactured by the Dollond firm of London, the instrument was made of brass, glass, and mercury, measured thirteen inches in length and five-eighths of an inch in width, and was hinged in the middle so it could be folded in half (*MB*, 1:614–6, 618, 621; Silvio A. Bedini, *Jefferson and Science* [2002], 31; TJ to Todd, 15 Aug. 1816).

Courtesy of the National Museum of American History, Smithsonian Institution.

WILLIS'S MOUNTAIN

Willis's Mountain, an isolated, cone-shaped elevation roughly 1,000 feet in height, is located some forty miles southeast of Monticello in Buckingham County. Because it was visible from his mountaintop home on clear days, Jefferson often used it as a point of reference when measuring other nearby features. Willis's Mountain also fascinated him because it exemplified the optical phenomenon of looming. In his *Notes on the State of Virginia* Jefferson revealed that the peak "sometimes subsides almost totally into the horizon; sometimes it rises more acute and more elevated; sometimes it is hemispherical; and sometimes its sides are perpendicular, its top flat, and as broad as its base. In short it assumes at times the most whimsical shapes, and all these perhaps successively in the same morning." Jefferson calculated the latitude of Willis's Mountain during on-site visits in November 1811 and December

1816. He presumably made this drawing during one of those expeditions. Mining operations have since substantially altered the landmark's appearance (Betts, *Garden Book*, 80, 84–5; *Notes*, ed. Peden, 80–1; Notes on the Latitude of Willis's Mountain, [ca. 19 Dec. 1811]; Field Notes and Calculations of Altitude of the Peaks of Otter, [10–ca. 17 Nov. 1815]; Calculations of Latitude of Willis's Mountain, 8–9 Dec. 1816; Francis Hall's Account of a Visit to Monticello, 7–8 Jan. 1817).

Courtesy of the Massachusetts Historical Society.

THOMAS JEFFERSON BY GIUSEPPE VALAPERTA

The Italian sculptor Giuseppe Valaperta arrived at Monticello on 16 Sept. 1816 with a letter of introduction from John Payne Todd, determined to take the ex-president's likeness. At some point over the next few days he executed a wax, bas-relief, life portrait of his host on black glass. By 19 Sept. Valaperta had brought the unfinished three-by-two-inch profile to Madison's Montpellier estate, where he completed it. He planned to reproduce the piece in ivory, but this scheme never came to fruition. No extant portraits can be shown to derive from this little-known artwork (Todd to TJ, 14 Sept. 1816; Bush, *Life Portraits*, 68–70; Montlezun, *Voyage fait dans les années 1816 et 1817, de New-Yorck a la Nouvelle-Orléans* [Paris, 1818], 1:71–2).

Courtesy of the New-York Historical Society.

Volume 10

1 May 1816 to 18 January 1817

JEFFERSON CHRONOLOGY

1743 • 1826

1743	Born at Shadwell, 13 April (New Style).
1760–1762	Studies at the College of William and Mary.
1762–1767	Self-education and preparation for law.
1769–1774	Albemarle delegate to House of Burgesses.
1772	Marries Martha Wayles Skelton, 1 January.
1775–1776	In Continental Congress.
1776	Drafts Declaration of Independence.
1776–1779	In Virginia House of Delegates.
1779	Submits Bill for Establishing Religious Freedom.
1779–1781	Governor of Virginia.
1782	Martha Wayles Skelton Jefferson dies, 6 September.
1783–1784	In Continental Congress.
1784–1789	In France on commission to negotiate commercial treaties and then as minister plenipotentiary at Versailles.
1790–1793	Secretary of State of the United States.
1797–1801	Vice President of the United States.
1801–1809	President of the United States.

RETIREMENT

1809	Attends James Madison's inauguration, 4 March.
	Arrives at Monticello, 15 March.
1810	Completes legal brief on New Orleans batture case, 31 July.
1811	Batture case dismissed, 5 December.
1812	Correspondence with John Adams resumes, 1 January.
	Batture pamphlet preface completed, 25 February; printed by 21 March.
1814	Named a trustee of Albemarle Academy, 25 March.
	Resigns presidency of American Philosophical Society, 23 November.
1815	Sells personal library to Congress.
1816	Writes introduction and revises translation of Destutt de Tracy, *A Treatise on Political Economy* [1818].
	Named a visitor of Central College, 18 October.
1818	Attends Rockfish Gap conference to choose location of proposed University of Virginia, 1–4 August.
	Visits Warm Springs, 7–27 August.
1819	University of Virginia chartered, 25 January; named to Board of Visitors, 13 February; elected rector, 29 March.
	Debts greatly increased by bankruptcy of Wilson Cary Nicholas.
1820	Likens debate over slavery and Missouri statehood to "a fire bell in the night," 22 April.
1821	Writes memoirs, 6 January–29 July.
1823	Visits Poplar Forest for last time, 16–25 May.
1824	Lafayette visits Monticello, 4–15 November.
1825	University of Virginia opens, 7 March.
1826	Writes will, 16–17 March.
	Last recorded letter, 25 June.
	Dies at Monticello, 4 July.

THE PAPERS OF
THOMAS JEFFERSON

From John Mackey

M[R] JEFFERSON— Philadelphia, May 1st 1816.

On the 18th day of last month, I addressed a packet to you, containing desultory views of education: and my motive for addressing those views to you was manifested in the concluding paragraph. If now you are not disposed to employ your influence and authority for promoting a circulation of those views in print, be pleased to send the Manuscript to me, at N[o] 42, Union Street, Philadelphia.

I am the person who superintended the erection of the Works at Harper's Ferry; and am now engaged in the business of a schoolmaster.

With much respect, JOHN MACKEY

RC (MoSHi: TJC-BC); addressed: "Thomas Jefferson Esquire Monticello Virginia"; endorsed by TJ as received 8 May 1816 and so recorded in SJL.

John Mackey (Mackie), public official and schoolteacher, was foreign-born. His tenure as the first paymaster and public storekeeper for the federal armory at Harpers Ferry, Virginia (now West Virginia), 1798–1800, ended amidst complaints that he showed bias in awarding contracts, kept poor records, and supplied inadequate rations to his workers. In 1804 TJ noted on a list of possible candidates for federal appointments in Louisiana that Mackey was "in customs" at Philadelphia, was "dimsighted," and had formerly resided in New Orleans. Later that year Mackey opened a school for girls in Philadelphia. He taught in that city until at least 1823. By 1825 Mackey had converted his school, then at 258 Mulberry Street, into a store, and he was listed there as a shopkeeper until 1835 (Merritt Roe Smith, *Harpers Ferry Armory and the New Technology: The Challenge of Change* [1977], 37–48; James McHenry to William Simmons, 31 Mar. 1800 [DNA: RG 94, PRWP]; List of Candidates, [26 Mar. 1804] [DLC: TJ Papers, 119:20570–1]; Philadelphia *Poulson's American Daily Advertiser*, 6, 29 Oct., 6 Nov. 1804 [Mackey's "Reflections on the method of teaching Grammar"], 30 July 1808; James Robinson, *The Philadelphia Directory* [Philadelphia, 1805]; Robert Desilver, *The Philadelphia Index, or Directory* [Philadelphia, 1823], 56; Thomas Wilson, *The Philadelphia Directory and Stranger's Guide* [1825]: 92; [1835]: 121).

For the PACKET, see TJ to Mackey, 9 May 1816, and note.

From Joseph Bringhurst

Esteemed & beloved fr[D] Wilmington Del: 5 Mo 2[d] 1816

The Wife of our mutual friend Isaac Briggs called on me yesterday to consult me respecting thy favour of the 17th ultimo to her husband. She dessired me to inform thee of the absence of her husband as an apology for the delay of a reply. Isaac has been obliged to attend Congress the greater part of the session for the purpose of obtaining a law for the settlement of his publick account—After some consideration it was postponed till the next meeting of the National Legislature. Our fr[d] thought it necessary to go immediately to W. City to obtain a Stay of the legal proceedings & he is yet there. When he shall return I have no doubt he [will][1] reply to thy favour. I hope he will accept thy proposition as I do not, at present, see any prospect of a preferable employment. I have known[2] Isaac from his youth & have always loved & esteemed him. There are several others here who are deeply interested in his welfare. He has[3] a Wife of uncommon moral excellence, & children possessing many valuable qualities for whom Jacob Alrichs & I have been exceedingly anxious. Dear Isaac, with all his extraordinary qualifications for usefulness, has not prosperd in his pecuniary concerns, & we have apprehended that the present [state][4] of manufactures & commerce[5] would prevent him from obtaining suitable employment for the support of his family. We [are][6] therefore earnistly solicitous that he should accept thy kind aid in procuring the station proposed by thee—We hope the salary will support his family in a humble mode of life— Permit me to embrace this opportunity of telling thee how much thy character & services in Publick have been esteemed by several friends here—Cyrus Newlin. Jacob Alrichs. W[m] Poole. John Reynold[s] & Isaac Starr—all men who [thou][7] wouldst love & esteem on personal knowledge, have often united with me in speaking, with approbation, of thy[8] publick services, & I am add[9] we all feel a very strong & tender interest in thy personal welfare—We are not men of the world—we mean what we say & thou mayst believe me to be with prayers for thy eternal happiness

thy sincere fr[d] Joseph Bringhurst

RC (MHi); edge trimmed; endorsed by TJ as received 9 May 1816 and so recorded in SJL.

Joseph Bringhurst (1767–1834), apothecary and public official, was a native of Philadelphia and a member of the Society of Friends. In 1793 he settled in Wilmington, Delaware, where he resided until his death. Bringhurst operated a drugstore on Market Street, and by 1822 he owned a cotton factory. He served as clerk of the borough, 1799–1800, and he was chairman of the Library Company of Wilmington in 1828. Bringhurst became postmaster of Wilmington during TJ's presidency in 1802 and held this position until his removal from office in 1820. His scientific publications included "Facts concerning the Efficacy of Alkalies in Diseases of the Alimentary Canal," *Medical Repository* 5 (1802): 413–5, and "On Officinal Tinctures," *Journal of the Philadelphia College of Pharmacy* 5 (1833): 19–20. Bringhurst was the author of a series of poems published under the pen name of "Birtha" in the Philadelphia *Gazette of the United States* between 23 Mar. and 6 July 1791, and he reputedly wrote a 1796 letter later published as a *Copy of a Letter from a Young Man, a Quaker, in Pennsylvania, to the late William Cowper, the Poet* (Chester, Eng., 1800) (Josiah Granville Leach, *History of the Bringhurst Family* [1901], 39–41; J. Thomas Scharf, *History of Delaware. 1609–1888* [1888], 2:637, 650, 652, 660, 886; Charles E. Bennett, "A Poetical Correspondence Among Elihu Hubbard Smith, Joseph Bringhurst, Jr., and Charles Brockden Brown in *The Gazette of the United States*," *Early American Literature* 12 [1977/78]: 277–85; Philadelphia *Claypoole's American Daily Advertiser*, 29 Aug. 1800; Robert J. Stets, *Postmasters & Postoffices of the United States, 1782–1811* [1994], 106; Bringhurst to TJ, 8 July 1803 [DLC]; *A Directory, and Register for the Year 1814 . . . of the Borough of Wilmington, and Brandywine* [Wilmington, 1813?], 12; Philadelphia *Poulson's American Daily Advertiser*, 19 June 1820; Wilmington *Delaware Patriot and American Watchman*, 4 Apr. 1828; gravestone inscription in cemetery of Wilmington Friends Meeting House).

[1] Omitted word editorially supplied.
[2] Manuscript: "know."
[3] Reworked from "had."
[4] Omitted word editorially supplied.
[5] Manuscript: "commercee," reworked from "commence."
[6] Omitted word editorially supplied.
[7] Omitted word editorially supplied.
[8] Manuscript: "the."
[9] Thus in manuscript.

From John Adams

Dear Sir. Quincy May 3. 1816

Yours Ap. 8 has long Since been rec^{d}

J. "Would you agree to live your 80 Years over again"?

A. "Aye![1] And Sanse Phrases."

J. "Would you agree to live your Eighty Years over again forever"?

A. I once heard our Acquaintance, Chew, of Philadelphia Say, "He Should like to go back to 25, to all Eternity": but I own my Soul would Start and Shrink back on itself, at the Prospect of an endless Succession of Boules de Savon, almost as much as at the Certainty of Annihilation. For what is human Life? I can Speak only for one. I have had more comfort than distress, more pleasure than paine, Ten to one, nay if you please an hundred to one. A pretty large Dose however of Distress and Paine. But after all, What is human Life? A Vapour, a Fog, a Dew, a Cloud,[2] a Blossom a flower, a Rose a blade of Grass, a glass Bubble, a Tale told by an Idiot, a Boule de Savon, Vanity of Vanities, an eternal Succession of which would terrify me, almost as much as Annihilation.

J. "Would you prefer to live over again rather than Accept the Offer of a better Life in a future State"? A. Certainly not. J. "Would you live again, rather than change[3] for the worse in a future State, for the Sake of trying Something new"? Certainly Yes.[4]

J. "Would you live over again once or forever, rather than run the risque of Annihilation, or of a better or a worse State at or after[5] death"?

A. Most certainly I would not.

J. "How valiant you are"? A. Aye, at this moment, and at all other moments of my Life that I can recollect: but who can tell what will become of his Bravery when his Flesh and his heart Shall fail him?

Bolinbroke Said[6] "his Philosophy was not Sufficient to Support him in his last hours." D'alembert Said "Happy are they who have Courage, but I have none." Voltaire the greatest Genius of them all, behaved like the greatest Coward of them all; at his death as he had like the wisest fool of them all in his Lifetime. Hume aukwardly affects[7] to Sport away all Sober thoughts. Who can answer for his last Feelings and Reflections? especially as the Priests are in possession of the Custom of making them the great Engines of their Craft. Procul este Prophani!

J. "How shall We, how can We, estimate the real Value of human Life"?

A. I[8] know not, I cannot weigh Sensations and Reflections, Pleasures and Pains, Hopes and Fears in Money Scales. But I can tell you how I have heard it estimated by Some Phylosophers. One of my old Friends and Clients, A Mandamus Counseller against his Will, a Man of Letters and Virtues without one Vice, that I ever knew or Suspected, except Garrulity, William Vassall, asserted to me, and Strenuously maintained that "<u>pleasure is no Compensation for Pain</u>." "An 100 Years of the keenest delights of human Life could not atone for one hour of Billious Cholic, that he had felt." The Sublimity of this Philosophy my dull Genius could not reach. I was willing to State a fair Account between Pleasure and Pain, and give Credit for the Ballance, which I found very great in my favour.

Another Philosopher, who as We Say, believed nothing, ridiculed the Notion of a future State. One of the Company asked "Why are you an Ennemy to a future State"? "Are you weary of Life"! "Do you detest Existence"?

"Weary of Life!—Detest Existence!"[9] Said the Philosopher, No, "I love Life So well, and am So attached to Existence, that to be Sure of Immortality I would consent, to be pitched about with forks by the Devils among flames of fire and Brimstone to all Eternity."

I find no Resources in my Courage, for this exalted Philosophy. I had rather be blotted out.

Il faut trancher Cet Mot! What is there in[10] Life to attach Us, to it; but the hope of a future & a better? It is a Craker, a Rocquett a Firework, at best.

I admire your Navigation and Should like to Sail with you, either in your Bark or in my own, along Side of yours; Hope with her gay Ensigns displayed at the Prow; fear with her Hobgoblins behind the Stern. Hope Springs eternal; and Hope is all that endures. Take away hope and What[11] remains? What pleasure? I mean, Take away Fear, and what Pain remains[.] $\frac{99}{100}$ths of the Pleasures and Pains of Life are nothing but Hopes and Fears.

All Nations, known in History or in Travels have hoped, believed, an[d] expected a future and a better State. The Maker of the Universe, the Cause of all Things, whether We call it, Fate or Chance or God has inspired this Hope. If it is a Fraud, We Shall never know it. We Shall never resen[t] the Imposition, be grateful for the Illusion, nor grieve for the disappointment. We Shall be no more.

Credat Grim, Diderot, Buffon, La Lande, Condorcet, D'Holbach, Frederick Catherine; Non Ego. Arrogant as it may be, I Shall take the Liberty to pronounce them all, Idiologians. Yet I would not persecute a hair of their Heads. The World is wide enough for them and me.

Suppose,[12] the Cause of the Universe, Should reveal to all Mankind, at once a Certainty that they must all die within a Century, and that death is an eternal Extinction of all living Powers, Of all Sensation and Reflection. What would be the Effect? Would there be one Man Woman or Child existing on this Globe, twenty Years hence? Would not every human Being be, a Madame Deffand, Voltaires "Aveugle clairvoiante," all her Lifetime regretting her Existance, bewailing that She had ever been born; grieving that She had ever been dragged without her Consent, into being. Who would bear the Gout the Stone the Cholick, for the Sake of a Boule de Savon when a Pistol a Cord, a Pond, or a Phyal of Laudanum was at hand? What would Men Say to their Maker,? would they thank him? No They would reproach him; they would curse him to his Face,

Voila! a Sillier Letter than my last.! For a Wonder, I have filled a Sheet. And a greater Wonder, I have read fifteen Volumes of Grim. Digito comesce Labellum. I hope to write you more upon this and other Topicks of your Letter. I have read also a History of the Jesuits in four Volumes. Can you tell me the Author or any Thing of this Work?

John Adams

RC (DLC); edge trimmed, with missing text supplied from FC; at foot of text: "President Jefferson"; endorsed by TJ as received 13 May 1816 and so recorded in SJL. FC (Lb in MHi: Adams Papers).

"Sans phrases" (SANSE PHRASES): "without reservations." BOULES DE SAVON: "soap bubbles." A TALE TOLD BY AN IDIOT quotes William Shakespeare, *Macbeth*, act 5, scene 5. The phrase VANITY OF VANITIES is from the Bible, Ecclesiastes 1.2.

As his death approached, Jean Le Rond D'ALEMBERT wrote "Ils sont bien heureux ceux qui ont du courage; moi je n'en ai pas" ("Happy are they who have courage; as for me, I do not") (Friedrich Melchior, Freiherr von Grimm and Denis Diderot, *Mémoirs Historiques, Littéraires et Anecdotiques, tirés de la Correspondance Philosophique et Critique, adressée au Duc De Saxe Gotha* [London, 1813], 3:126).

According to one account of the last days of VOLTAIRE, he confessed his belief in the divinity of Jesus Christ and thus died as a member of the Roman Catholic Church. At another time, however, when asked "Croyez-vous à la divinité de Jésu-Christ?" ("Do you believe in the divinity of Jesus Christ?"), Voltaire replied, "Au nom de Dieu, Monsieur, ne me parlez plus de cet homme-là, et laissez-moi mourir en repos" ("In the name of God, sir, do not speak to me anymore about that man, and let me die in peace") (Condorcet, *Vie de Voltaire* [(Kehl), 1789], 156–7).

During the last month of his life, David HUME reportedly conducted an imaginary conversation with Charon, the mythological Greek boatman who ferries the souls of the dead into Hades. According to Adam Smith's account, Hume at one point said "Have a little patience, good Charon, I have been endeavouring to open the eyes of the public. If I live a few years longer, I may have the satisfaction of seeing the downfal of some of the prevailing systems of superstition" (*The Life of David Hume, Esq. Written by Himself* [Dublin, 1777], 20–1).

PROCUL ESTE PROPHANI ("away! you that are uninitiated!") is from Virgil, *Aeneid*, 6.258 (Fairclough, *Virgil*, 1:550–1). A MANDAMUS COUNSELLER was one of thirty-six men appointed to the Massachusetts Council, heretofore an elected body, under "An Act for the better regulating the Government of the Province of the Massachuset's Bay, in New England," 20 May 1774 (14 George III, c. 45, *The Statutes at Large* [London, 1776], 12:84–9; *Massachusetts Gazette; and the Boston Post-Boy and Advertiser*, 1–8, 8–15 Aug. 1774). WILLIAM VASSALL was a notably litigious Bostonian who derived his wealth from plantations in his native Jamaica and fled to London as a Loyalist refugee in 1775 (*Sibley's Harvard Graduates,* 9:349–59).

IL FAUT TRANCHER CET MOT: "it is necessary to make a decision on this." HOPE SPRINGS ETERNAL is taken from line 95 of the first epistle of Alexander Pope, *Essay on Man* (*The Works of Alexander Pope, Esq.* [Edinburgh, printed for J. Balfour, 1764; Adams's copy in MBPLi], 2:12). In stating that the designated individuals CREDAT ("may believe it") while his own answer is NON EGO ("not I"), Adams is adapting Horace, *Satires*, 1.5.100–1 (Fairclough, *Horace: Satires, Epistles and Ars Poetica*, 72–3).

The marquise du DEFFAND, a correspondent of Voltaire and Horace Walpole, was the AVEUGLE CLAIRVOIANTE ("blind clairvoyant") (Hoefer, *Nouv. biog. générale*, 13:351–5). Digito compesce (COMESCE) Labellum ("button your lip with your finger") is from Juvenal, *Satires,* 1.160 (Susanna Morton Braund, ed. and trans., *Juvenal and Persius*, Loeb Classical Library [2004], 144–5).

[1] Omitted opening quotation mark editorially supplied.

[2] RC: "Clould." FC: "Cloud."

[3] RC: "chang." FC: "change."

[4] Word added in place of "Aye," which had been reworked from "not."

[5] RC: "affter." FC: "after."

[6] Preceding seven words not in FC.

[7] RC: "affect." FC: "affects."

[8] Unmatched opening quotation mark preceding this word editorially omitted.

[9] Omitted closing quotation mark editorially supplied.

[10] RC: "is." FC: "in."

[11] Preceding thirteen words not in FC.

[12] RC: "Supose." FC: "Suppose."

To William Wingate

Sir Monticello May 4. 16.

I recieved yesterday yours of Apr. 8. accompanied by a Manuscript volume of your interpretation of the Revelations, & their application to Napoleon Bonaparte. you request me to read it, to take minutes from it, to converse on it with Joseph Bonaparte, and to write to you the result. I am 400. miles from that gentleman, never was, and probably never shall be nearer to him. and my occupations do not allow me the time even to read it. I acknolege too that had I the time, I should prefer employing it on something more levelled to my capacity than the revelations. to understand them requires a head more sublimated than mine, and we derive no profit from reading what we do not understand. in returning the volume promptly therefore, I comply with the only part of your request in my power. I hope you will recieve it safely, and with it the assurance of my respects.

Th: Jefferson

PoC (MoSHi: TJC-BC); on verso of reused address cover of Archibald Robertson to TJ, 3 Apr. 1816; at foot of text: "Mr William Wingate"; endorsed by TJ. Enclosure not found.

JOSEPH BONAPARTE had fled Europe for the United States in the summer of 1815, arriving in New York City on 20 Aug. Early in 1816 he was maintaining homes in Philadelphia and at Lansdowne, a country estate outside that city (Patricia Tyson Stroud, *The Man who had been King: The American Exile of Napoleon's Brother Joseph* [2005], 1, 13, 15).

To William Short

Dear Sir Monticello May 5. 16.

On my return, the day before yesterday, I found here your favor of Apr. 23. and answer without delay the remaining question on your affair with mr Carter. the last payment I made him for you was by a draught of Aug. 3.[1] 1795. for 524.83 D the exact balance for the lands after the ascertainment of their contents by actual survey. consequently, in this was included the overpayment now to be refunded with interest from that date. legal interest was then 5. p.c. per ann. the law which raised it to 6. p.c. not coming into force till May 1. 97 and restraining the advance of interest strictly to contracts entered into subsequent to that day these data of course fix the date and rate of interest to be paid by mr Carter.

I am really sorry for La Motte's failure to obtain the Consulship of Havre. but no blame can be imputed to Monroe. disbanded officers, without means of subsistence, and favored by the public sentiment, as well as by that of the Executive, leave them without grounds of refusal, except of what is in actual possession of another. and even possession can scarcely hold it's own. I have had to make representations in favor of Cathalan of Marseilles and Appleton of Leghorn, my old friends, the one having been in office 35. years and the other 30. years. yet they were jeopardised by competitions founded on a military service of 3. years only. in a government proceeding as ours does, by general rules, little can be yielded to favor, either conscientiously, or safely. I am satisfied Monroe's wishes were with La Motte.

I am glad you have fallen in with my grandaughter Ellen. from a batchelor not keeping house she could[2] expect nothing more than the civil attentions which I am sure you have shewn her in society. I did not know beforehand of her visit to Philadelphia or I would have sent her letters for some of my friends there. she merits any thing I could have said of a good heart, good temper, a sound head, and great range of information. the small chat of the day is a thing of habit, and of familiarity with local characters and circumstances. on these a stranger must always be deficient. it is on general topics only their measure can be taken.

I have taken it for granted that the fugitives from France would only make of this their first lighting place, from whence they might look around and see in what other residence they could ultimately find society and safety. I imagine that in no country, except England, is the state of society less adapted, than in this, to the French character and habits. the security and freedom they find under the tutelary, & yet invisible hand of our government must appear like enchantment to them. of our maniere d'etre they may with justice say it is <u>different</u> from theirs.

You express a wish and a hope that I may have been writing memoirs of myself. while in public life, my whole time has been absorbed by the duties that laid me under; and now, when the world imagines I have nothing to do, I am in a state of as heavy drudgery as any office of my life ever subjected me to. from sunrise till noon I am chained to the writing table. at that hour I ride of necessity for health as well as recreation. and even after dinner I must often return to the writing table. were this correspondence confined to my real friends only, it would be no more than an amusement, and would be a delicious repast. but it is one equally foreign to my interests and inclinations, & yet forced on me by the courtesies of those to whom it is responsive. it precludes me entirely from the course of studies and reading which would make my hours pass lightly and pleasantly away. however it must cease ere long from physical necessity, my wrist beginning to stiffen so as to render writing painful & slow. the letters I have written while in public office are in fact memorials of the transactions with which I have been associated, and may at a future day furnish something to the historian. copies of some of those written during the revolutionary war have been preserved and communicated freely to one or two persons writing the history of the day. the copying press and polygraph have preserved all written in France and subsequently.

But you propose a more Quixotic task in the reformation of what may be deemed defective in our constitution. no, my dear friend; nothing could allure me again into the furnace of politics. while engaged in the various functions of the government, duty required me to go straight forward, regardless of the enmities and execrations it excited. I felt and deplored them as a man; but scouted them as a public functionary. still I wished that in retiring from my duties, I might retire also from their afflicting associates. to volunteer again into these scenes and sufferings would be to forget what I have undergone, to be insensible of what I feel of the moral and physical decline which the laws of our structure have ordained. I submit to these with entire contentment. tranquility is the softest pillow for the head of old age; and the good will of those around us the sweetest soother of our repose. in this state of being, seasoned by occasional communications with my friends, I shall pass willingly to that eternal sleep which, whether with, or without, dreams, awaits us hereafter. I leave, with satisfaction and confidence, to those who are to come after me, the pursuit of what is right, & rectification of what is wrong; convinced they will be as able to manage their own affairs, as we have been ours. I restrict my anxieties within the circle of my family and friends, among whom I feel constant and affectionate interest in your health and happiness.

TH: JEFFERSON

RC (ViW: TJP); ink stained, with obscured text rewritten by TJ; endorsed by Short as received 13 May 1816. PoC (DLC); ink stained, with obscured text rewritten by TJ; at foot of first page: "Mr Short"; endorsed by TJ.

TJ made a PAYMENT to William Champe Carter on 3 Aug. 1795 on behalf of Short for the latter's purchase of the Indian Camp tract in Albemarle County (*PTJ*, 28:430). LEGAL INTEREST was capped in Virginia at 5 percent by "An Act to make void certain Contracts for the paying excessive Usury," which took effect on 10 Nov. 1734. This rate was renewed by subsequent legislation until 23 Nov. 1796, when "An Act to amend the act, intituled, an act Against Usury" increased the maximum to 6 percent, effective 1 May 1797 (Hening, 4:395–7; *The Revised Code of the Laws of Virginia* [Richmond, 1819], 1:373n; *Acts of Assembly* [1796 sess.], 16–7). MANIERE D'ETRE: "way of life."

[1] Reworked from "23."
[2] TJ here canceled "neither."

From John Adams

Dear Sir Quincy May 6 1816

Neither Eyes Fingers or Paper held out, to dispatch all the Trifles I wished to write in my last Letter.

In your favour of April 8th You "wonder for what good End the Sensations of Grief could be intended"? You "wish[1] the Pathologists would tell Us, what the Use of Grief, in Our Œconomy, and of what good it is the Cause proximate or remote." When I approach Such questions as this, I consider myself, like one of those little Eels in Vinaigre, or one of those Animalcules in black or red Peper or in the Horse radish Root, that bite our Tongues So cruelly, reasoning upon the το παν. Of what Use is this Sting upon the Tongue? Why might We not have the Benefit of these Stimulants, without the Sting? Why might We not have the fragrance and Beauty of the Rose without the Thorn?

In the first place, however, We know not the Connections between pleasure and Pain. They Seem to be mechanical and inseperable. How can We conceive a Strong Passion, a Sanguine Hope Suddenly disappointed without producing Pain? or Grief? Swift at 70, recollected the Fish he had angled out of Water when a Boy, which broke loose from his hoock, and Said I feel the disappointment at this Moment. A Merchant places all his fortune and all his Credit in a Single India or China Ship. She Arrives at the Vineyard[2] with a Cargo worth a Million, in Order. Sailing round the Cape for Boston a Sudden Storm wrecks her, Ship Cargo and Crew all lost. Is it possible that the Merchant ruined, bankrupt Sent to Prison by his Creditors, his Wife and Children Starving, Should not grieve? Suppose a young Couple, with every Advantage[3] of Persons, fortunes and Connection on the Point of an indissoluble Union. A flash of Lightening, or any one of those millions of Accidents which are alloted to Humanity proves fatal to one of the Lovers. Is it possible that the other, and all the Friends of both Should not grieve? It Should Seem that Grief, as a mere Passion must necesarily be in Proportion to Sensibility.

Did you ever See a Portrait or a Statue of a great Man, without perceiving Strong Traits of Paine, & Anxiety? These Furrows were all ploughed in the Countenance, by Grief. Our juvenile oracle, Sir Edward Coke, thought that none were fit for Legislators and Magistrates, but "Sad Men." And Who were these Sad Men? They were aged Men, who had been tossed and buffeted in the Vicissitudes of Life, forced upon profound Reflection by Grief and disappointments and taught to command their Passions & Prejudices

But, All this, You will Say, is nothing to the purpose. It is only repeating and exemplifying a Fact, which my question Supposed to be well known, viz the Existence of Grief; and is no Answer to my question, "What Are the Uses of Grief." This is very true, and you are very right: but may not the Uses of Grief be inferred, or at least Suggested by Such Exemplifications of known facts? Grief Compels the India Merchant to think; to reflect upon the plan of his Voyage. "Have I not been rash, to trust my Fortune, my Family, my Liberty, to the Caprices of Winds and Waves in a Single Ship? I will never again give a loose to my Imagination and Avarice.[4] It had been wiser and more honest to have traded on a Smaller Scale upon my own Capital." The dessolated Lover and disappointed Connections, are compelled by their Grief[5] to reflect on the Vanity of human Wishes and Expectations; to learn the essential Lesson of Resignation; to review their own Conduct towards the deceased; to correct any Errors or faults in their future Conduct towards their remaining friends and towards all Men; to recollect the Virtues of the lost Friend and resolve to imitate them; his Follies and Vices if he had any and resolve to avoid them. Grief drives Men into habits of Serious Reflection Sharpens the Understanding and Softens the heart; it compells them to arrouse their Reason, to assert its Empire over their Passions Propensities and Prejudices; to elevate them to a Superiority over all human Events; to give them the Felicis Annimi immota tranquilitatem; in Short to make them Stoicks and Christians.

After all, as Grief is a Pain, it Stands in the Predicament of all other Evil and the great question Occurs what is the origin and what the final cause of Evil. This perhaps is known only to Omnicience. We poor Mortals have nothing to do with it, but to fabricate all the good We can out of all inevitable Evils, and to avoid all that are avoidable, and many Such there are, among which are our own unnecessary Apprehensions and imaginary Fears. Though Stoical Apathy is impossible, Yet Patience and Resignation and tranquility may be acquired by Consideration in a great degree, very much for the hapiness of Life.

I have read Grim, in fifteen Volumes of more than five hundred pages each. I will not Say, like Uncle Tobey "You Shall not die" till you have read him.[6] But you ought to read him, if possible. It is the most entertaining Work I ever read. He appears exactly as you represent him. What is most of all remarkable is his Impartiality. He Spares no Characters, but Necker and[7] Diderot; Voltaire, Buffon, D'Alembert, Helvetius Rousseau, Marmontel, Condorcet, La Harpe, Beaumarchais and all others are lashed without Ceremony. Their

Portraits as faithfully drawn as[8] possible. It is a compleat Review of French Litterature and fine Arts from 1753 to 1790. No Politicks. Criticisms very just. Anecdotes without number, and very merry. One ineffably ridiculous I wish I could Send you, but it is immeasurably long. D'Argens, a little out of health and Shivering with the cold in Berlin asked leave of the King to take a ride to Gascony his Native Province. He was absent So long that Frederick concluded the Air of the South of France was like to detain his Friend and as he wanted his Society and Services he contrived a Trick to bring him back. He fabricated a Mandement in the Name of the Archbishop of Aix, commanding all the Faithful to Seize The Marquis D'Argens, Author of Ocellus, Timæus and Julian, Works Atheistical, Deistical, Heretical and impious in the highest degree. This Mandement composed in a Style of Ecclesiastical Eloquence that never was exceeded by Pope, Jesuite, Inquisitor, or Sorbonite he Sent in Print by a courier to D'Argens, who frightened out of his Witts fled by cross roads out of France and back to Berlin, to the greater Joy of the Philosophical Court for the laugh of Europe which they had raised at the Expence of the learned Marquis.

I do not like the late Resurrection of the Jesuits. They have a General, now in Russia, in correspondence[9] with the Jesuits in the U.S. who are more numerous than every body knows. Shall We not have Swarms of them here? In as many Shapes and disguises as ever a King of the Gypsies, Bamfied More Carew himself, assumed? In the Shape of Printers, Editors, Writers School masters &c. I have lately read Pascalls Letters over again, and four Volumes of the History of the Jesuits. If ever any Congregation of Men could merit, eternal Perdition on Earth and in Hell, According to these Historians though like Pascal true Catholicks, it is this Company of Loiola. Our System however of Religious Liberty must afford them an Assylum. But if they do not put the Purity of our Elections to a Severe Tryal, it will be a Wonder.

J. ADAMS

RC (DLC); endorsed by TJ as received 23 May 1816 and so recorded in SJL. RC (MHi); address cover only; with PoC of TJ to Elisha Ticknor, 15 Aug. 1816, on verso; addressed by Susan B. Adams: "His Excellency Thomas Jefferson. Late President of the United States. Monticello Virginia"; postmarked Quincy, 10 May. FC (Lb in MHi: Adams Papers).

το παν: "totality; all." The anecdote by Jonathan SWIFT can be found in *The Works of Dr. Jonathan Swift, Dean of St. Patrick's, Dublin. with The Author's Life and Character* (Edinburgh, 1768; Adams's copy in MBPLi), 10:5–6. THE VINEYARD and THE CAPE: Martha's Vineyard and Cape Cod. SIR EDWARD COKE stipulates that juries of twelve SAD MEN from the king's household should investigate conspiracies to kill him or members of his council in *The Third Part of the Institutes of the Laws of England* (London, 1648, and other eds.; Sowerby, no. 1784), chap. 4.

FELICIS ANNIMI IMMOTA TRANQUILITATEM: "the imperturbable tranquillity of a happy heart." The fictional character of Uncle Toby (TOBEY) resolves that an ailing English officer "shall not die" in Laurence Sterne, *The Life and Opinions of Tristram Shandy, Gentleman* (Melvyn New and Joan New, eds., *The Florida Edition of the Works of Laurence Sterne* [1978; for edition owned by TJ, see Sowerby, no. 4336], 2:511). MANDEMENT: "a commandment or order" (*OED*). The Jesuit superior GENERAL was Tadeusz Brzozowski. Bampfylde Moore CAREW was a renowned swindler and impostor (*ODNB*).

[1] Omitted opening quotation mark editorially supplied.

[2] RC: "Viniard." FC: "Vineyard."

[3] RC: "Advantge." FC: "advantage."

[4] Superfluous closing quotation mark editorially omitted.

[5] Preceding three words interlined.

[6] Superfluous closing quotation mark editorially omitted.

[7] Preceding two words interlined.

[8] RC: "as as." FC: "as."

[9] RC: "corronspondence." FC: "correspondence."

From Marcus Dyson

DEAR SIR Richmond May 6. 1816

I hope you will pardon the liberty I have taken in addressing you, I have no other apology to offer except total unacquaintance with any person who could give me the information I desire, the eminent rank you hold in this Country, your acquaintance in Europe, & great reading, led me to hope you could, my enquiry is this,

whether oxygen gas can be pressed with same facility as atmospheric air,

whether the extreme pressure will not destroy its vitality, &

whether the passage of the expired air through the water, will absorb the carbon & render it fit for inspiration—

however to shew you I do not propose questions without a reason, I shall Subjoin a drawing of a machine, to be used by a person wishing to travel under the water, So as to leave his arms & legs at perfect liberty. this is but the outline of a machine, on which many improvements may be put & many alterations made for the better. I have taken the Standard of pressure @ 20 times & allowing 1 pint for inspiration & 20 pr minute $\frac{1}{10}$ consumed would be the actual consumption of 1 Quart pr minute, therefore this reservoir would support life 80 minutes. but this could be varied to any length of time by enlarging or contracting the reservoir the same principle applies to the pedestrian & boat Navigation, the whole question rests upon the above 3 points, & if they can be established, what a vast feild will be opened for Speculation, what immense advantages will mankind derive from the discovery, no longer can proud Navies approach our Shores and fill our Bays with impunity, nor the hidden treasures of the ocean remain undiscovered—

It has for a long time been considered a desidetarium, by me, to enjoy equal privileges with the inhabitants of the Ocean, on foot to explore the bottoms of our Bays & Rivers, or to navigate them & the ocean beneath the surface in boats. both of which I think I have accomplished,[1] & though I can have but little doubt on the Subject, Still the impossibility of procuring Suitable apparatus for the purpose of making experiments in this City, induced me to lay the whole plan before you (& you are the only person who knows it) & not only request your reply to my queries, but your advice & opinion upon the whole business, which will determine me in the further prosecution of it, I should be much more lengthy in my communication, were I not afraid of occupying too much of your time. your reply as Soon as convenient will much oblige

Your m° Ob^{t} Svt— MARCUS DYSON

RC (DLC); addressed: "His Excellency Thomas Jefferson Monticello Albemarle Virginia"; franked; postmarked Richmond, 10 May; endorsed by TJ as received 13 May 1816 and so recorded in SJL; with enclosure on both sides of address cover.

[1] Manuscript: "accomplised."

ENCLOSURE

Marcus Dyson's Drawing and Description of a Device for Breathing Underwater

[ca. 6 May 1816]

EXPLANATION

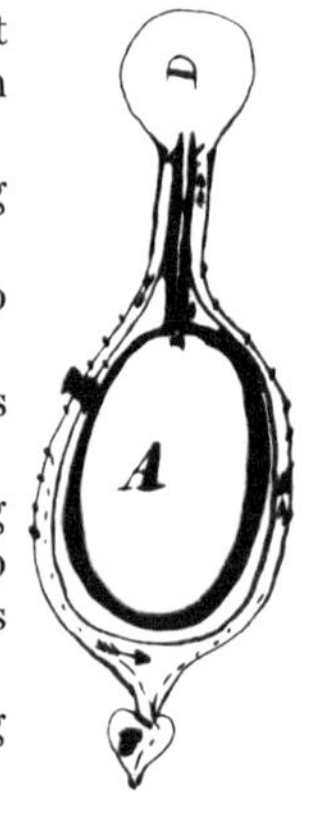

A. The reservoir made of copper in form of an half oval (flat Side next the body) capacity 4 Quarts, with an half inch opening

B The stop cock, inserted in the reservoir, which by turning the handle will emit air in any quantity wanted,

C A tube half inch diameter leading from the Stop cock into the half Globe **D**

D In form of a half Globe capacity 1 pint which closely covers nose & mouth

E a tube 1 inch diameter nearly circular one end commencing at **D**. with a Valve opening downward & the other end also joining **D** with Valve opening upwards having numerous Small holes

F in form of a pair of bellows, joining **E** with 2 Valves opening downwards

Experiment

having provided yourself with a water proof[1] covering, fix the Reservoir upon your breast (being filled with air) & the half Globe closely upon your face, turn the cock **B**. air will rush through the tube **C**. into Globe **D**. which you will inspire & again respire, which air having no other escape will be forced into the tube **E**. where the water coming through the small holes will absorb the carbon, & carry it off through the bellows **F**. by being opened & shut by the hand. the Valves preventing it returning, the air will pass on & be still further robbed of its carbon by the water trickling[2] down & pass through the Valve into the Globe **D** & be again inspired, the quantity of Oxygen therefore wanted will be but $\frac{1}{10}$ from the reservoir of the bulb of each inspiration

MS (DLC: TJ Papers, 207:36847); written entirely in Dyson's hand on both sides of address cover of covering letter; undated.

[1] Manuscript: "proff."
[2] Manuscript: "tricling."

From John P. Boyd

SIR Boston May 7th 1816

Permit me the honour of soliciting your perusal of the enclosd Documents and Facts, relative to the Military conduct of an Officer, who proudly Acknowledges your former patronage.

And has the honor to be with much respect Sir Your Obdt Ob'gd Sert

JNO P. BOYD

RC (MHi); endorsed by TJ as received 16 May 1816 and so recorded in SJL. RC (MHi); address cover only; with PoC of TJ to Charles Willson Peale, 17 Aug. 1816, on verso; addressed: "Thomas Jefferson Esq Virginia"; franked; postmarked Boston, 9 May. Enclosure: Boyd, *Documents and Facts, relative to Military Events, During the Late War* (Boston?, 1816; Poor, *Jefferson's Library*, 5 [no. 163]), in which Boyd, "anxious to vindicate his military character" (p. 1), describes his actions and decisions in 1813, especially during the American defeat at the Battle of Crysler's Farm on 11 Nov., and includes documents to support his assertions of competence.

John Parker Boyd (1764–1830), soldier, was a native of Newburyport, Massachusetts. After serving briefly in the state militia, 1786–87, he became a mercenary soldier in India in the service of native rulers allied with the British, in recognition of which the British government awarded him £6,000 in 1819. After Boyd returned to the United States in 1798, he resided in Boston and engaged in international trade and in land speculation in Maine. In 1808 TJ appointed him a colonel in command of the 4th Infantry Regiment, United States Army, and in 1811 he was second in command during the American victory at the Battle of Tippecanoe. Boyd was promoted to brigadier general at the start of the War of 1812 and charged with the defense of Boston. In 1813 he was assigned to western New York and subsequently assisted in the capture of Fort George, a British post in Upper Canada. Boyd's role later that year in the American defeat at the Battle of Crysler's Farm effectively concluded his active command duties, and he was discharged when the army was reduced in size shortly after the war ended. President Andrew Jackson appointed Boyd in 1830 the naval officer for the district of Boston and Charlestown, Massachusetts (*ANB*; *DAB*; Ronald Rosner, "John Parker Boyd: The Yankee Mughal," *Asian Affairs* 34 [2003]: 297–309; Thomas C. Hansard, comp., *The Parliamentary Debates* [London, 1812–20], 40:1416–9 [28 June 1819]; *The Boston Directory* [Boston, 1803], 23; John F. Sprague, "General John Parker Boyd and Judge Henry Orne, the Original

Proprietors of the Town of Orneville, Maine," *Sprague's Journal of Maine History* 1 [1913]: 43–7; Boston *New-England Palladium*, 17 Mar. 1807; Heitman, *U.S. Army*, 1:236; *JEP*, 2:97, 103, 107, 299, 302, 4:46, 79–80 [25 Jan., 2 Feb. 1809, 9, 10 Nov. 1812, 14 Jan., 24 Mar. 1830]; *Boston Courier*, 7 Oct. 1830).

From Isaac Briggs, with Postscript by Mary B. Briggs

MY DEAR FRIEND, Wilmington, 5mo–7–1816. (Delaware)

Thy kind favor, of Apr 17. 16, had been forwarded from Brookeville to this place, my present residence, during a second journey I have made to Washington City. I returned yesterday.

While in the Metropolis, I conceived an expectation, which[1] still exists, of an employment either in the survey of the line between the United States and the British possessions, from the source of St Croix to the river St Lawrence, or in the Survey of the coast—Or if these surveys should be so organised as to place the scientific operations under the special direction of one person to be stationed at some central point, to and from which the communication would be easy; this director to receive the notes and make all the calculations and maps—at my age, I should prefer such a station, leaving to younger men the more active and laborious operations of tracing lines and measuring bases, of taking angles and making astronomical observations. By the time this letter reaches thee, I expect our friend James Madison will be at Montpelier, I should be glad if thou and he could converse on the subject, and what you think best for me, that do—what you think best for our country, I am sure you will do.

I thank thee feelingly for thy wishes to engage me in the survey of Virginia—the circumstance of its bringing me often near to thee in body as I always am in mind, inclines me to it strongly; but whatever thou dost for me, I believe I shall think best.

I wish much for a careful examination of the ground between the nearest waters of James River and of the Cheat River—and between the nearest waters of the Potomak and of the Monongahela, as to its level, with a view to a future navigation across the Alegany mountains. I believe most firmly such a navigation is practicable, and that the consequences of it would be of great national importance.

I will consider with my best attention thy astronomical problem, and in a future communication, state the result.

My whole family join me in salutations of affectionate regard for our friend and benefactor. ISAAC BRIGGS.

My father has given me permission to add a few lines to his letter by way of Postscript—I joyfully accept it; and with a heart glowing with gratitude & affection I acknowledge the receipt of thy kind & highly-valued favor of 17th Inst. I wish it were possible to express to thee, the gratification,—the happiness it afforded me;—I shall ever prize it, as one of my dearest treasures. For the good wishes it contains—so flattering to my heart,—I feel something which I cannot describe,—a something more than gratitude—and my feelings, for the writer, claim a higher appellation than common esteem & love.

With all the energy of which my warm and grateful heart is capable, I shall ever offer prayers to Heaven for thee!—and with Sentiments of affectionate, regard I am thy friend,

MARY B BRIGGS

RC (DLC); endorsed by TJ as separate letters from Isaac Briggs and Mary B. Briggs received 16 May 1816 and so recorded in SJL. RC (DLC); address cover only; with PoC of TJ to Ashur Ware, 22 Aug. 1816, on verso; addressed by Isaac Briggs: "Thomas Jefferson, Monticello, Virginia"; franked; postmarked Wilmington, Del., 8 May.

Isaac Briggs apparently hoped for federal employment, either to work on the SURVEY OF THE LINE between Maine and British territory in Canada as mandated in Article 5 of the Treaty of Ghent, or to assist with the SURVEY OF THE COAST of the eastern United States as required by "An Act to provide for surveying the coasts of the United States," 10 Feb. 1807 (Miller, *Treaties*, 2:577–8; *U.S. Statutes at Large*, 2:413–4).

[1] Isaac Briggs here canceled "is not."

To Peter Cottom

SIR

Monticello May. 7. 16.

I recieved some time ago a letter from messrs Brooks and Ashley assignees of Bradford & Inskeep an application for the cost of the Portfolio for the year 1814. and lately one from Thomas de Silur as proprietor for the year 1815. percieving however that you are agent in Richmond for that publication, and there being difficulty in remitting small sums to other states, I prefer making the payments to you. I will pray you therefore to call on mr Gibson of the firm of Gibson & Jefferson in Richmond for the two year's payment, and hereafter to call on him annually for the yearly cost while I continue a subscriber, and he will be so kind as to pay the same on sight of this letter. accept the assurance of my respects.

TH: JEFFERSON

PoC (MHi); on verso of reused address cover of Francis Adrian Van der Kemp to TJ, 24 Mar. 1816; at foot of text: "Mr Peter Cottom"; endorsed by TJ.

The missing January 1815 LETTER from Samuel Brooks and Thomas Astley is recorded in SJL as a communication from "Brooks & Ashley" received 13 Apr.

1815 from Philadelphia. The ONE from Thomas Desilver to TJ of 18 Apr. 1816, not found, is recorded in SJL as written by "De Silur Thos" and received 3 May 1816 from Philadelphia. The YEARLY COST of the monthly *Port Folio* was $6 (Philadelphia *Poulson's American Daily Advertiser*, 27 Feb. 1815; *Prospectus of the Port Folio* [Philadelphia, 1809], 11; *MB*, 2:1337).

To John F. Dumoulin

SIR Monticello May. 7. 16.

Your favor of Apr. 12. is just recieved, and with it the two copies of your treatise on Naturalization and Allegiance: the one of which has been delivered, as you requested, to Col° Randolph; and for the other be pleased to accept my thanks. from a cursory view, I promise myself great pleasure in reading it, as well from it's logic as it's learning. on these subjects we cannot but think alike; and I permit myself to doubt whether there is a man in the world who thinks otherwise; provided he has thought at all on the subject, has turned inwardly on himself, and ascertained whether he has not there found the same innate feeling of right to live on the outside of an artificial geographical line as he has to live[1] within it: whether he finds there any stronger sentiment of right to use his own faculties at all, than of that to use them in whatever place he can do it to the greatest promotion of his own happiness; whether he feels any obligation to die by disease or famine in one country, rather than go to another where he can live?

The family accepts with thankfulness the kind expressions of your remembrance of them, and joins me in assuring you that we considered ourselves as the debtors for the visit you did us the favor to make the last autumn, and in assurances of great esteem and respect.

TH: JEFFERSON

PoC (DLC); on verso of reused address cover of Levin Gale to TJ, 30 Mar. 1816; at foot of text: "Mr J. F. DuMoulin"; endorsed by TJ. Tr (NHi: Albert Gallatin Papers); entirely in Dumoulin's hand; with full address presumably copied from missing RC: "mr J: F: Dumoulin pensylvania Avenue Washington"; subjoined to Dumoulin to Gallatin, 28 May 1817.

[1] Preceding two words not in Tr.

To Levin Gale

SIR Monticello May 7. 16.

Your favor of Mar. 30. came during an absence from home of considerable length, and the box of vine cuttings arrived soon after, in excellent order, and were immediately planted. I hope they will do well, as, judging from a sample of wine made from this grape and sent to me formerly by Maj^r Adlam, I expect to be gratified with the great desideratum of making at home a good wine. his was certainly equal to the best Burgundy I have ever seen; and they were tried together at the same time. the grape too, being native, is therefore preferable to anyone yet to be imported, acclimated, and tried with us. Accept my thanks for your kind attention to this object, and the assurances of my respect and esteem. TH: JEFFERSON

PoC (MHi); on verso of reused address cover of José Corrêa da Serra to TJ, 29 Mar. 1816; at foot of text: "Mr Levin Gale"; endorsed by TJ.

The VINE CUTTINGS were of the Alexander GRAPE (TJ to John Adlum, 13 Jan. 1816, and note).

From William Short

DEAR SIR Philadelphia May 7.—16

In consequence of an understanding between M^r H: & myself, that I would inclose to you his bond & mortgage,[1] when the payment was completed, I now take the liberty of inclosing his last bond & the mortgage—I have been informed by Mr Gibson that he has recieved for me from the agent of Mr H. at Richmond $170, being the sum to which this last bond was reduced by the deduction of the 68. acres—This affair is thus terminated—I cannot put the last hand to it without again renewing my thanks for all the trouble which you have been so good as to submit to in it for me, & which I can assure has made the proper impression on my mind—I must add also my hope that you will excuse this last liberty which I shall take in it, that of inclosing to you these two papers for M^r H.

I had the pleasure of writing to you on the 23. ul^to. That letter will await your return to Monticello, where I hope this will find you in good health.

The papers mention the appointment to the consulship at Paris, of the late incumbent at Havre—This removes one obstacle from the path of poor la Motte—& I observe also that an old incumbent at Cowes, I think, Mr Auldjo, who is an Englishman, is reappointe[d]—This would be an example or authorization also for la Motte—As I do not see his name however among the new appointments, I fear our Lord of the ascendant does not mean to take him up. This is strange & passing strange, as you have had the goodness to interest yourself in his behalf—I have been much tempted to write myself & urge the just claims of this old & faithful servant—but I take for granted that other motives must govern at Washington in such cases—I doubt whether my letter would produce any good effect with Mon: & I fear it would produce a bad effect with Mad:—I have never been rectus in curia with the latter since, on my first return from Europe, instead of subscribing to and confirming one [of][2] his fine dreams, that the Directory were a quintette of good honest souls—purely republican, & above all things desirous to be kind & affectionate to this sister Republic, I scouted the vision & assured him that they were really & bona fide, most consummate villains & having no other idea than power & plunder—Mad's idea was to me so new & so absurd & fell on me so abruptly that I probably betrayed some kind of ridiculing sneer, without intending me—but l'amour propre blessé seldom forgets & never forgives—so I must submit to the penalty of my inadvertence.

Under all circumstances & at all times believe me, dear sir, most sincerely & perfectly yours W: SHORT

RC (MHi); edge trimmed; endorsed by TJ as received 16 May 1816 and so recorded in SJL. RC (DLC); address cover only; with PoC of TJ to George Flower, 18 Aug. 1816, on verso; addressed: "Thomas Jefferson Monticello" by "mail to Milton Va"; franked; postmarked Philadelphia, 7 May.

MR H: David Higginbotham. For the enclosed BOND and MORTGAGE, see TJ to Short, 10 Feb. 1813, the enclosure printed there, and notes to both documents. On 20 Apr. 1816 the United States Senate confirmed the appointment of Isaac Cox Barnet to the CONSULSHIP AT PARIS and of Thomas AULDJO to that at Cowes, England (*JEP*, 3:43, 46 [16, 20 Apr. 1816]). Auldjo had previously served as vice-consul at the port of Poole, but the British government had allowed him to reside at Cowes (*PTJ*, 19:316). The LORD OF THE ASCENDANT was Secretary of State James Monroe (MON:), whom many correctly expected to succeed James Madison (MAD:) as president of the United States.

RECTUS IN CURIA: "free from charge or offense" (*Black's Law Dictionary*). Short's FIRST RETURN to the United States occurred in 1802. His conversation with James Madison about the French revolutionary DIRECTORY may have occurred in September 1802, when both men were guests at Monticello (*PTJ*, 38:400–1). L'AMOUR PROPRE BLESSÉ: "wounded self-esteem."

[1] Manuscript: "mortgge."
[2] Omitted word editorially supplied.

From Jean David

MONSIEUR Richmond le 8 mai 1816—

Je prends la liberté de vous adresser quelques ecrits que j'ai faits depuis que je Suis dans les Etats unis d'amerique ils Sont relatifs a La prosperité de ce pays.[1] Je les crois basés Sur les vrais principes de l'economie politique et de la justice. S'ils Sont tels ils peuvent être utiles à votre patrie. vous êtes mieux à même que tout autre de juger de leur merite. c'est ce qui m'a porté a vous les communiquer avant de quitter ce pays. Je souhaite que vous les trouviez dignes de votre suffrage

Je dois vous prevenir que ces divers ecrits ont été precedemment adressés à M[r] Le President des Etats unis, datés de Richmond et Signés un francais. Je les ai ensuite communiqués à Mr Girardin, il les a lus, (je crois) il m'en a fait l'eloge, peut être par politesse, mais il n'en a rien extrait pour inserer dans Sa Gazette, Soit qu'il ne les estime gueres on qu'il n'ait pas cru convenable de les produire. peut être aussi que Mr Girardin qui est un homme d'esprit très instruit et plein de connoissances, n'en a-t-il pas beaucoup en politique et en finance

quant à M[r] Le President des Etats unis, j'ignore S'il les a reçus et le cas qu'il en a fait Sur Le tout je n'ai pas voulu quitter ce pays Sans vous en presenter l'hommage. J'y parle peut être un peu trop librement et d'une maniére trop tranchante, mais qu'importe! Si les principes en Sont vrais et les consequences justes, C'est là l'essentiel. la façon dont une chose est dite me paroit alors assez indifferente.

J'ai eu l'honneur de vous ecrire le premier du mois de fevrier je vous entretenois de nouveau de lutilité de la culture de la vigne et j'avois joint à ma lettre un projet de petition au gouvernement, je reviendrai d'autant moins Sur Son contenu que devant partir incessamment celá Seroit tout a fait inutile. Cependant je Serois bien aise de Savoir Si ma lettre du 1er fevrier et surtout celle de ce jour vous Sont parvenues. Je vous Serois infiniment obligé Si vous vouliez dire un mot à ce Sujet à Mr Girardin lorsque vous lui ecrirez, car je pense que vous êtes en correspondance avec lui, et devant correspondre moi même avec Mr Girardin, j'aurai beaucoup de plaisir à être instruit par lui Si vous avez reçu mes deux lettres

Je vous Salue respectueusement D——

EDITORS' TRANSLATION

SIR Richmond, 8 May 1816—

I take the liberty of addressing to you a few things I have written since my arrival in the United States of America. They concern the prosperity of this country. I believe them to be based on the true principles of political economy and justice. If so, they may be useful to your homeland. You are in a better position than anyone else to judge their merit. This is what led me to communicate them to you before leaving this country. I hope that you will find them worthy of your approval

I must warn you that these various writings, dated at Richmond and signed a Frenchman, have been previously sent to the president of the United States. After that, I directed them to Mr. Girardin. He read them (I believe) and praised them, perhaps out of politeness, but he did not choose any passages for insertion in his newspaper, either because he does not value them or did not think it appropriate to publish them. It may also be that Mr. Girardin, who is a very educated and knowledgeable man, is not well-versed in politics and finance

As for the president of the United States, I do not know whether he has received them or what he thinks of them. I did not want to leave this country without offering them to you as a token of my esteem. In them I may speak a little too freely and in too cutting a manner, but what does it matter! If the principles therein are true and the consequences just, that is the main thing. In such a case, I feel that the way in which something is expressed is rather irrelevant.

On the first of February I had the honor of writing again to you about the usefulness of the cultivation of vineyards, and I enclosed with my letter a draft petition to the government. As I must leave soon, it would be quite useless to repeat its contents. I would be very pleased, however, to know if my letter of 1 February and, especially, the one I am sending you today have reached you. I would be most obliged to you if you could say a word on this subject to Mr. Girardin when you write to him, as I understand that he is a correspondent of yours. Since I need to correspond with Mr. Girardin myself, I would be very happy to learn from him whether you have received my two letters

I salute you respectfully D——

RC (DLC); with first enclosure on third and fourth pages of sheet folded to form four pages; at head of text: "Mr Ths Jefferson Monticello"; endorsed on last page of first enclosure as a letter from "David" received 13 May 1816 and so recorded (with added first initial "J") in SJL. Translation by Dr. Genevieve Moene.

David's letter to PRESIDENT James Madison was dated 22 Apr. 1816 (DLC: Madison Papers). Louis H. GIRARDIN published the *Daily Compiler and Richmond Commercial Register* from as early as 6 May 1815 until May 1816 and the Richmond *Virginia Argus* from 3 Feb. to 19 Oct. 1816 (Brigham, *American Newspapers*, 2:1137, 1142–3).

[1] Preceding three words interlined.

ENCLOSURES

I

Jean David's Memorandum on Treaties of Commerce

Sur les traités de commerce—fait en Decembre 1815—

un traité de commerce entre deux peuples ne m'a jamais paru être qu'un traité de Guerre, je veux dire un Sujet une occasion de Guerre attendu qu'un des deux peuples y est toujours la dupe de l'autre

Pourquoi donc faire un parait traité qui ne Sert qu'a nous donner des entraves. restons toujours les maitres de changer a notre gré nos droits de Douane et nos relations commerciales. S'il convient a deux nations de commercer ensemble, elles le fairont bien Sans qu'il existe de traité pour cet objet. un des meilleurs moyens de conserver la paix avec toutes les nations c'est de les traiter toutes egalement.

Mais outre ce motif majeur il en est un autre plus relatif à la chose même. C'est que moins vous mettrez de restrictions dans vos liaisons avec les etrangers en faveur de quelques uns d'eux, mieux vous Serez traités chez touts, plus ils abonderont dans vos ports, et plus votre commerce fleurira; de sorte que tout commande à une nation Sage de ne point faire de pareils traités.

Ces Sortes de traités ne conviennent qu'a l'angleterre qui n'existant que par le commerce et ne pouvant exister telle qu'elle est que par lui et par la guerre qui lui fournit le pretexte et les moyens d'avoir Sur pied une marine formidable Superieure à celle de toute l'Europe reunie, a tourné toutes Ses vues de ce coté. pour toutes les autres ils ne Sont bons qu'a leur nüire et a devenir pour elles ainsi que je l'ai dit plus haut un Sujet de guerre.

EDITORS' TRANSLATION

On treaties of commerce—composed in December 1815—

A treaty of commerce between two nations never seemed to me to be anything but a treaty of war, by which I mean a cause or an occasion for war, given that one of the two nations is always the dupe of the other

Why then make a treaty that only shackles us? Let us always remain free to change as we like our customs duties and commercial relations. If it suits two nations to trade with each other, they will do just as well without the existence of a treaty for this purpose. One of the best ways to preserve peace with every nation is to treat them all equally.

But besides this primary reason, another is more closely related to the thing itself. The fewer restrictions you place on your relations with foreigners by favoring some of them, the better you will be treated by all of them; the more they will frequent your ports; and the more your commerce will flourish. Everything, therefore, commands a wise nation to avoid such treaties.

These kinds of treaties are only suitable for England. Existing only through commerce and surviving as she does only through that and the wars that provide her with the pretext and means to maintain a formidable navy superior to that of all of Europe put together, England has turned all of her designs in that direction. For every other nation such treaties succeed only in inflicting harm and becoming, as I said above, a cause of war.

MS (DLC: TJ Papers, 207:36854); entirely in David's hand; partially dated; with covering letter on first and second pages of sheet folded to form four pages. Translation by Dr. Genevieve Moene.

II

Jean David's First Memorandum on American Banks

Sur les Banques des Etats unis d'Amerique—N° 1—8bre 1815

Lorsqu'une fois on a commencé à manquer à Ses obligations et par consequent à S'ecarter de la justice, il n'est aucune sorte d'abus qui ne puissent naitre de cette premiére faute. C'est ce qui est resulté de l'acte illegal par lequel presque toutes les Banques des Etats Unis ont decidé de ne plus payer leurs bills en espéces, ainsi qu'elles y etoient obligeés par leurs chartes, et par l'enoncé même de leurs bills.

J'avoue que cette mesure prise et executée Sans obstacle, dans un pays libre et qui Se vante de tenir dune maniére Sacrée à Ses engagements, m'a Surpris à un point inexprimable.

Je Sais qu'on a mis en avant quelques raisons plausibles pour pallier cette mesure, comme S'il pouvoit y en avoir quelqu'une qui autorisat à manquer à Ses engagements et à Sa foi publique; mais ces raisons tout injustes qu'elles Seroient quand même elles auroient operé le bien qu'on en attendoit, etoient encore mauvaises, puisque cet acte illègal, par la degradation du change qui en est resulté, tend à la ruine du Commerce.

quoi qu'il en soit, il ne s'agit plus aujourd'hui de raisonner Sur ce qu'on a fait, mais bien Sur ce qu'il convient de faire pour arreter le mal, qui va et ira toujours croissant, Si l'on n'y apporte un prompt remede:

on dit que les Banques S'occupent en ce moment des moyens de recommencer à payer en numeraire; je ne puis croire qu'elles y pensent Serieusement à moins de vouloir entierement Se perdre. elles ont fait une grande faute en cessant de payer en argent, elles en feroient une plus grande encore en recommençant le payement[.] la chose est impossible, et je le repete, je ne crois pas qu'elles y pensent Serieusement.

quel moyen y a-t-il donc, de reprimer l'agiotage et les inconvenients majeurs attachés à l'etat actuel des choses?—le voici—

C'est que toutes les Banques des Etats unis, (je dis les banques autoriseés par le gouvernement car je ne reconnois pas Les autres.) recoivent les bills les unes des autres et tiennent compte de leur montant, dans le pays ou elles Se trouvent et Sans aucune perte, à ceux qui les deposent chez elles. par ce moyen on detruira l'agiotage qui entrave le commerce et ruine les citoyens.

Mais dira-t-on; il y aura des Banques auxquelles il Sera du par d'autres des Sommes considerables; comment celles ci pourront elle[s] S'acquiter?

Par le même moyen et de la même maniére que le font les particuliers entre eux, lequel Se reduit en derniére analyse, à envoyer à celui à qui l'on doit, ou de l'argent ou de la marchandise

Mais celle mesure occasionera de la perte à certaines Banques! eh qui doit mieux supporter cette perte que ceux qui y ont donn[é] occasion par un acte arbitraire et illegal

Au reste le moyen que j'indique ici seroit, par Ses consequences, extrêmement avantageux aux banques. Si elles l'adoptent elles peuven[t] esperer de Se maintenir, Si non leur perte est inevitable car tr[ès] certainement le Gouvernement prendra des mesures pour obvier à Ces abus, et le Seul qu'il puisse employer, qui est detablir une banque nationale dont les bills auront cours dans touts les Etats unis, portera le coup de mort à toutes les banques particuliéres.

Le Gouvernement peut d'autant moins negliger d'adopter cette mesure, qu'il est inoui que jamais un Gouvernement ait existé, sans une monnoie réelle ou fictive, et cependant celui ci n'en a point puisqu'il donne et reçoit en payement comme monnoie, des bills des banques particuliéres. il est vrai qu'il est censé que ces bills Sont de l'argent, puisqu'il est dit qu'ils doivent être remboursés en argent au porteur! Lorsque reellement les Banques donnoient de l'argent à ceux qui en demandoient, la chose pouvoit être vraie, mais à present c'est une derision, puisque grace à l'acte illegal qu'elles Se Sont permises, la monnoie effective gagne jusques à vingt pour cent.—

Quant aux moyens d'améliorer le change avec l'etranger; il en est deux principaux.—

Le Premier est d'etablir une Banque nationale qui prendra l'engagement Solemnel de rembourser, dans touts les temps, Ses bills en numeraire effectif. cette mesure doit faire renaitre peu à peu la confiance Si necessaire chez une nation commerçante.

Le Second qui, j'ose le dire, est encore plus essentiel, est, que la balance du commerce des etats unis avec l'etranger, Soit en Sa faveur; c'est à dire que la Somme des exportations, excede celle des importations; Sans celà, plus on faira de commerce, et plus la nation S'appauvrira; car il faut necessairement payer Ses dettes. on commencera donc par lui enlever Son numeraire, ensuite Ses denrées même celles de premiére necessité, ce qui les faira hausser prodigieusement de prix, et produira dans les villes de commerce, et chez les fabriquants et les manouvriers un mecontentement general.

Les etrangers qui vous enleveront ces marchandises à des prix elevés, vous fairont necessairement payer les leurs à des prix exhorbitants; des faillites nombreuses auront lieu, la confiance Se perdra, et qui peut alors calculer jusqu'ou le mecontentement general pourroit Se porter, surtout s'il Survenoit une guerre etrangére.—

Sans doute qu'un Gouvernement Sage prudent et ferme, peut, en prenant à temps les mesures convenables, prevenir d'aussi funestes effets. Les moyens à employer Seroient trop long à deduire ici. J'ai indiqué les causes du mal, les remedes doivent être appliqués Suivant le temperament du malade; c'est à ceux qui le connoissent à fond, à le faire avec prudence et Sagesse.—

EDITORS' TRANSLATION

On the Banks of the United States of America—Number 1—October 1815

Once one starts failing to meet one's obligations and consequently deviating from the law, any abuse can flow from this primary transgression. This is what resulted from the illegal act by which almost all the banks in the United States decided to stop paying their bills in specie, as they were obliged to do by their charters and under the terms of their bills.

I confess that this measure, which was taken and executed without hindrance in a free country that boasts of holding its commitments sacred, surprised me inexpressibly.

I know that a few plausible reasons have been advanced to justify this measure, as if any reason could excuse the failure to keep one's engagements and the public faith. But these unfair reasons, even if they brought about the good expected from them, would still be bad, since this illegal act, through the degradation of trade resulting from it, tends to ruin commerce.

Be that as it may, the present need is certainly to stop debating past actions and, rather, to determine what can appropriately be done to arrest the evil that is and always will be increasing if we do not provide a prompt remedy:

At this moment the banks are said to be busy finding ways to resume paying in cash. I cannot believe that they are seriously considering this unless they wish to disappear completely. They made a big mistake by ceasing to pay in specie, and they would make an even bigger one by resuming payment. It is impossible, and I repeat that I do not believe they are seriously considering it.

How, then, do we repress speculation and the major disadvantages associated with the actual state of affairs?—Here is the answer—

All the banks in the United States (I mean the banks authorized by the government, because I do not recognize the others) should accept bills from each other at their own locations and keep track of their amounts, without any loss to those who deposit them there. This will destroy speculation, which impedes commerce and ruins citizens.

It will be said, however, that some banks will owe considerable sums to other ones. How will they be able to discharge these debts?

Through the same means and in the same way employed between individuals, which in the final analysis boils down to sending the person to whom a debt is owed either money or merchandise

But this measure will cause a loss to certain banks! Well, who is in a better position to bear this loss than the ones who caused it by an arbitrary and illegal act?

In any case the means that I advocate here would prove to be extremely advantageous to the banks. If they adopt it, they may hope to survive. If they do not, their ruin is inevitable, because the government will most certainly take measures to prevent these abuses, and the only measure open to it, the establishment of a national bank whose bills will be legal tender in the whole United States, would be fatal to all the private banks.

Neither can the government neglect adopting this measure. No known government ever existed without a currency, real or fictional, and yet this government does not have one, as it gives and receives bills from private banks as payment. It is true that these bills are assumed to be money, in that it is said they must be reimbursed in money to the bearer! When the banks actually gave money to those who asked for it, this might have been true, but now it is a charade, since thanks to the illegal act they allowed themselves to perform, the value of hard currency has increased by up to twenty percent.—

There are two principal means to improve our trade with foreign countries.

The first is to establish a national bank that will solemnly swear to reimburse, at all times, its bills in hard cash. This measure must gradually renew the trust so necessary in a commercial nation.

The second, which, I dare say, is even more essential, is that the balance of trade between the United States and foreign nations must be in its favor; that is to say, the sum of its exports must exceed the sum of its imports. Until this is true, the more commerce there is, the poorer the nation will become, because a positive balance is absolutely necessary to pay the nation's debts. Without one, its currency will first be taken away, followed by its products, even the essential ones, which will cause prices to rise prodigiously. In commercial towns this will give rise to a general dissatisfaction among the manufacturers and factory workers.

Foreigners, who will remove these goods at elevated prices, will inevitably charge exorbitantly for theirs. Numerous bankruptcies will take place; trust will vanish; and who can imagine how far the general discontent will lead, particularly if a foreign war were to occur.—

A wise, prudent, and firm government can certainly take suitable and timely measures that would prevent such disastrous effects. It would take too long to explain the means to be employed. I have indicated the roots of the disease. The remedies must be applied according to the patient's constitution. It falls to those who know it thoroughly to do so with prudence and wisdom.—

MS (DLC: TJ Papers, 207:36855–6); entirely in David's hand; partially dated; edge trimmed. Translation by Dr. Genevieve Moene.

III

Jean David's Second Memorandum on American Banks

Sur les Banques des Etats unis—N° 2—avril 1816.[1]—

Le Congrés vient de décréter l'etablissement d'une Banque nationale, cette mesure etoit indispensable pour detruire l'agiotage scandaleux qui existe Sur les bills des differentes Banques.[2] Mais remediera-t-elle au discredit du change avec l'etranger?[3]

J'oserois presque assurer qu'elle n'y apportera aucun changement, et que le mal ira toujours croissant comme il auroit été Sans cette mesure, jusqu'a ce que par la ruine d'un grand nombre de negociants[4] et de Banques le Commerce de ce pays ait eprouvé une crise qui l'ait placé dans la Situation où il doit être.

Deux causes principales contribuent au discredit du change avec l'etranger.

Le luxe qui vous rend Ses tributaires pour des Sommes enormes;

Et la quantité prodigieuse de banques qui existent dans les Etats unis, lesquelles en facilitant les operations commerciales Sont cause que l'on fait trop d'affaires.[5]

on ne doit pas juger du present et de l'avenir par le passé. Depuis l'epoque de la revolution francaise, jusqu'a la guerre qui a eu lieu entre les Etats unis et[6] l'angleterre en 1812, le pavillon americain etoit presque le Seul qui naviguât[7] librement. alors l'amerique n'ayant pas des capitaux Suffisants pour tout le commerce que les circonstances lui permettoient de faire, il etoit convenable de créer beaucoup de Banques pour en faciliter les operations. Mais ce qui etoit un bien alors, est devenu un grand mal depuis que le commerce des Etats unis a considerablement diminué, d'abord par l'effet de la derniére guerre et ensuite par la tranquilité de l'Europe—

aujourd'hui toutes les nations etant en paix et touts les pavillons pouvant naviguer librement, les americains Sont necessairement reduits a leur propre commerce, qui Sera très peu de chose en comparaison de celui qu'ils faisoient precedemment. en consequence Si le gouvernement veut prevenir la ruine totale des negociants, et je dirai même de l'Etat, il doit prendre le plutot possible les mesures convenables à ce Sujet. Voici celles qui me paroissent indispensables.—

Il faut Supprimer toutes les Banques particuliéres et qu'il n'y ait plus que la Banque nationale que l'on vient de décréter.

que cette Banque ait une Seule succursale dans chaque ville des Etats unis que ces succursales excomptent avec beaucoup de reserve qu'elles ne mettent des bank notes[8] en emission que pour un quart ou une demi au plus, du numeraire qu'elles ont[9] dans leurs caves—

et qu'elles payent en numeraire effectif toutes les fois qu'on l'exigera. Par ce moyen la masse des affaires diminuera considerablement et elles deviendront plus lucratives. peu à peu la confiance renaitra, le change avec l'etranger Se bonifiera, pourra venir au pair et peut etre même gagner.

il y auroit peut être un moyen plus Simple à employer.[10] ce Seroit de Supprimer toutes les Banques, et que les particulier[s] payassent eux mêmes leurs engagements en espéces; mais ce remede violent pourroit devenir dangereux; c'est a l'assemblée du congrès a juger le quel de ces deux moyens est preferable, mais il doit necessairement adopter l'un ou l'autre, s'il ne le fait pas le commerce S'appauvrira touts les jours, jusqu'a ce que le discredit etant porté à Son comble, une banqueroute generale aura lieu, et alors il est impossible de prevoir jusqu'ou le mal pourra Se porter.

aujourd'hui Je considere l'Etat comme un malade en danger mais qui cependant a encore assez de force pour supporter les remedes necessaires pour Sa guerison; Si on neglige de les lui administrer il est à craindre qu'il ne perisse.—

Je reviens aux[11] moyens de Bonifier le change avec l'etranger. il faut augmenter les droits de Douane Sur toutes les marchandises etrangéres et les porter S'il est possible à cent pour cent de leur valeur

il faut favoriser encourager dans les etats unis la culture et la fabrication de toutes les denrées et[12] marchandises que les etrangers leur fournissent[13]

il faut mettre des taxes considerables Sur tout ce qui Sert au luxe comme chevaux, voitures, domestiques &c[a] car le luxe poussé à l'excés comme il l'est dans ce pays, corrompt les mœurs et ruine les citoyens—

Je pense que par ces moyens reunis on preservera l'Etat de la crise terrible dont il est menacé.—

EDITORS' TRANSLATION

On the Banks of the United States—Number 2—April 1816.—

Congress has just ordered the establishment of a national bank. This measure was indispensable to put an end to the scandalous speculation in the bills of the different banks. But will it remedy the poor rate of exchange in your foreign trade?

I would almost dare to guarantee that it will change nothing and that the problem will get progressively worse, as it would have without this measure, until, through the ruin of many merchants and banks, commerce in this country endures a crisis that will put it in the position it deserves.

Two principal causes contribute to the poor rate of exchange in your foreign trade.

Luxury that drains away enormous sums from you;

And the prodigious quantity of banks that exist in the United States, which, by facilitating commercial operations, are the cause of too much business.

One must not judge the present and future by the past. From the time of the French Revolution until the war that took place between the United States and England in 1812, the American flag was almost the only one that sailed freely. Because America then lacked sufficient capital for all the commerce that circumstances allowed it to have, it was appropriate to create many banks to facilitate operations. But what was good then has become very bad since commerce in the United States has decreased considerably, first through the effects of the last war and then by the tranquillity of Europe—

Today, with all nations at peace and all flags able to sail freely, Americans are necessarily reduced to their own commerce, which will be very small compared to what preceded it. In consequence, if the government wishes to prevent the complete ruin of the merchants, and I would even say the state, it must, as soon as possible, take suitable measures on this subject. These seem indispensable to me.—

All private banks must be suppressed, leaving only the national bank that was just created by decree.

This bank must have only one branch in each city in the United States. These branches need to exercise great restraint in discounting. They must issue banknotes for only a quarter or, at most, half of the currency they have in their cellars—

And they must pay in hard currency whenever it is demanded. This will decrease the volume of business considerably, and it will become more profitable. Little by little, trust will return, foreign trade will improve and may become balanced, and exports may even exceed imports.

It might perhaps be simpler to suppress all banks and have individuals pay their commitments directly in specie. But this violent remedy could become dangerous. Congress will have to decide which of these means is preferable, but it must necessarily adopt one or the other. If it does not, commerce will become poorer every day, until the failure to extend credit peaks and a general bankruptcy takes place, at which point no one can predict how badly things will go.

Today, I consider the state to be dangerously ill, but it still has strength enough to bear the remedies necessary for its cure. If they are neglected, it is to be feared that it will perish.—

I return to the means of improving foreign trade. Duties on all foreign goods must be increased, to one hundred percent of their value if possible

The cultivation and manufacture of all commodities and merchandise that are currently provided by foreigners must be encouraged in the United States

Every luxury, such as horses, coaches, servants, etc., must be taxed heavily, because luxury pushed to an extreme, as it is in this country, corrupts morals and ruins citizens—

I believe that a combination of all these measures will protect the state from the terrible crisis that threatens it.—

MS (DLC: TJ Papers, 207:36857–8); entirely in David's hand; partially dated; edge trimmed. Translation by Dr. Genevieve Moene.

David enclosed a similar memorandum in his 22 Apr. 1816 letter to James Madison (both in DLC: Madison Papers).

The Second Bank of the United States (BANQUE NATIONALE) was established on 10 Apr. 1816 by "An Act to incorporate the subscribers to the Bank of the United States" (*U.S. Statutes at Large*, 3:266–77).

[1] Memorandum number and date not in Madison MS.

[2] Madison MS: "Sur les Bank notes des differentes places" ("in the banknotes of different places").

[3] Manuscript: "letranger."

[4] Madison MS: "la ruine entiére des negociants" ("the total ruin of the merchants").

[5] Madison MS here adds "ce qui tend à la ruine du commerce" ("which leads to the ruin of commerce").

[6] Madison MS substitutes "avec" ("with") for preceding five words.

[7] Madison MS: "put naviguer" ("could sail").

[8] Preceding three words interlined.

[9] Madison MS: "auront" ("will have").

[10] Preceding two words not in Madison MS.

[11] Madison MS here adds "autres" ("other").

[12] Madison MS substitutes "ces mêmes" ("these same") for preceding four words.

[13] Preceding five words not in Madison MS.

To Charles Willson Peale

DEAR SIR Monticello. May 8. 16.

I am indebted to you for two letters yet unacknoledged, to wit of June 18. and Dec. 23. 15. I pay three or four visits a year to a very distant possession I have in Bedford, where, being comfortably fixed, I pass a month or two at a time, so that it is almost a second home. it is in the finest part of our state for soil & climate, and near to Lynchburg; now the 2d town in the state for business, and thriving with a rapidity exceeding any thing we have ever seen. when I first visited that place 50 years ago, there was nothing but a ferry house. it may be considered as the out-port of Richmond, recieving all the produce of the S. Western quarter of our state, and of the upper part of N. Carolina, & transmitting it down the river 130 miles to Richmond. it furnishes me therefore good society while in that neighborhood. these absences must apologize for my tardy acknolegements of your letters.

In that of June 18. you promised yourself to visit Dr Allison's improvements in the small family machines for spinning. he published a drawing & description of one in the Emporium [wh]ich spun from the roll, & saved the intermediate operation of roving, which is $\frac{1}{3}$ of the labor. I formed a good opinion of it and wrote him a letter on the subject, which he kindly answered. if you have seen it work, I should like to know how it answers. and can you tell me how Janes's loom is approved in practice? it promised well. I concur with you in doubting whether the great establishments, by associated companies, are advantageous in this country. it is the houshold manufacture which is really precious; because the same children are employed in them, under the eye & care of their parents, where they are more correctly brought up, and have better opportunities of healthy exercise. this however is for coarse, and midling goods only. for the finest fabrics, we must depend on the associated establishments, or on foreign countries. this last has many serious inconveniences.—the fruit gatherer you describe I was in possession of, a little varied only in it's construction.—Dr Logan's drill is too complicated. I do not think it comparable to Martin's, which any carpenter can make. as yet it has been made to sow one row at a time only; but I am sure I can make it sow a breadth of 3.f. at a time in rows of what interval you please. it opens the furrow, sows the seed & covers it, & may be drawn by the weakest draught animal which can be used. in a former letter I mentioned to you that I had adapted a hemp break to my sawmill, which did good work. I have since fixed one to my threshing machine in Bedford, which breaks & beats about 80.℔ a day with a single horse. the horizontal horsewheel of the threshing machine drives a wallower and shaft, at the outer end of which shaft is a crank which lifts a common hemp-break the head of which is made heavy enough to break the hemp with it's knives, & to beat it with it's head. we suffer much here for want of nice workmen. the screws of the pencases of my polygraph are worn, so that I can with difficulty regulate the pressure of the off-pen: and we have no artist who can repair them.[1] we suffer in like manner[2] in our clocks & watches, being obliged to send the latter always to Richmond for repairs (75 miles) and the former being at rest for years sometimes, till some straggling pretender accidentally passes this way to repair or ruin them. yet Charlottesville would be a fine stand for one.[3] I wrote to mr Voigt once to ask of him to persuade one[4] of his young pupils, when turning out, and in quest of a place, to come here. the [popu]lation[5] is thick, & independant, and would furnish abundant employment [for a wat]chmender,[6] clockmaker and silversmith. it is also a very cheap sit[uation.[7] you wou]ld render us a great service by sending on such an one, <u>if sober</u>, he would need nothing but his tools for outfit. he would get an apartment & his board readily on credit, until he could begin to recieve money, which indeed would be immediately: and I would put him into the hands of such persons in Charlottesville as would efficiently patronise him.[8] ever & affectionately yours

Th: Jefferson

PoC (DLC); on reused address cover from Isaac Briggs to TJ; mutilated at seal, with three words rewritten by TJ and missing text toward end of document supplied from Tr; at foot of first page: "Charles W. Peale"; endorsed by TJ. Tr (MHi); extract in TJ's hand in PoC of his 8 Oct. 1816 letter to Joseph E. McIlhenney.

The DRAWING & DESCRIPTION of Burgess Allison's "domestic Machine for spinning wool" appeared in the *Emporium of Arts and Sciences* 1 (1813; Poor, *Jefferson's Library*, 14 [no. 920]): 461–3.

[1] Tr begins here.
[2] Preceding three words not in Tr.
[3] Tr: "for a good workman."
[4] Tr: "to recommend to one."
[5] Tr: "population of the country."
[6] Tr: "watchmaker."
[7] Tr: "a cheap place for articles of subsistence."
[8] Tr ends here.

To John Mackey

Sir Monticello May 9. 16.

I recieved yesterday your letter of May 2. on the 3[d] an anonymous writing had come to hand which bearing the date of Apr. 18 as now[1] mentioned by you, is I presume the paper called for. being anonymous

I knew not to whom to return it. this is now done on the presumption it is yours. I do not meddle in printing any thin[g.] my time of life requires rest of body and mind and that I should withdraw myself from all correspondence which no special duty makes incumbent on me. the existing generation posesses as much wisdom as that which preceded them, and will, I am confident, take as good care of their affairs. the paper inclosed is of their concern, and they will probably do it justice if you chuse to submit it to them. Accept my respec[ts]

TH: JEFFERSON

PoC (MoSHi: TJC-BC); on recto of reused address cover to TJ, with Dft on verso; edge trimmed; at foot of text: "M[r] John Mackey"; endorsed by TJ. Dft (MoSHi: TJC-BC); on verso of PoC; incomplete and canceled; dated Monticello, 10 May 1816, and reading "I recieved the day before yesterday your letter of the 1st inst but that of Apr. 18. which it mentions as having covered MS. views of education has never come to my hands. it may yet come, as these delays by mail sometimes occur. should it be recieved it shall be immediately re-incl."

Mackey's LETTER OF MAY 2. was actually dated 1 May. The enclosed ANONYMOUS WRITING of 18 Apr. 1816 is not recorded in SJL and has not been found.

[1] Word interlined.

To Eusebio Valli

SIR Monticello May 9. 16.

I am much indebted to the much esteemed Seignior Botta for furnishing me the occasion of addressing to you my salutations on your arrival in the United states, and of tendering my portion of the obligations all owe you for the dangers you voluntarily encounter to lessen theirs. while we are striving how best to preserve our own health, you immolate yours as the victim of safety for us. the disease to which you now propose to offer yourself is indeed a formidable one; yet happily of rare occurrence, and of very limited range of time and place. while our own physicians are divided in opinion as to it's contagious character, the unlettered may with less presumption entertain an opinion also. I think you will find, on exact enquiry, that it has never existed with us but in the cities, on tidewaters, beginning always at the water's edge, extending slowly from that, bounded as it advances by a line, which altho invisible but from it's effects, is as well defined as if by a street; that it is incommunicable by persons or goods, or otherwise than by going within the line of infection, never appearing till autumn, and disappearing with the first frost. the sick have often gone into the country, been nursed in the beds of the families there, have died and been buried, without a single well attested fact of the infection being communicated. I say well attested, for you will have insulated facts related to you by those who believe them, but who have not strictly verified them. caution too is requisite to distinguish this from kindred fevers; as other fevers have often been confounded with it. I believe that the true Yellow fever has never been known in these States, South of Alexandria, and as far as that but once. yet physicians have pronounced it to be among the mountains of my own neighborhood. the Southern towns on the seacoast, Norfolk, Charleston, New Orleans, have every autumn among them what has been called the Stranger's fever, which I have known for 60. years. it formerly prevailed as far up into the country as the heads of the tidewaters. a remarkable and distinguishing characteristic of this is that it attacks strangers only, & not the native or acclimated inhabitants; whereas the Yellow fever attacks natives and strangers, without distinction. I take the liberty of suggesting these remarks, merely to draw your attention to them, and as furnishing some outlines for the enquiries you will of course make for yourself. the absence of all medical theory and pretensions can alone claim any respect for the information from those unlearned, as myself, in the art.

I am much flattered and gratified by the prospect of the visit you propose to favor me with. the line of country from your present station to this place is worth seeing before you leave us. as it would be mortifying to me to lose by any occasional absence the pleasure of recieving you here, I take the liberty of mentioning that three or four times a year I visit a distant possession, & sometimes make considerable stays there. but as these visits are fixed to no particular times a previous notice of that which will best suit yourself will enable me to accomodate my movements to yours. no absence from the tidewaters can risk your losing any opportunity of observing the fever, until the commencement of autumn. indeed the occurrence of that disease is so rare that it may not offer itself to you for years. I pray you to accept the assurance of my high esteem and consideration.

TH: JEFFERSON

PoC (DLC); at foot of first page: "Doctor Valli."

From Theodorus Bailey

Dear Sir, New york 10. May 1816.

I have been duly favored with your Note covering a letter for Mr Van der Kemp—and in obedience to your wishes have forwarded the same by Post. Olden Barnevelt is in the Town of Trenton in the County of Oneida, about twelve miles from Rome.

I beg leave to add that I shall always take great pleasure in executing your commands in this City; and in rendering you any service in my power—

With great consideration and esteem, I am very truly yours,

Theodorus Bailey.

RC (MHi); endorsed by TJ as received 16 May 1816 and so recorded in SJL. RC (CSmH: JF-BA); address cover only; with PoC of TJ to Washington Society (of Boston), 22 Aug. 1816, on verso; addressed: "Thomas Jefferson Esqr Monticello V^a^"; franked; postmarked New York, 11 May.

From Patrick Gibson

Sir Richmond 10th May 1816

I have not had the pleasure of hearing from you since my letter of the 27th Ult^o^ advising you of the sale of your flour— Your note in bank becoming due on the 24th Ins^t^ I now inclose you a blank for your signature—

Your ob^t^ Servt Patrick Gibson

I hand you inclosed the Acco^t^ Sales of your Tobacco & flour N^t^ Proceeds $3128.77 which when received shall appear at your credit

RC (MHi); postscript written in a different ink; between dateline and salutation: "Thomas Jefferson Esqre"; endorsed by TJ as received 13 May 1816 and so recorded in SJL.

TJ had a $2,000 note in the Bank of Virginia, at Richmond. He signed the enclosed blank, not found, and dated it 24 May 1816 before returning it to Gibson in a letter of 15 May (*MB*, 2:1323).

ENCLOSURE

Account with Gibson & Jefferson for Tobacco and Flour Sales

Sales of 10 Hhds Tob^{o} Made on Account Thomas Jefferson Esqr

1816									
March 15th	to Peter F Smith	sh^{o}	1660.	152.	1290				
			1661.	150.	1328				
			1662.	156.	1170	3788 @	16.55		$626.91
"	to Wm Gilliat	refused	224.	169.	1235				
			225.	170.	1130				
			231.	154.	1220	3585 a	15		537.75
"	to J. M Warwick	passed	1709.	142.	1100		16		176.
28th	to Wm Muir	refused							
		Seab:	170.	137.	1228	Stem^{d}	14.90		182.97
"	to ditto		171.	1450.	1300				
			172.	1200.	1050	2350 a	13.95		327.82
									$1851.45
		charges							
	Inspection & Extra Coop^{e} 10 Hhds 6$ toll $4.17						10.17		
	dray^{e} $2.17[1] Cryer 50 Cents p Hhd $5						7.17		
	Com^{n} on $1851.45 at 2½ pCent						46.27[2]		63.61
		n^{t} proceeds 10 Hhds Tob^{o}							$1787.84

Sales of 265[3] Barrels flour made on Acc^{t} Thomas Jefferson

1816						
April 8th	to William H Hubbard					
	a 60^{d}/.	138 Bbls Superfine	6		$828.[4]	
24th	to Smith & Riddle d^{o}	81 " "	6¼		506.25	
		36 " Fine	5¾.		207.[5]	
					$1541.25	
	charges					
	Canal toll a 7^{d} $22.29 on 214 Bbls			$22.29.		
	Storage 214 Bbls		9^{d}	26.75		
	Insp^{n} 4.28[6] Coop^{e} & Lining Barrels 4.60.			8.88		
	freight 178 Barrels		3/6	103.83		
	Com^{n} on 1541.25 at 2½ pCent			38.57[7]	200.32	
	n^{t} proceeds flour				$1340.93	$1340.93
	30^{h} April 1816					$3128.77

E[.E.] J Lig[on]

MS (MHi); entirely in James Ligon's hand; ink stained.

sh^{o} (Shockoe) and seab: (Seabrook's) were tobacco warehouses in Richmond (*The Richmond Directory, Register and Almanac, for the Year 1819* [Richmond, 1819], 18). A crier (cryer) is "an agent who advertises or auctions another's goods" (*OED*). 60^{D}/.: "sixty days' sight." e.e.: "errors excepted."

[1] Omitted decimal point editorially supplied.

[2] Correct amount is $46.29.

[3] Correct number is 255.

[4] In pencil at lower right Ligon noted that this debt was "Due 10th June" 1816.

[5] In pencil at lower right Ligon noted that Smith & Riddle's total debt of "713.25" was due on 26 June 1816.

[6] Omitted decimal point editorially supplied.

[7] Correct amount is $38.53.

From Joseph Delaplaine

DEAR SIR, Philadelphia May 11th 1816.

I had the honour of duly receiving your obliging favour of the 9th of February last.

You have been pleased to correspond with me much on the subject of your portrait. Being very desirous to obtain it, and fearing that Mr Stuart will never be prevailed upon to give up yours, I avail myself of your kind offer to receive in your house, any Artist I might send to further my Work. Accordingly I have engaged one of our best portrait painters, Mr Otis of this City, who has Contracted, and made arrangements to set out for your Mansion on the First day of June next, for the express purpose of painting your portrait for my work. Mr Otis will take with him a volume of publick characters, a work you already mentioned to me, in which your biography is given. I take the liberty of sending it to you for the purpose of having it corrected, if it needs it; for I purpose to take great care that justice shall be done to your life. The alterations or corrections be pleased to give on a piece of paper if you see proper, & Mr Otis will take charge of them as well as the Book.

I cherish the hope that I may be enabled to accompany Mr Otis to your house. I shall endeavour so to do.

I beg you to have the goodness to inform me whether it will be your pleasure to receive Mr Otis at the time mentioned.

The late President Adams has lately sat for his portrait for me to young Mr Morse[1] who studied in London.—Mr Monroe sat to Mr Wood for me a few days ago, & the President promised to do the same. Mr Clay also sat. I take the liberty of enclosing a head of Columbus which be pleased to do me the favour to accept.

I remain with perfect respect & esteem Your obedt humle st

JOSEPH DELAPLAINE

P.S. In a few days I will have the pleasure of sending your Vespucius. The engraver has nearly done with it

RC (DLC); endorsed by TJ as received 18 May 1816 and so recorded in SJL. RC (DLC); address cover only; with PoC of TJ to William Wirt, 18 Aug. 1816, on verso; addressed: "Thomas Jefferson Esq[r] Monticello Virginia"; stamp canceled; franked; postmarked Philadelphia, 12 May.

The VOLUME containing TJ's biography was *Public Characters of 1800–1801* (London, 1801; Sowerby, no. 402). *Delaplaine's Repository* ceased publication before it could include the portrait of John Adams by Samuel F. B. MORSE now owned by the Brooklyn Museum. Contrary to Delaplaine's assertion, James MONROE had not sat for a portrait by Joseph Wood (Monroe to Delaplaine, 31 May 1816 [LNT: George H. and Katherine M. Davis Collection]). Delaplaine later displayed his large collection of portraits, including those of Adams, James Madison (THE PRESIDENT), Henry CLAY, and TJ in an art gallery that he opened in Philadelphia in 1819 (Delaplaine, *Prospectus of Delaplaine's National Panzographia for the reception of the Portraits of Distinguished Americans* [Philadelphia, 1818]; Philadelphia *Franklin Gazette*, 4 Oct. 1819; Georgetown, D.C., *Metropolitan*, 10 Feb. 1820). The enclosed engraving of COLUMBUS, not found, appeared in *Delaplaine's Repository*, vol. 1, plate opp. p. 1. The ENGRAVER of the Amerigo Vespucci portrait was Gideon Fairman.

[1]Reworked from "Morris."

From William Lee

SIR/: Bordeaux May 11. 1816.

I beg leave to inclose you a letter from Mr. Gard, professor at the Deaf and Dumb College in this city. He is considered in this country as a phenomenon for though deaf and dumb he is familiar with every branch of Science and literature—he wrote the inclosed himself, and brought it to me to correct but I thought it best to make no alteration in it. There is no one Sir who can appreciate his merits better than you, or who can determine how far those rare talents he possesses can be made useful in our country. I can assure you he is considered far Superior to the Abbé Sicard who has acquired so much celebrity in Europe in instructing the deaf and dumb;—Being but twenty eight years of age and of an excellent constitution he has a large margin for improvement, and if fixed in the United States would in all probability live to see his proposed institution carried to the highest perfection it is Susceptible of.

He will be highly flattered in receiving a line from you. I have led him to believe that if our Government to whom I have written on the subject should not think proper to favour his project he would find no[1] difficulty in procuring individual patronage.

I have the honor to be with high esteem and respect Your very humble Servant. W[M] LEE

RC (DLC); endorsed by TJ as received 10 July 1816 and so recorded in SJL. RC (DLC); address cover only; with PoC of TJ to William W. Hening, 15 Sept. 1816, on verso; addressed: "Thomas Jefferson Monticello Virginia" by "Mr Zantzinger U.S. Navy"; stamped "SHIP"; franked; postmarked Baltimore,

3 July. Enclosure: François Gard to TJ, 9 Apr. 1816.

The DEAF AND DUMB COLLEGE was the Institution Nationale des Sourdes-Muettes in Bordeaux (Adrien Cornié, *Étude sur l'Institution Nationale des Sourdes-Muettes de Bordeaux, 1786–1889* [1889], 1, 25).

[1]Manuscript: "no no."

From José Corrêa da Serra

DEAR SIR Philadelphia 12 May. 1816

Your Letter from Poplar forest reached my hands Last week, and with it i am enabled to follow with more cognizance the research of Capt. Lewis's papers. The only part which i had recovered i had forwarded to you by your excellent grand daughter when she was here.

Colonel Jones of the Guards who is going to Kentucky to dispose of his lands there, will present this to you. He wishes to have the honour of seeing you and conversing with you. I assure you that he is worthy of it. He is the whiggest of all whigs i have met, and bears a highly honorable character.

Be so kind to remember me to M^rs^ and Colonel Randolph, and receive the assurance of the sentiments with which i am

Sir Your most obliged obed^t^ servant J. CORRÊA DE SERRA

RC (MHi); endorsed by TJ as received 29 May 1816 and so recorded in SJL, which adds that it was delivered "by Col^o^ Jones."

TJ'S EXCELLENT GRAND DAUGHTER was Ellen W. Randolph (Coolidge).

From Pierre Samuel Du Pont de Nemours

EXCELLENT ET RESPECTABLE AMI, 12 may 1816

J'ai reçu avec une extrême reconnaissance votre lettre de Poplar-Forest.[1]

Ne croyez pas que j'aie la plus legere intention d'appliquer aux Etats-Unis aucune des idées que je devais employer pour la République Française; et que je crois bonnes à proposer à des Républiques naissantes, qui n'ont encore rien d'arrêté, Sont dans un Etat de matiere premiere,[2] et ont demandé mon avis pour en Sortir.

Ce n'est que Sur les Finances que je crois les Etats-Unis Susceptibles d'improvement; et il faudra longtems en exposer les principes, il faudra les y rendre familiers au petit nombre des Savans avant de rien essayer dans la pratique, qui a été commencée avec les préjugés de l'Angleterre et du Général Hamilton—

Vous êtes une nation Anglaise. Vous n'aspiriez lors de votre révolution qu'à vous élever à la constitution anglaise. Et Si le Parlement britannique avait voulu consentir à vous permettre d'avoir aussi un Parlement, ce que le Roi et Ses Ministres voulaient assez, vous n'auriez pas eu de révolution: vous seriez encore[3] Sujets du Roi d'Angleterre.

Si Washington n'avait pas été un homme vertueux, et dont la Vertu a été aidée, Soutenue par cinq ou Six hommes de Courage, vous auriez eu un Roi et des Pairs. C'est le regret de n'être pas des Pairs qui a Semé la graine de vos Fédéralistes.

Bénissez Dieu de n'avoir ni Roi, ni Pairs: c'est-à-dire de n'avoir pas confié l'éducation des Familles les plus influentes à la Flatterie qui est le plus mauvais Précepteur que l'on puisse imaginer.

Voila ce que vous avez de mieux que l'Angleterre. Vous avez conservé Ses mauvaises Loix civiles, et tous Ses mauvais usages.

un des pires est les Elections absolument populaires, où L'on a vu à Londres un Amiral faire venir les matelots de la Flotte avec de gros bâtons; à quoi Son compétiteur opposa les Bouchers armés de couperets, qui couperent en effet les épaules à une vingtaine de matelots et gagnerent la bataille.

J'ai vu en France des Elections à coups de chaise, et avec menace de la Lanterne.

Vous n'en êtes pas là, parce que vos Hommes Sont plus graves et plus doux que les Européens: mais les coups de poing ne Sont pas épargnés: et les Taverniers Sont les grandes Puissances, les Seigneurs du Pays, les nominateurs des magistrats.

Le Whiskey est un mauvais Souverain, les Boxeurs[4] Sont de mauvais ministres; et quand ils Se Sont emparés de l'Autorité ils la vendent aux dollars payeurs du Whiskey. La liberté romaine a été perdue par les Cliens, les capite censi,[5] les Tribus urbaines que les Patriciens, les Patrons, les anciens Proconsuls et les Généraux pillards Soudoyaient a leur retour des Provinces[6] et des Armées.

J'ai pris non Seulement dégoût, mais horreur, pour les Elections de Cabaret.

Peut-être Sont elles moins horribles dans votre Virginie; ce doit tenir, à un autre mal, c'est que vous avez des Esclaves; de Sorte que la derniere classe de vos Citoyens n'est pas la derniere Classe de la Société

C'est peut-être aussi ce qui fait que vous avez plus de gens de Lettres et d'Hommes propres au Gouvernement que la pluspart des autres Etats. Vos Hommes un peu bien élevés Sont plus riches, ont moins de travail forcé, moins d'affaires, plus de loisir, plus de tems pour Se livrer à l'étude.

Quand l'esclavage aura cessé, vous retomberez à cet égard au niveau des autres Etats: ce qui n'empêche pas qu'il faille tendre à terminer l'esclavage.

Mais, malheureux Enfans de l'Angleterre, vous êtes voués comme elle, pour plusieurs Siecles, peut-être pour toujours, aux plus mauvais principes d'Election. Et il ne faut pas Songer à y remedier;[7] il ne faut pas en beaucoup parler; il ne faut pas en écrire trop librement. Si cela changeait, votre Peuple Se croirait détrôné, il perdrait le Patriotisme; et votre Sureté politique, votre indépendance Seraient en danger.[8]

Dans des Sociétés neuves, ou dans une qui, comme la Nation française, Sort de la monarchie, de la distinction entre la Noblesse et la Roture, et de la Soumission au Sacerdoce, il faut être plus hardi; ne pas Souffrir la Tyrannie d'en haut, ne pas donner occasion et moyens à celle d'en bas. La première est plus perverse, la dernièr[e] est plus féroce. Toutes deux Sont insolentes, impitoyables et cruelles.

Comment Suis-je Sorti de là? En consultant la Justice, et lui donnant pour Conseiller, non pour maitre, l'Interêt public—

La Justice m'a dit que le droit naturel d'exprimer Sa pensée Sur toute chose, de vive voix ou par écrit, à la charge De n'insulter; ni calomnier personne, n'emporte aucunement celui de déliberer, de voter, de prononcer Sur les Affaires d'autrui, Si l'on n'en a pas reçu de cet Autrui la mission Spéciale: car la Société n'est faite que pour conserver à chacun ce qu'il a, et la faculté d'ameliorer ce qu'il a, Sans porter atteinte à la liberté, ni à la Propriété de qui que ce Soit.

La Justice m'a dit que chacun devant être le Maitre Sur Son Champ et dans Sa maison, ceux qui n'ont ni champ, ni maison, qui ne mangent que par Salaire, et ne logent que par contrat, ne Sont et ne doivent être dans aucune Société complettement les égaux de ceux dont ils ont Sollicité le toit et le pain, qui les hébergent et qui les nourrissent, de ceux à qui Dieu, le travail, les Capitaux qu'il a procurés, la Nature et l'équité, ont confié l'importante magistrature de produire les Récoltes, de les conserver pour l'interêt de tous, de les distribuer par de libres conventions.

Personne ne peut avoir que par délégation aucun droit Sur ce dont il n'est pas Propriétaire.

Tout Homme est propre à recevoir une délégation: C'est l'affaire de Son déléguant, ou de Ses déleguans que de la bien placer. L'Eligibilité est un droit naturel; et la non éligibilité Serait, est un tort fait aux

Electeurs. L'Electoralité n'appartient à Personne que pour l'administration de ce qui est à lui.

L'Homme qui ne posséde que Sa personne et des biens mobiliers ne peut avoir droit qu'à la liberté de Sa personne, à la propriété de Ses biens, à la faculté d'en disposer comme il l'entend.

Vous ne prétendriez pas que parce qu'il a besoin de manger, il eut le[9] droit d'obliger les Propriétaires de terre à cultiver pour le nourrir; car alors les Propriétaires ne seraient plus les Propriétaires, ils Seraient devenus des Esclaves de la Glèbe. Les Romains l'ont voulu et c'est ce qui a principalement favorisé contre eux les succès des Barbares. Mr Colbert en a fait l'objet de Sa politique. Et les Anglais ont adopté depuis Soixante ans cette politique injuste et périlleuse qui conjointement avec l'ignorance et la négligence des autres nations et avec le progrès du luxe, ont fait de l'Angleterre une immense ville, exposée à tous les dangers d'une Ville, ce dont elle commence à S'appercevoir aujourd'hui, et ce dont elle a une imbécile et inutile Surprise.

Les Droits des Hommes qui ne possédent que leur Personne et des effets mobiliers, doivent être religieusement respectés en tout pays, par toutes les nations, par tous les Gouvernemens. Aucune nation n'a le droit de conférer à Son Gouvernement le pouvoir de gêner la liberté, de violer la propriété d'aucun homme.

Il entre dans les droits de ces membres de la Classe des Salariés d'aller chercher leur Salaire où il leur plait, de le gagner comme il leur plait, de faire pour lui les conventions qui leur plaisent. Ils ne Sont réellement membres, ni sujets d'aucune nation qu'autant qu'il convient à leur interêt et à leur bienveillance.

Les Propriétaires du Sol au contraire tiennent nécessairement au Pays. Ils en Sont cosouverains,[10] car il est à eux. Ils peuvent l'exploiter à leur fantaisie. Ils peuvent le vendre; et ne Sauraient abdiquer leur part de la cosouveraineté qu'en vendant leur héritage—

Mais j'ai Senti que leur Souverainete ou Cosouverainété, quoique très juste et très incontestable, ne Serait pas très assurée, S'ils ne ralliaient pas à eux tous les Hommes d'esprit et jouissans d'une existence indépendante. C'est ce qui m'a fait inventer les Gentilshommes avoués qui ne Sont pas des Gens Sans aveu puisqu'un Seigneur de maison consent à leur céder, pour un tems convenu, le tout ou partie de Son Autorité dans Sa Seigneurie; et c'est aussi ce qui m'a fait appeller à leur conseil, au droit de concourir aux Elections de Magistrats et[11] aux plans d'amélioration. Les Gentilshommes honoraires et les Seigneurs dignitaires, qui le deviennent à raison de gradés mérites et[12] obtenus dans le Service civil ou militaire et dans les Professions lettrées.

La[13] belle idée de ne donner l'activité du droit de cité[14] qu'à ceux qui a une époque indiquée Sauront lire et écrire, n'est point aux Cortès d'Espagne. Elles l'ont puisée avec raison dans La Constitution de l'An Trois des Français qui fût un très bel ouvrage, auquel j'ai tâché de rallier la mienne, parce qu'elle est la Seule qui ait été adoptée librement, et que, renversée par la violence, elle devait en France être regardée comme encore obligatoire.

Cette Constitution de l'An Trois avait peu de défauts: dont le plus grave était de n'avoir assuré aucune retraite aux Membres du Directoire, pas même la place à vie dans le Conseil des Anciens où ils auraient été des Consulaires très utiles

Ce directoire nommé par le Canon de Buonaparte, et le Canon est un dangereux Electeur, a dit-on été vénal: cependant La Revelliere et Le Tourneur en Sont Sortis fort pauvres. Les autres ont fait le 18 Fructidor parce qu'ils avaient de la répugnance à passer du Trône au Grenier, a Sortir d'un magnifique Palais pour rentrer dans leur triste Cabinet de médiocres Avocats.

Dans ma Constitution, je n'ai rien ôté à personne, et j'ai mis tout citoyen à portée d'acquérir. Le moindre ouvrier, S'il est Sage, y peut Sur Ses vieux jours acheter une propriété fonciere et devenir membre actif du Souverain. Le moindre Homme de lettres, S'il S'applique à des études Serieuses, et Se distingue toujours entre Ses Pairs, peut devenir Membre de la Régence et Président de la République.

Aucun choix Important ne peut être mauvais, parce qu'aucune Assemblée n'est tumultueuse; et qu'une fois Sorti de sa Commune, on ne peut avancer que du Sein d'une élite à une plus haute élite.

En donnant le plus grand interêt d'Ambition et d'Amour propre à la Propriété territoriale, j'ai assuré le plus bas prix possible à l'Interêt de l'argent pour les manufactures, pour le commerce, pour les Emprunts publics. En animant la tête et le coeur, j'ai renforcé les bras.[15]

Je Suis bien aise que vous ayiez approuvé mes quatre mots magiques, la Liberté, la Vérité, la probité, l'honneur, consolidés par le droit d'être crûs Sur parole, tant que la fausseté n'est pas démontrée; et par l'affreuse peine de quitter la cocarde nationale S'il arrive qu'il Soit prouvé qu'on ait été de mauvaise foi, ou qu'on ait menti.

J'ai regardé comme une louable adresse, mais j'avoue bien que ce n'est qu'une adresse, d'avoir donné comme un privilege à ceux dont l'existence n'est pas indépendante l'exemption des Assemblées politiques, du service de la Garde nationale, et des fonctions de Juré.—Le vrai Sans doute est qu'il leur est avantageux et profitable de n'être pas dérangés de leur travail; comme aussi qu'ils Seraient dangereux dans le nôtre.[16]

Il est vrai encore que tous les maux causés par les ouvriers et Journaliers métamorphosés en Politiques, déguisés en membres du Souverain dont j'ai été le triste témoin en France, Seraient beaucoup diminués Si l'éducation publique était bonne; Si de bons livres classiques que les Enfans auraient eu à transcrire, même à apprendre par coeur, leur avaient profondément inculqué les principes de justice et de morale qu'ils ont tous dans leur premiere enfance, et qui ne s'obliterent que[17] par la faute des Parens et des Instructeurs.

Nous Sommes loin d'être à cet égard Sans reproche, mon respectable Ami, ni vous, ni moi.

Si j'avais eu le Courage d'apprendre l'anglais assez pour le pouvoir écrire, (mais je ne puis m'assujettir à étudier des mots qui ne Sont que des Synonimies et ne me donnent pas une Seule idée nouvelle, quand je me Sens un Si grand besoin d'apprendre des choses, et même d'en enseigner à ceux qui Sont encore plus ignorans que moi):

Ou Si vous aviez eu la bonté de faire traduire notre[18] petit Traité de l'Education nationale, quatre, cinq, ou Six ans auraient Suffi pour nous procurer les livres classiques; et il y aurait déja dix ou douze ans que nos Ecoles Seraient montées, et nous aurions aujourd'hui des Hommes de vingt ans d'une haute valeur, qui d'ici à dix ans auraient été dans les Etats Unis une inexprimable richesse, une impôsante Puissance à tout bien.

Mr Gilmer S'est mis à cette Traduction, et la fera très bonne. mais nous aurons perdu dix Sept ans, peut être vingt; car il faut bien trois ou quatre ans pour que Votre Souverain dont le Palais est dans un million de maisons, comme dit Si ingénieusement le bon Corréa, ait le tems de lire les mémoires de Ses Conseillers, celui de Se former une opinion, et de donner, dans le Sanctuaire des Tavernes, par le Pouvoir exécutif de quelques nez[19] cassés, de quelques yeux pochés, Ses instructions et Ses ordres à Ses délégués, Représentans, Sénateurs, Président et Ministres.

Rien n'est perdu, tout Se fait à la longue, mais tout Se fait tard; parce que les Hommes Sont négligens et indolens, S'amusent à dormir, à rire, à Se promener, à jouer aux échecs, ou au Wisk, à lire des Romans, à faire des Poëmes, à tuer le tems qui les tue.

Ce petit livre, quoiqu'imprimé deux fois en France, n'y a été d'aucune utilité, non pas même à la commission formée pour y établir la méthode d'éducation de Lancaster, mais qui ne passera pas d'un cheveu ce qu'on fait dans la divine ou détestable Angleterre.—Et je ne Souhaite pas même que notre ouvrage y ait actuellement de l'influence;

car, au lieu de livres classiques, on n'y ferait que des Livres catholiques,[20] et l'on reculerait les Hommes d'un Siecle avec l'instrument fait pour les avancer.

Je viens de vous dire que Mr Gilmer veut bien travailler pour moi, et devenir Savant en Economie politique. Ce m'est un grand bonheur.

Je lui envoie en feuilles volantes, à un cent la Feuille, les livres ou fragmens de livres qui me paraissent lui être le plus nécessaires, et Selon l'ordre des idées.

Je n'ai pas pu lui envoyer ainsi imprimé le petit Traité du droit naturel de M^r^ quesnay, qui a eu le premier le mérite de voir que les Hommes réunis en Société n'ont pas renoncé, comme on le croyait, à quelques uns de leurs droits naturels, et n'ont au contraire formé des Corps politiques que pour étendre et augmenter l'usage de tous leurs droits. J'ai été obligé de faire copier cet ouvrage très court et très rare. Je le joins ici, Voudrez vous bien le lui envoyer Sous votre contreseing. Je crois que vous Savez qu'il demeure à Winchester, dans votre Virginie.

une autre chose que je ne vous ai pas dite; et[21] qui m'afflige au plus profond du coeur,[22] est que je Serai vraisemblablement[23] obligé de retourner en France chercher la Calomnie, la persecution, d'en haut et celle d'en bas;[24] peut-être et Selon l'apparence la prison Suivie d'une mort violente, en Supposant que celle ci ne la précede pas.

Mais ma Femme est malade, même estropiée depuis dix Sept mois[25] d'une blessure à une jambe. Il parait qu'elle ne peut absolument pas venir ici. Elle me demande avec les plus vives instances.

Si elle persiste, et ne peut Se faire amener en chaise à porteurs ou Sur une chaise Longue de Paris au Havre, y être hissée Sur un Vaisseau, en descendre de même, et revenir à bras d'hommes dans la même chaise à notre Eleutherian, je ne pourrai me dispenser d'aller la rejoindre.—Il m'est plus aisé de me compromettre, de Sacrifier le reste de ma vie et ce que je puis encore faire de travail, et même de nous exposer tous deux car je lui Serai un danger de plus, que de lui écrire, je t'abandonne; vis ou meurs comme tu pourras; nous Sommes Séparés pour toujours.—Cela Serait entierement indigne de moi.—L'écriture dit: l'homme quittera Son Pere et Sa mere et S'attachera à Sa Femme.—Ces liens qui ont été volontaires Sont les plus Sacrés.—Je vous envoie la notice historique que j'ai faite pour le brave et bon Barlow: Dans la derniere phrase vous trouverez l'inviolable régle de ma conduite, que j'ai Suivie, non pas tout a fait depuis les Soixante Seize ans auxquels j'arrive, mais bien depuis environ Soixante.

Si je puis guérir ma pauvre Amie assez pour la rendre transportable, je la ramenerai dans notre Vallée: car je désire par dessus tout, et pour l'accomplissement de mes devoirs, donner mes derniers travaux aux Etats-Unis et aux autres Républiques américaines.

J'ai trois ouvrages à faire, qui ne peuvent guere être écrits, et certainement ne peuvent être imprimés que dans un Pays complettement libre.

Voici le Sujet du premier:

„Qu'est-ce que tous les Gouvernemens doivent pouvoir et vouloir faire?

Qu'est-ce qu'aucun Gouvernement ne doit pouvoir, et ce qu'aucune Nation n'a le droit d'autoriser Son Gouvernement à faire?„

Voici celui du Second:

„Comment Se fait-il que, depuis l'existence du monde, il n'y ait encore eu nulle part un bon Gouvernement, une bonne éducation,[26] ni une bonne Religion? tandis que toutes les Vérités, tous les Principes, toutes les maximes, qui fonderaient ces trois choses, lesquelles ne peuvent être complettes ni durables l'une Sans l'autre, Sont néanmoins dans toutes les têtes et dans tous les coeurs, et qu'il est assez facile de les y reconnaitre, de les en tirer.„

Voici celui du troisième dont j'ai fait le plan chez vous à mounticello:

„Quelles Sont les Loix naturelles du bon Gouvernement et de la bonne Administration d'une Famille isolée dans un désert?

Et comment peuvent-elles S'appliquer et S'étendre aux cinq cent millions de Familles qui doivent un jour peupler l'Amérique?„

Je vous Salue et vous embrasse avec tendresse et respect.

DuPont (de Nemours)

Mes respects à Madame Randolph, et à toutes Ses aimables dames et demoiselles, y comprise Miss Septimia.[27]

Je joins une petite brochure,[28] que je crois vous avoir donné[29] dans le tems mais Sur laquelle on me dit qu'on ne pourrait plus l'imprimer en France.[30]

EDITORS' TRANSLATION

Excellent and respectable Friend, 12 may 1816

I have received with extreme gratitude your letter from Poplar Forest.

Do not believe that I have the slightest intention of applying to the United States any of the ideas I used for the French Republic. I believe that they are only suitable to propose to newborn republics that have not yet settled on anything, are in a raw state, and have requested my advice to get them out of that condition.

Only with regard to finance do I believe the United States susceptible to improvement; and much time will be needed to expose it to the relevant principles. These must be made familiar to the few experts before trying anything in practice, which has been developed thus far in accordance with the prejudices of England and General Hamilton.

You are an English nation. During your revolution you only aspired to elevate yourself within the English constitution. If the British parliament had consented to allow you to have a parliament as well, which the king and his ministers were rather willing to accept, you would have had no revolution. You would still be subjects of the king of England.

If Washington had not been a virtuous man, and if his virtue had not been helped and supported by five or six courageous men, you would have had a king and peers. Regret at not being peers sowed the seed of your Federalists.

Thank God for having neither king nor peers; that is to say, for not having entrusted the education of the most influential families to flattery, which is the worst tutor that can be imagined.

This is what you have that is better than England. But you have kept its bad civil laws and all its bad customs.

One of the worst is completely popular elections. To one such in London, an admiral brought sailors of the fleet armed with large bludgeons, which his competitor opposed with butchers armed with cleavers and who indeed cleaved the shoulders of about twenty sailors and won the battle.

In France I have seen electoral battles with chairs and threats to hang people from the lampposts.

You have not reached this point, because your men are more serious and gentle than Europeans are: but punches are not spared: and tavern keepers are the highest power, the lords of the land, the nominators of magistrates.

Whiskey is a bad sovereign, and pugilists are bad ministers; and when they have seized authority, they sell it for the dollars they need to pay for whiskey. Roman liberty was lost by the clients, the capite censi, and the urban tribes, whom the patricians, patrons, former proconsuls, and pillaging generals bribed when they returned from the provinces and the army.

I have acquired not only a feeling of disgust, but of horror, for cabaret elections.

Perhaps they are less horrible in your Virginia; if so, it must be because of another evil, which is that you have slaves, so that the lowest class of your citizens is not the lowest class in society

Perhaps this is also why you have more scholars and men suitable to govern than most other states. Your men, raised somewhat better, are richer and not forced to work as much, have less business to attend to and more leisure time, and can devote more time to study.

When slavery ends you will fall back in this regard to the level of the other states: which makes it no less necessary to see to the abolition of slavery.

But, unfortunate children of England, you are doomed, like her, for several centuries and perhaps forever, to follow the worst electoral principles. One must not think of remedying the problem; one must not talk much about it; one must not write about it too freely. If that were to change, your people would believe that they had been dethroned; they would lose their patriotism; and your political safety and independence would be threatened.

In new societies or in one that, like the French nation, is just emerging from monarchy, from the distinction between nobles and commoners, and from submission to the priesthood, it is necessary to be bolder. One must neither suffer tyranny from the top nor give an opportunity or means for tyranny from below. The former is more perverse, while the latter is more ferocious. Both are insolent, merciless, and cruel.

How did I escape this? By consulting justice and giving it the public interest as an adviser, not as a master—

Justice told me that the natural right to express one's thoughts on all things, in speech or in writing, providing one does not insult or slander anyone, in no way confers a right to deliberate, vote, or pronounce on the affairs of other people, if one has not received a special assignment from them: because the main goal of society is to preserve to each person what he has and the faculty to improve what he has without undermining the liberty or property of anyone else.

Justice told me that, while each person must be master of his own domain and house, people who have neither land nor home, who put food on the table only through their salaries and are housed only through contract, are not and should not in any society be the complete equals of those from whom they solicit their room and board, who give them a roof over their heads and feed them, and to whom God, work, capital provided by work, nature, and equity have entrusted the important magistracy of producing crops, storing them in the interest of everybody, and distributing them through freely negotiated agreements.

No one can have the right to what he does not own, except through delegation.

Every man is eligible to receive a delegation: it is the responsibility of his delegator or delegators to act wisely. Eligibility is a natural right; and ineligibility would be, and is, unfair to the electors. The ability to elect belongs to nobody except as it pertains to the administration of what belongs to him.

A man who owns nothing but his own person and personal property can only be entitled to the freedom of his own person and property and the ability to dispose of it as he wishes.

You would not claim that because he needs to eat he has the right to force landowners to farm in order to feed him; because then landowners would no longer be landowners, they would have become slaves of the soil. The Romans wished it to be so, and this is what contributed more than anything to the success of the barbarians opposed against them. Mr. Colbert made it the object of his politics. The English have adopted this unfair and perilous policy for sixty years, which, combined with the ignorance and negligence of the other nations and the progress of luxury, has turned England into an immense city and exposed it to all the dangers of a city. That nation is beginning to notice this today, which stupidly and uselessly surprises it.

The rights of men who own nothing but their persons and personal property must be religiously respected in every country, by every nation, and by all governments. No nation has the right to confer on its government the power to hinder the freedom or violate the property of any man.

One of the rights of these members of the salaried class is to go and get their salary wherever they want, earn it as they please, and enter into whatever working arrangements they like. They really are members or subjects of any nation only inasmuch as it suits their interest and benevolence.

Landowners, on the contrary, are necessarily attached to the land. They are its co-sovereigns, because it is theirs. They may cultivate it as their fancy dictates. They can sell it; and they could only abdicate their portion of the co-sovereignty by selling their inheritance—

But I felt that their sovereignty or co-sovereignty, though very just and undeniable, would not be very secure if they did not rally around them all intelligent men who enjoy an independent life. This is what caused me to invent the concept of the avowed gentlemen, who are not untrustworthy, since a lord consents to cede them for an agreed-upon time all or a portion of his authority over his domain; and it is also what made me call for their advice and for their right to contribute to the election of magistrates and to projects of improvement. The honorary gentlemen and dignitary lords become so through grades of merit obtained in the civil or military service and the learned professions.

The beautiful idea of giving the right of citizenship to those who at a specified time know how to read and write does not belong to the Cortes of Spain. The Cortes was right to take it from the French constitution of the Year III; this was a very handsome work, to which I have tried to connect mine, because it is the only one that was adopted freely and, as it was overthrown by violence, it was still considered to be in force in France.

This constitution of the Year III had few defects, of which the gravest was the failure to insure any retreat to the members of the Directory, not even a lifetime seat in the Council of Elders, where they would have been very useful as consuls

This Directory was appointed by Bonaparte's cannon, and the cannon is a dangerous elector. It was said to be venal: La Révellière and Le Tourneur, however, came out of it very poor. The others staged 18 Fructidor because they were reluctant to move from throne to garret and leave a palace in order to enter their sad, second-rate lawyers' offices.

In my constitution I have taken nothing from anybody, and I have put every citizen within reach of acquiring property. Accordingly the humblest worker, if he is wise, can, in his old age, buy real estate and become an active member of the sovereign. The humblest man of letters, if he applies himself to serious studies and always distinguishes himself among his peers, can become a member of the regency and president of the republic.

No important choice can be bad, because no assembly is tumultuous; and once a man has left his commune, he can only advance from one elite to a higher one.

By giving ambition and self-esteem the greatest interest in owning land, I have insured the lowest possible price for the interest on money used for manufactures, commerce, and public loans. By animating the head and the heart, I have strengthened the arms.

I am happy that you have approved my four magic words, liberty, truth, probity, and honor, consolidated by the right to have one's word believed so long as falsehood has not been proven and by the horrible pain of being stripped of the national cockade if it is proved that one acted in bad faith or lied.

I have considered it a laudable and ingenious proposition, but only that, to have given, as a privilege, exemption from political assemblies, national guard service, and jury duty to those whose life is not independent.—In truth, it is probably advantageous and profitable not to disturb these people from their work; they would also be dangerous in ours.

It is also true that all the evils caused by workers and day laborers metamorphosed into politicians and disguised as members of the sovereign, evils I was sad to witness in France, would be greatly diminished if public education were good and if fine classical books that children would be required either to transcribe or even learn by heart had deeply instilled in them the principles of justice and morality that they all have in early childhood and that are only obliterated through the errors of their parents and instructors.

We are far from blameless in this regard, my respectable friend, neither you nor I.

If I had had the courage to learn enough English to be able to write in that language (but I cannot subject myself to the study of words that are just synonyms and do not give me a single new idea when I feel such a great need to learn things and even teach them to those who are even more ignorant than I am):

Or if you had had the kindness to have our little treatise on national education translated, four, five, or six years would have been enough for us to procure classical books, and our schools would have already been created ten or twelve years ago. Today we would have twenty-year-old men of high value, who ten years hence would have been for the United States a source of inexpressible wealth and an imposing force for everything good.

Mr. Gilmer has undertaken this translation and will do it very well. But we will have lost seventeen years, perhaps twenty, because it takes three or four years for your sovereign, whose palace is in a million houses, as the good Corrêa so cleverly says, to have time to read the memorandums of his advisers, form an opinion, and give, in the sanctuaries of taverns, through the executive power of a few broken noses and black eyes, his instructions and orders to his delegates, representatives, senators, president, and ministers.

Nothing is lost; everything gets done eventually, but all gets done late, because men, who are negligent and lazy, waste their time in sleeping, laughing, taking walks, playing chess or whist, reading novels, writing poems, and killing the time that kills them.

This little book, though printed twice in France, was completely useless there, even to the commission that was formed to establish Lancaster's method of education, but which will not surpass by a hair what is done in divine or detestable England.—And I do not even wish for our work to have any influence there, because instead of classical books, they would only make Catholic books and set men back a century with the tool made to push them forward.

I just told you that Mr. Gilmer is willing to work for me and become a scholar in political economy. It pleases me greatly.

I am sending him, at one cent per leaf, loose sheets of the books or fragments of books that to me seem most necessary to him, following the ideas in their order.

I was unable to send him, printed in the same manner, the little treatise on natural rights by Mr. Quesnay, who has the merit of having been the first to see that men united into societies have not renounced, as was believed, their natural rights, but have on the contrary formed political bodies only to spread and increase the use of all their rights. I had to have this very short and rare book copied. I am enclosing it here. Would you please send it to him under your countersignature? I believe you know he lives in Winchester in your Virginia.

Another thing that I have not told you and that afflicts me deep in my heart is that I probably will have to go back to France in search of slander, persecution from on high and below, and perhaps, more than likely, prison followed by a violent death, supposing that the latter does not precede the former.

But my wife is sick and has even been crippled for seventeen months by an injury to her leg. It seems that she absolutely cannot come here. She is pleading for me to go to her.

If she persists and cannot be brought on a sedan chair or a chaise longue from Paris to Le Havre, hoisted onto a ship and lowered in the same manner, and carried by men in the same sedan chair to our Eleutherian, I could not excuse myself from going and joining her.—It is easier for me to compromise myself, sacrifice the rest of my life and the work I am still able to do, and even endanger the two of us, because I will be for her an additional danger, than write to her: I am abandoning you; live or die as you can; we are separated forever.—This would be entirely unworthy of me.—The scripture says: man will leave his father and mother and become attached to his wife.—These bonds, because they are voluntary, are the most sacred ones.—I send you the historical notice I have written about the brave and good Barlow. In the last sentence you will find the inviolable rule of my conduct, which I have been following for not quite all of my seventy-six years, but for a good sixty.

If I am able to cure my poor friend enough to make her transportable, I will bring her back to our valley, because I desire above all, and for the fulfillment of my duties, to give my last works to the United States and the other American republics.

I have three to write, and they cannot be written and certainly cannot be printed in a country that is not completely free.

Here is the subject of the first one:

"What is it that all governments must be able and willing to do?

What is it that no government should be able to do and which no nation should have the right to authorize its government to do?"

Here is that of the second:

"How is it that, since the world began, there has not yet been a good government, a good education, or a good religion? Whereas all the truths, principles, and maxims that would establish these three things (which cannot be complete or lasting without each other) are, nevertheless, in every head and heart, easy to recognize, and draw out."

Here is the third, which I outlined at your house at Monticello:

"What are the natural laws for the good government and administration of a family isolated in a desert?

And how can they be applied and extended to the five hundred million families that must some day populate America?"

I salute and embrace you with tenderness and respect.

DuPont (de Nemours)

Give my regards to Madame Randolph and all her kind ladies and young ladies, including Miss Septimia.

I am including a little brochure that I think I gave you in the past, but which I am told could no longer be printed in France.

RC (DLC); edge chipped, with missing text supplied from FC; at head of text: "A Monsieur Jefferson"; endorsed by TJ as received 23 May 1816 from "Eleutherian" and so recorded in SJL. FC (DeGH: Pierre Samuel Du Pont de Nemours Papers, Winterthur Manuscripts); in a clerk's hand, with emendations by Du Pont. 1st Tr (DeGH: Du Pont Miscellany, Winterthur Manuscripts); posthumous copy by Eleuthera du Pont Smith, presumably based on a missing Dft); dated 16 May 1816; varies significantly from RC, with only the most important differences noted below. 2d Tr (DeGH: Papers of Descendants, Longwood Manuscripts); posthumous copy by Sophie M. Du Pont evidently taken from the same missing Dft, but with some omissions; dated 5 May 1816. Translation by Dr. Genevieve Moene. Enclosure: MS transcription, not found, of François Quesnay, *Le Droit Naturel* (Paris, 1765). Du Pont, as editor, had published this work twice: first, as "Observations sur le droit naturel des hommes réunis en société," *Journal de l'agriculture, du commerce et des finances* 2 (Sept. 1765): 4–35; and second, as "Le Droit Naturel," in *Physiocratie, ou Constitution Naturelle du Gouvernement le plus avantageux au genre human* (Paris, 1768; Sowerby, no. 2370), 1–38. TJ enclosed the transcription in his 7 June 1816 letter to Francis W. Gilmer.

CAPITE CENSI ("those counted by head") were citizens of ancient Rome who owned little or no property and were enumerated in the census by head rather than estate (*OCD*, 308, 1253). The French constitution DE L'AN TROIS DES FRANÇAIS ("of the French Year III") was adopted on 22 Aug. 1795 (5 Fructidor). The constitutional government was overthrown in a coup d'état by members of the French Directory with support from the military on 18 FRUCTIDOR, Year V (4 Sept. 1797) (William Doyle, *The Oxford History of the French Revolution* [1989], 318–9, 330–1).

L'HOMME QUITTERA SON PERE ET SA MERE ET S'ATTACHERA À SA FEMME ("Man will leave his father and mother and become attached to his wife") is based on the Bible, Genesis 2.24. The enclosed NOTICE HISTORIQUE, a tribute to the late American diplomat and poet Joel Barlow, has not been identified. Du Pont collaborated with Konrad E. Oelsner on one such essay, enclosed to TJ on 10 Feb. 1813, but other, longer Barlow memorials attributed to Du Pont were published in 1813 in various formats in Paris. The enclosed PETITE BROCHURE has also not been identified.

[1]In place of this paragraph, 1st Tr reads (with first bracketed passage not in 2d Tr, second and fourth bracketed passages supplied from 2d Tr, and third bracketed passage changed to "il ne la oté la victoire" ["he did not succeed"] in 2d Tr): "J'ai reçu hier, tres cher et excellent Ami, votre belle, bonne et grande lettre de la Foret des Peupliers, et du 24 Avril. Je vous en remercie très tendrement—[Je ne dispute pas avec mes maîtres. Je dirai mes motifs à mon ami.]—Vous dites très bien qu'il faut offrir aux Peuples les loix et les Constitutions qui leur conviennent, en approchant le plus que l'on peut de celles qui seraient éminement justes, et pourraient être données à un Peuple entierement neuf [si l'on etait comme Numa, capable de la ruse que je blame fort, de feindre une revelation et revetir de l'autorité usurpée que cette ruse peut donner] Le projet que je vous ai donné avait été fait pour la France, et aurait été éxécuté, si le brave Mallet, qui travaillait de son côté ne s'etait pas emparé, sans le savoir de mon moyen d'éxécution, et ne l'avait pas rendu pour l'avenir impraticable, et si, dans la suite, un de mes principaux Amis, n'avait pas préféré une monarchie à l'Anglaise, avec une Constitution parodieé de la Britannique, et qu'il n'a pas pu constituer tout à fait comme il la voulait à la Republique, dont je l'aurais pourtant fait un des Regents—Il était un grand Seigneur; il vivait avec de grands Seigneurs. Il a voulu un Gouvernement sous le quel les Grands Seigneurs fussent quelque chose, et [il en a été la victime]. Ma multitude de petits Seigneurs un par Maison, lui a paru une folie. Il prétendait qu'il n'y avait que moi de Republicain en France. La Nation l'etait; mais il ne voyait pas la Nation et les autres Republicains, il ne voyait que moi. Je ne le blame pas, parce qu'il a eu

de très bonnes intentions. Je le plains et l'aime, mais Je plains encore plus ma Patrie et mes Concitoyens.—Mes dernières espérances ont cessé immediatement après les belles paroles de l'Empereur de Russie, qui en descendant chez mon Ami, lui dit, en notre présence (nous etions quatre ou cinq personnes) Je ne viens point gèner la liberté des Français, ni leur imposer un Gouvernement. Je viens prèter ma force à leur volonté. J'appuyerai le Gouvernement qu'ils préférerons, Dites le moi. Mon Ami crut que c'etait une Monarchie constitutionelle sous la Famille de leurs Anciens Rois, auxquels on ne pensait pas encore [avant] le 20 mars, durant les negotiations de Chatillon. Ils ont été rappelés, ils ont regnés, et ils regnent encore par la grâce de Dieu, et de Talleyrand que leur Cour a fait disgraciér, voudrait faire fusiller, ou au moins bannir, en quoi il est très possible qu'elle parvienne" ("I received yesterday, excellent and very dear friend, your beautiful, good, and lengthy letter of 24 April from Poplar Forest. I thank you very tenderly for it—[I do not argue with my teachers. I will explain my motives to you, my friend.]—You say very well that it is necessary to offer people laws and constitutions that suit them and come as close as possible to those that would be eminently just and might be given to an entirely new people [if one were, like Numa, capable of the trick, of which I strongly disapprove, of feigning a revelation and assuming the usurped authority which that ruse can give]. The project I submitted to you was made for France and would have been executed if the brave Malet, who was working in this area on his own, had not inadvertently adopted my method of execution and made it impracticable for the future and if, after that, one of my best friends had not preferred an English-style monarchy with a parody of the British constitution. He did not succeed in establishing the constitution exactly as he wanted in the Republic, of which I would still have made him a regent—He was a great lord; he lived with great lords. He wanted a government under which the great lords amounted to something, and [was a victim of that]. My crowd of little lords, one per household, seemed like madness to him. He claimed that I was the only republican in France. The nation was republican, but he did not see the nation and the other republicans; he saw only me. I do not blame him, because he had very good intentions. I pity him and I love him, but I pity even more my country and my fellow citizens.—My last hopes ended immediately after hearing the beautiful words of the Russian emperor, who in coming down to my friend's house, told him in our presence (there were four or five of us): "I am not coming to disturb the liberty of the French people or impose a government on them. I am coming to lend my strength to their will. I will support the government they choose. Tell me about it." My friend believed that this government was a constitutional monarchy under the family of their former kings, whom they had not yet thought of [before] 20 March, during the Châtillon negotiations. They were recalled. They reigned and still reign by the grace of God and Talleyrand, whom their court dismissed and would like to execute or at least banish, which it will quite possibly succeed in doing."

[2] 1st Tr: "nature primitive" ("primitive nature"). 2d Tr: "matiere primitive" ("primitive matter").

[3] Word interlined.

[4] Trs: "buveurs" ("drinkers").

[5] Preceding three words not in Trs.

[6] Word interlined in place of "Gouvernemens" ("Governments").

[7] Preceding eight words not in Trs.

[8] Trs end here.

[9] RC: "le le."

[10] Word interlined in place of "souverains" ("sovereigns").

[11] Preceding three words interlined.

[12] Preceding two words interlined.

[13] Trs resume here.

[14] Trs: "citoyens" ("citizens").

[15] Paragraph not in Trs.

[16] Paragraph not in 2d Tr.

[17] In place of preceding eleven words, Trs substitute "n'acquerent pas dans leur premiere jeunesse" ("do not acquire in their first youth").

[18] Trs: "mon" ("my").

[19] RC and FC: "nés." 1st Tr: "nès." 2d Tr: "nez."

[20] RC and FC: "catholistiques." Trs: "catholiques."

[21] Preceding eight words not in Trs.

[22] In place of preceding five words, Trs substitute "veritablement" ("truly").

[23] Trs: "probablement" ("probably").

[24] 1st Tr omits remainder of paragraph.

[25] Preceding four words not in 1st Tr. 2d Tr substitutes "depuis mois" ("for months").

[26] In Trs remainder of paragraph reads "tandis que tous les principes, toutes les maximes qui les fondraient sont dans toutes les têtes & dans tous les cœurs" ("whereas all the principles and maxims on which they are based exist in every head and heart").

[27] Paragraph not in Trs.

[28] FC and Trs: "une bagatelle" ("a trifle").

[29] Trs: "envoyé" ("sent").

[30] Preceding two words not in 1st Tr. Paragraph added separately to RC and FC by Du Pont.

Wilson Cary Nicholas's Circular to the County Courts

COUNCIL CHAMBER,
Richmond, May 12*th,* 1816.

GENTLEMEN

The "Act to provide an accurate Chart of each County and a general Map of the Territory of this Commonwealth," directs the Executive "to cause such surveys to be made of the exterior boundaries of the Commonwealth, as may be necessary to ensure greater accuracy in the details of the preceding Charts where they present the boundaries of adjacent States, and to cause such surveys to be made of the great divisions of the Territory of the Commonwealth where the same are occasioned by chains of mountains or rivers." For the purpose of carrying into effect this part of the Act, contracts will be immediately entered into by the Executive. It would be a useless expence to have the same lines surveyed twice and in many instances three times. The respective County Courts are therefore requested to exclude from the contracts they may enter into for County Charts, the lines of their Counties that are a part of the boundary of the State, the Blue Ridge, North Mountain and Allegany Mountains, the Chesapeake Bay, and the following rivers and parts of rivers, to wit: Roanoke to the fork of Dan and Staunton; Dan to the North Carolina line above Danville and Staunton, to the junction of the North and South forks of Roanoke above Fort Lewis; Meherin to the Charlotte line; Nottoway to the line of Prince Edward; Black Water to the line of Prince George; Elizabeth River to Kempsville; Nansemond to Suffolk; Appomattox to its source; James River from its mouth to the point of Fork; the Rivanna from its mouth to the first fork above Charlottesville; the Fluvanna from its mouth to Jackson River; Jackson's River to the mouth of Dunlap's Creek; Chickahominy to its source; York River from its mouth to the junction of Mattapony and Pamunky; Mattapony to the Caroline line; Pamunky to North Wales; Northanna to the Orange line; Piankatank from its mouth, as far as it is the line of Essex; North River (Matthews) to its source; Rappahannock from its mouth to the fork above Fredericksburg; the North Fork to its source; the Rapidan to its source; Potomac to the South Branch; the South Branch to Moorefield; the North Branch to the Allegany; Shenandoah to Port Republic, Occoquon and Bull Run; Kanawha from the Ohio to the mouth of Gauley; Gauley from its mouth to the Harrison line; New River to the North Carolina line; Little Kanawha from the Ohio to the mouth of Gauley; Gauley from its mouth to the Harrison line; New River to the North Carolina line;—Little Kanawha from the Ohio to Salt Lick Creek; Monongalia to Buckhanan's River; West Fork to Clarksburg, and Cheat River to Chavers's Fork. As soon as the surveys of the boundaries, mountains and rivers aforesaid, are completed, under contracts with the Executive, the contractor for the County Charts will be furnished with such parts of the respective surveys as may be necessary to complete the said Charts.

I am, Gentlemen, with great respect, your humble servant,

FC (Vi: RG 3, Nicholas Executive Papers); printed broadside; endorsed in a clerk's hand: "Circular to the County Courts. May 12th 1816." Recorded in SJL as a 12 May 1816 "(Circular)" from "Nicholas Govr W. C." received 16 July 1816.

Nicholas first mentioned the ACT TO PROVIDE AN ACCURATE CHART OF EACH COUNTY to TJ in a letter of 22 Mar. 1816. TJ responded on 19 Apr. 1816 with his own ideas about surveying the state. MONONGALIA: Monongahela River. CHAVERS'S FORK: Shavers Fork.

From William Canby

ESTEEMED FRIEND
THOMAS JEFFERSON.— [ca. 13] 5mo 1816—

it was with concern I heard (think in the 2nd Year after I Recd thy answer & Remarks on my Note) that they were published in a Wilmington News paper, for tho' it was far from my intention, yet I think my weaknes might make Room for som to do it—as I have not for som Years kept a key, or done much busines, Yet using som handicraft industry—yet often feel the Want of Natural Ability or Supernatural perfection

farewel— WM CANBY

RC (MHi); partial dateline at foot of text; addressed: "Thomas Jefferson (Monticello) Esqr late President of the States of North America"; franked; postmarked Wilmington, Del., 13 May; endorsed by TJ as a letter of "May 1816" received 16 May 1816 and so recorded in SJL.

TJ's ANSWER & REMARKS to Canby of 18 Sept. 1813 and Canby's NOTE to TJ of 27 Aug. 1813 were both PUBLISHED in the Wilmington *Delaware Gazette*, 1 Nov. 1814.

From John Steele

DEAR SIR, Collectors office Philad[a] May 14. 1816

Stephen Cathalan Esq[r], Commercial & Navy Agent Marseilles, has consigned to me two Cases, one containing wine & the other Macarony with instructions to forward them to you by the first favourable opportunity

You will please to advise me, to what place and to whose care the Cases will be sent, & they will be forwarded accordingly

I am very respectfully,

Sir, Your Obed[t] Sv[t] JN[O] STEELE

RC (ViU: TJP-ER); endorsed by TJ as received 23 May 1816 and so recorded in SJL. RC (DLC); address cover only; with PoC of TJ to John Wood, 16 Aug. 1816, on verso; addressed: "Thomas Jefferson Esq[r] Monticello"; franked; postmarked Philadelphia, 14 May.

From Thomas Appleton

SIR Leghorn 15th may 1816.

My last respects were in date of the 15th of april, conveying to you at the same time, the legal Attestation of the death of m[r] mazzei; an attested copy of his will; together with a letter from the guardian of his daughter, as to the disposal of the property in your hands; all of which, were transmitted by the Brig Sphynx Capt: macomb for new York. I now inclose you, Sir, duplicates of these Acts.—By the letter of m[r] Carmigniani, you will observe, that they are desirous of recieving both principal & interest, as Soon as it shall be in your power to Remit them; but if delay must be allow'd for the former, that the amount of the latter should be forwarded to them as it falls due.—

Miss mazzei will give her hand in marriage to a m[r] Pini, as Soon as the customs of the country will permit her to lay aside her mourning vestments—her intended husband is a gentleman of respectability, good manners, and a competent income in Pisa—in this choice she has complied with the wishes of her father, and only hearkned to the dictates of reason, for she is a third of a century younger than m[r] Pini.

A few days ago, I reciev'd a letter from m^r Robert Dickey of n. York, covering a draft for fifty dollars, which has been duly paid, and is pass'd to your credit.

I mention'd also in my last letter, that the wine of montepulciano, owing to an uncommon Season, is greatly inferior to that usually made in that part of Tuscany; of course, I shall defer Sending you the wine you Request, until the next vintage—in the mean time, I am promis'd Some, of the villages of Carminiani & Ama, and should they prove of the quality I am assur'd they are, I purpose to Send you a hundred bottles on trial: the Sample I have tasted, appears to me very little inferior to the wines of montepulciano.—Accept, Sir, the expressions of my great esteem & Respect— TH: APPLETON

RC (DLC); at foot of first page: "Thomas Jefferson. esq."; endorsed by TJ as received 29 Aug. 1816 and so recorded in SJL. Enclosures: enclosures to Appleton to TJ, 15 Apr. 1816.

Appleton credited TJ with the payment of FIFTY DOLLARS in an account dated 3 May 1816: "C^r Thomas Jefferson esq^r for Cash Rec'd of Grant, Pillans & Co by an order of Robt Trueman jun^r in fav^r Robt Dickey fifty Spanish dollars.—@ £6 & 1/3— To be applied for purchasing wines" (entry in unidentified hand in MBPLi: Appleton Account Book). The Tuscan villages of Carmignano (CARMINIANI) and Casanuova di AMA both produced wine.

From John Martin Baker

SIR, Bordeaux, May, 15th 1816.

I have the Honor with due Respect to address you: and take the liberty to remit you, per the American Brig, General Ward, to the care of, D. Gelston, Esquire.—Newyork, a Case of Barsac white Wine, growth of the Estate, called Darancour, it is genuine, and ten years old, I have Seen it drawn and bottled in my presence, while there, I hope it may meet your approbation. Permit me Sir, to State, that I leave this tomorrow for Montpellier, where my family Reside at present owing to Mrs Baker's, late ill health, from thence, I proceed to my Consular Station, where, Praying for your Commands, I have the Honor to Be, with the Highest Respect, and Gratitude, Sir,

Your most obedient, faithful, humble servant.

JOHN MARTIN BAKER.

RC (MHi); at foot of text: "To The Most Honorable, Thomas Jefferson Monti-cello Virginia"; endorsed by TJ as received 1 Aug. 1816 and so recorded in SJL.

To Patrick Gibson

DEAR SIR Monticello May 15. 16.

On my return from Bedford on the 3[d] inst. I found here your favor of Apr. 27. and that of the 10th inst. is now recieved, inclosing an account of sales of my flour. I am glad it is so well sold, as I had begun to apprehend worse. while in Bedford I drew on you in favor of mr Robertson for 153. D 33 c and still owe there (for the last of the month)[1] 120.D. about the same period I shall need here for taxes & neighborhood debts about 200.D. which will I believe close my wants of the year till new resources come in. I return the note for the bank with my signature, and the assurances of my great esteem & respect TH: JEFFERSON

PoC (Mrs. T. Wilber Chelf, Mrs. Virginius Dabney, and Mrs. Alexander W. Parker, Richmond, 1944; photocopy in ViU: TJP); on verso of reused address cover of Jesse Torrey to TJ, 6 Apr. 1816; at foot of text: "M[r] Gibson"; endorsed by TJ. Enclosure not found.

TJ DREW an order in favor of Archibald Robertson for $153.53 on 30 Apr. 1816 for payment of $100.20 to Charles Clay for corn and $53.33 for expenses incurred in connection with the enrollment of TJ's grandson Francis Eppes at the New London Academy near Poplar Forest (*MB*, 2:1322).

[1]Omitted closing parenthesis editorially supplied.

From Charles Thomson

MY VERY DEAR, MUCH LOVED AS WELL AS ANCIENT FRIEND Lower Merion, near Philadelphia May 16. 1816

Your letter of the 9 of January last which did not reach me till the latter end of April was to me indeed a cordial. It recalled to mind the trying Scenes through which we passed with undessembled confidence, but in a particular manner rejoiced me as it informed me of the firm state of your health and the full enjoyment you have of your faculties both of body and mind and more especially of the precious little book you have composed and which you call the philosophy of Jesus, which is to you a document in proof that you are a real Christian, that is a disciple of the doctrines of Jesus and can look to the consummation of life with the composure of one qui summum nec metuit diem nec optat. For the good of our country I could wish that day to be distant; but on account of the infirmities with which age[1] is accompanied and which I experience, I dare not. Nothing but your earnest desire could induce me to trouble you with a detail of what I experience[2] and feel. Though I have reached and am near closing, my

87th year, my constitution was naturally not of the robust, but of a weak and delicate kind, subject to bilious complaints and fevers by which I have been several times brought to the gates of death and have (I may say miraculously) recoverd and with returning strength have found the powers of the mind restored. But that is not the case now. I find as I advance[3] in life that disorders of any kind make more lasting impressions. They dull the senses and stupify the mind so as to render it incapable of exercising its powers. I have parted with most of my teeth and[4] the few stumps that remain are unfit for mastication. My Eyes indeed (though in 1778 I almost lost the use of them by what the french call a Coup de Soleil) have been so far restored that I write and read without spectacles and use them only occasionally to ease the Eyes when tired or when the print is too small. My hearing is so dull that I can take no share in common conversation So that when my friends visit me and wish to communicate any thing or ask me a question they must sit near me and bawl. My memory is like a riddle—

But why should I proceed with this detail of weaknesses. How few at my age enjoy greater comforts. I am free from gout or stone or any acute disorder. My sleep is sweet, and when tired, whether by day or night I can, by laying my head on a pillow, enjoy that comfort. I read the news papers for amusement and glance over the debates of sages and am sorry to say I find more to disgust than to please. I lately met with Allen's history of Lewis and Clarks interesting expedition up the Missouri to its source, thence across the rocky mountains and down the river Columbia to the Pacific Ocean. It is a wonderful instance of persevering resolution I wish it had undergone another revision before it was committed to the press, and that it was accompanied with a better map.

I ought to have informed you that from an early period of life I have continued the constant use of the flesh brush, always in the morning and sometimes at night just before going to bed. This serves instead of riding and I have the benefit of an air bathe instead of a water bathe. But to finish this string of Egotisms I beg leave to assure you that I am with constant and[5] undessembled love your affectionate

Chas Thomson

RC (DLC); endorsed by TJ as received 29 May 1816 and so recorded in SJL. RC (MHi); address cover only; with PoC of TJ to John Payne Todd, 15 Aug. 1816, on recto; addressed: "Thomas Jefferson Esqr at Monticello Virginia"; stamp canceled; franked; postmarked Philadelphia, 21 May.

QUI SUMMUM NEC METUIT DIEM NEC OPTAT is a variant of "summum nec metuas diem nec optes" ("don't fear your last day, nor yet pray for it"), from Martial, *Epigrams*, book 10, poem 47, line 13 (Martial, *Epigrams*, trans. David R. Shackleton Bailey, Loeb Classical Library [1993; later printing with variant pagination], 2:360–1). COUP DE SOLEIL: "sunstroke; sunburn."

[1] Reworked from "old."

[2] Manuscript: "experienc."
[3] Manuscript: "advanc."
[4] Manuscript: "and and."
[5] Manuscript: "and and."

From John R. F. Corbin

D^R^ SIR May 17—1816

It is with Some degree of difidence I undertake to address you: I hope however you will not consider it impertinent in me, because I have not had the pleasure of an acquaintence with you.—My object is to learn of you (if in your power to instruct) any thing or some thing concerning the title, or claim, or interest in property generally known and call'd Birds Lottery, in which my Grand Mother Sally Jones, who was Sally Skelton had a considerable interest

Mr Wirt is of opinion the title is a clear one.—A letter address'd to me in winchester, will be thankfully received—

Yr: Very Ob^t^ Sv^t^ JOHN R. F. CORBIN

RC (MHi); endorsed by TJ as received 1 June 1816 and so recorded in SJL.

John R. F. Corbin was a son of Gawin Corbin and Elizabeth Jones Corbin, who was a daughter of Sally Skelton Jones and Thomas Jones (1726–ca. 1785). In 1814 he was a private in R. W. Carter's cavalry troop of the Virginia militia, attached to the 41st Regiment, from Richmond County. Corbin died between 1822 and 1830 (Stella Pickett Hardy, *Colonial Families of the Southern States of America* [1911], 180; Lewis H. Jones, *Captain Roger Jones of London and Virginia* [1891], 40, 55; "The Corbin Family," *VMHB* 30 [1922]: 403; Williamsburg *Virginia Gazette* [Purdie], 10 May 1776; *Muster Rolls of the Virginia Militia in the War of 1812* [1852], 202; DNA: RG 29, CS, Frederick Co., Stephensburg, 1820; *Burwell et al. v. Corbin et al.* [1822] [1 Randolph], *Va. Reports*, 22:131–64, esp. 132–3; Charles Town *Virginia Free Press and Farmers' Repository*, 21 July 1830).

The prizes in the 1768 drawing for the LOTTERY of William Byrd (1728–77) consisted of tracts laid off from his land at and near the falls of the James River. Subsequent problems with the allotment of the parcels prompted the Virginia General Assembly in 1781 to pass "An act to secure to persons who derive titles to lots, lands or tenements under the lottery . . . of the late William Byrd, esquire, a fee simple estate therein" (*DVB*, 2:470–2; Neal Elizabeth Millikan, "'A Taxation Upon All the Fools in Creation': Lotteries in the British North American Empire" [M.A. thesis, North Carolina State University, 2004], 27–8; Hening, 10:446–7).

To Nicolas G. Dufief

DEAR SIR Monticello May 17. 16.

On the 7th Ult. I inclosed you an order on mr Vaughan for 24. D 68 C the balance of my former account which I hope you recieved. I have just recieved from M. de la Fayette a request to send him two copies of the Review of Montesquieu published by Duane in 1811. in 8vo which I must ask the favor of you to procure and send for me. mr Gallatin I suppose is not yet gone, but must be on the eve of departure, and furnishes the safest opportunity of conveyance. I therefore inclose you two envelopes, addressed to him with my frank, and accomodated each to the size of the volume. I will pray you to put a copy into each cover and forward it to him by the first mail, wherever he is. this will be better known to you than to me, as I have never heard from what port he will embark. I hope the packages will reach him in time.

Will you be so good as to send me a copy of your dictionary, neatly bound, a good book deserving a good binding, also a copy of Mackay on the Longitude. I salute you with great esteem & respect

TH: JEFFERSON

PoC (DLC); on verso of reused address cover of John Vaughan to TJ, 13 Mar. 1816; at foot of text: "M. Dufief"; endorsed by TJ. Enclosures not found.

Lafayette's REQUEST of 21 Jan. 1816 was for Destutt de Tracy, *Commentary and Review of Montesquieu's Spirit of Laws*. Albert GALLATIN, the newly appointed American minister plenipotentiary to France, departed from New York on 11 June 1816 aboard the *Peacock*, a United States sloop of war bound for Le Havre (New York *National Advocate*, 13 June 1816).

To Lafayette

Monticello May. 17. 16

I recieved, my dear friend, yesterday evening only your letter of Jan. 21. and this day I write to a bookseller in Philadelphia to send immediately, for you, two copies of the Anonymous Review of Montesquieu, under cover to mr Gallatin, if he be not gone. in a letter to him lately, I begged of him to say to yourself and mr T. that I had not the courage to write to either of you, until I could send a copy of the work on Political economy which I have been so long endeavoring to get printed. I will state to you however the simple fact. I proposed to the same editor at Philadelphia to translate and print this, who had done the former work. he undertook it. after time enough had elapsed as I thought, to have heard of it's publication, I wrote to ask when it would appear? at such a time it was answered. it is needless[1] to repeat to you the subsequent reiterated applications, excuses & promises. they ended finally in a declaration that the work was translated, but that he could not print it. I then desired a return of the work. it was sent to me with the translation. I then engaged a person in Washing-

ton to print it, offering, if he would, to revise the translation myself. he has undertaken it. but when I came to look into the translation, I found it such as had never been seen. it had been done by a person who understood neither French nor English. I entered on the correction, and had got too far into it before I became sensible it would have been shorter for me to translate it anew. I spent five hours a day on it, for between two and three months. I was able at length to make it faithful to the text, but not elegant. le premier jet rendered that impossible. it has been in the hands of the editor about a month; but as he is to send me the proof sheets for correction, successively as they come out and by mail, it will employ the summer & autumn probably. nothing has been spared which depended on me; and had I resided where the publication was undertaken, I could, by daily attentions, have soon seen into the fact and cause of delay, and have remedied them. but at the distance of 300. miles from Philadelphia, unable to get information but such as the undertaker chose to give, and through the public mail, I was quite at his mercy. still I shall think my trouble and vexations well requited by possessing my countrymen of such a work. it's principles are so profound, so logically demonstrated, and so briefly expressed, that it must become the elementary book of the world for the science of Political economy, as the other will be of that of government. the very metaphysical character of the Prefatory pieces may deter some readers not in the habit of abstract contemplation, while it will be highly satisfactory to those who are
the indications however are sufficient which shew the former where the part of the work begins which will be interesting to them,[2] and levelled to comprehensions less exercised in speculations of this character. in this plain statement I hope yourself & your friend will find an apology for the delays which have taken place in sending you this work. with respect to the Commentary on Montesquieu there is a fact of some note. you are aware that the Edinburg review is considered as the ablest work of that kind which has ever been published. means were taken to place this work in the hand of the Editor. but while the work itself, & the principles of his Review permitted him to say nothing against it, it's being an American publication was ground enough to avoid saying any thing in it's favor. they have therefore not even mentioned it in their Monthly catalogue of new publications. such are the feelings of that country towards this.

Uncertain whether mr Gallatin is yet gone, & of course whether this letter will reach him in time, or go by some other conveyance, it is most prudent to say little on politics. that the violations of all rights committed on the Continent by France, under the direction of

Bonaparte, as well as those on the ocean by England, merited a proper measure of retaliation and punishment, I imagine yourselves are sensible. on England it is yet to come: and on France, had it proceeded but to a reasonable length, justice would not have condemned it. but it has past that term. the continuation of it becomes aggression: and the allies have gone on to commit equal violations on independant nations with those of Bonaparte. if there were another world to do it, the same crusade ought now to be undertaken against them, which they enlisted against France. still I believe the loss of the battle of Waterloo was the salvation of France. had Bonaparte obtained the victory, his talents, his egoism, and destitution of all moral principle, would have rivetted a military despotism on your necks. in your present situation, however afflicting and humiliating, I think it certain you will effect a constitution in which the will of the nation shall have an organised controul over the actions of it's government, and it's citizens a regular protection against it's oppressions. I dare add no more, but my prayers for the event, and that your steady pursuits of this object may be rewarded by the happiness of your seeing it realised before you sing your Nunc dimittas. TH: JEFFERSON

RC (ICN: Thomas Jefferson Letters); at head of text in an unidentified hand: "N° 3." PoC (DLC); at foot of first page: "M. de la Fayette"; endorsed by TJ. Tr (NNPM); in French. Tr (DLC: Lafayette Papers, La Grange microfilm); extract in English, consisting of final paragraph. Enclosed in TJ to Albert Gallatin, 18 May 1816.

TJ here discusses his involvement in the English translation of two works by Destutt de Tracy (MR T.), the *Commentary and Review of Montesquieu's Spirit of Laws* and the *Treatise on Political Economy*. William Duane was the SAME EDITOR, and TJ subsequently ENGAGED Joseph Milligan. LE PREMIER JET: "the first attempt." The EDITOR of the *Edinburgh Review* was Francis Jeffrey.

[1] Manuscript: "needess."
[2] Preceding two words interlined.

To David Bailie Warden

DEAR SIR Monticello May 17. 16

I recieved last night your favor of Feb. 20. and hasten to acknolege it by return of mail, in the hope it may be in time to reach mr Gallatin before his departure. I should have associated you myself with mr Ticknor in requesting the friendly office of purchasing some books for me, but at the time he left this country your letters had given me reason to believe you might be on a return to it. his visit to Germany too gave a chance of better editions of the classical books. I particularly requested of him, should you be still in Paris, to call on you in my name, as one whom I especially respected, and to consult you in the execution of my book-commission. in the application he has made to you on that subject he has but fulfilled my wishes, and I have now to thank you for your readiness in undertaking it, and to pray you to add to the catalogue I sent him, the 'Opere di Platone di Dardi Bembo,' published at Venice in 1601. in 5.v. 12mo and probably to be had in Paris.—of the several copies you sent me of Talleyrand's certificate, I made the best use in my power and sincerely regret it was to no better effect.—you will have seen from our papers the designation of our next president. there will be no republican opposition[1] to Monroe. the federal states of Connecticut & Delaware, & the feeble and declining federal majorities of Massachusets and Rhode island will oppose pro formâ only. he will certainly therefore be our next president. there is great and general content in this country with the conduct of our administration and the issue of the war. altho' our taxes this year have been five times greater than we ever paid before, they have been paid with unexampled chearfulness and punctuality. I hope therefore the debt contracted will be diminished rapidly. the great prices given for tobacco have produced great preparations for the present year, which however will be baffled by the weather. the spring has been unusually dry and cold. our average morning cold for the month of May in other years has been 63° of Farenheit. in the present month it has been to this day an average of 53° and one morning as low as 43°. repeated frosts have killed the early fruits and the crops of tobacco and wheat will be poor. about the middle of April they had at Quebec snow a foot deep. mr and mrs Randolph and our family are well, and desire me to place here their great esteem for you, to which I beg leave to add the assurances of mine and my best wishes for your health and welfare.

TH: JEFFERSON

RC (MdHi: Warden Papers); addressed: "David B. Warden esq. Paris"; endorsed by Warden. PoC (DLC); on reused address cover of Patrick Gibson to TJ, 18 Mar. 1816; endorsed by TJ.

[1] RC: "oppostion."

Addition to Note for Destutt de Tracy's *Treatise on Political Economy*

[ca. 18 May 1816]

To this a single observation shall yet be added. Whether property alone, and the whole of what each citizen possesses, shall be subject to contribution, or only it's surplus after satisfying his first wants, or whether the faculties of body and mind shall contribute also from their annual earnings, is a question to be decided. but, when decided, and the principle settled, it is to be equally and fairly applied to all. to take from one, because it is thought that his own industry and that of his father[s?][1] has acquired too much, in order to spare to others, who, or whose fathers have not exercised equal industry and skill, is to violate arbitrarily the first principle of association, 'the guarantee to every one of a free exercise of his industry, & the fruits acquired by it[.'] if the overgrown wealth of an individual be deemed dangerous to the state, the best corrective is the law of equal inheritance to all in equal degree: and the better as this enforces a law of nature, while extra-taxation violates one.

FC (DLC: TJ Papers, 206:36788); written entirely in TJ's hand on verso of his Note for Destutt de Tracy's *Treatise on Political Economy*, [ca. 6 Apr. 1816]; undated; edge trimmed. Enclosed in TJ to Joseph Milligan, 18 May 1816.

Despite Milligan's assurance in a letter dated 4 June 1816, this addition was not printed with TJ's note on page 202 of Destutt de Tracy, *Treatise on Political Economy*.

[1] Word trimmed at the letter "r," leaving it uncertain whether TJ wrote in the singular or plural.

To Albert Gallatin

Dear Sir Monticello May 18. 16.

I have just recieved a request from M. de la Fayette to send him two copies of the Review of Montesquieu, published in Philadelphia about 4. or 5. years ago, and have written to Dufief to forward them under cover to you, wherever you may be, which he will know better than I can. I pray you to be the bearer of them, with the letter for him now inclosed; and, if you have never read the work, that you will amuse yourself with it on the passage. altho' in some points it will not obtain our concurrence either in principle or practice, yet, on the whole, you have never seen so profound and so correct an exposition of the true principles of government. a work of equal distinction on the science of political economy is now in the press at Washington, profound, solid, and brief.

You are so much more in the way of recieving information of what is passing in the world, that it would be idle in me to offer you any. one fact perhaps can be better judged of in the country than in the cities; a belief expressed by every one I see (for I go little out, and meddle less with their opinions), that at the next election of representatives to Congress, there will be the most signal display which has ever been seen of the exercise by the people of the controul they have retained over the proceedings of their delegates. at least if those of the other states are cast in the same mould of their fellow citizens in this. and what is very remarkable is that this spontaneous and universal concurrence of sentiment has been produced without scarcely a word having been said on the subject in the public papers of this state. I consider this last circumstance as presenting an element of character in our people, which must constitute the basis of every estimate of the solidity & duration of our government. sincere prayers for your safe and pleasant passage, and a happy return in the fulness of time when your own wishes and the public good shall require.

TH: JEFFERSON

P.S. I trouble you also with a letter for mr Warden

RC (NHi: Gallatin Papers); addressed: "His Excellency Albert Gallatin esquire recommended to the care of mr Graham at the Office of State Washington"; franked; postmarked Milton, 22 May; endorsed by Gallatin; also erroneously endorsed in an unidentified hand: "Monticello 16 June 1816." PoC (DLC); endorsed by TJ. Enclosures: (1) TJ to Lafayette, 17 May 1816. (2) TJ to David Bailie Warden, 17 May 1816.

The WORK OF EQUAL DISTINCTION was Destutt de Tracy, *Treatise on Political Economy*.

To Joseph Milligan

DEAR SIR Monticell[o] May 18. 16.

On the 7th Ult. I wrote to you and forwarded at the same time the corrected translation of mr Tracy's book, with a request that you would forward to me for correction the proof sheets as they are struck off, and as we have three mails a week now from Washington, you will always recieve the sheet on the 5th day after it comes from your hands, perhaps sometimes on the 7th. having as yet recieved none I begin to be uneasy, and the more so on account of the great delay which that work has already so unfortunately experienced. will you drop me a line of information to relieve my anxiety[1]

In some part of the MS. I inserted a Note beginning with the words 'our author's classification'[2] Etc and ending 'weighty observations of our author.' will you add at the end of it what is on the inclosed paper? accept my best wishes and respects.

TH: JEFFERSON

PoC (DLC); on verso of portion of reused address cover to TJ; dateline faint; at foot of text: "Mr Millegan"; endorsed by TJ. Enclosure: TJ's Addition to Note for Destutt de Tracy's *Treatise on Political Economy*, [ca. 18 May 1816].

TJ's letter of THE 7TH ULT. was actually dated 6 Apr. 1816.

[1] Edge may be trimmed here, with possible loss of a question mark.

[2] Omitted closing quotation mark editorially supplied.

To John Steele

SIR Monticello May 18. 16.

A letter just recieved from mr Cathalan of Marseilles informs me he has sent me a case of Hermitage wine and a box of Maccaroni by the Pilot, Capt Dixon, and I learn by the public papers that that vessel is arrived at Philadelphia. I inclose you the bill of lading, and have copied on the back of it from mr Cathalan's invoice the quantity & cost of the articles. I have to ask the favor of you to drop me a line of information of the amount of the duties, freight & other charges which shall be immediately remitted to you. in the mean time if you will have the goodness to forward the two boxes by some safe vessel to Richmond, addressed to Messrs Gibson & Jefferson, then you will confer a great obligation on me. they will pay to the master of the vessel carrying the articles his freight & other charges.

I avail myself of this occasion to observe that having occasion to recieve from different parts of Europe, & at different times articles such as the above, books E^tc without being able to prescribe the port to which there may be an opportunity of sending them, they may sometimes come to that of Philadelphia. will you give me leave to hope that you will always drop me a line of the duties, freight & charges to be paid, under the assurance of a punctual and immediate remittance of them? the articles will always be to be forwarded to Richmond as above; and when they are wines the advance of the hot season may render their immediate transmission desirable to lessen the danger of spoiling. be pleased to accept the assurance of my thankfulness and respect. TH: JEFF[ERSON]

PoC (MHi); on verso of portion of reused address cover to TJ; signature faint; at foot of text: "The Collector of Philada"; endorsed by TJ. Recorded in SJL as a letter to "Steele John Genl Collector of Phila." Enclosure not found.

To Marcus Dyson

SI[R] Monticello. May 19. 16

Your favor of the 6th is [r]ecieved, and I am sorry to say I am not able to answer your chemical enquiries with satisfaction. the antient chemistry was in possession of the schools when I was a student in them, and when that was reformed by the nomenclature of Morveau, and the theories of Lavoisier, I had become too much engaged in public affairs and the practical business of life, to undertake a fundamental renovation of any branch of science. I contented myself therefore with a general knolege of the system of Lavoisier, and have at no time followed it up with such a degree of attention as would authorise me to hazard opinions where error would be serious. the best informed Chemist of our state, as far as my acquaintance goes, is Joseph C. Cabell of Warminster, Senator for our district. he passed a considerable time in Paris, applied himself while there with assiduity to this branch of science, and availed himself of all the advantages which that place offers for it's acquisition. were you to take the trouble of consulting him, he could probably satisfy your enquiries on grounds which would merit confidence. with a wish that your object may be accomplished, accept the assurance of my great respect

Th: Jefferson

PoC (DLC); two words faint; at foot of text: "Mr Marcus Dyson"; endorsed by TJ.

Following TJ's suggestion, on 27 May 1816 Dyson sent JOSEPH C. CABELL a letter and drawing similar to those he forwarded to TJ on 6 May 1816. According to Cabell's endorsement on his letter from Dyson (RC in ViU: JCC), in his response he declined "to give any advice upon the Subject" and referred Dyson to Thomas P. Jones, the "Professor of chemy in Wm & Mary."

To George Logan

Monticello May 19. 16.

It gives me the greatest pain, dear Sir, to make a serious complaint to you. from the letter which I wrote you on the 3d of Oct. 1813. an extract was published, with my name, in the newspapers, conveying a very just, but certainly a very harsh censure on Bonaparte. this produced to me more complaints from my best friends, and called for more explanations than any transaction of my life had ever done. they inferred from this partial extract an approbation of the conduct of England, which yet the same letter had censured with equal rigour. it produced too from the Minister of Bonaparte a complaint, not indeed formal, for I was but a private citizen, but serious, of my volunteering with England in the abuse of his sovereign. it was incumbent on me to explain, by declaring to a member of the government that the extract was partial, and it's publication unauthorised. notwithstanding the pain which this act had cost me, considering it on your part but as a mere inadvertence, on the reciept of your letter of

Aug. 16. 15. I wrote an answer of Oct. 13. & again on reciept of that of the 27th Ult. I had begun an answer, when the arrival of our mail put into my hands a newspaper containing at full length mine of Oct. 13. it became necessary then to ask myself seriously whether I meant to enter as a political champion in the field of the newspapers? he who does this throws the gauntlet of challenge to every one who will take it up. it behoves him then to weigh maturely every sentiment, every fact, every sentence and syllable he commits to paper, and to be certain that he is ready with reason, and testimony to maintain every tittle before the tribunal of the public. but this is not our purpose when we write to a friend. we are careless, incorrect, in haste, perhaps under some transient excitement, and we hazard things without reflection, because without consequence in the bosom of a friend. perhaps it may be said that the letter of Oct. 15. contained nothing offensive to others, nothing which could injure myself. it contained a reprobation of the murders and desolations committed by the French nation, under their leader Bonaparte. it contained a condemnation of the allied powers for seizing and taking to themselves independant & unoffending countries, because too weak to defend themselves. in this they had done wrong: but was it my business to become the public accuser? and to undertake before the world to denounce their iniquities? and do you not think I had a right to decide this for myself? and to say whether the sentiments I trusted to you were meant for the whole world? I am sure that on reflection you will percieve that I ought to have been consulted.

I might have manifested my dissatisfaction by a silent reserve of all answer: but this would have offered a blank, which might have been filled up by erroneous imputations of sentiment. I prefer candid and open expression. no change of good will to you, none in my estimate of your integrity or understanding, has taken place, except as to your particular opinion on the rights of correspondence: and I pray you especially to assure mrs Logan of my constant and affectionate esteem & attachment, the just tribute of a respect for the virtues of her heart & head.

TH: JEFFERSON

RC (PHi: Logan Papers); addressed: "Doctr George Logan Stenton near Philadelphia"; franked; postmarked Charlottesville, 22 May; endorsed by Logan. PoC (DLC).

TJ's ANSWER OF OCT. 13. to Logan was actually dated 15 Oct. 1815.

To Joseph Delaplaine

SIR Monticello May 20.

Your's of the 11th is just recieved, and with it the head of Columbus for which accept my thanks. it has been evidently taken at an earlier period of his life than that of the Florentine gallery, which I think you will deem worthy of taking additionally. I shall be happy to recieve mr Otis here, and yourself also should you conclude to come as intimated. I wish it may not be later than the 1st of June, as in the 2d week of that month I am to set out on a journey of some weeks absence. I have no doubt that the copy of my portrait at the President's residence in Orange (3. miles off the stage road) is as good as the original in the possession of Stewart. I own one by him which has been highly esteemed, original also, on strong paper, in water colours, a profile in the medallion stile, which I lent to Dr Thornton at Washington, & now there. I write to him for it's return if done with. but mr Otis can in any event see it there. you must judge for yourself whether a copy by Stewart himself (as that of the President's) whose name is without a rival would not be more valued than an original by any other however good. should mr Otis come in the stage, it may be convenient for him to know that the stage to Charlottesville which passes my gate, leaves Fredericksburg either the Saturday afternoon or Sunday morning (probably the latter) and arrives at Charlottesville Monday, at 8 P.M. coming but once a week. Accept the assurance of my respect TH: JEFFERSON

RC (LNT: George H. and Katherine M. Davis Collection); partially dated; addressed: "Mr Joseph de la Plaine Philadelphia"; franked; postmarked Charlottesville, 22 May; endorsed by Delaplaine as a letter of 20 May 1816. PoC (DLC); on verso of reused address cover of Wilson Cary Nicholas to TJ, 22 Mar. 1816; at foot of text: "Mr Joseph Delaplaine"; endorsed by TJ as a letter of 20 May 1816.

The COPY owned by James Madison may actually be the ORIGINAL TJ portrait produced by Gilbert Stuart (STEWART) in 1805. Stuart also painted the MEDALLION profile on loan to William THORNTON (David Meschutt, "Gilbert Stuart's Portraits of Thomas Jefferson," *American Art Journal* 13 [winter 1981]: 2–16; Bush, *Life Portraits*, 57–63).

To William Thornton

DEAR SIR Monticello May. 20. 16.

Mr Delaplaine of Philadelphia, being engaged[1] in a work of engravings of American characters, has engaged an artist to come on here, and perhaps will accompany him himself, to copy my Columbus, Vespucius, Cortez Etc. and he wishes to copy that also of myself by

Stewart which you have. but this must depend on the question whether you are done with it yourself. if it has answered your purposes, and can be returned by the stage, it may gratify mr Delaplaine's wish. but it should not be hazarded by the stage, unless in the care of some one coming on to Charlottesville, as it would be buckled behind with the baggage and be destroyed by rain or rubbing.   I thank you for your last annual report of the patents. I think the English must acknolege we excel them in the faculty of invention. there can be no better proofs than are furnished by your office & our newspapers; the former in things useful, the latter in lies. our family joins me in compliments to the ladies of yours, with which accept the assurance of my great esteem & respect.

TH: JEFFERSON

P.S. my grandaughter will be returning home thro' Washington this week, but as a bird of passage, without stopping but a night to roost & rest. she would[2] take good care of the portrait if done with.

RC (DLC: Thornton Papers); addressed: "Doct[r] William Thornton Washington Col."; franked; postmarked Charlottesville, 22 May. PoC (MHi); on verso of reused address cover of missing letter from William Short to TJ of 14 Mar. 1816 (see note to TJ to Short, 7 Apr. 1816); endorsed by TJ.

During his time in Europe, TJ commissioned copies of portraits of Christopher COLUMBUS, Amerigo Vespucci (VESPUCIUS), Hernán Cortés (CORTEZ), and Ferdinand Magellan in the Gioviana Collection of the Galleria degli Uffizi in Florence, Italy (*PTJ*, 14:440–1; TJ to Joseph Delaplaine, 3 May 1814; Susan R. Stein, *The Worlds of Thomas Jefferson at Monticello* [1993], 132–3). TJ's GRANDAUGHTER Ellen W. Randolph (Coolidge) was RETURNING to Monticello via Baltimore and Washington from an excursion that took her as far north as Philadelphia (Ellen W. Randolph [Coolidge] to Martha Jefferson Randolph, 6 Apr., 12 May 1816 [ViU: Coolidge Correspondence]).

[1] Manuscript: "enaged."
[2] TJ here canceled "offer a."

To Francis Eppes

Monticello May 21. 16.

I send you, my dear Francis, a Greek grammar, the best I know for the use of schools. it is the one now most generally used in the United States. I expect you will begin it soon after your arrival at the New London academy. you might, while at home, amuse yourself with learning the letters, and spelling and reading the Greek words, so that you may not be stopped by that when mr Mitchell puts you into the grammar. I think you will like him, and old mr & mrs Dehavens, from the character I have of them. I am sure mr Mitchell will do every thing for you he can; and I have no fear that you will not do full justice to his instruction. but, while you endeavor, by a good store of learning, to prepare yourself to become an useful and distinguished member of your country you must remember that this can never be, without uniting merit with your learning. honesty, disinterestedness, and good nature are indispensable to procure the esteem and confidence of those with whom we live, and on whose esteem our happiness depends. never suffer a thought to be harbored in your mind which you would not avow openly. when tempted to do any thing in secret, ask yourself if you would do it in public. if you would not, be sure it is wrong. in little disputes with your companions, give way, rather than insist on trifles. for their love, and the approbation of others will be worth more to you than the trifle in dispute. above all things, and at all times, practice yourself in good humor. this, of all human qualities, is the most amiable and endearing to society. whenever you feel a warmth of temper rising, check it at once, and suppress it, recollecting it will make you unhappy within yourself, and disliked by others. nothing gives one person so great advantage over another, as to remain always cool and unruffled under all circumstances. think of these things, practice them &[1] you will be rewarded by the love & confidence of the world. I have some expectation of being at Poplar Forest the 3^d week of June, when I hope I shall see you going on[2] cleverly, & already beloved by your tutor, curators, & companions as you are by your's affectionately

TH: JEFFERSON

RC (DLC). PoC (DLC); at head of text: "Francis Eppes"; endorsed by TJ.

The GREEK GRAMMAR has not been identified.

[1] Remainder of PoC written on verso after removal from polygraph.

[2] In PoC TJ here canceled "well."

To Joel Yancey

DEAR SIR Monticello May 21. 16.

I informed mr Darnell that[1] on account of the misfortunes of the last year, scarcely any thing made for market there or here, immense purchases of corn for bread here and some there, and unexampled taxes, I could not pay his wages till another crop should come in. he said he should be particularly in want of 50.D. which therefore I promised to send him. I have also to pay John Depriest for a horse 70.D. on the 1st of June. for these purposes I inclose a draught on Gibson & Jefferson for 120.D. in favor of mr Robertson, to enable him to make the payments for me. I shall send up the two coopers the last week in June to aid in your harvest. they are both cradlers. I think (without being certain) I shall be with you about the same time. drought and cold weather give us a wretched prospect here. I wish it may be better with you. Accept the assurance of my great esteem & respect. TH: JEFFERSON

PoC (MHi); at foot of text: "M[r] Joel Yancey"; endorsed by TJ. Enclosure not found.

The TWO COOPERS were TJ's slaves Barnaby Gillette and Nace (Yancey to TJ, 29 Aug. 1816).

[1]TJ here canceled "nothing."

To Peter Minor

TH:J. TO MR PETER MINOR Mont[o] May 22. 16. Wednesday.
Will you do us the favor to take peas & punch with us to-day? we did not know till last night that we should have either.

RC (photocopy in ViU: TJP); dateline at foot of text. Not recorded in SJL.

From John F. Watson

D SIR, Bank Germantown 24 may 1816—

A few days ago I forwarded you the 9th & now by this mail the 10th Vol of the Edinburg Review— Be pleased at your convenience to remit me a 5 D[rs] state Bank note of Richmond or Petes[bg] if attainable as pay for them— Yrs very respectfy

JOHN F WATSON

It occurs to me to mention that I have on hand a copy of the Quarterly Review from the commencement to the present its 26th N[os]—If you had any inclination to possess them I should give them at 25 ℔C[t] Reduction in price—I already know your low estimate of them: but for the sake of "audi alteram partem" & occasional reference, I have not known but you might be induced to give a reduced price for them—Perhaps [...]

RC (DLC); bottom of page trimmed; dateline beneath signature; addressed: "Thomas Jefferson Esq[re] Monticello V[a]"; franked; postmarked Germantown, 24 May; endorsed by TJ as received 1 June 1816 and so recorded in SJL.

From Charles Simms

SIR Alexandria 25th May 1816

Mr Stephen Cathalan commercial and navy agent of the United States at Marseilles, has consigned to my care, four Cases of red wine, which he requests to have forwarded to you by the first opportunity.

I have put them in store where they will be carefully preserved, to wait your further order, as to the mode of conveying them to Monticello.

Very respectfully I have the honor to be Sir yr obt Servt

CH. SIMMS

RC (MHi); in the hand of William D. Simms, signed by Charles Simms; endorsed by TJ as received 1 June 1816 and so recorded in SJL. RC (DLC); address cover only; with PoC of TJ to James Madison, 15 Aug. 1816, on verso; addressed by William D. Simms: "Thomas Jefferson Esquire Monticello (near) Charlottsville Virginia"; franked; postmarked Charlottesville, 31 May.

From Joseph Story

SIR Salem. Massachusetts. May 25. 1816.

I beg your acceptance of the enclosed Sketch of the life & character of Mr Dexter—It is a hasty composition, but, I trust, it will receive your indulgent consideration, as a token of the gratitude & respect, with which

I have the honour to be Your very obliged & obedient Sert

JOSEPH STORY

RC (MHi); at foot of text: "The Honorable Thomas Jefferson"; endorsed by TJ as received 4 June 1816 and so recorded in SJL. RC (DLC); address cover only; with PoC of TJ to Peter Derieux, 27 July 1816, on verso; addressed (trimmed): "The Honorable Thomas [...] Mo[...]." Enclosure: Story, *Sketch of the Life of Samuel Dexter, LL. D.* (Boston, 1816; Poor, *Jefferson's Library*, 5 [no. 163]).

Joseph Story (1779–1845), jurist, legal scholar, and educator, was a native of Marblehead, Massachusetts. He graduated from Harvard University in 1798, studied law, joined the bar in 1801, and established his legal practice in Salem, Massachusetts. Story declined TJ's appointment in 1803 as naval officer for Salem and Beverley, Massachusetts. He was in the state House of Representatives, 1805–08, and again in 1811, when he served as Speaker. As a member of the United States House of Representatives, 1808–09, Story adamantly opposed the Embargo Act of 1807, and TJ credited its repeal to his influence. President James Madison nominated Story to the United States Supreme Court in 1811 despite TJ's opposition. He took his seat on 3 Feb. 1812 as the youngest person ever appointed to the court and served until his death. A strong supporter of Chief Justice John Marshall, Story opposed states' rights and supported interpretations of the United States Constitution that strengthened and expanded the power of the federal government. In 1829 Story accepted the position of Dane Professor of Law at Harvard, which he also served as overseer,

1818–25, and fellow, 1825–45. During his tenure attendance at the law school increased dramatically, as did its prestige. Story was a member of the Massachusetts Historical Society, a fellow of the American Academy of Arts and Sciences and, from 1844, a member of the American Philosophical Society. His many scholarly publications included a series of influential treatises on technical legal subjects, with the *Commentaries on the Constitution of the United States*, 3 vols. (1833), being among the most important (*ANB*; *DAB*; R. Kent Newmyer, *Supreme Court Justice Joseph Story: Statesman of the Old Republic* [1985]; Story, *Miscellaneous Writings, Literary, Critical, Juridical, and Political* [1835]; William W. Story, ed., *Life and Letters of Joseph Story*, 2 vols. [1851]; *Harvard Catalogue*, 120, 181; *JEP*, 1:441, 446, 453, 2:189, 190 [4 Feb., 1 Mar., 11 Nov. 1803, 15, 18 Nov. 1811]; Story to TJ, 14 Jan. 1806 [MHi]; TJ to Henry Dearborn, 16 July 1810; TJ to Madison, 15 Oct. 1810; APS, *Proceedings* 4 [1844]: 37–9; *Boston Daily Atlas*, 12 Sept. 1845; Washington *Daily National Intelligencer*, 15 Sept. 1845).

From Anonymous

Respected Friend May 26th 1816

The numerous, vindictve and malicious Aspersions that have appeared in our public papers to lacerate your Character & reputation—by factious Harpies & party Zealots for the last twenty years have fill'd the breasts of your friends with sorrowfull feelings & vexatious indignation and of none more than the person who now takes the liberty of addressing you—it is a Tax laid on superior Talents & Virtue & exemplified in an eminent degree in the Redeemer of the World who committed no Sin—neither was Guile found in his mouth—the Writer of this has recd some Consolation in his own life's experience[1] in the reflection that he has seen many a Cur dog lift his leg—& water the outside of a Church which had no effect in defiling the Sanctity of the Temple & in this light he has uniformly[2] viewed the unceasing virulent attacks upon your Reputation—but in the numerous Conflicts & Controversies upon your Character—he has been hard set to Justify you upon the Subject of Slave Keeping after the energetic & forcible Expressions in your Notes on Virginia (extracts from which he has only seen) that the wonderfull Great-Almighty Creator—does not possess one Attribute that we could apply to in a Contingent Conflict with that People. I must confess upon this Subject your practice is indefensible—tho I have heard alledged by some of your best Friends—that you hold them as you would a Wolf by the Ears that he should do no mischief & by others better informed—that you owe them not only Liberty—but Education to qualify them for that Liberty—this is ingenious reasoning & satisfactory—provided—that no Motives of personal Convenience & Interest make a part of it—the Writer of this—makes no hesitation in declaring that if an immediate[3]

Abrupt & total Emancipation depended upon his (ipse dixit) he should withhold it as he conceives that it might do more Mischeif than Good but as the Evil has been introduced gradually—in the same way it ought to be gotten rid of & that in the first instance by Men Eminent for Talents—discernment & Disinterestness which would lead others Step by Step to abolish it without material Injury to the Mass of the Community—what a Continuance of Known Injury & injustice may finally lead to I will not in this place undetake to say but—what will Posterity say of the illustrious Author of the Declaration of our Independane should he leave a numerous Class of his fellow Men in the Abject & forlorn Conditn of Slaves who have never done either himself or his Country Injury—but have rec[d] heaped Measures of Insults & wrongs—Death before Slavery—is the Banner under which we fought in our Revolutiony War—where[4] our Civil & not personal Rights were in Controversy—& shal[l] we imitate the Case of the person in the Gospel whose Lord after releasing him from a great Debt—threw his fellow Servant into Prison for a penny—nay Keep in Bondge those who owe us Nothing—but who have clear'd our Lands & in various Ways—contributed to our Comfort & Support—let the Name of Tho[s] Jefferson after the Sentiments he has publicly expressd on this Subject—never be coupled or cited[5] with that of Bacon—the bribe'd Judge—The Writer of this could add numerous Arguments to shew the Absurdity & Wickedness of Robbing a Man of his person—depriving him of his Liberty & obstructing his Happiness & improvement & the political Evil to Society—but holds it superfluous to the Mind he is addressing—we hesitate at receiving Stolen Goods—Knowing them fraudulently taken—but make no hesitation at receiving what is incomparably more valuable than any Kind of Property—Human Souls—violating in the Seperation[6] of their Connections every feeling of Nature—Making us worse than Cannibals—this Justified by Legislation & Courts of Justice The Writer of this has seen with Frantic Feelings what he had no power to alleviate—the most heart Rending Seperations—but it has had the happy Effect to convince him of the Christian System—which from Some of the Absurdities mixed with it—he had almost doubted & recollecting that it makes part of the presents that you have expressed—I will venture to State tho it may make little impression on the Mind he is adressing—who no doubt has abler Views on the Subject—when I consider Man's original Stamina—what he proceeds from—when I see what a dolefull helpless Figure he makes in Infancy—unable to distinguish his Parents or what is Salutary or pernicious in his Food—how dependant & helpless—how ignorant for years—what instructions are necesary for his Conduct—how prone to Evil Habits & Cruelty his Spirts—that it takes one thrd of his Life to qualify him to act in the World when in the World under the domains of Propensities & passions—cheating & being Cheated—Robbing & being Robbed—destroying his Fellow Creatures & et[c]. see the Slavery of the West indies & the Southern States—see South America desolated by Spain & their County taken Millions of Men destroyd—See the East Indies—Millions Suffering by the Rapacity of British Merchents—look at the French Revolution—& the Crueties of it—see the enormites of Private Life—look at Man at the End of his Career—mixing with the Dust—then what is Man the Pompous Self Styled Governor of the World—but a thing of Night a worm—a wretch—contrast him with the Power—that could take the Mass of Matter in Your Estate from its foundation & move it to where[7] I am writing or take the Cities of Phila[a]—Baltimore London—Paris or Amsterdam & Remove them into your State—extend the Idea to the Mass of Matter betwixt this & Calcutta in the East Indies extend the Idea to the Planetary System (of which I have but an Imperfect Idea Myself) can you compehend the Power,—No—you cannot—Contemplate your own System from its foundation its progress & termination & ask whether you are not a living Miracale in Yourself—carry this to every thing around you—can You create Knowledg[e] no—every thing is Given to you—all Knowledge is Revelation—the Doctrines promulgated by Jesus Christ are Medicines—if taken—will cure the assort disorders of our System—they will destroy & root out the Evil propensitys of our Nature—they will Refine they will purify, they will place Man in that Situation he ought to be—considing his Weakness—his Ignorance & his Dependence & enable TJ to reject the Fiery darts & venomous Bites of his advesaries in the Soft Spirit of the Gospel with the Saying of Father forgive them for they Know not what they do—The Devil going about like a Roaring Lyon seeking whom he may devour—the Devils Getting into a herd of Swine & Going down a Steep place into the Sea—the Dead rising from their Graves Jesus being of the Liniage of David is not proved by Joseph being of that Line—the only begotten Son of that wonderfull immense Being is an unhapy Expression—these things I doubt—say disbelive—& these Pious Persons who see into these things I hope will have compassion on my Want of Sight—& not abuse—vilify—cudgell—hang or burn me for what I cannot help—but that the Mind of Jesus Christ was[8] again raized—Sanctified—prepared to go thro the Humiliations—Sufferings & trials—to exercise the Virtues that he practised—at the time he did & in the State the World then was for the Benefit & Redemption of

Mankind from the Pompous Ignorance—Wretchd Cruety & Depravity of his Nature I most firmly believe & I have no doubt if I partake while here a Sufficent Portion of the Spirt that actuated him that it will cast out & destroy every evil disposition & Propensity of my Nature—tranquilize my Mind & if I transmigrate from this State of Being prepare it for any[9] additonal Bounties that an all Wise & Powerfull Creator may extend to it

My hand tires & the bounds of a letter does not admit of amplyfying the Subjects I have introduced which I have been forced to condense in as Small a Compass as I well could I dout Some parts are unintelegable but if they Shoud Stir up your own Thoughts they will do more Justice to this than I have the Vanity to pretend to—As I concluded[10] all letters to you[11] are exempt from Postage I omit[12] the paymt of it—& I hope you will take this address in good part which woud be reviewed revised & corrected if there was a probability of the Writer ever being Known—it would however afford him Satisfaction to Know that this reached its Destination & if not too much trouble JT—of Virginia[13] (letters Received)—could acknowledge in Duane's Phila[a] Country Aurora—the receipt of a Washington Letter—without any thing further—

My Mind is in a State of vacill[ments][14] whether[15] to send or Retain this letter—it is so hastily &[16] slovenly written—but as it will travel, incog—it goes—

RC (DLC); edges trimmed and chipped; between dateline and salutation: "Thomas Jefferson"; endorsed by TJ as "Anon.," "religious," and received 1 June 1816 by "post," and so recorded (without specifying the manner of delivery) in SJL.

WHO COMMITTED NO SIN—NEITHER WAS GUILE FOUND IN HIS MOUTH is in the Bible (1 Peter 2.22). TJ's ENERGETIC & FORCIBLE EXPRESSIONS are probably those found in "Query XIV. Laws" of his *Notes on the State of Virginia* (*Notes*, ed. Peden, 138–43). TJ uses a slightly modified version of the expression WOLF BY THE EARS when discussing slavery and the Missouri Compromise in a letter to John Holmes, 22 Apr. 1820. The biblical CASE OF THE PERSON IN THE GOSPEL . . . INTO PRISON FOR A PENNY is from Matthew 18.23–34. The English parliament in 1621 impeached Francis BACON and convicted him of taking bribes while a judge (*ODNB*). STAMINA: "the rudiments or germs from which living beings or their organs are developed" (*OED*).

The author quotes from or alludes to the Bible several more times: FATHER FORGIVE THEM FOR THEY KNOW NOT WHAT THEY DO (Luke 23.34); THE DEVIL GOING ABOUT . . . WHOM HE MAY DEVOUR (1 Peter 5.8); THE DEVILS GETTING INTO A HERD . . . INTO THE SEA (Matthew 8.32 and Mark 5.13); THE DEAD RISING FROM THEIR GRAVES (Matthew 27.52–3 and perhaps also Revelation); JESUS BEING OF THE LINIAGE OF DAVID (Matthew 1.1–16 and Luke 3.23–31); and Jesus as God's ONLY BEGOTTEN SON (John 1.18, 3.16, 18).

Another anonymous letter to TJ, received 21 Nov. 1816 but not found, is recorded in SJL (with brackets in original) as "Anon. [corruptions of X[ty]] Leonard Jonathan. Mass."

[1] Preceding five words interlined.
[2] Word added in margin.

[3] Word interlined.
[4] Manuscript: "were."
[5] Preceding two words interlined.
[6] Manuscript: "Speration."
[7] Manuscript: "were."
[8] Manuscript: "but that the Mind of Jesus Christ—was But that the Mind of Jesus Christ was."
[9] Word interlined.
[10] Word interlined in place of "belive."
[11] Preceding two words interlined.
[12] Word interlined in place of "dispense with."
[13] Preceding two words interlined in place of "coud."
[14] Word illegible.
[15] Manuscript: "wheath."
[16] Preceding two words interlined.

From Joseph Delaplaine

DR SIR, Philad May 27: 1816.

I have just had the honour of receiving your obliging & kind favour of the 20: instant.—

I purposd to leave this[1] on Wednesday with Mr Otis, for your seat, & hope to be there by the first of June or thereabouts.—It is possible Mr Otis will go without me, but I will endeavor to accompany him. I return my thanks for your kind invitation.—

With the highest respect & esteem
I am your obedt hul st JOSEPH DELAPLAINE

RC (DLC); dateline beneath signature; endorsed by TJ as received 6 June 1816 and so recorded in SJL. RC (NjMoHP: Lloyd W. Smith Collection); address cover only; with PoC of TJ to Patrick Gibson, 12 July 1816, on verso; addressed: "Thomas Jefferson Esqr Monticello Virginia"; franked; postmarked Philadelphia, 27 May.

[1] Preceding two words interlined in place of "set out."

From Nicolas G. Dufief

MONSIEUR, A Philadelphie ce 27. May 1816

J'ai reçu ce matin la lettre dont vous m'avez honoré, & me Suis acquitté aussitôt de votre commission pour Mr Gallatin qui recevra demain À New York les deux exemplaires de l'ouvrage admirable que vous envoyez à Mr De la Fayette. Avant de lui adresser les deux paquets Je me Suis assuré par Mr Dallas qu'il était, à présent, dans cette ville-là. J'ai accompagné le tout d'une lettre d'avis. J'ai quelque envie de faire un voyage en Europe pour assortir mon magazin des bons livres qui lui manquent dans tous les Genres & dans les differentes langues: Dans huit jours je Saurai, Si Ce voyage aura lieu ou non. si j'ai le temps de vous en prévenir & de recevoir une réponse je le ferai, parce que Ce Sera toujours un vrai plaisir pour moi de vous procurer de par tout où j'irai, les choses qui pourraient vous être agréables ou utiles

Vous recevrez par la poste qui part demain le premier vol. de Mackay Sur la longitude & quelques jours après le Second. ensuite mon dictionnaire Quoique le prix de Mackay Soit de 18.25 vous ne le payrez cependant que 14.00. Mr Duane me fait payer cinq dollars les deux exemplaires de l'ouvrage Sur Montesquieu. Le dictionnaire vous coûtera 12.00 relié en Veau

Je vous ai crédité, dans le temps, de 24.68. Somme reçue de Mr J. Vaughan pour Balance de notre ancien compte

Je Suis avec le plus profond respect Votre très-dévoué Serviteur

N. G. Dufief

EDITORS' TRANSLATION

Sir, Philadelphia 27 May 1816

This morning I received the letter with which you honored me, and I immediately carried out your commission to Mr. Gallatin, who will receive tomorrow in New York two copies of the admirable work you are sending to Mr. Lafayette. Before dispatching the two packages, I made sure, through Mr. Dallas, that he was currently in that city, and I accompanied them with a written notification. I am tempted to take a trip to Europe to supply my store with the good books that it lacks in every genre and in the different languages. In eight days I will know whether this voyage will take place. If I have time to let you know about it and receive a reply, I will do so, because I will always take real pleasure in obtaining for you, wherever I go, things that you might find pleasing or useful

You will receive Mackay's first volume on longitude by the mail that leaves tomorrow and the second one a few days later. Then my dictionary. Although the price for Mackay is $18.25, you will only pay $14. Mr. Duane charges me five dollars for the two copies of the work on Montesquieu. The dictionary will cost you $12 bound in calf

I credited you some time ago with $24.68, the amount received from Mr. J. Vaughan to balance our old account

I am with the most profound respect your very devoted servant

N. G. Dufief

RC (DLC); notation at foot of text in TJ's hand: "14.
5.
12.
31."; endorsed by TJ as received 6 June 1816 and so recorded in SJL. RC (DLC); address cover only; with PoC of TJ to William H. Crawford, 27 July 1816, on verso; addressed: "Th: Jefferson, Esq[re] Monticello V[a]"; franked; postmarked Philadelphia, 27 May. Translation by Dr. Genevieve Moene.

From James Warrell

SIR Richmond 27th May 1816

The laudable zeal you have invariably manifested for the honour, dignity and improvement of your native country, induces me to hope that the Museum of Virginia, about to be established in this Metropolis, will find in you a patron—

I therefore take the liberty to forward to you the subjoined proposals, conceiving should I neglect to do so, that I would be deficient in respect to yourself and[1] attention to the establishment.

Permit me to tender you my acknowledgements for the polite attention I have personally received while your guest, and accept, Sir an assurance of my high consideration.

I have the honour to subscribe myself
your Obedient Servant JAMES WARRELL

RC (MoSHi: TJC-BC); subjoined to enclosure; addressed: "Thomas Jefferson Esqr Monticello"; franked; postmarked Richmond, 30 May; endorsed by TJ as received 1 June 1816 and so recorded (mistakenly dated 22 May 1816) in SJL.

James Warrell (b. ca. 1780), artist and museum proprietor, came to the United States in 1793 with his English parents to join a Philadelphia-based theatrical company. He appeared in numerous stage productions in Philadelphia and Baltimore before settling in Richmond by 1799. The following year he opened a dancing school there with his brother, Thomas Warrell. By 1808 a leg injury forced him to concentrate on painting. Warrell specialized in portraits, historical scenes, and theater scenery. He visited Monticello on 27 Dec. 1809, having professed a desire to see TJ's collection of paintings. Warrell moved regularly as he pursued his new career, with brief stays in Washington, Philadelphia, and Providence, Rhode Island, before returning to Richmond by 1812. The Virginia General Assembly granted him permission in 1816 to build the Virginia Museum on a portion of Capitol Square. The following year Warrell and Richard Lorton, his financial partner and brother-in-law, opened the new institution, which showcased both fine arts and natural history. Warrell bought his partner's share in 1819. Due to declining revenue, however, he could not pay for that share, and the museum reverted to Lorton in 1832. Even before he lost control of the museum, Warrell was forced to market his artistic skills elsewhere. Beginning in 1825 he moved about the United States, with intermittent residence in Richmond until at least 1846. Warrell died by 1854 (R. Lewis Wright, "James Warrell: Artist and Entrepreneur," *Virginia Cavalcade* 22 [winter 1973]: 4–19; George O. Seilhamer, *History of the American Theatre: New Foundations* [1891], 3:122, 136–7, 151, 202; *Federal Gazette and Philadelphia Daily Advertiser*, 28 Sept. 1793; Valentine Museum, *Richmond Portraits … 1737–1860* [1949], 235–9; Groce and Wallace, *Dictionary of Artists*, 662; Peter Hastings Falk, ed., *Annual Exhibition Record of the Pennsylvania Academy of the Fine Arts, 1807–1870* [1988 revision of a 1955 work by Anna Wells Rutledge], 1:242; Archibald Stuart to TJ, 25 Dec. 1809; Richmond *Enquirer*, 29 Sept. 1812; *Acts of Assembly* [1815–16 sess.], 26–7 [7 Feb. 1816]).

Warrell wrote a nearly identical letter this day to President James Madison, omitting the third paragraph (DLC: Madison Papers).

[1] Manuscript: "and and."

ENCLOSURE

James Warrell and Richard Lorton's Proposal for Construction of a Museum in Richmond

[ca. 27 May 1816]

THE MUSEUM.

The Legislature of Virginia, conceiving great advantages would result to the State by establishing

A MUSEUM

IN THE METROPOLIS, HAVE GIVEN SUFFICIENT GROUND TO JAMES WARRELL, TO ERECT A BUILDING FOR THAT PURPOSE, ON THE CAPITOL SQUARE.

One of the results of National prosperity, is the promotion of the Sciences and the Arts; and by a necessary reaction, the Sciences and the Arts, in their turn, stimulate industry, enlarge the sphere of social happiness, and embellish every scene of social life.

The multiplied advantages of the establishment which it is contemplated to form, might be minutely delineated, and developed in so clear and so forcible a manner, as to produce universal conviction. It would be easy to demonstrate, that a Museum, as it respects society at large, will subserve, at the same time, to the *necessities* and to the *elegancies* of life—that it will promote the interest of medicine, agriculture and commerce, and diffuse among the higher classes of citizens, and through their example ultimately among all orders of men, a delicate and refined taste, and a comparative innocency and purity of manners; that it will furnish delightful and manly entertainment for every member of society, stir up a spirit of useful enquiry and laudable emulation, collect to a proper focus the solitary rays of genius and knowlege, which beam here and there throughout Virginia, bring to light and convert to purposes of practical utility, a mass of treasures with which the bounteous hand of nature has enriched our forests, our plains, our shores and our mountains; and, by thus reacting in a greater or less degree, upon education, manners and industry, eminently contribute to the dignity of our national character, and to the agricultural and commercial prosperity of our country. But argument on this subject is deemed superfluous: the example of Europe and of many of our sister States, must be conclusive. Can it reasonably be supposed, that the liberal and the enlightened of almost every country, would throw away so many donations, so much time and laborious researches, on objects, captivating indeed, and highly ornamental, but of no practical use whatever in its ultimate result? The views which the subject opens, the ideas which it suggests, are boundless and impressive in the extreme. But it is needless to explore every part of this rich and immense field. Many among us are the men of mind, who fully understand the principle that "national industry is compounded of theory, application, and execution," and with whom the least recommendation of a Museum, is that it constitutes a pure and never-failing source of national amusement; who wish expansion of knowledge to keep pace with the considerable and rapid accessions lately made, and daily making to our national character—who, besides independence, excellent political institutions, and increased resources, ardently desire to bequeath to posterity scientific legacies, and to satisfy the claims of the rising generation on the wisdom and liberality of their fathers.

The only question then seems to be, whether the respectable and wealthy State of Virginia, has, or has not arrived at that stage of social refinement and improvement which will authorize a hope, that the *study of nature and the fine arts* will be zealously and liberally encouraged? Every fact leads to a decision of this question in the affirmative. Its citizens have taste, talents, energy, liberality, and opulence; men who possess, it is hoped, not only the disposition, but the means efficiently to patronize the contemplated institution. Under their auspices let it promptly rise! The grant of the Legislature is a powerful appeal to the wisdom and generosity of its inhabitants; let that appeal duly operate on every enlarged mind; let not the confidence which it implies, be frustrated. A *Museum* now looks up to Virginia for support, and, indeed, for existence, but, any aid it may receive will in time be returned with multiplied advantages to the State. In addition to the collection of minerals, fossils, anatomical studies, the curious productions of ingenuity, &c. &c. usually assembled in an establishment of this description, it is the intention of James Warrell (who will shortly visit Europe) to appropriate a gallery or galleries exclusively to portraits of eminently distinguished characters, historical subjects, and views of the sublime and beautiful in nature, together with casts from the finest models of antique sculpture.

In order to facilitate this object, he has associated Mr. Richard Lorton in the establishment.

JAMES WARRELL & RICHARD LORTON,

Have made arrangements to secure towards the establishment in contemplation, in money and materials, to be placed in the interior of the Museum, *a sum not less than ten thousand dollars*, which they propose to extend to that magnitude, if patronized, that will do honor to themselves, and be an ornament to the State.

TERMS OF SUBSCRIPTION.

A subscriber of 200 dollars will be entitled to a free admission ticket, for himself, lady and children in perpetuity, not transferrable, except in the following manner:

Subscribers of $200 will possess the privilege of selling their shares, but the admission ticket which constitutes the share cannot change its proprietor oftener than once in every six months.

A Subscriber of $100 will be entitled to a ticket of admission for himself and lady for life, and children, during their nonage.

A Subscriber of $50 dollars shall be entitled to a ticket of admission for ten years. Any individual subscribing 30 dollars, shall be entitled to a ticket of admission five years.

A subscriber of 20 dollars, shall be entitled to a ticket for three years.

And any person subscribing ten dollars shall be entitled to a ticket for one year; any ticket in the event of the demise of the subscriber may be sold, but is transferable in no other case.

There shall not be more than 50 subscribers at $200—and 50—at $100.

The money to be paid in the following manner to James Warrell and Richard Lorton, or their authorized agents:

The $200 shares to be paid as follows:

25, when the building is begun,
25, when the first story is up,
25, when the walls are finished,
25, when the house is covered in,
25, when the floors are laid and doors are hung,
25, when the house is fit for occupation,
25, when the Museum is opened,
And 25, in six months after the *Museum* is opened.

Those shares of $100 and $50, to be paid in the following manner:

25 per cent on the commencement of the building,
25 per cent when the first story is raised,
25 when the walls are finished,
And 25 when the building is fit for occupation.

All sums subscribed under fifty dollars, to pay one half on the commencement of the building, and the residue when the walls are raised.

James Warrell and Richard Lorton, reserve to themselves the privilege of purchasing all shares subscribed for, at the expiration of ten years, except those of 200 dollars. The materials purchased by the money subscribed, to remain forever with the building.

The public will recollect that the Legislature have sufficiently guarded this object. The building is to remain forever as a Museum; or, it is to be forfeited to the Commonwealth.

Printed circular (MoSHi: TJC-BC); undated; with covering letter subjoined.

Richard Lorton, artist and museum proprietor, belonged to a Petersburg Masonic lodge in 1802, was a member of the Society of Artists of the United States in 1813, and served as a public-school commissioner for Henrico County, 1827–28. When he and his brother-in-law James Warrell ended their partnership in the Virginia Museum on 15 Mar. 1819, Lorton received a lien on the museum in lieu of a cash payment. In 1832 he called in his lien and became sole owner of the museum. Lorton then offered the museum and all its "Paintings, Minerals, Fossils, and curiosities" for sale. It attracted no buyers. On 22 Mar. 1836, by an act of the Virginia General Assembly, Lorton surrendered the property to the state for $6,500, even though an 1818 fire insurance policy had valued the museum at $16,000 (*Proceedings of a Grand Annual Communication of the Grand Lodge of Virginia* [Richmond, (1802)], 38; "An Act to incorporate 'The Society of Artists of the United States,' by the name of the Columbian Society of Artists," *Acts of the General Assembly of the Commonwealth of Pennsylvania* [1812–13 sess.]: 73–6; D. E. Gardner, "History of Public Education in Henrico County," Superintendent of Public Instruction, *Annual Report* [1884–85]: 198; Valentine Museum, *Richmond Portraits . . . 1737–1860* [1949], 237–9; R. Lewis Wright, "James Warrell: Artist and Entrepreneur," *Virginia Cavalcade* 22 [winter 1973]: 10, 14, 16; *Richmond Enquirer*, 25 May 1832; "An Act to authorize Richard Lorton to surrender his interest in the museum property," *Acts of Assembly* [1835–36 sess.], 10–11; Mutual Assurance Society Declarations, no. 1073, 28 Feb. 1818 [Vi]).

In "An Act authorising the establishing a Museum on part of the public Square in the City of Richmond," 7 Feb. 1816, the Virginia General Assembly SUFFICIENTLY GUARDED the public's interest by stipulating that the museum building and the land on which it stood would be forfeited to the state if the museum ceased its operations (*Acts of Assembly* [1815–16 sess.], 26–7).

To John Taylor

Dear Sir Monticello May 28. 16.

On my return from a long journey, and considerable absence from home, I found here the copy of your 'Enquiry into the principles of our government' which you had been so kind as to send me, and for which I pray you to accept my thanks. the difficulties of getting new works in our situation, inland and without a single book store, are such as had prevented my obtaining a copy before; and letters which had accumulated during my absence, & were calling for answers, have not yet permitted me to give to the whole a thorough reading: yet certain that you and I could not think differently on the fundamentals of rightful government, I was impatient, and availed myself of the intervals of repose from the writing table, to obtain a cursory[1] idea of the body of the work. I see in it much matter for profound reflection; much which should confirm our adhesion, in practice, to the good principles of our constitution, and fix our attention on what is yet to be made good. the 6th section on the good moral principles of our government, I found so interesting and replete with sound principle, as to postpone my letter-writing to it's thoro' perusal and consideration. besides much other good matter, it settles unanswerably the right of instructing representatives, and their duty to obey. the system of banking we have both equally and ever reprobated. I contemplate it as a blot left in all our constitutions,[2] which, if not covered, will end in their destruction, which is already hit by the gamblers in corruption, and is sweeping away, in it's progress the fortunes & morals of our citizens. funding I consider as limited, rightfully, to a redemption of the debt within the lives of a majority of the generation contracting it; every generation coming equally, by the laws of the creator of the world, to the free possession of the earth he made for their subsistence, unincumbered by their predecessors, who, like them, were but tenants for life. you have succesfully and completely pulverised mr Adams's system of orders, and his opening the mantle of republicanism to every government of laws, whether consistent or not with natural right. indeed it must be acknoleged that the term republic, is of very vague application in every language. witness the self-styled republics of Holland, Switzerland, Genoa, Venice, Poland. were I to assign to this term a precise and definite idea, I would say that, purely and simply, it means a government, by it's citizens, in mass, acting directly and personally, according to rules established by the majority: and that every other government is more or less republican in proportion as it has in it's composition more or less of this ingredient of the direct action of the citizens. such a government is evidently restrained to very narrow limits of space and population. I doubt if it would be practicable beyond the extent of a New England township. the first shade from this pure element, which, like that of pure vital air cannot sustain life of itself, would be where the powers of the government, being divided, should be exercised each by representatives chosen by the citizens, either pro hâc vice, or for such short terms as should render secure the duty of expressing the will of their constituents. this I should consider as the nearest approach to a pure republic which is practicable on a large scale of country or population. and we have examples of it in some of our state-constitutions, which, if not poisoned by priest-craft, would prove it's excellence over all mixtures with other elements; and, with only equal doses of poison, would still be the best. other shades of republicanism may be found in other forms of government, where the Executive, Judiciary, and Legislative functions, and the different branches of the latter are chosen by the people more or less directly, for longer terms of years, or for life, or made hereditary; or where there are mixtures of authorities, some dependant, and others independant of[3] the people. the further the departure from direct and constant controul by the citizens, the less has the government of the ingredient of republicanism; evidently none where the authorities are hereditary, as in France, Venice E^tc. or self-chosen as in Holland; and little where for life, in proportion as the life continues in being after the act of election.[4]

The purest republican feature in the government of our own state is the House of Representatives. the Senate is equally so the 1st year, less the 2^d and so on. the Executive still less, because not chosen by the people directly. the Judiciary seriously antirepublican because for life; and the national Arm wielded, as you observe by Military leaders, irresponsible but to themselves. add to this the vicious constitution of our county courts (to whom the justice, the executive administration, the taxation, police, the military appointments of the county, and nearly all our daily concerns are confided) self appointed, self continued, holding their authorities for life, and with an impossibility of breaking in on the perpetual succession of any faction once possessed of the bench. they are in truth the Executive, the Judiciary, and the Military of their respective counties, and the sum of the counties makes the State. And add also that one half of our brethren who fight and pay taxes, are excluded, like Helots, from the rights of representation; as if society were instituted for the soil, and not for[5] the men inhabiting it; or one half of these could dispose of the rights, & the will, of the other half, without their consent.

'What constitutes a state?
Not high-rais'd battlements, or labor'd mound,
Thick wall, or moated gate:
Not cities proud with spires and turrets crown'd
No: Men, high-minded men;
Men, who their duties know;
But know their rights; and, knowing, dare maintain.
These constitute a state.'

In the General government the House of Representatives is mainly republican; the Senate scarcely so, at all, as not elected by the people directly, and so long secured even against those who do elect them. the Executive more republican than the Senate, from it's shorter term, it's election by the people, in practice, (for they vote for **A.** only on an assurance that he will vote for **B.**) & because, in practice also, a principle of rotation seems to be in a course of establishment. the Judiciary independant of the Nation, their coercion by impeachment being found nugatory.

If then the controul of the people over the organs of their government be the measure of it's republicanism, and I confess I know no other measure, it must be agreed that our governments have much less of republicanism, than ought to have been expected; in other words that the people have less regular controul over their agents than their rights & their interest required. and this I ascribe, not to any want of republican dispositions in those who formed these constitutions, but to a submission of true principle to European authorities, to Speculators on government, whose fears of the people have been inspired by the populace of their own great cities, and were unjustly entertained against the independant, the happy, & therefore orderly citizen of the US. much I apprehend that the golden moment is past for reforming these heresies. the functionaries of public power rarely strengthen in their dispositions to abridge it, and an unorganised call for timely amendment is not likely to prevail against an organised opposition to it. we are always told that things are going on well; why change them? 'chi sta bene, non si muove,' says the Italian, 'let him who stands well stand still.' this is true; & I verily believe they would go on well with us under an absolute monarch, while our present character remains, of order, industry & love of peace, and restrained as he would be by the proper spirit of the people. but it is while it remains such, we should provide against the consequences of it's deterioration.—

and let us rest in the hope that it will yet be done, & spare ourselves the pain of evils which may never happen.

On this view of the import of the term republic, instead of saying, as has been said, that 'it may mean anything or nothing,' we may say, with truth and meaning, that governments are more or less republican as they have more or less of the element of popular election and controul in their composition: & beleiving, as I do, that the mass of the citizens is the safest depository of their own rights, & especially that the evils flowing from the duperies of the people are less injurious than those from the egoism of their agents, I am a friend to that composition of government which has in it the most of this ingredient. And I sincerely believe with you, that banking establishments are more dangerous than standing armies; & that the principle of spending money to be paid by posterity, under the name of funding, is but swindling futurity on a large scale

Let me turn to a more engaging subject, the honest culture of the earth. it is a shame that I should ask you a 2[d] time for a little seed of the Swedish turnep, if you still preserve it. my absences from home at a distant possession, which is almost a second home, occasioned a failure to save seed the last year; and the Ruta baga is so much preferable for the use of the table, that I wish to recover it again. a little may come in a letter by mail, or more if you have a plenty by my grandaughter who says she is coming shortly. I salute you with constant friendship and respect. TH: JEFFERSON

RC (MHi: Washburn Autograph Collection); addressed: "John Taylor esquire at Hazlewood near Portroyal"; franked; postmarked Charlottesville, 29 May. PoC (DLC); first two pages only.

John Taylor (1753–1824), agriculturalist, author, and public official, often known as John Taylor of Caroline, was born in Orange or Caroline County and later resided at Hazelwood, his estate near Port Royal in the latter county. After attending the College of William and Mary, 1770–71, he studied law under his uncle Edmund Pendleton, and in 1774 he was admitted to the Caroline County bar. Taylor was an officer in the Continental army, 1776–79, and in the Virginia militia, 1780–81. He represented Caroline County in the Virginia House of Delegates, 1779–82, 1783–85, and 1796–1800, and he sat in the United States Senate, 1792–94, 1803, and 1822–24. Taylor sought TJ's opinion on a complicated legal case in 1782, and TJ corresponded with him on agricultural matters beginning in 1794. His distinctive version of republicanism is reflected in his political writings, which include *A Defence of the Measures of the Administration of Thomas Jefferson*, written under the pseudonym "Curtius" (Washington, 1804; Sowerby, no. 3316); *An Inquiry into the Principles and Policy of the Government of the United States* (Fredericksburg, 1814; TJ's Retirement Library Catalogue, p. 88 [no. 656] [MS in DLC: TJ Papers, ser. 7]); and *Construction Construed, and Constitutions Vindicated* (Richmond, 1820; Poor, *Jefferson's Library*, 11 [no. 652]). Taylor combined his political views and his interest in agricultural reform in *Arator; being a series of Agricultural Essays, Practical & Political* (Georgetown, 1813, and later eds.; Sowerby, no. 814; Poor, *Jefferson's Library*, 6 [no. 255]) (*ANB*; *DAB*;

Garrett Ward Sheldon and C. William Hill Jr., *The Liberal Republicanism of John Taylor of Caroline* [2008]; Robert E. Shalhope, *John Taylor of Caroline* [1980]; *William and Mary Provisional List*, 39; Heitman, *Continental Army*, 534; Leonard, *General Assembly*; *PTJ*, esp. 27: 724–7, 28:68–9; *Richmond Enquirer*, 24, 27 Aug. 1824).

WHAT CONSTITUTES A STATE? ... THESE CONSTITUTE A STATE is based on lines 1–4, 9, 13–4, and 17 of Sir William Jones, "An Ode in Imitation of Alcæus" (John Shore, Baron Teignmouth, ed., *The Works of Sir William Jones* [London, 1807], 10:389–90). TJ's GRANDAUGHTER was Ann C. Bankhead.

[1] TJ here canceled "view."
[2] Manuscript: "constituons."
[3] Manuscript: "on."
[4] PoC ends here.
[5] Preceding two words interlined.

From Caspar Wistar

D[R] SIR Philad[a] May 28 1816

The Bearer M[r] Otis is an Artist of rising Character who has been settled in Philad[a] Several years & has distinguished himself by his ingenuity as well as his obliging disposition. He has Several inventions which will interest you & if you have any Specimens of Natural History to Copy he will I believe give you great Satisfaction by his execution—Expecting to write again in a few days I only Renew the declarations of Sincere Regard & attachment which are uniformly felt by

Your obliged friend C WISTAR

RC (NNPM); dateline adjacent to signature; at foot of text: "His Excellency M[r] Jefferson"; endorsed by TJ as received 3 June 1816 and so recorded in SJL, which adds that it was delivered "by mr Otis."

Bass Otis (1784–1861), artist and lithographer, was born in Bridgewater, Massachusetts. He reputedly studied art with Gilbert Stuart in Boston before moving by 1808 to New York City. By 1812 Otis had settled in Philadelphia. That same year he was elected a member of the Society of Artists of the United States, and eight of his portraits were included in its annual exhibition. Otis received a patent on 14 Mar. 1815 for a "perspective protracter," a device that helps a portraitist keep a sitter's body parts in proportion. He is also credited with producing in 1818 the first lithograph made in the United States. Otis was engaged by the publisher Joseph Delaplaine in 1816 to create a series of paintings to be engraved for *Delaplaine's Repository*. Although he completed a number of portraits, TJ's likeness was the only one of his efforts ultimately used in this work. Otis later painted other portraits of TJ based on the original sitting, but it is this first version of June 1816 that is reproduced elsewhere in this volume. At a Philadelphia art show in 1818, he exhibited his *Portrait of Thomas Jefferson, late President of the United States of America*. Starting late in the 1830s, Otis painted portraits in cities across the northeastern United States, residing at times in Boston, New York City, and Wilmington, Delaware, before returning permanently to Philadelphia in 1858 (*ANB*; *DAB*; Groce and Wallace, *Dictionary of Artists*, 480; Gainor B. Davis and Wayne Craven, *Bass Otis: Painter, Portraitist and Engraver* [1976]; Thomas Knoles, "The Notebook of Bass Otis, Philadelphia Portrait Painter," *Proceedings of the American Antiquarian Society* 103 [1993]: 179–253; Gordon

Hendricks, "'A Wish to Please, and a Willingness to be Pleased,'" *American Art Journal* 2 [1970]: 16–29; *Second Annual Exhibition of the Society of Artists of the United States, and the Pennsylvania Academy. 1812* [Philadelphia, 1812], 15, 17–9, 21, 29; *List of Patents*, 150; Joseph Jackson, "Bass Otis, America's First Lithographer," *PMHB* 37 [1913]: 385–94; *Delaplaine's Repository*, 1:124; Bush, *Life Portraits*, 64–7; *Seventh Annual Exhibition of the Pennsylvania Academy of the Fine Arts* [Philadelphia, 1818], 10; *Philadelphia Inquirer*, 4 Nov. 1861).

From Thomas Appleton

Leghorn 30th may 1816.

My last letter to you, Sir, was in date, of the 10th of the present month, conveying duplicates of the legal Attestations of the death of mr mazzei; and which were forwarded by the Brig Silk-worm, Capt: Parker Burnham for Boston.—I then, likewise, mention'd that owing to the failure in quality, of the wine of montepulciano of the last vintage, I should defer Sending of the growth of that place, until the next Season.—In the mean time, I have procur'd from a friend, a barrel of Carmigniano wine, which though not equal to that of montepulciano, is nevertheless, one of the best flavour'd of Tuscany.—I have had it carefully bottled, and Seald with pitch, So that, I have good Reason to believe, it will arrive to you, free from injury.—One barrel contains fifty-seven bottles, which are pack'd in one Case, and Shipp'd on board the Schooner Fanny, Capt: Selby for new York, and address'd to the care of the Collector.—I cannot precisely Say the prices, as my friend is in the country, and the vessel will sail in the course of the day; but it will be at a very moderate expence.—towards the latter part of the next month, I have the promise of a barrel of Ama wine, to which none is Superior, except montepulciano; and in the estimation of many, they are on a level:—by the first vessel which will sail afterwards, I shall forward it to you.—these wines can always be procur'd, at a much less price than that of montepulciano, as they are convey'd by the Arno, while the latter is transported 150 miles over land.—

The commerce of the U: States in the mediterranean, since the period, which the allied Sovereigns of Europe, have denominated peace, has been [a]ttended with little or no benefit to the adventurers, owing to the unusual high prices of colonial produce in America.—this evil, however, is a partial one, and will, probably be compensated by the present reduc'd prices of those articles in the U: States: while the commerce of G: britain Seems rapidly declining to extinction.—I speak from a personal Knowledge of facts, as it Relates to all Italy, and I think I Can with much truth Say, that not a bale of british manufactur'd goods has been sold here, at a less loss, than from 25 to 50 ℘C[t] on the original invoice; while those of Germany & Switzerland meet with Ready and advantageous Sales.—It is certainly a most memorable event in the manufactures of Europe, that the fabricks of the continent have now advanc'd, as far beyond those of England, as the latter did of the former, twenty years ago.—the long prohibatory decrees on british manufactures, have produc'd the most fatal effects on their trade with the continent.—If it be true, that the necessary articles of Subsistance have greatly increas'd in England, while it certainly is, that provisions Remain as they were, on the continent; add to which, the Surprizing progress in the manufacturing arts, it will not appear extraordinary, that a Similar Result should have arisen.—The present political State of Italy, offers no well-founded hopes of a Speedy amelioration: and until the immense pecuniary obligations, of the legitimate Sovereigns are Cancell'd, no relief Can be expected from the intollerable burthens they now suffer.—the same system prevails from Turin to Naples, nor was there ever a period, when one common Sentiment pervaded every class of Society, as at the present time. to disappointment has succeeded disgust and contempt; and I have no hesitation in believing, that even the Standard of Mahomet, would now find followers.—It is Certainly to be wish'd, at least for the sake of the present generation, that thier patriotism may not be put to the test; but Should Such an event arrive, there is no extreme into which they might not be plung'd; even anarchy would be a gain.—Knowing, Sir, as I well do, how little truth is to be collected from the contemptible european gazettes, on the actual Situation of Italy; as likewise, how few travellers, either from the speed with which they run over it, or from an ignorance of the language, are capable of investigating truth from the appearance of it, I have Sketch'd this little tableau; it is only a miniature, but the features are discernible.—Accept, Sir, the Sincere expressions of my highest esteem & respect—

Th: Appleton

RC (DLC); hole in manuscript; at foot of text: "Thomas Jefferson, esquire monticelli"; endorsed by TJ as received 14 Aug. 1816 and so recorded in SJL; notation by TJ adjacent to endorsement: "N. York. 57. bottles Carmigniano." Enclosure: bill of lading, Leghorn, 30 May 1816, according to which "*One Case Cont*[g] *Wine*" was shipped for New York aboard the *Fanny*, John Selby master, to the care of "*the Collector of the port of New York*," David Gelston, who was to pay "freight for the said goods *as Customary*" (printed form in MHi; with blanks filled in a clerk's hand rendered above in italics, signed by Selby). Enclosed in David Gelston to TJ, 6 Aug. 1816.

Appleton's last letter was dated 15 May 1816, not the 10th.

From John Barnes

Dear Sir— George Town Co[a] 31st May 1816.

I have now the Hon[r] of Covering you Statem[t] of Sales Gen[l] Kosciuskos Treasury Notes and purchase therew[th] of B[k] Stock—as Noticed in my letter 22[d] March—Bal[e] in fav[r] of B. Stock $50\frac{35}{100}$ to the Debit of the Gen[ls] a/c—I hope & trust these will meet—your Approval: —still Anxious—but without a too severe Remedy I cannot—yet feel for the good Gen[ls] want of a Remittance but at a loss of 20 per Cent—is too much to sustain—when with a little more patience, will, I trust, Afford him relief—as from Appearances, the Banks generally, are emmerging from the restraints hitherto preventing a circulation of Specia the very first favorable Moment, that Offers: I shall eagerly embrace in a purchase of £400 Ster[g] a 3 a 10 days after sight if to be had.—

I had waited Miss Randolphs expected Return from Philad[a] to Offer her my Bank services—when 2 days since M[rs] Madison being[1] in G: T. informed me Miss Randolphs Arrival in Washington—(in M[rs] Madisons Absence at Annapolis—) had proceeded on to Monticello. of course, I had not the pleasure of paying my respects, nor Offer of Cash: but in replacing $20. Advanced Miss Randolph by M[rs] Madison—

The late Excursion to Annapolis—was truly Splendid—and highly gratifying to all parties—more especially so it must have been to the good President whom I presume have never before seen, even at a distance—a 74. That not only to Board so Compleat a <u>first Rate</u> But as Commander-in <u>Chief</u> of the US. Navy &[a] &[a] surrounded by his Principal Officers, both Civil & Military Foreign Ministers & Fellow Citizens &[a] How glowing—and Joyous must have been the feelings of this Assemblage And to the President—in particular—the most Exulting & Gratifying. May He live, many Years, to injoy that supreme satisfaction in having had so great a share in its present Establishment—Aided—in Example by his Predecessor—and may it—(should it become Necessary) increase and <u>Vie</u> with the most Splended European—at least so as to Secure a proper Respect from them—or Either of them—

with the greatest Esteem I am Dear Sir—Your most obed[t] serv[t]

John Barnes,

RC (ViU: TJP-ER); endorsed by TJ as received 7 June 1816 and so recorded in SJL. RC (MHi); address cover only; with PoC of TJ to Enoch Reynolds, 13 July 1816, on verso; addressed: "Thomas Jefferson Esquire Monticello—Virginia"; franked; postmarked (faint) Georgetown, [...] June.

Barnes's letter of 22^{D} MARCH was actually dated a day earlier. During their LATE EXCURSION TO ANNAPOLIS, on 21 May 1816 James Madison and Dolley Madison inspected and dined aboard the USS *Washington.* This 74-gun warship was constructed at Portsmouth, New Hampshire, under the authority of "An Act to increase the Navy of the United States," 2 Jan. 1813. The Madisons were joined by Secretary of the Navy Benjamin W. Crowninshield, former attorney general William Pinkney, General Winfield Scott, Commodore John Rodgers, Captain David Porter, Commodore Isaac Chauncey, and other dignitaries (*Baltimore Patriot & Evening Advertiser*, 27 May 1816; Howard I. Chapelle, *The History of The American Sailing Navy: The Ships and their Development* [1949; repr. ca. 1960], 283–6, 310, 557; *U.S. Statutes at Large*, 2:789).

[1] Manuscript: "beeing."

ENCLOSURE

John Barnes's Account (as Agent of Thomas Jefferson) with Tadeusz Kosciuszko

Dr Genl Thad^{s} Kosciusko In a/c with John Barnes, Agent to T. Jefferson Esqr for a/ Sales in US. Treasury Notes & purchase in Colum^{a} Bank Stock in the Name of said T. Jefferson

1816.			Dolls	Cents	1816			Dolls	Cents.
March 21st	To C^{t} Smith Cash^{r} of Farmers & Mechanic Bank for 46 whole shares of Columbia Bank Stock a $110.	5060			March 21st	By Clem^{t} Smith for Amo^{t} of Sales US. Treasury Notes bearing Int to and payable 21 April	4.500		
	½ ꝑCt Brokerage	25.30				By 11 M^{os} Int a 5⅖th	222.75.		
			5085.	30.		a 7½ ꝑCt advance	337.50.		
							5060.25.		
	George Town Dist of Co^{a} 21 March 1816					deduct ½ ꝑC^{t} Brokerage	25.30	5034.	95.

JOHN BARNES.					for Bal^{ce} fav^{r} B Stock car^{d} to the debit of Genl Kosciuskos $^{a}/_{c}$	EE	50.	35.
							5085.	30

MS (ViU: TJP-ER); entirely in Barnes's hand.

EE: "errors excepted."

From William H. Crawford

MY DEAR SIR Washington 31st May 1816

Your letter recommending Mr Bradbury was rece^{d} during a Serious indisposition with which I was afflicted in the course of the last winter, and has been mislaid So that I am not able to Refer to it more particularly. No Service of the kind for which that gentleman[1] was proposed, has been contemplated by the government.

Your letter in Reply to the one which you Rec^{d} from me whilst I was in Paris, was delivered to me in this place on my arrival in August last, and would have been immediately acknowledged, but for the Pressure of official duty incident to a new Station & which had long been provisionally filled.

A few days ago Mr Graham delivered to me a large packet of my own letters, written in Paris in the month of December 1814, which had been just Rec^{d} at the State department; in which was the enclosed letter to yourself. The Reasoning upon the then State of France, and of Europe which it contains, is at this moment destitute of interest. It is forwarded to you, not from a conviction, that it is worthy of your attention, but as an evidence of the high Respect I entertain of the liberality and candor with which you judge the opinions of your friends, when proven by subsequent events to be erroneous.

The letters Referred to in the Postscript[2] are not enclosed, as there is now no inducement to subject your patience to the task of Reading them.

Among the letters in the Packet, is a letter to a member of Congress which developes my views of the existing State of our affairs at that time, & of the policy which ought to be adopted at the Return of peace. I believe that there is no disposition in any class of politicians at this day, to adopt the System proposed in that letter. It is very far from my intention at this moment, to obtrude it upon the public, but I feel Some inclination to present it [for][3] your perusal. At one time during my Services in the Senate of the U. S. I had prevailed upon general Bradly to Consent to bring forward a bill for the Repeal of the Draw-back System; but Such was the distracted State of our Relations from the time I entered, until that of my quitting it, that the measure was postponed from time to time, under the hope that a more auspicious period would Shortly arrive. This favorable moment never Presented itself, and there is now but little probability that the attention of Congress will be called to consider of the policy of this measure.

Should the peace of Europe be Preserved for a longer period than usual, our attitude may be Such at the Recommencement of hostilities, as to preserve us from its baleful influence.

We have every thing to hope from time; to it therefore we must trust for an exemption of the probable Consequences of our insatiable Cupidity for foreign Commerce.

I am dear Sir your most ob^{t} & very humb^{e} Servt

WM H CRAWFORD

RC (DLC); endorsed by TJ as received 7 June 1816 and so recorded in SJL. RC (DLC); address cover only; with PoC of TJ to David Hosack, 13 July 1816, on verso; addressed: "Thomas Jefferson Late President of the United States Monticello Virginia"; franked; postmarked (faint): "[Washington], 4 June." Enclosure: Crawford to TJ, 12 Dec. 1814. Other enclosure printed below.

Crawford, at this time the secretary of war, served in the United States SENATE, 1807–14. Stephen R. Bradley (BRADLY) was a senator between 1791 and 1812 (*Biog. Dir. Cong.*).

[1] Manuscript: "gentlemen."
[2] Manuscript: "Postcript."
[3] Omitted word editorially supplied.

ENCLOSURE

William H. Crawford to Jonathan Fisk

DEAR SIR. Paris 8th Dec^{re} 1814

Your letter of the 9th of Oct. reached me on the 5th inst. From the letters & News Papers which I have Rec^{d} by the Fingal, & the Ajax, public spirit Seems to be good, every where, but in old Massachussetts.

The attempt to form a New England confederacy under the pretext, that the general government Refuses them protection, when they have labored assiduously to prevent the execution of the measures which were calculated to afford that protection, approaches the confines of treason. The execution of their threat to with hold their taxes, & to apply them for their defence, will be an overt act which will Rend the veil which their hypercritical canting has hitherto thrown over their insidious measures. Their mode of calling a convention is certainly irregular & unconstitutional. I do not believe that they will do more than menace. Whilst New york Remains Sound, the New England States dare not move, even if they were united. The federalism of Connecticutt, is constitutional, & will not be Seduced by the intentional flattery of Selecting one of its towns, for the assembling of this unconstitutional Convention. Independent of the Steady habits of Connecticutt, it is notorious that the majority in the other States, is a very inconsiderable one, upon general questions—upon the question of separation, or of Performing any act which amounts to treason or Rebellion, these majorities would immediately dwindle into Contemptible[1] minorities. There is therefore no danger of Rebellion or treason. The Essex Junto disappointed in all their Schemes of ambition; convinced of their incapacity to carry the People with them in their treasonable views, will not dare to act, but will continue to Snarl and Shew their teeth.

I sincerely Rejoice with you in the Reputation which our armies have acquired in many a well fought field, during the present campaign. This had become indispensably necessary for our national character. Six months ago we stood as low in the scale of Nations, in the estimation of Europe as it was possible. This opinion it is true, was Principally the Result of circumstances wholly unconnected with our military operations. Every nation in Europe was in the pay of our enemy, except France, where the revolution which had just taken place, & the Peculiar circumstances attending it, had given to public opinion so far as it was influenced by the government, a direction more inimical to our national Character, than any where else. It must be admitted that our military operations, were not calculated to counteract, the influence which[2] the English press, & British gold, So Skilfully exerted & profusely lavished, were calculated to produce to our injury. The Result of the Campaign, & the Relation which England now holds towards most of the nations of Europe, has performed wonders in our favor. If England had made peace with us in the month of May last, as She might have done, all Europe would have attributed it to the justice & magnanimity of her councils. The general opinion in France & indeed every where else, was that we must Submit to the terms which England Should think fit to impose. The Prince of Beneven[t] told Madame De Stael in the month of August last, that he would not give her one livre for her forty thousand pounds in the American funds. If we had made peace in May or June, we Should have been Compelled to engage in the first war which Should break out in Europe. The exclusive commerce which we Shall always carry on when the principal maritime States of Europe are at war, will So Strongly tempt the Stronger naval Belligerents to Commit aggressions upon it, that we shall always be in danger of being drawn into the war if it continues any considerable time. To diminish this danger one of two courses must be adopted. The inducement to depredate upon our commerce must be diminished, or it must be counteracted, by a constant state of Preparation to Repress that spirit of depredation. The first object will be obtained by the Repeal of the System of[3] drawbacks[4] which will keep our commerce Nearly on the Same footing as to extent that it[5] was in time of Peace. The Second can only be obtained by continuing a war establishment, & of course war taxes, from the Commencement to the close of every war, between the principal maritime States of Europe. Between these Systems, the Nation upon the Return of Peace, ought to make its election.

To adopt any other course, will be to subject the[6] government to continual irritation, and eventually to degradation or, war.

If we determine to become the carriers of the weaker belligerents, as we have heretofore done, & at the same time determine to avoid war, our commerce will be the Subject of general depredation, on the part of the Stronger Belligerents. This will produce Remonstrance which, if ineffectual, must be followed by war, or by national degradation. This was the Situation in which we were placed from 1805–6. to the year 1812. The national character Suffered much, & would have Suffered Still more, but for the Peculiar situation of Europe. To form a correct decision upon the Relative merits of the two courses, first pointed out, We ought to compare the profits arising from the prosecution of the trade of the weaker Belligerents, with the expences which the State of Preparation to protect that commerce, will cost the nation. The probability of being compelled ultimately to engage in the war, in spite of this Preparation, & consequently to lose, not only the profit of this Belligerent carrying trade, but the direct commerce of the country also, ought to enter into this estimation. I will not examine the effects which this increase of Public expenditure will have upon ourselves. The most enlightend, as well as the best men in the nation, differ upon this question. Admitting the correctness of the theory of those who believe that this effect will be beneficial in the highest degree, still I think there is Strong ground to prefer the first to the Second of these propositions. The Repeal of the draw-back-system will not prevent Some increase of our trade in time of war, between the Principal maritime States of Europe. In the year 1807, there was Re-exported not subject to draw-back, foreign merchandize to nearly the amount of ten millions of dollars. This Sum would probably have been considerably increased if no draw-backs had been allowed. The Repeal of this System[7] would convince the maritime States that our commercial System was not devised for the Purpose of becoming the [carriers of the][8] weaker Belligerents in Every European war. The increase of revenue Resulting from the duties paid upon foreign merchandize Re-exported, might with great propriety be applied to increase[9] our naval force kept in Service, during the same Period. The increase of naval force being in exact proportion to the increase of Commerce arising from the war, would be found equal to the Repression of the Spirit of Rapacity which this increase might excite. If this System Should be Rejected; we must then choose between the old policy of extending our commerce as widely as possible in time of war, relying upon the justice of the Belligerents and the efficacy of our diplomatic reasoning for its protection; or we must consent to Submit to war establishments, & war taxes during the periods of all the wars which break out between the principal maritime States of Europe. These two systems are So nicely balanced that it requires Some Power of[10] discrimination to form a correct choice between them. To insist upon the exercise of national Rights, and to suffer the habitual violation of those Rights, in the persons and property of American citizens, must degrade the national Character, & invite to aggressions of a more general & vital nature. To subject the whole nation to war taxes for the purpose of enabling a few hundred Capitalists[11] in Boston, Philadelphia, New york & Baltimore, to employ their Capital in carrying the Productions of France and Spain, to Europe, & bringing to those colonies, the European manufactures, which they may want in Return, is wholly unreasonable. I have constantly believed that the people of the Eastern & middle States, would no more consent to this State of things, if it was understood, than the people of the Southern & Western States. In a

Speech which I made in the winter of 1812 on the Navy bill, I endeavored in my feeble and indistinct manner to explain this Subject; but that Speech was not published north of the Capitol. The Representatives of the New England States with very few exceptions have devoted themselves to the Commercial system with an infatuation which is truly astonishing. If the nation is compelled to Submit to the System of extending our Commerce to supply the wants of the weaker Belligerents, & of placing ourselves in a State of Collision with their adversaries, I for one am for submitting to the depredations to which this intrusion will invite, without incurring war taxes, or abandoning the benefits of the legitimate commerce of the nation. I will not consent to forego the right of selling Cotton, rice, flour & provisions for the purpose of compelling England to permit our merchants to carry Rum, Sugar, Coffee &C &C from the Spanish & French Colonies, to France & Spain. I will not consent to jeopardize the former, by entering into any System of Restrictions, intended to obtain from England, an acquiescence in the colonial Carrying trade of her enemies, by our merchants. This is my Creed. I know it will be unpopular to the north of the Potomac, but it will be unpopular because it is not understood by the great body of the people. I know it is Said that this trade is directly beneficial, as the profits of it, are Realized in the towns & cities, & that it causes all the productions of the country to Rise in value, & Reduces foreign merchandize as low as it can be Sold. It is admitted that it does hasten the growth of our towns. It may have slight tendency to Raise the price of the productions of the country. But admitting the truth of all this, Still it does not prove that these advantages are equal to the burthens of a war establishment. If the loss which the direct commerce of the Country suffered by the depredations of the English, which were provoked by our becoming the carriers of her enemy, were substracted from the whole Profit of the carrying trade, I believe that the balance of that profit would be inconsiderable indeed. But when the danger of eventual war is considered, I cannot conceive how any Reasonable man can hesitate, viewing it as a mere question of interest. When we arrive at a Population of thirty millions, we may venture upon the enjoyment of this trade in the future wars of Europe, without incurring any great danger of being forced into the war. Whenever this can be done, I would do it. In the mean time I would enter into no engagements with foreign nations to abstain from it. The change in our policy Should be effected by the modification of our Revenue laws, which we can change at pleasure without giving Cause of offence to others.

I am afraid[12] that the new Secretary of the treasury will find great difficulty [getting?][13] his proposed bank into operation If the precious metals have disappeared from circulation, will this new bank Recal it? I am fearful that the Stoppage at the banks of the middle States has vitally affected the confidence which heretofore existed in bank Paper. If this is true it may well be doubted, whether the institution[14] of a national bank will Restore that confidence—If it Should not, it will afford no substantial Relief in the present exigency. Had a national bank been in operation, so long as the gold and Silver Remained in the Country it would have been able to have prevented the Stoppage which has unfortunately taken place in the middle States, by preserving the proper equlibrium in the different parts of the Nation. The beneficial effects which the operation of a national bank would produce upon the management of the State banks, were distinctly Pointed out by the friends of that institution in

1810–11. but were then disregarded. We are young as a nation, & must endeavor to profit, by experience. I look forward to the Conclusion of this war without[15] dismay. With the example which new York has Set her Sister States, we have nothing to fear. This Example will not be imitated by Massachusetts; but I hope it will be by Pennsylvania & the Southern States. The Republican States ought to emulate the Conduct of New york. I am sure they will do it. In this Struggle we must depend upon ourselves alone. In Europe public opinion is decidedly in our favor, but no government will move a finger in our cause, at least thro' the next year.

I am dear Sir with Sentiments of the highest Respect— Yours &C &C

(Signed) WM H CRAWFORD

Tr (DLC); entirely in Crawford's hand; edge trimmed; at foot of text: "Honbe Jonathan Fisk."

Jonathan Fisk (1778–1832), attorney and public official, was born in Amherst, New Hampshire. He later resided in New York City, where he studied law and in 1799 was secretary of the Independent Royal Arch Lodge No. 2, a Masonic organization. By 1800 he was living in Newburgh, New York. Fisk practiced law before the Supreme Court of the state of New York for several years. He served two full terms in the United States House of Representatives, 1809–11 and 1813–15. Shortly after the start of his third term in March 1815, Fisk resigned his seat in order to accept a recess appointment from President James Madison as the United States attorney for the Southern District of New York. Subsequently confirmed by the United States Senate, Fisk resigned the post in 1819 (*Biog. Dir. Cong.*; Daniel D. Tompkins, *Public Papers of Daniel D. Tompkins* [1898–1902], 3:559; *Longworth's New York Directory* [1799]: 134, 223; Edward Manning Ruttenber, *City of Newburgh. A Centennial Historical Sketch* [1876], 25–6, 52; DNA: RG 29, CS, N.Y., Newburgh, 1810–30; John W. Taylor and others to Madison, 15 Feb. 1815 [DNA: RG 59, LAR, 1809–17]; New York *National Advocate*, 20 Mar. 1815; New York *Commercial Advertiser*, 31 Mar. 1815; *JEP*, 3:18, 21 [8, 9 Jan. 1816]; *New-York Columbian*, 20 May 1819; Concord *New-Hampshire Statesman and State Journal*, 11 Aug. 1832; gravestone inscription in Old Town Cemetery, Newburgh).

The federal SYSTEM OF DRAWBACKS established conditions under which duties paid on imported goods could be refunded when those same goods were subsequently exported ("An Act making further provision in cases of Drawbacks," 29 Jan. 1795, *U.S. Statutes at Large*, 1:411–3). On 2 Mar. 1812 Senator Crawford gave a lengthy SPEECH in opposition to a proposal to increase the size of the United States Navy. The proposed amendment, defeated four days later, would have modified what became "An Act concerning the Naval Establishment," 30 Mar. 1812 (*Annals*, 12th Cong., 1st sess., 148–60, 164; *U.S. Statutes at Large*, 2: 699).

SUBSTRACTED is an obsolete form of "subtracted" (*OED*). The NEW SECRETARY OF THE TREASURY was George W. Campbell. The EXAMPLE set by New York may refer to that state's efforts, under the leadership of Governor Daniel D. Tompkins, to meet the militia quotas set by the federal government during the War of 1812 (Robert Malcomson, *Historical Dictionary of the War of 1812* [2006], 373–4).

[1] Manuscript: "Contemptble."

[2] Manuscript: "which the influence which."

[3] Preceding two words interlined.

[4] Crawford here canceled "duty."

[5] Preceding five words interlined in place of "in time of."

[6] Crawford here canceled "nation."

[7] Manuscript: "Sysem."

[8] Omitted words editorially supplied.

[9] Manuscript: "to increase to increase."

[10] Manuscript: "Some of Power of."

[11] Manuscript: "Capatalists."

[12] Manuscript: "fraid."

[13] Omitted word editorially supplied.

[14] Manuscript:"instition."

[15] Crawford here canceled "delay."

From John F. Dumoulin

SIR South fourth St Philadelphia May the 31st 1816—

On Sunday the 12th inst the eve of my departure from Washington I was flattered by the receipt of the letter you did me the honor of writing to me informing me of the receipt of the copies of my Essay which I had taken the liberty of sending you, In a few lines you have set in the strongest light the invaluable right which I had undertaken to advocate. Enlightened as this age and especially this country is in political science yet the difficulty interposed to the establishment of many principles of freedom is great and surprising. But looking back to the last century it is impossible not to be pleased with the situation in which we are placed. The yet remaining prejudices resulting from an English and aristocratic education will not allow the correctness of any principle which cannot be sanctioned by a precedent from Coke or supported by some dictum pronounced in an Age of ignorance and slavery. But these persons find themselves daily in a greater minority. Humanity receives continually accession to her cause from the rising generation while prejudice can hardly decoy a single recruit to her ranks. this is the never failing consequence of that principle and argument for toleration which you so long since laid down that for truth to triumph over error and prejudice it only required an equal and unrestrained freedom of discussion

I fear Sir I may appear rude or negligent in not having sooner acknowledged your letter—indeed since I was made happy by its receipt I have scarce had a moment of leisure—On my arrival at Baltimore I had to unpack a small library which had just arrived to me from the island of Trinidad and which I had on leaving the island committed to the care of an acquaintance—I found several of my most valuable books missing which by breaking many sets of works made my loss in reality much greater than it was numerically—the chagrin which I felt made me come to the resolution of going to the West Indies and no longer to depend on those who had[1] neglected me—the hopes of accomplishing this and returning before the hurricane months made me seize the first opportunity and hurried me in my preparations—I had taken my passage on board a Vessel about to proceed on her voyage immediately when the wishes of my friends added to the superior consideration that by leaving the Country even for a few months I would forfeit the period of probation for Citizenship which I have already served, I gave over my intended voyage and have changed it to one for New Orleans for which place I sail on Wednesday next in the Ship Tennessee.

I have here mentioned these little facts because the hurry and anxiety attending them are the causes of my not having sooner acknowledged the letter you did me the honor of addressing to me—

It is my present intention to settle myself in that country of whose liberty and independence you are the father and whose valuable and important emporium you sought to preserve from the extravagance of speculation—You will perhaps Sir, be surprised that I should prefer the seeming monotony of a Sea Voyage to the magnificent variety of the land and river passage—but this last is a feast which I wish to enjoy more at leisure and which I fear I would not have time to spare at present, being particularly desirous of being at New Orleans while Mr Robertson its strictly virtuous representative is there. If I went by the Ohio and Missipi the well known hospitality of the inhabitants of their bank[s] would not permit me to arrive at New Orleans for several months at least when I should not have the pleasure and advantage of Meeting either Mr Robertson or Mr Brown the Senator as they mentioned it was not their intention to remain longer in Louisiana than August.

I am proud in being recollected by the family at Monticello. May I beg you to make my respectful remembrances and believe

Sir Your very humble and devoted J: F: DUMOULIN—

I beg Sir you may pardon the incoherence of this letter, but yesterday arrived in this City I am now about leaving it for New York where I go for a day to go to make my Adieus to my friends of whom, Mr Emmet felt no small pleasure and pride at your recollection of him and was grateful for your kindness to me at Monticello.

RC (DLC); edge trimmed; endorsed by TJ as received 7 June 1816 and so recorded in SJL. RC (MHi); address cover only; with PoC of TJ to Charles Simms, 12 July 1816, on verso; addressed: "To Thomas Jefferson Esqr Monticello in Virginia"; franked; postmarked Philadelphia, 31 May.

[1]Manuscript: "had had."

Draft Agreement for Sale of Henderson Lands by John T. Wood

Articles of covenant and agreement[1] entered into and concluded between John Wood of the state of Kentucky on the one part and Thomas Jefferson of the county of Albemarle in the commonwealth of Virginia on the other part on the day of May one thousand eight hundred and sixteen.

The said John[2] Wood on his part covenanteth with the sd Thomas that in the lands which were the property of Bennet Henderson dec[d] around the town of Milton in Albemarle aforesaid, and adjacent thereto, he hath full title in feesimple to all the portion thereof which descended on Nancy Crawford[3] Henderson, one of the daughters of the said Bennet, now the wife of Matthew Nelson or which have otherwise come to her; which title he acquired by purchase and conveyance from the said Matthew and Nancy Crawford[4] his wife to him the said John Wood in feesimple. And that in his own right, and in that of Lucy[5] his wife, another of the daughters of the sd Bennet, he hath full title and power to sell and convey in feesimple all the portion of rights and interests whatsoever in the said lands which descended on the said Lucy his wife, or which have otherwise come to her or him, at any time, directly or indirectly.

And the said John Wood further covenanteth with the sd Thomas that on or before the day of next ensuing he and his said wife Lucy, by lawful deed to be executed and proved in the state of Kentucky or elsewhere in such way as that the same shall be admissible to record in the proper court of Virginia, and according to the laws of Kentucky & Virginia, and to be transmitted to the said Thomas, will convey to him the sd Thomas, a good and indefeasable estate in feesimple in all the rights, titles & interests of whatsoever nature they be, whether in claim, trust, possession, or reversion jointly or severally,[6] which descended on, or otherwise came directly or indirectly to the said Nancy Crawford and Lucy, or to their sd husbands, in the lands aforesaid around the town of Milton,[7] which were of the property of their said father at the time of his death.[8]

And the said Thomas, on his part, covenanteth for himself, his heirs executors and administrators, that he will pay to the said John Wood at the signing of these presents the sum of two hundred Dollars, and the conveyance aforesaid having been previously made and transmitted to the sd Thomas,[9] that he will pay to the said John Wood the further sum of one thousand dollars on or before the first day of April next ensuing the date of these presents[10]

MS (ViU: TJP); entirely in TJ's hand; partially dated; with wax from two seals on right side at foot of text. PoC (ViU: TJP). Dft (ViU: TJP); entirely in TJ's hand; undated; on reused address cover to TJ.

John T. Wood married Lucy L. Henderson (b. 12 Apr. 1790) in February 1812 (affidavit relating to the lands of Bennett Henderson, 22 Nov. 1815 [KyHi]).

These ARTICLES OF COVENANT AND AGREEMENT were never finalized. John T. Wood acquired FULL TITLE to the tract inherited by Nancy C. Henderson Nelson with a payment of $600 to her and Matthew Nelson on 26 Mar. 1816 (Albemarle Co. Deed Book, 20:57–8).

[1] Remainder of paragraph in Dft reads "between E^t^c."

[2] Blank left for first name in Dft.

[3] Preceding two words interlined in Dft in place of "Lucy."

[4] "Nancy C." interlined here in Dft in place of "Lucy."

[5] Word interlined in Dft in place of "Nancy Crawford," here and at next two instances below.

[6] Preceding three words not in Dft.

[7] Preceding five words not in Dft.

[8] In Dft, the following paragraph originally read "And the sd Thomas, on his part, covenanteth with the sd Wood that on rcciept of such conveyance, executed, proved, and admissible to record as aforesd he will execute and deliver, on the premisses, to the sd Wood or to his order a lawful bond obliging him the sd Thomas to pay to the sd Wood, his exrs admrs or assigns the sum of Dollars, at or before the expiration of one year from the date of these presents, and that he will faithfully pay the same accordingly." TJ later rewrote this paragraph on verso of Dft, with differences from MS noted below.

[9] Preceding four words not in rewritten Dft paragraph.

[10] Preceding five words not in rewritten Dft paragraph.

Draft Conveyance of Henderson Lands by John T. Wood and Lucy Henderson Wood

[ca. May 1816]

This indenture made on the day of one thousand eight hundred and sixteen between John Wood and Lucy his wife of the state of Kentucky on the one part, and Thomas Jefferson of the county of Albemarle in the commonwealth of Virginia on the other part witnesseth, that Whereas Bennet Henderson dec^d[1] father of the sd Lucy was at the time of his death seized and possessed in feesimple of a certain tract of land around the town of Milton in Albemarle aforesaid, & adjacent thereto, one child's portion whereof, on his death, descended in feesimple on[2] the sd Lucy, who is since intermarried with the sd John; and one other child's portion thereof descended in feesimple on Nancy Crawford Henderson, another of the daughters of the sd Bennet, who is since intermarried with Matthew Nelson, which said Matthew & Nancy Crawford his wife have in due form of law sold & conveyed the sd child's portion so descended on the sd Nancy Crawford to the sd John Wood in feesimple.

Now therefore the sd John & Lucy his wife, in consideration of the sum of two hundred dollars to them in hand paid by the said Thomas, and of the further sum of one thousand dollars secured to be paid, have given, granted, bargained and sold[3] unto the sd Thomas[4] the two portions of the sd lands and their appurtenances[5] held by the sd Bennet Henderson[6] around the town of Milton and descended on the sd Nancy Crawford & Lucy, and all their right, title, & claim therein & in every part thereof, whether divided, or undivided, in separate or joint parcels or[7] titles, in possession, reversion or action, or in any other manner or title whatsoever: To have and to hold the sd portions of the sd lands and their appurtenances,[8] and all rights therein to him the said Thomas and his heirs. and the sd John & Lucy his wife, jointly & severally,[9] their joint & several heirs, executors & administrators, the sd two portions of lands & appurtenances, and all rights therein to the sd Thomas & his heirs, will for ever warrant & defend. In witness whereof the sd John & Lucy his wife have hereto subscribed their names & affixed their seals on the day and year abovewritten.

Signed, sealed,
and delivered
in presence of }

MS (ViU: TJP); written entirely in TJ's hand on indented paper; partially dated; unsigned, but with wax from two seals on right side at foot of text. Dft (ViU: TJP); entirely in TJ's hand; on verso of reused address cover of Benjamin J. Campbell to TJ, 16 Mar. 1816; partially dated; endorsed by TJ: "Wood et ux to Jefferson} rough draught of deed delivered to Wood to be executed & transmitted."

[1] Word interlined in Dft.

[2] Reworked in Dft from "child's part whereof descended on."

[3] Word interlined in Dft in place of "conveyed."

[4] In Dft TJ here canceled "all."

[5] Preceding three words interlined in Dft.

[6] Reworked in Dft from "by their sd father."

[7] Preceding two words interlined in Dft.

[8] Preceding three words interlined in Dft.

[9] Word interlined in Dft in place of "separately."

Account with Frank Carr

[after 1 June 1816]

Thomas Jefferson in acct with Frank Carr

		Dr
1813		$
Decr	3. To visit negro woman at night from Monticello to Bacon's	2.00
	4. To bleeding &c Evelina 1.$ (1814 July 13.) visit &c Negro Woman (Minerva) 3$	4.00

1814				
July	14.	To visit &c Minerva 3.$ (16th) Visit &c Minerva 3.$ (17.) med: & adv: Minerva 2$		8.00
	19.	To visit &c Minerva 3$ (21) ditto ditto—ditto 3.$ (23) ditto ditto 3.$		9.00
	25	To[1] visit &c Minerva 3:$ (1815 Mar 3) Visit & bleedg Jesse 3$	29.	6.00
1815				
Mar	8	To[2] med: & adv: Jesse 2$ (10) Visit Jesse from Monticello 1.$ (18) passg visit do 1.50		4.50
May—	10	" Visit med: & adv: Aggy 3.$ (16) passing visit &c Aggy 1.50		4.50
	22	" Visit Aggy 3.$ large Box Ungt Merc: 75. 24 pill Merc: 1$		4.75
	27.	To visit Aggy 3.$ (June 1) visit &c Aggy 3.$ (4th) visit &c Aggy 3.		9.00
July	14.	To visit Negroes 3 med: & adv: Aggy & Jesse 4. (19th) visit med: & adv: Aggy. 3.		10.00
	22	To visit &c Aggy[3] 3. (24) ditto ditto ditto 3. (26) xii pulv: op: & Ipec: 50.		6.50
	29.	To visit &c Aggy 3.	42.25	3.00
1816				
Feby	6	To visit & reducing fractured thigh Boy Joe at Lego. reducing ditto twice displaced sundry medicines visits &c up to March 5th		30.00
	29.	To visit med: & adv: Sally at Bacon's—3.		3.00
Mar	7.	To passing visit Sally 1.50 lancing her breast 1.50 (14) visit do &c 3.		6.00
	15.	To ℥i Borax 37½ ℥i Corrosive Sublimate 1.25		1.62½
		xii pill op: &c Sally 50. Box long L. Cerate 37½		0.87½
	17.	To Reducing Moses' Fractured leg Sundry med: daily[4] visits & attentions to final Cure Apl 21.		25.00

	27. To visit Sally at Bacon's 3.$ xii pulv: Tonic &c 50		3.50
April.	9. To visit &c Sally 3.$ (May 15) visit &c Mrs Marks 3.$ (21) ditto do 3.		9.00
May.	23. To ℥i Flour Sulph: & Cream: Tart. 75. (June 1.) Pulv: Col: 37½: Ungt Herp: 50.	80.62½	1:62½
			$151 87½

MS (ViU: TJP-CC); in Carr's hand, with three underlined annual sums in penultimate column written by TJ; undated; notation by Carr on verso: "mr Thos Jefferson with Frank Carr} acct $151.87½"; endorsed by TJ: "Carr Dr Frank. 1813. Dec. 3.–1816. May 23 151.87½ D"; with additional calculations by TJ beneath endorsement: "1814 29
1815 42.25
1816 80.62½
151.87½
11.64 interest
163.51."

TJ reworked his calculation of interest on the verso from $9.90 to $11.64 and the total owed from $161.77 to $163.51. He probably arrived at the revised figures about 2 June 1817, when he gave Carr an order on Gibson & Jefferson "for 164.D. amount of his medical account" (*MB*, 2:1334).

Unguent of mercury (UNGT MERC:) was used to treat symptoms of venereal disease. Pulverized opium (PULV: OP:), on its own or mixed with lard, provided a soothing dressing. IPEC:: "ipecac." ℥ is the apothecary symbol for a troy ounce, which is approximately 31.1 grams. Mercuric chloride (CORROSIVE SUBLIMATE) was used to treat venereal disease. Lead cerate (L. CERATE), flores sulphuris (FLOUR SULPH:; sublimed sulphur), and cream of tartar (TART.), when mixed with molasses, could all be taken orally to remedy skin diseases and eruptions. Pulverized colocynth (PULV: COL:), made from the dried fruit of *Citrullus colocynthis*, was used as a cathartic (John Hunter, *A Treatise on the Venereal Disease*, 3d ed. [London, 1810], 41, 261, 310–2; Edward S. Lang, *Medicine Chests: with Suitable Directions* [Salem, Mass., ca. 1800]; William T. Brannt and William H. Wahl, eds., *The Techno-Chemical Receipt Book* [1887], 167; Oscar Oldberg, *A Manual of Weights, Measures, and Specific Gravity* [1885], 96–100; John S. Billings, *The National Medical Dictionary*, 2 vols. [1890]; *OED*).

[1] Superfluous ditto mark in front of this word editorially omitted.

[2] Superfluous ditto mark in front of this word editorially omitted.

[3] Carr here canceled "& Jesse."

[4] Word interlined.

From Joseph Lakanal

MONSIEUR ET ILLUSTRE CITOYEN

Gallatin Contry par Vevay
indian Contry, le 1r Juin 1816.

J'ai l'honneur de vous adresser deux Lettres que J'esperois avoir l'inappréciable avantage de Vous présenter; des événemens que Je n'ai pu maîtriser ont Changé la direction que Je Voulois prendre. me Voici Sur les bords de l'ohio, dans des propriétés que J'ai acquises, Gallatin Contry, en face de la Colonie française de Vevay: Je vais, dans Cette douce retraite, partager mon tems entre la Culture de mes terres et Celle des Lettres. Je me propose d'écrire l'histoire des etats-unis pour laquelle Je ramasse des matériaux depuis dix ans. le Spectacle d'un peuple libre et heureux, Supportant, avec docilité, le Joug Salutaire des Lois, temperera l'amertume que J'éprouve en m'éloignant de ma patrie; elle Seroit heureuse Si vôtre génie pacifique avoit dirigé Ses destinées. l'ambition d'un Seul homme a précipité Sur nous, les nations Courroucées, tandis que vous attachiez à la belle amérique, les tribus indiennes, par le lien durable des bienfaits. ma patrie avilie ruinée, mais frappée de la Sagesse de vôtre administration, Vous envie au nouveau monde.

Jespère, qu'en écrivant l'histoire de vôtre mémorable administration, et de vos prédecesseurs plus ou moins Célèbres, le tableau Se ressentira du Charme qu'éprouvera le peintre, et que Soutenu par la beauté du Sujèt, bien plus que par mes propres forces, Je pourrai, avec un poëte Célèbre de l'antiquité, m'écrier à la fin de mon ouvrage,

"exegi monumentum ære perennius"

J'ai l'honneur d'être Monsieur et illustre Citoyen,
Vôtre très humble et très obéïssant serviteur

Lakanal
de l'institut de france
et de la Légion d'honneur

EDITORS' TRANSLATION

Gallatin Contry near Vevay
indian Contry, 1 June 1816.

Sir and illustrious Citizen

I have the honor of sending you two letters that I had hoped to have the invaluable advantage of presenting to you personally; events beyond my control have changed my preferred course. I find myself on the banks of the Ohio River, on properties I have acquired in Gallatin Contry, opposite the French colony of Vevay. In this peaceful retreat I will divide my time between the cultivation of my lands and the humanities. I propose to write a history of the United States for which I have been gathering material for ten years. The sight of a free and happy people, docilely tolerating the salutary yoke of the law, will moderate my bitterness at leaving my homeland. She would be fortunate if your peaceful genius had directed her destinies. The ambition of a single man hurled onto us all the wrathful nations, even as you were binding the Indian tribes to noble America through the lasting bonds of kindness. My country, degraded, ruined, but struck by the wisdom of your administration, envies you in the New World.

I hope that in writing the history of your memorable administration and of your more or less famous predecessors, the picture will reflect the charm felt by its painter, and that, sustained by the beauty of the subject much more than my own strength, I will be able to exclaim at the end of my work, along with a famous poet of antiquity, "exegi monumentum ære perennius"

I have the honor to be, Sir and illustrious Citizen,

Your very humble and very obedient servant

LAKANAL
of the Institut de France
and the Légion d'honneur

RC (MoSHi: TJC-BC); dateline at foot of text; endorsed by TJ as received 10 July 1816 from "Vevay. Indiana," and so recorded in SJL. Translation by Dr. Genevieve Moene. Enclosures: (1) André Thoüin to TJ, 18 Dec. 1815. (2) Lafayette to TJ, 28 Dec. 1815.

GALLATIN CONTRY: Gallatin County, Kentucky. VEVAY was in adjacent Switzerland County, Indiana Territory (INDIAN CONTRY). The SEUL HOMME was Napoleon. EXEGI MONUMENTUM ÆRE PERENNIUS: "I have finished a monument more lasting than bronze" (Horace, *Odes*, 3.30.1, in *Horace: Odes and Epodes*, trans. Niall Rudd, Loeb Classical Library [2004], 216–7).

On this date Lakanal also sent a similar letter to President James Madison (DLC: Madison Papers).

From John Steele

SIR, Collectors office Philad[a] June 1st 1816

Yours of the 18th instant came duly to hand—I had, previously, received a letter from M[r] Cathalan containing a Bill of lading, and had written to you for advice where to send the goods

They[1] are now laden on board the Sc[r] Five Sisters, which will Sail on tomorrow, and consigned agreeably to your instructions

The Box, which M[r] Cathalan informs me had, in mistake, been shipped without an outside wrapper, was somewhat injured when I rec[d] it from the vessel. I had it matted & expect it will reach you in safety

Enclosed are Bills of lading & freight with a statement of duty & charges

It will always give me pleasure to render you any service, that my situation here will afford me opportunity to perform

With most respectful Consideration yours &C. JN[O] STEELE

RC (ViU: TJP-ER); endorsed by TJ as received 7 June 1816 and so recorded in SJL. RC (DLC); address cover only; with PoC of TJ to Joseph C. Cabell, 13 July 1816, on recto and verso; addressed: "Thomas Jefferson Esq[r] Monticello"; franked; postmarked Philadelphia, 1 June. Enclosure: bill of lading, Philadelphia, 28 May 1816, according to which Steele had shipped to TJ, bound for Richmond aboard the schooner *Five Sisters* under Michael Fisher, "*One Case containing fifty bottles Hermitage Wine*" and "*One matted Box containing Macarony*," to be delivered to Gibson & Jefferson in Richmond, with that firm to pay freight "at the rate of *12½ Cents pr* [*hw[t]*?] with primage and average accustomed" (printed form in ViU: TJP-MJ; with multiple blanks filled by Steele and one, the rate of freight, apparently by Fisher, all rendered above in italics; signed by Fisher; one word illegible). Other enclosures not found.

[1] Manuscript: "The."

To John R. F. Corbin

Sir Monticello June 2. 16.

Your favor of May 17. came to hand yesterday only: and I am sorry I cannot give you the information you ask relative to the tickets of mrs Jones in Byrd's lottery. on the death of mr Wayles I assorted all his papers, and every paper he had passed then thro' my hands, and notice, and I am tolerably certain no such tickets were among them. all the papers were delivered to mr F. Eppes of Eppington in Chesterfield, who had the settlement of all mr Wayles's affairs. it is possible mr Wayles may have sold tickets for Col^o Byrd. in that case he will have entered it in his acc^t with that gentleman, which is in his Ledger. this may be known by your dropping a line to mr Archibald Thweat at Eppington near Richmond, who is in possession of all mr Wayles's papers. Accept the assurance of my esteem and respect

Th: Jefferson

PoC (MHi); at foot of text: "John R. F. Corbin esq."; endorsed by TJ.

From Donald Fraser

Respected Sir. N. York June 2^d 1816

Some days ago I did myself the honour of transmitting a letter to You, wherein I intimated sending a piece wherein Your name was mentioned. It has just Struck me that I did not enclose the piece, as intended[1]— .. Here it follows .....

Mr Philips

I have read a number of anecdotes, the following one is, in my opinion, very applicable to the present State of parties in this country. A certain wealthy English Baronet who had an only Son, a mere Dolt, his father Sent him to Several eminent Teachers; none of whom could make a Schollar of this heir apparent to an ancient family...... The father applied to the late accomplished Earle of Chesterfield, to recommend him a proper Tutor for his Son: The Earl pointed out to him, Dr B..... "What, exclaimed the Baronet, with Surprize, Don't Your Lordship Know? that D^r B,— is a whig, & a violent opposer of our Party? I can't think of trusting my Son to his care:—As he might poison his mind with his own principles" Chesterfield, "D^r B, is a very honest & learned man, he'll do justice to Your Son; he has, invariably adhered to his party, in worst & best of times, & never changed Sides....... When in office, I endeavoured to retain it, by every method in my power: When out of office, I tried hard to Get in again; wrote & Spoke against my opponents, right or wrong."

Now, the erudite Editor of the "Evening-Post," has certainly followed Chesterfield's maxims in politics; as he has uniformly for fifteen Years past, Calumniated A Jefferson, a Madison & now a Tompkins, whether from Patriotic or Selfish motives, that is best Known to himself. I am conscious,[2] that their are Some Good men; & Genuine Patriots, in the Federal ranks; whom I Should be Sorry to See, any Republican Editor, treat with personal abuse, as Wm Coleman, has, the most respectable Patriots on[3] the Republican Side.

A friend to the People.

[My first piece in Defence of Govr Tompkins]
To the Editor of the "National Advocate"
Sir .... Upon perusing Mr Coleman's Strictures of Friday last, & Your Remarks on Monday—Relative a certain pecuniary transaction, wherein Govr Tompkins, was an: I was Struck with Mr C's attempts, to hold forth one of our most incorruptible & excellent Patriots, (a man of irreproachable character in every Stage of his public life) as a Swindler.

I am, an old man, & remember Several adages; I'll Give You a common one "Never estimate any man's character, from the applause of his friends, nor the Defamation of his enemies."

If my memory serves me, the following Sentiments are contained in letters which I received, from two, great & Good Patriots—now no more!
The letters I possess, & can be produced if necessary.

"I have noticed Your remarks on Party-Spirits they are well-founded# ... It is greatly to be lamented, that Party politicans are So little inclined to do justice to their opponents merits"

"Benjn Rush"

A Thorough-paced party politican, censures measures, that he approves of:[4] He confides in men, whom he heartily—despises:—He opposes [the measures][5] of his antagonists, tho, his reason tells him they are proper."

"Robt R. Livingston"

[Coleman's remarks on the foregoing piece—In the Evening-Post Novr 8th 1815.]

I wrote a Pamphlet fifteen years ago, entitled "Party-Spirit exposed" or, "Remarks on the Times" You never Saw the thing.

"A writer in the 'National Advocate,"[6] under the Signature of 'an old Citizen,' Quotes with Great form & ceremony, the Sayings of D[r] Rush & Chancellor Livingston; in order to assist Governor Tompkins, on the present occasion; whom he calls an incorrupti[ble][7] & excellent Patriot.—I tell these people again, the Advocate, its editors & correspondents, that I will not be diverted from my object"

I have the honour to be, venerable Sir, with Great respect & Esteem, Your obd[t] humble Servant. DONALD FRASER SEN[R]

RC (MHi); dateline at foot of text; ellipses and first and third sets of brackets in original; addressed: "Tho[s] Jefferson Esq[r] Late President of the U.S. Monticello Virg[a]"; franked; postmarked New York, 1 July; endorsed by TJ as received 10 July 1816 and so recorded in SJL. Fraser's subsequent letter of 27 June 1816 was probably enclosed in this one.

The earlier LETTER to TJ is not recorded in SJL and has not been found. The first item quoted here was addressed to the publisher Naphtali PHILIPS and printed in his newspaper, the New York *National Advocate*, 11 Nov. 1815. The ERUDITE EDITOR of the *New York Evening Post* was William Coleman. Fraser's DEFENCE, addressed to the editor of the *National Advocate*, Andrew Caldwell Mitchell, appeared in the 8 Nov. 1815 issue (Brigham, *American Newspapers*, 1:631, 672). Coleman issued his STRICTURES in the *New York Evening Post*, 3 Nov. 1815, and Mitchell replied in the *National Advocate*, MONDAY, 6 Nov. 1815.

1 Manuscript: "intened."
2 Manuscript: "conscois."
3 Manuscript: "on on."
4 *National Advocate*: "concurs in many measures that he does not approve."
5 Omitted words supplied from *National Advocate*.
6 Omitted closing quotation mark editorially supplied.
7 Word partially lost due to mutilation at seal.

To Charles Simms

SIR Monticello June 2. 16.

I recieved yesterday your favor of May 25. and am thankful to you for the favor of notifying me, as I have not been yet advised by mr Cathalan of the actual dispatch of the wine. I expected 2. parcels from him, the one of 200. bottles of wine of Nice (red) the other a wine of Roussilon, a somewhat larger quantity, but I do not exactly know how much, because it depended on the price. which parcel this is I know not, but I imagine the former as there are 4. cases of, I expect, 50. bottles each. I must ask the favor of you to drop me a line of the amount of duty and any other expences which have attended it, which I will immediately have remitted to you: and as the advance of the season endangers injury to the wine, I will ask the favor of you to forward it to Richmond addressed to the care of Mess[rs] Gibson & Jefferson of that place by any vessel going to Richmond which you may think safe. the master will recieve his freight & any other expences from them.

In ordering these little importations from Europe, as it is impossible for me to know what vessels may be in their harbor, and to what place destined, I am always obliged to take the liberty of desiring their consignment to the Collector of whatever port they may be coming to; and I am to request that if at any time hereafter like consignments should happen to come to you, that you will have the goodness to recieve them & notify me, & the promptest care shall be taken to remit you the duties & costs. with my thanks for the present kindness accept the assurance of esteem & respect TH: JEFFERSON

PoC (MHi); on verso of reused address cover of James Ligon (for Patrick Gibson) to TJ, 27 Apr. 1816; at foot of text: "Col° Charles Simms"; mistakenly endorsed by TJ as a letter of 2 June 1817, but recorded under correct date in SJL.

The deputy collector at Alexandria eventually notified TJ of THE AMOUNT OF DUTY AND ANY OTHER EXPENCES as requested here (William D. Simms to TJ, 1 July 1816).

To James Warrell

SIR Monticello June 2. 16.

I recieved yesterday your favor of May 27. and thank you for this mark of attention: but a desire to close all worldly concerns and to be free from cares forbids me to engage in any new undertakings: indeed I fear that neither the population nor pursuits of Richmond are as yet such as to support a museum; with my wishes however that it may reward your zeal for endeavoring to give to the inhabitants so reasonable a resource for amusement and information I pray you to accept the assurance of my great esteem and respect.

TH: JEFFERSON

PoC (MoSHi: TJC-BC); on verso of reused address cover of Stephen Cathalan to TJ, 6 Jan. 1816; at foot of text: "Mr James Warrell"; endorsed by TJ.

To John F. Watson, with Watson's Receipt

SIR Monticello June 2. 16.

I had recieved the 9th vol. of the Edinb. Review some days ago, and yesterday the 10th came to hand, with your favor of May 24.[1] and in compliance with that I now inclose you a 5. Dollar note of the bank of Virginia, and salute you with esteem and respect.

TH: JEFFERSON

Rec[d] Germantown June 7. 1816 from Thomas Jefferson Esq[r] Five dollars in full for the 9 & 10 Vol[s] of the Edin[bg] Review

JOHN F. WATSON

RC (DLC); in TJ's hand adjacent to his signature: "M[r] John F. Watson"; with subjoined receipt in Watson's hand; addressed by Watson: "Thomas Jefferson Esq[re] Monticello V[a]"; franked; postmarked Germantown, 11 June; endorsed by TJ as a "rec[t] for 9. & 10. Ed. review" received 19 June 1816. FC (DLC); entirely in TJ's hand; lacking salutation and subjoined receipt; edge torn; endorsed by TJ: "Watson John F. June 2. 16."

[1] Reworked from "27."

Corrections to Biography in *Public Characters*

[ca. 3 June 1816]

pa. 220. line 3. born Apr. 2. 1743.

12. as Minister plenipot[y] in July 1784. & returned Dec. 1789.

221. at bottom. if I have had any merit as a member of our legislature it was in drawing and introducing the following laws, some of which were adopted when proposed & some afterwards.

1. a law forbidding the future importation of slaves.
2. converting estates tail into fee-simple.
3. annulling the laws of primogeniture & establish[g] the descent of property equally on all in equal degree.
4. establishing schools for general education.
5. sanctioning the right of expatriation.
6. confirming the rights of freedom of religious opinions.
7. proportioning crimes & punishments, which last under a different modification was past at a subsequent period.

to the above may be added the draught of the Declaration of Independance.

223. l. 2. I was never a member of the board of Agriculture of England, nor of any other society of any kind in that country.

17. I did not <u>propose</u> the declaration of Independence nor did I take any very leading part more than many others, to whom that merit equally belongs.

26. Dr Franklin was the first Minister Plenipo. to France.
31. fill the blank with British.

228. * the case of Col^o^ Cresap has been established on unquestionable ground in a letter to mr Henry of Maryland, annexed to the editions of the Notes on Virginia, subsequent to 1797.

229. appointed Govr of Virginia in 1779. reappointed in 1780. and resigned in 1781.

230. my plan of a Constitution does not deserve much eulogium. it was a new business to us all, & I believe my draught was the very first made by any person in America. I was in Congress at the time the Virginia convention were establishing their constitution, and my draught did not reach them till the day the one they had prepared was to recieve it's last vote. having been long contested & debated till every one was tired they could not re-open it for anything they might have liked in mine; but they adopted my preamble in a lump & prefixed it to their Constitution.

pa. 232. line 6. from bottom. I was never appointed Ambassador to Spain nor was I in Congress in 1782.[1] my diplomatic appointments have been as follows. in 1778. after Independance declared and the Confederation agreed to by every state except Maryland, Congress determined to propose to France treaties of Alliance & Commerce, and Dr Franklin, mr Adams & myself were appointed plenipotentiaries for that purpose; but I declined it from circumstances in the state of my family, & from a conviction I could be more useful here, our affairs then laboring under their greatest difficulties.

About the close of 1782. Congress having recieved information from their ministers in Europe that there was a prospect of concluding the war by a treaty of peace I was appointed a minister to join those in Europe for settling the conditions of the treaty. I repaired to Philadelphia in Jan. 1783 in order to proceed to Europe. the Minister of France offered me the French frigate Romulus, then at Baltimore, for my passage, and while I was waiting there the breaking up of the ice in which she was blocked up, we recieved informn that preliminary articles were signed between Great Britain and us, to be valid only in the event of peace concluded with the other powers. I wrote to ask of[2] Congress whether the occasion of my service was not past, & they accordingly dispensed with my proceeding.

Peace being established in 1783. & a general commerce opened, Congress thought it advisable to propose treaties of commerce with all the powers of Europe with whom we wer[e] likely to have intercourse. plenipotentiary commissions wer[e] accordingly given to mr Adams, Dr Franklin & myself, severally addressed to the several powers of Europe, and I sailed for Europe in July 1784. these commissions all proved abortive except that to Prussia, after the signing of which Dr Franklin returned to America, & I was appointed his successor as Minister plenipotentiary to Fran[ce.] a little before the expiration of the joint commissions I crosse[d] over from Paris to London to see jointly with mr Adams, whether that government was disposed to enter into close & cordial connections, and we made up our minds to offer an exchange of naturalisation for our citizens & vessels as to every thing relating to commerce or commercial navigation. Ld Carmarthaen recieved us to present our commission, but evaded every attempt at any conference; so that 3. or 4. days only before the expiration of our commission & after 7. weeks attending, I returned to Paris.

I continued in France until Oct. 1789. & having obtained leave of absence for a while I arrived in Norfolk about the end of Nov. and on my way home met an express from Genl Washington bringing me a Commission to be Secretary of Stat[e.] I answered by an expression of my preference of returning to France but left to himself the ultimate decision. he agreed that I should return if I declined the other appointment but expressing a much stronger desire that I should take a par[t] in the government, I acquiesced and proceeded to N. York in April where I entered on the office of Secretary of state & continued in it until the new year's day of 1794. when I resigned, and retired to private life.

While residing at Paris, there was little to be done. a free reception of our whale oils, & salted fish, our flour, rice and tobacco into France & of our fish and flour into their West-India islands was obtained and continued until their revolution.

---

page 244. line 7. from bottom. the medal was not struck by any publick authority, but by the artist on his own free will.

MS (LNT: George H. and Katherine M. Davis Collection); entirely in TJ's hand; undated; edge trimmed.

The conjectural date of this document is based on the arrival of Bass Otis at Monticello on 3 June 1816 with a copy of

Public Characters of 1800–1801 (London, 1801; Sowerby, no. 402), pp. 220–45 of which contained the biography on which TJ based the above set of corrections (Joseph Delaplaine to TJ, 11 May 1816; note to Caspar Wistar to TJ, 28 May 1816).

When TJ was BORN, Great Britain and its American colonies used the Julian calendar. In 1752 the British government adopted the Gregorian calendar, thus moving TJ's birth date forward by eleven days to 13 Apr. For numbers 1 and 2 of the FOLLOWING LAWS, see respectively *PTJ*, 2:22–4, 1:560–2. For items 3–7 see bills numbered 20, 79, 55, 82, and 64 in a grouping of documents on "The Revisal of the Laws 1776–1786" (*PTJ*, 2:391–3, 526–35, 476–9, 545–53, and 492–507, respectively). TJ addressed the CASE of Michael Cresap in a letter to John Henry, 31 Dec. 1797 (*PTJ*, 29:600–4). The letter was published first in Jefferson, *An Appendix to the Notes on Virginia Relative to the Murder of Logan's Family* (Philadelphia, 1800; Sowerby, nos. 3225, 4051), and then as the fourth appendix to *Jefferson's Notes, on the State of Virginia; with the Appendixes—complete* (Baltimore, 1800, and other eds.), pp. 29–32 of the appendices.

TJ wrote three drafts of a proposed PLAN OF A CONSTITUTION for Virginia in 1776 (*PTJ*, 1:329–65). Anne César, chevalier de La Luzerne, was the MINISTER OF FRANCE who offered TJ the use of a French frigate in 1783 (*PTJ*, 6:227–8, 237–8). For the meeting of TJ and John Adams with Francis Osborne, 5th Duke of Leeds (styled the Marquess of Carmarthen [CARMARTHAEN] until he succeeded to the dukedom in 1789), see *PTJ*, 9:406–9.

The MEDAL commemorating TJ's first presidential inauguration was struck in 1801 by John Reich, an engraver at the United States Mint (R. W. Julian, *Medals of the United States Mint: The First Century, 1792–1892*, ed. N. Neil Harris [1977], 77). *Public Characters*, 244, states that TJ's "countrymen have done themselves honour by striking a medal to commemorate the services he has rendered them."

[1] Preceding seven words interlined.
[2] Preceding two words interlined.

To William D. Meriwether

SI[R] Monticello June 3. 1816.

I have concluded to accede to your proposition of purchasing the rights of mr and mrs[1] Hornsby in the lands of her father around the town of Milton, on the valuation of persons to be chosen by us, and payment to be made at the end of two years, but with interest during the second year. but as it is inconvenient to me to go out much, and I shall shortly have a long absence in Bedford, I have authorised my grandson Thomas J. Randolph to act for me in the whole business, and I hereby confirm whatever he shall do in it, as if done by myself, and oblige myself to execute whatever he shall agree to on my behalf. Accept my respectful salutations. TH: JEFFERSON

PoC (DLC); on verso of portion of reused address cover of William Thornton to TJ, 22 Mar. 1816; mutilated at seal; at foot of text: "Cap[t] William D. Meriwether"; endorsed by TJ.

[1] TJ here canceled "Hende." Frances Hornsby's maiden name was Henderson.

To Thomas Eston Randolph

Dear Sir Monticello June 3. 16.

In my letter of the other day I mentioned that the credit of 122.50 D for corn formerly bought from mr Bankhead as mentioned by Col° T. M. Randolph, was correct, and reduced our balance to 176.26½ D since that, having occasion to pay mr Fagg 49.58 D and not having the money, he told me it was due to you, & that an order on you would answer his purpose, which accordingly I gave him, & it reduces our balance to 126.68 ever & affectionately

Your's Th: Jefferson

PoC (MHi); on verso of reused address cover of John Tayloe Lomax to TJ, 11 Mar. 1816; between closing and signature: "T. E. Randolph esq."; endorsed by TJ.

TJ's letter of the other day is not recorded in SJL and has not been found. The payment to John fagg on Randolph's account was for 85 bushels of oats and is listed elsewhere as $53.12½ (*MB*, 2:1324; TJ to Randolph, 18 June 1816).

From Stephen Cathalan

My Dear Sir & as much
Respected as Beloved Friend! Marseilles the 4th June 1816

I hope that my Letters of the 15th febry & 19th march Last, with the Containts of my Several Invoices, therein Inclosed, will have Reached you before this Day;

your Favor of the 1st February last Reached me on the 7th ult° — many Thousand Gratefull Thanks—for your kind Expressions towards me! & I cannot better Express them to you, than by my Continued Endeavours to desire the Continuation of the Confidence placed in me by the Executive Government of the united states;

This will Reach you by the Ship Lothair[1] of norfolk John Stones[2] Master Bound for norfolk & Ready for Sea, on which I have Shipped as pr Bill of Loading, (which I have Inclosed in my Letter of this Day to the Collector of the District of norfolk) one Cask Containing one Barrel of about 38 Gallons or 120 Litres old Roussillon wine,[3] which Mr Fois Durand of Perpignan, has at last Sent to me, assuring me to be the Exact quality you wished, & by the Bottle he Sent me at Same time to taste it, I Took it, at first, for its flavour[4] & Taste for old Madeira wine, however with Some Difference Easily Perceived after;—he has an one other Barrel to Send me, but wished before, to have my opinion, whether it's quality Should be Satisfactory & I am writing him to Send it to me as Soon as Possible.[5]

he has not Sent me the Invoice of this 1st Barrel, but it will not Cost on[6] Board, one hundred & Fifty franks

I have had Lately in this Road, (& under my Country house)[7] the U.s. Frigate United States, Commodore John Shaw, who Sailed on the 29th Ulto

we have now her Royal Highness the Dutchess of Berry[8] arived on the 21st Ulto into this Lazareto, & had her Free Pratick on the 30th ditto;—She is Just Returned from Toulon at one half past Ten at night;—herewith[9] the Ceremonial of her Reception here & at Toulon;

Everything appears now quiet,[10] & it is hoped we Shall at Last enjoy of a Lasting Tranquility;

meantime I may write you more fully, Please to accept my best & Sincerest wishes for your happiness & good health, having the honor to be with great Respect;

my Dear sir Your most obedt Servt STEPHEN CATHALAN.

Dupl (MHi); at head of text: "2ta"; with RC of Cathalan to TJ, 19 June 1816, subjoined; at foot of first page: "Thomas Jefferson Esqr &ca &ca Monticello"; endorsed by TJ as received 28 Aug. 1816 and so recorded in SJL. RC (MHi); dated 1 June 1816; endorsed by TJ as received 2 Sept. 1816 and so recorded in SJL. Enclosure: Anne Joachim Joseph, marquis de Rochemore, *Cérémonial Pour la remise, la réception et le séjour de Madame la Duchesse de Berri, a Marseille, Et son voyage à Toulon* (Marseille, 1816), which describes the receptions given at Marseille and Toulon in honor of Marie Caroline Ferdinande Louise de Bourbon, Duchesse de Berry.

The COLLECTOR OF THE DISTRICT OF NORFOLK was Charles K. Mallory. On her arrival at the port of Marseille on 21 May 1816, the DUTCHESS OF BERRY entered a lazaretto (LAZARETO), a quarantine hospital, where she remained until given a pratique (PRATICK), a clearance of good health (Arthur Léon Imbert de Saint-Amand, *The Duchess of Berry and the Court of Louis XVIII*, trans. Elizabeth Gilbert Martin [1900], 27–53).

1 Word rewritten by TJ above the line for clarity.

2 RC: "Stone."

3 In left margin of RC Cathalan added: "J
No 1."

4 RC substitutes "as by its Colour" for preceding three words.

5 TJ noted in left margin, perpendicular to text: "150.*f* @ $5\frac{1}{3}$ *f* to the D. = 28. D 11 c 38. galls for 28.11 D is .74 cents per galln or .18½ the quart, or .15 cents pr bottle."

6 Dupl: "one." RC: "on."

7 Parenthetical phrase not in RC.

8 RC: "Berri in this City."

9 RC: "herein I enclosed."

10 RC here adds "in this kingdom."

From Joseph Milligan

DEAR SIR Georgetown June 4th 1816

Your esteemed favour of the 18th May was[1] received on the 25th,

I received the manuscript but it was not in time to issue the prospectus before the end of the Session of Congress, as it was longer in coming than I expected I engaged to print the laws of the last Session of Congress for the department of State that will keep me employed to the 4th of July, about that time I will issue a prospectus and Commence the work and get it out as Soon as practicable The enclosure[2] in yours of the 18 May shall be duly attended to

I have Suffered much inconvenience by a weakness in my Eyes ever since November last which prevents me from writing by candle light and my other Engagements are So many[3] during the day that I frequently fail in attending to the writing part of my business as I could wish

With esteem your obedient Servant

RC (DLC); endorsed by TJ as a letter from "Millegan Joseph" received 17 June 1816 and so recorded in SJL.

Milligan was ENGAGED TO PRINT the *Acts passed at the First Session of the Fourteenth Congress of the United States* [Georgetown, 1816].

[1] Milligan here canceled "duly."
[2] Manuscript: "exclosure."
[3] Manuscript: "may."

From Francis Adrian Van der Kemp

SIR! Oldenbarneveld 4 June 1816.

Accept mÿ Sincerest thanks for the distinguished proof of your confidential esteem, with which you have been pleased to gratifÿ me. I Suppose, I consult your wishes, to copÿ it, and Send it in mÿ handwriting to mÿ friend in England, for publication in the Month. Repos. of Theol. with the expressed request, that neither he or his friends by insinuation or allusion Should drop a hint with respect to the presumtive Author—but invite a fair discussion of this interesting Subject—except leave to act in a contrarÿ course was obtained from me in expressed words.

I know from experience—my master Van der Marck Prof. at Law—having been a victim to a persecuting clergÿ—not because he was not Orthodox—which he was indeed in a Superlative[1] degree, but because he resisted the Hierarchy, and would not Submit to clerical power—and, had I not received this lesson in my youth, the warnings of my friend Adams—before I crossed the Atlantic—not to meddle here with topics of controversy—would have been Solemn enough, to make me avoid that rock—and generally—with one or two exceptions—I Steered free. A Sketch of the hist. of Calvin and Servetus was inserted in the V vol. of the Month. Repos. for 1810—but—yet—incedis[2] per ignes—

An estimate of the doctrine of Jezus—and a view of his historÿ—on the proposed plan are two desirable Subjects—requiring more candour than learning—an unbiassed mind—and ardent love of truth. Such an investigation, even if it is not at first, carried to perfection must effectuallÿ promote the Gospel-cause, which—in my opinion—Stands Stedfast, on a rock.

All heterogeneous materials ought to be carefullÿ Set aside—nothing precariously assumed, and from one undisputed or proved fact proceeded to the next. The Sublime doctrine of a first wise—and good Being—the pure and elevated moral doctrine—with the certainty of a future life contain the Summarÿ of the Christ: Revelation—the remaining are hay and Stubbles. You presume, that according with this plan, I have adopted the Divine interposition—miracles—the revival of a man—died on the cross—without this last point, I can not perceive, that with all the excellence of that doctrine above others—we have advanced one Single Step farther than before—Immortality remains desirable—but cannot be proved.

On this Subject you will permit me a few words more—In my youth—educated as others—but Surrounded with young men of Superior Talents—I Soon rejected what—though not examined—appeared absurd—inquired for myself—and ransacked all, that was written on the Subject in France and England: Soon I was convinced that truth was not the only aim of the opposers—neither was allways at their Side An utter Stranger to polemical Divinity, as what I had learnd from the catechism—well armed with preparatory knowledge of Languages—hist. and Antiquities—I resolved—to enquire in the truth. I became persuaded of the hist. truth of christianity—now I proceeded to examine its doctrine. If it had a divine origine, it must be So plain „that any man, of the meanest capacities—but with a Sound head and honest heart, could discover it with ease„ With this axiom—taken for granted—I Supposed—the four Evang: and Acts must contain this doctrine: these I would endeavour to read, as if theÿ were Send me, and I had lived in those times—however with the allowance—that even now—they ought to have the Same effect. All what I did not[3] plainly understand—at first—by an attent perusal—I passed bÿ—This was Not for me. At the end of mÿ enquiry—the doctrine, I had gathered—was plain and Simple—I renewed the perusal—

Several times—without further progress—and have Since forty years —having more than once repeated this critical examination—not gathered a more ample Stock; by this, you must perceive—that I am no proper person to enter the list of the Champions of divinity—neither am I longing to obtain that distinction.

I hope—your life maÿ be Spared—to finish your plan—of which I anticipate, that it must do good. Several years past I Send to my old friend Dr. Toulmin a life of Jezus—which—as he informed me then, never reached him—I cannot repair that loss—as by the Sale of my large Libraryÿ—before I left Europe, retaining only a few remnants of ancient and modern Literature and history and Philosophy, I would be unable to retrace that plan—but—as I possess manÿ Separate fragments—relating to this Subject, if my days are prolonged—I may yet, and it is my intention, institute an Inquirÿ—„what there is in the Jewish writings about a Messiah—what opinions the cotemporaries of Jezus—friends and foes had of him—and what he instilled in his disciples—what they learned of him in Public.„[4] You will Say—this is not an easÿ task—and In this I agree—but I deem it feasible.

I include a copÿ of the Letter—which I send to England—to accompany it and am confident, that my Correspondents Shall make no abuse of it bÿ any hints—even the most distant.

Are you acquainted with Goëthens ingenious conjecture—„that not one word—of what we call the Decalogus, was written on the two Tables„?—it is in IV vol. of his Schrïften. if unknown to you, and you wish to See it, I Shall make a translation, as Soon [as][5] the Season of labouring—to which I Must Submit is over—and the fall or winter permits me to return to my Studÿ.

Permit me to Sollicit the continuance of your favourable regard and believe, that I remain with Sentiments of high respect

Sir! Your most obed: and obliged Ser[t]

Fr. Adr. vander Kemp

RC (DLC); dateline adjacent to closing; endorsed by TJ as received 19 June 1816 and so recorded in SJL, which adds that Olden Barneveld was located "near Trenton Oneida." RC (DNAL: Thomas Jefferson Correspondence, Bixby Donation); address cover only; with PoC of TJ to John Campbell White, 24 Aug. 1816, on verso; addressed: "Thomas Jefferson L L D at his Seat Monticello Virginia"; franked; postmarked Trenton, N.Y., 6 June.

Van der Kemp's SKETCH was published in a series of eight letters under the pseudonym of "Candidus" ("Sketch of the Life of Servetus, in Letters to the Rev. Jedediah Morse, D. D.," *Monthly Repository of Theology and General Literature* 5 [1810]: 105–8, 163–8, 222–6, 277–82, 328–31, 377–87, 430–5, 525–9). "INCEDIS PER IGNES suppositos cineri doloso" ("fires still burning beneath the treacherous ash") comes from Horace, *Odes*, 2.1.7–8, in *Horace: Odes and Epodes*, trans. Niall Rudd, Loeb Classical Library (2004), 96–7. For Johann Wolfgang von Goethe's (GOËTHENS) argument against the generally accepted text of the biblical Ten Commandments, see John Adams to TJ, 14 Nov. 1813, and note.

[1] Manuscript: "Superlatve."
[2] Manuscript: "incedi."
[3] Word interlined.
[4] Omitted closing quotation mark editorially supplied.
[5] Omitted word editorially supplied.

ENCLOSURE

"Sincerus" (Francis Adrian Van der Kemp) to Robert Aspland

SIR! O … d[1] 1 July [June?] 1816.

Pleased with the liberal plan, which you have adopted in your Review[2]—I deemed it a duty to contribute to its Success—as far as mÿ retirement would permit it. The only thing I regret, is, that I find it not more generally encouraged. Every lover of truth is interested in its Success—and a fair defence of any reprobated opinion ought to meet an equallÿ ready admittance, as an unadorned exposition, of what is reputed a Revelation from heaven: The truth of the Gospel-Doctrine is built[3] on a rock, and can not want the feeble or crafty Support of frail men—and infidelity Shall blush—when Struck by its native purity and lustre, it discovers, that its darts were aimed at human inventions only. Perhaps you Shall not disagree with me, that infidels—moderns as well as Ancients—did in their most virulent and artful attacks upon the religion of Jezus less injury to it, than its reputed friends by bigotry and false zeal. It is from this conviction, that I have long time Since wished, to See the uncontrovertible facts of the gospel-history placed in one lucid point of view—and—in a Similar manner—the Gospel-doctrine fully explained, without the Smallest mixture of any controverted tenet. or—even the incidental admission or allusion,[4] embraced bÿ any christian Sect; when, this Solid basis—having once been adopted by friend and foe, gradually might be proceeded to a discussion of collateral topics.

In this mood I was gratified with the perusal of a Letter and Sketch—which bears the Stamp of candour and that of profound researches. He would deserve well of his country, and the gospel-doctrine, could he find leisure to execute the plan, whose outlines he So masterly delineated. But—accept it as it is; there are, I hope manÿ in our[5] happy Isle equal to this task; in this question a Churchman is as much interested as a Dissenter, and He, who Shall have accomplished it, Shall have done more in defence of the religion of Jezus—than a host of well-meaning though misguided Apologists.

SINCERUS.

Tr (DLC: TJ Papers, 207:36940); entirely in Van der Kemp's hand; misdated; dateline at foot of text; at head of text: "Copÿ." Printed in *Monthly Repository of Theology and General Literature* 11 (1816): 573–4; dated 1 July 1816.

Robert Aspland (1782–1845), minister and editor, was born at Wicken, Cambridgeshire, England. He was ordained in 1801 by a General Baptist congregation at Newport, Isle of Wight. Aspland gradually changed his religious convictions to those of Unitarianism, and in 1805 he accepted an appointment to the Gravel Pit Chapel at Hackney, a London suburb, where he remained until his death. His numerous publications were often based on his sermons, and he started two major Unitarian periodicals: the *Monthly Repository*, which he edited 1806–26, and the *Christian Reformer*, which he edited from 1815 until his death. Aspland also founded several important religious societies: the Unitarian Fund, which encouraged missionary work, in 1806; the Christian Tract Society in 1809; and the Association for the Protection of the Civil Rights of Unitarians in 1819. He merged the first and third societies with the Unitarian Society in 1825 to form the British and Foreign Unitarian Association, the central body of the denomination. Thoughout his life Aspland was a leading proponent of and activist for religious liberty in Great Britain (*ODNB*; R. Brook Aspland, *Memoir of the Life, Works and Correspondence of the Rev. Robert Aspland, of Hackney* [1850]).

In the Bible, Jesus likened those who heard and followed his teachings to a wise man who built his house ON A ROCK (Matthew 7.24; Luke 6.48).

When he printed the material forwarded by Van der Kemp, Aspland followed the text above with TJ's LETTER to Benjamin Rush of 21 Apr. 1803 (*PTJ*, 40:251–5). He identified the author only as Crito. In the eponymous dialogue by Plato, Crito, a supporter of Socrates who has arranged for the latter's escape after his condemnation, is thwarted when the reasoning of Socrates rebuts Crito's plea that he save himself (Plato, *Euthyphro, Apology, Crito, Phaedo, Phaedrus*, trans. Harold North Fowler, Loeb Classical Library [1914; repr. 1990], 1:148–91).

The accompanying SKETCH by TJ was published as a "Syllabus of an Estimate of the Doctrine of Jesus, compared with those of others." For other versions see *EG*, 332–6.

Aspland combined all three items under the title "Letter, &c. on the Doctrine of Jesus, by an Eminent American Statesman," preceded by the following introductory paragraph: "We have received a packet of valuable communications from a venerable Correspondent in America, of which the following is a part. No. I. is an introductory Letter by our Correspondent, who adopts the signature which he affixed to Letters on the Life of Servetus, in our Fifth Volume. Nos. II. and III. are a Letter and Syllabus, by an eminent American Statesman, whose name we are not at liberty to mention, but who will probably be recognized by such of our readers as are acquainted with the characters of the leading men in the American revolution. Other communications from our valuable Transatlantic Correspondent will follow" (*Monthly Repository* 11 [1816]: 573–6).

[1] *Monthly Repository*: "*Oldenbarneveld, S. of New York.*"

[2] *Monthly Repository*: "Repository."

[3] Tr: "build." *Monthly Repository*: "built."

[4] *Monthly Repository* here adds "to any one."

[5] *Monthly Repository*: "your."

To José Corrêa da Serra

Monticello June 5. 16.

I had determined, my dear Sir, to have withdrawn at the close of this year from all subscriptions to newspapers, and never to read another. but the National Intelligencer of the 1st inst. has given me so much pleasure that I shall defer for a year longer my resolution. it announced your appointment from your new king, to be his minister to this country. if this is acceptable to you, I congratulate you sincerely, but still more my countrymen to whom I know it will be most acceptable. I hope this fixes you with us for life, and that you will continue to visit your old friends as before; and be contented that we recieve and treat you as our friend, keeping out of sight [your?] political character. particularly I hope it will not disappoint [us?] of the visit we should shortly have expected. I leave this for Bedford on the 20th inst. and shall return the 1st week of July, in the hope of the expected pleasure of recieving you here at your own convenience.—my grandaughter delivered me the MS. volume of Capt Lewis's journal, & I hope the others, & most especially his observations of Long. & Lat. will be found. Colo Jones passed a few days with us, and did justice to your recommendations. we found him a plain, candid man, knowing all our European acquaintances, able to give us their history & present situation, and to give us new information of many characters which have figured on the wonderful drama of our day. I have rarely met with a more interesting or agreeable acquaintance, and he left us with impressions which will follow him thro' life. I salute you with constant & affectionate esteem & respect.

TH: JEFFERSON

PoC (DLC); on verso of reused address cover to TJ; mutilated at seal; at foot of text: "Mr Correa"; endorsed by TJ.

News of the APPOINTMENT of Corrêa da Serra as minister plenipotentiary by John VI, the NEW KING and former prince regent of Portugal, appeared in the Washington *Daily National Intelligencer*, 31 May 1816.

From George Logan

DEAR SIR — Stenton June 5th: 1816

your Letter of the 19th: ult: duly came to hand. I sincerely regret to find by it, that a measure adopted by me, to defend your character against the slanders of your political enemies, has given you a moment of uneasiness.[1] you well know that individuals have been engaged for years, in accusing you as the advocate and friend of Bonaparte—even at the moment he was devastating with fire and sword the whole continent of Europe. And also of your being an enemy to the christian religion. Having an opportunity under your own signature, to remove from the minds of your fellow citizens; the effects of such slanders; I considered it my duty, as your friend, to publish your opinion on these important subjects; and it is with pleasure I inform you, that the publication on both subjects, has removed prejudices highly injurious to you; from the minds of many of the best citizens of the U States.

Had your communications to me been made under an injunction of secrecy, no consideration would have tempted me to have violated your confidence. I judge of the feelings of others by my own: and I should think it criminal in a friend to suppress any information from the public; calculated to remove unmerited slanders from my own[2] character. To do otherwise under any false notions of delicacy, is to act the hypocrite—it is the grimace of friendship—the honest heart has no share in the business.

During an acquaintance of many years I have at all times, communicated my sentiments to you without disguise; in terms of plain truth.[3] I am therefore particularly gratified by that part of your Letter, in which you say "I prefer candid and open expression. No change of good will to you, none in my estimate[4] of your integrity, or understanding, has taken place, except as to your particular opinion on the rights of correspondence." I hope the present communication will remove from your mind even the exception.

If I am mistaken in the opinion, that you set more value on the lasting esteem of posterity than on the ephemeral[5] applause of pretended friends; I shall at least receive[6] the approbation of my own mind; in having uniformly followed the impulse of honor, and of an unshaken attachment to your welfare.

On the present occasion, trusting to your candour and integrity, I am satisfied, that on taking a comprehensive view of the whole subject; you will yet consider me as your best friend.

My wife unites with me in best respects to yourself & amiable family

Geo Logan

RC (DLC); at foot of text: "Thos Jefferson Esqr"; endorsed by TJ as received 12 June 1816 and so recorded in SJL. FC (PHi: Logan Papers); in Logan's hand; correctly dated, but endorsed by Logan as a letter of "June 6th: 1816."

IT IS THE GRIMACE OF FRIENDSHIP—THE HONEST HEART HAS NO SHARE IN THE BUSINESS quotes directly, adding the word "honest," from *The Works of Cornelius Tacitus*, trans. Arthur Murphy, 6 vols. (1st American ed., Philadelphia, 1813), 4:25 (for the original, see Tacitus, *Histories*, 1.15, in *Tacitus: The Histories, Books I–III*, trans. Clifford H. Moore, Loeb Classical Library [1925; repr. 2006], 30–1).

1 FC: "anxiety."

2 Word not in FC.

3 Omitted period supplied from FC.

4 RC: "estimation." FC and TJ to Logan, 19 May 1816: "estimate."

5 RC: "ephimeral." FC: "ephemeral."

6 RC: "recive." FC: "receive."

To Charles Simms

SIR Monticello June 5. 16.

I wrote to you on the 2[d] inst. in answer to yours of May 25. and requested you to forward the 4. cases of wine from mr Cathalan to Richmond to the address of Mess[rs] Gibson & Jefferson of that place, and to be so good as to drop me a line of information of the duties & charges which should be remitted immediately. since that mr Cathalan's invoice is come to hand, of which I now inclose a copy, not knowing whether our duties may not be ad valorem on non-enumerated wines. I also add an extract from his letter requesting a return of his acquit à caution, and, to save you all possible trouble of returning it, if you will be so good as to put it under cover to me I will undertake that office. I presume there is a French Consul in Alexandria who will certify the landing of the wine, and if you will add his fee of office (if any) to the bill of duties & costs to be sent to me all shall be remitted together. I pray you to accept the assurance of my great respect & esteem.

TH: JEFFERSON

PoC (MHi); on verso of reused address cover of Emmor Kimber to TJ, 22 Mar. 1816; at foot of text: "Col[o] Simms"; endorsed by TJ.

Neither the COPY of Stephen Cathalan's invoice nor the EXTRACT from his letter to TJ of 19 Mar. 1816 has been found. An ACQUIT À CAUTION is a French customhouse bond.

From Eusebio Valli

MIO SIGNORE Trenton li 5 Giugno 1816—

Sono oltre modo sensibile alla gentile, e generosa accoglienza, che Ella mi fa, e ricevo come un dono la communicazione[1] delle sue idea sulla così detta febbre gialla:

Parlandomi di questo morbo crudele, che forma il soggetto delle attuali mie ricerche, VS: a avuto la segreta intenzione di farmi cicalare. Obbedisco volentieri all'impulsione datami, perche ho speranza d'ottenere da Lei ulteriori lumi e cognizione—

Comincio dal confessarle candidamente, che L'origine prima di questa pestilenza é un problema per mé. Forse dessa é nata in Oriente, come vi son nate la peste, le variole, la rosolìa—Il S[re] Hombolt assicura, che da tempo immemorabile regna nel messico, e che ivi si riproduce annualmente[2] in forza delle cause Locali—Peraltro noi sappiamo dall'Abbate Calvigero, che é solo nell'Anno[3] 1725, che la malattia si manifestó per la prima volta in quella parte di mondo, il che ci porta a credere, che vi fu trasportata da paese straniero. Ció che son per dirle toglie ogni dubbio su questo punto—

La Vera-Crux é stata riguardata, e si riguarda anch'oggi, come L'Emporio della febbre gialla, ed in fatti riunisce in sé tutte le condizioni, credute atte a generarla—I calori vi sono eccessivi, i contorni di una ariditá estrema, coperti di una sabbia moventesi, che si accumula su diversi luoghi, e forma dei piccoli monticelli di dodici a quindici metri di altezza, i quali riflettono un calore sì considerabile, che il termometro centigrado affossato in quella sabbia nei mesi di Luglio e Agosto monta da 48 a 50—Ed é appunto in questa stagione che la febbre si trova in tutta la sua possanza[4]—Il celebre Viaggiatore, da cui traggo questa nozione, il S[e] Hombolt fedele, quant'altro mai, nel riferire i fatti, c'informa nel medesimo tempo, che dal 1776 sino al 1791 non era occorso neppure un esempio di febbre gialla in Veracruz,[5] quantunque il concorso degl'Europei, e dei marinari provenienti dall'interiore fosse considerabile, e che i Marinari non acclimatati si abbandonassero agl'eccessi, che gli si rimproverano—Il ritorno dell'Epidemia dopo un intervallo di 18 anni coincide con l'arrivo colá di tre bastimenti da guerra, il Vascello Elmino, la Fregata la Venus e L'hourque St[a] Vibiana, che nel tragitto avevano toccato Porto-Ricco, ove il vomito[6] regnava—

L'errore invalso nel Messico, sin dalla prima apparizione del contagio, che desso fosse il prodotto dei venti di Sud-Est apportatosi di un caldo infernale, questo errore diede campo alla malattia di stabilir lá uno di suoi piu tirannici Imperj—Dal messico e specialmente da Veracruz[7] si propagó come da un centro commune, all'Havana, e di qui alle Antille, alla nuova Inghilterra, all'Europa—In Europa non vi ha, che La Spagna, che sia stata percossa a piu riprese da questo flagello—Cadice nel 1731 e Malaga nel 1741 furono le prime a risentirne i funesti effetti—

La malattia si mostró di nuovo a Cadice nel 1764 e 1800—In quest'ultima invasione, dopo aver devastata la Cittá, passó a Seviglia e di lá si dilató, quali incendio, in quasi tutta L'Andalusia, portando ovunque la desolazione, e la morte—Ricordo una costituzione, che forma epoca nei fasti della febbre gialla, e sulla di cui origine e progressi abbiamo nelle opere dei medici, che vi trovarono sul campo d'onore, i migliori dettagli possibili—Permetta che io li richiami alla di lei memoria—

Ai 6 di Luglio entró nella rada di Cadice la Corvetta il Delfino, Capitano Guillaume Jaskal, proveniente dall'Havana e che aveva approdato a Charles-town, ove aggiunse quatr'Uomini d'equipaggio, dé quali due morirono di febbre gialla nel tragitto—Al suo arrivo furono messe a bordo due guardie, che caddero immediatam[e] ammalate—Il Visitatore della dogana, la guardia della porta di mare, e il Cancelliere del bureau di sanitá, che avevano communica[to] con la gente di questo naviglio perirono in breve[8]—Il Luogo tenente visitatore Don Francisco de Paulo Carrion si trasportó esso pure al bastimento, e cadde ben tosto ammalato e communicó il contagio a tutta La famiglia—La malattia fece paura per qualche settimana, per riprodursi in Scena verso la metá di Luglio—Limitata in principio al Sobborgo di St[a] Maria vi soggiornó qualche tempo, dilatandosi passo a passo, senza mai andar di salto; E se mai inoltrossi in quartieri lontani, fú sempre per l'intermezzo di persone venute a vedere i loro parenti o amici ammalati—Sul finir d'Agosto la malattia, che andava ogni dí crescendo, penetró nel centro della Cittá, ed in Settembre si rese pressoche generale, ed eravi confusamente somma mortalitá—Vi furono delle famiglie, che essendosi sequestrate nelle loro Case, e rompendo ogni specie di communicazione con qualunque siasi persona, rimasero illese[9] dal contagio, mentre La morte spigionava tutt'all'intorno le abitazioni vicine—

Seviglia che continuava le sue relazioni commerciali con questa disgraziata cittá si vide ben tosto afflitta dalla medesima piaga—É a Triana, Sobborgo ove vivono i Marinari, che si sentirono i primi attacchi, e dacché la malattia si fu impadronita di tutto quel quartiere, la si diffuse al Sobborgo de Los-Humeros frequentato da marinari e che giace al di lá del fiume e in faccia di Triana—Da Los-Humeros si avvanzó nella Cittá, seguendo nella sua progressione quella Legge, che osservava a Cadice—

—Molti furono i barcajoli del Guadalviquir, che s'isolarono nelle Loro barche, e il fuoco divoratore non ne investì alcuno—I fuggitivi da Cadice come da Seviglia i quali si rifugiarono nei villaggi vicini alle due Cittá[10] divennero tanti Seminarj d'infezione[11]—Cordova se ne difese, mettendo in pratica quelle precauzioni sanitarie, che la polizia medica e governativa prescrivono in momenti così perigliosi[12]—(Piguillem—Villelva[13]—Berthe—Bally)

Malaga non ricevette in quest'anno che un insulto leggere ma nel 1803, e piu nel 1804 soffrì d'una maniera orribile[14]—Ecco come il male vi nacque ai 14 di Luglio 1803[15]—Certo[16] Felix Munos Contrabandiere (e la Spagna regurgita di questa esecrabile genia)[17] si transportó nascostam[e] a bordo della nave il giovine Nicolas, ove fece acquisto di tabacchi e di calze di cotone—Partendo di lá Egli provó i primi segnali della malattia, e ai 20 dello stesso mese, morì—Dopo trenta sei giorni Cristofano[18] Verduras altro[19] Contrabandiere, che aveva nascosto in sua Casa un marinaro impestato, e la di cui malattia il condusse alla tomba, Verduras cadd[e] infermo, e successivamente un suo figlio, sua madre, due fratelli ed il restante della Casa, che si componeva di 8 individui—Il Sig^e[20] Buzon che aveva assistito senza fortuna il marinaro incognito, ed il curato che diede sepoltura al morto contrassero ambedue L'infezione, e soccombettero—I medici di consulta Mammelli e Gimal incontrarono la medesima sorte, e

()Arejula— Lasciarono in seno delle Loro desolate famiglie il germe distruttivo—() É facile adesso seguire col pensiere i passaggi successivi della malattia, e la sua diffusione nella Cittá I rigori dell'inverno posero fine a questa costituzione, ma fatalmente si rinnovelló nell'autunno del 1804[21] con un apparato molto piu terribile: E Malaga dopo essere stata vittimata e rimasta quasi vidua super terram divenne il punto centrale della contagione, d'onde si sparse in tutta la costa del meditarraneo Spagnolo[22]—I medici della Penisola non perdendola mai di vista hanno potuto tracciare le vie cui essa percorse per portarsi su questo, o quel punto, ed é alla lettura delle loro Oper[e][23] non meno che a quelle di Bally, d'Hombolt, di Berthe, di Caillot,[24] che rimando coloro, che dubiterebbero ancora del carattere contagioso della febbre gialla di Spagna—

Si é detto che le pestilenze, le quali hanno regnato negli Stati-uniti sotto il nome di febbre gialla non appartengono nullamente a questa famiglia come quelle osservate in Spagna, peraltro se noi, Spogliandoci di ogni prevenzione confrontiamo Le une con le altre rileveramo: o che esse sono egualmente corredate dei Sintomi, che voglionsi chiamare patognomonici, come il vomito nero,[25] il colore itterico &&& o che prendendo la maschera e il tipo di malattie di un ordine qualunque esse presentano costantemente delle tinte caratterische communi, e mi si lasci dire, La fisonomia della razza infame, da cui derivano—Medesime insidie, e perfide calme—medesimo L'ordine, o il disordine nella Successione dei Sintomi; nel giro delle rivoluzioni—medesime le marche esterne impresse sulle vittime immolate—medesimi i danneggiamenti portati su questo o quel viscere, o su piu visceri insieme—Negli Stati uniti come in Spagna la malattia[26] ha attaccati di preferenza gl'Uomini i piu robusti, i pletorici, i biliosi—meno degl'Uomini le donne, e meno ancora i ragazzi ed i teneri bambini. Ha investito di rado e per lo piu fiaccamente i macellari, i conciatori di pelle, i pelliciaj: ha rispettato religiosam^e i coloni e quelli che avevano soggiornato lungo tratto di tempo alle Isole—negli Stati Uniti come in Spagna ha lasciato generalmente negl'individui piu o meno malmenati garanzia da nuovi attacchi, e bene spesso un fondo migliore di Salute[27]—Il d^e Rush assicura che dopo l'epidemia del 1793 i convalescenti avevano una tendenza straordinaria all'atto venereo, e che si era fatto un numero sorprendente di matrimonj—osservazione che ci Scopre un punto di contatto[28] della peste d'oriente con la febbre gialla—A Mantova nel 1506 tale era il trasporto dei pestiferati convalescenti per il bel sesso,[29] e tante le violenze da essi commesse, che il magnifico Messer Alessio Becaguto Luogo tenente Capitano della Cittá fu costretto di far erigere un pajo di forche, onde por termine a quel commercio scandaloso—Hodges racconta che dopo la peste di Londra del 1664–65 le donne che in avanti erano state riconosciute Sterili, divennero madri dappoi,[30] cosiché ben presto Si vide riempito il deficit occasionato dalla malattia—„A Messina fu tale il furore dei matrimonj, che se fosse stato possibile abbreviare il termine di parti la Cittá si sarebbe veduta ben tosto piena di popolo„ (Forne.)

Per quanto dall'insieme delle cose dette resultino le prove dell'identitá delle due pesti, Americana e Spagnola, pure VS: di cui conosco gl'intimi pensieri non converrá meco facilmente su quest'articolo di fede—Per convertirla, sembra a me, che non mi resti altra operazione a eseguire, che non quella di provarle, che gli Stati Uniti hanno tratto il germe funesto dalle medesime sorgenti che la Spagna—

Il primo Cuadro,[31] sulla febbre gialla americana, dipinto col pennello dell'arte e dietro natura, é quello del Dr Lining, il quale ebbe l'opportunitá di osservarla a Charles-town nel 1732—L'illustre Autore in quest'occasione c'informa „that the yellow fever had prevailed in that Country[32] four times within twenty five years, and that whenever the disease appeared here,[33] it was easily traced to some person, who was Lately arrived from some west India Islands, where it was epidemical„

Tale altresì fu il parere del Collegio medico di Filadelfia sull'origine e il genio della pestilenza che dominó nel 1793 codesta Cittá. É nell'Anno istesso che apparve in Grenada nel mese di maggio „soon after the arrival of a Guinea Ship from Sierra Leone, the crew of which had been so sickly, that most of the Sailors died of the yellow fever, either in the voyage, or soon after the arrival of the Ship—It suddenly spread over the other Leward Islands, and from thence was carried to Philadelphia, Hispaniola, and Jamaica„—Così scrive William Wright—Erano arrivati effettivam^e^ nel porto di Filadelfia alcuni bastimenti da quella parte dopo la metá di Luglio, e i membri rispettabili, che componevano il Collegio si assicurarono che il contagio aveva lá il suo fomite—

La malattia si manifestó alla fine di Luglio „it first appeared in Water Street between Mulberry and Sassafras Streets, and all the cases of this fever, were, for two or three weeks[34] evidently traced to this particular Spot—a considerable part of the city, Northern Liberties, and district of South wark became gradually infected, and it was not until the coming of the frost that the disease subsided, after having proved fatal to nearly [five] thousand persons„[35]

In queste poche linee VS: vede L'immagine viva della febbre gialla—Non vi é che dessa o la peste, che trasportate in un porto di mare, o altrove abbino per costume di covare nella loro prima Stazione, di progredire lentissimamente, e di cadere come per incantesimo, all'apparire di una data Stagione—

Il Collegio dopo avere indicati alcuni dei tratti originali della malattia, La distinse dalle sue analogue per l'alto grado di malignitá, che possedeva, per La rapiditá del suo corso, e per la resistenza invincibile che oppose a quei rimedj, da quali sono vinte generalmente le remittenti biliose del paese—Le misure che desso propose sia per impedire l'ulteriore propagazione del contagio, sia per garantirsi da successive irruzione, erano le meglio intese e le piu Saggie—ma: Alas!: non se ne sentì tutta L'importanza—Le Leggi delle quarantine e i regolamenti interni furono trascurati, così la Cittá fu di bel nuovo investita negl'Anni 1797–98[36]—In quest'ultimo anno particolarmente erano arrivati nei mesi di Luglio e Agosto molti bastimenti partiti dal Cap Nichola More, jeremie, e Port-au-Prince dell'Isola della Hispaniola e di St. Domingo, dove regnava il vomito, e donde erano partiti in somma fretta „On the fifth day of july last six or eight of those vessels, having a large number of passengers[37] on board, of course a quantity of cloathing, bedding &c. brought[38] off in the greatest haste, themselves exposed to all these circumstances, which are allowed to produce contagious fever: in this situation they arrived at the fort, where they [were][39] detained on board[40] for twenty days—On the arrival at the city, they generally lay at the wharves between Walnut and Spruce Street—and it is well known, that at this part of the City, the fever first appeared about the latter end of july and beginning of August—On the evening of the eighth of july the armed Ship Deborah, Captain Edward yard arrived at the fort from jeremie—She buried eight persons during her stay there and return, and sent six sick[41] to the marine[42] hospital„

Il Collegio fissó specialmente i suoi sguardi sul Deborah, che ai 28 di Luglio was moved a Kensington, nelle di cui salubri rive si cercherebbero invano dei fonti d'infezione—Resulto dalle loro piu scrupolose indagini, che gl'individui i quali travagliarono sul bastimento o vicino a quello contrassero la febbre, e che questi seminarono il contagio in diversi punti della Cittá. =Facts and obs. on pestilent. fever which prevailed in Philadelpia in 1793–97–98 by the College of physicians of Philadelphia= L'opera che accenno offre tanto piu d'interesse, in quanto che, oltre le eccellenti riflessioni, che vi sono sparse quá e lá, é arricchita di testimonianze e di osservazioni of several respectable characters physicians and others—

Malgrado tanta evidenza di fatti e di ragioni il partito d'opposizione continuó a sostenere che Le cause locali erano bastanti a creare la così nominata febbre gialla, e che era follia il farla procedere dalle Indie—Così nell'A° 1802 essendosi riprodotta la medesima calamitá si fecero giuocare coteste forze immaginarie, idea accarezzata dagli Speculatori, e abbracciata ciecamente dal popolo macchina—

In medicina del pari che nelle Scienze esatte si puo ritrovare La cagione dell'errore in cui Si é caduti—Per mancanza di una cifra l'analista sbaglia il suo calcolo, e l'astronomo non presagisce giustamente la comparsa o il ritorno d'una Cometa—A Messina, a Marsiglia, a Venezia, ove La peste erasi introdotta furtivamente, i Medici scordarano di mettere in conto uno degl'elementi i piu essenziali: quello: cioé: dell'arrivo di bastimenti sporchi dal Levante, e il loro calcolo di probabilitá si trovó erroneo—

—In affari tanto gelosi, come quelli che concernono la vita e la felicitá dei popoli, tutto deve essere esaminato senza preoccupazione, tutto deve essere sottoposto ad un'analisi rigorosa—Regolati da questi principj i SS^i Currie e Cathrall pervennero a discoprire la vera sorgente della malattia insorta a Filadelfia nell'anno di cui io parlavo poc'anzi—Dopo le prove che essi ne hanno date, non é permesso di dubitare, che il contagio non fosse stato apportato dal bastimento il Paquet, il quale arrivava dal Cap—Come dal Paquet si communicasse al Brigantino della Speranza e dai marinari di ambi i bastimenti ad altri individui, e cosí di mano in mano, é inutil cosa che io il dica—

La febbre gialla che apparve in New york nel 1791 vi fu introdotta egualmente da un Vascello, che veniva dalle Indie (Hosack[43]) Simile sempre a Se Stessa la malattia restó stazionarja nel Luogo ove nacque „near Peck-Slip. Here it raged a considerable time: it then began to spread, as some attendants on the sick became infected, who lived in other neighbourhoods[44]—By this means it was carried to other families, and most generally could be traced to this source. It likewise proved more particularly fatal near the place, where it first appeared,[45] than in [any][46] other part—Thus at length[47] it spread through the city until the middle of October, when the weather growing a little cooler, the disease[48] greatly abated, and in a short time disappeared„[49]—(Addoms)—Questa malattia per confessione dello stesso Addoms era precisamente la stessa, che la febbre gialla da lui osservata piu volte[50] nell'Isola di St[a] Crux (Hosack—Obs. on contag. diseas—)

New-york fu novamente attaccata dal contagio[51] nel 1795–98[52] all'arrivo di bastimenti dall'Indie[53]—()In quest'ultimo anno l'estensione della malattia fu cosí circoscritta, che in generale si credette originata da cause domestiche,[54] e segnatamente da provvisioni putride, ma il dotto Hosack dimostra con l'ultima evidenza, che La febbre si era dichiarata avanti che coteste cause esistessero—Quando anche avessero preesistito non si potevano creder capaci di generare la febbre gialla[55]—Allorche i gas, i quali provengono dalla putrefazione dei corpi organici, si combinano con qualche principio sparso nell'atmosfera, sì da comporre dei miasmi specifici, questi miasmi conservando la loro natura volatile circolano insiem con l'aria e i venti, e affettano simultaneamente una moltitudine d'individui, cosí che Le malattie, cui danno luogo, Sono, quasi direi, generali sino dal loro primo nascimento—Altre di ció cotesti miasmi non imprimono nell'organismo vivante la facoltá di riprodurre un veleno simile a Loro—

()Hosack—Dr. M.Knight

Queste ragioni sole, quando io non avessi altri fatti avanti di me, mi condurrebbero a negare L'influenza delle carni salate guaste, delle ostriche imputridite,[56] e della corruzione d'ogni genere di sostanze nella generazione del morbo, di cui trattiamo—

La febbre gialla, egualmente che la peste d'Oriente sua Sorella, é il prodotto d'un germe deleterio sui generis: pesante, lordo, non percorre[57] gli spazi sulle ali dei venti—E se l'aria gli serve alcuna volta di conduttore ció non si verifica che a picciolissime distanze e solamente quando questo fluido se ne trova impregnato—In generale si communica o per mezzo dei corpi che gli servono di ripostiglio, o pel contatto degl'infetti, generatori e fonti di contagio—[58]

Questa é oggi mai L'opinione di tutta L'Europa culta,[59] ed é pur quella d'un gran nümero di medicine dotti della nuova Inghilterra[60]—Vi ha egualmente, il só, Uomini Sommi in America,[61] che sostengono acremente l'opinione contraria, appoggiandosi ad un osservazione, che trovo ripetuta nella di lei lettera, ed é che negli stati uniti, la malattia, cui hanno data la denominazione di febbre gialla[62] non si é mai propagata dalla Cittá alla Campagna, il che esclude tutt'a fatto l'idea di contagio—

Rispondendo a Lei, mio Signore, avró risposto a tutti—nel tempo che la febbre gialla infieriva a Malaga nel 1803 non vi furono nei piccoli villaggi che circondano La Cittá, a Churiano, a Alhauriz, al grande e piccolo Coin, a Torre del mare altri ammalati che i fuggitivi, o quelli tra gl'abitanti, che andando a Malaga, avevano L'imprudenza di passarvi La notte—Cartagena che in meno di tre o quattro mesi perdette quasi la metá della sua popolazione per la pestilenza ricevuta da Malaga, non infettó ne i luoghi vicini, ne i bastimenti del porto—In Alicante la malattia non portó la menoma offesa alle Case isolate, che si trovano tra le due Mura, onde La Cittá é attorniata, ne a quelle separate dai sobborghi fuori del recinto—A Palamo, ove si lava la biancheria d'Alicante non vi fu un sol esempio di contagio, come neppure a St^{a} Fax, che é a mezza lega dalla Cittá, ne a Mucha-Michel, che n'é men lontano ancora—Fenomeno tanto piu sorprendente, in quanto che Pena-Serada separata da Mucha-Michel per un sol cammino, St. joan che é a cinque quarti di lega da Alicante, e Tabarca che ne é distante circa quattro leghe ricevettero L'infezione—A Vera nel 1811 fu osservato, che i contagiati, i quali si rifugiavano presso i loro amici, o parenti, che vivevano sotto Le tende a pochi passi dallo Spedale, non inocularono La malattia[63] a veruno—Termineró con un fatto accaduto nell'armata francese sotto gl'ordini del famoso maresciallo Soult,[64] allorché i roversci del gran Capitano al nord del Continente, lo forzarano d'abbandonare[65] l'andalusia—Il General Conrou, che comandava una divisione arrivato nelle vicinanze di Cesara fu prevenuto dai principali della Cittá, i quali furono al suo incontro, che la febbre gialla mieteva il Loro paese—A tale avviso il Generale invió il Suo Chirurgo maggiore per esaminare cotesta malattia—Il rapporto dell'offiziale di sanitá fu, che La febbre, la quale dominava, era una remittente biliosa costituzionale—In allora il Sr Conrou diede ordine alla truppa di marciare, ed entró nel Luogo, e Lá gli offiziali, e le persone addette all'amministrazione presero alloggio—La truppa bivaccó—All'indomani la divisione si rimise in marcia, ma poche ore dopo, gl'ajutanti di Campo del Generale cominciarono a lagnarsi di dolori alle articolazioni, di prostrazione di forze & & & e il giorno appresso altri ancora caddero ammalati, ma solo quelli che avevano communicato davvicino con gl'abitanti, che avevano, ed avevano avuto pestiferati nelle loro famiglie—In vista di questo inatteso avvenimento il Generale fece far alto a jecla, dove fu stabilito uno Spedale provvisorio—La malattia, che si era di gia spiegata percorse velocissimamente i suoi stadj, presentando i sintomi piu pronunziati della febbre gialla: cioé: il vomito nero, le dejezioni atro-sanguigne fetentissime, emorragie incoercibili, ictero & Il Dr Peysson medico d'infinito merito,[66] mi diceva non aver veduta mai una malattia così orribile e rovinosa—Tale certamente dovette essere, poiche non lasció tra gl'infetti, che un solo in vita, François Musicien, e questo morí dopo una convalescenza piu penosa ancor che la morte—Eppure i medici i

Bally opinion ur la ntag. de fiéve une)

chirurghi, gl'infermieri che erano allocati al servizio nauseabundo e periglioso di quello Spedale sortirono dal pelago Sani e Salvi, attoniti peró e spaventati sempre—

Scorrendo la Storia delle Epoche piu memorabili della peste in Europa, si trova che alcuni borghi, o Cittá, o parti di provincia sono state rispiarmate da questo mostro, scegliendo egli altro tempo[67] per esercitare le sue furie[68] anche Su queste stesse popolazioni—(And vea Gratiolo di Salò—Tuano—Muratori—Mead) Esempj di tal fatta sono frequentissimi nel Levante ottomanno, come io stesso ho avuto campo di osservarlo[69] sia a Smyrna, sia nell'interno dell'Asia minore, e ne ho lasciata memoria

Esistono talora sciolti e fluttuanti nell'aria atmosferica incogniti principj, i quali o si combinano col germe contagioso, ossivero il tengono in dissoluzione sì da favorire il giuoco delle affinitá reciproche tra il germe istesso e l'ossigeno dell'atmosfera:[70] É questo il nostro caso.

I medici in ogni tempo si sono lusingati di ottenere con l'arte quello che vedevano operarsi nel piu profondo segreto della natura—I loro sforzi non furono sempre senza sucesso—Lind, per parlare dei tempi vicini a noi, distrusse il fomite della febbre gialla e col fuoco e col fumo—Có suffumigi d'acido muriatico L'illustre Gujton Morveau arrestó la malattia insorta a Dijon pel dissotteramento dei Cadaveri della Cattedrale—Il Signor Smith con mezzi appresso a poco eguali estinse la febbre nervosa, che erasi manifestata nel Vascello Ospedale L'Unione

—Questi metodi sono divenuti inseguito universalissimi, ma bisogna convenire che non sempre hanno corrisposto alla nostra espettazione[71]—Verrá peró un giorno in cui l'esperienza e L'osservazione ci condurranno alla Scoperta luminosa[72] d'ogni Specie di miasmi—In allora le pestilenze tutte spariranno[73] dalla terra, meno i Tiranni—

Le condizioni atmosferiche sfavorevoli alla febbre gialla Sono ben Spesso accidentali, e per consequenza l'indennitá di Luoghi, ov'esse sonosi incontrate, non é che precarja—Il contagio che non aveva potuto svilupparsi a Medina-Sidonia nel 1800, malgrado che ella vi fosse involta, Vi scoppió nell'anno successivo, e rapì quasi i tre quinti della totalitá degl'ammalati. E Velez-Malaga, Àntequerra, che nulla avevano sofferto durante il primo regno della febbre gialla nella Loro capitale, con la quale mantennero sempre corrispondenza, furono crudelmente maltrattate da quella peste medesima nel 1804—

Cosa degna di rimarca é che alcune contrade, il di cui clima é oltre ogni dire, iniquo e pestifero vadino esenti dal vomito nero—Non é stato mai osservato nelle maremme di Pisa, di Siena, nelle palude pontine, ne in Batavia, ne in tutta la Costa occidentale del messico „A

Acapulco, dice Mr Caillot, les habitans sont tourmentés par des ouragans fréquens: Ils respirent un air embrasé et vicié par les émanations putrides, qui s'exhalent des mares voisines, dont l'eau croupissante disparaît chaque année, et laisse à nu la vase, dans laquelle pourrissent une innombrable quantité des poissons et d'insectes—Les vapeurs olivâtres qui s'enlévent sont si épaisses,[74] que Le Soleil a de la peine à les traverser, et les dissiper—cependant on n'y a jamais vu le vomite„[75]—

Queste osservazioni devono mettere in un brutto imbarazzo quei medici, che nel caso, di cui é questione, fanno giuocare il principale anzi L'unico rôle ai calori ardenti,[76] alle putride esalazioni && Io credo bene che queste cause, sotto particolari circostanze indeterminabili, decidono Lo sviluppo del germe, e gli servino di pascolo e d'alimento, ma son lontano dal pensare, che desse sieno essenzialmente necessarie alla dilui esistenza—Medina-Sidonia, Carmona, Couvas, vera, dove si respira l'aria piu pura e piu salubre del mondo, poiche esse sono situate sulle montagne, o sulle Alture, lontane dal mare, dalle paludi, dai Laghi, queste popolazioni che non conoscono, se non di nome i mali endemici, e epidemici,[77] sono state anch'esse flagellate al pari di Cadice, di malaga, d'Alicante, di Cartagena, di Murcia[78] &

Sembra che negli Stati uniti la febbre gialla non siasi estesa, come nella grande Penisola d'Europa, e ció senza dubbi per mancanza d'opportunitá atmosferica—Niente di meno i Non-Contagisti di buona fede son forzati a confessare,[79] ché anche nel Loro Paese il contagio é passato alcune volte per via delle communicazioni ordinarje[80] dalle Cittá alle Campagne—É di questo modo che si communicó a Huntingdon[81] in Long Island nel 1795:[82] a Swedeborough negl'anni 1797–98–99—in New Hampshire, a Connecticut, a Germanton nel 1798—in Staten Island nel 1799—

Temando che questi rapidi cenni non faccino nel di lei animo bastante impressione, le trasmetto copia di Due Documenti, relativi al soggetto, irrefragabili documenti,[83] l'uno dei quali é segnato dal Dr. Wistar onore dal sua patria:—e l'altro dal rispettabile Dr. Richard Moore[84]—

Convinto dal carattere contagioso della febbre gialla[85] io mi propongo d'inocularmi la malattia[86] col sudore degli agonizzanti, e la bile degli estinti, modificando il veleno con quei reattivi medesimi, che hanno servito alle mie esperienze sulla peste d'Oriente—Se mai é scritto nel Libro del Destino, che io cada Vittima nel gran cimento, la mia morte non Sará senza gloria, ed i Filantropi di questa fortunata Regione correranno in folla a spargere fiori odorosi sulla mia tomba—

Pieno intanto di venerazione e di stima ho l'onore di dirmi Suo Dev° Servitore

Valli—

EDITORS' TRANSLATION

SIR Trenton 5 June 1816—

I am extremely moved by the kind and generous welcome that you extend to me, and I receive as a gift the communication of your ideas on the so-called yellow fever:

In speaking to me of this cruel disease, which forms the subject of my current research, you had the secret intention of making me jabber. I gladly comply with this impulsion because I hope to obtain further enlightenment and knowledge from you—

I begin by candidly confessing to you that I regard the ultimate origin of this pestilence as problematic. Perhaps it came from the Orient, where the plague, smallpox, and measles were born—Mr. Humboldt assures us that from time immemorial yellow fever has reigned in Mexico and that it reproduces annually there, thanks to local causes—On the other hand, we know from Abbot Clavigero that the disease first manifested itself in that part of the world only in the year 1725, which leads us to believe that it was transported from a foreign country—That which I am about to tell you removes any doubt on this point—

Veracruz has been considered and is still considered today as the emporium of yellow fever, and in fact it unites within itself all of the conditions believed capable of generating it—The heat there is excessive, and the surroundings are of an extreme aridity, covered by shifting sands that accumulate in different places and form little hills from twelve to fifteen meters high, which reflect a heat so considerable that a centigrade thermometer buried in that sand in the months of July and August rises to 48 or 50°—And it is precisely during this season that the fever is most potent—The famous traveler from whom I derive this notion, Mr. Humboldt, faithful as no other in his reporting of facts, informs us at the same time that from 1776 to 1791 not one case of yellow fever occurred in Veracruz, even though the convergence of Europeans and sailors coming from the interior was considerable, and the sailors who were not acclimated abandoned themselves to reproachable excess—The return of the epidemic after an interval of eighteen years coincides with the arrival there of three warships, the vessel El Mino, the frigate la Venus, and the hourque Santa Vibiana, which in their journey had called at Puerto Rico, where the vomit reigned—

The mistaken idea that the infernal heat carried by southeastern winds caused the disease, a notion widespread in Mexico since the contagion first appeared, enabled it to establish there one of its most tyrannical empires—From Mexico and especially from Veracruz it spread, as from a common center, to Havana, and from there to the Antilles, New England, and Europe—In Europe no other place has been struck by this scourge more often than Spain—Cádiz in 1731 and Málaga in 1741 were the first to experience its deadly effects—

The disease appeared again in Cádiz in 1764 and 1800—During this last outbreak, after devastating the city, it moved to Seville, and from there it spread like a fire to almost all of Andalusia, bringing desolation and death everywhere—I remember an occurrence that is a landmark in the annals of yellow fever, whose origin and development we find in the best possible detail in the works of the doctors in this honorable field—Permit me to recall them to your memory—

On 6 July the corvette Dolphin, Captain William Haskel, entered the roadstead of Cádiz, having originated in Havana and called at Charleston, where four men joined the crew. Of these, two died of yellow fever on the journey—On its arrival two guards were put on board, and they immediately fell ill—The customs inspector, the guard of the seaport, and the chancellor of the bureau of health, who had interacted with the people on the ship, perished shortly thereafter—The lieutenant inspector, Don Francisco de Paula Carrion, also went aboard, and he very soon fell ill and communicated the contagion to his whole family—The disease caused a scare for some weeks, reappearing around the middle of July—Confined at the beginning to the suburb of Santa Maria, it remained there for a time, spreading step by step without ever skipping a beat. And if it penetrated distant neighborhoods, it was always by means of a person coming to see their sick relatives or friends—At the end of August the disease, which was growing by the day, penetrated the center of the city, and in September it became nearly universal. The death toll was calculated with confusion—Some families, having sequestered themselves in their houses and broken off all communication with anyone else, remained unscathed by the contagion while death spilled forth all around the nearby dwellings—

Seville, which continued its commercial relations with this unfortunate city, quickly became afflicted by the same plague—The first attacks were felt in Triana, the suburb where sailors live, and from there the disease took charge of that entire quarter. It spread from there to the suburb of Los Humeros, which is frequented by sailors and lies on the other side of the river facing Triana—From Los Humeros it advanced to the city, following in its progression the same law it observed in Cádiz—

Many boatmen of the Guadalquivir isolated themselves on their boats, and the devouring flame attacked none of them—The fugitives from Cádiz as well as those from Seville, who found refuge in the villages near the two cities, became so many disseminators of infection—Cordova defended itself from this by putting into practice those sanitary precautions that the public health officials and the police prescribe in such dangerous times—(Piguillém—Villalba—Berthe—Bally)

Málaga received only a slight injury that year, but in 1803 and again in 1804 it suffered horribly—Here is how the evil was born there, on 14 July 1803—A certain smuggler Félix Muñoz (and Spain is overflowing with this despicable breed) hid himself aboard the ship the Young Nicolas, where he acquired tobacco and cotton stockings—He experienced the first signs of the disease as he departed from there and died on the 20th of the same month—After thirty-six days another smuggler, Cristóbal Verduras (who had hidden in his house a sailor infected with the plague, which conducted him to the tomb), fell ill, followed by his son, his mother, two brothers, and the rest of the household, which was composed of eight individuals—Mr. Buzon, who had the misfortune of assisting the unknown sailor, and the curate who buried the dead man, both contracted the infection and succumbed—The consulting doctors Mamely and Gimel met the same fate and left the destructive germ in the bosom of their desolate families—()In one's mind it is easy now to follow the subsequent routes of the disease and its dissemination in the city. The rigors of the winter put an end to this situation, but unfortunately it deployed itself much more terribly in the autumn of 1804. And Málaga, after having been victimized and left quasi vidua super terram, became the focus

jula—

of the contagion, from where it spread along the entire Mediterranean coast of Spain—Never losing sight of it, the doctors of the Peninsula were able to chart the routes that it traveled to this or that place, and I refer those who still doubt the contagious nature of the yellow fever of Spain to their works, as well as those of Bally, Humboldt, Berthe, and Cailliot—

Some say that the pestilences that have reigned in the United States under the name of yellow fever do not at all belong to the same family as those observed in Spain. However, if we, divesting ourselves of every prejudice, compare the ones with the others, we will notice either that they both come with the symptoms that we call pathognomonic, such as black vomit, jaundice, etc., etc., etc., or that, taking on the appearance of any of several classes of disease, they consistently present the same characteristic undertones and, permit me to say, the features of the vile stock from which they derive—the same pitfalls and perfidious calmness—the same order or disorder in the succession of the symptoms and in their cycle—the same external marks impressed on the sacrificed victims—the same damages to this or that organ or to many organs at once—In the United States as in Spain the disease particularly attacked the most robust men, the plethoric, the bilious—fewer women than men, and still fewer adolescents and young children. It seldom assailed, and when it did only in the lightest way, butchers, leather tanners, and furriers. It religiously spared the settlers and those who had long stayed on the islands—In the United States as in Spain it generally left moderately affected individuals with protection against new attacks, and quite often with better underlying health—Dr. Rush maintains that after the epidemic of 1793 the convalescents had an extraordinary tendency to the venereal act and that a surprising number of marriages occurred—an observation that reveals a commonality between the Oriental plague and yellow fever—In Mantua in 1506 such was the enthusiasm of the plague convalescents for the fair sex and so numerous the acts of violence committed by the former that the magnificent Sir Alessio Becaguto, lieutenant captain of the city, was obliged to cause a couple of gallows to be erected in order to end that scandalous business—Hodges reports that after the London plague of 1664–65 women who had been previously deemed sterile became mothers, so that soon the deficit caused by the disease was made good—"In Messina the marriage frenzy was such that, if it had been possible to shorten the length of pregnancy, the city would have quickly seen itself full of people" (Fornés.)

All that has been said so far evidences the similarity between the two plagues, American and Spanish. And yet you, whose intimate thoughts I know, will not easily agree with me on this article of faith—To convert you, it seems to me that my only recourse is to prove that the United States contracted the deadly germ from the same source as Spain—

The first description of American yellow fever, painted from nature with an artistic brush, is that of Dr. Lining, who had the opportunity to observe it in Charleston in 1732—On this occasion the illustrious author informs us "that the yellow fever had prevailed in that Country four times within twenty-five years, and that whenever the disease appeared here, it was easily traced to some person, who was Lately arrived from some west India Islands, where it was epidemical"

Such was also the opinion of the Medical College of Philadelphia on the origin and character of the pestilence that dominated that city in 1793. It appeared that same year in Grenada in the month of May, "soon after the arrival of a Guinea Ship from Sierra Leone, the crew of which had been so sickly, that most of the Sailors died of the yellow fever, either in the voyage, or soon after the arrival of the Ship—It suddenly spread over the other Leeward Islands, and from thence was carried to Philadelphia, Hispaniola, and Jamaica"—so writes William Wright—In fact, a few ships from those parts had arrived in the port of Philadelphia in the second half of July, and the college's respectable members assured themselves that the contagion had thereby originated—

The disease manifested itself at the end of July, "it first appeared in Water Street between Mulberry and Sassafras Streets, and all the cases of this fever, were, for two or three weeks evidently traced to this particular spot—a considerable part of the city, Northern Liberties, and district of South wark became gradually infected, and it was not until the coming of the frost that the disease subsided, after having proved fatal to nearly five thousand persons"

In these few lines you see the living image of yellow fever—It and the plague are unique in that, having been carried to a seaport or elsewhere, they are likely to incubate at their first stop, progress very slowly, and decline as if by witchcraft at the beginning of a given season—

The college, after having indicated some of the unique characteristics of yellow fever, distinguished it from similar diseases by its high degree of malignancy, the rapidity of its course, and the invincible resistance that it puts up to those remedies that generally defeat the bilious remittent fevers in the country—The measures that it proposed, both to prevent further propagation of the contagion and guard against subsequent outbreaks, were the best intentioned and wisest—but alas! their full importance was not felt—The quarantine laws and the local regulations were disregarded, so that the city was assailed all over again in the years 1797–98—Especially in this last year many ships had arrived in the months of July and August from Cape Môle Saint-Nicolas, Jérémie, Port-au-Prince on the island of Hispaniola, and Saint Domingue, where the vomit reigned, and from where they had departed with the utmost haste. "On the fifth day of july last six or eight of those vessels, having a large number of passengers on board, of course a quantity of cloathing, bedding &c. brought off in the greatest haste, themselves exposed to all these circumstances, which are allowed to produce contagious fever: in this situation they arrived at the fort, where they were detained on board for twenty days—On the arrival at the city, they generally lay at the wharves between Walnut and Spruce Street—and it is well known, that at this part of the City, the fever first appeared about the latter end of july and beginning of August—On the evening of the eighth of july the armed Ship Deborah, Captain Edward yard arrived at the fort from Jeremie—She buried eight persons during her stay there and return, and sent six sick to the marine hospital"

The college kept its eyes especially on the Deborah, which on 28 July was moved to Kensington, on whose salubrious banks one would search in vain for sources of infection—Their extremely scrupulous investigations demonstrated that the individuals who worked on or near the ship contracted the fever and spread the contagion to different parts of the city. "Facts and obs. on pestilent. fever which prevailed in Philadelpia in 1793–97–98 by the College of physicians of Philadelphia"   The work I am referring to offers much more of interest, because in addition to the excellent reflections scattered here and there, it is enriched by testimonies and observations of several respectable characters, physicians and others—

Despite so much factual and rational evidence, the opposing party continued to claim that local causes were enough to create the so-called yellow fever and that it was madness to establish its origin in the Indies—Thus in the year 1802, when the same calamity reproduced itself, these imaginary forces were called into play, and this explanation was an idea entertained by speculators and blindly embraced by the machine-like population—

The cause of the error into which they fell can be found both in medicine and the exact sciences—A dropped number causes the mathematician to err in his calculation and the astronomer to predict incorrectly the appearance or return of a comet—In Messina, Marseille, and Venice, where the plague had introduced itself furtively, the doctors neglected to take into account one of the most essential elements, that is, the arrival of filthy ships from the Levant, and their calculation of probability proved erroneous—

In affairs so closely guarded, such as those which concern the life and happiness of the people, everything must be examined calmly; everything must undergo a rigorous analysis—Regulated by these principles, Messrs. Currie and Cathrall discovered the true source of the disease that arose in Philadelphia in the year of which I was speaking a little earlier—After the evidence that they have given it is impossible to doubt that the contagion was brought by the ship Packet, which was coming from the Cape—How it was communicated from the Packet to the brigantine Esperanza, and from the sailors of both ships to other individuals, and so forth, little by little, I need not say—

The yellow fever that appeared in New York in 1791 was likewise introduced by a vessel, which came from the Indies (Hosack). As usual, the disease remained stationary in the place where it was born "near Peck-Slip. Here it raged a considerable time: it then began to spread, as some attendants on the sick became infected, who lived in other neighbourhoods—By this means it was carried to other families, and most generally could be traced to this source. It likewise proved more particularly fatal near the place, where it first appeared, than in any other part—Thus at length it spread through the city until the middle of October, when the weather growing a little cooler, the disease greatly abated, and in a short time disappeared"—(Addoms)—This disease, by the admission of the same Addoms, was precisely the same as the yellow fever observed by him more than once on the island of Saint Croix (Hosack—Obs. on contag. diseas—)

()Hosack—Dr. McKnight

New York was again attacked by the contagion in 1795–98 on the arrival of ships from the Indies.—()In this latter year the disease's extension was limited enough that it was generally believed to have originated from domestic causes, namely from rotten provisions, but the learned Hosack patently demonstrates that the fever had declared itself before these causes even existed—Even if they had preexisted, they could not have generated yellow fever—Whereas the gases derived from the decomposition of organic bodies combine with some principle scattered in the atmosphere and thereby create specific miasmas, which, conserving their volatile nature, circulate with the air and winds and simultaneously affect a multitude of individuals so that the diseases to which they give rise are, let us say, generalized from their first inception—Other miasmas do not imprint in the living organism the power to reproduce poisons similar to themselves—

These reasons alone, even with no other facts in front of me, would lead me to deny the influence of the spoiled salted meats, of the rotten oysters, and of the decay of every kind of substance in the generation of the disease with which we are concerned—

Yellow fever, like its sister the Oriental plague, is the product of a deleterious, sui generis germ: heavy, filthy, it does not travel on the wings of the wind—And if the air serves sometimes to conduct it, that happens only for very short distances and when this fluid is impregnated with it—In general it is communicated either by substances carrying it or by contact with the infected, who act as generators and sources of contagion—

This is today the opinion of all of educated Europe, and it is also that of a great number of doctors and scholars in New England—I know that there are also outstanding men in America who bitterly support the contrary opinion, based on an observation, which I find repeated in your letter, that in the United States the disease to which they gave the denomination of yellow fever never propagated itself from the city to the countryside, which completely excludes the idea of contagion—

By responding to you, Sir, I will respond to everyone—at the time when yellow fever was raging in Málaga in 1803, in the little villages that surround the city—in Churriana, Alhaurín, the big and little Coín, and Torre del Mar—no one was ill except the fugitives or those among the inhabitants who, in traveling to Málaga, had the imprudence to spend the night there—Cartagena, which in less than three or four months lost almost half its population to the pestilence received from Málaga, infected neither the places nearby nor the ships in the port—In Alicante the disease did not bring the least offense to the isolated houses located between the two walls that surround the city nor to those set apart by the suburbs outside the enclosure—In Palamo, where the linen of Alicante is washed, there was not a single example of the contagion, neither in Santa Faz, which is half a league from the city, nor at Mutxamel, which is even less distant—A phenomenon which was that much more surprising because Peñacerrada, which is separated from Mutxamel by a single path, Saint Joan, which is five quarter-leagues from Alicante, and Tabarca, which is about four leagues distant from it, were all infected—In Vera in 1811 it was observed that the infected who sought refuge in the homes of friends or relatives who lived a few steps away from the hospital did not transmit the disease to anyone—I will conclude with an event that happened in the French army under the command of the famous Marshal Soult, when the great captain's reversals in the north of the continent forced him to abandon Andalusia—General Conroux, who commanded a division arriving in the vicinity of Cesara, was warned by the city leaders who came to meet him that yellow fever was decimating their town—On receiving this warning the general sent his senior surgeon to examine this disease—The report of the health official was that the prevailing fever was a remittent bilious constitutional one—Conroux immediately ordered the troops to march and enter the place, and there the officers and administrators took lodging—The troops bivouacked—The next day the division continued its march, but a few hours later the general's aides-de-camp started to complain of joint pains, exhaustion, etc., etc., etc., and the next day still more fell ill, but only those who had had close contact with those inhabitants who then or previously had sick persons in their families—In light of this unexpected event the general ordered a stop at Yecla, where a provisional hospital was established—The disease, which had already spread, went very quickly through its stages, presenting the most pronounced symptoms of yellow fever, that is, black vomit; very fetid, dark, and bloody feces; unstoppable hemorrhages; jaundice; etc. Dr. Peysson, a physician of infinite merit, told me that he never saw such a horrible and destructive disease—That it surely was, since it left only one alive among the infected, François Musicien, and even he died after a convalescence more painful still than death—And yet the doctors, surgeons, and nurses who had been assigned to the nauseating and dangerous service in that hospital left the sea of troubles safe and sound, albeit astonished and ever fearful—

Going through the story of the most memorable periods of the plague in Europe, one finds that some villages, cities, or parts of provinces were spared this monster, which chose another time to exercise its fury on these same populations—(See Gratiolo di Salò—Turriano—Muratori—Mead). Examples of such an occurrence are very frequent in the Ottoman Levant, as I have had occasion to observe both in Smyrna and in the interior of Asia Minor, and of which I have left my recollection

Unknown principles sometimes exist, loose and fluctuating in the atmosphere, which either combine with the contagious germ or keep it dissolved so as to favor the interplay of the reciprocal affinities between the germ and the oxygen in the atmosphere. This is our case.

In every age doctors have congratulated themselves on achieving with art what they saw working in nature in deepest secrecy—Their efforts did not always fail—Lind, to speak of recent times, destroyed the fomite of yellow fever with both fire and smoke—The illustrious Guyton de Morveau used fumigations of muriatic acid to stop the disease caused in Dijon by disinterring cadavers at the cathedral—Mr. Smyth, with more or less identical methods, extinguished the nervous fever that had manifested itself in the hospital ship Union

These methods subsequently became universal, but it must be agreed that they have not always met our expectations—One day, however, experience and observation will lead us to the brilliant discovery of every type of miasma—And then all of the pestilences except tyranny will disappear from the earth—

The atmospheric conditions unfavorable to yellow fever are often fortuitous, and consequently the security of the places where they occur is nothing if not precarious—The contagion that was unable to develop in Medina-Sidonia in 1800, despite its being surrounded by the illness, erupted the next year and carried off almost three-fifths of the sick. And Vélez-Málaga and Antequera, which had suffered no cases during the first reign of yellow fever in their capital (with which they always maintained communication), were cruelly mistreated by this same plague in 1804—

It is noteworthy that some regions, whose climate is unspeakable, evil, and pestiferous, have been spared the black vomit—It has never been observed in the marshlands of Pisa or Siena, nor in the Pontine Marshes, Batavia, or along the entire western coast of Mexico. "In Acapulco," says Mr. Cailliot, "the inhabitants are tormented by frequent hurricanes: They breathe an air inflamed and contaminated by putrid emanations, exhaled by the nearby seas, whose stagnant water disappears every year leaving naked the mud in which an innumerable quantity of fish and insects rot—The olive-green vapors that rise up are so thick that the sun has difficulty crossing and dissipating them—nevertheless one has never seen the vomit there"—

These observations must put in a very awkward situation those doctors who maintain that blazing heat, putrid exhalations, etc., etc., play the principal or only role in the case in question. I strongly believe that these causes, under particular, undetermined circumstances, cause the germ to develop and serve as its pasture and nourishment, but I am far from thinking that they are fundamentally necessary for it to exist—Even Medina-Sidonia, Carmona, Cuevas del Almanzora, and Vera, where one breathes the purest and healthiest air in the world (since they are situated in the mountains or high up, far from the sea, swamps, and lakes) and where people know endemic and epidemic diseases only by name, have been scourged as badly as Cádiz, Málaga, Alicante, Cartagena, Murcia, etc.

In the United States yellow fever does not seem to have spread as it has in the large European peninsula, and this is undoubtedly due to the lack of atmospheric opportunity—Nevertheless, noncontagionists of good faith must admit that even in their country the contagion passed a few times via ordinary communications from the city to the countryside—It was transmitted in this way to Huntington, Long Island, in 1795, to Swedesboro in the years 1797–98–99, to New Hampshire, Connecticut, and Germantown in 1798, to Staten Island in 1799—

Fearing that these hasty accounts may not make an adequate impression on your mind, I send you a copy of two documents pertinent to the subject, irrefutable documents, one of which is signed by Dr. Wistar, the pride of your country, and the other by the respectable Dr. Richard Moore—

Convinced of the contagious character of yellow fever, I offer to inoculate myself with the disease using the sweat of the dying and the bile of the deceased, and to modify the poison with those same reactives that were used in my experiments on the Oriental plague—If it is written in the Book of Fate that I should fall victim to this great trial, my death will not be without glory, and the philanthropists of this happy land will run en masse to scatter fragrant flowers on my tomb—

Meanwhile, full of veneration and esteem, I have the honor to call myself your most devoted servant

VALLI—

RC (DLC); edge chipped; endorsed by TJ as received 19 June 1816 and so recorded in SJL. Tr (PPAmP: APS Archives); entirely in Valli's hand; undated. Translation by Dr. Christina Ball and Dr. Jonathan T. Hine.

In a communication to Peter S. Du Ponceau dated Trenton, New Jersey, 28 June 1816, Valli described the above letter as his answer "all'Eretico Sr Jefferson sull'articolo di fede relativamente al contagio della febbre gialla" ("to the heretical Mr. Jefferson on the article of faith concerning the contagion of yellow fever") and asked Du Ponceau to translate it for Caspar Wistar (RC in PPAmP: APS Archives; addressed: "Al Sig. Avvocato du Ponceau—a Filadelfia"; endorsed by Du Ponceau as received 30 June 1816).

Alexander von Humboldt (HOMBOLT) reviewed the origin and causes of yellow fever in Mexico in his *Essai Politique sur le Royaume de la Nouvelle-Espagne* (Paris, 1808–19; Sowerby, no. 4157), 2:750–88. The Jesuit priest Francisco Javier Clavijero (Francesco Saverio Clavigero) (CALVIGERO) claimed in his history of Mexico that the so-called black vomit did not enter the Mexican port of Veracruz before 1725 (Clavigero, *Storia Antica del Messico* [Cesena, 1780–81; Sowerby, no. 4121], 1:117). Humboldt asserted that the RITORNO DELL'EPIDEMIA to Veracruz coincided with the arrival of three ships that had recently stopped at Puerto Rico (*Essai Politique*, 2:783). A HOURQUE, French for "hooker," is a round-sterned ship (Alan Moore and R. Morton Nance, "Round-Sterned Ships. No. II. The Hooker," *Mariner's Mirror* 1 [1911]: 293–7).

The American ship *Dolphin* (DELFINO), under Captain William Haskel (GUILLAUME JASKAL), was suspected of bringing yellow fever to Cádiz in 1800 (James Fellowes, *Reports of the Pestilential Disorder of Andalusia, which appeared at Cadiz in the years 1800, 1804, 1810, and 1813* [London, 1815], 424, 433; Charleston *South-Carolina State Gazette, and Timothy's Daily Advertiser*, 3 June 1800; Newburyport, Mass., *Merrimack Magazine and Ladies' Literary Cabinet*, 12 Oct. 1805). Valli based his account of the arrival of yellow fever in Cádiz and other parts of Spain on the works of the Spanish physicians Francisco Piguillém (PIGUILLEM), "De la Propiedad Contagiosa de la Calentura amarilla," in Piguillém and others, *Memoria sobre la Calentura Amarilla de las Américas* (Barcelona, 1804), 15–34, and Joaquín de Villalba (VILLELVA), *Epidemiologia Española ó Historia Cronológica de las Pestes, Contagios, Epidemias y Epizootias* (Madrid, 1802), 1:333–8, as well as those of the French doctors Jean Nicolas BERTHE, *Précis Historique de la Maladie qui a régné dans l'Andalousie en 1800* (Paris, 1802), 52–65, and Victor François BALLY, *Du Typhus d'Amérique ou Fièvre Jaune* (Paris, 1814), 71–4, 429–33.

José Mamely (MAMMELLI) and Guillermo Gimel (GIMAL) served on Málaga's board of health during the city's 1803–04 yellow fever epidemic (Josef Mendoza, *Historia de las Epidemias Padecidas en Malaga en los años de 1803 y 1804* [Málaga, 1813], esp. 20–5; Bally, *Du Typhus d'Amérique*, 81–4; "Half-Yearly Retrospect of Spanish Literature," *Monthly Magazine; or, British Register* 14 [1803]: 604). Valli's marginal note suggests that he also consulted Juan Manuel de Aréjula (AREJULA), *Breve Descripcion de la Fiebre Amarilla Padecida en Cadiz y Pueblos Comarcanos en 1800, en Medinasidonia en 1801, en Malaga en 1803 … y varias otras del Reyno en 1804* (Madrid, 1806), 264–78.

QUASI VIDUA SUPER TERRAM ("as a widow left on the Earth") recalls a similar description of the ruins of Jerusalem in the Bible (Lamentations 1.1).

Louis Cailliot (CAILLOT), the chief physician at the French port of Cherbourg, supported the proposition that yellow fever is contagious in his *Traité de la Fièvre Jaune* (Paris, 1815).

The sexual drive and fecundity of survivors of yellow fever and bubonic plague is discussed, respectively, by Benjamin RUSH in *An Account of the Bilious remitting Yellow Fever, as It Appeared in the City of Philadelphia, in the year 1793* (Philadelphia, 1794), 67–8, and by the British physician Nathaniel HODGES in *Loimologia: or, an Historical Account of the Plague in London in 1665* (3d ed., London, 1721), 27–8. The Italian city of MESSINA suffered an outbreak of bubonic plague in 1743 (Orazio Turriano, *Memoria Istorica del Contagio della Città di Messina Dell'anno MDCCXLIII* [Naples, 1745]).

Within quotation marks Valli paraphrases, quotes, and rearranges an account by John LINING of the 1748 epidemic in Charleston, South Carolina ("A Description of the American Yellow Fever, in a Letter from Dr. John Lining," *Essays and Observations, Physical and Literary. Read before a Society in Edinburgh* 2 [1756]: 372–3). Information about the ORIGINE E IL GENIO of yellow fever in Philadelphia and GRENADA in 1793 is quoted from a report by the College of Physicians of Philadelphia, *Facts and Observations relative to the Nature and Origin of the Pestilential Fever, which Prevailed in this City, in 1793, 1797, and 1798* (Philadelphia, 1798; Sowerby, no. 924), 4, 21–2, 25, 30. This report includes an extract of a letter from the Scottish physician WILLIAM WRIGHT to Maxwell Garthshore, a physician in London, 10 Dec. 1794 (pp. 28–32), printed earlier in *Medical Facts and Observations* 7 (1797): 1–25.

William CURRIE and Isaac CATHRALL discussed the 1802 Philadelphia yellow fever epidemic in *Facts and Observations, relative to the Origin, Progress and Nature of the Fever … of Philadelphia in the summer and autumn of the present year, (1802.)* (Philadelphia, 1802).

In support of his statement that the 1791 yellow fever epidemic in New York City started NEAR PECK-SLIP, David Hosack quotes from Jonas Smith ADDOMS, who experienced this outbreak and a later one on the West Indies island of Saint Croix (ST^A CRUX). Hosack also discusses the 1795 and 1798 New York City epidemics, arguing that the disease was both imported and contagious (Hosack, *Observations on Contagious Diseases*, 24–8; Addoms, *An Inaugural Dissertation on the Malignant Fever, which prevailed in the city of New-York ... in the year 1791* [New York, 1792], 7). Valli had also encountered a letter from John McKnight (M.KNIGHT) to Hosack, printed as an "Account of the Origin of the Yellow Fever which prevailed in the City of New-York in the Summer of 1798," *American Medical and Philosophical Register* 3 (1814): 293–8. Valli refers to Bally's OPINION as well (Bally, *Opinion sur la Contagion de la Fièvre Jaune* [Paris, 1810]).

GRAN CAPITANO: Napoleon. During an 1812 campaign in Andalusia, the French marshal Nicolas Jean de Dieu Soult appointed the military physician Jean Claude Anthelme PEYSSON president of an advisory commission on yellow fever ("Nécrologie," *Journal de Médecine de Lyon* 16 [1848]: 314–5). Peysson eventually published his experiences in *Histoire de la fièvre jaune qui fut observée parmi les troupes françaises, en Espagne, en 1812* (Paris, 1818).

Commenting on the bubonic plague that had earlier spread throughout Europe, Valli refers to the works of the Italian authors Andrea GRATIOLO DI SALÒ, *Discorso di Peste* (Venice, 1576), Turriano (TUANO), *Memoria Istorica del Contagio della Città di Messina*, and Lodovico Antonio MURATORI, *Del Governo della Peste* (Rome and Modena, 1714), as well as that of the British doctor Richard MEAD, *De Peste Liber* (London, 1723). Valli's MEMORIA of plagues in the Ottoman Levant is in his *Memoria sulla Peste di Smyrne del 1784* (Lausanne, 1788) and *Sulla Peste di Costantinopoli del MDCCCIII* (Mantua, 1805).

The Scottish physician James LIND advocated the use of fire and smoke to combat yellow fever in *An Essay on Diseases Incidental to Europeans in hot Climates* (London, 1768), 136–7, 160–1. The French chemist Louis Bernard Guyton de Morveau (GUJTON MORVEAU) claimed that his method of fumigation with muriatic acid (now more commonly called hydrochloric acid) aborted the fever that erupted in 1773 after the opening of the tombs under the church of Saint-Médard at DIJON in "Nouveau Moyen De purifier absolument & en très-peu de temps une masse d'air infectée," *Observations sur La Physique* (Paris, 1773), 1:436–41, and *Traité des Moyens de Désinfecter l'Air* (Paris, 1801), 6–11. The British physician James Carmichael Smyth (SMITH) promoted the use of nitrous acid to stop contagion in *An Account of the Experiment made ... on board the Union Hospital Ship, to determine the effect of the Nitrous Acid in Destroying Contagion, and the safety with which it may be employed* (London, 1796), esp. 7–35.

After noting that yellow fever had not been observed in several areas, including BATAVIA (present-day Jakarta) and towns on the west coast of Mexico, Valli provides more detail on conditions in ACAPULCO by quoting in French from Cailliot, *Traité de la Fièvre Jaune*, 126–7.

[1] Tr: "partecipazione" ("announcement").

[2] Tr: "quasi annualmente" ("almost annually").

[3] RC: "A." Tr: "Anno" ("Year").

[4] Tr: "vigore" ("vigor").

[5] RC: "St^a Crux." Tr: "Vera-Crux." Humboldt: "Vera-Cruz."

[6] Tr: "vomito nero" ("black vomit").

[7] RC: "St^a Crux." Tr: "Vera-Crux." Humboldt: "Vera-Cruz."

[8] Tr: "prontamente" ("promptly").

[9] RC:"illesi." Tr: "illese."

[10] Preceding ten words interlined.

[11] Sentence in Tr reads "I fuggitivi da Cadice come da Seviglia i quali si ritirarono in disordine nei Villagi o borghi vicini alle due Città, vi sparsero il seme del contagione, il terrore ed il lutto" ("The fugitives from Cádiz as well as those from

Seville, who fled in disorder to the villages near the two cities, transmitted the seed of the contagion along with terror and mourning").

[12]Tr: "critici" ("critical").

[13]Name not in Tr.

[14]Tr: "durissima" ("very harsh").

[15]RC: "14 di Luglio 1783." Tr: "14 di Luglio."

[16]Word not in Tr.

[17]Parenthetical phrase not in Tr.

[18]Tr: "Cristoforo."

[19]Tr here adds "famoso" ("famous").

[20]Tr: "Dottor" ("Doctor").

[21]RC and Tr: "—84."

[22]Tr here adds "e nelle parti interne del Paese" ("and in the interior of the country").

[23]Tr here adds "interessantissime, preziose" ("very interesting, valuable").

[24]Preceding two words not in Tr.

[25]Tr here adds "L'emorragie passive" ("the passive hemorrhages").

[26]Tr: "febbre gialla" ("yellow fever").

[27]Tr here adds "e fiamme di lussuria" ("and flames of lust").

[28]Remainder of sentence in Tr reads "della febbre gialla con la peste, malattie Sorelle" ("of yellow fever with the plague, sister diseases").

[29]Preceding four words not in Tr.

[30]Remainder of paragraph not in Tr.

[31]Tr: "quadro."

[32]Tr: "City." Lining: "town."

[33]RC and Tr: "whenever apparead there." Lining: "whenever the disease appeared here."

[34]RC: "wee weeks." Tr and College of Physicians version: "weeks."

[35]RC: "thousand person." Tr: "thousand persons." College of Physicians version: "five thousand persons."

[36]RC: "1792–93." Tr: "1797–98," which correctly reflects events in the referenced text.

[37]RC and Tr: "passangers." College of Physicians version: "passengers."

[38]RC: "& brougth." Tr: "&& brougth." College of Physicians version: "&c. brought."

[39]Omitted word supplied from College of Physicians version.

[40]Preceding two words, interlined in RC, are not in Tr.

[41]RC and Tr: "six sicks." College of Physicians version: "*six* sick."

[42]Word not in Tr.

[43]RC: "neighboourhoods." Tr: "neighboorhoods." Addoms: "neighbourhoods."

[44]Tr here adds "on contagious diseases."

[45]RC: "apparead." Tr and Addoms: "appeared."

[46]Omitted word supplied from Addoms.

[47]RC and Tr: "lenght." Addoms: "length."

[48]RC and Tr: "diseases." Addoms: "disease."

[49]Omitted closing quotation mark editorially supplied.

[50]Preceding two words not in Tr.

[51]In place of preceding three words, Tr substitutes "in preda della malattia" ("prey to the disease").

[52]Phrase from "nel" interlined.

[53]Tr here adds "(v. Hosack and statement of facts on this subject by the Rev. Dr. M[c]Knight in the Amer. Med. and phil. Reg. vol. 3.)," followed by "E qual altra costituzione di febbre gialla si puo rammentare che non Sia derivata dal di fuori? (v. Currie)" ("And what other occurrence of yellow fever can be recalled that does not derive from outside? [see Currie]").

[54]For remainder of sentence Tr substitutes "Povera ragione per opinar così—Nella peste di Antiochia (nel 540 della nostra Era) mentre La malattia Signoreggiava in alcuni quartieri della Cittá, gl'altri godevano d'una salute intiera—Nella Cittá popolose della Turchia Si vedono ogni giorno questi Strani fenomeni—Direm noi per questo che La peste non é contagiosa? Il Dr. Hosack nel rammentare la febbre gialla del —98—osserva, che Le cause, cui si voleva attribuire, non erano contemporanee, ma posteriori al nascimento del morbo" ("This is not a good argument—in the plague at Antioch [in 540 of our era], while the disease reigned in some quarters of the city, others enjoyed perfect health. One sees such strange phenomena every day in the populous cities of Turkey. Would we say for this reason that the plague is not contagious? Recalling the plague of 1798, Dr. Hosack observes that

the causes to which it was attributed occurred not contemporaneously with but after the appearance of the disease"). In the left-hand margin next to this passage, Tr adds "Evagrio," indicating that this passage derives from the Byzantine historian Evagrius (*Ecclesiastical History*, book 4, chapter 29, in *The Ecclesiastical History of Evagrius Scholasticus*, trans. Michael Whitby [2000], 229–30).

[55] In place of preceding three words Tr substitutes "il vomito nero" ("the black vomit").

[56] For remainder of paragraph Tr substitutes "del café avariato &&& della generazione della febbre gialla" ("of spoiled coffee etc. etc. etc. in the generation of yellow fever").

[57] In place of preceding two words Tr substitutes "inatto perció a percorrere" ("thus unsuited to travel").

[58] In place of this sentence Tr substitutes "Per L'ordinario si receve L'infezione o pel contatto delle sostanze, che gli servono di ripostiglio, o per quello degl'infetti, i quali sono come altrettanti laboratorj di nuovo identico miasma" ("One usually receives the infection either by contact with substances carrying it, or by contact with the infected, who are like so many other laboratories producing new, identical miasmas").

[59] In place of preceding three words Tr substitutes "tutti i medici d'Europa" ("all the physicians in Europe").

[60] Tr here adds "a quali io vado dietro ma non come le pecorelle, che uscendo dal chiuso, corrono Su i passi delle prime in moto e lo perche non sanno" ("after whom I come, although not like sheep who, coming out of their enclosure, first run in place and only seem to be advancing, and they do not know why").

[61] Tr: "questa Contrada" ("this region").

[62] In place of section from "l'opinione contraria" to this point, Tr substitutes "che La febbre gialla, o almeno quella che si chiama cosí, perché ne ha tutti i caretteri nosologici, é malattia originaria del paese, e non giá esotica—Essi s'appoggiano in modo particolare sopra un'osservazione, che trovo ripetuta nella dilei Lettera, ed é che la febbre, o diciam meglio, peste Americana" ("that yellow fever, or what is thus called, since it has all its nosological characteristics, is a disease originating inside the country, not exotic—They rely in particular on an observation that I see repeated in your letter, that the fever, or rather, the American plague").

[63] RC: "malatti." Tr: "malattia."

[64] RC: "Soulth." Tr: "Soult."

[65] RC: "d'abandonare." Tr: "d'abbandonare."

[66] In place of preceding three words Tr substitutes "Soggeto molto distinto pé suoi talenti" ("individual much distinguished for his talents").

[67] Tr here adds "piu propizio" ("more propitious").

[68] For preceding four words Tr substitutes "scagliarsi" ("to lash out").

[69] For remainder of paragraph Tr substitutes: "e no ho lasciata memoria nel mio Opusculo sulla peste di Smyrne del 1784" ("and of which I have left my recollection in my article on the plague of Smyrna in 1784").

[70] Tr here adds "Ora come i miasmi sì nell'una che all'altra ippotesi vengono ad esser neutralizzati, così non possono piu aver azione Sull'organismo animale" ("Now, since in both hypotheses the miasmas become neutralized, they cannot act on the animal organism").

[71] Tr here adds "alle nostre speranze" ("to our hopes").

[72] Tr here adds "degl'antidoti" ("of the antidotes").

[73] RC: "sparirann." Tr: "spariran."

[74] Word, illegible in RC, supplied from Tr and Cailliot.

[75] Omitted closing quotation mark editorially supplied.

[76] Tr here adds "alle variazioni brusche dell'atmosfera" ("to sudden atmospheric changes").

[77] Preceding twelve words not in Tr.

[78] Preceding two words not in Tr.

[79] In place of preceding twelve words Tr substitutes "Peraltro é forza il convenire" ("However, we must recognize").

[80] Preceding five words not in Tr.

[81] RC: "Huntingondon." Tr: "Huntingdon."

[82] Tr: "1795–98."

[83] Preceding two words interlined.

[84] In place of preceding five words Tr substitutes "from the right Rev. Dr. Richard Channing Moore."

[85] Tr here adds "Americana" ("American").

[86] Preceding two words not in Tr.

ENCLOSURES

I

Richard Channing Moore to David Hosack

DEAR SIR Staten-Island Octob. 20 1806.

The discordant opinions which are held by physicians of the first reputation, upon the Subject of yellow fever, have prevented me from Replying to your letter of january last, lest the information which I may offer should give rise to such observations as would necessarily involve me in a medical controversy—From frequent conversations with my worthy[1] preceptor, the late Mr. Richard Bayley, as well as from the perusal of those tracts, which had fallen under my notice, I for many years entertained the opinion, that the yellow fever, which has proved a scourge to our Cities, originated exclusively within their [e]nclosures, and was confined to the impurity of their immediate atmosphere

One of the first circumstances which excited in my mind an impression [o]f the infectious nature of the disease, and which induced an alteration in my views, was the illness and subsequent death of Dr Wynant and his wife—This gentleman had been called to take the charge of a man from New-york, ill with yellow fever, upon the north side of this island—The Doctor, after an examination of the case, Judged it expedient to bleed the patient, and while engaged in the performance of that operation, the man was seized with violent puking, and discharged the contents of his Stomach upon his physician's clothes—From the appearance of the matter so discharged, Dr Wynant expressed his apprehensions with respect to his own safety; he continued, however, his attendance faithfully, until the patient expired—A few days after the death of the person alluded to, Dr Wynant was taken seriously ill: the usual remedies were applied, from the use of which he imagined himself relieved, and expressed a conviction of his recovery—At this moment [he][2] was visited by Dr. Henderson and myself—When we entered his room, which was a fine, airy, comfortable apartament, he declared to us his expectation of being restored in a little time; the danger of the disease he concluded to be completly removed, and he was then in the use of bark and wine—His wife, an amiable woman, was sitting at his bed side, to all appearance in full health, elated with the prospect of her husband's recovery—She, however, Soon discovered that her hopes were premature. the next day, the companion of her bosom was wrested from her arms by that fatal disease[3]—Upon the day[4] Mrs. Wynant was attacked with the same fever, which had terminated the life of her husband, and within [the][5] space of[6] five days from its commencement she fell a victim to its malignant, deadly influance—

Il D^r^ parla in seguito della malattia, che egli medesimo contrasse in occasione che fu chiamato a visitare un Parrocchiano preso da febbre gialla, che aveva guadagnata a New-york, e aggiunge altri casi dalla stessa natura av[evano] in Staten-Island—.

Tr (DLC: TJ Papers, 207:36908); extract entirely in Eusebio Valli's hand, consisting of opening of letter; with following enclosure subjoined; edge chipped; at head of text: "Letter addressed to David Hosack M.D. from the right Rev. Dr. Richard Channing Moore." The complete letter, containing other accounts of yellow-fever victims instead of the final paragraph in Italian, is printed in Literary and Philosophical Society of New-York, *Transactions* 1 (1815): 266–8, and in Hosack, *Observations on Contagious Diseases*, 70–2.

Richard Channing Moore (1762–1841), Episcopal bishop, was born in New York City. After studying medicine under Richard Bayley, he had a brief career as a physician in New York City and on Long Island. Moore then studied for the Episcopal ministry and was ordained in 1787. He served successively as rector at Saint Andrew's Church on Staten Island starting in 1789 and at Saint Stephen's Church in New York City from 1809. Moore was elected bishop of Virginia in 1814 and moved to Richmond, where he also served as rector of Monumental Church and from 1819–23 acted as bishop of North Carolina. He was aided by William Meade as coadjutor bishop from 1829 but remained at the head of the diocese until his death in Lynchburg (*ANB*; *DAB*; John P. K. Henshaw, *Memoir of the Life of the Rt. Rev. Richard Channing Moore* [1843]; John N. Norton, *The Life of the Right Reverend Richard Channing Moore, D.D., Bishop of Virginia* [1857]; *Lynchburg Virginian*, 15 Nov. 1841; gravestone inscription in Hollywood Cemetery, Richmond).

IL D[R] PARLA IN SEGUITO ... IN STATEN-ISLAND: "The doctor speaks subsequently about the illness he himself contracted while calling on a parishioner who had contracted yellow fever in New York, and he added other cases of the same nature from Staten Island."

[1] Manuscript: "whorty."
[2] Omitted word supplied from printed versions.
[3] Printed versions here add "the force of which she had flattered herself was subdued."
[4] Printed versions here add "in which the doctor died, which was the 13th of October, '99."
[5] Omitted word supplied from printed versions.
[6] Manuscript: "of of."

II

Caspar Wistar's Statement on Yellow Fever

Statement of facts tending to prove the contagious nature of the yellow fever, at Germantown, in the year 1798. by C. Wistar M.D. Professor of Anatomy in the University of Pensylvania E[t]c

---

The disease which produced the fatal effects now to be related, commence[d] in the family of Elizabeth Johnson, widow who lived in the main Street of the village of Germantown, about six and a half miles from Philadelphia—

The person first affected was her child, Betsey Johnson, who had been in Philadelphia from the third to the seventh of August, in a neighbourhood where several cases of the fever had already appeared. She returned home the seventh, and on the ninth of the same month was attacked with the yellow fe[ver,] which terminated fatally in four days—Fourteen days after her death, viz. Augu[st] 27th, mrs. Duy, the next neighbour of mrs. Johnson, who had visited Betsey several times during her illness, was attacked with a fever supposed to be of the same kind, and died at the end of four days—

On the thirtieth of August, the wife of Charles Hubbs, who also lived near to mrs. Johnson, and had visited both Betsey and mrs. Duy, once at least, during their respective indispositions, but had not been in Philadelphia for many months, was attacked with unequivocal symptoms of the yellow fever, in its most malignant form, and died the 2d of September—

Mr. Duy, husband of the above-mentioned mrs. Duy, was attacked sixteen days after the death of his wife, viz. September 18, and died also after an illness of six days—

A few days after the death of mrs. Duy, an English gentleman and his wife, of the name of Fisher, who had fled from Philadelphia on account of the fever, went to board with mr. Duy, and were placed in the Chamber occupied by his late wife during her illness. they were also attacked with fever—mrs. Fisher was taken, 7ber 19th, and recovered in a few days, but mr. Fisher, who was attacked four days after his wife, died with the black vomit the 27th of September—

At the same time, the disease re-appeared in Mrs. Johnson's family, in a young female servant, who was very ill, but recovered. Soon after the attack of this girl, Mrs. Johnson herself was taken ill with the same disease: She had visited both of her neighbours, mrs. Duy and mrs. Hubbs, while they were sick: She also had assorted the clothes of her deceased daughter, four or five days before her own attack commenced, but had not been in Philadelphia for a month—Her disorder continued eight days, and terminated the 28th September, with convulsions and the black vomit—

A few days before the death of mrs. Johnson, Elisabeth[1] Stern, a woman, who lived in the family, was attacked with the fever, and became very yellow—Her symptoms appeared moderate at first, but after lingering a fortnight she also died.—The wife of a tenant of mrs. Johnson, who lived in a separate part of the house, but used the same yard, was attacked before the death of Elisabeth Stern, and recovered with great difficulty—

The last victim to be mentioned, was one Stephen post, an old man, who lived at a distance, but worked in mr. Duy's barn, while the bed was there, on which mrs. Duy died—He was also attacked with fever, and died in a few days—

These melancholy circumstances occurred in a Village, which has long been remarkable for its salubrity, at a time when the other Inhabitants enjoyed their usual health—In most of the cases, the disease appears to have been contracted at the house of Mrs. Johnson, which, before this distressing period, had been eminently distinguished by the health and longevity of its inhabitants—The family were extremely neat, and it may be asserted with confidence, that the premises were never more clean, than they were at the time of this truly affecting catastrophe—

What cause but contagion is adequate to the production of such a disease among persons so situated? Philadelphia Dec. 15, 1805—

Tr (DLC: TJ Papers, 207:36908–9); edge chipped; entirely in Eusebio Valli's hand; subjoined to preceding enclosure. Printed in Literary and Philosophical Society of New-York, *Transactions* 1 (1815): 268–9, and in Hosack, *Observations on Contagious Diseases*, 72–3.

[1] Manuscript: "Elisabet." Printed versions: "Elizabeth."

From Franclieu

Monsieur Ancien president, Senlis (oise) 6 juin 1816./.

des malheurs ont passé Sur la france. votre Cœur genereux vous y aura fait Compatir. francais, le desir de les prevenir me dicta quelques ecrits.

jai l'honneur de Vous les Soumettre, de Vous en faire hommage.

les principes vrais que jai Voulu Saisir Sont de tous les lieux et les tems.

agreez je Vous prie lexpression de ma Respectueuse Consideration

Le Cte De Franclieu.
ancien Capt de dragons Francais.

1er Ces feuills plates devaient vous avoir été adressées./.

EDITORS' TRANSLATION

Mr. former president, Senlis (Oise) 6 June 1816./.

Misfortunes have befallen France. Your generous heart must have made you sympathetic. As a Frenchman, the desire to prevent them moved me to write a few pieces.

I have the honor to submit them as an homage to you.

The true principles I wanted to grasp belong to all places and times.

Accept, I pray you, the expression of my respectful consideration

Comte de Franclieu.
former captain of the French dragoons.

1st These humble sheets should have been addressed to you./.

RC (DLC); dateline above postscript; at head of text: "A Monsieur Jefferson Ancien president des Etats unis damerique"; endorsed by TJ as received 19 Sept. 1816 and so recorded in SJL. Translation by Dr. Genevieve Moene. Enclosed in John Graham to TJ, 16 Sept. 1816.

Louis Henri Camille Pasquier, comte de Franclieu (b. 1763), soldier and political writer, was by 1785 a captain of the Bourbon-Dragoons, later the 3d Regiment of Dragoons, and a member of the Order of Malta in 1799. He was active in French politics and wrote several tracts, including *Opinion et Project de Loi sur la Liberté de la Presse* (Paris, 1817) and *Du Principe des Gouvernemens. Des Progrès de l'Espirit Humain* (Paris, 1824) (Jean Baptiste de Junquières, *Une Famille Senlisienne. Les Junquières* [1915], 92; Nicolas Viton de Saint-Allais, *Nobiliaire Universel de France, ou Recueil Général des Généalogies Historiques des Maisons Nobles de ce Royaume* [1873–74], 4:93; René Louis de Roussel, *Etat Militarie de France pour l'année 1789* [Paris, 1789], 383; Constant Antoine Serrure, *Histoire de la Souveraineté de 'S Heerenberg* [1859], 2:47; Saint-Allais, *L'Ordre de Malte: ses Grands Maitres et ses Chevaliers* [1839], 311).

The ecrits here enclosed have not been identified. Franclieu had by this time authored several works, including the pamphlets *Réflexions Rapides de L.-H.-C. de Franclieu* (Senlis, 1791) and *Opinion sur la Charte qui nous est Annoncée* (Paris, 1815). TJ had at least one of Franclieu's publications bound in a volume of "Political, foreign" pamphlets (Poor, *Jefferson's Library*, 11 [no. 680]).

From Albert Gallatin

Dear Sir New York 7th June 1816

I have received your's of 16th ulto, and, from Dufief, the work of Mr Tracy, for La Fayette. I had become acquainted with Mr T. at Paris, think highly of him and of his book, and will be anxious to See that on political economy.

I do not precisely understand what is the subject to which you allude, when speaking of the feeling excited in Virginia by Some proceedings of Congress. But whatever that may be, I must believe that such feeling if spontaneous is correct.

We expect to sail on Sunday next. Your letters will be duly delivered. Accept the assurance of my respectful attachment and best wishes. Your obedient Servant Albert Gallatin

RC (DLC); at foot of text: "Mr Jefferson"; endorsed by TJ as a letter of 9 June received 17 June 1816 and so recorded in SJL.

The letter Gallatin received from TJ was dated 18 May 1816, not the 16th.

To Francis W. Gilmer

Dear Sir Monticello June 7. 16.

I recieved, a few days ago, from mr Dupont, the inclosed MS. with permission to read it, and a request, when read, to forward it to you, in expectation that you would translate it. it is well worthy of publication for the instruction of our citizens, being profound, sound, and short. our legislators are not sufficiently apprised of the rightful limits of their powers: that their true office is to declare and enforce only our natural rights and duties, & to take none of them from us. No man has a natural right to commit aggression on the equal rights of another; and this is all from which the laws ought to restrain him: every man is under the natural duty of contributing to the necessities of the society; and this is all the laws should enforce on him: and, no man having a natural right to be the judge between himself and another, it is his natural duty to submit to the umpirage of an impartial third. when the laws have declared and enforced all this, they have fulfilled their functions, and the idea is quite unfounded that on entering into society we give up any natural right. the trial of every law by one of these texts would lessen much the labors of our legislators, & lighten equally our municipal codes. there is a work of the first order of merit now in the press at Washington, by Destutt-Tracy, on the subject of political economy, which he brings into the compass of 300. pages 8vo. in a preliminary discourse on the origin of the right of property he coincides much with the principles of the present MS. but is more developed, more demonstrative. he promises a future work on morals, in which[1] I lament to see that he will adopt the principle of Hobbes, so humiliating to human nature, that the sense of justice & injustice is not derived from our natural organisation, but founded on convention only. I lament this the more as he is unquestionably the ablest writer living on abstract subjects.[2] assuming the fact that the earth has been created in time, and consequently the dogma of final causes, we yield of course to this short syllogism. Man was created for social intercourse; but social intercourse cannot be maintained without a sense of justice; then man must have been created with a sense of justice. there is an error into which most of the speculators on government have fallen, and which the well known state of society of our Indians ought before now to have corrected. in their hypotheses, of the origin of government, they suppose it to have commenced in the patriarchal, or monarchical form. our Indians are evidently in that state of nature which has past the association of a single family; & not yet submitted to the authority of positive laws, or of any acknoleged magistrate. every man, with them, is perfectly free to follow his own inclinations. but if, in doing this, he violates the rights of another, if the case be slight, he is punished by the disesteem of his society, or, as we say, by public opinion; if serious, he is tomahawked as a dangerous enemy. their leaders conduct them by the influence of their character only; and they follow, or not, as they please, him of whose character for wisdom or war they have the highest opinion. hence the origin of the parties among them adhering to different leaders, and governed by their advice, not by their command. the Cherokees, the only tribe I know to be contemplating the establishment of regular laws, magistrates and government, propose a government of representatives elected from every town. but of all things they least think of subjecting themselves to the will of one man. this the only instance of actual fact, within our knolege, will be then a beginning by republican, and not by patriarchal or monarchical government, as speculative writers have generally conjectured.

We have to join in mutual congratulations on the appointment of our friend Correa to be Minister or Envoy of Portugal here. this I hope will give him to us for life. nor will it at all interfere with his botanical rambles or journies. the government of Portugal is so peaceable and inoffensive that it has never any altercations with it's friends. if their minister abroad writes them once a quarter that all is well, they desire no more. I learn, tho' not from Correa himself,[3] that he thinks of paying us a visit as soon as he is through his course of lectures. not to lose this happiness again by my absence, I have informed him I shall set out for Poplar Forest about the 20th inst. and be back the first week of July. I wish you and he could concert your movements so as to meet here, and that you would make this your head quarters. it is a good central point from which to visit your connections; and you know our practice of placing our guests at their ease, by shewing them we are so ourselves, & that we follow our necessary vocations, instead of fatiguing them by hanging unremittingly on their shoulders. I salute you with affectionate esteem and respect. TH: JEFFERSON

RC (CLU-C); at foot of first page: "Francis W. Gilmer esq." PoC (DLC). Enclosure: essay by François Quesnay enclosed in Pierre Samuel Du Pont de Nemours to TJ, 12 May 1816.

[1] Manuscript: "in-which."

[2] Word interlined in place of "principles."

[3] Inconsistent closing parenthesis editorially changed to a comma.

From Hugh Nelson

SIR, Belvoir June 7th

During the late session of Congress, there was committed to my Care for you, the small package herwith Sent, and addressed to you—by a Senator of the U.S—On leaving the City this package was put up in my Trunk and brought by me to Fredericksburg—There changing my route to the lower Country instead of coming directly home, I entrusted the Trunk to an agent who was to forward it as soon as he coud conveniently—The Trunk was not brought home until the last Evening—I therefore hasten to forward it immediately to you—I also send a small parcel for Your daughter Mrs Randolph which was committed to my Care at Washington—this being put up in my Trunk, did not get to hand until yesterday with my Baggage—This will account for my Seeming inattention to these commissions—Accept assurances of my high Consideration HUGH NELSON

RC (DLC: TJ Papers, 207:36920); partially dated; endorsed by TJ as a letter of 7 June 1816 received one day later and so recorded in SJL.

The SMALL PACKAGE sent to TJ by an unnamed United States senator may have included Hosea Humphrey to TJ, 31 Dec. 1815, and its enclosures, which reached TJ the same day as this letter. The PARCEL conveyed to Martha Jefferson Randolph has not been identified.

To Patrick Gibson

Dear Sir Monticello June 8. 16.

In July last you were so kind as to remit for me to John Vaughan 550.D. this was for wines and books I ordered from Marseilles, Leghorn & Paris. these articles are just now beginning to arrive in different ports of the US. 2. boxes (one containing wine) which had arrived from Marseilles in Philadelphia were shipped by the Collector from thence the 2^d^ instant, consigned to you. 4. other boxes have arrived at Alexandria from the same place, and are by this time shipped for Richm^d^. one more parcel is still expected from thence, one from Leghorn, & some packages of books from Paris. there will be duties & port charges on each, for remittances of which I shall be obliged to trouble you. for the parcel from Philadelphia there is due 16. D 80 C which I must pray you to have paid to John Steele Collector of that port, and at the same time 31.D. to Nicholas G. Dufief, bookseller at that place, who being about to go to France, I wish him to be paid before his departure. for the parcels still expected, I will, in like manner, as they shall be made known to me communicate to you with a request to have them paid. I should wish these parcels to be sent up by Johnson or Gilmer, & to be trusted to no other person. by Johnson, who will be down in a few days, I shall be obliged to you to send me a hogshead of Molasses. I shall go to Bedford within a fortnight & be absent three weeks. I salute you with affectionate esteem & respect. Th: Jefferson

PoC (DLC: TJ Papers, ser. 10); on verso of reused address cover of Albert Gallatin to TJ, 1 Apr. 1816; at foot of text: "Mr Gibson"; endorsed by TJ.

To Joseph Darmsdatt

Dear Sir Monticello June 9. 16.

I understand you have on hand a good supply of excellent fish. I will therefore pray you to send me my annual supply which is of 6. barrels of herrings to Lynchburg to the care of mr Archib^d^ Robertson, and 6. barrels of herrings, and one of shad to this place, which mr Johnston a boatman of Milton will call on you for within a few days. the immediate dispatch of those to Lynchburg is of importance that they may have them for their harvest. I ask nothing about price, confident you will charge me as you do others who like myself pay sooner or later as they can. with my best wishes for your health accept the assurance of my great esteem and respect. Th: Jefferson

PoC (MHi); on verso of a portion of a reused address cover from George Logan to TJ; at foot of text: "Mr Darmsdatt"; endorsed by TJ.

TJ did not PAY for the fish until the following May, when he ordered another thirteen barrels (TJ to Darmsdatt, 7 May 1817; TJ to Daniel Call, 13 May 1820).

To Nicolas G. Dufief

DEAR SIR Monticello June 9. 16.

Your favor of May 27. is but just now come to hand, and I write this day to request messrs Gibson & Jefferson to remit you from Richmond 31.D. the amount of the books, in the hope you may recieve it before your departure for France should you definitively decide to go. Mckay's two volumes are recieved. Accept my best wishes for a pleasant and safe voyage & return, with the assurance of my great esteem & respect TH: JEFFERSON

PoC (DLC); on verso of reused address cover of Gideon Fitz to TJ, 20 Mar. 1816; at foot of text: "Mr Dufief"; endorsed by TJ.

Not on THIS DAY but the previous one, TJ made his REQUEST for a remittance to Dufief (TJ to Patrick Gibson, 8 June 1816).

From Hugh Nelson

SIR, June 9th 1816. Belvoir

This will be presented to you by Mr Kingsberry who is about entering on the laudable pursuit of imparting to our Indian Brethren, such portion of civilized improvement as he may find them calculated to receive, and circumstances may enable him to bestow—To you it is only necessary to communicate his object, to ensure your aid and advice—Nothing can hereafter, in the page of the Historian, throw more light on a life devoted to the Good of your Country, than the undeviating and philanthropic zeal which has ever distinguished your course towards the untutored Man of the Wilderness—

With high Consideration I am yr hule st HUGH NELSON

RC (DLC); endorsed by TJ as received 10 June 1816 and so recorded in SJL, which adds that it was delivered "by mr Kingsberry."

Cyrus Kingsbury (1786–1870), Congregational clergyman and missionary, was born in Alstead, New Hampshire. After graduating from Brown University in 1812, he entered Andover Theological Seminary that same year. On 29 Sept. 1815 Kingsbury was ordained at Ipswich, Massachusetts, and shortly thereafter he was commissioned to serve as a missionary in Tennessee. Early in 1816 he spent time in Washington, where he conferred with Secretary of War William H. Crawford and obtained a commitment of federal support for missionary efforts to convert and "civilize" Native Americans. By

3 Aug. Kingsbury was in Tennessee arranging to set up a mission station among the Cherokee Indians, and early the following year he opened the Brainerd School near Chattanooga. In 1818 he was sent to work with the Choctaw Nation in western Mississippi. When the administration of President Andrew Jackson had many Native Americans expelled from the eastern United States, Kingsbury followed the Choctaw westward and eventually established a new mission in 1836 at Pine Ridge in present-day Oklahoma, where he remained until his death (Arminta Scott Spalding, "Cyrus Kingsbury: Missionary to the Choctaws" [Ph.D. diss., University of Oklahoma, 1974]; William G. McLoughlin, *Cherokees and Missionaries, 1789–1839* [1984]; Clara Sue Kidwell, *Choctaws and Missionaries in Mississippi, 1818–1918* [1995]; Andover Theological Seminary, Society of Inquiry Respecting Missions, *Memoirs of American Missionaries* [1833], 41, 164–6; Arthur H. DeRosier Jr., "Cyrus Kingsbury—Missionary to the Choctaws," *Journal of Presbyterian History* 50 [1972]: 267–87; *Historical Catalogue of Brown University, 1764–1904* [1905], 109; *ASP, Indian Affairs*, 2:477–8; Boston *Recorder*, 24 Sept. 1816).

In a memoir dated 4 May 1869, Kingsbury recalled that during his 1816 visit to Monticello he discussed the "condition and prospect of the colored people" in a "brief conversation" with TJ, whom he quoted as saying that "I had hoped the present Generation would take some measures in relation to this Subject, but I now despair of it untill they are compelled to do Something" (MS in OkHi: Sue L. McBeth Collection; in an unidentified hand).

To John Steele

Monticello June 9. 16.

Your favor of the 1st instant is just now recieved, and I have immediately requested messrs Gibson & Jefferson, my correspondents at Richmond, to remit you the sum of 16.80 D the amount of the duties & charges on the two cases you have been so kind as to forward for me to them; which sum[1] they will readily find the means of remitting from that place. Accept my thanks for your kindness and the assurance of my great esteem & respect Th: Jefferson

PoC (MHi); on verso of reused cover of an otherwise unidentified account of David Higginbotham with TJ; at foot of text: "Mr John Steele"; endorsed by TJ.

[1] TJ here canceled "you."

From William Thornton

Dear sir City of Washington 9th June 1816.—

I have received your very friendly Letter, & I really feel ashamed at putting you to the necessity of writing for the Paintings you were so kind as to lend me to copy;—but still more so to offer any apology for not immediately sending them: however I must do it, for they are yet here. The Head by Stewart I really think one of the finest I ever saw,

& having commenced it, I was in hopes of finishing it before the departure of the President & his Lady, & of sending it by them or M[r] Todd, but my public Duties are so oppressive in consequence of the long sickness and inability of my Clerk to render me any aid that I have not finished it, and after keeping it so long I should feel like a sinner for leaving the work undone, and I mean to dedicate every spare moment to it till I make it worthy of the original if possible.—I should be very sorry to delay the work of M[r] Delaplaine: but in his return if he will favor me with his Company he can make a Copy of it here before it be sent back, and examine mine. I hope to be able to get it modelled hereafter, & it is therefore necessary to equal the original if possible. I shall afterwards seek for such an opportunity of sending them as will ensure their safety.—

We had not the pleasure of seeing your charming & accomplished Grand Daughter in her return.—I know that she had made several Conquests before she left Washington, & if she keep a list of the dying & wounded I query whether she will not soon equal Gen[l] Jackson's.—She is very much admired, & very much beloved—she could not be otherwise, being handsome, accomplished & very amiable.—

I am, dear Sir, with the highest respect, consideration, & esteem Yours very sincerely &[c] William Thornton—

RC (MHi); endorsed by TJ as received 17 June 1816 and so recorded in SJL. RC (MHi); address cover only; with PoC of TJ to Thomas Eston Randolph, 21 June 1816, on verso; addressed: "Hon-or[ble] Thomas Jefferson Monticello Virg[a]"; franked; postmarked Washington City, 10 June.

From Dabney C. Terrell

Dear Sir Geneva. June. 12th 1816.

It would be ill repaying the interest you have taken[1] in me were I not to inform you of my prospects, now that I have arrived at the place of my destination. I believe I wrote you from Baltimore that as there was no vessel in that port sailing for any part of France, I had taken my passage to Amsterdam. I remained in Holland and the Pays-Bas about three week. At the Hague I met with M[r] Eustis, the American Embassidor, from whom I experienced every attention during the few days that I was there. I afterwards saw him and M[rs] Eustis at Paris, where I left them. After leaving Brussels[2] I proceeded directly to Paris, where I arrived the 1st of May. I immediately presented the letters which you had been so good as to give me to Mr. Warden and D[r] Jackson. Both of these gentlemen were extremely attentive to me. M[r] Warden took a fatherly care of me; he indicated and conducted me to whatever he considered most worthy of observation in this famous capital. I remained a month there. In all this time my advancement in speaking French was scarcely perceptible; but since I have been here it surpasses my most sanguine expectations. The day after my arrival I presented your letter to M[r] Pictet He immediately arranged every thing for me; and with respect to the studies that I shall pursue he thinks I can enter a class which will take the degree of A.M. in two years. They have nothing more to do with the classics. The studies of the class will be confined chiefly to moral and natural philosophy and the mathematics. I know nothing of philosophy and in this respect I am on an equality with the rest who are just entering this department. I believe I am somewhat more advanced in mathematics than they are, and this may perhaps give me time to compleat my knowledge of the Latin and to learn the Greek; in which case I will graduate at the same [time?][3] that the class does; and if I cannot do it the time will at all events have been well employed. It is with the deepest[4] regret that I have read some articles in the Moniteur which arrived[5] here this evening. If all that I see there be true the cause of the Patriots both in Mexico and South America is totally lost. But I still hope that the report of a Spanish General which is found among other things, on the same subject has either been writen at Madrid or that it is much exaggerated by the General himself. If the war in Mexico is prolonged untill I leave Europe I shall repair there immediately on my arrival in America. I should like very much to spend 8 or 9 months in Spain and above all at Madrid if that would be practicable.

Perhaps M[r] Pictet will write by the same opportunity[6] that I do. Pray, Sir, present my best respects to M[rs] Randolph and the rest of the family, and believe me ever

Sir, ever, your most grateful and obedient[7] servant

DABNEY C. TERRELL

P.S. I have waited several days for M[r] Pictet to write, but as he has not done it yet I dispatch this. DCT.

RC (ViU: TJP-CC); endorsed by TJ as received 12 Aug. 1816 and so recorded in SJL. RC (ViU: TJP-ER); address cover only; with PoC of TJ to John Bankhead, 14 Oct. 1816, on verso; addressed: "Thomas Jefferson Esq. Monticello Virginia"; with notes by John A. Morton: "Rec[d] & forw[d] Bord[x] 25th June 1816, by Your ob[t] Serv[t] John A. Morton" and "Sch[r] Spartan via New York"; stamped "SHIP"; franked; postmarked New York, 7 Aug.

PAYS-BAS: literally "Low Countries," the name given to a region consisting of the modern nations of Belgium, Luxembourg, and the Netherlands (*The New Pocket Dictionary of the French and English Languages* [New York, 1817], 120; *OED*).

[1] Preceding three words interlined.
[2] Manuscript: "Brusses."
[3] Omitted word editorially supplied.
[4] Manuscript: "depeepest."
[5] Manuscript: "arriveded."
[6] Manuscript: "opportuni-."
[7] Manuscript: "obdient."

From Benjamin W. Crowninshield

SIR, Navy Department June 13th 1816.

In compliance with your request by letter of the 30th January last, I now have the pleasure to inform you I have transmitted a Midshipman's Warrant to Mr Thomas M. Randolph, being one of the first issued since that date.

I should be happy at the same time to order Mr Randolph into service, but the present state of our Navy affords employment to a few only of our numerous Officers of this grade. His wishes in this respect will be favorably considered, when occasion shall present of giving him orders for active service.

Permit me Sir, to tender you the assurances of my unfeigned, and most cordial respect. B W CROWNINSHIELD

RC (DLC); in a clerk's hand, signed by Crowninshield; at foot of text in clerk's hand: "Mr Jefferson"; endorsed by TJ as received 19 June 1816 and so recorded in SJL. FC (Lb in DNA: RG 45, LSNO).

From "Henry Tompkinson" (Samuel Kercheval)

SIR N. T. Stephensg 13th June 1816

Altho I have not the honor of being personally known to you, and it is more than probable I never shall, You will have the goodness to pardon the liberty I have taken, of enclosing to you a pamphlet I have lately publishd; shewing the necesity of calling a convention for the revision and amendment of our State constitution.

This subject excites considerable interest in this section of the State, and I trust will draw the attention of our eminent men, in every quarter of the Commonwealth—Will you pardon me Sir for requesting that you will favor me with your opinion of the merits and demerits of the work enclosed for your inspection.

I have the honor to be Sir Your Most Obt Svt

H. TOMPKINSON

RC (DLC); addressed: "The Honble Thomas Jefferson Monticello"; endorsed by TJ as a letter from "Tompkinson H." received 19 June 1816 from "Newtown Stephensbg. Frederick" and so recorded in SJL, which adds that Tompkinson was a pseudonym for Samuel Kercheval. Enclosure: [Kercheval], *Letters addressed to the people of Virginia showing the necessity of Immediately calling a convention for the revision and amendment of our state constitution. By Henry Tompkinson, a citizen of Virginia* (Winchester, 1816), not found (Virginia State Library, *A Record of Virginia Copyright Entries [1790–1844]* [1911], 18).

Newtown (N. T.) and Stephensburg (STEPHENS[G]) either separately or together are variant names for present-day Stephens City in Frederick County (Garland R. Quarles and Lewis N. Barton, eds., *What I Know About Winchester: Recollections of William Greenway Russell 1800–1891* [1953], 179; Linden A. Fravel and Byron C. Smith, *Stephens City* [2008], 7–8, 30).

To Hosea Humphrey

SIR Monticello June 15. 16.

I recieved exactly a week ago your favor of Dec. 31. which may explain the tardy date of this acknolegement, and of my thanks for the copy of your Inquiries concerning the laws of nature, which accompanied it. on these you ask my observations, 'as well on their errors, as on what I may approve.' the range of these enquiries takes in the whole field of physics, and also of Medecine and it's kindred sciences. on the last I could offer nothing new to one of the faculty: and as to Physics I percieve that many of the fundamental principles, heretofore supposed established, are deemed erroneous, and others proposed as substitutes. I am an advocate for freedom of challenge of every fact and principle which any one may suspect to be founded in error. one man's opinion being as free as another's, neither is to controul or to be controuled by the other. on the contrary, the freer the enquiry, the more favorable to truth. but when a whole system is proposed to be reformed, the undertaking is for the young, not for the old. the latter have not time to resume their enquiries de novo, and to learn over again all the lessons they have learnt in their preceding life. having once fully enquired, and maturely made up their minds, they must leave to future investigators the advantages of correcting, or of still further advancing the boundaries of science. it has been said, as you know, that no physician in Europe, then 40. years of age, ever became a convert to Harvey's discovery of the circulation of the blood. but I, my good Sir, am 73. I have not then either time or energy enough to undertake the settlement of new questions, or the correction of old ones: and while I give you credit for the freedom &

ingenuity of the ideas I find in your book, I am sure of your permission to leave them to younger & more vigorous minds for scrutiny at the bar of reason & fact. I hope you will be so good as to accept of this apology for my declining to say any thing, yea, or nay, on these profound subjects. On that of the Long talk which accompanied the other publication I am happy to percieve that what has been the creed of my youth, and is now matured by age, has the further sanction of your sentiments, for which, on this as well as the other subjects, I tender you the assurance of my high respect.

TH: JEFFERSON

PoC (DLC); at foot of text: "Doct[r] Hosea Humphrey"; endorsed by TJ.

IT HAS BEEN SAID ... CIRCULATION OF THE BLOOD is paraphrased from David Hume, *The History of England, from the Invasion of Julius Cæsar to The Revolution in 1688* (London, 1790–91, and other eds.; Sowerby, no. 370), 7:347.

From José Corrêa da Serra

DEAR SIR Philadelphia 16. June. 1816

Your kind Letter of the 5 of this month reached me in due time, and i must entreat your forgiveness for not answering it sooner, neither my health, nor the hurry to finish the botanical course in which i was engaged without defrauding my hearers of any of the promised Lectures have given me a moment's rest. Under severe rhumatic pains, i have Lectured almost every day in the afternoon, and gone to the fields in a gig every morning to collect the necessary plants. I feel very sensible to your congratulations, as to every sign of kindness from you, as to the thing itself though i must value it, does not make a great impression on me. It is somewhat Like Persimmon fruit, comes Late, and has been ripened by hard frosts. One of the clear advantages i find in it, is that by keeping me in America, it ensures me a greater number of pilgrimages to Monticello. Three other pocket books of Capt. Lewis have been found among the papers of D[r] Barton, and that was all that existed in the D[rs] hands, but all the remaining papers concerning that expedition i have found deposited with M[r] Nicholas Biddle, who tells me he is ready to give them, on receiving an intimation to do so, from Gen[l] Clarcke from whom he had them. You see that i have done every thing in my power to satisfy your wishes, and you may be sure that will be the case in every occasion to serve you.

Lately, Litterary presents from Paris, after long delays, have at Last reached my hands, in them i have found the prescription of a new impenetrable cement, which i enclose in this Letter. M[r] Blainville has published a Little memoir of ingenious conjectures to show that your Megalonyx is the Grisly Bear of the Missouri. what he says is very cleaver, but not sufficient to bring conviction, and he himself avows it. This memoir is printed in the journal de physique, and is not among the presents i received, otherwise i would have sent it to you. My best respects to M[rs] and Mr Randolph, and souvenirs to all your family. I expect to be able to renovate them personally in a few weeks.

I remain with the highest esteem and respect

Most sincerely yours J. Corrèa de Serra

RC (DLC); endorsed by TJ as received 10 July 1816 and so recorded in SJL. RC (DLC); address cover only; with PoC of TJ to Joseph Milligan, 8 Sept. 1816, on recto; addressed: "Thomas Jefferson Esqr Monticello Albemarle C[ty] Virginia"; franked; postmarked Philadelphia, 19 June.

The enclosed PRESCRIPTION OF A NEW IMPENETRABLE CEMENT has not been identified. For cement recipes received from Corrêa, see his letter to TJ of 12 Feb. 1816 and note. Henri Marie Ducrotay de BLAINVILLE commented on the megalonyx in "Note sur l'ours gris d'Amérique" and "Des Fossiles," *Journal de Physique, de Chimie, d'Historie Naturelle et des Arts* 81 (1815): 416–9; 82 (1816): 34–5. SOUVENIRS is French for "regards; recalling to one's memory." RENOVATE: "to renew; resume" (*OED*).

From John Meer

Sir Philadelphia June 18th 1816

I have taken the liberty to enclose you a coppy of my Bank Note, Which I believe to be superiour in many respects to any other hitherto used. It is engraved on a Steel plate (mostly with a Hair pencil) It will print ten times more coppies than any copper plate, and will come at the same price of copper plates in general made for Bank notes. This mode of work produces great strength and richnes of colouring, and a boldnes of expression not to be obtained by any other means, yet the most delicate tints may be produced; and it is susceptible of an infinite variety of pattern and design. This invention is most likely to secure Bank Notes and all kinds of Official and confidential papers from forgery.

I shall be happy to supply any of the Governmental departments, and the Bank with plates.

If you will favour me with your recommendation you will confer a great obligation

On Sir Your's Most Respectfully John Meer

This specimen is not sent as a highly finished work of the artist, but to show the principle of the invention you will see by this first and hasty specimen,[1] that it is capable of very great improvement in the execution, I wish to have an opportunity of exemplifying this assertion.

RC (CSmH: JF-BA); adjacent to signature: "Thos Jefferson"; endorsed by TJ as received 18 July 1817 but correctly recorded a year previously in SJL.

John Meer (1756–1831), artist and inventor, immigrated to the United States from his native Wolverhampton, England. By 1790 he had settled in Philadelphia, where in 1798 he became a naturalized citizen. In 1795 Meer exhibited flowers painted on the back of glass and five flower pieces "in imitation of Enamel." He served as the president of the Society of Artists and Manufacturers in 1804, and in 1813 both he and TJ were incorporators of the Columbian Society of Artists, formerly the Society of Artists of the United States. Meer was the regulator of weights and measures for Philadelphia, 1809–18, and in 1812 he contracted to paint canteens and knapsacks for the United States Army. He received a patent in 1815 for graphic plates used for banknotes and another in 1818 for an improvement in bookbinding. Meer also developed a type of kaleidoscope by 1819, created a chemical process to harden argillaceous stone for use in sharpening razors and other cutting instruments in 1823, and improved varnishes used in japanning (Groce and Wallace, *Dictionary of Artists*, 437; P. William Filby, ed., *Philadelphia Naturalization Records* [1982], 461; *The Exhibition of the Columbianum or American Academy of Painting, Sculpture, Architecture, &c.* [Philadelphia, 1795], nos. 55, 56; Cornelius William Stafford, *The Philadelphia Directory for 1798* [Philadelphia, 1798], 98; Philadelphia *Aurora General Advertiser*, 31 Mar. 1804; Philadelphia *Tickler*, 24 May 1809; Thomas Sully to TJ, 22 Dec. 1811, and note; *Acts of the General Assembly of the Commonwealth of Pennsylvania* [Philadelphia, 1813], 73–6; *Kite's Philadelphia Directory for 1814* [Philadelphia, 1814]; John Adems Paxton, *The Philadelphia Directory and Register, for 1818* [Philadelphia, 1818]; John Armstrong, *Letter from the Secretary of War, transmitting A Statement of the Contracts which have been made during the year 1812* [Washington, 1813]; *List of Patents*, 153, 194; *City of Washington Gazette*, 16 Jan. 1819; *Boston Daily Advertiser*, 21 Aug. 1822; Washington *Daily National Intelligencer*, 23 July 1823; Thomas P. Jones, "On Japanning and Varnishing," *Franklin Journal, and American Mechanics' Magazine* 2 [1826]: 32; gravestone inscription in Norris Stanley Barratt, *Outline of the History of Old St. Paul's Church Philadelphia, Pennsylvania* [1917], 250–1).

[1] Manuscript: "speimen."

ENCLOSURE

John Meer's Sample Banknote

[ca. 18 June 1816]

Engraving (CSmH: JF-BA); undated.

From Thomas Eston Randolph

DEAR SIR Ashton 18th June 1816

As I am prevented from riding, by indisposition, I beg leave to enclose the agreement between yourself and T. M. and T. E. Randolph respecting the lease of Shadwell Mill—and will thank you to state therein, that the Rent for the ensuing year is payable in flour—This is only necessary in consequence of my having made arrangements with a very good Miller to give him an interest in the business instead of paying him wages—and it is my wish that he understands perfectly the nature of my obligations to you respecting the Rent—Permit me also to suggest to you, that it has frequently happen'd that we have not begun to grind 'till late in Septr and we rarely have water to carry produce to market before the month of December, under those circumstances it would be impossible for me to comply with that part of the agreement stipulating for the Flour to be deliver'd or paid quarterly—if therefore you will make 113⅓ barrels of Flour payable at the end of 6 months, say the 1st Jany 1817—the remaining 100 barrels shall be paid to suit your convenience and in any event I will promise to pay it in due time—

I am with great respect and afft regards Yrs

THOS ESTON RANDOLPH

RC (MHi); dateline beneath signature; addressed: "Thomas Jefferson Esqre"; endorsed by TJ as received 18 June 1816 and so recorded in SJL. Enclosure not found.

The VERY GOOD MILLER was Daniel Colclaser (Randolph to TJ, 4 Mar. 1817; TJ to Colclaser, 8 Aug. 1817).

To Thomas Eston Randolph

DEAR SIR Monticello June 18. 16.

I have subjoined to the lease an acknolegement that the rent of the next year is payable in flour as you desired. I wish I could, even by possibility postpone the October payment to January. but I shall not have one Dollar through the remainder of this year but the rent of the mill, having exhausted all other funds, even of credit, in the purchase of corn, and oats, by the total failure of my overseers both here & in Bedford the last year, and I have more still to buy. I hope I shall not live to see such another year. but I trust you will find no difficulty in delivering the 1st quarter's rent at the mill, and I will see to the getting it down.

The balance of rent to Apr. 1. since you rendered the account is by subsequent credits reduced to 63.54 D to wit

		D
Balance as stated in your account		299.16½
By corn from Carlton on acct of T M Randolph	122.50	
my order in favor of Fagg	53.12½	
cash recd from Th: J. Randolph on your account	60.	
balance remaining due	63.54	299.16½

Of that which will be due July 1st Th: J. Randolph advanced me 240.D. on your account, for which I gave him an order on you payable Sep. 1. so that there will be due for this quarter but 80.D. more. ever & affectionately your's TH: JEFFERSON

P.S. I set out for Bedford on Saturday next.

PoC (MHi); on verso of reused address cover to TJ; postscript adjacent to signature; at foot of text: "Thomas E. Randolph esq."; endorsed by TJ.

From Benjamin Waterhouse

SIR— Cambridge, 18th June, 1816

Finding that Mesrs. Rowe & Hooper are about sending you a copy of "a Journal of a young man of Massachusetts," who was captured by the British, and confined during the war, at Halifax, at Chatham, and at Dartmoor, I cannot refrain, because I think it is proper, giving you more information relative to its publication than what appears on the face of the book—

This smart young man put his manuscript Journal into my hands, when I questioned him on each and every part of it, and felt satisfied of its authenticity. At his request, and at the request of the printers, I undertook to prepare this narrative for the eye of the American and British[1] public. The raw material is here worked up into one uniform warp, woof and coloring; making, I hope, no bad specimen of American manufacture. Or to change the figure, the young surgeon brought me all the stones and the bricks, while I designed, and built up the structure, finding the mortar or connecting material. Alexander Selkirk, who resided several years on a desert Island, put his manuscript into the hands of the famous Dan[l] De Foe, who out of it made the renowned history of Robinson Crusoe: This book may in some measure resemble it, provided De Foe never suppressed, or added any important facts. I believe every representation in this little book to be true; but the painter, aiming to make an agreeable picture, has used a free and rapid brush, which, now and then betrays marks of an incorrect manner, without ever once violating the truth of the story.

This production was the amusement of my lonesome evenings the past winter; and was sent to the press without ever reviewing a paragraph or line of it.

Sentiments of respect, and ideas of propriety forbad me to allow the book to be presented to you, without this explanation; although the public have no idea of the painter.

I remain, dear sir, with a high degree of respect, your obedient servant.

BENJ[N] WATERHOUSE

RC (DLC); in an unidentified hand, signed by Waterhouse; at foot of text in Waterhouse's hand: "Honorable Tho[s] Jefferson"; endorsed by TJ as received 10 July 1816 and so recorded in SJL.

The book being sent to TJ by the Boston publishing firm of ROWE & HOOPER was Waterhouse, ed., *A Journal, of a Young Man of Massachusetts, late a surgeon on board an American privateer, who was captured at sea by the British, in May, Eighteen Hundred and Thirteen, and was confined first, at Melville Island, Halifax, then at Chatham, in England, and Last, at Dartmoor Prison. Interspersed with Observations, Anecdotes and Remarks, Tending to Illustrate the Moral and Political Characters of Three Nations. To which is added, A Correct Engraving of Dartmoor Prison, representing the massacre of American prisoners. Written by Himself* (Boston, 1816). The SMART YOUNG MAN who wrote this journal was probably Amos G. Babcock, surgeon of the privateer schooner *Enterprise* at the time of its capture by British warships in May 1813 (Henry R. Viets, "'A Journal of a Young Man of Massachusetts . . . written by Himself.' Boston: 1816, and a Note on the Author," *Yale Journal of Biology and Medicine* 12 [1980]: 605–22, esp. 608–9).

Waterhouse apparently reconsidered his decision against REVIEWING A PARAGRAPH OR LINE of the *Journal*, because a second edition he published in Boston later in 1816 contained "considerable Additions and Improvements."

[1] Preceding two words interlined.

From Stephen Cathalan

DEAR SIR Marseilles the 19th June 1816—

What Preceeds is a Copy of my last Respects of the 4th Inst by the Ship Lothair of norfolk;[1]

I have now the honor of Informing you that on the 4th Inst I have Shipped on the Brig Ocean of New york Capn Nel S. Bond[2]—

Two Cases of 12 Bottles Each Red wine of Paillerols,

& 1 Basket Maccaroni

& on the 14th Inst on the Brig General Marion of new york[3]

one Box Containing 30 Bottles Red Wine of Lédenon.[4]

Both vessels Sailed[5] the next morning after I had Shipped Said Wine & maccaroni, which prevented me of Informing you, by the Same of opportunity I have Consigned them to the Collector of the District of new-york, where Bound for, to be forwarded to you by him, as you will observe it by the Inclosed Bills of Lading;

The quality of the wine of Paillerols is not yet Generaly known, but I Beg your Refference to the Printed Paper inserted in the Said cases,

as to the wine of Lédenon, it is from a Vilage at 3[6] miles distant of the famous, antic, Pont du Gard,[7] about 11 Miles from nismes, going to the Pont du Snt Esprit Route du Bas Languedoc to Lyon, Paris &a you tasted of that Sort of wine at dinner at my house in the year 1787—which I called vin de ma Tante, as the Sister of my Father had the best vin[e]yards, on that Cottage,[8] & when alive, used to Send yearly Some for our own use; you found it Good & being more Liquoreux[9] than the Claret, I had; you Preffer[e]d it to the vin de Bordeaux I had;—She Died in the year 1794—at 88. of age! by which Event, we lost with her our yearly Stock of this wine, her landed Property was Sold, & now[10] one Mr Tourneyzon a Switz who has Purchased Some vineyards at Lédenon, has established there un choix, & purchases the 1st qualities of the wines of Lédenon;[11] it is then from him, that I have procured that wine, mentioning that I wanted the Best & Genuine as it was for you;[12] hoping he has (tho' wine's Sellers[13] are not Generaly to be trusted, many being Called Monsieur Melange,) Served me faithfully & being encouraged, as well as the owner of the vineyards of Paillerols, that if those wines, Proves Satisfactory to your Palate, they will be demanded by the Connoisseurs of the united States,

I beg you to accept These Two Samples of wine, to be drinked with your family & Friends, if it turns out to your Taste.

In Talking about wines with you, you remember, I dare Say, of the Famous choix of Mr henry Bergasse at Marseilles, where we dinned together in 87—he Left this Place Soon after the 23[d] april 1789—when the Populace of Marseilles, Rised a Riot on that Day,[14] asking to the Mayor & aldermans[15] of this City to Lower the Pr[i]ce of Bread at 2 Sols, Fresh Beef & mouton at 6 Sols P[r] ℔. & Wine at 4 Sols p[r] bot; Pretending that Since Bergasse had emproved the quality of the wines of Proven[c]e, very near as good as Bordeaux claret,[16] they had too much risen in Price, & they Threatned to distroy his choix; it was fortunately preserved, but he never Returned here, & died Some years ago at Lyons; other Wine's merchants purchased his Large Casks, & his Branch of Commerce to which this Country is endebted to him has Since much encreased;—his Son who had under his tuition Continued in that Branch at Lyons, has Risen Such an Stablishment here, & has rented 18 months ago my own house for 6 years where I Lodged in the year 1787—the Same you visited with Whare houses adjacents to it for that Purpose; he will Soon have old Wine, that quality is well known in the united States, where it is Drunk as Claret, it Cost here only one Frank per Bottle, Box included, Three Years old.—

I will Ship the[17] wine of Roussillon as Soon as it will Reach me, & Send you it's Invoice.

The Basket Maccaroni ammounts to *f*35– to your Debit.

I am allways at your Commands & with Great Respect Dear sir your most obed[t] & Devoted Serv[t] STEPHEN CATHALAN.

Th[s] Jefferson Esq[r] to Stephen Cathalan	Deb[or]
for 1 Basket Maccarony by the Brig ocean Bound for New-York as p[r] Bill of Lading of the 4th June 1816[18]	
Weighing ℔ 54 net[19] at *f*55– p[r] quintal[20]	F 29–70
Canvas, Packing, Portering, Custom's Duty & Craftage on Board[21]	5–30
	F 35–

RC (MHi); damaged at fold, with obscured letters supplied from Dupl; subjoined to Dupl of Cathalan to TJ, 4 June 1816; notation by TJ perpendicular to postscript: "Maccaroni 54. ℔ cost 35 fr which is .18 cents p[r] ℔"; endorsed by TJ as received 28 Aug. 1816 and so recorded in SJL. Dupl (MHi); at head of text: "Copy 2[ta]"; at foot of first page: "Tho[s] Jefferson Esq[r] &[ca] &[ca] Monticello"; endorsed by TJ as a "Duplicate" received 16 Oct. 1816; enclosed in Cathalan to TJ, 12 July 1816. Enclosures not found.

David Gelston was the COLLECTOR at New York City. LIQUOREUX: "liqueur-like; sweet and strong." UN CHOIX: "a selection of the best." MONSIEUR MELANGE: "Mr. Blending." TJ visited Henri Joachim BERGASSE in 1787 during a tour of southern France and northern Italy (*PTJ*, 11:428).

[1] Dupl here adds "Cap[n] John Stone."

[2] Dupl here adds "Master" and "**B TJ** N[o] 1 & 2."

[3] Dupl here adds "Ruben Brumley Master."

[4] Dupl adds to left of this line "C N[o] 1."

[5] Dupl here adds "for new York."

[6] Dupl: "5."

[7] Dupl here adds "an aquedut & Bridge built by the Romans."

[8] RC: "Cotage." Dupl: "Cottage."

[9] Dupl: "having more Liquour or Sprit."

[10] Preceding seven words replaced in Dupl with "We having not Inherited of that Property it has been Sold (& out of my Family) to."

[11] Preceding ten words not in Dupl.

[12] Dupl here adds "who had Long Since tasted it."

[13] RC: "Salers." Dupl: "Sellers."

[14] Dupl here adds "(which was the 1st Spark, which Set in Fire the Revolution all over France &[ca])."

[15] Preceding two words interlined.

[16] Dupl here adds "by their great Consomption a Broad."

[17] Dupl here adds "2[d] B[el] of."

[18] In Dupl, postscript to this point reads "The 4th June 1816 Invoice of one Baskett Containing Maccaroni Shipped on Board the Brig ocean of New York Nath[el] Smith Bond Master, to be Consigned to the Collector of the District of New-York, to be forwarded to Tho[s] Jefferson Esq[r] at Monticello being by his order, for his Account & Risk viz—."

[19] Dupl here adds "ancient Marseilles Weight."

[20] Dupl: "100 lb."

[21] Adjacent to this line on Dupl TJ wrote ".12 p[r] ℔."

From Nicolas G. Dufief

MONSIEUR, A Philadelphie ce 19 Juin 1816

J'ai été très-sensible à l'attention que vous avez eu d'écrire à Richmond pour qu'on me fit passer la petite somme de 31 d[lls] afin que je la reçusse avant mon départ pour France. Je me flatte toujours d'avoir le temps de vous demander vos ordres. Le 3ème et d[er] volume du dictionnaire a été mis à la poste Samedi 15 du c[t]. Ainsi, J'espère que vous avez tout l'ouvrage à présent & que vous êtes content de la reliûre

J'ai l'honneur d'être Monsieur, très-respectueusement Votre très-dévoué Serviteur N. G. DUFIEF

EDITORS' TRANSLATION

SIR, Philadelphia 19 June 1816

I was very touched by the care you took in writing to Richmond to have the small sum of 31 dollars forwarded to me so that I would receive it prior to my departure for France. I flatter myself that I always have time to call for your orders. The third and final volume of the dictionary was put in the mail on Saturday, the fifteenth of this month. Therefore, I hope you are now in possession of the entire work and that you are happy with the binding

I have the honor to be Sir, very respectfully your very devoted servant

N. G. DUFIEF

RC (DLC); endorsed by TJ as received 10 July 1816 and so recorded in SJL. Translation by Dr. Genevieve Moene.

TJ's communication to RICHMOND was his letter to Patrick Gibson of 8 June 1816.

To Joseph Story

Monticello. June 19. 16.

I thank you, dear Sir, for the eulogy of mr Dexter, which you have been so kind as to send me; and I subscribe with sincerity to the testimonies it bears of his merits. no one rendered more justice to his virtues & talents than myself; and if, in political matters we entertained some differences of opinion, they were on both sides the result of honest conviction, and held by both as inoffensive as differences of feature. his loss was a real affliction to the friends of our Union; & especially at a crisis when a successor was in question to the important magistracy for which he was proposed. I am fond however of believing that the majority with you will still return to the sacred principle of fidelity to the union, and will see in the duties which he would have inculcated their own most important interests. Accept the assurance of my great esteem and respect.

Th: Jefferson

PoC (MHi); on verso of a reused address cover from Joseph Milligan to TJ; at foot of text: "The honble Judge Story"; endorsed by TJ.

Samuel Dexter (1761–1816), attorney and public official, was a native of Boston who studied law after graduating from Harvard University in 1781. He sat in the Massachusetts House of Representatives, 1788–90, the United States House of Representatives, 1793–95, and the United States Senate, 1799–1800. In the final year of John Adams's presidency, Dexter served successively as secretary of war and secretary of the treasury. He was prominent in the legal profession and frequently argued before the United States Supreme Court. Dexter supported the War of 1812 even though he opposed the Embargo and Nonintercourse acts adopted during TJ's administration. He ran unsuccessfully for governor of Massachusetts as a Republican in 1814, 1815, and 1816. Dexter died during a visit to Athens, New York (*DAB*; Story, *Sketch of the Life of Samuel Dexter, LL. D.* [Boston, 1816; Poor, *Jefferson's Library*, 5 (no. 163)]; *PTJ*, 33:24; Boston *Independent Chronicle*, 17 Feb. 1814; Boston *Repertory*, 28 Feb. 1815; Boston *Recorder*, 14 Feb. 1816; Hudson, N.Y., *Northern Whig*, 7 May 1816).

To William H. Crawford

Dear Sir Monticello June 20. 16.

I am about to sin against all discretion, and knowingly, by adding to the drudgery of your letter-reading, this acknolegement of the reciept of your favor of May 31. with the papers it covered. I cannot however deny my self the gratification of expressing the satisfaction I have recieved, not only from the general statement of affairs at Paris, in your's of Dec. 12. 14. (as a matter of history which I had not before recieved) but most especially and superlatively, from the perusal of your letter of the 8th of the same month to mr Fisk, on the subject of draw backs. this most heterogeneous principle was transplanted into ours from the British system, by a man whose mind was really powerful, but chained by native partialities to every thing English: who had formed exaggerated ideas of the superior perfection of the English constitution, the superior wisdom of their government; and sincerely believed it for the good of this country to make them their model in every thing: without considering that what might be wise and good for a nation essentially commercial, and entangled in complicated intercourse with numerous and powerful neighbors, might not be so for one essentially agricultural, & insulated by nature from the abusive governments of the old world. the exercise by our own citizens of so much commerce as may suffice to exchange our superfluities, for our wants, may be advantageous for the whole. but it does not follow that, with a territory so boundless, it is the interest of the whole to become a mere city of London, to carry on the business of one half the world at the expence of eternal war with the other half. the agricultural capacities of our country constitute it's distinguishing feature: and the adapting our policy & pursuits to that, is more likely to make us a numerous and happy people than the mimicry of an Amsterdam, a Hamburg, or a city of London. every society has a right to fix the fundamental principles of it's association, & to say to all individuals that, if they contemplate pursuits beyond the limits of these principles, and involving dangers which the society chuses to avoid, they must go somewhere else for their exercise; that we want no citizens, & still less ephemeral & Pseudo-citizens on such terms. we may exclude them from our territory, as we do persons infected with disease. such is the situation of our country. we have most abundant resources of happiness within ourselves, which we may enjoy in peace and safety, without permitting a few citizens, infected with the Mania of rambling & gambling, to bring danger on the great mass engaged in innocent and safe pursuits at home. in your letter to Fisk, you have fairly stated the alternatives between which we are to chuse; 1. licentious commerce, & gambling speculations for a few, with eternal war for the many: or 2. restricted commerce, peace, and steady occupations for all. if any state in the union will declare that it prefers separation with the 1st alternative, to a continuance in union without it, I have no hesitation in saying 'let us separate.' I would rather the states should withdraw, which are for unlimited commerce & war, and confederate with those alone which are for peace & agriculture. I know that every nation in Europe would join in sincere amity with the latter, & hold the former at arm's length by jealousies, prohibitions, restrictions, vexations & war. no earthly consideration could induce my consent to contract such a debt as England has by her wars for commerce, to reduce our citizens by taxes to such wretchedness as that, laboring 16. of the 24. hours, they are still unable to afford themselves bread, or barely to earn as much oatmeal or potatoes as will keep soul and body together. and all this to feed the avidity of a few millionary merchants, and to keep up 1000. ships of war for the protection of their commercial speculations. I returned from Europe after our government had got under way, and had adopted from the British code the law of draw-backs. I early saw it's effects in the jealousies and vexations of Britain; and that, retaining it; we must become, like her, an essentially warring nation, and meet, in the end, the catastrophe impending over her. no one can doubt that this alone produced the orders of council, the depredations which preceded, and the war which followed them. had we carried but our own produce, and brought back but our own wants, no nation would have troubled us. our commercial dashers then have already cost us so many thousand lives & so many millions of Dollars, more than their persons and all their commerce was worth. when war was declared, and especially after Massachusets, who had produced it, took side with the enemy waging it, I pressed on some confidential friends in Congress to avail us of the happy opportunity of repealing the draw-back: and I do rejoice to find that you are in that sentiment. you are young, & may be in the way of bringing it into effect. perhaps time, even yet, & change of tone (for there are symptoms of that in Massachusets) may not have obliterated altogether the sense of our late feelings & sufferings; may not have induced oblivion of the friends we have lost, the depredations & conflagrations we have suffered, and the debts we have incurred, & have to labor for through the lives of the present generation. the earlier the repeal is proposed, the more it will be befriended by all these recollections & considerations. this is one of three great measures necessary to ensure us permanent prosperity. this preserves our peace. a 2^d should enable us to meet any war, by adopting the report of the war department, for placing the force of the nation at effectual command; and a 3^d should ensure resources of money by the suppression of all paper circulation during peace, and licensing that of the nation alone during war. the metallic medium of which we should be possessed at the commencement of a war would be a sufficent fund for all the loans we should need thro' it's continuance: and if the National bills issued, be bottomed (as is indispensable) on pledges of specific taxes for their redemption within certain & moderate epochs, and be of proper denominations for circulation, no interest on them would be necessary, or just, because they would answer to every one the purposes of the metallic money withdrawn & replaced by them.

But possibly these may be the dreams of an old man, or that the occasions of realising them may have past away without return. a government regulating itself by what is wise and just for the many, uninfluenced by the local and selfish views of the few who direct their affairs, has not been seen perhaps on earth. or if it existed, for a moment, at the birth of ours, it would not be easy to fix the term of it's continuance. still, I believe, it does exist here in a greater degree than any where else; and for it's growth and continuance, as well as for your personal health and happiness, I offer sincere prayers with the homage of my respect and esteem. TH: JEFFERSON

PoC (DLC); at foot of first page: "William H. Crawford. Secretary at War."

Alexander Hamilton was the MAN WHOSE MIND WAS REALLY POWERFUL. The United States Congress first ADOPTED the practice of a drawback with "An Act for laying a Duty on Goods, Wares, and Merchandises imported into the United States," 4 July 1789 (*U.S. Statutes at Large*, 1:24–7). TJ favored the principles of the 17 Oct. 1814 REPORT OF THE WAR DEPARTMENT written by James Monroe during his tenure as secretary of war (note to John H. Cocke to TJ, 6 Nov. 1814; TJ to Tadeusz Kosciuszko, 3 July 1815).

To George Logan

DEAR SIR Monticello June 20. 16.

Your favor of the 5th is now recieved. I never doubted the purity of your intentions in the publications of which I complained; but the correctness only of committing to the public a private correspondence not intended for their eye.[1] as to federal slanders, I never wished them to be answered, but by the tenor of my life, half a century of which has been on a theatre at which the public have been spectators, and competent judges of it's merit. their approbation has taught a lesson, useful to the world, that the man who fears no truths has nothing to fear from lies. I should have fancied myself half guilty had I condescended to put pen to paper in refutation of their falsehoods, or drawn to them respect by any notice from myself. but let all this be forgotten. knowing now my repugnance to take any part in public discussions, I shall be confident in future of being spared that pain, and avail myself freely of every occasion of renewing to mrs Logan and yourself the assurance of my sincere & friendly remembrance, respect and attachment. TH: JEFFERSON

RC (PHi: Logan Papers); addressed: "Doct[r] George Logan Stenton near Philadelphia"; franked; postmarked Milton, 21 June; endorsed by Deborah Norris Logan. PoC (DLC).

[1] Preceding two words reworked from "them."

From Robert Patterson

SIR Philadelphia June 20, 16.

You have no doubt been informed, at least thro the medium of News-papers, of M[r] Peale's complete success in illuminating his Museum with gas-lights, & presuming that it would not be uninteresting to you, I shall do myself the pleasure of giving you a description of his apparatus & process for generating & distributing the gas.

It is well known that any substance containing hydrogen will, by decomposition, produce an inflammable gas. Pure hydrogen gas is, perhaps, the most inflammable; but the light it produces is of a pale bluish colour. When combined with other inflammable substances, particularly carbon, the light is greatly improved. This carburetted hydrogen gas may be obtained, by heat alone, from various substances: bituminous pit-coal yields it in great abundance; but contaminated with sulphuretted hydrogen, & other matters which give it a very offensive smell, from which it is difficult to purify it. M[r] Peale, after various unsatisfactory attempts with other substances, now makes use of pitch; from which, by simple distillation, he extracts a gas that gives a brilliant white light, perfectly free from any smell.

His apparatus consists of two cast iron matrasses, or Retorts, of a cylindrical form, each 36 inches long & 10 in diameter; placed horizontally, along-side of each other, in a close fire place of masonry; their ends, projecting a few inches beyond the masonry; being closed with plates of sheet copper, fastened on with screw & flanch. From one end of each issues a copper cyphon, thro which the gas is conveyed to a box of tin or copper, surrounded with water, where a small proportion of the gaseous product is condensed into an oily liquid of the colour & consistence of mollasses. In this oily substance,[1] the pitch, after being melted, is dissolved, before it is introduced into the Retorts for distillation.

The gas, thus purified, is conveyed thro another tube into the gasholder, without passing thro any portion of the water in which it is immersed; and from the gas-holder it is distributed, by small tin tubes, to the several burners.

But the enclosed sketch, drawn by M[r] Peale, will, it is believed, give you a sufficiently clear idea of the whole process & apparatus

Explanation

AA two Retorts of cast iron, inclosed in masonry
BB Necks or tubes opening into the Retorts, to convey the dissolved pitch into the Retorts, previously made Red hot
CC Funnels, furnished with
DD Stop-cocks, for the purpose of admitting, by little & little, the dissolved pitch into the Retorts.
EE Tubes to convey the gas from the Retorts, into
F The condensing vessel, surrounded with
G A box filled with water, which seldom requires renewing.
H A tube, with its stop-cock, to convey the depurated gas from the condenser **F** to
I The gas-holder, made of sheet copper, in a cylindrical form, its open mouth plunging downwards, into
J A cistern containing water, & lined with thin sheet lead.
K A distributing tube, conveying the gas to the burners.
L A curvated tube to carry off the oily liquid from the condenser into
M A square box lined with sheet lead; when full it runs over into
N A box in which the oil & melted pitch are mixed together; & thence by
O A hand-pump transferred to
P The Reservoir from which the funnels are occasionally supplied.

Remarks

1. The gas-holder may be made of any convenient form, whether square or cylindrical, at pleasure; and the cistern containing it may be a single vessel wholly filled with water, where the weight (as when sunk under ground) would be no inconvenience.
2. To commence the process, before any oil is obtained, simple melted pitch may be used.
3. The proportion of the oil obtained by condensation may be increased or diminished, according as more or less of the dissolved pitch is let into the Retort at a time
4. A pot, in which the pitch is melted, is placed along-side of the Retorts, in the same masonry; and when the distillation of the gas

is nearly finished, the fire is drawn from the Retorts, & placed under the pot.

5. From the experience of some weeks, Mr Peale has furnished me with the following results.
   (1) One barrel of pitch will produce 2000 cubic feet of gas, besides oil sufficient to dissolve an equal quantity of fresh pitch.
   (2) After the Retorts are made red hot, they will generate 100 cubic feet of gas per hour.
   (3) One cubic foot of gas, under a moderate pressure, will supply light for one hour, equal to that of 5 spermaceti candles[2] of 4 to the pound.
   (4) Every barrel of pitch will require 5 bushels of Stone coal, & 4 of wood coal to generate the gas.
   (5) Mr Peale has two gas-holders, one containing about 100 cubic feet & the other about 300
   (6) The Museum is illuminated by 250 burners, equal to 500 candles, about 3½ hours every night ☞ The whole expense of gas being about ⅞ of a dollar per night ☜

☞ As the above information is given with the knowledge & approbation of Mr Peale, it is perfectly at your service, to make what use of it you shall think proper.

Mr Peale gives credit to Dr Kugler for his present system of gas-lights; for which, I understand, he has obtained a patent.

If any further improvements, relative to this subject, should come to my knowledge, I shall take great pleasure in communicating them.

I have the honour to be, Sir, with the greatest Respect & esteem Your Most obed^t Servt

R^T PATTERSON.

RC (DLC); at foot of text: "Thomas Jefferson"; endorsed by TJ as received 10 July 1816 and so recorded in SJL.

Both Charles Willson Peale and his son Rembrandt Peale had SUCCESS IN ILLUMINATING their respective museums in Philadelphia and Baltimore with gaslights in 1816. The enclosed description, however, depicts the APPARATUS & PROCESS used by the elder Peale (Charles Willson Peale to TJ, 9 Aug. 1816; Philadelphia *Poulson's American Daily Advertiser*, 18 Apr. 1816; *Baltimore Patriot & Evening Advertiser*, 12 June 1816).

MATRASSES are flasks with round or oval bodies and long necks, usually used in chemical distillation; FLANCH is a variant of "flange"; DEPURATED: "freed from impurities"; STONE COAL is anthracite coal; and WOOD COAL is charcoal (*OED*). Benjamin KUGLER obtained a patent for "Making carburated hydrogen gas" on 23 Apr. 1816 (*List of Patents*, 165).

[1] Manuscript: "substances."

[2] Manuscript: "candes."

ENCLOSURE

Charles Willson Peale's Sketches of an Apparatus for Gas Lighting

[ca. 20 June 1816]

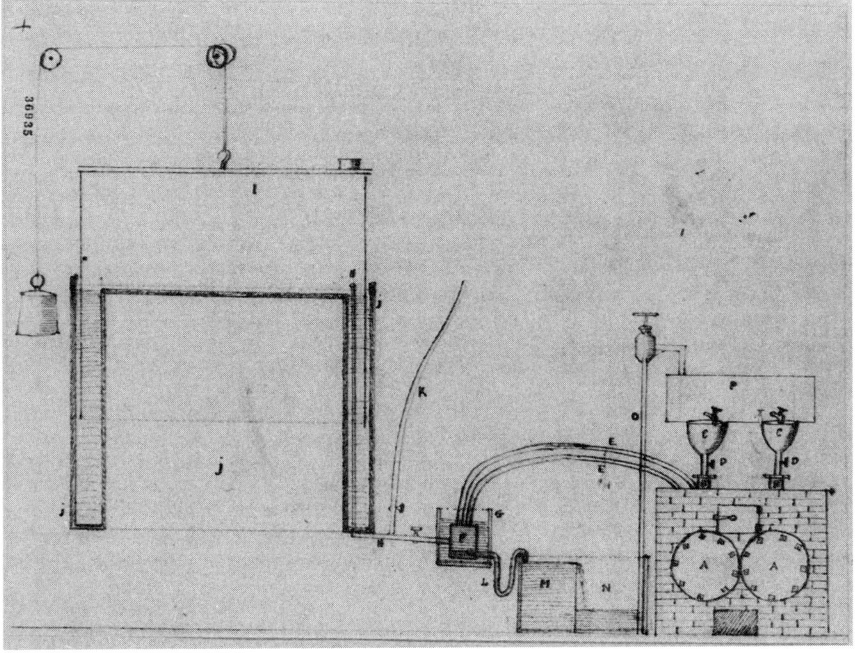

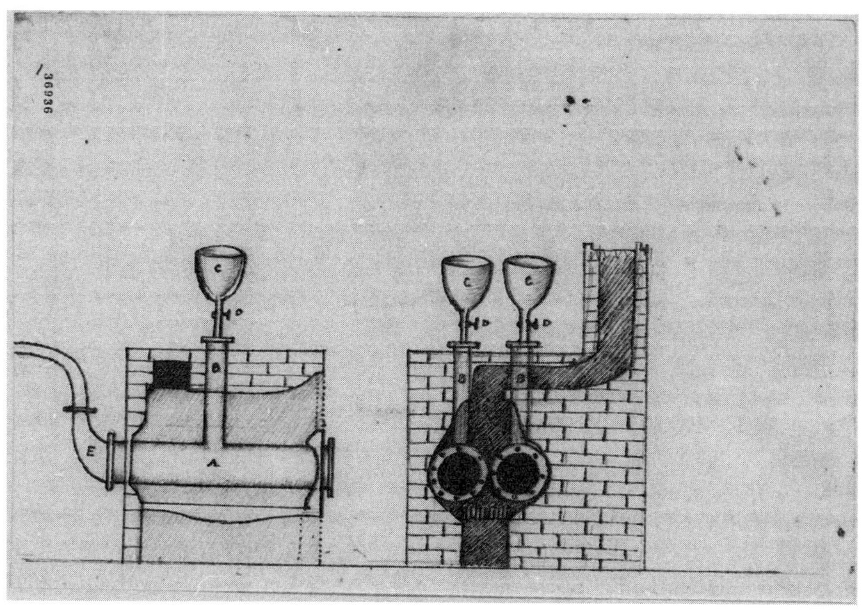

MS (DLC: TJ Papers, 207:36935–6); entirely in Peale's hand; undated.

From Thomas Eston Randolph

DEAR SIR Ashton 20th June 1816

I am much obliged to you for your kind attention in sending Mr Crowninshield^{s} letter—Mann received his warrant by the last Mail—and immediately wrote to the Sect^{y} of the Navy soliciting to be order'd into active service—of which there appears no prospect.

From the date of his acceptance his pay (half pay) commences, and could he be order'd on duty as a supernumery, he would be willing to serve without additional pay—Will you have the goodness to inform me if there will be any impropriety in making an application to that effect he is anxious to gain experience in his profession and from my knowledge of the service, I am aware that he has no time to lose—your advice will be received with many thanks—

With respect to the application which I made to you to give me additional time to pay the first quarters Rent in Flour—for the Mill, it was made in consequence of my fears that a sufficiency of Wheat would not be sent into the Mill to enable me to pay the customers their dues and leave a surplus equal to the discharge of the Rent—which is payable the 1st of Oct^{r}—the profits of 2000 bushels with very good grinding will leave a small deficiency—all that I wanted to guard against, was, that I should not be obliged to buy Flour at an extravagant price to pay a Rent which the Mill cannot make at that early period—I hope you will do me the justice to believe that I do not wish to derive any undue advantage or to make difficulties where none exist—I lament that the payments of Rent have lately been made with much irregularity, and have been fearful that you have suffer'd some inconvenience therefrom—but I confidently hope such will not be the case hereafter—for which reason I have taken a Miller into partnership with me—who is fully competent to his business, and disposed to do justice and be accomodating to the customers—

With this explanation suffer me to add, that I do not mean to be troublesome, but on the contrary that I wish to avoid it by a perfect understanding in the outset—after which I trust every thing will go on smoothly—very Affectionately Yours

THO[s] ESTON RANDOLPH

RC (MHi); dateline beneath signature; addressed: "Thomas Jefferson Esq[e] Monticello"; endorsed by TJ as received 20 June 1816 and so recorded in SJL.

MANN: Thomas Mann Randolph (1798–1835), Thomas Eston Randolph's son. The MILLER was Daniel Colclaser.

To George Watterston

DEAR SIR Monticello June 20. 16.

I have formerly mentioned, either in some letter written to you, or in a note in the MS. catalogue, that I had cut the print of Americus Vespucius out of the book containing his life, & lent it to mr Delaplane to be copied. it is just now returned to me, very much sullied: but as it is the original, it should be pasted again into the work, for which purpose I now inclose it. you will readily find at the beginning of the book the remains of the leaf from which it was cut. Accept the assurance of my esteem & respect TH: JEFFERSON

PoC (DLC); on verso of portion of reused address cover of James Monroe to TJ, 28 Apr. 1816; at foot of text: "M[r] Watterston"; endorsed by TJ. Enclosure: frontispiece to Stanislao Canovai, *Elogio d'Amerigo Vespucci* (Florence, 1788; Sowerby, no. 4163).

To Thomas Eston Randolph

Dear Sir Monticello June 21. 16.

In answer to the enquiry of yesterday, I think that the proposition for Mann to serve on his half pay until a vacancy may entitle him to whole pay, may be very properly made to the Secretary of the navy either by Mann or yourself, on the reasonable ground of unwillingness to let him be idle, and a preference that he should be learning what is to be the business of his life. still, as they must act by general rules, it may perhaps be declined. but there is no impropriety in the trial.

On the subject of the flour for Oct. 1. I did not dream of your being obliged to purchase, because I knew I could deliver you my own crop in time, and shall be glad to do it as early as you will recieve on the condition of delivering equivalent flour, ground after the first frost, and delivered in November, or December as I should call for it. we shall probably get out our whole crop in August, & can deliver it as it is got out if you will recieve it. Affectionately Yours

Th: Jefferson

PoC (MHi); on verso of reused address cover of William Thornton to TJ, 9 June 1816; at foot of text: "Tho[s] E. Randolph esq."; endorsed by TJ.

To John Wayles Eppes

Dear Sir Poplar Forest June 24. 16.

I am this moment arrived here with Ellen & Cornelia, and find Francis who arrived last night. I will take care and attend him to the Academy & see to every thing necessary for him. we will keep him with us as long as we stay (a week or 10. days) and rub him up in his French. I learn with great concern the state of your health, but can prescribe nothing but patience & the springs with good nursing & no Doctors. should you go to the springs, make this your resting place. mr Yancey will have you taken care of here. Francis tells me mr Baker would send his son as soon as he should know he could be recieved at the boarding house. no enquiry is necessary for this, as they have but 8. and could lodge twice as many. I will engage a reception for him immediately—subject to mr Baker's determination whether he will send or not. Accept my prayers for your better health, and with my respects to mrs Eppes the assurance of my affect[te] attachment.

Th: Jefferson

PoC (MHi); at foot of text: "J. W. Eppes"; endorsed by TJ. Mistakenly recorded in SJL in the column for letters received.

TJ's granddaughters ELLEN W. Randolph (Coolidge) and CORNELIA J. Randolph accompanied him to Poplar Forest, where they joined their cousin FRANCIS Eppes, who soon would enroll at the nearby New London ACADEMY.

From A. D. Saunders

SIR Tattnall County Georgia 26. June 1816

After twenty five years Study and various experiments I have at length discovered a new principle in Mechanics or rather have made A new application of the established principles which I feel confident will answer all the purposes of water or Steam, the power is produced by the gravity of A horizontal wheel So constructed as to continue to Seek its resting place but is never able to change its position, the quantum of[1] power depends on the weight applied which may be added or diminished at pleasure and the machine regulated at pleasure, I have demonstrated the principle fully to my Satisfaction, and Intend aplying for A patent if none has been granted, the remoteness of my Situation puts it out of my power to inform myself whether there is any thing of the kind in use in this or any other Country, nor do I know what name to call it by—I have taken the liberty to address you on the Subject knowing you to be the most Scientific Character our Country can boast of, and ever willing to aid and protect genius,—the object of this letter is to obtain Such information as you may possess on the Subject,—I am an operative Mechanic but have not the advantage theoretically to understand the principles, and terms used by authors, having no books that treat on the Subject of Mechanism—

Shall Esteem it A particular favour when leisure will admit to drop me A line, and please Say whether you think that your state Legislature would grant me an excluse right of navigating its waters with boats propelled by those Machines for fourteen or twenty years, the united states patent law is either too ambiguous, or not Explicit Enough to Secure rights, to Invention, as Slight variations are often decide[d] on to be new Inventions by Jurors who are Seldom competent Judges. any Ideas as to the proper name, or other matter will be thankfully recivd by your ob H s[t] A, D, SAUNDERS

RC (MHi); endorsed by TJ as received 28 July 1816 from "near Tattnall C.H. Georgia" and so recorded in SJL. RC (DLC); address cover only; with PoC of

TJ to Alexander H. Everett, 19 Sept. 1816, on verso; addressed: "Thomas Jefferson Esqr Monticello virginia"; stamped; postmarked Tattnall, Ga., 26 June.

[1] Preceding two words interlined.

From Donald Fraser

SIR New York June 27th 1816.

I beg leave to present for the honor of Your acceptance, a copy of my latest Publication. I am conscious, that it contains little, if any, Novelty to a person of Your extensive reading..... It is presented as a Small tribute of respect for Your Superior talents, & well Known Patriotism.—The fourth of July is near at hand, & the venerable Author of the Declaration of Independence, will not be forgotten at the approaching anniversary.... Nor, I trust, for centuries to come.—

Occasionally I Send Some pieces to the "National Advocate," an ably conducted paper, printed here, & other Republican papers.—The following piece which appeared in that paper, was written in defence of my Benevolent friend, Governor Tompkins. It proved a Bar, to mr Coleman's malignant[1] attacks on that truly worthy & Patriotic Character; at least, he did not think proper to make any remarks thereon... — .... The piece previous to this, in which I introduced extracts from letters of two of my most respectable correspondants, The late Hon. Chancellor Livingston & Dr Rush, relative to party Spirit [I wrote a pamphlet on that Subject Some Years ago.][2] .... He, with his accustomed asperity wrote Some remarks upon that piece... If it would not be encroaching too much upon retirement, I Shall, at a future period, Send the piece & Coleman's remarks thereon.....

Mr Philips ..

If You think proper, You'll oblige a patron of Your[3] paper, by giving the following piece a place in Your paper, I have read a number of anecdotes; the following one, in my opinion is[4] very applicable to the present State of parties in this country. A certain wealthy English Barronet, who had an only Son, a mere Dolt; his father, Sent him to Several eminent Preceptors; none of whom could make a Schollar of him,—Altho, the heir apparent to an ancient family, The father applied to the accomplished Earl of Chesterfield, to recommend[5] him a proper Tutor for his Son: Chesterfield, pointed out to him Dr B— "What exclaimed the Baronet, with Surprize, don't Your Lordship know, that B— is a whig, and a warm opposer of our Party; I can't

think of trusting my son to his care, as he might poison his mind with his own whiggish principles"[6]—Chesterfield replied, Dr B... Is a very honest & learned man; he will do justice to Your son; he has invariably adhered to his party, in the worst & best of times..
When I was in office,[7] I endeavored to retain it by every method in my power: When out of office, I tried hard to get in again: Wrote & Spoke, true or[8] false, againest my opposers.
Now, me thinks, that the erudite Editor of the Evening-Post, has certainly adopted Chesterfield's maxims, in politics; as he has for fifteen Years past, uniformly calumniated a Jefferson, a Madison & now a Tompkins: whether, from political & Selfish motives, that's best known to himself...... I am conscious, that there are Some genuine Patriots in the Federal ranks; for instance, John Jay, &c. Whom, I Should be Sorry to See any Republican Editor abuse, as Wm Coleman, has done, the most respectable & incorruptible Patriots, on the Republican Side.
Novr 11th 1815.[9] A friend to the People,

Being well[10] informed of the Urbanity of Your Disposition I write with freedom,[11] as I have been in the habit of doing to other [e]minent characters ... Your good Sense will induce You to pardon the verbosity of an old man of Sixty eight Years ... I have two Sons in the army of the U.S. one of whom (Donald) has Distinguished himself and won the approbation of his commanders: .. He received four or fiv[e] wounds, in as many different actions— ... He has been aide camp to Generals Pike, Boyd, Porter & now to Genl Brown: He is a very felial Son, having allowed me one Dollar a Day for three Years past, out of his knowng that I have lost by misplaced confidence, the fruits of nearly a whole life of industry:—And not now able to follow my former profession; from Physical causes.

I have the honor to be, Venerable Sir, with the highest respect & consideration, Your Obedient[12] humble Servant

Donald Fraser Senr

P.S. I am no Poet, But can write Rhymes with[13] facility— .. —The following light effusions of an old Republican[14] may afford You a few moments[15] amusements[16] after Deep Study.—

N York Septr 3^d 1814.[17] One of the Masonic Bretheren (about 700 attended[18] to build "Fort Masonic")[19]—A member of Mount Moria lodge,[20] Spoke the following lines extemporally—

1st Hail children of light, whom the charit[ies] Se[nd]
Their country, their wives, & fire-Sides to defend:

May the flame Patriotic, which nothing can Smother,
Burn bright in the breast, of each true loving Brother:
2^d As Masons, as men, we'll proudly oppose,
The Secret or open attacks of our foes....[21]
Like his Honor, our present Grand-Master & Mayor.
3^d For me, whose dismissal must Shortly arrive,
May I never America's freedom Survive:
And, if that is maintain'd by[22] powder & Guns,
May my memory live, in the fame of my Sons.

Lines[23] Spoken Brooklyne-heights, when working with the Teachers of this City—Septr 2^d 1815.[24]

1. Well, when our Day's labor's done,
Which will be at the Setting Sun;
Molasses, Pork, & punkin pie
I vow, we'll [eat][25] before we die:
2^d You must not think us barren fools,
Because we are pent up in Schools:
And, Should the foe, but make a Breach,
We Shall, to them Good manners teach:
3^d Our country Shall continue free,
As long as we, teach, A. B. C......
And, if the foe, Should tread our Sod,
They'll find how we can use the rod.

There's, Pike, Porter, Scot, & Brown we know,
Where-e'er they met, they beat the foe:
May Columbia, ever have Such men,
To Show John-Bull, what Yankeys Ken!

RC (MHi); dateline at foot of text; edge trimmed and ink stained; ellipses in original; addressed: "Thomas Jefferson Esqr, Late President of the United States Monticllon V^a"; endorsed by TJ as received 10 July 1816 and so recorded in SJL. Enclosure: Fraser, *An Interesting Companion for a Leisure Hour: or, an Historical, Geographical, and Chronological Compendium: containing a brief but comprehensive history of England, Ireland, Scotland, and Holland: together with a variety of curious articles, both miscellaneous and Masonic, not generally known* (New York, 1814; Poor, *Jefferson's Library*, 4 [no. 124]; TJ's copy in Vi, with Fraser's inscription "To Thos Jefferson Esqr late President of these U. States—As a Small testimony of respect, for his Talents & Patriotism. From Donald Fraser N. York June 27th 1816"). Probably enclosed in Fraser to TJ, 2 June 1816.

Fraser included in his previous letter to TJ of 2 June 1816 excerpts from two PIECES sent to the New York *National Advocate*—the DEFENCE of Daniel D. Tompkins, which is repeated here, and EXTRACTS FROM LETTERS of Robert R. Livingston and Benjamin Rush. The earlier PAMPHLET was Fraser, *Party-Spirit Exposed, or Remarks on the Times: to which is added Some Important Hints to the Ladies* (New York, 1799).

Fraser was the OLD REPUBLICAN and ONE OF THE MASONIC BRETHEREN who made the first poetic recitation above on 1 Sept. 1814 at the site of Fort Masonic in Brooklyn, New York. Various groups of citizens in and around New York City donated time and materials to assist in the construction of this fort during August and September 1814. DeWitt Clinton was the Masonic GRAND-MASTER for New York State and the MAYOR of New York City in 1814 (Rocellus S. Guernsey, *New York City and Vicinity during The War of 1812–'15* [1889–95], 2:294–5; New York *Mercantile Advertiser*, 3 Sept. 1814).

[1] Fraser here canceled "remarks."
[2] Brackets in original.
[3] Manuscript: "of Your of Your."
[4] Manuscript: "is is."
[5] Manuscript: "recommed."
[6] Manuscript: "princiciples."
[7] Manuscript: "When I was in office, When in office."
[8] Manuscript: "of."
[9] Manuscript: "1816."
[10] Manuscript: "weel."
[11] Manuscript: "freedon."
[12] Manuscript: "Obdient."
[13] Manuscript: "Rhynes wih."
[14] Preceding four words interlined.
[15] Word interlined.
[16] Manuscript: "amusements amusements."
[17] Manuscript: "1816."
[18] Manuscript: "attended attended."
[19] Omitted closing parenthesis editorially supplied.
[20] Manuscript: "loge."
[21] New York *Mercantile Advertiser*, 3 Sept. 1814, gives the line omitted here as "And act towards all on the compass and square."
[22] Manuscript: "by by."
[23] Fraser here canceled "written."
[24] Manuscript: "1816."
[25] Omitted word editorially supplied.

From Enoch Reynolds

SIR, Washington City 27th June 1816

Permit me the honor to enclose you a Prospectus of a very Splendid work now in the hands of the artists,

The publisher having appointed me his agent to procure subscriptions and deliver the plates, I avail myself of this early opportunity of Soliciting your patronage, Should you be inclined to grant my request, I Shall be obliged by your naming Some person in the District to whom the engraving Shall be delivered,

With the greatest respect I have the honor to be Sir Your obedt Servant ENOCH REYNOLDS

RC (MHi); endorsed by TJ as received 10 July 1816 and so recorded in SJL. RC (DLC); address cover only; with PoC of TJ to Albert Gallatin, 8 Sept. 1816, on recto and verso; addressed: "Thomas Jefferson Esquire Monticello Va"; franked; postmarked Washington, 27 June.

Enoch Reynolds (1776–1833), civil servant, was born in Norwich, Connecticut. By 1799 he had migrated to Luzerne County, Pennsylvania, where he was a shopkeeper. Reynolds had relocated by 1804 to Philadelphia, and in 1809 he helped found the Third Baptist Church of Philadelphia. By 1813 he was in Washington, D.C., serving as a clerk in the Department of War's Office of the Superintendent General of Military Supplies, and by 1816 he was chief clerk. In 1818 Reynolds was chief clerk in the Second Comptroller's Office in the Treasury Department, a position he held until his death. He sat on Washington's Board of Common Council, 1818–19, and was a justice of the peace, 1821–33. Reynolds was among the founders of Columbian College (later George Washington University) in 1821, and he served on its board of trustees as secretary, 1821–26, and as treasurer, 1827–33 (Marion H. Reynolds, *The History and Descendants of John and Sarah [Backus] Reynolds of Saybrook, Lyme and Norwich, Conn., 1655–1928* [1928], 21–2, 28–9; Emily C. Blackman, *History of Susquehanna County, Pennsylvania* [1873], 12, 121, 217; Philadelphia *Aurora General Advertiser*, 31 Oct. 1804; David Spencer, *The Early Baptists of Philadelphia* [1877], 175; John Armstrong, *Letter from the Secretary of War, transmitting a Statement Showing the Names of the Clerks Employed in the War Department* [Washington, 1814]; George Graham, *Letter from the Acting Secretary of War transmitting Statements of the Clerks Employed in the Departments of War* [Washington, 1817], 11; William H. Crawford, *Letter from the Secretary of the Treasury, transmitting a List of the Clerks employed in the Treasury Department* [Washington, 1819], 7; William A. Weaver, *Register of all Officers and Agents, Civil, Military, and Naval, in the Service of the United States, on the Thirtieth September, 1833* [1833], 13; *City of Washington Gazette*, 2 June 1818, 13 Nov. 1819; *JEP*, 3:236, 242, 449, 456, 4:154, 169 [23 Jan., 10 Feb. 1821, 13, 20 Dec. 1825, 14 Feb., 2 Mar. 1831]; Howard L. Hodgkins, *Historical Catalogue of the Officers and Graduates of The Columbian University* [1891], 6, 29–31; Washington *Globe*, 15 Oct. 1833).

The PROSPECTUS, not found, was also enclosed to TJ in a printed circular from the publisher John Binns, in which Binns advised that he would be "publishing a Splendid Edition of the Declaration of Independence" that was "purely national" and "executed in a manner worthy of the nation," for which he solicited patronage (DLC: TJ Papers, 207:36937; signed by Binns; dated "Philadelphia, June, 1816"; addressed: "Th^os^ Jefferson Esq. Monticello. [Va]"; franked; postmarked Philadelphia, 18 June; endorsed by TJ without date of receipt, but recorded in SJL as a "circular" received 10 July 1816).

From Charles Clay

C. CLAY TO M^R^ TH. JEFFERSON — Petty Grove Jun. 29. 16

Cyrus brings for your inspection the last Act of Assembly Respecting Appeals from interlocutary decrees of County & Corporation Courts—I have no Idea of Justice from the County Court, & if I must Contend I would wish to take Such Steps & file Such exceptions as might Carry the business Speedily before the Courts above where it might be fully and fairly investigated, as it were de novo, or an original Case—I say Speedily for the waste they are Committing is enormous—every good piece of Tob. land is put under lease, & one only of them had last year a considerable length of time twenty hands employed in getting timber for the Lynchburg Markett &c & others of them have not been idle in that way—accept my friendly & Respectful Salutations

RC (MHi); dateline at foot of text; addressed: "Tho. Jefferson Esqre Poplar Forest"; endorsed by TJ as received 29 June 1816 and so recorded in SJL, in which it mistakenly appears in the column for letters written by TJ.

Clay sent his son CYRUS B. Clay to TJ with a copy of "An Act, concerning appeals and proceedings in Chancery," 26 Feb. 1816. The statute facilitated appeals from INTERLOCUTARY DECREES OF COUNTY & CORPORATION COURTS to the Superior Courts of Chancery for the pertinent districts, stipulated that when such appeals were successful the case could not be remanded to the lower court, and provided for appeals from the superior chancery courts to the Virginia Court of Appeals (*Acts of Assembly* [1815–16 sess.], 17–23, esp. 17–8).

To Charles Clay

DEAR SIR Poplar Forest July.[1] 1. 16.

Having never had an entire view of the facts & proceedings in the partition of mr Davis's estate, & percieving it has become entangled by some irregularities, I can only give detached opinions on certain parts of them, & these too under the risk that they may be affected by circumstances of which I am not apprised.

On the general subject of Hotchpot I may safely say that, as regards the real and personal property of a decedent, these two masses are to be considered and divided as separately and distinctly as if they had come from two different ancestors. no law has made either a fund for correcting inequalities in the partition of the other.

The law of Hotchpot as to lands arose under the Common law, at a time when personal estate was so generally inconsiderable, that the law noticed it no otherwise than as a fund to pay debts, abandoning the surplus, if any, to the administrator, for pious purposes. it was not till the statute of Distributions that the rights of relations to the personal property of a decedent were recognised and sanctioned by the legislature, the portions of each defined, and the principles of hotchpot introduced into the distribution of that species of property also. but this statute respected personal estate only; taking into account no advancement from any other fund. our act of distribution is an exact copy of that statute, and confines itself by express words to personal property only.

At the Common law there could be no occasion for hotchpot in the descent of lands to the eldest male in the line of inheritance it was only therefore when they descended to, or through, females that the law had provided that each parcener, on partition, should bring into hotchpot any lands she had recieved, by way of advancement, from the decedent in his lifetime: and it was confined strictly to advancement in lands. when we changed the course of descents, & made lands partible equally, among males and[2] females, we extended the law of hotchpot equally to partitions among both sexes. but the act expressly confines itself to advancement in lands only; taking no notice of personal estate; this having been provided for in another act, and as a distinct subject. these two classes of property therefore being under the regimen of different laws, and going, in some cases, in different courses of succession, have, on partition, no relations with each other, and are subject to hotchpot, each within itself only, and separately from the other.

The bond given to mr Clay by mr Davis in his lifetime, was an advancement of personal property,[3] the law not enquiring from what source the decedent had raised that money, whether by the profits or sale of lands, or how otherwise; and it is to be brought into hotchpot on a distribution of the personal estate only, and according to the sum actually recieved. for had it never been recovered, it would have been no advancement at all, nor would have had any value to be brought into account: or had a part only been recovered, that part alone must have come into hotchpot, and, as so far only, an advancement. but I think the whole sum recieved must be taken into account, without any deduction for interest on the instalments not then due. for mr Davis only gave the debt as he held it; without obliging himself to make it ready money, or even to ensure it's recovery at all. in like manner no subsequent inter[est] on the sums recieved is to be brought into hotchpot, the law requiring the principal only to be brought into account.

The selection of Commissioners, and some of their proceedings, have been obviously exceptionable: and will doubtless be corrected on an appeal from the final decree: and altho' the act of the last session does not give an appeal from any interlocutory decree pronounced before it's passage, yet should new occasion offer, or be produced, for another interlocutory decree, an appeal from that may be taken under the new law, and the whole[4] proceedings be removed to the superior court: and as that court is now to retain and finish the cause, they will, of course, as a basis for a correct decree, rectify all errors in the preceding stages.

If any new matter of fact has come to light, which was not known, or could not be obtained, when depositions were taken in the cause, or when the bill was filed, it may be availed of, either by an amended bill, or by a bill of Review.

I recollect no advantages which a proceeding by Supersedeas, rather than by Appeal, would have in this case. but, in matters of practice especially, I distrust my memory, and may say generally, and truly,

—obstat mihi tarda vetustas;
Multaque me fugiunt primis spectata sub annis;
Alia tamen memini.—

You must accept these ideas therefore, with all their doubts about them, not as rescripts of certain law, but as testimonies of my wishes, by any suggestions within my present reach, to aid in disentangling the perplexities of your case, and of my sincere friendship and esteem.

TH: JEFFERSON

PoC (DLC); corner torn; at foot of first page: "M[r] Clay"; endorsed by TJ. Mistakenly recorded in SJL in the column for letters received.

Clay had a financial interest in the PARTITION OF MR DAVIS'S ESTATE through his wife, Editha Landon Davies Clay (*DVB*). Her father, Henry L. Davies, died intestate in 1808 (*Arthur Davies et al. v. Benjamin C. Davies et al.* [Vi: Bedford Co. Chancery Causes, case 1812–001]). The British STATUTE OF DISTRIBUTIONS, enacted in 1670, was "An Act for the better setling of Intestates Estates" (*The Statutes: Revised Edition* [1870–], 1: 767–8). Virginia's ACT OF DISTRIBUTION of October 1705 was "An act for the distribution of intestates estates, declaring widows rights to their deceased husbands estates; and for securing orphans estates" (Hening, 3:371–6). Late in the 1770s TJ drafted a statute adopted in 1785 that changed the COURSE OF DESCENTS and ended the use of primogeniture in cases of intestacy in Virginia (*PTJ*, 2:305–24, 391–3).

OBSTAT MIHI ... ALIA TAMEN MEMINI ("time has blurred my memory, though many things which I saw in my young years have quite gone from me, still can I remember much") varies only slightly from Ovid, *Metamorphoses*, 12.182–4 (Ovid, *Metamorphoses*, trans. Frank Justus Miller, Loeb Classical Library [1916], 2:192–3).

[1] Reworked from "June."

[2] Word interlined in place of "as well as."

[3] TJ here canceled "only."

[4] Word interlined.

From Ira Ingram

VENERABLE SIRE, Charlottesville July 1st 1816.—

Pardon a young man for interrupting the late chief magistrate of our Republic, in the enjoyment of that sweet and solacing retirement, so long an object of his anxiety, and so recently realized.—Imbibing, at an early age, his political principals from the writings of a Washington, a Jefferson, a Franklin and a Rush, it is natural that he should entertain a respect, approaching to veneration, for the merits and memories, the lives and labours, of those pillars of our liberties and worthies of the revolution. Neither of these great Men, has it ever been the lot of the obscure individual now addressing you, to behold.—Visiting Virginia for the purpose of obtaining subscribers for an American edition of Nicholson's Encyclopædia, he is instructed by the Company whose Agent he is, to visit Monticello, and solicit the patronage and Name, of its great Proprietor.—It is for this end, as well as to gratify a laudable curiosity to see the seat and person of President Jefferson, that the subscriber has presumed to intrude upon the repose of our retired Statesman & Philosopher. The American Publishers being aware of the just influence of a name, deserving and receiving the high respect[1] of their Countrymen, are doubly anxious to obtain its sanction to the undertaking now presented to the public for patronage. A prospectus is enclosed—As it is presumed M[r] Jefferson is well acquainted[2] with the Work, it is thought needless to exhibit a sample.—

Please to overlook the errors of this note, as the writer has had the advantages, only, of a plain English education at a country Academy. His Father is a poor man, the Parent of Nine children, who have, and will be compelled, to educate themselves and labour for a living.

That the remainder of your days may be sweetened by the society of your friends[3] and relatives, the enjoyment of a rational and benign religion, and that the choicest of heaven's blessings may accompany your decline to the tomb and the mansions of eternal rest hereafter, is the sinsere and unfeigned prayer, of your

obedient, and very humble servant IRA INGRAM

RC (MHi); addressed: "Honourable Thomas Jefferson Esquire Late President of the United States—Present"; endorsed by TJ as received 10 July 1816 and so recorded in SJL. Enclosure not found.

Although TJ was not listed as a subscriber, at some point he acquired William NICHOLSON's *American Edition of the British Encyclopedia, or Dictionary of Arts and Sciences*, 6 vols. (Philadelphia, 1816–17; Poor, *Jefferson's Library*, 14 [no. 931]). The AMERICAN PUBLISHERS were Samuel A. Mitchell and Horace Ames.

[1] Manuscript: "repect."
[2] Manuscript: "acquinted."
[3] Manuscript: "fieneds."

From William D. Simms

SIR Collectors Office Alexandria 1st July 1816

In the absence of the Collector I have the honour to inform you, that I have this day laden on board, the Sloop Fair play, Charles Brown, master, & consigned to Mess[rs] Gibson & Jefferson, Richmond four Cases of wine received from M[r] Cathalan at Marseilles.—The present is the only opportunity that has occurred to forward the wines, since the receipt of your letter, directing the disposition of them.—every precaution I believe has been taken for their preservation

At present there is no french Consul at this Port.—the arrival of one is however daily expected, & I shall take the earliest opportunity to obtain his certificate to the landing of the wine, & will remit the acquit a caution, to M[r] Cathalan, by the first vessel which sails from this or any of the adjoining ports to a port in France.

I enclose the Bill for the freight—the amount of Duties is $27.30¢. Very respectfully I have the honor to be sir y obt ser[t]

W D Simms D C

RC (MHi); endorsed by TJ as received 10 July 1816 and so recorded in SJL; notation by TJ on verso: "July 12. wrote to P. Gibson to remit 40.70." RC (MHi); address cover only; with PoC of TJ to Charles Pinckney, 3 Sept. 1816, on verso; addressed: "Thomas Jefferson Esquire @ Monticello. (near) Charlottesville Virginia"; franked; postmarked. Enclosure not found.

William Douglass Simms (d. 1822), attorney and public official, graduated in 1801 from the College of New Jersey (later Princeton University). In 1805 he opened a law office in Alexandria. Simms was married in 1807 in Pittsburgh, near which his father, Charles Simms, owned land. Simms served as deputy customs collector for the Alexandria district under his father, and he was a captain in the President's Horse Guards in 1819. The following year President James Monroe appointed him register of the land office at Arkansas, in Arkansas Territory. After the death of his wife, Emily Neville Simms, in 1821, Simms resigned this position and returned to Alexandria. Monroe nominated him as the navy agent at Pensacola, Florida Territory, in 1822, but withdrew the nomination before its confirmation. Simms later died at Pensacola of yellow fever (*General Catalogue of Princeton University 1746–1906* [1908], 113; *Alexandria Daily Advertiser*, 26 Aug. 1805; *Pittsburgh Gazette*, 10 Nov. 1807; Appleton Morgan, *A History of the Family of Morgan* [1902], 35; Alexandria City Will Book, 2:358–61 [father's will]; *Alexandria Gazette & Daily Advertiser*, 27 Apr., 20 Nov. 1819, 8 May 1820; *JEP*, 3:205, 293, 308 [5 Apr. 1820, 15 Apr., 7 May 1822]; *Terr. Papers*, 19:158, 284, 22: 489–90; *Arkansas Gazette*, 17 Mar. 1821; *Alexandria Herald*, 20 Sept. 1822).

From Joseph C. Cabell

Dear Sir, Warminster. 4th July. 1816.

I saw General Cocke on his way to Norfolk, early in June, and had a conversation with him on the subject of Hedges: in the course of which he informed me that you were under the impression that Maine's method of preparing Haws, so as to make them vegetate quickly, had died with him. It affords me pleasure to furnish you with it, in an extract of a Letter written by Maine to M[r] James Henderson of Williamsburg at the time that the latter purchased of him about 10,000 of his Thorns. I was making enquiries in the month of may, with the view of collecting information as to the practicability & expediency of introducing live fences into Virginia, when I accidentally got sight of Maine's letter to m[r] Henderson. It differs from all other methods I have yet heard of: and is more expeditious by one winter than that of m[c]mahon, who follows the English & Scotch methods; and is the quickest of all the processes that have come to my knowledge, unless it be that of immersing the Haws in fermenting bran, as recommended by Sir Isaac Newton. I have no where, read of a successful experiment on a large scale, of the latter method—and have seen it merely suggested as recommended by Sir I. Newton. Maine's method is simple, quick, & well suited to common practice. I should be glad to know why Maine selected the Maple-leaf Thorn in preference to all others. It does not appear to me to be as vigorous in its growth, or as strong in its appearance, as the Laurel Leaf Thorn: nor do I know whether it is to be found in this part of the country. In crossing Willis's River on my way up the country, I found a Thorn in great abundance, which from the shape of the Leaf, appeared to be the maple Leaf Thorn. There may, however, be other varieties with a leaf of the same shape. you planted some years ago, a hedge around your House, of Maine's thorn. I should be happy, before I commence experiments in this line, to know your impressions as to the practicability of making Hedges of real use in this country, where Hogs, are suffered to run at large: and as to the relative advantages of the Holly, the Cedar, and the thorn, for that purpose. I should also be much indebted to you for a reference to such authors as treat best on the subject. I have consulted Dobsons Encyclopædia, Lord Kames, maine's Pamphlet, & the articles in the ordinary books on agriculture. I have been informed by a young gentleman who attended the Lectures of the Abbe Corea in Philadelphia, that the Abbe expressed the opinion that Hedges would not succeed in this country, because we have not the right kind of plant, and that the proper plant when imported, degenerates. The same person told me that the Hedges about Wilmington in Delaware, seemed to be declining. These are discouraging circumstances. Still I have a strong desire to go on. I had a Cedar[1] Hedge of about two miles in length planted on the Rappahannock low grounds, some years ago. It grew handsomely and promised well. But during the war, it was neglected, & beaten down by stock, in many places. A part of it, about 500 yards in length, is now entire & very beautiful. But whether it will be ultimately a secure fence, I am unable to say. As an object of ornament, I think it remunerates for the care & trouble it has cost: and it is of real use, in breaking the force of the violent winds that often sweep those plains. I propose to renew it where it is defective, and to extend it to 4 miles in length. The Holly is scarcely to be found in the woods of the upper country. Still I suppose it would succeed with the aid of cultivation, and I am about trying it as an enclosure for a yard & Lots.

I mentioned to you in a letter last winter, I had a thought of attempting a translation of Say's political economy. my health is now improving, but being still very much reduced by a severe disease of some month's continuance, I shall be unable to enter upon such an undertaking in the course of this summer or fall. I perceive from the newspapers that a Catechism of political economy by Say has been translated into English, and this being a later work, I presume his former work must also have been translated. I have sent to England for it; and shall ascertain whether I am correct by the month of Dec^r—

I am appointed one of the members of a Committee of three persons to enquire & report to the Court of this county such information as we may be able to procure, to enable them to carry into successful execution the act of the Last assembly, directing an accurate chart of each county in the state to be taken. Could you do me the favor to recommend a man that ought to be employed on such an occasion? There is not one in this county. I have thought it would be well for several counties to join in the employment of the same man—so as to unite economy, & uniformity in the execution of the maps. We are to make our report to the Court of this county on the 4th monday of August. If we cannot do better, I shall recommend it to the court, to adopt the map of this county, made, in the year 1809, by the late Captn Varnum, son of the Genl, in order to ascertain the most convenient point for the establishment of the public buildings.

I am, dear Sir, with great respect & regard y^rs

JOSEPH C. CABELL

RC (ViU: TJP-PC); addressed: "Thomas Jefferson Esq. Monticello"; stamped; postmarked Warminster, 4 July 1816, and Charlottesville, 10 July; endorsed by TJ as received 10 July 1816 and so recorded in SJL.

The MAPLE-LEAF THORN was also known as the Washington hawthorn (*Farmer's Monthly Visitor* 1 [1839]: 84). For A HEDGE comprised of Washington hawthorns planted at Monticello from seedlings purchased from Thomas Main, see note to Main to TJ, 10 Jan. 1810. The British judge and author Henry Home, LORD KAMES, wrote *The Gentleman Farmer. Being An Attempt to improve Agriculture, By subjecting it to the Test of Rational Principles* (Edinburgh, 1776, and other eds.; Sowerby, no. 710). Main's PAMPHLET was *Directions for the Transplantation and Management of young Thorn or other Hedge Plants, preparative to their being set in Hedges* (Washington, 1807; Sowerby, no. 723).

Cabell had considered ATTEMPTING A TRANSLATION of Jean Baptiste Say, *Traité d'Économie Politique*, 2 vols. (Paris, 1803; Sowerby, no. 3547; Poor, *Jefferson's Library*, 11 [no. 697]). The CATECHISM by Say was *Catéchisme d'Économie Politique* (Paris, 1815), which was translated by John Richter as *Catechism of Political Economy* (London, 1816). THIS COUNTY was Nelson. The ACT OF THE LAST ASSEMBLY was "An Act to provide an accurate chart of each county and a general map of the territory of this Commonwealth," 27 Jan. 1816 (*Acts of Assembly* [1815–16 sess.], 39–42).

[1] Word interlined.

E N C L O S U R E

Thomas Main to James Henderson

[1811]

"The Hedge Thorn Plants are the best that ever left my Nursery of one year old, and the Pyracantha are equally excellent.

You will, I am certain, scarce believe that such plants could be raised at once from the seed gathered from my Hedges last year—1810—and now fit to plant in the Hedge row. As soon as the plants come to hand they are to be taken out of the boxes and submersed in cool water, for an hour or two. After which they may remain with their roots only in the water until they are planted in the hedge. But if they cannot be planted immediately or for four or five days they had better be laid in a trench and covered well with mould to keep them moist untill they be planted: four and an half inches apart is the best distance for the Hedge Thorn and from two to three feet asunder for the Pyracantha. In my opinion it will be best to plant the gooseberry cuttings in a long shallow box, and keep it in the House continually damp until they are rooted. I lost every one of my Gooseberry cuttings last year by the extraordinary dryness of the season. The Chinese Arbor Vitae is a beautiful evergreen & grows to a considerable height.

The seed of the Hedge Thorn (Crataegus Cordata) may be gathered any time after they are fully ripe. Put them in a trough and pound or crush the Haws or berries until the stones are completely separated (taking care to proportion the strokes of the pestle so as not to break the stones) turning over the mass repeatedly until the whole of the berries are mashed. The stones are then to be washed from the pulp, and deposited in a box or other convenient vessel in the coolest situation (out of doors) that can be had. They are to be kept in a damp or humid condition through the winter (or frozen). At the commencement of vegetation in the Spring they must be inspected every 3 or 4 days, and when they begin to feel slimy on being handled it is an indication that they are about to open. The ground must then be prepared for their reception. And as soon as the little white point or rootlet of some of them appears protruded, then is the critical time to sow them as soon as the state of the soil & weather will permit. I commonly mix them plentifully with Plaister of Paris at the time of sowing—an inch apart is the best distance. Cover them with half an Inch of fine mould as evenly as practicable. The stones may be[1] cleaned from the pulp any time in the winter before march."

Tr (DLC: TJ Papers, 147:25565); extract in Joseph C. Cabell's hand; undated, with year conjectured from internal evidence; at head of text: "Extract of a Letter from Thomas Main of the District of Columbia to James Henderson esq. of Williamsburg"; notation by Cabell at foot of text: "Thomas main's method of preparing Haws"; endorsed by TJ: "Agriculture. Thorn Hedges. Maine's process."

James Henderson (1764–1818), Episcopal minister and educator, emigrated from Scotland to America in 1785. He was ordained by Bishop William White in Pennsylvania on 19 Dec. 1788. Henderson served successively as rector of Westover Parish, Charles City County, from at least 1790 to 1792, and of Yorkhampton Parish, York County, from 1793 until at least 1797. He was appointed an adjunct professor of humanity in 1792 at the College of William and Mary. In 1796 Henderson was named a director of the Public Hospital, Williamsburg's institution for the insane later known as the Eastern State

Hospital. From about 1800 he resided at the corner of England and Nicholson streets in Williamsburg. Henderson's father-in-law was United States Supreme Court justice John Blair. At the time of his death Henderson owned stock in bank, canal, insurance, and land companies, as well as Blair Park, an estate in Albemarle County. His will freed two slaves and stipulated that, in the sale of slave families, spouses were not to be separated and young children were to remain with their mothers (G. MacLaren Brydon, "A List of Clergy of the Protestant Episcopal Church Ordained after the American Revolution, who served in Virginia between 1785 and 1814 …" *WMQ*, 2d ser., 19 [1939]: 407, 426, 434; *The History of the College of William and Mary from its Foundation, 1660, to 1874* [1874], 81; Lyon Gardiner Tyler, *Williamsburg, The Old Colonial Capital* [1907], 244, 250; Eastern State Hospital, *Annual Report* 143 [1916]: 54; DNA: RG 29, CS, York Co., 1810; Henderson Family Bible Record, 1795–1872 [Vi]; Mary Blair Andrews to TJ, 16 Oct. 1815, and note; Henderson's will in Bernard M. Caperton, "Three Williamsburg Wills," *Virginia Genealogist* 29 [1985]: 205–12; *Virginia Patriot, and Richmond Daily Mercantile Advertiser*, 15 Dec. 1818; gravestone inscription in Bruton Parish Cemetery, Williamsburg).

CRATAEGUS CORDATA: Washington hawthorn, also classified as *Crataegus Phaenopyrum* (*Hortus Third*, 329–31).

[1] Cabell here canceled "cleared."

From Joseph Delaplaine

DEAR SIR, Philad[a] July 6: 1816.

The first half volume of the Repository will be published in a few days. The second half volume is preparing for publication. Among others, for the second half volume, the life & Portrait of yourself & of the late celebrated Peyton Randolph Eq[r] will be given. The engraving of his portrait is already executed. It is done from his portrait in Peale's Museum. It is said to be a pretty good likeness, but the painting is certainly very indifferent.

I want, as soon as possible, the facts of Peyton Randolph's life. Judge Tucker of Williamsburg in his letter to me says, "M[r] Jefferson is probably the only man alive that can do justice to the character of this truly great & good man."—

May I beg the favour of something from you on this subject, if there is any thing in your possession. Or, if it will be not inconvenient,[1] may I request your influence to obtain the facts from his son Peyton Randolph Esq[r] of Richmond.—

I enclose the frontispiece for my work for your acceptance & beg you to show it to the ladies

M[r] Otis painted for me the portraits of M[rs] & M[r] Madison. The likeness of each gave entire satisfaction.

With my kind remembrance to your excellent family, I remain, D[r] sir with great regard your obed. hu[e] s[t] JOSEPH DELAPLAINE

P.S. As soon as my work appears I shall beg you to accept a copy, as a token of my respect.

RC (DLC); endorsed by TJ as received 17 July 1816 and so recorded in SJL. RC (MHi); address cover only; with PoC of TJ to Joel Yancey, 13 Sept. 1816, on verso; addressed: "Thomas Jefferson Esq[r] Monticello Virginia" and "In case of his absence To be forwarded to Bedford"; franked; postmarked Philadelphia, 8 July.

The ENGRAVING of Peyton Randolph (ca. 1723–75) by the Philadelphia firm of Charles Goodman & Robert Piggot was probably based on a 1774 portrait by Charles Willson Peale that was later destroyed in a fire. A similar painting, however, is now in the collection of Independence National Historical Park, Philadelphia, while a miniature made by Peale from the original portrait is owned by the Carnegie Museum of Art in Pittsburgh (*Delaplaine's Repository*, vol. 1, plate opp. p. 107; William S. Baker, *American Engravers and Their Works* [1875], 72–3, 135–7; Peale, *Papers*, 1:171; Charles Coleman Sellers, *Portraits and Miniatures by Charles Willson Peale* [1952], 177–8; Doris Devine Fanelli, *History of the Portrait Collection, Independence National Historical Park* [2001], 267).

The portrait of Dolley Madison by Bass OTIS is owned by the New-York Historical Society. Otis's depiction of James Madison is known from an engraving by either James Neagle or John Neagle (Gordon Hendricks, "'A Wish to Please, and a Willingness to be Pleased,'" *American Art Journal* 2 [1970]: 16–7, 23–5; Fielding, *Dictionary*, 254–5; Thomas Knoles, "The Notebook of Bass Otis, Philadelphia Portrait Painter," American Antiquarian Society, *Proceedings* 103 [1993]: 236; Theodore Bolton, "The Life Portraits of James Madison," *WMQ*, 3d ser., 8 [1951]: 32–3).

[1]Manuscript: "incovenient."

ENCLOSURE

Frontispiece from *Delaplaine's Repository*

[by 6 July 1816]

Printed in *Delaplaine's Repository*, vol. 1; undated.

Thomas Birch (1779–1851), artist, was born in England, the son of the enamel painter and engraver William Birch. By 1800 he had settled in Philadelphia, where he assisted his father in the production of *The City of Philadelphia, ... as it appeared in the Year 1800* (Springland Cot, Pa., 1800; Sowerby, no. 4161). Originally a profile painter, the younger Birch later turned to landscapes and seascapes, and he portrayed a number of naval engagements from the War of 1812. He was keeper of the Pennsylvania Academy of the Fine Arts, 1812–17, and often exhibited there (Jane Turner, ed., *Encyclopedia of American Art before 1914* [2000], 42–3; Fielding, *Dictionary*, 29; Philadelphia *North American and United States Gazette*, 14, 15 Jan. 1851).

Alexander Lawson (1772–1846), engraver, was a native of Scotland. He immigrated to the United States in 1794 and soon settled in Philadelphia, where he worked for the engraving firm of Thackara & Valance for two years before beginning a successful career on his own. Lawson is best known as the engraver for Alexander Wilson, *American Ornithology; or, The Natural History of the Birds of the United States*, 9 vols. (Philadelphia, 1808–14; Sowerby, no. 1022), and Charles Lucian Bonaparte, *American Ornithology; or, The Natural History of Birds Inhabiting the United States, not given by Wilson*, 4 vols. (Philadelphia, 1825–33) (Townsend Ward, "Alexander Lawson," *PMHB* 28 [1904]: 204–8; Fielding, *Dictionary*, 211; Bayard H. Christy, "Alexander Lawson's Bird Engravings," *Auk* 43 [1926]: 47–61; Philadelphia *North American*, 28 Aug. 1846).

Lawson, the engraver of this frontispiece, worked from a drawing by Birch (PPAN: Lawson Scrapbooks, item 1:92a).

From Peter Derieux

MONSIEUR Richmond ce 6 Juillet 1816.

Ayant eté informé par L'Enquirer du 26. Juin que Mr Mazzei etoit mort a Pisa le 19. mars d^er je prends la Liberté de vous supplier de voulloir bien me marquer si vous avés appris qu'il eut fait un Testament et L'etat de sa succession, me croyant authorisé a y réclamer mes droits, en conséquence de mon mariage avec sa belle fille.

Ce fut en consequence de ce mariage qu'en L'année 1780. Mr Mazzei etant à Paris, y Signa un acte en presence des conseillers du Roy Notaires au Chatelet; par le quel il institua ma femme, L'héritiere universelle de tous les Biens qu'il laisseroit au jour de son decés, en meubles ou immèubles, en quelque lieux quils seroient Situés et sans aucune reserve, il ajouta cependant quil auroit la Liberté d'en disposer par Testament; mais je ne crois pas que cette restriction seroit valable en Loi, parcequil declara alors en presence du Comte de Jaucourt, quil n'avoit mis cette clause que pour nous faire le bien traiter dans son vieux age, car Son intention positive etoit qu'aprés sa mort, La fortune qu'il Laisseroit devint La notre. Je puis donc esperer d'aprés ces principes de justice, que Si même il avoit fait un Testament; il ny aura pu reprendre dune main ce quil nous avoit donné de Lautre, ny oublié combien il me fut prejudiciable de n'avoir trouvé dans ce quil nous avoit donné d'effectif qu'une terre mauvaise et inculte, dont cependant par Larticle 9. de notre contrat il déclara consentir que le produit en discontinueroit d'avoir Lieu a Son profit aussitot que nous viendrions en Virginie.

Comme vous pouriés penser, Monsieur que la raison qui L'empecha de nous faire pendant sa vie tout le bien que nous en esperions, provenoit peut etre de ce que le mariage n'avoit pas recu son approbation, et que j'ai a coeur de pouvoir vous persuader que ce ne fut pas le cas, je prends la liberté de vous envoyer une de Ses lettres au Cte de Jaucourt ou vous trouverés Jespere que Son attention a lui annoncer quil en avoit fait part a l'ami du Comte de Vergennes demontre assés quil Lui avoit eté agreable.

Je vous supplie Monsieur en consideration des droits que je me crois fondé a reclamer et me propose de faire valloir dans la Succession de Mr Mazzei, de voulloir bien me rendre le Service de retenir dans vos mains ce que vous pouvés y avoir encore a Lui appartenant Jusqu'a ce que les affaires de sa Succession soient terminés et que les Loix ayent prononcé Sur La validité de mes pretentions; J'espere qu'alors mes esperances n'auront pas eu le même Sort que dans La fortune de Me Bellanger, et que je jouirai de La Satisfaction de pouvoir vous rembourser des avances que vous avés eu la bonté de me faire en different tems dont je conserve toujours le plus reconnaissant souvenir; et qu'enfin j'obtiendrai peut être avant de mourir la consolation que je demande a Dieu de pouvoir procurer un peu damelioration dans La Situation de mes enfants, qui depuis tant danneés Languissent comme moi Sous le poids de L'infortune.

J'ose esperer, Monsieur que vous voudres bien continuer de m'honorer de vos Bontés et protection et etre persuadé des Sentiments du plus profond respect et reconnaissance avec les quels J'ai L'honneur d'être

Monsieur

Votre très humble et trés obeis[t] Serviteur P. Derieux

EDITORS' TRANSLATION

Sir Richmond 6 July 1816.

Having been informed by the *Enquirer* of 26 June that Mr. Mazzei died in Pisa on 19 March last, I take the liberty of begging to know if you have learned whether he made a will and the situation of his estate, as I believe I am authorized to claim my rights under it, in consequence of my marriage to his stepdaughter.

Mr. Mazzei was in Paris in 1780 because of this marriage, and he signed there a document in the presence of the king's councilors and notaries at the Chatelet. In it, he appointed my wife the sole heir of all the assets he left at the time of his death, both personal property and real estate, wherever they may be located, and with no reservation. While he added that he would be at liberty to dispose of his possessions through a will, I do not believe this restriction to be legally valid, because he declared at the time in the presence of the comte de Jaucourt that he had only added this clause to make us treat him well in his old age, as his positive intention was that his fortune should be ours after his death. Therefore, I hope, under the principles of justice, that even if he made a will, he could not have taken back with one hand what he had given with the other. Forgetting how harmful it was for me to find out that he had, in fact, given us only poor and barren land, for which he nevertheless declared, in the ninth article of our contract, that he would consent to relinquish his profits as soon as we came to Virginia.

As you might think, Sir, that he did not do us all the good we had hoped for during his lifetime because he had not approved of the marriage, and that I am intent on persuading you to the contrary, I take the liberty of sending you one of his letters to the comte de Jaucourt. In it I hope you will find proof enough that the marriage pleased him in the fact that he chose to advise the comte that he had sent news of it to the friend of the comte de Vergennes.

In consideration of the rights in Mr. Mazzei's estate to which I believe myself entitled and that I intend to claim, I beg you, Sir, kindly to retain in your hands what you may still have that belongs to him until the business of the succession is settled and the law has pronounced on the validity of my claim. I hope then that my expectations will not suffer as they did with regard to the fortune of Madame Bellanger and that I will be happily enabled to reimburse you for the advances you were so kind as to make me at various times and for which I remain extremely grateful. I will finally, perhaps, obtain before I die the consolation I ask God to grant me of being able to improve the situation of my children, who for so many years have languished, as I have, under the weight of misfortune.

I dare hope, Sir, that you will be willing to continue honoring me with your kindness and protection, and I ask you please to accept my most profound respects and the gratitude with which I have the honor to be

Sir

Your very humble and very obedient servant P. DERIEUX

RC (DLC); dateline at foot of text; addressed: "The Hon[ble] Th[s] Jefferson Monticello. Albemarle County—Virginia"; endorsed by TJ as received 22 July 1816 and so recorded in SJL. Translation by Dr. Genevieve Moene. Enclosure not found.

In a family Bible record, Derieux listed his marriage as having occurred in PARIS on 14 Oct. 1780, at which time Philip Mazzei was in Florence, Italy (Derieux family Bible [photocopy in ViHi]; Mazzei, *Writings*, 1:246–9).

From Charles Willson Peale

DEAR SIR Belfield July 7th 1816.

By my inquiries amongst the Watch-makers in the City, I have found a young man of good Character, just out of His apprentiship, who seems disposed to go into Virginia, I have read to him, the contents of your letter on that subject—and I have left him time to make up his mind, probably he will give me his Answer, when I go into the City; a few days hence—and then I will write again— I am now under great anxiety of mind to know what I shall do with the Museum, for since the City of Philad[a] have purchased the State House—and the Garden, a committee has been appointed to settle what rent

I must pay, and at a meeting I had with them, they tell me that I must pay 1600$ ℔r Year, insure the Building, take care of the Clock and ring the Bell in cases of fire—In the session before the last, the Legislature enacted a law, authorising the county commissioners to receive from me 400$ pr Year in case I choose to continue the Museum in the Building, I have paid a half years rent—and I have thought 400$ as much as I ought to Pay, as the Museum is by every body considered a valuable Institution and in many points of view of great utility to the City—several of my friends are of oppinion that the Counsils will not adopt the report of their committee. and I am now writing an address, which I intend to read before the Corporation of the City, the Phylosophical Society, Trustees of the University and other Citizens, who may be friends to the Museum—In this Address I give the rise and progress to its present magnitude, the utility of such an Institution, and now the Absolute necessity of measures to prevent its destruction, by a division of it, in the case of my Death. The Gas lights having brought much company together on the evenings of illumination, has given it the semblance of bringing me immence wealth. especially by those who cannot calculate the Cost of my labours & expences—and the City being much in debt & obliged to borrow 70.000$ to pay for the state-House & lot—hence, this extraordinary demand on me—which I cannot pay, therefore if the Citizens do not step forward and relieve me, I shall endeavor to sell the Museum. It has cost me 31 Years labour—and with the same industry in many other persuits, I certainly could have acquired much wealth. My fondness for mechanic's has robed me of much precious time—and I very much regret my neglect of the Pensil—my late paintings are on all hands esteemed better than my former works. I have several[1] subjects to write on that may occasion another letter soon from your much esteemed friend C W PEALE

RC (DLC); at foot of text: "Thos Jefferson Esqr"; endorsed by TJ as received 17 July 1816 and so recorded in SJL. PoC (PPAmP: Peale Letterbook).

The Pennsylvania LEGISLATURE expressed a "preference" that the upper part of the State House be rented to "the proprietor of the Museum" for $400 per year in "An Act providing for repairing the State House in the city of Philadelphia," 13 Mar. 1815 (*Acts of the General Assembly of the Commonwealth of Pennsylvania* [1814–15 sess.], 162–3). Peale delivered his ADDRESS on 18 July 1816 (Peale, *Papers*, 3:411–23). The PHYLOSOPHICAL SOCIETY was the American Philosophical Society.

[1] Manuscript: "sevrral."

From William Plumer

DEAR SIR, Epping (N.H.) July 9th 1816

On my return from an active and interesting session of our legislature, permit me to present you with a copy of my speech to them at the commencement of their session. I offer this as a tribute of respect to your exalted talents & public services,[1] and as an exposition of my own principles[2] & views of government.

I have the honor to be with much respect and esteem Dear Sir, your most obedient humble servant[3] WILLIAM PLUMER

RC (MHi); at foot of text: "Hon. Thomas Jefferson Montecello Virginia"; endorsed by TJ as received 18 July 1816 and so recorded in SJL. FC (Lb in DLC: Plumer Papers); in Plumer's hand. Enclosure: Plumer's gubernatorial address to the New Hampshire legislature, 6 June 1816, celebrating the return of peace to the United States while reminding his audience that it is "our duty in time of peace to make the necessary preparations for war" (p. 14); calling for legislation to make the state's militia requirements conform with national law; recommending the encouragement of manufacturing by exempting pertinent property from state taxes for "a certain number of years" (p. 17); suggesting that the state be divided into "equal and compact" congressional districts (p. 17) and that presidential electors be chosen by popular vote; advocating changes to the state judicial system; proposing a reduction in the salaries of the governor, supreme court justices, and treasurer; urging state protection of the "rights of conscience and of private judgment in religious matters" (p. 24); and calling for more state oversight of Dartmouth College, with his declaration that governments have "the right to amend and improve acts of incorporation of this nature" (p. 27) (*Journal of the Honorable Senate, of the State of New-Hampshire* [June 1816 sess.], 13–30; also printed in Concord *New-Hampshire Patriot*, 11 June 1816, and other newspapers).

[1] Preceding three words not in FC.
[2] RC: "priniples." FC: "principles."
[3] Preceding two words not in FC.

From Francis W. Gilmer

DEAR SIR. Winchester, 10th July 1816

I have delayed until now the acknowledgement of your favour of June 7th inclosing the 'traité du droit naturel' par Mr. Quesnay, from Mr. DuPont; under the expectation that you would not return from Bedford 'till about this time. I can but feel myself flattered by your very polite invitation to meet our 'admirable friend the Abbé,' as Mr. DuPont, calls him, at Monticello; and from the last intelligence which I had of him, I hope to accompany him to Albemarle from Winchester.

I have read Quesnay's treatise & the comments contained in your letter with equal pleasure. I thought myself happy in finding two such advocates of an opinion which I had often defended in conversation.

I have generally found those who contend for the hypothesis that man surrenders part of his natural rights on entering into civil society, argue entirely from the matter of fact as it is found to exist in the two states, without considering that it may, & indeed often must happen, in a natural society, that individuals exercise powers which cannot be derived from natural right: such as killing their fellow creatures merely from resentment. &c. And that we should always inquire in a civil Society, when a power is exercised in violation of our natural rights, whether such power be really conferred on the body politic on entering into the social compact, or whether it be not just as much an usurpation as the killing is in the other case.

It seems to have been generally admitted that men have even their natural rights better secured in civil societies than in natural ones; that their natural rights are enjoyed with a greater extent, for what Cicero says, 'Legum denique idcirco omnes servi sumus, ut liberi esse possumus,' has never been contradicted;[1] and I could never yet be convinced, that man on entering into social relations gave up any portion of his natural rights, in order as is commonly said,[2] to secure the rest. They who affirm that he has relinquished this portion, say, that in a natural society, individuals may lawfully exercise the right of killing a trespasser[3] with their own hands. But in a civil society death or some other adequate punishment is equally inflicted,[4] and all that can be said is, that the remedy is changed, which does not affect the right. But say they, the privilege of applying the remedy with ones own hands is a part of the right. Denying as I do, the correctness of this position, it cannot be overlooked, that in every civil society conformable to the nature of things, a law is, but the expression of the general will, and that general will being conformable to the rules of justice, is the will of each particular individual who thinks justly; whatever then is done by a just[5] law, is as much in conformity to the will of a just man, as if he himself had dictated the law: and every punishment inflicted on the perpetrator of a crime by such law, is as much his act as if he himself had inflicted it. And if he does not think as a just man, he could have no more right to gratify such a will in a natural, than in a civil society; since there is no state in which one can have a right, to do wrong. and all that the right of inflicting punishment with our own hands can be worth, is the pleasure of gratifying the will, which is better gratified in civil than in natural societies, because the injured party has the co-operation of the whole community in executing his will.

The advocates of this doctrine next object, that men on entering into societies submit themselves to pains & punishments[6] for crimes against the body politic as such, which did not exist in the natural state, & that therefore they give up a portion of their natural rights. Now to relinquish a right implies, that we enjoyed it before it was relinquished; but as there was no civil society in the natural state, & men could consequently commit no offence against such society, it is hard for me to conceive, what right we relinquish in subjecting ourselves to punishment for offences which we had neither right, nor power to commit in the natural state. But to consider the subject more according to its own nature than to these objections, which tho' made are out of nature; is it not manifest, that men in a natural state have a right to govern their actions as they please, provided that they violate none of the rights of others? And all the laws which are made to enable a society to maintain itself, are only to prevent such society from being subjected to the controul of particular individuals instead of that of the general will. Thus the laws against Treason, are to prevent the exercise of powers not conceded by the people: and as men cannot govern themselves without such laws; to enact them to secure the right of self government, is doing only in another way, what was previously done in the natural state, where men vindicated their right of exemption from the controul of others by force, instead of convention. But as men in a natural state had no right to controul the actions of others, they surely relinquish none in being punished for usurping such a right.[7]

I can therefore find no right at all belonging to men in a natural state which is relinquished on entering into a civil one; & if men are less free in the latter than the former, it is either because the government is an usurpation; or because a licentiousness exists in the natural state which has not the sanction of reason, or of justice, & is therefore not a natural right, but a natural wrong.

Your remarks on the opinion of Hobbes, that justice is a merely conventional thing, appear to me very[8] satisfactory. I regret with you that Mr. Tracy should have adopted such an hypothesis. This doctrine of the Philosopher of Malmesbury has always appeared to my mind, with many others of his, to spring entirely from a very bad opinion of mankind, & from a love of paradox. If Justice be conventional, I should be glad to know what governs that agreement on right & wrong;[9] for if it depends entirely on an arbitrary & capricious will, its rules could not be so constant as they are admitted to be. 'Justitia est constans & perpetua,' are almost the first words I believe in the Civil Law. Are not right & wrong in reality, whatever we may think of them, relations in themselves absolute & independent of all convention? If so, for men to agree that certain things are just & others unjust, when their agreement cannot alter the nature of these things, is agreeing to nothing more than that men on entering into social relations may if they please tolerate injustice; a power which no body ever denied them physically, or can ever concede to them morally.

If Hobbes contend that the sense of justice[10] is the effect of convention, he appears to me equally in an error. For what is this justice whether it be conventional or not, but a fitness between a moral action & the moral good which is its end? Now what is good or bad for man depends upon his wants, & his wants depend upon his[11] organization both physical & moral; & what can best gratify these wants[12] depends on the nature of things & not upon the will. Therefore justice not being controuled by the will, but depending upon the order of nature, if the sense of justice be different from this order it is a false sense, & alters not the nature of the thing itself; and if on the other hand, the sense be conformable to this order, it cannot be merely conventional because controuled by such order: and what Hooker[13] says, is evident[14] 'choice there is not, unless the thing we take be so in our power, that we might have refused & left it.' But in this case, justice being necessarily[15] conformable to the nature of things, & the nature of things independent of us, it cannot be said that justice is dependent on our wills.

we have moreover great authorities with us against Hobbes & Mr. Tracy. Aristotle has said that man is ζῶον πολιτίκον., and so indeed we have every where found him. Can it be supposed that a being from his very necessities subject to civil & social relations, is[16] without a moral sense to govern him in such relations? Would not the society be broken up for want of the only element which holds it together, before men became[17] enlightened enough[18] to discover it by the light of reason?[19] There are other 'politic animals' beside man, which must be endowed with instincts to enable them to sustain the part which as individuals they bear to the whole; for otherwise having no reason to guide them in establishing conventional standards of moral propriety,[20] their society would perish from defect of a convention to settle their reciprocal obligations: and what Hobbes has said of man out of society—would apply to them just as strongly in it. 'negari non potest quin status hominum naturalis antequam in societatem coiretur bellum fuerit.' If then even insects are created with such instincts, is it any thing unreasonable to suppose[21] that man whose relations to his fellow beings are so much more complicated, should be endowed with a similar & an higher sense,[22] to govern him in the twilight of his reason, & contribute to perfect it? The doctrine of Justinian that nature has taught all animals their natural rights, is much more agreable to my feelings & opinions: and what is justice but the observance of those rights?[23] 'jus naturale est quod natura omnia animalia docuit, nam jus istud non humani generis proprium est, sed omnium animalium.'

But I am troubling you with very crude opinions on a subject which you have already studied. I will in my first leizure hours translate the treatise of Quesnay. For a few weeks I shall be at the Bedford Springs to recruit my languid health: & may perhaps in that interval find time, if I can retirement enough, to pay Mr. DuPont that small piece of attention in return for his kindness[24] in sending me many books & letters.

with sentiments of admiration and esteem yours sincerely &c.

F. W. GILMER.

RC (MoSHi: Gilmer Papers); at foot of first page: "Thomas Jefferson esq[r]"; endorsed by TJ as received 24 July 1816 and so recorded in SJL. Dft (MoSHi: Gilmer Papers); addressed: "Thomas Jefferson esquire Monticello Albemarle County."

CICERO wrote "legum denique idcirco omnes servi sumus, ut liberi esse possimus" ("all of us in short—obey the law to the end that we may be free") in *Pro Cluentio*, 53.146 (*Cicero: Pro Lege Manilia ... Pro Rabirio Perduellionis*, trans. H. Grose Hodge, Loeb Classical Library [1927; undated reprint], 378–9). Thomas Hobbes was from MALMESBURY, England (*ODNB*). JUSTITIA EST CONSTANS & PERPETUA ("justice is constant and perpetual") is the opening statement of book 1, chapter 1, of Justinian, *D. Justiniani Institutionum libri quatuor. The Four Books of Justinian's Institutions*, ed. and trans. George Harris (London, 1761, and other eds.; Sowerby, no. 2191), 5.

CHOICE THERE IS NOT ... REFUSED & LEFT IT is from Richard Hooker, *The Works Of that Learned and Judicious Divine, M[r] Richard Hooker, in Eight Books of Ecclesiastical Polity* (London, 1676), 78. ARISTOTLE wrote that man is by nature a ζῶον πολιτίκον ("political animal") in his *Politics*, 1.1.9 (*Aristotle: Politics*, trans. Harris Rackham, Loeb Classical Library [1932; rev. ed. 1944; undated reprint], 8–9). In his *Historia Animalium*, 1.1, Aristotle asserts that, BESIDE MAN, bees, wasps, ants, and cranes are social animals (*Aristotle: Historia Animalium*, trans. Arthur L. Peck, Loeb Classical Library [1965], 1:14–5).

Hobbes argued that NEGARI NON POTEST ... BELLUM FUERIT ("it cannot be denied but that the natural state of men, before they entered into Society, was a mere War") in *De Cive*, 1.12 (Hobbes, *Elementa Philosophica De Cive* [Amsterdam, 1669; Sowerby, no. 2388, TJ's copy in DLC], 15; Hobbes, *Philosophicall Rudiments Concerning Government and Society* [London, 1651], 14). JUS NATURALE ... SED OMNIUM ANIMALIUM ("The law of nature is not a law to man only, but likewise to all other animals") is from book 1, chapter 2 of Justinian, *D. Justiniani Institutionum*, 6.

[1] Preceding four words not in Dft.
[2] Preceding four words not in Dft.
[3] Preceding two words not in Dft.
[4] TJ wrote "negatur" ("deny") in left margin opposite this phrase.
[5] Dft: "general."
[6] Dft substitutes "punishment" for preceding three words.
[7] Sentence not in Dft.
[8] Dft here adds "just &."
[9] Remainder of this and following sentence not in Dft.
[10] Dft: "right & wrong."
[11] Preceding five words not in Dft.
[12] Dft substitutes "advance this good" for preceding three words.
[13] Dft here adds "justly."
[14] Preceding two words not in Dft.
[15] Word not in Dft.
[16] Dft here adds "created."

[17]Dft from "without a moral sense" to this point reads "to sustain his part in those relations, before his reason is."

[18]Word interlined.

[19]Dft substitutes "direct him in his duty" for preceding seven words.

[20]Remainder of sentence in Dft reads "it might be said of their political associations as Hobbes has said of the state of man before he entered into society."

[21]Preceding two words interlined in RC and absent from Dft.

[22]Remainder of sentence not in Dft.

[23]Sentence in Dft to this point reads "Justinian too has said."

[24]Sentence from this point in Dft reads "for many books & letters which he has done me the honor to send me."

From John Taylor

Dear Sir Caroline Port Royal July 10. 1816

A bad state of health, the diagnostick of which evidently is, that I must 'ere long shake hands with time, has compelled me to postpone an acknowledgment of the pleasure I reaped from yours of May last, to an interval of temporary convalescence. And give me leave to Say, that no Small portion of this pleasure, was derived from the absence of any indication of old age or instability of hand, in your letter.

Having been unable to read the Enquiry since it was printed, much ill health having intervened, and it having been written long ago, I cannot Say what I should think of it upon a revision now. As an acknowledgment for some pecuniary success in Society, I imposed upon myself many years past, the three tasks of attempting to do something towards advancing agriculture, education and political knowledge; and the Enquiry was written to discharge the last; though a duty I was the least qualified to discharge. The chief object as well as I recollect, is to prove that civil liberty is unlikely to be lasting, except by placing government under the coercion of good moral principles, and by counteracting the Subversion of Such principles as are established by political or constitutional law, with the lever of civil law. For I think that "the controul of the people over the organs of their government" cannot be Safely deposited in election alone, any more than in tumultuous meetings of a whole nation; and that the controul of good moral principles, enunciated by conventions, is a powerful ally to that of election. In ordinary or civil legislation, majorities are sometimes so far from being in fact a genuine national organ, as to be the meer creatures of an individual a junto or a faction, and Seduced as engines of minorities into acts, Seldom or never perpetrated by conventions. As a System of political law for the restraint of governments, is dictated by more virtue and judgment, than civil or ordinary legislation, which is oftener warped from the publick good by the temporary interests of individuals or factions; it ought to be regarded with more veneration, and to constitute both a barrier against immoral civil legislation, and a beacon to alarm nations against those gradual Subversions of their fundamental political laws, which occur under every form of government. Against these, the widest range of election, Seems to be an insufficient security, even within the experience of the United States; for priestcraft and papercraft have Succeeded better under it, than under election Systems more contracted. A corrupt influence over election may easily by fraudulent laws, be extended Sufficiently to countervail the right however unlimited, and rotten laws may operate here as rotten boroughs do in England. It may be deceived and Seduced by banking fanaticism self interest fashion ambition and faction. A genuine influence over election may be destroyed by artifice and fraudulent civil laws, and I discern no better remedy against the Evil, than a constitutional code of political law, compounded of good moral principles. By some modes of corrupting election, the honest influence of the landed interest even in this state, Seems to be already destroyed or greatly impaired; and the circumstance brings to my mind the policy of taxing agriculture to advance manufacturing, about which I fear we differ in opinion. In my view, it endows paper capital, with a strong auxiliary to her already too competent power, for corrupting election; nor do I think it consistent with our constitutional or political law, with good moral principles, or with republican institutions, that government Should thus contaminate election, favour particular districts, and distribute wealth or poverty to individuals, in place of leaving to each his own fig tree, or without a figure, the enjoyment of his own earnings. We also differ in our ideas of the county courts of this state. I think them the most fortunate institution for dividing patronage, that was ever hit upon. Acting without pay, and seldom advanced to a higher station, the members are as little exposed to bad views as men can be; and as they make all their appointments from a personal knowledge, Such appointments can hardly be worse, than those made by wiser people without this knowledge. It is true that they are something like a cluster of states, but I do not See why the federal principle may not apply as forcibly, and as Successfully to Such a cluster, as to that of the United States themselves.

The Enquiry I believe has sold but slowly, and the best ground: next to what you are pleased to say of it, I have for Supposing it may possess some Small Share of merit, is, that Mr: Adams has favoured me with a long criticism upon it. This when finished I promised with his permission to publish, but he Some time ago stopt writing to me,

Suggesting another avocation, which I heard was a correspondence with you. Thus the good which the Enquiry might have done, in bestowing on the publick his more valuable political labours, is I fear likely to be lost.

As Soon I received your letter, I forwarded a bag of the Sweedish turnip Seed to Doctor Bankhead's for you, but I afterwards understood that your grand-daughter had previously departed for Monticello. If it Should not come to hand, or if there Should be too little of it, I will with great pleasure Send you more. With the highest respect and Esteem, I am Your mo: ob[t] Ser[t] JOHN TAYLOR

RC (MoSHi: TJC-BC); addressed: "Thomas Jefferson esquire at Monticello"; stamp canceled; franked; postmarked Port Royal, 9 July; endorsed by TJ as received 17 July 1816 and so recorded in SJL.

In the Bible "saith the king of Assyria, Make an agreement with me by a present, and come out to me, and then eat ye every man of his own vine, and every one of his FIG TREE, and drink ye every one the waters of his cistern" (2 Kings 18.31). John Adams provided a LONG CRITICISM of Taylor's *An Inquiry into the Principles and Policy of the Government of the United States* (Fredericksburg, 1814; TJ's Retirement Library Catalogue, p. 88 [no. 656] [MS in DLC: TJ Papers, ser. 7]) in thirty-two letters to the author, beginning on 15 Apr. 1814 (Charles Francis Adams, ed., *The Works of John Adams* [1850–56], 6:447–521). TJ's GRAND-DAUGHTER was Ann C. Bankhead.

From George Ticknor

DEAR SIR, Göttingen July 10. 1816.

The vessel, which carries this to my father, carries him also for you the following books—

Homerus Heyne	8. 8vo.
Virgilius Heyne	4. 8vo.
Æschylus Schultz	3. 8vo.
Juvenalis Ruperti	2. 8vo.
Tacitus Oberlini	4. 8vo
	21. 8vo—cost $35.55.

This sum, with the charges my father will pay on it in Boston, you can, as may be most convenient—to you repay to him there or to me—in Paris, or in any other[1] way you may designate.—I send them unbound, because binding here is expensive & poor—and you will observe that I have used the Virgil a little, as I send you my own copy, rather than lose a good opportunity by waiting for the one I ordered for you above two months since but which has not yet arrived.

Loesner's Hesiod is not to be had here, but I shall probably be able to pick it up somewhere—

Coray's editions are so dear here that I think you would prefer to have me purchase them in Paris, which I shall do unless you direct otherwise

I hesitate about purchasing the German Herodotus, till I know, whether Mr. Warden has purchased the Oxford one.—

These are all the books mentioned in your's of Feb. 8. which I received April 19.—

When you have looked through these, I think you will like the German editions, & if you should think proper to order any more of them in the course of the winter, I can without inconvenience, send them with my own books, which I shall in ye spring[2] forward from here through Hamburg.—At any rate, I must in the spring of 1817 be in Paris & in the winter of 1818–19 in Florence, Rome, & Naples—and whatever commissions you or Col. Randolph may have that I can execute in France or Italy, I shall do with great pleasure & ease,—as I shall be continually purchasing & sending out books for myself.—

I remain, with great respect, Yrs. etc. GEO: TICKNOR.

RC (MHi); at head of text: "No. VII."; endorsed by TJ as received 21 Nov. 1816 and so recorded in SJL. PrC (MHi); edge trimmed; endorsed by TJ as received 12 Dec. 1816. Enclosed in Elisha Ticknor to TJ, 1 Nov. 1816.

[1]Manuscript: "othe."

[2]Preceding three words added in margin.

From John Travers

SIR Lisbon 11th July 1816

Inclosed I have the honor to hand you a letter of introduction from my particular friend mr Miligan of George Town, and I regret extremely that circumstances should have arisen when I was in Richmond to prevent my delivering it, as it would I assure you [have][1] been a source of infinite satisfaction to me to have made the personal acquaintance of one so much the friend of his Country and whom I esteem above all his countrymen.

My object in sending this letter at this late period is merely to assure you that should an opportunity occur wherein I could be useful in this place, I pray you to do me the honor to command me when it will be gratifying to me to execute any commissions you may be pleased to entrust to my care

I have the honor to be

sir Your most obedient humble Servt JOHN TRAVERS

RC (MHi); between dateline and salutation: "To Thomas Jefferson Esqre Monticello Virginia"; endorsed by TJ as received 5 Oct. 1816 and so recorded in SJL. Enclosure: Joseph Milligan to TJ, 28 Aug. 1815.

[1] Omitted word editorially supplied.

From Elizabeth Trist

My Valued Friend Bird wood 11th July—16

If I had obey'd the impulse of my heart I shou'd long ere now have express'd my thanks for your favor of the 28th of April but the fear of being troublesome to my friends often deters me from writing, altho the last Winter and Spring almost incapasatated me from making the attempt my Spirits flag'd and I retain'd only the remembrance of what had occasion'd me unhappiness, and constantly in a state of Somnolency induced me to believe I shou'd become inanimate but thank God I am better, tho I daily feel the effects of age I need not assure you how much it revived me to have proof of your being in existance and in good health and on Peacheys Return from Albemarle he confirmd the glad tidings to us, that he never saw you in better health or in as good spirits God grant that the blessing may be long continued to you The news paper of last week announces the Death of our friend Hawkins I was not surprised for his life has been prolong'd beyond my expectation, but the loss of a friend can not but excite emotions, I believe he has done a great deal of good in melioration of the Savage life—tho I believe he made many enemies among the white Settlers in establishing the Rights of the Indians but time will do justice to his memory and acknowledge his Philanthrophy—I was surprised to see Charles Thompsons name in the paper for I was under the impression of his being defunct some years, have you ever seen his translation of the Bible? I want an Edition of that Holy Book printed with a large letter pray recommend to me what edition you think the best I think your predictions will Soon be verified with regard to France and England if the News papers are to be depended upon. a Storm is gathering which will revolutionize england and emancipate france from her present oppressors—I agree with you that it wou'd have been better for the happiness of mankind If Bonaparte had been a Prisoner in St Helena instead of destroying the human race by his ambitious projects, I used to consider him in a very advantagious point of view till he made that campaign in Russia never was any thing more horrid then the description given by Labaume of the sufferings misery and Death of 400 thousand Souls that composed the french Army besides the destruction they caused in Russia, and the misery they have entail'd on that people So much for large standing armies, for it appears that the state of the french Army made it necessary to undertake somthing to appease the discontent which prevaild in consiquence of their inactive state, Pillage and promotion seem'd to be the general motive that led to that campaign and perhap[s] it is well for mankind that they met so severe a check God grant that we may never keep up a large Army in time of Peace we have much to be thankful for that our destinay has removed us from the Neighbourhood of such Sanguinary people, M[r] Gilmer and my Neice join me in wishing you long life and health and every other blessing that can rend[er] the evening of your days pleasant and happy and believe me your Sincere friend E, TRIST

RC (MHi); edge trimmed; endorsed by TJ as received 11 Aug. 1816 and so recorded in SJL.

Peachy R. Gilmer, on his RETURN from Albemarle County, confirmed TJ's good health. The longtime federal Indian agent and former United States senator Benjamin HAWKINS died on 6 June 1816 (Washington *Daily National Intelligencer*, 25 June 1816). Eugene LABAUME wrote a *Relation Circonstanciée de la Campagne de Russie* (Paris, 1814, and other eds.). Trist's niece (NEICE) was Mary House Gilmer.

A letter from Trist to TJ's granddaughter Ellen W. Randolph (Coolidge), not found, was enclosed in this letter (see Trist to TJ, 10 Oct. 1816).

From Stephen Cathalan

MY DEAR SIR— Marseilles the 12th July 1816

I have the honor of Remitting you herein Inclosed the 2ta of my Last Respects of the 19th ult[o] via Bordeaux, whereof M[r] D. Strobel in the absence of W[am] Lée Esq[r] & acting in his Stead as Consul of the U.s.—has acknowledged me Receipt by his Letter of the 2[d] Ins[t]— which he was forwarding by the Ship-Tontine to Sail for new york with first fair wind;

This will Reach you by Cap[n] Isaac Doane of the Brig David Moffit of Philad[a] Ready to Sail from this Port for hyeres near Toulon to take in a Cargo of Salt for Philad[a];

I Intrusted Said Cap[n] with one Small Box Containing Immortelles, or Eternal Flowers (cassidony) which I have Gathered in the 1st days of this month at my Country Seat, directed to you under Cares & Thro' the Collector of Philad[a] to whom Said Cap[n] has Promised to deliver it, with my Letter of advice, to him, on his Safe arival.

when this Box will Reach you, I Beg your Leave to offer it to your Grand Daughters, as the only Flowers of my Garden worth to be Sent & offered to them in a Good State at Such a Great distance, tho'

I am as much as Possible Situated at hand, as the U/ States Frigate United states Commodore John Shaw, was anchored Twice at one half Gun Shot, distance where Gathered from the 29th april to the 5th may & from the 22d do to the 29th Last may; & in that Intervall I had the Pleasure of his Company on that mountanious Spot & we Drank together to your Good & Lasting health;—

if Such flowers are Acceptable I Engage myself to Send them Yearly a fresh & even larger Supply, I am not Certain whether Such a plant Grows in virginia, but if next Spring there is here an American vessel Bound for norfolk or alexandria or any Port in the cheasapeack I will Send you Some Plants in vases, also Some Layers or Twigs in a Terrine, hopping that Provided the Capn Takes Care of them in the Passage, they may Succeed & propagate very fast at Monticello with but Little Care, at Least into a Summer house in winter; here tho' we have in that Season 4 to 6 Degrées of Frost they Succeed very Easily into dry & poor Earth, where they are Cultivated with Great advantage not only as an ornment in our Parterres but Even in Small fields, without being need to water them in the Summer & Dry Season, & Since Peace with England that flower being Purchased at advantageous Prices for the planters & those of my Country Seat are preffered to any others of my neighbourghs, I am Encreasing their Plantation yearly, observing it becomes an yearly Revenue to me & my Gardner (Joint account) the English and northern Countries purchasing them at Good Prices, I am Glad to Draw a Tribute tho' Small as it may be from the British, a very Short Compensation indeed for the Losses I have Suffered by them during the war, & for what we have Still to pay to them Since they Returned into France with their allies, to have Let Scape the Destructor of mankind from the Island of Elbe in March 1815; Regretting, no Doubt, their pretended[1] Generosity by the Treaty of 1814—being moved by Self Interest & Machiavelism,!

how has Behavied their Lord Exmouth, lately, toward the Dey of algiers,! I do not pretend to plead in favour of their chief of Pirates, but why before entering into further negotiations with him, why he did not fullfill the Payment of the napolitan Captives &a he had Redeemed by a Treaty, Shamefull perhaps for his honor & of his nation, the God neptun;—it was Reserved to the united States to Shew to all Europe & christian Powers, how to treat with Success with the Powers of Barbary, but when,? when the treaties were Brocken or unexecuted by Such powers, but not by a foolish or sottish & Matchiavelick agression, as he has done;—

we will Soon See if the Result of their chalenge under Command of their Same admiral with Great forces, will be So Prompt & Successfull as the one of Commodore Ducatur ariving last year with only one Division of the u. states Frigates, without waiting for Superior forces with or by the 2[d] Division under Commodore Bainbridge; as I have not yet any official account from our Cons[l] G[al] &[a] at algiers,[2] this is Confidentialy hazarded on the Reports direct or the British news Papers.

but what digression from my 1st topic, the Immortelles Flowers! which made me forget, that of the 1st ones I Gathered in the year 1804 I made a garland over the Bust in Marble of the Immortal Gen. Washington your Predecessor President, which I Possess, & this Garland is as yet as Fresh as if it was of this Season.

Pray, how has Succeeded the Plantation of olive Trées in south Carolina?

I hope now to Receive soon, & probably by our Ministers Messrs Galatin or Pinkney, a Letter from you, acknowledging the Receipt of my 1st Invoice;—

I hope also to be honored with a Letter from the Secretary of State, in answer to my claims, also the acts of Congress Respecting Consuls &[a] which may have been issued & not Received Since the term of your Presidency Expired.

as to the 2[d] B[el] of wine of Roussillon I Just Receivd, at Last, a Letter from M[r] Durand of Perpignan in answer to mine of the 2[d] June, Informing me that he is on the eve of Sending it to me, by the 1st opportunity and of the Same q[ty] of the 1st B[el]; his Letter is of the 9th Ins[t] & I had wrote him again on that Same Day, to Recall this object to his memory;

I Received by this Same mail a Letter from henry Jackson Esq[r] our chargé d'affairs at Paris of the 6th Ins[t]—Informing me of M[r] Gallatin's arival at havre on the 3[d] Ins[t] in the Peacock Sloop of war, to be at Paris on the 9 or 10th Ins[t], he had not yet forwarded to him the Letters & packets for him, he has therefore as yet no Information to Communicate—

begging you to Excuse my Prolixity, bad Hand & Tedious Style I apprehending to have abused in this, of the Friendship you are So kind as to honor me with.

I remain with Great Respect & veneration my Dear sir your most obed[t] & Devoted Servant STEPHEN CATHALAN.

RC (MHi); at foot of first page: "Tho[s] Jefferson Esq[r] V[a] Monticello"; endorsed by TJ as received 16 Oct. 1816 and so recorded in SJL.

CASSIDONY is *Lavandula Stœchas*, commonly called French lavender (*OED*). John Steele was the United States customs COLLECTOR at Philadelphia. The escape of Napoleon (the DESTRUCTOR OF MANKIND) from the ISLAND OF ELBE (Elba) in February 1815 overturned the 30 May 1814 peace TREATY of Paris (Clive Parry, ed., *The Consolidated Treaty Series* [1969–81], 63:172–96).

In the spring of 1816 Edward Pellew, first Viscount EXMOUTH, concluded treaties with the Barbary States of Tunis and Tripoli to end the enslavement there of captured Christian sailors and fishermen. He failed to reach a similar agreement with Omar bin Muhammad, dey of Algiers, and shortly after the departure of the British fleet Algerian troops killed about two hundred fishermen on the Barbary coast. Exmouth was then sent back to Algiers to retaliate, after which he obtained an agreement with the dey (*ODNB*; Robert L. Playfair, *The Scourge of Christendom: Annals of British Relations with Algiers prior to the French Conquest* [1884], 251; John Murray [firm], *A Handbook for Travellers in Algeria* [1873], 24; C. Northcote Parkinson, *Edward Pellew* [1934], 424–69).

Commodore Stephen Decatur (DUCATUR) successfully negotiated treaties for the United States with all three Barbary powers in the summer of 1815 (*ANB*; Miller, *Treaties*, 2:585–94). William Shaler was the consul general (CONS^{L} G^{AL}) of the United States at Algiers (*DAB*; *JEP*, 3:20, 21 [8, 9 Jan. 1816]). Beginning in 1788 and continuing early into the 1790s, TJ helped procure OLIVE trees for cultivation in South Carolina. In 1800 he included this activity in his "Summary of Public Service" (*PTJ*, esp. 13:180–1, 20:333, 32:122–5). James Monroe was the current SECRETARY OF STATE.

[1] Word interlined.

[2] Preceding two words interlined.

To Patrick Gibson

DEAR SIR Monticello July 12. 16.

In my letter of June 8. I mentioned the arrival from Marseilles of some wines for me at Philadelphia and Alexandria on which there would be some duties, freight & port charges to pay, which I must ask the favor of you to remit for me. the 2 boxes from Philadelphia I presume have come to hand; and I have just recieved a letter from Col^{o} Simms the Collector of Alexandria informing me he put the 4. boxes rec^{d} there on board the sloop Fairplay, Charles Brown master, on the 1st inst. consigned to you, that he had paid the freight from Marseilles 13.40 D [a]nd that the duties were 27.30 D making together 40.70 D which I must ask the f[a]vor of you to remit him with as little delay as convenient, as the advance of [t]he freight was a favor on his part, requiring immediate replacement. I wish the boxes may have got to hand in time for Johnson who is now down.

I returned from Bedford two days ago. while there I drew on you in favor of Joel Yancey for 32.25 D I inclose you a renewal of my Note in bank which will be out in the course of this month. I salute you with friendship & respect. TH: JEFFERSON

PoC (NjMoHP: Lloyd W. Smith Collection); on verso of reused address cover of Joseph Delaplaine to TJ, 27 May 1816; three words faint; at foot of text: "M[r] Gibson"; endorsed by TJ.

The 1 July 1816 letter was actually written by William D. Simms on behalf of his absent father, COL[o] Charles Simms. The draft of 5 July 1816 in favor of Poplar Forest superintendent JOEL YANCEY reimbursed his payment of $32.25 "to John Depriest for plank." The enclosed RENEWAL, not found, was for a $2,000 note from the Bank of Virginia in Richmond (*MB*, 2:1324, 1325).

From John F. Oliveira Fernandes

DEAR SIR! Norfolk 12th July 1816

My Last respects to you, from Newyork in April Last, were in answer to your much esteemed favour, of the 24 January Last—

Although I have not had as yet, M[r] Richardsons acc[t] in full of all the charges on, the Tenerife-wine; I know now; that the Cost freight; duties & &—will bring the price for the Quarter Cask, you had—to $63.81—; for which, I will draw, within 2 or 3 weeks on Mess[rs] Gibson & Jefferson of Richmond; to whom you will have the goodness to inform of it, before Same.—

These Gentlemen will forward to you, a Small bundle, containing a book, which in all probability, will amuse you, a little; in your Solitude.

To avoide, however, your just Censure, for having taken this liberty; I will offer to you my apology— A french book Seller, newly Stablished in Newyork; having received a new provision of books, while I was there; it So happened, that I visited his Shop, in the moment, he was opening Some of the boxes—

Among them, was—this „L'Angletterre vue A Londres; et dans Ses Provinces—par Le Marechal de Camp—Pillet—„

Curiosity; as well as my inveterated[1] Aversion to that Cabinet, induced me to purchase, a Copy, which I perused with avidity & horror!

I was immediatly persuaded that the English at Paris, would not like it at all—and of Course Some Police-measure would be adopted to forbid its perusal; (which I knew, in Philad[a], it had already taken place in Paris)—I purchased in the very next day the only 5 remaining[2] Copies, out of 6. imported.—Sent 4—to Some of my Friends at the Court[3] of Rio de Janeiro; Kept one for You, & other for me—

My books and other objects having arrived on the 8th instant from Newyork—it was only yesterday that I had the opportunity, to have it delivered to a Safe hand to Carry it to Mess[rs] G & J—

Consequently the Circumstance of the book being extremely Scarce, was my reason for taking the liberty of Sending it to you—

I remain—very respectfully Dr Sir Your mo: obt Servt

JOHN F. OLIVEIRA FERNANDES

RC (DLC); at foot of text: "Thomas Jefferson Esquire"; notation by TJ beneath endorsement: "Mar. 24."; endorsed by TJ as received 16 July 1816 and so recorded in SJL.

René Martin PILLET, chevalier de Saint Louis, relied on a four-year residence in England to create an unfavorable description of English government, society, and manners in his *L'Angleterre Vue a Londres et dans ses Provinces, pendant un séjour de dix années, dont six comme prisonnier de guerre* (Paris, 1815; Poor, *Jefferson's Library*, 7 [no. 329]). He also described the cruelty and hardships he suffered during six years as a prisoner of war on a British pontoon off the coast of England (*Biographie universelle*, 15:248). Reviews of Pillet's book appeared in London in the *Quarterly Review* 13 (1815): 442–8, and in such American newspapers as the *Richmond Enquirer*, 18 May 1816.

[1] Manuscript: "inverated."
[2] Manuscript: "remainin."
[3] Manuscript: "Cout."

Proposals to Revise the Virginia Constitution

I. THOMAS JEFFERSON TO "HENRY TOMPKINSON" (SAMUEL KERCHEVAL), 12 JULY 1816

II. THOMAS JEFFERSON'S NOTES ON REVISING THE VIRGINIA CONSTITUTION, [CA. 1816?]

EDITORIAL NOTE

Virginia adopted its first written constitution by a unanimous vote on 29 June 1776 at a convention held in Williamsburg. Not surprisingly, considering the new state's experiences as a British colony, the charter greatly restricted executive power and gave the legislature the authority not only to pass laws, but to appoint the governor, Council of State, attorney general, and all state judges. To the dismay of many Virginians, however, representation in the General Assembly was not based on population. Instead, the members were allotted under a system that more and more favored the commonwealth's smaller, eastern counties. Each county sent two representatives to the House of Delegates, while districts composed of several adjacent counties chose state senators. As Virginia's population grew in size and expanded westward following the American Revolution, the upland counties increasingly perceived the need for and right to more proportionate legislative representation. On 1 June 1816 deputies from eleven western counties called for a preliminary meeting to pave the way for a statewide convention "to reform defects in the constitution of the state." The ensuing gathering, which was held in Staunton from 19–24 Aug., failed to achieve even this modest goal.

EDITORIAL NOTE

Thomas Jefferson's 1816 correspondence with Samuel Kercheval, which originated with a missive Kercheval wrote Jefferson under the assumed name of "Henry Tompkinson" on 13 June, grew out of the effort to reform Virginia's constitution at this time. The ex-president's letters show conclusively, particularly when read in conjunction with his undated notes on the subject printed below, that he supported a substantial overhaul of his native state's political system. Jefferson favored, among other things, the calling of a convention to make the required constitutional changes; universal suffrage for white males in elections for the House of Delegates; freehold suffrage for the Senate of Virginia; "equal" (presumably meaning proportional in some way to population) legislative representation; biennial elections; the elimination of the Council of State; direct gubernatorial elections; the election of judges, justices, jurors, and sheriffs; and the division of the state into wards. While advocating reform privately, he expressly declined being drawn into a public discussion of the subject.

Following Jefferson's death on 4 July 1826, at least two newspapers published his 12 July 1816 letter to "Tompkinson" and his follow-up communication of 5 Sept. 1816 to Kercheval. An introductory letter by Kercheval to the editor of the Woodstock *Sentinel of the Valley*, dated 21 Nov. 1826, accompanied the correspondence into print. He explained therein that, after consulting "a number of the most intelligent individuals," he had concluded that it was his duty to publish Jefferson's letters. The former president's earlier objection to publication was thought to have been nullified by his passing. In addition, far from harming his reputation, Kercheval asserted that "it will add, if any addition can be made, to the transcendant character of this great apostle of the freedom and happiness of his fellow-citizens." Three years later, in 1829 he published a pamphlet containing both of the abovementioned letters and an extract from Jefferson's letter to Kercheval of 8 Oct. 1816. Kercheval prefaced this work with an introductory letter "To the People of Virginia" of 31 Mar. 1829 containing a similar explanation of his reasons for printing the correspondence.

Despite the efforts of Kercheval and others, the Virginia constitution remained unchanged prior to the state constitutional convention of 1829–30. Indeed, the resulting revised constitution of 1830 did nothing to alter the basic structure of the government, although the western counties obtained a slightly larger share of the seats in the General Assembly. Only under a later Virginia constitution, adopted in 1851, was the governor chosen by popular vote, the Council of State abolished, property qualifications for voters removed, enough of the legislature given to western Virginia to shift the balance of political power, and local officials elected within each county (William J. Van Schreeven, Robert L. Scribner, and Brent Tarter, eds., *Revolutionary Virginia, the Road to Independence: A Documentary Record* [1973–83], 7:649–54; Emily J. Salmon and Edward D. C. Campbell Jr., eds., *The Hornbook of Virginia History* [1994], 30–1, 41–2; Jacob N. Brenaman, *A History of Virginia Conventions* [1902], 33–8, 43–8; *Journal of the Proceedings of a Convention, begun and held at Staunton* [Staunton?, 1816]; Woodstock *Sentinel of the Valley*, 25 Nov. 1826; Kercheval, *Jefferson's Letters*; *Richmond Enquirer*, 5 Dec. 1826, 7 July 1829; *Proceedings and Debates of the Virginia State Convention, of 1829–30. To which are subjoined, The New Constitution of Virginia, and the Votes of the People* [1830]).

I. Thomas Jefferson to "Henry Tompkinson" (Samuel Kercheval)

Sir Monticello July 12. 16.

I duly recieved your favor of June 13. with a copy of the letters on the calling a Convention, on which you are pleased to ask my opinion. I have not been in the habit of mysterious reserve on any subject, nor of buttoning up my opinions within my own doublet. on the contrary, while in public service especially, I have thought the public entitled to frankness, and intimately to know whom they employed. but I am now retired: I resign myself, as a passenger, with confidence to those at the present helm, and ask but for rest, peace and good will. the question you propose, on equal representation, has become a party one, in which I wish to take no public share. yet, if it be asked for your own satisfaction only, and not to be quoted before the public, I have no motive to withold it, & the less from you, as it coincides with your own. at the birth of our republic, I committed that opinion to the world, in the draught of a Constitution annexed to the Notes on Virginia, in which a provision was inserted for a representation permanently equal. the infancy of the subject at that moment, and our inexperience of self-government occasioned gross departures, in that draught, from genuine republican canons. in truth, the abuses of monarchy had so much filled all the space of political contemplation that we imagined every thing republican which was not monarchy. we had not yet penetrated to the mother-principle that 'governments are republican only in proportion as they embody the will of their people, and execute it.' hence, our first constitutions had really no leading principle in them. but experience & reflection have but more & more confirmed me in the particular importance of the equal representation then proposed. on that point then I am entirely in sentiment with your letters; and only lament that a Copy-right of your pamphlet prevents their appearance in the newspapers, where alone they would be generally read, and produce general effect. the present vacancy too of other matter would give them place in every paper, and bring the question home to every man's conscience.

But, inequality of representation, in both houses of our legislature is not the only republican heresy in this first essay of our revolutionary patriots at forming a constitution. for let it be agreed that a government is republican in proportion as every member composing it has his equal voice in the direction of it's concerns, (not indeed in person, which would be impracticable beyond the limits of a city, or small township, but) by representatives chosen by himself, & responsible to him at short periods, and let us bring to the test of this Canon every branch of our constitution.

In the legislature, the House of Representatives is chosen by less than half the people, and not at all in proportion to those who do chuse. the Senate are still more disproportionate, and for long terms of irresponsibility.—In the Executive, the Governor is entirely independant of the choice of the people, & of their controul; his Council equally so, and at best but a fifth wheel to a waggon.—In the Judiciary, the judges of the highest courts are dependant on none but themselves. in England, where judges were named, & removable at the will of an hereditary Executive, from which branch most misrule was feared, and has flowed, it was a great point gained, by fixing them for life, to make them independant of that Executive. but in a government founded on the public will this principle operates in an opposite[1] direction, & against that will. there too they were still removable on a concurrence of the Executive and legislative branches. but we have made them independant of the nation itself. they are irremovable but by their own body for any depravities of conduct, and even by their own body for the imbecilities of dotage.—the justices of the inferior courts are self-chosen, are for life, and perpetuate their own body in succession forever, so that a faction once possessing itself of the bench of a county can never be broken up, but hold their county in chains, forever indissoluble. yet these justices are the real Executive, as well as judiciary in all our minor and most ordinary concerns. they tax us at will; fill the office of sheriff, the most important of all the executive officers of the county, name nearly all our military leaders, which leaders, once named, are removable but by themselves.—The Juries, our judges of all fact, and of law when they chuse it, are not selected by the people, nor amenable to them. they are chosen by an officer named by the Court and Executive. chosen, did I say? picked up by the Sheriff from the loungings of the court yard, after every thing respectable has retired from it.—where then is our republicanism to be found? not in our constitution certainly, but merely in the spirit of our people. that would oblige even a despot to govern us republicanly. owing to this spirit, and to nothing in the form of our constitution, all things have gone well. but this fact, so triumphantly misquoted by the enemies of reformation, is not the fruit of our constitution, but has prevailed in spite of it. our functionaries have done well, because generally honest men. if any were not so, they feared to shew it.

But it will be said it is easier to find faults than to amend them. I do not think their amendment so difficult as is pretended. only lay down true principles, and adhere to them inflexibly. do not be frightened into their surrender by the alarms of the timid, or the croakings of wealth against the ascendancy of the people. if experience be called for, appeal to that of our 15. or 20. governments for 40. years, and shew me where the people have done half the mischief in these 40. years, that a single despot would have done in a single year; or shew[2] half the riots and rebellions, the crimes & the punishments which have taken place in any single nation, under kingly government, during the same period. the true foundation of republican government[3] is the equal right of every citizen in his person, & property, & in their management. try by this, as a tally, every provision of our constitution, and see if it hangs directly on the will of the people. reduce your legislature to a convenient number for full, but orderly discussion. let every man who fights or pays exercise his just and equal right in their election. submit them to approbation or rejection at short intervals.—let the Executive be chosen in the same way, & for the same term, by those whose agent he is to be; and leave no screen of a council, behind which to skulk from responsibility.—it has been thought that the people are not competent electors of judges learned in the law. but I do not know that this is true, and, if doubtful, we should follow principle. in this, as in many other elections, they would be guided by reputation, which would not err oftener perhaps than the present mode of appointment. in one state of the Union at least it has been long tried and with the most satisfactory success. the judges of Connecticut have been chosen by the people every 6 months for nearly two centuries, and I believe there has hardly ever been an instance of change; so powerful is the curb of incessant responsibility. if prejudice however, derived from a monarchical institution, is still to prevail against the vital elective principle of our own, and if the existing example among ourselves of periodical election of judges by the people be still mistrusted, let us at least not adopt the evil & reject the good of the English precedent; let us retain amovability on the concurrence of the Executive and legislative branches, and nomination by the Executive alone. nomination to office is an executive function. to give it to the legislature, as we do, is a violation of the principle of the separation of powers. it swerves the members from correctness by temptations to intrigue for office themselves, & to a corrupt barter of votes; and destroys responsibility by dividing it among a multitude. by leaving nomination in it's proper place among executive functions the principle of the distribution of power is preserved, and responsibility weighs with it's heaviest force on a single head. The organisation of our county administrations may be thought more difficult.

but follow principle, & the knot unties itself. divide the counties into Wards of such size as that every citizen can attend when called on, and act in person. ascribe to them the government of their wards in all things relating to themselves exclusively. a justice chosen by themselves, in each, a constable a military company, a patrole, a school, the care of their own poor, their own portion of the public roads, the choice of one or more jurors to serve in some court, & the delivery, within their own wards, of their own votes for all elective officers of higher sphere will relieve the county administration of nearly all it's business, will have it better done, and by making every citizen an acting member of the government, & in the offices nearest & most interesting to him, will attach him by his strongest feelings to the independance of his country, and it's republican constitution. The justices thus chosen by every ward, would constitute the county court, would do it's judiciary business, direct roads and bridges, levy county and poor-rates, and administer all the matters of common interest to the whole county. these Wards, called townships, in New England, are the vital principle of their governments, and have proved themselves the wisest invention ever devised by the wit of man for the perfect exercise of self-government, and for it's preservation. We should thus marshal our government into 1. the General federal republic, for all concerns foreign & federal; 2. that of the State for what relates to our own citizens exclusively. 3. the County republics for the duties & concerns of the county, and 4. the Ward-republics, for the small, and yet numerous & interesting concerns of the neighborhood: and in government, as well as in every other business of life, it is by division and subdivision of duties alone, that all matters, great & small, can be managed to perfection. and the whole is cemented by giving to every citizen personally a part in the administration of the public affairs.

The sum of these amendments is 1. general suffrage. 2. equal representation in the legislature. 3. an Executive chosen by the people. 4. judges elective or amovable. 5. justices jurors, and sheriffs elective. 6. Ward-divisions. & 7. periodical amendment of the Constitution.

I have thrown out these, as loose heads of amendment, for consideration & correction: and their object is to secure self-government by the republicanism of our constitution, as well as by the spirit of the people; and it is to nourish and perpetuate that spirit. I am not among those who fear the people. they and not the rich, are our dependance for continued freedom. and, to preserve their independance, we must not let our rulers load us with perpetual debt. we must make our election between economy & liberty, or profusion and servitude. if we run into such debts as that we must be taxed in our meat and in our drink, in our necessaries & our comforts, in our labors & our amusements, for our callings and our creeds, as the people of England are, our people, like them, must come to labor 16. hours in the 24. give the earnings of 15. of these to the government for their debts and daily expences; and the 16th being insufficient to afford us bread, we must live, as they now do, on oatmeal & potatoes; have no time to think, no means of calling the mismanagers to account; but be glad to obtain subsistence by hiring ourselves to rivet their chains on the necks of our fellow sufferers. our land holders too, like theirs, retaining indeed the title and stewardship of estates called theirs, but held really in trust for the treasury, must wander, like theirs, in foreign countries, and be contented with penury, obscurity, exile, and the glory of the nation. this example reads to us the salutary lesson that private fortunes are destroyed by public, as well as by private extravagance. and this is the tendency of all human governments. a departure from principle in one instance becomes a precedent for a 2d that 2d for a 3d and so on, till the bulk of the society is reduced to be mere automatons of misery, to have no sensibilities left but for sinning and suffering. then begins indeed the bellum omnium in omnia, which some philosophers observing to be so general in this world, have mistaken it for the natural, instead of the abusive, state of man. and the forehorse of this frightful team is Public debt. taxation follows that, and in it's train wretchedness and oppression.

Some men look at Constitutions with sanctimonious reverence, & deem them, like the ark of the covenant, too sacred to be touched. they ascribe to the men of the preceding age a wisdom more than human, and suppose what they did to be beyond amendment. I knew that age well: I belonged to it, and labored with it. it deserved well of it's country. it was very like the present, but without the experience of the present: and 40. years of experience in government is worth a century of book-reading: and this they would say themselves, were they to rise from the dead. I am certainly not an advocate for frequent & untried changes in laws and constitutions. I think moderate imperfections had better be borne with; because when once known, we accomodate ourselves to them, and find practical means of correcting their ill effects. but I know also that laws and institutions must go hand in hand with the progress of the human mind. as that becomes more developed, more enlightened, as new discoveries are made, new truths disclosed, and manners and opinions change with the change of circumstances, institutions must advance also, and keep pace with the times. we might as well require a man to wear still the coat which fitted him when a boy, as civilised society to remain ever under the regimen of their barbarous ancestors. it is this preposterous idea which has lately deluged Europe in blood. their monarchs, instead of wisely yielding to the gradual changes of circumstances, of favoring progressive accomodation to progressive improvement, have clung to old abuses, intrenched themselves behind steady habits, and obliged their subjects to seek, thro' blood & violence, rash & ruinous innovations, which, had they been referred to the peaceful deliberations, & collected wisdom of the nation, would have been put into acceptable and salutary forms. let us follow no such examples, nor weakly believe that one generation is not as capable as another of taking care of itself, and of ordering it's own affairs. let us, as our sister-states have done, avail ourselves of our reason and experience to correct the crude essays of our first and unexperienced, altho' wise, virtuous, & well meaning councils. And lastly, let us provide in our constitution for it's revision at stated periods. what these periods should be Nature herself indicates. by the European tables of mortality, of the Adults living at any one moment of time, a majority will be dead in about 19. years. at the end of that period then a new majority is come into place; or in other words a new generation. each generation is as independant of the one preceding, as that was of all which had gone before. it has then, like them, a right to chuse for itself the form of government it believes most promotive of it's own happiness: consequently to accomodate to the circumstances in which it finds itself that recieved from it's predecessors; and it is for the peace and good of mankind that a solemn opportunity of doing this every 19. or 20. years should be provided by the constitution; so that it may be handed on, with periodical repairs, from generation to generation to the end of time, if any thing human can so long endure. it is now 40. years since the constitution of Virginia was formed. the same tables inform us that, within that period, two thirds of the Adults then living are now dead. have then the remaining third, even if they had the wish, the right to hold in obedience to their will, and to laws heretofore made by them, the other two thirds who, with themselves compose the present mass of Adults? if they have not, who has? the dead? but the dead have no rights. they are nothing; and nothing cannot own something. where there is no substance, there can be no accident. this corporeal globe, and every thing upon it, belongs to it's present corporeal inhabitants, during their generation. they alone have a right to direct what is the concern of themselves alone, and to declare the law of that direction: and this declaration can only be made by their majority. that majority then has a right to depute representatives to a Convention, and to make the Constitution what they think will be best for themselves. but how collect their voice? this is the real difficulty. if invited by private authority to County or district meetings, these divisions are so large that few will attend, and their voice will be imperfectly, or falsely pronounced. here then would be one of the advantages of the Ward-divisions I have proposed. the Mayor of every Ward, on a question like the present, would call his ward together, take the simple Yea or Nay of it's members, convey these to the County court, who would hand on those of all it's wards to the proper general authority, and the voice of the whole people would be thus fairly, fully, & peaceably expressed, discussed & decided by the common reason of the society. if this avenue be shut to the call of sufferance it will make itself heard thro' that of force, and we shall go on, as other nations are doing, in the endless circle of oppression, rebellion, reformation; & oppression, rebellion, reformation again, and so on forever.

These, Sir, are my opinions of the governments we see among men, & of the principles by which alone we may prevent our own from falling into the same dreadful track. I have given them at greater length than your letter called for. but I cannot say things by halves; and I confide them to your honor, so to use them as to preserve me from the gridiron of the public papers. if you should approve & enforce them, as you have done that of equal representation, they may do some good. if not, keep them to yourself as the effusions of withered age and useless time. I shall, with not the less truth, assure you of my great respect and consideration. TH: JEFFERSON

PoC (DLC); at foot of first page: "H. Tompkinson esq.," with TJ's adjacent note in a different ink that this was "a pseudonomy for Samuel Kerchival." Printed in Woodstock *Sentinel of the Valley*, 25 Nov. 1826, and Kercheval, *Jefferson's Letters*, 3–10. Enclosed in TJ to Joseph C. Cabell, 14 July 1816, and probably returned in Cabell to TJ, 4 Aug. 1816.

For TJ's DRAUGHT OF A CONSTITUTION ANNEXED TO THE NOTES ON VIRGINIA, see *PTJ*, 6:294–308. AMOVABILITY: "liability to dismissal" (*OED*). TJ proposed division into WARDS on multiple occasions (TJ's 1778 Bill for the More General Diffusion of Knowledge [*PTJ*, 2:526–35]; Draft Bill to Create Central College and Amend the 1796 Public Schools Act, [ca. 18 Nov. 1814]; TJ to Cabell, 2 Feb. 1816; TJ to Wilson Cary Nicholas, 2 Apr. 1816). Thomas Hobbes used the phrase BELLUM OMNIUM IN OMNIA (omnes) ("a war of all against all") in his *Elementa Philosophica de Cive* (Amsterdam, 1669; Sowerby, no. 2388), chapter 1, section 12, and chapter 8, section 10. WHERE THERE IS NO SUBSTANCE, THERE CAN BE NO ACCIDENT: TJ is contrasting the Aristotelian concepts of substance, "the essential element underlying phenomena," and accident, "something that does not constitute an essential component" (*OED*).

[1] Preceding two words interlined in place of "a contrary."

[2] *Sentinel of the Valley* and *Jefferson's Letters* have "here" at this point.

[3] Reworked from "true principle of republicanism."

II. Thomas Jefferson's Notes on Revising the Virginia Constitution

[ca. 1816?]

Convention by the people
general suffrage for Delegates
freeholders for Senate
equal representn.
seat of govmt every 10th year.
100. members. both houses older[1]
pay to be fixed
biennial elections
Govr elected by people.
no council
appt all officers except of legislrs,
judges reappntble 6 years with approbn Senate
opns seriatim entd of record.
division into wards

MS (ViU: Peter Coolidge Deposit); written entirely in TJ's hand on one side of a small scrap; undated.

OPNS SERIATIM ("opinions seriatim"): on more than one occasion TJ roundly condemned the judicial practice "of cooking up a decision in Caucus, & delivering it by one of their members as the opinion of the court, without the possibility of our knowing how many, who, and for what reasons each member concurred.… [justices] would, were they to give their opinions seriatim and publicly, endeavor to justify themselves to the world by explaining the reasons which led to their opinion." The fact that, under Chief Justice John Marshall, the United States Supreme Court habitually adhered to the caucus model did little to endear it to the former president (TJ to James Pleasants, 26 Dec. 1821 [quote]; TJ to William Johnson, 27 Oct. 1822).

[1] Preceding three words interlined in place of "Senators older."

To Charles Simms

SIR Monticello July 12. 16.

I have just now recieved from mr William D. Simms of your office his letter of the 1st inst. informing me he had shipped my wines for Richmond, that you had been so kind as to pay the freight from Marseilles 13.40 D and that the duties were 27.30 D I have therefore by this day's mail requested messrs Gibson & Jefferson of Richmond to remit you without delay 40.70 D which I hope you will immediately recieve; and with my thanks for your kindness &

attention in this business I pray you to accept the assurance of my great respect Th: Jefferson

RC (University Archives, Stamford, Conn., 1996); at foot of text: "Col° Charles Simms." PoC (MHi); on verso of reused address cover of John F. Dumoulin to TJ, 31 May 1816; endorsed by TJ.

From Gerardus Vrolik

Amsterdam ce 12e Juillet 1816.

Je suis chargé de vous communiquer que Sa Majesté le Roi à donné à l'Institut établi à Amsterdam, le titre d'Institut Royal des Sciences, des belles lettres et des beaux Arts des Pays-bas. Elle avait au préalable chargé cette compagnie de revoir ses règlemens, et d'y faire les changemens utiles ou nécessaires pour repondre au dessein qu'avait Sa Majesté de donner à cet établissement plus de developpement en y ajugeant comme membre des Savans des provinces méridionales du Royaume. Sa Majesté a approuvé ce règlement à très peu de choses près tel qu'il Lui a été offert;—Le nombre des membres regnicoles de la première Classe sera dorénavant de quarante cinq au lieu de trente. Enfin Sa Majesté a confirmé par son décrêt du 28 mai tous les membres actuels, et en a nommé de nouveaux: ceux-ci sont pour la première Classe M.M. Le Commandeur de Nieuport, Burtin, van Mons, Sentelet, et Dequin à Bruxelles; Wauters et Zerbeck, à Gand; Roucel, à Alost; Parmentier, à Enghien; Utenhove, à Jutphaas pres d'Utrecht; Minkelers à Maastricht; et Kluiskens, à Gand.

Si nous avons travaillé avec constance même à des epoques qui rendaient l'existance de l'Institut incertaine ou précaire, nous nous sentons animés d'un nouveau Zêle actuellement que nous sommes definitivement organisés; et nous nous flattons, Monsieur, que vous voudrez bien prendre part à nos travaux, et coopérer ainsi avec nous aux Vues bienfaisantes de Sa Majesté pour le perfectionnement des Sciences, et la propagation des lumières

G: Vrolik.
Secrétaire perpétuel de la première
Classe de l'Institut Royal des Sciences
des belles lettres et des beaux Arts
des Pays-bas.

EDITORS' TRANSLATION

Amsterdam 12 July 1816.

I have been charged with communicating to you that His Majesty the king has given the institute established in Amsterdam the title of Royal Institute of Sciences, Belles Lettres, and Fine Arts of the Low Countries. He had previously commanded this society to review its rules and make useful or necessary changes to them, in accordance with the plan of His Majesty to expand this establishment by enrolling as members scholars from the southern provinces of the kingdom. His Majesty approved this new regulation almost in the form that it was presented to him. From now on there will be forty-five first-class members from the kingdom instead of thirty. Finally, His Majesty confirmed in his decree of 28 May all the current members and nominated new ones. These are, for the first class, Messrs. Commandeur de Nieuport, Burtin, van Mons, Sentelet, and Dequin from Brussels; Wauters and Zerbeck, from Ghent; Roucel, from Aalst; Parmentier, from Enghien; Utenhove, from Jutphaas near Utrecht; Minckelers from Maastricht; and Kluyskens, from Ghent.

If we have worked steadily even when the existence of the institute was uncertain or precarious, we feel animated by a new zeal now that we are definitely organized, and we flatter ourselves, Sir, that you will be willing to take part in our work and, thus, cooperate with us toward achieving the benevolent designs of His Majesty for perfecting the sciences and propagating enlightenment

G: VROLIK.
Perpetual secretary of the first
class of the Royal Institute of Sciences,
Belles Lettres, and Fine Arts
of the Low Countries.

RC (MoSHi: TJC-BC); at foot of first page: "Monsieur Jefferson, Membre associé de la première Classe de l'Institut Royal des sciences, des belles lettres et des beaux Arts des Pays-bas"; addressed: "Monsieur Jefferson, Membre associé de l'Institut Royal des Sciences des Belles lettres et des beaux Arts des Pays-bas; Monticello en Virginie dans l'Amérique"; stamped "SHIP"; franked; postmarked Baltimore, 16 Nov.; endorsed by TJ as received 11 Dec. 1816 and so recorded in SJL. Translation by Dr. Genevieve Moene.

From David Bailie Warden

DEAR SIR, Paris, 12 July, 1816.

our minister, mr. Gallatin, has arrived at Paris, and handed me your letter of the 17th of may. Finding that the Peacock does not return directly to the United States, I have requested a friend of mine, mr Carere of Baltimore,[1] to have your Books sent from Havre for that port, on board of a vessel in which he proposes to embark. I inclose a copy of the invoice of the Books, amounting to nineteen hundred francs; and will send you the receipt as soon as the Booksellers have received a note of the expences of carriage &c. I hope that you will be pleased with the selection. The Debure, who are the sons of the well-known Debure, have the reputation of being honest[2] in their business. They promise to procure the work in question; and any others which you may wish to possess.[3] Since the late change of politicks[4] in france, classical works have increased in price, while those on Science, and politicks[5] have greatly diminished.

I pray you to accept my thanks for your friendly interference in my behalf; and to present my respects to mr. & mrs. Randolph and family. I find that I must now Seek other means of existence.[6]—It would appear that Europe is far from being tranquil. The will of Sovereigns is not that of the enlightened class of people: and it is doubtful whether the former, with all their military apparatus, will succeed even for a time, in reestablishing[7] an order of things to which the latter are strongly opposed. England was never in a more critical situation than at this moment.

I am, dear Sir, with great respect your most obed[t] Sert

D. B. WARDEN.

RC (DLC); at foot of text: "Thomas Jefferson Esquire, monticello"; endorsed by TJ as received 18 Sept. 1816 and so recorded in SJL. FC (MdHi: Warden Letterbook); entirely in Warden's hand; lacking closing and signature. Enclosed in TJ to David Gelston, 19 Sept. 1816, and Gelston to TJ, 26 Sept. 1816.

The members of the de Bure (Debure) family were eminent publishers, booksellers, and bibliophiles active in Paris during the eighteenth and nineteenth centuries. Guillaume François de Bure (1731–82) published *Bibliographie Instructive: ou Traité de la Connoissance des Livres Rares et Singuliers* (Paris, 1763–68), a seven-volume bibliographical treatise on rare books. After his death, his brother Jean François de Bure de Saint-Fauxbin (1741–1825), a noted Hellenist, and their cousin Guillaume de Bure (1734–1820) led the firm. They strengthened its reputation by specializing in rare books, composing excellent catalogues, and publishing French classics such as works by François Rabelais. They were succeeded in turn by Guillaume de Bure's two sons, Jean Jacques de Bure (d. 1853) and Jacques de Bure (d. 1847), who continued the family business under the name of de Bure Frères until they sold it in 1834 (Hoefer, *Nouv. biog. générale*, 13:295–7; *Biographie universelle*, 10:245–7; Gustave Chaix d'Est-Ange, *Dictionnaire des Familles Françaises Anciennes ou Notables A la fin du XIXe siècle* [1903–29], 7:392–3).

[1] Preceding two words not in FC.
[2] FC: "very honest."
[3] Sentence not in FC.
[4] Preceding two words not in FC.
[5] FC: "those of mere Science."
[6] Preceding two sentences not in FC.
[7] RC and FC: "reestabling."

E N C L O S U R E

Invoice of Books for Thomas Jefferson Purchased from de Bure Frères

facture des Livres remis en une caisse Cordeé et emballeé en toile grasse et Maigre; Marqueé. Libri. ✗ I. M. T. J. adresseé a Mrs Hottinguer et cie, negociants au Havre.

1816		*f*
Mai—30.	flavii josephi opera, gr. et lat. lipsiæ, 1782, 6 vol. in 8o, dem. vel.	72
	thucydidis opera, gr. et lat. Biponti, 1788, 6 vol. in 8o, v. j.[1]	80
	arriani expeditio alexandri et historia indica, gr. et lat. 1757, in 8o, velin	16
	diogenes Laertius, gr. et lat. excud. H. Stephanus, 1570, in 8o, v. f.	11
	diodorus siculus, gr. et lat. Biponti, 1793, 11 vol. in 8o, v. j.	124
	titus Livius, cum notis clerici, 1710, 10 vol. in 12, v. b.[2]	21
	cæsaris commentarii, in usum delphini, Londini, 1788, in 8o, v. porph.[3]	12
	taciti opera, cum not. variorum, amst. 1672, 2 vol. in 8o,[4] velin	48
	xiphilini epitome rerum romanarum, gr. Lutetiæ, 1551, in 4to,[5] dem. vel.	11
	Herodiani historiæ, gr. et lat. oxoniæ, 1678, in 8o, velin	9
	eutropii Breviarium. historiæ romanæ, Lugd. bat. 1762, in 8o, v. f.[6]	15
	zozimi historiæ, gr. et lat. oxonii, 1679, in 8o, v. b.	12
	geoponica, gr. et lat. ed. Niclas, lipsiæ, 1781, 4 tom. en 2 vol. in 8o, v. m.	36
	histoire des animaux d'aristote, en grec et en franç. par Camus, 2 vol. in 4to, v. j.[7]	30
	æschinis socratici dialogi tres, gr. et lat. amst. 1711, in 8o,[8] v. j.	10
	Senecæ philosophi et Senecæ rhetoris opera,[9] argentorati, 1809, 6 vol. in 8o, v. j.	48
	œuvres de seneque, trad. par la grange, paris, 1795, 6 vol. in 8o, v. rac.	30
	vetus testamentum græcum, Londini, 1653, petit in 8o, v. b.[10]	10
	historia et concordia evangelica, paris. 1660, in 12, v. b.	2
	etat des etoiles fixes, de ptolemeé, trad. par Montignot, Strasbourg, 1787, in 4to vel.[11]	7

dionysii orbis descriptio, gr. et lat. Londini, 1688, in 8°, v. b.[12]	9
Homeri opera, gr. et lat., ed. j. a. Ernesti, lipsiæ, 1759, 5 vol. in 8°, vel.[13]	125
apollonii rhodii argonautica, gr. et lat. ed. shaw, oxonii, 1779, in 8°, v. j.	19
poetæ minores græci, gr. et lat. ed. wintertone, Lond.[14] 1712, in 8°, v. b.	9
juvenalis et persii satyræ, cum not. var. Lugd. bat. 1671, in 8°, velin	8
Sophocles, gr. et lat. cum notis t. johnson, Etonœ, 1788, 2 vol. in 8°, v. j.[15]	24.
oratores græci, gr. ed. reiske, lipsiæ, 1770, 12 vol. in 8°, v. j.	220
Hederici lexicon græcum, ed. ernesti, lipsiæ, 1796, in 8°, cart.	21
le jardin des racines grecques, paris, 1694, in 12, vel.[16]	4
dictionnaire histor. de Ladvocat, avec le supplement, paris, 1777, 4 vol. in 8°,[17] v. m.	24
tablettes chronologiques de Lenglet dufresnoy, paris, 1778, 2 vol. in 8°, vel.[18]	14
	1081[f]
Micali,[19] l'italia avanti il dominio dei romani, firenze, 1810, 4 tomes vel. en 2 vol. in 8°, v. ec. et atlas in fol. dem. vel.	54
Sismondi, republiques Italiennes du moyen age, paris, 1809, 11 vol. in 8°, v. ec.	83
davila,[20] guerre civili di francia, Londra, 1801, 6 vol. in 8°, v. j.	47
Memoires[21] de Sully, Londres,[22] 1767, 8 vol. in 12, v. m.	22
tableau histor. de l'europe, par de segur, paris, 1810, 3 vol. in 8°, v. porph.	17
Botta, guerra d'america, 4 vol. in 8°, veau porphire, la reliure seulement	8
traité de la culture de la vigne,[23] paris, 1801, 2 vol. in 8°, v. porph.[24]	15
Lavoisier, traité element. de chimie, paris, 1789, 2 vol. in 8°, v. porph.[25]	11
cabanis, degrè de certitude de la medecine, paris, 1803, in 8°, v. rac.	7–50
______ coup d'oeil sur les revolutions de la medecine, paris, 1804, in 8°, v. rac.	7–50
Synopsis plantarum, aut. persoon, paris. 1805, 2 vol. in 12,[26] v. porph.	22
traité elementaire d'histoire naturelle, par dumeril, paris, 1807, 2 vol. in 8°, v. porph.[27]	13–50
Condorcet, progrès de l'esprit humain, paris, 1798, in 8°, v. m.	4

cabanis, rapport du physique et du moral de l'homme, 1815, 2 vol. in 8°, v. porph.[28]	17
Calvini lexicon juridicum, coloniœ, 1734, in fol. v. b.	21
histoire des mathematiques, par Montucla, paris, an VII, 4 vol. in 4to, v. rac.	66
Bezout, cours de Mathematiques, publ. par peyrard, 5 vol. in 8°, v. rac.	33
tables of Logarithms,[29] by Callet, 1808, in 8°, v. j.	17–50
astronomie physique, par Biot, 1810, 3 vol. in 8° v. ec.	30
astronomie, par Lalande, paris, 1792, 3 vol. in 4to, rel.[30]	80
l'astronomie, poeme, par gudin, 1810, in 8°, v. porph.	5
Bibliotheque d'architecture, par jombert, paris, 1766, 4 vol. in 8°, v. m.	27
grammatica castellana, en madrid, 1781, in 12, dem. vel.	4–50
dictionnaire espagnol, par Cormon, Lyon, 1803, 2 vol. in 8°, v. rac.	13
______ de la langue française, par Boiste, paris, 1811, in 8°, oblong, v. rac.	16
abregé de l'histoire de france du pres. Henault, paris, 1775, 5 vol.[31] in 8°, v. rac.	27
histoire de france depuis la revolution, par toulongeon, paris, 1801, 7 vol. in 8°, v. j.	57–75
fabri thesaurus eruditionis scholasticæ, lipsiæ, 1726, in fol. velin	15
frais de caisse, d'emballage, du douane, etc.	35[32]
	1857^f^–25^c.^

articles oubliés

Horace de dacier, 10 vol. in 12, v. b.[33]	22^f^	43
Botta, guerra d'america, 4 vol. in 8°, brochés[34]	21	
		1900^f^–25^c.^[35]

J. Duryee
E. Seabury

MS (MHi); in an unidentified hand, signed by J. Duryee and Edmund Seabury; at foot of first page: "la suite de l'autre part" ("continues on the other side"); repeated sum at head of second page editorially omitted; endorsed by TJ at head of text: "1816. May"; notation by TJ at foot of text: "fr.
$5\frac{1}{3}$ = 1.D.
fr. c
24.93 = 1.£ sterl."
Also enclosed in TJ to David Gelston, 19 Sept., and Gelston to TJ, 26 Sept. 1816.

TJ received two other versions of this book list, which vary slightly in sequence and contain fewer details: (1) a packing list (MS in MHi; in an unidentified hand; at head of text: "Memoires des livres Contenus dans cette Caisse" ["Records of the books contained in this crate"] and, in TJ's hand: "1816. May 30."; a small check mark, probably by TJ, appears to the left of each book title; endorsed by TJ: "1816. May 30."). (2) a receipt (MS in DLC: TJ Papers, 207:36954–5; in an unidentified hand, signed "de Bure freres"; at head of text: "Memoire des livres remis en une Caisse cordée et emballée en toile grasse et maigre, marquée, Libri. ⨳ **I. M. T. J.** adressée a Mrs Hottinguer et Cie Negociants au Havre" ["Record of books sent in a crate tied with rope, wrapped in a thin oilcloth, and labeled Libri. ⨳ **I. M. T. J.** addressed to Messrs. Hottinguer & Co., merchants at Le Havre"] and "1816 Mai–30"; at foot of text: "Reçu composé a paris ce 6 aout 1816" ["Receipt written at Paris 6 Aug. 1816"]; enclosed in David Bailie Warden to TJ, 9 Aug. 1816). Significant differences between the three lists are described in the textual notes below.

After selling his library to the United States Congress in 1815, TJ set out to rebuild his book collection, and this invoice represents a significant early step in that process. Most of the books detailed here were in TJ's library at Monticello at the time of his death and are listed in Poor, *Jefferson's Library*. A bound MS in TJ's hand (DLC: TJ Papers, ser. 7) provides a more detailed catalogue of TJ's retirement library at Monticello. With rare exceptions the titles are the same as those listed in Poor and in the same organizational sequence. Other books that TJ kept in his library at Poplar Forest are found in Leavitt, *Poplar Forest*. The books on the invoice printed above are in most cases readily identifiable in the Editors' index under author, editor, translator, or title. Exceptions are listed below, as are titles for which the location of TJ's copy is known.

The following abbreviations and terms are used above to indicate the page sizes of each book: "fol." or folio, in which a standard printing sheet is folded once to produce two leaves, or four pages; "4[to]" or quarto, in which a sheet is folded twice to produce four leaves, or eight pages; "8[o]" or octavo, in which a sheet is folded three times to produce eight leaves, or sixteen pages; and "12 mo." or duodecimo, in which a sheet is folded four times to produce twelve leaves, or twenty-four pages. In general, the more pages a sheet makes, the smaller the book. The invoice uses the following French terms and abbreviations to describe the covers of the books: "bas." and "baz." for basanne (basil/bazil: vegetable-tanned, sheep- or lambskin); "brochés" (sewed; stitched); "cart." for cartonné (boards); "dem. vel." for demi vélin (half vellum); "pet." for petit (small); "rel." for relié (bound); "v. b." for veau bleu (blue calf); "v. br." for veau brun (brown calf); "v. ec." for veau écaille (tortoise calf); "vel." and "velin" for vélin (vellum); "v. f." for veau fauve (plain calf); "v. j." for veau jaspé (mottled calf); "v. m." for veau marbré (marbled/mottled calf); "v. Porph." for veau porphyre (porphyry calf); and "v. rac." for veau racine (tree calf, in which brown calf is stained with acid to resemble the branches of a tree) (Matt T. Roberts and Don Etherington, *Bookbinding and the Conservation of Books: A Dictionary of Descriptive Terminology* [1982], 18–9, 28, 35, 45, 268; Edwin Hamlin Woodruff, "A List of Abbreviations Used in Book Catalogues," *Library Journal* 12 [1887]: 187–92; *OED*, cf. "tree").

FACTURE: "invoice." LIPSIÆ: Leipzig. BIPONTI: Zweibrücken.

Arrian (ARRIANI), *Arriani Nicomedensis Expeditionis Alexandri Libri Septem et Historia Indica Græc. et Lat. cum Annotationibus* . . ., ed. George Raphel (Amsterdam, 1757; Poor, *Jefferson's Library*, 3 [no. 9]; TJ's copy in MBAt; same ed., Sowerby, no. 25).

Excudebat (EXCUD.): "printed."

DIODORUS SICULUS, *Διόδωρος. Bibliothecae Historicae Libri qui Supersunt*, eds. Pieter Wesseling, Christian G. Heyne, and Jeremias N. Eyring, 11 vols. (Zweibrücken, 1793–1807; Poor, *Jefferson's Library*, 3 [no. 17]; TJ's copy in MoSW; another ed., Sowerby, no. 37). CUM NOTIS: "with notes."

Tacitus (TACITI), *C. Cornelii Taciti Opera, quæ exstant*, ed. Johann Friedrich Gronovius and Jacob Gronovius, 2 vols. (Amsterdam, 1672; Poor, *Jefferson's Library*, 3 [no. 44]; TJ's copy in DLC; another Latin ed., Sowerby, no. 80, was interleaved by TJ with Tacitus, *The Works of Tacitus*, ed. Thomas Gordon, 4 vols. [London, 1737], to form 9 vols.). VARIORUM: "of various people."

LUTETIÆ: Paris. OXONIÆ: Oxford. Lugduni Batauorum (LUGD. BAT.): Leiden. ARGENTORATI: Strasbourg.

Seneca (SENEQUE), *Oeuvres de Séneque le philosophe*, trans. Nicolas de La Grange, 6 vols. (n.p., [1795]; Poor, *Jefferson's Library*, 8 [no. 445]; TJ's copy of vols. 1–3 in ViCMRL and vols. 2 and 5 of a duplicate set owned by TJ in ViU; same ed., Sowerby, no. 1324).

Dionysius Periegetes (DIONYSII), *Διονυσίου Οἰκουμένης Περιήγησις, μετὰ τῶν Εὐσταθίου Ὑπομνημάτων. Dionysii Orbis Descriptio*, eds. Eustatius of Thessalonica, Henri Estienne, and William Hill, 2 vols. (London, 1688; Poor, *Jefferson's Library*, 7 [no. 310]; TJ's copy in DLC; another ed., Sowerby, no. 3818).

Homer (HOMERI), *Ὁμήρου ἅπαντα. h. e. Homeri opera omnia*, eds. Samuel Clarke and Johann August Ernesti, 5 vols. (Leipzig, 1759–64; Poor, *Jefferson's Library*, 12 [no. 733]; TJ's copy in DLC).

SOPHOCLES, *Αἱ τοῦ Σοφοκλέους τραγῳδίαι ἑπτά. Sophoclis Tragoediæ Septem*, ed. Thomas Johnson, 2 vols. (Eton, 1788; TJ's Retirement Library Catalogue, 100 [no. 758] [MS in DLC: TJ Papers, ser. 7]; TJ's copy in PSC; same ed., Sowerby, no. 4520).

Jean Baptiste LADVOCAT, *Dictionnaire Historique et bibliographique portatif*, 4 vols. (Paris, 1777–89; Poor, *Jefferson's Library*, 3 [no. 67]; TJ's copy in ViCMRL, with vol. 1 and supplement on deposit ViU; same ed. without supplement, Sowerby, no. 146).

Giuseppe MICALI, *L'Italia avanti il dominio dei Romani*, 4 vols. in 2 (Florence, 1810; Poor, *Jefferson's Library*, 3 [no. 23]; TJ's copy, lacking atlas, in MoSW). FIRENZE: Florence.

Enrico Caterino DAVILA, *Storia delle Guerre Civili di Francia*, 6 vols. (London, 1801–02; Poor, *Jefferson's Library*, 4 [no. 73]; TJ's copy in MoSW; another ed., Sowerby, no. 198).

Louis Philippe Ségur (SEGUR), *Tableau Historique et Politique de l'Europe, depuis 1786 jusqu'en 1796*, 3 vols. (3d ed., Paris, 1810; Poor, *Jefferson's Library*, 4 [no. 86]; TJ's copy in Vi).

TRAITÉ DE LA CULTURE is Jean Antoine Chaptal and others, *Traité théorique et pratique sur la Culture de la Vigne*, 2 vols. (2d ed., Paris, 1801; Poor, *Jefferson's Library*, 6 [no. 258]; same ed., Sowerby, no. 787).

Pierre Jean Georges CABANIS, *Du Degré de Certitude de la Médecine* (rev. ed., Paris, 1803; Poor, *Jefferson's Library*, 5 [no. 186]; TJ's copy in MoSW; another ed., Sowerby, no. 861), and *Coup d'Oeil sur les Révolutions et sur la réforme de la Médecine* (Paris, 1804; Poor, *Jefferson's Library*, 5 [no. 187]; TJ's copy in MoSW; same ed., Sowerby, no. 862).

COLONIŒ Allobrogum: Geneva.

Paul Philippe GUDIN de la Brenellerie, *L'Astronomie, Poëme en quatre chants* (Paris, 1810; Poor, *Jefferson's Library*, 7 [no. 375]; TJ's copy in MoSW; same ed., Sowerby, no. 4495).

Charles Antoine JOMBERT, ed., *Bibliothèque portative d'Architecture élémentaire, a l'usage des Artistes*, 4 vols. (new ed., Paris, 1764–66; Poor, *Jefferson's Library*, 12 [no. 723]; TJ's copy in MoSW; same ed. of vols. 2 and 4, Sowerby, nos. 4215–6; other eds. of vols. 1 and 3, Sowerby, nos. 4177–8).

Charles Jean François Hénault (HENAULT), *Nouvel Abregé Chronologique de l'Histoire de France*, 3 vols. (rev. ed., Paris, 1775; Poor, *Jefferson's Library*, 4 [no. 79]; TJ's copy in DLC; same ed., Sowerby, no. 215).

François Emmanuel, vicomte de TOULONGEON, *Histoire de France, depuis la Révolution de 1789*, 7 vols. (Paris, 1801–10; Poor, *Jefferson's Library*, 4 [no. 88]; TJ's copy in MoSW; same ed., Sowerby no. 240).

Basilius Faber (FABRI), *Basilii Fabri sorani Thesaurus Eruditionis Scholasticæ* (Leipzig, 1726; Poor, *Jefferson's Library*, 13 [no. 865]; another ed., Sowerby, no. 4765).

FRAIS DE CAISSE, D'EMBALLAGE, DU DOUANE: "cost of the crate, packing, customs." ARTICLES OUBLIÉS: "omitted items."

[1] Packing list: "vel. en veau."

[2] Packing list: "veau Br."

[3] Packing list: "v. j."

[4] Receipt: "in 4°."

[5] Listed as "8vo" in TJ's Retirement Library Catalogue, 4 (no. 50).

[6] Receipt adds "cum not. var." for "cum notis variorum."

[7] Packing list: "v. m."

[8] Receipt: "in—4°."

[9] Packing list adds "Biponti."

[10] Packing list describes this book as "Biblia græca" (Greek Bible). Receipt omits "petit" and describes binding as "v. br."

[11] Packing list and receipt: "dem. vel."

[12] Receipt: "v. br."

[13] Packing list and receipt: "dem. vel."

[14] Packing list: "Cantab." for Cantabrigiæ (Cambridge, England).

[15] Packing list: "v. m."

[16] Packing list and receipt: "bas."

[17] Poor, *Jefferson's Library*, 3 (no. 67), and Retirement Library Catalogue, 10 (no. 68), describe this item as a duodecimo. Packing list adds "pet."

[18] Packing list: "Baz."

[19] Receipt: "Mocoli."

[20] Entry beginning with this word is preceded by a "#" symbol in packing list.

[21] Entry beginning with this word is preceded by a "#" symbol in packing list.

[22] Packing list: "Paris."

[23] Packing list precedes title with author's name: "Chaptal."

[24] Packing list: "v. j."

[25] Packing list: "v. f."

[26] Packing list and receipt: "in 18."

[27] Packing list: "v. j."

[28] Packing list: "v. j."

[29] Packing list adds "en Anglais" ("in English").

[30] Receipt: "vel." Packing list: "baz. R."

[31] Packing list adds "petit."

[32] Receipt substitutes "frais de transport, au havre &c. 25–25" ("cost of transport, to Le Havre, etc. 25–25") for preceding nine words. Packing list omits this expense altogether.

[33] Packing list omits this book.

[34] Packing list omits this book. Receipt combines this entry and an earlier listing for "la reliure seulement" ("the binding only") of a book by Botta into a single entry for Botta's work at a cost of 29*f.*

[35] TJ calculated to the left of this figure that the sum was equal to "356.29 D."

To Joseph C. Cabell

Dear Sir Monticello July 13. 16.

I thank you for Maine's recipe for preparing the haw, inclosed in your favor of the 4th. I really thought it lost with him, and that the publication of it would be a public benefit. I do not know that his hedgethorn is to be found wild but in the neighborhood of Washington. he chose it, I think, for it's beauty. I have extensive hedges of it, which I have too much neglected. the parts well grown appear rather weak against cattle; yet when full grown will probably be sufficient. he proposed to keep out hogs by a couple of rails passed along the bottom, and I think it will be sufficient; and that should the upper part prove too weak for very strong cattle, a pole run horizontally through will bind them together & make them sufficient. Colo Randolph thinks the Cockspur hawthorn (our common one) would be preferable as being stronger. my grandson Jefferson Randolph found one common about Willis's mountains which he thinks eminently preferable to all others. the Pyracanthus which I got from Maine is a beautiful plant, but not fit for a hedge. he tried the honey-locust meaning to keep it down by the shears, but I thought it too straggling. the holly certainly will not do with us, because all but impossible to make live in our climate. I have one tree 44. years old, not yet taller than a hedge should be. of the Cedar I have no experience but of the difficulty of either transplanting it, or raising it from the berry.

on the whole I think nothing comparable with the thorn, and that they may be made to answer perfectly with the aids I have mentioned.   I am sorry you hesitate about the translation of Say's Political economy. I have not supposed his catechism was a work of note, but rather an occasional criticism on English practices. but I have not seen it, and I think you should not wait for it.

I think your idea a good one of employing a single person for half a dozen counties. I am sure the state does not furnish one for every county, qualified & willing. there is a son of Cap[t] W. D. Meriwether's in this county who has had a collegiate education and possesses geometry enough for this operation. he has expressed a willingness to undertake our county, & perhaps would yours, for a sufficient allowance.   but what may be deemed a competent reward I know not; nor whether our court will employ mr Meriwether or the county surveyor. if the county surveyors are generally employed, the work will not be worth a copper, as few of them know any thing of geometry, but depend altogether on platting.

I salute you with great friendship & respect. TH: JEFFERSON

P.S. Col[o] Randolph tells me he has repeatedly heard mr Correa say that our Cockspur hawthorn (Crataegus cruxgalli) was the best for hedges he had ever met with.

RC (ViU: TJP); addressed: "Joseph C. Cabell esq. Warminster"; franked; endorsed by Cabell as a letter concerning "Hedges" answered 4 Aug. PoC (DLC); on verso of reused address cover of John Steele to TJ, 1 June 1816; mutilated at seal, with some missing words rewritten by TJ; endorsed by TJ.

William Woods was the Albemarle COUNTY SURVEYOR.

To David Hosack

[S]IR Monticello July 13. 16.

Uninformed of the persons particularly connected with the Botanical garden of N.Y. I hope I shall be pardoned for this address to yourself. I have just recieved from my antient friend Thouin, director of the king's garden at Paris a packet of seeds selected by him as foreign to the US. they are of the last year's gathering, but he informs me that if they arrive (as they have done) too late to be committed to the earth this year, most of them will be still good for the ensuing year. not believing I could make a better use of them than by presenting them to the Botanical garden of N. York, I have taken the liberty of sending the packet to your address by mail, and, altho' large, I have thought the object justified my franking it. I have not opened the packet knowing I could not pack them so well again; but coming from Thouin I am sure they are worthy the acceptance of the garden. Accept the assurance of my great respect & consideration.

Th: Jefferson

PoC (DLC); on verso of reused address cover of William H. Crawford to TJ, 31 May 1816; salutation incomplete due to polygraph malfunction; at foot of text: "Dr Hosack"; endorsed by TJ.

Hosack founded the Elgin Botanic garden in 1801 just outside what was then the boundary of New York City. In 1810 ownership of the garden was transferred to the state of New York (Hosack, *A Statement of Facts relative to the Establishment and Progress of the Elgin Botanic Garden* [New York, 1811]).

To Enoch Reynolds

Sir Monticello July 13. 16.

Absence from home has occasioned my not recieving till lately your favor of June 27. I have for some time declined becoming a subscriber for any new work, on the general wish to avoid every possible new engagement. I return you the inclosed however with my subscription for a copy of the Declaration of Independance, I will ask the favor of mr John Barnes of Georgetown to recieve the copy when ready, and to pay for it.

Accept the assurance of my respect. Th: Jefferson

RC (MHi); with subjoined receipt from Joseph Reynolds to John Barnes, 28 Jan. 1820 (see TJ to Barnes, 23 Mar. 1820); beneath signature: "Mr Enoch Reynolds." PoC (MHi); on verso of reused address cover of Barnes to TJ, 31 May 1816; endorsed by TJ. Enclosure not found.

To Joseph C. Cabell

Th:J. to mr Cabell. July 14. 16.

You have sometimes thought my political ramblings worth the time and trouble of reading. I inclose you a letter lately written on a subject now much agitated in our state. I will ask the favor of it's early return by mail as I have no other copy. I salute you with friendship & respect.

RC (ViU: TJP); dateline at foot of text; addressed: "Joseph C. Cabell esq. Warminster"; franked; postmarked Milton, 18 July; endorsed by Cabell. Not recorded in SJL. Enclosure: TJ to "Henry Tompkinson" (Samuel Kercheval), 12 July 1816.

Joseph Delaplaine by John Wesley Jarvis

Thomas Jefferson by Bass Otis

Engraving of Thomas Jefferson by James or John Neagle

TO

Thomas Jefferson,

THE OBLIGING NEIGHBOUR,

THE WARM, KIND, INDULGENT FRIEND,

AS WELL AS

THE ACTIVE PATRIOT,

THE ABLE STATESMAN,

AND

THE LIBERAL PHILOSOPHER,

THE FOLLOWING CONTINUATION OF

The History of Virginia

ORIGINALLY AND JUSTLY

DEDICATED TO HIM,

IS RESPECTFULLY INSCRIBED,

BY

L. H. GIRARDIN.

Book Dedication by Louis H. Girardin

Greenhouse at Monticello

Spherical Sundial

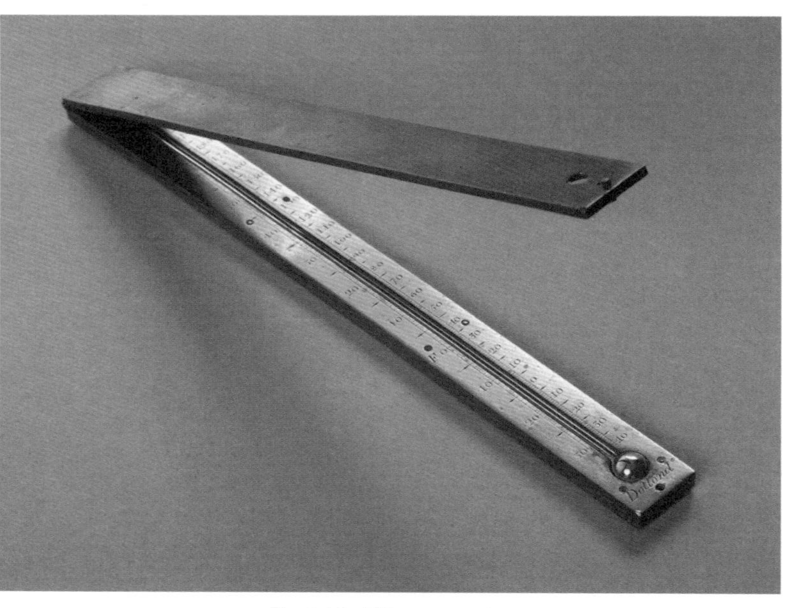

Portable Thermometer

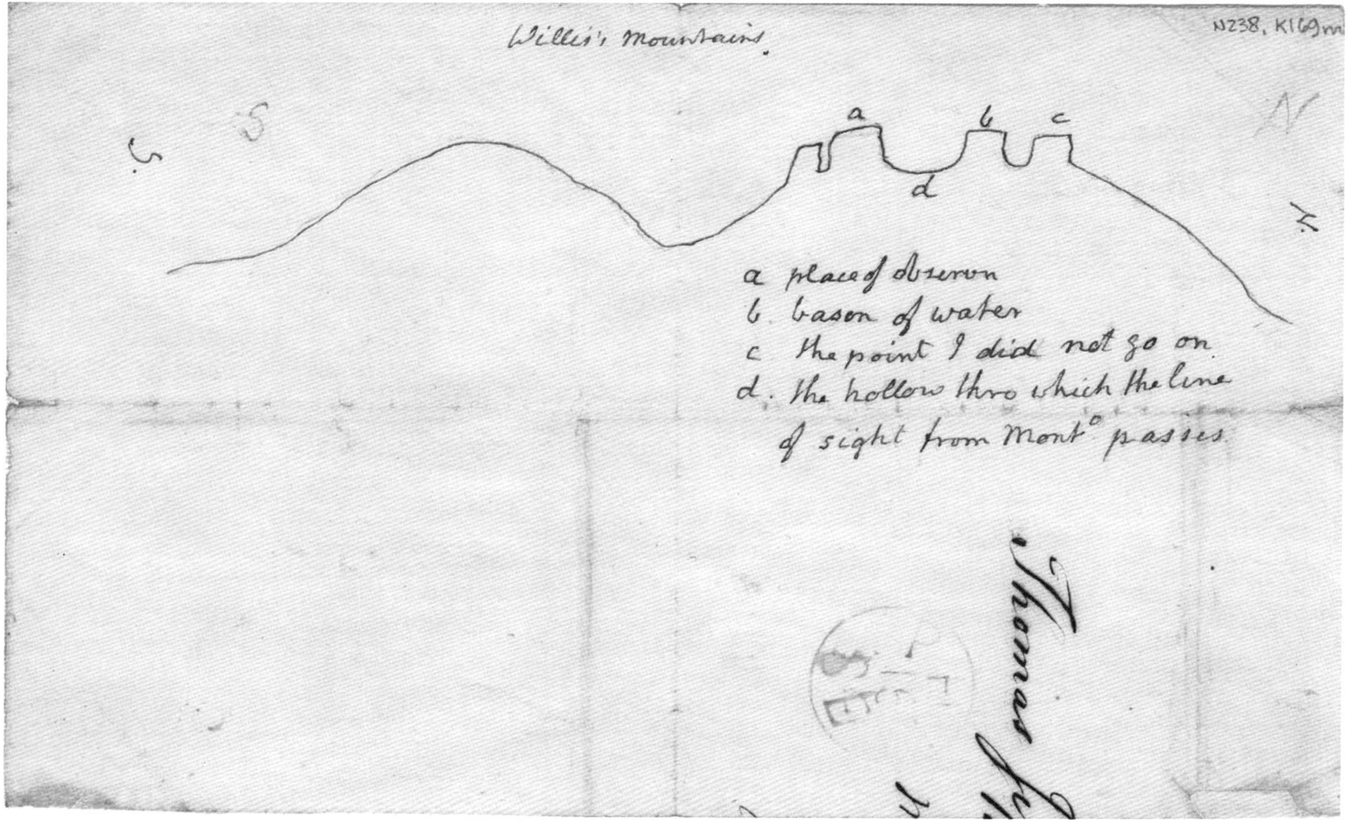

N238, K169m

Willis's Mountains.

S. S

a b c

d

N.

a place of observon
b. bason of water
c the point I did not go on.
d. the hollow thro which the line
of sight from Monto passes

Thomas Je

Willis's Mountain

Thomas Jefferson by Giuseppe Valaperta

From Francis Adrian Van der Kemp

SIR Olden barneveld 14 July 1816.

The distinguished proof of your esteem, with which you favoured and gratified me, when you honoured me with your Letter of apr. 25. induces me to take the liberty of Sending you a few lines more[.] I am pleased to Suppose, that my last has not been unacceptable, and that you approved the course, which I have taken with the papers with whom I was entrusted. These are now on their way to Old England. Since I wrote my last I received a highly valuable parcel of books from there—of which I doubt not, or Several would[1] be perused by you with delight: they are written in that Spirit which recommend themselves to elevated minds. Among these were Kenricks discourses and Several of Belsham's works. Was I So fortunate to live in your neighbourhood, I Should not hesitate with their communication, in the full confidence, that this would be acceptable. But the Same unavailing wish I have often indulged with my old friend at Quinceÿ—and yet—I was once, unexpectedly—blessed with the opportunity of visiting him.

Among these Theological works is one excentric production—which I regret, that I cannot communicate to either of you—As it is a masterly performance, in burlesque, viz. a defence of the orthodox System against Unitarian Hereticks „a new way of answering old heresies by Basanistes„ He not only defends a Triune God—but defends a Quaternity—Moses is the fourth person! The third ed: has appeared.

Did I live nearer your residence I Should flatter myself, that you might communicate with me your proposed lucubrations—for your next winter amusement—now I hope, when you have accomplished this momentous task, you will condescend to favour me with its outlines. Permit me now a few words on the Syllabus, which I have perused again and again, and I do not retract my former favorable opinion of it—I hope, it may be Seen in the Same point of view by my Brittish friends—and I am Satisfied—its publishing must eventually have a good effect.

upon what grounds do you assert—that the Mosaic Religion did imbue degrading and injurious ideas of God and his attributes?

Why do you Suppose that the reason of Jezus had not attained the maximum of his energy?

in what point was his System of moral duties deficient? and in what point were his doctrines defective?

How could he emphatically—by which I understand—to a clear conviction—preach the doctrine of a future State—if his death[2] and resurrection are not above Suspicion?
To my last query it is required—that I explain, that In my opinion it is the basis of the Christian revelation—the ground of all my future hopes. As I am persuaded, that man perish by death—as well as beast—it may be desirable—it may be made plausible—that he Should be immortal—but this too is the utmost, and I See no incongruity, that it takes no place even admitting—an intelligent good Being—governing the universe—but a dark veil on the human existence is drawn away—if his existence is to be continued—if he Shall revive again—with his former consciousness—of this gospel truth I am firmly persuaded. but the ground of my conviction is—that Jezus was a man—in every respect—that he proclaimed true doctrine—that he died—and was—in its confirmation—restored again to life.
I know not—if we Shall agree in So far—but then I have one Solid Ground of consolation more—or Some arguments must have made a deeper impression on your mind, which lost their efficacy on mine. It matters not in my opinion—if we adopt the Souls immateriality or not—whatever this may be—without the evidence of Jezus resurrection—I Should believe that Both are perishable—or, to Soften this harsh language—I Should not be able to foster my Solid hope—upon my continued existence—although I might long[3] for it.

If mÿ friend Dr W. Willoughby returns next winter to Congress—it might not be amiss—to give him Basanistes as a guide to Monticello—He wished—to pay his respect to you, and deserves in every regard to be favoured with your kind reception—being a man of Sterling worth.

Grant me the privilege, that I may continue to assure you that I remain with high consideration

Sir! your most obed: and obliged Ser^{t}

FR. ADR. VAN DER KEMP.

RC (MHi); edge trimmed; dateline at foot of text; endorsed by TJ as received 26 July 1816 and so recorded in SJL, which gives its place of origin as "Olden barneveld (Trenton N.Y.)."

Van der Kemp's FRIEND AT QUINCEŸ was John Adams. The EXCENTRIC PRODUCTION is "Basanistes," *Αἱρέσεων ἀνάστασις or, A New Way of Deciding Old Controversies*, 3d ed. (London, 1815). The author's pseudonym is taken from the Greek word βασανστης meaning "tormentor" (James Strong, *The New Strong's Exhaustive Concordance of the Bible* [1990], Greek entry no. 930).

[1] Manuscript: "vould."
[2] Manuscript: "dead."
[3] Manuscript: "loung."

From David Bailie Warden

DEAR SIR, Paris, 14 July, 1816.

I had the honour of writing to you, on the 12th Instant, inclosing the invoice of your Books, which mr. Carere of Baltimore had promised to have shipped on board his vessel about to sail for that port: but the house of Hottinguer has since informed me, that they have been put on board of the ship united states, bound to New york, and addressed to the Collector of that port. I inclose the Bill of lading and account of charges.—

It gave me much pleasure to see mr. Terril, whom you were pleased to introduce to me. He is a young Gentleman of great promise. Baron Humboldt bids me present you his respects: he has, on several occasions, expressed his regret in not hearing from you for a long time. The London quarterly review of may last, contains a severe attack against him excited probably by the liberal principles of all his writings, and the praise which they have recieved from the Edinburgh Reviewers.[1] I am, dear Sir, very respectfully

Your obliged Servant D. B. WARDEN

RC (DLC); at foot of text: "Thomas Jefferson Esquire"; endorsed by TJ as received 18 Sept. 1816 and so recorded in SJL. FC (MdHi: Warden Letterbook); entirely in Warden's hand. Enclosures: (1) Hottinguer & Compagnie's Bill of Lading for Books Shipped to TJ, 28 June 1816, stating that the firm had placed on the ship *United States*, under the master Destebecho and bound from Le Havre for New York City, "*One Case Containing Library*" marked "**MTJ** N° 1./." to be delivered to the collector of New York, who will pay "freight for the said *Goods fifteen dollars per tun measurement & 10 p% primage*" (printed form in DLC: TJ Papers, 207:36946; with blanks filled in an unidentified hand rendered above in italics). (2) Hottinguer & Compagnie to David Gelston, Le Havre, 1 July 1816, informing him in his capacity as collector of New York that "The ship United States, captain Destebecho, will convey to you a Box marked, **MTJ**—Containing books—This Package is from Mr Bure of Paris with instructions to address it to your care for the late President the Hon[ble] Tho[s] Jefferson—Enclosed you receive the Bill of lading with which please do the needful—For the amount of our expences as p[r] note on the other Side in *f*25–25¢ we shall understand ourselves with our Paris friend" (Dupl in MHi; in a clerk's hand, signed by a representative of Hottinguer & Compagnie; in red ink at head of text: "Dup[e] 1st P[r] United States"; conjoined with Hottinguer & Compagnie's Bill for Carriage of a Box of Books, 1 July 1816 (printed below); addressed: "To The Collector of the Port of New York New York Dup: ℘ Hesperus"). (3) Hottinguer & Compagnie's Order on Warden, Le Havre, 9 July 1816, addressed to him at the "place de l'abbaie N° 8. près la rue du Colombier," Paris, asking that he pay in Paris, at sight and to the firm's order, *f*25.25 for value received (MS in DLC: TJ Papers, 207: 36947; in French; written on a small scrap in two different hands, with address and signature in the hand of a representative of the firm; at foot of text: "H & C N: 3369"; endorsed in an unidentified hand: "30eme August hottinguer"). (4) Hottinguer & Compagnie to Warden, Le Havre, 9 July 1816, enclosing nos. 1 and 3 and observing that, since "Every thing here wears an extreme dull aspect, and the news from England is replete with Statements of Commercial distresses," they "can only wait for better times with patience" (RC in DLC: TJ Papers, 207: 36945; in the hand of a representative of the firm and signed by him; between dateline and salutation: "Paris D. B. Warden Esq[ue]"; endorsed by Warden). Other enclosure printed below. Enclosed in TJ to David Gelston, 19 Sept. 1816, and Gelston to TJ, 26 Sept. 1816.

Hottinguer & Compagnie, a powerful French merchant-banking firm, was founded in 1786 under the name of Rougemont, Hottinguer & Compagnie by Denis de Rougemont and Jean Conrad Hottinguer (1764–1841), a businessman from Zurich who immigrated to Paris in 1784. After a series of false starts and name changes, the company established itself in 1798 under the sole leadership of Hottinguer. Originally specializing in the coffee and cotton trades, Hottinguer & Compagnie soon became an important adviser and financier of the French state. In 1803 Hottinguer was appointed regent of the recently established Bank of France. By 1815 the firm had achieved a high national and international standing, with branches in Nantes, Le Havre, Marseille, and New York. Hottinguer & Compagnie played a prominent role in managing France's war debt following Napoleon's fall in 1815, and after 1826 it became an important lender to the Bank of the United States. The company continued to thrive thanks to its participation in the crucial financial events of the time, from the establishment of European railway systems in the second half of the nineteenth century to the two world wars and the Great Depression. More recently the firm split into several companies, collectively known as the Hottinguer Group and specializing in administering the accounts of individual investors, corporate finance, and international investment policy (*DBF*, 17: 1315–6; Max Gérard, *Messieurs Hottinguer, Banquiers à Paris*, 2 vols. [1968–72]; *The American Almanac and Repository of Useful Knowledge for the year 1830* [1830], 1:208; *The American Annual Register; for the years 1827–8–9* [1830], 577; Washington *Daily National Intelligencer*, 9 Nov. 1839; Paul Jacques Lehmann, "Les Hottinguer, Banquiers classiques de la haute banque," *La Vie Financière*, 26 Aug.–1 Sept. 2005, 44–7; *Commerce International*, July 2007, 1–4; *L'Agefi*, 1 June 2010, 4).

The London *Quarterly Review* 14 (Jan. 1816; published 18 May 1816): 368–402, contained a SEVERE ATTACK on Alexander von Humboldt, *Personal Narrative of Travels to the Equinoctial Regions of the New Continent, during the years 1799–1804. by Alexander de Humboldt, and Aimé Bonpland* (London, 1814), trans. Helen Maria Williams, vols. 1–2 (for TJ's French ed., see Sowerby, no. 4157). The same work received PRAISE in the *Edinburgh Review* 25 (1815): 86–111.

[1] FC ends here.

ENCLOSURE

Hottinguer & Compagnie's Bill for Carriage of a Box of Books

Charges and Disbursements on *1.* Package sundry Goods, marked and numbered as in the Margin, received by HOTTINGUER & C[o] from *M[r] Bure*—at *Paris* and shipt on Board the *United States* Captain *Destebecho* to the address[1] of *the Collector of the port of New-york. for account & risk of the late President the Hon[ble] Th[s] Jefferson.*

MTJ.	*1.* PACKAGE			
	Carriage from *Paris* to Havre	F.	*15*	*40*
	Journeymen housing and unhousing			*75*
	Cartage to Store, Customhouse and Vessel		*1*	*05*
	Storage			*75*
	Permit and Customhouse-Clearance		*2*	*30*
	Officer's fees			
	Postage of Letters and Customhouse-Acquits	}	*5*	
	Commission on Receipt and Shipping			
	Errors excepted	F.	*25*	*25*
	HAVRE, *July 1st 1816.*			
	HOTTINGUER & Co			

Printed form (MHi); with blanks filled in by a clerk rendered in italics above; brace also added by a clerk; signed by a representative of Hottinguer & Compagnie; on first page of a sheet folded to form four pages, with enclosure no. 2 to covering letter on third and fourth pages. Also enclosed in TJ to David Gelston, 19 Sept. 1816, and Gelston to TJ, 26 Sept. 1816.

[1] Clerk here canceled "and for account and Risk."

From Peyton Randolph (d. 1828)

SIR Richmond July 16. 1816

I hope the subject of this letter will be deemed a sufficient apology for the liberty I have taken in writing to you.

M. Delaplaine, who has undertaken to publish the biography of the eminent men of America, has requested me to furnish him with some facts respecting my uncle Peyton Randolph. I have felt great regret at not being able to gratify his desire in a manner worthy of the subject and of his work; for altho' I hold the memory of my uncle in great reverence, my age will not enable me to contribute any thing more than family anecdotes. Written documents cannot be referred to for[1] more than a few public and notorious acts. In this dilemma I have seen no other means of rescuing his life from total oblivion, but to apply to the few of his remaining cotemporaries, who, knew him personally, acted with him in public life, and may have treasured up incidents which would throw light on his biography. In all these particulars, I believe that you Sir are more competent to give satisfactory information than any person now living. The points to which M. Delaplaine calls my attention are the following;—his birth—parentage—education—profession—offices—times of holding them—public & private life generally—and any other facts which I may think proper to furnish. If you can find leisure to communicate to me your knowledge on any of these subjects, it will be duly appreciated and most thankfully recieved by Sir

Yr. mo. ob. serv[t] PEYTON RANDOLPH.

RC (MHi); endorsed by TJ as received 24 July 1816 and so recorded in SJL. RC (MHi); address cover only; with PoC of TJ to David Gelston, 19 Sept. 1816, on verso; addressed: "Thomas Jefferson esq[r] Monticello Near Charlottesville" by "Mail"; franked; postmarked Richmond, 18 July, and Charlottesville, 24 July.

Peyton Randolph (d. 1828), attorney and public official, was the son of Edmund Randolph, the first attorney general of the United States, and the grandnephew of Peyton Randolph (ca. 1723–75), the first president of the Continental Congress. Randolph attended the College of William and Mary in 1798 and by 1804 had established his residence in Richmond, where he joined a Masonic lodge and practiced law. TJ considered but decided against nominating him as the federal district attorney for Virginia in 1803. Randolph sat on the Virginia Council of State, 1809–12, and when Gov. George W. Smith died on 26 Dec. 1811, Randolph, as senior member, was the acting governor until 2 Jan. 1812. He served as the official reporter for the Virginia Court of Appeals, 1821–28, and in this capacity authored vols. 22–27 of the *Va. Reports*, 1823–29 (Jonathan Daniels, *Randolphs of Virginia* [1972], xviii; Robert Isham Randolph, *Randolphs of Virginia* [1936], 197–8; R. Gaines Tavenner, "Peyton Randolph," in W. Hamilton Bryson, ed., *Virginia Law Reporters Before 1880* [1977], 47–8; *William and Mary Provisional List*, 33; TJ to John Wayles Eppes, 19 Nov. 1803, letter not found, but with its subject noted in SJL as "Peyton Randolph to be distr Atty v. T. Nelson dec[d]"; *Proceedings of a Grand Annual Communication of the Grand Lodge of Virginia* [Richmond, 1804], 42; David Robertson, *Reports of the Trials of Colonel Aaron Burr* [Philadelphia, 1808], 1:374; *The Richmond Directory, Register and Almanac, for the Year 1819* [Richmond, 1819], 64; *Richmond Enquirer*, 6 Dec. 1821, 30 Dec. 1828; Washington *Daily National Intelligencer*, 31 Dec. 1828).

[1] Randolph here canceled "any thing."

To Patrick Gibson

DEAR SIR Monticello July 17. 16

In a letter of Mar. 24. I mentioned that I should have occasion to draw on you in favor of Doct[r] Fernandes of Norfolk for the am[t] of one or two quarter casks of wine. one only has been furnished, and I have just recieved a letter from him of July 12. informing me the price was 63. D 81 C for which he would draw on you. be so good as to pay his draught & accept the assurance of my great esteem & respect

TH: JEFFERSON

PoC (DLC: TJ Papers, ser. 10); at foot of text: "M[r] Gibson"; endorsed by TJ.

To John F. Oliveira Fernandes

Dear Sir Monticello July 17. 16.

I recieved yesterday your favor of the 12th inst. I had so long ago as the 24th of March advised mr Gibson of the call for the cost of the cask of Teneriffe which would be made on him, and have written to him this day to remind him of it and to desire the payment of your draught.

I thank you for the book you have been so kind as to send me. I had seen some extracts from it in the newspapers which had excited my curiosity, and I shall read it with gratification. the world begins now to be apprised of the jesuitical politics of the court of St James, the paradoxical composition of liberty & oppression in their g[over]nment, their ostentatious grandeur & real meanness, their commercial avarice under the cloak of kindness and generosity. still may there be peace between them & us until we are more advanced in growth & strength. in 20. years we shall be 20. millions and in 40. years 40 millions. I look forward to those days with triumph altho' I shall live to see neither. have you seen the Journal of the young man of Massachusets? it is one of the most attaching narratives I ever read, and will pierce deeply & irresistably into the British character. he gives side blows as he goes along to French, Spaniards and Portuguese, acknoleging he knows nothing of them but from his fellow prisoners of those nations, but of the British he speaks knowingly & experimentally. I expect very soon, without knowing exactly when, a visit from your learned countryman Correa, now minister of Portugal; I wish you could find motives for meeting him here. as his visit will be of some weeks I would gladly give you notice of his arrival. should you recieve a supply of genuine port, unbrandied, & such as you could recommend I should be glad to take a quarter cask of it

I salute you with great esteem and respect. Th: Jefferson

PoC (DLC); ink stained; at foot of text: "Doctr Fernandes"; endorsed by TJ.

To Thomas Appleton

[D]ear Sir Monticello July 18. 16.

Your letters of Mar. 20. & Apr. 15. are both recieved: the former only a week ago. they brought me the first information of the death of my antient friend Mazzei, which I learn with sincere regret. he had some peculiarities, & who of us has not? but he was of solid worth; honest, able, zealous in sound principles moral & political, constant in friendship, and punctual in all his undertakings. he was greatly esteemed in this country, and some one has inserted in our papers an account of his death, with a handsome and just eulogy of him, and a proposition to publish his life in one 8vo volume. I have no doubt but that what he has written of himself during the portion of the revolutionary period he passed with us, would furnish some good materials for our history, of which there is already a wonderful scarcity: but where this undertaker of his history is to get his materials, I know not, nor who he is.

[I] have recieved mr Carmigniani's letter requesting the remittance of his money in my [h]ands. how and when this can be done I have written him, in the inclosed [lett]er, which I leave open for your perusal; after which be so good as to stick a wafer in it, & have it delivered. I had just begun a letter to Mazzei, excusing to him the non-remittance the present year, as requested thro' you by his family. and I should have stated to him, with good faith, that the war-taxes of the last year, almost equal to the amount of our whole income, and a season among the most unfavorable to agriculture[1] ever known, made it a year of war as to it's pressure, & obliged me to postpone the commencement of the annual remittances until the ensuing spring. the receipt of your letter, and of mr Carmagnani's, only rendered it necessary to change the address of mine. the sale was made during the war, when the remittanc[e] of the price was impossible: nor was there here any depot for it at that time which would have been safe, profitable, and ready to repay the principal on demand. I retained it therefore myself to avoid the risk of the banks, to yield the profit the treasury would have given, and to admit a command of the principal at a shorter term. it was of course therefore that I must invest it in some way to countervail the interest and being but a farmer recieving rents and profits but once a year, it will take time to restore it to the form of money again, which I explained to mr Mazzei in the letter I wrote him at the time. Exchange is much against us at present, owing to the immense importations made immediately after peace, and to the redundancy of our paper medium. the legislatures have generally required the banks to call in this redundancy. they are accordingly curtailing discounts, & collecting their debts, so that by the spring, when the first remittance will be made, our medium will be greatly reduced, and it's value increased proportionably. the crop of this year too, when exported, will so far lessen the foreign debt & the demand for bills of exchange. these circumstances taken together promise a good reduction in the rate of exchange; which you can more fully explain in conversation to mr Carmagnani.

I am happy to inform you that the administrator of mr Bellini has at length settled his account, and deposited the balance 635. Dollars 48. cents in the bank of Virginia at Richmond. I think it the safest bank in the US. and it has been for some time so prudently preparing itself for cash payments, as to inspire a good degree of confidence, & I sha[ll] moreover keep my eye on it. but the money while there bears no interest; and I did not chuse to take it myself on interest reimbursable on demand. it would be well then that mr Fancelli should withdraw it as soon as he can. his draught on me shall be answered at sight to the holder, by one on [t]he[2] bank. in the present state of our exchange, & the really critical standing of our merchants, at this time, I have been afraid to undertake it's remittance, because it could only be done by a bill of some merchant here on his correspondent in England, and both places are at this time a little suspicious. I know nothing so deplorable as the present condition of the inhabitants of Europe, and do not wonder therefore at their desire to come to this country. laborers in any of the arts would find abundant employ in this state at 100.D. a year & their board and lodging. and indeed if a sober good humored man, understanding the vineyard & kitchen garden would come to me on those terms, bound to serve 4. years, I would advance his passage on his arrival, setting it off against his subsequent wages. but he must come to the port of Norfolk or Richmond, & no where else. if such a one should occur to you, you would oblige me by sending him. I remark the temporary difficulty you mention of obtaining good Montepulciano; and prefer waiting for that, when to be had, to a quicker supply of any other kind which might not so certainly suit our taste. it might not be amiss perhaps to substitute a bottle or two as samples of any other wines which would bear the voyage, and be of a quality and price to recommend them. you know we like dry wines, or at any rate not more than silky. I salute you with constant friendship and respect.

TH JEF[FERSON]

PoC (DLC); on a reused address cover from Hugh Nelson to TJ; salutation faint; edge trimmed and torn at seal, with several words rewritten by TJ; signature incomplete; at foot of first page: "M[r] Appleton"; endorsed by TJ. Enclosure: TJ to Giovanni Carmignani, 18 July [1816]. Enclosed in TJ to John Graham, 19 July 1816.

An ACCOUNT of Philip Mazzei's life and death and a PROPOSITION to publish the "Life of Philip Mazzei" in "a handsome octavo volume of 250 pages" appeared respectively in the Washington *Daily National Intelligencer*, 20, 29 June 1816. John Bracken was the ADMINISTRATOR of the estate of Charles Bellini.

[1] Preceding two words interlined.
[2] Word faint.

From John Barnes

DEAR SIR— George Town Co[a] 18th July. 1816.

Thro the politeness of M[r] Monroe—I am fav[rd] with the inclosed. Viz Gen[l] Kosciuskos letter dated Soleure 15 April the Contents of course—his pressing wants of a seasonable Remittance, which from the extreme advance of exchange—I cannot bring myself to comply with without your express consent & Approbation—

and altho' the present Balance in my hands viz $1400—do not warrant a Bill of Ex. for £400[1] Ster[g]—the Amo[t] I proposed to remit him—still his growing Int: would in Course of a few M[os] Cover that Amo[t]—Nevertheless—with your Assent I propose to Remit—at this Critical Juncture—£200 Ster[g] or Nearly $1100—towards his present pressing wants: and in Course of a few M[os] the like sum—

And M[r] Monroe whom I waited on this Morning to thank him for his politeness—has Obligingly Assured me—(at my Request) to forward any letters &[ca] I may occasionally have to forward to the good Gen[l]—

Most Respectfully—and truly—Sincerely—Your Obed[t] serv[t]

JOHN BARNES,

PS I pray you to fav[r] me with a letter to Gen[l] K. to Accompany Mine—mean time, I shall endeavour to engage a Bill of exchange for the Sum proposed say £200[2] Sterling—

RC (ViU: TJP-ER); beneath signature, at foot of recto: "Thomas Jefferson Esq[r] Monticello"; postscript on verso; endorsed by TJ as received 26 July 1816 and so recorded in SJL. Enclosure not found.

[1] Manuscript: "$400."

[2] Reworked from "$200."

To Giovanni Carmignani

SIR Monticello in Virginia July 18. 1817. [1816]

Within these few days I have recieved your favor of April 7. with certificates of the death of my estimable friend Philip Mazzei, and a copy of his Will. I learn this event with great affliction, altho' his advanced age had given reason to apprehend it. an intimacy of 40. years had proved to me his great worth; and a friendship, which had begun in personal acquaintance, was maintained after separation, without abatement, by a constant interchange of letters. his esteem too in this country was very general; his early & zealous cooperation in the establishment of our independance having acquired for him here a great degree of favor.

Having left under my care the property which he had not been able to dispose of and to carry with him to Europe, it is some years since I had been able to settle all his affairs here, and to have the whole proceeds remitted to him,[1] except for his house and lot in Richmond. this being in the possession of another, a course of law became necessary to recover it: and after the recovery,[2] it was some time before it could be disposed of at a reasonable price. very favorable circumstances however occurring at length, I was enabled to get for it a sum very far beyond what had ever been expected or asked. this was in the time of our late war with England, while a close blockade of our harbors cut off all commercial intercourse with Europe, and rendered a remittance of the price impossible. the question then arose what could be done with the money? our banks, which had been heretofore considered as safe depositories of money, had excited alarm as to their solvability, by the profuse emission of their notes; and in fact they declared, soon after, their inability to pay their notes, in which condition they still continue; and could they have been trusted with the money, no interest would have been allowed by them. it might have been lent to the government, who would have paid an interest; but then the principal could not have been demanded under 15. or 20. years, the terms of their loans.[3] I concluded therefore to retain it myself, at our legal interest of 6. per cent per annum, as the only means of avoiding the risk of the banks, of yielding the profit which the treasury offered, with the command of the principal at a shorter period. but to indemnify myself for the interest I should have to pay it was necessary I should invest it in some profitable course: and to restore it again to the form of money, would require some time after the close of the war. I explained this in a letter to Mr Mazzei, and then supposed it might be done at two or three annual instalments, counting from the close of the war. altho' the cessation of hostilities took place in the spring of the last year, yet the war contributions continued thro the year, aggravated by the most calamitous[4] season for agriculture almost ever known. our term of peace then really began with the present year. I was about informing mr Mazzei that, counting from that period, the principal and interest should be remitted him in three annual instalments, when I recieved the information of his death. I had been led to propose to him this delay the less unwillingly, as I had received from his family, thro' mr Appleton, a request not to remit the principal, which they feared he would dispose of to loss.

I have thought this much necessary, Sir, to explain to you the present state of this fund, and the reasons why it cannot be remitted but by successive instalments. a third with it's interest shall be paid the ensuing spring: and the remainder in equal portions the two springs following that. the channel of remittance must depend on the circumstances of the times. the exchange with London at present is much against us. but the calls of the banks on their debtors, now rapidly going on, by reducing the redundancy of our medium,[5] and the produce of agriculture this year, which, as an article of remittance, will lessen the demand, & consequently the price, of bills of exchange, will probably produce, by the next spring, a more favorable state of exchange for the first remittance. in the mean time I shall recieve & execute with pleasure & punctuality any instructions you may think proper to give me as to the channel and mode of remittance: and, recieving none, I will certainly do the best I can for the benefit of mr Mazzei's family, to whom I will render every service in my power with the same zeal I would have done for my deceased friend, of which I pray you to give them assurance with the homage of my great respect, and to accept yourself the tender of my high[6] consideration.

TH: JEFFERSON

RC (DLC: Philip Mazzei Papers); misdated. PoC (DLC: TJ Papers, 207: 36961–2); at foot of first page: "Mr Giovanni Carmigniani, Professor of law in the Imperial university of Pisa and Advocate in the courts of Florence. Pisa"; misdated, but endorsed by TJ as a letter of 18 July 1816 and so recorded in SJL. Tr (ItPiAFM); in Italian; misdated 10 July 1817. Enclosed in TJ to Thomas Appleton, 18 July, and TJ to John Graham, 19 July 1816.

Philip Mazzei acquired his HOUSE AND LOT in Richmond from Edmund Randolph, placed them under the trusteeship of Foster Webb when he left America in 1784, and had them conveyed back to himself by Webb in 1806. The following year a Mr. Taylor, possibly the eventual purchaser Thomas Taylor, was in POSSESSION of the two half-acre lots, and resort to a COURSE OF LAW was needed to eject him (Lewis Harvie to TJ, 24 Feb. 1807 [DLC]; TJ to Mazzei, 10 Feb. 1809 [Philip D. Sang, Chicago, 1961]; Deed of Lots in Richmond from Mazzei to Taylor, 17 May 1813 [Henrico Co. Deed Book, 13:315–9], enclosed in TJ to Randolph, 17 May 1813, but located after that document was published above).

[1] Remainder of sentence rendered in Tr as "eccetto quelli della casa di Richmond ed altri averi" ("except for the house in Richmond and other assets").

[2] Remainder of sentence rendered in Tr as "occorse ancora del tempo prima che arrivassi a vendere tutto" ("then it was some time before I managed to sell it all").

[3] Preceding five words not in Tr.

[4] Tr: "orribile" ("horrible").

[5] Sentence to this point rendered in Tr as "ma lo stato delle nostre banche andando megliorando sollecitamente" ("but the state of our banks is rapidly improving").

[6] Tr: "più alta" ("highest").

From William Short

Dear sir Philadelphia July 18 —16

Your favor of May 5. is the last I have had the pleasure of recieving from you. It crossed on the road one I wrote to you of May 7. This last was to inclose to you, as agreed on with Mr Higginbotham, his mortgage & last bond. I hope & take for granted they were recieved by you & that Mr H. has disposed of them to his satisfaction. I am the more certain of this, as he would certainly have written to me on the subject had he not recieved them. This terminates the affair between Mr H. & me. I wish I could say the same of Mr Carter. I always apprehended delay & difficulty with him—& in this I am not disappointed—To my first letter he sent an answer after so long a delay that I had despaired of it, expressive in general terms of his good disposition—I then wrote to him to state the acc^t as I understood it with the interest at 5. p^ct & requested him if he found it accurate to send me a bond or some specialty for it—To this I got no answer—after waiting a month, I wrote a second time on the 1st inst.—To this I have no answer either, & now I do not expect one—So that I have got already to a non plus. I did not apprehend so much difficulty in getting a bond or written promise—I thought that would come at the time of realizing the paper. I know not how I am to procure from him this specialty—He seems fully aware of the advantage of witholding it.—To pay 5. p^ct—on the simple sum, is of course much better than 6. p^ct on the compound sum of principal & interest.

Some time ago M. de Grouchy told me he was going with his friend Genl Clausel to make you a visit at Monticello, & requested me if I should write to you, to mention it. I learned at that time from M. Correa that you were in Bedford—And this I mentioned to Grouchy—He is as you know the brother of M^de de Condorcet—I did not understand from him whether his visit was grounded on her former acquaintance with you, or whether he had a letter from lafayette, with whom he is intimate, or whether he went on the principle generally of paying respect to you—The French you know form to themselves duties of this kind. I have been also requested by a person of a perfectly opposite character, to mention to you when I should write, that it had been his intention when he lately waited on the President at Montpelier, to have extended his visit to Monticello in order to pay his respects to you—but he learned at M^r M's that you were not at home. It is his intention however to do himself that honor on some future occasion. This is M. Hide de Neuville, the new French minister, He & poor Grouchy are in very different situations, but each has had his vicissitudes. Neuville is also a member of the house of Deputies & represented as one of the Ultra Royalist party. Political or party spirit may blind him to a certain degree, but his heart is most excellent.

I have kept for la bonne bouche to inform you that Correa & Dr Wistar purpose going together to visit you during this summer. The former as you know of course, is entering on the diplomatic career—He was giving us a course of botanical lectures when the information was first recieved here. He did not abandon it, but has now just finished the course—His translation to Washington will be a real loss to us inhabitants of Philadelphia—Still we joy in his joy.

I am really sorry to learn that you are so much overwhelmed & obliged to be anchored to a writing table—You are certainly entitled to "the softest pillow for the head of old age"—I was far from wishing to throw you again into "the furnace of politics." I thought that the tracing your own memoirs might be a soothing labor, & a most valuable legacy to your country, peculiarly useful & instructive to those who from the nature of things must always, at least during the present constitution, govern this country—I mean the organs of the democratic party. If your own experience has induced you to change or modify any of your political opinions, & it is the wise man particularly who is enlightened by experience, you might leave this as a legacy to your successors—For instance if you think it a dangerous policy to admit foreigners into our political rights,[1] if you think it would increase the love & pride of country to make birth the sole & exclusive door of entry into this sanctuary, if you think that this Republic may be, as Rome was, lost by this kind of bastard amalgamation, your voice & solemn warning would, I think be listened to: You are now beyond the power of party influence, & it would therefore respect you—But already such is the power & influence of foreign editors in this country, that no man who is a candidate for popular favor can advise a reformation with impunity—See what has happened to Crawford—I know nothing of the man—I never saw him, but it is evident that he is lost by the mere hint that he gave, which indeed was done in a very unnecessary manner. The ideas that I recollect to have read in your notes on Virginia, appear to me to be perfect on that subject—(I have lost my copy of this work—If you have one to spare I will be much obliged to you for it.) There are other changes that are desirable in our constitution—It is impossible that your experience should not have discovered some I should think—& I think a recommendation from you either given now or left as a legacy would be listened to with pleasure & certainly with profit. The idea of having been useful to your country not only during your whole life, but to continue to be so after your death must be a motive worthy of you—However I will urge nothing more, being persuaded that whatever you may do in this behalf will be rightly done.

What I have asked I asked for your country's sake—one thing more I will ask for your sake—I know your sentiments on the infamous traffic in human flesh—many others know them also—but there are some who do not—& all know you inhabit a slave State & are an owner of slaves, which the candid will acknowlege to be the unavoidable lot of an inhabitant of such a state—Congress have taken some steps towards the preventing their subjects from being involved in this foul traffic—but experience shews it is not sufficient—I could wish you would in some public way urge on them the rooting out this infamous evil—There are scoundrels living in Rhode Island particularly, who openly carry it on & make so much the more profit that many[2] are prevented from engaging in it—Adieu my dear sir—God bless & preserve you. Believe me ever & for ever your friend

W SHORT

RC (MHi); endorsed by TJ. RC (DLC); address cover only; with PoC of TJ to James Monroe, 9 Oct. 1816, on verso; addressed: "Thomas Jefferson Monticello mail to Milton—Virginia"; franked; postmarked Philadelphia, 19 July. Recorded in SJL as received 28 July 1816.

LA BONNE BOUCHE: "the best for last."

In an official letter of 13 Mar. 1816 to John Gaillard, the president pro tempore of the United States Senate, William H. CRAWFORD argued that federal policy might better incorporate Native Americans into "the great American family of freemen" rather than continuing "to receive with open arms the fugitives of the old world, whether their flight has been the effect of their crimes or their virtues." This MERE HINT that some immigrants were fugitives from European justice proved controversial (*ASP, Indian Affairs,* 2:26–8; Chase C. Mooney, *William H. Crawford, 1772–1834* [1974], 85–9). In his related IDEAS in the *Notes on the State of Virginia*, TJ suggested that it was impolitic for the government to encourage mass immigration from countries with monarchies (*Notes*, ed. Peden, 83–5).

Congress had taken SOME STEPS to discourage the transatlantic slave trade by passing a 2 Mar. 1807 law forbidding the importation of slaves into United States territory effective 1 Jan. 1808 (*U.S. Statutes at Large*, 2:426–30).

Letters from David Higginbotham to TJ of 4 and 5 July, not found, are both recorded in SJL as received 10 July 1816, the latter from Charlottesville. SJL also lists a missing letter from Higginbotham to TJ of 14 Sept. 1816, received from Milton that same day.

[1] Word interlined in place of "family."
[2] Word interlined in place of "others."

To John Graham

Sir Monticello July 19. 16.

I take the liberty in which you have so often & so kindly indulged me of requesting you to send the inclosed to mr Appleton by the first safe conveyance by which you may send official dispatches to him, and with my assurance of a due sense of this favor accept those of my great esteem & respect. Th: Jefferson

PoC (DLC); at foot of text: "Mr John Graham"; endorsed by TJ. Enclosures: TJ to Thomas Appleton and TJ to Giovanni Carmignani, both 18 July 1816.

To John Meer

Sir Monticello July 19. 16.

I recieved yesterday only your favor of June 18. which I mention as an explanation of the delay of this answer, and regret that, late as it is, it cannot be more satisfactory. but I am entirely unqualified to judge of the merit of your engraving, & consequently to undertake it's recommendation. the art of the engraver is one I have never attended to. I know it's effects only as an object of taste, but not at all as to the difficulties it may contrive against imitation. you must be so good therefore as to accept this apology with the assurance of my respect. Th: Jefferson

PoC (CSmH: JF-BA); at foot of text: "Mr John Meer"; endorsed by TJ. Not recorded in SJL.

To José Corrêa da Serra

Dear Sir Monticello July 20. 16.

I returned from Poplar Forest about a week ago, and found here your favor of June 16. I learn with sincere regret your rheumatic indisposition; and the more as it strikes so directly at your summum bonum of botanical rambles. would it not be well to direct these towards the Augusta springs, which we consider as specific for that complaint? they are but about 80. or 90. miles from Monticello. but of this we will say more when we have the pleasure of seeing you here; which from the 'few weeks' of your letter of June 16. we daily hope. mr Gilmer is also daily expected by his friends. I am very glad to learn that 3. more of Capt Lewis's volumes are found, and hope the rest will reappear in time, as no one could think of destroying them. as to the Astronomical observations & the Vocabularies, I will write to Gen[l] Clarke to obtain his order for their delivery to the war-office, to which they belong. besides the notoriety of the fact that the expedition was under public authority, at public expence, & for public objects and consequently that all it's results are public property, in the XIVth page of the life of Cap[t] Lewis prefixed to the History of his expedition, it will be seen that the Astronomical observations were expressly directed to be rendered to the War office for the purpose of having the calculations made by proper persons within the US. if on these considerations mr Biddle would think himself authorised to deliver these papers to the order of the Sec[y] at war, I will sollicit such an order to be given in favor of such person as the Secretary may engage to make the calculations. but if mr Biddle[1] has any scruples of delicacy with respect to Gen[l] Clarke I shall not press it, but wait an answer from him, which will only add 3. or 4. months to the delay already incurred. I hope my anxieties and interference in this matter will be excused, when my agency in the enterprise is considered, and that the most important justification of it, still due to the public depends on these astronomical observations, as from them alone can be obtained the correct geography of the country, which was the main object of the expedition.

I thank you for the new recipe for the cement. I think it more easily practised than the former one, which, by the bye I have recovered. I had stuck the paper into a little Cornelius Nepos which I had in my pocket at the Natural bridge, and had replaced the volume on it's shelf at Poplar Forest without observing the paper. I am in the daily hope of seeing you, and the more anxiously lest the recurrence of my calls to Bedford should repeat the last year's misfortune. but as the next visit to that place has nothing to fix it to a day, it can be accomodated to your movements if known without the least inconvenience. ever & affectionately yours Th: Jefferson

PoC (DLC); on reused address cover from Caspar Wistar to TJ; at foot of first page: "M. Correa de Serra"; endorsed by TJ.

TJ wrote the LIFE of Meriwether Lewis printed in Biddle, *Lewis and Clark Expedition*, 1:vii–xxiii (TJ to Paul Allen, 18 Aug. 1813, Document I in a group of documents on TJ's biography of Meriwether Lewis). William H. Crawford was the SEC[Y] AT WAR. The work by the biographer CORNELIUS NEPOS was part of TJ's petit format classical library at Poplar Forest (Leavitt, *Poplar Forest*, 38–9 [no. 647]).

[1]Manuscript: "Biddel."

From William Thornton

MY DEAR SIR City of Washington 20th July 1816.

I lamented very much when you wrote to me for the Portrait by Stewart, that I had not finished a Copy of it; for I was in hopes that the Gentlemen who were engaged in taking the Heads of our worthies, would have done more justice than I could do: but when I saw, on their return, the Portraits of yourself of Mr & Mrs Madison, I beheld them with amazement.—I did not admire them, but I admired at them. Never was such injustice done to you, except by Sign Painters, and Genl Kosciusko; than which last nothing can be so bad, and when I saw it, I did not wonder that he lost Poland—not that it is necessary a Genl should be a Painter, but he should be a man of such Sense as to discover that he is not a Painter.—After this Proemium, equal to one of the long Sentences of President Adams, I will proceed to say that I rejoice in having preserved the Portrait here, for no Engraving should be made from the Paintings of the Gentleman whose works I saw: and I lament that Mr D: is not a better Judge of Paintings when he undertakes so laudable a work. I am also very sorry that the Artist who appears so amiable a man should have failed so much: for it is not in yr Portrait alone but in the President's & his Lady's—The draperies are very well done, but the Faces are really very bad.—I think Stewart cannot be exceeded, & the Engraving of the Presidt is capital—Nothing better can be wished f[or.] If your Portrait by Stewart were engraven, it would be equally good; for fortunately it is one of his best Productions.—Mrs Madison's Head by Stewart is good, but the Figure bad.—I have copied your Head by Stewart, in Swiss Crayons, & a superb Frame is now preparing.—I had nearly finished it when the Gentlemen were here, & I would have shewn it to them, but they did not call as they promised & set out very soon on their Journey.[1]—Some, to whom I have shewn it, think it mor[e] like than the original, though I have deviated very little from it. I think it so like the original that I am not ashamed of it; and for two weeks past I have daily been giving it some more last touches.—I lament it is not in Oil, but the Straining Frame & Canvas[2] which I got prepared for Oil, a month ago, is not dry yet. I mean to attempt to model[3] it in fine washed Clay, that I have got from the Head of Elk, in Maryland; and if I succeed as well in that, as I have done in Crayons, I shall be delighted.—I mean to place my Crayon Picture in the Library of Congress, and if I succeed in Oil, to give one of them to Congress.—But if it would be more agreeable to you to have it at home now, than to leave it longer (for it has been here a long time) I will send it by a safe opportunity; and with it the Sketch by West. In the mean time they are kept with the utmost care;—& for the loan I return a thousand thanks.—I am,

dear Sir, with consid^{n}, esteem, & with the highest respect y^{rs} &c

WILLIAM THORNTON—

RC (DLC); damaged at fold; addressed: "Honorable Thomas Jefferson Monticello"; franked; endorsed by TJ as received 22 July 1816 and so recorded in SJL.

Bass Otis was the GENTLEMAN engaged by Joseph Delaplaine (M^{R} D:) to produce portraits of TJ, James Madison, and Dolley Madison (Caspar Wistar to TJ, 28 May 1816, and note). M^{RS} MADISON's portrait, which was completed by Gilbert Stuart in 1804, is currently in the White House art collection (William Kloss and others, *Art in the White House: A Nation's Pride* [2d ed., 2008], 78–9).

[1] Preceding eight words interlined.
[2] Preceding two words interlined.
[3] Preceding two words interlined.

To Benjamin Waterhouse

Monticello July 20. 16.

I thank you, dear Sir, for the new Robinson Crusoe you have been so good as to send me. the name of it's hero, like that of the old, merits to be known as should that also of the new Defoe. I have read it with avidity, for a more attaching narrative I have not met with; and it may be truly said of the whole edifice, that the bricks and the mortar are worthy of each other, and promise to be a lasting monument of British character. Pillet's work had already broken that character on the wheel. this gives it the coup de grace. Govr Strong too, with his band of Anglo-feds cannot but sympathise with the sufferings of their dear friends, their idolised bulwark, with which they took such pious and affectionate part in it's war against their native country.—but if they repent, let us give them quarter, let us forget all, & henceforward become a cordial & incorporated nation. if Unitarianism, as a tertium quid, can fuse us with a part of them, let us yield to that Amalgam. it will reduce the mass so far, and the Trinitarian residuum may hereafter perhaps find some other principle, physical or moral, religious or civil, which may solve it's refractory particles also, and make all homogeneous. how goes the weather between these conflicting schismatics? we hear nothing of the storm at this distance, and are contented to be honest, without presuming to scan the nature of the being who made us what we are. I salute you with great friendship and respect. TH: JEFFERSON

RC (MBCo: Waterhouse Papers); with upward-pointing fist in an unidentified hand adjacent to signature; at foot of text: "Doct[r] Waterhouse." PoC (DLC); on verso of portion of reused address cover to TJ; endorsed by TJ.

To Joseph Milligan

Dear Sir Monticello July 21. 16.

In your letter of June 4. you informed me you would be ab[le] to begin Tracy's work by the 4th of July. my responsibility to m[r] Tracy makes me expect with anxiety the Prospectus & proof sheets. I hope soon to begin to recieve them. they shall meet no delay from [me.] will you be so good as to send me the Miniature editions of Homer['s] Iliad & Odyssey, and of Dryden's Virgil, handsomely bound. I rec[ol]lect that the latter was advertised by Conrad. these volumes are [so] small that they may come by mail. Accept my respects & bes[t] wishes.

Th: Jefferson

PoC (DLC); edge trimmed; at foot of text: "M[r] Millegan"; endorsed by TJ.

miniature editions of Homer, *The Iliad*, in 2 vols., and John Dryden, *The Works of Virgil* (Philadelphia, 1814), were respectively advertised in the Washington *Daily National Intelligencer*, 6 Mar. 1815, 4 Jan. 1816.

To William Plumer

Monticello July 21. 16.

I thank you, Sir, for the copy you have been so good as to send me of your late speech to the legislature of your state, which I have read a second time with great pleasure, as I had before done in the public papers. it is replete with sound principles, and truly republican. some articles too are worthy of peculiar notice. the idea that institutions established for the use of the nation, cannot be touched nor modified, even to make them answer their end, because of rights gratuitously supposed in those employed to manage them in trust for the public, may perhaps be a salutary provision against the abuses of a monarch, but is most absurd against the nation itself. yet our lawyers and priests generally inculcate this doctrine; and suppose that preceding generations held the earth more freely than we do; had a right to impose laws on us, unalterable by ourselves; and that we, in like manner, can make laws, and impose burthens on future generations, which they will have no right to alter: in fine that the earth belongs to the[1] dead, & not the living—I remark also the phaenomenon of a chief magistrate recommending the reduction of his own compensation. this is a solecism of which the wisdom of our late Congress cannot be accused. I, however, place economy among the first and most important of republican virtues, and public debt as the greatest of the dangers to be feared. we see in England the consequences of the want of it: their laborers reduced to live on a penny in the shilling of their earnings, to give up bread, & resort to oatmeal & potatoes for food; and their landholders exiling themselves to live in penury and obscurity abroad, because at home the government must have all the clear profits of their land. in fact they see the feesimple of the island transferred to the public creditors, all it's profits going to them for the interest of their debts. our laborers and landholders must come to this also, unless they severely adhere to the economy you recommend. I salute you with entire esteem & respect. TH: JEFFERSON

RC (NjP: Andre deCoppet Collection). RC (University Archives, Stamford, Conn., 1996, catalog 122, item 60); address cover only; addressed: "His Excellency William Plumer Governor of New Hampshire Epping"; franked; postmarked Milton, 24 July. PoC (DLC).

The LATE CONGRESS, in "An Act to change the mode of compensation to the members of the Senate and House of Representatives, and the delegates from territories," 19 Mar. 1816, substituted annual salaries for the previous daily stipend awarded each member while in attendance. The Senate's president pro tempore and the Speaker of the House each received $3,000 and the other congressmen got $1,500, with proportional deductions for each day's absence (*U.S. Statutes at Large*, 3:257–8).

[1]TJ here canceled "living."

From Margaret Bayard Smith

DEAR SIR. New York—July 21. 1816.

Will you allow me to recall to your mind one, whom a long absence may have almost obliterated from your reccollection,—One, who never had any claim to your kind regard, but what she derived from a sensibility to that worth, which once to know, is never to forget.—Yes dear Sir, for the enthusiasm inspired by great talents, or the veneration awaken'd by the union of great virtue, to talent, may be deaden'd by absence from the object which gave them birth; but one who has been as happy as I have been, to have seen you in the bosom of your family, surrounded by objects & circumstances which excited the best affections of the heart, & whose sympathies in those affections have been awaken'd as mine have been,—never can forget,—So constantly is your venerated idea present to my mind, so habitualy is my tongue familiar with your name, that I can scarcely believe that so many years have elaps'd since I have seen your face, or heard your voice.

After an absence of fourteen years I am once more in the circle of beloved relations & dear & enlighten'd friends.—They naturaly enquire & listen with interest to events, & characters with which I was acquainted during that time; & those occurences in which your name is introduced, or your character delineated, awaken the most lively interest.

At present a more than usual degree of interest is awaken'd, by a rumour which has lately become the topic of conversation; which is, that in a letter which you have written to Mr Charles Thompson, you have express'd opinions so highly favorable to the christian religion, that they amount to a profession of faith.

The public mind has of late years, been much turn'd to plans for the diffusion of the Christian faith; Bible societies, sunday schools, & various charitable institutions have been form'd, which whatever may be their result, owe their existence to a zeal for religion which pervades all ranks of society; the rich & the gay, the ignorant & the poor; & which has in no age of the church been more ardent or more universal. Sunday schools, both here & in Philadelphia, have been establish'd on a broad & liberal bassis & vagabonds of all ages, sexes, or colours, are collected in well regulated schools, where they are instructed not from the love of money but from the love of God. In the present state of the public mind, when so much zeal for religion is awaken'd, it is not surprising that the rumour to which I have alludeed, should excite attention & enquiry—When enquired of, as to the truth of this report, I can only answer that as I am certain you never was the enemy of the christian religion, I can easily believe you to be its friend. You have no idea Sir what an interest is excited in the minds of zealous christians, & how pleasing to them[1] & how glorious to the cause, it would be, to see the name of one of the greatest of Statesmen & Philosophers enrol'd among that of Christians!—

It would be highly gratifying to me my dear Sir, to be able to give satisfactory answers, to all the enquiries that I hear, & [if?] amidst the felicities of domestic life, & the [occu]pations of your ever busy mind, you could find a few moments to answer this, you would confer a degree of pleasure, I will not attempt to describe.

And, will you too? say something of the dear family of Monticello, every individual of whom inspires an interest far beyond that of acquaintance, & near akin to the most affectionate friendship.—I was delighted to see Ellen last winter, & my only regret was that I saw her so seldom; Her name, accompanied with the highest praises, was familiar to me in Philadelphian circles, where I often met with her warm admirers—But her friends there complain sadly of her silence & accuse her of having totaly forgotten them.—Accept Sir, of an expression of sentiments of affectionate respect & veneration, from yours, M. HARRISON SMITH.

If I should have the pleasure of an answer to this, please to direct it to the Care of Sam[l] Boyd. Pine Street New York—as I shall not return to Washington for some time.

RC (MHi); mutilated at seal; postscript on address leaf; addressed: "Thomas Jefferson Esq[r] Montecello Virginia"; franked; postmarked New York, 22 July; endorsed by TJ as a letter from "Smith M. Harrison" received 1 Aug. 1816 and so recorded in SJL.

[1]Manuscript: "then."

To John Taylor

DEAR SIR Monticello July 21. 16.

Yours of the 10th is recieved, and I have to acknolege a copious supply of the turnep seed requested. besides taking care myself, I shall endeavor again to commit it to the depository of the neighborhood, generally found to be the best precaution against losing a good thing.—I will add a word on the political part of our letters. I believe we do not differ on either of the points you suppose: on education certainly not: of which the proofs are my bill 'for the diffusion of knolege,' proposed near 40. years ago; and my uniform endeavors to this day to get our counties divided into wards, one of the principal objects of which is the establishment of a primary school in each. but education not being a branch of municipal government, but, like the other arts and sciences, an accident only, I did not place it, with election, as a fundamental member in the structure of government.—nor, I believe, do we differ as to the county courts. I acknolege the value of this institution; that it is in truth our principal Executive & Judiciary, and that it does much for little pecuniary reward. it is their self-appointment I wish to correct; to find some means of breaking up a Cabal, when such a one gets possession of the bench. when this takes place, it becomes the most afflicting of tyrannies, because it's powers are so various, and exercised on every thing most immediately around us. and how many instances have you and I known of these monopolies of county administration! I knew a county in which a particular family (a numerous one) got possession of the bench, and for a whole generation, never admitted a man on it who was not of it's clan or connection. I know a county now of 1500. militia, of which 60. are federalists. it's court is of 30. members, of whom 20. are federalists (every third man of the sect) wherein there are large and populous districts, without a justice, because without a federalist for appointment, and the militia as disproportionably under federal officers; and there is no authority on earth which can break up this junto short of a general convention. the remaining 1440 free, fighting & paying citizens are governed by men neither of their choice nor confidence, & without a hope of relief. they are certainly excluded from the blessings of a free government for life, & indefinitely for ought the constitution has provided. this solecism may be called any thing but republican, and ought undoubtedly to be corrected. I salute you with constant friendship and respect.

TH: JEFFERSON

RC (MHi: Washburn Autograph Collection); addressed: "Col° John Taylor Hazel-wood near Portroyal Virginia"; franked; postmarked Milton, 24 July; endorsed by Taylor. PoC (DLC).

TJ cited as PROOFS his 1778 Bill for the More General Diffusion of Knowledge (*PTJ*, 2:526–35) and such other efforts to GET OUR COUNTIES DIVIDED INTO WARDS as his Draft Bill to Create Central College and Amend the 1796 Public Schools Act, [ca. 18 Nov. 1814].

To Louis H. Girardin

DEAR SIR Monticello July 23. 16.

I think I once saw in your hands a copy of the approbatory[1] resolution of our assembly, past after the enquiry instituted by mr Nicholas, in the session of 1781.1782. you will oblige me much by a copy of it by return of mail, as I have immediate occasion to quote it. have you not a letter of mr Page's on the skirmish at Norfolk, which I think I loosened from it's place & sent you? I do not ask the question with a view to it's return if you are not done with it, but from a desire only to reinstate it when done with. I salute you with constant esteem and respect.

TH: JEFFERSON

RC (PPAmP: Thomas Jefferson Papers); addressed: "Mr Girardin Richmond"; franked; postmarked Charlottesville, 24 July.

The Virginia General Assembly passed a RESOLUTION on 12 Dec. 1781 thanking TJ for his services as governor. A House of Delegates resolution of 12 June 1781 had called for an ENQUIRY into TJ's conduct in that office during the previous twelve months (*PTJ*, 6:88–90, 97, 133–7). John Page's letter to TJ of 11 Nov. [1775] describes the SKIRMISH at Norfolk (*PTJ*, 1:256–9).

[1] Word interlined.

To George Logan

DEAR SIR Monticello July 23. 16.

I have recieved and read with great pleasure the account you have been so kind as to send me, of the interview between the emperor Alexander and mr Clarkson, which I now return, as it is in MS. it shews great condescension of character on the part of the emperor, and power of mind also to be able to abdicate the artificial distance between himself and other good and able men, and to converse as on equal ground. this conversation too, taken with his late Christian league seems to bespeak in him something like a sectarian piety. his character is undoubtedly good, and the world, I think, may expect good effects from it. I have no doubt that his firmness in favor of France, after the deposition of Bonaparte, has saved that country from evils still more severe than she is suffering, & perhaps even from partition. I sincerely wish that the history of the secret proceedings at Vienna may become known, and may reconcile to our good opinion of him his participation in the demolition of antient and independant states, transferring them & their inhabitants, as farms & stocks of cattle at a market to other owners, and even taking a part of the spoil to himself. it is possible to suppose a case excusing this, & my partiality for his character encorages me to expect it; & to impute to others, known to have no moral scruples, the crimes of that Conclave, who, under pretence of punishing the atrocities of Bonaparte, reacted them themselves, & proved that with equal power they were equally flagitious.—but let us turn with abhorrence from these sceptered Scelerats, and, disregarding our own petty differences of opinion about men and measures, let us cling in mass to our country & to one another, & bid defiance as we can if united, to the plundering combinations of the old world. present me affectionately and respectfully to mrs Logan, and accept the assurance of my friendship and best wishes. TH: JEFFERSON

RC (PHi: Logan Papers); signature, clipped, supplied from PoC; addressed: "Doct[r] George Logan Stenton near Philadelphia"; franked; postmarked Charlottesville, 24 July; endorsed by Logan. PoC (DLC). Enclosure: "Thomas Clarksons account of his conference with the Emperor of Russia at Paris on the 23[d] Sep[r] 1815," in which the British abolitionist reported that during his private interview with Alexander I of Russia, the emperor declared, speaking in English, that he "had always been an enemy to the slave trade," that he considered it "an outrage against human nature: and this alone had made him a determined enemy to the traffic," and that "when he had seen the print of a slave ship he felt he should be unworthy the high station he held, if he had not done his utmost in all the late political conferences on the subject, to wipe away such a pestilence from the face of the earth" (pp. 3–4); that Clarkson then expressed his disappointment "in finding that the allied Sovereigns at the congress at Vienna had not proclaimed the slave trade—piracy," to which the emperor replied that the "one great object" of the Congress was "the future safety, peace, and tranquility of Europe," that he expected future progress in abolishing the slave trade, and that he "would not desert the cause of the injured Africans" (pp. 5–7); that Alexander also spoke of his "high regard" for the Society of Friends, whose members, in his opinion, "approached nearer the primitive Christians than any other people," not only in their dress and manners but also in their religious doctrines, and declared that "I embrace them more than any other people, I consider myself as one of them" (p. 8); and that the emperor asserted, after Clarkson's brief summary of the merits of the British educational system and the efforts of some British Quakers to introduce this system to other nations, that he "should be glad to promote the system in Russia" (p. 11) (Tr in PPL, on deposit PHi: Logan Family Papers; entirely in Logan's hand; with his subjoined, signed note dated Stenton, 11 July 1815 [1816]: "The character, and sublime vews of the present Emperor of Russia, merit the serious attention of the Kings of Europe, and of the statesmen of the United States").

The CHRISTIAN LEAGUE, better known as the Holy Alliance, was created when Alexander joined the sovereigns of Austria and Prussia in signing at Paris a treaty of alliance on 26 Sept. 1815 pledging "to take for their sole guide the precepts of that Holy Religion, namely, the precepts of Justice, Christian Charity, and Peace, which ... must have an immediate influence on the councils of Princes, and guide all their steps, as being the only means of consolidating human institutions and remedying their imperfections" (Edward Hertslet, *The Map of Europe by Treaty* [1875], 1:317–9). Scelerates (SCELERATS) are "atrociously wicked" people (*OED*).

To Joseph Delaplaine

DEAR SIR Monticello July 26. 16.

In compliance with the request of your letter of the 6th inst. with respect to Peyton Randolph, I have to observe that the difference of age between him and myself admitted my knowing little of his early life; except what I accidentally caught from occasional conversations. I was a student at College, when he was already Attorney General; at the bar, and a man of established years; and I had no intimacy with him until I went to the bar myself, when, I suppose he must have been upwards of 40. from that time, and especially after I became a member of the legislature, until his death, our intimacy was cordial; and I was with him when he died. under these circumstances I have committed to writing as many incidents of his life as memory enabled me to do: and to give faith to the many and excellent qualities he possessed, I have mentioned those minor ones which he did not possess; considering true history, in which all will be believed, as preferable to unqualified panegyric, in which nothing is believed. I avoided too the mention of trivial incidents, which, by not distinguishing, disparage a character. but I have not been able to state early dates. before forwarding this paper to you, I recieved a letter from Peyton Randolph, his great nephew, repeating the request you had made. I therefore put the paper under a blank cover, addressed to you, unsealed, and sent it to Peyton Randolph, that he might see what dates, as well as what incidents, might be collected, supplementory to mine; and correct any which I had inexactly stated. circumstances may have been misremembered, but nothing, I think, of substance. this account of Peyton Randolph therefore you may expect to be forwarded by his nephew.

You requested me, when here, to communicate to you the particulars of two transactions, in which I was myself an agent, to wit, the coup de main of Arnold on Richmond, and Tarleton's on Charlottesville. I now inclose them, detailed with an exactness on which you may rely, with entire confidence. but having an insuperable aversion to be drawn into controversy, in the public papers, I must request not to be quoted either as to these or the account of Peyton Randolph. Accept the assurance of my esteem and respect.

Th: Jefferson

RC (LNT: George H. and Katherine M. Davis Collection); at foot of text: "Mr Delaplaine." PoC (DLC). Enclosures: (1) TJ to George Washington, 10 Jan. 1781 (Tr in LNT: Davis Collection, in TJ's hand, with Trs of nos. 2–3 subjoined, at head of text: "Copy of a letter to Genl Washington"; PoC in DLC: TJ Papers, 207:36976–7, at head of text: "To General Washington" and "previously copied"; these versions, which omit a section praising Gen. Friedrich Wilhelm von Steuben, were not accounted for in *PTJ*, 4:333–5). (2) 1816 Version of TJ's Diary and Notes of 1781, [31 Dec. 1780–11 Jan. 1781] (*PTJ*, 4:262–8). (3) William Tatham to William Armistead Burwell, 13 June 1805 (*PTJ*, 4:273–7).

To Peyton Randolph (d. 1828)

Dear Sir Monticello July 26. 16.

Before the reciept of your letter of the 16th I had recieved one from mr Delaplaine requesting answers to the same enquiries made in yours, and I had accordingly prepared and was about forwarding them to him. the difference of age between your uncle & myself admitted my knowing little of his early life, except what was accidentally caught from occasional conversations. I was a student at College, when he was already Attorney General, at the bar, and a man of established years: and I had no intimacy with him until I went to the bar myself, when I suppose he must have been upwards of 40. from that time, and especially after I became a member of the legislature, until his death, our intimacy was cordial, and I was with him when

he died. under these circumstances, I have committed to writing as many incidents of his life as memory enabled me to do: and, to give faith to the many and excellent qualities he possessed, I have mentioned those minor ones which he did not possess: considering true history, in which all will be believed, as preferable to unqualified panegyric, in which nothing is believed. I have avoided too the mention of trivial[1] incidents which, by not distinguishing, disparage a character. but I have not been able to state early dates. these, I am in hopes, you may, by enquiry, be enabled to supply. for example
what were the dates of his birth?
of his first return from England?
of his marriage?
of his appointment as Attorney General?
of his 2^d voyage to England? [examine the Journals of the H. of B.]
of his expedition with the Blues?
had he any, and what command in that corps? if his papers do not shew this, Col^o Byrd's or General Washington's will.
All subsequent to this date, I have been able to state.

I inclose you this paper, in order that you may furnish Mr Delaplaine with every thing you can collect supplementory, and worthy of being noted in your uncle's life, and especially the dates: and that you may also correct any thing I may have inexactly stated. circumstances may be misremembered; but nothing, I think, of substance. be so good as to put a wafer into the cover of this paper addressed to mr Delaplaine, and forward it to him thro' the mail, as I shall advise him to expect; and accept the assurance of my great esteem & respect.

Th: Jefferson

PoC (DLC); brackets in original; at foot of first page: "Peyton Randolph esq."

H. OF B.: House of Burgesses.

[1] Word interlined in place of "trifling."

ENCLOSURE

Biography of Peyton Randolph (ca. 1723–75)

[ca. 26 July 1816]

Peyton Randolph was the eldest son of Sr John Randolph of Virginia, a barrister at law, and an eminent practitioner at the bar of the General court. Peyton was educated at the college of W^m & Mary in Williamsburg, & thence went to England, & studied law at the temple. at his return he intermarried with Elizabeth Harrison, sister of the afterwards Governor Harrison, entered into practice in the General court, was afterwards appointed the king's Attorney General for the colony;[1] and became a representative in the House of Burgesses (then so called) for the city of Williamsburg.

Governor Dinwiddie having, about this period, introduced the exaction of a new fee on his signature of grants for lands, without the sanction of any law, the House of Burgesses remonstrated against it, and sent Peyton Randolph to England, as their agent, to oppose it before the King & Council. the interest of the Governor, as usual, prevailed against that of the colony, and his new exaction was confirmed by the king.

After Braddock's defeat, on the Monongahela in 1755. the incursions of the Indians on our frontiers spread panic and dismay thro' the whole country; insomuch that it was scarcely possible to procure men, either as regulars or militia, to go against them. to counteract this terror, and to set good example, a number of the wealthiest individuals of the colony, & of the highest standing in it, in public as well as in their private relations, associated under obligations to furnish[2] each of them two able bodied men, at their own expence, to form themselves into a regiment, under the denomination of the Virginia blues, to join the colonial force on the frontier, and place themselves under it's commander, George Washington, then a Colonel. they appointed William Byrd, a member of the council, Colonel of the regiment, and Peyton Randolph, I think, had also some command. but the original associators had more the will than the power of becoming effective soldiers. born and bred in the lap of wealth, all the habits of their lives were of ease, indolence and indulgence. such men were little fitted to sleep under tents, and often without them, to be exposed to all the intemperances of the seasons, to swim rivers, range the woods, climb mountains, wade morasses, to skulk behind trees, and contend as sharp shooters with the savages of the wilderness, who in all these scenes and exercises would be in their natural element. accordingly the Commander was more embarrassed with their care, than reinforced by their service. they had the good fortune to see no enemy, and to return at the end of the campaign rewarded by the favor of the public for this proof of their generous patriotism & good will.

When afterwards in 1764. on the proposal of the Stamp-act, the House of Burgesses determined to send an Address against it to the king, and Memorials to the Houses of Lords & Commons, Peyton Randolph, George Wythe, and (I think) Robert C. Nicholas, were appointed to draw these papers. that to the king was by Peyton Randolph, and the Memorial to the Commons was by George Wythe. it was on the ground of these papers that those gentlemen opposed the famous resolutions of mr Henry in 1765. to wit, that the principles of these resolutions had been asserted and maintained in the Address & Memorials of the year before, to which an answer was yet to be expected.

On the death of the Speaker Robinson in 1766. Peyton Randolph was elected Speaker. he resigned his office of Attorney General, in which he was succeeded by his brother John Randolph, father of the late Edmund Randolph, and retired from the bar. he now devoted himself solely to his duties as a legislator, & altho' sound in his principles, and going steadily with us in opposition to the British usurpations, he, with the other older members, yielded the lead to the younger, only tempering their ardour, and so far moderating their pace as to prevent their going too far in advance of the public sentiment.

On the establishment of a Committee, by our legislature, to correspond with the other colonies, he was named their Chairman,[3] and their first proposition to the other colonies was to appoint similar committees, who might consider the expediency of calling a general Congress of deputies in order to procure a harmony of proceedure among the whole. this produced the call of the first Congress, to which he was chosen a delegate, by the House of burgesses, and of which he was appointed, by that Congress, it's President.

On the receipt of what was called Ld North's conciliatory proposition, in 1775. Ld Dunmore called the General Assembly, & laid it before them. Peyton Randolph quitted the chair of Congress, in which he was succeeded by mr Hancock,[4] and repaired to that of the house which had deputed him. anxious about the tone and spirit of the answer which should be given (because being the first it might have effect on those of the other colonies) and supposing that a younger pen would be more likely to come up to the feelings of the body he had left, he requested me to draw the answer, and steadily supported and carried[5] it thro' the House, with a few softenings only from the more timid members.

After the adjournment of the House of burgesses he returned to Congress and died there of an Apoplexy on the 22^{d} of October following, aged, as I should conjecture, about 50. years.

He was indeed a most excellent man; and none was ever more beloved and respected by his friends: somewhat cold and coy towards strangers, but of the sweetest affability when ripened into acquaintance. of Attic pleasantry in conversation, always good-humored and conciliatory. with a sound and logical head, he was well-read in the law; and his opinions, when consulted, were highly regarded, presenting always a learned and sound view of the subject, but generally too a listlessness to go into it's thoro' developement: for being heavy and inert in body, he was rather too indolent and careless for business, which occasioned him to get a smaller proportion of it at the bar than his abilities would otherwise have commanded. indeed, after his appointment as Attorney General, he did not seem to court, nor scarcely to welcome business. in that office he considered himself equally charged with the rights of the colony, as with those of the crown; and in criminal prosecutions, exaggerating nothing, he aimed at a candid and just state of the transaction, believing it more a duty to save an innocent than to convict a guilty man. altho' not eloquent, his matter was so substantial that no man commanded more attention; which, joined with a sense of his great worth, gave him a weight in the House of Burgesses which few ever attained. he was liberal in his expences, but correct also; so as not to be involved in pecuniary embarrasments. and, with a heart always open to the amiable sensibilities of our nature, he did as many good acts as could have been done with his fortune, without injuriously impairing his means of continuing them. he left no issue; and gave his fortune to his widow and nephew, the late Edmund Randolph.

MS (LNT: George H. and Katherine M. Davis Collection); entirely in TJ's hand; undated; corner damaged, with missing text supplied from PoC. PoC (DLC: TJ Papers, 207:36974–5).

Peyton Randolph (ca. 1723–75), attorney and public official, was probably born at Tazewell Hall, his father's estate in Williamsburg. After attending the College of William and Mary, he went to London, where he was admitted to the Middle Temple in 1739. Randolph was called to the bar in London in 1744, and later that year he was appointed attorney general of Virginia, a post he held, with one brief interlude, until 1766. He became a member of the House of Burgesses, representing Williamsburg, 1748–52 and 1758–75, and the College of William and Mary, 1752–58. The burgesses voted late in 1753 to send Randolph as their agent to England in an unsuccessful bid for repeal of a fee that the royal lieutenant governor had begun to impose for affixing the colony's seal to official documents. In 1756 Randolph led the "Patriot Blues," a volunteer unit of attorneys and other gentlemen that rode to Winchester to assist George Washington in the defense of Virginia's frontier. He was Speaker of the House of Burgesses, 1766–75, chairman of the Virginia Committee of Correspondence in 1773, and presiding officer of the first three Virginia revolutionary conventions, 1774–75. As part of the Virginia delegation in 1774, Randolph was chosen president of the First Continental Congress. He was also elected president on 10 May 1775 when the Second Continental Congress convened, but he resigned in June and returned to Virginia later that month in order to preside over what turned out to be the last meeting of the House of Burgesses. Randolph resumed his seat in Congress in September and died in Philadelphia the following month (*ANB*; *DAB*; *ODNB*; *William and Mary Provisional List*, 33; *The Journal of the House of Burgesses* [Williamsburg, 1753], 85; Washington, *Papers, Colonial Ser.*, 3:86, 87; Henry Timberlake, *The Memoirs of Lieut. Henry Timberlake* [London, 1765], 2; Philadelphia *Story & Humphreys's Pennsylvania Mercury, and Universal Advertiser*, 27 Oct. 1775).

The biography of Randolph that appeared in *Delaplaine's Repository*, 1:106–23, draws on TJ's essay and in places adopts his wording, with especially heavy use of the concluding paragraph.

For the response of the House of Burgesses to the STAMP-ACT of 1765 and its later reaction to Lord North's CONCILIATORY PROPOSITION of 27 Feb. 1775, see TJ to William Wirt, 14 Aug. 1814, 5 Aug. 1815, and notes. For TJ's ANSWER to the latter, see *PTJ*, 1:170–4.

[1] Remainder of sentence interlined.
[2] Word interlined in place of "take."
[3] Reworked from "the first member."
[4] Preceding eight words interlined.
[5] Preceding two words interlined.

From Theodorus Bailey

DEAR SIR, New york 27th July. 1816.

The letter under cover has remained in this Office unclaimed for a considerable time—We know not where to send it to meet its address—I have therefore thought it most advisable to return it to you. I should have mentioned that it has been advertised.

I embrace this occasion to renew to you the Assurance of my sincere respect and regard. THEODORUS BAILEY.

RC (MHi); endorsed by TJ as received 11 Aug. 1816 and so recorded in SJL. RC (DLC); address cover only; with PoC of TJ to Patrick Gibson, [8] Oct. 1816, with Jefferson's Note, on verso; addressed: "Thomas Jefferson Esqr Monticello Va"; franked; postmarked New York, 28 July. Enclosure: TJ to John Bradbury, 29 Feb. 1816.

To William H. Crawford

Dear Sir Monticello July 27. 16.

You will percieve that the inclosed papers of Jacob Koontz, are from a very ignorant man, who supposes I am still at Washington, and the proper person to be addressed. under this supposition he has even forwarded his original papers on which his all depends. in rigor I ought to return them to him, but on so distant a transmission by mail they would run risks, and I would rather at once place him under the protection of your goodness by inclosing them to you, and praying you to put them into the proper channel for his relief. I know all the irregularity of this, but we must not be too regular to do a good act, and there is no danger of the precedent; for we shall never find another in the US. who shall be ignorant of the name of his President 7. years after the change. I shall drop him a line of what I have done, & placing him under your patronage I pray you to accept assurances of my great esteem & consideration.

Th: Jefferson

RC (DNA: RG 94, PRWP); at foot of text: "M[r] Crawford"; addressed (trimmed): "William H[...]"; postmarked Milton, 31 July. PoC (DLC); on verso of reused address cover of Nicolas G. Dufief to TJ, 27 May 1816; endorsed by TJ. Recorded in SJL, with notation: "(Koontz' papers)." Enclosure: Jacob Koontz to TJ, 14 July 1816, recorded in SJL as received 24 July 1816 from Annville, Pa., but not found. Other enclosures not found.

To Peter Derieux

Dear Sir Monticello July 27. 16.

Your favor of the 6th came to hand on the 22[d] inst. only. I had recieved some time before an account of the death of mr Mazzei, of which I should have informed you but that I saw it immediately in the newspapers, announced by some other person. I recieved at the same time an authenticated copy of his will, by which after some legacies to the poor E[t]c he bequeaths his whole fortune to his wife and daughter. the executor too, who forwarded the documents to me, desired that the money for which his house in Richmond had been sold, should be remitted to him. the sale having been made during the war, the remittance could not then be made, & the money was retained by myself on interest, and an undertaking to remit it by instalments after the peace. the first instalment will go the ensuing spring.

It would have been very pleasing to me had mr Mazzei directed a part of it to relieve your wants, as I had pressed him to do: but the smallness of the gratuity he desired me to pay to you, left little hope of any more. on the subject of any legal reclamations you may propose to make, I, of course, can with propriety say little. yet a sincere regard for your welfare induces me to express the wish that you may be well advised before you plunge into the abyss of expence which that will occasion. I can candidly say that in the paper on your marriage I see nothing more than a promise of something should he not otherwise dispose of his fortune: and altho' this might truly express his favorable intentions under his then circumstances, yet on his subsequent marriage and having a daughter, a reasonable change was of course produced and their claims assumed a natural preference over yours. but in this I must leave you to your own government, pursuing on my part the duties which the law imposes on me. the advances of money which I have at different times made you, & which you in your letter [ex]press a wish to be able to refund, were meant by me as gratuitous, & never expected [or wi]shed to be refunded. be so good therefore as to permit me to enjoy the gratification of supposing that I may have been of some service to you, and to add the assurance that I could under no circumstances recieve any retribution. I return you mr Mazzei's letter inclosed in yours and tender to mrs Derieux & yourself the assurance of my great respect TH: JEFFERSON

PoC (DLC); on verso of portion of reused address cover of Joseph Story to TJ, 25 May 1816; hole in manuscript; at foot of text: "M[r] Derieux"; endorsed by TJ. Enclosure not found.

The NEWSPAPERS that printed identical notices of Philip Mazzei's death included the Washington *Daily National Intelligencer*, 20 June 1816, and the *Richmond Enquirer*, 26 June 1816. Giovanni Carmignani was the EXECUTOR of Mazzei's 3 Dec. 1814 will, enclosed in Thomas Appleton to TJ, 15 Apr. 1816.

To Jacob Koontz

SIR Monticello July 27. 16.

I have recieved your letter of the 14th inst. and the papers inclosed, solliciting me to have justice done you on your claims for military service. from the address of your letter to me at Washington, I have presumed you were under some error as to the proper channel for the prosecution of your claim. rather however than that your papers should run the risks of the mail at such a distance as you are I have undertaken to inclose them to the Secretary at war directly & to pray him to put them into the proper channel to have justice done you. perhaps it would be well for you to get the favor of your delegate in

Congress to enquire into this matter when he repairs to the next session. Accept my best wishes for your health and relief.

Th: Jefferson

PoC (MoSHi: TJC-BC); with salutation and part of another word rewritten by TJ to correct a polygraph malfunction; at foot of text: "Mr Jacob Koontz Anneville Pensva"; endorsed by TJ.

Jacob Koontz (b. ca. 1778), carpenter, was a native of Dauphin County, Pennsylvania. He enlisted in the summer of 1812 as a private in the 5th Infantry Regiment, United States Army. Koontz was admitted to a military hospital on 14 Feb. 1814, released on 28 July, ordered two days later to Plattsburgh, New York, and subsequently checked into the hospital at Burlington, Vermont. Suffering from "Dropsy and debility," he was discharged from military service as unfit for duty on 9 Dec. 1814 (register entitled "Records of Men Enlisted in the U.S. Army Prior to the Peace Establishment, May 17, 1815," p. 125, record no. 1143 [DNA: RG 94, RUSAE]).

To William Thornton

Dear Sir Monticello July 27. 16

Your favor of the 20th is recieved, and I take up my pen merely to assure you I had not mentioned the return of the paintings from any hurry to recieve them, but merely to make known a safe occasion of sending them if done with. I thank you for the offer to place a copy of one of them here in oil; but Stewart's original takes as much room on the walls as the thing is worth. with respect to the merit of Otis's painting I am not qualified to say any thing: for this is a case where the precept of 'Know thyself' does not apply. the ladies from the study[1] of their looking glasses may be good judges of their own faces; but we see ours only under a mask of soap-suds and the scrapings of the razor. Accept always the assurance of my great esteem & respect

Th: Jefferson

PoC (MHi); on verso of reused address cover of Edward Caffarena to TJ, 5 Sept. 1814; at foot of text: "Dr Thornton"; endorsed by TJ.

[1] Reworked from "studies."

From Thomas Appleton

Leghorn 30th July 1816.

My last respects, Sir, were in date of the 30th of May, and which went by the Schooner Fanny, Capt: Selby for New York; at the Same time I shipp'd to the care of the collector for that port, in order to be forwarded to you, a Case containing 57 bottles of Carmigniano wine.—I have now shipp'd on board the ship Von-Hollen Capt: Ralph Porter, bound to Baltimore, two Cases of Tuscan-wine—N° 1. contains 57 bottles of Artiminiano—N° 2, contains an equal number of bottles of Chianti-wine, this latter is of a very high flavour; and both are directed to the care of the Collector for that port—by the next vessel, I am in hopes, to be able to forward the Ama; a wine of a very Superior quality, indeed.—The vessel unexpectedly departing in the course of the day, allows me only the time, to Renew the expressions of my very Sincere Respect & esteem. TH: APPLETON

RC (DLC); at foot of text: "Thomas Jefferson esq—"; endorsed by TJ as received 5 Oct. 1816, accompanied via "Baltimore" by "N° 1. 57. bottles Artimigniano N° 2. 57. d° Chianti" and so recorded in SJL.

The COLLECTOR for the port of New York City was David Gelston. His counterpart at BALTIMORE was James H. McCulloch.

From Benjamin Galloway

Hagers Town Washington County
SIR. Maryland July[1] 30th 1816.

I have taken the liberty of placing under cover to you a Letter for your amiable daughter, Mrs Randolph; which, I shall be much obliged to you, to deliver into her hands: Should she be with you at Monticello, when you receive this—If Mrs R should be absent, I must beg the favour of you, Sir, to break the seal, peruse the contents, and comply with a sollicitation contained therein, at an early day; which will confer a favour on me—I have enjoyed perfect health, ever since I took my departure from your house, with the exception of a short, but, dangerous illness, with which I was attacked, in September last; whilst I was on a visit to my friends in Ann Arundel: since, which; I have been gaining flesh, almost daily, and am thirty pounds heavier, than I weighed, when, at your house: I hope, that you, and your kind family, have enjoyed the same blessing—

Mr Johnson, the Watch & Clock Maker, who, I did suppose, would have eagerly embraced the very favourable offer, that, you authorized me make to him; as an inducement to remove his family to Charlotteville: tho' he was seemingly anxious, to better his situation, when I set off from Hagers Town to Monticello; like too many others, was unwilling to encounter the trifling difficulties, with which such an undertaking, would have been accompanied: but promised to use his endeavours to persuade some fit young man of the trade to settle in your part of the country: and has repeatedly informed me, that he has recieved promises so to do, in abundance: but, the characters, have never come forward: which, has been in no slight degree, painfull to me; because, I gave you confident assurance, of the practicability of engaging a good workman to accept your very generous offer—I find, on enquiry, that the Clock, and Watch makers business, is, so rapidly encreasing in the western counties of our state: that I almost despair of succeeding in my said undertaking: I will, however, keep a sharp look out; and, if I should be so fortunate, as to meet with a proper character; who, may be willing to accept your offer; I will inform you: and afford every aid and assistance towards his removal—

Mrs Galloway joins me in Compliments—

I am, Sir with lively esteem and due respect—Yours &

Benjamin Galloway

RC (MHi); endorsed by TJ as received 11 Aug. 1816 and so recorded in SJL. Enclosure not found.

[1] Reworked from "June."

To Joseph Lakanal

Sir Monticello July 30. 16.

Your favor of June 1. with the letters it covered was recieved a few days ago only; and had your worth been less known, the testimony of my friend La Fayette would have been a sufficient passport to my esteem and services. the affliction of such a change of scene as that of Paris for the banks of Ohio, I can well concieve. but the wise man is at home every where, and the mind of the Philosopher never wants occupation. I weep indeed for your country; because, altho' it has sinned much, (for we impute of necessity to a whole nation the wrongs of which it permits an individual to make it the instrument) yet it's sufferings are beyond it's sins; and their excesses are now become crimes in those committing them. we revolt against them the more too, when we see a nation equally guilty wielding the scourge, instead of writhing under it's inflictions, at the same stake. but this cannot last. there is a day of judgment for that nation, and of resurrection for yours. my greatest fear is of premature efforts. it is an affliction the less for you, that you now see them from a safe shore: for to remain amidst sufferings which we cannot succour is useless pain. I am happy that in your retirement the subject to which you propose to avert your mind is an interesting one to us. we have not as yet a good history of our country, since it's regenerated government. Marshall's is a mere party diatribe, and Botta's only as good as could have been expected from such a distance. I fear your distance from the depositories of authentic materials will give you trouble. it may perhaps oblige you at times to travel in quest of them. should your researches bring you into this section of the country, and any thing here be worth your notice, we shall be glad to recieve you as a guest at Monticello, and to communicate freely any thing possessed here. with every wish for your happiness in the new situation in which you are placed, I salute you with perfect esteem & respect.

TH: JEFFERSON

RC (RHi, 1978); addressed: "Mons[r] Lakanal of the Institute of France and Legion of honor near Vevay, Indiana"; frank clipped; postmarked Milton, 1 Aug. PoC (DLC).

THE WISE MAN IS AT HOME EVERY WHERE is from Seneca, *De Consolatione ad Helviam*, 9.7 (Seneca, *Moral Essays*, trans. John W. Basore, Loeb Classical Library [1932; repr. 1970], 2:446–7).

YOUR COUNTRY: France. The NATION EQUALLY GUILTY was Great Britain.

To Francis Adrian Van der Kemp

DEAR SIR Monticello July 30. 16.

Your favor of July 14. is recieved, and I am entirely satisfied with the disposition you have made of the Syllabus, keeping my name unconnected with it, as I am sure you have done. I should really be gratified to see a full and fair examination of the ground it takes. I believe it to be the only ground on which reason and truth can take their stand, and that only against which we are told that the gates of hell shall not finally prevail. yet I have little expectation that the affirmative can be freely maintained in England. we know it could not here. for altho' we have freedom of religious opinion by law, we are yet under the inquisition of public opinion: and in England it would have both law and public opinion to encounter. the love of peace, and a want of either time or taste for these disquisitions induce silence on my part as to the contents of this paper, and all explanations & discussions which might arise out of it; and this must be my apology for observing the same silence on the questions of your letter. I leave the thing to the evidence of the books on which it claims to be founded, and with which I am persuaded you are more familiar than myself. Altho' I rarely waste time in reading on theological subjects, as mangled by our Pseudo-Christians, yet I can readily suppose Basanistos may be amusing. ridicule is the only weapon which can be used against unintelligible propositions. ideas must be distinct before reason can act upon them; and no man ever had a distinct idea of the trinity. it is the mere Abracadabra of the mountebanks calling themselves the priests of Jesus. if it could be understood it would not answer their purpose. their security is in their faculty of shedding darkness, like the cuttle[1] fish, thro' the element in which they move, and making it impenetrable to the eye of a pursuing enemy. and there they will skulk, until some rational creed can occupy the void which the obliteration of their duperies would leave in the minds of our honest and unsuspecting brethren. whenever this shall take place, I believe that Christianism may be universal & eternal. I salute you with great esteem and respect. TH: JEFFERSON

RC (NBuHi: Van der Kemp Papers); address cover clipped, with loss of frank and part of address; addressed: "[...] [Va]nderkemp at Oldenbarneveld near Trenton. New York"; postmarked Milton, 31 July. PoC (DLC).

[1] RC: "scuttle." PoC: "<*s*>cuttle."

From David Gelston

DEAR SIR, New York July 31st 1816.

I have received by the Ship Genl Ward from Bordeaux a case said to contain 25 bottles sautern wine, shipped by John Martin Baker esq: the wine I have in store for your order—

I have not yet been able to ascertain the expenses attending, but probably shall in a short time, when you will be advised of the amount—

With very great regard and esteem—I am, Sir, your obedient servant DAVID GELSTON

RC (MHi); endorsed by TJ as received 11 Aug. 1816 and so recorded in SJL, which has the additional notation (brackets in original): "[Barsac] 25.b." RC (DLC); address cover only; with PoC of TJ to John Barnes, 12 Oct. 1816 (first letter), on verso; addressed: "Thomas Jefferson Esquire Monticello"; franked; postmarked New York, 31 July.

To Louis H. Girardin

DEAR SIR Monticello July 31. 16.

Your favor of the 27th is recieved, covering the resolution I had asked, which I now return with thanks for the use of it. I learn with pleasure that we are not to lose the benefit of your labors on our history, which I had begun to fear from it's delay. Your letter gives me the first information of the state of your health, and I am sensible of the power of the paternal motives which induce you to think still of continuing in the lower country. I have no doubt you can make more money there. but would it not be better for your family that your life and health should be continued with less profit, than with greater gains under the present risk? and would not the combination of the business of a bookseller and editor of a paper at Staunton or Winchester, or of the writing for a paper, and taking perhaps a few Mathematical students, ensure more permanently the good of your family with the preservation of your life, health & happiness? of these things you are the best judge. I can only assure you of my best wishes for them all.

TH: JEFFERSON

RC (PPAmP: Thomas Jefferson Papers); addressed: "M[r] L. H. Girardin Richmond"; franked; postmarked Milton, 2 Aug. Enclosure: Resolution of Thanks to Jefferson by the Virginia General Assembly, 12 Dec. 1781 (*PTJ*, 6:135–7).

Girardin's FAVOR OF THE 27TH, not found, is recorded in SJL as received 29 July 1816 from Richmond.

To A. D. Saunders

SIR

Monticello July 31. 16.

I have just recieved your favor of June 26. mentioning your invention of a horizontal wheel so constructed as that it's gravity shall make it continue to seek it's resting place, yet never to change it's position, and enquiring whether I know of any thing of the kind in this or any other country. I know of no such thing any where; and as what is said leaves an idea of impossibility, so I must suppose there is something not said which would remove the impossibility. I would certainly advise you to trust to no demonstrations on paper, nor conceptions of the mind, but to execute the thing in large & see it work before you commit yourself to the public. the effects of friction & imperfection of workmanship must exhaust some power & are beyond calculations & conceptions.

I think our state has never given a patent for any invention since the federal constitution gave that power to Congress. were they to do it it might produce conflict and question between the two authorities. but the Congressional law altho' it involves the people in dangers and impositions, seems abundantly to secure to the patentee his own principle. another may improve upon the principle; yet he cannot use the principle itself without paying for it. he cannot add his improvement till he has purchased the use of the principle on which it is engrafted.

Accept my good wishes for your success.

TH: JEFFERSON

PoC (MHi); at foot of text: "M[r] A. D. Saunders"; endorsed by TJ.

Article I, section 8 of the United States CONSTITUTION gives Congress the power to issue patents. The patent LAW was "An Act to promote the progress of useful Arts; and to repeal the act heretofore made for that purpose," 21 Feb. 1793, which was modified in 1800 to extend the right of patenting to foreign nationals with two years' residency (*U.S. Statutes at Large*, 1:318–23, 2:37–8).

To Sir John Sinclair

DEAR SIR Monticello July 31. 16.

Your favor of Nov. 1. came but lately to my hand. it covered a prospectus of your Code of health and longevity, a great and useful work, which I shall be happy to see brought to a conclusion. like our good old Franklin, your labors and science go all to the utilities of human life.

I reciprocate congratulations with you sincerely on the restoration of peace between our two nations. and why should there have been war? for the party to which the blame is to be imputed, we appeal to the 'Exposition of the causes & character of the war,' a pamphlet which, we are told, has gone thro' some editions with you. if that does not justify us, then the blame is ours. but let all this be forgotten; and let both parties now count soberly the value of mutual friendship. I am satisfied both will find that no advantage either can derive from any act of injustice whatever, will be of equal value with those flowing from friendly intercourse. both ought to wish for peace and cordial friendship; we, because you can do us more harm than any other nation; & you, because we can do you more good than any other. our growth is now so well established by regular enumerations thro' a course of 40. years, and the same grounds of continuance so likely to endure for a much longer period, that, speaking in round numbers, we may safely call ourselves 20. Millions in 20. years, & 40. Millions in 40. years. many of the statesmen now living saw the commencement of the first term. and many now living will see the end of the second. it is not then a mere concern of posterity: a third of those now in life will see that day. of what importance then to you must such a nation be, whether as friends or foes. but is their friendship, dear Sir, to be obtained by the irritating policy of fomenting among us party discord, and a teasing opposition; by bribing traytors, whose sale of themselves proves they would sell their purchasors also, if their treacheries were worth a price? how much cheaper would it be, how much easier, more honorable, more magnanimous & secure, to gain the government itself, by a moral, a friendly, and respectful course of conduct, which is all they would ask for a cordial and faithful return. I know the difficulties arising from the irritation, the exasperation produced on both sides, by the late war. it is great with you, as I judge from your newspapers; and greater with us, as I see myself. the reason lies in the different degrees in which the war has acted on us. to your people it has been a matter of distant history only, a mere war in the Carnatic: with us it has reached the bosom of every man, woman and child. the maritime parts have felt it in the conflagration of their houses, and towns, and desolation of their farms; the borderers in the massacres & scalpings of their husbands, wives & children; and the middle parts in their personal labors and losses in defence of both frontiers, and the revolting scenes they have there witnessed. it is not wonderful then, if their irritations are extreme. yet time and prudence on the part of the two governments may get over these. manifestations of cordiality between them, friendly and kind offices made visible to the people on both sides, will mollify their feelings, and second the wishes of their functionaries to cultivate peace, and promote mutual interest. that these dispositions have been strong on our part, in every administration from the first to the present one, that we would at any time have gone our full half-way to meet them, if a single step in advance had been taken by the other party, I can affirm of my own intimate knolege of the fact. during the first year of my own administration, I thought I discovered in the conduct of mr Addington some marks of comity towards us; and a willingness to extend to us the decencies & duties observed towards other nations. my desire to catch at this, and to improve it for the benefit of my own country, induced me, in addition to the official declarations from the Secretary of state, to write, with my own hand, to mr King, then our Minister Plenipotentiary at London in the following words.—'I avail myself of this occasion to assure you of my perfect satisfaction with the manner in which you have conducted the several matters committed to you by us; and to express my hope that through your agency, we may be able to remove every thing inauspicious to a cordial friendship between this country, and the one in which you are stationed: a friendship dictated by too many considerations not to be felt by the wise and the dispassionate of both nations. it is therefore with the sincerest pleasure I have observed on the part of the British government various manifestations of just and friendly disposition towards us: we wish to cultivate peace and friendship with all nations; believing that course most conducive to the welfare of our own: it is natural that these friendships should bear some proportion to the common interests of the parties. the interesting relations between Gr. Britain and the US. are certainly of the first order, and as such are estimated, and will be faithfully cultivated by us. these sentiments have been communicated to you from time to time, in the official correspondence of the Secretary of state: but I have thought it might not be unacceptable to be assured that they perfectly concur with my own personal convictions, both in relation to yourself, and the country in which you are.'—my expectation was that mr King would shew this letter to mr Addington, and that it would be received by him as an overture towards a cordial understanding between the two countries. he left the ministry however, & I never heard more of it, and certainly never percieved any good effect from it. I know that in the present temper, the boastful, the insolent, and the mendacious newspapers, on both sides, will present serious impediments. ours will be insulting your public authorities, and boasting of victories: and yours will not be sparing of provocations & abuses of us. but if those at our helms could not place themselves above these pitiful notices, and throwing aside all personal feelings, look only to the interests of their nations, they would be unequal to the trusts confided to them. I am equally confident, on our part, in the administration now in place, as in that which will succeed it; and that if friendship is not hereafter sincerely cultivated, it will not be their fault. I will not however disguise that the settlement of the practice of impressing <u>our citizens</u> is a sine quâ non, & a preliminary, without which treaties of peace are but truces. but it is impossible that reasonable dispositions on both parts should not remove this stumbling block, which, unremoved, will be an eternal obstacle to peace, and lead finally to the deletion of the one or the other nation. the regulations necessary to keep your own seamen to yourselves are those which our interests would lead us to adopt, & that interest would be a guarantee of their observance; and the transfer of these questions from the cognisance of their naval commanders to the governments themselves, woul[d] be but an act of mutual, as well as of self respect.

I did not mean, when I began my letter, to have indulged my pen so far on subjects with which I have long ceased to have connection. but it may do good, and I will let it go. for altho' what I write is from no personal privity with the views or wishes of our government, yet believing them to be what they ought to be, and confident in their wisdom and integrity, I am sure I hazard no deception in what I have said of them. and I shall be happy indeed if some good shall result to both our countries, from this renewal of our correspondence and antient friendship. I recall with great pleasure the days of our former intercourse, personal and epistolary, and can assure you with truth that in no instant of time has there been any abatement of my great esteem and respect for you. TH: JEFFERSON

PoC (DLC); edge trimmed; at foot of first page: "Sir John Sinclair."

TJ evidently sent this letter to John Graham, chief clerk of the State Department, who in turn forwarded it to John Quincy Adams, United States minister plenipotentiary to Great Britain. Adams received it on 8 Oct. 1816 and delivered it to Sinclair that same day (Adams Diary, 30:84–5 [MS in MHi: Adams Papers]).

The excerpt of THE FOLLOWING WORDS is from TJ to Rufus King, 13 July 1802 (*PTJ*, 38:54–7).

From Jacob Griswold

SIR, *NEW-YORK, JULY* 1816.

I take the liberty of enclosing to you two copies of Proposals for founding a New Institution for Promoting Useful Knowledge; and, should the Plan meet your approbation, I would most respectfully solicit your patronage and influence in support of the same. Pray, sir, have the goodness to pardon the freedom I use, and to believe, that not merely self-interest has induced me to offer to you and the public a proposition of the kind. I would also beg the favor of you to inform me, in the course of a month from the receipt of this, what are your sentiments respecting the undertaking, and what is the prospect of patronage in your vicinity.

Should any thing be offered as capital, it may, in the first instance, be put down on the half sheet for pasting up, and afterwards regularly subscribed to a duplicate of the contract contained in the pamphlet; which duplicate can be forwarded whenever desired.

Wishing prosperity to our rising republic, and being desirous to put forth one hand for the advancement of knowledge, and to add one stone to the edifice of true national glory,

I remain, Sir, respectfully your, and the public's, most obedient servant, JACOB GRISWOLD, JUN.

Note. Should Stereotype Plates be procured for the Commentary Bibles mentioned in the pamphlet herewith inclosed, the one may be afforded in Numbers for $9, and the other for $18. The Comment of the first is about the length of the Text, and of the other about three times as much. Fine vellum paper of a superior quality, may be procured for the one for $4.50, and the presswork would be $1. The expense in the same respects for the other would be double.

Those desirous of procuring either of those most excellent Family Bibles, or other books, will do well to furnish some capital, as in this way they may promote an excellent institution, and procure books at a quarter less expense than they otherwise would. The Stereotype Plates possess this peculiar advantage over other type, a set will last good a man's life-time.—Surely the object is important; why may it not be accomplished? J. G.

Printed circular (DLC: TJ Papers, 207:36989); partially dated; endorsed by TJ as a "(Circular)" received 1 Aug. 1816 and so recorded in SJL. Enclosures not found.

Jacob Griswold, shopkeeper and educator, operated a dry-goods store at 6 Chatham Street in New York City in 1816. Two years later he advertised the establishment of the Washington Academy on Grand Street. Griswold moved his school twice in the next three years, and in 1821 he attempted to found a Society for Promoting the Education of Youth. He remained in New York City until at least 1828 (*Longworth's New York Directory* [1816]: 229; [1828]: 285; New York *Mercantile Advertiser*, 16 May 1818; New York *Commercial Advertiser*, 9 Oct. 1819; DNA: RG 29, CS, N.Y., New York, 1820; New York *Patron of Industry. Agricultural, Manufacturing, Commercial*, 31 Mar., 2 June 1821).

To John Adams

Dear Sir Monticello Aug. 1. 16

Your two philosophical letters of May 4. and 6. have been too long in my Carton of 'Letters to be answered.' to the question indeed on the utility of Grief, no answer remains to be given. you have exhausted the subject. I see that, with the other evils of life, it is destined to temper the cup we are to drink.

Two urns by Jove's high throne have ever stood,
The source of evil one, and one of good;
From thence the cup of mortal man he fills,
Blessings to these, to those distributes ills;
To most he mingles both.

Putting to myself your question, Would I agree to live my 73. years over again for ever? I hesitate to say. with Chew's limitations from 25. to 60. I would say Yes; and might go further back, but not come lower down. for, at the latter period, with most of us, the powers of life are sensibly on the wane, sight becomes dim, hearing dull, memory constantly enlarging it's frightful blank and parting with all we have ever seen or known, spirits evaporate, bodily debility creeps on palsying every limb, and so faculty after faculty quits us, and where then is life? if, in it's full vigor, of good as well as evil, your friend Vassall could doubt it's value, it must be purely a negative quantity when it's evils alone remain. yet I do not go into his opinion entirely. I do not agree that an age of pleasure is no compensation for a moment of pain. I think, with you, that life is a fair matter of account, and the balance often, nay generally in it's favor. it is not indeed easy, by calculation of intensity and time, to apply a common measure, or to fix the par between pleasure and pain: yet it exists, and is measurable. on the question, for example, whether to be cut for the stone? the young, with a longer prospect of years, think these overbalance the pain of the operation. D[r] Franklin, at the age of 80, thought his residuum of life, not worth that price. I should have thought with him, even taking the stone out of the scale. there is a ripeness of time for death, regarding others as well as ourselves, when it is reasonable we should drop off, and make room for another growth. when we have lived our generation out, we should not wish to encroach on another. I enjoy good health; I am happy in what is around me. yet I assure you I am ripe for leaving all, this year, this day, this hour. if it could be doubted whether we would go back to 25. how can it be, whether we would go forward from 73? bodily decay is gloomy in prospect; but of all human contemplations the most abhorrent is body without mind. perhaps however I might accept of time to read Grimm before I go. 15. volumes of anecdotes and incidents, within the compass of my own time and cognisance, written by a man of genius, of taste, of point, an acquaintance the measure and traverses of whose mind I knew, could not fail to turn the scale in favor of life during their perusal. I must write to Ticknor to add it to my catalogue, and hold on till it comes.—there is a mr Vanderkemp of N.Y. a correspondent I believe of yours, with whom I have exchanged some letters, without knowing who he is. will you tell me?—I know nothing of the history of the Jesuits you mention in 4. vols. is it a good one? I dislike, with you, their restoration; because it marks a retrograde step from light towards darkness. we shall have our follies without doubt. some one or more of them will always be afloat. but ours will be the follies of enthusiasm, not of bigotry, not of Jesuitism. bigotry is the disease of ignorance, of morbid minds; enthusiasm of the free and buoyant. education & free discussion are the antidotes of both. we are destined to be a barrier against the returns of ignorance and barbarism. old Europe will have to lean on our shoulders, and to hobble along by our side, under the monkish trammels of priests & kings, as she can. what a Colossus shall we be when the Southern continent comes up to our mark! what a stand will it secure as a ralliance for the reason & freedom of the globe! I like the dreams of the future better than the history of the past. so good night! I will dream on, always fancying that mrs Adams and yourself are by my side marking the progress and the obliquities of ages and countries. TH: JEFFERSON

RC (MHi: Adams Papers); endorsed by Adams as answered 9 Aug. 1816. PoC (DLC); at foot of first page: "Mr Adams."

Adams's letter OF MAY 4 is actually dated 3 May 1816. TWO URNS BY JOVE'S HIGH THRONE . . . TO MOST HE MINGLES BOTH is from book 24, lines 663–7, of Alexander Pope, trans., *The Iliad of Homer* (London, 1750; Sowerby, no. 4264), 6:174–5. The surgical removal of a kidney STONE was risky as well as painful, which is why Benjamin FRANKLIN chose instead to use laudanum to dull the pain from his stones (Walter Isaacson, *Benjamin Franklin: An American Life* [2003], 439–40, 462). RALLIANCE: "rallying," the first recorded use of this word (*OED*).

From John Graham

DEAR SIR Dept of State. 1st Augt 1816.

It was not until yesterday that I had the pleasure to receive your Letter of the 19th Ulto covering one for mr appleton at Leghorn.

I am happy to inform you that I shall soon have it in my power to forward the Letter to Mr appleton by a safe conveyance, as there is now a Public Vessel waiting at New York to take Despatches to the Mediterranian. These would have been ready before this time; but they have been delayed by the difficulty of getting a translation of a Letter from the Dey of Algiers to the President. That difficulty is now surmounted or soon will be, as we have found a Person who reads the Arabic and Turkish Languages in both of which the Letter is written. The Vessel will therefore, I presume, sail before the Middle of the Month or about that time. Should you have other Letters for that part of the World, they will yet be in time for this conveyance; and if you do me the favor to send them to me, I will take care to have them forwarded in the way most likely to ensure their safety.

I beg to offer my best wishes for the continuance of your Health: and the assurance of the sincere & Respectful Regard with which

I am Dear Sir your mo obt Sert JOHN GRAHAM

RC (DLC); endorsed by TJ as received 11 Aug. 1816 and so recorded in SJL. RC (DLC); address cover only; with PoC of TJ to Fitzwhylsonn & Potter, 12 Oct. 1816, on verso; addressed: "Thomas Jefferson Esqr Monticello Virginia" via "Post Office Milton"; franked; postmarked Washington City, 2 Aug.

The transmission of DESPATCHES to nations bordering the Mediterranean Sea was delayed in order to accommodate President James Madison's 21 Aug. 1816 response to a letter of 24 Apr. 1816 from Omar bin Muhammad, DEY OF ALGIERS (Gardner W. Allen, *Our Navy and the Barbary Corsairs* [1905], 335–9).

From David Hosack

SIR New york august 1. 1816

Accept my thanks for your favour of the 17th July with the seeds accompanying it—I am also indebted to you for a former favour of the Same nature—the seeds are in good order but it is too late to sow them in the present season—with the aid of manganese most of them will probably grow the next year—you know that this stimulus will excite the smallest remains of the vital principle which seeds may possess—It gives me pain to State to you that altho new york has done herself great credit by the purchase of the Botanic Garden She has made no provision whatever for the Support or the improvement of it—I hope however that measures are now about[1] to be taken to recover it and to augment the collection it at present contains—in that case it is my intention immediately to begin the Flora of our country particularly of those plants that have not yet been figured or described—I propose to do it in ye manner of the English Botany—I only wait for the corporation of our city to give me the facilities I ask, to begin this much wanted work—mr Elliott of So Carolina—mr Le Compte of Georgia my nephew Dr Eddy will give me great aid—I have Just received an interesting letter from my friend Dr Francis—I Subjoin an extract from it which will gratify you as it is to you we are indebted for ye valuable work to which it relates

I am Sir with great respect
yours DAVID HOSACK

RC (DLC); at foot of text: "Thomas Jefferson Esqr"; endorsed by TJ on verso of enclosure as received 11 Aug. 1816 and so recorded in SJL. RC (DLC); portion of address cover only; with PoC of TJ to James Freeman, 10 Oct. 1816, on verso; addressed: "Thomas Jef[...] &c Mon[...]"; postmarked New York, 4 Aug. Enclosure: extract from John W. Francis to Hosack, London, 26 May 1816, stating that "The Population of the U.S. as a whole are more enlightened than that of any other Country; they possess more enterprise than any other people under the canopy of Heaven; they are inferior to no people in regard to physical and intillectual capacity. This is not the opinion of an humble individual; all who have studied with impartiality the Character of our people must give their assent to the truth of what is now advanced. I remember so distinc[t]ly and with so much pleasure the assertions of a Philosopher whose reputation is preeminen[t]ly great and who on a Subject of this kind must be acknowledged to be a most competent Judge that I cannot but give them to you—They were uttered by your friend, the learned president of the Royal Society during one of those morning visits at his residence that I have so often and so advantageously made After some questions put me relative to the state of the physical Sciences in America, Sir Joseph [Banks] observed 'your country has lately given us the travels of Lewis & Clark: I have just finished the perusal of their work; its a great performance we have nothing like it—Our voyages and our travels are very inferior when compared with their exploratory Tour—It was a wonderful expedition, wisely projected, and ably executed. Sir, the fatigues of a Single day which those Travellers endured would have killed almost any European'—Such is the language which this distinguished man employed and I might add similar opinions from other high authorities" (Tr in DLC: TJ Papers, 207:36880; in an unidentified hand; bracketed material editorially supplied; at head of text in Hosack's hand: "Extract of a Letter from D[r] John W. Francis to D Hosack dated London May 26. 1816").

TJ's FAVOUR was actually dated 13, not 17 July 1816. ENGLISH BOTANY: James Edward Smith and James Sowerby, *English Botany; or, Coloured Figures of British Plants, with their Essential Characters, Synonyms, and Places of Growth*, 36 vols. (London, 1790–1814). John Eatton Le Conte (LE COMPTE) summered in New York or New Jersey and spent the rest of the year at Woodmanston, his Georgia plantation (John Hendley Barnhart, "John Eatton Le Conte," *American Midland Naturalist* 5 [1917]: 135).

[1]Word interlined.

To James Madison

DEAR SIR Monticello Aug. 2. 16.

M[rs] Randolph, Ellen & myself intended before this to have had the pleasure of seeing mrs Madison and yourself at Montpelier as we mentioned to mr Coles; but three days ago mrs Randolph was taken with a fever, which has confined her to her bed ever since. it is so moderate that we are in the hourly hope of it's leaving her and, after a little time to recruit her strength, of carrying our purpose into execution, which we shall lose no time in doing. in the mean time I salute mrs Madison & yourself with unceasing affection & respect

TH: JEFFERSON

RC (Christie's, New York City, 2012); at foot of text: "The President of the US." PoC (MHi); on verso of reused address cover to TJ; endorsed by TJ.

ELLEN: Ellen W. Randolph (Coolidge).

From John Wood

DEAR SIR Lynchburg 2[d] August 1816

I received a letter by last mail from M[r] John Tyler, member of the executive, informing me that I was appointed to survey the principal rivers of Virginia, from their mouths up to their falls, and afterwards to ascertain Latitudes and Longitudes of such places as they may hereafter name. He says, it is not expected that an actual survey of the rivers is to be made by running the chain, but by means of base lines. The compensation they have fixed at two dollars per mile, and I am to find every thing attendants, boat, instruments &c.—

I have written for information upon other particulars, before I agree. viz to define what species of survey is wanted 1st If the distances are desired to be accurately laid down as well as the courses. 2d If the depths and breadths are require'd, and in how many points; whether they are to be expressed at every variation and at every course? 3d Whether the courses and distances of only one side of the river, or if both sides are to be taken. 4th If both sides are to be taken whether $2 per mile is to be allowed for each side.

As I am at present unprovided with proper instruments; I have to request if you conveniently could do me the favour to loan me your surveying compass and Sextant for three months; and I assure you the greatest care will be taken of them. If you have not a large Sextant, the small pocket[1] one will answer. It is my intention to accomplish the whole by water. If all the particulars which I have stated are required I think $2 per mile is too little unless they mean $2 per mile for each side.—

I shall not leave this if I undertake the business previous to the 24th of September as I wrote to the Executive soon after my arrival in this place that from my health & other circumstance I could not commence if I were appointed before the 1st of October. I shall therefore have the pleasure of seeing you at Popler Forest before I go down and shall be obliged to you to suggest any ideas concerning the survey which you may deem important. Requesting my respects to be given to Mr Jefferson Randolph,—

I remain with respect and esteem your obliged Servant

John Wood

RC (DLC); endorsed by TJ as received 11 Aug. 1816 and so recorded in SJL. RC (DLC); address cover only; with PoC of TJ to William W. Hening, 12 Oct. 1816, on verso; addressed: "Thomas Jefferson Esqr Monticello near Charlottesville"; franked; postmarked Lynchburg, 3 Aug., and Charlottesville, 7 Aug.

JOHN TYLER, later tenth president of the United States, was currently a MEMBER of Virginia's Council of State, which shared executive authority with the governor (*ANB*).

[1]Manuscript: "pcket."

To Pierre Samuel Du Pont de Nemours

Dear Sir Monticello Aug. 3. 16.

I have just recieved a letter from M. de la Fayette, inclosing me the copy of one to you from M. Tracy dated Jan. 30. he is, as you now know, the author of the Review of Montesquieu. he sent it to me in the fall of 1809. but it was not until the spring of 1810. that I could engage the translating & printing of it. Duane then undertook both;

which he did not complete till July 1811. on the 10th of that month, he sent me a single copy, which I inclosed to La Fayette for mr Tracy the same day, that it might get into the hands of mr Warden, then on the point of sailing for France. I had subscribed for ten copies for myself, with a view of sending them to my friends in Europe. these came to me some time after. but our non-intercourse law first, and then the war rendering the transmission of them across the sea impracticable, I distributed them among my friends in the different states, that they might bring this excellent book into notice. learning, this last spring, mr Gallatin's appointment to Paris, I ordered mr Dufief of Philadelphia to procure and inclose two copies to M. de la Fayette, which he accordingly did, and had them delivered to mr Gallatin. the French original is in my hands, and I have it much at heart that it should be printed: but my situation renders it difficult. yours is more favorable, and if you can effect it I will send it to you. it is due to the author & the world to give it in his own words.

The IVth volume on Political economy came to my hand in the spring of 1812. the same editor undertook it's translation and publication. two years were lost in enquiries and urgencies on my part; excuses and promises on his; until a letter of Aug. 11. 1814. declared to me that, altho' he had had it translated, it was not in his power to publish it. I then requested a return of the original. he claimed the price of the translation, which I immediately paid him; but did not recieve the work till July or August 1815. three years being thus lost. I first proposed the printing it to mr Ritchie of Richmond. but he required so long a time for it's execution that I thought it better to accept the offer of mr Millegan of George town to print it immediately, promising to revise the translation myself if he would. a very long visit to Bedford, a journey to the Peaks of Otter, and some geometrical operations in which I engaged to ascertain the height of these our highest mountains, with the business I found accumulated on my return in the winter, put it out of my power to begin the revision of the translation until January last. this is the only period of time delayed in my hands. I found the translation a very bad one indeed; done by one who understood neither French nor English: and I had proceeded too far before it became evident that I could have translated it myself in less time than the revisal cost me. I devoted to it five hours a day for between two & three months; and on the 6th of April only was able to send it to mr Millegan. instead of printing it immediately however, he now informed me he could not begin it till the 4th of July. that day being past, and no proof sheet coming to me (for I have undertaken to supervise them) I wrote to him on the 21st of July, to which I have yet no answer.

To compleat the proof that these unaccountable delays have not happened thro' any remissness of exertion on my part, I will now add the dates of my letters written to these printers purely on the subject of this IVth volume.

to Duane. 1812. Aug. 4.	to Ritchie. 1814. Sep. 27.	to Millegan. 1814. Oct. 17.
Oct. 1.	1816. Mar. 8	Oct. 29.
1813. Jan. 22.	Apr. 6.	Nov. 24.
Apr. 4.		1815. June 25.
Sep. 18.		Aug. 17.
1814. July 3.		Oct. 27.
Aug. 17.		1816. Feb. 11.
Nov. 24.		Apr. 6.
1815. Feb. 10.		May 18.
		July 21.

you will thus see, my dear friend, what scenes of mortification I have gone thro' with these printers. Mr Tracey has the greatest reason to suppose inattention in me. in May last I wrote la Fayette (for I really had not the courage to write mr Tracy) some account of the causes of the delay of this work: but I did not go into particulars minutely, preferring an imperfect justification to the risk of giving uneasiness to M. Tracy by detailing the course of labor and vexation I had gone thro'. but I would have gone through ten times more to procure for the world the publication of this inestimable volume. I have done chearfully, and will yet do what still remains, only regretting the apparent cause which mr Tracy has of dissatisfaction with me. if from these materials, you, who know our printers, their position and mine, can make up something more of a justification of me, without disquieting M. Tracy, you will render me a most acceptable service; for his merits as a great author & a good man make me set a very high value[1] indeed on his esteem.—but when I shall be able to get the translation out, I cannot tell. Millegan has already shaken my confidence by his delays, and I know not where they are to end. I now wish I had given it to Ritchie, altho' the same delays perhaps might have taken place with him. I salute you affectionately.

Th: Jefferson

RC (DeGH: Pierre Samuel Du Pont de Nemours Papers, Winterthur Manuscripts). PoC (DLC); at foot of first page: "M. Dupont de Nemours"; endorsed by TJ.

William Duane enclosed a single copy of Destutt de Tracy, *Commentary and Review of Montesquieu's Spirit of Laws* in his letter to TJ of 5 July 1811, which TJ received five days later. The

NON-INTERCOURSE LAW of 1 May 1810 was "An Act concerning the commercial intercourse between the United States and Great Britain and France, and their dependencies, and for other purposes" (*U.S. Statutes at Large*, 2:605–6). The letter to Joseph Milligan of JUNE 25 was actually dated 26 June 1815.

[1]Word interlined in place of "opinion."

To David Gelston

DEAR SIR Monticello Aug. 3. 16.

I have just recieved a letter from John Martin Baker, our Consul, in which he informs me he had shipped a case of Barsac wine for me from Bordeaux by the American brig Gen[l] Ward addressed to your care. will you have the goodness to reship it to Richmond to the address of Mess[rs] Gibson and Jefferson of that place who will pay all charges which can be referred to them. such as cannot, I will ask the favor of you to notify to me, by mail, and they shall be promptly remitted.

In my calls for different articles from Europe, the want of constant opportunities of transmission from their ports to any particular one of ours, obliges me to request my correspondents to ship to any port of the US. addressing the articles to the Collector of the port. some of these will of course sometimes come to the port of N. York. may I hope the favor of you in like manner to reship them to Richmond always to the same address, who will pay all costs which can be referred to them, and to notify me by post of such as cannot which shall always be promptly replaced. Accept the assurance of my constant esteem and respect. TH: JEFFERSON

RC (ViU: TJP). RC (Grace Floyd Delafield Robinson, Greenport, N.Y., 1947); address cover only; addressed: "David Gelston esquire New York"; franked; postmarked Milton, 7 Aug.; endorsed by Gelston. PoC (MHi); on verso of portion of reused address cover of Sir John Sinclair to TJ, 1 Nov. 1815; endorsed by TJ.

From Joseph C. Cabell

DEAR SIR, Edgewood. 4th Aug[t] 1816.

I beg you to accept my sincere thanks for your favor of the 13th ins[t], and for the communication of the accompanying letter on the propriety of calling a convention to amend the constitution of Virginia. The information you give me on the subject of Hedges is very acceptable; it will exempt me from the mortification of failures in experiments that extend thro so large a portion of human life. I have about a half bushel of Holly seed now lying in my garden undergoing the process of preparation for the seed bed—but since the receipt of your letter I have determined to throw them aside, or to make but very small use of them. I shall direct my future attempts in this line towards the thorn, & to the variety you recommend, unless I should be able to procure that of which m[r] Jefferson Randolph Speaks so highly, for which purpose I have sent him the enclosed letter of enquiry. I presume he alludes to a Thorn in the old fields about Hendrick's Tavern, the strength & density of which have frequently been mentioned to me by gentlemen who had been travelling that way. It is not certain, altho' it is probable that maine's Recipe will succeed with all the different thorns.

I have written to m[r] meriwether on the subject of surveying this county. The law authorizing a chart of the State passed hastily thro' both Houses of Assembly, at the close of the session, and is defective. I regret that the county Courts have any thing to do with the business: for tho' some may make judicious contracts, I am confident many of them will employ incompetent agents, and the map will be a half formed party colored affair. In my opinion, it would be a commendable course, if the executive would defer acting on any of the contracts till the meeting of the Assembly, when we might amend the Law, by appointing a Surveyor General, who with the aid of deputies chosen by himself under proper checks, would make a map of which the State might justly be proud. If, as is to be apprehended, this well intended scheme, should be spoilt in the execution, the people, already dissatisfied with so large an appropriation for such an object, may in a fit of disgust, insist on the repeal of the Law for internal improvement. The difficulties which must, by this time, have been encountered in every county of the state, in the attempt to procure suitable agents, have probably prepared the public mind for such an exercise of power on the part of the executive. I have written nothing on this subject, as any suggestions of mine would be entitled to but little attention on the part of the Executive: but I wish some gentleman possessing the confidence of the Executive would take the subject in hand.

I am extremely obliged to you for the perusal of your letter on the state constitution. many of the views are new; some in conflict with my previously-formed opinions: and all in the highest degree interesting. I wish this letter could have fallen into my hands some years ago. Wishing to give to its various topics the fullest consideration, I have taken the liberty to retain a copy, & unless you should forbid it,

I will take the further liberty of shewing it to a few of my friends, who will not disregard the injunctions contained in a certain part of the Letter.

For eight years I have been contending with factions in the county of Nelson & this Senatorial District. During all that time, I have seen the people as often made the dupes of unprincipled intriguers, that I acknowledge I have gradually glided into the ranks of the friends of the freehold Law. In the same series of years I have served in the Assembly: where I have been disgusted by often witnessing what I deemed to be the most unjustifiable efforts in the western Delegation to throw the pecuniary burthens of the commonwealth upon the eastern people. In the hottest of the war, when the British army were laying waste all the shores of the Chesapeake, this temper often displayed itself. They demand a convention, & drop the project so soon as a reassessment of Lands is coupled with it. Last winter, Doddridge & others, finding we would not charter their 15 banks, said to us—We (meaning the federalists of the west) have heretofore been enemies to a Convention; but now we will let you see we will have one. Accordingly the Staunton Convention originated among Bank Stockholders, & officers, about Winchester. Viewing it in the light of a Hartford Convention, I declined attending a Small meeting at Nelson Court House in July, when two gentlemen of this county were appointed to go to Staunton in August.—A Series of circumstances like this, has made me heretofore hostile to a Convention. If one is to be held, I hope it will be taken out of the Hands of Speculators, & brought forward under the auspices of the friends of the people. I will reconsider my opinions on these subjects, and sincerely thank you for your letter.

I enclose for the perusal of yourself & Col: Randolph two interesting papers relative to the two Banks in Virginia, which were communicated to the last Assembly: I will thank you for the return of them by the 1st Octr—

Doct Smith has adopted the Review of montesquieu as the text book on the Principles of govt for the Students of Wm & mary. He will adopt either Say or Tracy on political economy, as the one or the other may appear best, when the latter comes out. We hear nothing of it. Owing to the weak state of my health, I shall be tardy about the translation of Say, you recommend me to undertake. Perhaps I shall not be competent—but I will make the attempt, as soon as my health will permit.

I am dr sir, most respectfully & truly yours

Joseph C. Cabell

RC (ViU: TJP-PC); endorsed by TJ as received 5 Aug. 1816 and so recorded in SJL. RC (DLC); address cover only; with PoC of TJ to John Wood, 6 May 1817, on verso; addressed: "Mr Jefferson Monticello"; postmarked Warminster, 4 Aug.

The ACCOMPANYING LETTER, probably enclosed herein and originally sent by TJ on 14 July 1816, was TJ to "Henry Tompkinson" (Samuel Kercheval), 12 July 1816. Cabell's ENCLOSED LETTER OF ENQUIRY to Thomas Jefferson Randolph has not been found. The EXECUTIVE of Virginia was Governor Wilson Cary Nicholas.

Cabell represented NELSON County in the House of Delegates, 1809–10 and 1831–35. In the Senate of Virginia, 1810–29, he served Nelson County and a changing array of nearby counties. His current SENATORIAL DISTRICT consisted of Albemarle, Amherst, Buckingham, Fluvanna, and Nelson counties (Leonard, *General Assembly*). The TWO GENTLEMEN representing Nelson County at the Staunton Convention were Landon Cabell and William C. Rives (Norfolk *American Beacon and Commercial Diary*, 30 Aug. 1816).

The TWO INTERESTING PAPERS enclosed were probably the letter of 22 Jan. 1816 from John Brockenbrough, the president of the Bank of Virginia, to Alfred H. Powell, chairman of a joint committee of the General Assembly, with its "exhibit, in a tabular form, of 'the condition of the Bank of Virginia and its several offices of discount and deposit, on the 1st of January of each year since the period at which the first dividend was declared,'" and a letter of 25 Jan. 1816 from Benjamin Hatcher, president of the Farmers' Bank of Virginia, to Charles Fenton Mercer, chairman of a House of Delegates committee, stating that "the suspension of specie payments still continues" because "the Northern Banks" refuse to pay their debts to his bank in specie (*JSV* [1815–16 sess.], 43 [3 Feb. 1816]).

From John Barnes

DEAR SIR— Geo: Town—5th Augst 1816.

On recpt of your favr 27th Ult in Ansr to mine of the 18th I judge it proper to present you with a View or statemt of Genl K. resources with me; in Order to favr a Simi Annual remittance to him.

1816			
1st Jany	To his Bale due as Remitted to him And acknowed by his later lettr 17th Aprl	1080.65.	
Aprl 4th	By his quarterly Int. recd on his $12.500 6 ⅌Ct Stock Net	182.82.	
July 2d	By d d do	182.82.	
		1446.29.	
Mar. 21st for 46 Shares.	from this sum deduct the difference between JB. purchase of Coa Bank Stock and Sale of US. Certificates & Int. &a &a therein—viz.	50.	1396.29.
Sepr 20th	By (to receive[1] presume) on said 46 whole shares Bank of Columa say on $4600—for $100 Each		

	presume—8 ℔Ct—$184.		
	Negt 4.60	179.40.	
Octr 1t	By (to receive)[2] 3 Mos Int. on the above 6 ℔Ct Net	182.82.	362.22.
			1758.51.

Over Anxious to remit the good Genl and fearing some Accident might delay your Ansr I sought every opporty to avail my self of a sett of ex—and on the 25th Ult the Only One that offered—of which I inclose you the 3d sett at 30 days Only—most favble and hastened—thro favr of Mr Monroe to whose Care I deposited 1t & 2d sett together with my Letter to Genl K. under Cover of each to Messrs Baring Brothers & Co London—of which you herewith Receive Duplicates—

I have now to deduct from the above sum viz—

July 25.	Smith & Riddle (of Richmond) a Sett of Ex. for £200. Sterg drawn By A P. Heinrich Esqr (of Baltimore) on John Rapp Esqr of London a 30 days in favr and endorsed by themselves.—a 20 ℔er Cent advance Amot	1066.66.	
	Negotn &a &a	21.33.	1087.99.
	leaves (the presumed) Amot in hand the 1t		$670.52.

Octr would not purchase, at the present rate of Ex—more than £123. pound Sterg Nevertheless—it is not probable this extra ex. will Continue long—with Reference to transferring his 6 ℔Ct Certificates & Bank Stock—in his Name, I shall endeavour to effect & advise you but from the present unsettled State of the Public & Bank Stock—generally it will require some time to judge of the expedience—the profit & loss Attending it—to which I shall pay every Attention—and Advise you—

You will please Notice to deduct from the above	$670.52
the presumed—recd sums 20 Sep & 1 oct Amt	362.22
leave a Bale in my hands—at this present—of	$308.30 only

with the Greatest Esteem—I am Dear Sir your most Obedt

JOHN BARNES,

RC (ViU: TJP-ER); with repeated sum at head of second page editorially omitted; at foot of text: "Thomas Jefferson Esqr Monticello"; endorsed by TJ as received 11 Aug. 1816 and so recorded in SJL. Enclosures: (1) Barnes to Tadeusz Kosciuszko, Georgetown, 31 July 1816, acknowledging receipt on 17 July of Kosciuszko's letter of 15 Apr. 1816 (not found); reporting that the delay in sending a remittance earlier in the year was due to the "very Extra Exchange" rate of 20 to 25 percent, but that since the rate had not subsequently declined, he had made "the first favorable purchase—a Sett for £200 Sterling a 30 days sight Only—and this day inclosed to Mess[rs] Baring & Brothers in London—to whose Care this is addressed with particular request to remit you the proceeds by the Earliest Conveyance—in the Hope that the Ex: between London & Soleure—may be in your fav[r]"; and promising another remittance in the ensuing autumn as soon as a favorable opportunity offers (Tr in ViU: TJP-ER; entirely in Barnes's hand and signed by him; at head of text: "Copy"; at foot of text: "Gen[l] Thad[s] Kosciusko at Soleure Switzerland in Care of Baring & Brothers London"). (2) Barnes to Baring Brothers & Company, Georgetown, 31 July 1816, enclosing the preceding; stating that while he was "Anxious to remit" £400 sterling, the high exchange rate of 20 to 25 percent induced him to send for the enclosed bill of exchange of "A P. Heinrich Esq[r] on John Rapp Eq[r] of London a 30 days in fav[r] of and endorsed—by Smith & Riddle—for two hundred pound sterling—which I trust will be duly Hon[d] and soon as paid the Net proceed thereof—you will have the goodness to transmit to Gen[l] Kosciusko at Soleure—in Switzerland"; hoping that "a more favorable ex. from London may fav[r] y[r] Remittance"; and asking to be notified when the bill is "Recd—and Accepted—or Noted for Non-Acceptance—to advise for my Goverment" (Tr in ViU: TJP-ER; entirely in Barnes's hand and signed by him; at head of text: "Copy"; at foot of text: "Mess[r] Baring & Brothers London"). Other enclosure not found.

TJ's FAV[R] to Barnes of 27 July 1816 is recorded in SJL but has not been found.

[1] Manuscript: "recive."

[2] Manuscript: "recive." Omitted closing parenthesis editorially supplied.

From William Duncanson

SIR Washington City 5th August 1816—

I trust you will excuse the liberty I take of thus addressing you nor would have taken Such a liberty, but well knowing that the warmest friendship at all times Subsisted between yourself and my late Uncle William Mayne Duncanson have taken this method therfrom of Seeking your friendship for myself & family as well as thre fine Children of my Uncle's whom I have taken under my Charge to assist them through[1] the world with my owin—

I believe Sir you were not unacquanted as to the Embaresed State of my poor Uncles fortune. Surrounded as he was by a Set of Villains he gave himself up to despondency by which not only his owin fortune but that which my farther his Brother left in his hands was Compleatly dispoiled. In Consequence of which I am left to make the best Shrift I Can—

I cannot See one friend Comming forward to giv any assistence; I have long Intertained the Idia of addressing you for the very purpose of Seeking your Patronage—my Uncle has often told me that Your heart was formed to Sempethise in the misfortunes of your fellow Creatures, Pardon me Sir, but I cannot hear omit what I have been told by him, and it is not altogether the motives which I write you on that would lead me to flatter—

as I have observed not one friend Comes forward to take me by the hand, they are either ashamed of their then Conduct toward my Uncle; or are Calious to all kind of human feelings—

I must now make you acquanted with the nature of my address. altho with much diffidence I presume to write to a Charicter of your Exaulted Talents—

your Interest with your friend the Honourable James Madison might procure me a Lecrutive Situation, eather In the Navy or War department Coustom house's or any other Situation by which I Could Support my heavy Charge and mantain the Respectibility of our Ancient and very honourable Name—

The zeal and assiduety which I Should at all times Shew in the faithfull discharge of my duty Should never Cause you one moment of painful Reflection to be Sorry for the Confidince you may be Induced to bestow on me by your Recomendation of me to Mr Madison and from him to the future President of the United States, according as my Merrits may be Seen,

Should you honour me with your friendship; In Conjunshen with my family we will ever pray that you may live many, many, Years in the ful Injoyment of every earthly blessing and when you leav this world that you meet with every heavenly blessing allow me to begg the honour of an answer when most convenient &

I am Sir with Sentiments of Respect and Esteem Yr Most obd[t] H[ble] s—

WILLIAM DUNCANSON

RC (DLC: James Madison Papers); endorsed by TJ as received 11 Aug. 1816 and so recorded in SJL. RC (MHi); address cover only; with PoC of TJ to Timothy Banger, 10 Oct. 1816, on verso; addressed: "Thomas Jefferson Esqr Montpelier Virginia" by "Mail"; franked; postmarked Washington City, 6 Aug. Enclosed in TJ to James Madison, 15 Aug. 1816.

The author's uncle, WILLIAM MAYNE DUNCANSON, lost a considerable fortune through land speculation and other failed business ventures in Washington, D.C. In 1807 TJ decided against appointing him either the librarian of Congress or the United States marshal for the District of Columbia (Allen C. Clark, "William Mayne Duncanson," *Records of the Columbia Historical Society* 14 [1911]: 1–24; TJ to Henry Dearborn, 21 Apr. 1807 [DLC]; William Mayne Duncanson to TJ, 15 Dec. 1807 [DNA: RG 59, LAR, 1801–09]).

[1]Manuscript: "though."

From George Flower

Dear Sir Mechanic Hall. New York Aug[t] 6–1816.—

I do not apologize altho' an entire stranger to you for addressing you with the utmost simplicity & freedom.

Just arrived from England I am about to proceed through the United States in search of a healthy & pleasant spot, whereupon I may pursue Agriculture and enjoy the pleasures of domestic life, free'd from those anxieties that were once confined to commercial speculations but now unfortunately invade every rural retreat in England.

I reserve to myself the pleasure of presenting to[1] you two letters, one from my good friend Lasteyrie (of Paris) & the other from La Fayette which they kindly sent me from france for the purpose of introducing me to you.

I am free to confess, that feeling myself rather perplexed to know what course exactly to pursue I am anxious for the assistance of your advice before I set out on my intended tour.

Trusting to your kindness to plead a sufficien[t] excuse for this hasty & abrupt communication permit me to subscribe myself, with the greatest

respect & sincerity your ob[dt] Ser[t]— George Flower

PS Letters address'd to me at Mess[rs] Warder & Brothers Philadelphia I shall receive with certainty.

If nothing extraordinary occurs, to prevent my intention, I mean to stop in the above mentioned City on Tuesday Night.

RC (MHi); edge trimmed; endorsed by TJ as received 16 Aug. 1816 and so recorded in SJL. RC (MHi); address cover only; with PoC of TJ to David Gelston, 18 Oct. 1816, on verso; addressed: "Thomas Jefferson Esq[r] Monticelo Virginia"; stamp canceled; franked; postmarked New York, 7 Aug.

[1]Manuscript: "to to."

From David Gelston

Dear Sir, New York 6. Aug: 1816.

The enclosed was received this day, under cover from M[r] Appleton from Leghorn—presuming it gives you the information, of his having Shipped 57 bottles wine for you, by the Ship Fanny, just arrived, I need not say more, than, that, I shall pay every necessary attention—received the wine in store, and wait your orders—

with great respect & regard I am sir, your obedient servant,

David Gelston

RC (MHi); endorsed by TJ as received 14 Aug. 1816 and so recorded in SJL, which has the additional notation (brackets in original): "[Carmigniano] 57.b." RC (DLC); address cover only; with PoC of TJ to Joseph Miller, 14 Oct. 1816, on verso; addressed: "Thomas Jefferson Esquire Monticello"; franked; postmarked New York, 6 Aug. Enclosure: Thomas Appleton to TJ, 30 May 1816, and enclosure.

To Patrick Gibson

[DE]AR SIR Monticello Aug. 6. 16.

Understanding that the 4. cases of wine shipped for me from Alexandria are arrived with you, and the state of our river rendering it improbable that it can be brought up that under a month or six weeks, I send the bearer with a small cart, and pray you to deliver to him two cases. the other two may wait for either Johnson or Gilmore. if you can procure for me & send by him also a cheese or two, it will much oblige me. I have understood it has been scarce in Richmond; but I see some now advertised there by Ralston and Pleasants, and some about 10. days ago advertised by some other firm. American is preferred, if to be had. if not, then of any other country.

Your's with great esteem & respect TH: JEFFERSON

PoC (DLC: TJ Papers, ser. 10); on verso of reused address cover of Eusebio Valli to TJ, 26 Apr. 1816; salutation faint; at foot of text: "Mr Gibson"; endorsed by TJ.

TJ's slave Wormley Hughes, the BEARER, was sent to Richmond this day and returned on 12 Aug. 1816 (*MB*, 2:1325).

To Margaret Bayard Smith

Monticello. Aug. 6. 16

I have recieved, dear Madam, your very friendly letter of July 21. and Assure you that I feel with deep sensibility it's kind expressions towards myself, and the more as from a person than whom no other's could be more in sympathy with my own affections. I often call to mind the occasions of knowing your worth, which the societies of Washington furnished; and none more than those derived from your much valued visit to Monticello. I recognise the same motives of goodness in the solicitude you express on the rumor supposed to proceed from a letter of mine to Charles Thomson on the subject of the Christian religion. it is true that, in writing to the translator of the Bible and Testament, that subject was mentioned: but equally so that no adherence to any particular mode of Christianity was there expressed;

nor any change of opinions suggested. a change from what? the priests indeed have heretofore thought proper to ascribe to me religious, or rather antireligious sentiments, of their own fabric, but such as soothed their resentments against the Act of Virginia for establishing religious freedom. they wished him to be thought Atheist, Deist, or Devil, who could advocate freedom from their religious dictations. but I have ever thought religion a concern purely between our god and our consciences, for which we were accountable to him, and not to the priests. I never told my own religion, nor scrutinised that of another. I never attempted to make a convert, nor wished to change another's creed. I have ever judged of the religion of others by their lives: and by this test, my dear Madam, I have been satisfied yours must be an excellent one, to have produced a life of such exemplary virtue and correctness. for it is in our lives, and not from our words, that our religion must be read. by the same test the world must judge me. but this does not satisfy the priesthood. they must have a positive, a declared assent to all their interested absurdities. my opinion is that there would never have been an infidel, if there had never been a priest. the artificial structures they have built on the purest of all moral systems, for the purpose of deriving from it pence and power, revolts those who think for themselves, and who read in that system only what is really there. these therefore they brand with such nicknames as their enmity chuses gratuitously to impute. I have left the world, in silence, to judge of causes from their effects: and I am consoled in this course, my dear friend, when I percieve the candor with which I am judged by your justice and discernment; and that, notwithstanding the slanders of the Saints, my fellow-citizens have thought me worthy of trusts. the imputations of irreligion having spent their force, they think an imputation of change might now be turned to account as a boulster for their duperies. I shall leave them, as heretofore to grope on in the dark.

Our family at Monticello is all in good health; Ellen speaking of you with affection, and mrs Randolph always regretting the accident which so far deprived her of the happiness of your former visit. she still cherishes the hope of some future renewal of that kindness; in which we all join her, as in the assurances of affectionate attachment and respect.

TH: JEFFERSON

RC (DLC: J. Henley Smith Papers); addressed: "M[rs] M. Harrison Smith to the care of mr Samuel Boyd Pine street Philadelphia"; franked; postmarked Charlottesville, 7 Aug.; with "Dead Letter" and "not found AR" written in two different hands on address leaf. PoC (DLC).

From Philip P. Barbour and William F. Gordon

Dear sir Charlottesville 7th Augt 1816

On the Subject of the writ of Right, which we have been requested to issue, in Your name & other claimants we have to inform you that on investigating the manner of instituting the Suit, we find that altho' the property has been conveyed[1] in joint tenancy, not Subject to Survivorship; yet that the Joint tenancy has been destroyed both by alienation & descent. That as tenants in Common Cannot maintain a joint action, we should have proceeded to institute Suits in the names of the several tenants[2] in common who are known to us, but that we are not in possession of the names of the persons claiming the adversary freehold title, or of the boundaries of the land. We therefore have troubled you by inclosing you a Writ with your own name as demandant of two Sixths of the land. & have to ask the favor of you to insert the names of the Tenants and the boundaries of the Land. We have the honor to be respectfully

Yr obt Serts P. P. Barbour

Wm F Gordon

RC (MHi); in Gordon's hand, signed by Barbour and Gordon; addressed by Gordon: "mr Jefferson Monticello"; endorsed by TJ as received 15 Aug. 1816 and so recorded in SJL. Enclosure not found.

A writ of right, also termed a writ of course, was "issued as a matter of course or granted as a matter of right" (*Black's Law Dictionary*). TJ owned a one-third undivided share of a 400-acre parcel on property known as the Limestone Survey and situated along the Hardware River in Albemarle County. The persons making an adversary claim to this land were Charles Hudson and John Hudson (TJ to Mary Stith, 7 Mar. 1811, and note; TJ's List of Landholdings and Monticello Slaves, [ca. 1811–1812]; TJ's Statement of Albemarle County Property Subject to State Tax, Mar. 1815).

[1] Word interlined in place of "devised."

[2] Reworked from "of all the tenants."

From LeRoy, Bayard & Company

Sir Newyork the 7 August 1816.

In reply to the communication we made to Mess. N. & J & R. Van Staphorst on the Subject of your last favor to us under date of the 7 of May, whereby you proposed to discharge the amount due them in three annual installments, these friends have written to us as follows, we quote their own words, Viz "Our intention in this advance having allways been to oblige mr Jefferson we will allow him every facility to discharge the amount due to us in the manner heretofore mention'd (within three years from 7 May last) and readily consent to the arrangement proposed which we request you to bring in due order. We beg you will communicate it to that Gentleman together with the assurance of our true regard" and while we acquit ourselves with pleasure of this Commission we make free to repeat for good understanding[1] Sake that in compliance with your proposal we Shall calculate on Successive payments under

dates of 7 May 1817 $2083.20 }
7 May 1818 " 2083.20 } with interest @ 6% ℔ ann^m from the 1 Day of January 1816 to the respective periods.
7 May 1819 " 2083.20 }

We have the honor to Subscribe with great respect Sir Your obed^t h^l S^t

LeRoy Bayard & Co
Successors to
LeRoy Bayard & McEvers

RC (DLC); in the hand of a representative of LeRoy, Bayard & Company; at head of text: "The Honble Thomas Jefferson Monticello"; endorsed by TJ as received 14 Aug. 1816 and so recorded in SJL.

TJ's last favor was dated 7 Apr. 1816, not the 7 of may.

[1] Manuscript: "undestanding."

From James Mease

Dear Sir — Philadelphia 7th Augt 1816

I contemplate collecting and publishing a volume or more of the letters addressed by my late friend Dr Rush to various persons on political, religious, and miscellaneous subjects, and as I know he had the pleasure to correspond with you, I will deem myself much obliged by being favoured with such as you may have in your possession. I will Carefully return them if so desired.—

I am with very Sincere respect
Your most obedient and obliged Servt — James Mease

RC (DLC); endorsed by TJ as received 15 Aug. 1816 but recorded in SJL as received a day earlier. RC (MHi); address cover only; with PoC of TJ to William Short, 14 Oct. 1816, on recto and verso; addressed: "Thomas Jefferson Monticello"; franked; postmarked Philadelphia, 7 Aug. Probably enclosed in Richard Rush to TJ, 13 Nov. 1816.

From Isaac H. Tiffany

Sir. Schoharie, N.Y. 8 Aug. 1816.

Will you be so good as to assist me from a doubt. Mr Gillies, historiographer to the king for Scotland has translated Aristotle's works into english. I have not seen the original, nor a translation into any other language than the beforementioned; but from the introductions to the Several books "on polities," & the notes, remarks & conclusions, altogether foreign from the text, of the great author, I am desirous to know, whether the translation is full & fair? Would it not be well, could a pure original be found, that the republican author should be translated by a republican? We regard with anxious & scrupulous suspicion, the precious relics which have passed through unhallowed hands. And if the productions of the "deepest thinker of all antiquity" shall have suffered by time by tyranny or barbarism, Who can restore the pristine proportion solidity & polish but the deepest thinker of all the moderns—

Sir please to receive my wishes & respects—

Isaac H. Tiffany.

RC (DLC); dateline at foot of text; endorsed by TJ. RC (DLC); address cover only; with PoC of TJ to Peter Derieux, 22 Nov. 1816, on verso; addressed: "Thomas Jefferson, Esq[r] Monticello—Vir[ga]"; franked; postmarked Schoharie Bridge, 8 Aug. Recorded in SJL as received 23 Aug. 1816.

Isaac Hall Tiffany (1778–1859), attorney, was born in Keene, New Hampshire. After graduating from Dartmouth College in 1793, he studied law successively under Aaron Burr in New York City and his own brother George Tiffany at Schoharie. Tiffany then established his own law practice, first at Cobleskill about 1798 and then in 1800 at Lawyersville, both villages in Schoharie County. He was also an officer in the county militia, 1800–04. Tiffany ran unsuccessfully as a Federalist candidate for the United States House of Representatives in 1806. He moved his practice to Albany in 1809, but by 1820 he had returned to Schoharie County, where in 1822 he was a judge of the court of common pleas and in 1825 the postmaster at Esperance. Having impoverished himself as a breeder of sheep for fine wool, by 1834 Tiffany moved to the town of Glen in Montgomery County. He represented that county in the New-York State Society for the promotion of Internal Improvements in 1836. Tiffany died in the village of Fultonville, Montgomery County (George T. Chapman, *Sketches of the Alumni of Dartmouth College* [1867], 71; William E. Roscoe, *History of Schoharie County, New York* [1882], 417; *Historical Magazine, and Notes and Queries, concerning the Antiquities, History and Biography of America* 10 [1866]: suppl. 2, p. 46; *Military Minutes of the Council of Appointment of the State of New York, 1783–1821* [1901–02], 1:520, 728, 755; *Albany Gazette*, 7 Apr. 1806, suppl.; New York *Republican Watch-Tower*, 17 June 1806; Albany *Balance, And New-York State Journal*, 28 Nov. 1809; Madison, *Papers, Pres. Ser.*, 5:613; *New-York Columbian*, 17 May 1820; *Albany Argus*, 19 Apr. 1822; *Table of Post-Offices in the United States* [Washington, 1825], 29; Edwin Williams, *The New-York Annual Register for … 1834* [1834], 338; *American Railroad Journal, and Advocate of Internal Improvements* 5 [1836]: 22; *History of Montgomery and Fulton Counties, N.Y.* [1878], 122–3).

John gillies, royal historiographer for Scotland under king George III, had published *Aristotle's Ethics and Politics, comprising his Practical Philosophy, Translated from the Greek*, 2 vols. (London, 1797; 2d ed., London, 1804; Poor, *Jefferson's Library*, 11 [no. 640]). In this work he described Aristotle as the DEEPEST THINKER of antiquity (2:53).

From John Adams

DEAR SIR Quincy August 9. 1816

The Biography of M[r] Vander Kemp would require a Volume which I could not write if a Million[1] were offered me as a Reward for the Work. After a learned and Scientific Education he entered the Army in Holland and Served as a Captain, with Reputation: but loving Books more than Arms he resigned his Commission and became a Preacher. My Acquaintance with him commenced at Leyden in 1780. He was then M[in]ister of the Menonist Congregation the richest in Europe; in that City where he was celebrated as the most elegant Writer in the Dutch Language.[2] He was the intimate Friend of Luzac and De Gyselaar. In 1788 when the King of Prussia threatened Holland with Invasion, his Party insisted on his taking a Command in the Army of defence and he was appointed to the Command of the most exposed and most important Post in the Seven Provinces. He was Soon Surrounded by the Prussian Forces. But he defended his Fortress with a Prudence Fortitude Patience and Perseverence, which were admired by all Europe, Till, abandoned by his Nation, destitute of Provisions and Ammunition,[3] Still refusing to Surrender, he was offered the most honourable Capitulation. He accepted it. Was offered very Advantageous Proposals, but despairing of the Liberties of his Country, he retired[4] to Antwerp determined to emigrate to New york; wrote to me in London requesting Letters of Introduction. I Sent him Letters to Governor Clinton and Several others of our little great Men. His History in this Country is equally curious and affecting. He left Property in Holland, which the Revolutions there, have annihilated and I fear is now pinched with Poverty. His head is deeply learned and his heart is pure. I Scarcely know a more amiable Character. A Gentleman here asked my opinion of him. My Answer was, he is a Mountain of Salt of the Earth.

He has written to me, occasionally and I have answered his Letters in great haste. You may well Suppose that Such a Man has not always been able to Understand our American Politicks. Nor have I. Had he been as great a Master of our Language[5] as he was of his own he would have been at this day one of the most conspicuous Characters in the U.S.

So much for Vanderkemp: now for your Letter of Aug. 1.
Your Poet, the Ionian I Suppose, ought to have told Us, whether Jove in the distribution of good and Evil from his two Urns, observes any Rule of Equity or not. Whether he thunders out flames of eternal Fire on the Many, and Power Glory and Felicity on the Few, without any consideration of Justice.?

Let Us State a few Questions, Sub rosâ.

1. Would you accept a Life, if offered You, of equal pleasure and Pain?[6] E.G. one million of moments of Pleasure and one Million of Moments of Pain?

   1,000,000 Pleasure = 1,000,000 Pain. Suppose the Pleasure as exquisite as any in Life and the Pain as exquisite as any. E.G. Stone, Gravel, Gout, Head Ache, Ear Ache, Tooth Ache, Cholick. &c. I would not. I would rather be blotted out.
2. Would you accept a Life of one Year of incessant Gout, Head Ache &c for Seventy two Years of Such Life as you have enjoyed? I would not.

   1 Year of Cholic = 72. of Boule de Savon. pretty but unsubstantial. I had rather be extinguished. You may vary these Algebraical Equations at pleasure and without End. All this Ratiocination Calculation, call it what you will, is founded on the Supposition of no future State.

Promise me eternal Life free from Pain, tho' in all other respects no better than our present terrestrial Existence, I know not how many thousand Years of Smithfield fires I would not endure to obtain it.

In fine, without the Supposition of a future State, Mankind and this Globe appear to me the most Sublime and beautifull Bubble and Bauble that Imagination can conceive.

Let us then wish for Immortality at all hazards and trust the Ruler with his Skies. I do: and earnestly wish for his Commands which to the Utmost of my Power Shall be implicitly and piously obeyed.

It is worth while to live to read Grimm, whom I have read. And La Harpe and Mademoiselle D'Espinasse the fair Friend of D'Alembert[7] both of whom Grimm Characterises very distin[ctly] are I am told in Print. I have not Seen them but hope Soon to have them.

My History of the Jesuits is not elegantly written but is Supported by unquestionable[8] Authorities, is very particular and very horrible. Their Restoration is indeed "a Step towards Darkness" Cruelty Perfidy Despotism Death and ——! I wish We were out of "danger of Bigotry and Jesuitism."! May We be "a Barrier against the Returns of Ignorance and Barbarism"! "What a Colossus Shall We be"! But will it not be of Brass Iron and Clay? Your Taste is judicious in like-ing better the dreams of the Future, than the History of the Past. Upon this Principle I prophecy that you and I Shall Soon meet and be better Friends than ever. So wishes JOHN ADAMS

RC (DLC); ink stained and mutilated at seal, with missing text supplied from FC; addressed by Susan B. Adams: "Thomas Jefferson Esq[re] Late President of the US. Monticello. Virginia"; franked; postmarked Quincy, 9 Aug.; endorsed by TJ as received 23 Aug. 1816 and so recorded in SJL. FC (Lb in MHi: Adams Papers).

MENONIST: Mennonite. In London on 6 Jan. 1788, Adams wrote a letter of introduction to New York governor George CLINTON on behalf of Francis Adrian Van der Kemp (DLC: John Pierpont Morgan Collection, Signers of the Declaration of Independence). Adams alludes playfully to TJ's alleged belief that the Louisiana Purchase included a large MOUNTAIN OF SALT (note to TJ to Benjamin Waterhouse, 9 Mar. 1813). Homer was the IONIAN poet.

BOULE DE SAVON: "soap bubble." During the reign of the Tudors, religious dissenters were burned at the stake in the London neighborhood of SMITHFIELD (Walter Thornbury, *Old and New London* [1872–78], 2:339). In the Bible, BRASS IRON AND CLAY, along with silver and gold, were "broken to pieces together, and became like the chaff of the summer threshingfloors; and the wind carried them away, that no place was found for them" (Daniel 2.35).

1 RC: "Milion." FC: "Million."
2 RC: "Languge." FC: "language."
3 RC: "Amunition." FC: "Ammunition."
4 FC: "returned."
5 RC: "Languge." FC: "language."
6 Here and in next three instances, RC: "Paine"; FC uses correct spelling.
7 RC: "D'Allembere." FC: "D'Alembert."
8 RC: "unquestiable." FC: "unquestionable."

From David Gelston

DEAR SIR, New York August 9th 1816.

I have received bill of lading for 2 boxes, 12 bottles each, red Paillerole wine and one basket maccaroni, from Marseilles by the Ship Ocean just arrived, shipped by M[r] Cathalan—

I Shall pay every attention, put the whole in Store, await your orders—and remain, with great respect,

sir, your obedient servant— DAVID GELSTON

RC (MHi); at foot of text: "M[r] Jefferson"; endorsed by TJ as received 16 Aug. 1816 and so recorded in SJL, which has the additional notation: "Paillerole wine 24.b. & maccaroni."

From Charles Willson Peale

DEAR SIR Belfield Aug[t] 9th 1816.

some time past I thought that I had found a young man in the Watch making line, that would have gone to settle as you proposed, but I have since heard that he has gone towards Bethlehem—and I have requested several Watch makers in the City to make inquiries for me by which means I shall have a chance of hearing if any young Man can be found suitable to recommend to your notice, I have required that he must have a good character, & perfectly Sober—

as often as I visit the City will I attend to this Business—and having resumed my Pencil my visits to the City in future will be frequent—At present I have been much perplexed to know what ought to be done with the Museum—Since the Corporation have purchased the State-house, a Committee from the Councils have requird of me a rent of 1600$ P^r^ An^m^ insure the Building &c &c which I consider, if the report is adopted by the Councils, as a total expultion of the Museum, I now think it a fortunate circumstance, as had they only required a small rent, I might have gone on neglectful of futurity—and if droped into my grave the Museum would most assuredly be divided by my Children in one year after my decease, and thus totally lost—Being alarmed at such an exhorbatant rent, I hastily drew up an address to the Corporation & other Citizens which I delivered the 18th Ul^t^ asking advice & aid to obtain a permanant foundation—In consequence a number of Gentlemen, have drawn up a Memorial & are getting the Signatures of many respectable Citizens—what will be the result I cannot yet divine—The Corporation have very limited powers, and they are very much in debt—I would much like to get less than the Value of the Museum according to the Annual income by Visitations—rather than undertake to have a Building made for its reception even should rich men lend me Money at a small Interest—I am now too old to expect to get through with any expensive undertaking—and it will be grevious to me to think of leaving my family of Numerous Children &c in imbarrassed Circumstances.

I will enclose my address, which now is in the press—It is a subject that I might have made much more interresting, if I had taken more time to have digested the subjects—but I was alarmed under the impression that the Councils would meet speedily—and however imperfect it might be, yet it might give Idea's to some men who perhaps had never thought on such subjects—

I have thought a great deal on the follies of my life—how much time I have consumed in mechanic labours—how much better it would have been for me to have choosen my other imployment than indulged my fancies in making various Machines, and doing work that I had not been accustomed to do. even at this moment I have to exert my resolutions to withstand temtations to oblige friends who ask my aid, or resist the impulse of doing whatever I want done—Within a short time I have studied effects I have seen in Landscapes which I had not noticed before, therefore in that line as well as in Portraits I conceive I can[1] make considerable improvements on my former practice—I have weighed the consequences of certain modes of execution with Colours—by judging of the consequences of not only the use of certain colours, but also the quantity of oils, or varnishes imployed to produce certain effects. an earlier turn of the mind to these studies might have enabled me to produce works of some importance—but at my time of life I cannot promise myself a continuance of good Eye sight, even should my days be lenthened.

However I have this satisfaction in view, that if I can produce some good Paintings imbracing such effects as may merrit admiration, that I may shew to those practicing the art, such rules as may to them be advantagous.

I have heard that wheat this year weighs 67 ℔ ℘ B:, equal it is said to English[2] wheat. I dont know why our wheat should not always be equally good—unless the heat of our Summers are generally too hot, and therefore too much hastens the harvest before it get a full growth of Grain. I have found that the Hessian Fly has very much injured wheat that was early sown—I have had this verified.

13th I find that much is said, both pro- & con, on the subject of my proposal to vest the corporation with a control on the Museum—and I very much suspect that some members composing that Body are taking this method to sound the disposition of the Citizens towards this institution—I do not intend to make any reply to any thing published—The corporation last week had a meeting, which I had no Notice of,[3] or I would most certainly have sent them some proposals of what I supposed might put the business in train—Their committee made no report about my rent—This helps to confirm my oppinion that they want time to feel the pulse of the People—for I find that some of the pieces published has made some of them sore—But the committee can only be blamed for a want [of][4] Liberality—At this season of the Year it is difficult to form a quoram in any public Body—besides short Evenings do not admit of much business being done—My present Idea is, that if they demand any considerable sum as rent—that I shall most certainly make[5] some efforts, either to sell the Museum in some manner, or get it remooved elswere. If you have any Idea's of what may be done, you will very much oblige me with your advice. There is no part of the Museum but can receive additions & great improvements, without very considerable expence—except of labour & time, and I am still zealous for its increase—The preserved subjects are generally as perfect as they were when first put into the Museum—Our mode of preservation in practice is easey, but where so many departments of Animals are imbraced, all cannot be brought to imbrace every spieces, but by a long course of exertions with very favorable circumstances—a certain sum to be paid for admission—, not exceeding the average price of a ℔ of Butter—given to those who superintend a Museum will secure their attention to preserve it in the best order for use or amusement—I need not say any thing more on this subject, as the Address notices these views—

I expect that Mr Patterson has given you every thing particular respecting the Gas-lights at the Museum, as some short time past he was making particular inquiries of my Son Rubens on[6] the expences &c attending the process &c—My Son Rembrandt ingaged in the plan of lighting the Streets of Baltimore is progressing fast with that work—The pipes, making of Copper to be screwed togather as in the mode practiced[7] in the fire-hose—and the branch pipes also to be screwed on—They will begin to lay them down as soon as a roof is put on the Building now erecting for the Furnaces & Gazometers—The manner in which Rembrandt has contrived his retorts appears to me well adapted to save trouble, in the replacing those that are burnt out—It is simply a pot with a flange[8] round the top thus:

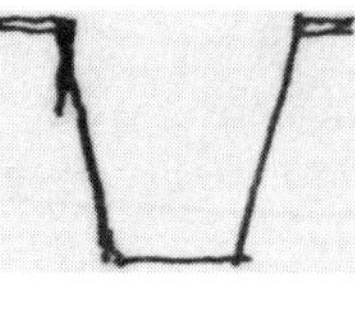

to which is screwed a copper lid with the Tubes, hard soldered on it—To give you a better Idea of the apparatus I will make a sketch on the other side.

a. The funnel to receive the Pitch—
b The Cock to let it down
c a hollowed plate to catch any of the droping of pitch & oil, to prevent its falling on the lid of the pot, where it would flame.
d. the tube coming to the center of the pot within 4 Inches of the bottom. e. The Tube 4 Inches diameter to carry the Gas to the Gazometer—f & g. flanges screwed togather by small hand vices, so that the pieces of joint (h) may be easily taken off in order to clean out the joint (e) when necessary, and making it more convenient to remoove the whole cover of the pot, to take out the coke, or rather charcoal, The Whole body of the pot is supported by the flanges—and the coal is thrown in by remooving an Iron plate level with the top of the pot—The grate at the bottom is not small nor but a little distance from the bottom of the pot—There are 3 flues near to

the top of the pot with a damper, connected into one flue going to the Chimney. Should you desire any further explanation I may give it in my next letter. I have given this to shew[9] how easey it is to supply the place of a retort burned out.

with my best wishes for your health—I am ever yours

C W PEALE

RC (DLC); endorsed by TJ as received 20 Aug. 1816 and so recorded in SJL. PoC (PPAmP: Peale Letterbook); at foot of text: "Thos Jefferson Esqre." Enclosure: Peale, *Address delivered by Charles W. Peale, to the Corporation and Citizens of Philadelphia, on The 18th Day of July, 1816, in Academy Hall, Fourth Street* (Philadelphia, 1816; Poor, *Jefferson's Library*, 6 [no. 223]; TJ's copy in DLC; reprinted in Peale, *Papers*, 3:411–23), in which Peale makes an "attempt to illustrate the importance of the study of Natural History, by the aid of a Museum," noting that the task was laborious and difficult and one "promising so little recompense" (p. 5); reviews the expense and effort involved in building his collection of mammoth bones, thus giving "knowledge to the world, what species of animal these huge bones belonged to" (p. 7); acknowledges the numerous donations of other gentlemen; emphasizes the museum's "constant drain upon the profits of my profession as a portrait painter" (p. 8); asserts that, by attracting visitors to Philadelphia, the museum provides a "means of bringing wealth into our city" (p. 10); declares that the museum provides city residents an opportunity to educate themselves about the natural world and scientific principles; explains that, far from being a financial success, establishing and maintaining the museum for thirty-one years has cost him "a fortune" (p. 15); indicates that the recent proposal that he pay a yearly rent of $1,600 to continue housing the museum in the statehouse newly acquired by the city "will bring me into distress" (p. 20); and solicits help from "the more enlightened portion" of Philadelphians "in devising some plan by which the Museum may be rescued from its difficulties" (pp. 22–3).

[1] Manuscript: "cam."
[2] Manuscript: "Enlish."
[3] Manuscript: "off."
[4] Omitted word editorially supplied.
[5] Manuscript: "make my," with "make" interlined.
[6] Manuscript: "or."
[7] Manuscript: "practrice."
[8] Manuscript: "falange," and "falanges" on two occasions below.
[9] Manuscript: "chew."

From David Bailie Warden

Place de L'abbaye, no. 8. (ter) par la rue du Colombier. Paris, 9 august,

DEAR SIR,

I had the pleasure of writing to you, on the 12th of last month, by mr Carere of Baltimore, concerning the Books forwarded to you, of which I now Send you the Booksellers receipt. I preferred Debure because he was highly[1] recommended to me by my friends mr. Chevallier, Librarian[2] of the Pantheon Library—and mr. Van Präet of the Royal Library. It will give me great pleasure to execute any commissions for you during my residence at Paris. Not receiving any favourable communication from our minister mr gallatin, I have offered my services as agent for the Settlement of claims, and hope to find in this employment some means of existence.

I am, dear Sir, with great Respect,
your most Obed[t] Ser[t] D B. WARDEN.

P.S. mr. Terril has entered the College at Geneva, and is in good health. I take the liberty of enclosing a copy of my circular Letter.

RC (DLC: TJ Papers, 207:37007); partially dated; at foot of text: "Thomas Jefferson Esquire"; endorsed by TJ as a letter of 9 Aug. 1816 received 21 Nov. 1816 and so recorded in SJL. Enclosures: (1) Receipt from de Bure Frères, 6 Aug. 1816, described at enclosure to Warden to TJ, 12 July 1816. (2) de Bure Frères to Warden, Paris, 7 Aug. 1816, stating with regret that the firm is unable to reduce the amount of the bill for books recently purchased; that it always charges the exact price at which it must sell; that it treats all of its customers similarly; and that it is confident that the shipment is satisfactory, because the firm has supplied only good editions (RC in DLC: TJ Papers, 207:36998; in French; addressed: "A Monsieur Monsieur Warden, Rue de furstenberg, a paris"). (3) Circular letter by Warden, Paris, 9 Aug. 1816, offering his services in obtaining compensation for, or recovery of, American property that has been seized by French authorities; expressing his "Intention to take charge of any other American Commercial Interests in relation to this Government, or its Subjects; of Affairs of litigation existing between them and American Citisens, and of Claims against the latter residing in France"; and promising that he will ask only "a Very moderate Commission or Recompence" (RC in DLC, in a clerk's hand, signed by Warden). (4) Carlo Botta to TJ, 10 Jan. 1816. (5) Destutt de Tracy to TJ, 4 Feb. 1816.

[1] Manuscript: "highlly."
[2] Manuscript: "Librarrian."

From John Barnes

DEAR SIR— George Town Co[a] 10th Aug[t] 1816.

Yesterday I waited on M[r] whann Cash[r] of Bank of Colum[a] as well M[r] Nourse Register of the Treasury respecting the Transfers you proposed in the Name of Gen[l] Thad[s] Kosciusko—now standing in your Name. The question I proposed was to Know Whether—or not—I could receive the Int & dividend as at present—when transfered—To which they both Answer'd—Neither you—(of course your substitute[1]) could not—
to which difficulty I submitted a proposition viz—that you inclose to me the Gen[ls] Original power—(or Copy) to you together, with his late letter to you—a Request to same purport.

and from these premises the Att[y] Gen[l] would determine Whether or not the transfer proposed could not be Accomodated to Afford the Object wish[d2] for—and by depositing a sett each—in B of C. and Treasury Offices—together with your substitution I might be Allowed to receive the Int. & Dividend—rather—than wait the Uncertain Risque & delay &[a] in Receiving a New and formal power from Switzerland—a letter from you to the Att[y] Gen[l] I persuade my self would close the Scruples of the Cash[r] and Treasur[y] departm[t]—with great Respect

I am Dear Sir—yr most obed[t]

JOHN BARNES,

RC (ViU: TJP-ER); at foot of text: "Thomas Jefferson Esq[r] Monticello"; endorsed by TJ as received 16 Aug. 1816 and so recorded in SJL.

Tadeusz Kosciuszko's ORIGINAL POWER of attorney is dated 30 Apr. 1798 (*PTJ*, 30:313–5). The ATT[Y] GEN[L] was Richard Rush.

[1]Manuscript: "substitue."
[2]Manuscript: "Object[d] wish."

From John F. Oliveira Fernandes

DEAR SIR! Norfolk 10th August 1816

Your favour of the 17th ultimo was recived, in Course of mail. The disagreable visit of fever[1] tertians, in the commencement of June, & July, together with the necessity of attending some Family; which, I could not with propriety, dismiss; have kept me weak enough.

I value highly the honour of your repeated invitation; of which I will do my self the pleasure to accept, for a day, or two, towards the end of this month, or the commencement of the next; in my passage to the Springs—because, calculatting it, as an impossible, to attend regularly my own health, in the place, I have resolved to travel a little—

For this reason, I will probably Lose the agreable Opportunity of meeting M[r] Correa de Serra, probably, detained as yet, in Philadelphia, with his Literary engagements.

Mess[rs] J. & w– Southgate, have Lately recived by their Ship from Lisbon few Q. Cask of wine for their own use I hope however, to have one for you; if you Say So—

I expect Some Porto—for my own use—I will cheerfully divide with you—

I remain with Sincere respect
D[r] Sir—Your Mo: ob[t] Servant

JOHN F. OLIVEIRA FERNANDES—

RC (DLC); between dateline and salutation: "Thomas Jefferson Esquire"; endorsed by TJ as received 17 Aug. 1816.

TERTIANS: fevers or agues "characterized by the occurrence of a paroxysm every third day" (*OED*). The SHIP *General Washington* brought "10 quarter casks very old Lisbon Wine" (Norfolk *American Beacon and Commercial Diary*, 8 Aug. 1816).

[1]Manuscript: "feve."

To William Short

Dear Sir Montpelier Aug. 10. 16.

Your favor of the 18th ult. after loitering unaccountably on the road, reached my hands on the eve of a visit to the President from whose seat therefore the present is written. I am much gratified by the prospect you hold up to me of a visit from Marshal Grouchy and Genl Clausel; and the pleasure will be heightened should the country thro' which they will pass, and the people whom they will see, of a character so novel to them, furnish[1] matter of compensation for so long a journey. be so good as to assure them I shall recieve them with great pleasure, and feel deeply sensible of this mark of their respect. you flatter me too with the hope of seeing Dr Wistar whom I have not seen for many years, and to whom a very long intimacy has affectionately attached me. I wish you could have been tempted to add your own name to the bonne bouche. it would have added much to the feast of friendship. I have been for some time expecting our excellent friend Correa. but I learn from a letter he has written to the President that he is confined by an attack of rheumatism. he was to come by the way of Winchester and to bring on with him mr Gilmer, whom I believe you know. I lost the pleasure of their visit by my absence in Bedford the last year, as lately that of M. de Neufville whom I should have been so happy to have recieved, and to whom I pray you to express my regards for the past, and my hopes for the future that according to the adage of his country 'tout ce qui est differé n'est pas perdu.'[2] to avoid a repetition[3] of loss with Correa and Gilmer, I had informed them that I had a visit of 6. weeks to make to Poplar forest, some time in autumn, the particular time of which however whether a month sooner or later was entirely immaterial: that if it should suit their convenience to take their journey before the 1st of Sep. they would find me at home and quite at leisure to enjoy the happiness of their company as long as they would give it to me; and that if they should not come before that day, I should conclude that a later season suited them better, and should immediately depart, have my visit over, and be ready to recieve them by the latter part of October. I must request you to explain this same state of things to Messrs Grouchy & Clausel, and save me the great mortification of being out of place on an occasion so gratifying to me. the delay of your letter on the road has unfortunately shortened the period from this to the 1st of September.[4]

To your encouragements to take up the political pen, I must turn a deaf ear. my repugnance to that is insuperable, as the thing itself is unnecessary. the present generation will be as able, as that which preceded them to do for themselves what is necessary for their own happiness; and that which shall succeed them will do what they shall leave undone. constitutions & laws should change with the changes of times and circumstances. those made now may as little suit our descendants, as we should be suited by those of our Gothic ancestors. the concerns of each generation are their own care.

I am sorry I have not a copy of the Notes of Virginia but a single one which I have made the depository of some additional annotations.

I think you had better employ mr Greene to collect the money from Carter. his commission will be a cheap riddance of the trouble you will have. ever and affectionately yours. TH: JEFFERSON

RC (ViW: TJP); edge trimmed and text faint, with missing and illegible letters supplied from SC; endorsed by Short as received 23 Aug. 1816 "at Ballston." SC (DLC); at foot of first page: "Wm Short"; endorsed by TJ.

José Corrêa da Serra mentioned his RHEUMATISM in a 10 July 1816 letter to President James Madison (DLC: Madison Papers). TOUT CE QUI EST DIFFERÉ N'EST PAS PERDU: "not all that is postponed is lost." TJ made ADDITIONAL ANNOTATIONS, including some written on inserted pieces of paper, to his copy (now in ViU) of the *Notes on the State of Virginia* (London, 1787).

[1] Manuscript: "shall furnish."
[2] Omitted closing quotation mark editorially supplied.
[3] Manuscript: "repetion."
[4] In RC TJ here replaced "period" with "September." Change not made in SC.

From William Wirt

DEAR SIR. Richmond. August 10. 1816.

I suppose it proceeds from the circumstances of my having lived in your neighbourhood, for several years; the brotherly intimacy and affection which has always subsisted between your nephews, the M[r] Carrs, and myself; and the paternal kindness with which you have always treated me, that I feel a sort of filial right to be more troublesome to you, than my judgment can entirely approve: but I beg you to be assured that the same feeling which prompts my applications to you, will dispose me to acquiesce, with undiminished respect and affection, in any refusal on your part to yield to them.

In the rare intervals of professional duties, and domestic avocations imposed upon me by a large and growing family, I have made such progress in my sketches of Henry's life, as to justify the hope that they will be ready for the press this autumn. I am very desirous, if it comport entirely with your convenience and inclination, that the manuscript should pass through your hands before it goes to the press:

but I repeat my entreaty that you will not yield to this wish, if it will be attended with any sacrafice of your convenience or ease. Besides the advantage to the work and to my self from your previous perusal, & corrections,[1] I am d[e]sirous that you should see whether I may not have made a freer use of your communications than you intended.

The work is now copying by my clerk; if you can accede to my wish, the manuscript shall be forwarded to you, in detachments, as the copy shall be finished. The whole, I presume, will not exceed an hundred and fifty pages; of which, perhaps, one hundred will have been copied, by the time I can receive your answer.

I beg you to accept the assurance of my unvarying respect and affection. WM WIRT

RC (DLC); edge chipped, with missing text supplied from Tr; endorsed by TJ as received 17 Aug. 1816. RC (DLC); address cover only; with PoC of TJ to Maximilian Godefroy, 11 Nov. 1816, on verso; addressed: "Thomas Jefferson esq^r Monticello" by "mail"; franked; postmarked Richmond, 15 Aug. Tr (MdHi: Wirt Papers).

[1] Preceding two words interlined.

From T. H. Pasley

SIR Chatham 12 Augt 1816

I have taken the liberty to enclose you a Statement of the possibility to attain a Natural Standard for Weights & Measures that appears more perfect & determinate than that the Pendulum is capable of—The Subject has been under partial consideration here but nothing has been concluded on respecting it And Nothing proposed at the time but ye Pendulum

Should the Opinions I have formd on the Subject be correct[1] they will no doubt under your Auspices[2] be converted to the Public good—

With Sentiments of the greatest respect I remain

Sir Your Most Obed^t Humb Servt T H PASLEY

RC (MHi); dateline at foot of text; adjacent to closing: "To Thos Jefferson Esq"; endorsed by TJ as received 5 Mar. 1817 from "Chatham Dockyard" and so recorded in SJL. Enclosure not found.

T. H. Pasley was probably with the Corps of Royal Engineers stationed at Chatham, England, the site of major British naval and military bases and the location of the Royal Dockyard. His publications on a wide variety of scientific topics included *A Treatise on Heat, Flame, and Combustion* (London, 1820), *A Paper on the Dry Rot in Timber* (Chatham, 1820), *A Theory of Natural Philosophy on Mechanical Principles, divested of all immaterial Chymical Properties, Showing for the First Time the Physical Cause of Continuous Motion* (1836), *A Paper Showing the Use of the Spleen* (1839), and *The Philosophy which shows the Physiology of Mesmerism, and explains the Phenomenon of Clairvoyance* (1848). In later years Pasley evidently resided on the isle of Jersey (Pasley to J. C. Robertson, 12 Aug. 1842, *Mechanics' Magazine, Museum, Register, Journal, and Gazette* 37 [1842]: 183).

[1] Manuscript: "correect."
[2] Manuscript: "Auspics."

From John Campbell White

SIR Baltimore 13th Augt 1816

Two of my sons travelling in England through the favour of Sir John Sinclaire, received some Melon seed, of two species, brought from Persia by Sir Gore Ousely, it has a high character. I have therefore much pleasure in sending a portion of it, to the first character in the United States

I am Sir with great respect JOHN CAMPBELL WHITE

RC (DNAL: Thomas Jefferson Correspondence, Bixby Donation); dateline at foot of text; at head of text: "Thomas Jefferson Esqr"; endorsed by TJ. Recorded in SJL as received 23 Aug. 1816.

John Campbell White (ca. 1757–1847), physician and merchant, was a native of Ireland. After receiving a medical degree from the University of Glasgow in 1782, he moved to Belfast, assisted his brother's export firm of Campbell & Tenant, and helped lead the efforts of Irish Catholics to mitigate British colonial policies perceived to be oppressive. By 1798 White had immigrated to the United States. As of the following year he had settled in Baltimore, where he practiced medicine, established the mercantile firm of John Campbell White & Sons, and started a distillery. White was an officer of the Medical and Chirurgical Faculty of Maryland in 1802; a founder and first president of the Baltimore Benevolent Hibernian Society in 1803; a founder and trustee of Baltimore College in 1803, later managing a fundraising lottery in 1808 and serving as president of the board of trustees in 1830; and a consulting physician for the Baltimore Hospital in 1812 and 1818. He became a naturalized United States citizen on 7 Mar. 1839 (W. Innes Addison, *A Roll of the Graduates of the University of Glasgow* [1898], 641; *PTJ*, 29:45, 39:405–6; *Historical Collections relative to the Town of Belfast from the Earliest Period to the Union with Great Britain* [Belfast, 1817], 285–9, 311–7, 363–5, 432–3; New York *Daily Advertiser*, 13 Dec. 1798; *Federal Gazette & Baltimore Daily Advertiser*, 18 June 1799; *The New Baltimore Directory, and Annual Register; For 1800 and 1801* [Baltimore, 1800], 98; Baltimore *Maryland Gazette*, 15 July 1802; Baltimore *Republican, or Anti-Democrat*, 19 Oct. 1803; Bernard O. Steiner, *History of Education in Maryland* [1894], 245–7; Baltimore *North American, and Mercantile Daily Advertiser*, 19 Feb. 1808; Washington *National Intelligencer*, 11 July 1812; *Alexandria Gazette & Daily Advertiser*, 9 Sept. 1818; *Baltimore Patriot & Mercantile Advertiser*, 12 Mar. 1834; DNA: RG 21, NPM; *Liverpool Mercury and Lancashire, Cheshire, and General Advertiser*, 5 Oct. 1847).

To William Duncanson

SIR Monticello Aug. 15. 16.

I recieved your favor of Aug. 5. on my return from a visit to the President, and regretted it had not come 3. or 4. days sooner, as I might have made it the subject of a conversation with him instead of a letter. I knew well the worth of the late Wm M. Dunca[n]son your uncle, his loyal principles to our republican government, & his great merit towards the city of Washington, towards the establishment of which he expended a handsome fortune; and I set a just value on the pleasures and advantages of his society. I will willingly bear testimony to his worth in a letter to the President this day, which, in the absence of all personal knolege of yourself, is the only service I can render you. Accept my best wishes for your success and the tender of my respects TH: JEFFERSON

PoC (DLC); one word faint; on verso of a reused address cover from José Corrêa da Serra to TJ; at foot of text: "Mr Wm Duncanson"; endorsed by TJ.

To David Gelston

DEAR SIR Monticello Aug. 15. 16.

Your favors of July 31. and Aug. 6. are both at hand. I considered that of July 31. as answered by mine of Aug. 3. altho' not then recieved: and indeed the general request I made you in that, anticipated the subject of your last letter also; by requesting all articles recieved for[1] me to be consigned to mess^rs Gibson & Jefferson of Richmond, drawing on them for whatever articles of expence may be referred to them, and notifying me of any others. if the bank paper of Richmond is recievable with you I could always myself make prompt returns to you by mail. if not recievable I should always be obliged to remit thro' my correspondents at Richmond. I shall often[2] be needing apologies for these troubles to you, which I hope you will excuse and be assured of my great esteem and respect TH: JEFFERSON

RC (Bruce Gimelson, Garrison, N.Y., 2003). RC (Grace Floyd Delafield Robinson, Greenport, N.Y., 1947); address cover only; addressed: "David Gelston esq. New York"; franked; postmarked Milton, 16 Aug.; endorsed by Gelston. PoC (MHi); endorsed by TJ.

[1] Word interlined in place of "from."
[2] Word interlined.

To LeRoy, Bayard & Company

Gentlemen Monticello Aug. 15. 16.

Your favor of the 7th is recieved, and I shall endeavor to comply as exactly as in my power with the instalments with which messrs Van Staphorsts are so kind as to indulge me. my resources are those of a farmer, depending on the produce of my farms, which is usually sold in April or May, but sometimes necessarily on some credit to avoid sacrificing it, which I am sure the kind motives of the loan would spare were these causes at any time to oblige me to overrun the exact day. Accept my thanks for your friendly intermediation in this business and the assurance of my great esteem and respect.

Th: Jefferson

PoC (DLC); on verso of reused address cover to TJ; at head of text: "Messrs Leroy and Bayard"; endorsed by TJ.

To James Madison

Dear Sir Monticello Aug. 15. 16.

I do not know whether you were acquainted with the late Major Duncanson of Washington, uncle of the writer of the inclosed letter. he was one of the earliest adventurers to the city of Washington. he had made a princely fortune in the E. Indies, the whole of which he employed in the establishments of that city and finally sunk. his political merits were a most persevering republicanism in the worst of times, having been one of the four only republicans in Washington & George town in the time of mr Adams. when I first went there, a stranger, I found him often useful for information as to characters, and I always believed him an honest & honorable man, altho' the warmth of his temper made him many enemies. these are the merits of the uncle. of the nephew I know nothing, and have therefore informed him I could render him no other service than that of stating to you what I knew of his uncle, considering it as a duty to bear testimony to truth. I salute you with affectionate attachment and respect

Th: Jefferson

RC (DLC: Madison Papers); at foot of text: "The President of the US."; endorsed by Madison. PoC (DLC); on verso of reused address cover of Charles Simms to TJ, 25 May 1816; endorsed by TJ. Enclosure: William Duncanson to TJ, 5 Aug. 1816.

To Elisha Ticknor

Sir Monticello. Aug. 15. 16.

I have recieved two letters from your son, mr George Ticknor, dated Mar. 15. and Apr. 23. from which I learn with pleasure that he enjoys health and is so much satisfied with his situation at Gottingen that he has concluded to prolong his residence there a year. the account he gives me of the German literature is very interesting, and such as I had not been before apprised of. it seems well worthy of his avail and he is accordingly sowing the seed of what with his genius & industry will yield a rich harvest. he informs me he is about sending you some books, and that he will at the same time send a parcel for me to your address. it is this which gives you the trouble of this letter to request you will be so good on their arrival[1] as to reship them to Richmond consigned to Messrs Gibson and Jefferson, my correspondents there, who will pay all articles of duties and charges which can be referred to that place: and indeed the freight & other charges from Europe if they can be referred to them wi[ll] perhaps be more promptly replaced: if this cannot be done and you will be so good as to drop me a line by mail, they shall be remitted immediately by myself if Richmond bank paper is recievable with you; if not recievable I will have the remittance made from Richmond. the kind office you hold between your son and myself requires many apologies and thanks which I must pray you to accept with indulgence, and to be assured of my great esteem & respect Th: Jefferson

PoC (MHi); on verso of reused address cover of John Adams to TJ, 6 May 1816; mutilated at seal; at foot of text: "Elisha Ticknor esq."; endorsed by TJ.

[1] Preceding three words interlined.

To John Payne Todd

Monticello Aug. 15. 16.

You have given me, my dear Payne, a very handsome keep-sake which has amused me much, and not the less by the puzzle it has afforded me, to find out the method of rectifying it. I at length discovered it, and that it was only necessary to loosen a little a single screw to throw it out of geer, and to throw it in again after setting the index. it was exactly 10° wrong. it is indeed a very convenient travelling thermometer.

You must now accept a keep-sake from me, which may suit you as a sportsman, better than myself who have ceased to be one. I send by the stage, to be lodged for you at Orange C. H. a box containing a pair of Turkish pistols. they were originally with wheel-locks, which not being convenient, I had locks of the modern form substituted, but so that they can be changed for the former in a moment. they are 20. inch barrels so well made that I never missed a squirrel 30. yards with them. I fixed one in a wooden holster to hang in the loop of the pommel of my saddle to be handily taken out & in, having used it daily while I had a horse who would stand fire. I had other holsters also made for both to hang them at the side of my carriage for road use; & with locks & staples to secure them from being handled by curious people. one of the wheel locks is a little out of order, and will require a skilful gunsmith to put to rights it is now cocked, and I could not find out how to discharge it.

the key is with them; and they wind up to the right, or with the sun. in the hope they will afford you sport in your daily rides, I pray you to accept the assurance of my friendship & respect and to present the same to the president and mrs Madison. TH: JEFFERSON

RC (Christie's, New York City, 1990; facsimile, lacking address cover, in its catalogue of *Printed Books and Manuscripts including Americana*, 8 June 1990, lot 91; photocopy including address cover from NUt, 1955, in TJ Editorial Files); addressed: "Payne Todd esq. at the President's near Orange C. H."; franked; postmarked Milton, 16 Aug. PoC (MHi); on recto of reused address cover of Charles Thomson to TJ, 16 May 1816; mutilated at seal; endorsed by TJ.

For TJ's acquisition of the PAIR OF TURKISH PISTOLS from Isaac Zane, see TJ to Jacob Rinker, 27 June 1803 (*PTJ*, 40:620).

To Benjamin Galloway

DEAR SIR Monticello Aug. 16. 16.

Your favor of July 30. came to hand on the 11th inst. I had already concluded that the clockmaker you had contemplated for us was not willing to displace himself, and had taken measures to obtain one from Philadelphia, in which we are like to succeed.[1]

On the subject of your letter[2] to mrs Randolph I have only to say that generally I am averse to be quoted in the public papers,[3] because there are bigots, religious and political always ready and disposed to make every word from me a text for perversions and ribaldry; and I am now at that time of life which asks repose and tranquility. but as the principles of the letter in question are those I have always avowed, and wished that every one should understand to be mine,[4] and especially as you think it will remove imputations to which the transaction it relates to has given rise, I consent with chearfulness and approbation[5] to [its] publication;[6] and for this purpose I return the copy you sent with some [fin?]al corrections, to make it scrupulously what it professes to be.

Our family joins me in assurances of great esteem and respect.

TH: JEFFERSON

PoC (DLC); torn at seal, with first missing word supplied from newspaper versions below; on verso of reused address cover to TJ; at foot of text: "Benjamin Galloway esq."; endorsed by TJ. Reprinted from an unidentified issue of the Fredericktown (later Frederick), Md., *Political Examiner & Public Advertiser* in the 18 Sept. 1816 issues of the *Richmond Enquirer* and the Washington *Daily National Intelligencer*.

A version of the LETTER IN QUESTION, TJ to Galloway, 2 Feb. 1812, was printed in the above newspapers, along with Galloway's letter to "Philip [Thomas] Northmore, Esq. England," 17 June 1812, in which Galloway enclosed TJ's 2 Feb. 1812 letter, described TJ as "now in the enjoyment of *otium cum dignitate*," and asserted that the United States wished to maintain peaceful relations with Great Britain.

[1] Sentence not in newspapers.

[2] Newspapers substitute "yours" for preceding two words.

[3] Newspapers substitute "newspapers" for preceding two words.

[4] Newspapers: "sincere."

[5] PoC: "appobation." Newspapers: "approbation."

[6] Remainder of paragraph not in newspapers.

From Samuel Kercheval

SIR N. T. Stephens[g] 16th Aug[t]—16

I received[1] your truly interesting letter, on Monday last; and have shewn it to several gentlemen of both political parties, who unite in the opinion with me, that its importance to society at the present crisis, is of that imperious nature as to counter ballance all consideration of delicacy—and your opinions on the subject of calling a convention so interesting to the Western people particularly it is with difficulty I can restrain my own anxiety as well as that of others from giving its contents to the publick

The solemn injunctions however under which you have[2] placed me, not to "quote[3] it as authority before the publick" must be paramount to the interest of our common country; unless indeed you will consent to its publication.

Your lucid and candid exposition of republican canons—have taken strong hold on the minds of several gentlemen, heretofore your political opponents—And if I may judge by the voice of the few individuals to whom I have taken the liberty to shew it—it is fair to conclude that it will make the same impression upon the minds of a vast majority of our fellow citizens

I pray you—Sir—I conjure you by all that is dear to our common country to permit me to publish your letter—The pamphlet enclosed to you in June last was written by me—the name of H— Tompkinson assumed from motives of timidity in my own judgement and talents to discuss a question of such vital importance—I however find the work is generally approved of, and popular, and it is no longer necesary to conceal my name from the publick—I trust you will pardon the fraud I committed,[4] in addressing you under a feignd name—if indeed it deserves the name of fraud I hope you will view it as an innocent one

Accept Sir the assurances of my high regard

SAM[L] KERCHEVAL.

RC (DLC); endorsed by TJ as received 28 Aug. 1816 and so recorded in SJL. RC (DLC); address cover only; with PoC of TJ to Stephen Kingston, 25 Sept. 1816, on verso; addressed: "The Honble Thomas Jefferson Monticello Virg[a]"; franked; postmarked New Town Stephensburg, Va., 17 Aug. 1816.

[1] Manuscript: "receved."
[2] Manuscript: "have d <*p*> have."
[3] Manuscript: "qoute."
[4] Kercheval here canceled "on you."

From Lafayette

MY DEAR FRIEND La Grange August 16[h] 1816

Your Letter of May 17[h] Has Afforded me Every kind of Gratification. I Had not for a Long time Heard from you and was very Anxious for intelligences of your welfare. Certain Leanings of the Liberal opinion on the other Side of the Channel and Atlantic waters Appearing to me Not Quite Correct I Have Been much pleased to find you were Sensible of the dangers we Had to Encounter from Both Quarters. Yet it Behoved a patriot to Give His Whole Weight on the Scale of defence Against foreign invasion and influence. that a Longer Resistance Has not Since taken place is Still my Regret and Has not Been my fault.

I Have Had the pleasure to See m[r] Gallatin at my friend m[r] parker's Country Seat, And am in Hopes of His visit next month at La Grange. He was So kind as to indulge my Reluctance for the town where I Have not Been Since the Ennemy Have Evacuated this[1] Rural place of Retirement. Here I am with my numerous family Quite Stranger to the politics which Now divide the two fractions of one party. Our friend Tracy is for the present At An Estate of His in the departement de L'allier; I Gave Him an Extract of your letter for which He Has Been very thankful, and am now Sending the letter itself. He is almost Blind. There are Hopes of a Cataract which might Be Extracted.

I thank you, my dear friend, for the Cheering Good wishes and Expectations Contained in your much Esteemed favour. I am Sanguine also. notwithstanding[2] present Appearances the true doctrines Have made Great progress. There are Axioms at Which we Have Seen, you and I, not thirty years Ago philosophers and patriots Stare, and which are now Common place Sayings. There is no Stability for things and men, not only in france, But in the Neighbouring Countries, Unless their Governments are founded upon our primitive principles of freedom.

this Letter Having not Been writen in time for the departure of m[r] Vail from paris, I Let it Run its chance through the post offices to the Havre: But would not miss this Occasion to Express to you the Grateful, affectionate Attachment and Regard of your old friend

LAFAYETTE

RC (DLC); endorsed by TJ as received 17 Oct. 1816 and so recorded in SJL. RC (DLC); address cover only; with PoC of TJ to Patrick Gibson, 22 Nov. 1816, on verso; addressed: "Thomas Jefferson Esq. Monticelo State of Virginia favour'd By m[r] Vail."

THE TOWN: Paris.

[1] Reworked from "my."
[2] Manuscript: "notwistanding."

To John Wood

DEAR SIR Monticello Aug. 16. 16.

Your favor of the 2[d] inst. is recieved, and I congratulate you sincerely on your appointment to the survey of the rivers. I had been afraid that your late rheumatic affections would have rendered you unequal to the bodily labors it will call for. I recollect nothing in the manner of execution but what we have already talked over; but should any thing occur I will communicate it freely, when I shall have the pleasure of seeing you at Poplar Forest, which will be in the first week of September. I will bring with me my pocket sextant, as I possess no large one. my surveying compass is also at your service, but I think it will not answer your purpose. I bought it in London, and altho' well-executed, it is in miniature only for the pocket, being but of 1. inch radius. I have found it very defective in it's traverses from the shortness of it's needle. the longer the needle the more strongly and certainly it takes it's direction. as every surveyor has a better one, I shall not take this with me to Bedford, unless you signify to me that it will answer your purpose; in which case it shall be at your command. Accept the assurance of my great esteem & respect

Th: Jefferson

PoC (DLC); on verso of reused address cover of John Steele to TJ, 14 May 1816; at foot of text: "Mr John Wood"; endorsed by TJ.

To James Mease

Dear Sir Monticello Aug. 17. 16.

I have duly recieved your favor of the 7th inst. requesting me to communicate to you such letters from the late Dr Rush to myself as I possess, on political, religious & miscellaneous subjects, with a view to their publication. I possess but few such; but these were of extraordinary confidence; insomuch that, on his death, I requested from his family a return of my letters to him on subjects of this character; which they kindly and honorably did return. had I died first, I think it probable he would have made the same request from my family, & with the same view, that of preventing the publication of his letters, or their getting into hands which might expose him, living, or his character when dead, to obloquy from bigots in religion, in politics, or in medecine. when we are pouring our inmost thoughts into the bosom of a friend, we lose sight of the world, we see ourselves only as in confabulation with another self; we are off our guard; write hastily; hazard thoughts of the first impression; yield to momentary excitement; because, if we err, no harm is done; it is to a friend we have committed ourselves, who knows us, who will not betray us; but will keep to himself what, but for this confidence, we should reconsider, weigh, correct, perhaps reject, on the more mature reflections and dictates of our reason. to fasten a man down to all his unreflected expressions, and to publish him to the world in that as his serious & settled form, is a surprise on his judgment and character. I do not mean an inference that there is any thing of this character in Doctor Rush's letters to me: but only that, having been written without intention or preparation for publication, I do not think it within the office of a friend to give them a publicity which he probably did not contemplate.

I know that this is often the form in which an author chuses to have his ideas made public. when the occasion, the subject, the chastened style evidently indicate this, it may be as good evidence of intention, as direct expression. but, in the present case, the occasions were special, the persons and subjects most confidential, and the style the ordinary careless one of private correspondence. under these circumstances, I hope, my dear Sir, you will see in my scruples only a sentiment of fidelity to a deceased friend, and that you will accept assurances of my great esteem and respect TH: JEFFERSON

RC (Anonymous, New York City, 1984). PoC (DLC); at foot of text: "Doctor Mease." Probably enclosed in Richard Rush to TJ, 13 Nov. 1816.

To Charles Willson Peale

DEAR SIR Monticello Aug. 17. 16.

In your's of July 7. you informed me you had found a young watchmaker of good character disposed to come here, who had taken time to consider of it. hearing nothing further of him, & being now within a fortnight of departure to Bedford where I shall be 6. weeks I am anxious to know of a certainty; because were he to come during my absence he might not[1] find the same facilities for first establishment as were I here. I have a good deal also which might employ his first days until work should come in. I am sorry to be troublesome to you, but rely on your often experienced goodness for apology. ever & affectionately Yours TH: JEFFERSON

RC (TxU: Thomas Jefferson Collection); at foot of text: "Mr Peale." PoC (MHi); on verso of reused address cover of John P. Boyd to TJ, 7 May 1816; top half of text faint; endorsed by TJ.

[1] Word interlined.

To William Clark

DEAR SIR Monticello Aug. 18. 16.

The bearer of this letter, mr Robert Sthreshley, for some time a neighbor of mine has sold his possessions adjoining me and proposes to remove with his family to St Louis. as he will be an entire stranger there he naturally wishes to be known to some one whose countenance may be a recommendation & introduction into the society of the place. he is a man of property, careful, correct, industrious, and under all circumstances of perfect[1] integrity; an amiable neighbor, and with a wife equally so, and worthy of him. any notice or attentions you can shew him will be meritoriously placed and will be considered as an obligation on myself. I salute you always with affectionate esteem & respect. TH: JEFFERSON

PoC (MHi); at foot of text: "Genl William Clarke"; endorsed by TJ. Recorded in SJL, with the additional notation that it was sent "by mr Sthreshly."

[1] Reworked from "in."

From Pierre Samuel Du Pont de Nemours

Mon très respectable Ami, 18 Aoust 1816.

Il m'a paru que je ne pouvais faire aucun meilleur usage de votre Lettre relative à Mr de Tracy que de lui en envoyer copie. C'est ce que j'ai fait.

Quant à la partie de Son ouvrage qui n'était pas encore traduite, qui ne l'a pas bien été par la Personne à qui Mr Duane en a remis le travail, et que vous avez ou retraduite ou corrigée, je Suis assez d'avis que vous la donniez à imprimer à Mr Milligan, qui, conjointement avec Mr R. Chew-Weightman a fait à George Town une Superbe édition de Malthus.

Mais je vous demanderai Si ce nouveau Volume est une continuation du Commentaire Sur l'Esprit des Loix, ou un Traité particulier d'Economie politique, mis Simplement à la Suite de l'autre ouvrage par analogie des Sujets.

Si c'est le premier cas, il vaut mieux assortir les deux Editions.

Si c'est le Second, il n'y a pas d'inconvénient de rendre l'Edition de cet ouvrage, entierement propre à l'Auteur, plus belle que ne l'a été celle de Son Commentaire Sur le travail d'un autre Ecrivain: quelque justes qu'aient été les Succès et du Commentateur et de l'Auteur primitif.

Il me paraît que vous aviez Songé à en donner aussi une Edition française. Si vous persistiez dans cette idée, je me chargerais volontiers d'en corriger les épreuves. C'est tout ce à quoi je pourrais Servir: Car vous avez vu combien je Suis loin de pouvoir être utile à aucune édition anglaise.

Je resterai un Ecrivain Français Supportable; Je ne pourrai jamais devenir un bon Ecrivain anglais; et pressé par mon âge de jetter Sur le papier Ce que je puis avoir encore d'idées Sur les Gouvernemens en général, et les Républiques nées ou à naitre en particulier, je ne peux plus mettre à l'étude des mots la force dont je n'ai pas de trop pour la Science des choses. Je Suis obligé d'employer la langue dans laquelle j'écris avec facilité.

Combien je regrette, mon cher Ami, que vous n'ayiez pas fait traduire il y a Seize ans mon ouvrage Sur l'Education dans votre Pays.

Elle y Serait présentement en pleine vigueur. Nous avons perdu dix années d'utilité publique.

On ne peut plus faire les Livres classiques en Europe. Ils y Seraient Souillés par les Prêtres.

Le Gouvernement des Etats unis ne voudra pas les payer. Celui des Républiques de l'Amérique espagnole ou portugaise Sera encore quelques années agité par des guerres auxquelles le véritable Peuple du Pays ne prend interêt, ni part. Et même après la victoire de la liberté politique, les chaines du Catholicisme, du Christianisme[1] même qui depuis dix huit Siecles n'est plus la Religion de Jesus-Christ, péseront Sur la raison, Sur la morale, Sur la philosophie, Sur le bon Sens, Sur l'équité, gêneront plus ou moins la Liberté religieuse, continueront de calomnier Dieu et les Hommes.

Ne nous dégoutons pas, ne nous désolons pas, mon excellent Ami. Travaillons tant que la nature nous en laissera la force.

Nous ne pouvons encore Semer que du gland Sur des terres assez mal préparées. Il poussera des Chênes, Sous lesquels, quelques Siecles après nous, les Hommes et les Animaux Se promeneront, peupleront avec Sureté, avec abondance, avec délices.

Je présente mes hommages à Madame votre Fille, et à Ses aimables Filles y comprise Septimia.

Et je vous embrasse avec respect et tendresse.

DuPont (de nemours)

Je ne quitterai plus l'Amérique. Ma Femme Sera ici au mois de mai prochain. Je n'aurai pas le bonheur que ma mort fût utile à la France. Il faut tâcher que le reste de ma vie le Soit aux Etats Unis et au monde. Utinam![2]

Nous aurons à faire les livres classiques par Souscription. Cela ne coutera que douze mille dollars. Il nous Suffira de cent personnes.[3]

N'est-il pas à craindre que les cruautés réciproques entre les Espagnols d'Europe et les Espagnols créoles, ne fassent naitre, chez les véritables indigênes et les Sang-mêlés, l'idée de laisser les hommes blancs S'affaiblir et S'exterminer; puis de les achever tous une nuit ou un matin, et de ne conserver que des Hommes rouges? Triste uniforme que celui de la peau!

Une telle pensée peut germer chez un Peuple timide, longtems insulté, longtems opprimé par une Race étrangere.

On ne peut trop Se hâter d'admettre au plus complet droit de cité les Hommes de Sang rouge ou mêlé; ou au moins ceux d'entre eux qui sont Propriétaires de terres et le deviendront: C'est le meilleur moyen d'exciter au travail, d'inspirer l'esprit public, de tenir au plus bas taux possible l'interêt des Capitaux, partant de favoriser le commerce et l'industrie

Notre Science de l'Economie politique S'avance, et demande encore beaucoup de travail.[4]

Celle des Finances est faite, mais n'est pas crue; elle est[5] loin d'influer Sur l'opinion publique.

Elle n'a pas du tout germé chez votre race anglaise, qui[6] a encore le mauvais Sang et le mauvais Sens de Ses Peres.

Mon Ami, nous Sommes des Limaçons et nous avons à monter Sur les Cordilieres. Par dieu il y faut monter!

EDITORS' TRANSLATION

My very respectable Friend, 18 August 1816.

It seemed to me that I could make no better use of your letter about Mr. de Tracy than to send him a copy of it. I have done so.

Regarding the part of his book that has not yet been translated or which had been badly translated by the person to whom Mr. Duane had given the work and that you had either retranslated or corrected, in my opinion you should give it to Mr. Milligan for printing. He produced in Georgetown, along with Mr. R. Chew Weightman, a superb edition of Malthus.

But, I will ask you, is this new volume a continuation of the Commentary and Review of Montesquieu's Spirit of Laws or a distinct treatise on political economy placed at the end of the other work simply because of the similarity of subject matter?

In the first case, it is better for the two editions to match.

In the second, there is no objection to making the edition of this work, written entirely by the author, more beautiful than his commentary on the work of another writer, however successful the commentator and the original author may have been.

It seems to me that you had also contemplated producing a French edition. If this is still your idea, I would willingly take on the responsibility for correcting the proofs. This is all I can do to help; you have seen how useless I am to any English edition.

I will remain a tolerable writer in French. I will never be a good one in English. Pressed by age to throw down on paper any ideas I might still have on governments in general and, in particular, on republics in existence or still to come, I can no longer apply to the study of words the limited strength that I can still bring to the science of things. I am obliged to employ the language in which I write with ease.

How I regret, my dear friend, that you did not have my work on education in your country translated sixteen years ago.

It would now be fully in force. We have lost ten years of public usefulness.

Classical books can no longer be published in Europe. They would be defiled by the priests.

The government of the United States will not want to pay for them. Those of the republics of Spanish or Portuguese America will continue for some years to be agitated by wars in which their true people take no interest or part. Even after winning their political liberty, the chains of Catholicism, even Christianity, which has not been the religion of Jesus Christ for eighteen centuries, will weigh down reason, morality, philosophy, common sense, and equity, hinder religious freedom to a greater or lesser degree, and continue to slander God and men.

Let us not be disgusted or distressed, my excellent friend. Let us work as long as nature grants us sufficient strength.

For now we can only sow acorns on rather poorly prepared soil. Oak trees will grow, under which, a few centuries after us, men and animals will walk and multiply in safety, abundance, and delight.

I send my regards to Madam your daughter and her kind daughters, including Septimia.

And I embrace you with respect and tenderness.

DuPont (de Nemours)

I will not leave America again. My wife will be here next May. I will not have the happiness of knowing that my death proved useful to France. I must try to make the rest of my life of use to the United States and the world. Utinam!

We will do the classical books by subscription. It will only cost twelve thousand dollars. One hundred people will be sufficient for us.

Should we not fear that the reciprocal cruelties of the European and the creole Spaniards will create among the indigenous peoples and those of mixed blood the idea of letting the whites become weaker through their extermination of one another and then of finishing them all off one night or morning and only preserving red men? Skin is a sorry uniform!

Such a thought can form among timid people who have long been insulted and oppressed by a foreign race.

Complete citizenship rights cannot be given too soon to men of red or mixed blood or, at least, to those who are or will become landowners. This is the best way to motivate people to work, inspire public spirit, keep interest rates on capital as low as possible, and thereby promote commerce and industry

Our science of political economy is progressing, but it still requires a lot of work.

That of finance is mature, but it is not believed; it is far from having any influence over public opinion.

It has not taken root at all with your English race, which still has the bad blood and opinions of its fathers.

My friend, we are snails, and we have to climb cordilleras. By God, we must climb them!

RC (DLC); dateline beneath signature; endorsed by TJ as received 29 Aug. 1816 and so recorded in SJL. RC (MHi); address cover only; with PoC of TJ to Hutchins G. Burton, 1 May 1817, on verso; addressed: "Thomas Jefferson, Late President of the United States, Monticello, Virginia"; franked; postmarked Wilmington, Del., 26 Aug. FC (DeGH: Pierre Samuel Du Pont de Nemours Papers, Winterthur Manuscripts); in a clerk's hand, with emendations by Du

Pont. Tr (DeGH: Du Pont Miscellany, Winterthur Manuscripts); posthumous copy by Eleuthera du Pont Smith; dated 18 Aug. 1816. Tr (DeGH: Du Pont Miscellany, Winterthur Manuscripts); posthumous copy by Eleuthera du Pont Smith; mistakenly dated 18 Aug. 1815. Tr (DeGH: Papers of Descendants, Longwood Manuscripts); posthumous copy by Sophie M. Du Pont; dated 18 Aug. 1816. Translation by Dr. Genevieve Moene.

The SUPERBE ÉDITION was Thomas R. Malthus, *An Essay on the Principle of Population; or, a View of its Past and Present Effects on Human Happiness*, first American ed., 2 vols. (Washington City, 1809; see also Sowerby, no. 2938). UTINAM: "If only." Du Pont's reference to snails (LIMAÇONS) at high altitudes recalls TJ's remark in his *Notes on the State of Virginia* that "It is said that shells are found in the Andes, in South-America, fifteen thousand feet above the level of the ocean" (*Notes*, ed. Peden, 31).

[1] Preceding two words canceled in FC.

[2] Word interlined by Du Pont in FC in place of "Utiparte" ("How to bring forth").

[3] Paragraph added by Du Pont perpendicularly in left margin of third page of RC.

[4] In FC Du Pont here adds "Say y est très faible. Il la borne comme Smith à celle des richesses" ("Say's work on this is very feeble. He, like Smith, limits himself to the study of wealth"). Trs follow FC.

[5] In RC Du Pont here canceled "encore" ("still").

[6] Word interlined in RC in place of "Elle" ("it").

To George Flower

SIR Monticello Aug. 18. 16.

Your favor of the 6th came to hand the day before yesterday. independant of the moral considerations which dictate to us to be useful to one another, the letters of Messrs La Fayette and Lasteyrie would have been a sure passport to any service I can render you. if, as I presume, your purpose is to fix yourself in the US. my first advice to you would be not to be hasty in doing it, but to examine for yourself places, climates & societies, and chuse what suits best your own habits physical & moral, your own inclinations and pursuits. all our middle climates, say from 40.° to 36.° of Lat. are comfortable and healthy above the tide-waters. beyond these there is too much of either winter or summer. should you conclude to take such a survey, I would recommend that your rout from Washington shall be by Prince William Courthouse, Fauquier C. H. Culpeper C. H. Orange C. H. to this place, and hence by Nelson C. H. and Amherst C. H. to Lynchburg on James river. if you should reach this place during this month I shall be here, happy to recieve you; if later than the 1st day of Sep. I shall be gone on with my family to a possession I have near Lynchburg where I shall stay 6. or 8. weeks. I shall be glad that you become one of my family at either place, and make a station of it for contemplating what further you will conclude to do. on your return to Philadelphia I would recommend your passing along the valley between the blue ridge & North mountain, that is to say by the Peaks of Otter, Natural bridge, Staunton, Winchester Harper's ferry, Frederictown & Lancaster. you will thus have seen the two by far most interesting lines of Country of this state. with the tender of my services in any way in which they can be useful I pray you to accept assurances of my best wishes for your success & of my great respect.

TH: JEFFERSON

PoC (DLC); on verso of reused address cover of William Short to TJ, 7 May 1816; at foot of text: "George Flower esquire"; endorsed by TJ.

From Jonas Humbert

RESPECTED SIR New York Augt 18th 1816

I doubt not your goodness will Readily find an excuse for the liberty taken by a stranger in addressing a few lines to your friendly attention: but particularly so when the contents of this Communication is impartially considered.

Permit me to Say, respected Sir, that it is many years since I became conversant with your sentiments on public concerns, and I have often been pleased, as well as instructed, in noting those Republican maxims and sentiments which have uniformly characterised the whole career of your public life. Happy shall we be in future times if our chiefs shall pursue the example you are going to leave your country; and I sincerely hope and pray that your exit from transitory Scenes[1] may be abundantly Compensated with those Joys which spring from the prospect of a glorious immortalitty.

My political principles have alway been Republican, and by birth I am an American. In 1800. amongst others, in our ranks, I was warmly interested in the election of Mr Jefferson: our Success gave me high satisfaction, as I was confident your best efforts would be exerted to maintain our Republican System in all its purity. When our foreign concerns became critical and it was thought prudent to lay an Embargo Mr Jefferson will well recollect how much contention there was concerning that measure and other's connected in the general administration. In this City, you will have perceived a spirit of opposition to yourself and the government that was highly incompatible with republican principles. A Strong interest was attempted to be made in our own ranks against administration Connected with the nomination of Mr Madison;—and, Mr Jefferson will well recollect the hostile character and calumniating spirit of the "American Citizen"; he and his abettors charged you with being under the "dictation" of the french Emperor; these charges were made with all the malevolence of the bitterest anglo-federalists. At that period I was a member of the Republican general Committee. Here I was connected with men who had been your warm advocates in 1800.[2] I listened, and marked their conversation: how they should be So soon altered in their opinions concerning Mr Jefferson was a matter of some surprise to me. A difference of sentiment on a public act I did not think any Crime, but to hear you so shamefully impeached and treated with so much contempt, by these men, as well as that press, made me, somewhat indignant. Honor, Duty, as well as Justice, prompted me to espouse your Cause in the Committee: I was told such conduct would make a rend in the party. I wanted to know if a life of upwards of forty years devoted to the cause of republicanism and interests of our Country was now to be trampled under foot with as little[3] Ceremony as we should pay to existence of a lilly-put. At that time I held a situation which gave me a genteel living, about twenty three to twenty five hundred dollars a year: however, such were my impressions of the rectitude of administration that I was determined to use my best efforts to vindicate the government.

In this place there was no paper friendly to the government except the "Public Advertiser"; the Editors were young men and inexperienced: there were Some persons capable with a pen, but hesitated, others dreaded the violence and biting sarcasm of the "Citizen," who lacerated the government, and imputed to you and Mr Madison conduct and motives, as though you was disposed to immolate the honor of our Country at the shrine of a foreign despot. I told the Editors of the "Public Advertiser" I would commence against the Citizen if they would publish my pieces. I belive My Essays were the first that could claim any Notice for systematic defence of the administration: I was Sensible of the power of my antagonist, but the cause of truth, and a firm conviction of the Rectitude of government, inspired me with confidence. Those misguided Republicans smarted under the lash—their unprincipled editor began to loose his influence, and then, and not till then did any one dare to come out in defence of administration. These effusions were[4] honored with some Considerabl[e] attention in different parts of the Union, but they cost me the loss of the Situation I held. Such is the spirit of intollerence. I was well known to have been always uniform in politics, by those who cut me off, and I am certain If I had not written in defence of administration that I should Not have been disturbed. I will mention here the honorable testimony in favour of my humble efforts, by Some of the heads of "Department" while at Table in Washington, in a conversation had with one of the

Editors of the "Public Advertiser" Mr Geo. White. He was asked if Mr Emmet of this city, Counseller at law, was not the writer of Certain Numbers? he told, Mr Madison, No: the interogatory was continued—who then?—, the answer was given. I have informed the President of my treatment, and had the matter substantiated by respectable gentlemen, who have known me many years, and certify'd my moral character and efforts previous to, as well as during the late war. Mr Munroe has their testimonies if they have not been witheld by some of the clerks.

I have solicited a situation now vacant—that of Marshall of this District; and if Mr Jefferson could Render me a favour, by a line to the President it will lay me under the strongest obligations. If the President shall see the testimonies, and he considers how shamefully I was treated, I think he will be inclined to do something for an injured man.

I have the honor, Sir to Subscribe my Self your Sincere friend and obedient Servant JONAS HUMBERT

RC (DLC); edge trimmed; at foot of text: "Thos Jefferson Esqr"; endorsed by TJ as received from "Humbal Jonas" on 28 Aug. 1816 and so recorded (as from "Humbul Jonas") in SJL.

Jonas Humbert (1764–1847), baker and political writer, was a native of New Jersey. By 1775 he was a resident of New York City, and after several years of apprenticeship he established his own bakery by 1787. Humbert was the city's inspector of flour, 1809–10, until accusations of extortion led to his dismissal. He wrote several articles on the subject of flour, and he was a member of the Society for the Promotion of Useful Arts, in the State of New-York. Humbert was active in the local Republican party and in 1808, along with two other officers, sent TJ a letter of support from the Tammany Society, or Columbian Order, of which he was secretary, 1807–09. In the latter year he ran unsuccessfully on the "Madisonian" ticket for sixth-ward councilman, and in 1830 he was a failed candidate for lieutenant governor on the Agrarian Party ticket (David C. Franks, *New-York Directory* [1787], 18; *Longworth's New York Directory* [1807]: 79, 216; [1809]: 215; Tammany Society of New York to TJ, [11 Jan. 1808] [DLC]; Gustavus Myers, *The History of Tammany Hall*, rev. ed. [1917], 23–5, 60; New York *Mercantile Advertiser*, 9 June 1809; New York *Public Advertiser*, 21 Nov. 1809, 9 Apr. 1810, 22 May 1811; *New-York Evening Post*, 25 Nov. 1809; New York *Columbian*, 27 Nov. 1809; Humbert, "A Paper On the Importance of regulating the Inspection of Flour, &c. in the State of New-York," "Communication On the Utility and Advantage of Ventilating and Storing Grain," and "Observations On the Culture of Wheat, and the Manufacture of Flour, in the State of New-York," in *Transactions of the Society for the Promotion of Useful Arts, in the State of New-York* 3 [1814]: 178–86, 261; 4, pt. 1 [1816]: 38, 55–61; 4, pt. 2 [1819]: 33–49; *New-York Morning Herald*, 8 Sept. 1830; New York *Evening Post*, 3 June 1847).

The publisher of the New York AMERICAN CITIZEN was James Cheetham, who referred to Humbert as "Diodorus Dough-Head" while accusing him of misconduct. Originally a strong Republican who supported TJ, Cheetham opposed the election of James Madison in 1808 (Brigham, *American Newspapers*, 1:608–9; New York *American Citizen*, 31 Oct. 1808; Noble E. Cunningham Jr., *The Jeffersonian Republicans in Power: Party Operations, 1801–1809* [1963], 119–21, 237; Andrew Burstein and Nancy Isenberg, *Madison and Jefferson* [2010], 371, 413, 458–9). Jacob Frank and George White were the EDITORS of the New York *Public Advertiser* in 1808 (Brigham, *American Newspapers*, 1:682–3).

In an 8 July 1811 letter to President Madison, Humbert emphasized his loyalty to the Republican party, complained of mistreatment by his political foes, and described his published PIECES: "I wrote five of the first Numbers over the Signature of 'Diodorus Siculus' the whole Series Nineteen: after which I continued defending the administration, in 'Zenophon' Six Numbers, and other detached pieces" (DLC: Madison Papers). For Humbert's "Diodorus Siculus" and "Zenophon" essays, see *Public Advertiser*, 12–14, 17, 21 May, 22 July, 1–2 Aug., 7, 19, 28 Sept. 1808. The TESTIMONIES in support of Humbert's unsuccessful effort to become federal marshal for the district of New York included Humbert to James Monroe, 2, 19, 24 July, Humbert to Madison, 24 July, 1 Aug., James R. Mullany to Monroe, 24 July, and a recommendation by Henry J. Feltus, Cave Jones, and James McKeon, 25 July 1816 (DNA: RG 59, LAR, 1809–17).

[1] Manuscript: "Scences."
[2] Manuscript: "1810."
[3] Manuscript: "littee."
[4] Manuscript: "where."

To John F. Oliveira Fernandes

DEAR SIR Monticello Aug. 18. 16.

I recieved the last night your favor of the 10th and I hasten to express the pleasure I shall have in recieving you here, and the wish that this may meet with no delay. you propose to us the hope that you will be here towards the end of this month, or the commencement of the next; and the object of this is to express my anxiety that it may be within the present month, because arrangements are already fixed for the departure of myself and family to a possession I have near Lynchburg, and where I am to pass six or eight weeks: and I write this on the bare possibility that it may reach you in time to anticipate your departure a day or two if your affairs permit it. I should be mortified to lose the pleasure of your visit by this metachronism. mr Correa will not be with us till the latter end of October. the supplies of wine which I had ordered from different ports of Europe & which have now begun to arrive, have greatly relieved my wants. but a quarter cask of unmixed Port[1] will be a very acceptable addition when you shall have it to spare. I salute you with great esteem & respect

TH: JEFFERSON

PoC (DLC); on verso of reused address cover to TJ; at foot of text: "Dr Fernandes"; endorsed by TJ.

METACHRONISM: "An error in chronology, *esp.* the placing of an event later than its real date" (*OED*).

[1] Word interlined.

From John Preston

SIR Charlottesville 18th. August 1816.

With much pains and trouble mingled with anxiety I have compiled a Lancastrian Spelling book and caused the same to be printed: I have also written an Introduction to Arithmetic[1] on a similar plan as you will perceive by the manuscript accompanying this note. The embarrasments I have brought on myself by this assiduous task, the flattering recommendations given by some of our first American Characters, and the enthusiasm I have ever possessed for the diffusion of rudimental knowledge, make me anxious to publish this work.

If a general diffusion of knowledge is expedient and will be the means of prolonging a free government,[2] I am compelled to believe that every improvement which facilitates the attainment of our first principles in literature, must be an individual and public acquisition worthy of patronage.

If by examining the manuscript you find agreement of opinion with Mr Clinton, the other Gentlemen and yourself, I will consider your additional certificate as an important favour. It is impracticable to give every man time to examine a work of this nature, if they were disposed to undergo the task; therefore if the publication deserve that encouragement which is certified, then I consider it my duty to present Gentlemen with such authorities as will do away hesitancy in subscribing.

Being a stranger, please to excuse my boldness—I have a few books to dispose of in this Village—By tuesday evening will ask the liberty to call on you personally as I must prepare to take Stage for Washington on Wednesday at two o'Clock P.M.

Meanwhile am Sir

Your most obedient friend And humble servant

JOHN PRESTON

P.S. A short note by the Bearer will be thankfully received.

RC (MHi); postscript written perpendicularly in left margin; at foot of text: "Mr Thomas Jefferson." Enclosure not found.

John Preston (ca. 1755–1842), educator, was born in Connecticut and served as a private in the New York Continental Line during the Revolutionary War. By 1790 he was in Albany County, New York, having settled at Van Leuven's Corners in the present-day township of Westerlo. Here Preston ran a tavern and an establishment that tanned and curried leather. He also began teaching at a nearby Quaker school. Preston championed the instructional methods established by the English-born educator Joseph Lancaster, under whose system older students tutored younger ones and inexpensive visual aids replaced textbooks. Adherents established numerous Lancasterian schools in the United States early in the nineteenth century. In 1812 Preston borrowed $500 from the state of New York to assist in publishing Lancasterian spelling-book cards and an arithmetic textbook. Some of this material was in circulation early the following year, but in 1816 Preston admitted that his efforts had failed and that he could not repay the loan. He had, however, written another arithmetic book, which he expected to be more successful. Preston included a survey of schools and wrote on the importance of education in his *Statistical Report of the County of Albany, for the Year 1820* (2d ed., Albany, 1824), 7–8, 28–9. As late as 1835 he petitioned the New York legislature to implement the Lancasterian system throughout the state (National Society of the Daughters of the American Revolution, *DAR Patriot Index* [2003], 3:2172; *The Pension Roll of 1835* [1835; indexed ed., 1992], 2:355; *A Census of Pensioners for Revolutionary or Military Services* [1841], 73; DNA: RG 29, CS, N.Y., Albany Co., 1790–1840; George R. Howell and Jonathan Tenney, eds., *Bi-Centennial History of Albany. History of the County of Albany, N.Y., from 1609 to 1886* [1886], 265, 921, 924, 927; *Journal of the Senate of the State of New-York* [Albany, 1812], 220, 228, 254, 270 [2, 3, 10, 13 June 1812]; *Albany Register*, 12 Jan. 1813; *Journal of the Assembly, of the State of New-York* [Albany, 1816], 397, 430, 440, 495 [21, 25, 26 Mar., 1 Apr. 1816]; Preston, *Every Man His Own Teacher; or, Lancaster's Theory of Education, Practically Displayed; being An Introduction to Arithmetic, written in thirteen parts. to which are annexed, Thirty-Two Cards of Lessons, to be suspended in the school-room conformably to the Lancaster Plan* [Albany, 1817]; *Documents of the Assembly of the State of New-York* [1835], 1–4; gravestone inscription and memorial plaques in Westerlo Rural Cemetery).

[1] Manuscript: "Arithmeti."
[2] Manuscript: "govermment."

To William Wirt

Dear Sir — Monticello Aug. 18. 16.

I will with pleasure undertake the perusal of your work and with the frankness to which you are entitled will make the observations to which it may give occasion, and this I will do on the condition and confidence that you will shew you think me worthy of equal frankness by regarding the observations I shall hazard exactly as much only as your own judgment shall dictate on severe examination: that you will be entirely at ease in rejecting, & thereby place me at ease in offering my remarks. the work is yours, to your account the world will place it's merit and demerit. and the ultimate decision is of right there where the responsibility is. I shall go to Poplar forest near Lynchburg on the 1st of the ensuing month and remain there 6. or 8. weeks, so that you must be so good as to address the sheets to me here or there according to the times of your transmitting them. ever an[d] affectionately your's — Th: Jefferson

PoC (DLC); on verso of reused address cover of Joseph Delaplaine to TJ, 11 May 1816; mutilated at seal, with missing text supplied from Tr; at foot of text: "William Wirt esquire"; endorsed by TJ. Tr (MdHi: Wirt Papers).

From John Preston

SIR 19th Aug. 1816

Impressed with an idea that you have not seen my note of 18th. Instant, I beg leave to present my Manuscript a second time—I consider Sir, if you should acquiesssce with those who have recommended the work, that your separate Recommendation will be of great importance

With due Respect
am Sir your and my Country's friend JOHN PRESTON

RC (MHi); at foot of text: "Honourable Thomas Jefferson"; endorsed by TJ as received from Charlottesville on 19 Aug. 1816 and so recorded in SJL.

To John Preston

SIR Monticello Aug. 19. 16.

The Lancastrian system of education was proposed w[hen?] I was too much engaged in business to attend to it; and after my retirement I considered it as the commencement of a system which was to go into operation with another generation and with which of course I should have nothing to do. I have therefore neve[r] read a sentence on the subject, nor know a single element of [it?] consequently am totally unqualified to recommend it to others, an[d] were[1] it moral to recommend what I know nothing about, it would only degrade myself without honoring your bo[ok.] under these circumstances you must be so good as to excus[e] my declining it, and with my best wishes for it's success if it b[e] really useful, I tender you the assurance of my respect TH: JEFFERSO[N]

PoC (MHi); on verso of portion of a reused address cover from George Logan to TJ; mutilated at seal and edge trimmed; at foot of text: "Mr John Preston"; endorsed by TJ.

[1] TJ here canceled "I to do it."

From David Gelston

SIR, New York 20th August 1816.

I have this day received in Store one case, said to contain thirty bottles red wine shipped by Mr Cathalen from Marseilles—this with the preceding I shall Ship by the first good opportunity for Richmond agreeably to the request in your letter of the 3d instant—

With great respect I am sir your obedient servant,

DAVID GELSTON

RC (MHi); endorsed by TJ as received 26 Aug. 1816 and so recorded in SJL, which has the additional notation: "30. b. red wine Ledanon Cathalan." RC (MHi); address cover only; with PoC of TJ to John Burke, 22 Nov. 1816, on verso; addressed: "Thomas Jefferson Esquire Monticello"; stamp canceled; franked; postmarked New York, 21 Aug.

From Charles Pinckney

DEAR SIR [by 21] August 1816 In Charleston

It being discovered great pains had been taken to circulate & reprint the Pamphlet against our excellent & worthy friend Colonel Monroe in all the federal papers in North Carolina & in this & the neighbouring States it has been Thought adviseable by his friends here that I should answer it & that copies should be transmitted to our friends in the northern States—Inclosed is one which I hope will meet your Approbation & that this will find You in health & enjoying Your full share of such comforts as are bestowed on the happiest among us & that You may continue to do so as long as You wish or is agreeable to you is the sincere prayer of

dear sir With affectionate regard Your's Truly

CHARLES PINCKNEY

RC (MHi); dateline at foot of text; partially dated; addressed (with cover divided between verso of this letter and PoC of TJ to George Logan, 24 Nov. 1816, resulting in some loss of text): "To The Honourable Thomas Jefferson (To the care of Doctor Tucker or Joseph Anderson Esquire) City of Washington Who are requested t[o] forward it on to M[r] Jefferson"; franked; postmarked (faint) [Charleston], 21 Aug.; endorsed by TJ as a letter of "Aug. 1816" received 29 Aug. 1816 and so recorded in SJL. Enclosure: "A South-Carolinian" [Pinckney], *Observations to shew the propriety of the nomination of Colonel James Monroe, to the Presidency of the United States by the Caucus at Washington* (Charleston, 1816), which refutes the notion that the presidency should be rotated among the states, with no Virginians to be elected in future until other parts of the nation have provided presidents; commends Monroe's character and qualifications in a biographical essay that emphasizes the numerous federal appointments he has held successfully and shows "the superiority of his claims in every respect to any opponent" put forth by other Republicans (pp. 30–1); and defends the practice of congressional caucuses recommending presidential candidates, asking, in such a large country, "how will it be possible for the people or State Legislatures, to know any thing of the principles, talents and conduct of the candidates, but through the members of Congress" (p. 37).

A PAMPHLET entitled *Exposition of Motives for Opposing the Nomination of M[r] Monroe for the office of President of the United States* (Washington, 1816) had been reprinted in full in the Raleigh *Star, and North-Carolina State Gazette*, 24 May 1816.

From Joseph Miller

HONRE^D FREND Norfolk Augt 22 1816—

I Rec^d your Frendly Letter yeasterday an for the Truble I have Given you I am ashamed of I intend Coming up as Soone as the Court is over I am not Able to Sell aney Part at Pressent I have tried all I Can But no buyers one House that Cost $6000 Building I offered it for $4000 and the Ground along with it I Could wish you to Lett Old Peeter Get Sume Grain to work Soone Hops in New York is one Doll^r pr ℔ by the Bale

I Rem your Humbl &^c JOSEPH MILLR

RC (DLC); at head of text: "Mr Jafferson"; endorsed by TJ as received 26 Aug. 1816 and so recorded in SJL.

TJ's FRENDLY LETTER is not recorded in SJL and has not been found. OLD PEETER: Peter Hemmings.

To Ashur Ware

Monticello Aug. 22. 16.

Th: Jefferson not knowing how otherwise to address the inclosed to the Washington society in Boston, has taken the liberty of putting it under cover to mr Ware, and of requesting it's delivery by him. he does this the more willingly as it furnishes him an opportunity of expressing the pleasure he has recieved from the perusal of mr Ware's oration on the 4th of July and from the evidence it affords that the sun of freedom of Independance and Union, without having ceased to illumine the West, promises to beam again in the horizon of the East, in it's pristine splendor.

PoC (DLC); on verso of reused address cover of Isaac Briggs to TJ, with postscript by Mary B. Briggs, 7 May 1816; dateline at foot of text; endorsed by TJ as a letter to "Ware mr <*Rich^d*>." Recorded in SJL as written to "Ware Asa." Enclosure: TJ to Washington Society (of Boston), 22 Aug. 1816.

Ashur Ware (1782–1873), newspaper editor and public official, was born in Sherborn, Massachusetts, and graduated from Harvard University in 1804. After stints as an assistant at Phillips Exeter Academy in New Hampshire and as a private tutor, in 1807 Harvard appointed him a tutor in Greek. In 1811 he was promoted to professor of Greek, resigning in 1815 to pursue legal studies. Ware was admitted to the bar of Suffolk County in 1816 but devoted most of his time to journalism. He coedited the Boston *Yankee*, a Republican newspaper. Moving in 1817 to the Maine district of Massachusetts, Ware edited the Portland *Eastern Argus*, which he used to promote statehood for Maine. When this goal was achieved in 1820, he became Maine's first secretary of state. In 1822 President James Monroe appointed Ware the United States district judge for Maine, a post he held until 1866. During his judgeship he became a noted expert on maritime law. Ware served as a trustee of Bowdoin College, 1820–44, and was a founder in 1826 of the Portland Athenæum, serving as its president in 1832. He was president of the Exchange Bank in 1832 and a director of the Androscoggin and Kennebec Railroad Company in 1850. On the 1870 census Ware declared ownership of real estate valued at $2,000 and a personal estate worth $10,000 (*DAB*; William Willis, *A History of The Law, The Courts, and The Lawyers Of Maine* [1863], 634–46; George F. Talbot, "Ashur Ware. A Biographical Sketch," Maine Historical Society, *Collections and Proceedings*, 2d ser., 1 [1890]: 409–21; *JEP*, 3:273, 274 [15 Feb. 1822]; Ware, Edward H. Daveis, and George Freeman Emery, *Reports of Cases Determined in the District Court of the United States for the District of Maine ... by Ashur Ware, District Judge*, 3 vols. [1849–74]; *Catalogus Senatus Academici ... Collegio Bowdoinensi* [1864], 4; *Private Acts of the State of Maine, passed by the Sixth Legislature, at its Session, held in January, 1826* [Portland, 1826], 692–3; Portland *Eastern Argus*, 10 Jan., 8 May 1832; *Boston Daily Atlas*, 15 Aug. 1850; DNA: RG 29, CS, Me., Cumberland Co., 1870; *Boston Daily Advertiser*, 11 Sept. 1873).

The title page of Ware, *An Oration, delivered before the Washington Society, in Boston, on the Fourth of July, 1816* (Boston, 1816; Poor, *Jefferson's Library*, 13 [no. 826]; TJ's copy in ViU) gives the author's first name as "Asher" and bears an inscription (trimmed), in an unidentified hand: "Thom[s] Jefferson [esqr]—presented by the Washington Society." In this work Ware asserts that the Declaration of Independence "was an act of that moral sublimity, that finds few parallels in the history of nations," that it was intended "to defend the equal rights of a whole people," and that the nation's success "now inspires with fortitude the patriots of South America" (pp. 3–5); that from its principle of the "natural and inborn right of man to self-government," a "scheme of civil polity" was erected (p. 6); that a minority of Americans managed "to place themselves at the head of a powerful and respectable party, to whose eyes liberty never appears so lovely, as when she is reposing under the shadow of a throne" (p. 10); that victory in the late war, however, put an end to "the glories of federalism" (p. 14); that the "storm that threatened to prostrate our liberty in eternal destruction, only shook its branches, and caused its roots to strike deeper and more firmly in the soil"; and that "the tree of Liberty, watered by the blood of heroes and martyrs, shall continue to flourish and look green in the chosen land of law and freedom, till the thunders of the last trumpet shall be heard resounding over the fragments of a ruined world" (p. 16).

To Washington Society (of Boston)

Monticello Aug. 22. 16.

Th: Jefferson presents his respects to the Washington[1] society in Boston, and his thanks for the copy of mr Ware's eloquent oration, forwarded him by their order. he is particularly happy to see the revered name they have chosen for their designation restored to it's genuine principles of Union and Independance, to no other than which was it's authority or countenance ever lent.

RC (Seth Kaller, Inc., White Plains, N.Y., 2005); dateline at foot of text; endorsed in an unidentified hand: "Th. Jefferson's Letter." PoC (CSmH: JF-BA); on verso of reused address cover of Theodorus Bailey to TJ, 10 May 1816; endorsed by TJ. Printed in *An Historical View of the Public Celebrations of the Washington Society, and those of the Young Republicans. from 1805, to 1822* (Boston, 1823), 93. Enclosed in TJ to Ashur Ware, 22 Aug. 1816.

The Washington Society (of Boston) originated in 1805 when some of the city's Republicans formed the Young Republicans of Boston, a group determined to celebrate the anniversary of American independence with a commemorative oration designed to counterbalance the Fourth of July orations offered by Federalists "who merely used the name of liberty to deride its qualities and to excite jealousies and animosities between different sections of our happy land." In 1811 the organization changed its name to the Washington Society, whose "prime object" was to "encourage, disseminate and support such sentiments as are contained in that correct standard of American political principles, 'Washington's Farewell Address to the people of the United States.'" At the Washington Society's 4 July 1816 celebration at Dow's Hotel, the ninth of eighteen toasts honored TJ: "His character is the boast of philanthropy, his talents the delight of philosophy, and his name the pride of America." Members of the group regularly offered similar toasts to TJ at its Independence Day events (*Historical View*, esp. iii–iv, 5, 45–7, 91; *Boston Patriot*, 13 July 1811).

The REVERED NAME was that of George Washington.

[1]Manuscript: "Washingto."

From David Gelston

DEAR SIR, New York August 23[d] 1816.

I have this day shipped by the Sloop Alpha, Coffin, Master to Mess[rs] Gibson & Jefferson the five cases wine & basket of Macaroni— not yet being able to collect all the expenses, I have not drawn on them only for freight from this to Richmond—when the amount of charges is received it Shall be forwarded to you—

With very great regard I am Dear Sir, truly yours

DAVID GELSTON

RC (MHi); endorsed by TJ as received 29 Aug. 1816 and so recorded in SJL, which has the additional notation: "has forward[d] the 5. cases wine & 1. of Maccaroni." RC (DLC); address cover only; with PoC of TJ to Joseph Delaplaine, 11 Nov. 1816, on verso; addressed: "Thomas Jefferson Esquire Monticello"; franked; postmarked New York, 23 Aug.

To William Lee

DEAR SIR Monticello Aug. 24. 16.

Your letters of Dec. 20. 14. and May 11. 16. are yet to be aknoleged: and my thanks to be returned for the book which accompanied the former on the subject of Great Britain and America. that able exposition prepared the European mind for receiving truths more favorable to us, and subsequent events have furnished facts corroborating those views. I believe that America, & by this time England also are more justly appreciated. some greatly enlightened minds in Europe are in science far beyond any thing we possess; but leaving them out of the account (& they are but few) the mass of their people, within which term I include from the king to the beggar, is returning to Gothic darkness while the mass of ours is advancing in the regions of light. during the paroxysm of Anglomany lately raging in Bordeaux you must have had a mortifying time. that rage cannot last. the English character is not of that cast which makes itself be loved. I was just about publishing mr Garde's letter when I saw in the newspapers that addressed to D[r] Mitchell. his position in a populous city, and convenient to others, being so much more favorable than mine for the views of M. Garde, I rejoiced to see his letter in so good hands and surceased medling in it myself, my inland & rural situation affording me no facilities for promoting it's object. should you have occasion to write to mr Garde, I will thank you to throw in a line of explanation and to tender him my respects & best wishes for his success.

Not doubting that after so long a residence in France your wishes are still there, I heartily sympathise with them and hope the circumstances are not very distant, which may render your return agreeable and useful. Accept my salutations and assurances of perfect esteem and respect. TH: JEFFERSON

PoC (DLC); on verso of reused address cover to TJ; at foot of text: "W[m] Lee esq."; endorsed by TJ.

From Charles K. Mallory

SIR Collector's Office Norfolk August 24th 1816

A cask of Wine has arrived here for you in the ship Lothair Cap[t] Stone from Marseilles, consigned to my care by the Commercial & Navy Agent of the United States at that place. I inclose you the Bill of lading therefor & will thank you to inform me in what way I shall send it to you. An estimate of the duty & charges shall be made out & forwarded so soon as the Wine is landed. A Small package brought by the same vessel, addressed to you, is herewith transmitted.

I have the honor to be with the highest respect your ob[t] serv[t]

CHA[s] K. MALLORY

RC (MHi); at foot of text: "Thomas Jefferson Esq[r] Monticello"; endorsed by TJ as received 2 Sept. 1816 and so recorded in SJL, which identifies the sender as "Mallory Cha[s] F." and has the additional notation: "a cask of Roussillon." Enclosures not found.

Charles King Mallory (ca. 1781–1820), attorney and public official, was born in Elizabeth City County, attended the College of William and Mary late in the 1790s, and became a lawyer. He represented his native county in the Virginia House of Delegates, 1804–09 and 1810–11, and he sat on the Council of State, 1811–14, serving as its president and thus as lieutenant governor, 1812–14. Mallory became the federal collector for the District of Norfolk and Portsmouth in 1814, and he held this position until his death ("The Mallory Family," *VMHB* 15 [1907]: 99–100; will of Mary Mallory, 20 Jan. 1789, proved 24 Apr. 1789, Elizabeth City Co. Wills, Etc., 1701–1904 [Vi microfilm]; *William and Mary Provisional List*, 27; Leonard, *General Assembly*; *CVSP*, 10:97; *Alexandria Daily Advertiser*, 18 Dec. 1807; New York *Columbian*, 31 July 1812; Benjamin Bates, *The Virginia Almanack for 1813* [Fredericksburg, 1812]; *JEP*, 2:450 [7, 10 Jan. 1814]; *American Beacon and Norfolk & Portsmouth Daily Advertiser*, 17 Apr. 1820).

The COMMERCIAL & NAVY AGENT at Marseille was Stephen Cathalan.

From Charles Willson Peale

DEAR SIR Belfield Aug[t] 24. 1816.

Last evening I received your letter of the 17th Instant, and I suppose before this time you have received one from me dated the 9th & 13th in which I stated that the young man I had spoken to, had gone to the neighbourhood of Bethlehem—I have been with several Watchmakers in the City since I wrote, who all have promised me notice if any discreet young man offers—within two days I shall again be in the City and will then make the rounds & I will then visit a silver-smith of my acquaintance that I have confidence will endeavor to serve me & in whose judgement I can rely on—my letter alluded to above, imbraced several subjects, and also contained an Address which I made to the Citizens on 18th Ul[t]—I suppose you get our Philad[a] papers, if so I need not detail any thing about the publications respecting my Museum—

I have wrote a letter to each of the Councils of the City, which will be delivered at their next meeting—If they do not Patronize the Museum—The City of Philad[a] may loose the benefit of all my labours—The tenor[1] of my letter implies that I have full confidence that they will do all I ask of them. Whatever may be the result, I will communicate to you soon after. An ingenious mechanic (M[r] Lukens) is making a Galvanic apparatus to ring bells—It is said one of the kind has been in continual operation in London more than 3 years—and it is supposed that it will continue to attract & repel a claper as long as the material will last—and being dry, the metals will last a long time. M[r] Lukens[2] has made it very handsome, & I hear that he intends to give it a place in the Museum—a slight Sketch may be acceptable.

a, a, Bells—supported by hollow Glass Pillars—in which are plates of Zink, paper & silvered paper alternatly placed over each other in number as I understand about 5000, a connection from base to base of the Pillars of Tin foil—[3] which punched out of the plates of thin Zinc—& paper by a harness makers punch. b, b, Bases of the pillars. c, c, bases of 2 low Pillars—with a small pit on each for what I shall call the Pendelum,[4] made thus: (d) a cross with points to rest in the pitts of the small Pillars, so that the vibration is perfectly[5] easy from Bell to Bell.

Perhaps all this may be familiar to you, by your correspondance, or receipts of periodical works from Europe[6]—however I have the pleasure[7] of the attempt to amuse you, at the samc time the copies of my letters, will leave to posterity the various remembrances of machines, with my Idea's at the same time.

If I can find any thing satisfactory to say respecting a watch-maker or silver-smith, I shall immediately write after I go to Philad^{a}—I am with the highest reguard your friend. C W PEALE

PS. My Son Franklin says that in Mr Lukens machine that there is not 2 stands to support the Pendelum, but only the back one from that an arm with a ring thus. in which ring are the pivot holes on opposite sides.

RC (DLC); endorsed by TJ as received 29 Aug. 1816 and so recorded in SJL. PoC (PPAmP: Peale Letterbook).

Peale WROTE A LETTER jointly addressed to the Select Council and the Common Council of Philadelphia sometime between 1 and 24 Aug. 1816 (Peale, *Papers*, 3:441–4).

[1] Manuscript: "tenure."

[2] Manuscript: "Lukins."

[3] The diameter of the circle depicted here is approximately five-eighths of an inch.

[4] Manuscript: "Pendetum."

[5] Manuscript: "perfetly."

[6] Manuscript: "Eurpope."

[7] Manuscript: "peasure."

To John Campbell White

Monticello Aug. 24. 16.

Th: Jefferson presents his salutations and respects to mr White with his thanks for the Persian melon seed he has been so kind as to send him. he will endeavor to do it justice by his attentions, and especially to disperse it among his most careful acquaintances. it is by multiplying the good things of life that the mass of human happiness is increased, and the greatest of consolations to have contributed to it.

RC (MdHi: White Papers); dateline at foot of text; addressed: "Mr John Campbell White Baltimore"; franked; postmarked Milton, 28 Aug.; endorsed by White as received 1 Sept. 1816. PoC (DNAL: Thomas Jefferson Correspondence, Bixby Donation); on verso of reused address cover of Francis Adrian Van der Kemp to TJ, 4 June 1816; endorsed by TJ.

From William Wirt

DEAR SIR. Richmond. August 24. 1816.

I accept, with gratitude, the terms on which you are willing to remark on my manuscript—and send herewith three sections, ninety one pages. There will be an advertisement prefixed to it, stating the authorities on which the narrative is founded, and appealing to the candor and indulgence of the public on account of the peculiar disadvantages under which the work has been written. This, I confess, is a kind of beggarly business which I abhor very much—but I can still less bear to have it believed that the work is the offspring of profound leisure and a mind at ease, when the truth is that no one sheet of it, scarcely, has been written without half a dozen professional interruptions which have routed my ideas as compleatly, each time,[1] as Don Quixote's charge did the flock of sheep—I make no doubt that you will perceive the chasms caused by these interruptions, and the incoherence as well as crudeness of the whole mass. When I was engaging with Mr Webster, last summer, with respect to the publication I refused expressly to bind my self [to] furnish it at any particular period—foreseeing[2] the extreme un[cer]tainty as to the time of its completion, from the interference of professional duties and wishing to reserve to my self also, full leisure, to revise, correct and retouch at pleasure—But he has made such an appeal to my humanity on account of the expensiveness of the materials which he has laid in for the publication, and his inability to remain longer without some reimbursement, that I am much disposed to let the work go in its present general form, if you think it can be done without too much sacrifice. What I mean is that I think the whole work might be re-cast to advantage—but then it must be written, wholly anew, which would illy suit M[r] Websters alleged situation—and my disposition, therefore, is to let the form of the work remain, correcting the composition, statements &[c] where it shall be suggested and thought proper—If you think the publication of the work, will do me an injury with the public, I beg you to tell me so, without any fear of wounding my feelings—I am so far from being in love with it my self, that I should be glad of a decent ret[reat] from the undertaking—I confide implicitly in your fr[ankness] and friendship, and beg you to believe me dear Sir, with the greatest respect & affection, your friend & servant

W[m] Wirt

I observe that Webster has advertised in the Virginia papers, and I suppose, in those of other states, in which he has subscribers, that the work will probably be ready for the press in two or three months—I should be glad to have it in my power to fulfil this promise—and altho' it is of the utmost importance to me that you should take full time for your remarks, yet as I shall most probably have to make material alterations after the return of the sheets from your hands; I hope it may suit your convenience to favor me with them, in such time, as to enable me to avoid disappointing him—There will probably be about as many pages as those now sent—

RC (DLC); lower corner of first two pages torn, with missing text supplied from Tr; addressed: "Thomas Jefferson esq[r] Monticello"; endorsed by TJ as received 28 Aug. 1816 and so recorded in SJL. Tr (MdHi: Wirt Papers). Enclosure: manuscript, not found, of a portion of Wirt, *Patrick Henry*.

DON QUIXOTE'S CHARGE at a flock of sheep appears in Miguel de Cervantes, *Don Quixote*, pt. 1, chap. 18 (Cervantes, *Don Quijote de la Mancha*, ed. Francisco Rico [2004; for editions owned by TJ, see Sowerby, no. 4347; Poor, *Jefferson's Library*, 12 (nos. 746–7); one of TJ's copies in ViCMRL], 154–65). The Philadelphia publisher James Webster ADVERTISED earlier in August that Wirt, *Patrick Henry*, would be available in "a few months" (*Richmond Enquirer*, 10 Aug. 1816).

[1] Preceding two words interlined.
[2] RC: "foreseing." Tr: "foreseeing."

To Peter Minor

Dear Sir Monticello Aug. 25. 16.

The present state of things at the Shadwell mills & at the lock requiring some new order to be taken respecting them, I must request the favor of a meeting of the Directors of the Rivanna company; in order that what is necessary may be done in concert between us. the small proportion of business which has been done at the mills heretofore, rendered the stoppages which took place from time to time, and the constant waste of water by leakage, not so injurious as to make it necessary to call the attention of the Directors to them. but the quantity of wheat now coming & engaged makes the sacrifice heavier than can reasonably be expected. what requires to be now rectified will be better understood by stating what has past formerly. the 1st proposition between us was that whenever the water requisite for the locks should occasion a stoppage of the mills, the time their operations were suspended should be paid for at such reasonable rate as should be agreed on. this seemed to be admitted as just, but was willingly abandoned by all, as likely to be troublesome & litigious from the difficulty of keeping a precise account of these fragments of time. the 2d and correct arrangement was that the bed of the bason, from which the vessels were to be recieved into the locks, should be so high above the bed of[1] our forebay as that there should always be water enough to continue the mills in operation; so that the surplus water only should be abandoned to the locks. a constant head of 2. feet was deemed necessary. this surplus water, with the use of my canal was certainly the extent of what I ever contemplated as indulging to the locks, and this was the ground on which I believe we all considered the use of the locks ultimately & properly to stand. but mr Meriwether suggested a 3d expedient, which was to make so[2] large a bason below the cut leading to the locks as to hold water enough to keep the mills going while a vessel was passing the locks. the trial of that was assented to, it has been partly made, has no sensible effect, and evidently no bason practicable there can ever have the effect proposed. the great increase of business at the mills requiring now more exactness of proceeding, I ask the favor of you to request a meeting of the Directors at their convenience, but I should hope it might be on some day of the present month, as on the 1st of the ensuing I go to Bedford, and shall be absent 6. or 8. weeks. I will attend any day or hour you will be so good as to notify me I salute you with affectionate respect.

TH: JEFFERSON

PoC (ViU: TJP); at foot of text: "Peter Minor esq."; endorsed by TJ. Tr (Junius R. Fishburne, Charlottesville, 1973; photocopy in ViU: TJP); in TJ's hand; mutilated at folds; at head of text: "No 11."; endorsed on verso in an unidentified hand: "Jefferson vs The Rivanna Co } Exhibits." Enclosed in TJ's Bill of Complaint against the Rivanna Company, printed below at 9 Feb. 1817, and in TJ to Chapman Johnson, 9 Feb. 1817.

[1] Preceding three words interlined.
[2] Word interlined in place of "a."

To Isaac H. Tiffany

SIR Monticello Aug. 26. 16.

In answer to your enquiry as to the merits of Gillies's translation of the Politics of Aristotle, I can only say that it has the reputation of being preferable to Ellis's, the only rival translation into English. I have never seen it myself, and therefore do not speak of it from my own knolege. but so different was the state of society then, and with those people, from what it is now & with us, that I think little edification can be obtained from their writings on the subject of government. they had just ideas of the value of personal liberty; but none at all of the structure of government best calculated to preserve it. they knew no medium between a democracy (the only pure republic, but impracticable beyond the limits of a town) and an abandonment of themselves to an aristocracy, or a tyranny, independant of the people. it seems not to have occurred that where the citizens cannot meet to transact their business in person, they alone have the right to chuse the agents who shall transact it; and that, in this way, a republican, or popular government, of the 2^d^ grade of purity, may be exercised over any extent of country. the full experiment of a government democratical, but representative, was and is still[1] reserved for us. the idea (taken indeed from the little specimen formerly existing in the English constitution, but now lost) has been carried by us, more or less, into all our legislative and Executive departments; but it has not yet, by any of us, been pushed into all the ramifications of the system, so far as to leave no authority existing not responsible to the people: whose rights however to the exercise & fruits of their own industry, can never be protected against the selfishness of rulers not subject to their controul at short periods. the introduction of this new principle of representative democracy has rendered useless almost every thing written before on the structure of government: and in a great measure relieves our regret if the political writings of Aristotle, or of any other antient, have been lost, or are unfaithfully rendered or explained to us. my most earnest wish is to see the republican element of popular controul pushed to the maximum of it's practicable exercise. I shall then believe that our government may be pure & perpetual. Accept my respectful salutations. TH: JEFFERSON

RC (MHi: Washburn Autograph Collection); addressed: "Mr Isaac H. Tiffany Schoharie. N.Y."; franked; postmarked Milton, 28 Aug.; endorsed by Tiffany as received 11 Sept. 1816. PoC (DLC).

The RIVAL TRANSLATION was William Ellis, *A Treatise on Government. Translated from the Greek of Aristotle* (London, 1778; Sowerby, no. 2357).

[1] Preceding three words interlined.

To Benjamin Henry Latrobe

Dear Sir Monticello Aug. 27. 16.

As you were so kind as to give me your invention[1] of the handsome and peculiarly American capital, I must give you mine of the new Dial to which that Capital has led. I had placed the Capital on a pedestal of the size proper to it's diameter, and had reconciled their confluence into one another by interposing plinths successively diminishing. it looked bald for want of something to crown it. I therefore surmounted it with a globe and it's neck, as is usual on gate posts. I was not yet satisfied; because it presented no idea of utility. it occurred then that this globe might be made to perform the functions of a dial. I ascertained on it[2] two poles, delineated it's equator and tropics, described meridians at every 15° from tropic to tropic, and shorter portions of meridian intermediately for the half hours quarter hours, and every 5. minutes. I then mounted it on it's neck, with it's axis parallel to that of the earth by a hole bored in the Nadir of our latitude, affixed a meridian of sheet iron, moveable on it's poles, and with it's plane in that of a great circle, of course presenting it's upper edge to the meridian of the heavens corresponding with that on the globe to which it's lower edge pointed. I then meridianised the globe truly, and presenting the outer edge of it's moveable meridian to the sun, the shade of it's thin plane, as a thread, designates on the hour lines of the globe, the meridian of the heavens on which he then is.

My globe is of locust, $10\frac{1}{2}$ I. diameter, equal to the collar of the capital, & enables me to judge within one or two minutes of the solar time. this device may be usefully applied to the ornamental balls on gate-posts; or mounted on a balluster, or the frustum of a column, for the purpose of an ordinary dial. it is easily made by a common turner, with materials which every one possesses, and requires no calculation of hourlines, being adapted to every latitude by only fixing it on the point corresponding with the Nadir of the place.—perhaps indeed this may be no novelty. it is one however to me, and I offer it to you as an architectural embellishment which you may sometimes perhaps find occasion to use in your profession, and as a testimony of my readiness to embrace every occasion of renewing to you the assurances of my constant esteem & respect.

Th: Jefferson

PoC (DLC); at foot of text: "B. H. Latrobe esq." Dft (DLC); incomplete; with PoC of TJ to Mathew Carey, 1 Sept. 1816, on verso. PoC of incomplete Dft (MHi); with PoC of TJ to Charles K. Mallory, 1 Sept. 1816, on verso.

For the PECULIARLY AMERICAN maize capital sent by Latrobe, see Latrobe to TJ, 28 Aug. 1809. A photograph of the NEW DIAL as it was reconstructed at Monticello in 2001 is reproduced elsewhere in this volume.

[1]Dft ends here, with the variant of the drawing of the sundial (depicted here in right-hand column), on a pedestal but lacking the capital, in lower left-hand corner.
[2]Preceding two words interlined.

From John F. Oliveira Fernandes

DEAR SIR Norfolk 27th August 1816—

Your much esteemed favour, dated 18th Inst. (and Post marked 21st) came to hand but yesterday, after the departure of the mail. I am Sorry, that letters within our own State take Sometimes longer, to reach their destination than those from Boston or Savannah:

Slave as I am, had I received it Sooner, I would have made such arrangements, as to be from Norfolk four or five days, before the time I had calculated; but now, considering the necessity of your departure from Monticello & the shortness of time of your residence there—I will postpone the honour of paying my respects to you, for another occasion; if Circumstances will permit me that agreable opportunity.

I will not forget to forward the Quarter Cask of choiced Port Wine, as Soon as a Small parcel, recommended for my use, will arrive. Permit me to Subscribe myself

with the highest respect & esteem Dear Sir your mo: obt Servant

JOHN F. OLIVEIRA FERNANDES

RC (DLC); between dateline and salutation: "Thomas Jefferson Esqre"; endorsed by TJ as received 2 Sept. 1816 and so recorded in SJL.

From Charles Willson Peale

DEAR SIR Philada Augt 27th 1816

Calling on a Watchmaker to day, he told me of a young man who is an excellent artist, that is now in Virginia, I do not recollect at what place, but I believe I was told at Petersburgh, that he did not like the place—I then waited on his brother son of Mr Mcilhany—who has promised me to write by tomorrows post to his brother and request him to call on you at Monticella—The Brother seemed much pleased when I told him where you wanted a Watchmaker to settle—and that you had something to do for you, and he believes his Brother will be willing to settle at Charlotteville. Therefore I do not deem it necessary to make enquiry further at present—Young Mr Muckilhany told me that you knew his father.

I have seen Mr Luken's Galvanic Machine today, & it had motion but too little power to give sound to the Bells—Mr Lukens said that the vibration ought to be 6 Inches—Dr Jones Professor of Chemistry &c of Williamsburgh Colledge, says that he suspects that the Zinc was not sufficiently free from oxidation, and they probably will take them[1] out to clean & then replace them.

I write in haste yours &c C W Peale

RC (MHi); with faint words enhanced by Peale; at foot of text: "Thos Jefferson Esqre"; endorsed by TJ as received 4 Sept. 1816 and so recorded in SJL. PoC (PPAmP: Peale Letterbook).

[1] Manuscript: "then."

To James Monroe

Th:J. to Colo Monroe. Monticello. Aug. 29. 16.

I sent to mr Divers to-day to ask a dinner for mr Correa, Dr Wistar, mr Gilmer & myself for tomorrow. I did not venture to add your name and mr Rush's not knowing your convenience; but I am sure he will be rejoiced to see you both. Affectionate salutations to yourself & mr Rush.

RC (DLC: Monroe Papers); dateline at foot of text; addressed: "Colo Monroe." Not recorded in SJL.

In a letter to André Daschkoff written 7 Sept. 1816 at Charlottesville (ViU), José Corrêa (correa) da Serra mentioned his visit to Monticello and stated that he expected to be in Philadelphia within ten or twelve days.

From James Monroe

Jas Monroe's best respects to mr Jefferson. 29. augt 1816.

mr Rush has just left me to bid you farewell, intending, when he departed, to set out on his return to washington tomorrow. If you can keep him, I will be happy to join with him, the party, from your house, on the visit to mr Divers. But if he proceeds on his journey, it is possible that my engagments with him, may prevent me. I will join you if in my power, & at an early hour.

RC (DLC); dateline at foot of text; addressed: "Mr Jefferson. Monticello"; endorsed by TJ as received 29 Aug. 1816 and so recorded in SJL.

On 31 Aug. 1816 Monroe wrote to James Madison from "Albemarle" that "I presume there will be no call, in relation to the literary institution, contemplated by Mr Jefferson. I shall dine with him tomorrow & write you respecting it, again in the evening; the cause is imputable to the failure of the proposed arrangme[nt] in the Executive" (RC in DLC: Madison Papers, Rives Collection; edge trimmed). Monroe wrote Madison on 4 Sept. 1816 that "Mr Jefferson, mentiond to me, on monday that he expected you up, notwithstanding the particular object had failed" (RC in DLC: Madison Papers).

From Louis Pio

ce 29. Aout 1816.

Monsieur Rue St honoré, no 284. près S. Roch. à Paris.

Quoique nous soyons séparés par un immense océan; quoique chacun de nous placé dans deux mondes différens, laissant à vous de nommer le votre l'ancien, ou le nouveau, je conserve, monsieur, et je conserverai tout le peu de vie qui me reste le souvenir de la candeur de votre ame, et celui de la bienveillance particuliere, avec la quelle vous m'avez honoré si long tems dans ce païs-ci. Jusqu'à present j'ai gardé le silence, premierement pendant la tyrannie de L'Usurpateur; en second lieu parce que je ne savais comment vous faire parvenir mes Lettres. Enfin votre nouvel Ambassadeur m'invite très honnêtement à Lui confier ma Lettre, et même il m'ecrit qu'il sera charmé de faire ma connoissance. Je suis flatté de pouvoir présenter mes hommages à un de vos Successeurs. Je n'ai pas beaucoup[1] compté dans le tems sur les faveurs de feu Mr Barlow, homme d'esprit; mais voilà tout ce[2] qu'on pouvait dire de lui. Il reste ici un Mr Parker, qui me connaît bien; mais qui n'est entouré que de mauvais sujets. moi je finis ma carriére tranquillement; mais privé de fortune je suis obligé de courir cette populeuse ville tous les jours pour donner des Leçons de Langue italienne, seule ressource pour me procurer une existence quelconque très précaire. Le Roy de Naples, que j'ai servi 21. ans ne veut plus de moi à cause de la démission de son service, que je fus forcé de donner au commencement de la Revolution, parce que j'eus le malheur de me trouver en opposition avec la façon de penser de Mr de Circello, pour lors ambassadeur ici, et actuellement premier ministre à Naples. Ce Circello est inexorable; il s'est réfusé meme aux instances que lui a fait faire en ma faveur S. A. R. la Duchesse d'Orléans, qui est, comme vous savez, la fille de Ferdinand IV. N'importe, vous me restez, monsieur, et c'est assez pour mon coeur. conservez vous pour vous, et pour L'humanité entiére, car on sçait tout le bien, que vous avez fait dans votre Présidence, et que vous faites encore par vos conseils. Donnez moi, je vous en supplie, de vos nouvelles, et si je[3] puis mériter vos ordres de telle façon que cela soit, ne m'en privez pas, je suis un instrument faible, et cassé, mais le nom de Jefferson m'electrisera, et je serais celui de trente ans auparavant.

Agreez, monsieur, mes salutations philosophiques, mais très cordiales, et tres sinceres. PIO

EDITORS' TRANSLATION

29. August 1816.
SIR Rue St. Honoré, number 284. near St. Roch. in Paris.

Although we are separated by an immense ocean and live in two different worlds, leaving it up to you to call yours the old or the new, I keep, Sir, and will preserve, for the rest of the short time left to me, the memory of the candor of your soul and the special kindness with which you honored me for so long while in this country. Until now, I have kept silent: first, during the tyranny of the Usurper; second, because I did not know how to get my letters to you. At last, your new ambassador invites me very honorably to entrust my letter to him, and he even writes that he will be delighted to make my acquaintance. I am flattered to be able to pay my respects to one of your successors. I did not much count, at the time, on the favors of the late Mr. Barlow, who was a man of intellect, although this is all that could be said of him. There remains here a Mr. Parker, who knows me well, but he is surrounded by nothing but poor specimens. I am finishing my career peacefully, although, being deprived of resources, I am obliged to run around this populous city every day giving lessons in Italian. This is my only option for providing myself with a very precarious living. The king of Naples, whom I served for twenty-one years, no longer wants me. I was forced to resign from his service at the beginning of the Revolution because I had the misfortune of opposing the opinions of Mr. de Circello, who was ambassador here at the time and is currently prime minister in Naples. This Circello is inexorable; he has even refused the entreaties made on my behalf by Her Royal Highness the duchesse d'Orléans, who is, as you know, the daughter of Ferdinand IV. I do not mind. I still have you, Sir, and that is enough for my heart. Stay well, for yourself and for all humanity, because everybody knows the good that you did during your presidency and that you still do through the advice you offer. I beg you to give me news of yourself, and if I may be deserving of your orders of any kind, do not deprive me of them. I am a weak and broken instrument, but Jefferson's name will electrify me, and I will become the person I was thirty years ago.

Please accept, Sir, my philosophical, but very cordial and very sincere salutations. PIO

RC (ViW: TC-JP); dateline at foot of text; endorsed by TJ as received 21 Nov. 1816 and so recorded in SJL. Translation by Dr. Genevieve Moene.

Louis Pio, diplomat and language instructor, was born in Italy. By 1780 he was employed as secretary and then in 1781 as chargé d'affaires at the Paris embassy of the Kingdom of Naples, over which Ferdinand IV reigned. In this capacity he became acquainted with TJ in 1784. Pio was active in the French Revolution, eventually allying himself with the the Jacobins, renouncing his title of chevalier, and in 1790 becoming a French citizen. After losing his diplomatic appointment, Pio worked first at the passport bureau, then as an emigration commissaire, and later at the war office before being imprisoned for his political views, 1794–95. After obtaining his freedom he remained in Paris, where he earned his living as a translator and teacher of Italian. He authored *Lettere Italiane di Piu Distinti Scrittori* (Paris, 1807) under his birth name of Luigi Pio (Albert Mathiez, "Le Chevalier Pio," *Annales Révolutionnaires* 11 [1919]: 94–104; *Biographie Nouvelle des Contemporains* [Paris, 1820–25], 16:340–1; Alessandro Cutolo, "Da Diplomatico a Giacobino: La vita di Luigi Pio atrraverso il suo carteggio inedito," *Rassegna Storica del Risorgimento* 22 [1935]: 396–413; *New-York Daily Gazette*, 11 June 1790; *PTJ*, esp. 7:423–4, 17:643).

The USURPATEUR was Napoleon. Albert Gallatin was the NOUVEL AMBASSADEUR to France. Tommaso di Somma, marchese di CIRCELLO, was the Neapolitan ambassador at Paris, 1786–90, and the then current prime minister and secretary of state for foreign affairs in Naples (Alberto M. Ghisalberti and others, eds., *Dizionario Biografico degli Italiani* [1960–], 40:283–8).

[1] Manuscript: "beacoup."
[2] Manuscript: "cee."
[3] Manuscript: "jee."

From Joel Yancey

DEAR SIR Poplar Forest August 29th 1816

I have had Several conversations with Capt Mitchel, with respect to grinding your wheat but could never learn from him possitively what he ment to do, until a few days past, he declines taking your wheat upon the terms you proposed, and Says he cannot alter the general rule, but he will buy your barrels at 2/– ℘ barrel delivered in Lynchburg, which I think is not enough, Barnaba and Nace have been getting Staves, building spring House & coopers Shop Since Harvest and will begin to set up flour barrels next week, we finishd getting out the wheat on 20th Inst the grain is fine and I hope it will turn out tolerably well, but our crops of corn and Tobacco are ruin,d by the Drought, a great many refuse to sell their wheat in consequince of it, I hope it is better with you, I think we are rather more than half done fallawing at both places, and shall get done in good time if we have rain, the current price of wheat in Lynchburg is 8/3, and 9/– might have been got for your crop about 10 days ago but I have heard that it has fallen since—your People are all well except Bess, who appears to be much the Same as when you were here, I see Francis very often he is in good health and Spirits, and very anxious for your return to the Forest his Cousin W. Baker is with him. accept my best wishes for your Happiness JOEL YANCEY

P.S

Cap[t] Martin has disappointed me in not having your timber Ready, he has alwa[ys] told me he could Saw it at any time and that you should have it time enough, but he has put it off, and now he has taken his Dam down and can,t tell when he can Saw or grind, all your timber is lying there untouch[d]. the amount of your State Taxes 133 dollars & 83 cents—

J YANCEY

RC (MHi); edge trimmed; endorsed by TJ as received 4 Sept. 1816 and so recorded in SJL.

TJ's grandson FRANCIS Eppes and Eppes's COUSIN John Wayles Baker attended school at the nearby New London Academy.

From David Gelston

DEAR SIR, New York August 31. 1816.

I have received bill of lading &[ca] enclosed, but have no invoice, if you can furnish the inv[o] it will save much trouble—when completed I shall forward the case to Richmond—

Very truly & sincerely your's

DAVID GELSTON

RC (MHi); mistakenly endorsed by TJ as received 17 Aug. 1816. RC (MHi); address cover only; with PoC of TJ to George Cabell, 1 May 1817, on verso; addressed: "Thomas Jefferson Esquire Monticello"; franked; postmarked New York, 31 Aug. Recorded in SJL as received 17 Sept. 1816.

For the enclosed BILL OF LADING &[CA], see David Bailie Warden to TJ, 14 July 1816. The 30 May 1816 INVOICE for TJ's recent book purchase from de Bure Frères is printed above at Warden to TJ, 12 July 1816.

To James Monroe

TH:J. TO COL[O] MONROE. Aug. 31. Saturday.

Will you join mr Divers here at dinner tomorrow? and can you tell me the name of the Collector at Norfolk?

RC (facsimile in Gerard A. J. Stodolski, Inc., spring 1985 catalogue, item 96); partially dated at foot of text. Not recorded in SJL.

The COLLECTOR AT NORFOLK was Charles K. Mallory.

From John Payne Todd

My Dear Sir, Mont Pelier Augt 31st 16.

A week after the valuable letter you honored [me][1] with, I received your highly prized present, a p^{r} of Turkish Pistols of curious workmanship which shall be preserved with all that devotedness of respect and affection I feel for you—Until the present moment I had hoped to have paid you my respects and thanked you in person but learning from Mr Rush of your intended visit to Bedford I am induced to pospone this pleasure; in the mean time I beg you to be assured of my wishes for a continuance of your health [and][2] of my very affectionate tho' respectful attachment. J. Payne Todd.

RC (MHi); at foot of text: "Th: Jefferson Esqre"; endorsed by TJ as received 2 Sept. 1816 and so recorded in SJL.

[1] Omitted word editorially supplied.

[2] Omitted word editorially supplied.

To Mathew Carey

Sir Monticello. Sep. 1. 16.

Mr Correa has favored me with a copy of your catalogue of Dr Priestly's library, on which I have found the articles underwritten, which I will pray you to forward to me, or such of them as remain on hand, to Richmond to the address of Messrs Gibson & Jefferson merchants there, who will pay the freight. I believe there are few weeks or days without a vessel sailing from Philadelphia for Richmond. so soon as you will be so good as to inform me of the amount of those on hand & forwarded, it shall be remitted to you. Accept the assurances of my continued esteem & respect. Th: Jefferson

page
7. Bedae ecclesiastica historia. 18mo 0. D 75 c
23. the Lord's prayer in 100. languages. 4to 3.
26. Metaphrasis psalmorum. à Duport. 12mo 1.
31. Priestley's harmony of the Evangelists. Greek. 4to 5.D.
37. Van Dale super Aristaea. 4to 2.D.
40. Abercrombie on plants & trees. 2. v. 12mo 1.25
41. Bonnycastle's Algebra. 12mo .50
52. Potter's Mathematics 8vo 1.25
58. Aristotelis de poeticâ. Gr. Lat. .75
Anacreon à Barnes. Gr. Lat. 18mo .50
61. Buffier traité des premiers verités. 12mo .75
62. Bruckeri institutiones historiae Philos. 8vo 2.D.

71. Grotius's Annals. Eng. 12mo 1.25
Grammatica Anglo-Saxonica Hickesii. 4to 3.50
78. Kusterus de verbis mediis. 12mo .50
82. Mair's Tyro's dictionary. 12mo .62½
86. Potter's antiquities. 2. v. 8vo 4.
Portroyal Greek primitives. 8vo 1.75
91. Schrevelii Lexicon. 8vo 2.
Somneri Vocabularium Anglo-Sax. à Benson. 8vo 2.D.
92. Thucydides, Platonis, et Lysiae orationes. Gr. Lat. 8vo 1.75
93. Polydori Virgilii Angl. hist. 8vo 2.D.

RC (NjMoHP: Lloyd W. Smith Collection); with book list, clipped, supplied from PoC; addressed: "Mr Matthew Cary Bookseller Philadelphia"; franked; postmarked Milton, 4 Sept.; endorsed by Carey as received 8 Sept. and answered 12 Sept. PoC (DLC); on verso of Dft of TJ to Benjamin Henry Latrobe, 27 Aug. 1816; endorsed by TJ.

The ARTICLES UNDERWRITTEN were drawn from the *Catalogue of the Library of the late Dr. Joseph Priestley, containing Many very scarce and valuable Books, for sale by Thomas Dobson* (Philadelphia, 1816). THE LORD'S PRAYER IN 100. LANGUAGES: *Oratio Dominica ... Nimirum, Plus Centum Linguis, Versionibus, aut Characteribus Reddita & Expressa* (London, 1713). PORTROYAL GREEK PRIMITIVES: Claude Lancelot, Antoine Arnauld, and Pierre Nicole, *The Primitives of the Greek Tongue ... Translated from the French of Messieurs de Port Royal, with considerable Improvements*, ed. and trans. Thomas Nugent (London, 1748).

To Charles K. Mallory

SIR Monticello Sep. 1. 16.

By a letter of June 4. from mr Cathalan at Marseiles (our Consul) I am informed he had shipped a barrel of 38. gallons of wine of Roussillon in France for me, on board the ship Lothair, John Stone master, bound for Norfolk, and consigned to the Collector of the port for me, and that the vessel was to sail the next day. I do not know whether she has arrived at Norfolk; but whenever she does, I will ask the favor of you to forward the cask to mess[rs] Gibson & Jefferson at Richmond[1] by a captain who can be depended on against it's adulteration, and to draw for freight, duties, & all expences on them, and they will pay your draught on sight on my account.

Having occasion from time to time to import articles (particularly wines and books) from different ports of Europe, & especially of the Mediterranean, from which conveyances to any particular port of the US. are not always to be had, I am obliged to desire my correspondents to ship them to any of our ports, consigned to the Collector of the port; trusting that these gentlemen will notify me and draw on my correspondents above named for expences & duties. this will sometimes happen to draw such consignments on you, and I hope you will do me the favor to recieve them, forward them without further order to mess[rs] Gibson & Jefferson, and to draw on them for all expences & duties, only dropping me a line notifying their arrival, and that you will be so good as to excuse this liberty from the necessity of the case, as I have no particular correspondent at Norfolk. with this apology for the trouble I have taken the liberty to give you I pray you to accept the assurance of my great esteem & respect

TH: JEFFERSON

PoC (MHi); on verso of PoC of Dft of TJ to Benjamin Henry Latrobe, 27 Aug. 1816; at foot of text: "Charles K. Mallory esq."; endorsed by TJ.

[1] Preceding two words interlined.

From John Adams

DEAR SIR Quincy Sept[r] 03. 1816

D[r] James Freeman, is a learned, ingenious, honest and benevolent Man, who wishes to See President Jefferson, and requests me to introduce him. If you would introduce Some of your Friends to me, I could with more confidence introduce mine to You. He is a Christian,[1] but not a Pythagorian a Platonick or a Philonick Christian. You will ken him and he will ken You: but you may depend, he will never betray, deceive or injure You.

Without hinting to him, any Thing which had passed between You and me, I asked him, your Question "What are the Uses of Grief"? He Stared. Said "the question was new to him." All he could Say at present was that he had known in his own Parish, more than one Instance of Ladies, who had been thoughtless, modish, extravagant in a high degree; who upon the death of a Child, had become thoughtfull, modest, humble, as prudent amiable Women as any he had known. Upon this I read to him your Letters and mine, upon this Subject of Grief, with which he Seemed to be pleased. You See I was not afraid to trust him: and you need not be.

Since I am, accidentally, invited to write to You, I may add a few Words upon Pleasures and Pains of Life. Vassall thought, an hundred Years, nay an eternity of Pleasure was no Compensation for one hour of billious Cholic. Read again Mollieres Spsyke. Act. 2. Scene 1st On the Subject of Grief.[2]

And read in another place "On est payé de mille Maux Par un heureux moment." Thus differently do Men Speak of Pleasures and Pains.

Now, Sir, I will tease you with another Question. What have been the Abuses of Grief?

In Answer to this question, I doubt not, you might write an hundred volumes. A few hints may convince You that the Subject is ample.

1 The Death of Socrates excited a general Sensibility of Grief in Athens, in Attica and in all Greece. Plato and Xenophon two of his Disciples took Advantage of that general Sentiment, by employing their enchanting Style to represent their Master to be greater and better than he probably was. And What have been the Effects of Socratic, Platonick which were Pythagorean, which was Indian Philosophy, in the world?[3]

2. The Death of Cæsar, Tyrant as he was, Spread a general Compassion which always includes Grief, among the Romans. The Scoundrel M. Anthony availed himself of this momentary Grief to destroy the Republick, to establish the Empire, and to proscribe Cicero.

3. But to Skip over all Ages and Nations for the present, and descend to our own Times. The Death of Washington, diffused a general Grief. The Old Tories, the Hyperfederalists, the Speculators, Sett up a general Howl. Orations Prayers Sermons Mock Funerals, were all employed, not that they loved Washington, but to keep in Countenance the Funding & Banking Systems; And to cast into the Background and the Shade all others who had been concerned in the Service of their Country in the Revolution.

4. The Death of Hamilton, under all its circumstances, produced a General Grief. His most determined Enemies[4] did not like to get rid of him, in that Way. They pitied too his Widow and Children. His Party Seized the moment of publick Feeling to come forward with Funeral orations and printed Panegyricks reinforced with mock Funerals and Solemn Grimaces, and all this by People who have buried Otis, Sam. Adams Hancock[5] and Gerry in Comparative[6] Obscurity. And Why? Merely to disgrace the Old Whiggs, and keep the Funds and Banks in Countenance.

5. The Death of Mr Ames excited a general Regret. His long Consumption his amiable Character and respectable Talents[7] had attracted a general Interest, and his Death a general Mourning. His Party made the most of it, by Processions orations, and a Mock Funeral. And Why? To glorify the Torys, to abash the Whiggs, and maintain the Reputation of Funds, Banks and Speculation. And all this was done in honour of that insignificant Boy; by People who have let a Dana a Gerry and a Dexter go to their Graves without Notice.

6. I almost Shudder at the thought of alluding to the most fatal Example of the Abuses of Grief, which the History of Mankind has preserved. The Cross. Consider what Calamities that Engine of Grief has produced.! With the rational Respect that is due to it, knavish Priests have added Prostitutions of it, that fill or might fill the blackest and bloodiest Pages of human History. I am with[8] ancient friendly Sentiments JOHN ADAMS

RC (DLC); at foot of text: "President Jefferson"; endorsed by TJ as received 5 Oct. 1816 and so recorded in SJL. FC (Lb in MHi: Adams Papers).

Philonic (PHILONICK): of or relating to the beliefs of the Hellenistic Jewish philosopher Philo Judaeus (*OED*). The brief interlude between the third and fourth acts of Molière's *Psyche* (MOLLIERES SPSYKE), a 1670 tragicomedy, includes the phrase ON EST PAYÉ DE MILLE MAUX PAR UN HEUREUX MOMENT ("a happy moment costs a thousand bad ones").

[1] RC: "Christion." FC: "Christian."
[2] Preceding nine words added by Adams in a different ink.
[3] Sentence added by Adams.
[4] RC: "Ennemies." FC: "Enemies."
[5] RC and FC: "Handcock."
[6] RC: "Comparitive." FC: "comparative."
[7] RC: "Tatents." FC: "Talents."
[8] Word, interlined in RC, not in FC.

To Joseph C. Cabell

DEAR SIR Monticello Sep. 3. 16.

I am afraid I have kept your papers longer than you expected. mr Randolph's absence till within these two days has been the cause of it. they are valuable documents, and are now returned. with respect to the copy of my letter, I know it is safe in your hands, and I rely on your effectual care that it be kept out of the public papers. affectionately your's TH: JEFFERSON

RC (ViU: TJP); at foot of text: "Joseph C. Cabell esq."; endorsed by Cabell. PoC (MHi); on verso of reused address cover of otherwise unlocated letter from Joel Yancey to TJ of 8 June 1816 (addressed: "Mr Thomas Jefferson Monticello Near Milton"; franked; postmarked Lynchburg, 12 June, and Charlottesville, 19 June; recorded in SJL as received 19 June 1816 from Lynchburg); endorsed by TJ.

For the enclosed VALUABLE DOCUMENTS, see Cabell to TJ, 4 Aug. 1816, and note. Cabell had made a COPY of TJ's 12 July 1816 letter to "Henry Tompkinson" (Samuel Kercheval).

From Micajah Davis

HONORED SIR Elysian Fields Miss. Ter. 3rd Sep. 1816

Often times hath the Record of the public expression of your praise met Mine eyes and as often hath a feeling involuntarily pervaded my Mind which testified to the justice of the merited Sentiment & rare it is that an occasion occurs that a grateful country does not pay you that tribute so justly due is it possible that a human being Can possess a more Soothing Reward of Recompense. is it not the beginning of your Heaven whilst you are yet on earth the foretaste of things which are to come

Many of those who have held the reins of Government in their hands have outshone you in pomp & Splendor & the abundant means placed in their hands have secured to them their flatterers but where is the crowned head that can recline upon So downy a pillow as yours, These few Sentiments are Solemn & Serious, the offspring of impressions repeatedly made on my mind I am very well aware how far you are above any thing in the Stile of flattery & too well know how far it is out of my power were I vain enough to attempt it all that I have in view is to afford you the addetion of one more testimony of approbation & myself the honor of Rendering it to the man who in my judgment has always deserved it in the first degree

Very Respectfully your devoted friend MICAJAH DAVIS

RC (DLC); endorsed by TJ as received 5 Oct. 1816 and so recorded in SJL, where TJ mistakenly entered it as a letter of 24 Sept. 1816. RC (MHi); address cover only; with PoC of TJ to John Wayles Eppes, 24 Jan. 1817, on verso; addressed: "Mr. Thomas Jefferson Monticello Va." by "mail"; franked; postmarked "Elysian Fields, M.T.," 3 Sept.

Micajah Davis (ca. 1753–1821), merchant, was a Virginia native who lived in Louisa and Hanover counties as a young man. In 1782 he relocated with his wife and growing family to Campbell County, where he operated a store and mill. Davis represented Virginia at a national convention of abolition societies in Philadelphia in 1796. Having returned to the Richmond area by 1799, he continued his mercantile business and served as a penitentiary inspector, 1801–03. In 1805 Davis was expelled from the Society of Friends for allowing his eldest daughter to marry outside the Quaker faith. Within two years he had migrated to the Mississippi Territory, where he served in the territorial legislature, 1807–10, became chief justice of Amite County in 1809, and was a deputy postmaster eight years later (National Society of the Daughters of the American Revolution, *DAR Patriot Index* [2003], 1:709; William Wade Hinshaw and others, *Encyclopedia of American Quaker Genealogy* [1936–50; repr. 1969–77], 6:171, 240, 306–7; Ruth H. Early, *Campbell Chronicles and Family Sketches Embracing the History of Campbell County, Virginia, 1782–1926* [1927], 53, 89–90; *Minutes of the Proceedings of the Third Convention of Delegates from the Abolition Societies Established in different Parts of the United States, assembled at Philadelphia* [Philadelphia, 1796], 4; *CVSP*, 9:295, 297, 373; Richmond *Enquirer*, 2 June 1804; *Missisippi Herald & Natchez Gazette*, 8 Sept., 21 Oct. 1807; Dunbar Rowland, ed., *Mississippi* [1907], 1:80, 111; *Terr. Papers*, 6:33–4, 152; *A Register of Officers and Agents, Civil, Military, and Naval, in the Service of the United States, on the thirtieth day of September, 1817* [Washington City, 1818], 22; Natchez *Mississippi State Gazette*, 6 Feb. 1819).

To Charles Pinckney

DEAR SIR Monticello Sep. 3. 16.

your favor of August has been duly recieved, with the pamphlet it covered.[1] Col° Monroe happened to be at his seat adjoining me and to dine with me the day I recieved it. I thought I could not make better use of it than, by putting it into his hands, to let him know his friends. you say nothing in your letter of your health which, after so long an interval,[2] cannot but be interesting to a friend. I hope it continues firm. as for myself, I weaken very sensibly, yet with such a continuance of good health as makes me fear I shall wear out very tediously, which is not what one would wish. I see no comfort in outliving one's[3] friends, and remaining a mere monument of the times which are past. I withdraw myself as much as possible from politics, and gladly shelter myself under the wings of the generation for which in our day,[4] we have labored faithfully to provide shelter.

Your's with continued friendship & respect[5] TH: JEFFERSON

PoC (MHi); on verso of reused address cover of William D. Simms to TJ, 1 July 1816; at foot of text: "Charles Pinckney esq."; endorsed by TJ. Printed with partial date of Sept. 1816 in the New York *National Advocate*, 30 Nov. 1818.

James Monroe's SEAT ADJOINING Monticello was his Highland estate.

[1] *National Advocate* here adds "in defence of Colonel Monroe's nomination to the Presidency, written by yourself."

[2] Preceding five words not in *National Advocate*.

[3] *National Advocate*: "our."

[4] Preceding three words not in *National Advocate*.

[5] *National Advocate*: "Your truly, and with continued friendship."

To Thomas Ritchie

SIR Monticello Sep. 3. 16.

I have just had sight of a statistical document so very curious that I am exceedingly anxious to obtain a copy of it. it is entitled 'a statement of the revenue tax for the year 1815 arising on lots land and other property' a two sheet table printed in your office. if you can procure me a copy you will greatly oblige me. Accept assurances of my friendly respect. TH: JEFFERSON

PoC (MHi); on verso of a reused address cover from David Higginbotham to TJ; at foot of text: "Mr Ritchie"; endorsed by TJ.

From Alexander H. Everett

Philadelphia. 4 Sept. 1816.

Mr. Everett. Secretary of Legation in Holland. presents his best respects to Mr. Jefferson with a copy of the Programme of the Haerlem Society of Sciences which he was requested by Dr Van Marum the Secretary of the Society to convey to him. Mr. E. will take it as a great favour if Mr. Jefferson will acknowledge the receipt of the programme by a line addressed to Mr. Everett at Boston.

RC (DLC); dateline at foot of text; addressed: "President Jefferson. Monticello. Virginia"; franked; postmarked Philadelphia, 4 Sept.; endorsed by TJ as a letter from "Everett" received 17 Sept. 1816 and so recorded in SJL. Enclosure: *Programme de la Société Hollandoise des Sciences, à Harlem, pour l'année 1816*, reporting at the meeting of 25 May 1816 on what had been received in the preceding year; acknowledging answers to specific questions posed by the society; judging each submission and announcing the prizes awarded to the best replies; reporting that medals and money had been given to the authors of works on an improved hernial bandage and on the invention, in Haarlem before 1440, of printing using movable type; recirculating queries for further consideration and raising new issues, with deadlines of 1 Jan. 1817 and 1 Jan. 1818; asking that responses be in Dutch, French, Latin, or German; and requesting that the papers be left unsigned, adhere closely to their topic, and be clearly and succinctly written (printed circular in DLC: TJ Papers, 209:37210–1; in French; undated; addressed by the Dutch scientist Martin [Martinus] van Marum "à Mr Jefferson ancien President de la société Philosophique à Philadelphia").

Alexander Hill Everett (1790–1847), diplomat and man of letters, was born in Boston and graduated from Harvard University in 1806. After teaching Greek at Phillips Exeter Academy, 1806–07, he studied law under John Quincy Adams. During Adams's tenure as minister plenipotentiary to Russia, 1809–11, Everett was his private secretary. Thereafter he served as secretary of the American legation in the Netherlands, 1815–16, as chargé d'affaires there, 1818–24, and as United States envoy extraordinary and minister plenipotentiary to Spain, 1825–29. A prolific writer, Everett purchased a controlling interest in the *North American Review* in 1830 and edited the journal for the next five years. During the 1830s he also sat for several terms in the Massachusetts legislature as a Whig, won election to the American Philosophical Society, and was briefly an American agent in Cuba. Everett held the presidency of Jefferson College in Louisiana, 1841–44. Having shifted his party allegiance to the Democrats, he was America's first commissioner to China, 1845–47. He died shortly after arriving in Canton (*ANB*; *DAB*; *Harvard Catalogue*, 186; *General Catalogue of the Officers and Students of the Phillips Exeter Academy. 1783–1903* [1903], vii; *New-York Gazette & General Advertiser*, 3 Aug. 1809; *JEP*, 2:605, 3:143, 150, 436, 445, 4:52, 6:399, 433, 443 [21, 24 Jan. 1815, 27, 30 Nov. 1818, 5, 9 Mar. 1825, 3 Feb. 1830, 26 Feb., 12, 13 Mar. 1845]; APS, Minutes, 15 Apr. 1831 [MS in PPAmP]; Washington *Daily National Intelligencer*, 21 Apr. 1841; Everett, *Critical and Miscellaneous Essays*, 2 vols. [1845–46]; Baltimore *Niles' National Register*, 23 Oct. 1847).

To William Wirt

Dear Sir Monticello Sep. 4. 16.

I have read with great delight the portion of the history of mr Henry which you have been so kind as to favor me with, and which is now returned: and I can say from my own knolege of the cotemporary characters introduced into the canvas, that you have given them quite as much lustre as themselves would have asked. the exactness too of your details has in several instances corrected the errors in my own recollections where they had begun to faulter. in result, I scarcely find any thing needing revisal. yet to shew you that I have scrupulously sought occasions of animadversion, I will particularize the following passages which I noted as I read them.

pa. 11. line 17. to bottom. I think this whole passage had better be moderated. that mr Henry read Livy thro' once a year is a known impossibility with those who knew him. he may have read him once, and some general history of Greece; but certainly not twice. a first reading of a book he could accomplish sometimes, and on some subjects; but never a second. he knew well the geography of his own country, but certainly never made any other his study. so as to our ancient charters, he had probably read those in Stith's history. but no man ever more undervalued chartered titles than himself. he drew all natural rights from a purer source, the feelings of his own breast. he never, in conversation or debate, mentioned a hero, a worthy, or a fact in Greek or Roman history, but so vaguely & loosely as to leave room to back out, if he found he had blundered. the study and learning ascribed to him in this passage would be inconsistent with the excellent and just picture given of his indolence thro' the rest of the work.

pa. 27. l. 12. if the professor of the college was the writer of the pamphlet, his name was Graham, not Greeme. he was my master, & intimately known to me.

pa. 33. l. 4. enquire further into the fact alleged that Henry was counsel for Littlepage. I am much persuaded he was counsel for Dandridge. there was great personal antipathy between him and Littlepage, and the closest intimacy with Dandridge, who was his near neighbor, in whose house he was at home, & as one of the family, who was his earliest and greatest admirer and patron, and whose daughter became afterwards his second wife. it was in his house that during a course of Christmas festivities, I first became acquainted with mr Henry. this, it is true, is but presumptive evidence, and may be overruled by direct proof. but I am confident he could never have undertaken any case against Dandridge. considering the union of their bosoms, it would have been a great crime.

pa. 37. l. 13. & pa. 55. l. 6. from bottom. there was but one clear & sound bottom on which the separation of the chair and the treasury was decided. the legislature made all their levies of money payable into the hands of their speaker, over whom they had controul. the only hold the Gov[r] had on him was a negative on his appointment as Speaker at every new election, which amounted consequently to a negative on him as treasurer, and disposed him so far to be obsequious to the Governor.

pa. 57. l. 11. strike out Starke. he was nobody; a mere lounger at the bar, without business, without knolege, and without principle. John Blair is omitted here, one of the purest men then living, a well read lawyer, logical reasoner, & only kept down by his insuperable diffidence.

These are the only passages which I thought might be worthy of further enquiry; and are so unimportant as scarcely to be worth a defacement of the MS. by alteration.—I shall set out for Bedford on the 8th return a fortnight after to pass a week here, and shall then go back to Bedford to remain till the last of October. this knolege of my movements will enable you to give a proper direction to any further communications you may wish to make. accept the assurance of my constant friendship & respect

TH: JEFFERSON

RC (ViU: TJP); at foot of first page: "William Wirt esq." PoC (DLC); endorsed by TJ. Tr (MdHi: Wirt Papers). Enclosure: manuscript, not found, of a portion of Wirt, *Patrick Henry*.

With regard to the 1764 election of one of the burgesses for Hanover County, disputed between James Littlepage and Nathaniel West Dandridge, Wirt ultimately agreed with TJ that "Mr. Henry was on this occasion employed by Mr. Dandridge," HIS NEAR NEIGHBOR and the eventual loser in the contest (Wirt, *Patrick Henry*, 38–9; Leonard, *General Assembly*, 92). TJ's paragraph beginning THERE WAS BUT ONE CLEAR & SOUND BOTTOM is printed as a note from an unidentified "correspondent" in Wirt, *Patrick Henry*, 69.

From David Isaacs

Septr 5th 1816

David Isaacs returns M[r] Jefferson many thanks for the kindnes he has just bestowed on him and in return, he will acceept I hope of the Perusal of a Sermon which is just come to hand from a friend in Baltimore—Preached to the congregation in Philadelph on the same subject by the rever[d] M[r] Carvalho & with his best wishes for M[r] Jeffersons long life and a happy one—

RC (MHi); dateline at foot of text; endorsed by TJ as received 5 Sept. 1816. Enclosure: probably Emanuel N. Carvalho, *A Sermon, Preached on Sunday, . . . July 7, 1816, on occasion of the death of the Rev. Mr. Gershom Mendes Seixas, Pastor of the Hebrew Congregation at New York* (Philadelphia, 1816).

TJ may have BESTOWED ON Isaacs, a member of Charlottesville's small Jewish community, information about the death of Pastor Seixas contained in one of the newspapers to which TJ subscribed (Washington *Daily National Intelligencer*, 24 Aug. 1816).

To Samuel Kercheval

SIR Monticello Sep. 5. 16

Your letter of Aug. 16. is just recieved. that which I wrote to you under the address of H. Tompkinson was intended for the Author of the pamphlet you were so kind as to send me, and therefore, in your hands, found it's true destination. but I must beseech you, Sir, not to admit a possibility of it's being published. many good people will revolt from it's doctrines, & my wish is to offend nobody, to leave to those who are to live under it the settlement of their own constitution and to pass in peace the remainder of my time. if those opinions are sound, they will occur to others, and will prevail by their own weight, without the aid of names. I am glad to see that the Staunton meeting has rejected the idea of a limited convention. the article however, nearest my heart, is the division of the counties into Wards. these will be pure & elementary republics, the sum of all which, taken together, composes the state, & will make of the whole a true democracy as to the business of the Wards, which is that of nearest and daily concern. the affairs of the larger sections of counties, of states, & of the Union, not admitting personal transaction by the people, will be delegated to agents elected by themselves; and representation will thus be substituted where personal action becomes impracticable. yet, even over these representative organs, should they become corrupt and perverted, the division into wards, constituting the people, in their wards, a regularly organised power, enables them, by that organisation, to crush, regularly and peaceably, the usurpations of their unfaithful agents, and rescues them from the dreadful necessity of doing it insurrectionally. in this way we shall be as republican as a large society can be; and secure the continuance of purity in our government by the salutary, peaceable, and regular controul of the people. no other depositories of power have ever yet been found which did not end in converting to their own profit the earnings of those committed to their charge. George III. in execution of the trust confided to him, has, within his own day, loaded the inhabitants of Great Britain with debts equal to the whole fee-simple value of their island, and under pretext of governing it, has alienated it's whole soil to creditors who could lend money to be lavished on priests, pensions, plunder & perpetual war. this would not have been so, had the people retained organised means of acting on their agents. in this example then let us read a lesson for ourselves, and not 'go, and do so likewise.'

Since writing my letter of July 12. I have been told that, on the question of equal representation, our fellow-citizens in some sections of the state claim peremptorily a right of representation for their slaves. principle will, in this, as in most other cases, open the way for us to correct conclusion. were our state a pure democracy, in which all it's inhabitants should meet together to transact all their business, there would yet be excluded from their deliberations 1. infants, until arrived at years of discretion. 2. women; who, to prevent depravation of morals, and ambiguity of issue, could not mix promiscuously in the public meetings of men. 3. slaves, from whom the unfortunate state of things with us takes away the rights of will and of property. those then who have no will could be permitted to exercise none in the popular assembly; and of course could delegate none to an agent in a representative assembly. the business, in the first case, would be done by qualified citizens only; and in the second by the representatives of qualified citizens only.   It is true that, in the General constitution, our state is allowed a larger representation on account of it's slaves. but every one knows that that constitution was a matter of compromise, a capitulation between conflicting interests and opinions. in truth, the condition of different descriptions of inhabitants in any country is a matter of municipal arrangement, of which no foreign country has a right to take notice. all it's inhabitants are men as to them. thus, in the New England states, none have the powers of citizens but those whom they call freemen; and none are free men until admitted by a vote of the freemen of the town. yet, in the general government these non-freemen are counted in their quantum of representation, and of taxation. so slaves, with us, have no powers as citizens; yet in representation in the General government they count in the proportion of 3. to 5. and so also[1] in taxation. whether this is equal is not here the question. it is a capitulation of discordant sentiments and circumstances, and is obligatory on that ground. but this view shews there is no inconsistency in claiming representation for them from the other states, & refusing it within our own.

Accept the renewal of assurances of my respect.

TH: JEFFERSON

PoC (DLC); at foot of first page: "Mr Samuel Kercheval." Printed in Kercheval, *Jefferson's Letters*, 10–2.

Jesus uses the phrase GO, AND DO SO LIKEWISE in the Bible (Luke 10.37). Under the United States Constitution, article 1, section 2, each slave state was ALLOWED A LARGER REPRESENTATION ON ACCOUNT OF IT'S SLAVES, each of whom was to be counted as three-fifths of a person.

[1]Preceding two words interlined in place of "as 5." (see postscript to TJ to Kercheval, 8 Oct. 1816).

From Nicholas H. Lewis

SIR September 5th 1816

The Rivanna company request that you will meet them at Shadwell Mills next saturday You will be so good as to let me know by boy whether you can attend

I am yours &a N, H, LEWIS

RC (MHi); dateline at foot of text; addressed: "Mr Thos Jefferson ℔ boy"; endorsed by TJ as received 5 Sept. 1816.

Nicholas Hunter Lewis (1789–1840), farmer, was a nephew by marriage of William D. Meriwether. He served in 1812 on an Albemarle County jury that agreed with TJ that a tract of his land near Milton had been improperly seized. Lewis was an officer of the Rivanna Company into the 1830s. He was a member from 1817 until at least 1828 of the Agricultural Society of Albemarle, which awarded him prizes on several occasions, and in 1818 he subscribed $300 toward the establishment of Central College. Lewis owned fifty-eight slaves in 1820. In 1835 he sold his property in Albemarle County and moved to Missouri, where he died (Sarah Travers Lewis Anderson, *Lewises, Meriwethers and their Kin* [1938], 73–4; Woods, *Albemarle*, 272–3; Jury Findings regarding Land Seized by David Michie, 30 July 1812; True, "Agricultural Society," 271, 313, 315, 344; Master List of Subscribers to Central College, [after 7 May 1817], document 5 in a group of documents on The Founding of the University of Virginia: Central College, 1816–1819, printed at 5 May 1817; TJ to Lewis, 26 June 1819; *Richmond Enquirer*, 17 Apr. 1832, 26 June 1835; DNA: RG 29, CS, Va., Albemarle Co., 1820, 1830; Mo., Lincoln Co., 1840; Albemarle Co. Will Book, 15:523; gravestone inscription in Elmwood Cemetery, Lincoln Co., Mo.).

To Nicholas H. Lewis

Sep. 5. 16.

Th: Jefferson presents his compliments to mr Lewis and will attend the Rivanna company on Saturday at the Shadwell mills.

RC (CtHi: Hoadley Collection); dateline at foot of text; addressed: "Mr Nicholas H. Lewis"; endorsed by Lewis. Not recorded in SJL.

From Nicolas G. Dufief

MONSIEUR À Philadelphie ce 6 7bre 1816

Après vingt-cinq années de réflexions & d'expériences presque continuelles, je suis parvenu, autant que mes faibles talens me le permettent, à simplifier & à rendre commun l'art d'enseigner les langues, d'une telle manière que la partie la plus pauvre et la plus nombreuse de la société, bornée, dans les pays où le Gouvernement est le plus libéral, à savoir à peine lire et écrire, pourra y recevoir la même éducation, (et peut-être une meilleure) Sous le rapport de leur langue & celui de plusieurs autres, que la classe la plus riche, lorsqu'on y aura introduit la méthode développée dans le manuscript que je vous adresse, & que je me suis fait un honneur et un devoir de Soumettre à votre examen.

Il a fallu, Monsieur, que je fusse bien convaincu de vos bontés inaltérables pour moi, du zèle qui ne cesse point de vous animer pour le bien général, de la puissance des nouveaux moyens que je propose d'après l'expérience, & Surtout des effets qui en résultent pour le bonheur et le perfectionnement de la société, pour oser troubler le repos qui vous est si justement acquis après tant d'années de consacrées à la chose publique & aux plus utiles travaux. Ainsi, sans chercher à m'excuser davantage de la démarche que je fais auprès de vous, je vais entrer dans quelques détails relatifs à la 4ème Edition de "Nature Displayed" que je projette, de cet ouvrage que l'encouragement puissant de votre approbation m'enhardit à livrer à l'impression, il y a environ treize ans. Elle doit être Stéréotypée a New York où il y a trois fonderies d'établies. Les deux pages qui Sont dans le manuscrit, vous donneront une idée des progrès que l'art admirable de la Stéréotypie a faits dans notre patrie. J'ai du apporter, en conséquence, l'attention la plus soutenue, à purger l'ouvrage des fautes des éditions précédentes. A l'égard de celles qui pourraient Se glisser dans l'édition Stéréotype, on a inventé un procédé ingénieux pour les corriger après même que les planches ont été fondues

Le corps de l'ouvrage restera invariablement le même. L'ordre des matières, a, cependant, été un peu changé; par exemple, le second vocabulaire du 1er Vol. Se trouve être le premier, & le 2[d] vol. commence par la Conjugaison du verbe avoir, au lieu de l'analysis of the parts of speech. J'en ai donné la raison.

sur les 103 pages de la préface manuscrite, il y en a 53 Sur les premières desquelles il suffit de jeter un coup d'œil pour en connaître l'usage, ainsi il est seulement nécessaire d'en lire cinquante, qui imprimées en feront à peu près vingt-cinq, pour pouvoir embrasser la méthode dans toute son étendue. Au lieu de l'épigraphe de Bacon qui est en tête Je me propose d'y Substituer les deux suivantes:

"'Tis the last key-stone
That makes the arch: the rest that there were put
Are nothing till that comes to bind and Shut.
Then Stands it a triumphal mark! then men
Observe the Strength, the height, the why and when
It was erected; and Still walking under
Meet some new matter to look up and wonder!"

The most certain means of rendering a people free and happy, is to establish a perfect method of education.

Beccaria

J'ai trouvé la première à la fin d'une lettre de Horne à Junius, mais Sans nom d'Auteur. Aucun de nos hommes de lettres que j'ai consultés à ce sujet n'a pu me dire qui il est. La Seconde appartient, comme vous Savez, à l'excellent ouvrage sur Montesquieu, sorti des presses de Mr Duane

Aussitôt que vous aurez eu la bonté de me renvoyer le manuscript, Je commencerai à faire mes dispositions pour imprimer l'édition Stéréotype de "Nature Displayed"

J'ai l'honneur d'être, Monsieur, avec les Sentimens qui vous sont dus à tant de titres, & en fesant les vœux les plus ardens pour la conservation de votre Santé Votre très-dévoué & très-respectueux Serviteu[r] N. G. Dufief

EDITORS' TRANSLATION

Sir Philadelphia 6 September 1816

After twenty-five years of almost continual reflection and experience, I have succeeded, so far as my feeble talents allow, in simplifying and <u>making accessible</u> the art of teaching languages in such a way that the poorest and most numerous part of society (which is limited, even in countries where the government is very liberal, barely to knowing how to read and write) will be able to receive the same education (and perhaps a better one) with regard to their own language and several others, as the richest class, once the method developed in the manuscript I am sending you (and that I considered it an honor and a duty to submit to your examination) is introduced.

Sir, I had to be completely convinced of your unfailing kindness toward me, of the zeal for the common good that continues to animate you, of the power of the new means that I propose from experience and, most of all, of the beneficial effects they will have on the happiness and improvement of society to dare trouble the repose you have so justly earned after so many years devoted

to the public good and the most useful works. Therefore, without apologizing further, I will enter into a few details about the fourth edition of "Nature Displayed" that I am planning. The powerful encouragement of your approbation emboldened me to submit this book for publication about thirteen years ago. It will be stereotyped in New York, where there are three established foundries. The two pages that are enclosed in the manuscript will give you an idea of the progress that the admirable art of stereotypography has made in our country. In consequence, I had to pay the closest attention in order to purge the book of the mistakes of the preceding editions. Regarding the ones that might infiltrate the stereotyped edition, they have invented an ingenious procedure of correcting them even after the plates have been cast
The body of the book will remain invariably the same. The order in which the topics are presented, however, has changed a little. For example, the second vocabulary of the first volume now comes first, and the second volume starts with the conjugation of the verb avoir, instead of the analysis of the parts of speech. I have given the reason why.

Of the handwritten preface's 103 pages, it is enough to glance at the first 53 to know how to use the work. Thus, one need only read fifty pages, which, once printed, will be about twenty-five, to understand the method in its entirety. Instead of Bacon's epigraph, which appears at the beginning, I propose to substitute the following two:

"'Tis the last key-stone
That makes the arch: the rest that there were put
Are nothing till that comes to bind and Shut.
Then Stands it a triumphal mark! then men
Observe the Strength, the height, the why and when
It was erected; and Still walking under
Meet some new matter to look up and wonder!"

The most certain means of rendering a people free and happy, is to establish a perfect method of education.

Beccaria

I found the first at the end of a letter from Horne to Junius, but without the author's name. Not one of the men of letters I consulted on the subject was able to tell me who he is. The second belongs, as you know, to the excellent work on Montesquieu, which came off Mr. Duane's printing presses
As soon as you will be so kind as to send the manuscript back to me, I will begin making arrangements to print the stereotyped edition of "Nature Displayed"

I have the honor to be, Sir, with the sentiments due to you for so many reasons and the warmest wishes for the preservation of your health, your very devoted and very respectful servant N. G. Dufief

RC (DLC); edge trimmed; addressed: "Th: Jefferson, Esq[re]"; endorsed by TJ as received 14 Sept. 1816 and so recorded in SJL. Enclosure: manuscript and sample stereotyped pages, not found, of a forthcoming edition of Dufief, *Nature Displayed, in her Mode of Teaching Language to Man*, 2 vols. (Philadelphia, 1804, and later eds.; Sowerby, no. 4819; Poor, *Jefferson's Library*, 14 [no. 879]; vol. 1 of TJ's copy of 1806 ed. in ViCMRL, on deposit ViU). Translation by Dr. Genevieve Moene.

AVOIR: "to have." The lines 'TIS THE LAST KEY-STONE . . . LOOK UP AND WONDER!, which appeared in *The Genuine Letters of Junius* (London, 1771, and other eds.; Sowerby, nos. 2741–2), 298, are taken from Ben Jonson's "An Epistle to Sir Edward Sacvile, now Earle of Dorset" (Jonson, *Under-Woods: Consisting of Divers Poems* [London, 1640], 181). The quotation by Cesare Bonesana BECCARIA, which is printed on the title page of Destutt de Tracy, *Commentary and Review of Montesquieu's Spirit of Laws*, is apparently adapted from a passage in the Italian author's *Dei Delitti e delle Pene* (Leghorn, 1764; first English ed. London, 1767, and other eds.; Sowerby, no. 2349; Poor, *Jefferson's Library*, 11 [no. 629]).

To Madame de Staël Holstein

Monticello. Sep. 6. 16.

A request, dear Madam in your letter of Jan. 6. gives you the trouble of reading this. you therein ask information of the state of things in S. America. this is difficult to be understood even to us who have some stolen intercourse with those countries: but in Europe I suppose it impossible. that mendacity, which Spain, like England, makes a principal piece in the machine of her government, confounds all enquiry, by so blending truth and falsehood, as to make them indistinguishable. according to Spanish accounts they have won great victories in battles which were never fought, and slaughtered thousands of rebels whom they have never seen: and, as in our revolution, the English were perpetually gaining victories over us until they conquered themselves out of our Northern continent, so Spain is in a fair way of conquering herself out of the Southern one. even our information of the state of things in the Spanish colonies is far from being distinct or certain; so that I can give you but a general idea of it. to do this we must throw that country into masses, considering Brazil as a nucleus, around which they are thus disposed.

1. Buenos Ayres, & the country South of Brazil.
2. Chili, Tucumana, & Peru, West of Brazil, & on the Pacific ocean.
3. Caraccas, & the country North of Brazil, on the gulf of Mexico.
4. Mexico, in the Northern continent.

---

1. Buenos Ayres has established it's independance, as the Spanish functionaries themselves admit. it was for some time embarrassed by

the ambition of Monte-Video on the other side of La Plata, which claimed to be the principal place, & endeavored to maintain it by arms: but they have finally come to an arrangement which has re-united them, and they have formed their regular government. Spain, conscious that they are irrecoverable, is, as we are told, bartering them with the court of Brazil for Portugal. whether Spain can court, or conquer Portugal from hatred to love, you can best judge. the transfer of a people, like cattle, with their soil, seems to be growing into a part of the jus gentium of Europe: but it is not likely to be received here where we consider the cattle as owners of the soil. surrounded, as Brazil is, with revolutionary countries and principles, and having at times participated in them, it is possible this may turn out to be a gift of Brazil to Buenos Ayres, instead of a transfer of Buenos ayres to Brazil.

2. Chili, Tucumana and Peru, at one time were entirely ascendant. they have since suffered some reverses, and Buenos[1] Ayres, we are told, is gone to their assistance. the mother country can do little on that coast.

3. the Caraccas are the most accessible to the arms of Spain; & there accordingly successes have been most diversified. the Patriots & Royalists have been victors and vanquished by turns. lately the patriots carried all before them; but now there is reason to believe they have suffered serious discomfiture; and it is here the most atrocious cruelties have been exercised. the Patriots have in vain endeavored to end them by examples of moderation; the Royalists answer by examples of extermination. yet difficult as is the contest this country too will be ultimately revolutionised.

4. Mexico. the Royalists still hold the city of Mexico and the port of Vera cruz, the only one of that province; while it is understood that the Patriots prevail over the country. the siege of Vera Cruz now believed to be begun, or about to be begun, is supposed to be the cause why Apodaca, the new Viceroy of Mexico, who lately sailed for that port from Havanna, has been obliged to return, without venturing to land at Vera Cruz. this, first of all the Spanish possessions, and superior to Spain itself in extent, fertility, population, riches and information, has nothing to fear from the pigmy power of Spain.

So far then all would seem well. but their real difficulties are not how to repel the efforts of the mother country, but how to silence and disarm the schisms among themselves. in all those countries, the most inveterate divisions have arisen, partly among the different casts, partly among rival-leaders. constitution after constitution is made and broken, and in the meantime every thing is at the mercy of the military leaders. the whole Southern continent is sunk in the deepest ignorance and bigotry. a single priest is more than a sufficient opponent to a whole army; and were it not that the lower clergy, as poor and oppressed as the people themselves, has very much taken side with the revolutionists, their cause would have been desperate from the beginning. but, when their independance shall be established, the same ignorance & bigotry will render them incapable of forming and maintaining a free government: and it is excruciating to believe that all will end in military despotisms under the Bonapartes of their regions. the only comfortable prospect which this clouded horizon offers is that, these revolutionary movements having excited into exercise that common sense which nature has implanted in every one, it will go on advancing towards the lights of cultivated reason, will become sensible of it's own powers, and in time be able to form some canons of freedom, and to restrain their leaders to an observance of them. in the meantime we must pray to god as most heartily we do for your country, that 'he will be pleased to give them patience under their sufferings, and a happy issue out of all their afflictions.'

Your resolution not to revisit your own country, while under foreign force, is worthy of you. no patriotism requires us to incur the pain of witnessing miseries which we cannot remedy or alleviate, and towards which, even in absence, your pen may do more than your presence. that such a country and such a people can never be kept permanently prostrate on the earth is a decree of heaven, which will not pass away. our great anxiety is lest they should lengthen their sufferings by premature and abortive attempts to end them; and our wish that they may have patience, yet a while, until dissensions among their enemies may give them a choice of friends. in general it is sinful, but now pious, to pray for war and strife among nations, as the only means of dissolving their criminal combinations.

I congratulate you on the happy union of your daughter with a peer and patriot of France: and should your son realise the hope you hold up to us of visiting this sanctuary of the unfortunate of every country where 'the wolf dwells with the lamb, and the leopard lieth down with the kid,' he will be hailed as the son of M[de] de Staël and grandson of M. Necker, and will see an example, in the peaceable reunion here of so many discordant worthies of his own country, how much more happy the tolerant principles of his great ancestor might have made them at home.

Permit me here to renew the assurances of my high consideration and esteem. TH: JEFFERSON

RC (Archives du Château de Broglie, Haute-Normandie, France, 1948); with dateline altered by an unidentified hand to "Sep. 16. 16."; mutilated at seal, with missing text supplied from PoC. PoC (DLC); at foot of first page: "M^{de} la baronne de Staël Holstein"; endorsed by TJ as a letter of 7 Sept. 1816. Tr (StEdNL); at head of text: "Copy." Tr (NO-OsNB); in French; lacking drawing; at head of text: "Copie Lettre de Mr Jefferson à Mme de Stael." Recorded in SJL as a letter of 6 Sept. 1816 delivered "thro A. Gal. & Sec^{y} state." Enclosed in TJ to Albert Gallatin, 8 Sept. 1816.

The phrase HE WILL BE PLEASED ... THEIR AFFLICTIONS is from "A Collect or Prayer for all conditions of men" in *The Book of Common Prayer* (London, 1662, and other eds.; Sowerby, no. 1507; Poor, *Jefferson's Library*, 9 [nos. 514–5]). Following Napoleon's defeat at Waterloo, France was reduced to its 1789 borders and forced to pay an indemnity of 700 million francs. To ensure payment and the preservation of peace, the country's northern and eastern frontiers were to be garrisoned by a large FOREIGN FORCE for between three and five years (Alfred Cobban, *A History of Modern France* [1965], 2:70). The PEER AND PATRIOT OF FRANCE was Achille Charles Léonce Victor, duc de Broglie. THE WOLF DWELLS WITH THE LAMB, AND THE LEOPARD LIETH DOWN WITH THE KID is in the Bible (Isaiah 11.6).

[1]Manuscript: "Bueons."

From Thomas Ritchie

DEAR SIR — Richmond September 7th 1816.

I need scarcely say, that a Request from you is a Command upon me—I obey it with pleasure.

I have forwarded you by mail, not only the Document you ask for, but the entire Journal of the last House of Delegates, of which that Document forms a part.—The Journal may furnish additional Documents, which you may find interesting.

I beg leave to add the Acts of the last Legislature—being, in my humble judgment, one of the most honorable Monuments, of the public Spirit of our Legislature.

With the highest Respect,

Yours Sincerely, THOMAS RITCHIE

RC (MHi); endorsed by TJ as received 17 Sept. 1816 and so recorded in SJL.

THE DOCUMENT TJ had requested, "A Statement of the Revenue Tax for the Year 1815, arising on Lots, Land and other Property," is reprinted in the unpaginated appendix at the end of *JHD* (1815–16 sess.). Copies of three of the items in this section, including this one, were bound with TJ's set of the reprinted proceedings of Virginia's revolutionary conventions (see Philip Doddridge to TJ, 17 Jan. 1816, and note). This volume, which is listed in Poor, *Jefferson's Library*, 10 (no. 576), is now in Vi.

To William Clark

DEAR SIR Monticello Sep. 8. 16

The travelling journal of Govr Lewis and yourself having been published some time ago, I had hoped to hear that something was doing with the astronomical observations, the Geographical chart, the Indian vocabularies, and other papers not comprehended in the journal published. with a view to have these given to the public according to the original intention, I got a friend to apply for them to mr Biddle, in whose hands I understood them to be, referring him for authority[1] to the instructions inserted in the life of Govr Lewis prefixed to the journal. he said he could not deliver them even to the War-office, without an order from you. it is to sollicit this order that I now trouble you, and it may be given in favor either of the war office or of myself. if the latter, I should deliver the Astronomical observations to the Secretary at War, who would employ some one to make the calculations, to correct the longitudes of the map, and to have it published thus corrected; and I should deliver the papers of Natural history & the Vocabularies to the Philos. society at Philadelphia, who would have them properly edited, and I should deposit with them also for safekeeping the travelling pocket journals as originals to be recurred to on all interesting questions arising out of the published journal. I should recieve them only in trust for the War office to which they belong, and take their orders relating to them. I have recieved from Dr Barton's exrs[2] 4. vols of the travelling pocket journals, but I think there were 11. or 12. the rest I suppose mr Biddle has. I hope the part I have had in this important voyage, will excuse the interest I take in securing to the world all the beneficial results we were entitled to expect from it, and which would so fully justify the expences of the expedition incurred by the United states in that expedition. I salute you with constant friendship and respect.

TH: JEFFERSON

RC (MoSHi: Clark Papers); addressed: "General William Clarke Governor of Missouri St Louis"; franked; postmarked Charlottesville, 9 Sept.; endorsed by Clark as answered 10 Oct. 1816. PoC (DLC); on verso of reused address cover of Thomas Appleton to TJ, 20 Mar. 1816; torn at seal; endorsed by TJ.

TJ's FRIEND was José Corrêa da Serra. The PHILOS. SOCIETY AT PHILADELPHIA was the American Philosophical Society.

[1] Preceding two words interlined.
[2] Preceding four words interlined.

From Henry Clay

D[R] SIR Lexington 8th Sept. 1816

Mr. Alvan Stewart, who will deliver to you this letter, being desirous of the honor of your acquaintance, and of visiting Monticello, has asked of me a letter of introduction. Altho' I am sure, with his objects, it is altogether unnecessary, I have no hesitation in Soliciting your favorable reception of him. I comply the more readily with his request as it affords me an opportunity of tendering to you assurances of my high respect and Consideration. H. CLAY

RC (DLC); endorsed by TJ as received 15 Oct. 1816 and so recorded in SJL. RC (DLC); address cover only; with PoC of TJ to Patrick Gibson, 12 Dec. 1816, on verso; addressed: "Thomas Jefferson Esq[r] Monticello."

Henry Clay (1777–1852), attorney and public official, was a native of Hanover County. Having studied law under George Wythe in Richmond, he was admitted to the bar in 1797. Shortly thereafter Clay moved to Kentucky, where he established a legal practice. During a long political career, he served in the lower house of the Kentucky legislature, 1803–06 and 1807–10; the United States Senate, 1806–07, 1810–11, 1831–42, and 1849–52; the United States House of Representatives, 1811–14, 1815–21, and 1823–25 (holding the post of Speaker throughout these discontinuous terms); as one of the Ghent peace commissioners, 1814–15; and as secretary of state, 1825–29. Clay lost bids for the presidency in 1824, 1832, and 1844. A staunch nationalist, he was successively a leader of the National Republican and Whig parties. Consistently favoring protective tariffs, a strong central bank, and government-sponsored internal improvements, Clay also supported war with Great Britain in 1812, Latin American independence, the gradual elimination of slavery through compensation and colonization, and political compromise as a way to preserve the Union. His efforts during controversies over Missouri statehood, the Nullification crisis, and the debate over the admission of territories acquired as a result of the Mexican War helped to save the United States from civil war during his lifetime. Clay died of tuberculosis in Washington (*ANB*; *DAB*; Clay, *Papers*; Robert V. Remini, *Henry Clay: Statesman for the Union* [1991]; David S. Heidler and Jeanne T. Heidler, *Henry Clay: The Essential American* [2010]; Washington *Daily National Intelligencer*, 30 June 1852).

Alvan Stewart (1790–1849), attorney and abolitionist, was born in South Granville, New York. After attending several sessions at the University of Vermont and working for a number of years as an educator in Vermont, Canada, and New York, he undertook a journey, 1815–16, that took him to Kentucky, where he met Clay, and Virginia, where he visited TJ at Monticello. Stewart returned thereafter to New York, was admitted to the bar, and resided first in Cherry Valley and, from 1832, in Utica. In his latter years he tirelessly promoted the cause of abolition. Stewart helped organize and served as president of the New York State Anti-Slavery Society, raising money, giving speeches, and advocating more aggressive tactics than the moral suasion favored by William Lloyd Garrison. In an 1845 test case before the supreme court of New Jersey, he forcefully challenged the constitutionality of slavery. A fervent supporter of protectionism, a national bank, public education, federally funded internal improvements, and temperance, Stewart ran unsuccessfully for governor of New York on the ticket of the abolitionist Liberty Party in 1840 and 1844. He died in New York City (*ANB*; *DAB*; Levi Beardsley, *Reminiscences* [1852], 167–8; Luther Rawson Marsh, ed., *Writings and Speeches of Alvan Stewart, on Slavery* [1860]; New York *Weekly Herald*, 5 May 1849).

To Albert Gallatin

Dear Sir Monticello Sep. 8. 16.

The jealousy of the European governments rendering it unsafe to pass letters thro' their post-offices, I am obliged to borrow the protection of your cover to procure a safe passage for the inclosed letter to M^{de} de Staël, and to ask the favor of you to have it delivered at the hotel of M. De Lessert without passing thro' the post office.

In your answer of June 7. to mine of May 18. you mentioned that you did not understand to what proceeding of Congress I alluded as likely to produce a removal of most of the members,[1] & that by a spontaneous movement of the people, unsuggested by the newspapers, which had been silent on it. I alluded to the law giving themselves 1500.D. a year. there has never been an instance before of so unanimous an opinion of the people, and that thro' every state of the union. a very few members of the first order of merit in the house will be re-elected, such as R. M. Johnson who has been reelected, Clay of Kentucky by a small majority & a few others. but the almost entire mass will go out, not only those who supported the law, or voted for it, or skulked from the vote, but those who voted against it, or opposed it actively, if they took the money; and the examples of refusal to take it were very few. the next Congress then, federal as well as republican, will be almost wholly of new members.

We have had the most extraordinary year of drought & cold ever known in the history of America. in June, instead of $3\frac{3}{4}$ I. our average of rain for that month, we had only $\frac{1}{3}$ of an inch, in Aug. instead of $9\frac{1}{6}$ I. our average, we had only $\frac{8}{10}$ of an inch. and it still continues. the summer too has been as cold as a moderate winter. in every state North of this there has been frost in every month of the year; in this state we had none in June & July. but those of Aug. killed much corn over the mountains. the crop of corn thro' the Atlantic states[2] will probably be less than $\frac{1}{3}$ of an ordinary one, that of tob^{o} still less, and of mean quality. the crop of wheat was midling in quantity, but excellent in quality. but every species of bread grain taken together will not be sufficient for the subsistence of the inhabitants; and the exportation of flour, already begun by the indebted and the improvident, to whatsoever degree it may be carried, will be exactly so much taken from the mouths of our own citizens. my anxieties on this subject are the greater, because I remember the deaths which the drought of 1755. in Virginia, produced from the want of food.

There will not be the smallest opposition to the election of Monroe and Tompkins; the republicans being undivided, & the federalists desperate. the Hartford convention, and peace of Ghent, have nearly annihilated them.

Our state is becoming clamorous for a convention & amendment of their constitution, and I believe will obtain it. it was the first constitution formed in the US. and, of course the most imperfect. the other states improved in theirs in proportion as new precedents were added, & most of them have since amended. we have entered on a liberal plan of internal improvements, and the universal approbation of it will encourage and ensure it's prosecution. I recollect nothing else domestic worth noting to you, and therefore place here my respectful and affectionate salutations. TH: JEFFERSON

RC (NHi: Gallatin Papers); holes in manuscript, with missing text supplied from PoC; endorsed by Gallatin. PoC (DLC); on reused address cover of Enoch Reynolds to TJ, 27 June 1816; mutilated at seal, with some missing text rewritten by TJ; at foot of first page: "Albert Gallatin"; notation by TJ at foot of text: "thro' the Sec^y of state's office"; endorsed by TJ. Enclosure: TJ to Madame de Staël Holstein, 6 Sept. 1816.

The members of Congress voted themselves a salary of 1500.D. A YEAR in lieu of a per diem in "An Act to change the mode of compensation to the members of the Senate and House of Representatives, and the delegates from territories." This law was enacted on 19 Mar. 1816 and repealed less than a year later, on 6 Feb. 1817 (*U.S. Statutes at Large*, 3:257–8, 345). TJ correctly predicted that the next Congress would be composed ALMOST WHOLLY OF NEW MEMBERS (*Biog. Dir. Cong.*). TJ's figures for the usual amount of RAIN in his home state in June and August are from his *Notes on the State of Virginia* (*Notes*, ed. Peden, 74).

[1]Preceding two words reworked from "them."

[2]Preceding two words interlined in place of "US."

To Joseph Milligan

Monticello Sep. 8. 16.

You must excuse me, dear Sir, if I trouble you with my inexpressible anxieties about the delay of publication of mr Tracy's book, as I hear nothing of it's commencement altho' you assured me it should be begun the 4th of July. mr Tracy's complaints of me give me a right to complain highly of mr Duane, and now turn to you. pray let me hear from you, and say only what I may depend will be done, & communicate to him as my justification. Accept my best wishes & respects.

TH: JEFFERSON

PoC (DLC); on recto of reused address cover of José Corrêa da Serra to TJ, 16 June 1816; at foot of text: "Mr Joseph Millegan"; endorsed by TJ.

From Francis Adrian Van der Kemp

Dear Sir! Olden barneveld 8 Sept. 1816.

In answer to your favour of July the 30—I must once more return to the papers, which I Send to England for publication; and am Satisfied with the precautions, I deemed requisite, to conceal the author. Since I received last week information from London of the Sudden desease of mr joÿce—whom I had intrusted with the business I then directly adressed mr. Belsham, Solliciting him to inquire about these papers by the heirs of mr. Joyce, take these under his care—and publish these with the Same precautions, and am fully persuaded, that, although he—from having published in 1812 in Lendsey's Mem: its chief parts with your Letts to Dr Priestley.[1]—Can not be mistaken in the author, he Shall not betraÿ his trust. I fully agree with you that a fair and impartial examination of this Subject—on the ground laid by the author must eventually promote truth and establish religion on a basis, which can not be Shaken.

If I am not mistaken in the character of my friends—and I had no hesitation about mr. joyce, there can be no Scruples fostered about its publication in a country, where Basanistes is printed and reprinted—The Liberty of the press is pretty unlimited there—and in it nothing is ridiculed; Here it would be foolishness to try it, as bigotry and intolerance, tho they might not Succeed in persecuting the publication openly, would decry him at least an Atheist, and endeavour to expose him to the insults of a fanatic Rabble. Our young minister has republished here from England a Small tract against the Trinity, Seasoning it, against my entreaties, with Some harsh reflections on one and other of the clergÿ, and Shall, I doubt not gather a harvest of obloquy, as I predicted—It will cool his ardent zeal for truth—and then he Shall become more circumspect, and consequently usefull—I acknowledge however—that forty years ago I Should not have listened much to a doctrine, which I now endeavoured to instil. It is not fear, which makes me reluctant to imitate the hornets—but my peace is at my age too costly a possession to have it disturbed. When thus I intend Something for the Public—I Send it to my friends in England.

I can not blame you, Sir! for waving the answer on Some questions of mÿ Letter—I had no right to ask it, and am not known enough, to be treated with that indulgence. Permit me, however, to observe, that neither a vain curiosity or a Spirit to enter into a controversial correspondence—had the Smallest Share in my inquirÿ—I was lead to it, by what I perused from you, and Seemed to make those answerings desirable. Although I am averse of polemicks, nevertheless, after having perused Some of[2] Belsham masterly performances—and bold advances, I was astonished—to find that he maintained yet a Theses—inadmissible in my opinion—with his fundamental Doctrine of the worship of one God—„that J. could work miracles at pleasure„ I have Send him mÿ objections—and urged their discussion—in one of his next publications.

Basanistes is now on a visit to Quincÿ—I Send another work to N. England—from which, with perfect Safety, a Refutation of the doctrine of the Trinity could be copied—being a careful examination of all the passages—brought forward in its defence—and all rejected, peremptorily by one or more learned Trinitarians.

This winter I Shall endeavour to chalk out a Sketch of the life, proposed bÿ you, and Shall Send you the outlines—to Submitt these to your criticisms.

mr. A: mentions in one of his Last one Tucker's light of nature—I Suppose he is a Virginian—is he a layman?

Permit to request the favour of your remembrance, while I assure you that I am with Sentiments of high respect

Dear Sir your most obed: and obliged Servant

FR: ADR. VAN DER KEMP.

RC (DLC); dateline adjacent to closing; endorsed by TJ as received 5 Oct. 1816 and so recorded in SJL. RC (DLC); address cover only; with PoC of first letter from TJ to Joseph Delaplaine of 25 Dec. 1816 on verso; addressed: "Thomas Jefferson LLD. Monticello Virginia"; franked; postmarked Trenton, N.Y., 10 Sept.

TJ was THE AUTHOR of the writings on Jesus's doctrines. The SMALL TRACT AGAINST THE TRINITY was probably the recently published first American edition of Richard Wright's pamphlet, *An Answer to the Question, Why are you not a Trinitarian?* ([Utica, N.Y.], 1816).

Of MIRACLES, Thomas Belsham wrote that Jesus "possessed a voluntary power of working miracles: but his mind was so disciplined by his temptation, and by other circumstances, as to exercise these powers only upon proper occasions" (*A Calm Inquiry into the Scripture Doctrine concerning the Person of Christ* [London, 1811], 174). In his letter to Van der Kemp of 14 Aug. 1816 (PHi), John Adams (MR. A:) referred to the magnum opus of the English author and LAYMAN Abraham Tucker (*ODNB*).

Van der Kemp advised Adams in a letter dated 7 July 1816 of his plan to publish TJ's syllabus anonymously in England. He stressed the need for secrecy on TJ's authorship (MHi: Adams Papers).

[1] Section from "from having" to this point interlined.

[2] Preceding two words interlined.

From Elizabeth Ticknor

September 10th 1816.

Your favour Sir, of the 15–16th of August was received yesterday.—My husband being an overseer of the University, in which he was educated, is now absent on business for that institution, but, in all probability will return before the arival of the books.—If he does not, I have a friend, who will address them according to your order, and take every possible care, that they are safely sent on to Richmond.—It is with pleasure Sir that I inform you of the receipt of your letter, as its contents are of consequence to you, and as it affords me an opertunity of making a gratefull acknowledgment of the benevolent and friendly favours you shew our son, while he was under your hospitable roof.—Be assured Sir they were felt, sensibly felt, by Mr Ticknor and myself, as well as by our son.

He was well, the 30th of June, and desired an affectionate rememberance to all, who mentioned his name.

Therefore, be so good as to accept it from him, by the hand of his mother, who with due consideration and esteem, has the honor of subscribing herself

your much obliged, and very humble servant

ELIZABETH TICKNOR

RC (MHi); endorsed by TJ as received 19 Sept. 1816 and so recorded in SJL. RC (MHi); address cover only; with PoC of TJ to Charles Willson Peale, 24 Dec. 1816, on recto and verso; addressed: "Honorable Thomas Jefferson Esqr Monticello"; franked; postmarked Boston, 11 Sept.

Elizabeth Billings Curtis Ticknor (1753–1818) was born in Sharon, Massachusetts, where she worked as a schoolteacher. During the Revolutionary War she married Benjamin Curtis, a physician, and had four children with him prior to his death in Boston in 1784. She then resumed her former career and continued it for a time even after her marriage in 1790 to Elisha Ticknor. Her only child by her second marriage was George Ticknor (*DAB*, 9:524; George S. Hillard, ed., *Life, Letters, and Journals of George Ticknor* [1876], 1:3–4; Boston *Massachusetts Centinel*, 27 Nov. 1784; *Boston Daily Advertiser*, 28 Jan. 1819).

TJ's FAVOUR of 15 Aug. 1816 was addressed to Elisha Ticknor. He had recently been named an OVERSEER of his alma mater under New Hampshire statutes of 1816 that superseded the charter of 1769, asserted state control, created new officers, and renamed Dartmouth College as a UNIVERSITY. The United States Supreme Court struck down the acts in 1819 in *Dartmouth College v. Woodward* (Hanover, N.H., *American*, 10 July 1816; Marshall, *Papers*, 8:217–39).

From William Wirt

Dear Sir. Richmond. Sept. 10. 1816

I thank you for the remarks with which you have been so good as to accompany the return of the sheets. The story of Livy I had from Judge Nelson who gave it as a declaration to him from Mr Henry himself. I think with you that the statement must be inaccurate: his indolence forbad it and Livy I find is not among the books left by him, of which I have a catalogue—I have moderated the passage but know not how to reject altogether the statement of a fact so authenticated.—I can tell you with very great sincerity that you have removed a mountain load of despondency from my mind by the assurance that you could find entertainment in those sheets.—I trouble you now with others and beg leave to call your attention particularly to what relates to Mr Pendleton. The passage has given me pain—but truth and the justice due to Mr Henry seemed to require it. If you think it wrong, I am sure you will tell me so, and will suggest some expedient by which equal justice can be done to Mr H. with more delicacy to Mr Pendleton.

I entreat you not to spare your remarks on account of the defacement of the manuscript. I had rather commence it de novo than lose the advantage of your freest criticisms. If you think the narrative too wire-drawn, or the style too turgid (points about which I have, myself, strong fears) I depend on your friendship to tell me so—much better will it be to learn it from you, in time to correct it, than from the malignity of reviewers, when it shall be too late.

There is an anecdote in circulation on the authority of the late Maj^r^ scott which if true I should like to weave in, and if true you will certainly remember it. It is said that about the year 1769, Mr Henry, spoke, in the House of Burgesses, on some question of public grievance, with so much power that the people in the lobby and gallery were excited to a kind of frenzy, rushed to the top of the capitol, tore down the royal standard which usually waved there during the session, tore it into fragments and scattered[1] to the winds—Will you be so obliging as to say whether you recollect, at any time, an occurrence of this sort?

most respectfully and affectionately, yours. W^M^ Wirt

RC (DLC); at foot of text: "Mr Jefferson"; endorsed by TJ as received 26 Sept. 1816 and so recorded in SJL. Tr (MdHi: Wirt Papers). Enclosure: manuscript, not found, of a portion of Wirt, *Patrick Henry*.

Wirt ultimately decided not to reject a passage asserting that Patrick Henry read Livy "through, once at least, in every year, during the earlier part of his life," but he included a footnote crediting the story to a conversation between Henry and a "Judge Nelson" (Wirt, *Patrick Henry*, 13).

[1] Tr here adds "it."

From Samuel Butler (for Hezekiah Niles)

SIR Baltimore 11th Sept. 1816.—

On the rec^t of your very polite and friendly favor of 7h Sept I had a serch made into my last years books and old letters—and have the mortification to state, that you made a remittance, as you mention, in march last of Ten dollars which through hurry of business had been neglectted to be passed to your credit, and which with the Five in your last letter pays your subscription up to September next Year—all that can be done is to beg your pardon for the past, and to be more correct in future, but out of 3000 small accounts it would be almost miraculous if some errors did not creep in amongst them—

I [am][1] much pleased and gratified to find that the proposed Index meets your approbation—

With sentiment of respect and esteem I am your Humble Servt

for H. Niles

S. BUTLER

RC (DLC); at foot of text: "Honbl Thos Jefferson Esqr"; endorsed by TJ as a letter concerning "Newspapers" from "<*Butler S.*> Niles H." received 18 Sept. 1816. Recorded in SJL as received 18 Sept. 1816 from Butler, with the entry canceled and a new one added giving Niles as the author.

Samuel Butler (ca. 1765–1826), bookseller, moved by 1800 to Baltimore, probably from Portsmouth, New Hampshire. He operated his own bookshop for a decade after his arrival and worked for Niles from about 1816 until at least 1818. Butler died in Baltimore (DNA: RG 29, CS, Md., Baltimore, 1800; *The New Baltimore Directory, and Annual Register; for 1800 and 1801* [Baltimore, n.d.], 24; Butler to William W. Woodward, 30 Mar. 1807 [PPL]; William Fry, *The Baltimore Directory for 1810* [Baltimore, 1810], 42; Butler [for Niles] to TJ, 16 Dec. 1818; *Baltimore Patriot & Mercantile Advertiser*, 2 Sept. 1826; *Portsmouth Journal of Literature & Politics*, 16 Sept. 1826).

TJ's missing FAVOR OF 7H SEPT is entered in SJL as a letter of 6 Sept. 1816 to "Niles Henry." TJ recorded his payment of $5 to Niles "for Weekly register to Sep. 1817" as having been made on 7 Sept. 1816, however. He had remitted $10 on 22 Mar. 1815, not IN MARCH LAST (*MB*, 2:1307, 1326).

Niles proposed in the 25 Feb. 1815 issue of his journal to publish a general INDEX for its first ten volumes. A quotation from TJ supporting this idea, which was presumably taken from the missing letter of 6 or 7 Sept. 1816 noted above, was printed in *Niles' Weekly Register* on 23 Nov. 1816: "I am much pleased to find you propose to make a *general index*. That alone is wanting to complete the utility of the work."

[1] Omitted word editorially supplied.

From Mathew Carey

SIR, Philad[a] Sept. 12. 1816

Your favour of the 1st inst. which I Rec[d] a few days since, is before me.

Of the whole list of Books you wish, there are only three remain, of which I annex the Invoice. They shall be sent by the first opportunity in a Box to Fitzwhylsonn & Potter, my correspondents at Richmond, with directions to deliver them to Mes[rs] Gibson & Jefferson.

I remain, respectfully, Your ob[t] h[ble] serv[t] MATHEW CAREY

RC (MHi); dateline at foot of text; with enclosure on verso of address leaf; addressed (in a clerk's hand): "Thomas Jefferson Esq[r] Monticello V[a]"; franked; postmarked Philadelphia, 12 Sept.; endorsed by TJ as received 19 Sept. 1816 and so recorded in SJL.

ENCLOSURE

Mathew Carey's Invoice for Books

Phil[a] 12[h] sep[r] 1816

Tho[s] Jefferson Esq[r]
Bo[t] of Mathew Carey

To Vandale Super Arest	$2
Bonnycastle's Algebra	.50
Potters Mathematics	1.25
	$3.75

MS (MHi); written in a clerk's hand on verso of address leaf of covering letter.

From Stephen Kingston

SIR Philadelphia 12 Sept[r] 1816

In the pursuit of Justice no excuse is necessary for addresing it's general advocate I therefore take the liberty of inclosing the papers herewith. As the principle at issue has been under your consideration, permit me to entreat you will have the goodness to peruse those documents & favor me with your opinion whether this case is not within the spirit of the treaty of 1783? I need not add the high sense with which the favor solicited will be received.

With great sincerity of Respect and consideration I have the honor to subscribe Sir Your most Obedient and humble servant

STEPHEN KINGSTON

Be kind enough to return M[r] Harris's letter.

RC (DLC); between dateline and salutation: "Thomas Jefferson Esqr"; postscript adjacent to closing and signature; endorsed by TJ as received 19 Sept. 1816 and so recorded in SJL.

Stephen Kingston (d. 1836), merchant, was born in Ireland and immigrated to the United States as a minor by 1783. He settled in Philadelphia shortly thereafter. President James Madison appointed Kingston United States consul at Havana in 1812, but the Spanish government there soon forced him to leave the island. He subsequently returned to his adopted hometown, and he retired from trade in the mid-1820s (Philadelphia *Independent Gazetteer; or, the Chronicle of Freedom*, 16 Apr. 1785; DNA: RG 29, CS, Pa., Philadelphia, 1790, 1830; *PTJ*, 25:626–8; Madison, *Papers, Pres. Ser.*, 4:79; *JEP*, 2:240, 241 [24, 25 Mar. 1812]; Kingston to James Monroe, 12 Sept. 1812 [DNA: RG 59, CD, Havana]; Kingston to John Rhea, 25 Jan. 1814 [DNA: RG 59, LAR, 1809–17]; Thomas Wilson, ed., *The Philadelphia Directory and Stranger's Guide, for 1825* [Philadelphia, 1825], 79; Philadelphia *Poulson's American Daily Advertiser*, 9 Feb. 1836).

The enclosed PAPERS, not found, accompanied a note from Kingston that reads "Mr Jefferson is respectfully requested to return the inclosed to S.K." (MS in DLC: TJ Papers, 208:37062; undated; unsigned; endorsed by TJ as received 19 Sept. 1816 and so recorded in SJL). The documents apparently pertained to a controversy over a piece of land in Philadelphia that Kingston had purchased in 1807 "from William and John Oxley and others in the island of Barbadoes." A question "whether the wills of said Oxley's ancestors have been proved conformable to the laws of Pennsylvania" later cast doubt on Kingston's title. The case dragged on in the courts until November 1823, when the state supreme court confirmed Kingston's right to two-thirds of the property. Five years later the Pennsylvania legislature affirmed his title to the final third (*Journal of the Senate of the Commonwealth of Pennsylvania* [1813–14 sess.], 95; *Facts, and Observations on the Facts, originating the bill, entitled "An Act for the Relief of Stephen Kingston"* [Philadelphia, 1815]; Thomas Sergeant and William Rawle Jr., *Reports of Cases adjudged in the Supreme Court of Pennsylvania*, 3d ed. [1851–75], 10:382–91; *Laws of the Commonwealth of Pennsylvania, from the fourteenth day of October, one thousand seven hundred* [1810–44], 10:143 [10 Apr. 1828]).

Kingston seems to be referring to the fifth article of the TREATY of Paris of 1783, which dealt with "the Restitution of all Estates, Rights and Properties" owned by British citizens that had been seized during the Revolutionary War (Miller, *Treaties*, 2:154).

To Patrick Gibson

DEAR SIR Monticello, Sep. 13, 16

Since sending you my letter of the 10th to the post office a call of 200 D. is made upon me which had been agreed to be delayed until my produce should have been sold in the next spring but the party assigned it to another who now required it without regard to that arrangement. I am obliged to draw for it on you in favor of Branham & Jones of Charlottesville. I do this with reluctance because I am sure the state of my account with you does not authorize me. I will immediately after the expiration of the present month hurry down flour both from here and Bedford to cover this, as well as the draughts for my taxes for both places which will soon come upon us, as mentioned in my former letter.

Accept the assurances of my great esteem and respect

TH. JEFFERSON

Typescript (ViHi: Thomas Jefferson Papers); adjacent to signature: "Mr. Gibson"; with the manuscript from which this transcript was taken reportedly on verso of a reused address cover to TJ and endorsed by him.

TJ's letter to Gibson OF THE 10TH is recorded in SJL but has not been found. He summarized it at that date in his financial records: "Renewed my note in bank for 2000.D. date Sep. 24. Desired P. Gibson to pay to Sheriff Henrico 42.29 taxes on my 4. lots in Beverly town from 1787. to 1797 inclusive" (*MB*, 2:1326).

A missing letter from Bramham & Jones to TJ of 12 Sept. 1816 is recorded in SJL as received the same day. On 17 Sept. 1816 TJ indicated that he had been OBLIGED TO DRAW an "order on Gibson & Jefferson for 200.D. in favr. Branham and Jones assees. of my note to Elijah Ham ante Mar. 24," a debt resulting from Ham's service as overseer at TJ's Lego plantation (*MB*, 2:1321, 1326).

To Joel Yancey

DEAR SIR Monticello Sep. 13. 16.

Yours of Aug. 29. came to hand on the 4th inst. I had packed and was to have set off for Pop. For. with mrs Randolph and some of the family on Monday the 2d inst. but on the Sunday recieved a visit which detained us till these rains begun. they still continue & were they now to stop it will be still some days before we can cross James river: I therefore find it necessary to write, as some things are pressing. for the taxes which you mention, as well as those here to the State & general government which will all be soon upon us, I must pray you to get down some flour, if it be only a single load to recruit my funds with mr Gibson whereon to draw for the taxes. also as we cannot have the benefit of our offal there[1] by finding barrels, & here I can engage any quantity of offal at it's present price in exchange for barrels at 43. cents equal to 2/8, I have actually engaged for 1000. bushels over and above my own in exchange for barrels to be delivered as quick as possible. I must therefore pray you to send off Barnaby [and] Nace immediately, hoping they have done your hogsheads: if they have not let them do them without delay & come off. we will determine what to do with the barrels & staves they have prepared when I come up.—I had planted here as much corn ground as, in an ordinary year, would have made about 700. barrels. but no part of the country suffered with the drought as much as this neighborhood, as far as I have heard. of the fine rain you had the 1st of June, which detained me, not a drop fell here. so that my expectations here were reduced to 150. barrels when these rains commenced. it is possible they may advance now to 250. it is thought the price here will start at 5.D. I hope you have these rains & that they will give you corn enough for the year. there has already fallen between 9. & 10.I. with us, & it is still raining. your letter relieves me as to Francis. having never had a line from him I had become quite uneasy. I shall feel Cap[t] Martin's disappointment very heavily. as we shall be obliged to get our stocks sawed by hand & to work them green & for outside work too. John Hemings & his two aids will set out so as to be at Poplar forest the evening before us. I salute you with great friendship & respect

TH: JEFFERSON

PoC (MHi); on verso of reused address cover of Joseph Delaplaine to TJ, 6 July 1816; mutilated at seal; at foot of text: "M[r] Yancey"; endorsed by TJ.

TJ was at Poplar Forest at the beginning of July 1816 but not THE 1ST OF JUNE (*MB*; SJL). FRANCIS: Francis Eppes.

[1]Word interlined.

From John Payne Todd

MY DEAR SIR Mont Pelier 14th Sep[r] 16.

I take the liberty of introducing[1] to you, M[r] Valaperta, an artist of considerable merit and reputation.

His object in visiting Monticello, should he be so fortunate as to find you at home, is to ask your permission to take your bust in clay, or your profile in Wax with a view to work it afterwards in ivory, to perform either, he says will be attended with little trouble to you, and the latter particularly may be done in two sittings, and those not long ones.

with the highest Consideration and respect y[r] very devoted S[t]

JOHN P. TODD

RC (MHi); at foot of text: "Th: Jefferson Esq[re]"; endorsed by TJ as a letter from "Todd Paine" received 16 Sept. 1816 and so recorded in SJL, which adds that it was delivered "by Vallaperta."

Giuseppe Valaperta (d. 1817?), sculptor, was born in Milan and worked in Italy, in Spain, and in France at Napoleon's imperial residence of Malmaison. Having been convinced to visit the United States by William Lee, the American consul at Bordeaux, he arrived in Washington in the autumn of 1815 armed with Lee's letters of introduction. By early in February 1816 Valaperta had agreed to help refurbish the United States Capitol. He designed and executed the American eagle on the entablature frieze in the Hall of the House of Representatives. Valaperta also created wax bas-relief portraits of James Madison, James Monroe, TJ, and other notables. His likeness of TJ is reproduced elsewhere in this volume. A contemporary newspaper reported, however, that Valaperta's "health and mind were much impaired" by his labors; that "After a short illness, he became completely deranged"; and that "He often repeated, that he had worked enough, and that it was time for him to rest." On 4 Mar. 1817 Valaperta disappeared from his lodgings. He was presumed to have committed suicide, although his body was never found (Alexander J. Wall, "Joseph Valaperta, Sculptor," *New-York Historical Society Quarterly Bulletin* 11 [1927]: 53–6; Groce and Wallace, *Dictionary of Artists*, 643; Latrobe, *Papers*, 3:719, 726–7; Bush, *Life Portraits*, 68–70; Washington *Daily National Intelligencer*, 4 Nov. 1815, 29 Nov. 1816, 10 Mar., 28 Apr. 1817).

[1]Manuscript: "intrducing."

To William W. Hening

Dear Sir Monticello Sep. 15. 16.

The Committee of Congress, on the purchase of my library having chosen to take it as stated in the Catalogue, I was not at liberty to retain a single volume. consequently those of your collection of the laws, which you had been so kind as to send me, all went. I have therefore to ask the favor of you to send me a compleat collection of all the volumes you have published, and to have the bill presented to mr Gibson who will pay it. they will come safely by the Charlottesville mail-stage, if put on board in the moment of it's departure; otherwise they will let it lie in their stage office for months neglected. address it to the Postmaster at Milton. will you also be so good as to tell me when you think the next volume will be out, and how low it will come down as I wish to make now [a com]pleat collection from that date to the present day. indeed [I s]hould be glad to know how low you will continue it. why not to the present day? I salute you with esteem & respect. Th: Jefferson

PoC (DLC); on verso of reused address cover of William Lee to TJ, 11 May 1816; torn at seal; at foot of text: "Mr Wm W. Hening"; endorsed by TJ.

The committee of congress was the Joint Library Committee.

To Nicolas G. Dufief

Dear Sir Monticello Sep. 16. 16.

Your favor of the 6th with the MS. accompanying it comes to hand just as I am preparing to set out on a journey of considerable time and distance. I am therefore able to give it but a hasty perusal. this added to my want of familiarity with the technical methods of conveying instruction makes me an inadequate judge of that you propose. I have not indeed heretofore made myself acquainted, but very generally, with those of Pestalozzi & Lancaster. they are calculated for cities or large towns, but not at all for the sparse settlements in the country I inhabit. I have neglected them therefore as useless to us. I believe they have only been proposed for elementary instruction in the mother tongue. your idea, if I rightly comprehend it is to extend a method of somewhat similar effect to the acquisition of foreign languages. such an abridgment of the ordinary process would certainly be very beneficial, and the reduction of the expence [of] instruction to a few shillings would incalculably[1] extend the advantages of education. but of the probability of it's success I must repeat that I am an incompetent judge. of the value of your Nature displayed and of your Dictionary, I have before fully expressed my high estimate; and have further proved it by the many copies of both which I have purchased & given to those in whose education I take an interest; and altho to us in the country the process now proposed would be inapplicable, I sincerely wish it success for the benefit of those in towns as well as for your own. I now return the MS. with the assurance of my great esteem & respect.

TH: JEFFERSON

PoC (DLC); on verso of a reused address cover from Benjamin Waterhouse to TJ; mutilated at seal, with one of the two damaged words rewritten by TJ; at foot of text: "M. Dufief"; endorsed by TJ. Enclosure: enclosure to Dufief to TJ, 6 Sept. 1816.

[1] Manuscript: "incalculaby."

From John Graham

Dept of State 16th Sepr 1816.

J Graham presents his most Respectful Compliments to mr Jefferson, and in transmitting to him the enclosed Packet which has just been received at this Dept has the pleasure to inform him, that his Letter to mr Gallatin was forwarded under Cover with Despatches for that Gentleman, the day after it was received.

RC (DLC); dateline at foot of text; endorsed by TJ as received 19 Sept. 1816 and so recorded in SJL. Enclosure: Franclieu to TJ, 6 June 1816, and enclosures.

From Lafayette

MY DEAR FRIEND La Grange 7ber 16h 1816

I Cannot Let gal Bernard Embark with His Amiable Lady and family for America without a line to You. that Eminent officer Has Been Honour'd with the only Exception to the determination of Government Not to Employ foreigners in the Army of the U.S. I think He deserves the Confered distinction, Not only on Account of His Great talents, and deep knowledge in His Line, But also Because I Never Saw a disposition of mind more Unassuming, disinterested, and Conciliatory. Emperor Napoleon Struck with the Abilities and Economy He display'd in fortifying Antwerpt Surprised Him with an Invitation to Become His aid de Camp, in which Capacity He Remained a Stranger to the intrigues, Rewards, and principles of the Court. an avowed patriot, He is Confessed by all parties to Be the Excellent man whom I pourtray to You. I Believe He may Render great Services as An Engineer, and am also persuaded, from the intentions He Has Expressed in His visit to me, that His Companions will Love Him for His Eagerness to adjust matters in the way the Most Agreable to them. I Shall only add that we are all well, children, grandchildren, and myself. this Short letter is posting after g[al] Bernard to the Havre. You know the Sentiments of Your Affectionate friend

LAFAYETTE

RC (DLC); endorsed by TJ as received 27 Feb. 1817 and so recorded in SJL. RC (MoSHi: TJC-BC); address cover only; with PoC of TJ to Jethro Wood, 23 Mar. 1817, on verso; addressed: "Thomas Jefferson [Esq.] Monticelo Virginia favour'd By g[al] Bernard." Enclosed in Simon Bernard to TJ, 21 Feb. 1817.

Simon Bernard (1779–1839), military engineer, was a native of Dole, France, and graduate of the École Polytechnique in Paris. He entered the French army as a lieutenant of engineers in 1797 and was promoted to captain three years later. Bernard helped to fortify Antwerp, 1810–12, and he became one of Napoleon's aides-de-camp in 1813. He served the emperor faithfully until the latter's downfall the following year. Although Bernard accepted a military appointment under the restored Bourbons, he rejoined Napoleon during the Hundred Days and fought with him at the Battle of Waterloo. Following his arrival in the United States, on 16 Nov. 1816 Bernard became an assistant engineer in the United States Army with the pay of a brigadier general, and he sat on the War Department's board for improving border and coastal defenses, 1816–31. During the 1820s he also labored on the government's internal improvements board, where he helped to plan roads and canals. After Louis Philippe ascended the French throne in 1830, Bernard resigned his post on 10 Aug. 1831 and returned to his native land. There he was promoted to lieutenant general, raised to the peerage, made inspector general of engineers, and employed as minister of war, 1834 and 1836–39 (*ANB*; *DAB*; *DBF*; Charles Mullié, *Biographie des Célébrités Militaires des Armées de Terre et de Mer de 1789 a 1850* [1851], 62; Heitman, *U.S. Army*, 1:214; Washington *Daily National Intelligencer*, 9 Dec. 1839; gravestone inscription in the Cimetière de Montmartre, Paris).

From Joseph E. McIlhenney

DEAR SIR Winchester Septr 17th 1816

Mr Peale of Philad[a] called upon my brother, and told him, he had reacieved a letter from you, requesting him to procure a young man, who would be willing to settle in Charlottsville. He, as a particular friend of my brothers, advised him to communicate the circumstance to me; which he did in a letter of the 5th Instant. I immeadiately answer'd his letter, and requested him to inform Mr Peale, I would with pleasure except of the offer. He wrote me that mr Peale would inform you of my intended visit. He also advised me, (as a preliminary step) to address a fiew lines to you with a view of knowing wether you had return'd to Monticello; which place you had left (as he acquainted me) on a journey. Mr Peale represents the place as a very good cituation for a Watch Maker.

I am respectfully Yours &Ca— Jos E McIlhenney

P.S. I shall remain in this place untill I reaceive an answer. I have been abcent from Phlada during the summer; and was on the point of returning when I reacd the above intelegance. J E McI—

RC (MHi); endorsed by TJ as received 5 Oct. 1816 and so recorded in SJL. RC (MHi); address cover only; with PoC of TJ to Chapman Johnson, 26 Dec. 1816, on verso; addressed: "Thoms Jefferson, Esqr Monticello Va"; franked; postmarked Winchester, 28 Sept.

Joseph E. McIlhenney (ca. 1795–1873), clockmaker and dentist, was a native of Pennsylvania. He soon decided against moving to Charlottesville and returned instead to Philadelphia, where he lived thereafter. He worked as a clock- and watchmaker, both alone and in partnership with Thomas G. West, until at least 1825. Later in the 1820s McIlhenney became a dentist, in which profession he amassed a considerable fortune. He owned real estate worth $25,000 in 1850 and $45,000 twenty years later (Charles Willson Peale to TJ, 28 Feb. 1817; John Adems Paxton, *The Philadelphia Directory and Register, for 1818* [Philadelphia, 1818]; Philadelphia *Poulson's American Daily Advertiser*, 2 Oct. 1820; Philadelphia *Saturday Evening Post*, 7 Aug. 1824; Thomas Wilson, ed., *The Philadelphia Directory and Stranger's Guide, for 1825* [Philadelphia, 1825], 90; *Philadelphia Directory and Stranger's Guide, 1829* [1829], 122; DNA: RG 29, CS, Pa., Philadelphia, 1850, 1870; *Philadelphia Inquirer*, 25 Mar. 1873).

To David Gelston

Dear Sir Monticello Sep. 18. 16.

Your favor of Aug. 31. did not come to hand but by yesterday's mail, delayed I presume by the late extraordinary floods. it brings me the first notice of the arrival of my books which I have been 3. or 4. months expecting. but I have not yet recieved either invoice or letter. as we ought to suppose they came by the same ship, tomorrow's mail may perhaps bring them, in which case you shall have the invoice instantly. the day after tomorrow I shall set out on a journey of 3. weeks, which, if it arrives afterwards may occasion that delay in your receipt of it. in the mean time it may not be amiss that the books should remain with you till the equinoctial weather is over, as their loss would be a great affliction to me they are what I wrote for as most necessary on parting with my library to Congress. I return the bill of lading & Hottinguer & co's letter and salute you with friendly esteem and respect. Th: Jefferson

RC (CLjC, 2002). RC (Grace Floyd Delafield Robinson, Greenport, N.Y., 1947); address cover only; addressed: "David Gelston esq. New York"; franked; postmarked Milton, 18 Sept.; endorsement by Gelston reads, in part, "Books." PoC (MHi); on verso of a reused address cover from George Logan to TJ; mutilated at seal, with some words rewritten by TJ; endorsed by TJ. Enclosures: enclosures to Gelston to TJ, 31 Aug. 1816.

Heavy, incessant rainfall earlier this month had caused extraordinary floods in Virginia (*Richmond Enquirer*, 14 Sept. 1816).

To Alexander H. Everett

Monticello Sep. 19. 16.

Th: Jefferson returns to mr Everett his thanks for the care he has been so good as to take of the Programme of the Harlaem society of sciences, recieved from mr Van Marum, and now come safe to hand: and he avails himself with pleasure of this occasion of assuring him of his great esteem and respect.

RC (MHi: Everett-Peabody Family Papers); dateline at foot of text; addressed: "M[r] Everett Boston"; franked; postmarked Milton, 20 Sept. PoC (DLC); on verso of reused address cover of A. D. Saunders to TJ, 26 June 1816; endorsed by TJ.

To James Fishback

Sir Monticello Sep. 19. 16.

Presuming that a copy of your oration delivered in Lexington on the 4th of July last, which came inclosed to me yesterday, may have come from yourself, I take the liberty of addressing to you my thanks for this mark of attention. I have read it with satisfaction, a single paragraph only in the following words excepted. 'mr Jefferson, it is said, declared that when he was in Paris, atheism was the common table-talk of the French bishops.' I protest to you, Sir, that I never made such a declaration; and that as far as my knolege of that order of clergy enabled me to judge, it would have been entirely untrue. when speaking of the religious freedom, in matters of opinion, and conversation, practised in that country, in opposition to laws never put in execution but against what is printed, I may have said, what was true, that 'I had heard the doctrines of atheism maintained at table in mixed company,' but never by a bishop, nor even in presence of a bishop. such rudeness would not have been committed by any man of decent manners, nor witnessed without offence by any society. the importance of religion to society has too many founded supports to need aid from imputations so entirely unfounded. I am persuaded of the innocence with which you have introduced this matter of report: but being myself quoted by name, and in print too, as the author of such a calumny on a respectable order of prelates, I owe to them, as well as to myself, to declare that no such declaration, or expression, was ever uttered by me. trusting it will be as acceptable to yourself to recieve this truth, as it has been incumbent on me to testify it, I pray you to accept the assurance of my great respect.

TH: JEFFERSON

RC (NNGL, on deposit NHi); mutilated at seal, with missing text supplied from PoC; at foot of text: "M[r] James Fishback." PoC (DLC).

The recently received ORATION was Fishback's *An Oration delivered in the First Presbyterian Church in the Town of Lexington, Ky. On the 4th day of July, 1816* (Lexington, Ky., 1816; Poor, *Jefferson's Library*, 13 [no. 826]; TJ's copy in ViU is inscribed by the author to "Thos Jefferson"). The work was dedicated "To the Christian Republicans in these United States, the *real* friends of American Independence." Just prior to the sentence about atheism being a common topic of conversation among French bishops, Fishback argued that "It was the corruption of religion, or rather its destruction, with a correspondent profligacy of manners, which caused the sanguinary scenes of the French revolution, and incapacitated that nation for civil liberty" (p. 19).

To David Gelston

DEAR SIR Monticello Sep. 19. 16.

I wrote yesterday morning in answer to yours of Aug. 31. and in the evening recieved the Invoice you requested, which I now inclose with mr Warden's letters & other papers. I will thank you for the return of these when they shall have answered your purpose. as I presume the usual apprehensions from Equinoctial gales are not of many days, I will request you to forward the books to Richmond as usual as soon as you think it safe; and the rather that they may get up our river before winter sets in. if you will have the goodness to drop me a note of the amount of expences attending these, & the cases of wines, they shall be immediately remitted. I salute you with great esteem & respect

TH: JEFFERSON

RC (ViU: TJP); addressed: "David Gelston esquire New York"; franked; postmarked Milton, 20 Sept.; endorsement by Gelston reads, in part, "Books." PoC

(MHi); on verso of reused address cover of Peyton Randolph to TJ, 16 July 1816; endorsed by TJ. Enclosures: (1) David Bailie Warden to TJ, 12 July 1816, and enclosure. (2) Warden to TJ, 14 July 1816, and enclosures.

OUR RIVER: the Rivanna River.

Agreement with Thomas Eston Randolph & Company, with Jefferson's Note

Shadwell Mill 19th Septr 1816—We agree to deliver to the order of Thos Jefferson Esqr Six hundred bushels of Shipstuff at eighteen-pence ℘er bushel to be deducted from the first quarters Rent—and to be deliver'd vizt 200 bushels in the second week of October next,—200—on the 1st Novr and the remaining 200 on the 1st Decr

THOS ESTON RANDOLPH & CO

[*Note by TJ:*]
1816. Oct. 18. there being a misunderstanding as to the within, we rescinded it, and agreed that I should be furnished by mr T. E. Randolph with 600. bushels certain of shipstuff, and that I should have the offer of as much more as he shall have to spare all to be paid for at two shillings the bushel, cash or barrels @ 40. cents as should suit me. TH:J.

MS (MHi); written on a small scrap, with recto in Randolph's hand and verso in TJ's hand, including his endorsement: "Randolph Thos E."

SHIPSTUFF is inferior wheat flour (*OED*).

From John Payne Todd

DEAR SIR Mont Pelier Sepr 19th—16.

I take the liberty of mentioning that Mr Labarshette, who will have the honor of paying his respects; brought a letter from Genl Lafayette to the President, and carries with him, a certificate from the same, of services rendered by his father and himself during our Revolution; which are titles certainly to civility.

I have the honor to be with the most profound respt yr St

JOHN P. TODD.

RC (MHi); endorsed by TJ as received 20 Sept. 1816 and so recorded in SJL. RC (DLC); address cover only; with PoC of TJ to James Barbour, 19 Jan.

1817, on recto; addressed: "Thomas Jefferson Esqre Monticello" by "Mr Labarshette."

MR LABARSHETTE was Barthélémy Sernin du Moulin, baron de Montlezun de Labarthette.

Montlezun's Account of a Visit to Monticello

Vendredi 20 *septembre* 1816.[1] *Voyage de Montpellier à Monticello* (*Albemarle*).

A sept heures du matin, je suis parti de Bentivoglio, Couper's-Tavern; et de nouveau, traversant les bois, j'ai passé à trois milles de là, devant la maison du juge Gordon, d'où je suis allé franchir à gué le North-River, près de Milton, très-petit village.

A trois milles plus loin est situé Monticello, sur une élévation considérable, d'où l'on domine l'horizon à quarante-cinq milles de distance. J'y suis arrivé à deux heures, au moment où l'ex-président Jefferson allait se mettre à table, devant partir aussitôt après, et se rendre à une autre terre qu'il possède près de New-London, en Virginie.

M. Jefferson, après m'avoir montré les principaux points de vue à la ronde, et aussi plusieurs objets très-curieux, m'a invité à dîner.

Au sortir de table, et après m'avoir poliment engagé à rester chez lui, malgré son départ, il est monté en calèche à quatre chevaux, accompagné de madame Randolph et de deux de ses petites filles.

Je suis rentré avec M. Randolph fils, qui m'a fait voir le muséum, situé à l'entrée de la maison. Il s'y trouve des choses excessivement rares, et d'autres que l'on ne trouverait nulle part ailleurs, entre autres la mâchoire supérieure du mammouth. Elle a été trouvée dans le Kentucky. C'est d'après elle que M. Péale a fait exécuter le *fac-simile* avec lequel il a complété son mammouth du muséum de Philadelphie. La tête est complette, mais la mâchoire inférieure n'est pas du même individu. Deux autres pièces infiniment curieuses sont: 1° un tableau indien représentant une bataille; il est sur peau de bufle, d'environ cinq pieds carrés. Il y a quatre lignes de combattans. Sur chaque ligne sont des chevaux peints en rouge et en vert, opposés un contre un, de même que les guerriers, armés et costumés à la manière des sauvages. 2° Une carte géographique, aussi sur peau de bufle, de six pieds carrés, sans le moindre défaut. Elle représente une partie du cours du Missouri, et ne laisse pas que d'être bien entendue, quoique grossièrement tracée. Les explications ont été écrites en français par des interprètes.

On y voit aussi une défense de mammouth, et une d'éléphant, avec une dent de ce dernier animal pour faire voir combien elle diffère de celles du mammouth; ces dernières étant coniques, et désignant un animal carnivore, tandis que l'autre, plate et rayée au couronnement, caractérise le frugivore.

Une tête de bélier gigantesque; on suppose que l'animal dont elle faisait partie appartient à la race primitive qui existait dans l'Amérique du nord.

M. Randolph m'a ensuite fait voir les tableaux et portraits qui ornent les différentes salles.

Les portraits de Washington, LaFayette, Adams, Francklin, Walter-Raleigh, Améric-Vespuce, Colomb, Bacon, Locke, Newton, etc., etc.

En tableaux: un mort sortant du tombeau pour rendre témoignage;

La reddition de Cornwallis en octobre 1781, à Yorck-Town, en Virginie;

Diogène cherchant un homme;

Alexandre et Diogène;

Démocrite et Héraclite, etc., etc., etc.

J'ai vu en outre:

Une griffe d'ours, du Missouri. Cette espèce est de plus grande taille et beaucoup plus féroce que les autres;

Une défense de mammouth;

Plusieurs dents du même animal;

L'os de la cuisse du même.

La tête du mammouth que l'on voit ici, est formée, comme je l'ai déjà dit, de la mâchoire supérieure qui est parfaite, et de deux demi-mâchoires inférieures provenant d'individus différens; l'une de ces dernières est de plus forte dimension que l'autre.

Cote de maille européenne, dont se servaient, dans le principe, ceux qui faisaient la guerre contre les Indiens. Ils étaient, par ce moyen, sans danger d'être blessés par leurs flèches.

Bois de l'élan d'Amérique, et d'autres animaux du même genre. Ceux des premiers sont très-considérables; ces animaux, ainsi que les bufles et plusieurs autres, ont été détruits dans les parties de la Virginie où la population s'est pressée. On les retrouve sur le territoire de l'Ohio, où la grande quantité de chasseurs les a forcés de se reléguer.

Deux bustes en pierres sculptés par les sauvages; l'un représentant un homme, l'autre une femme. Les figures sont hideuses, et très-grossièrement travaillées. Elles étaient sans doute consacrées au culte, et ne laissent pas que d'avoir infiniment de rapport avec ces divinités des Égyptiens et des Orientaux, dont les images sont gravées dans la plupart des livres qui traitent de ces peuples.

Petite hache indienne en espèce de porphyre poli; le dessus en forme de pipe;

Figure d'animal, de la même qualité de pierre;

Pétrifications diverses.

Des arcs, des flèches, des lances et une foule d'objets fabriqués par les sauvages;

Statue en marbre, grandeur de nature, semblable à celle de Cléopâtre. Elle est couchée; un serpent est roulé autour de son bras gauche. Copie d'après l'antique.

M. Jefferson pense qu'elle représente Ariane.

Dent d'éléphant. Cette dent, qui annonce un animal graminivore, diffère totalement de celles du mammouth. Néanmoins, on pense généralement que ce dernier n'est autre que l'éléphant.

Quoi qu'il en soit, je suis et demeure convaincu que M. Peale (de Philadelphie) a commis un contre-sens impardonnable et choquant, lorsqu'il a placé ses défenses les pointes contre terre, en pose inverse de l'éléphant.

Je n'ai aucun doute que ce ne soit contre sa persuasion intime; mais par des vues intéressées, il a voulu présenter au public un animal particulier, extraordinaire et inconnu, afin d'attirer un plus grand nombre de curieux, regardant et payant. *In omnibus respice finem*:

> En todo caso convenia mirar el fin.
>
> HERRERA.

En voyant le squelette de mammouth, du muséum de Peale, j'aurais volontiers écrit dessus ces quatre vers:

> Votre mammouth, ainsi que le voilà,
> N'est qu'une choquante imposture;
> En redressant ces deux défenses-là,
> Vous imiterez la nature. . . .[2]

Le muséum (qui est à l'entrée de la maison de M. Jefferson) est hors de proportion avec elle, et la fait paraître encore plus petite qu'elle n'est. Au-dehors règne une plateforme en gazon, d'où la vue s'étend au loin de toutes parts, excepté vers le sud-est, où se trouve un morne beaucoup plus élevé que Monticello, qu'il domine de très-près.

Précisément dans la ligne du sud on aperçoit, à quatorze ou quinze lieues, la hauteur dite *Wallace's-Mountain;* elle a précisément la forme, l'élévation, et les dimensions de la grande pyramide d'Égypte; laquelle, vue à la même distance que cette hauteur, isolée au milieu de vastes plaines, paraîtrait exactement comme cette dernière vue de Monticello.

De Wallace's-Mountain, jusque vers le nord-est, s'étend une immense plaine qui semble confiner à la mer. L'horizon est à la distance de quarante-cinq milles.

Vers le nord, est une autre plaine limitée par les montagnes bleues. Au nord-est, on aperçoit quelques montagnes du Maryland, et la chaîne de celles dites du sud-ouest, en ligne parallèle des montagnes bleues.

Au nord-ouest, est située Charlotte-Ville, très-petit endroit au centre d'un pays plat, et peu distant de North-River.

M. Jefferson est âgé de soixante-treize ans, et n'a pas l'air d'en avoir plus de soixante-trois. Son petits-fils, qui a six pieds quatre pouces, me disait que, parmi les habitans des montagnes dans les environs, il était de la taille ordinaire. Les femmes que j'ai eu occasion de voir dans cette contrée, sont jolies, fraîches et de grande taille.

M. Randolph m'a montré une carte particulière, indiquant le voyage des capitaines Lewis et Clarke, qui, suivis de quarante-quatre hommes, traversèrent la totalité du vaste territoire qui s'étend de l'Atlantique à la mer du Sud....[3]

A quatre heures, j'ai pris congé de M. Randolph pour me rendre chez M. Monroe, qui habite à trois milles de la résidence de l'ex-président Jefferson.

J'y suis arrivé à six heures; et le colonel, secrétaire-d'état, m'a très-civilement accueilli.

EDITORS' TRANSLATION

Friday 20 September 1816. Trip from Montpellier to Monticello (Albemarle).

I departed from Bentivoglio, Couper's-Tavern, at seven o'clock in the morning; and, once again going through the woods, I passed, three miles from there, Judge Gordon's house, where I crossed the North-River at the ford near the very small village of Milton.

Monticello is situated on a considerable elevation three miles farther on, from whence one towers over the horizon for a distance of forty-five miles. I arrived at two o'clock, just as former president Jefferson was sitting down to eat. Soon afterwards he was to travel to another piece of land he owns near New-London, Virginia.

After showing me the principal vistas and also several very curious objects, Mr. Jefferson invited me to dine.

After leaving the table and politely urging me to remain at his house despite his departure, he climbed into a four-horse carriage with Mrs. Randolph and two of his granddaughters.

I went back inside with Mr. Randolph fils, who showed the museum in the entrance hall of the house to me. It contains both extremely rare items and others that you could find nowhere else, among them the upper jaw of a mammoth. It was discovered in Kentucky, and Mr. Peale used a *copy* of it to complete his mammoth at the Philadelphia Museum. The head is complete, but the lower jaw is not from the same individual. Two other infinitely curious pieces are: 1. An Indian painting representing a battle; it is on buffalo hide, about five feet square, and shows four lines of combatants. Each facing line has horses painted red and green and warriors armed and dressed in the manner of the savages. 2. A geographical map without the slightest flaw, also on buffalo hide and six feet square. It depicts a section of the Missouri River, and, although roughly drawn, is easy to understand. The explanations have been written in French by interpreters.

One also sees there a tusk from a mammoth and one from an elephant, with a tooth from the latter animal to show how different it is from those of the former, which are conical and designed for a carnivorous animal, whereas the others have flat and scratched crowns, as is characteristic of a frugivore.

A head of a gigantic ram; one supposes that it is from the primitive breed that used to live in North America.

Mr. Randolph next showed me the pictures and portraits that decorate the different rooms.

The portraits of Washington, Lafayette, Adams, Franklin, Walter Raleigh, Amerigo Vespucci, Columbus, Bacon, Locke, Newton, etc., etc.

Pictures: a dead man emerging from the tomb to tell his story;

The surrender of Cornwallis in October 1781 at Yorktown, Virginia;

Diogenes looking for a man;

Alexander and Diogenes;

Democritus and Heracleitus, etc., etc., etc.

I also saw:

A bear's claw from Missouri. This species is larger and much more ferocious than the others;

A mammoth's tusk;

Several teeth from the same animal;

The thighbone of the same.

The mammoth's head is constituted, as I said before, of a perfect upper jaw and two lower half-jaws from different animals; one of the latter is much larger than the other.

A European coat of mail used by those who fought the Indians early on. With it, they were in no danger of being wounded by their arrows.

Antlers of the American elk and other animals of that sort. Those of the elk are considerable; these animals, as well as the buffalo and several others, have been killed off in the parts of Virginia where the population is densest. One may find them in the Ohio territory, to which the large number of hunters have relegated them.

Two stone busts sculpted by the savages, one representing a man and the other a woman. The faces are hideous and quite coarsely made. They were no doubt used for worship and have a lot in common with the Egyptian and oriental divinities, whose images are engraved in most of the books that deal with those peoples.

A small Indian hatchet made from a kind of polished porphyry, with the top in the shape of a pipe;

A figure of an animal in the same type of stone;

Various petrifactions.

Bows, arrows, spears, and lots of objects made by the savages;

A life-size marble statue similar to that of Cleopatra. She is lying down, and a snake encircles her left arm. This is a copy from the ancients.

Mr. Jefferson believes that she represents Ariadne.

An elephant's tooth, which, being from an herbivorous animal, is totally different from those of the mammoth. Nevertheless, it is generally thought that the latter is just a kind of elephant.

Whatever it may be, I am convinced that Mr. Peale (of Philadelphia) has committed an unforgivable and shocking misinterpretation by placing its tusks with their points turned toward the ground, which is the opposite of what one sees in the elephant.

I have no doubt that this is contrary to his private opinion; but, for reasons of self-interest, he wanted to offer to the public a unique, extraordinary, and unknown animal, so as to attract an even larger number of curious, paying visitors. *In omnibus respice finem*:

En todo caso convenia mirar el fin.
Herrera.

Upon seeing the skeleton of the mammoth at Peale's Museum, I wanted to write these four lines above it:

Your mammoth, as he is here,
Is just a shocking imposture;
By turning his two tusks upright,
You will imitate nature....

The museum (which is in the entrance hall of Mr. Jefferson's house) is disproportionate to it and makes it look even smaller than it really is. Outside is a grassy platform from which the view extends in every direction except toward the southeast, where a nearby hill, much higher than Monticello, looms over it.

Fourteen or fifteen leagues due south is the height called *Wallace's-Mountain.* It has precisely the shape, elevation, and dimensions of the Great Pyramid in Egypt, which, if seen from the same distance and placed by itself in the middle of a vast plain, would appear exactly as this mountain does from Monticello.

To the northeast of Wallace's-Mountain is an immense plain that seems to stretch all the way to the sea. The horizon is forty-five miles away.

Toward the north is another plain bounded by the Blue Ridge Mountains. To the northeast one perceives some mountains in Maryland and the chain called the Southwest Mountains, which runs parallel to the Blue Ridge Mountains.

To the northwest lies Charlottesville, a very small place in the center of a flat country, not far from the North-River.

Mr. Jefferson is seventy-three years old, but he does not appear more than sixty-three. His grandson, who is six feet four inches tall, told me that, among the inhabitants of the neighboring mountains, he was of ordinary size. The women whom I had occasion to see in this country are pretty, fresh-faced, and tall.

Mr. Randolph showed me an unusual map of the travels of captains Lewis and Clark, who, accompanied by forty-four men, crossed the whole of the huge territory extending from the Atlantic to the Pacific Ocean....

At four o'clock I took leave of Mr. Randolph and went to the home of Mr. Monroe, who lives three miles from the residence of former president Jefferson.

I arrived there at six o'clock; and the colonel, secretary of state, welcomed me very politely.

Printed in Montlezun, *Voyage fait dans les années 1816 et 1817, de New-Yorck a la Nouvelle-Orléans* (Paris, 1818), 1:74–94; ellipses indicate editorial omissions. Translation adapted from J. M. Carrière and L. G. Moffatt, "A Frenchman Visits Albemarle, 1816," *MACH* 4 (1943/44): 45–52.

Barthélémy Sernin du Moulin, baron de Montlezun de Labarthette (1762–after 1839), soldier and author, was born in Gascony, France, and educated at the royal military school in Sorèze, 1773–74. After a sojourn in Saint Domingue, in 1781 he fought alongside his father, the lieutenant colonel of the Touraine Regiment, at the Battle of Yorktown. Montlezun was appointed a second lieutenant in the French army in June 1782 and promoted to first lieutenant three years later. When the French Revolution broke out, he joined the royalist forces and, after they disbanded, he expatriated himself to London. Montlezun had returned to the land of his birth by the time Napoleon fell from power in 1814. Neglected by the Bourbons and troubled by the emperor's return to France early in 1815, he set sail for America. Following a brief tour of New York City and Philadelphia in September and October 1815, Montlezun left for the West Indies. During the following year he spent nearly five months in the United States, a trip that included visits to TJ, James Madison, and James Monroe in Virginia and travels to Baltimore, Washington, Philadelphia, New York, and New Orleans. After a visit to Cuba, Montlezun was in Charleston, South Carolina, in March 1817. He then returned to France, where he published two books the following year detailing his adventures in the western hemisphere (Edgar Erskine Hume, ed., *General Washington's Correspondence concerning The Society of the Cincinnati* [1941], opp. p. 112, 345–8, 375; tablet listing alumni of the Abbaye-École de Sorèze; *Les Combattants Français de la Guerre Américaine 1778–1783* [1905], 320; L. G. Moffatt and J. M. Carrière, "A Frenchman Visits Norfolk, Fredericksburg and Orange County, 1816," *VMHB* 53 [1945]: 101–23, esp. 101–7; Henry du Moulin de Labarthete, *La Vie en Armagnac et en Tursan* [1970], 59).

In his one subsequent reference to Monticello in the work quoted above, Montlezun remarks that the number of slaves there far exceeded the more than three hundred residing at James Madison's Montpellier estate (1:107).

NORTH-RIVER: the Rivanna River. Martha Jefferson Randolph (MADAME RANDOLPH) and her daughters Virginia and Mary accompanied TJ on his September 1816 trip to Poplar Forest (note to TJ to William Wirt, 29 Sept. 1816). M. RANDOLPH FILS was Thomas Jefferson Randolph.

IN OMNIBUS RESPICE FINEM: "In all things, look to the end." EN TODO CASO CONVENIA MIRAR EL FIN, a Spanish version of the preceding phrase, appears in book 8, chapter 1, of Antonio de Herrera y Tordesillas's *Historia General de los Hechos de los Castellanos en las Islas, y Tierra Firme del Mar Oceano* (Madrid, 1601–15, and other eds.; Sowerby, nos. 4107–8).

The hill (MORNE) overlooking Monticello to the southwest is Montalto. WALLACE'S-MOUNTAIN: Willis's Mountain.

[1]Printed text: "1815."

[2]A section editorially omitted here, which is found on pages 80–4 of Montlezun's book, is an edited translation into French of John E. Caldwell, *A Tour through Part of Virginia, in the summer of 1808* (New York, 1809), 26–9. This passage from Caldwell's book also appeared in the Wilmington, N.C., *Cape-Fear Recorder* and other newspapers in 1816–17 (Washington *Daily National Intelligencer*, 10 Oct. 1816; Wilmington, Del., *American Watchman*, 5 July 1817).

[3]A section editorially omitted here, which is printed within quotation marks on pages 86–94 of Montlezun's book, is an account of the Lewis and Clark Expedition.

From William W. Hening

SIR, Richmond 23rd Septr 1816

Your letter of the 15th was delivered to me, after the arrival of the last mail only; and I have not lost a moment in complying with its contents.—I send you by the Charlottesville stage-driver, the three first volumes of the Statutes at large.—Unfortunately the sheets of the 4th Vol. which had been sent to Petersburg, to be bound, were all destroyed by the dreadful conflagration at that place; so that none of the impression were saved except those copies which had been previously bound for public use. It will be immediately reprinted.—The 5th Vol. is printed, except the Index.—With this volume, I will send you the 4th which will shortly be reprinted. My original plan contemplated the bringing down the Statutes at Large to the end of the year 1792, when our last Revisal was made. But, should it be found expedient, they will be continued to a later period.

I have still, in my possession, the M.S. Vol. of laws, which I received, from the late Edmund Randolph Esqr, and which, from the description you gave, I had no doubt was your property. I do not recollect, that you gave me any specific directions, in relation to it.—Will you have it sent to you; or shall I send it to Washington?—and, if to the latter place, to whose address?

With much esteem & respect, I am Yrs WM: W: HENING

RC (DLC); endorsed by TJ as received 5 Oct. 1816 and so recorded in SJL. Enclosure: Hening, vols. 1–3.

Despite Hening's prediction that the fourth volume of his *Statutes at Large* would be IMMEDIATELY REPRINTED, a second edition did not appear until 1820. The unpaginated preface to that tome states that "THE first edition of this volume was printed in 1814, by the late *Mr. Samuel Pleasants*, printer to the commonwealth, by contract with the editor, and the sheets sent to *Petersburg* to be bound. As many copies as were subscribed for by the state, at that time, and a few over, were finished and delivered, the remaining sheets were all burnt, in the dreadful fire which happened in that town on the 16th day of July, 1815." The 5TH VOL. was published in Richmond in 1819.

From Dabney Carr

My Dear Sir. Winchester. Sep 24th 1816

I have hesitated for some time, whether I should write to you, on the subject of this letter. I am sure you will do me the justice to believe that what I shall say is dictated by an anxiety[1] for your repose.

I have seen in pretty free circulation here, a letter written by you to a Mr Kercheval, on the subject of calling a convention, & discussing the topicks which would probably come before it. I say in free circulation, because it was in the hands of a printer here—I heard several speak of having seen it, & the idea was, that it was refused to none who asked for it. I got it from Judge Holmes, who having heard of it, had applied to the printer for it. On reading it, & remarking the earnestness with which you deprecate a publication; I remarked to the Judge, that I feared there was some danger, of our printer (who is not over scrupulous) publishing it—he said he would speak to him on the subject—which he did—& told me that the printer observed, that he did not mean to publish it, without leave; but that he had written, or would write (I am not positive which) & try to obtain permission from you. If he has written & you have given leave, my letter comes too late—if you have refused, I do not think he would publish: but perhaps you have not yet decided on the subject; if so, will you pardon me the liberty of advising, that you Should refuse permission. The subjects which the letter discusses, interest deeply, the minds, & the feelings, of the people in this quarter—most are for a convention—but some, with limited powers, merely to make amendments; others with full powers to cast the whole government anew—in this state of things, those of the latter opinion, will eagerly catch at the weight of your arguments, & your name—& those on the other side, feeling that weight, will too probably, with an illiberality which so often marks & disgraces political opposition, resort to abuse instead of reasoning. I trust I need not express the perfect conviction I feel; that no wish for additional fame as a writer, would mingle with the motives, which might induce you to consent to a publication—I know well, that of honour, you have enough; & that all you ask of the present generation is, that you may be permitted to close your useful & honorable course, in peace & quiet. But I know that you have long been in the habit of disregarding personal consequences, when the publick good was in View; & I did not know, but that if urged on this ground, you might consent to have the letter published. I confess I am selfish enough (if I may use the word) to prefer your ease & repose, to the chance of benefit from enlightening publick opinion on these subjects—for after all, most men, will be guided as to them[2] by preconceived opinions or prejudices.

While my pen is in my hand, I will say a word on another subject—I feel a good deal of anxiety about the figure which my father is to make in Mr Wirt's life of Henry I copied & sent to him, the sketch you drew of his character; since which I have had no letter from him—I would like very much to know the manner in which he will treat it—whether he will insert your picture without alteration, or will change it in any thing. As you reside so much nearer Richmond than I do, I have Supposed it not improbable that you might have some information on these points—if so, & the request be not improper, I should be very glad to hear how these things are—I have myself a high opinion of Mr Wirt's talents, but this is an untried field—I hope he will not disappoint publick expectation.

My family are well. With best wishes to your self, & household. believe me truly yrs &C D CARR

RC (DLC); addressed: "Thomas Jefferson Esqr near Milton Albemarle" by "Mail"; franked; postmarked Winchester, 27 Sept.; endorsed by TJ as received 5 Oct. 1816 and so recorded in SJL.

TJ addressed his letter of 12 July 1816 to Samuel KERCHEVAL under the latter's pseudonym of "Henry Tompkinson." TJ included a SKETCH of Dabney Carr (1743–73) in his 19 Jan. 1816 letter to the younger Carr.

[1] Manuscript: "anxeity."
[2] Preceding three words interlined.

To Stephen Kingston

SIR Poplar Forest near Lynchburg. Sep. 25. 16

Your letter of the 12th inst. was recieved in the moment of my setting out on a long journey, and is therefore answered from a very distant place. the case to which it relates appears to be now in the courts of Pensylvania, and before it's legislature. it cannot be doubted that both of these authorities will, in their respective functions do what is right and just: for a private individual therefore, and of another state, without pretence of any call, official, professional, or personal, to volunteer an opinion in such a case, would be very derogatory from the respect and confidence due to those magistracies, and sincerely believed by me to be justly due to them. this consideration alone would, I am persuaded, be deemed by you a sufficient justification for my declining to give any opinion in the case. but to this may be truly added a sense of my incompetence. I have indeed been once of the profession of the law. but retired from it now between 40.

and 50. years, all familiarity with it is lost, and I no longer meddle with questions of law. and altho' a treaty is supposed to enter into your case, yet a treaty is but a law of the land, and as such is cognisable by the judiciary and legislative authorities. I return therefore all the papers printed and manuscript which you were pleased to inclose to me, and, with my regrets that the situation of the case does not admit my being useful to you, I pray you to accept the assurance of my respect. TH: JEFFERSON

PoC (DLC); on verso of reused address cover of Samuel Kercheval to TJ, 16 Aug. 1816; at foot of text: "Mr Stephen Kingston"; endorsed by TJ. Enclosures: enclosures to Kingston to TJ, 12 Sept. 1816.

From James H. McCulloch

SIR Custom House Baltim^o Coll^ts Off^e Sep^t 25 1816

I yesterday received a bill of lading of two cases Tuscan wine for your order, in a letter from Mr Thomas Appleton of Leghorn. The vessel has just entered that bears the consignment & it may be some days before they are landed. It will enable me to forward them to you in the most convenient manner, if you can give me some directions as to the route in which they will be least exposed by a land carriage. It is presumable this will be by shipment to Richmond: but it is desireable to wait your direction.

Agreeably to the wish made known heretofore at this office, a statement is given of the duty & charges below, by estimation: If left to ourselves it would be esteemed something like a duty to transmit them as free as your letters. It must only be added further, that as long as the present Collector is in a situation to render any services, he hopes that the pleasure will be afforded him by your making that use of him which your occasions may require.

I am Sir with sincere respect Your ob^t serv^t

JA^S H M^CCULLOCH

Tuscan wine in bottles 114 bottles Gall^s 22 @ 70 Cts D^s 15.40
$\frac{3}{4}$ gro' @ 144 Cts 1.10
M^r C F Kalkman owner of the vessel charges no freight

RC (DLC); endorsed by TJ as received 7 Oct. 1816 and so recorded in SJL, which has the additional notation: "Tusc^n 114. bot."; note by TJ beneath endorsement: "2. cases Tuscan wine 16.50." RC (DLC); address cover only; with PoC of TJ to Gouverneur Morris, 20 Oct. 1816, on verso; addressed: "Thomas Jefferson Esqr Monticello near Milton Albemarle County Virginia"; franked; postmarked Baltimore, 28 Sept.

James Hugh McCulloch (1756–1836), merchant and public official, graduated from the College of New Jersey (later Princeton University) in 1773 and apparently then joined his father in a mercantile firm in his native Philadelphia. He relocated to Maryland by 1782 and settled permanently in Baltimore the following year. A friend and political ally of Samuel Smith (of Maryland) and an "undeviating Republican," McCulloch served in the Maryland House of Delegates in 1800 and in the state senate, 1801–05. With Smith's backing, in 1808 he secured an appointment from TJ as collector of the port of Baltimore, a highly lucrative post that he retained until his death. During the War of 1812, McCulloch was wounded and captured during service as a volunteer at the September 1814 Battle of North Point. Having invested in privateers during this conflict with Great Britain, in the decade that followed he helped to frustrate federal efforts to end similar but illegal activities against Spanish ships by Baltimore vessels claiming to promote South American independence. McCulloch died at his home near Baltimore (*Princetonians, 1769–75*, pp. 320–4; Trustees' Minutes, College of New Jersey, 29 Sept. 1773 [NjP: Princeton University Archives]; Papenfuse, *Maryland Public Officials*, 1:42, 143; McCulloch to TJ, 14 Oct. 1806 [MHi]; Smith to TJ, 29 Dec. 1806, 4 Apr. 1808 [DNA: RG 59, LAR, 1801–09]; *JEP*, 2:79, 4:375, 392 [6, 7 Apr. 1808, 22 Mar., 24 Apr. 1834]; Baltimore *Niles' Weekly Register*, 12 Nov. 1836).

The vessel carrying the CONSIGNMENT of wine was the *Von (Van) Hollen*. GRO': "gross."

From William Wirt

Richmond—Sept. 25. 1816.

W^m[1] Wirt, with respectful compliments to Mr Jefferson, sends a few more sheets of the biography—and thinks he may venture to add the consoling assurance that a few more pages, (20, or at the most 30) will put an end to the trouble to which Mr Jefferson has been so kind as to subject himself.

RC (MHi); dateline at foot of text; endorsed by TJ as received 1 Oct. 1816 and so recorded in SJL. Tr (MdHi: Wirt Papers). Enclosure: manuscript, not found, of a portion of Wirt, *Patrick Henry*.

[1]Tr: "M^r."

From Timothy Banger

SIR, Phil^a Sepr 26. 1816

Duty required me to write the enclosed for the Commissary General, but gratitude compels me not to lose the present favourable opportunity of thanking you for your kindness to me, when I arrived in this Country in the year 1793. The temporary employment you was so good as to give me, on the application of my good friend the late Doctor Rush, laid the foundation for my continued employment to this day, and under the blessings of Providence, I have done well.

The freedom I have taken you will no doubt excuse; & believe me, when with sincere wishes for your health & happiness, I subscribe myself

Your faithful friend & obliged Servant TIMOTHY BANGER

It would afford me great pleasure, if I could be useful to you in this place, in any way.

RC (MHi); postscript adjacent to closing and signature; at foot of text: "His Excellency Thos Jefferson late Pres^t^ of the U. States"; endorsed by TJ as received 5 Oct. 1816 and so recorded in SJL. Dft (DNA: RG 107, LRSW); lacking postscript; filed with Banger to John C. Spencer, 1 Feb. 1842. Enclosure: Banger (for Callender Irvine) to TJ, 26 Sept. 1816.

Timothy Banger (1773–1847), Universalist preacher and government clerk, was born in London, England, and immigrated in 1793 to Philadelphia, where he lived thereafter. After working at the Treasury Department register's office, 1794–97, he served as a War Department clerk under the superintendent of military stores, held a similar position at the federal arsenal in his adopted hometown, and from at least 1814 until 1840 was chief clerk at the commissary general's office (Abel C. Thomas, *A Century of Universalism in Philadelphia and New-York* [1872], 55–6; John F. Meginness, ed., *History of Lycoming County, Pennsylvania* [1892], 741; Joseph Nourse to Samuel Hodgdon, 16 Feb. 1797 [DNA: RG 94, PRWP]; Harold C. Syrett and others, eds., *The Papers of Alexander Hamilton* [1961–87], 23:92n; *Philadelphia Gazette & Daily Advertiser*, 3 May 1802; DNA: RG 29, CS, Pa., Philadelphia, 1810–30; *Muster Rolls of the Pennsylvania Volunteers in the War of 1812–1814* [1880], 736, 738–9; *A Register of Officers and Agents, Civil, Military, and Naval, in the Service of the United States* [Washington City, 1822], 58; *Letter from the Secretary of War, transmitting A report of the number of persons employed in the public service . . . with the names of persons removed from office between 4th March, 1829, and 30th September, 1841* [27th Cong., 2d sess., Executive Documents, no. 58], 50; Philadelphia *Public Ledger*, 2 June 1847).

From Timothy Banger (for Callender Irvine)

SIR, Comm^y^ Generals Office Philadelphia Sepr 26.[1] 1816

There has been recently discovered in the Military[2] Stores near this City, a Box addressed to you,—contents unknown. How this Box Came into the Store; when, or by whom it was delivered, no person there can tell;—it is probable it may have lain there some years. Mr Irvine, being at Erie,[3] I have, in obedience to his instructions,[4] shipped it on board the Schooner Hamlet, bound to Norfolk, with directions to have it delivered to Edwin Starke Esqr Ass^t^ Commissary there; and have requested him to embrace the earliest opportunity of forwarding it to you.

with the highest respect I have the honor to be, Sir, Yr: mo: ob[t] Servant

TIMOTHY BANGER,
for CALLENDER IRVINE,
Comm[y] General

RC (MHi); at foot of text: "His Excellency Tho[s] Jefferson late President U. States"; endorsed by TJ as received 5 Oct. 1816 and so recorded in SJL. Dft (DNA: RG 107, LRSW); dated 25 Sept. 1816; filed with Banger to John C. Spencer, 1 Feb. 1842. FC (Lb in DNA: RG 92, ROQG). Enclosed in Banger to TJ, 26 Sept. 1816.

Callender Irvine (1775–1841), public official, graduated in 1794 from Dickinson College in his home state of Pennsylvania. He was a captain in the United States Army's 2d Regiment of Artillerists and Engineers, 1798–1801, and a federal Indian agent, 1802–03. Irvine subsequently served as the nation's superintendent of military stores, 1804–12, and as commmissary general of purchases, 1812–41. Having joined the Hibernian Society of Philadelphia in 1815, he was its vice president, 1829–41. Irvine died in Philadelphia (Nicholas B. Wainwright, *The Irvine Story* [1964], 12, 18–9, 52; *Dickinson College General Catalogue, 1787–1891* [1892], 7; Heitman, *U.S. Army*, 1:40, 564; *JEP*, 1:277, 278–9, 2:300, 303 [29 May, 1 June 1798, 9, 10 Nov. 1812]; *PTJ*, 38:274, 628; TJ to James Madison, 18 Aug. 1803 [DLC: Madison Papers, Rives Collection]; John H. Campbell, *History of the Friendly Sons of St. Patrick and of the Hibernian Society for the Relief of Emigrants from Ireland* [1892], 197, 435; Philadelphia *North American and Daily Advertiser*, 12 Oct. 1841).

The contents of the BOX have not been identified.

1 Reworked from "25."
2 FC: "public."
3 Dft: "being absent."
4 Preceding five words interlined in Dft.

From David Gelston

DEAR SIR, New York September 26. 1816.

Your letters of the 18 & 19th instant I have received, and immediately caused an entry to be made of the books by the invoice, am[o] of duties paid 58^{\underline{40}}$ the invoice—&[ca] I now enclose—I also enclose an account of the expenses I have paid, I have not been called upon for all the freights, perhaps I shall not be, it will be time enough to charge them when paid—I now shall wait only a few days to remove all apprehensions from the equinoctial gales, & shall then improve the first good opportunity to send the package of books to Richmond—

with great affection & esteem I am—Sir—your obedient servant.

DAVID GELSTON

RC (MHi); at foot of text: "M[r] Jefferson"; endorsed by TJ as received 7 Oct. 1816 and so recorded in SJL; in TJ's hand beneath endorsement: "350 D : 58.40 D :: 100 : 17. p[r] cent." Enclosures: enclosures to TJ to Gelston, 19 Sept. 1816. Other enclosure printed below.

E N C L O S U R E

Account with David Gelston

M[r] Jefferson

			To David Gelston— D[r]	
	for cash			
paid	duties	on wine by	Fanny from Leghorn	8.70
d[o]	d[o]	d[o] "	Gen: Ward—Bordeaux	3.94
d[o]	freight	"	d[o] d[o]	3.85
d[o]	duties	on Wine &	Macaroni. Ocean Marseilles	4.29
d[o]	fre[t]	"	" " "	4.98
d[o]	duties	on wine	Gen: Marion Marseilles	4.95
d[o]	d[o]	on books	United States—Havre	58.40
				$89:11

New York
Sep: 26. 1816.

MS (MHi); in Gelston's hand and endorsed by him: "Acc[t]—$89[11]."

From Thomas Appleton

SIR Leghorn 27th September 1816.

I had the honor of addressing you on the 20th of march, announcing the death of m[r] mazzei.—my next, was in date of the 15th of April, conveying to you the legal Attestations of his decease, with other Relative documents; indeed, it was a letter of unpardonable length.—I wrote again on the 10th of may following, inclosing duplicates relating to the deceas'd.—also on the 30th of the Same month, and by this conveyance, I forwarded to the care of the collector of new-York, a Case of 57 bottles of Carmingniano wine, by the sch[o] Fanny Captain Selby of that port.—my last Respects were on the 30th of July by the Ship Van-Hollen, Capt: Ralph Porter bound to Baltimore, by which vessel, I Sent to the care of the Collector, two cases of 57 bottles each of Tuscan wine, N[o] 1—artiminiano, & N[o] 2. chianti.—I have now shipp'd on board the Brig Saucy-Jack, Richard Humfries, master and to the Care of the collector of Charleston, S[o] Carolina two Cases of Ama wine N[o] 1. containing 57 bottles & N[o] 2.—30.—inclos'd is your little account, which you will percieve precisely balanc'd for the fifty dollars you Remitted me for this purpose.—the last mention'd wine, is esteem'd the first quality of all I have Sent, and the next, after Montepulciano.—The late Season has been the most extraordinary one, Remember'd by the oldest & most observing farmer. there has not been a Single day, in which Farenheit's thermometer has risen above

75—generally it mark'd from 65 to 70 degrees; the usual heat in Summer, is from 75 to 83.—Our harvest of wheat, has been much below middling: the Indian corn has been So blasted, that it does not exceed one tenth part of the usual crops.—Oil is absolutely Nullity.—the greatest part of our grapes have dropp'd from the vines; and the remainder, have not, even yet, arriv'd at perfect maturity; So that, our wine will be dear, and of a very indifferent quality.—.—I, very lately reciev'd from the Secretary of State, a letter Requesting my Attention to the Sculpturing a Statue of General washington, for the State of North-Carolina; the particular instructions relating to it, I have Reciev'd from m^r^ King, Secretary to the legation to Russia, and now at Naples.—I have accepted this commission with a very Sincere gratification, and every Attention on my part, Shall be paid to its accomplishment, in a manner Suitable to the confidence, which is thus reposed in me.—I have written to m^r^ Canova at Rome, to execute the Statue, and in his Reply are the following expressions—"Signore, rispondo subito alla graziosa lettera con cui ella Si compiace offerirmi l'essecuzione della marmorea Statua dell'immortale Washington; per un governo degli Stati uniti di America—Veramente le molte opere alle quali sono per diversi Anni obligato, vorebbero che jo la ringraziassi di quest'onorato incarico; ma l'ammirazione mia, al Genio operatore di Si alte Cose, per la Salute e libertà della sua nazione, Vogliono, che jo adoperi ogni sforzo, onde assecondare la di lei gentile domanda. Accetto adunque la commissione."[1] &^c^ &^c^

The Senate-hall of Carolina, I find is only Sixteen feet in heighth, which it Should Seem, would not admit an erect figure, larger than life, fix'd on its proportionate base; for you will at once percieve, Sir, that it would nearly touch the cieling, and thus violate all the rules of just proportion.—Mr Canova is of opinion, it ought to be Sitting, not merely from this consideration, but likewise from the place & purpose for which it is intended.—here, there is no appeal from his judgement.—I have Reciev'd, likewise, from m^r^ King, a drawing and inscription, which are directed to be sculptur'd on the piedestal.—It is a maxim, you Know, Sir, in Sculpture, as it is in painting, that Unity of Subject Should be Scrupulously observ'd.—the drawing contains two figures, one Sitting, & the other erect; on the left is the Godess of liberty, and that on the right, I presume, was intended for Ceres; but the latter is by no means, correct with mythology.—it is delineated in a fashionable modern dishabille-dress, with a wreathe of flowers round the head; in the right-hand, a Cornucopia of the Same, and in the left, an ear of grain; this figure then combines two Subjects.—the Godess to be correctly express'd, the vestments should be heroic, with a wreathe of wheat round the head; the right-hand is usually extended with poppies, a plant of extraordinary fecundity, and the left, supporting her drapery.—if the figure is intended for Flora, which it certainly more Resembles, the Cornucopia Should be in the left hand; the right, Should Support an ample heroic drapery, with a wreathe of flowers; but She Should not be ornamented with any of the Attributes of Ceres.—pardon me, Sir, if I have enter'd thus minutely on this Subject, as it may possibly be, that you have no work near you, containing the figures delineated.—to Return then to the maxim of Unity of Subject.—Were I consulted, I Should most certainly Recommend, instead of the Godesses in question, to have Sculptur'd on the base, some expressive traits in the life of the General, which would at once lead to the recollection of the numerous virtues, with which he was Singularly adorned; and this, I believe, would not only be consistent with the usage of the most enlighten'd ages of Antiquity, but conformable also, to the universal practice of modern times.—I Should then propose, that the inscription, Should be on the front of the base; and the historic-traits of the General, on the two visible sides; and indeed on three, if the place where it is to be erected in the hall, Should Require it.—I have taken the liberty to communicate my Sentiments to Governor Miller, but whatever may be his final decision, it Shall, on my part, be most scrupulously Adher'd to.—

In my letter, Sir, of the 15th of april, I, perhaps, too much enlarg'd on the Subject of the Capitals contracted for at Carrara by mr Andreis, but my Single motive was, that our government might not be led a Second time, into a Similar error, in any future commissions.—there has Since arriv'd all the evils, & even more than I had anticipated.—At the time the contract was made, there were few commissions for marble in the place, the prices were therefore fix'd exceeding low; but they were So much So, that it was impossible they could be deliver'd, without a positive loss to the undertakers; this, I was appris'd of by an intelligent friend of Carrara, but as the contractors with Studious Care avoided consulting me, I was as cautious on my part, of intruding advice.—had a fair price been Stipulated, they would have been compleated in three months; twelve have now nearly expir'd, and the Sculptors have finally instituted a process against mr Andreis, urging that the work is not Sufficiently paid for; they will, I am inclin'd to believe, gain their cause, as the fact will be establish'd, and the tribunal will be dispos'd to favor their Citizens, in preference to foreigners; at least, this is their usual mode of administring justice.—besides, finding themselves deluded in their hopes of gain, the only remedy then, was, to compensate it by coarse & unfinish'd work.—this mode they have pursued, and from a friend of mine, who lately examin'd them with Attention, and is himself an eminent professor in the art, I am told, they would discredit the meanest workmen; this is the more to be lamented, as the ornaments of washington, will be the Standards, which our young artists will copy as models of Sculpture.—From the great delay, has resulted another inconvenience.—The Princess sovereign of Carrara, has a few days Since, increas'd the duty on exporting of marble-work, about five fold—there will then result to the government, considering the expence of Conveying here, from the U.S. Mr Andreis's family in the frigate John Adams: two years of Salary, Augmentation of duties, with a variety of other contingent expences, that it may be fairly calculated, for every dollar the government would have paid, had they Simply Sent a written order for the capitals, they will now, probably cost three.—.—The number of applicants to go to the U. States, has become incalculable; from professors of the highest Sciences, down to the labouring peasant; and had they the means; as they have the will, Italy would be half depopulated.—You will naturally infer, Sir, from thence, that there is no amelioration in the political State of the country; on the contrary, it is progressing to that Sort of maturity, which must terminate in an universal convulsion: this is not a partial evil, but extends to the utmost limits of Italy.—Such is the fatal blindness of the Sovereigns, that they Augment the impositions on their Subjects, in about the Same proportion, as their means decrease to pay them, and one would be almost led to believe, that their object was, to Reduce them to desperation.—what infinitely adds to their misery is, that the money does not again Return into circulation, but is transported far from their country.—under the late government, an immense internal traffic extended its benefitts to all the useful members of Society, but this is now extinguish'd; and the commerce which is carried on in the few Sea-ports of Italy is little advantageous, except to a very inconsiderable portion of the community.—

October 1st

I have this day reciev'd from Mr Canova, a letter, of which the following is the translation.—

To Thomas Appleton }
Consul. Leghorn }

SIR Rome 28. September 1816.

"I now Reply to your most esteem'd favor of the 20th instant.—I have thus the honor to observe to you, that my desire of executing the

Statue Sitting, is occasion'd, not wholly from the necessity of proportioning it to the heighth of the hall; but likewise, because in this attitude, there is infinite more dignity, and if I may be allow'd the expression, I Can give a greater force to my feeble genius.—if I consulted only my own ease & interest, I Should have adopted the erect figure, as Requiring less labour; but animated with the ardent Zeal with which I am, to apply every effort, to Render me worthy of so great a Subject, I have much preferr'd the Sitting posture.—I have the honor &c—
Antonio Canova.—"[2]

In my letter, & by this opportunity, to Governor miller, I have taken the liberty to write him nearly what is contain'd in the present one, on the Subject of the figures, intended for the piedestal; as I have, likewise, Sent him the translation of the last letter from mr Canova, Relating to the attitude of the Statue.—On my Recieving the decision of the Governor, I shall give the final answer to mr Canova.—

Accept, Sir the renewal of my very Sincere Respect & esteem

Th: Appleton

P.S.—about a month Since, miss Bettina mazzei gave her hand in marriage to mr Pini, of Pisa.—

RC (DLC); endorsed by TJ as received 12 Jan. 1817 and so recorded in SJL. RC (MHi); address cover only; with PoC of TJ to Jerman Baker, 25 Jan. 1817, on verso; addressed: "Thomas Jefferson, esquire monticelli Virginia U.S. America ℔ Brig Othello Capt: Gladding of Providence"; stamped "SHIP"; franked; postmarked Providence, 31 Dec.

Appleton's letter of THE 10TH OF MAY was actually dated 15 May 1816. The COLLECTOR OF NEW-YORK was David Gelston, while those of BALTIMORE and CHARLESTON, So CAROLINA, were James H. McCulloch and Simeon Theus, respectively. The SECRETARY OF STATE was James Monroe.

SIGNORE, RISPONDO SUBITO ALLA GRAZIOSA LETTERA ... ACCETTO ADUNQUE LA COMMISSIONE: "Sir, I reply immediately to the gracious letter in which you were pleased to offer me the execution of the marble statue of the immortal Washington for a government of the United States of America. Truthfully, because of the many works I have been obligated for several years to do, I should refuse this assignment with thanks. My admiration for the genius who has accomplished such lofty things and for the health and freedom of your nation, however, induces me to indulge your kind request. Therefore, I accept the commission."

As completed, Canova's statue of a seated George Washington did not include the GODESSES IN QUESTION (modern copy of destroyed original in rotunda of North Carolina State Capitol, Raleigh). The PRINCESS SOVEREIGN OF CARRARA was Maria Beatrice d'Este, duchess of Massa. UNDER THE LATE GOVERNMENT, prior to 1814, the Italian peninsula had been divided into thirds, administered by France directly and by the Napoleonic satellite kingdoms of Italy and Naples. The arrangement facilitated internal commerce and trade. Leghorn had been in the French section.

[1] Omitted closing quotation mark editorially supplied.

[2] Omitted closing quotation mark editorially supplied.

ENCLOSURE

Account with Thomas Appleton

Leghorn 28 May [ca. 27 Sept.] 1816[1]

Thomas Jefferson—D^r from Frulani		
To a barrel of Carmigniano Wine	£45	
To 57 bottles for the Same at 4. crazie	19	
To a Case	4.13.4	
To Corks, bottling, Straw, Cord, & packing	4.13.4	73. 6.8
Sent by the Sch^o fanny Capt. Selby for N. York—		
from ombrosi		
To a barrel of florence Wine	£28.	
To 57 bottles for the Same @ 4 crazie	19	56. 6.8
To a Case	4.13.4	
To Corks, bottling Straw, Cord & packing	4.13.4	
The above is artimino Wine—N° 1		
To a barrel of chianti Wine	£40.	
To 57 bottles for the Same @ 4 crazie	19	
To a Case	4.13.4	
To Corks, bottling Straw & pack^g & Cord	4.13.4	68. 6.8
The two last[2] barrels above mention'd are Shipp'd on board the Von Hollen, Ralph Porter master & Shipp'd to the Care of Collector for Balt^o—& Sail'd 3. August—		
To 2 Cases Cont^g 87. Bottles of Ama wine	£77	
Bottles, Cork, Cases, & bottling &^c	37. 3.4	114. 3.4
		£312. 3.4
Porterage of 5 Cases, in the 3 Shipments on board		4.10
		£316.13.4
C^r		
By 50. dollars as Credited on the last page @ £6⅓ each		£316.13.4

FC (MBPLi: Appleton Account Book); entirely in Appleton's hand.

For the transactions described in this account, see the covering letter and Appleton to TJ, 15, 30 May, 30 July 1816. The account is expressed in lire (£). CRAZIE were silver coins used in Tuscany (Patrick Kelly, *The Universal Cambist and Commercial Instructor; being a full and accurate treatise on the Exchanges, Monies, Weights, and Measures, of all Trading Nations and their Colonies* [London, 1821], 1:130, 199–201). The COLLECTOR of Baltimore was James H. McCulloch.

[1] Dateline taken from top of page of account book, with "28" repeated at head of account; editorially redated based on internal evidence.

[2] Word interlined.

From Isaac H. Tiffany

Venerable Sir. Schoharie 27 Sept. 1816.

While reading the "Spirit of Laws," at College, my curiosity was highly excited to become acquainted with Aristotle, by the mention made of him by the author. The illustrious Grecian had thought[1] so much & written so well, that the lapse of 2000 years has enabled Montesquieu to add but scanty improvements. Aristotle teaches to develope & establish many permanent, uniform & universal truths. It is unfortunate that the presidents & professors of our Seminaries of learning are seldom adequately acquainted with the existing municipal laws of the nations of the earth & their administration, to form qualified & correct opinions relative to the fundamental laws which exist only in form & fame, but are dead in act & force. Thus unversed, & unaware of the importance of this distinction between form & fact, made by both the above authors, & particularly applied by the latter to England, the teachers do not sufficiently impress it on the student's mind, & a graduate carries the bias received from Montesquieu[2] & Delolme, confirmed by Coke, Blackstone & others, to the bench & into the capitol itself. Years of active experience may wipe away the Stain; but from the pulpit, it is more indelible. An American, finding no established system of education, pursuing his researches from generals to particulars, from effects to causes, & from terminations, through history, to origins of courts & Systems, Seizes[3] on authors recommended[4] by reputation or presented by chance. The works of British novelists & reviewers, pensioned to decieve & powerful to persuade, find votaries in every eye that Can read; every bosom that can feel—They kindle the imagination; expel the Bible, & usurp the dominions of reason & religion. The influence of the British muse is still more irresistible. Dear maid, She has her hour of bloom & song—

"Yet hence O Heaven! convey that fatal face
And from destruction save the Trojan race."

And She Shews evident Symptoms of decline. Her Sisters of Greece & Rome have ceased their tuneful lays. Each has Sung Sweetest in her country's cause. Columbia's muse is yet to rise; must yet begin her song. Asia was first, America will close the circle of the muses. The era of the invention or discovery of the representative principle has been considered problematical. Gillies denies it to be of modern date.[5] Some seek it's origin in the woods of Germany. The author of Publius or the Federalist, supposes it to have been recognized & practised in the executive & legislative departments of antient; democratical governments;[6] but that it not being then understood to exclude the collective body of the people from these departments, it was therefore necessarily confined in operation to cities & their Suburbs. And Aristotle, thought it probable that "political, like all other inventions, have been often discovered and often lost; and that many institutions have been laid aside and revived, times without number." The American constitution is a new order of Structure, associating with admirable skill & intelligence the estimable parts of[7] successful & celebrated political fabrics of every age, with new principles, arrangements & combinations, all fitted to the expansive scale of thought & action in America. We confidently trust for its duration in the Simple and Safe contrivance for its amendment, from time to time, as the people may will. Ye who achieved this, will be blessed forever.

In the judiciary department, there yet exists authority not subject to the Controul of the people, at Short periods; & to this I have presumed to refer the earnest wishes expressed in your letter. The test or term of "Good behaviour" is equivocal. The intricacy of forms; the length, expense & difficulty of proceeding by impeachment; the strict rules of testimony & the technical Constructions of law, may secure an occupant upon the bench, when his faculties are impaired by age, disease or prejudice. He may be in contemp[t] yet lord over an insulted people. The objections of Publius to periodica[l] appointments are hypothetical & argumentative; they are but illy Supported by the example of England, which he cites. Besides, the history & reasoning which would be applicable there, would not be, here. Uniformity of decision are not inconsistant with such appointments when decisions are reported & judges are, as Publius presumes they ought to be, Selected from the bar. That hopes & fears have influenced the judge exposed to the passions of a tyrant or a city populace, who, in a breath could elevate or destroy him, all history discloses; but that the[8] judiciary of the U. States, should corruptly Seek popularity among a nation scattered over 600 mil[lions] of acres, is an imaginary alarm. Popularity, in the apprehended view, might be more easily secured by irresponsibility of power in Salary, for life. The constitution of N. York superannuates a judge at 60. Experience has amply attested the prudence of this provision, though it may have been doubted, or disapproved, when Publius wrote. Illustrious examples of the force of mental faculties to the term of prolonged life, are but favoured exceptions from the ordinary course of nature.

Your actual experience of oppresive, anarchical & imbecile governments before, during & subsequent to, the revolutionary war,—in the Construction of the present constitution, Service in Several of its departments, & finally direction[9] & presidency over all, without expectancy of future employment in any, entitles your opinion of its excellencies or defects, to unrivalled[10] authority. Nothing Could be more interesting to be known.

Receive my acknowledgements for what you have pleased to communicate, for I listen to your counsels with reverenced rapture.

May God long preserve your health & life— I. H. Tiffany.

RC (DLC); edge trimmed and chipped; dateline at foot of text; addressed: "Thomas Jefferson, Esqr—Monticello—Va."; stamp canceled; franked; postmarked Schoharie Bridge, 27 Sept.; endorsed by TJ as received 10 Oct. 1816 and so recorded in SJL.

yet hence … trojan race is from book 3, lines 209–10, of Alexander Pope's translation of Homer's *Iliad* (*The Iliad of Homer* [London, 1750; for eds. owned by TJ, see Sowerby, no. 4264, and TJ's copy of vol. 1 of 1750 London ed. in ViCMRL], 1:182). The historian John gillies asserted that no one with "the least tincture of learning" could maintain that "the Greeks were totally unacquainted with representative government" (Gillies, *Aristotle's Ethics and Politics* [London, 1797; 2d ed., London, 1804; Poor, *Jefferson's Library*, 11 (no. 640)], 2:64).

James Madison, writing as "Publius" in the federalist, number 63, contended that the superiority of the American form of government to that practiced in ancient Greece lay primarily in the former's "*total exclusion of the people in their collective capacity* from any share" in governance (Madison, *Papers, Congress. Ser.*, 10:544–50, quote on p. 548). Aristotle's comment about political inventions is from his *Politics*, 7.9.4 (Gillies, *Aristotle's Ethics and Politics*, 2:233; *Aristotle: Politics*, trans. Harris Rackham, Loeb Classical Library [1932; rev. ed. 1944; undated reprint], 580, 581).

The United States Constitution, article 3, section 1, stipulates that "judges, both of the supreme and inferior courts, shall hold their offices during good behaviour." Alexander Hamilton cited the English example while arguing against periodical appointments in *The Federalist*, number 78 (Harold C. Syrett and others, eds., *The Papers of Alexander Hamilton* [1961–87], 4:655–63, esp. 656, 663).

1 Manuscript: "thougt."
2 Manuscript: "Monstequieu."
3 Manuscript: "Seizeses."
4 Manuscript: "recmended."
5 Sentence interlined.
6 Manuscript: "goverments."
7 Manuscript: "of of."
8 Manuscript: "the the."
9 Manuscript: "directin."
10 Manuscript: "urivalled."

To William Wirt

Dear Sir Poplar Forest Sep. 29. 16.

I found, on my arrival here the 2^d parcel of your sheets, which I have read with the same avidity and pleasure as the former. this proves they will experience no delay in my hands, and that I consider them as worthy every thing I can do for them. they need indeed but little, or rather I should say nothing. I have however hazarded some suggestions on a paper inclosed. when I read the former sheets, I did not consider the article of style as within my jurisdiction. however since you ask observations on that, and suggest doubts entertained by yourself on a particular quality of it, I will candidly say that I think some passages of the former sheets too flowery for the sober taste of history. it will please young readers in it's present form, but to the older it would give more pleasure and confidence to have some exuberances lightly pruned. I say lightly; because your style is naturally rich and captivating, and would suffer if submitted to the rasp of a rude hand. a few excrescences may be rubbed off[1] by a delicate touch; but better too little than too much correction. in the 2d parcel of sheets, altho' read with an eye to your request, I have found nothing of this kind. I thus comply with your desire; but on the condition originally prescribed, that you shall consider my observations as mere suggestions, meant to recall the subject to a revision by yourself, and that no change be made in consequence of them but on the confirmed dictates of your own judgment. I have no amour-propre which will suffer by having hazarded a false criticism. on the contrary I should regret were the genuine character of your composition to be adulterated by any foreign ingredient. I return to Albemarle within a week, shall stay there 10. days, come back and pass here October and part of November. I salute you affectionately. TH: JEFFERSON

RC (ViU: TJP); at foot of text: "Mr Wirt." PoC (DLC); edge trimmed. Enclosure: manuscript, not found, of a portion of Wirt, *Patrick Henry*. Other enclosure printed below.

TJ's daughter Martha Jefferson Randolph accompanied her father to Poplar Forest and subsequently received a communication of 27–30 Sept. [1816] written by her daughter Ellen at Monticello, which detailed numerous family occurrences; complained of the large number of visitors there, including, among others, Maximilian Godefroy and his family, a party of "impudent and ungenteel" North Carolinians, and some "dashing but not genteel Carolinians," who "made a great noise asked many silly questions and at last went away leaving papa and myself weary & disgusted"; expressed her happiness that thanks to TJ's absence he had escaped their "gigling impertinence"; remarked that her father had assisted her "in doing the honors of the house"; sent her love to TJ, her mother, and her sisters Virginia and Mary; asked that TJ be informed that she had "not forgotten to wind up his clocks, and will take good care of his wines, when they arrive"; and passed along news of various members of the enslaved community (RC in ViU: Ellen Wayles Randolph Coolidge Correspondence; unsigned; partially dated; addressed: "Mrs Randolph Poplar Forest").

[1]Manuscript: "of."

ENCLOSURE

Notes on William Wirt's Biography of Patrick Henry

[ca. 29 Sept. 1816]

page 92. there is one circumstance in my letter here quoted which may not perhaps be exactly correct, to wit, whether Govr Livingston produced Jay's draught in the House of Congress, or in the Committee to which Lee's draught was recommitted? the latter seems most agreeable to usage; and lest I should have erred in this particular, I have so modified the quotation as to adapt it to either fact. this anecdote will probably draw on me the wrath of the family & friends of mr Lee, who are exceedingly jealous of the fame of their eminent relation. it will only add however a bouche à feu the more to the battery of obloquy which, reared in 94, has been incessantly directed on me, but without changing my course a single point. mr Jay's rude address to mr Lee in my presence, which I immediately diverted from him would have been a mortifying addition to the anecdote: but this does not belong to history.

pa. 92. Capt Foy was private Secretary to Ld Dunmore, lived with him in the palace, was believed to be the chief instigator of all his violences, and being very ill-tempered, haughty & presumptuous, was very obnoxious.

pa. 110. Was not William Nelson still living? if he was, he was the President. I thought he retired to Hanover and died there some time after these transactions. his brother Thomas, the Secretary, succeeded as President[1] only on his death, whenever that took place.

pa. 128. that mr Henry wanted personal courage was the very general belief of all his acquaintances, strengthened perhaps by inference from the fact that his brother William, and half brother Syme were notorious cowards. but I know nothing of the facts on which this opinion of mr Henry was founded; nor do I recollect having heard except a single one related to me by Govr Page, then a member of the Committee of safety. this was that while mr Henry's corps was encamped near Williamsburg, a nocturnal alarm took place, on a false[2] report that the enemy had landed, I believe, at Burwell's ferry: and were on their march to the city. mr Henry was so panic struck as to be incapable of giving an order, and the next in command was obliged to array the men, and take the necessary measures for defence. the belief therefore that mr Henry was no souldier, which prevailed with the Committee of safety, and also with our own members of Congress, might justify them in not confiding to him the military destinies of the state. the same doubt occasioned a refusal of command sollicited by Col^o^ Byrd, one of our highest citizens in rank & wealth, who had been Col^o^ of a regiment in the war of 1755. it is true indeed that mr Henry and mr Pendleton each, thought they saw in the character of the other something which they condemned; of which those who knew both more intimately than either did the other, acquitted both. and[3] this distrust they never dissembled in their private conversations. they were always polite to each other, but nothing affectionate. possibly some of this grudge might have incorporated itself with mr Pendleton's judgments on the military merit of mr Henry: but since this trait in mr Henry's character has at least been believed, and no fact has been produced to prove it ill-founded (for his march to Williamsburg proved civil courage only, but not military, as he knew there was no enemy to meet him) why bring it into view at all? mr Henry's transcendent eminence as an Orator & Statesman, and especially his unquestioned primacy in bringing on the revolution give him a mass of fame sufficient to satisfy any ambition. to claim for him questionable merits detracts more than it adds in the estimate of his character. Demosthenes like Henry, was unquestioned as an Orator & Statesman, but doubted as a soldier. but is it not found that, on the former grounds alone the Graecian is placed as high as mortal man can be? the danger is that if this point be urged it may produce contradiction and proof, which would die away if not excited. I was as intimate, and more cordial with mr Henry in those days, than perhaps any other of those with whom he acted on the higher stage of affairs; and my settled opinion was this. when mr Henry found that the business of Congress had got into a regular train of action, in which he could no longer maintain his eminence, it became his wish to withdraw; and the military command in Virginia, which was conferred on him while absent at Philadelphia, appeared to him as a god-send to justify his retirement from Congress. I accompanied him to Virginia on his return, which gave me some opportunity of estimating his views on the occasion. I did not observe that they were directed to military fame, or that he thought his appointment had put him into the line of splendid utility. indeed I doubted from his conversation, whether he meant to accept it. add to this that his mind was not formed for subordination, even to a Committee of safety, or a Convention. he became anxious therefore to withdraw from his military station, after it had served the purpose of procuring him a decent retreat from his Congressional one; and the question about rank furnished him plausible cause. of this he availed himself, and thus got back to that ground on which nature had formed him to command. he returned to our civil councils which were his natural element, and in which his eminence at once placed him at their head. this I did then, and do still verily believe was the train of views on which mr Henry acted. I think that he felt himself at home in civil affairs and soaring above all: but not at all so in military things: that he never had a wish or a thought of pursuing that career, in which there was already a croud of Generals, who must for ever be above him, and that his apparent resentment covered really a secret wish. mr Henry was not a man who, on a nice punctilio of honor, would have withdrawn from a post of his choice in a cause in which he was so ardent.

If this be a true view of the question between mr Pendleton & mr Henry, it would seem that all difficulty may be avoided by striking out the whole of what relates to this incident, and leaving it blank to bury the question as to both in oblivion. while this would leave in quiet the admirers of both parties, it would remove from the page of history an example of sacrificing so holy a cause, and at so early a period of it, to personal passions and interests; which it is distressing, in such a case, to suppose but on notorious fact.

pa. 137. Can this preamble be correctly copied from the printed one? it is not grammar. my original draught did not run so, as may be seen if examined.

pa. 144. I think that Congress only authorised Gen[l] Washington to extend military law (which always prevails within a camp & to gunshot distance beyond the line of centinels) to the distance of twenty miles around his camp. but I am not sure of this, and it ought to be enquired into; for it is not useful that examples should be strained to furnish precedents for so execrable a measure as the establishment of a dictator.

Of the anecdote of popular violence on the flag of the General assembly in 1769. I never before heard, nor can I believe it true. I was in Williamsburg during the 4. courts of Apr. June, Oct. & Dec. of that and of some years preceding & subsequent, and also during the autumn session of the legislature of the same year, and do not remember to have heard a word of such an act of insurgency of our people; and had I ever heard it, I could not have forgotten so unique a fact. it would have been the first instance of actual riot, in our country below the mountains since Bacon's rebellion. the previous assemblages of people to ask their stamp masters to resign were entirely peaceable. in 1769 the people were yet entirely submissive to the laws, and would have been unquestionably punished for any daring breach of them.

MS (ViU: TJP); entirely in TJ's hand; undated. PoC (DLC).

In this document TJ cites page numbers from a manuscript, not found, of Wirt, *Patrick Henry*.

For the LETTER HERE QUOTED, see the enclosure to TJ to Wirt, 12 Apr. 1812. An extract from that document is printed without attribution in Wirt, *Patrick Henry*, 108–9. BOUCHE À FEU: "gun; cannon." TJ had faced a BATTERY OF OBLOQUY from the Lee family since 1794, in part, perhaps, because of his opposition to the Jay Treaty, which they favored. In addition, in that year Henry Lee had passed on to George Washington a secondhand account of a dinner-table remark by TJ that Lee regarded as insulting to the president (*PTJ*, 28:433; Washington, *Papers, Pres. Ser.*, 16:572–3). TJ's description of Edward Foy as the CHIEF INSTIGATOR of Lord Dunmore's VIOLENCES is inserted parenthetically and without attribution in Wirt, *Patrick Henry*, 134.

Wirt ultimately glossed over doubts about Henry's PERSONAL COURAGE by stating that "His personal bravery, so far as I have heard, has never been called in question; or if it has, it has been without evidence" (Wirt, *Patrick Henry*, 177). Edmund Pendleton's low opinion of Henry's MILITARY MERIT was merely one manifestation of his longstanding opposition to the famed orator, whom he considered a demagogue. Pendleton also disapproved of his 1765 Stamp Act resolutions, resisted his military advancement during the Revolutionary War, and supported, in 1788, Virginia's ratification of the United States Constitution, which Henry opposed (*ANB*; *DAB*). Henry ostensibly resigned from his MILITARY STATION early in 1776 because Congress would not give him the rank of brigadier general in the Continental army (Wirt, *Patrick Henry*, 179–80).

TJ had forwarded from Philadelphia a draft of what became the PREAMBLE to Virginia's constitution by the end of June 1776 (*PTJ*, 1:329–86; see also Wirt, *Patrick Henry*, 196n). On several occasions during the Revolutionary War, Congress gave George Washington vast powers to control the region AROUND HIS CAMP, a territory that was defined in 1777 as "such parts of these states as may be within the circumference of 70 miles of the head quarters of the American army" (Worthington C. Ford and others, eds., *Journals of the Continental Congress, 1774–1789* [1904–37], 6:1027, 1045–6, 8:752). Nathaniel Bacon (1647–76) led a REBELLION against royal authority in Virginia in the year of his death (*DVB*).

[1] Preceding two words interlined.

[2] Word interlined.

[3] Word interlined in place of "but."

From John Adams

Dear Sir Quincy Sept. 30. 16

The Seconds of Life, that remain to me, are So few and So Short; (and they Seem to me Shorter and Shorter every minute) that I cannot Stand upon Epistolary Ettiquette: And though I have written two Letters, yet unnoticed I must write a third. Because I am not acquainted with any Man on this Side of Montecello, who can give me any Information upon Subjects that I am now analysing and investigating; if I may be permitted to use the pompous Words now in fashion.

When I read Dr Priestleys Remarks upon "Du Puis," I felt a Curiosity to know more about him. I wrote to Europe and engaged another to write. I had no Idea of more than one or two Volumes in 8o or 12mo

But Lo! I am overwhelmed[1] with 8 or ten Volumes[2] and another of Planches!

Sixteen years of Research the Author acknowledges, and as he quotes his Authorities I would not undertake to verify them in 16 years, If I had all his Books which Surely are not to be found in America.

If you know any Thing of this "Monsieur Dupuis"[3] or his "origine de tous les Cultes"; candidus imperti.

I have read only the first Volume. It is learned and curious. The whole Work will afford me Business, Study and Amusement for the Winter.

Dr Priestley pronounced him an Atheist, and his Work "The Ne Plus ultra of Infidelity." Priestley agrees with him, that the History of the Fall of Adam and Eve, is "an Alegory," a Fable, an Arabian Tale, and So does Dr Middleton, to account for the origin of Evil; which however it does not

Priestly Says that the Apocalypse,[4] according to Dupuis is the most learned Work that ever was written.

With these brief Fletrissures, Priestly Seems to have expected to annihilate[5] the Influence of Dupuis Labours; as Swift destroyed Blackmore with his

"Did off Creation with a Jerk
And of Redemption made damn'd Work." And as he disgraced Men as good at least as himself by his

"Wicked Will Whiston,
And Good, Master Ditton."

But Dupuis is not to be So easily destroyed.

The Controversy between Spiritualism and Materialism between Spiritualists and Materialists, will not be Settled by Scurrilous Epigrams of Swift, nor by dogmatical Censures of Priestly.

You and I have as much Authority to Settle these Disputes as Swift Priestley or Dupuis, or The Pope.

And if you will agree with me, We will issue our Bull,[6] and enjoin upon all these Gentlemen to be Silent, till they can tell Us, What Matter is and What Spirit is! And in the mean time to observe the Commandments and the Sermon on the Mount. J. ADAMS

RC (DLC); endorsed by TJ as received 7 Oct. 1816 and so recorded in SJL. RC (MHi); address cover only; with PoC of TJ to Thomas Eston Randolph, 20 Oct. 1816, on verso; addressed by Susan B. Adams: "Thomas Jefferson Esq[re] Late President of the US. Monticello Virginia"; postmarked Quincy, Mass., 30 Sept. FC (Lb in MHi: Adams Papers).

PLANCHES: "plates; illustrations." CANDIDUS IMPERTI: "pass it on, my good fellow," from Horace, *Epistles*, 1.6.67 (Fairclough, *Horace: Satires, Epistles and Ars Poetica*, 290–1).

Joseph Priestley referred to Charles François Dupuis, *Origine de Tous les Cultes: ou, Religion Universelle*, 12 vols. in 7 (Paris, year III [1794/95]; Adams's copy in MBPLi), as THE NE PLUS ULTRA OF INFIDELITY in his *A Comparison of the Institutions of Moses with those of the Hindoos and Other Ancient Nations; with Remarks on Mr. Dupuis's Origin of all Religions* (Northumberland, Pa., 1799), 301. Flétrissures (FLETRISSURES) are "blots" or "stains."

DID OFF CREATION WITH A JERK AND OF REDEMPTION MADE DAMN'D WORK is from Jonathan Swift, "Verses To be placed under the Picture of England's Arch-Poet: Containing a compleat Catalogue of his Works" (*Miscellanies. Consisting of Verses by Dr. Swift, Dr. Arbuthnot, Mr. Pope, and Mr. Gay* [London, 1742], 4:254). The couplet satirizes Sir Richard Blackmore and his poems on *Creation* (1712) and *Redemption* (1722). WICKED WILL WHISTON, AND GOOD, MASTER DITTON, drawn from Swift's "Ode, for Musick. On the Longitude" (*Miscellanies*, 4:145), ridicules a proposal by the mathematicians William Whiston and Humphry Ditton that rockets fired from a network of ships at known positions could be used to determine a seagoing vessel's longitude (*ODNB*).

[1] RC: "overwhilmed." FC: "overwhelmed."

[2] RC: "Volums." FC: "volumes."

[3] Omitted closing quotation mark editorially supplied.

[4] RC: "Apocalypes." FC: "Apocalypse."

[5] RC: "annilate." FC: "annihilate."

[6] RC: "Bulle." FC: "bull."

From James Monroe

DEAR SIR Albemarle Sepr 30. 1816

The inclosed was left with me by M[r] Rush, for your opinion, of the propriety of the measure proposed. I retaind it, in the hope of finding you alone, before we separated, for a moments conversation on the subject. The first[1] question is, whether such a notice of the occurrence, which it is proposed to commemorate, is proper, or silent contempt, will be, more expressive, & dignified? You will have the goodness to inclose the papers to me, at your leisure, with your sentiments on the project, at washington. with my best and affectionate wishes for your health & welfare, I am dear sir

your friend & servant JAS MONROE

RC (DLC); addressed (trimmed): "[...]as Jefferson Monticello"; endorsed by TJ as received 5 Oct. 1816 and so recorded in SJL.

For the likely subject of the enclosed PAPERS, not found, see TJ to Monroe, 16 Oct. 1816.

[1] Word interlined.

From Wilson Cary Nicholas

MY DEAR SIR Richmond Sept. 30. 1816

I feel great reluctance at asking of you what from its nature I fear cannot be very agreeable. I am confident I ought not to impoze so much trouble upon you. I trust however you will pardon me if it shou'd not be agreeable to you to interest yourself for a family, with which I am nearly connected. my Eldest sister you know married Mr Norton & had the fairest prospects in point of fortune. The revolutionary war swept off the whole of her husbands great fortune, so that his children have not received one cent from his estate. His second daughter a beautiful delicate & amiable woman married a Mr Armistead, who was bred a merchant, but was unfortunate and obliged to retire into the Country, where he has supported his family for several years by his labour. The issue of a law suit about the land on which he lived being unfavorable, has thrown him & his helpless family upon the world without a home. M^r^ A— I am informed is well qualified to discharge the duties of a clerk in any of the departments[1] at Washington. His connexions are highly respectable. He is the brother of Col Armistead who defended the fort at Baltimore, and of one or two other officers of great merit who were lost in the service. If you cou'd procure such[2] employment for him you wou'd add greatly to the obligations I am under to you & wou'd save an amiable woman & children and I believe a worthy man from distress. In any event I trust my Dear Sir, you will forgive the liberty I have taken in making this application. a letter addressed to M^r^ A at Hay market prince William County will get to hand. I hope the next time I go to Albemarle to have it in my power to pay my respects to you at monticello. I have only a moment to assure you of the very great respect & regard of

Dear Sir

Your hum. Servant W. C. NICHOLAS

RC (DLC); endorsed by TJ as received 7 Oct. 1816 and so recorded in SJL. RC (DLC); address cover only; with PoC of TJ to Alexander J. Dallas, 20 Oct. 1816, on verso; addressed: "Thomas Jefferson Esqr monticello milton va."; stamp canceled; franked; postmarked Richmond, 3 Oct.

William Armistead (ca. 1773–1840) was married to Ann (Anne) Cary Norton, a daughter of Nicholas's eldest sister, Sarah Nicholas Norton. The owner of a dozen slaves in 1810, in the same year he patented a method of "destroying the Hessian fly and Weavel, or preventing it from injuring wheat or grain." His brother, United States Army major George Armistead, commanded Baltimore's Fort McHenry during the British bombardment of 13–14 Sept. 1814, and two other siblings, Addison Bowles Armistead and Lewis G. A. Armistead, lost their lives during the War of 1812. William Armistead, who had been ejected from the farm on which he lived in Prince William County in March 1815, was hired as a clerk in the office of the War Department's accountant on 4 Dec. 1816. He transferred to a similar position in the Treasury Department's third auditor's office early the following March. Having labored there until at least the end of 1818, Armistead served as post sutler at Fort Monroe, Virginia, 1820–40 (Louise Pecquet du Bellet, *Some Prominent Virginia Families* [1907; repr. 1976], 2:317, 664; William S. Appleton, *The Family of Armistead of Virginia* [1899], 13; *List of Patents*, 87; Wilmington *American Watchman and Delaware Republican*, 25 Sept. 1811; DNA: RG 29, CS, Prince William Co., 1810; Heitman, *U.S. Army*, 1:169; *Chapman v. Armistead* [1815], *Va. Reports*, 18 [4 Munford]: 382–98; *Letter from the Acting Secretary of War transmitting Statements of the clerks employed in the Departments of War* [Washington, 1817], 8; *Letter from the Secretary of the Treasury, transmitting a Statement of the names of the clerks in the Treasury Department* [Washington, 1818], 10; *Letter from the Secretary of the Treasury, transmitting a List of the Clerks employed in the Treasury Department* [Washington, 1819], 12; Robert L. Meriwether and others, eds., *The Papers of John C. Calhoun* [1959–2003], 5:212–3, 286, 9:545; Washington *Daily National Intelligencer*, 6 Apr. 1840; Washington *Army and Navy Chronicle*, 9 Apr. 1840).

On this date Nicholas also asked President James Madison to find a position for Armistead (DLC: Madison Papers).

[1]Manuscript: "departmentments."
[2]Nicholas here canceled "appoint."

From Jethro Wood

FRIEND THOMAS JEFFERSON Aurora 10mo 1st 1816

The Firm of which I am a partner requests thy acceptance of a plough, as a respectfull tribute to thy Ingenuity in improving that important Instrument.[1] We shall feel ourselves amply recompenced by thy approbation; or, additionally obliged by any suggestion which may tend to render it more Complete.

By an accident occasioned by the warping[2] of the wooden patern the edges are raised $\frac{1}{3}$ of an Inch too[3] high. The plough is now gone for new york and will be forwarded to thee as soon as possible.

With the greatest Respect I am thy friend JETHRO WOOD

RC (MoSHi: TJC-BC); addressed: "Thomas Jefferson Montisello Late President of the united states"; franked; postmarked Poplar Ridge, N.Y., 17 Oct., and

Washington City, 29 Oct.; endorsed by TJ as received from "Woods? Jethro" on 7 Nov. 1816 and so recorded in SJL.

Jethro Wood (1774–1834), inventor, was born in either Massachusetts or New York and raised in Washington County, New York. He moved permanently to Cayuga County in about 1800. Wood later became a proprietor of a female boarding school in Aurora, corresponding secretary of the Cayuga County Agricultural Society, and postmaster of Poplar Ridge. He is best known, however, for the patents he received for improved plows on 1 July 1814 and 1 Sept. 1819. Having partnered with Elias Rogers to manufacture his invention, he sent samples of their handiwork to both TJ and Emperor Alexander I of Russia. The machine was widely copied, especially in the North. Wood is sometimes credited as inventor of the cast-iron plow, but earlier examples used this material. His invention owed its popularity to a combination of design features, including longitudinal straight lines, good balance, ease of use, interchangeable parts, strength, and affordability. Although his 1819 grant was extended a further fourteen years in 1832, Wood and his family seem to have derived little financial benefit from the invention due to widespread patent infringement (*DAB*; New York *Commercial Advertiser*, 5 Nov. 1819; Boston *Agricultural Intelligencer, and Mechanic Register*, 28 Apr. 1820; Elliot G. Storke and James H. Smith, *History of Cayuga County, New York* [1879], 441–2, 458; *List of Patents*, 140, 206; *Cherry-Valley* [N.Y.] *Gazette*, 4 Feb. 1819; *U.S. Statutes at Large*, 6:486; *Documents relating to the improvements of Jethro Wood in the Construction of the Plough* [1838]; *New-Bedford* [Mass.] *Mercury*, 24 Oct. 1834).

[1] Manuscript: "Instrumment."
[2] Manuscript: "worping."
[3] Manuscript: "to."

To Christopher Clark

TH: JEFFERSON TO MR CLARKE. Poplar Forest Oct. 2.

Reflecting on the case of mr Robertson, which I think a very cruel one, a doubt has occurred to me, which probably has to you also; but lest it should not, I will suggest it. I do not think that information, given in to a grand jury (even if it were false) is perjury in law. a grandjury is no magistracy, no tribunal, has not therefore the power of administering an oath. it is a body merely for enquiry and accusation. they can try nothing. they are merely to say that they have reason to believe that A.B. has committed an illegal act, and that he ought to be put on his defence before a tribunal which can try him. they are formed into a body, that they may fear nothing either for themselves or those who give information to them, & therefore they are sworn to keep their proceedings secret, that the individual among themselves, or who gives them information may not be known or exposed to the enmity or persecution of another. Blackstone (for I have no other law book here) defines perjury, from Ld Coke, to be an offence 'when the suit is <u>past it's commencement</u>, and <u>come to trial</u>.' but the information given to a grandjury is before any suit is commenced. it is an affidavit given out of court, and relating to nothing in court. Blackstone says further that the matter sworn must be 'material to the issue'; but here is no issue joined, nor as yet any proceeding in court determined on; it is as yet entirely extrajudicial.—again, how does the information of mr Robertson become known? by the disclosure of a grandjuror of course. then that grandjuror is perjured, for he was[1] sworn in court not to disclose the transactions before them, and this is specially intended for the safety & assurance of the individual, whether one of themselves or a witness who gives information. it is a high misprision in him for which he ought to be fined & imprisoned. 4. Black. 126. and can that disclosure, which is itself an act of perjury, fix perjury on another[?] does it not destroy itself and render itself null, as being an oath against an oath? the grandjuror, I am sure, has done this unwittingly. so did mr Robertson. both have been unguarded, and said or done what neither meant. mr Robertson was asked a question the true answer to which would have accused himself, and the law authorised him to say 'I know nothing of it which you have a right to require me to say, and therefore to you, in your office, I have a right to say I know nothing about it.' with this paraphrase & explanation, what he said was true, and to the grandjuror, immediately after when out of his official character, he gave this very explanation, which proved the sense in which he gave the answer to him officially. the grandjuror has need of much more paraphrase & explanation to exculpate himself. he can only say that in making the disclosure he had forgotten the oath of secresy he had just taken and was breaking by that disclosure. the oath says further that they will present no one thro malice. is this presentment clear of that ingredient? I am sorry mr Robertson permits this persecution to afflict him. his whole life as well as the impossibility of any rational motive in this case,[2] has given it the lie, and proved it calumnious; and I am persuaded he will find that the interest it has excited in his behalf will increase the attachment of his friends, and place him on firmer ground than he occupied before. nor is it possible to fear any thing from our judges or jurors. their character in our country is the reverse of straining constructions to infer guilt. the difficulty with us is how to bring the guilty to punishment, and not how to oppress the innocent; and whatever a grandjury may think itself obliged to do, as hearing but one side, I have no fear but that our judges & jurors, hearing both sides, and combining with the formal testimony, the evidence of circumstances, characters & motives, will prove the light in which the prosecution is held. a perfect confidence myself in the character of mr Robertson & a supposition that you are his counsel, have induced me to hazard these suggestions, to which I will only add my friendly salutns. TH: JEFFERSON

P.S. surely no Grandjuror would yield to be exam[d] on the trial as to what passed before the grandjury, because he would be forsworn; nor would a judge in his discretion permit a witness to forswear himself even if he were so disposed.

PoC (DLC); partially dated; edge trimmed; ink stained, with obscured word rewritten by TJ; postscript written perpendicularly in left margin of first page; endorsed by TJ as a letter of 2 Oct. 1816 and so recorded in SJL.

MR ROBERTSON was most likely the Lynchburg merchant Archibald Robertson, the only correspondent of TJ's with that surname living near Poplar Forest. William Blackstone DEFINES PERJURY in his *Commentaries on the Laws of England* (Oxford, 1765–69; Sowerby, nos. 1806–7; Poor, *Jefferson's Library*, 10 [no. 553]), 4:136–7. In doing so he drew on Edward COKE, *The Third Part of the Institutes of the Laws of England* (London, 1644; Sowerby, no. 1784), chap. 74. 4. BLACK. 126: Blackstone, *Commentaries*, 4:126.

[1] Manuscript: "was was."
[2] Preceding twelve words interlined.

From James Freeman

Octo. 2. 1816.

M[r] Freeman of Boston has visited Monticello, that he might have the honour of seeing M[r] Jefferson, and of enjoying the high pleasure of hearing him converse; and he regrets that his professional duties as a clergyman compel him to quit his hospitable mansion without indulging himself in the delight, which has long been the object of his ardent desire. He tenders his best respects to M[r] Jefferson, and wishes him much health and happiness.

RC (DLC); endorsed by TJ as a letter from "Freeman James. rev[d]," written at Monticello and received 5 Oct. 1816, and so recorded in SJL. RC (DLC); address cover only; with PoC of TJ to Patrick Gibson, 28 Dec. 1816, on verso; addressed: "Mr Jefferson."

James Freeman (1759–1835), Unitarian minister, was born in Charlestown, Massachusetts, and graduated from Harvard University in 1777. He joined King's Chapel, an Anglican church in Boston, as a reader in 1782 and promoted the revision of its prayer book and adoption of Unitarianism over the next several years. Although Freeman's rejection of the Trinity prevented him from being ordained by the Episcopal Church, he received a lay ordination from his congregation in 1787. He remained the pastor of King's Chapel until 1826, when he retired for health reasons. During his long career Freeman was a member of the local school committee and the American Academy of Arts and Sciences, and he represented Boston at the state constitutional convention of 1820–21. He was also a founder of the Massachusetts Historical Society and served as its recording secretary, 1793–1812. Freeman died in Newton, Massachusetts (*ANB*; *DAB*; *Harvard Catalogue*,

171; *The Act of Incorporation, Bye-Laws, Catalogue of Members, and Circular Letter of the Massachusetts Historical Society* [Boston, 1813], 9, 13; *Journal of Debates and Proceedings in the Convention of Delegates, chosen to revise the Constitution of Massachusetts* [Boston, 1821]; *New-Bedford Mercury*, 20 Nov. 1835; gravestone inscription at East Parish Burying Ground, Newton).

From William Wirt

DEAR SIR. Richmond. Oct. 2. 1816

I sent you about three or four weeks ago a second, and by the last mail, a third parcel of my biographical M.S.—Not having heard of their arrival and having had frequent proofs of the irregularity of the mails, I begin to be[1] fearful that the packets have miscarried.—I beg you to be assured that it is not with the most distant intention of hurrying you in the kind and obliging office[2] which you have been so good as to undertake for me, that I trouble you with this note—but singly and sincerely to ascertain whether the packets[3] have arrived—because if they have not, I will have them immediately recopied and forwarded through a private channel,[4] and shall thus save time which might[5] otherwise be lost, on the supposition that the papers[6] have miscarried.—So far[7] from hurrying you I feel myself most sensibly[8] obliged by every hour of the time which you are so good as to devote to this little business of mine,[9] and am much more disposed to[10] Enlarge than to contract your opportunity for remark.

Respectfully and affectionately—Yours WM WIRT

RC (MHi); at foot of text: "Thomas Jefferson esq^{r}"; endorsed by TJ as received 24 Oct. 1816 and so recorded in SJL. Dft (ViU: TJP); with apparently unrelated computations by Wirt on verso. Tr (MdHi: Wirt Papers); follows RC.

1 Dft: "I am."

2 Remainder of phrase in Dft reads "you have undertaken for me, that I drop this note."

3 Dft: "parcels."

4 Preceding four words not in Dft.

5 Dft: "w^{d}."

6 Dft: "<*the packets*> they."

7 Dft here adds "indeed."

8 Dft: "myself much."

9 Preceding two words not in Dft.

10 Dft: "and had much rather."

From John Barnes

MY DEAR SIR,— George Town 3^{d} Octr 1816,

I am Anxiously waiting receipt of your expected fav^{r} in Answer to my Letters of the 5th & 10th of Aug^{t}—the first Covered: a rough statem^{t} of Genl Kosciusko^{s} ℀ with me whilst that of the 10th respected the difficulty in transferring and Consolidating his several Stocks into Govern[t] security—and in his Own—proper Name—and presuming—these transfers to be Effected—it would still be unavailing—in point of my Authority—to receive[1] his dividends—or Int. without his proper power of Attorney—to you, and substitution thro you to me—to be lodged in the Departm[t]—wherever the Int &a—is made payable.—I called Yesterday at Bank of Colum[a]—in Order to receive the 6 M[os] Dividend—on the Gen[ls] 46 Shares a 8 ℔Ct—but could not receive it—(though in your Name) Unless your power of Atty to me—is lodged there—which please send me: at your first Leisure hour—with Respect to Consolidating the several Stocks in the Gen[ls] Name—you will be Obliged—to direct him to forward you his general power—such a one—as will eventually serve the wish[d] for purpose—

I pray, no Unforeseen Accident has happened, to deprive me, the pleasure & satisfaction of receiving—your long wished for favours—

Most Respectfully and Affectionately

Dear Sir, Your Obed[t] humble servant JOHN BARNES.

RC (ViU: TJP-ER); endorsed by TJ as received 11 Oct. 1816, but recorded in SJL as received a day earlier. RC (DLC); address cover only; with PoC of TJ to Wilson Cary Nicholas, 16 Oct. 1816, on verso; addressed: "Thomas Jefferson Esqr—Monticello—Virginia"; stamped; postmarked (faint) Georgetown, 4 [Oc]t.

[1]Manuscript: "recive."

From John F. Watson

Bank of Germantown Oct 4. 1816

Thomas Jefferson Esq[re]

1816 To John F Watson Dr—

Oct 4 for the 11 to 14 Vol[s] of the Edinb[g] Review now forwarded in 2 packets ℔ mail & which close the sub[on] 10 D[rs]

SIR

Be pleased to remit me the amo[t] ℔[1] mail in Richmond notes as heretofore

Yrs very respectfully JOHN F WATSON

I determine to send only one vol ℔ Each successive mail— W

RC (DLC); dateline beneath full signature; postscript written perpendicularly in left margin of address leaf; addressed: "His Excellency Tho[s] Jefferson Esqre Monticello V[a]"; franked; postmarked Germantown, 5 Oct.; endorsed by TJ as received 10 Oct. 1816 and so recorded in SJL.

SUB[ON]: "subscription."

[1]Manuscript: "℔r."

From Thomas Bingham

Anville, Lebanon County,
MAY IT PLEASE YOUR EXCELLENCY, Octr 7th 1816.

The writer of this was a Soldier in the Army of the United States, was enlisted under the command of Captain Evans & Lieutenant Luthar Scott in the 2nd Corps of heavy Artillery on the 5th day of February 1813 and remained in the Service until the 18th day of August 1815. I made application for my discharge to Major Nourse who got my papers and retains them until the present. I was under the necessity of applying to the Civil Authority for the same—before I could obtain it, and after a Severe examination & strict scrutiny they could not find that I was enlisted for a longer term than five years or during the War. I served for nine Months under the Command of Major Robert Deau Topographical Engineer, returned[1] from the Pea patch to Fort Mifflin[2] where I did duty until I obtained my clearance from the Civil Authority.—Major Robert Deau can and will certify for my good behaviour during the time I was under his Command. I never received more than one payment during the term of my Service. there remains due to me fifteen months and eighteen days pay due to me from the United States.—My reliance & confidence is placed in your[3] Excellency that you will exert your influence in behalf of a poor Soldier who has a wife and Small family to support I have the honor[4] to be

Your Excellencies devot Servant THOMAS BINGHAM.

RC (MHi); addressed: "His Excellency Thomas Jefferson Esquire late President of the United States City of Washington," with the last word canceled by a postmaster and replaced with "Milton V"; franked; postmarked Annville, 8 Oct., and Washington, 11 Oct.; endorsed by TJ as received 16 Oct. 1816 and so recorded in SJL.

Thomas Bingham (ca. 1774–1851) was born in County Down, Ireland, and immigrated with three of his brothers to New York City in 1793. By 1801 he had moved to Lancaster County, Pennsylvania, where he married and started a family. Bingham relocated by 1808 to Annville in Lebanon County, and he lived there until at least 1830. He was still trying as late as 1844 to obtain $121.06 due him for his service as a private in the War of 1812. In his last years Bingham resided in Philadelphia County (Theodore A. Bingham, comp., *The Bingham Family in the United States* [1927], 813, 828–9; *JHR*, 39:449 [23 Feb. 1844]; U.S. House of Representatives, 28th Cong., 1st sess., H.R. 397 [7 June 1844]; DNA: RG 29, CS, Pa., Annville, 1820, 1830, Philadelphia Co., 1850).

MAJOR ROBERT DEAU was Isaac Roberdeau.

[1] Manuscript: "rturnd."
[2] Preceding three words interlined.
[3] Manuscript: "yur."
[4] Manuscript: "hononor."

To Dabney Carr

DEAR SIR Monticello Oct. 8. 16.

I found here on my late return from Bedford, your favor of Sep. 24. and am very thankful for the information it conveys.
I recieved in the summer, a pamphlet and a letter under the name of H. Tompkinson. I knew no such person; but the pamphlet was sensibly & temperately written, on the subject of a convention, and as my sentiments on it were sollicited, and I thought such a writer might make good use of the matter without the name, I communicated them fully & freely. he acknoleged the reciept of my letter under his real name of Sam[l] Kerchival, and pressed me to permit the publication of my letter. I instantly repeated to him my entreaties to prevent the possibility of that; and, still confiding in his honor, I added some matter supplementory to the former. your letter is the first notice of the breach of my injunctions, and I now inclose a 3[d] letter to him, and pray you, after it's perusal, to stick a wafer in it, and to put it into the post office. can you do me the further favor of telling me who mr Kerchival is? for I know nothing of him but from his pamphlet. I have sometimes thought of coming to a resolution never to answer a letter from a person whom I do not know. yet, to consider every man as unworthy of confidence, because some are found to be so, is a Machiavelism so contrary to my opinion of the human character generally, that I cannot act upon it. I believe it is better to suffer sometimes by breaches of confidence, than to suspect all and, by a jesuitical reserve, to become suspected of all.

Before the reciept of your letter I had attended to the other subject mentioned in it, and I have reason to believe that not only the testimony, but the very words of my letter to you are used as you wished them. Affectionately Yours TH: JEFFERSON

PoC (DLC); at foot of text: "the honble Dabney Carr"; endorsed by TJ. Enclosure: TJ to Samuel Kercheval, 8 Oct. 1816.

To Patrick Gibson, with Jefferson's Note

DEAR SIR Monticello Oct. [8]. 16.

The navigation of our river above M[c]Gruder's locks having been suspended by their being out of order for 2. or 3. weeks past, and likely to continue so some days longer, I am obliged to send a small cart for a part of the wines which I expect have been lodged with you for me from Alexandria, New york & Norfolk. I give to the bearer a paper of directions what parcels I would prefer that he should bring. what he cannot bring will be called for by Gilmore or Johnson as soon as they can pass the locks. I have had flour waiting in our mill for some time which will go on as soon as the locks can be passed. I am the more anxious for this as calls for our taxes are now coming on us, and it is the season for favorable purchases of corn, which the scanty crop will render scarce and high. Accept the assurance of my great esteem & respect TH: JEFFERSON

[*Note by TJ:*]

The following articles are, as I expect, now deposited with mr Gibson.

from Alexandria. 2. cases of wine, 50. bottles in each. there were 4. two of which the bearer brought away before.

from Norfolk. 1. barrel 38. gallons.

from New York. 2. cases B. N° 1. and 2. TI. of 12. bottles each.
1. d° C. N° 1. of 30. bottles.
1. d° 25. bottles
1. d° 57. bottles
1. basket Maccaroni.

there will come further from New York a package of books.
& from Baltimore 2. cases of wine 57. bottles each.

PoC (DLC); on verso of reused address cover of Theodorus Bailey to TJ, 27 July 1816; ink stained; at foot of text: "Mr Gibson"; endorsed by TJ as a letter of 8 Oct. 1816 and so recorded in SJL.

McGRUDER'S LOCKS were located on the Rivanna River near the boundary between Albemarle and Fluvanna counties. Wormley Hughes was the BEARER (*MB*, 2:1327). The PAPER OF DIRECTIONS has not been found. OUR MILL was TJ's flour mill at Shadwell.

To Samuel Kercheval

SIR Monticello Oct. 8. 16.

A friend in your part of the country informs me that he has seen, in pretty free circulation, a letter from me to yourself on the subject of a Convention, that it was in the hands of a printer, that he had heard several speak of having seen it, and the idea was that it was refused to none who asked for it. I cannot but be alarmed at this information. my letter of July 12. was expressly confided to your honor, to be so used as to be kept from the public papers; and that of Sep. 5. further pressed my request that you would not admit a possibility of it's being published. I did expect, and had no objections, that you should be at liberty to[1] communicate it's contents to particular friends in whom you had confidence; but not that you would permit it to go out of your own hands, still less into those of a printer, to be shewn to every one, perhaps to be copied and finally published. I must, Sir, reiterate my prayers to you to recall the original, and the copies, if any have been taken.

the question of a Convention is become a party one with which I shall not intermeddle. I am willing to live under the constitution, as it is, if a majority of my fellow-citizens prefer it; altho' I think it might be made better, and, for the sake of future generations (when principles shall have become too relaxed to permit amendment, as experience proves to be the constant course of things) I wished to have availed them of the virtues of the present time to put into a chaste & secure form, the government to be handed down to them. but I repeat that if a majority of my fellow citizens are contented with what will last their time, I am so also, and with the more reason as mine is nearly out.[2] I again throw the quiet of my life on your honor, and repeat the assurances of my respect. TH: JEFFERSON

P.S. on revisal of my letter of Sep. 5. I discover an error which be pleased to correct with the pen, by striking out of the 5th line from the close, the words 'as 5' and inserting 'so also.'

PoC (DLC); at foot of text: "Mr Samuel Kerchival"; endorsed by TJ. Enclosed in TJ to Dabney Carr, 8 Oct. 1816. Extract printed in Kercheval, *Jefferson's Letters*, 12.

TJ'S FRIEND IN YOUR PART OF THE COUNTRY was Dabney Carr.

[1] Preceding four words interlined.

[2] Extract in Kercheval, *Jefferson's Letters*, consists of paragraph to this point, plus dateline, closing, and signature.

To Joseph E. McIlhenney

SIR Monticello Oct. 8th 16.

On my return from a journey I found here your letter of Sep. 17. in answer to which I will previously make an extract from my letter to mr Peale which led to it. 'we suffer in our clocks & watches; being obliged to send the latter always to Richmond (75. miles) for repairs. and the former being at rest for years sometimes till some straggling pretender accidentally passes this way to repair or ruin them. yet Charlottesville would be a fine stand for a good workman[1] I wrote to mr Voigt once to ask of him to recommend to one of his young pupils when turning out and in quest of a place, to come here. the population of the country is thick, & independant, & would furnish abundant employment for a good watchmaker, clock maker and silversmith. it is also a cheap place for articles of subsistence. you would render us a great service by sending such an one. if sober, he would need nothing but his tools for outfit. he would get an apartment and his board readily on credit, until he could begin to recieve money, which indeed would be immediately: & I would put him into the hands of such persons in Charlottesville as would efficiently patronize him.'

Facts are still as they were at the date of this letter to mr Peale, & I sincerely wish you had happened to come on; because I am obliged to leave this place in a few days, and to be absent a month or 6. weeks. it would be much better that I should be here when you arrive, as I could make you known and smooth difficulties which might embarras a stranger; and indeed I could employ you in my own house for some time, during which you could visit Charlottesville daily and be providing a situation for yourself, without being at expences in a tavern. I am sure that I could so much facilitate your commencement here, were I here myself, that I would recommend, if you can, to employ yourself a month otherwise, so as to be here about[2] the 1st day of December, you will find me at home, and ready to do whatever I can towards your introduction to business here. I would wish you to come directly to my house where we can at leisure look out for your establishment in Charlottesville. I tender you my best wishes for your success.

TH: JEFFERSON

PoC (MHi); ink stained, with portion of dateline rewritten by TJ for clarity; at foot of first page: "Mr Joseph E. Mc-Ilhenny"; endorsed by TJ.

[1] Preceding three words reworked from "one" and "a good."

[2] Word interlined.

To William Wirt

DEAR SIR Monticello Oct. 8. 16.

I recieved your 3d parcel of sheets just as I was leaving Poplar Forest, and have read them with the usual pleasure. they relate however to the period of time exactly, during which I was absent in Europe. consequently I am without knolege of the facts they state. indeed they are mostly new history to me. on the subject of style they are not liable to the doubts I hazarded on the 1st parcel, unless a short passage in page 198. should be thought too poetical. indeed as I read the 2d & 3d parcels with attentions to style and found them not subject to the observations I made on the first, (which were from memory only, & after I had parted with them) I have suspected that a revisal might have corrected my opinion on the 1st. of this however you will judge. one only fact in the last sheets was within my knolege, that relating to Philips, and on this I had formerly given you explanations. I am very glad indeed that you have examined the records, and established truth in this case. how mr Randolph could indulge himself in a statement of facts, so solemnly made, the falsehood of every article of which had been known to himself particularly; and how mr Henry could be silent under such a perversion of facts known to himself, agreed on at a consultation with members whom he invited to the palace to advise with on the occasion, and done at his request according to what was concluded, is perfectly unaccountable. not that I consider mr Randolph as mistating intentionally, or desiring to boulster an argument at the expence of an absent person: for there were no uncordial dispositions between him & myself; and as little do I impute to mr Henry any willingness to leave on my shoulders a charge which he could so easily have disproved. the fact must have been that they were both out of their heads on that occasion: still not the less injuriously to me, whom mr Randolph might as well have named, as the journals shewed I was the first named of the Committee. would it be out of place for you to refer by a note to the countenance which judge Tucker has given to this misrepresentation, by making strictures on it, in his Blackstone, as if it were true? it is such a calumny on our revolutionary government as should be eradicated from history, and especially from that of this state, which justly prides itself on having gone thro the revolution without a single example of capital punishment connected with that. ever affectionately yours

Th: Jefferson

RC (ViU: TJP); at foot of first page: "Mr Wirt." PoC (DLC). Presumably enclosing the manuscript, not found, of a portion of Wirt, *Patrick Henry*.

TJ defended the 1778 bill of attainder against Josiah PHILIPS at length in his letter to Louis H. Girardin of 12 Mar. 1815, an extract of which he forwarded to Wirt on 12 May 1815. THE PALACE was the governor's residence in Williamsburg. To correct St. George Tucker's alleged MISREPRESENTATION of the Philips case, Wirt duly added a section entitled "Note C." to pp. ix–xii of the appendix of Wirt, *Patrick Henry*.

To William H. Crawford

Dear Sir Monticello Oct. 9. 16

I rebut as steadily as is in my power applications to join in sollicitations for appointment. but circumstances sometimes render it impossible. a mr Armistead of this state who married a neice of our governor, has a family, and is reduced to extreme want by unsuccesful commerce wishes to be appointed a clerk in some of the offices at Washington. he is represented as a very worthy man, and entirely qualified for the duties of such an appointment. he is brother to the Col^o Armistead who defended the fort at Baltimore, and of one or two other officers of great merit who were lost in the service. should any such vacancy happen within your appointment, I verily believe you would acquire an useful subject in mr Armistead,[1] and it would be peculiarly grateful to our governor & his family. I hope you will pardon me for becoming the channel of application which circumstances forbade me to decline, & that you will be assured of my great esteem and respect. TH: JEFFERSON

P.S. mr Armistead's[2] Christian name has not been given to me. it shall however be forwarded to you.

PoC (DLC); on verso of reused address cover to TJ; at foot of text: "<*Govr Nicholas*> Wm H. Crawford esq."; endorsed by TJ.

[1] Manuscript: "Armstead."
[2] Manuscript: "Armstead's."

To Benjamin W. Crowninshield

DEAR SIR Monticello Oct. 9. 16.

The inclosed sollicitations for a midshipman's place for William Henry Kennon of this state, are from his mother and uncle, both well known to me as persons of merit. the latter is Clerk of our House of delegates. the father Genl Kennon was a valuable character, of whose services I wished much to have availed the public in instituting the new government at St Louis. of the grounds which would befriend mr W. H. Kennon's wish, I have no information but from the letters I inclose, in the truth of which I have entire confidence. a favorable presumption however always arises that a person so peculiarly anxious for a particular career has some natural instincts suited to it's duties. with the request that you will pardon my having consented to become the channel of this sollicitation I pray you to accept the assurance of my perfect esteem & high consideration.

TH: JEFFERSON

RC (NjP: Andre deCoppet Collection). PoC (DLC); on verso of a reused address cover from Louis H. Girardin to TJ; at foot of text: "<*Wm Munford esq.*> B. W. Crownenshield"; endorsed by TJ. Enclosures: (1) Elizabeth B. Kennon to TJ, 18 Sept. 1816, not found, but recorded in SJL as received 7 Oct. 1816 from Norfolk. (2) William Munford to TJ, 29 Sept. 1816, not found, but recorded in SJL as received 7 Oct. 1816 (RC in DLC; address cover only; with PoC of TJ to James

Monroe, 10 Jan. 1817, on verso; addressed: "Thomas Jefferson Esq[r] Monticello, Albemarle County"; franked; postmarked [faint] Richmond, 2[9] Sept.).

William Henry Kennon (1800–43), naval officer, was the son of Richard Kennon and Elizabeth Beverley Munford Kennon. Having attended the College of William and Mary in 1814, he was appointed a midshipman in the United States Navy on 1 Jan. 1817. Kennon was promoted in 1828 to lieutenant, to date from 28 Apr. 1826, and he resigned his commission on 16 Dec. 1840. He then retired to his Norwood estate in Powhatan County, where he died (John McGill, comp., *The Beverley Family of Virginia* [1956], 616–7, 639; *William and Mary Provisional List*, 24; Callahan, *U.S. Navy*, 311; *JEP*, 3:595, 599, 5:334 [1, 19 Feb. 1828, 3 Feb. 1841]; *Richmond Enquirer*, 23 Dec. 1843; Powhatan Co. Will Book, 12:236–7).

In 1804 TJ appointed Richard Kennon a commandant with the rank of colonel in the NEW GOVERNMENT of the Louisiana Territory, but he declined the position due to poor health (*Terr. Papers*, 13:46–7, 74).

To James H. McCulloch

SIR Monticello Oct. 9. 16.

I am much indebted for the trouble you have been so good as to take in informing me of the arrival of the 2. cases of wine from mr Appleton, and I now inclose the amount of duties stated in your letter at 16. D 50 c in bank paper, such as I understand to be passable at Baltimore. and I return my thanks to m[r] Kalhenon for his voluntary care of these things the value of which is in it's testimony of dispositions personally kind. I will ask the favor of you to have the 2. cases shipped by some vessel going to Richmond to be delivered to Mess[rs] Gibson & Jefferson there, who will receive them, and pay freight & other charges.

I am particularly thankful for the offer of[1] your kind offices at Baltimore, of which I may happen to have need in cases like the present. I make annually small importations of books from Paris, and wines from Marseilles & Leghorn: and as from these places vessels cannot always be had bound to any particular port of the US. my correspondents put them on board the first bound to any American port consigned to the Collector of the port. in these cases I will ask the favor of you to give me notice of the arrival, & the amount of duties, freight and other charges which I will immediately remit; and that you will be so good as to reship the articles to Richmond to the address of Gibson & Jefferson, who will always pay the charges from your port. I pray [you][2] to accept the assurance of my perfect esteem & respect

TH: JEFFERSON

RC (NjP: Andre deCoppet Collection); addressed: "James H. M[c]Culloch esq. Baltimore"; franked; postmarked Milton, 9 Oct.; endorsed by McCulloch: "Presid[t]

Jefferson of Wine in Shp Von Hollen rec[d] 14 Oct[o] 1816." PoC (DLC); on verso of reused address cover to TJ; mutilated at seal, with one word rewritten by TJ; endorsed by TJ.

M[R] KALHENON: Charles F. Kalkman.

[1] Preceding three words interlined.
[2] Omitted word editorially supplied.

To James Monroe

DEAR SIR Monticello Oct. 9. 16.

A mr Armistead,[1] who married a neice of our governor, who is brother to the Col[o] Armistead[2] that defended the fort at Baltimore and of one or two other officers of great merit lost in the service, and who is reduced to poverty by unsuccesful commerce, wishes to get bread for his family as clerk in an office at Washington. he is represented as a very worthy man and entirely competent to the business. if a vacancy should happen within your gift I believe you would acquire an useful servant in him. I wish this the more in your office because it would tend to restore dispositions between two characters which ought never to have been alienated. between[3] persons so reasonable as yourself and the Governor it is impossible either can be in the wrong. the one, or the other, or perhaps both, must therefore have acted properly, but on wrong information. I have often wished I could be the mediator of restoring a right understanding but, as unsuccesful essays sometimes make things worse, I have feared a formal step towards it. yet you are both made to esteem one another, and esteem is so much sweeter to both parties than it's contrary, that you should both open yourselves to it. should there be any present vacancy, I should value it the more as it would furnish you an occasion of shewing to my other friend what I know myself,[4] how much you are above every thing which is not generous and frank. this object, more than any other, has induced me to the present sollicitation. God bless and preserve you for the eight years to come especially.

TH: JEFFERSON

RC (NN: Monroe Papers); at foot of text: "James Monroe"; endorsed by Monroe. PoC (DLC); on verso of reused address cover of William Short to TJ, 18 July 1816; endorsed by TJ.

Monroe and OUR GOVERNOR, Wilson Cary Nicholas, became ALIENATED during the 1808 presidential campaign. In June of that year Nicholas, who supported James Madison for the Republican nomination, published a harshly worded circular to his congressional constituents questioning Monroe's competence as a diplomat. Later in 1808 he called in a personal loan in such a way, Monroe thought, as was intended to inconvenience him. Despite TJ's efforts the rift between the two men was never entirely healed (Harry Ammon, *James Monroe: The Quest for National Identity* [1971], 275–6; Noble E. Cunningham Jr., ed.,

Circular Letters of Congressmen to Their Constituents, 1789–1829 [1978], 2:601–16). TJ correctly anticipated that Monroe would be president for THE EIGHT YEARS TO COME.

[1] Manuscript: "Armstead."
[2] Manuscript: "Armstead."
[3] TJ here canceled "such."
[4] Manuscript: "mysef."

To Wilson Cary Nicholas

DEAR SIR Monticello Oct. 9. 16.

I am very happy in any opportunity of endeavorin[g] to be useful to one of mrs Norton's family, with whom I had great intimacy at that period of life when impressions are strongest & longest retained. I fear however that a birth in the offices at Washington will be uncertain. they are rarely vacated but by death. I have written however to the two heads of departments with whom I am more at ease in solliciting than with the others. these are the departments of war & state. but it will be necessary for you to furnish me with mr Armistead's[1] Christian name, which was not given in your letter. an increasing stiffness in the wrist, the effect of age & an antient dislocation begins to render the use of the pen painful [& s]low. I can therefore only add the pleasure with which I shall always see you at Monticello, and the hope that I may not be disappointed[2] of it by my visit to Bedford, to which place I set out on the 19th to remain there a month or 6. weeks. Accept my friendly and respectful salutations.

TH: JEFFERSON

PoC (DLC); on verso of reused address cover of Lafayette to TJ, 17 Feb. 1816; edge trimmed and damaged at seal, with some missing text rewritten by TJ; at foot of text: "Governor Nicholas"; endorsed by TJ.

TJ had dislocated his right WRIST in 1786 while living in Paris (*PTJ*, 10:600).

[1] Manuscript: "Armstead's."
[2] Manuscript: "dispointed."

Richard Rush's Account of a Visit to Montpellier and Monticello

DEAR INGERSOLL. Washington October 9. 1816.

I have never seen Mr Madison so well fixed any where as on his estate in Virginia, not even before he was burnt out here. His house would be esteemed a good one for any of our country seats near Philadelphia, and is much larger than most of them. The situation is among mountains, and very beautiful. A fine estate surrounds him, at the head of which he appears to eminent advantage, as well in his great as in his estimable qualities. He has the reputation of being an excellent manager, and is a model of kindness to his slaves. He lives with profuse hospitality, and in a way to strike the eye far more agreeably, than while keeping tavern here. on the fourth of July I was told ninety persons dined with him. To be sure it was a special occasion; but not a week, scarcely a day, passes that he is not doing hospitality in a large way. He was never developed to me under so many interesting lights; as during the very delightful week I spent under his roof. Perhaps I should add, that French cookery, and Madeira that he purchased in Philadelphia in :96 made a part of every day's fare!

Monticello is a curiosity! artificial to a high degree; in many respects superb. If it had not been called Monticello, I would call it Olympus, and Jove its occupant. In genius, in elevation, in the habits and enjoyments of his life, he is wonderfully lifted up above most mortals. The fog I was told never rises to the level of his mountain; and it is just so with what the newspapers say of him. Further: the dew does not fall on it; nor are there any insects there; nor, by consequence, any birds! Now, figure to yourself a house exalted upon such an eminence as all this bespeaks, and that house, thus as it were in the sky, decked off with art and wealth, and you have Monticello. I saw nothing so cheap as a print on his walls; nothing but paintings or statuary, with curious assemblages of artificial or natural objects forming quite a museum.

He lamented to me the loss of his library, and expects an importation of books this fall from Europe. His chief reading is the antient classicks, in the originals. He admitted that they were of no use; but he exclaimed, "they are such a luxury." He reads, he says, no longer for knowledge, but gratification. I need not tell you with what open doors he lives, as you well know that his mountain is made a sort of Mecca.

Poor Alston. And Huger—seven children, you six, and I but three. If Governor Tompkins attempts to play governor and Vice president too, he will be ruined. But I do not believe it.

Adieu—Yours always R. RUSH.

RC (PHi: Charles Jared Ingersoll Collection); endorsed by Ingersoll.

Rush's visit to Montpellier and Monticello took place late in August 1816. POOR Joseph Alston (who had recently died), Charles J. Ingersoll, and Daniel Elliott HUGER all attended the College of New Jersey (later Princeton University) with Rush during the latter half of the 1790s (*DAB*, 1:229; *ANB*, 11:647; *General Catalogue of Princeton University 1746–1906* [1908], 111, 112).

To Timothy Banger

Sir Monticello Oct. 10. 16.

I thank you for the disposition you have made of the box found in the Military stores addressed to me. I know nothing of it, nor of it's contents. it is probably something which has long been considered as lost. I will write a line to mr Starke to forward it to Richmond to my correspondents there, mess[rs] Gibson & Jefferson, who will receive it and pay all costs.

The length of time you have continued in your present employment is a proof you have deserved it. if I have been instrumental to your obtaining it, you are indebted for it to your own merit only, and my reward is the satisfaction of having contributed to the procuring an useful servant to the public. Accept the assurance of my respect.

Th: Jefferson

RC (DNA: RG 107, LRSW); addressed: "M[r] Timothy Banger Philadelphia"; franked; postmarked Milton, 11 Oct.; endorsement in an unidentified hand reads, in part, "respecting Box found in Military Stores"; filed with Banger to John C. Spencer, 1 Feb. 1842. PoC (MHi); on verso of reused address cover of William Duncanson to TJ, 5 Aug. 1816; endorsed by TJ.

From William Clark

Dear Sir Saint Louis October 10th 1816

I had the honor of Receiving your letter of the 8th of Sept[r], by the Mail, and with Much pleasure comply with the contents.

It has ever been my wish, that the Travelling journal of Gov[r] Lewis & Myself, the astronomical Observations, the Geographial Chart, the Indian Vocabularies and all Subjects of Natural history Should be given to the public in the best possible manner, and agreeably to the Original intention—. and for that purpose I have been twice to Phil[a] and have used all the Means which have been in my power without the Success Contemplated.—

The Naritive has been published, but I have not been So fortunate as to precure a Single Volum, as yet. after the death of my friend Gov[r] Lewis, finding the arrangements he had made relative to the publication had failed, and the greater part of the astronomical observations with the plates and drawings which he had directed to be made, were not to [be][1] found a new Contract was made with Mess[rs] Bradford & Inskep, to print & publish that part, and the Cientific part also, which was to have been (by Contract) prepared in Six months from the time by Doct^r^ Barton—in these arrangements I have been also disappointed.

Since the failure[2] of Bradford & Inskep, and the death of Doct^r^ Barton my Agent Mr Nicholas Biddle has been Requested to Collect all the Books, papers, Specimens &^c^—

Previously to my making the last Arrangement, I had Conversation with the then Secretary of War on the Subject of publishing Lewis & Clarks Journal map &^c^, he thought it important, but Could promis no assistance at that time.—

It is with pleasure that I inclose you an Order on my friend Mr Biddle for the papers in his possession Relating to the Astronomical Observations, the Geographial Charts, the Indian Vocabularies, and other papers not Comprehended in the journal of Lewis & Clarks Travels laterly published, and the Specimins which were left in the possession of Doct^r^ Barton—also the Traveling pocket Journals.—

From the mortification[3] of not haveing Succeeded in giving to the world all the Results of that expedition, I feel Relief &[4] greatitude for the interest which You are Willing to take, in effecting what has not been in my power to accomplish.—

Some time ago, I requested Mr Biddle to deliver to Mrs Markes's Order, the half of all the Books he may have Received in my behalf—The Map from which the plate was made, is in my possession at this place; it is Rough and has not been Corrected and Comprehends the Connection of Country from Lat. 34° to 50° N. If you think it adviseable?, I will make a new map of the Same Size of the one I have, Corrected by Such materials as I have precured Since the last was made, otherwise I Shall take the liberty of Sending the one I have to you.

The Missouri River on which there is Such emence tracts of fine Country Calculated for rich & populous Settlements, and watering an emence Space in which there is much welth in furs, Peltres, minerals, dies &^c^ is tolerably well understood but not in Sufficient use—The Lands on the lower portion of that River is Settling fast, the middle portion (or as high up as the Big Bend or White River) is Crouded with Traders, but the upper and richer portion has had No American Citizen Since the failure[5] of the Missouri C^o^ in 1811 and I am under great apprehentions that the British will take possession of that Rich Tract by the Way of Assinniboin & Saskassoin Rivers as they have done at the mouth of Columbia, and on Lewis & Clarks Rivers—: If a large and over bearing Company Cannot be formed of American Citizens with Sufficient[6] Capital to keep them Out I think Such a Co. Could be formed with Some Count[rimen] and a little aid from the government.

The present population of this Territory would most probably amount to about 35 or 40,000 Soles Since peace was made with the Indians on the Mississippi the emogration has been emence bending their Course to the Missouri principally. Landed property has risen which has inrichened the Old inhabitants and reconsiled them to our Government much more than formerly.

In this excercise of Gov[r] of this Territory I have Suceed in the worst of times with more approbation than I had expected. laterly a Small and disappointed party has Sprung up deturmined to vex & Tease the executive.

I am happy to have it in my power to Say to you that I Succeed in keeping the Indians[7] of this Territory (exceept those high up the Mississippi) in peace, The Torments of this frontier was perducd by the Tribes East of the Missippi & high up that River—The dificueltes & responsibilities however were great, and in Some instancs I was Compeled to vary from principal, and Let the Missouri Tribes at war against those of the Mississippi to prevent the British influence amongst[8] the Missouri tribes as also to prevent a Coeleition which would have destroyed our Settlements at a blow.

Please to accept the assurence of my highest Respect and veneration and best wishes for your health and hapiness

Yours Most Sincerly Wm Clark

RC (PPAmP: Thomas Jefferson Papers); one word illegible; at foot of text: "Mr Jefferson Monticello"; endorsed by TJ as received 21 Nov. 1816 and so recorded in SJL. Enclosure: Clark to Nicholas Biddle, Saint Louis, Missouri Territory, 10 Oct. 1816, consisting, besides salutation, dateline, close, and signature, of one sentence following almost verbatim the pertinent paragraph of the covering letter (RC in NjP: Biddle Collection; printed in Donald Jackson, ed., *Letters of the Lewis and Clark Expedition, with Related Documents, 1783–1854* [2d ed., 1978], 2:623). Enclosed in TJ to Peter S. Du Ponceau, 7 Nov. 1817 (first letter).

The NARITIVE was Biddle, *Lewis and Clark Expedition*. The THEN SECRETARY OF WAR may have been William Eustis (Jackson, *Letters of Lewis and Clark*, 2:580). On 31 Mar. 1816 Clark asked Biddle to deliver HALF OF ALL THE BOOKS he had received for him to Meriwether Lewis's mother, Lucy Marks (DLC: Biddle Papers; printed in Jackson, *Letters of Lewis and Clark*, 2:609–10).

MISSOURI Co: the St. Louis Missouri Fur Company. CLARKS River in present-day Oregon later became known as the Deschutes River. The INDIANS ON THE MISSISSIPPI signed peace treaties with the United States at Portage des Sioux, a village near Saint Louis, between July and September 1815 (Robert Malcomson, *Historical Dictionary of the War of 1812* [2006], 432).

1 Omitted word editorially supplied.
2 Manuscript: "falue."
3 Clark here canceled "& regret."
4 Preceding two words interlined.
5 Manuscript: "falue."
6 Manuscript: "Suffcient."
7 Manuscript: "Indins."
8 Manuscript: "amogst."

To James Freeman

Monticello Oct. 10. 16.

Th: Jefferson presents his respects to the reverend mr Freeman, and his regrets at having lost the favor of his visit to Monticello, at which place he arrived three days after mr Freeman's departure. his family testify amply the pleasure he should have recieved from his acquaintance had he been fortunate enough to have been at home. he prays him to accept his salutations and assurances of his high consideration.

PoC (DLC); on verso of portion of reused address cover of David Hosack to TJ, 1 Aug. 1816; dateline at foot of text; endorsed by TJ as a letter to "Freeman D^r^" and so recorded in SJL.

To William Munford

Sir Monticello Oct. 10. 16.

According to the request of mrs Kennon and yourse[lf] I have written to the Secretary of the Navy to sollicit the place of a midshipman for her son. but having no personal acquaintance with the Secretary much cannot be expected from my application. the number of midshipmen is limited by law; the places are always full, and a long list of candidates entered on the roll, every one expecting to be called in his turn to fill the[1] vacancies as they happen[.] I mention these circumstances to prevent too immediate expectations of mr Kennon's being called into employment. an increasing stiffness in the wrist, the effect of age & an antient dislocation rendering the use of the pen painful and slow, I must pray you to communicate the above to mrs Kennon with the tender of my great respect, and to accept the assurance of it for yourself Th: Jefferson

PoC (MoSHi: TJC-BC); on verso of a reused address cover from Benjamin Galloway to TJ; edge trimmed; at foot of text: "Wm Munford esq."; endorsed by TJ.

William Munford (1775–1825), public official, author, and court reporter, was born in Mecklenburg County and attended the College of William and Mary, 1790–94, where he studied law under George Wythe and St. George Tucker. He represented his home county in the Virginia House of Delegates, 1797–98 and 1800–02, and sat in the Senate of Virginia, 1802–06. With his election in 1806 to the Virginia Council of State, Munford relocated permanently to Richmond. In 1811 he left the Council to become clerk of the House of Delegates, an office he held until his death. During his lengthy public career, he also wrote poetry and a play, published ten volumes of decisions of the Virginia Court of Appeals between 1807 and 1821 (the first four as coeditor with William W. Hening), and translated Homer's *Iliad* into blank verse. Munford died in Richmond (*ANB*; *DAB*; *William and Mary Provisional List*, 29; Leonard,

General Assembly; Munford, *Poems and Compositions in Prose on Several Occasions* [Richmond, 1798]; *Va. Reports*, vols. 11–20; Sowerby, no. 2093; *Richmond Enquirer*, 24 June 1825).

[1] Word interlined in place of "any."

From Bernard Peyton

MY DEAR SIR, Richmond 10 October 1816

I have just returned to this City and established myself permanently in business, where I am always to be found, and shall be ever happy to serve you and your good family in any possible way—your commands shall at all times be executed with promptitude, and to the best of my judgment should you think proper to favor me with them.—Be pleased to make this known to the different branches of your family with my affectionate regards—for yourself sir accept assurances of the high respect and esteem of:

Your Very Obd: Hub: Servt: BERNARD PEYTON

RC (MHi); endorsed by TJ as received 15 Oct. 1816 and so recorded in SJL. RC (MHi); address cover only; with PoC of TJ to Elisha Ticknor, 12 Dec. 1816, on verso; addressed: "Thomas Jefferson Esq[r] Monticello near Milton" by "Mail"; stamped; postmarked Richmond, 12 Oct.

To Edwin Stark

SIR Monticello Oct. 10. 16.

M[r] Timothy Banger of Philadelphia informs me that a box found in the military stores addressed to me, & so long there as that neither it's contents, or when it came there is known, has been sent to you to be forwarded. I am equally ignorant of the box & it's contents; but if you will have the goodness to send it to Richmond to Mess[rs] Gibson & Jefferson, my correspondents there, they will receive it and pay all expences which have attended it. Accept my apology & thanks for the trouble it costs you & the assurance of my respect.

TH: JEFFERSON

PoC (MHi); on verso of portion of reused address cover to TJ; at foot of text: "M[r] Edwin Starke"; endorsed by TJ.

Edwin Stark (ca. 1769–1830), public official, was a longtime resident of Norfolk who was appointed a collector of the federal direct tax and internal duties in 1813. He served as a military storekeeper, 1813–21, and as a customs measurer from about 1823 until his death. Stark owned fifteen slaves in 1810, ten a decade later, and seven in 1830. He left a personal estate valued at almost $900, including three slaves (*WMQ*, 1st ser., 4 [1896]: 271; DNA: RG 29, CS, Norfolk, 1810–30; *JEP*, 2:438, 442 [13, 23 Dec. 1813]; Heitman, *U.S. Army*, 1:916; *A Register of*

Officers and Agents, civil, military, and naval, in the Service of the United States [Washington City, 1824], 51; [1830], 58; Norfolk Hustings and Corporation Court Will Book, 5:190–1, 192–5; *American Beacon and Norfolk and Portsmouth Daily Advertiser*, 3 July 1830; gravestone inscription in Saint Paul's Episcopal churchyard, Norfolk).

From Elizabeth Trist

MY DEAR SIR Bird Wood, Henry C^ty^ 10th October—16

In consiquence of a letter I received from my Daughter of 28th August, in which She mentions that in the calamitous State of Orleans in consiquence of the inundation She had sent for the Boys home. and they do not wish to return to that place again which detirmines Mr Tournillon to make every exertion in his power to send them to this section of the US in the Spring to finnish their education; she requests me to ask the opinion of those friends whoes judgement I have the most confidence in which will be the most eliguble College to Place them in. Peachey thinks that under the present regulations William and Mary combine as Many advantages as any of the Colleges in the U.S. and I shoud certainly prefer it to Princeton or any of the N England seminaries but for its unhealthy situation Peachey has been so kind as to assure me that it wou'd give him pleasure for them to spend the vacation with us which commences in July and continues four months as he has a good collection of Books they can read four hours in a day and have sufficient time for recreation, the advantage it will be to their health and the pleasure it wou'd give me to have them with me, wou'd, I believe add to my existence but I wou'd not let Selfish considerations influence me to their disadvantage therefore beg the favor of you to let me know your opinion

I hope you enjoy good health also Mrs Randolph and all the family pray how has the drouth effected your crop? it occasion'd at one time great depression but the late rains have help'd the corn and Tobacco very much tho many will not make sufficient corn to[1] supply them through the Winter, Peachey as well as all those who have farms on the Horse pasture was favord with partial Showers tho at one time we feard the consiquences anticipated but we never ought to despair We have more corn and fodder than we ever had and the Tobacco has turnd out better than was expected a farmers life is more replete with anxiety than a seamans tho attended with less personal danger. fortunatly for N Orleans the Mississippi, began to fall earlier than any of the oldest inhabitants can remember Saw mills that used to saw till the middle of august had to stop the latter end of May, but I cant learn that the country is unhealthy—tho my Grandson Nicholas was Ill of the fever soon after he got home and M[rs] Tournillons little Son was near Dying but they were on the recoviry when I last heard from there—I wrote you last July directed to Poplar Forest with one enclosed for Miss Ellen presume they did not reach you tho the loss is not of much consiquence, I wish'd to know from you which of the Holy Bibles you most approve of as I heard you had all the New Editions, and if you had ever Seen that which was translated by Charles Thompson and to enquire of Ellen after M[rs] Bache but I have since had a letter from her. M[r] Gilmer is attending the Chancery Court at Lynchburg M[rs] G Unites with me in affectionate love to M[rs] Randolph and all the family with sincere wishes for yours M[r] Randolphs and Jeffersons prosperity and happiness

I am your affectionate and obliged Friend E, TRIST

RC (MHi); endorsed by TJ as received 21 Nov. 1816 and so recorded in SJL.

Trist had recently received conjoined letters of 28 Aug. 1816 from her DAUGHTER-in-law, Mary Trist Jones Tournillon, and grandson Hore Browse Trist (NcU: NPT). The latter discussed the INUNDATION of New Orleans the preceding May after a levee on the Mississippi River broke a few miles above the city (*Alexandria Herald*, 12 June 1816).

THE BOYS: Nicholas P. Trist and Hore Browse Trist. PEACHEY was Peachy R. Gilmer. MISS ELLEN: Ellen W. Randolph (Coolidge). M[R] GILMER was probably Francis W. Gilmer. JEFFERSONS: Thomas Jefferson Randolph's.

[1]Manuscript: "to to."

From David Gelston

DEAR SIR, New York October 11. 1816.

Believing now we have nothing to apprehend from the equinoctial gales, and a good opportunity offering, I have this day Shipped by the Sch[o] William, E Williams Master, your case of books, to the care of Mess[rs] Gibson & Jefferson at Richmond

since my letter to you of the 26 ult: enclosing my

Account of	$89.11
I have paid the freight of the books from Havre	6.60
	$95:71

I wish the books safe to hand and am,

with very great regard,[1] Dear Sir, your obedient servant

DAVID GELSTON

RC (MHi); endorsed by TJ as received 17 Oct. 1816 and so recorded in SJL. RC (DLC); address cover only; with PoC of TJ to William Wirt, 12 Nov. 1816, on recto and verso; addressed: "Thomas Jefferson Esquire Monticello"; franked; postmarked New York, 12 Oct.

[1]Manuscript: "regad."

To John Barnes

DEAR SIR Monticello Oct. 12. 16.

Your favors of Aug. 10. & Oct. 3. are now before me. the difficulties you find in transferring the stock of Genl Kosciuzko standing in my name to his own, puzzle me exceedingly, because I do not understand them. it is a business I am not familiar with. both the General's wish and mine is that the stock should stand in his own name to avoid difficulties in case of my death, but that the powers of acting on it for him should still continue under his original Power of attorney to me. I inclose you that original which is as comprehensive as words can make it, and would seem, after transferring the stock to him, to leave in me a full power to act on it.

I send also the General's private letter expressing this wish, in which I have marked with a pencil the passage relating to it. be so good as to return both these papers to me, copies of which may be retained by the Treasury or bank of Columbia authenticated as they think best. if the transfer can be m[a]de and my authority to act for the General under this power of Attorney still continue, then let it be done. but if that transfer should be a revocation of the power of Attorney (which I cannot concieve) then I must avail myself of the power of Attorney to sell out the whole stock, and with the proceeds buy good bills of exchange on Amsterdam, payable to the house of the Van Staphorsts for the General; as it is indispensable that his property be in his own name, and[1] that it be where he can draw the interest himself, if it cannot be done here by the present power. a new one would be long coming, & he would be on sufferance in the mean time. be so good, dear Sir, as to act on these alternatives, as I leave this place for Bedford on the 19th & shall be absent 6 weeks. I send[2] you a special power to recieve the dividends at the bank of Columbia; but I thought you had a general power of attorney from me, to[3] act on all the General's funds. if you have not, I will send you one. ever and affectionately yours TH: JEFFERSON

PoC (DLC); on verso of reused address cover of David Gelston to TJ, 31 July 1816; mutilated at seal, with most missing text rewritten by TJ; at foot of text: "Mr Barnes"; endorsed by TJ. Enclosures: (1) Power of Attorney from Tadeusz Kosciuszko to TJ, 30 Apr. 1798 (*PTJ*, 30:313–5). (2) Kosciuszko to TJ, Apr. 1816.

[1] TJ here canceled "if he can."

[2] Thus in manuscript, with some variant of "I would send" probably intended.

[3] TJ here canceled "do."

To John Barnes

Monticello Oct. 12. 16.

Mr Millegan undertook to print a work put into my hands for that purpose. it was to have been begun on the 4th of July last. I have written him letter after letter, and can get no answer. if he cannot print the work, I wish him to say so, and to return it to me. will you do me the favor to apply to him personally, and to procure for me a definitive answer?

Th: Jefferson

FC (DLC); written in TJ's hand on a small scrap; dateline at foot of text; between signature and dateline: "Mr Barnes." Only one letter to Barnes of this date is recorded in SJL.

To Fitzwhylsonn & Potter

Messrs Fitzwhylson and Potter Monticello Oct. 12. 16.

During the life of the late mr Pleasants of Richmond I usually applied to him for such books as I had occasion to call for from that place. as these calls still occur at times I will take the liberty, with your approbation, to address them to yourselves. Mr Gibson, of the firm of Gibson & Jefferson, will pay your bills at such epochs as you shall chuse to present them, as I trust has been done for the Edinburgh Reviews which have come to me I believe through your channel. I am in possession of the 14.[1] republished volumes of that work, bringing it down to No 28. I am in want of No 29. to 43. inclusive, and of Nos 47. & 49. and I send you by the stage Nos 43. 44. 45. 46. 48. 50 which with the Nos wanting as above, I will pray you to have half bound and returned to me. I have No 51. but do not send it because it will make part of a vol. with No 52. not yet recieved.

I will pray you also to send me the 2d vol. of Pleasant's Collection of the Acts of Assembly (I have the 1st vol.) and as compleat a collection as can be made of the Sessions acts from the end of Pleasant's collection down to the present day, except of the last session of 1815.16. which I have. these to be half bound in vols of convenient size, lettered & dated on the back. if you can have this commission executed for me by the last of November it will be in time, as I shall leave home on the 19th to be absent until then. when ready, they are to be forwarded by the stage to Milton. but it will be necessary to see them put into the stage, for if[2] put into their office only they may lie there for months. a bill of costs sent to me at the same time, I will send you a special order on mr Gibson with a general one as to future supplies. I salute you with respect Th: Jefferson

PoC (DLC); on verso of reused address cover of John Graham to TJ, 1 Aug. 1816; mutilated at seal, with missing text rewritten by TJ; endorsed by TJ.

The *Edinburgh Review* was REPUBLISHED in New York City by Ezra Sargeant until his death in 1812 and thereafter by Eastburn, Kirk & Company (note to TJ to Sargeant, 3 Feb. 1812; Sowerby, no. 4733).

[1]Number interlined in place of "12," which TJ left uncanceled.
[2]Manuscript: "it."

From Maximilian Godefroy

Monsieur: Du Pont Naturel. 12. oct^{bre} 1816.

Si vous n'etiez vous même un Amateur Si distingué des beautés de la Nature, je devrais certainement craindre que la liberté que je prends en me faisant L'Honneur de vous adresser cette Lettre ne vous parût une indiscrétion, Etrange peut être, lorsque le motif qui l'inspire vous Sera connu.

Depuis une Douzaine de jours que je Suis ici aucun, excepté celui cy, ne S'est passé Sans que j'allasse Etudier L'Effet imposant de ce pont, merveille que les notes Sur la virginie, non moins que la Nature, rendent Si justement célebre. forcé de m'eloigner bientôt de ce lieu solennel Si propre à la méditation; Si analogue au Caractère et de mes souvenirs et des affections profondes de mon âme; j'ai voulu du moins tâcher d'en Emporter une image plus correcte que toutes celles que J'avais pu en voir jusques ici, pour Servir de pendant, dans mon Cabinet, à la vue de Harper's ferry, que j'ai déjà faite depuis quelques années. J'Exprimais il y a quelques jours mes Regrets de me trouver bientôt Separé de cette grande Scène, lorsque quelques habitans du voisinage auxquels je les communiquais me donnerent a croire que peut être ne Serait il pas impossible que d'après L'offre que vous aviez faite précedemment à l'un d'eux de lui céder le Lot qui comprend ce beau lieu, vous ne voulussiez encore consentir, Monsieur, a vous en désaisir, Surtout Si c'etait en faveur du culte des Beaux arts et pour assurer la préservation de cette noble Solitude contre la Hache impitoyable d'une aveugle mais Barbare industrie.

Si, comme il est vrai, la discrétion Seule peut me prescrire en quittant Charlotteville de ne pas y laisser un mot d'Hommage et L'Expression de tout le Regret que Mme Godefroy (fille du feû Doct^{r} Crawford de Baltimore) avait Eprouvé, ainsi que moi, d'avoir manqué L'Honneur de vous rencontrer dans votre Temple des Muses, ainsi que nous nous en etions flattés en entreprenant notre visite à la Virginie; vous Jugerez, Monsieur, que ce ne peut être Sans hésitation et Sans quelque embarras que j'ose me permettre de vous présenter ma Timide pétition—Elle ne peut manquer d'être Telle, puisque, par ce qui précede, vous avez déjà prévu, Monsieur, que Son objet est de vous prier, au cas où effectivement vous ne tiendriez pas particulierement à cette possession, de vouloir bien m'accorder la préference pour m'en transmettre la propriété, conformément au Titre original, et aux Conditions que je prends la Liberté de vous solliciter de vouloir bien me faire connaître.

Ma démarche exige, je crois quelques developpemens; je vais me permettre de les ajouter rapidement.—Elle ne naît d'aucun Esprit de Spéculation, car je Suis trop parfaitement Etranger au génie mercantile; et quant à la petite Factory qu'on a etabli sur le Pont elle ne paraît pas pouvoir Se Soutenir dans les circonstances actuelles. un tel pas de ma part est donc une affaire que le vulgaire appelera Caprice, mais qu'un homme Sensible à la poésie de la Nature et à Ses effets Jugera Certainement d'une maniere plus favorable.—Balloté d'une Etrange maniere pendant 29 anneés par la varieté des Caprices du sort et de L'Inconséquence[s] humaines, Je Suis déterminé depuis plusieurs années a mourir Citoyen Americain et a vivre le Reste de mes jours Sous L'Egide d'une Liberté raisonnable qui n'existe, et ne peut plus exister pour longtems, ailleurs qu'Ici Sur Notre malheureux Globe—D'Après L'accueil flatteur que j'ai reçu des Habitans de Richmond,—J'ai quelque lieu de croire que je pourrai venir me fixer en Virginie et y respirer un air[1] plus fait pour moi que ne l'a eté celui qui, pendant 10 années de Constance et d'Efforts inouis a presque epuisé mes forces physiques et mon courage dans ce Baltimore "Sur lequel (pour user d'une phrase qui ne vous est pas inconnüe) le génie du goût avait Semblé avoir jetté Sa malédiction"; du moins jusques à ces derniers momens.—

or—dans L'Hypothèse, probable, de ce changement de Situation, peut être pourrais-je employer quelques Soins dans mes momens de loisir pour rendre quelques legers Services à la petite contrée du Pont Naturel, Si toutefois, Monsieur, vos dispositions à son Egard sont telles qu'elles m'ont eté représentées

D'Après ces considérations Sur lesquelles je vous prie; Monsieur, de m'excuser de vous avoir trop arrêté peut être, j'ose me décider en partant pour Baltimore a vous adresser cette Lettre, Esperant que ma démarche trouvera une assez ample Apologie auprès de vous pour me[2] mériter, à votre loisir, la faveur d'un mot de Réponse Sur cet objet et l'absolution de mon indiscrétion Si, effectivement, j'ai pu en commettre une. Dans ce cas je vous prierai de L'oublier en Considération de L'Enthousiasme que m'inspirerent toujours les grandeurs de la Nature, et du prix que je mettrais aussi a posseder un lieu que vous avez chanté avec tant de charmes.

Je Saisis avec Empressement, Monsieur, cette occasion de vous prier d'agreér Les Hommages Respectueux de ma famille, qui me charge d'avoir L'Honneur de la rappeler au Souvenir de la votre, et je vous prie de vouloir bien accepter L'assurance de tous les Sentimens de Respect avec lesquels

J'ai L'Honneur d'être parfaitement Monsieur, Votre Très Humble et obeissant Serviteur MAXIM[AN] GODEFROY

Hanover Street. Baltimore.

EDITORS' TRANSLATION

SIR: Natural Bridge. 12 October 1816.

If you were not yourself such a distinguished connoisseur of the beauties of nature, I would certainly fear that the liberty I am taking in doing myself the honor of addressing you this letter would seem indiscreet to you. Strange, perhaps, once you know the motive that inspires it.

In the twelve days I have been here, not a day, except this one, has passed without my considering the imposing effect of this bridge, a marvel that the Notes on the State of Virginia, no less than nature, renders so justly famous. Forced to depart soon from this solemn place, which is so conducive to meditation and analogous to the character of my memories and the deepest affections of my soul, I wanted, at least, to take away with me a more correct picture of it than I had so far seen to serve as a counterpart to the one in my study of Harper's ferry that I made a few years ago. While recently expressing my regret at finding myself so soon separated from this grand scene, the local inhabitants with whom I spoke gave me to understand that, because of the offer you had previously made to one of them to give up the piece of land including this beautiful place, you might still be willing, Sir, to part with it, especially if it were for the sake of the fine arts and to assure the preservation of this noble solitude against the merciless ax of blind, barbaric industry.

If, and this is true, discretion alone prevented me, on departing Charlottesville, from leaving there a word of tribute and expressing all the regret that Mrs. Godefroy (daughter of the late Dr. Crawford, of Baltimore) and I felt at missing the honor of meeting you at your Temple of the Muses, as we had flattered ourselves we would when we undertook our visit to Virginia, you will judge, Sir, that it is not without hesitation and some embarrassment that I dare present my timid petition to you. It cannot fail to be so, as from what I have written above, you have already anticipated, Sir, that its object is to ask you, if you do not particularly value this possession, to be so kind as to grant me the preference in transferring the ownership of it, in accordance with the original title and the conditions that I take the liberty of asking you to make known to me.

I believe that my request requires some explanation, which I will add in short order. It is not at all motivated by the spirit of speculation, because a mercantile bent is totally foreign to me. Regarding the small factory that has been established on the bridge, it seems unable to sustain itself under current circumstances. Such a step on my part is, therefore, what ordinary people might call a whim, but a man sensitive to the poetry of nature and its effects will certainly judge it in a more favorable light.—Tossed about in a strange manner for 29 years by the caprices of fate and the inconsistencies of mankind, I have determined for several years to die an American citizen and to live the remainder of my days under the protection of a reasonable freedom, which does not and cannot exist for long anywhere else on our unhappy globe—Because of the flattering welcome I received from the residents of Richmond, I have reason to believe that I could settle in Virginia and breathe there an air that is better suited to me than that which has, during 10 years of constant and extraordinary effort, almost exhausted my physical strength and courage in Baltimore, "On which (to use a phrase that is not unknown to you) the genius of taste seemed to have cast its malediction." At least until now.—

Assuming this probable change of situation, perhaps I could render in my moments of leisure some small services to the area around the Natural Bridge, if, Sir, your dispositions regarding it are such as have been represented to me

From these considerations, for which I beg you, Sir, to excuse me for perhaps having taken up too much of your time, I dare send you this letter on my departure for Baltimore, in the hope that my request will contain sufficient apology to deserve, at your convenience, the favor of a word of reply on this subject and your absolution for my indiscretion, if in fact I have committed one. In that case, I ask you to forget it in consideration of the enthusiasm that the grandeurs of nature have always inspired in me and also of the price I would be willing to pay to own a place you have sung about so charmingly.

I eagerly seize this occasion, Sir, to ask you to accept the respectful regards of my family. They entrust me with the honor of recalling them to your family, and I pray you to accept the assurance of all the sentiments of respect with which

I have the honor to be in every way, Sir, your very humble and obedient servant

MAXIM[AN] GODEFROY
Hanover Street. Baltimore.

RC (DLC); edge trimmed; addressed: "Thomas Jefferson Esq[re] &c &c Monticello Charlottesville Virginia"; endorsed by TJ as received 7 Nov. 1816 and so recorded in SJL. Translation by Dr. Genevieve Moene.

Maximilian Godefroy (1765–1848), architect and educator, grew up in France and served in that nation's army from about 1782 until 1803. During his military service he attained the rank of colonel and was wounded three times. Godefroy fell under suspicion of opposing the Napoleonic regime in 1803, was imprisoned, and eventually secured his release only by agreeing to go into exile in the United States. He arrived there in the spring of 1805 and settled in Baltimore, where he taught art, architecture, and military engineering at Saint Mary's College (later Saint Mary's Seminary and University) until 1817. During his years in Baltimore, Godefroy designed a number of churches, was a pioneer in introducing the Gothic Revival to American architecture, helped strengthen the United States defenses at Fort McHenry, and drew up the plans for the monument commemorating the repulse of the 1814 British attack on the city during the War of 1812. He also worked with Benjamin H. Latrobe on the construction of the merchants' exchange in his adopted hometown and provided the blueprint for a new courthouse in Richmond. Having fallen out with Latrobe and facing declining prospects, Godefroy sailed for London in 1819. Eight years later he returned to France. Godefroy died in a suburb of Paris (*ANB*; *DAB*; David Karel, *Dictionnaire des Artistes de Langue Française en Amérique du Nord* [1992], 354–5; Godefroy to TJ, 10 Jan. 1806 [DLC]; Latrobe, *Papers*; Robert L. Alexander, *The Architecture of Maximilian Godefroy* [1974]).

TJ discusses the Natural Bridge in his NOTES SUR LA VIRGINIE (*Notes*, ed. Peden, 24–5). Early in his retirement he had offered to sell the LOT containing this geological formation to William Jenkings (see TJ to Jenkings, 1 July 1809). The PHRASE that Godefroy thought TJ would find familiar is adapted from the *Notes on the State of Virginia*: "The genius of architecture seems to have shed its maledictions over this land" (*Notes*, ed. Peden, 153).

[1] Preceding two words interlined.
[2] Word interlined.

To William W. Hening

DEAR SIR Monticello[1] Oct. 12. 16.

I thank you for the 3. first volumes of your statutes which are safely recieved, as I shall also do for succeeding ones as they come out. with respect to the MS. volume in your hands, as it belongs to Congress, it will be best when you are done with it, to forward it by the stage to Washington, addressed to mr George Watterston, librarian of Congress. you would oblige me at the same time by dropping me a line of information, as it would be satisfactory to me to know that I stand there discharged from my obligations. Accept the assurance of my esteem & respect TH: JEFFERSON

PoC (DLC); on verso of reused address cover of John Wood to TJ, 2 Aug. 1816; at foot of text: "William W. Hening esq."; endorsed by TJ.

[1] Manuscript: "Monticllo."

From Gilbert J. Hunt

RESPECTED SIR, New York Oct. 12 1816

I had the honor of recieving[1] Your answer to my note, with its enclosure; and now, at this late hour, with pleasure, fulfil my obligation, by forwarding the enclosed copy of the Late War in the Scriptural Style.

It should not have been So long delayed had my pecuniary resourses been adequate to its accomplishment. Though but a trifle, it is received here with flattering marks of approbation.

The question might be delicate; and the answer troublesome; but, if I may presume so much, a line from you, expressive of your opinion of the publication, whatever may be the result, will be a pleasure to him whose best wishes for your health and happiness can only cease with life.

Though no stern religionist myself; a professor of no particular Sect; not bound by fetters whorse than the clanking chains of criminals—the fetters of the mind; but free to act and reason; yet I would be liberal to all classes:—And perhaps if rightly appreciated, this little volume might be made, as Such would think, a benefit to the children of the most religious class, and be an inducement to them to read the scripture as well as to strengthen their belief in it.—

With due respect & esteem G. J. HUNT

NB. I should have sent you a copy on blossom paper, but I thought you would prefer the hot-prest copy on white.—

RC (MHi); endorsed by TJ as received 17 Oct. 1816 and so recorded in SJL. RC (MHi); address cover only; with PoC of TJ to Elizabeth Trist, 23 Nov. 1816, on verso; addressed: "Thos Jefferson Esq Late President U States Monticello." Enclosure: Hunt, *The History of the Late War between the United States and Great Britain. Written in the ancient historical style* (New York, 1816; Poor, *Jefferson's Library*, 5 [no. 144]).

BLOSSOM PAPER is a soft, spongy type of stationery often used for preserving pressed botanical specimens (*Encyclopædia Perthensis; or Universal Dictionary of the Arts, Sciences, Literature, &c.* [2d ed., Edinburgh, 1816], 17:621).

1 Manuscript: "recievig."

To John Adams

Monticello Oct. 14. 16

Your letter, dear Sir, of May 6. had already well explained the Uses of grief, that of Sep. 3. with equal truth adduces instances of it's abuse; and when we put into the same scale these abuses, with the afflictions of soul which even the Uses of grief cost us, we may consider it's value in the economy of the human being, as equivocal at least. those afflictions cloud too great a portion of life to find a counterpoise in any benefits derived from it's uses. for setting aside it's paroxysms on the occasions of special bereavements, all the latter years of aged men are overshadowed with it's gloom. whither, for instance, can you and I look without seeing the graves of those we have known? and whom can we call up, of our early companions, who has not left us to regret his loss? this indeed may be one of the salutary effects of grief; inasmuch as it prepares us to lose ourselves also without repugnance. Dr Freeman's instances of female levity cured by grief are certainly to the point, and constitute an item of credit in the account we examine. I was much mortified by the loss of the Doctor's visit by my absence from home. to have shewn how much I feel indebted to you for making good people known to me would have been one pleasure; and to have enjoyed that of his conversation, and the benefits of his information so favorably reported by my family, would have been another. I returned home on the third day after his departure. the loss of such visits is among the sacrifices which my divided residence costs me.

Your undertaking the 12. vols of Dupuis is a degree of heroism to which I could not have aspired even in my younger days. I have been contented with the humble atchievement of reading the Analysis of his work by Destutt-Tracy in 200 pages 8vo. I believe I should have ventured on his own abridgment of the work in one 8vo volume, had it ever come to my hands; but the marrow of it in Tracy has satisfied my appetite: and, even in that, the preliminary discourse of the Analyser himself, and his Conclusion, are worth more in my eye than the body of the work. for the object of that seems to be to smother all history under the mantle of allegory. if histories so unlike as those of Hercules & Jesus, can by a fertile imagination, and Allegorical interpretations, be brought to the same tally, no line of distinction remains between fact and fancy. as this pithy morsel will not overburthen the mail in passing and repassing between Quincy and Monticello, I send it for your perusal. perhaps it will satisfy you, as it has me; and may save you the labor of reading 24 times it's volume. I have said to you that it was written by Tracy; and I had so entered it on the title-page, as I usually do on Anonymous works whose authors are known to me. but Tracy had requested me not to betray his anonyme, for reasons which may not yet perhaps have ceased to weigh. I am bound then to make the same reserve with you. Destutt-Tracy is, in my judgment, the ablest writer living on intellectual subjects, or the operations of the understanding. his three 8vo volumes on Ideology, which constitute the foundation of what he has since written, I have not indeed entirely read; because I am not fond of reading what is merely abstract, and unapplied immediately to some useful science. Bonaparte, with his repeated derisions of Ideologists (squinting at this author) has by this time felt that true wisdom does not lie in mere practice without principle. the next work Tracy wrote was the Commentary on Montesquieu, never published in the original, because not safe; but translated and published in Philadelphia, yet without the author's name. he has since permitted his name to be mentioned. altho' called a Commentary, it is in truth an elementary work on the principles of government, comprised in about 300. pages 8vo. he has lately published a third work on Political economy, comprising the whole subject within about the same compass; in which all it's principles are demonstrated with the severity of Euclid, and, like him, without ever using a superfluous word. I have procured this to be translated, and have been 4 years endeavoring to get it printed. but, as yet, without success. in the meantime the author has published the original in France, which he thought unsafe while Bonaparte was in power. no printed copy, I believe, has yet reached this country. he has his 4th and last work now in the press at Paris, closing, as he concieves the circle of metaphysical sciences. this work which is on Ethics, I have not seen, but suspect I shall differ from it in it's foundation, altho not in it's deductions. I gather from his other works that he adopts the principle of Hobbes, that justice is founded in contract solely, and does not result from the construction of man. I believe, on the contrary, that it is instinct, and innate, that the moral sense is as much a part of our constitution as that of feeling, seeing, or hearing; as a wise creator must have seen to be necessary in an animal destined to live in society: that every human mind feels pleasure in doing good to[1] another; that the non-existence of justice is not to be inferred from the fact that the same act is deemed virtuous and right in one society, which is held vicious & wrong in another; because as the circumstances and opinions of different societies vary, so the acts which may do them right or wrong must vary also: for virtue does not consist in the act we do, but in the end it is to effect. if it is to effect the happiness of him to whom it is directed, it is virtuous, while in a society under different circumstances and opinions the same act might produce pain, and would be vicious. the essence of virtue is in doing good to others, while what is good may be one thing in one society, & it's contrary in another. yet, however we may differ as to the foundation of morals, (and as many foundations have been assumed as there are writers on the subject nearly) so correct a thinker as Tracy will give us a sound system of morals. and indeed it is remarkable that so many writers, setting out from so many different premises, yet meet, all, in the same conclusions. this looks as if they were guided, unconsciously, by the unerring hand of instinct.

Your history of the Jesuits, by what name of the Author, or other description is it to be enquired for?

What do you think of the present situation of England? is not this[2] the great and fatal crush of their funding system, which, like death, has been foreseen by all, but it's hour, like that of death, hidden from mortal prescience? it appears to me that all the circumstances now exist which render recovery desperate. the interest of the national debt is now equal to such a portion of the profits of all the land and the labor of the island as not to leave enough for the subsistence of those who labor. hence the owners of the land abandon it and retire to other countries, and the laborer has not enough of his earnings left to him to cover his back, and to fill his belly. the local insurrections, now almost general, are of the hungry and the naked, who cannot be quieted but by food & raiment. but where are the means of feeding and clothing them? the landholder has nothing of his own to give, he is but the fiduciary of those who have lent him money: the lender is so taxed in his meat, drink, and clothing, that he has but a bare subsistence left. the landholder then must give up his land, or the lender his debt, or they must compromise by giving up each one half. but will either consent peaceably to such an abandonment of property? or must it not be settled by civil conflict? if peaceably compromised, will they agree to risk another ruin under the same government unreformed? I think not; but I would rather know what you think; because you have lived with John Bull, and know, better than I do the character of his herd. I salute mrs Adams & yourself with every sentiment of affectionate cordiality and respect.

TH: JEFFERSON

RC (MHi: Adams Papers); at foot of first page: "Mr Adams"; endorsed by Adams as answered 4 Nov. 1816. PoC (DLC); lower corner of second page torn. Enclosure: Destutt de Tracy, *Analyse Raisonnée.*

Destutt de Tracy's recently printed THIRD WORK ON POLITICAL ECONOMY, *Traité de la volonté et de ses effets* (1st ed. Paris, 1815; 2d ed. Paris, 1818; Poor, *Jefferson's Library*, 8 [no. 454]), was later published in the United States as Destutt de Tracy, *Treatise on Political Economy*. HIS 4TH AND LAST WORK was *Principes Logiques, ou Recueil de Faits relatifs a l'Intelligence Humaine* (Paris, 1817; Poor, *Jefferson's Library*, 8 [no. 455]). Thomas Hobbes postulates that JUSTICE IS FOUNDED IN CONTRACT SOLELY in *Leviathan, or, The Matter, Form, and Power of a Common-wealth Ecclesiastical and Civil* (London, 1651), 71.

[1] TJ here canceled "others."
[2] Manuscript: "is not this is not this."

To John Bankhead

DEAR SIR Monticello Oct. 14. 16.

It is most painful to me to be always addressing on a distressing subject one whom I so highly esteem, and who merits so much to be spared every possible pain. but your request, my promise, and the happiness of us all require it. mr Bankhead stood his ground firmly until Monday last (the 8th) our district court day, when he went to Charlottesville, and all his resolution gave way. when the spell was once broke he went into full indulgence. on Thursday he engaged a Fredericksburg hack, returning empty, to carry him to that place: but the driver stopping at Milton to feed, he got so overpowered with liquor that the driver percieving he could never get him to Fredericksburg, brought him here. he went to bed immediately & kept it chiefly for two days during which we succeeded in keeping liquor from him in the hope that he might cool and recover his resolution. but in the mean time he was trying every means of procuring whisk[ey] & on Saturday succeeded. this stimulus raised him from his languer; he went to Charlottesville (as we suppose) returned here at night, and has been ever since in a state of strong intoxication, and the consequent aberration of mind which you have probably witnessed.

Oct. 16. a glimmering of hope that mr Bankhead would consent to pay you a visit, on our offer to send him down, suspended the closing my letter. that however has vanished, and he has continued in the same state.

in the mean time mr Randolph says the plantation is going to ruin, no wheat sowing or other preparation making for another year. on these facts your affections and knolege of the case will dictate what is best to be done. with sentiments of sincere esteem & respect for mrs Bankhead and yourself I am Dr Sir Th: Jefferson

PoC (ViU: TJP-ER); on verso of reused address cover of Dabney C. Terrell to TJ, 12 June 1816; mutilated at seal, with most missing words rewritten by TJ; at foot of text: "Dr Bankhead"; endorsed without date by TJ. Recorded in SJL as a letter of 16 Oct. 1816.

Charles L. Bankhead's Carlton estate was GOING TO RUIN. His letter of 4 Aug. 1816 to TJ, not found, is inconsistently recorded in SJL as received from Carlton the previous day.

To Joseph Miller

Dear Captain Monticello Oct. 14. 16.

I returned from Bedford a few days ago, which has delayed the commencement of our malting till three days ago. altho I shall set out for Bedford again on the 19th to continue there to the first[1] of December, yet I shall take measures to enable Peter to go on with his malting and brewing.

not to be too late again in providing corks, as I was last year, and fearing I should get bad ones at Richmond, I will ask the favor of you to procure 8. gross for me of the best, and forward them to mr Gibson who will answer your draught for them, or if you will note the cost to me I will inclose it to you in Richmond bank bills, unless you should come here and recieve it as we had heretofore hoped. I salute you with friendship and respect. TH: JEFFERSON

PoC (DLC); on verso of reused address cover of David Gelston to TJ, 6 Aug. 1816; at foot of text: "Cap[t] Miller"; endorsed by TJ.

PETER: Peter Hemmings.

[1] Word interlined in place of "end."

From Elijah Rosson

HON[R] SIR, Richmond Penitentiary Oct: 14th 1816.

Having had the great Pleasure of being acquainted with Your Excellency, and although brought to this place of Misery, I hope you will grant me the favour of trubling your hon[r] with a few lines.

It is true, and I shall confess my faults to your hon[r] I possesed a great Love for that fair Sex the Women, and what young man would not, should I therefore be deprived of Liberty?

had it not been for prejudice, I would now be at home, and I have no doubt, Your hon[r] has been by this time informed of all the circumstance of my trial. I assure your Excellency that my two apprentices was bribed, which I was told by M[r] Harris, one of my Venir and I can now prove it by M[r] Jasper Anderson, to whom they confest all, and had there been sufficient proof of harbouring that Girl, was there Law to send me here?

Convincet of your tender feelings for the distressed, and particular towards me, give me hopes, as I expect there will be a Petition drawn for me, for your hon[r] to sign it; and should not, do pray and send on here a Letter, to my present Keeper M[r] Sam[l] P. Parsons, and let him Know the circumstance as far as your Consience will permit, and also my Character, Your hon[r] having Knowing me long enough and satisfyd never to heard any thing that would stain my Character, as dishonesty or to defraud any person.

Not acquainted wether the jury was prejudice, or not, I only objected one Gentlemen, which I since belive would have been in my favour.

Now inclined of life, I wont to be relieft of this place, so that I may comulate some Property agin for my old age if it should please you therefore, to do the above request for me, I have no doubt as I have the favour of my Keepers; to git my Liberty, and by your hon[r] so doing, I shall always be with gratitude your hon[r] unfort. Serv[t]

in haste ELIJAH ROSSON

RC (MHi); addressed: "Thomas Jefferson E[sqr] Mounticello near Charlottville Albermarle County V[a]"; franked; postmarked Charlottesville, 23 Oct.; endorsed by TJ as received 7 Nov. 1816 and so recorded in SJL.

Elijah Rosson (b. ca. 1792), carriage maker, had worked in Charlottesville since at least 1812. He was convicted in 1813, but not imprisoned, for allowing an unlawful "faro bank to be exhibited in his house," and in the spring of 1814 he did the finishing work on TJ's landau. Having been found guilty two years later of an undetermined felony, Rosson authorized James Rosson and John M. Perry to manage his affairs in Albemarle County during his incarceration. Following his release from the Richmond penitentiary in 1817 under a gubernatorial pardon, he settled for a time in nearby Henrico County. By mid-century he resided in Buckingham County, still working as a coach-maker (Rosson to Philip P. Barbour, 18 Nov. 1812 [ViU: Ambler Family Papers]; Albemarle Co. Law Order Book [1809–21], 182; *MB*, 2:1298n, 1300; List of Prisoners, 1 July 1816 [Vi: RG 42, Records of the Virginia Penitentiary, 1796–1991]; Albemarle Co. Deed Book, 20:26, 21:414–5; *Report of the Joint Committee appointed to examine into the state of the Penitentiary Institution* [1827], 22; DNA: RG 29, CS, Henrico Co., 1820, Buckingham Co., 1850).

To William Short

DEAR SIR Monticello Oct. 14. 16.

A circumstance has occurred here which will occasion a drawback of about 30.D. in mr Higgenbotham's last payment to you. a law was past here some 2. or 3. years ago subjecting lands to be sold for any payment of taxes uncredited on the sheriffs books without limitation of time, unless the party could produce proof of payment; and 10. p.c. interest required from the date. and no notice was required to be given to the party to produce his proofs. the extent of injury perpetrated by this law is incalculable. I heard by mere accident that your land was advertized to be sold for nonpayment of taxes for the year 1799. being 17. years ago. I attended court, proved by several persons who had been sheriffs that I had always paid your taxes with my own, and included in the same draught on Richmond. I proved a draught of 106.64 D on Gibson & Jefferson for taxes that year, & the sheriffs rec^{t} but it did not specify that it included yours (for none of my draughts for any year did that) the sheriff declared in court that he was new in office that year, did not know that I acted for you, that he did not apply for[1] the taxes, nor recieve them. I was absent a great part of that year at Philadelphia, and think it very possible they were not paid. I observe they were not charged in my account with you; but the mass of business I was always engaged in, and my absences from home prevented[2] a rigorous attention to making these entries,[3] altho' the Sheriff's books prove your taxes were paid every other year. they were about 10.D. for the year 99. and with interest at 10. p. cent per annum the court gave judgment for about 30.D. which mr Higgenbotham paid.

I got home from Bedford on the 5th inst. and shall return there on the 19th to remain until the 1st of December. I was happy to recieve Correa's & Dr Wistar's visits before I went, and foresee that the season will be too much advanced when I return to expect or ask that of Marshal Grouchy. mais tout ce qui est differé n'est pas perdu. when the pleasant season returns the Marshal may probably find it agreeable to take a tour thro' our country, on which it would give me great pleasure to recieve and possess him here as long as his own convenience would permit. we should wish to make it his home, from which as a center he could make his excursions in every direction. I salute you with affectionate esteem and respect.

Th: Jefferson

RC (ViW: TJP); edge frayed, with missing text supplied from PoC; at foot of first page: "Mr Short"; endorsed by Short as received 19 Oct. 1816. PoC (MHi); on reused address cover of James Mease to TJ, 7 Aug. 1816; torn at seal, with missing text rewritten by TJ; endorsed by TJ.

David Higginbotham's last payment toward the purchase of Short's Indian Camp property had been made the preceding May (enclosure to TJ to Short, 10 Feb. 1813). The law passed some 2. or 3. years ago was the 9 Feb. 1814 "Act to amend and explain the Act, entitled 'An act concerning Taxes on Lands'" (*Acts of Assembly* [1813–14 sess.], 15–27, esp. 21). TJ attended court to settle Short's tax obligations on 5 Aug. 1816 (Albemarle Co. Order Book [1816–18], 18).

On 17 Sept. 1799 TJ gave Albemarle County sheriff Edward Garland an order "on G. Jefferson for 106.64" for taxes that year (*MB*, 2:1006). mais tout ce qui est differé n'est pas perdu: "but not all that is postponed is lost."

1 Preceding two words interlined in place of "recieve."

2 TJ here canceled "my."

3 Reworked from "making entries, as they."

To Mathew Carey

Dear Sir Monticello Oct. 16. 16.

I was very unlucky indeed in being in time for so small a portion only of the books I had wished of Dr Priestly's library. there was one in particular (Benson's Saxon Vocabulary) I would rather have given double price for than have missed. the amount of the 3. vols on their way to me being 3.75 D I inclose you 4.D. in Virginia bank notes, which I understand pass with you. the difference of amount may make up that of exchange, if any. I salute you with great esteem & respect.

Th: Jefferson

RC (NHi; tipped into John B. Moreau's extra-illustrated copy of Jared Sparks, *The Life of George Washington* [1849], vol. 3, opp. p. 480); at foot of text: "Mr M. Carey"; endorsed by Carey as received 20 Oct. 1816 and answered two days later. PoC (DLC); on verso of portion of reused address cover to TJ; endorsed by TJ.

To David Gelston

Dear Sir Monticello Oct. 16. 16.

Your favor of Sep. 26. was recieved a few days ago, and I have this day written to my correspondents in Richmond, mess[rs] Gibson & Jefferson to desire them to remit you the amount of the account you inclosed me, to wit 89.11 D which I trust they will do without delay. I am very thankful to you for your kind offices on this & similar occasions which I could with much difficulty arrange without them, because of the uncertainty of the port to which the shipments will be made. with my thanks be pleased to accept the assurance of my great esteem & respect Th: Jefferson

RC (NjP: Delafield Family Papers); at foot of text: "David Gelston esq." PoC (MHi); on verso of a reused address cover from John Payne Todd to TJ; endorsed by TJ.

To Patrick Gibson

Dear Sir Monticello Oct. 16. 16.

Johnson's boat, and one of mr Eston Randolph's went off yesterday afternoon with between 90 & 100 barrels of flour for me & would haul their boats round Magruder's locks, which by unloading & reloading, they say, is practicable. Johnson on his return will take off another load for me. in Bedford as we are 11. miles from the Lynchburg mills, and our horses all engaged in putting in wheat I could direct only one boat load at present, which mr Yancey promised to have sent off without delay. this & those which went from here yesterday will be with you before the last day of this month, & the other from here nearly by the same time. my desire is that so much of these may be sold at the current price as will answer my bills on you, which will be presented about the last day of this month chiefly. to wit

Oct. 1. in favor of the sheriff of Bedford 133.80.

Oct. 15. (yesterday) sheriff of Albemarle 163.51

Th: J. Randolph will have a draught for about 360. or 370 D.

in all November I shall be called on for my federal taxes which I suppose will be between 2. & 300.D. and some purchases of corn. I must moreover request the favor of you to remit to David Gelston Collector of N. York 89. D 11 C freight, charges & duties due him on my wines & books. I will ask immediate attention to this because I consider these as debts of honor, the Collectors being so kind as to advance the freight & charges for me for whatever arrives for me in their ports, &

to be answerable for the duties also, without waiting to bond them. in general I will request you to pay our boatmen for water carriage whenever they require it. at present Johnson wishes to draw from you the hire of his hands. as I set out for Bedford in 3. or 4 days to be absent 6. weeks, I have thought it safest to send a renewal of my note in bank for next month. I salute you with sentiments of friendship & respect

Th Jeff

PoC (DLC); on verso of portion of reused address cover to TJ; signature incomplete, likely due to polygraph error; at foot of text: "M[r] Gibson"; endorsed by TJ. Enclosure, not found, described by TJ as "a renewal of my note in bank for 2000.D. dated Nov. 24" (*MB*, 2:1327).

Instead of oct. 1., TJ indicated elsewhere that on 3 Oct. 1816 he "Gave ord. on Gibson & Jeff. in favr. sheriff Bedford 133.80 taxes." On oct. 15. TJ drew on that firm again "in favr. Clifton Harris for Benj. Harris sher. Alb. for 163.51 for taxes & tickets" (*MB*, 2:1327).

th: j. randolph loaned TJ $211.25 on 7 Oct. ($11.25 of which was given to Edmund Bacon "for tallow"), $19 on 8 Oct., $15 on 12 Oct., $123 on 16 Oct., and $30 on 20 Oct. 1816. On the latter date TJ repaid the debt to his grandson by giving him an order on Gibson & Jefferson for $400 (*MB*, 2:1327–8).

On 10 Feb. 1817 Randolph paid TJ's 1816 federal taxes on his properties in Albemarle County, which came to $141.20 (*MB*, 2:1330).

From George Logan

Dear Sir Stenton Octb[r] 16; 1816

I contemplate with great satisfaction the publication of your system of ethicks extracted from the holy scriptures, as tending to support the correct maxim—that religion should influence the political as well as the moral conduct of man, strictly complying with the sacrid injunction, of doing unto others whatever we desire others to do unto us.

However sincerely attached a christian statesman may be to his country; he will regard the great family of mankind as brethren; and therefore will never sacrifice the happiness and prosperity of other nations, to the trifling ephemeral advantage of his own. He will derive all his politicks as well as all his morals from the oracles of God—he will forget for a time, the place of his birth and the opinions of worldly wisdom—He will banish every thought of inordinate selfishness, of deceitful honours and of aspiring ambition—in fine, he will act in the high and holy character of a Christian. No acuteness of intellect, no diligence of research, no extent of erudition, will suffice to understand this subject unless the heart sanctified by the grace of God cherishes principles of submission to the ruler of nations to such a degree, as to prefer his doctrines to the councils of cabinets, and the prosperity of his kingdom to the triumphs of human empires.

It is to be lamented that there exists even among professed christians a disinclination to have their political maxims and transactions subjected to the rules of christianity. This fact, whilst it is an evidence that religion is opposed to the general plans of worldly minded men, is not surprising. Christianity hitherto (except in a few instances) has suffered by its connection with civil policy: and from the very nature of civil society, it must suffer in such connection; until both learning and power are transferred into the hands of virtuous men, and made subservient to piety.[1] If vicious statesmen incorporate religion with the government of kingdoms, such a form will be given to religion as may suit the selfish views of the ambitious and profligate. Under such circumstances, it is safer for the genuine[2] christian to struggle in poverty against the frowns of power, than to become the stipendiary of corrupt statesmen.

Attention to the principles and moral instruction of the bible, is increasing every day, and mankind have many inducements in the present convulsed state of the world, to fly for refuge to that book which contains the only correct view of the principles which will bless the nations with peace and happiness.

Such is the[3] pride and cupidity of man, that I am confident (as I mentioned to you in a former Letter) that nothing but the spirit of the christian religion influencing our public councils, can preserve our country from anarchy and ruin.

Accept assurances of my friendship GEO LOGAN

RC (DLC); endorsed by TJ as received 7 Nov. 1816 and so recorded in SJL. RC (MHi); address cover only; with PoC of TJ to William D. Meriwether, 30 Dec. 1816, on verso of left half of cover and PoC of TJ to Craven Peyton, 30 Dec. 1816, on verso of right half; addressed: "Thomas Jefferson Esq[r] Monticello virginia"; franked; postmarked Philadelphia, 16 Oct. FC (PHi: Logan Papers); entirely in Logan's hand and endorsed by him.

Jesus's SACRID INJUNCTION known as the Golden Rule is in the Bible (Matthew 7.12; Luke 6.31). Logan's FORMER LETTER is probably that to TJ of 21 Oct. 1815.

[1] Omitted period supplied from FC.
[2] Logan here canceled "states."
[3] In FC Logan here canceled "natural."

To James Monroe

[D]EAR SIR Monticello Oct. 16. 16

If it be proposed to place an inscription on the Capitol, the lapidary style requires that essential facts only should be stated, and these with a brevity admitting no superfluous word. the essential facts in the two inscriptions proposed are these

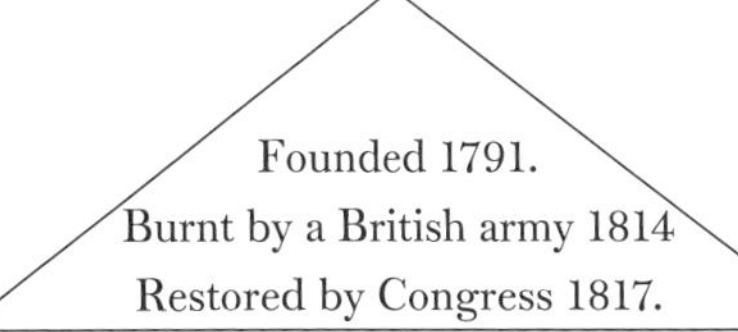

the reasons for this brevity are that the letters must be of extraordinary magnitude to be read from below; that little space is allowed them, being usually put into a pediment or in a frize, or on a small tablet on the wall; and, in our case a 3[d] reason may be added, that no passion can be imputed to this inscription, every word being justifiable from the most classical examples.

But a question of more importance is Whether there should be on[e][1] at all? the barbarism of the conflagration will immortalise that of the nation[.] it will place them for ever in degraded comparison with the execrated Bonaparte who, in possession of almost every capital in Europe, injured no one. of this, history will take care, which all will read, while our inscription will be seen by few. Great Britain, in her pride and ascendan[cy] has certainly hated and despised us beyond every earthly object. her hatred may remain,[2] but the hour of her contempt is past; and is succeede[d] by dread; not a present, but a distant and deep one. it is the greater, a[s] she feels herself plunged into an abyss of ruin from which no human mea[ns] point out an issue. we also have more reason to hate her than any nati[on] on earth. but she is not now an object for hatred. she is falling from h[er] transcendant sphere, which all men ought to have wished; but not th[at] she should lose all place among nations. it is for the interest of all tha[t] she should be maintained nearly on a par with other members of th[e] republic of nations. her power, absorbed into that of any other, would [be] an object of dread to all; and to us more than all, because we are accessible to her alone, and thro' her alone. the armies of Bonaparte, with the fleets of Britain, would change the aspect of our destinies. Under these prospects, should we perpetuate hatred against her? should we not on the contrary begin to open ourselves to other, and more rational dispositions? it is not improbable that the circumstances of the war, and her own circumstances may have brought her wise men to begin to view us with other, and even with kindred eyes. should not our wise men then, lifted above the passions of the ordinary citizen, begin to contemplate what will be the interests of our country, on so important a change among the elements which influence it? I think it would be better to give her time to shew her present temper, and to prepare the minds of our citizens for a corresponding change, of disposition, by acts of comity towards England, rather than by commemorations of hatred. these views might be greatly extended. perhaps however they are premature, and that I may see the ruin of England nearer than it really is. this will be matter of consideration with those to whose councils we have committed ourselves, and whose wisdom, I am sure, will conclude on what is best. perhaps they may let it go off on the single and short consideration that the thing can do no good, and may do harm. ever & affectionately yours. TH: JEFFERSON

PoC (DLC); salutation faint and edge frayed; at foot of first page: "The Secretary of State."

No inscription was ultimately placed in or on the United States CAPITOL to commemorate its destruction by British forces during the War of 1812.

[1] Word faint.
[2] Reworked from "hatred remains."

To Wilson Cary Nichols

DEAR SIR Monticello Oct. 16. 16.

I learn that you have recieved Dr Byrd's journal on the survey of our Southern boundary, from mr Harrison of Barclay. it is a work I have wished to see, and if you think yourself at liberty, when done with it, to trust it in my hands for perusal only, it shall be promptly and safely returned by mail. if you do not feel entirely free to do this, I will write to request it of mr Harrison. I set out within 3. or 4. days for Poplar forest to remain there 6. weeks. it would come by the Lynchburg mail as safely to that as this place. I salute you with affection & respect TH: JEFFERSON

RC (MHi); at foot of text: "Govr Nicholas"; endorsed by Nicholas. PoC (DLC); on verso of reused address cover of John Barnes to TJ, 3 Oct. 1816; endorsed by TJ.

William Byrd (1674–1744) composed two histories of his 1728 expedition to survey Virginia's SOUTHERN BOUNDARY. The first, which was evidently prepared with the intent of publication, was finally printed in an 1841 collection of his works as *The History of the Dividing Line betwixt Virginia and North Carolina*. TJ received through Nicholas by January 1817 the second manuscript version, Byrd's secret narrative, which was a more frank, critical, and even satirical account (*DVB*; Louis B. Wright, ed., *The Prose Works of William Byrd of Westover* [1966], 1–2, 19–20, 417–23; TJ to Peter S. Du Ponceau, 26 Jan. 1817; TJ to Nicholas, 19 Mar. 1817).

Benjamin Harrison lived at Berkeley (BARCLAY), his family's estate in Charles City County.

To John F. Watson

Sir Monticello Oct. 16. 16.

Your favor of the 4th is recieved & also the 4. vols of Edinburgh review, and I now inclose you a Virginia bank note of 10.D. with the assurance of my respects Th: Jefferson

PoC (DLC); on verso of a reused address cover from Thomas Appleton to TJ; at foot of text: "Mr John F. Watson"; endorsed by TJ.

To Henry A. S. Dearborn

Monticello Oct. 17. 16.

Th: Jefferson presents his compliments and his thanks to mr Dearborne for the copy he has been so kind as to send him of his translation of De Lasteyrie's learned & valuable work on the Pastel or Woad. he hopes the translation will encorage and promote the culture of that useful plant in the US. a long absence from home must apologise for this late acknolegement of the receipt of the work.

RC (Remember When Auctions, Inc., Los Angeles, 1995); dateline at foot of text. FC (DLC); written in TJ's hand on a narrow sheet, on verso of portion of a reused address cover from John Barnes to TJ; at head of text: "Dearborn H. A. S."

From William D. Meriwether

Dear Sir October 17th 1816

Understanding by your grandson Mr Randolph, that you have declined to take the property claimed by the legatees of Bennett Henderson Decd, as it was valued to you, by Martin Dawson, I am desirous of knowing explicitly, whether or not, you will give up the property so claimed by them, and pay the rents due thereon, peaceably, and without my having recourse to law to obtain the same: but I assure you, I prefer Setling all the points in controversy, in an amicable way, and will with pleasure submit them, to the decision, of two or more disinterested persons, as you may prefer. Give me your answer to this as speedily as possible accept assurance of my esteem &c

W D Meriwether

RC (MHi); addressed: "Honbl. Thomas Jefferson Monticello"; endorsed by TJ as received 30 Oct. 1816 and so recorded in SJL.

The legatees of bennett henderson in question were Frances Henderson Hornsby, Lucy Henderson Wood, and Nancy C. Henderson Nelson. Meriwether had acted since 1811 as legal counsel for Hornsby and her husband in the Henderson CONTROVERSY (TJ to Craven Peyton, [12 May 1811]).

To Bernard Peyton

DEAR SIR Monticello Oct. 17. 16.

Your favor of the 10th is recieved and communicated to the family, and we all join in thankfulness for the kind offers of service. these we shall accept with frankness if occasion occurs, because we are assured of the good will with which they are offered, and we shall never be happier than when we can be useful to you. we are in the hope that your business will permit you occasionally to visit your friends in this neighborhood, and I pray you to make Monticello your head quarters when you come. I think I could suggest to you an article of commerce which might make a part of your business, and just as small or great as you should find worthwhile, in which you could not soon have a rival. but this can be explained only in conversation, and only here also, where samples can be shewn. I set out in 2. or 3. days for Bedford, to be absent 6. weeks. I salute you with great friendship and respect.

TH: JEFFERSON

PoC (MHi); on verso of reused address cover to TJ; at foot of text: "Capt Peyton"; endorsed by TJ. Mistakenly recorded in SJL in the column for received letters.

From Thomas Eston Randolph

DEAR SIR 17th Novr [Oct.] 1816

If it should not be convenient to you to meet me at the Mill tomorrow at 10 O'Clock, I will do myself the pleasure to call on you about 11 O'Clock—in the meantime I will examine the Mill books and see what offal is due to the customers—and if it is possible to furnish you with the quantity you want I will inform you—I am sorry there should have been any misunderstanding on the subject of offal—if my note written at a moment when I was much engaged, and suffering violent bodily pain, was not sufficiently explicit—Mr Bacon could have explain'd the nature of the bargain, which as he came with a verbal message, I particularly express'd to him—I did not dream of any advantage arising to us farther than what the rise in the Shipstuff afforded us which would have been 33 ℔Cent—the rise at that time on flour (slow at $8.—) offer'd only an eqivalent—

With very sincere esteem THOS ESTON RANDOLPH

RC (MHi); misdated; dateline at foot of text; addressed: "Thomas Jefferson Esqr"; mistakenly endorsed by TJ as received 17 Nov. 1816. Recorded in SJL as received 17 Oct. 1816.

For Randolph's NOTE, see Agreement with Thomas Eston Randolph & Company, 19 Sept. 1816, with TJ's Note of 18 Oct. 1816.

To David Gelston

DEAR SIR Monticello Oct. 18. 16.

Your favor of the 11th came to hand last night. supposing that mr Gibson will have sent on the former sum of 89.11 as mentioned in my letter of the 16th before I could advise him to enlarge it, I have thought it best to inclose to you directly the additional sum of 6.60 D in Richmond bank notes which we understand to be at par in N. York, or if not exactly so the fractional cents on the inclosed may perhaps make up the difference. with a repetition of my thanks accept that of the assurance of my great esteem and respect. TH: JEFFERSON

RC (Skinner Auctioneers & Appraisers, Boston, 2010); addressed: "David Gelston esq. New York"; franked; postmarked Milton, 23 Oct. PoC (MHi); on verso of reused address cover of George Flower to TJ, 6 Aug. 1816; endorsed by TJ.

FRACTIONAL CENTS: TJ enclosed "7.D. for 6.60 freight of books" (*MB*, 2:1328).

From Wilson Cary Nicholas

SIR, Council Chamber, Richmond, October 18th 1816.—

I have the honor to inform you that you are appointed one of the Visitors of the Central College in Albemarle, and to forward you the enclosed commission. It is hoped that it will not be inconvenient for you to undertake the execution of this office.

I am, Sir, With great respect, Your Humble Servant

W. C. NICHOLAS

RC (DLC); in a clerk's hand, signed by Nicholas; at foot of text: "Thomas Jefferson, Esq."; endorsed by TJ as received 31 Oct. 1816 and so recorded in SJL.

Nearly identical versions of this letter were sent to the other appointees. Those to Joseph C. Cabell, John H. Cocke, James Madison, and James Monroe are each conjoined with a copy of their respective commission (see enclosure printed below).

ENCLOSURE

Commission Appointing Central College's Board of Visitors

Virginia, to wit:—

Whereas, by an Act of the General Assembly, Passed the 14h day of February 1816, intitled, "An act for establishing a College in the County of Albemarle," it is made the duty of the Governor for the time being, as Patron of the said College, to appoint Visitors thereof—Therefore, I, Wilson C. Nicholas, Governor of the Commonwealth of Virginia, do, in pursuance of the authority vested in me by the said Act, hereby constitute and appoint, Thomas Jefferson, James Madison, James Monroe David Watson (of Louisa) General John H. Cocke and Joseph C. Cabell, Visitors of the said College, with all the powers vested in the office of Visitor by the Act of the General Assembly aforesaid—And you are hereby authorised to proceed in the execution of the said office according to law.—

In witness whereof I have hereunto subscribed my name as Governor aforesaid, this eighteenth day of October, in the year of our Lord, one thousand eight hundred and sixteen. W. C. NICHOLAS

MS (DLC); TJ's copy; in a clerk's hand, signed by Nicholas. MS (ViU: JCC); Cabell's copy; in a clerk's hand, signed by Nicholas; conjoined with covering letter similar to that received by TJ; addressed: "Joseph C. Cabell, Esq Nelson"; with endorsement by Cabell reading, in part, "appointing me Visitor of the Central College." MS (ViU: JHC); Cocke's copy; in a clerk's hand, signed by Nicholas; conjoined with covering letter similar to that received by TJ; at foot of cover letter: "Genl John H. Cocke Fluvanna"; with endorsement by Cocke reading "Commission as Visitor of the Central College." MS (DLC: Madison Papers); Madison's copy; in a clerk's hand, signed by Nicholas; conjoined with covering letter similar to that received by TJ; addressed: "James Madison, Esq President of the U. States. Washington City"; with endorsement by Madison reading, in part, "Feby 14. 1816." MS (NN: Monroe Papers); Monroe's copy; in a clerk's hand, signed by Nicholas; conjoined with covering letter similar to that received by TJ; addressed: "James Monroe, Esq Secr'y of State Washington City"; with endorsement by Monroe reading, in part, "accademy."

Statement of Account with Thomas M. Randolph & Company

[ca. 19 Oct. 1816]

Entries taken from Day Book kept by J Kuhn

1816

April 4 Thos Jefferson To 4 barrels of Flour, sent to the Mountain by Isaac

12th ditto " 1 ditto made of unmerchantable Wheat

May 22 ditto " 1 ditto ℔ verbal order of E Bacon deliverd to Jerry

ˣditto " 3 ditto 2nd quality remaining in the Mill

(A) 9

ˣnote—This entry I suppose was made the day previous to J. Kuhn's leaving the Mill—by way of closing the Mill accounts—and the present Millers say the Flour has since been deliver'd

(A)—Those 9 barrels; added to 268. Bars 154 ℔ (as per your statement) will make the amount stated in the account furnish'd by TMR & Co, vizt 277. Bars 154 ℔, leaving a balance due to the Mill of 8. bars 175 ℔ Flour—

With respect to the difference in the cash balance between the last acct furnish'd you, and a former acct for 1814/15—it arose from neglecting to include the charges for freight of 5 barrels of Flour of crop 1814[1] carried to Richmond for you by T E. Randolph's boat—And the charge for freight of 36 bars is also correct—those 36 barrels were part of the last load sent for you to Gibson—deliverd to Wm Johnson 20th Feby 1816—vizt 16 bars on acct of Crop the freight of which was recd by Wm Johnson—36 bars on account of Rent—on which no freight was received—other arrangements being since made for payment of Rent the 52 were all consider'd as deliver'd on acct of Wheat crop—

The account deliver'd to Th: Jefferson by TMR & Co is defective only on the Debtor side—charge Th: Jefferson with 63. dolls 54 Cts paid him by Th: J. Randolph, and the balance due on acct of Rent will appear to be $56.08, agreeing with Th: Js statement—

MS (MHi); entirely in Thomas Eston Randolph's hand; undated; addressed: "Thomas Jefferson Esqe"; with Randolph's penciled note on address leaf: "Colo TMR [Thomas Mann Randolph] will please to deliver this to Mr Jefferson"; endorsed by TJ: "Randolph Thos E. Oct. 19. 16."

THE MOUNTAIN was Monticello. Daniel Colclaser was one of the PRESENT MILLERS at TJ's Shadwell mills. Neither TJ's current version of the account (YOUR STATEMENT) nor the most recent ACCOUNT FURNISH'D BY TMR & CO has been found.

On 22 June 1816 TJ received $63 from his grandson TH: J. RANDOLPH "& gave him verbal ord. on Thos. E. Randolph for the same, being the balce. of rent to Apr. 1." (*MB*, 2:1324).

[1] Preceding three words interlined.

From Thomas Appleton

SIR Leghorn 20th October 1816.

I have shipp'd on board the Brig Saucy-Jack, Capt: Humphrys for charleston. S. Carolina—two Cases containing together 87. bottles of Ama wine, which I hope you will find greatly to your Satisfaction.—

By the brig Othello Capt: Gladding, & who Sail'd 10 days Since, I wrote you very fully on various Subjects; and especially Relating to the Statue, whic[h] I am directed to have sculptur'd, for the State of North-Carolina.—at the Same time, I inclos'd your little account for the wines Sent, which you will percieve exactly balanc'd by the two Cases now Sent.—I have written Gov: miller in relation to the attitude of the Statue, which m[r] Canova Strongly urges should be in a Sitting-posture, considering the lowness of the Senate-chamber, & the place for which it is intended.—I have also greatly Recommended to the Governor, that the figures in basso-relievo on the piedestal, should represent some great traits in the life of the General, instead of the fabulous Goddesses of antiquity which he has Sent me for this purpose.—I inclos'd you, likewise, copies of the letters of m[r] Canova.—I frequently see m[rs] mazzei & her daughter, who appear desirous of withdrawing their money from the u.S. in order to put it at interest in this country.—

I shall only now renew the expressions of my great respect & esteem

TH: APPLETON

RC (DLC); edge chipped; endorsed by TJ as received 30 Dec. 1816 and so recorded in SJL. RC (MHi); address cover only; with PoC of TJ to Fernagus De Gelone, 7 Mar. 1817, on verso; addressed: "Thomas Jefferson esq. Monticello Virginia fav[d] by Capt: Humphreys Via Charleston"; stamped "SHIP"; stamped again and postmarked Charleston, 18 Dec.

THE GENERAL: George Washington.

To Alexander J. Dallas

DEAR SIR

Monticello Oct. 20. 16.

On the establishment of the offices of Assessor & Collector of the land tax, the first being all-important to us, I recommended, on a consultation with others a mr Peter Minor for it: but the office of Collector being given to an inhabitant of this county the principle of geographical distribution prevailed for the other[1] in favor of a mr Armistead. the present Collector now resigning I wish to recall your recollection to my letter of 1814 and to refer to a previous one written to your predecessor with the character of mr Minor which I now confirm in every point.

having made that recommendation without his knolege, and thereby turned his attention & expectations to what he had never before thought of, I feel myself in duty bound to repeat my sollicitation for his appointment to the other office now become vacant.

The office will probably be asked for by mr Southall who has acted as deputy. for integrity and capacity to execute the office he is certainly unobjectionable. the points of difference are that mr Minor has a handsome estate which secures his responsibility, while mr Southall's will have no dependance but on that of his sureties; and again that the latter is a young lawyer, growing in fame, already having much business, and daily gaining more so that the execution of the duties must rest solely on the deputy he may appoint. Accept the assurance of my great esteem & respect TH: JEFFERSON

P.S. I refer again to Col° Monroe's personal knolege of mr Minor, and perhaps the President's.

PoC (DLC); on verso of reused address cover of Wilson Cary Nicholas to TJ, 30 Sept. 1816; adjacent to signature: "Alexr Dallas esq. Secy of the Treasury"; endorsed by TJ.

TJ had recommended Peter Minor for the post of land-tax ASSESSOR in a 23 Aug. 1813 letter to President James Madison. The OFFICE OF COLLECTOR of Virginia's nineteenth collection district was briefly held by TJ's son-in-law Thomas Mann Randolph early in 1814. Randolph was succeeded thereafter by his son Thomas Jefferson Randolph, the PRESENT COLLECTOR (*JEP*, 2:456, 461, 511, 515 [18, 21 Jan., 16, 26 Mar. 1814]; TJ to Dallas, 26 Feb. 1816 [first letter]).

TJ's 1814 LETTER to Dallas concerning Minor was dated 7 Dec. No PREVIOUS communication on the same subject from TJ to either of Dallas's predecessors as secretary of the treasury, Albert Gallatin and George W. Campbell, has been found. TJ may have arrived at Minor's name WITHOUT HIS KNOLEGE, but he soon gained his agreement to serve if appointed (TJ to Minor, 15 Aug. 1813; Minor to TJ, 16 Aug. 1813).

[1] Preceding three words interlined.

To Gouverneur Morris

DEAR SIR Monticello Oct. 20. 16

On the eve of departure to a possession 90. miles Southwestwardly from hence, where my affairs will keep me until the end of the next month, I learn from a letter of mrs Morris's that we may expect the pleasure of a visit from her and yourself in this quarter. I shall be really mortified if I lose my share in it by absence. but an inference from the letter that your departure from New York was still at some little distance, encourages me to hope that by the time you reach this point in the circle of the friends you have to visit in this state, I may be returned. I shall be very happy indeed to recieve you here and to give you personally assurances of my continued esteem. you will find me enjoying general good health, but much enfeebled by age, as at that of 73. ought to be expected. should I however not be returned, my daughter your quondam acquaintance in Paris, now surrounded by her children and grandchildren will be happy in the opportunity of renewing old acquaintance with you, and the more as she will be charged, to pay to you, as my representative the friendly attentions, I should so much rather have done myself. we shall still regret that your visit is not in our belle saison, as to the general unpleasantness of cold our winter adds deep and miry roads. with my respects to mrs Morris accept the assurance of my great consideration and esteem.

TH: JEFFERSON

RC (NNC: Morris Papers); salutation and dateline added separately to RC and PoC; addressed: "Gouvernier Morris esquire Morrisania near New York"; franked; postmarked Milton, 23 Oct. PoC (DLC); on verso of reused address cover of James H. McCulloch to TJ, 25 Sept. 1816; mutilated at seal; endorsed by TJ.

Gouverneur Morris (1752–1816), public official and diplomat, was born at his family's Morrisania estate in what is now the Bronx, New York City, educated at King's College (later Columbia University), 1764–68, and admitted to the bar three years after graduation. During the American Revolution he helped frame New York's constitution and represented that state in the Continental Congress, 1778–79. After leaving office Morris remained in Philadelphia, resumed his legal practice and, later, worked as an assistant to Superintendent of Finance Robert Morris (no relation), 1781–84. In 1787 Morris was an influential Pennsylvania delegate to the Federal Convention, where he favored a strong executive, centralized government, and a free-market economy. He is credited with editing the resulting United States Constitution into its final form and supplying the preamble. In 1788 Morris departed for Europe, where he pursued business interests in Paris, labored as an unofficial American emissary to Great Britain in 1790, and served as United States minister plenipotentiary to France, 1792–94. Morris returned to the United States in 1798, settled at Morrisania, which he had purchased from his family in 1787, and represented New York as a Federalist member of the United States Senate, 1800–03. Although he supported the Louisiana Purchase, he opposed most of the Republican platform, including the War of 1812. Late in life Morris promoted the construction of the Erie Canal (*ANB*; *DAB*; William Howard Adams, *Gouverneur Morris: An Independent Life* [2003]; Morris, *A Diary of the French Revolution*, 2 vols., ed. Beatrix Cary Davenport [1939]; Melanie Randolph Miller, ed., *The Diaries of Gouverneur Morris: European Travels, 1794–1798* [2011]; *PTJ*, 15:79; *JEP*, 1:92, 96, 157 [22 Dec. 1791, 12 Jan. 1792, 27 May 1794]; *New-York Evening Post*, 6 Nov. 1816).

In 1809 Morris married Ann Cary Randolph, a sister of TJ's son-in-law Thomas Mann Randolph. No LETTER OF MRS MORRIS's to TJ from this period has been found, and none is recorded in SJL. She may have written instead to her brother or his wife. BELLE SAISON: "beautiful season; summer."

To Thomas Eston Randolph

DEAR SIR   Monticello Oct. 20. 16.

The account rendered to-day is perfectly satisfactory, as the not having known of the 9. barrels of family flour subsequent to the last account, had alone excited doubt and a wish for you to examine it. I inclose you a statement as I suppose the account now to stand

your's affect[ly]   TH: JEFFERSON

PoC (MHi); on verso of reused address cover of John Adams to TJ, 30 Sept. 1816; at foot of text: "Mr T. E. Randolph"; endorsed by TJ. Enclosure not found.

The account RENDERED TO-DAY is printed above at 19 Oct. 1816. For the LAST ACCOUNT, see the enclosure to Thomas M. Randolph & Company to TJ, 12 Mar. 1816.

From John Barnes

DEAR SIR— George Town 21h Octr 1816.

Your much Esteemed favr so Anxiously expected together with the inclosiers—Viz the good Genls Letter dated Soleure April last, as well his Original and general power of Attorney to you, with substitution &c—all of which shall be duly Attended to.—and no doubt with me—can be Obtruded—or raised—against their being Admitted to be of suff: Validity, for me to receive[1]—thro you—the present and future Interest or Dividends Arising from his present Stocks—Nor shall I suffer the Genls original power of Atty—out of my hands. but Attested Copies thereof—to be lodged—at the several Offices—or Banks from whence I am to receive[2] all such Int or dividends.[3] and to return to you the Originals together, with the generals private Letter to you—

The Necessary proceedings to effect these desirable[4] objects will require some time. mean while I am preparing my self to effect a further Remittance of £200 Ster at all events (tho short of his Nt balle in hand) ℔ 1h favble Opportunity: that offers in a purchase and Conveyance—

I judged it Necessary—at this Instant to Acknowledge these receipts—and when Matured—to advise you the Result

Most Respectfully and with greatest Esteem.

I am Dear Sir your Obedt servant. JOHN BARNES.

PS. your Note to Mr Milligan I handed to him & Ansr inclosed

RC (ViU: TJP-ER); at foot of text: "Thomas Jefferson Esqr Monticello"; endorsed by TJ as received 31 Oct. 1816 and so recorded in SJL.

The MUCH ESTEEMED FAVR SO ANXIOUSLY EXPECTED was TJ's first letter to Barnes of 12 Oct. 1816. For the GOOD GENLS LETTER, see Tadeusz Kosciuszko to TJ, Apr. 1816. NT BALLE: "net balance." The NOTE concerning Joseph Milligan was probably TJ to Barnes, 12 Oct. 1816 (second letter).

[1] Manuscript: "recive."
[2] Manuscript: "recive."
[3] Manuscript: "divendends."
[4] Manuscript: "desiable."

ENCLOSURE

Joseph Milligan to John Barnes

Georgetown Oct 21st 1816

in answer to your Note I enclose you a page of the book which I engaged to print for Mr Jefferson I would have answered his Letter but having failed in beginning to print the book I would not write until I Could Send him an evidence that I had begun: The enclosed page was set up to determine the size; next week I will send him a proof of the first Eight pages

yours JOSEPH MILLIGAN

RC (DLC); addressed: "John Barnes Esqr"; endorsed by TJ as a letter from Milligan to Barnes received 31 Oct. 1816 by TJ. Enclosure not found.

From James Ligon (for Patrick Gibson)

SIR Richmond 21st Octr 1816

I inclose you your account Current up to the 1st Septr balanced by $878.91 in my favor which I trust you will find Correct— Flour 8½ & 8¾$— respectfully

yr ob servt

PATRICK GIBSON
p JAS LIGON

your favor of the 16th is just recd the dfts & remittance you direct shall be attended to.

RC (ViU: TJP-ER); in Ligon's hand; addressed by Ligon: "Thomas Jefferson Poplar Forest near Lynchburg"; stamped; with TJ's description of the missing enclosure on address cover: "1816. Jan.—Aug."; endorsed by TJ as a letter from Gibson received 25 Oct. 1816 and so recorded in SJL.

From Mathew Carey

SIR, Philada Oct. 22. 1816

Your favour with four[1] Dollars, I have duly Recd. I enclose 25 cents.

By a letter of yours to Charles Thompson, Esqr I find you have been collating the Morality of the New Testament. Do you intend it for publication? If so, wd you be willing to let me have the MS. & on what terms?

With due respect

Your obt hble servt MATHEW CAREY

RC (MHi); dateline at foot of text; endorsed by TJ as received 7 Nov. 1816 and so recorded in SJL. RC (DLC); address cover only; with PoC of TJ to Joseph Milligan, 6 Jan. 1817, on verso; addressed (in a clerk's hand): "Thomas Jefferson

Esqr Monticello V^{a}"; franked; postmarked Philadelphia, 22 Oct. Enclosure: Carey's prospectus, Philadelphia, 25 Sept. 1816, for an eighth edition of his publication, *The Olive Branch: or, Faults on Both Sides, Federal and Democratic*, enclosing "proposals" (not found) and indicating that the seventh edition has almost sold out; that a subscription for the new edition will remain open until 1 Dec.; that it will be printed within two months once five hundred copies are subscribed for; and that he has been induced to prepare a new edition because "Time, calm reflection, and the suggestions of judicious friends, have pointed out errors in it, which I am desirous of having an opportunity of correcting" (broadside in MWA). A fuller version of the prospectus in the Washington *Daily National Intelligencer*, 5 Nov. 1816, adds that the work will cost $2.75; offers a free copy to anyone who procures nine subscriptions; lists those authorized to accept orders; and contends that, contrary to what some have said, the author has guarded against "undue bias" and tried to be impartial.

[1] Word interlined in place of what appears to be "five."

From Nicolas G. Dufief

MONSIEUR, A Philadelphie ce 22 Octobre 1816

J'ai bien des remerciemens à vous faire pour la bonté que vous avez eu de parcourir le manuscrit que je vous envoyai[1] le mois passé. Je m'empresse, maintenant, de vous adresser le Prospectus de l'ouvrage. La méthode, comme vous y verrez, est applicable à l'enseignement même d'un seul individu; Sans cela, elle eût été défectueuse, et ne pouvait convenir comme vous l'avez, Justement, observé, qu'à l'enseignement des villes. J'ai fait des efforts inouis pour la rendre la plus complète possible. Beaucoup de personnes croyant qu'elle avait de l'affinité avec celle de Lancaster, j'ai cru devoir les éclairer à ce sujet, car non-Seulement elle ne lui ressemble en rien, mais même ce qui est très-Singulier elle[2] en est l'antipode comme la lecture du Prospectus Suffira pour en convaincre

J'ai l'honneur d'être, Monsieur, avec le plus profond respect & la plus haute considération votre très-dévoué & très-reconnaissant serv^{r}

N. G. DUFIEF

EDITORS' TRANSLATION

SIR, Philadelphia 22 October 1816

Thank you very much for having the goodness to skim the manuscript I sent you last month. I now hasten to send you the prospectus of the work. The method, as you will see, applies even to the education of a single individual. Without that, it would have been defective and only suitable, as you justly observed, to teaching townspeople. I have made unprecedented efforts to render it as complete as possible. As many people believed it was similar to Lancaster's system, I thought it my duty to enlighten them on this subject, because, not only does it not resemble it in any way, but, and this is very remarkable, it is diametrically opposed to it, as a reading of the prospectus will suffice to convince anyone

I have the honor to be, Sir, with the most profound respect and the highest consideration, your very devoted and very grateful servant

N. G. Dufief

RC (DLC); endorsed by TJ as received 7 Nov. 1816 and so recorded in SJL. RC (MHi); address cover only; with PoC of TJ to Robert Patterson, 1 Jan. 1817, on verso; addressed: "Th: Jefferson, Esquire Monticello V[a]"; franked; postmarked Philadelphia, 22 Oct. Translation by Dr. Genevieve Moene.

The enclosed PROSPECTUS, not found, was probably similar to the "Proposal" that Dufief inserted in the newspapers two months later, wherein he discusses the need for an improved edition of his *Nature Displayed, in her Mode of Teaching Language to Man*; stresses that his plan is "effectually adapted to the instruction of a single scholar, of several, or of thousands at the same time, by one teacher only"; explains that his method not only teaches proper pronunciation and grammar, but also helps to prepare its students for mathematical work; denies that his system is at all like "*the Lancasterian plan of tuition by the aid of monitors*"; hails the use in his work of stereotyping, which Dufief describes as "the art of printing on solid pages"; and announces that subscribers will receive two handsome, octavo volumes on fine paper, each about six-hundred pages long, at a total cost of $5 (*Boston Daily Advertiser*, 11 Dec. 1816, and elsewhere).

[1] Reworked from "adressai" ("addressed").

[2] Manuscript: "ell."

From James Monroe

Dear Sir Washington Octr 22[d] 1816.

It would give me real[1] pleasure to be useful to m[r] armistead,[2] for the reasons which you have stated, if I had the power, but there is no vacancy in the dep[t] of State, and so closely beset are all the dep[ts], by applicants for clerkships, that opportunities rarely occur of introducing into either, any person whom we wish, however deserving of it. I have spoken to the President in m[r] armisteads[3] favor, and Shall speak to the gentlemen in the other dep[ts], as soon as they arrive, so that I hope he may be provided for. To gov[r] Nicholas's family I have been friendly, particularly to those in the military line, and especially while in the dep[t] of war, when I had the means.[4] Towards him personally, I thought that I had serious cause of dissatisfaction, some years past, but that feeling has long since subsided, and never could have been a motive for injuring or slighting his connections.[5] When in Richmond, shortly after the peace, I calld on him, thereby evincing my willingness, to restore a friendly intercourse.

Your sentiments relating to an inscription on the Capitol[6] correspond strictly with my own: our friends will I doubt not be satisfied with it.[7]

m[r] daschkoff has pushed his demand of reparation, for what he calls an insult to the Emperor, by the arrest & confin'ment of his consul gen[l] at Phil[a], on the charge of committing a rape there, with the utmost degree of violence, of which the case was susceptible. By the stile of his last[8] notes, we have reason to expect, that he will announce the termination of his mission, in obedience to o[r]ders given him by his gov[t], while acting under an excitment produc'd by his misrepresentations, and before a correct statment reached our chargé des aff[rs], at S[t] Petersburg. A collision with him, which he invited from the commenc'ment, by declaring the arrest & confin'ment of the consul, a violation of the law of nations, was carefully avoided, without making any concession, and still is, tho' the effect which he sought to produce with his gov[t], has unfortunately been too fully accomplished. It is hope[d] that the delusion of his gov[t] will be momentary, & presumed, whenever it ceases, that the reaction will be felt by himself. The incident is a disagreeable one; the gov[t] knew nothing of it, till after the consul had been arrested, & releasd, from confinment, and it has imposed on the gov[t] the painful duty only, of exerting itself, to prevent its producing mischief at Petersburg, without making any sacrifice of principle here. with m[r] de Neuville we have some respite, procurd by some jarring, which he ought to have avoided. The Spaniards in the gulph of Mexico, seem to invite, a rupture, which their gov[t] cannot be prepard for or desire. From Algiers we have heard nothing lately.

with great respect affec[y] your friend JA[S] MONROE

RC (DLC); edge chipped and trimmed; endorsed by TJ as received 7 Nov. 1816 and so recorded in SJL. RC (MHi); address cover only; with PoC of TJ to Jerman Baker, 1 Jan. 1817, on verso; addressed: "Thomas Jefferson Monticello"; franked; postmarked Washington City, 23 Oct. Dft (NN: Monroe Papers); incomplete; endorsed by Monroe.

Late in November 1815 the Russian CONSUL GEN[L] at Philadelphia, Nicholas Kosloff, was charged with raping a teenage servant girl in his employ and briefly imprisoned. The Russian minister André Daschkoff immediately protested against what he viewed as a serious breach of international law. Although the complaint against Kosloff was dismissed in January 1816 when the local court of oyer and terminer concluded that state tribunals lacked jurisdiction over cases involving consuls, Daschkoff continued to press the issue. On 23 Aug. 1816 he wrote Monroe demanding reparation for the actions taken against Kosloff and, two months later, he threatened to leave the country. Word having reached Saint Petersburg of the imbroglio, the Russian government asked the United States CHARGÉ d'affaires there, Levett Harris, not to appear at the imperial court until the matter was resolved. After further diplomatic wrangling, relations were patched up early in November 1816 (John C. Hildt, "Early Diplomatic Negotiations of the United States with Russia," *Johns Hopkins University Studies in Historical and Political Science*, ser. 24, nos. 5–6 [1906]: 91–107; Thomas Sergeant and William Rawle Jr., *Reports of Cases adjudged in the Supreme Court of Pennsylvania* [Philadelphia, 1818–29], 5:545–52; Philadelphia *Weekly Aurora*, 9 Dec. 1816).

Monroe had denied the request of the French ambassador Jean Guillaume Hyde DE NEUVILLE that John S. Skinner be removed from his office as Baltimore postmaster for making disparaging remarks about Louis XVIII the previous Fourth of July. In explanation of this decision, Monroe commented that "If a foreign Minister can dictate measures to the United States, especially in a case so intimately connected with the vital principles of their government, their Independence is gone" (Monroe to Albert Gallatin, 10 Sept. 1816, and enclosures [NHi: Gallatin Papers]).

[1] Word not in Dft.

[2] Manuscript: "armstead."

[3] Manuscript: "armsteads."

[4] In Dft Monroe here canceled "There is nothing that I abhor more in any one, than to see him, make a personal difference with another, the ground or motive of annoying his connections. The opposite course is more gratifying to the feelings of a generous mind, and more likely to elevate the character of him who pursues it."

[5] Dft substitutes "his friends" for preceding four words.

[6] Preceding three words not in Dft.

[7] Dft ends here.

[8] RC: "lats."

From Elisha Ticknor

SIR, Boston, 22d Octo. 1816.

Your favour of the 15th August last reach'd Boston, in my absence, on a long journey in the country. I returned two days ago and found your letter, which informs me, that my son is "about sending me out Books" and at the same time will forward "a parcel" to me to be forwarded to you. These Books have not yet arrived, and since he has resolved to continue another year in Göttingen I have supposed he would be a little more tardy in collecting books for himself than he otherwise, would have been. But, I am sure he wont fail exactly and punctually (if possible) to execute your orders agreeably to your wishes. It has, in my absence, been rumoured, that your <u>Books</u> and <u>his</u> were ship'd on board the Brig Abeona at Hamburg. I did not on hearing it, believe it was true. This vessel as probably you have heard was lost soon after she left Hamburg. The letters from my son have in no instance from the 1st Jany last to the 6th July, stated to me his intentions of sending out books, 'till after he had visited many of the principal cities in Germany and attended some of the Book-Fairs, at which he had made strong calculations to be able to furnish himself with such books as he wanted for his own Library as well as execute the orders of his friends. After thus premising I have two strong circumstances to induce me to believe, that neither your books nor his were on board the Abeona at the time she was lost; viz. 1st those Merchants of this town, who had goods on board, have received their Invoices. I have received none. 2d A Mr Clark, a young Merchant of this town also, who had ship'd at Hamburg personally many goods on board the Abeona, call'd on me yesterday to inform me, that, on his way from Hamburg to Paris, he stopt a few hours[1] at Gottingen and call'd on my son, who was well about the 8th August. I inquired of him very particularly, whether my son had shipt merchandize of any kind on board the Abeona? He informed me, he was confident he had not as he was much with his Commission Merchant as well as with the Captain of the Vessel. I think, therefore, we may fairly conclude, that no loss has happened either to yourself or to my son. when the books arrive, you may rely on my strictest attention to your orders, than which nothing will give me more pleasure than to serve the father and friend of my Country. Sir, the following lines in your letter give me much courage and satisfaction. "The account he gives me of the German literature is very interesting and such as I had not been before apprised of. It seems well worthy of his avail and he is accordingly sowing the seed of what with his genius and industry will yield a rich harvest." Such lines and opinion, sir, considering the source whence they came—his experience and age—his judgment and foresight, console and calm the heart of a father, who, at times, has almost regretted the enterprise he suffered his son to undertake. Please to accept, sir, for the confidence you have reposed in him, the thanks and highest consideration of

Your most obedient And very humble servant,

ELISHA TICKNOR.

RC (MHi); addressed: "Honourable Thomas Jefferson, Monticello, Virginia"; franked; postmarked (faint) Boston, 2[3?] Oct.; endorsed by TJ as received 21 Nov. 1816 and so recorded in SJL.

The BRIG ABEONA hit a sandbank near the mouth of the Elbe River on 9 Aug. 1816 and sank. Although most of its cargo was lost, the vessel's crew returned safely to Hamburg (New York *Commercial Advertiser*, 29 Oct. 1816). It did not carry any of TJ's book purchases (Boston *Independent Chronicle*, 4 Nov. 1816). Before this was confirmed, however, at least one newspaper reported that "a large part of the new Library purchased for Mr. Jefferson in Paris and Germany" might thereby have been lost, that many of the books were "elegant editions of Classical Works from the German Press.—These late editions are perhaps the most beautiful in the world," and that "Mr. Jefferson has lately received some of them, which he highly prizes." The unidentified correspondent added that "I should be sorry, indeed, that any of his literary importations of this cast should miscarry; as he has nearly abandoned the field of polemical politics—and draws the principal and purest sources of his pleasure from the antient Classics and Mathematics. A gentleman who visited him in July last, arrived at his farm at sunrise, and found that after rising at day-break, and riding round his farm, he had sat down to the perusal of a Greek Poet.—How many men in Virginia, of Mr. J's age, rise at day-break to enjoy an antient Classic?—The loss of the Library in the Abeano would indeed be a 'loss to literature'" (Norfolk *American Beacon and Commercial Diary*, 19 Oct. 1816).

[1] Word interlined in place of "days."

From John F. Watson

SIR, [ca. 22 Oct. 1816]

I have lately seen some books in this place which are for sale low & which might be desireable to you to possess—They belong to the Estate of Benjn Davis,[1] an old friend, whom you may remember as among the first members of the Philosophical society—I will add a description of a few of those most curious or rare—Should you think well to enquire further respecting them, I will fulfil you any service respecting them gratis—or you might refer yourself to our friend Doct Geo Logan, who equally knows all the parties.

very good preservation—

26 vol^s—small 4to in calf—of a "Genl history (by J Phillips) of Europe contained in the historical & political monthly mercuries from the Revolution of 1688 to 1716[2]—giving an acco^t of all the Public & private occurrences in every Court &^ca &^ca—with Political Reflections upon every State—Done from the originals published at the Hague"— These might be had for about 2½ D^s ℔ vol—

14 vol^s Universal mag^ze 1786 to 1792—about 2 D^rs[3]

10 vol^s of the Repertory of the Arts 8vo—about 2½ D^rs

Lahontans voyages to N^o Am^ca 2 vol^s—very ancient—

Caesars Commentaries & reflections by C Edmonds—do—folio—

Huets Commerce of the Ancients—Defence of Emigrants—

Hoopers Recreations—Easton on Longevity—

Ayeen Akbery or Institutes of Emperor Akber

Nobles memoirs of Cromwell—

many old vol^s of news Papers—

& many Political, works & national histories—

Y^rs respectfully J F WATSON—

[*At head of text:*]

Received Oct. 22. 1816 from Thos Jefferson Esqre (℔ mail) Ten dollars being full payment for the 11th to 14th vol^s of the Edinburgh Review J F WATSON—

RC (DLC: TJ Papers, 208:37130); date of letter conjectured from that of conjoined receipt and TJ's endorsement; addressed: "Thomas Jefferson Esqre Monticello V^a"; franked; postmarked Philadelphia, 29 Oct.; endorsed by TJ as a letter of 22 Oct. 1816 received 21 Nov. 1816 and so recorded in SJL.

The Philadelphia merchant Benjamin Davies was an early member of the American PHILOSOPHICAL SOCIETY and its predecessors (Whitfield J. Bell Jr., *Patriot-Improvers: Biographical Sketches of Members of the American Philosophical Society* [1997–], 1:306–7).

[1] Reworked from "Davies."

[2] Reworked from "1715."

[3] Reworked from "about 2 to 2½ Ds."

From Thomas H. Palmer

Sir, Philadelphia, Oct. 23, 1816.

I hope you will pardon the liberty I am taking of enclosing a letter to my brother, who is at present on his way from Lexington K^{y} to Petersburg, V^{a}. The letter which I enclose will be useless unless it reach him before he gets to Petersburg & Monticello is the only place he has mentioned of his route. If G. P. has not yet reached Monticello, you will oblige me by keeping the letter for him; if he has already passed, by throwing it in the fire. I am Sir,

with high consideration Respectfully Yours,

Thos H. Palmer

RC (MHi); endorsed by TJ as received 7 Nov. 1816 and so recorded in SJL. RC (DLC); address cover only; with PoC of TJ to Joseph C. Cabell, 1 Jan. 1817, on verso; addressed: "Thos Jefferson Esq. Monticello Milton Virginia"; franked; postmarked (faint) Philadelphia, [23] Oct. Enclosure not found.

G. P.: George Palmer.

From William Wirt

Dear Sir Richmond October 23. 1816

I now submit to you the last sheets of my sketches of Mr H.[1] which I am sorry to find more numerous than I expected, and I pray you to forgive the very great trouble which I am sincerely ashamed of having imposed on you.—Your remarks have been of great service to me not only by enabling me to correct mistakes in fact, but by putting me on a severe inquisition of my style which I am perfectly aware is too prone to exuberance.—I am afraid that the whole plan is too loose and the narrative too diffuse. Has it struck you in this light and do you think it would gain, in point of animation & interest, by retrenchment & compression?

I have another question to ask to which I entreat an unreserved answer, and I hope you think too well of my understanding to suppose that I shall be hurt by the answer, whatever it may be. Would you, as a friend, advise me to publish this book or not? It has been written under circumstances so extremely disadvantageous, amid such perpetual interruptions arising from my profession, at almost every step, too, invita Minerva, and I peruse it myself with so little satisfaction, that I am seriously apprehensive it may make shipwreck of what little reputation I possess as a writer. I am not obliged to publish, and I shall be governed on this head by the advice of my friends, who must, from the nature of things be much better qualified to judge of the subject than I am, and who, I hope & believe, think too justly of me to with-hold the expression of their opinions from motives of delicacy.

Your repose shall never be endangered by any act of mine if I can help it. Immediately on the receipt of your last[2] letter and before the manuscript had met any other eye, I wrote over again the whole passage relative to the first congress, omitting the marks of quotation and removing your name altogether from the communication. If there be any other passage for which I have quoted you and which you think may provoke the strictures of malice or envy, I beg that you will be so good as to suggest it. I am conscious of having made a very free use of your communications. It was natural for me to seek to give this value to my work: but it would be most painful to me to be, in any manner, instrumental in subjecting you to the renewed attacks of your political enemies. It is not enough for me that you despise those attacks: I have no right much less have I the disposition to make this call upon your fortitude: and, besides, the shaft which cannot reach you, never fails to wound and irritate your friends. This was one of the leading causes which made me anxious to submit my manuscript to you first.—Quæ.[3] have I not quoted some passages from you, of which the descendants of our landed aristocracy may take it into their heads to complain? This did not occur to me 'till Mr Wm H. Cabell (than whom you have not a warmer friend) made the suggestion. I have great dependance on his judgment and if the matter occurs to you in the same light, I will send up again the sheets which contain those quotations and get the favor of you to alter them to your own taste.

My[4] friends, here, concur in the opinion that every thing personal to Mr Pendleton shall be stricken out; and I shall do it with the greater pleasure, because it would have been very painful to me had I found it my duty to cast a shade upon his memory.

You will perceive that I have borne very lightly on the errors of Mr Henry's declining years. He did us much good in his better days and no evils have resulted from his later aberrations. Will not his biographer then be excused[5] in drawing the veil over[6] them and holding up the brighter side of his character, only, to imitation?

Most respectfully & affectionately Your friend & servant,

WM WIRT

RC (DLC); at foot of text: "Mr Jefferson"; endorsed by TJ as received 31 Oct. 1816 and so recorded in SJL. Tr (MdHi: Wirt Papers). Enclosure: manuscript, not found, of a portion of Wirt, *Patrick Henry*.

Wirt's reference to TJ's LAST LETTER actually pertains to his communication of 29 Sept. 1816 and its enclosure.

[1] Tr: "Henry."

[2] Word interlined.

[3] Tr: "Quære."
[4] Wirt here canceled "other."
[5] Tr: "excusable."
[6] Preceding four words interlined in place of "forgetting."

From William Lee

REVERED SIR/. New York Octr 25th 1816

The letter you did me the favor to write me under date of the 24th of August after having travelled from Boston to Philadelphia and then back to Boston found me here a few days since which will account for my not having acknowledged the receipt of it before this. I have not forgotten Sir the great obligations I am under to you and that I have lived so much in your memory as to have merited this amiable mark of your regard is particularly gratifying. Your opinion of my book is very flattering, it did some good while it drew upon me all the venom of the party at which it was aimed and has been the great cause of my abandoning a situation which was in every point of view agreeable to me.—I shall succeed here for Mr Garde. we have had two meetings composed of enlightened patriotic men who are digesting a plan for his establishment in this vicinity. I will not fail to make known to him your friendly sentiments.—Your observations on the State of things in Europe are very just, the best informed of all nations in that section of the globe are looking towards us with wishful eyes particularly those of the french kingdom. The languishing state of our infant fabricks and the prevalent opinion on our Sea board that we cannot become a manufacturing people for ages may check in a degree for a moment their imigration but as that opinion will prove erronious we shall not fail to reap great advantages from the gothic strides of legitimacy. That we cannot for many years become a manufacturing nation is certain that we may not become so for a lapse of time is desirable but that the germs of useful fabricks producing from our raw materials articles of the first necessity ought to be protected and encouraged will not be denied.—The seeds of the dissolution of European governments which the Commercial despotism of England has sown to her own and their inevitable destruction have taken such a deep root of late that the most superficial observers must see the consequences. The crimes of the legitimates begin to operate on this country by the throngs of useful artisans who are daily arriving in our cities in the Same manner as the Edict of nantz operated in favor of England who at that period was considered the bulwark of freedom. The french people at the commencement of their revolution threw off[1] a part of the scum of their population, napoleon when he became the champion of privileged orders called them back and the consequence has been that they in Revenge have warred against the people who in their turn are forced by a vindictive[2] policy to seek an asylum in other Countries. The result of this struggle is favorable to America. The first emigration from France to this Country was of the worst kind, so much so as to prejudice our people against that nation. The men who then came over brought from France & her colonies only their idleness, ignorance debauchery and decorations "the engines of the woes of men" while those who now come among us bring the arts sciences & manufactures, even the Dukes Counts and generals who were created by napoleon are very different men from most of those of the ancient french school, they rose by their merit not by hereditary right. Having received their education in the walks of private life we find them here returning with ease to the source from which they came and to the dignity of useful citizens. Look Sir at the Crowd of civilians, chymists, mineroligists, naturalists engineers, Geographers, mechanicians engravers sculptors dyers opticians weavers of cloth and Stocking Knit, gold beaters, hatters tanners, gun & lock smiths cutlers distillers—gilders in wood & metal, founders, glove makers, fringe makers, glass makers, gardeners Vignerons cultivators, Lampists Surgeons & dentists which have passed through Bordeaux only and been patronized by my small means and I am sure you will find your wise predictions fully confirmed. I brought over with me in the Same Ship sixty nine of this list for all of whom I have found employment & happiness. The received new England opinion that European emigrants bring only their vices with them cannot certainly be applied to the French. They are undoubtedly the most virtuous nation in Europe. The middling and lower classes are sober, amiable & industrious. The vulgar vices of swearing, drinking, fighting & petty larceny is unknown among them, there is a degree of civilization and good manners in their social intercourse which is very pleasing and when contrasted with their neighbours highly honorable to them. You must have observed an essential difference between them and all other emigrants. They never interfere improperly in affairs that do not concern them. If you will examine the conduct of the respectable french merchants artists & manufacturers settled in Baltimore, Philadelphia & N York you will scarcely find an instance of their meddling in our party disputes or making a bustle at an election, if they have acquired rights they exercise them with a moderation & decency which seems to say this people have received us among them we must not abuse their indulgence. We ought to cherish such men & I am happy to find public opinion is growing up in their favor—I hope this winter to have it in my power to present my respects to you in person & at the same time to present to you my friend & inmate Marshal Grouchy. I have taken the liberty to give to the celebrated ex legislator M[r] Penieres a letter of introduction to you he is one of the best informed men of the age and will let you more into the secrets of the late affairs in France than any other man can do. He is at the head of the company now forming for an establishment on the Ohio to be composed of Frenchmen altogether. My paper scarcely[3] gives me room enough to say with how much veneration and respect I have; Sir the honor to be your obliged humble Servant

W[M] LEE

RC (DLC); endorsed by TJ as received 7 Nov. 1816 and so recorded in SJL.

The revocation at Fontainebleau in 1685 of the EDICT OF NANTZ (Nantes) of 1598, which had previously mandated religious toleration, led many Protestants to leave France.

[1] Manuscript: "of."
[2] Manuscript: "vinditive."
[3] Manuscript: "scarcly."

Extract of Cornelia J. Randolph to Virginia J. Randolph (Trist)

poplar Forest. Oct. 25. 16

As sister Ellen is writing to mama my Dear Virginia, I will write also by this opportunity, to you, for I suppose you will expect a letter in return for the one you favour'd me with when you were here. we arriv'd here in safety after a journey pleasant enough, for the weather was very fine except being rather cold, mornings & evenings, but we were well wrapt up, having a cloak apiece of grand papa's besides our own things, the roads were not so good as we expected to find them, owing to a much greater quantity of rain having fallen in Buckingham, & Campbell than in Albemarle. the first day we were out till past seven oclock in the evening. I should have been very well pleas'd at M[r] Patterson's if I had not made a very ridiculous blunder from forgetfulness & inattention. On the road we stopt at Noah Floods to breakfast, & found that to be the best house on the road to stop at meals; & at night we were better accomodated at Hunters than we were any where else.

RC (NcU: NPT); extract consisting of opening of unsigned letter; addressed: "Miss Virginia Randolph." In the unextracted portion of this letter, Randolph mentions that she has mistakenly left several items at Monticello: a small roll of tape, "a corset lace," "a slip of homespun to put gores & bone-case to my corset," some darning cotton, and "a little English dictionary" that she wished to present to

John Hemmings; hopes that either her father, Thomas Mann Randolph, "if he comes to Linchburg as he said," or her brother Thomas Jefferson Randolph will bring these items to her; requests that Virginia Randolph collect and put away five letters from various family members that she left lying around the house; sends her love to the family members left behind at Monticello and Carlton; fears that Priscilla Hemmings was upset that she left without saying goodbye and explains that she "could not go up stairs after grand papa call'd me to go"; and asks her sister to "pray burn this scratch."

Virginia Jefferson Randolph (Trist) (1801–82), the sixth child of Thomas Mann Randolph and TJ's daughter Martha Jefferson Randolph, was born and lived at Monticello until the time of the first estate sale in January 1827. Like her sisters Ellen and Cornelia Randolph, Virginia occasionally accompanied her grandfather to his Poplar Forest retreat. An accomplished musician, she sang and played the harpsichord, piano, and guitar. Soon after Nicholas P. Trist met her in 1817, he asked her mother for permission to court her, but Martha persuaded him to wait. They were finally married at Monticello in September 1824, and their daughter Martha, the first of their three children, was born there just two months before TJ's death. Her husband's career led to extended residences in Washington, D.C., and Havana, Cuba. In 1839 Virginia Trist and her unmarried sisters Mary and Cornelia took two of the Trist children to be educated in Saint Servan, France, while the elder son Thomas Jefferson Trist attended a school for the deaf in Philadelphia. Leaving France in 1841, Virginia Trist rejoined her husband in Havana. The Trists subsequently lived in Washington, in New York, and in Pennsylvania, where Virginia and her sisters briefly operated a boarding school. The Trists were living in the Alexandria home of their daughter and son-in-law when they died, with Nicholas P. Trist predeceasing his wife in 1874 (Nicholas P. Trist to Martha Jefferson Randolph, 18, 20 Sept. 1818, Martha Jefferson Randolph to Nicholas P. Trist, [ca. 19 Sept. 1818], Cornelia J. Randolph to Virginia J. Randolph Trist, 21 Nov. 1826, Robley Dunglison to Nicholas P. Trist, 3 Jan. 1837 [1838], Virginia J. Randolph Trist to Nicholas P. Trist, 15 Mar., 10 May 1839, 30 Nov., 6 Dec. 1841, Ellen W. Randolph Coolidge to Virginia J. Randolph Trist, 23 July 1855, Martha J. Trist Burke to [Mary J. Randolph], 2 Nov. 1873 [all in NcU: NPT]; Shackelford, *Descendants*, 1:100–13, 231–2, 2:155; Helen Cripe, *Thomas Jefferson and Music* [1974; rev. ed. 2009], 41, 53–4, 63–7; *Richmond Enquirer*, 21 Sept. 1824, 3 Nov. 1826; *ANB*, 21:832–4; gravestone inscription in Ivy Hill Cemetery, Alexandria).

WHEN YOU WERE HERE: Virginia Randolph and her mother had accompanied TJ to and from Poplar Forest a few weeks earlier (*MB*, 2:1327; note to TJ to William Wirt, 29 Sept. 1816). During their 22–24 Oct. 1816 journey to his Bedford County estate, TJ and his granddaughters Cornelia and Ellen Randolph spent the night at Gibson's ordinary in Buckingham County and Robert HUNTERS establishment in Campbell County (*MB*, 2:1328).

From Joseph Delaplaine

DEAR SIR, Philadelphia October 26. 1816.

I have the honour to acknowledge the receipt of your most obliging & kind letter of July 26: together with the particulars of two transactions, and a sketch of Peyton Randolph's life. These papers I consider entirely confidential & shall never go out of my hands. Of course, you will never be quoted relative to their contents. I am happy to mention this because you have enjoined it on me to use the papers for my work as facts, but in no other way.

I trust that my work will be so conducted, invariably, as that the world shall have no room to find fault. The first half volume has given great satisfaction to all parties. The Repository shall in no instance be suborned to the purpose of party, influenced by party views, or discoloured[1] by political partialities. It shall be national throughout.

Nothing shall appear in the pages of the Repository in the least like reflections against other nations. Let us endeavour to exalt our own nation & act magnanimously towards others. I shall conduct the Repository in this particular manner whilst I am its proprietor.

I send to you by this mail the first half volume of the Repository with which I trust you will be pleased.—I have expended on it already upwards of Eleven thousand Dollars, and have been engaged in it more than three years. On its cover I mentioned that your likeness I caused to be painted by Mr Otis. I send to you also a pamphlet, at the end of which you will perceive I have stated that your portrait is now engraving by Mr Leney.

I shall receive from a number of respectable characters their opinions of the merits of the Repository, which I purpose to print with the second half volume. The President has most obligingly favoured me with his opinions of the work which are very highly flattering. May I beg dear sir, that you will after a week, furnish me with your opinion of the Repository. Relative to its paper, printing, engraving, literary part, and something of the plan & importance of the undertaking. I will not trouble you for more than a dozen lines.—

I am preparing the second half volume of the Repository for the press;—In this with five others, your life & portrait will be given.—I think I cannot publish it before January next.

With the highest respect & esteem, I remain, Dr sir, Your obedt & most huml st JOSEPH DELAPLAINE

P.S. I beg leave to have my most respectful compliments made to Mrs Randolph, Colo Randolph, & the young ladies.—

RC (DLC); endorsed by TJ as received 7 Nov. 1816 and so recorded in SJL. RC (DLC); address cover only; with PoC of TJ to John H. Cocke, 1 May 1817, on verso; addressed: "Thomas Jefferson Esqr Monticello Virginia"; franked; postmarked Philadelphia, 27 Oct.

The two works that Delaplaine forwarded to TJ BY THIS MAIL were *Delaplaine's Repository*, vol. 1, pt. 1, and [Delaplaine], *The Author Turned Critic; or The Reviewer Reviewed; being a Reply to a feeble and unfounded attack on Delaplaine's Repository, in the Analectic Magazine and Naval Chronicle, for the Month of September 1816* ([Philadelphia, 1816]). Notwithstanding the announcement in the latter, TJ's portrait in *Delaplaine's Repository* was engraved by James or John Neagle, not William Satchwell LENEY.

James Madison gave HIS OPINIONS OF THE WORK in a letter to Delaplaine of 22 Oct. 1816. He considered these remarks to be so inconsequential, however, that he asked that they not be published (DLC: Madison Papers).

[1]Manuscript: "discolured."

From John Steele

SIR, Collectors office Philad[a] Oct[r] 26. 1816

I have recieved, consigned to me by Stephen Cathalan Esq[r] at Marseilles, a small Box by the Brig David Maffet, and a double Cask of Wine by the Ship Prosperity, both of which I have shiped on board the Sc[r] Hilan Capt. Hand, consigned to Mess[rs] Gibson & Jefferson at Richmond, as ℔ Bill of lading enclosed

M[r] Cathalan informs me there are about twenty Gallons of Wine, & on that quantity I have charged duty, as I could not have it guaged

On the enclosed Bill of frieght are endorsed the duty & charges which I have paid

I am very respectfully
Sir your Obed[t] Ser[t]

JN[O] STEELE

RC (MHi); endorsed by TJ as received 7 Nov. 1816 and so recorded in SJL. RC (DLC); address cover only; with PoC of TJ to Philip I. Barziza, 1 Jan. 1817, on verso; addressed: "Thomas Jefferson Esq[r] Monticello"; franked; inconsistently postmarked Philadelphia, 25 Oct. Enclosure: bill of lading, Philadelphia, 25 Oct. 1816, according to which Steele had shipped to TJ, bound for Richmond aboard the schooner *Hilan* under John Hand Jr., "*One double Cask Wine*" (marked "***T*** *N° 4*") and "*one small wooden Box*" (marked "*Thomas Jefferson Esq[r] Monticello*"), to be delivered to Gibson & Jefferson in Richmond, with that firm to pay freight charges of $1.25 "with primage and average accustomed" (printed form in CSmH: JF; with multiple blanks filled by Steele rendered in italics; signed by Hand). Other enclosure not found.

From Peter Derieux

MONSIEUR Richmond ce 27. oct. 1816.

Depuis la Lettre dont vous avés eu la bonté de m'honorer le 31. Juillet, J'en ai recu de mes parents en France, qui me croyent toujours dans L'espoir de la fortune de m[r] mazzei; J'en ay appris aussi que depuis le retour du Roi, Le neveu du Cte de Jaucourt mon beau pere, avoit eté nommé Ministre de La Marine, et comme ce fut principalement en consideration de mon alliance a cette famille que m[r] mazzei Se mit plus particulierement en avance de promesses Verbales vis a vis d'elle, je desire Lui envoyer copie de Son Testament afin de prouver a ma famille combien Ses esperances et les miennes ont eté frustrées, malgré La fortune qu'il a Laissé, et vous serais infiniment obligé Monsieur Si vous voulliés bien me faire La grace de me l'envoyer pour en tirer copie, et jaurai l'honneur de vous le remettre par La poste Suivante; ne pouvant Sans indiscretion me permettre d'esperer que vous voudriés bien prendre la peine de transcrire ce Testament dont La teneur peut etre très Longue. Dans Le nombre de parents qui me restent encore; il en est plusieurs qui malgré la Revolution, Jouissent toujours de beaucoup de Biens, et il ne Seroit pas impossible que ce dernier outrage de La fortune [à mon] egard, ne les interesse de quelque manière en ma faveur.

Me Derieux toujours aussi Sensible que reconnaissante aux assurances flatteuses de votre Souvenir prend La Liberté de vous presenter Son Respect, et J'ai L'honneur d'être dans Les Sentiments du plus respectueux attachement et reconnaissance;

Monsieur

Votre trés humble et trés obei[ss] Serviteur P. DERIEUX

EDITORS' TRANSLATION

SIR Richmond 27 Oct. 1816.

Since receiving the letter you were so kind as to honor me with on 31 July, I have gotten one from my relatives in France, who still believe that I hope to inherit Mr. Mazzei's fortune. I also learned from it that since the return of the king, the nephew of the comte de Jaucourt, my stepfather, has been appointed minister of the navy. As it was mainly in consideration of my union with this family that Mr. Mazzei pointedly gave advance verbal assurances, I would like to send him a copy of Mr. Mazzei's will so as to prove to my family how both their hopes and mine have been frustrated, despite the large estate he left. I would be infinitely obliged to you, Sir, if you would do me the favor of sending it to me so that I can make a copy of it. I will have the honor of returning it to you by the next post, as I cannot, without indiscretion, allow myself to hope that you would be so kind as to take the trouble of transcribing this will, the contents of which are, perhaps, very long. In spite of the Revolution, several of the relations left to me still enjoy great wealth, and this last insult of chance might possibly interest them in my favor in some way.

Mrs. Derieux, who is always appreciative and grateful for the flattering assurances of your regard, takes the liberty of sending you her respects, and I have the honor to be, with feelings of the most respectful attachment and gratitude;

Sir

Your very humble and very obedient servant P. DERIEUX

RC (DLC); torn at seal; dateline at foot of text; endorsed by TJ as received 21 Nov. 1816 and so recorded in SJL. RC (DLC); address cover only; with PoC of TJ to Fitzwhylsonn & Potter, 3 Dec. 1816, on verso; addressed: "The Honble Th[s] Jefferson Monticello Albemarle C[ty] V[a]"; franked; postmarked Richmond, 31 Oct. Translation by Dr. Genevieve Moene.

The letter Derieux apparently received from TJ on 31. JUILLET was dated 27 July 1816.

Arnail François, comte de Jaucourt, a nephew of Derieux's stepfather, Armand Henri de Jaucourt, served as Louis XVIII's MINISTRE DE LA MARINE from July to September 1815 (Eugène Haag and Émile Haag, *La France Protestante ou Vies des Protestants Français* [1846–59], 6:51–2; Bessie E. L. Price, *Some Extracts from the Correspondence of Justin Pierre Plumard Comte de Rieux* [1913]; Ministère de la Marine, *Annuaire de la Marine* [1900]: xxix).

Philip Mazzei's last will and TESTAMENT is printed above at Thomas Appleton to TJ, 15 Apr. 1816.

From William H. Crawford

DEAR SIR Washington 28th oct. 1816

Your letter recommending Mr Armistead for an appointment in the war department has been duly Recd by the mail. Several vacancies exist in the Accountants office, but owing to the unfortunate death of Colo Lear will Not be filled until that office is filled.

Mr Armistead will be Recommended to the Person vested with the Right of appointment, as Soon as he is Known

His baptismal name has been communicated by Governor Nicholas.

Your letter of the 20th inst to my Predecessor in office, has also been Received. As Soon as the Resignation of Mr Armistead is Recd Mr Minor will be appointed, unless objections should be made by the President, which is highly improbable.

As long as I remain in the cabinet it will afford me great pleasure to receive any communications from you, even if they should be confined to recommendations for office.

I have the honor to be with Sentiments of the highest respect your most obt & very humbl Servt WM H CRAWFORD

RC (DLC); endorsed by TJ as received 7 Nov. 1816 and so recorded in SJL. RC (DLC); address cover only; with PoC of TJ to Nicolas G. Dufief, 1 Jan. 1817, on verso; addressed: "Thomas Jefferson late President of the U.S. Monticello Virginia"; franked; postmarked Washington City, 29 Oct.

At the time of his death on 11 Oct. 1816, Tobias Lear was accountant to the War Department. James Madison appointed William Lee to fill THAT OFFICE the following January (*ANB*; *JEP*, 3:70, 73 [16, 28 Jan. 1817]). Crawford had recently given up the post of secretary of war and become secretary of the treasury. His PREDECESSOR in the latter office was Alexander J. Dallas (Washington *Daily National Intelligencer*, 21 Oct. 1816).

From Joseph Delaplaine

D^R SIR, Octob^r 28^h 1816.

I have already written to you by this mail, & at the same time sent you a pamphlet. I now send your n^o of the Repository.—

I hope it will be convenient & agreeable to you to give me, if it is only a dozen lines, your opinion of the paper, typography, engravings & plan & importance of the Repository.—I have already mentioned that your opinion with that of Mr Madison & others, are to appear with the second half volume which is now preparing for the press & which will contain with others your life & portrait.—

I am Your obed. & very hum^l st JOSEPH DELAPLAINE.

I refer you to my letter of this mail for several particulars.

RC (DLC); written on a small scrap; dateline at foot of text; postscript adjacent to signature and dateline; at head of text: "Thos Jefferson Esqr"; endorsed by TJ as received 11 (reworked from 12) Dec. 1816 and so recorded in SJL, which mistakenly describes it as a letter of 2 Oct. Enclosure: *Delaplaine's Repository*, vol. 1, pt. 1.

From Christopher Clark

Grove 29 October 1816

mr Jeffersons Reasoning in the case of the wittnessth against Robertson for perjury is strong and Conclusive for the defendant if he is Right in his premisses, and even if it Shall be found erroneous in matter of law the length of time which has pased away since his attention was particularly caled to legal inquiry and the absence of books will be an ample apology for a Sketch proceeding from motives deserving every Commendation

Perjury

Its true definition is "taking a false oath in some Judicial proceeding, before a competent jurisdiction: in a matter material to the question depending." It must also have the two necessary ingredients "Wilful" and "corrupt" In a "Judicial proceeding" the enquiries of a Grand Jury must come within the term "Judicial proceeding" They are Sworn to "enquire and true presentment make" of all such matters & things &C to enquire they must examine evidence their duty is not limited to offences within their own knowledge, they have a Right and invariably exercise it to send for witneses The witness is Sworn in Court the "truth and the Whole truth to speak of such Matters and things as may be enquired of him by the Grand Jury" he is then sent for examination to their chamber they Submit the interrogotories, these must however be confined to Matters and thing Cognazable before them questions of this character and when the Response does not implicate the Witness he is bound to Answer and if he answer untruly with a Malum animum must be guilty of perjury

as far as events with in the observation of the Author of these Remarks it always has been considered and praetendan that the Offence[1] may be commited before a G Jury Two Cases at this time Occur to him in one of [w]hich he was Counsel and every effort unavailingly exerted to Save the defendant this comenced when it began in Court comwealth agt Hughes superior Court of Bedford Judge Winston defendant convicted broke Jail and now at large The other against Ward Cobel County Judge Allen This case Require more attention from its[2] analogy The defendant was caled to give evidence to a Grand Jury of what he knew of certain persons gaming he Stated he "knew nothing" he "saw none" "was in the Room" "discovered[3] no[4] gaming nor the instruments of gaming" It afterwards appeared that he himself had played several games at Cards and had lost two dollars by betting on the hands of others that were playing on this he was convicted and a new trial on his application Refused; errors in arrest of Judgment overruled; an Appeal to the clemency of the Executive Rejected; his petition to the Legislature thrown out. This is the strongest case that can be formed perhaps even by the imagination and the law must now be considered as Setled

The conduct of the Jury

For the last 20 years or there about that part of the G Jurymans Oath which formerly obtained "your and your fellow Council you Shall keep" has been Ousted by act of assembly and the law now directs that when a presentment Shall be made by the knowledge of any of the G Jury the name of the Juror Shall sit at the foot of the presentment more effectually to make a prosecution It is therefore no Misprision nor is it any immorality in a Juror to promulge what pased before them Even the old Rule was never extended to the protection of Witneses it only protected their own body they Were not at liberty to disclose Who wished such an enquiry Who gave notice of an offence or who Voted for or against Such a matter. In the most enlarged understanding of the Casses: it could go no further it would be opposed to both policy and law

Was it Wilful and Corrupt?

On this point is mr Jeffersons Reasonings clear and satisfactory and on this ground[5] does mr R Counsel intend to place him with the most Confident hopes of success it will be to him as safe and it will be Reputabl there could be no improper motive the Oath Could not be corrupt it could have proceeded only from a mistaken mode of Self protection to avoid implicating himself there was nothing immoral nothing contrary to the severest law An acquital on this ground will it is to be most sincerly hoped Reinstate him in his proper grade in Society Restore him to his friends and place him above the snarls even of his enemies

The Counsel for mr R Returns his thank to mr Jefferson for the observation submited to him he Read as he always does every thing that comes from his pen with great pleasure knowing that it endeavoured to maintain some exploded and untenable matter he think it a duty due to a friendship on which he set so high a Value frankly to submit the forgoing Remarks Relying on the Candor of his friends to appreciate the motive CHRIS CLARK

RC (DLC); dateline beneath signature; top of second page chipped; endorsed by TJ as received 29 Oct. 1816 and so recorded in SJL.

ROBERTSON was quite possibly the Lynchburg merchant Archibald Robertson. William Blackstone refers to perjury as a WILFUL and CORRUPT crime in his *Commentaries on the Laws of England* (Oxford, 1765–69; Sowerby, nos. 1806–7; Poor, *Jefferson's Library*, 10 [no. 553]), 4:136. Malo animo (MALUM ANIMUM): "malice or evil intent" (*Black's Law Dictionary*). Praetentam (PRAETENDAN): "alleged."

The ACT OF ASSEMBLY ending the requirement that Virginia grand jurors keep their deliberations secret was "An Act concerning Grand Juries, Petit Juries, and Venire-men," enacted 29 Nov. 1792. This law also directed grand juries to add to each presentment "the name and surname of the prosecutor or informer," not THE NAME OF THE JUROR (*Acts of Assembly* [1792–93 sess.], 11–2). PROMULGE: "publish or proclaim formally" (*OED*).

[1]Manuscript: "Office."
[2]Manuscript: "s it."
[3]Omitted opening quotation mark editorially supplied.
[4]Word interlined.
[5]Manuscript: "gound."

To William D. Meriwether

SIR Poplar Forest Oct. 30. 16.

I recieve this instant, and at this place your letter of the 17th the property of the three younger children of Bennet Henderson decd sold to me by their guardians, paid for while they were under age, and of which I am possessed, I am ready to give up, in consequence of their refusing confirmation; and I left directions accordingly with my grandson on leaving home. I will also pay any rents legally due thereon from me; and if we differ in opinion as to what rents are due

I will concur in referring the decision to two or more disinterested persons as you propose. I tender you the assurance of my respects.

TH: JEFFERSON

RC (PWacD: Sol Feinstone Collection, on deposit PPAmP); addressed: "Cap[t] William D. Meriwether Albemarle." PoC (MHi); on verso of a reused address cover from TJ to Thomas Appleton; endorsed by TJ.

The THREE YOUNGER CHILDREN of Bennett Henderson were Frances Henderson Hornsby, Lucy Henderson Wood, and Nancy C. Henderson Nelson. Elizabeth and James L. Henderson were THEIR GUARDIANS. TJ's GRANDSON was Thomas Jefferson Randolph.

From Edwin Stark

SIR Assistant Comm[ys] office Norfolk 30th Oct[r] 1816

On my return last evening to this place I found your letter of the 10th Inst

I have the pleasure to inform you the box shipt by M[r] Banger of Phil[a] to my care was on the day of its arrival here forwarded to M[r] Richard Thweatt of Petersburg with a particular request that he would send it on with as little delay as possible

I am Sir with g[t] respect Your hb[l] Serv[t] EDWIN STARK

RC (MHi); endorsed by TJ as received 21 Nov. 1816 and so recorded in SJL. RC (MHi); address cover only; with PoC of TJ to Martha Jefferson Randolph, 3 Dec. 1816, on verso; addressed: "Thomas Jefferson Esquire Milton Post office Albemarle"; franked; postmarked Norfolk, 2 Nov.

From Noah Worcester

SIR, Brighton Octo. 31. 1816

As, in pursuing the cause of peace, I make a free use of your name And your writings, it is but just that I should Submit what I publish to your inspection. For this reason I put into the post office directed to you No's 4 And 5 of the Friend of Peace, And shall now Send No. 6. It is my Aim to be impartial, but I Am liable to misapprehend. If in Any thing I have mistaken your meaning, or said any thing of your opinions which you disapprove, I will thank you to point out my error that I may correct it in a future No.

The friends of Peace multiply, And I have the most perfect confidence that their efforts will not be in vain. I rejoice in considering your name as on the list of my friends in Such a cause. Whatever you may do in its favor will be remembered with gratitude.

I would, Sir, gladly present to the American Philosophical Society a copy of all the No's of the Friend of Peace, could I be assured that they would be Acceptable, And informed to whom they should be directed.

With great respect. Noah Worcester

RC (DLC); endorsed by TJ as received 21 Nov. 1816 and so recorded in SJL. RC (DLC); address cover only; with PoC of TJ to John Trumbull, 10 Jan. 1817, on recto and verso; addressed: "Hon. Thomas Jefferson Monticello Virginia"; franked; postmarked Boston, 2 Nov.

The Friend of Peace, no. 6. ([Cambridge, Mass., 1816]; Poor, *Jefferson's Library*, 9 [no. 488]) contains an article entitled "Interesting Reflections on War, by Mr. Jefferson," pp. 18–20, wherein Worcester quotes from and comments on a portion of TJ's letter to Sir John Sinclair of 23 Mar. 1798 (*PTJ*, 30:197–209, quote on p. 206).

From George Logan

Dear Sir Stenton Novb[r] 1: 1816

Knowing your anxiety to promote the agriculture of your country, as the most stable support of the best interests of civil society I herewith send you a specimen of dressed flax, which I lately received from my friend Sir John Sinclair He says nothing respecting the mode of its preparation; but I am informed it is accomplished by beating and friction, without its being previously rotted. When I become acquainted with the whole process, I will do myself the pleasure of[1] communicating it to you. I also at the same time received from him the inclosed account of the astonishing production of the mangel wurzel which merits your attention.

In Sir John's Letter to me he says "I rejoice exceedingly at the restoration of peace between the two countries. It was neither your fault nor mine, that a war so unfortunate for both countries was not prevented." How much more honorable, how much more beneficial to the whole family of mankind are such communications, than mutual acts of violence and bloodshed; instigated by the cupidity of merchants or the ambition of statesmen.

My Wife unites with me in sentiments of respect to yourself and amiable family

Accept assurances of my friendship Geo Logan

What do you think of the inclosed delineation of Sir John's plough which he has politely forwarded for my consideration? G L

RC (DLC); at foot of text: "Tho[s] Jefferson Esq[r]"; endorsed by TJ as received 21 Nov. 1816 and so recorded in SJL; notation by TJ adjacent to endorsement: "dress[d] flax S[r] J. S. plough Mangel worzel." Enclosure: George Turnbull, *Mangel Wurzel. Account of a Crop of this most valuable Root grown in the Year 1815, in the Garden Ground at Bedfords, the Seat of John Heaton, Esq near Romford, in Essex*, dated Bedfords, 1 Jan. 1816, in which Turnbull, writing as Heaton's gardener and planter, states that mangel-wurzel seed was sown on one plot of ground on 6 May; indicates that most of the leaves were removed from half of the plants on 27 July to determine "what degree of injury the roots would receive by taking off the leaves in summer"; announces that at harvest on 6 Nov. the roots of those plants weighed "12 tons 11cwt. 48lbs" less than those that had been left unmolested; concludes from this that "*taking off the leaves does impede the growth of the root*"; and provides harvest results for plants that were transplanted from the plot to a garden on 13 June and harvested on 2 Nov. (printed circular in DLC: TJ Papers, 205:36578–9; addressed by Sinclair: "Dr Logan Stenton Pensilvania"). Other enclosure not found.

Sinclair's LETTER to Logan was dated Edinburgh, 20 July 1815 (PHi: Logan Papers; printed in James Wilkinson, *Memoirs of My Own Times* [Philadelphia, 1816], 1:462–3).

[1]Manuscript: "of of."

From Elisha Ticknor

SIR, Boston, 1st Nov. 1816.

I inclose you a letter and an Invoice of a parcel of Books, received yesterday from my son, in the Ship Cordelia from Hamburg. On receiving the Books, which will probably be in the course of eight or ten days, I will as soon as possible reship them to Messrs Gibson and Jefferson, your Correspondents in Richmond. As soon as I can get at the amount of duties, freight &c. I will forward it to you, and also, to Messrs Gibson and Jefferson.

I am, sir, With all due respect, your most obedient servant,

ELISHA TICKNOR.

RC (MHi); endorsed by TJ as received 21 Nov. 1816 and so recorded in SJL. RC (MHi); address cover only; with PoC of TJ to Archibald Thweatt, 14 Jan. 1817, on recto and verso; addressed: "Honorable Thomas Jefferson, Monticello, Virginia"; franked; postmarked Boston, 3 Nov. Enclosure: George Ticknor to TJ, 10 July 1816. Other enclosure not found.

From Francis Adrian Van der Kemp

DEAR SIR! Oldenbarneveld 1 Nov. 1816.

Reperusing your interesting Syllabus I have recalled in my mind a train of thoughts—which I brought in writing about twenty years past and Send then—for his criticisms—to my old friend Joshua Toulmin of Taunton—father of the judge in the Missisippi Territory—which treatise has been irrecoverably lost on its passage to England.

Having hurted my right leg—in my garden—by carelessness—which through neglect of it has compelled me, to leave off[1] working for a few days—I employ'd this leisure time in digesting a plan, upon which—en gros—with any desirable modifications—an interesting work might be executed—I Shall Send a copy to Mss-bay—it might be—that one of its worthies was willing to undertake the task.—It would require—a thorough acquaintance with ancient history—an unbiassed mind—and willingness to pay homage to truth—whatever it might be discovered—a vast deal of time—and a well provided Librarÿ: from these requisites, to which you might join others—you perceive I can not be the man.

I did not hesitate to use your own expressions—as the Syllabus was in manÿ respect the ground-work—and Shall be gratified, if You can find it proper—to remove the defects—and Supply the weak parts with props—By this—another may be enabled—to raise an elegant Superstructure

Dr. W. Willoughbÿ, member of Congress—eminent as a Physician and respected bÿ all parties, and beloved by all who knew—desired to be introduced to Monticello. Perhaps I Shall be So free—in Sending him a Letter Of introduction, when he returns to Washington.

Permit me to assure you—that I remain with high respect And consideration

Dear Sir! Your obed—and obliged S[t]

FR. ADR. VANDERKEMP

P.S. May I Sollicit, if you published any thing else besides your Valuable Notes—to gratifÿ me with a copÿ?

RC (DLC); dateline adjacent to signature; endorsed by TJ as received 21 Nov. 1816 and so recorded in SJL; notation by TJ beneath endorsement: "Syllabus Dr Willoughby any thing except Notes?" RC (MHi); address cover only; with PoC of TJ to John Patterson, 27 Nov. 1816, on verso; addressed: "Thomas Jefferson LLD. Monticello Virginia"; franked; postmarked Trenton, N.Y., 2 Nov.

EN GROS: "roughly; in general." Van der Kemp corresponded regularly with John Adams, of Massachusetts Bay (MSS-BAY). TJ's VALUABLE NOTES were his *Notes on the State of Virginia* (*Notes*, ed. Peden).

[1]Manuscript: "of."

ENCLOSURE

Francis Adrian Van der Kemp's Synopsis of a Proposed Book

[ca. 1 Nov. 1816]

Memoirs
respecting the person and doctrine of J.C.
compiled
from
S.S.[1]

Outlines

Part. i

Præliminarÿ discussions

Developement of the general principles of nat: Religion.

Inquirÿ in the authenticity of the S.S.—of the Jewish writings[2]—the lxx.—Examination of Astruc's hypothesis—arguments—objections—of Goethen's.

Delineation of the Jewish nation—character—remarquable periods—under the Patriarchs—the Legislation of Mozes—under the judges—kings—before, in, and after the Babylonian captivity—after the destruction of Jeruzalem,—degradation—dispersion and preservation as a distinct People.

Religion of the Jews

Theism—morality

Examination of their principles and correctness.

General view of the heathen world before the christian æra

Ancient Philosophers—Oriental—Greece—Rome—Indian—Chinese.

Merits and defects.

comparison with the Jews

Part. ii

Life—character—doctrine of Jezus.

Præliminarÿ observations

Inquiry in the authenticity of the S.s. Arguments—objections.

Particular discussions—Inspiration &c Rules of criticism &c

concise view of the various Systems of Divinity among christians.

Inquirÿ in the authenticity of the first Chapt. of matthew and Luke.

Apparition of angels—hymns of Simeon—Anna—

Miraculous conception and birth.

Inquiry in its necessity—usefulness—[3]

Chronological observations with regard to the time of the birth of Jezus.

Discussion of the arguments—pleaded. for Jezus being more than a man—of being a Spiritual head of the pious—being a proof of his high dignity.

Examination of various passages of S.s. 2 King. iv. 16. Ies. ix. 5/6 &c of God preparing him a bodÿ—not according the ordinarÿ Laws of nature Hebr. x. 5. made of a woman Gal. iv. 4. not of a Virgin Matth. xi. 9. &c.

General observation.

„All, what is necessary to believe and to do—to Secure our happiness—must have been So clearly revealed, as to be understood without anÿ difficulty by any one of a Sound judgment and a Sincere heart.„

Consequences.

Discussion

i. what Messiah was expected by the Jews?

a. consideration of the Jewish Prophecies.

b. application of these.

ii What ideas entertained the Jews of Jezus?

a. His enemies—and impartial observers

b. his friends and disciples.

iii With what ideas did Jezus imbue his Disciples about himself?

iv. causes of the different conceptions among his followers.

oriental Philosophÿ—Gnosticism—Platonism.

Corollarÿ

The fundamental part of the Christian Revelation is, the Divine mission of Jezus—not his person—character—

Requisites—Examination.

Part. iii

Life of Jezus of nazareth

Great outlines

His person, character, views, doctrine—Success

i. was he really a man?

Conclusion from Adam's creation considered Luke i. 1/2.

Where is thy Father Jo. viii. 19 comp. with 27. He followed his Father's trade Marc. vi. 3. his progress in mental endowments, though without a liberal education,[4] gradual Luc. ii. 42/52 ii Sam. 2 vs. 21–26, 1 Cor. xv. 22 comp: with Gen: ii. 7.

Did Jezus exist before his birth? Examination of Jo. i. 18 εἰς τον κολπον „In conviviis dilectissimi Solebant in Sinu ejus accumbere, qui convivii Princeps esset„[5] (Grotius, Elsner) εν κολπῳ τινος εἰναι. by which Summa familiaritas et censi horum cum aliquo communicatio is intended. It is used of married Deut xiii. 6. xxviii. 54–6.

ii Had Jezus a human body and Soul? was he man—an Angelic being or Man-God?

Concessions—by Orthodox—Skeptics.

§18. That Jezus had a real human nature—with all its frailties—Sin excepted—having been[6] conceived in the body of the beatified Virgin Mary, by the power of the holy ghost—without the concurrence of man, and has not only adopted human nature in regard to the body—but a real human Soul too, to become a real man, because this was necessary, as bodÿ and Soul were lost.

§19. Jezus human nature did loose nothing of her properties by her inseparable union and junction with the Godhead, but he remained a creature—had a beginning of existence—being of a finite nature, preserving everÿ thing, which belongs to a real body, and, though by its resurrection it became immortal, the reality of his human nature was not altered—because—our Salvation and resurrection were depending from the reality of the body.

But these two natures have been So conjointed in one person, that even by the death of Jezus they have not been Separated: So was, what he, dying, recommended in the hands of his Father—a real human Spirit, who departed from his body: but, in the mean time, the Godhead remained allways conjoined with the human part—even then—as it laid in the tomb, and the Godhead did not cease to be in him, even as, She was, when he was a Babe, although She for Some time did not reveal herself.

Confess: of the Ref: Church Synod. Dord. 1618/9

That he in body and Soul, during his whole life, but particularly at the end of his life bore the wrath of God against the Sin of the whole human race.

Heidelb. catech. answ. to Q 37.

Comp: with the 2. art, of the church of England 1562

For if the divine essence, or godhead, did not enter into the womb of the Virgin, when was it, that that fulness of the Godhead, which dwelled in him bodily col. ii. 9. did enter into him.

Rob. Clayton Bish. of Clogher's vindic. of the O. & N.T.
Lett. v. Pag. 446. Lond. 1759.

(b) Skeptics—Eulogiums.

ii Character of Jezus—the most innocent—the most benevolent the most eloquent and Sublime.

His courage—prudence—wisdom—humility—Philanthropy.

Consideration of his forbidding to declare himself the Messiah
Matth xii. 20 Marc. xviii.[7] 29/30 Luc. ix. 20–25

His devout temper—in prayer—compassion—filial obedience
Luc. ii. 42 Love and delight in the Service of God.

iii His views and doctrine.

Personal—in regard to mankind.

Pure Theism—nature and attributes of God.

Perfect morality—the most benevolent and Sublime that ever was taught.

Comparison with that of other Philosophers: ancient
modern:—with Mozes and Mahomet.

Belief in a future State
unquestionable proof of its certainty.

Miracles: definition—Requisites—end—not for ostentation but—to attain a great end—to evince beyond doubt the interposition of All-mighty power.

Their defence—extent.

iv. Success of his enterprize.

obstacles—disadvantages

Præjudices among the great—the Scientific—the Vulgar—

His doctrine not committed in writing—his disciples illiterate men—

Consideration of the State of Christianity upon the hypothesis—„that he was an Enthusiast or Impostor—So too his disciples„.

Conclusion—Prognostic.

MS (MHi); entirely in Van der Kemp's hand; undated. Tr (MHi: Adams Papers); entirely in Van der Kemp's hand; undated; enclosed in and filed with Van der Kemp to John Adams, 4 Nov. 1816.

J.C.: "Jesus Christ." THE LXX: the Septuagint. Jean ASTRUC's *Conjectures sur les Memoires Originaux Dont il paroit que Moyse s'est servi pour composer le Livre de la Genese* (Brussels, 1753) suggested that Moses compiled the biblical book of Genesis from earlier documentary sources. For the HYMNS OF SIMEON—ANNA (Hannah), see Luke 2.28–32 and 1 Samuel 2.1–10, respectively. IES. IX. 5/6 possibly refers to Isaiah 9.6–7.

εἰς τον κολπον ... PRINCEPS ESSET: "In the bosom: At banquets the favorites used to recline in the bosom of the one who presided over the banquet" (*EG*, 380n). εν κολπῳ τινος εἶναι ... COMMUNICATIO: "To be in someone's bosom: by which the closest possible intimacy and the sharing of the wealth of these with someone" (*EG*, 380n). Jesus committed his spirit into THE HANDS OF HIS FATHER in Luke 23.46.

The HUMAN SPIRIT of Jesus is considered in the eighteenth and nineteenth articles printed in *The Confession of Faith, of The Reformed Churches in the Netherlands* (Amsterdam, 1689). THAT HE IN BODY AND SOUL ... THE SIN OF THE WHOLE HUMAN RACE is the answer to the thirty-seventh question in *The Heidelberg Catechism* (London, 1720, and other eds.). It is similar in substance to the second of the Thirty-Nine Articles, which codified the theological doctrines of the CHURCH OF ENGLAND (*Articles whereupon it was agreed ... in the Convocation holden at London in the yere of our Lorde God, 1562* [London, 1571], 3–4).

[1] Abbreviation for "Sacred Scriptures," here and below.

[2] Word interlined in place of "Religion."

[3] Preceding two words initially reversed in MS. Van der Kemp then changed the sequence by placing a "2" above "usefulness" and a "1" above "necessity." The words are in the revised order in Tr.

[4] In Tr Van der Kemp here interlined "astonishing but."

[5] Omitted closing quotation mark editorially supplied.

[6] MS: "bein." Tr: "been."

[7] The biblical book of Mark has only sixteen chapters. Van der Kemp probably intended Mark 8.29–30.

From John Adams

DR SIR Quincy Nov. 4 1816

Your Letter of Oct. 14 has greatly obliged me. Tracys Analysis, I have read once; and wish to read it a Second time. It Shall be returned to you. But I wish to be informed whether this Gentleman is of that Family of Tracys with which the Marquis La Fayette is connected by intermariages.?

I have read, not only the Analysis, but Eight Volumes out of 12 of The origine de tous les Cultes, and if Life lasts will read the other four.

But, my dear Sir, I have been often obliged to Stop; and talk to myself like the Reverend, Alegorical, Hierogriphical and Apocalyptical[1] Mr John Bunyan; and Say "Sobrius esto John![2] Be not carried away by Sudden blasts of Wind, by unexpected flashes of Lightening, nor terrified by the Sharpest Crashes of Thunder.!"

We have now, it Seems a National Bible Society to propagate King James's Bible, through All Nations. Would it not be better, to apply these pious Subscriptions, to purify Christendom from the Corruptions of Christianity; than to propagate those Corruptions in Europe Asia, Africa and America.!

Suppose, We Should project a Society to translate Dupuis into all Languages and offer a Reward in Medals and Diamonds to any Man or Body of Men who would produce the best answer to it.

Enthusiasms,[3] Crusades, French Revolutions are Epidemical or Endemial Distempers, to which Man kind are liable. They are not tertian or Quartan Agues. Ages and Centuries are Sometimes required to cure them.

It is more worth your while to live to read Dupuis than Grim. Of all the Romances,[4] and true Histories I ever read, it is the most entertaining[5] And instructive, though Priestley calls it "dull."

Conclude not from all this, that I have renounced the Christian Religion, or that I agree with Dupuis in all his Sentiments. Far from it. I See in every Page, Something to recommend Christianity in its Purity, and Something to discredit its Corruptions.

If I had Strength, I would give you my Opinion of it in a Fable of the Bees.

The Ten Commandments and The Sermon on the Mount contain my Religion.

I agree perfectly with you, that "The Moral Sense is as much a part of our Constitution as that of Feeling," and in all that you Say, upon this Subject.

My History of the Jesuits, is in 4. Vol: in twelves, under the Title of "Histoire Generale de la naissance et des progres, de la Compagnie de Jesus, et l'analyse de Ses Constitutions et Ses Privileges."[6] printed at Amsterdam in 1761.

The Work is anonymous; because, as I Suppose, the Author was afraid as all the Monarks of Europe were at that time of Jesuitical Assassination. The Author however[7] Supports his Facts by authentic Records and known Authorities which the Publick may consult.

This Society has been a greater Calamity to Man kind than the French Revolution or Napoleons Despotism or Idiology. It has obstructed the Progres of Reformation and the Improvement of the human Mind in Society much longer and more fatally.

The Situation of England may be learned from the enclosed Letter, which I pray you to return to me.

Little reason as I have to love the old Lady, I cannot but dread that She is going after France, into a Revolution which will end like that of England in 1660 and like that of France in 1816. In all Events, our Country must rise. England cannot.

We have been long afflicted with a Report that your Books and Harvard Colledge Books,[8] and John Q. Adams's Ouranologia were lost at Sea. But lo! The Astronomy has arrived in one Ship and Colledge

Books in another. We hope your Books are equally Safe: but Should be glad to know.
It seems that Father and Son have been employed in contemplating The Heavens. I Should like to Sitt down with him and compare Du Puis with his Uranologia

I have been disappointed in the Review of Sir John Malcoms History of Persia. Those cunning Edinburgh men break off, at the Point of the only Subject that excited my Curiosity the ancient modern Religion and Government of Persia. I Should admire to read an Edinburg or a Quarterly[9] Review of Du Puis 12. Volumes. They have reviewed Grim who is not of half the importance to Mankind. I Suspect the Reviewers evaded the Religion of Persia for fear they Should be compelled to compare it with Du Puis.

A Scrap of an English Paper in which you are honorably mentioned and I am not much abused must close this Letter from your Friend

JOHN ADAMS

RC (DLC); at foot of text: "President Jefferson"; endorsed by TJ as received 21 Nov. 1816 and so recorded in SJL; notation by TJ beneath endorsement: "Tracy?—bible society—fable of the bees. my books.—uranologia." FC (Lb in MHi: Adams Papers). Enclosures not found.

Lafayette's son George Washington Lafayette joined Destutt de Tracy's FAMILY in 1802 by marrying Françoise Émilie Destutt de Tracy, the daughter of the author and TJ correspondent (*PTJ*, 38: 615, 616, 724). HIEROGRIPHICAL: possibly related to hierography, the description of religions or sacred things (*OED*). SOBRIUS ESTO JOHN: "Be sober, John." The American Bible Society (NATIONAL BIBLE SOCIETY) was founded in New York City in May 1816 (*Constitution of the American Bible Society* [New York, 1816]).

Joseph Priestley described Charles François Dupuis, *Origine de Tous les Cultes: ou, Religion Universelle*, 12 vols. in 7 (Paris, year III [1794/95]; Adams's copy in MBPLi), as DULL in his *A Comparison of the Institutions of Moses with those of the Hindoos and Other Ancient Nations; with Remarks on Mr. Dupuis's Origin of all Religions* (Northumberland, Pa., 1799), 303. A FABLE OF THE BEES refers to a work by Bernard Mandeville, *The Fable of the Bees: or, Private Vices Publick Benefits* (London, 1714; Sowerby, no. 1259). OURANOLOGIA: Johann Elert Bode, *Uranographia sive Astrorum Descriptio* (Berlin, 1801). A review of SIR JOHN Malcolm's *The History of Persia, from the Most Early Period to the Present Time*, 2 vols. (London, 1815), appeared in the *Edinburgh Review* 26 (1816): 282–304.

[1] RC: "Apocatiptical." FC: "Apocalyptical."

[2] Superfluous closing quotation mark before the exclamation point editorially omitted.

[3] RC: "Enthusiams." FC: "Enthusiasms."

[4] RC: "Romancs." FC: "romances."

[5] RC: "entertaing." FC: "entertaining."

[6] Omitted closing quotation mark supplied from FC.

[7] RC: "honever." FC: "however."

[8] Word interlined.

[9] RC: "Quarly," with the missing letters interlined in an unidentified hand. FC: "Quarterly."

From Benjamin Henry Latrobe

Dear Sir Washington Novr 5^{t} 1816

When your letter of the 27^{t} of Augt arrived, I was confined to my bed by a bilious fever. After my recovery two long absences from the city, and as much occupation as filled all my time, prevented my acknowledging the favor you have done me in communicating to me the very simple, & valuable invention it discribes. But what renders your letter more valuable, is the assurance it gives me of your continued kindness towards me.—

In respect to your Dial,—I can only say that its principles are so plain, & its construction so easy, that dials on Your construction might be brought into very general use, if once known & introduced. They could be made so cheap, that they might be[1] sold at every turner's, with a hole to be bored in the Nadir of the Latitude of the place at which they are wanted at the time of purchasing them. The only difficulty which an unskilful person would find would be to place them in the true Meridians. But a little instruction, which might be given by a bill delivered with the Dial, would enable any farmer to accomplish that object. Every common Almanack would enable him to convert Solar into common time.—

You have done my Capital much honor in making it the support of your Dial. The Columns & Capitals as executed, and standing in the Vestibule of the North wing of the Capitol on the Ground floor, were not much injured by the British, so little indeed that,—as I wish some part of the building to remain as they left it,—I do not propose to repair them, unless the president shall order it to be done. By the suggestion of the Senate, I devised a very material alteration of their accomodations; especially a great enlargement of the Chamber itself. The great Staircase must give way to this improvement. You probably recollect that, as a curious & difficult combination of admirably executed Stonework, it was one of the most remarkable parts of the Capitol. But it was much injured by the Lanthorn which being of wood, fell burning thro' the opening of the Dome, & resting on the Stairs burst many of the principal Stones.—The Staircase has now another situation. It will be less curious, but have, I think, more beauty. The Area of the Stairs will be occupied by a Vestibule, in the Center of which a circular Colonnade will support a dome for the purpose of admitting light.—The Columns of this Rotunda, 16 in number, must be more slender than the Ionic order will admit, & ought not to be of the Corinthian, because the Chamber itself is only of the Ionic order. I have therefore composed a Capital of the Leaves

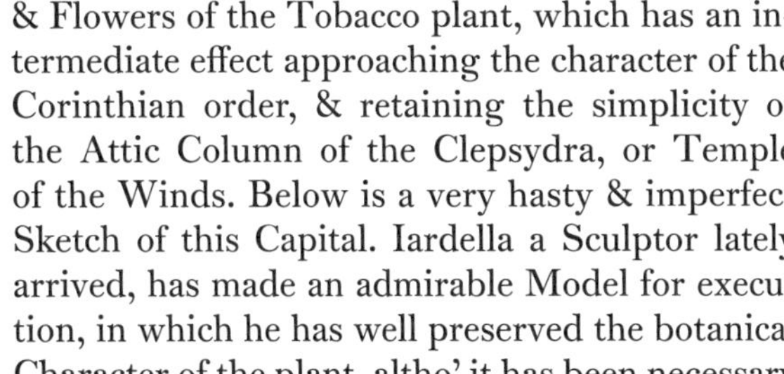

& Flowers of the Tobacco plant, which has an intermediate effect approaching the character of the Corinthian order, & retaining the simplicity of the Attic Column of the Clepsydra, or Temple of the Winds. Below is a very hasty & imperfect Sketch of this Capital. Iardella a Sculptor lately arrived, has made an admirable Model for execution, in which he has well preserved the botanical Character of the plant, altho' it has been necessary to enlarge the proportion of the flowers to the Leaves, & to arrange them in clusters of three. When we have done with the model, I will take the Liberty to forward it to You.—

I have neglected so long to answer your very kind letter, that I must entreat you to attribute my silence to any thing but the diminution of my respect & attachment. Believe me that it never can cease.

Yrs very respectfully B HENRY LATROBE

RC (DLC); edge trimmed, affecting one drawing; addressed: "Thomas Jefferson Esqr Monticello"; stamped; postmarked Washington, 7 Nov.; endorsed by TJ as received 21 Nov. 1816 and so recorded in SJL.

The TEMPLE OF THE WINDS in ancient Athens was a marble, octagonal tower that received its name from the sculpted images of the various winds that adorned it. It had sundials on its outer walls, a clepsydra inside, and a weather vane on top (W. H. Davenport Adams, *Temples, Tombs, and Monuments of Ancient Greece and Rome* [1871], 62–5). Francisco IARDELLA was a native of Carrara, Italy, which was famed for its marble (Groce and Wallace, *Dictionary of Artists*, 338).

[1] Latrobe here canceled "made."

From John Burke

Richmond, **November 7h** *1816*

Having suspended the publication of the "Virginia Argus" it becomes necessary for me, to call upon those indebted to the Establishment, for payment.

Accompanying this, you have your account stated—Being desirous to close my business, you will much oblige me by remitting the amount by mail, or if more convenient, by some private conveyance.

I am, very respectfully your obdt. servt. *JNO. BURKE.*

RC (MHi); printed circular, with portions filled in by Burke rendered in boldface above; endorsed by TJ as a letter of 19 Oct. 1816 received 21 Nov. 1816 and so recorded in SJL; with enclosure subjoined. RC (MHi); address cover only; with PoC of TJ to Robert Rives, 27 Nov. 1816, on verso; addressed: "Thomas Jefferson Esq[r] Milton V[a]"; stamped; postmarked Richmond, 9 Nov. Enclosure: Burke's Account with TJ, Richmond, 19 Oct. 1816, charging him $6.25 for his "Subscription to the V[a] Argus, from 25[h] March 1815, to 19[h] Oct[r] 1816, @ $4 p[r] Annum" (printed form in MHi; with blanks filled in by Burke, including the phrase quoted here).

John Burke, printer and journalist, worked in Richmond at the printing office of Samuel Pleasants and also saw service during the War of 1812. In partnership with Philip DuVal, he purchased the *Virginia Argus* from the Pleasants estate by mid-February 1815. Shortly thereafter DuVal left the firm. In February 1816 Burke formed a partnership with Louis H. Girardin, who remained with him at the *Argus* until its demise in October of that year. Burke also established a separate printing shop by the spring of 1815 and conducted it until January 1817 with a series of business associates: Arthur G. Booker, DuVal, and lastly, his own brother David Burke. Neither venture prospered, and by early in 1821 Burke had left both the United States and his creditors behind (A. Paull Hubbard Jr., "Notes on the Book Trade in Richmond, Virginia, together with a Preliminary Checklist of Richmond, Virginia, Imprints: 1780–1860" [1987], fascicle 1; Hugh Nelson to an unidentified correspondent, 12 Dec. 1816 [DNA: RG 59, LAR, 1809–17]; Brigham, *American Newspapers*, 2:1143; Norfolk *American Beacon and Commercial Diary*, 24 Oct. 1816; *Richmond Enquirer*, 3 May 1822).

From James Maury

DEAR SIR, Liverpool 7th Nov[r] 1816

My last letter was of the 9th Sep[r] 15. A State of war, for about twenty five years, appears to have so disqualified us for the sober habits of peace as to have occasioned great reverses in the affairs of many classes of persons in this country:—much so, even with the owners of the Soil; but, particularly, with merchants & Bankers, the failures of which last, I consider almost unprecedented,[1] as well for number of houses as for the magnitude of the sums they have been deficient: probably you may have heard that your correspondent M[r] Roscoe is among the bankers: he was my banker: his overthrow appears to me owing much[2] to a certain benevolence of disposition; which, however amiable, too frequently mislead those who trade.

Nevertheless his house has made a compromise with their creditors for paying <u>all</u> by installments, with interest too; & I hope, nay rather expect, they will pay all. M[r] R's conduct on the afflicting occasion has been exemplary: his Library Pictures &C have been sold at auction; &, as I supposed, you might like to see a catalogue of his books, I send you one. They produced £5,100.

The late summer has been the coldest I ever have experienced—has been most unfavorable for Grain & the prices have been rising for some time past. at this place wheat now sells for a Guinea ℔ bushel of 70 ℔ equal to 4 dollars ℔ Winchester of 60 ℔: however, as the ports must open on the 15th instant: there will, in all probability, soon follow considerable importations from foreign countries; &, no doubt the farmers of Virginia will be benefited by this disaster.

The cidevant Staple of our State has, by no means, decreased as much in value as I expected—the best Crops of James river Inspections[3] being still worth 10d a 12d ℔ ℔, & stemed about the same.

My Son informed us of your hospitable attentions to him, for which accept my acknowlegements.

I expect I am soon to be deprived of the society of a most valued friend, who has resided in this place about six years: 'Tis a Mr Gwathmey, originally of King William County; but, for some years previous to his coming here, of Richmond: he is a very intelligent merchant & judicious in his observations. I think you would like to see him; &, when he returns, I shall give him a line of introduction, desiring him to give you a call at Monticello as he goes up the country.

I wish to know if you still continue in the good health you have so long been remarkable for. I think I have heard it said that, after we have reached half a century or thereabouts, every seventh year is frequently a critical one, and I well remember that the two last seventh years have proved so with respect to myself: last winter I was three score & ten: and it indeed was a trying one: but I have of late regained my Statu quo & my health unusually good for which I thank God. I have resumed my cold bath, & while it agrees with me, I intend to continue it.

As For political information you have such stores of it from various, & other much better, sources that I will not enter on the subject.

Accept, I pray you, the sincere good wishes of your old & obliged friend JAMES MAURY

RC (DLC); endorsed by TJ as received 5 Jan. 1817 and so recorded in SJL. RC (MHi); address cover only; with PoC of TJ to John H. Peyton, 8 Feb. 1817, on verso; addressed: "Thomas Jefferson &c &c Monticello"; stamped "SHIP"; franked; postmarked New York, 29 Dec. Enclosure: *Catalogue of the very select and valuable Library of William Roscoe, Esq. which will be sold by auction* ([Liverpool], 1816).

The failure of ROSCOE's Liverpool bank earlier in 1816 forced him to auction off his large personal collection of books, manuscripts, and artworks, the sale of which ultimately netted more than £11,000 (*ODNB*). The standards of WINCHESTER measure were originally deposited in the English city of that name (*OED*). Virginia's CIDEVANT STAPLE was tobacco.

[1] Manuscript: "uprecedented."
[2] Word interlined.
[3] Manuscript: "Inspetions."

Calculations of Latitude of Poplar Forest

	Nov. 8.		Nov. 9.		Nov. 12.		Nov. 13.		Nov. 15.[1]	
		° ′ ″		° ′ ″		° ′ ″		° ′ ″		° ′ ″
½ observed altitude of ⊙		36– 1–30		35–44– 0		34–55–30		34–37–45[2]		34– 0– 6
–½ error of instrument		1–11½		1–11½[3]		1–11½		1–11½		1–11½
true observed altitude		36– 0–18½		35–42–48½		34–54–18½		34–36–33½		33–58–54½
– refraction + parallax		1–10½		1–11½		1–14½		1–15½		1–16½
true altitude of ⊙'s center		35–59– 8		35–41–37		34–53– 4		34–35–18		33–57–38
⊙'s declinn Greenwich	16–38–30		16–55–47		17–45–52		18– 1–57		18–33–11	
+ at Poplar Forest 79°–46′	3–42	16–42–12	4– 5	16–59–52	3–26	17–49–18	3–22	18– 5–19	3–13	18–36–24
true height of Æq. at P.F.		52–41–20		52–41–29		52–42–22		52–40–37		52–34– 2
		90–		90		90		90		90–
zen. dist. Æq. = Lat. of P.F.		37–18–40		37–18–31		37–17–38		37–19–23		37–25–58
	Nov. 21[4]		Nov 22		Nov. 23		Dec. 3			
		° ′ ″		° ′ ″		° ′ ″		° ′ ″		° ′ ″
½ observed altitude of ⊙		32–39–30		32–30–30		32–15–45		30–35–15[5]	Dec. 3.[6]	37–16–26
½ error of instrument		1–11½		1–11½		1–11½		1–11½	Nov. 22.	37–17–33

true observed Alt.		32–38–$18\frac{1}{2}$		32–29–$18\frac{1}{2}$		32–14–33		30–34– $3\frac{1}{2}$	12.	37–17–38
– refraction + parallax		1–$21\frac{1}{2}$		1–$22\frac{1}{4}$		1–$22\frac{1}{4}$		1–28	9.	37–18–31
true alt. of ⊙'s center		32–36–57		32–27–$56\frac{1}{4}$		32–13–11		30–32–35	8.	37–18–40
⊙'s declinn Greenwich[7]	19–58–48		20–11–50		20–24–29		22– 9–15		13.	37–19–23
+[8] at Poplar Forest	2–46	20– 1–34	2–41	20–14–31	2–36	20–27– 5	1–44	22–10–59	23.	37–19–44
true height of Æq. at P.F.		52–38–31		52–42–27		52–40–16		52–43–34	21.	37–21–29
		90		90		90		90		298–29–24
Zen. dist. of Æq. = Lat. P.F.		37–21–29		37–17–33		37–19–44		37–16–26	$\frac{1}{8}$	37–18–40

MS (MHi); filed with TJ's Weather Memorandum Book, 1802–16; written entirely in TJ's hand on one side of a sheet, with his Calculations of Latitude of Willis's Mountain, 8–9 Dec. 1816, on verso; partially dated.

Æq.: "equator."

[1] Entry for this date canceled by TJ with a diagonal line.

[2] Number inserted by TJ in place of "69–15–30."

[3] Manuscript: "1–11–$11\frac{1}{2}$."

[4] Number inserted by TJ in place of "20?"

[5] Number inserted by TJ in place of "61–10–30."

[6] At head of this column TJ canceled "Dec. 4" and readings of 30°–51′–45″ for half the observed altitude and 1′–$11\frac{1}{2}$″ for half the instrument error. In addition, TJ entered another reading for half of the observed altitude along the verso's lower lefthand margin: "Dec. 5. 30°–15′–45″."

[7] Manuscript: "Greewich."

[8] Editorially corrected from minus sign in manuscript.

Ellen W. Randolph (Coolidge) to Martha Jefferson Randolph

My dear Mama [ca. 10 Nov. 1816]

We were a good deal disappointed at not recieving letters from some of the family in the large pacquet which came to Grandpapa from Monticello; one of the girls might have written to let us know that you were all[1] well—We[2] expect to be with you the last of the Month and in the mean time are making very good use of our time; I have got through the Syntax, & have finished Corderi. Cornelia has been equally industrious—fortunately we have not been much interrupted by company—Mrs Yancey & Mrs Radford called a few days after our arrival & Mrs Johnson Mrs Penn Mrs Grimes & Miss Wormley formed our next party of Visitors—except these ladies & a few gentlemen who have visited Grand Papa we have seen no body—Cornelia & myself discovered a great likeness between Mrs Johnson and Mrs Carter, we were a little surprized at your admiring her so much for she appeared to us awkward & affected—her Sister Mrs Penn is the very quintessence of vulgarity—Upon the whole however I like this place & neighbourhood very much & should be well pleased to pass a part of my time here every year—

Grandpapa has probably informed you (in his letter) that we are to have Marshall Grouchy & Mr Lee the Consul at Bourdeaux, at Monticello in the course of the winter—that delightfull season for visitors—Mr Godefroi was so much delighted with the Natural Bridge that he has written to propose the purchase of it—(the offer as you may suppose was declined) Jane will scream when she hears of this and[3] conclude that the purchase money is to be deducted from the 70 dollars which formed the fortune of the family the last time we heard of them—Jeffersons visit was one of the most agreable surprizes we could have recieved—I fear he will not give us such another whilst we continue here—[4]

Grandpapa talks of taking Uncle Eppes in his way home—we shall also call at Warren—perhaps stay all night there—in case of this double visit I fear our finances will scarcely hold out—if you could send me[5] one or two dollars[6] to distribute on the road, it would be quite enough with what we have—Adieu my dearest Mother—give my love to all the family and kiss the ladies for me—John Hemmings makes frequent enquiries after Septimia—& told me the other day that last year when he left Monticello to come here—he had cried for about five miles of the road after taking leave of her—if

Mammy Critty & Aunt Priscilla enquire after their husbands say they are well.

Most affectionately your daughter

do not let any body see this letter for I have really "out done all my former outdoings" in it, and if I could spare paper would really write another—

Cornelia begs you will send some black berry flags by the boys. Adieu once more—

RC (ViU: Coolidge Correspondence); undated; written at Poplar Forest.

CORDERI was most likely an unidentified edition of Mathurin Cordier's *Colloquia*, a Latin work first printed in Geneva in 1563 and subsequently published a number of times with accompanying translations into French (Sowerby, no. 4791).

CORNELIA was Cornelia J. Randolph, while JANE was Jane H. Nicholas Randolph. Thomas Jefferson Randolph's (JEFFERSONS) visit to Poplar Forest had been an agreeable surprise. SEPTIMIA: Septimia A. Randolph (Meikleham).

MAMMY CRITTY (Critta Colbert) and AUNT PRISCILLA (Priscilla Hemmings) were slaves belonging to the Randolph family. THEIR HUSBANDS were TJ's slaves Burwell Colbert and John Hemmings, respectively. THE BOYS were John Hern and Randal Hern.

[1] Word interlined.
[2] Reworked from "Grandpapa."
[3] Here is canceled "wonders."
[4] Here is canceled "however, now that the time is fixed for our return I fear."
[5] Preceding two words interlined in place of "get."
[6] Here is canceled "from papa."

To Martha Jefferson Randolph

Poplar Forest Nov. 10. 16.

We are all well here, my dear Martha, and thinking of our return home which will be about the 30th or perhaps a day or two sooner. it is necessary therefore that the boys, Johnny & Randall with the mules should set off from Monticello on the 19th or 20th to take the cart and baggage. I must pray you to desire mr Bacon to let them have a good mule and geer in addition to Tilman and his. tell Wormley also to send some Calycanthus plants well done up in moss and straw, and about a bushel of Orchard grass seed out of the large box in the Green house. would it be possible for you so to make up some of the hardy bulbous roots of flowers as to come safely on the mule? daffodils, jonquils, Narcissuses, flags & lillies of different kinds, refuse hyacinths Etc. with some of the small bulbs of the hanging onion. I think if wrapped & sewed[1] up tight in two balls, one to come in each end of a wallet with nothing else in it to bruise them, they would come safe. present me affectionately to mr Randolph, kiss all the young ones for me & be assured of my most tender affection.

TH: JEFFERSON

P.S. Ellen writes to you more fully & I write to Jefferson. the boys must come to Gibson's the 1st night, Hunter's the 2d & here the 3d

RC (NNPM); endorsed by Randolph. PoC (MHi); on verso of a reused address cover from Christopher Clark to TJ; at foot of text: "Martha Randolph"; endorsed by TJ.

JOHNNY & RANDALL: John Hern and Randal Hern. An image of TJ's GREEN HOUSE at Monticello is reproduced elsewhere in this volume. An undated letter from ELLEN W. Randolph (Coolidge) to her mother is printed above at this date. TJ's letter to Thomas JEFFERSON Randolph of 10 Nov. 1816, not found, is recorded in SJL.

[1]Manuscript: "sowed."

To Mathew Carey

DEAR SIR Poplar Forest near Lynchburg Oct. [Nov.][1] 11. 16.

I recieve here (where I pass a good deal of my time) your favor of Oct. 22. covering a Prospectus of a new edition of your Olive branch: I subscribe to it with pleasure, because I believe it has done & will do much good, in holding up the mirror to both parties, and exhibiting to both their political errors. that I have had my share of them, I am not vain enough to doubt, and some indeed I have recognised. there is one however which I do not, altho' charged to my account in your book, and as that is the subject of this letter, & I have my pen in my hand, I will say a very few words on it. it is my rejection of a British treaty without laying it before the Senate. It has never, I believe, been denied that the president may reject a treaty after it's ratification has been advised by the Senate. then certainly he may before that advice: and if he has made up his mind to reject it it is more respectful to the Senate to do it without, than against their advice. it must not be said that their advice may cast new light on it. their advice is a bald resolution of yea, or nay, without assigning a single reason or motive.

You ask if I mean to publish any thing on the subject of a letter of mine to my friend Charles Thompson? certainly not. I write nothing for publication, and last of all things should it be on the subject of religion. on the dogmas of religion as distinguished from moral principles,[2] all mankind, from the beginning of the world to this day, have been quarrelling, fighting, burning and torturing one another, for abstractions unintelligible to themselves and to all[3] others, and absolutely beyond the comprehension of the human mind. were I to enter on that arena, I should only add an unit to the number of Bedlamites. Accept the assurance of my great esteem and respect

TH: JEFFERSON

RC (PPAmP: Thomas Jefferson Papers); misdated; signature and part of closing torn away, with missing text supplied from PoC; addressed: "Mr Matthew Carey Philadelphia"; frank clipped; postmarked Lynchburg, 13 Nov.; endorsed by Carey as received 19 Nov. PoC (DLC); on verso of a reused address cover from John F. Oliveira Fernandes to TJ; mutilated at seal, with most of the missing text rewritten by TJ. Recorded in SJL as a letter of 11 Nov. 1816.

Carey had criticized TJ in earlier editions of the OLIVE BRANCH for his unilateral rejection of the 1806 Monroe-Pinkney Treaty with Great Britain: "This was a mighty and a fatal error. It may be doubted whether it were not a violation, at least of the spirit of the constitution. It was, at all events, a case that probably did not enter into the conceptions of the framers of that instrument. If it had, it is likely they would have provided against its occurrence" (Carey, *The Olive Branch: or, Faults on Both Sides, Federal and Democratic*, 7th ed. [Philadelphia, 1815; Sowerby, no. 3539], 57–8).

TJ's letter to Charles Thomson (THOMPSON) was dated 9 Jan. 1816.

[1]Month corrected by TJ to "Nov." in PoC.

[2]Preceding five words interlined.

[3]Word added in left margin.

To William H. Crawford

DEAR SIR Poplar Forest near Lynchburg. Nov. 11. 16

I recieve here, where I pass much of my time, your favor of Oct. 28. and thank you for it's kindness. the object of my adding this to the mass of your labors in letter-reading, is lest I should have been misunderstood in my application on behalf of mr Minor I proposed him as successor to Thos J. Randolph, our collector who has resigned, or will immediately, and not as successor to mr Armstead the Assessor, as seems to have been understood by your letter. Armstead, I believe, has no intention of resigning. I will close the trouble I give you with assurances of my great esteem and respect TH: JEFFERSON

PoC (DLC); on verso of reused address cover to TJ; at foot of text: "Mr Crawford, Secy of the Treasury"; endorsed by TJ.

William Armistead (ARMSTEAD), of Amherst County, had been principal assessor of Virginia's nineteenth collection district since late in 1813 (*JEP*, 2:441, 443 [21, 23 Dec. 1813]).

To Joseph Delaplaine

Dear Sir Poplar Forest near Lynchburg. Nov. 11. 16.

I recieve here your favor of Oct. 26. the half volume of the Repository is probably recieved at Monticello where it will await my return. the objections to your work appear to be perfectly answered in the pamphlet you have been so kind as to inclose me. you had a right certainly to chuse your own scale of biography more or less extended, and the shorter as merely an Appendix to your main object, the portraits of American characters. the objections of the Critic seem to have been to the Appendix rather than to the principal work. I salute you with esteem and respect Th: Jefferson

RC (LNT: George H. and Katherine M. Davis Collection); addressed: "M[r] Joseph Delaplaine Philadelphia"; franked; postmarked Lynchburg, 13 Nov.; endorsement by Delaplaine reads, in part, "ans[d] twice." PoC (DLC); on verso of reused address cover of David Gelston to TJ, 23 Aug. 1816; endorsed by TJ.

To Maximilian Godefroy

Sir Poplar Forest near Lynchburg. Nov. 11. 16

I recieve here your favor of Oct. 12. written from the Natural bridge, and am not at all surprised at the sensations expressed by you as produced by that great object, and the attachment excited. as a place of retirement and contemplation I know none in the world which would be so delightful, were not it's solitude so incessantly interrupted by the curiosity of the world, and constant succession of visitors. but these would render it impossible for any one to live there but in some line of business which would turn their visits to account. there was a moment when I would have parted with it. when about to retire from the Presidency I found myself considerably in debt on winding up my affairs, and an individual from the neighborhood of the bridge happened to call on me at that moment, & proposed to buy. I told him I would consider of it and write to him. I did so & wrote him an offer which he never answered. had he accepted, it would have been gone, and I should now have been repenting it. the momentary motive having been relieved from other resources, has never again arisen. I consider myself as guardian only for the public of this first of all natural curiosities, and in the permission I gave to the little establishment there, I strictly guarded against defacing or masking the object. I regret very much that my absence from Monticello deprived me of the pleasure of seeing you when M[de] Godefroi and yourself[1] did me that of calling there. I should have recieved you with great satisfaction and have endeavored to render to you in person the assurances which I can now give by letter only of my great respect and esteem. TH: JEFFERSON

PoC (DLC); on verso of reused address cover of William Wirt to TJ, 10 Aug. 1816; mutilated at seal, with missing text rewritten by TJ; at foot of text: "M. Godefroi"; endorsed by TJ.

The INDIVIDUAL FROM THE NEIGHBORHOOD OF THE BRIDGE was William Jenkings (see TJ to Jenkings, 1 July 1809). TJ's 2 Dec. 1814 agreement to lease Natural Bridge to Philip Thornton and allow the establishment of a shot manufactory there prohibited him from DEFACING OR MASKING the site.

[1] Preceding two words interlined.

To John Steele

SIR Poplar Forest near Lynchburg Nov.[1] 11. 16.

I recieved at this place (100. miles S.W. from Monticello) your favor of Oct. 26. informing of the reciept of a cask of wine and a box from mr Cathalan, and of having forwarded them to Richmond, for which accept my thanks. I now inclose a 10.D. note of the bank of Virginia at Richmond which I understand pass at Philadelphia, to replace the duty and charges. the fraction need not be regarded; perhaps indeed there may be a difference of exchange which it may meet. I pass a considerable portion of my time, here, which I mention because it may sometimes happen to occasion delays in answering your favors. be pleased to accept the assurance of my great esteem & respect TH: JEFFERSON

PoC (Thomas Jefferson's Poplar Forest, on deposit ViU: TJP); on verso of portion of reused address cover; at foot of text: "Mr John Steele"; endorsed by TJ.

[1] Word interlined in place of "Oct."

To George Logan

DEAR SIR Poplar Forest near Lynchburg. Nov. 12. 16.

I recieved your favor of Oct. 16. at this place, where I pass much of my time, very distant from Monticello. I am quite astonished at the idea which seems to have got abroad; that I propose publishing something on the subject of religion. and this is said to have arisen from a letter of mine to my friend Charles Thompson, in which certainly there is no trace of such an idea. when we see religion split into so many thousands of sects, and I may say Christianity itself divided into it's thousands also, who are disputing, anathematising, and where the laws permit, burning and torturing one another for abstraction[s] which no one of them understand, and which are indeed[1] beyond the comprehension of the human mind, into which of the chambers of this Bedlam would a man wish to thrust himself. the sum of all relig[ion], as expressed by it's best preacher, 'fear god and love thy neighbor,' conta[in]s no mystery, needs no explanation. but this won't[2] do. it gives no scope to make dupes; priests could not live by it. your ideas of the moral obligations of governments are perfectly correct. the man who is dishonest as a statesman would be a dishonest man in any station. it is strangely absurd to suppose that a million of human beings collected together are not under the same moral laws which bind each of them separately. it is a great consolation to me that our government, as it cherishes most it's duties to it's own citizens, so is it the most exact in it's moral conduct towards other nations. I do not believe that in the four administrations which have taken place, there has been a single instance of departure from good faith towards other nations. we may sometimes have mistaken our rights, or made an erroneous estimate of the actions of others, but no voluntary wrong can be imputed to us. in this respect England exhibits the most remarkable phaenomenon in the universe in the contrast between the profligacy of it's government and the probity of it's citizens. and accordingly it is now exhibiting an example of the truth of the maxim that virtue & interest are inseparable. it ends, as might have been expected, in the ruin of it's people. but this ruin will fall heaviest, as it ought to fall, on that hereditary aristocracy which has for generations been preparing the catastrophe. I hope we shall take warning from the example and crush in it's birth the aristocracy of our monied corporations which dare already to challenge our government to a trial of strength, and to bid defiance to the laws of their country. present me respectfully to mrs Logan an[d accep]t yourself my friendly & respectful salutation[s.]

Th: Jefferson

PoC (DLC); on a reused address cover from John F. Oliveira Fernandes to TJ; edge trimmed and mutilated at seal, with two words rewritten by TJ; at foot of first page: "Doct^r Logan."

Jesus, here described as religion's best preacher, says in the Bible that people should fear god (Luke 12.5) and love thy neighbor (Matthew 5.43).

[1] Word interlined.

[2] Manuscript: "w'ont."

To William Wirt

Dear Sir Poplar Forest Nov. 12. 16.

Your's of Oct. 23. was recieved here on the 31st with the last sheets of your work. they found me engaged in a business which could not be postponed and have therefore been detained longer than I wished. on the subject of our antient aristocracy, I believe I have said nothing which all who knew them will not confirm, and which their reasonable descendants may not learn from every quarter. it was the effect of the large accumulations of property under the law of entails. the suppression of entails reduced the spirit of the rich[1] while the increased influence given by the new government to the people, raised theirs, and brought things to their present level from a condition which the present generation, who have not seen it, can[2] scarcely believe or conceive. I believe I have named none particularly: that would be wrong. you ask if I think your work would be the better of retrenchment? by no means; I have seen nothing in it which could be retrenched but to disadvantage: and again whether, as a friend, I would advise it's publication? on that question I have no hesitation, on your own account as well as that of the public. to the latter it will be valuable and honorable to yourself. you must expect to be criticised, and by a former letter I see you expect it. by the Quarterly reviewers you will be hacked and hewed by the tomahawk and scalping knife. those of Edinburgh, with the same anti-American prejudices, but sometimes considering us as allies against their administration, will do it more decently. they will assume as a model for biography the familiar manner of Plutarch, or scanty matter of Nepos, and try you perhaps by these tests. but they can only prove that your style is different from theirs, not that it is not good. I have always very much despised the artificial canons of criticism. when I have read a work in prose or poetry, or seen a painting a statue E^t^c. I have only asked myself whether it gives me pleasure, whether it is animating, interesting, attaching? if it is, it is good for these reasons. on these grounds you will be safe. those who take up your book will find they cannot lay it down, and this will be it's best criticism. You have certainly practised rigorously the precept of 'de mortuis nil nisi bonum.' this presents a very difficult question, whether one only, or both sides of the medal should be presented. it constitutes perhaps the distinction between panegyric and history. on this opinions are much divided, and perhaps may be so on this feature of your work. on the whole however you have nothing to fear, at least if my views are not very different from the common, and no one will see it's appearance[3] with more pleasure than myself, as no one can with more truth give you assurances of great respect & affectionate attachment

TH: JEFFERSON

RC (ViU: TJP); addressed: "William Wirt esquire Richmond." PoC (DLC); on reused address cover of David Gelston to TJ, 11 Oct. 1816; mutilated at seal, with missing text rewritten by TJ; endorsed by TJ. Tr (MdHi: Wirt Papers). Presumably enclosing the manuscript, not found, of a portion of Wirt, *Patrick Henry*.

Wirt referred to "the malignity of reviewers" in his FORMER LETTER to TJ of 10 Sept. 1816. DE MORTUIS NIL NISI BONUM: "speaking no ill of the dead."

[1] Reworked from "their spirit."
[2] Word interlined in place of "will."
[3] RC: "appeance." Tr: "appearance."

From Joseph Delaplaine

DEAR SIR, Philadelphia November 13h 1816.

Upwards of a week ago your No of the Repository was sent by the Mail. I shall be glad to hear, if it is not giving you too much trouble, whether You have received it in a perfect state of preservation.—

I am happy to inform you that the President has given me his opinion of the work. He also has done me the honour to send, in his own hand writing, the facts of his life.—

My work is not, neither shall it be, while I am its proprietor, a party work. Politics ought not, neither shall they enter into it. What can be fairer than this? Democrat & Federalist,[1] all share alike.

I am Dr sir with the highest respect & esteem your obedt & most huml st

JOSEPH DELAPLAINE

RC (DLC); at foot of text: "Thos Jefferson Eqr"; endorsed by TJ as received 11 Dec. 1816 and so recorded in SJL.

President James Madison sent Delaplaine a memorandum giving THE FACTS OF HIS LIFE in September 1816 (Dft in NjP: Andre deCoppet Collection).

[1] Manuscript: "Federalit."

To Wilson Cary Nicholas

DEAR SIR Poplar Forest Nov. 13. 16.

I wrote to the Secretary of State on the subject of mr Armistead,[1] and have recieved his assurance that if there is a vacancy, or should be one in any of the departments, he will exert himself to procure it. I wrote to him of preference, because more intimate with him than with any other of the heads of departments, and for a reason still more interesting, which I will explain to you as I did to him. I had observed that between you and him the former friendly intercourse had ceased for some time. something of this was visible to myself, but rendered more certain by the information of our beloved friend Peter Carr. the causes of it I never knew, nor wished to know. I only know it to be impossible that either of you could have been in the wrong. your characters assure that. it follows then that one or both must have been misled by wrong information. but two such men should not be at variance, should not be at the mercy of the passions of others. I stated this to Monroe. he answered me by acknoleging he once thought he had reason to complain of you; but that that sentiment had vanished long ago, and that he had called on you in Richmond as testimony of it; and he expresses such sentiments towards you as could not fail to merit and produce a return of them on your part. I think mr Carr mentioned some act of personal slight from Monroe to yourself directly. be it so. who can say what tale had been carried to him, what innocent expression of[2] yours had been distorted into the most injurious one? a man of his consideration does not act without a cause. but suppose him surprised into a momentary error. is a single error to have no forgiveness in this world? this is not your character. I hope then, knowing that this cloud has passed away, and mutual good will has resumed it's place with both, that both will awake from this dream of error, & conscious it has been a dream, go on together as heretofore, without considering it as needing or worthy of an explanation. perhaps this has already taken place; that his visit has been followed by the cordiality it invited, and I may be writing about a state of things long since done away; for I hear little of the ordinary occurrences of society. I shall rejoice if it is so. you have both too long to live, & to be useful, to make your want of harmony a matter of indifference[3] to your friends or your country. if it is not so, let it be so; and lose no opportunity of embracing each other.

I wrote also to mr Crawford, a man who has a heart also. he tells me there are two vacancies in the accountant's office, and that as soon as an accountant is appointed, mr Armistead[4] shall be named to one of them. consider this matter then as settled, and love me and my friends, as I do you and yours. TH: JEFFERSON

RC (facsimile in Sotheby's catalogue of *Fine Printed and Manuscript Americana*, 13 May 1987, lot 75); edge trimmed, with missing text supplied from PoC; at foot of first page: "Govr Nicholas"; endorsed by Nicholas. PoC (DLC); endorsed by TJ.

[1] Manuscript: "Armstead."
[2] TJ here canceled "his."
[3] Manuscript: "indiffence."
[4] Manuscript: "Armstead."

From the Philadelphia Society for Promoting Agriculture

11th mo. (*Nov.*) 13*th*, 1816.

AT a Special Meeting of "*The Philadelphia Society for promoting Agriculture*," held October (10th mo.) 30th, 1816,

It was resolved, unanimously,

THAT the Curators, with the assistance of the Secretary and Assistant Secretary, and any other Member or Members of the Society, who will procure and give information, collect facts relating to Agriculture and Horticulture, and of all circumstances connected therewith, which have occurred through the extraordinary season of 1816; and particularly the effects of Frost on vegetation, so far as it shall be in their power to acquire a knowledge of them. In performing this useful service, they will designate the Trees, Grasses and other Plants, and especially those cultivated, on which the Season has had either beneficial or injurious influence, and the local situations in which it has operated more or less perniciously, with the view to ascertain, (among other beneficial results,) the hardy or tender Grains, Grasses, or Plants, most proper for situations exposed to droughts, wet, or frost. In their inquiries, they will endeavour to discover the stages of growth in which cultivated crops have been more or less affected, and the state of products both of Grains, Grasses, and fruit. The addition of any facts, as to insects and vermin usually or occasionally preying on cultivated plants, and whether more or less injury has been done by them in this, than in ordinary seasons, would also be useful. The result of such inquiries to be drawn into the form of a report, to be made by the Curators at our annual Meeting in January next, subjoining such observations as they shall deem proper to furnish, not only with the view to present information, but to record for future instruction, the uncommon occurrences, and the consequences attending them, which have marked this anomalous period.

Published by order of the Society,
RICHARD PETERS, *President.*
ROBERTS VAUX, *Secretary.*

☞ The Curators of the Philadelphia Society for promoting Agriculture, will thankfully receive any information on the subjects of the foregoing Resolution, from any of their Agricultural, or other Fellow-Citizens, who may be pleased to afford it—Any Meteorological Observations made during the present year, will also be acceptable.

Letters sent by Post, or otherwise, addressed to SOLOMON W. CONRAD, No. 87 Market-street, Philadelphia, will be gratefully attended to.

RC (DLC: TJ Papers, 208:37141); printed broadside; dateline at foot of text; at head of text: "AGRICULTURAL"; addressed: "Thomas Jefferson Esq Monticello Virginia"; stamp canceled; franked; postmarked Philadelphia, 22 Nov.; endorsed by TJ as a "Circular" from Peters received 11 Dec. 1816 from Philadelphia and so recorded in SJL.

The Philadelphia Society for Promoting Agriculture was founded in 1785. Richard Peters, one of its founding members, headed the organization from 1805 until his death in 1828 (Simon Baatz, *"Venerate the Plough": A History of the Philadelphia Society for Promoting Agriculture, 1785–1985* [1985], 4, 16, 51; *Minutes of the Philadelphia Society for the Promotion of Agriculture, from its Institution in February, 1785, to March, 1810* [1854], 1, 78).

Roberts Vaux (1786–1836), Quaker philanthropist, established a dry-goods store as a young man in his hometown of Philadelphia. The death of a beloved sister in 1812 and his mother two years later, however, convinced him to give up business and devote himself and much of his considerable inheritance to philanthropic endeavors. Vaux was involved in a host of charitable and educational organizations, including the American Philosophical Society and the Philadelphia Society for Promoting Agriculture, which he joined in 1812 and served as secretary. In addition, he argued against slavery and in favor of free public education, temperance, penal reform, and the better treatment of the blind, deaf, mute, and mentally ill. A staunch opponent of the Second Bank of the United States, Vaux was also a member of the Philadelphia Common Council, 1814–16, president of the Philadelphia school board, 1818–31, and a judge on the local court of common pleas from 1835 until his death (*ANB*; *DAB*; Joseph J. McCadden, *Education in Pennsylvania, 1801–1835, And Its Debt to Roberts Vaux* [1937; repr. 1969]; APS, Minutes, 15 Jan. 1819 [MS in PPAmP]; Baatz, *"Venerate the Plough,"* 42; Philadelphia *Poulson's American Daily Advertiser*, 8 Jan. 1836).

From Richard Rush

DEAR SIR. Washington November 13. 1816

I have to offer many apologies for detaining so long the letters you were kind enough to put into my hands, and which I now return. When I got back from my short, though most pleasant and gratifying excursion as far as Monticello, I sent them on to Philadelphia. Intending to go there in the course of the autumn, I did not ask that they should be transmitted back to me, preferring to bring them with me on my return from thence, which I have lately done.

The views you have been so good as to take of Doctor Mease's request, are very grateful to the feelings of my mother, as well as to the whole family of an age to estimate their delicacy and force. They all acquiese, (and you will permit me, sir, to be a party,) with respectful and warm acknowledgements, in the decision to which your letter points.

If, when I had the pleasure to see you, I understood you rightly, you were also so obliging as to say, that the letters of my father in question should, on the expression of a wish that such a course would be agreeable, be transferred to my hands. Allow me now to add, that if, quite at your own convenience, this were done, it would augment the favor which all of us feel has already been conferred upon the family.

With the highest respect, I pray you to believe me, dear sir, most faithfully your obedient servant RICHARD RUSH.

RC (MHi); endorsed by TJ as received 11 (reworked from 12) Dec. 1816 and so recorded in SJL. RC (DLC); address cover only; with PoC of TJ to Archibald Thweatt, 14 Dec. 1816, on recto and verso; addressed: "M[r] Jefferson Monticello"; franked; postmarked Washington City, 14 Nov.

The documents placed in Rush's HANDS during his recent visit to Monticello and now returned to TJ were evidently James Mease to TJ, 7 Aug., and TJ to Mease, 17 Aug. 1816.

From James Freeman

SIR, Boston. Nov. 14. 1816.

I have lately returned to Boston, where I had the pleasure of finding the note of October the 10th, which you did me the honour to address to me. I still regret, as do all my friends here, that I had not the opportunity of hearing you speak. But I shall always remember with gratitude the hospitality of those members of your family, whom I had the satisfaction of seeing; and I rejoice in particular, that by becoming acquainted with your granddaughters, I have obtained the knowledge of two elegant and well-educated young ladies, whom I may propose as models to my granddaughter, nieces, and other female friends, whom I wish to improve in the eloquence of conversation, in purity of language, in delicacy of manners, in knowledge, and in virtue. To Miss Ellen Randolph I take the liberty of presenting, with your permission, a small volume, which I published a few years ago.

With high respect, I am, Sir, your most obedient servant.

JAMES FREEMAN.

RC (DLC); dateline at foot of text; addressed: "M[r] Jefferson Monticello Virginia"; endorsed by TJ as received 11 Dec. 1816 and so recorded in SJL.

The SMALL VOLUME for Ellen W. Randolph (Coolidge) was Freeman's *Sermons on Particular Occasions* (Boston, 1812; repr. Boston, 1814).

From William Short

Dear sir Philad[a] Nov: 16—16

Your kind letter of Octob: 14. was recieved here the 19th the very day you fixed as that of your departure for Bedford to remain there until the 1st of Dec:—I did not therefore attempt to answer it at the moment, as it would have remained at Monticello, until your return—And this I count will get there some time before you & recieve you at your debotter. I write thus early because I am anxious to express to you my concern for the new trouble which my land has given you. In all cases which act as a deduction on it, & which give trouble, my first & only impression of pain is really the idea of the trouble being all yours. I can never express to you sufficiently how much I feel myself indebted to you for the unvarying kindness you have showed on the subject of this land. I will hope that this is the last scene of the kind for your sake particularly—I am obliged to M[r] H. for having paid the $30—& shall be glad to re-imburse him in any way he will point out to me. I will either pay it to his correspondent here if agreeable to him—or when I may have any money in Richmond, will pay it there if more agreeable—or in fine adopt any other measure he may prefer—and shall wish to know his wishes.

This makes me fear I shall have suffered also at Norfolk where I have 1000 acres of land purchased an age ago from Co[l] Harvie, under the idea that the city would extend to it in time—Since my return to America I have learned that it never can be of much value—A friend of mine at Norfolk who had promised to attend to the payment of the taxes & who did so for some years, has latterly become hypochondriac & not attended to his own affairs; of course, I apprehend, not to mine—& probably the taxes are now going on at 10: p[ct]—I met with Mr Myers of Norfolk last summer who kindly promised to look into this business—as yet I have not heard from him.

Although I have now but a small pecuniary interest remaining in Virginia, I have retained & shall always retain one of a much more powerful kind—that which belongs to "des coeurs bien nés." & to whom under all circumstances "la patrie est chere." I have therefore been made very uneasy by reports which I heard of a revolutionary spirit having gone ahead there—the ostensible object, or at any rate the certain effect, of which would be to destroy the unique principle existing there of having placed the sovereignty in the soil & not in the persons of its inhabitants.—It is to this principle I think that may be fairly attributed the decided superiority in talents & moral & commanding qualities which the individuals of the State of Virginia have hitherto held over those of the other States—According to my limited view of the subject I saw great danger approaching, but my apprehensions have been much diminished lately by learning that the whole business in contemplation meets with your unqualified approbation—If I were sure of this I should be inclined to suppose that my long absence from home might have made me take a false view of matters—but I know how little we can rely on what is attributed to you—& I refused absolutely to believe my informant who affirmed you had written a letter to one of the Mr Tuckers, I know not which, recommending the following changes in the constitution of Virginia—1st suffrage without a freehold—2. all the offices of government to be appointed by the people at large, excepting only the judiciary appointments—3. these to be made by the legislature & to be revoked by them at will.—I told my informant you had been so often reported to have written letters which you never thought of & to express sentiments the direct opposite of your own, that he must excuse me if for the present I could not give credence to this—& particularly as he did not pretend to have seen it himself, & only to have heard of it from others—I added that I knew you were acquainted with Judge Tucker & therefore it was highly probable you might have written to him; that I did not doubt therefore the fact of the letter—but its contents.—

From a recollection of a late letter of yours to me I did not believe you would again carry your counsel into the uncertain & troubled waves of political arrangements—I regretted that you should have adopted this kind of retreat even as to counsel—I thought you owed the results of your long experience to your country—& by your country I understood the United States. It appeared to me that your experience & your views resulting therefrom, as to what would be the probable effects of the democratic principle when left to itself to operate purely & Simply, on our liberties, might be invaluable to our country (I am sorry I cannot say to our posterity)—& would be to you monumentum aere perennius. I did wish therefore that you in your wisdom would make us now sensible, of what time will teach us perhaps at a great expence, the essential difference of the democratic principle when uncontrolled—& the same when used as a counteractor in feudal institutions.

If you think there is no danger to be apprehended from the Convention in contemplation, pray tell me so, that I may fear no more—for the word Convention carries something in it most aweful to my ear—This perhaps may proceed from my having once assisted at the birth of a monster of that name—& though the name be the same the animal may be different; but I would wish to know it from good authority.

Poor Grouchy, of whom you speak, is so unsettled in his plans that it is impossible to say where he is, or where he will be at any given time. The last I heard of him was that he was on a visit to Gen[l] Brown, & that he had purchased some land in that quarter. I hope this is not true. We think he will certainly be here in the course of the winter. I shall have great pleasure when I see him to mention what you say, & I know it will give him great pleasure.

God bless you my dear sir, & preserve[1] your health & happiness—Believe me as ever

most faithfully your friend & servant W: SHORT

RC (MHi); endorsed by TJ as received 11 Dec. 1816 and so recorded in SJL.

AT YOUR DEBOTTER (débotter): "at the moment of your arrival." MR H. was David Higginbotham, the purchaser of Short's Indian Camp estate. The phrases DES COEURS BIEN NÉS ("the well-bred hearts") and LA PATRIE EST CHERE ("the fatherland is dear") are adapted from the opening line of Voltaire's 1760 tragedy *Tancrède*, act 3, scene 1.

TJ had sent several letters in 1816 to Samuel Kercheval, not ONE OF THE MR TUCKERS, proposing changes to Virginia's constitution. TJ's LATE LETTER to Short was that of 5 May 1816. THE WORD CONVENTION troubled Short because of its association with the body which, under that name, directed the French Revolution, 1792–95, oversaw the trial and execution of Louis XVI, purged its moderate political elements, and instituted the Reign of Terror (Owen Connelly and others, eds., *Historical Dictionary of Napoleonic France, 1799–1815* [1985], 133).

Emmanuel, marquis de Grouchy, did purchase SOME LAND near the possessions of Jacob Brown in Jefferson County, New York (Franklin B. Hough, *A History of Jefferson County in the State of New York* [1854], 445; *ANB*, 3:682–3).

[1]Manuscript: "preseve."

From Elisha Ticknor

SIR, Boston 16th Nov. 1816.

A few days ago I forwarded to you a second letter from my Son, and now have the pleasure to inclose to you another copy of the Invoice of your Books as received from him, with the amount of freight and duties, paid by me in this port, viz.

					D c
Homerus	8	8vo	th.	20,16/[1]	=15.50
Juvenalis	2	8vo	"	6,04.	4.50
Virgilius	4	8vo	"	8,06.	6.
Tacitus	4	8vo	"	5,08.	3.75
[Æ]schylus[2]	3	8vo	"	7,00.	5.25[3]
				47,10.	= $35,55
Freight, Duties &c.					9,70.
					$45,25.

The above Books are enclosed in a Box, mark'd Honorable[4] Thomas Jefferson, Monticello, Virginia, and shipt [on boar]d the Brig Polly, Capt. David Snow, bound to [Richmo]nd. The Box of Books I consign'd to Messrs [Gibson &] Jefferson, your Correspondents there as you requested in your letter of the 15th Aug. last. I can inform my son of the amount of the above freight and duties, &ca being $9,70[5] which he may charge to you in his account, or if it be more agreeable to you, it may be paid to me in Boston.

I am, sir, With high esteem and respect, Your most obedient servant. ELISHA TICKNOR.

N.B. The Books were put on board the Brig Polly this day as pr Capt. D. Snow's Receipt.

RC (MHi); with lower corner of sheet torn away; endorsed by TJ as received 11 Dec. 1816 and so recorded in SJL. RC (MHi); address cover only; with PoC of TJ to William D. Meriwether, 16 Dec. 1816, on verso; addressed: "Honorable Thomas Jefferson, Monticello Virginia"; franked; postmarked Boston, 17 Nov. Enclosure not found.

[1] TJ here wrote "24," the number of groschens in a thaler (taler).

[2] Word partially obscured by foxing.

[3] Column to this point inserted by TJ, with the above entries totaling $35.

[4] Manuscript: "Honorble."

[5] Preceding three words interlined.

From John Prout

Thomaston (Maine) Novr 17th 1816,

Memoir. On a new invention for fertilizing the various products of the soil.

Inscribed to the Honorable Thomas Jefferson,

Imitate the Gods: say the priests of all nations. Imitate Nature: say the Enlightened, not interested in deceiving, nor disposed to live on the labor of others further than their services may merit.

As a few precepts faithfully instilled by the Moral Teacher into the minds of a rising generation would be of more extensive utility to mankind than all the shelfy lumber of a rabbi, priest, or iman, so would a few plain directions benefit the mere practical farmer more than the many voluminous tracts written on Agriculture.

What intelligent & contemplative person that has observed the copious effusion of the farina of some plants, hemp, & sorrel for instance, on being agitated by the wind or other causes, but must conjecture, that as Nature does nothing in vain would men but observe, this is intended as well to promote the growth of the plant as to fecundate the female blossoms? This natural process is to be imitated.

The use of wood ashes on the sea coast and of gypsum in the interior by strewing on the ground, experience has tested to cause more abundant crops than can be otherwise obtained: experience also ascertains that these articles by forcing the soil render it afterward inert without fresh applications. The cause & manner of operation seem not to be generally known even where most practiced. Similes similibus trahuntur. The saline particles in these manures forcibly attract to the surface the nitrous inherent in the earth, exhausting the superficies until renovated by a deeper tillage. A deep plowing & well pulverised soil are but little affected by the greatest drought, In these grounds the dews will be more abundant & useful than rains in shallower, tillage. A proper agent is wanted to co-operate.

Lime, gypsum, chalk, &c having a common animal origin must with the like preparation possess similar properties. Clay, marle, &c, being the residuum of animal bodies as the others are the concretion of shells, whether deposited 5000. or 100.000 years since, is immaterial, must also contain a saline tincture & with the like preparation have the same effects. Any of these being caused to adhere to the plant in place of being strewed on the ground, will naturally attract the nitrous effluvia exhaling at the close of the day & continuing till after sun-rise in greater or less proportion according to the state of the atmosphere causing that fertility so much to be desired as the reward of labor. the atmospheric atoms serving as the common pabulum, a proportion of the electric element more or less according to their various natures, most copiously in evergreens, giving animation, and these articles operating as invigorating stimulants like aromatics to the human sense, and to be used with like moderation the nitrous effluvia by their softening somnific quality opening the pores, inclining to repose, & serving to digest & assimilate their various elements.

And if these articles of native produce shall be experienced on a fair trial to serve as well as gypsum, what a national saving may it cause of money & labor!

These ideas revolving in the Writer's mind for a few years since, induced him to make an experiment the season of 1815 on a small mowing field of 4 acres rented with the buildings of Dr. E. Dodge of Thomaston (Maine). It is to be observed that the common produce in this part of the District is about half a ton of hay per acre, in many places not more than a quarter, and that a ton is reckoned a very good crop: the lands in general are capable of producing with good management 3 or 4 fold; this field the preceding year, had the common produce, that is 2 tons, much the same as the adjacent grounds. By using the process with lime & ashes, now to be related 7 tons were obtained: had it been repeated as oft as it might, it is expected more would have bee[n] had. Not renewing the lease nor the land receiving any assistance, the produce of the past [season?] was much the same as in the neighboring fields. One circumstance occurred worth noting, that spots Winter killed, where the ice had lain till late & not a spire of vegetation appeared, became thick set with white clover.

A copy of the process to be observed as annexed
to the petition to His Excellency the President
for the grant of a patent for this discovery,

Having a gentle breeze precedent to an approaching rain or a moist state of the atmosphere, nearly fill a common meal sieve, or an instrument that may be constructed on the principles of a barber's leather powder puff with a broad mouth face or sifter, with clean dry wood ashes, or pulverised lime, gypsum, chalk, clay, marle, creek or flat mud, all having the common property of the saline tincture, stepping in a zigzag line over the ground intended to be dressed, with greater or less celerity as the state of the wind may require, shaking lightly with your hand the sieve or puffer as you go, so that the dust or atoms will be equally wafted on the grass, grain, hemp, flax, vines, roots &c, on their first germination, recruiting the sieve or puffer when needed, repeating the process during the time of growth in the moderate manner that stimuli should be used: on going over a large field having regard to the length of the diagonals so as not to be too far distant from the opposite angular points; and this is to be governed by the state of the wind that the dust may reach from the one to the other & no further, to prevent the plants being overcharged; the intention being that all the plants may have as equal a share as may be and that the dust shall adhere to the plant in place of being strewed on the ground: this will cause the grass to become thick-set & well bottomed, and this & all other articles of culture to have a rapid growth & abundant produce; the harvesting to be much earlier, and without impoverishing the soil in the manner experienced by the Southern planters in their use of gypsum.

The Writer conceiving that by virtue of the act of Congress relative to new improvements, &c he is intitled to a patent for the exclusive right of vending the privilege of using these articles in this mann[er] has petitioned the President of the U.S. for this purpose. But as the subject may be deemed of more general national interest than the common applications which appear chiefly calculated for the purpose of private emolument, it is possible that the Government would be desirous of having it thoroly investigated by some Scientific Characters previous to a grant, the high estimation in which the Hon. M[r] J. is held, especially for his experimental agricultural knowledge, induces the Writer, tho entirely a stranger to inscribe to him this memoir, hoping that with his patronage & the assistance of his friends engaged in this most beneficial Science, that such a prospectus may be given of this improvement as to obtain what he conceives to be a legal right, and to induce the Citizens of the U.S. to adopt what he believes to be the cheapest & easiest, the most profitable & effectual mode of filling their basket & their store.

Leaving Mystery to that Order that cannot subsist nor exist without it, the Writer has endeavored to be as explicit & distinct in his theory & practice as his imperfect knowledge & experience would permit. With the twofold proper principles of our nature he makes this confidential disclosure that as the Community may be benefited, so may himself. Should any theoretic idea or expression appear improper he would esteem it as a great favor to have it corrected before publication, it being his intention that the mere farmer shall know & understand why & wherefore he will adopt the practice.

The armorial motto of his ancestors is, Prout meruit virtus, which he hopes will be realized by the Report that the Hon. M[r] J, & his agricultural friends may be pleased to make on the subject to the Executive Department who are vested with the discretionary power of dispensing that right he presumes to claim.

With every sentiment of deference & respect he is, Sir, Your most obedient servant, JOHN PROUT

RC (DLC); edge trimmed and chipped; one word illegible; dateline at foot of text; endorsed by TJ as received 30 Dec. 1816 and so recorded in SJL. RC (DLC); address cover only; with PoC of TJ to David Hosack, 19 Jan. 1817, on verso; addressed: "The Honorable Thomas Jefferson, Monticelli, Virginia"; franked; postmarked (faint) [...] Dec.

SIMILES SIMILIBUS TRAHUNTUR: "like attracts like." Prout never received a United States patent for his DISCOVERY. The ACT OF CONGRESS RELATIVE TO NEW IMPROVEMENTS was the 21 Feb. 1793 "Act to promote the progress of useful Arts; and to repeal the act heretofore made for that purpose" (*U.S. Statutes at Large*, 1:318–23). PROUT MERUIT VIRTUS: "Inasmuch as virtue has earned."

From Joseph Delaplaine

DEAR SIR, Philad[a] November 20th 1816

I have this moment had the honour of receiving your obliging favour of the 11 instant dated at Poplar Forrest.

I am much gratified to find you take so much interest in my work. No work that has ever been published in America, has been so much reviewed & criticised upon, so much censured & praised as the Repository.

The Aurora & every other Newspaper in this City, and in different parts of America praise it highly, except The Baltimore Patriot, which, if I can judge correctly, suppose, very wrongly, that the Repository leans a little towards Federalism. This is false, & until this paper was put in possession of the truth on this subject, it should not have attempted to injure the only National work now publishing in this Country. However, I shall have an opportunity to convince that paper & the public at large, that my work is impartial & national throughout. I have now[1] expended all my fortune in it, & it will keep me poor for a very long time.

Your life is preparing for the Repository. It is possible, dear sir, that I may have occasion to trouble you for a few more facts. I shall soon know.

I presume the life of the President will not be given till the 3d half volume is ready.—In that I hope also to give the Lives of Dr Franklin—Hopkinson &c &c—

I am Dr sir with unfeigned regard & respect Your obed: & most huml st

JOSEPH DELAPLAINE

RC (DLC); endorsed by TJ as received 11 Dec. 1816 and so recorded in SJL, which mistakenly describes it as a letter of 16 Nov. 1816. RC (MHi); address cover only; with PoC of TJ to Richard Rush, 16 Dec. 1816, on verso; addressed: "Thomas Jefferson Esqr Monticello Virginia"; stamped; postmarked Philadelphia, 21 Nov.

Delaplaine inferred that the *Baltimore Patriot & Evening Advertiser* of 23 Oct. 1816 was accusing his publication, *Delaplaine's Repository*, of a bias TOWARDS FEDERALISM. The newspaper criticized it for "its '*catch-penny*' character, its *party* arrangements and *spirit*," and "the wretched looseness, extravagance, and pomposity of the style of its biography"; added "that FRANKLIN, GATES, GREEN, HENRY, HANCOCK, and a number of other patriots, heroes, orators or statesmen, should have preceded AMES, HAMILTON, or RUSH"; and urged Delaplaine to recall the serial and "begin the work anew."

[1] Word interlined.

From Martha Jefferson Randolph

MY DEAREST FATHER Monticello Nov. 20, 1816

We recieved your letters last night only, and the necessary preparations for the boy's Journey would take up so much of the day that we determined not to send them till to morrow morning 21st Wormley will see to every thing but the bulbous roots. the kinds you mention are all growing at present and could not be moved with out destroying them but I have sent you a number of off sets of tulips and hyacinths some blooming roots and some that will not bloom till the ensuing year but I believe all of the finest kinds they were intended to have been planted in the borders last fall but were kept out waiting for a bed to be prepared for them. the others can be dug up at the proper season and planted next summer or fall. you will have seen by the papers the death of Gouverneur Morris. his loss will be irreparable to his wife by lessening the little consequence that I am afraid she had, and exposing her unprotected to the persecution of his heirs who have been dissapointed by the birth of her child of his large possessions. I wrote to her upon the occasion althoug[h] we had not previously corresponded, but poor creature she is surrounded by ennemies and never in more need of the countenance[1] of her family than at present. adieu My Dearest Father we are All well but poor Ann Mr Bankhead[2] has returned and recommencd his habits of drunkeness Mr Randolph has taken in to his own hands the mannagement of his affairs and if his family are much disturbed or endangered will take at once the steps necessary for their protection, as circumstances may require. sending him to the mad house is but a temporary remedy, for after a few weeks he would be returned with renewed health to torment his family the longer. I really think the best way would be to hire a keeper for him to prevent his doing mischief, and let him finish him self at once. his Father is utterly in dispair, and told Aunt Marks that but for Ann and the children he never wished to see his face again. he so entirely threw off all respect for the old gentleman as to tell him he would be master in his[3] own house and called for a decanter of whiskey and drank off[4] two draughfts to his face the more to brave him, Adieu My Dearest Father

with tender and unchangeable love Your affectionate Daughter

M RANDOLPH

the large crown imperial root is for Mrs Eppes, if you go that way the smaller ones are not blooming roots yet, but will be in a year or 2. the tulips & hyacinths are mixed but Cornelia knows them all. I have sent you besides the first letters 3 I believe of which I altered the direction 3 packets enclosing many letters[5] each the second via Richmond and the 3 went off[6] yesterday 19th before I recieved your letter, for they close the mail on Monday. which will accou[nt] for one packet going by Richmond, the mail being closed before my letters were sent to Charlottesville I have also sent all the weekly registers as I recieved them 4

RC (MHi); edge trimmed; endorsed by TJ as received 23 Nov. 1816 and so recorded in SJL. RC (DLC); address cover only; with PoC of TJ to Francis Adrian

Van der Kemp, 24 Nov. 1816, on verso; addressed: "Thomas Jefferson Poplar Forest."

THE BOY'S JOURNEY was to be undertaken by John Hern and Randal Hern. Flower BORDERS had encircled Monticello's West Lawn since late in TJ's presidency (Betts, *Garden Book*, opp. 335). An undated Dft of the letter Randolph WROTE TO Ann Cary Morris about this time is in NcU: NPT. TJ's granddaughter CORNELIA J. Randolph was with him on this visit to Poplar Forest.

A letter from Edmund Bacon to TJ of this date, not found, is recorded in SJL as received 23 Nov. 1816 from Monticello at Poplar Forest.

[1] Reworked from "support."
[2] Manuscript: "Bankead."
[3] Manuscript: "hi."
[4] Manuscript: "of."
[5] Manuscript: "letter."
[6] Manuscript: "of."

To John Burke

SIR Poplar Forest near Lynchburg. Nov. 22. 16.

Your favor of Oct. 19. is just now recieved, and at this place. I have always had a standing request with mr Gibson to pay for the gazettes and Reviews recieved at Richmond, annually, as the accounts should be presented. under this arrangement the Argus has been paid for ever since I was a subscriber, and if you will have the goodness to present your bill to mr Gibson he will be so kind as to pay you the 6. D 25 c due for it to the time of it's discontinuance. Accept the assurance of my respect TH: JEFFERSON

PoC (MHi); on verso of reused address cover of David Gelston to TJ, 20 Aug. 1816; at foot of text: "Mr John Burke"; endorsed by TJ.

Burke's FAVOR OF OCT. 19. is printed above at 7 Nov. 1816. TJ had been a SUBSCRIBER to the Richmond *Virginia Argus* since 1797 (*MB*, 2:958; Sowerby, nos. 576–8).

To Peter Derieux

DEAR SIR Poplar Forest near Lynchbg Nov. 22. 16

I received last night only, and at this place, where I have been a month, your favor of Oct. 27. I return to Monticello in a few days, where I will avail myself of the first moments of leisure to send you a copy of mr Mazzei's will, praying you to accept in the mean time the assurances of my respect and esteem. TH: JEFFERSON

PoC (DLC); on verso of reused address cover of Isaac H. Tiffany to TJ, 8 Aug. 1816; at foot of text: "Mr Derieux"; endorsed by TJ.

To Patrick Gibson

Dear Sir Poplar Forest Nov. 22. 16.

I have been here about a month and shall now within a day or two set out on my return to Monticello. on winding up here I find my debts amount to 222.D. which sum I recieve from mr Robertson, and draw for the same on you in his favor.

I found on my arrival here that mr Yancey had preferred employing the teams in getting the new crop sown, rather than in carrying the old to Lynchburg: so that he had not sent the boat load of flour[1] down which I expected. I shall not regret it, if enough has been sent from Albemarle to cover my deficit with you. we are told of a wonderfully sudden rise in the price at Richmond. I shall wonder mor[e] if in the course of the winter & spring it does not rise to a considerab[ly] higher price than has ever before been given. Europe & N. America were never before within my memory so destitute of bread. I am for holding up until the market opens on the breaking up of the ice in the spring of the year.—our crop of tobacco here is short. Yancey ha[d] calculated on 20,000. he now wavers as low as 15,000. of which he assures me one half will be prime, and the other good. this will be down in Jan. & Feb. and I see no reason for holding it up after it gets to market. of this however you will be the best judge and will sell when you think best.

Your's with great friendship Th: Jefferson

P.S. I must pray you to send a bale of cotton for the use of this place to mr Yancey by such boat or person as he shall direct to call for it. the smallest bale over 100. ℔ will be sufficient

PoC (DLC); on verso of reused address cover of Lafayette to TJ, 16 Aug. 1816; edge trimmed; mutilated at seal, with missing word rewritten by TJ; between closing and signature: "Mr Gibson"; postscript adjacent to signature; endorsed by TJ.

Archibald robertson was making the following payments for TJ: $45 to Joseph Slaughter "for a horse"; $20 to a Mr. Butler "for <*leather*> wheels"; $7 to Alexander Bridgeland (Bridgland) for "87. ℔ beef"; and $150 to Robertson himself "for corn" (*MB*, 2:1329). A missing letter from TJ to Bridgeland of 25 Oct. 1816 is recorded in SJL.

[1] Preceding two words interlined.

To Richard N. Thweatt

Dear Sir Poplar Forest Nov. 22. 16.

I received yesterday, and at this place, a letter from mr Edwin Starke of Norfolk of Oct. 30. when he had but just rec[d] one from me of Oct. 10. in which he informs me he had forwarded a box recieved for me from Europe to yourself at Petersburg to be forwarded to Monticello. I regret this terrible mistake of mr Starke in the geography of Monticello more for the trouble it has brought on you, than the delay of my box. I cannot get you out of the scrape otherwise than by praying you to send it by some vessel going round to Richmond to the address of messrs Gibson & Jefferson who will pay all charges, and repay any with which you may have been taxed by this error.

I have been here a month, and shall set out for Monticello the day after tomorrow, taking Millbrook in my way, as I hear that mr Eppes's health is very low.

I am indebted to this aberration of my box for the opportunity, of which I always avail myself with pleasure of renewing to mrs Thweatt & yourself the assurance of my affectionate esteem & respect

Th: Jefferson

PoC (MHi); on verso of a reused address cover from William Wirt to TJ; mutilated at seal, with missing text rewritten by TJ; at foot of text: "Rich[d] Thweatt esq."; endorsed by TJ.

Richard Noble Thweatt (ca. 1780–1835), planter, killed a man in a duel in 1802, was summoned for jury service during Aaron Burr's 1807 treason trial, and in 1809 married Mary "Polly" Eppes, a sister of TJ's son-in-law John Wayles Eppes and niece of TJ's wife, Martha Wayles Skelton Jefferson. President James Madison appointed Thweatt a federal tax assessor in 1816. He owned fifty-three slaves in Dinwiddie County in 1820 and sixty-five at his roughly 1,100-acre estate in Chesterfield County a decade later. Thweatt died in the latter county and was buried in the family cemetery at Eppington (John Frederick Dorman, ed., *Ancestors and Descendants of Francis Epes I of Virginia [Epes-Eppes-Epps]* [1992–], 2:410; *Alexandria Advertiser and Commercial Intelligencer*, 6 Sept. 1802; David Robertson, *Reports of the Trials of Colonel Aaron Burr* [Philadelphia, 1808], 1:422; note to TJ to Archibald Thweatt, 13 Jan. 1810; *JEP*, 3:27, 29 [29 Jan., 9 Feb. 1816]; DNA: RG 29, CS, Dinwiddie Co., 1820, Chesterfield Co., 1830; Chesterfield Co. Will Book, 13:210–2; *Richmond Enquirer*, 19 May 1835; gravestone inscription in Eppington graveyard, Chesterfield County).

Bad weather delayed TJ's departure for monticello until 6 Dec. 1816 (TJ to Martha Jefferson Randolph, 3 Dec. 1816; *MB*, 2:1329).

From Joseph Delaplaine

Dear sir, Philadelphia November 23[d] 1816.

I have already had the honour of answering Your obliging favour dated at Poplar Forest.

The Biographer, under my inspection, is busily engaged in preparing a sketch of your life for my National work.

As soon as circumstances will permit, I shall be happy to receive your candid opinion of the Repository. I beg you not to be scrupulous or delicate. I desire to profit by your remarks & suggestions. Whatever faults it may have, I wish you to point out. I shall be peculiarly pleased to know what you think of the plan, the general arrangement, whether the memoirs are long enough, or too long. the style & literary part generally—The engravings, each one separately.—The paper—& The type, &c &c &c.

If there are any facts connected with your life, that have occurred recently, & which you may suppose will be of service to me, I will thank you to furnish them. On no account will you be quoted. This it is impossible to do with the least propriety indeed.

I think we shall want more matter for your life.—

I have been several times recently, to see the Venerable Charles Thomson. He spoke of you freely. It appears that one of your letters gave him great delight. It is that, in which you speak of the scriptures &c. after this, I will not conceal from you the fact, and it is now no secret, that your letter to M[r] Thomson as well as one to another gentleman in another quarter, near Philad[a], has been quoted. Gen[l] Wilkinson said to me a few days ago "Sir, I am happy to learn that M[r] Jefferson has written to a gentleman that he has become a disciple or follower of Jesus Christ." To be brief; it is in general circulation, & a current opinion & belief, that you have avowed yourself a perfect believer in the Christian Religion & that you believe in the Divinity of Our saviour.—This has gained such ground that Gen[l] Wilkinson, has given it a place, he told me a few days ago, in his work which will be published in 2 or 3 weeks.—

I mention these things, dear sir, in a frank, open manner, to enable you to know, if you have not already heard, what the people say in this quarter on this subject. And I can say that the Religious world in this quarter, are daily congratulating each other, on what they call, your happy change of Religious belief.

On this subject, dear sir, I beg leave to say one word. I have been requested by their possessors & others to look at these letters spoken of, but from my great regard for you, have declined doing so, unless

I should receive your approbation which I shall not ask for. But I beg leave to say, dear sir, that inasmuch as the respectable gentlemen to whom you have written, believe that your letters justify & authorize them to promulgate what has been mentioned, can I ask from you on the subject of Religion precisely that which you believe for the purpose of introducing it in your life, not for the world, however, in the way of quotation, but in general terms. I know well, that if the change in your Religious faith, as spoken of by these gentlemen, is mentioned in the Repository, it will give a tone & currency to the book, in a certain quarter, and in the Religious world, that will produce great & lasting benefit to me. Still I shall do nothing on this subject 'till I hear from you, for, as you possess great confidence in me, & as I hold you in the highest esteem, I am determined never to do any thing, that shall incur your displeasure. I will have justice done to your life.—

Have the goodness to give the enclosed to Col° Randolph, & be pleased to send the other letter to Col° Coles. I know not his direction, & therefore beg you to forward it.

Hoping to receive a letter from you in reply, as soon as you can conveniently give it, I remain

with the most perfect respect & esteem D[r] sir your obed[t] ser[vt]

JOSEPH DELAPLAINE

P.S. I beg you to inform me, how far your knowledge of the different languages extends—of Musick—of Mathematics & other branches of science.—If you feel any delicacy in giving this, pray do not do it.—

RC (DLC); beneath signature: "(Over)," with postscript on verso of address leaf; addressed: "Thomas Jefferson Eqr Monticello V[a]"; endorsed by TJ as received 11 Dec. 1816 and so recorded in SJL. Enclosures not found.

For *Delaplaine's Repository*, Charles Caldwell was THE BIOGRAPHER (*Autobiography of Charles Caldwell, M.D.* [1855], 274). The GENTLEMAN IN ANOTHER QUARTER was most likely George Logan or Robert Patterson. The WORK WHICH WILL BE PUBLISHED IN 2 OR 3 WEEKS, James Wilkinson's *Memoirs of My Own Times*, 4 vols. (Philadelphia, 1816), did not mention TJ's religious beliefs.

From John Melish

DEAR SIR, Philadelphia 23 nov 1816

I have the pleasure of presenting You with a Copy of my new map and Description of the United States and Contiguous Countries, which I respectfully Submit to Your attention. As it is the first map that professes to give a display of all that is known of Louisiana, in Connection with the United States, it will probably be gratifying to

You who Contributed so much towards procuring that very interesting region for the use of the inhabitants of these States. When I first laid the materials together, so as to form a picture of that Country, I was delighted with its appearance, and have often reflected with pleasure in the anticipation of its giving similar sensations to you.—

You will observe that I have given a view of the present State of the Geography of the Country at the close of the Statistical Account of the United States; and being very desirous of engaging the respective State Governments in the business of promulgating[1] it, I have printed a number of Setts of the Geographical Intelligence Separately, and intend to transmit one, with a Circular letter, to the Governor of each State. I have enclosed you a Copy of each of these papers. You will observe that the Legislature of this State passed an Act on the Subject. The Governor of new Jersey writes me that a Committee are appointed to Consider of the best mode of Constructing a map of New Jersey. I have written to the Governor of Virginia by this post. I shall forthwith address the Governors of the other States, so as the subject may Come before the respective Legislatures the ensuing Sessions, and am in hopes that each State will eventually have its own map, supported & kept Correct at the Public expence; and thus pave the way for the execution of a Splendid National map or Atlas.

It will give me pleasure to have your opinion of the present work, and with best wishes for Your happiness, I have the honour to be—very respectfully

Your friend JOHN MELISH

RC (DLC); addressed: "Thos Jefferson Esq Monticello"; franked; postmarked Philadelphia, 23 Nov.; endorsed by TJ as received 11 Dec. 1816 and so recorded in SJL. Enclosures: (1) Melish, *Map of the United States with the contiguous British & Spanish Possessions* (Philadelphia, 1816). (2) Melish, *A Geographical Description of the United States, with the contiguous British and Spanish Possessions* (Philadelphia, 1816; Poor, *Jefferson's Library*, 7 [no. 355]). (3) Melish, *Geographical Intelligence* ([Philadelphia, 1816]; Poor, *Jefferson's Library*, 6 [no. 223]; TJ's copy in DLC: Rare Book and Special Collections). (4) printed circular (TJ's copy in DLC: Rare Book and Special Collections; filed with preceding enclosure; at head of text in Melish's hand [trimmed]: "Copy Circular Sent to the Gov[ernors o]f each State"); which indicates that the former publication contains lists of both his published and proposed geographical works, "an account of the present situation of the State Maps" and "an opinion as to what these maps should be," general reflections on the geography of the United States, and information about a forthcoming map of Pennsylvania; stresses the importance of local surveys; asks that public support for such surveys be considered by state legislatures; and concludes with a note in Melish's hand presumably intended for TJ: "In the respective letters Sent a few remarks are added applicable to the respective States. The great object in view is to impress the idea—that—1 Each State should have its own map 2^{d} That it Should be always kept Correct 3 That all the States should Concur in one plan."

The LEGISLATURE OF THIS STATE passed "An Act directing the formation of a Map of Pennsylvania" the preceding winter, and Governor Simon Snyder signed it into law on 19 Mar. 1816 (*Acts of the General Assembly of the Commonwealth of Pennsylvania* [1815–16 sess.], 185–8; Melish, *Geographical Description*, 176–8). The GOVERNOR OF NEW JERSEY at this time was Mahlon Dickerson, while the GOVERNOR OF VIRGINIA was Wilson Cary Nicholas.

[1]Melish here canceled "the Geography."

From Horatio G. Spafford

RESPECTED FRIEND— Albany, 11 Mo. 23, 1816.

After a long delay, occasioned by adverse events, I Send thee, by this day's mail, another No. of the American Magazine. The Essay, partially read by thee, concerning the establishing a New School at Washington, & new modeling the Patent system of the United States, is in type, & will be published in a few days. I am in hopes this Paper will engage the attention of the Administration.

In 3 or 4 weeks, I shall publish an Essay on the errors of philosophical Science, embracing Some novel opinions of my own. This Paper, I have ventured to Dedicate to thyself, Dr Mitchill, & Count Volney, with whom I have the pleasure of a Correspondence.

I have frequently been solicited to publish Some extracts from thy Letter to me, of March 17, 1814: & to gratify many of my friends, I now very respectfully Solicit permission to do So. The Letter is the one acknowledging the receipt of my Gazetteer, & I wish to extract that part relating to the pernicious influence of our professional crafts, including the Lawyers, the Clergy, & the Merchants.

Some Gentlemen in Virginia, have recently applied to me to know on what terms I would undertake to write a Gazetteer of that State, & I hesitate about my answer. I am poor—&, if I execute such a Work, must do it for others, who have capital to employ in this way. I know, perfectly, the liberal character of Virginia & Virginians, & I Should be particularly well pleased with Such an undertaking, if I could make it Subservient to my own interest. Were I to write a Gazetteer of Virginia, I must spend as much as one year, travelling through that State: and it would take nearly another year to arrange my materials, & prepare the Copy for the press. Pray, my venerated Friend, would Such a Work be likely to be well patronised? My Gazetteer of New York, is nearly out of print, though I published an edition of 6250 copies. It has sold well; & had I not lost So much by Booksellers, I should[1] have been well paid for my labor. Thy opinion, in this matter, would be of Such value to me, that I venture to use the freedom of asking it.

If I could prevail on the President, to give me Some office, at Washington, I could the better Succeed in this object. The Patent Office, regulated as I have proposed, in the Essay, mentioned above, would be, of all others the most agreeable; but I would accept of any that I might be thought to merit Thy goodness will pardon this liberty, wrung from me by events & fears & hopes. If thou couldest aid me in buoying up my hopes, 'twould Serve a noble purpose: for, truly, I am almost disheartened. Very respectfully, thy friend,

H. G. SPAFFORD.

P.S. In a few days, I shall ask thy acceptance of an Anonymous Work of mine—a Novel;—designed as a vehicle for certain sentiments & opinions, that I could nowhere else introduce.

RC (MHi); postscript added separately at foot of text; endorsed by TJ as received 11 Dec. 1816 and so recorded in SJL. RC (MHi); address cover only; with PoC of TJ to Francis W. Gilmer, 17 Dec. 1816, on verso; addressed: "Thomas Jefferson, LL.D. Monticello, Va."; stamp canceled; franked; postmarked Albany, 24 Nov.

Spafford forwarded BY THIS DAY'S MAIL a copy of the *American Magazine, a monthly miscellany*, vol. 1, no. 7 (Dec. 1815). His ESSAY ON THE ERRORS OF PHILOSOPHICAL SCIENCE, "Thoughts, on Philosophical Science, on Creation, and the order and constitution of Nature," appeared under the pseudonym "Franklin" in the *American Magazine*, vol. 1, nos. 11–2 (Apr.–May 1816): 388–401, 411–21. The NOVEL, by "Maria-Ann Burlingham" [Spafford], was *The Mother-In-Law: or Memoirs of Madam de Morville* (Boston, 1817).

[1] Spafford here canceled "now."

To Elizabeth Trist

DEAR MADAM Poplar Forest Nov. 23. 16.

Your favor of Oct. 10. travelled to Monticello, thence to Richmond, thence to Lynchburg, and came to me here on the same day with one of the same date from Genl Clarke at St Louis. this must apologise for a late answer, as it's finding me in the act of packing up for my return must for a short one. as far as I am acquainted with the colleges and academies of the US. and I will say more especially of Princeton, which you name I have found their method of instruction very superficial & imperfect, carrying their pupils over the ground like racehorses, to please their parents and draw custom to their school. this was never the character of W^{m} & Mary while I knew it, nor do I suppose it so now. whatever they learned, they learned thoroughly, and the principles in which it was founded. for the languages therefore, for Mathematics and Natural philosophy I prefer it to any college I know, except that of Philadelphia; and for boys to that also, because that is a great city while Williamsburg is but an academical village. in the months of Aug. Sep. & Oct. it is liable to bilious fever, but these are exactly the months of vacation, when the students can be withdrawn to places free from that objection. after the first frost in October, Williamsburg has been found to be a very healthy situation. —we heard from Monticello a few days ago. all were well. Ellen and Cornelia are with me here, where we have been a month. we are all packing for an early departure tomorrow morning. they join me in affectionate and respectful souvenirs to yourself, mr & mrs Gilmer and many wishes for your health and happiness.

TH: JEFFERSON

PoC (MHi); on verso of reused address cover of Gilbert J. Hunt to TJ, 12 Oct. 1816; at foot of text: "Mrs Trist"; endorsed by TJ.

Trist later stated that TJ held the College of New Jersey (later PRINCETON University) "in great contempt as being the most licentious and unruly seminary on the continant" (Trist to Catharine Wistar Bache, 12 Sept. 1817 [RC in PPAmP: Bache Papers]). The school at PHILADELPHIA was the University of Pennsylvania. ELLEN AND CORNELIA were TJ's granddaughters Ellen W. Randolph (Coolidge) and Cornelia J. Randolph. SOUVENIRS: "regards; remembrances."

To DeWitt Clinton

DEAR SIR Nov. 24. 16.

I thank you for the copy of your discourse which you have been so kind as to send me, and have read with pleasure the luminous view you have presented of the value of the Fine arts in human society. the example of Athens which you adduce, is certainly a weighty one, shewing the splendor to which they raised so small a territory & within so short a period of time. I rejoice to see the spirit of science manifesting itself so strongly in the city of New York. it is worthy the station she holds among us to distinguish among the fruits of commerce and wealth, the luxuries of science as well as of the sensualities.

The papers recently announce to us the death of my old acquaintance Gouverneur Morris. genius has lost in him one of it's distinguished subjects. it is a consolation to understand that he leaves his family in affluent circumstances. I salute you with great esteem and respect.

TH: JEFFERSON

RC (NNC: Clinton Papers); addressed: "De Witt Clinton esq. New York"; franked; postmarked Lynchburg, 27 Nov.; endorsed by Clinton. PoC (DLC); on verso of a reused address cover to David Bailie Warden, postmarked Le Havre, 11 July 1816; endorsed by TJ.

A letter from Clinton to TJ of 31 Oct. 1816, not found, is recorded in SJL as received from New York at Poplar Forest on 21 Nov. 1816. It apparently enclosed a COPY of *A Discourse, delivered before the American Academy of the Arts, by the Honourable De Witt Clinton, LL. D. (President.) 23d October, 1816* (New York, 1816; Poor, *Jefferson's Library*, 6 [no. 223]; TJ's copy in DLC).

To George Logan

DEAR SIR Poplar Forest Nov. 24. 16.

I recieve your favor of Nov. 1. here, as I am about setting out on my return to Monticello for the winter. the specimen of flax from Sr John Sinclair is exquisite. we have learned from the newspapers that a new method of preparing flax has been discovered in England. I presume this is an example. about 25. years ago Sr John Sinclair sent me a specimen of Virginia wool which he had picked up accidentally, and had finely prepared, to shew that we have among us native sheep with wool equal to the Merino. now & then in a flock we find such wool; but have never made the selection of the breed an object, because, in our houshold manufactures, (& we have no other) we make only coarse woollen clothing for our laborers. for the same reason we are retiring from the Merinos, for whose wool we have neither use nor market. even our houshold cotton manufactures which are innate and nearly coeval with the state, are laboring under a difficulty. originally, and till within 30. years, we raised our own cotton. about that time our emigrants to Georgia & the upper part of S. Carolina carried the culture there, and could raise it there so much easier, that we nearly gave up the culture, and procured our supplies from them thro' our merchants. these last finding our houshold manufactures shorten their sales of what is imported, have suddenly ceased to import the cotton wool of the South, and we are suddenly without a pound, and forced to go to the stores for imported substitutes. this trick will succeed for one year. & with the high price of the article is putting us on a resumption of the culture.—the account you send me of the Mangel-wurzell would encourage one to undertake it, even if it requires the culture of the spade. this plant was all the rage while I was in France; but soon went out of vogue, I know not why.—I think Sr John Sinclair's plough appears too bluff in front, and too close pinched at the side. I apprehend it would cause much resistance in the draught, and does not expand itself enough to turn the furrow over compleatly. I have had a plough ready for mr Peale upwards of a year, which the difficulty of forwarding has still retained, but I will find means shortly. it is a light 2. horsed plough, for a furrow 6.I. deep & 9.I. wide, & on the principle of the least resistance possible. I think it will be liked, and may be enlarged or diminished, still preserving it's principle. I tender friendly and respectful souvenirs to mrs Logan & yourself.

TH: JEFFERSON

PoC (DLC); on portion of reused address cover of Charles Pinckney to TJ, [by 21] Aug. 1816; at foot of first page: "Doct[r] Logan"; endorsed by TJ.

American newspapers had reported thus on a new English METHOD OF PREPARING FLAX: "Mr. [James] Lee, an English gentleman, has lately obtained a patent for machinery on a new construction, which prepares flax and hemp, in a few hours, for all the purposes of manufacture, without the tedious and disagreeable process of watering and grassing, as is the present practice. By this plan, the quantity of dressed flax is increased, the quality improved, and the seed saved" (Philadelphia *Weekly Aurora*, 13 Sept. 1815).

SOUVENIRS: "regards; remembrances."

To Francis Adrian Van der Kemp

DEAR SIR Poplar Forest near Lynchburg Nov. 24. 16.

I recieve your favor of Nov. 1. at this place at which I make occasionally a temporary residence; and I have perused with great satisfaction the magnificent skeleton you inclose me of what would indeed be a compleat Encyclopedia of Christian philosophy. it's execution would require a Newton in physics a Locke in metaphysics, and one who to a possession of all history, adds a judgment and candor to estimate it's evidence and credibility in proportion to the character of the facts it presents[1] and he should have a long life before him. I fear we shall not see this canvas filled in our day, and that we must be contented to have all this light blaze upon us when the curtain shall be removed which limits our mortal sight. I had however persuaded myself to hope that we should have from your own pen, one branch of this great work, the mortal biography of Jesus. this candidly and rationally written, without any regard to sectarian dogmas, would reconcile to his character a weighty multitude who do not properly estimate it; and would lay the foundation of a[2] genuine christianity.

You ask if I have ever published any thing but the Notes on Virginia? nothing but official State papers, except a pamphlet at the commencement of our difference with England & on that subject, and another at the close of the revolution proposing the introduction of our decimal money, of neither of which do I possess a copy.—should a curiosity to see our part of the union tempt your friend D[r] Willoughby to come as far as Monticello, I shall be very happy to recieve him there and to shew my respect for his worth as well as for your recommendation of it. Accept the assurance of my great esteem and consideration.

TH: JEFFERSON

RC (NBuHi: Van der Kemp Papers); addressed: "Mr Fr. Adr. Vanderkemp at Oldenbarneveld State of New-York"; franked; postmarked (faint) Lynchburg, 2[7] Nov.; with notes in Van der Kemp's hand relating to his letter to TJ of 2 Feb. 1817: "Porter le ruban gris-de-lin Voy. du Chev. de Parny. P. 146 & 153. Epicurean dress. La grappe de raisin Couronné de myrthe— Constit. of the Un. Neth:." PoC (DLC); on verso of reused address cover of Martha Jefferson Randolph to TJ, 20 Nov. 1816; mutilated at seal, with missing text rewritten by TJ; endorsed by TJ.

TJ's earlier PAMPHLET was *A Summary View of the Rights of British America* (Williamsburg, [1774]; Sowerby, no. 3085; *PTJ*, 1:121–37), while his work calling for the introduction of DECIMAL MONEY was entitled *Notes on the Establishment of a Money Unit, and of a Coinage for the United States* ([Paris, 1785]; Sowerby, no. 3755; *PTJ*, 7:175–88).

[1] Remainder of sentence interlined, with superfluous terminal punctuation editorially omitted.

[2] Word interlined.

From Charles Yancey

DR SIR. Richmond 24th Novr 1816

I have always conceived it my duty when in the legislature, to give You all the information I could & Should have written to You, before now, but Seeing Stenographers Admited within the Bar of our house I thought it useless as You Could be More fully informed by the papers. I expect from the present temper of our house, Some more Banks, to the west, will be Chartered. we have upwards of 100 New Members, in the Lower house This Session. enclosed is a Statement, Showing the Situation of the banks here &c that you May have happy days in Your well earned retirement is the Sincere wish of Your friend & mo ob Servant CHARLES YANCEY

RC (DLC); endorsed by TJ as received 11 Dec. 1816 and so recorded in SJL. RC (DLC); address cover only; with PoC of TJ to Joseph Dougherty, 13 Dec. 1816, on verso; addressed: "Thos Jefferson Esqr Monticello"; franked; postmarked Richmond, 28 Nov. Enclosure: *Statements concerning the Bank of Virginia and Farmers' Bank of Virginia, November, 1816*, which lists their assets and liabilities, both in general terms and broken down by branch bank, with the Bank of Virginia possessing just over $5 million of the former on 8 Nov. 1816 and the Farmers' Bank of Virginia having in excess of $4.7 million three days later (printed circular in DLC: TJ Papers, 208:37178; partially dated; at head of text: "Printed by Order of the House of Delegates").

To John Adams

Poplar Forest. Nov. 25. 16.

I recieve here, dear Sir, your favor of the 4th just as I am preparing my return to Monticello for winter quarters; and I hasten to answer to some of your enquiries. the Tracy I mentioned to you is the one connected by marriage with La Fayette's family. the mail which brought your letter brought one also from him. he writes me that he is become blind & so infirm that he is no longer able to compose any thing. so that we are to consider his works as now[1] closed. they are 3. vols of Ideology. 1 on political economy. 1. on Ethics, and 1. containing his Commentary on Montesquieu, and a little tract on education. altho' his Commentary explains his principles of government, he had intended to have substituted for it an elementary and regular treatise on the subject: but he is prevented by his infirmities. his Analyse de Dupuys he does not avow.

My books are all arrived, some at New York, some at Boston; and I am glad to hear that those for Harvard are safe also; and the Uranologia you mention, without telling me what it is. it is something good, I am sure, from the name connected with it, and if you would add to it your Fable of the bees, we should recieve valuable instruction as to the Uranologia both of the father & son; more valuable than the Chinese will from our bible-societies. these Incendiaries, finding that the days of fire and faggot are over in the Atlantic hemisphere, are now preparing to put the torch to the Asiatic regions. what would they say were the Pope to send annually to this country colonies of Jesuit priests with cargoes of their Missal and translations of their Vulgate, to be put gratis into the hands of every one who would accept them? and to act thus nationally on us as a nation?

I proceed to the letter you were so good as to inclose to me. it is an able letter, speaks volumes in few words, presents a profound view of awful truths, and lets us see truths more awful, which are still to follow. George the III[d] then, and his minister Pitt, and successors, have spent the fee-simple of the kingdom, under pretence of governing it. their sinecures, salaries, pensions, priests, prelates, princes and eternal wars have mortgaged to it's full value the last foot of their soil. they are reduced to the dilemma of a bankrupt spendthrift who, having run thro' his whole fortune, now asks himself what he is to do? it is in vain he dismisses his coaches and horses, his grooms, liveries, cooks and butlers. this done, he still finds he has nothing to eat. what was his property, is now that of his creditors. if still in his hands, it is only as their trustee. to them it belongs, & to them every farthing of it's profits must go. the reformation of extravagancies comes too late. all is gone. nothing left for retrenchment or frugality to go on. the debts of England however, being due from the whole nation, to one half of it, being as much the debt of the creditor as debtor, if it could be referred to a court of Equity, principles might be devised to adjust it peaceably. dismiss their parasites, ship off their paupers to this country, let the landholders give half their lands to the moneylenders,

& these last relinquish one half of their debts. they would still have a fertile island, a sound and effective population to labor it, and would hold that station among political powers, to which their natural resources and faculties entitle them. they would no longer indeed be the lords of the ocean, and paymasters of all the princes of the earth. they would no longer enjoy the luxuries of pyrating and plundering every thing by sea, and of bribing and corrupting every thing by land; but they might enjoy the more safe and lasting luxury of living on terms of equality, justice and good neighborhood with all nations. As it is, their first efforts will probably be to quiet things awhile by the palliatives of reformation; to nibble a little at pensions and sinecures; to bite off a bit here, and a bit there to amuse the people; and to keep the government agoing by encroachments on the interest of the public debt, 1. percent of which, for instance, witheld, gives them a spare revenue of 10 millions for present subsistence, and spunges in fact 200. millions of the debt. this remedy they may endeavor to administer in broken doses of a small pill at a time. the first may not occasion more than a strong Nausea in the moneylenders; but the 2^d^ will probably produce a revulsion of the stomach, borborisms, and spasmodic calls for fair settlement and compromise. but it is not in the character of man to come to any peaceable compromise of such a state of things. the princes & priests will hold to the flesh-pots, the empty bellies will seize on them, & these being the multitude, the issue is obvious, civil war, massacre, exile as in France, until the stage is cleared of every thing but the multitude, and the lands get into their hands by such processes as the revolution will engender. they will then want peace and a government, and what will it be? certainly not a renewal of that which has already ruined them. their habits of law & order, their ideas almost innate of the vital[2] elements of free government, of trial by jury, habeas corpus, freedom of the press, freedom of opinion, and representative government, make them, I think, capable of bearing a considerable portion of liberty. they will probably turn their eyes to us, and be disposed to tread in our footsteps, seeing how safely these have led us into port. there is no part of our model to which they seem unequal, unless perhaps the elective presidency; and even that might possibly be rescued from the tumult of elections, by subdividing the electoral assemblages, into very small parts, such as of wards or townships, and making them simultaneous. but you know them so much better than I do, that it is presumption to offer my conjectures to you.

While it is much our interest to see this power reduced from it's towering & borrowed height, to within the limits of it's natural resources, it is by no means our interest that she should be brought below that, or lose her competent place among the nations of Europe.

the present exhausted state of the continent will, I hope, permit them to go through their struggle without foreign interference, and to settle their new government according to their own will. I think it will be friendly to us, as the nation itself would be were it not artfully wrought up by the hatred their government bears us. and were they once under a government which should treat us with justice & equality I should myself feel with great strength the ties which bind us together, of origin, language, laws and manners: and I am persuaded the two people would become in future, as it was with the antient Greeks, among whom it was reproachful for Greek to be found fighting against Greek in a foreign army. the individuals of the nation I have ever honored and esteemed, the basis of their character being essentially worthy: but I consider their government as the most flagitious which has existed since the days of Philip of Macedon, whom they make their model. it is not only founded in corruption itself, but insinuates the same poison into the bowels of every other, corrupts it's councils, nourishes factions, stirs up revolutions, and places it's own happiness in fomenting commotions and civil wars among others, thus rendering itself truly the hostis humani generis. the effect[3] is now coming home to itself. it's first operation will fall on the individuals who have been[4] the chief instruments in it's corruptions, and will eradicate the families which have, from generation to generation been fattening on the blood of their brethren: and this scoria once thrown off, I am in hopes a purer nation will result, and a purer government be instituted, one which, instead of endeavoring to make us their natural enemies, will see in us, what we really are, their natural friends and brethren, and more interested in a fraternal connection with them than with any other nation on earth. I look therefore to their revolution with great interest. I wish it to be as moderate & bloodless, as will effect the desired object of an honest government, one which will permit the world to live in peace, and under the bonds of friendship and good neighborhood.

In this tremendous tempest, the distinctions of whig & tory will disappear like chaff on a troubled ocean. indeed they have been disappearing from the day Hume first began to publish his history. this single book has done more to sap the free principles of the English[5] constitution than the largest standing army of which their patriots have been so jealous. it is like the portraits of our countryman Wright, whose eye was so unhappy as to sieze all the ugly features of his subject, and to present them faithfully; while it was entirely insensible to every lineament of beauty. so Hume has consecrated, in his fascinating style, all the arbitrary proceedings of the English kings, as true[6] evidences of the constitution, and glided over it's whig principles as the unfounded pretensions of factious demagogues. he even boasts, in his life written by himself, that of the numerous alterations suggested by the readers of his work, he had never adopted one proposed by a whig.

But what, in this same tempest, will become of their colonies & their fleets? will the former assume independance, and the latter resort to pyracy for subsistence, taking possession of some island as a point d'appui? a pursuit of these would add too much to the speculations on the situation and prospects of England, into which I have been led by the pithy text of the letter you so kindly sent me, and which I now return. it is worthy the pen of Tacitus. I add therefore only my affectionate and respectful souvenirs to mrs Adams and yourself.

TH: JEFFERSON

RC (MHi: Adams Papers); edge chipped and torn at seal, with missing text supplied from PoC; addressed: "John Adams late President of the US: Quincy. Mass."; franked; postmarked Lynchburg, 4 Dec.; endorsement by Adams reads, in part, "Ans. Decr 15 [16] 1816." PoC (DLC). Enclosure not found.

Destutt de Tracy's work ON ETHICS was *Principes Logiques, ou Recueil de Faits relatifs a l'Intelligence Humaine* (Paris, 1817; Poor, *Jefferson's Library*, 8 [no. 455]).

The book on URANOLOGIA was Johann Elert Bode, *Uranographia sive Astrorum Descriptio* (Berlin, 1801). The NAME CONNECTED WITH IT was John Quincy Adams. Borborygms (BORBORISMS) are "rumblings in the bowels" (*OED*). HOSTIS HUMANI GENERIS: "enemy of the human race" (*Black's Law Dictionary*).

David Hume FIRST BEGAN TO PUBLISH HIS HISTORY of the British Isles in 1754. He BOASTS in his autobiography that "though I had been taught by experience, that the Whig party were in possession of bestowing all places, both in the state and in literature, I was so little inclined to yield to their senseless clamour, that in above a hundred alterations, which farther study, reading, or reflection engaged me to make in the reigns of the two first Stuarts, I have made all of them invariably to the Tory side" (*The Life of David Hume, Esq. written by himself* [London, 1777], 22–3).

SOUVENIRS: "regards; remembrances."

[1] Word interlined.

[2] TJ here canceled "principles."

[3] Word interlined in place of "principle."

[4] TJ here canceled "practising."

[5] TJ here canceled "government."

[6] Word interlined in place of "the."

From Joseph Dougherty

SIR Washington City Nov. 25th 1816

While in Washington you received excellent cider from virginia—from Whom—or, from what part of the State I do not now recollect.

as I am in the habit of bottling, and Selling the best of liquors—it would be an advantage to me to have such as you formerly had while President of the U.S.

You will sir (in addition to numberless other favours) much oblige me by giving me the names, and residence of those who furnished you with good cider.

I hope the family are all well—It will give me infinite pleasure[1] to know that they are.[2]

I wish to know if Mrs Randolph rec^d^ two pieces of music which I sent by Mrs Madison last Spring.

Your Hble. Servt JO^S^ DOUGHERTY

RC (DLC); endorsed by TJ as received 11 Dec. 1816 and so recorded in SJL. RC (MHi); address cover only; with PoC of TJ to Thomas H. Palmer, 16 Dec. 1816, on verso; addressed: "Thos Jefferson Esqr Late President of the U.S. Monticello va."; franked; postmarked Washington City, 26 Nov.

[1] Manuscript: "plasure."
[2] Manuscript: "ar."

George Flower's Account of a Visit to Poplar Forest and Natural Bridge

Monday 24 [25 Nov. 1816]
Took a parting glass of Toddy with my travelling companions and rode to Poplar Forest Mr Jefferson was at home and two Miss Randolphs his grand'^trs^

Tuesday 25— [26 Nov. 1816]
A Quiet day of rest: spent in leisurely[1] conversations with m^r^ J & the Ladies.— If the inhabitants had not spoken English I should have imagined myself in a french house[2] I have often had occasion to remark, in houses of the higher classes in America, that the arrangment is more of french than English

Wednesday 26 [27 Nov. 1816]
Left Poplar Forest about Noon and assisted by the direction of Mr J. I went as far as Douglasses at[3] the foot of the Mountain on my way to the Natural Bridge

Thursday 27— [28 Nov. 1816]
Rode over a mountainous road for 20 Miles—to Rock Bridge.[4]—This Singular piece of natural architecture is composed of limestone. It is an arch of Stone over a chasm in the mountains of immense height.[5] A Stream of water flows[6] below. The sensacions when standing on the arch are fearful—on approaching the side to look down apprehension increases and it seems impossible to avoid seizing hold

upon the nearest[7] tree or Stone to prevent the magical power of the giddy height[8] from precipitating us to the bottom.—
Viewing it from below, all painful sensacions of fear vanish and we are reveled in admiration at the sight of an earthly arch set in the heavens. This singular Scene—produces sensations as singular as itself.[9]
During the War a manufactory of shot was carried on here. Returnd to James River ferry to Sleep.[10]
a particular description of this Natural Bridge is to be found in m[r] Jeffersons Notes on Virginia—[11]

MS (ICHi: Flower Diary, vol. 3); in Flower's hand; partially and incorrectly dated. MS (ICHi: Flower Diary, vol. 2); in Flower's hand; partially and incorrectly dated.

In a manuscript he compiled in or before 1860, Flower wrote of his visit to the ex-president's home in Bedford County: "I found M[r] Jefferson at his 'Poplar Forest' estate, in the western part of the state of Virginia. His house was built after the fashion of a French Chateau. Octagon rooms, floors of polished oak, lofty ceilings, large Mirrors, betokened his French taste, acquired by his long residence in France. M[r] Jefferson's figure was rather majestic; tall, (over six feet) thin, and rather high-shouldered—Manners simple, kind, and courteous. His dress in colour and form was quaint and old fashioned, plain and neat—a dark pepper-and-salt coat cut in the old quaker fashion, with a single row of large metal buttons, Knee-breeches, gray worsted stockings, shoes fastned by large metal buckles—such was the appearance of Jefferson when I first made his acquaintance, in 1816. His two Granddaughters—Miss Randolphs—well-educated and accomplished young ladies, were staying with him at the time" (MS in an unindentified hand, with corrections and emendations by Flower, in ICHi: Flower Family Papers; printed in Flower, *History of the English Settlement in Edwards County Illinois, Founded in 1817 and 1818, by Morris Birkbeck and George Flower* [1882], 43, with introductory material on p. 7).

The TWO MISS RANDOLPHS who accompanied TJ to Poplar Forest were Cornelia J. Randolph and Ellen W. Randolph (Coolidge). For TJ's DESCRIPTION OF THIS NATURAL BRIDGE in his *Notes on the State of Virginia*, see Peden, *Notes*, 24–5.

[1] Word not in vol. 2 MS.

[2] Remainder of entry not in vol. 2 MS.

[3] In vol. 2 MS, "to" is substituted for preceding five words.

[4] Sentence not in vol. 2 MS.

[5] Vol. 3 MS: "heigth." Vol. 2 MS omits preceding two words and begins next sentence with "Trees grow upon the top, and."

[6] Vol. 2 MS: "runs rapidly."

[7] Remainder of paragraph in vol. 2 MS reads "object; Tho' grasping it with all the force that a fearful apprehension will bestow it seems scarcely sufficient to prevent the magical influence of fear from precipitating one to the bottom."

[8] Vol. 3 MS: "heigth."

[9] Sentence not in vol. 2 MS.

[10] Sentence in vol. 2 MS reads "Pass'd the night at Green Lees ferry."

[11] Sentence not in vol. 2 MS.

From William Plumer

SIR Concord (NH.) Nov[r] 25. 1816

Permit me to congratulate you on the success of the Republicans in this State in the choice of Electors & Representatives to Congress; and of the prospect of great unanimity in the approaching interesting presidential election.

I avail myself of this opportunity of presenting you with a copy of my speech to the legislature at the opening of their present session.

I have the honor to be with much respect and esteem, Sir, your most obedient humble servant WILLIAM PLUMER

RC (MHi); at foot of text: "Hon. Thomas Jefferson Monticello V[a]"; endorsed by TJ as received 11 Dec. 1816 and so recorded in SJL. Enclosure: Plumer's gubernatorial speech to the New Hampshire legislature, 20 Nov. 1816, congratulating that body "on the peace and security of our country, the improved and flourishing state of our national finances, and the increasing confidence of the people in our general government" (p. 7); requesting additional funding for the construction of the new statehouse in Concord; describing his efforts to obtain money, arms, and equipment owed to the state from the federal government because of its participation in the War of 1812; remarking that he had made his recess judicial appointments on the basis of talent, not party spirit; expressing dismay at and offering ways to overcome resistance to reform by some of the trustees of Dartmouth College; reporting on the precarious condition of the state's finances; complaining that the fees collected by various state officers are often too high or unequally distributed; positing that taxes "should be appropriated solely to useful, necessary, public purposes" and that "We ought studiously to avoid extreme parsimony on the one hand, and extravagance on the other"; and declaring that restraining the propensity of the few to live at the expense of the many is one of the duties "of a free and enlightened legislature" (p. 22) (*Journal of the Honorable Senate, of the State of New-Hampshire, at their session, begun ... on the Third Wednesday of November, Anno Domini, 1816* [Concord, 1817], 7–23; also published in Amherst, N.H., *Farmers' Cabinet*, 23 Nov. 1816, and elsewhere).

At the recent election in New Hampshire, the REPUBLICANS had won all of the state's congressional seats and presidential electoral votes (Concord *New-Hampshire Patriot*, 12 Nov. 1816).

From William Sampson

SIR New York 26. Nov[r] 1816

An antient colleague and fellow student of mine has, in sending me as an authors gift several Copies of his political works, made it a request that I should present one of them to you; entitled "On National Government." I have so recently received these donations that I have not had time yet to peruse them, nor should I willingly presume to forestall your better judgement upon the merit of the work which he has dedicated to you If the author had no other merit it would be enough for me that he is zealous in the Cause of my unfortunate Country, that I have known him in my former days for a Gentleman and a scholar, and that he evinces his Respect for the character of one esteemed Respected and admired by us all. I therefore pray you, Sir, to accept the volume transmitted as a token of that Respect and to Receive the assurances of my sincere veneration as its accompanyment

WILLIAM SAMPSON

RC (MHi); endorsed by TJ as received 24 Dec. 1816 and so recorded in SJL, which has the additional notation that it was delivered "by D[r] J. Bradner Stuart of N. York." Enclosure: George Ensor, *On National Government*, 2 vols. (London, 1810; Poor, *Jefferson's Library*, 10 [no. 627]).

William Sampson (1764–1836), attorney and author, was born in Londonderry and educated at Trinity College, Dublin, and later at the Inns of Court in London. In 1790 he returned to Ireland, where he established a successful legal practice, played a role in the Irish nationalist movement, and published numerous literary, political, and satirical pieces. Sampson was arrested and charged with treason in 1798. Although he was never tried, he agreed to go into exile late that year. After spending the following seven years on the continent of Europe, Sampson returned to Great Britain in 1806, but he was immediately arrested and deported, at government expense, to New York City. He quickly rose to the top of the American legal profession and published his memoirs, a copy of which he sent to TJ in 1807. In his later writings and at the bar, Sampson denounced British policy toward Ireland; advocated common-law reform, personal rights, and the codification of law in the United States; and supported the interests of his fellow Irish expatriates. He died in New York City (*ANB*; *DAB*; *ODNB*; Sampson to TJ, 12 Dec. [1807] [DLC]; Sowerby, no. 441; New York *Evening Post*, 29 Dec. 1836; Washington *Daily National Intelligencer*, 2, 7 Jan. 1837).

One of the enclosed volumes became separated from the other and may never have reached TJ. In addition, at this time or shortly thereafter, Sampson decided to send TJ a copy of Ensor's *Defects of the English Laws and Tribunals* (London, 1812). This work also apparently did not find its way to Monticello (Sampson to TJ, 30 Nov. 1816; TJ to Sampson, 30 Dec. 1816).

From Francis W. Gilmer

DEAR SIR. Winchester Nov. 27. 1816

I owe many apologies both to you and to Mr Dupont for having delayed until now the translation of the treatise of Mr. Quesnay. I have however almost ever since I received it, been engaged in the courts: having recently commenced the practice of the profession, I have found the forms of judicial proceedings require much of my attention, I have too, to make my way thro' a thick rank of counsel of well established reputation, and some of them certainly of no mediocrity of abilities. All these circumstances have conspired, together with the necessity of much exercise & recreation on account of my health, to suspend almost entirely every literary labour. Even now, I have been compelled to eke out the translation on the evenings of our Chancery court, after the morning has been devoted to the irksome details of depositions, cross bills &c. I confess to you too, I was somewhat dismayed in undertaking a work entirely new to me, under the disadvantages of reading a badly written manuscript, in a foreign language, on one of the most difficult and abstruce branches of elementary politics. If under all these discouraging circumstances I have succeeded in any tolerable degree in giving the meaning of the author, it is all to which I can aspire. To infuse into the translation the elegant precision, and nervous brevity of the original, would require much more attention (if indeed it be attainable at all in English) than I can hope to bestow on it. I have only aimed at giving the meaning as accurately as I could, without even an attempt at grace or beauty of composition.

Will you do me the favour to read over the translation at your leisure, make such alterations as the sense, or propriety of expression seem to require, and return it to me, that I may correct, & transcribe it for Mr Dupont? I should not presume to ask of you this favour, if I were not desirous of addressing the translation to you (by your permission) and should regret its being entirely unworthy the patronage of your name.

If your engagements will not allow you to spare the small portion of time necessary to this revision, I must ask that service of Mrs. Randolph's kindness: one which I hope she will not be unwilling to shew an early pupil of hers in French, and who regrets that his other pursuits, and indeed his want of critical knowledge of the language, allow him to reflect so little honor on his disinterested patroness.— accept the assurance of my admiration and esteem. F. W. Gilmer.

P.S. I do not send the French manuscript, because I am unwilling even to ask of you the trouble of comparing word with word. I only wish your correction as to the general meaning, as you retain it, from the perusal you gave the French; with any verbal inaccuracies which may strike you. There is however part of a sentence the french of which I have written with a pencil at the bottom of page 5. which I have translated (except a single expression) in the first sentence of the 3[d] paragraph of the page. I can remember no word for the French 'surprises' which satisfies the tact of my mind. Your complete mastery of both languages will no doubt enable you to render the meaning precisely.

RC (MoSHi: Gilmer Papers); at foot of text: "Thomas Jefferson esq[r]"; endorsed by TJ as received 11 Dec. 1816 and so recorded in SJL. Enclosure: Gilmer's manuscript translation, not found, of François Quesnay's short treatise on natural law (see notes to Pierre Samuel Du Pont de Nemours to TJ, 12 May 1816, and TJ to Gilmer, 17 Dec. 1816).

Defendants in lawsuits use CROSS BILLS to combat allegations made in the plaintiffs' original complaints (*Black's Law Dictionary*).

To John Patterson

DEAR SIR Poplar Forest Nov. 27. 16.

The bearer of this mr George Flower is an English gentleman farmer, on a tour thro' the US. to look for a settlement for his family and friends. he wishes to see what we consider the best course of farming as adapted to the particular circumstances of our country. on this ground I address him to yourself and mr Randolph. in return for any information you give him of that kind he will give you that of Europe generally, & of England most particularly, being well informed of the men and things of the day. he was the travelling companion of Birkbeck in his tour thro' France which you have seen, and brings me letters of recommendation from the M. de la Fayette and M. de L'Asteyrie the agricultural writer, who speak in the highest terms of his worth. assured that you will be gratified with his conversation & acquaintance I consign him to your attentions & myself to your friendship TH: JEFFERSON

RC (Harold Anthony Caccia, London, 1962); at foot of text: "John Patterson esq." PoC (MHi); on verso of reused address cover of Francis Adrian Van der Kemp to TJ, 1 Nov. 1816; torn at seal; endorsed by TJ. Recorded in SJL as sent "by mr Flower."

John Patterson (ca. 1784–1851), planter, was born in Maryland into a wealthy Baltimore family of merchants. The brother of Elizabeth Patterson Bonaparte, in 1806 he married Mary Buchanan Nicholas, the daughter of Wilson Cary Nicholas and future sister-in-law of TJ's grandson Thomas Jefferson Randolph. The couple spent the next dozen years in Albemarle County. Patterson was active in the Agricultural Society of Albemarle, 1817–18, and he subscribed $1,000 toward the establishment of Central College. By early in 1819, however, he had sold his Virginia landholdings and returned to Maryland. Patterson owned real estate worth $40,000 at the time of his death at his Atamasco estate in Baltimore County (Louise Pecquet du Bellet, *Some Prominent Virginia Families* [1907; repr. 1976], 2:317; Richmond *Virginia Argus*, 17 June 1806; Woods, *Albemarle*, 305; True, "Agricultural Society," 263, 280; Master List of Subscribers to Central College, [after 7 May 1817], document 5 in a group of documents on The Founding of the University of Virginia: Central College, 1816–1819, printed at 5 May 1817; TJ to Patterson, 31 Jan. 1819; DNA: RG 29, CS, Md., Baltimore Co., 1850; Baltimore *Sun*, 3 Jan. 1851).

To Thomas Mann Randolph

Dear Sir Poplar Forest Nov. 27. 16.

The bearer mr George Flower is an English gentleman farmer, on a tour of the US. to look for a settlement for his family and friends. he was the travelling companion of mr Birkbeck thro' France in the tour we possess, and brings me letters from M. de la Fayette and de Lasteyrie who speak in the highest terms of his worth. he is well informed of the affairs of Europe, and particularly of England, on [w]hich he will give you much information. besides examining our soil, climate and other circumstances, he wishes to become acquainted with that scale of farming which experience has proved to us best adapted to the particular circumstances of the country. for this I recommend him to your attention particularly, and assure you that in return for any information you may give him you will have a rich return from his fund. I hope to find him at Monticello, for which the rain having now ceased, we shall set out in two or three days, and be six days on the road. I salute you affectionately Th: Jefferson

RC (PHarH); mutilated at fold; addressed (hole in manuscript): "Col° Thomas M. Randolph in his absence t[o] be opened by mrs Randolph or Th: J. Randolph. Monticello by mr Flower"; endorsed by T. M. Randolph: "Thos Jefferson Dec. 1816"; with penciled note in an unidentified hand on address leaf: "Presented by N. P. Trist to David Mc-Conkey together with a lock of hair Cut fm head of Mr. Jefferson the day of his death."

To Robert Rives

Dear Sir Poplar Forest Nov. 27. 16.

The bearer mr George Flower is an English gentleman, a farmer, looking out for a position in the US. to which he may bring a family from that country. he is on his return from the Westward and I have advised him to take his course thro the rich country below the blue ridge, and add the liberty of recommending him to your attentions. he was the travelling companion of mr Birkbeck whose tour thro' France you may have seen. he is well informed of the state of Europe, and particularly of England. he brings me letters from M. de la Fayette, who speaks of his worth in the highest terms; and I think you will be gratified by the fund of information he possesses. accept the assurance of my great esteem & respect Th: Jefferson

PoC (MHi); on verso of reused address cover of John Burke to TJ, 7 Nov. 1816; at foot of text: "Robert Rives esq."; endorsed by TJ. Recorded in SJL as sent "by mr Flower."

From James B. Pleasants

Brookeville Novr 28 1816

I have been informed that the State of Virginia is about to improove the facility of intercourse between[1] its Citizens, on this subject I have spent much thought & should give the preference to roads over canals. I do not mean to dogmatise; & I know my name will give no sanction to my theory, if I do not give rational conclutions, from clear facts, I do not call for attention, the expence however of testing the experiment is trifling and I want nothing for it.

I find that many well informed persons are of opinion that double force will give double velosity through[2] the water; I find it takes four times the force to give double the velosity, if the force of one pound propel a boat two yards in ten seconds it will require four pounds to propel a Boat 4 yards in the same time and so on in the same ratio, being 120 times more force to carry a Boat $5\frac{1}{6}$ miles pr Hour, than it would have required[3] if double force produced double velocity, this loss is so important that at the rate of 200 Miles pr hour, land carriage is superior to water, through bad roads,

Under certain circumstances increas'd velosity on land requires[4] less force, as any person may know by drawing a Gigg by hand

The Boats in Holland are drawn by a Horse from Amsterdam to the Hague in $10\frac{1}{2}$ Hours, a distance of 30 miles, (being something less than 3 miles an hour), with 60 passengers, which at an average of 150 ℔ for each[5] person will make for each boatload 9000 ℔[6] so

that if	1 Horse will carry	9000 ℔	3 miles Pr Hour
	1 do	do only 2222.	6 do do
	1 do	do only 555	12 do do

But it is probable the Horse would not stand the severe exercise of troting at the rate of twelve miles pr Hour (, applying the same force as when he only traveled three), more than half an hour in forty eight, Indeed it is believd no horse, or very few, could do as much, which would require 42 Horses to perform this service, but at the rate of 3 miles pr Hour one Horse is sufficient, it therefore appears that the loss of force is great, and a rapid passage through the water unattainable but to a great disadvantage

On turnpike roads four Horses will draw 4800 ℔ 20. Miles pr day, load and unload, which in favor of Boating (say 10 to one) it is believ'd that the sum of the actual resistance overcome by a waggon at 3 miles pr Hour,[7] and the resistance that a Boat meets with at the same rate, is not materially different, I say the sum, because the turnpike not being a plain, the resistance is unequal, if there were no hills I think there would be a practical equality, however the result of our enquiries will not depend on this assumption

On a fine surface of Iron it is beyond a doubt true that a Cylinder with a good Iron surface, with 40 Tons burden, can be propeled by one horse at the rate of 2 miles p^r Hour, I think I might say 100 Tons, for a loaded Cylinder is not obstructed by friction, A Cylinder sufficiently large to carry 40 Tons would soon make a turnpike road nearly if not quite equal to an Iron surface, for so large a surface to act on

If one Horse give 2[8] miles, 4 Horses will give 8, & twelve 24 miles p^r Hour, for 40 tons, this will be equal to twenty tons, carried by 6 Horses, 24 miles p^r Hour,

A Horse cannot travel more than 6 miles Pr Hour without any Burthen, but 6 Horses can give velosity to machenery, walking at the rate of 2 miles p^r Hour, equal to 24 miles.

These observations are made on the supposition that the country is perfectly level, as this is out of the question, we must either make great allowance for unequal ground, or by other means cause the effect in another way, this effect may be nearly produced[9] by Either steam, or Horse power, if in either case, the force applied shall opperate decending, asscending, on even ground, & the velosity Gained in the descent, will be nearly sufficient to gain[10] the next assent, it will be perciev'd that the Horse traveling on the road could not give the necessary[11] velosity, his force must be applied by means of cog wheels, to give 12 times his motion, which will be 24 miles p^r Hour, for 6 Horses, with 20 Tons,

A Cylinder is a bad form to pass rapidly through the Atmostphere, it must therefor have a light inclosure suspended on its axis, to which you may give the form[12] best adapted to pass through the air, and a Wheel to direct its course,

Steam will be equally convenient for this purpose, and perhaps more so

A Horse can carry 400 ℔s on a common road, what can he carry on smooth road, firm, & level, certainly the difference must be very great, on the proposed plan the effect is the same as if there were no hills,

To carry 9000 ℔ three miles an Hour, is equal only to the carriage of 1125 ℔ 24 miles an Hour, our calculation is more than three Tons or 60 Hundred, suppose we have not the practical result, and you can only carry 1000 ℔ 24 miles per Hour, the difference of cost between canals & roads, together with the many advantages attending quick conveyance, especially for persons, will make very decidedly in favour of roads

There is however another method, or rather an improovement on this method, that would be worth trying, and I believe would be found much superior, which I can on some future occation Explain,[13]

If thou should think any thing useful to the community might be produced,[14] Thou art at liberty to use the above[15] in any way thou may think most conducive to that end JAMES B PLEASANTS

I think that turnpike Roads may be made at one half the expence they are made by any method nowe in use and much better

RC (ViW: TC-JP); composed in two sittings; dateline between signature and postscript; endorsed by TJ as received 11 Dec. 1816 and so recorded in SJL. RC (MHi); address cover only; with PoC of TJ to Thomas Mann Randolph (1792–1848), 16 Dec. 1816, on verso; addressed: "Thomas Jafferson Near Charlottsville Montecello Virginia"; franked; postmarked Baltimore, 28 Nov.

James Brooke Pleasants (ca. 1762–1847), inventor, was born and raised a Quaker in Goochland County, but he relocated to Maryland by the mid-1780s. He wrote to Benjamin Franklin on the subject of balloons in 1788 and to George Washington and TJ two years later about Englehart Cruse's patent pretensions. In 1819–20 Pleasants forwarded to James Madison his thoughts on improving the navigation of the James River. Although a Maryland resident for about sixty years, at the time of his death he owned more than 775 acres in the county of his birth. Pleasants died at his son's home near Brookeville, Montgomery County, Maryland (Lawrence Buckley Thomas, *The Thomas Book* [1896], 219, 222; William Wade Hinshaw and others, *Encyclopedia of American Quaker Genealogy* [1936–50; repr. 1969–77], 6:264; Pleasants to Franklin, 1 Oct. 1788 [PPAmP: APS Archives]; Washington, *Papers, Pres. Ser.*, 5:384–6; *PTJ*, 16:412–3, 17:320; Madison, *Papers, Retirement Ser.*, 1:445–6, 586–7; Clayton Torrence, ed., *The Edward Pleasants Valentine Papers* [1927; repr. 1979], 2:1006–7; Washington *Daily National Intelligencer*, 6 Nov. 1822, 2 Mar. 1847).

On 5 Feb. 1816 the VIRGINIA General Assembly passed "An Act to create a Fund for Internal Improvement," which was "to be applied, exclusively, to the purpose of rendering navigable, and uniting by canals, the principal rivers, and of more intimately connecting, by public highways, the different parts of this Commonwealth" (*Acts of Assembly* [1815–16 sess.], 35–9).

[1] Manuscript: "btween."
[2] Manuscript: "throagh."
[3] Manuscript: "requred."
[4] Manuscript: "requirs."
[5] Manuscript: "eact."
[6] Preceding two words interlined.
[7] Preceding nine words interlined.
[8] Reworked from "4."
[9] Manuscript: "poduced."
[10] Preceding three words interlined in place of "equal th."
[11] Manuscript: "necessasary."
[12] Manuscript: "fom."
[13] Remainder of letter written in a different ink.
[14] Manuscript: "produed."
[15] Pleasants here canceled "observations."

From Robert Turner

SIR Richmond Nov. 29th 1816

Although I have not the honour of being personally acquainted with you, I have taken the liberty of enclosing to you, a paper containing my ideas concerning the earth, which were lately published in this Town. As you have no doubt thought much on the same subject, I shall consider it a great favour, if you will examen the theory[1] in the enclosed, and honour me with your opinion of its correctness. If any reasonable objections can be suggested, I shall be as ready as any man to admit them. Perhaps it will be said that no theory of the earth, can ever be proved, but it appears to me as susceptible of being reduced to certitude, as many other theorys, which are now universally allowed to be correct.

You will please Sir, to pardon this intrusion, in one who is sincerely in search of truth.

Yours with great respect, ROBT TURNER

RC (ViHi); endorsed by TJ as received 18 Dec. 1816 and so recorded in SJL. RC (MHi); address cover only; with PoC of TJ to William Sampson, 30 Dec. 1816, on verso; addressed: "The Hon. Thos Jefferson Monticello Albermarl V,a,"; stamp canceled; franked; postmarked Richmond, 12 Dec., and Charlottesville, 18 Dec. Enclosure: "Examinator" [Turner], "Concerning the Earth," asserting that "We have daily new proofs of the Atlantic parts of the middle and southern states having been lately formed by alluvion"; revealing the discovery at Richmond of "a variety of bones, wood, marine shells, sharks' teeth, &c." and smooth pebbles deep within the earth; dismissing explanations of this phenomenon that are based on the biblical deluge; contending that "the ocean has progressively occupied all parts of our earth"; and hypothesizing that both the formation of mountains through volcanic activity and natural weathering affect the tilt of the planet over time, which causes water to flow from one part of the globe to another (undated essay in *Virginia Patriot, and Richmond Daily Mercantile Advertiser*, 16 Nov. 1816, with TJ's clipping in ViHi; extract dated Richmond, 10 Nov., printed in Boston *New-England Palladium & Commercial Advertiser*, 26 Nov. 1816, and elsewhere).

A Robert Turner between the age of twenty-six and forty-four resided in Richmond with his family and four slaves in 1820 (DNA: RG 29, CS, Richmond, 1820).

[1] Manuscript: "theoy."

From William Sampson

SIR New York Novr 30 1816

Mr Geo Ensor An old friend fellow student and Colleague of mine, whom I formerly knew for a gentleman and scholar, sent me lately in memory of our antient friendship, several works of his pen. He requested me if I thought such a gift Could be acceptable to you to forward a Copy of that entitled, "Defects of the English Law," and one of that entitled "on National Government."

In looking for some person by whom to forward them to Washington, I was introduced by a friend to Mr Lovett member of Congress from this State. As I since learned that Gentleman is not of the same political opinions with me nor with the author I feared I had been possibly freer than was wellcome, but it was too late to retract or apologize as he went off So Soon after I Saw him. One of the Volumes was in paper and a Sealed letter enclosed, the two others were unpacked by a mistake, through hurry, I having been all that morning engaged in business, and unable to pay due attention. I begged of M Lovett as I understood he had not the honor of being personally acquainted with you to deliver them to Some member of Congress from your District, and doubt not but he will have the politeness to do so as he was good enough to promise; but I should be very thankful to have the assurance that they Came safe to your hands. And beg leave to repeat the sentiments of respect and admiration with which I am

Sir Your most obedt Sevant William Sampson

RC (MHi); endorsed by TJ as received 11 Dec. 1816 and so recorded in SJL. RC (DLC); address cover only; with PoC of TJ to Nicolas G. Dufief, 14 Dec. 1816, and FC of TJ to Dufief, 30 Dec. 1816, on recto; addressed: "Mr Jefferson Monticello"; franked; postmarked New York, 1 Dec.

From Richard N. Thweatt

Dear Sir, Petersburg N^ov^ 30th 1816

Yours of the 22nd inst. I received only three days ago—Being abscent in the country with my family prevented my receiving it before—With respect to your box, I had previously Sent it to Richmond, addressed to the care of Mr Gibson, whom I had seen, and who informed me that he would contrive it to you if I would send it over to him[1]—I trust by this time it has reached you in Safety—I assure you it gave me great pleasure to execute this little office for you, and your anxiety with respect to the little trouble it might give me is the only circumstance I regret, as that trouble, if it could be called so, was undertaken with great pleasure and Satisfaction.—

Mrs Thweatt joins me in presenting you our most Sincere and profound[2] respect

yours & & Richard N. Thweatt

RC (MHi); at foot of text: "Thomas Jefferson Esqr"; endorsed by TJ as received 15 Dec. 1816 from "Thweate Richd N." and so recorded in SJL.

[1] Word interlined in place of "you."
[2] Manuscript: "profund."

From John D. Vaughan

HONOURED SIR Pittsburgh Pennsylvania Nov. 30th 1816.

I fear you will think me bold in thus addressing a gentleman who does not know me; and who perhaps has never seen me. But upon your benevolence and your intimacy with my father, *Doctor John Vaughan of Wilmington Delaware I rely. Sir upon this ground I am emboldened to write to you and ask a favour which if granted shall never be forgotten. I wish to enter the Navy and I solicit you Sir to speak to the Secretary thereof in my behalf. I am at present studying medicine[1] with an uncle in this place. I have just completed my fifteenth year, am very healthy and I hope I will not be a disgrace to the Navy. I presume there are no persons in this place who have any influance with Government but I have no doubt any of the Gentlemen from Delaware or †Peter Little of Baltimore would speak favourably of me. But if you| will be so kind as to speak to the Secretary of the Navy in my behalf and let me know as soon as convenient I shall ever remember you with Gratitude. Believe Honourable Sir that nothing but circumstances under which I labour, your friendship for my father, my ardent desire to enter the Navy and my high opinion of your benevolence could have prevailed upon me to have thus addressed you and ask a favour which I have no just right to expect. With the most profound sentiments of respect I subscribe[2] myself.

Your most obedient Humble Servant JOHN D. VAUGHAN

* Who died in 1807.

† A distant relation.

| Under the patronage of a gentleman of your standing I cannot fail.

RC (MHi); endorsed by TJ as received 18 Dec. 1816 and so recorded in SJL. RC (DLC); address cover only; with PoC of TJ to John Barnes, 31 Dec. 1816, on verso; addressed: "Thomas Jefferson Esqr. Late President of the United States. Montecello"; franked; postmarked Pittsburgh, 1 Dec.

John Dickinson Vaughan (1800–34), attorney, was a son of John Vaughan, a physician in Wilmington, Delaware. Receiving no military appointment, he returned by 1819 to his hometown, where he married, started a family, and helped organize and administer a local fire company. By 1827 Vaughan had moved to Wayne County, Indiana, and become a lawyer. He passed away in Richmond, Indiana, from an "Inflammation of the Brain, preceded by an attack of Asiatic Cholera" (Gilbert Cope, comp., *Genealogy of the Sharpless Family* [1887], 622–3; Philadelphia *Friends' Intelligencer*, 20 Oct. 1900; J. Thomas Scharf, *History of Delaware. 1609–1888* [1888], 1:493, 2:676; Henry Clay Fox, ed., *Memoirs of Wayne County and the City of Richmond Indiana* [1912], 1:273; *Baltimore Patriot & Mercantile Advertiser*, 5 Sept. 1834).

[1] Word interlined.
[2] Manuscript: "subscibe."

From John Barnes

DEAR SIR, George Town, 2[d] Dec[r] 1816.

from the receipt of your last fav[rs] date, 12[h] Oct[r] your proposed Absense from Monticello for six weeks, via Bedford—from the 19th my present,—would probably meet your return—I have now to detail—the several, unexpected distressing Vexsatious tryals, my feelings and patience, has experiencd: sufficiently[1] roused by the former,—and withal—to sooth the painfull and tedious sufferance—of the latter.—On the 20th Ult[o] to my very great surprize & Mortification I recd Mess[r] Baring & C[os] letter of the 16th Sep[r] Covering 1st sett of Ex: for £200 Ster[g] purchased of Mess[s] Smith & Riddle of Richmond 25th July, of which you were duly advised—with protest for Non-payment—on this extreme—unlooked Occurance and distress,—it must have Occasioned the good Gen[l]—in the deranged state of his finances.—I hesitated not a moment in Risquing my Own—in Order, if possible to Alleviate, the unavoidable painfull sensations he must have to experience[2] for a series of time—ere a suitable, remittance—of Relief could be Obtaind from you—thro me—By the following Mail, I Ventured to Write my Occasional Correspondent Mess[rs] Buckley & Abbott—of New York, not personally known to—or By—stating to them—my Extreme—Anxiety to Reinstate the good Gen[l] without loss of time—and withal pressing my Request to prepare to engage Conditionally a sett of Ex: from a safe hand for £300 Ster[g] at a short date. if to be had to be in Readiness—and that, by the following Mail—I would most Assuredly—place in their hands prompt &[3] sufficient funds for their purchase—and withal—not to transmit them here for my signature—but, to have the goodness to Address the 1[t] & 2[d] Bills under Cover of their Letter—to Mess[rs] Baring & C[o] stating it to be, at the express—desire of me,—and for the sole Use and Benefit of Gen[l] Thadd[s] Kosciusko at soleure in Switzerland.—all which, has been happily effected—as by their very friendly letter here inclosed: will I trust confirm and prove Mutually satisfactory to all the parties Concern'd—And on a Review of all circumstances, claim particular Notice. The very extraordinary[4] dispatch of the unfortunate Sett a

30 days—to & from esspecially the latter: had Only, 23 days run of it which to 100 Vessels might not again happen in seven years.—and but a few days Elapsed from the Arrival & date of my receiving the protested one to the day of Repurchase[g] the One of £300 Ster[g] direct, on its passage,—the additional £100—was added—as a soothing Cordial to the irritated Bosom of our Venerable—Valuable—suffering Friend—whose exhausted Patience must still continue on the stretch—untill the Arrival—of this last dispatch—may it be speedy—safe, and its contents duly honor'd—

at my better leisure I shall prepare and transmit to you state of these Acco[ts] and therewith the expected settlem[t] with Mess[r] Smith & Riddle—with whom I have exchanged two letters: and expect a full settlem[t]—With their friend, D[d] English Cash[r] of the Union Bank—to my intire satisfaction

with every sentim[t] of Respect and Esteem,
I am always, D[r] Sir Yr mst. Ob[t] John Barnes,

PS. I beg again to request you would be pleased to fav[r] me—with the Original Certificates of the $12.500—6 ℔Ct US. Stock in y[r] Name in Order to their being Cancell'd—and Renewd in the Name of Thad[s] Kosciusko—as well, your two powers—for me to receive the Ins[t5] on the above Stock—at the Treasury and The Dividend on the 46 Share Bank of Colum[a]—One to be deposited—in each—Departm[t]—will be required and when Recd, your Original power—(two copys of which[6] must also be deposited—as above)—I shall inclose to you together with the good Gen[ls] private letter—

RC (ViU: TJP-ER); adjacent to closing and signature: "T. Jefferson Esq[r] Monticello"; endorsed by TJ as received 11 Dec. 1816 and so recorded in SJL. Enclosure not found.

The good gen[ls] private letter was Tadeusz Kosciuszko to TJ, Apr. 1816.

[1] Manuscript: "sufficently."
[2] Manuscript: "experienc."
[3] Preceding two words interlined.
[4] Manuscript: "extra," with an expansion mark over it.
[5] Abbreviation for "Interest."
[6] Superfluous closing parenthesis editorially omitted.

From Ambrose Spencer

Sir Albany Dec[r] 2[d] 1816

This will be delivered to you by Doc[t] Stewart of this City; he has requested of me, an introduction to you & I have presumed on the small acquaintance I had the honor to form with you twelve years ago, to comply with this request.

Doc[t] Stewart is a gentleman of respectable standing & acquirements, & any acts of civility you may shew him will be thankfully & gratefully received.

I cannot close this letter without expressing to you my ardent prayer for your continued health & happiness—

with high respect & esteem Your Obd[t] serv[t] A. SPENCER

RC (MHi); endorsed by TJ as received 24 Dec. 1816 and so recorded in SJL, which has the additional notation that it was delivered "by D[r] J. Bradner Stuart of N. York." RC (ViU: TJP); address cover only; with last page of Dft of TJ's Notes on the Rent Claims of the Heirs of Bennett Henderson, [by 30 Dec. 1816], on verso; addressed: "Hon. Thomas Jefferson" by "Doc[t] Stewart."

Ambrose Spencer (1765–1848), public official and judge, was born in Salisbury, Connecticut, studied at Yale, and graduated from Harvard University in 1783. He relocated to the state of New York, read law, and was admitted to the bar five years later. Spencer served in the New York State Assembly, 1794, and the State Senate, 1796–1802. He switched from the Federalist to the Republican party in 1798 and became a political ally and, later, brother-in-law of DeWitt Clinton. A powerful force in New York politics for many years, Spencer was the state's attorney general, 1802–04, and he sat on its supreme court, 1804–23, the last four years as chief justice. Though his influence waned thereafter, he was mayor of Albany, 1824–25, a member of the United States House of Representatives, 1829–31, and the president of the Whig national convention in 1844. Spencer moved in 1839 to Lyons, New York, where he died (*ANB*; *DAB*; *PTJ*, 38:501–2; *Harvard Catalogue*, 173; Franklin B. Hough, *The New-York Civil List* [1858], 90, 116–8, 168; *Albany Gazette*, 4 Feb. 1802, 6 Feb. 1804; *Albany Argus*, 12 Feb. 1819; Washington *Daily National Intelligencer*, 2 May 1844; *New York Herald*, 15 Mar. 1848).

To Fitzwhylsonn & Potter

Poplar Forest near Lynchburg

MESS[RS] FITZWHYLSON & POTTER Dec. 3. 16

I wrote to you from Monticello about the middle of October requesting to have some books bound and to be furnished with some others. I am now about returning to that place and shall be very glad to find them there on my arrival, or to recieve them as soon as possible afterwards. I shall most pressingly have occasion immediately for the collection of Virginia laws I requested. Accept the assurance of my respect. TH: JEFFERSON

PoC (DLC); on verso of reused address cover of Peter Derieux to TJ, 27 Oct. 1816; endorsed by TJ.

To Martha Jefferson Randolph

Poplar Forest. Tuesday Dec. 3. 16.

We have been, my ever dearest Martha, now weather bound at this place since Sunday was sennight. we were then[1] to have set off on our return home, but it began to rain that day, and we have had three regular N.E. rains successively, with intermissions of a single day between each. during the first intermission, mr Flower left us for Monticello, but by the way of the Natural bridge. by him I wrote to mr Randolph that we should set out in 2. or 3. days; but the 2^d storm set in the next day, and the 3^d cleared up last night, leaving us a snow of 4. inches on the ground. we shall wait 2. or 3. days for that to go off, the roads to harden, and the waters to fall, and we shall be 6. days on the road, that is to say, 2. days to Millbrook, 2. there and 2. home; so that I suppose we shall be at Monticello about this day or to-morrow sennight, allowing in addition for any further bad weather. Johnny Hemings & co. will set off on Thursday & be at home on Sunday. it is well that during our delay we have been in comfortable quarters. our only discomfort is the not being with you. the girls have borne it wonderfully. they have been very close students, and I am never without enough to do to protect me from ennui. god bless you all.

TH: JEFFERSON

RC (NNPM); at foot of text: "Mrs Randolph"; endorsed by Randolph. PoC (MHi); on verso of reused address cover of Edwin Stark to TJ, 30 Oct. 1816; mutilated at seal; endorsed by TJ.

The skilled woodworker JOHNNY HEMINGS (Hemmings) and his two assistants were at Poplar Forest doing finishing work at the main house (*MB*, 2:1328). THE GIRLS who had accompanied TJ on his visit to Bedford County were his granddaughters Cornelia J. Randolph and Ellen W. Randolph (Coolidge).

[1] Word interlined.

From Christopher Clark

DEAR SIR Grove Decr 5 16

We are Verry much obliged by your friendly enquire of this morning Mrs Clark is I trust better: the fever we have Rebuked if not Removed her debility is yet excessive but will sincerly hope be Restord by time The baby is well and thriving

I avail myself of this occasion to express my deep Regret that the situation of the family has deprived us of the society of yourself and the young Ladies during this Visit It will not be the case we fondly hope the next time you come up our endeavours then will be exerted to make their time more agreeable Can only now bid you a Melancholy farewell

CHRIS CLARK

RC (MHi); addressed: "Thomas Jefferson esquir Poplar Forest"; endorsed by TJ as received 5 Dec. 1816 and so recorded in SJL.

THE YOUNG LADIES were TJ's granddaughters Cornelia J. Randolph and Ellen W. Randolph (Coolidge).

From Joseph Miller

HONOR[ED] FRIND Norfolk Dec[r] 6–1816—

I this day have Shiped on Board the Sch[r] Resolution Cap[t] Cole a Small Bale of Corks which I hope will Come Safe to hand I am a Fraid you will think me Neglectfull in So Long Delay but Coold not Please myselfe heare I Sent to New york for them I hope thay Will Please

I woold have been up Before now but Owing to a Scever Pain in my Ancless not Able to Walk for 8 weeks

Times heare is Very Dull all that is Dowing of Momment is Lumber to the Wes[t] Indes but in hopes the Spring will Bring Better Times—I intend Coming up as Soone as yeare Turns—I Remain in the Same way not Able to Sell Eaney Part for one halfe its Value

I Conclude with my Evere Esteme To you and all the Famuly

JOSEPH MILLER

my Respts to Old Peter

RC (DLC); endorsed by TJ as received 13 Dec. 1816 and so recorded in SJL. RC (MHi); address cover only; with PoC of TJ to John Wood, 14 Apr. 1817, on verso; addressed: "Tho[s] Jefferson E[sqr] Monticello Milton Albemarl C[ty]"; franked; postmarked Norfolk, 6 Dec.

OLD PETER: Peter Hemmings.

Calculations of Latitude of Willis's Mountain

Willis's mountain. Long. W. from Greenwich. 78°–49′–31″ observations with Borda's circle.

	Dec. 8. 1816	Dec. 9. 1816.
		° ′ ″
1816. Dec. 8. $\frac{1}{2}$ observed alt. ☉	29–49–30	29–44–30
– error of instrum[t]	1–11$\frac{1}{2}$	1–11$\frac{1}{2}$

true observ^{d} alt.		29–48–18½	29–43–18½	
– refract^{n} + parallax		1–30	1–30	
true Altitude of ⊙		29–46–48	29–41–48	
decln Greenwich	22–45–51			22–51–51
more for 79° W.	1–15	22–47– 6	22–53– 6	1–15
true height of Æquator		52–33–54	52–34–54	
		90–	90	
Zenith dist. = lat.		37–26– 6	37–25– 6	

note the observn of Dec. 9. was compleatly perfect & satisfactory.

MS (MHi); filed with TJ's Weather Memorandum Book, 1802–16; written entirely in TJ's hand on verso of his Calculations of Latitude of Poplar Forest, 8 Nov.–3 Dec. 1816.

On a separate, narrow sheet, TJ recorded his key finding on these days: "observns with Borda W's. Mount. 1816.

		° ′
Dec.	8. mer. alt. ⊙	59–39/ 29
	9	59–29½

note this last was a most perfect observn. the 1st not perfect" (MS in MHi; filed with TJ's Weather Memorandum Book, 1802–16; entirely in TJ's hand, with his related calculations of instrument error for his Borda's circle, headed "1816. Nov. Dec. error of Borda," on verso).

From Fitzwhylsonn & Potter

Sir, Richmond Decr 11. 1816.

Your favor of October 11 was received in due course of Post, and that of the 3^{d} Current, yesterday. We have made repeated applications, at the Stage Office, for the package, mentioned in the former, which we have constantly expected, by the Stage, but it has never arrived, nor is it in our power to gain any information respecting it. As soon as it is received, the binding shall be executed without loss of time.

We commenced, sir, with sending the Edinburg Review, at N° 32 and every succeeding number has been forwarded. N° 52, the last number republished,[1] in this country, is just come to hand, and will accompany the 2nd Vol: of Pleasants' edition of the laws of Virginia, as soon as a safe opportunity presents itself of sending them to Monticello, or Charlottesville.

As soon as the Sessions Acts, ordered by you, can be gotten they shall be forwarded.

We shall be thankful, sir, to you for your orders and shall give to them the earliest attention.

We are, sir, with the utmost respect Your Obedient Servants

Fitzwhylsonn & Potter

RC (MHi); in William H. Fitzwhylsonn's hand; endorsed by TJ as received 18 Dec. 1816 and so recorded in SJL. RC (DLC); address cover only; with PoC of TJ to William H. Crawford, 24 Dec. 1816, on verso; addressed: "His Excellency Thomas Jefferson Monticello"; franked; postmarked Richmond, 12 Dec., and (faint) Charlottesville, 1[ ] Dec.

TJ's letter to Fitzwhylsonn & Potter RECEIVED IN DUE COURSE OF POST was actually dated 12 Oct. 1816.

[1]Reworked from "published."

From John Adams

DEAR SIR Quincy Dec[r] 12 1816

I return the Analysis of Dupuis with my thanks for the loan of it. It is but a faint[1] Miniature of the original.

I have read that original in twelve Volumes, besides a 13th of plates.

I have been a Lover and a Reader of Romances all my Life. From Don Quixotte and Gill Blas to the Scottish Chiefs and an hundred others.

For the last year or two I have devoted myself to this kind of Study: and have read 15 Volumes of Grim, Seven Volumes of Tuckers Neddy Search and 12 Volumes of Dupuis besides a 13th of plates And Traceys Analysis, and 4. Volumes of Jesuitical History! Romances all! I have learned nothing of importance to me, for they have made no Change in my moral or religious Creed, which has for 50 or 60 years been contained in four Short Words "Be just and good." In this result they all agree with me.

I must acknowledge however, that I have found in Dupuis more Ideas that were new to me, than in all the others.

My Conclusion from all of them is Universal Tolleration.

Is there any Work extant So well calculated to discredit Corruptions and Impostures in Religion as Dupuis.

I am Sir, with Friendship, as of old JOHN ADAMS

RC (DLC); at foot of text: "President Jefferson"; endorsed by TJ as received 25 Dec. 1816 and so recorded in SJL. FC (Lb in MHi: Adams Papers). Enclosure: enclosure to TJ to Adams, 14 Oct. 1816.

The volume of PLATES was Charles François Dupuis, *Planches de L'Origine de Tous les Cultes* (Paris, year III [1794/95]). GILL BLAS: Alain René Le Sage, *Histoire de Gil Blas de Santillane* (Paris, 1715–35, and later French and English eds.; Sowerby, no. 4346). TUCKERS NEDDY SEARCH: under the pseudonym of Edward Search, the English philosopher Abraham Tucker published *The Light of Nature Pursued*, 3 vols. in 9 (London, 1768–77).

[1]RC: "feignt." FC: "faint."

George Flower's Account of a Visit to Monticello

Thursday 12 [Dec. 1816]—
Morning Showery[1]—Rode to Monticello 14 miles.[2] Met Mr Jefferson—Miss Randolphs & Mrs Randolph.—

Friday 13—
Morn'g fine[3]—Read papers containing copious extracts from English Journals—
The Nottingham petition & the southwark speeches[4] given at full length.[5]

Rode to Mr Randolphs Farm.[6] dined at Monticello In the Evening after tea Mr J. gave us many amusing anecdotes relating to attempts in the early days of the American constitution to introduce the etti-quette & forms of an European Court.[7]
So strongly were a certain party attached to Royalty at N York a Throne was made &[8] they placed Gen Washington & Mrs Washington[9] upon it.
Two members from Massetuchets,[10] waited upon Gen Washington in their official capacity. As they entered his house, they espied Mrs Washington crossing the Hall.
with most respectful hommage they enquired of her "if his Majesty was at home." After this question was twice repeated with profound respect Martha Washington said, the Gen'l is up Stairs.[11]
M^r^ J always opposed every thing like the[12] mimickry of European Courts.
During his own presidency it was expected that the old levees w^d^ be kept up—he tho't the most easey way to get rid of them w'd be to ride out[13] on levee mornng & stay out till a late hour.

Upon his return to dinner a cluster of persons near the house were waiting in full dress. He dismounted and civily[14] shaking them by the hand he invited[15] them to walk in to dinner. So ended the last of the levees. He broke up in like manner all formal announcements to dinner according to Rank by sitting promiscuously amongst the company & often at the lower end of the Table—[16]

Saturday 14
Rode to Charlotsville in the morning and visited Mr Randolphs Farm. Good farming pays ten or twelve pr Cent for money invested in land and stock After the expences of a large family are deducted.[17]

In the course of conversation in the evening I was sorry to hear three disgraceful anecdotes of Lord Cornwallis when he commanded the British troops during the revolutionary war.
When admiring a silver[18] flat candlestick very much, the [host?][19] appologised to him for not being able to present it to him as it was an old favourite family piece of plate. but his lordship put it in his pocket without much cerimony His lordship[20] distroyed a county seat of Mr Jefferson's—broke the furniture, destroyed the library & committed every act of wanton distruction Admiral Cockburn by his activity in stealing pigs and poultry he has acquired for himself the title of "Admiral Henroost"

Sunday 15th
Wrote to Mr Davies of Montreal

Monday 16—
Left Monticello at Noon

MS (ICHi: Flower Diary, vol. 3); in Flower's hand; partially dated. MS (ICHi: Flower Diary, vol. 2); in Flower's hand; partially dated.

The NOTTINGHAM PETITION of September 1816 called on the British prince regent George (later George IV) and parliament to support policies aimed at "reducing the army, abolishing all sinecures, pensions, grants, and emoluments, not merited by actual public services; of bringing the charges of the civil list, within such moderate bounds as the circumstances of the country will enable it to meet; and restoring to the people their undoubted rights, a full, fair, and equal representation in the commons house of parliament" (*Richmond Enquirer*, 23 Nov. 1816). A large, public meeting held in mid-October in SOUTHWARK, England, authorized the presentation of a similar petition to the prince regent (*Alexandria Herald*, 29 Nov., 2 Dec. 1816).

TJ's country seat (COUNTY SEAT) was Elk Hill in Goochland County. For TJ's description of the devastation of its crops and livestock and the carrying off of its slaves in June 1781 by British troops commanded by Charles, 2d Earl Cornwallis, see *PTJ*, 13:363–4.

Although Flower LEFT MONTICELLO on 16 Dec. 1816, later that month he returned to TJ's mountaintop home for a week, and he spent most of February 1817 there as well. However, his diary covering these later visits (the vol. 3 MS) adds nothing of consequence about the ex-president and his life at Monticello. In a later account Flower recalled that "The greater part of the winter I passed at Monticello the permanent residence of Mr Jefferson, in Charlotte C^o^ [Albemarle County]—The chief charm of the visit was in the evening conversations with Mr Jefferson, who gave me the inner history of events, before only known to me, as to the world generally, in the published record or outside history, which is all that the public is generally allowed to see" (MS in ICHi: Flower Family Papers, in an unindentified hand, with corrections and emendations by Flower; printed in Flower, *History of the English Settlement in Edwards County Illinois, Founded in 1817 and 1818, by Morris Birkbeck and George Flower* [1882], 44–5).

[1] Preceding two words not in vol. 2 MS.
[2] Vol. 2 MS: "12. Miles."
[3] Preceding two words not in vol. 2 MS.
[4] Vol. 2 MS: "petition."

[5] Flower here inserted a page, not in vol. 2 MS, containing information about a 1,000-acre farm owned by the Maupin family of Albemarle County. A repeated "Friday 13," editorially omitted, appears at the start of the next paragraph.

[6] Vol. 2 MS: "Rode to Edge hill farm with Col. Randolph."

[7] Sentence in vol. 2 MS reads "M[r] J. gave us many amusing anecdotes of the early days of American freedom." Following sentence not in vol. 2 MS.

[8] Preceding eight words interlined in place of "that."

[9] Manuscript: "Washngton."

[10] Vol. 2 MS: "one of the northern states."

[11] Sentence in vol. 2 MS reads "Martha Washington replied, the Gen'[ls] up stairs if you mean him."

[12] Flower here canceled "mockery."

[13] Sentence to this point in vol. 2 MS reads "During his presidency—he wished to get rid of a leve—he rode out."

[14] Vol. 2 MS: "familliarly."

[15] Vol. 2 MS: "politely asked."

[16] Sentence in vol. 2 MS reads "Formal arrangements at dinner according to rank were broken thro'—by—paying no attention to them and sitting promiscuously."

[17] Sentence in vol. 2 MS reads "A farm well managed pays 12–pr C[t] after deducting the expences of a family." Vol. 2 MS ends here.

[18] Word interlined.

[19] Omitted word editorially conjectured.

[20] Flower here canceled "burn't and."

To Patrick Gibson

DEAR SIR Monticello Dec. 12. 16.

On my return from Bedford yesterday, I found here a letter from mr Elisha Ticknor of Boston informing me he had on the 16th of Nov. shipped a small package of books recieved for me from Europe on board the brig Polly, Cap[t] Snow, to your address, the cost of which were 45. D 25 C as he has been kind enough to advance this money for me some time ago, I must request the favor of you to remit it to him without delay, of which I give him notice this day. as the box of books is probably not over 18.I. cube, it will come quicker & safer by the stage than by water; and especially if taken within the stage. I will therefore pray you to have it carried to the stage office with such directions. I salute you with friendship and respect

TH: JEFFERSON

PoC (DLC); on verso of reused address cover of Henry Clay to TJ, 8 Sept. 1816; at foot of text: "M[r] Gibson"; endorsed by TJ.

To Elisha Ticknor

SIR Monticello Dec. 12. 16.

I returned yesterday to this place after an absence of two months, and find here your three favors of Oct. 22. Nov. 1. and 16. this will explain, and apologise, I hope for the delay of the answer. the alternative you are so kind as to offer of paying the amount of the books in Boston, instead of remitting it to Europe, is a great accomodation, as my situation in the interior of the country, far remote from any place of foreign commerce, where bills of exchange on Europe can be procured, renders that kind of negociation very difficult. I therefore write this day to my correspondents in Richmond, mess[rs] Gibson & Jefferson, desiring them to remit to you immediately the sum of 45. D 25 C stated in your letter, with many thanks for the trouble you have been so good as to take in this business. as your son mentions that he will be in Paris in the spring I shall suspend writing to him till then; and I believe were I 20. years younger, instead of writing, I should meet him there and take with him his classical voyage to Rome, Naples & Athens. I wish him all the happiness & information, and they will be very great, which he will derive from it, and to yourself the sublimer one of seeing your youth renewed and honored in him, and add the assurance of my great esteem & respect.

TH: JEFFERSON

PoC (MHi); on verso of reused address cover of Bernard Peyton to TJ, 10 Oct. 1816; mutilated at seal, with missing word rewritten by TJ; at foot of text: "Elisha Ticknor esq."; endorsed by TJ.

To Joseph Dougherty

DEAR SIR Monticello Dec.[1] 13. 16.

On my return here two days ago after an absence of two months in Bedford, I found here your letter of Nov. 25. the cyder which I used to procure from Norfolk was obtained thro' the channel of Col[o] Newton member of Congress from that district. he always purchased and shipped it for me. the difficulty I experienced was in getting it brought without being watered by the sailors. I have no doubt Col[o] Newton will be so kind as to advise you how to get the best, and put you into the hands of a good correspondent, one who will furnish you with what is good and at the market price. I salute you with my best wishes for your success and happiness.

TH: JEFFERSON

PoC (DLC); on verso of reused address cover of Charles Yancey to TJ, 24 Nov. 1816; at foot of text: "M[r] Joseph Dougherty"; endorsed by TJ.

Thomas Newton procured CYDER for TJ from Norfolk in 1802 and 1803 (*MB*, 2:1064, 1065, 1103; *PTJ*, 36:269–70; Newton to TJ, 11 Dec. 1807 [DLC]).

[1] Word, ink stained, rewritten by TJ for clarity.

From Robert Patterson

SIR Philadelphia Dec[r] 13, 16.

A considerable time ago, you made some enquiries relative to a good clock & watch-maker, who, you suggested, might advantageously settle in your neighbourhood. Neither then, nor since, till the other day, could I hear of one that I could recommend, who was willing to make the trial.

From the enclosed letter, you will be able to judge whether the persons therein Recommended by m[r] Hassler, would be likely to succeed in the place you mentioned. Any agency which I could exercise in this business, you may freely command.

I am, Sir, with the greatest Respect & esteem, Your most obed[t] serv[t]

R[T] PATTERSON

RC (MHi); endorsed by TJ as received 30 Dec. 1816 and so recorded in SJL. RC (CSmH: JF); address cover only; with PoC of TJ to John Wayles Eppes, 6 Mar. 1817, on verso; addressed: "Thomas Jefferson Monticello V[a]"; stamp canceled; franked; postmarked Philadelphia, 13 Dec.

For TJ's inquiry regarding A GOOD CLOCK & WATCH-MAKER for Charlottesville, see TJ to Thomas Voigt, 9 Apr. 1813, and Patterson to TJ, 24 Apr. 1813.

ENCLOSURE

Ferdinand R. Hassler to Robert Patterson

DEAR SIR! NewArk New Jersey 2[d] Dec[r] 1816.

M[rs] Hassler told me You had mentioned her last Summer that it was desired a good Watchmaker[1] would establish himself in the neighbourhood of President Jefferson. She made then the offer to a new arived Swiss who declined.

In Elisabethtown is a Swiss gentleman, with whom I got acquainted in London on his passage here, where he was made prisoner of war with all his family, being taken on the passage, his name is Montandon he has several sons, daughters, & a son in Law with him, all working in the watchmaking line, from its first till the boxes, which they are now since their arival in this country, engaged very assiduously to make and of all forms & fashions, gold & Silver &c to the great number of movement which he has brought with him. They are properly intended to settle on Land in the Interior, after being well acquainted with the country & language, & having realised the stock of watches &c which they brought with, they are a very industrious and agreable family; the old gentleman says his son in Law is as good a watchmaker in every part as may be found in their Country, the mountains of Neufchatel. As he would have sufficient means to begin an establishment, if he could find a good locality for so doing, and is desirous of it, he would be a man suitable and well recomandable for a situation like mentioned, but would of course wish some nearer particulars & need some direction for the begining upon the proper place of his settlement & the Kind of work or comerce in his line which he would have provide with particularly; if the place You have mentioned is not yet occupied You would oblige me by more particular informations upon the Subject which I would communicate to him.

I hope the present cold weather has not yet affected You with colds & all the usual consequences as we have some instances of it in our house, though none dangerous for generally speaking we are all prety well.

Please to present all our best wishes to Your whole family

I am in daily expectation of an answer from the Treasury Dep^t to my first Report upon the Survey & hope it will enable me to move again out for it which will procure me the pleasure to see You

I remain with most perfect esteem & attachment

Your most affectionate F: R: HASSLER

RC (MHi); at foot of text: "Robert Patterson Esqre Philadelphia."

Pierre Henry Montandon's SON IN LAW was Louis A. Leschot.

[1] Manuscript: "Watchmacker."

From Philip I. Barziza

MOST HONORABLE SIR Williamsburg the 14th D^br 1816

It was in vain that till now I flattered myself with the illusion of having the honour of Coming in Person to pay you my respects, my circumstances, or my fate, have prevented me from enjoying such an advantage, and what it is worst is that through the same reasons I shall be deprived yet a while.

Menwhile permit me Sir to acquaint you that though I have soon after received your order, Commissioned your books I have not yet received an answer, and as I Supposed that my Letters might have been Lost, its three months since I have written the second time; so that I hope if no sinister accident hapens, you will certainly receive them next march to come.

As to my affairs I am very sorry to say that I am not far advanced, except that M^r McCandlish my Guardian has stop^t the rents of the Lands in the hands of the Tenants, and presented a petition to the General assembly for the purpose of prayng to relinquish all claims (if any) in my favour: it is in this Circumstance, Sir, that I dare to take the Liberty of beging the favour of your assistance, as I Know, and I am firmely persuaded that I Cannot choose a more powerful protector and though I have no rights I am Sure that you will not refuse to grant to a young foreigner Fatherless Gentleman, to Whose Relations you have been Such a Kind freind; what you are in the habitude of according everyday; your fame, your goodness and above all your constant, and Generouse disposition of doing good, all these makes me Sure of what I have humbly asked

Your most humble, and most obed^{t} Servant

PHILIP I. BARZIZA

P.S. My petition has been presented and reffered; my Counselor in Richmond is Mr William Worth;

RC (DLC); with postscript on verso of address leaf; addressed: "To the Hnourable Thomas Jefferson & & & Charlottesville Monticello"; franked; postmarked Williamsburg, 16 Dec., and (faint) Charlottesville, [ ] Dec.; endorsed by TJ as received 30 Dec. 1816 and so recorded in SJL.

On 21 Nov. 1816 William McCandlish, the "att^{y} in fact for John L Barziza and Guardian of Philip I Barziza," presented A PETITION on their behalf to the Virginia House of Delegates. The House referred it on that day to its Committee for Courts of Justice (Vi: RG 78, Legislative Petitions, Miscellaneous; *JHD* [1816–17 sess.], 37).

WILLIAM WORTH: William Wirt.

To Nicolas G. Dufief

DEAR SIR Monticello Dec. 14. 16.

I have occasion for the execution of a little commission which will be somewhat troublesome, but your experienced kindness encourages me to ask it of you. it is to get me an English bible, whose printed page shall be as nearly as you can find one, of the size of the paper inclosed, and whose type shall be of such size as that the number of pages shall correspond with the numbers expressed on the same paper, as nearly as you can find one. the object is that it's leaves may be taken asunder and interleaved with those of a particular Greek bible I have, corresponding as nearly as may be. I will request you to send me also a copy of Enfield's history of philosophy. be so good as to send each volume separately at the distance of a week apart each. it will occur to you that as the Bible is to be cut up, it's binding will be disregarded. I salute you with friendship & esteem.

TH: JEFFERSON

P.S. be so good as to send me 2. copies of the Nautical Almanac for 1817. and two for 1818. also if to be had, and by the return of the first mail, as the new year is close at hand.

P.S. Dec. 16. I have opened my letter to pray you to send me also the Connoissanc[e] des tems for 1817. & 1818 which I this moment see advertised at the Bureau of the Abeille Americaine of M. Chaudron.

PoC (DLC); on recto of reused address cover of William Sampson to TJ, 30 Nov. 1816; edge trimmed; adjacent to signature: "M. Dufief"; with FC of TJ to Dufief, 30 Dec. 1816, subjoined; endorsed by TJ. Enclosure not found.

To Archibald Thweatt and Jerman Baker

DEAR SIR Monticello Dec. 14. 16.

There is a petition before the legislature for establishing a turnpike road from Rockfish gap through Charlottesville to Moore's ford on the Rivanna, in which I am much interested, and as I have outlived all my Legislative acquaintances, I must request the favor of yourself and mr Baker (to whom this letter is meant to be equally addressed) to pay some attention to it. but I ask you to do in it nothing more than what you think right. the case is this. the road from Moore's ford where this road proposes to terminate leads downwards[1] thro' the lands of a mr Sampson, mr Randolph, Jefferson Randolph his son & myself, and occasions us 7. miles of fencing. it runs across the spurs of the mountain, very hilly. I have been 4. or 5. years opening, a level road along the bank of the river to substitute for it. this leads from Charlottesville across the Secretary's ford downwards, uniting with the present road about 3½ miles below the ford. there is an opposition to this change by a Capt Meriwether ch[i]efly on account of a family interest in a ferry at Moore's ford, and he gets some persons in Charlottesville & some others who care little about it to back him. the road I have made at an expence of 1500.D. (so much rock was to be blown) is so much superior to the present one that they know there is not a man in the world who will not say it is infinitely preferable. this petition is a mere trick the[re]fore to fix Moore's ford by law, so that it may not be in the pow[er] of the court to adopt the better road over the Secretary's ford. from Rockfish gap to Charlottesville is 24. miles. Moore's ford is but $\frac{3}{[4]}$ of a mile further. their natural termination then would be Charlottesville, and it is carried the other $\frac{3}{4}$ of a mile to Moore's for[d] merely to fix the old road, and defeat the new one. if they g[et] the law past their whole object is accomplished, and there nev[er] be a stroke struck on this turnpike. turnpikes cost from 1000 to 5000 D. a mile. the distance of 24. miles then will cost from 24,000 to 112,000.D.[2] I do not believe, on my soul, that they could possibly raise 1000 D. for this object, and they know it themselves; but this is a device of Meriwether's as a last desperate effort to defeat the road. Sampson, mr Randolph, Jefferson Randolph & myself have sent down a counterpetition, not opposing their turnpike, but praying that it may either stop at Charlottesville, or if continued to the river, that the decision whether it shall go to Moore's or the Secretary's ford may be left to the courts in whose possession the case now is, and out of whose hands it ought not to be wrested by this side wind. I refer you to the counterpetition, which states facts with perfect accuracy as our delegates mr Maury & Col^{o} Yancey can vouch. I write to them, but [d]o not know what course they may steer themselves. but [I hope?] [t]he legislature will not suffer itself to be made a tool of to change the regular course of law which leaves the dispute between Meriwether and the counterpetitioners to the courts. Accept for yourself & mr Baker my affectionate & respectful salutations.

TH: JEFFERSON

PoC (DLC); on reused address cover of Richard Rush to TJ, 13 Nov. 1816; mutilated at seal and with some text lost at right margin of first page due to polygraph misalignment; at foot of first page: "Archibald Thweatt esq."; endorsed by TJ as a letter to Thweatt.

THE COUNTERPETITION, not found, was read in the Virginia House of Delegates on 31 Dec. 1816 and referred to the select committee charged with considering the route of the proposed turnpike road from Rockfish Gap to the Rivanna River (*JHD* [1816–17 sess.], 116).

[1] Word interlined.

[2] The correct figure is $120,000.

To Charles Yancey and Thomas W. Maury

SIR Monticello Dec. 14. 16.

On my return from Bedford after an absence of 7. weeks I find here your favor of Nov. 24. for which I thank you & for the information it contains. during my absence I expect a petition to the assembly from mr Sampson, Col^{o} T. M. Randolph, Jefferson Randolph and my self was sent to yourself and mr Maury (whom I pray to consider this letter as addressed to him as well as to yourself) on the subject of the petition from Capt Meriwether & others for permission to establish a turnpike road from Rockfish gap thro' Charlottesville to Moore's ford. you both know the road which I have opened from Charlottesville across the Secretary's ford down the North bank of the river to the mouth of the Chapel branch where it meets the present road, which we have petitioned the court to substitute for the present one across[1] Moore's ford th[ro] our lands to the mouth of the chapel branch, and which every [body?] knows will be preferred as unquestionably the best. we consider this petition for a turnpike as a mere trick of Capt Meriwether and a last, desperate expedient to get the worse established instead of the better road. but we hope you will not suffer this case to be taken out of the hands of the courts of justice. to their turnpike we make no opposition as far as Charlottesville but let it end there, or leave it's course from thence to the river which is only $\frac{3}{4}$ of a mile, either to Moore's or the Secretary's for[d] to the decision of the courts. I am sure if the legislature know th[at] the object of the petition is merely to fix the road to Moore's ford, so [that?] it may be taken out of the power of the courts of justice, they will not suffer themselves to be made the tools of injustice: and this we [trust?] mr Maury and yourself, will take care of, as our representativ[es] as well as of the petitioners: I salute you both with friendship & resp[ect]

TH: JEFFERSON

PoC (MHi); on verso of a reused address cover from Joseph Delaplaine to TJ; mutilated at seal and with some text lost at right margin due to polygraph misalignment; at foot of text (polygraph misaligned): "C[ol]° [Yancey]"; endorsed by TJ as a letter to Yancey.

[1] Word interlined in place of "from."

From Abigail Adams

DEAR SIR Quincy December 15th 1816

My good Husband has call'd upon me for Some Letters, written to me by my Son, when he was last in paris, in 1815[1] in which he gives me a particular account of the Family of Count de Tracy and of the circumstances which introduced him to their acquaintance.

Beleiving that it will give you pleasure to become acquainted with this happy Domestic circle, I readily embrace this opportunity of transmitting them to you, with two or three other Letters which follow in Succession, and are interesting, as they describe the Novel and importent events, to which mr Adams was an Eye witness.

I rely upon your known care and punctuality to return them to me. I need not add how valuable they are to me.[2] They may also afford Some entertainment to your Grandaughter Miss Ellen Randolph, whose praises are in the mouths, of all our Northern Travellers, who have been so happy as to become acquainted with her.—they bring us also: such delightfull accounts of Monticello and its inhabitants that I am tempted to wish myself twenty years younger, that [I mi]ght visit them, but I am so far down Hill, that I must only think of those pleasures which are past, amongst which, and not the least is my early acquaintance with, and the continued Friendship of the phylosopher of Monticello—to whom are offerd the respectfull attachment

of Dear Sir Your Friend ABIGAIL ADAMS

RC (MHi); mutilated at seal, with missing text supplied from FC; endorsed by TJ as received 30 Dec. 1816 and so recorded in SJL. FC (MHi: Adams Papers); entirely in Adams's hand; beneath signature: "Mr Jefferson," with dateline beneath that; note by Adams at foot of text: "The occasion of writing this Letter was a Letter from mr Jefferson with a Booke written by Count de Tracy call'd an annalysis of the writings of Dupuis origin of all Religions"; endorsed by Adams.

The enclosed letters from Adams's SON John Quincy Adams probably included missives he wrote his mother from Paris on 21 Feb., 19 Mar., and 22 Apr. 1815 (MHi: Adams Papers). The first discusses Destutt de Tracy's HAPPY DOMESTIC CIRCLE and the goodwill engendered by the younger Adams's efforts to obtain the release of Victor Destutt de Tracy, a French officer captured during Napoleon's ill-fated 1812 invasion of Russia. The other letters detail the emperor's return to power in France early in 1815.

[1] Preceding two words not in FC.
[2] Sentence not in FC.

To John Barnes

DEAR SIR Monticello Dec. 15. 16.

On my return from Bedford after an absence of 7. weeks I find here your favor of the 2d inst. covering a letter from Buckley & Abbot which I now return. in your P.S. you request 1. the original Certificates of the 12,500.D. 6. p.c. US. stock, 2. two powers for you to recieve the interest of the stock at the Treasury and dividends at the bank of Columbia. 3. my original power from Kosciusko that copies of it may be deposited in the bank and Treasury.

1. I never saw the original certificate of the 12,500.D. nor has it been sent to me. in your's of Jan. 10. 1815. to me you say 'the above recited certificates (N° 10. for 11,363.63 D and N° 10. also for 1136.99[1] D)[2] are lodged in safe custody in the Custom house iron chest,' where I presume you will find them

2. I now inclose 2. powers for you to receive the interest at the Treasury, and dividends on the 46. shares in the bank of Columbia.

3. my original power from Kosciuzko. I inclosed this to you [in?] my letter[3] of Oct. 12. as was requested in yours of Oct. 3. you probably have it yourself or have left it at the bank or Treasury to be copied. hoping you will find these papers, and that with those now inclosed they will enable you to do every thing necessary, I salute [...]

TH: JEFFERSON

PoC (DLC: TJ Papers, 208:37188); on verso of a reused address cover from Joseph Delaplaine to TJ; torn at seal; closing faint; at foot of text: "Mr Barnes"; endorsed by TJ. Enclosure: enclosure to Barnes to TJ, 2 Dec. 1816. Other enclosures printed below.

[1] Thus in manuscript. The correct figure is 1136.36.

[2]Mismatched closing square bracket editorially changed to a parenthesis.

[3]Second vowel, missing probably due to a polygraph malfunction, editorially supplied.

ENCLOSURES

I

Power of Attorney to John Barnes for United States Stock Interest

Know all men by these presents that I Thomas Jefferson of Monticello in Albemarle, by virtue of the powers to me given by Thaddeus Kosciuzko, late a General in the armies of the United States, do hereby constitute and appoint John Barnes of George town in the district of Columbia lawful attorney under my self, of the said Thaddeus with full powers to recieve for the sd Thaddeus and in his name all sums of interest due or to become due on any stock standing or which may hereafter stand in the name of the sd Thaddeus in the books or funds of the United States, and for the same to give discharges and acquittances in the name of the sd Thaddeus, which shall be equally valid, and are hereby confirmed, as if given by myself. Witness my hand and seal at Monticello aforesd this fifteenth of December 1816.

TH: JEFFERSON

Witness

PoC (DLC: TJ Papers, 208:37187); written entirely in TJ's hand on verso of reused address cover to TJ; mutilated at seal, with missing words rewritten by TJ; with PoC of second power of attorney to Barnes of this date on other side of sheet. Possibly also enclosed in Barnes to TJ, 13 Jan. 1817, and TJ to Barnes, 28 Jan. 1817.

II

Power of Attorney to John Barnes for Bank of Columbia Dividends

Know all men by these presents that I Thomas Jefferson of Monticello in Albemarle county of the state of Virginia, by virtue of the powers to me given by Thaddeus Kosciuzko late a General in the army of the United States, do hereby constitute and appoint[1] John Barnes of Georgetown in the district of Columbia lawful attorney under my self of the sd Thaddeus, with full power to recieve for the sd Thaddeus, and in his name, all dividends of interest or profit due, or hereafter to become due on shares in the bank of Columbia, which are or may hereafter be holden or owned by the sd Thaddeus in the sd bank, and for the same to give discharges and acquittances, which shall be equally valid, and are hereby confirmed as if given by my self. Witness my hand and seal at Monticello aforesd this 15th day of December 1816.

Witness
JAMES L. JEFFERSON

TH: JEFFERSON
his seal[2]

MS (Catherine Barnes Autographs & Signed Books, Philadelphia, 1998); in TJ's hand, signed by TJ and Jefferson. PoC (DLC: TJ Papers, 208:37187); on recto of reused address cover to TJ; mutilated at seal; with PoC of first power of attorney to Barnes of this date on other side of sheet.

[1] PoC: "appoin." RC corrected to "appoint," probably by a later hand.

[2] In MS these words are followed by wax from a seal.

From Horatio G. Spafford

Albany, 12. 15, '16.

The Essay which thou wast kind enough to wish to See in print, is commenced in this No., & I anxiously hope the spirit & plan of it may meet thy approbation; & that I may be favored with the assurance.

It is venturing a good deal, but not more, in my opinion, than the circumstances of the times demand. For the good of our Country, it is neccessary that the Men of the South express their liberality, in respect to Religious opinions. Theology, every where, is of Monarchical tendency. The people of the South really know little of what is going on in the N. & East. God grant they may, & in good time. They have an independence of mind, & a freedom of opinion,[1] far more noble & manly than those of the North. Oh Orthodoxy, how I hate thy reign!—

Always, with great esteem, thy friend, H. G. SPAFFORD.

RC (MHi); at foot of text: "Hon. T. Jefferson"; endorsed by TJ as received 30 Dec. 1816 and so recorded in SJL.

Spafford's ESSAY on establishing a national, secular school of science and the mechanic arts and improving the United States patent system appeared under the pseudonym "Franklin," as a letter to the editor dated 10 Dec. 1815, in the *American Magazine, a monthly miscellany*, vol. 1, nos. 8–9 (Jan.–Feb. 1816): 289–97, 313–26.

[1] Spafford here canceled "which the Theologi."

From John Adams

Quincy Decr 16th 1816

Your Letter dear Sir of Nov. 15 from Poplar Forrest was Sent to me from the Post Office the next day after I had Sent "The Analysis"[1] with my Thanks to you.

"3. Vol^{s} of Idiology!" Pray explain to me this Neological Title! What does it mean? When Bonaparte used it, I was delighted[2] with it, upon the Common Principle of delight in every Thing We cannot understand. Does it mean Idiotism? The Science of Non compos menticism. The Science of Lunacy? The Theory of Delirium? Or does it mean the Science of Self Love? of Amour propre? or the Elements of Vanity?

Were I in France, at this time, I could profess Blindness and Infirmity and prove it too. I Suppose he does not avow the Analysis, as Hume did not avow his Essay on human Nature. That Analysis however does not Show a Man of excessive Mediocrity. Had I known any of these Things two Years ago I would have written him a Letter. Of all Things, I wish to See his Idiology upon Montesquieu. If you, with all your Influence have not been able to get your own translation of it with your own Notes upon it, published in four Years, Where and What is the Freedom of The American Press.? Mr Taylor of Hazel Wood[3] Port Royal can have his voluminous and luminous Works published with Ease and dispatch.

The Uranologia, as I am told, is a Collection of Plates, Stamps Charts of the Heavens Upon a large Scale representing[4] all the Constellations. The Work of Some Professor in Sweeden. It is said to be the most perfect that ever has appeard. I have not Seen it. Why Should I ride 15 miles to See it When I can See the original every clear Evening; and especially[5] as Dupuis has almost made me afraid to enquire after any Thing more of it than I can See with my naked Eye in a Starlight night.?

That the Pope will Send Jesuits to this Country[6] I doubt not; and the Church of England, Missionaries too. And the Methodists, and the Quakers and the Moravians, and the Sweedenburgers and the Menonists, and the Scottish Kirkers, and the Jacobites and the Jacobins and the Democrats and the Aristocrats and the Monarkists and the Despotists of all Denominations And every Emissary of every one of these Sects will find a Party here already formed, to give him a cordial Reception;[7] No Power or Intelligence less than Raphaels Moderator can reduce this Chaos to order.

I am charmed with the fluency and rapidity of your Reasoning on the State[8] of Great Britain. I can deny none of your Premisses: but I doubt your Conclusion. After all the Convulsions that you forsee, they will return to that Constitution which you Say has ruined them, and I Say has been the Source of all their Power and Importance. They have as you Say too much Sense and Knowledge of Liberty, ever to Submit to Simple Monarchy or absolute despotism on the One hand: And too much of the Devil in them ever to be governed by popular Elections of Presidents, Senators and Representatives in Congress. Instead of "turning their Eyes to Us," their innate Feelings will turn them from Us. They have been taught from their Cradles to despize Scorn, insult and abuse Us. They hate Us more Vigorously, than they do the French. They would Sooner adopt the Simple Monarchy of France than our republican Institutions. You compliment me, with more knowledge of them than I can assume or pretend. If I Should write you a Volume of Observations I made in England You would pronounce it, a Satyre. Suppose, the "Refrein" as the french call it, or the Burthen of the Song as the English express it; Should be, the Religion, the Government[9] the Commerce the Manufactures, the Army and Navy of G.B. are all reduced to the Science of Pounds Shillings and Pence. Elections appeared to me a mere commercial Traffick; mere bargain and Sale. I have been told by Sober Steady Freeholders, that "they never had been and never would go to the Poll, without being paid for their Time, Travel and Expences." Now Suppose an Election for a President of the British Empire. There must be a Nomination of Candidates by a National Convention, Congress,[10] or Caucus, in which would be two Parties, Whigs and Tories. Of course two Candidates at least would be nominated. The Empire is instantly divided into two Parties at least. Every Man must be paid for his Vote, by the Candidate[11] or his Party. The only Question would be, Which Party has the deepest Purse. The Same Reasoning will apply to Elections of Senators and Representatives too. A Revolution might destroy the Burroughs and the Inequalities of Representation and might produce more toleration, and these Acquisitions might be worth all they would cost. But I dread the Experiment.

Britain will never be our Friend, till We are her Master. This will happen in less time than you and I have been Struggling with her Power—provided We remain United. Aye! there's the rub! I fear there will be greater difficulties to preserve our Union, than You and I, our Fathers Brothers Friends Disciples and Sons have had to form it.

Towards G.B. I would adopt their own Maxim An English Jocky Says "If I have a wild horse to brake I begin by convincing him that I am his Master. And then I will convince him that I am his Friend."[12] I am well assured that nothing will restrain G.B. from injuring Us, but fear.

You think that "in a revolution the distinction of Whig and Tory would disappear." I cannot believe this. That distinction arises from nature and Society; is now and ever will be time without End among Negroes Indians and Tartars as well as Federalists and Republicans. Instead of "disappearing Since Hume published his History," that History has only increased the Tories and diminished the Whigs. That History has been the Bane of G.B. It has destroyed many of the best Effects of the Revolution of 1688. Style has governed the Empire. Swift, Pope and Hume have disgraced all the honest Historians. Rapin and Burnet Oldmixen and Coke, contain more honest Truth than Hume and Clarendon and all their disciples and Imitators. But Who reads any of them at this day? Every one of the fine Arts from the earliest times has been inlisted in the Service of Superstition and Despotism. The whole World at this day Gazes with Astonishment at the grossest Fictions because they have been immortalized by the most exquisite Artists. Homer and Milton Phidias and Raphael. The Rabble of the Classic Skies and the Hosts of Roman Catholic Saints and Angells are Still adored[13] in Paint and Marble, and verse

Raphael has Sketched the Actors and Scenes in all Apuleus's Amours of Psyche and Cupid. Nothing[14] is too offensive to morals delicacy or decency, for this Painter

Raphael has painted in one of the most ostentatius Churches in Italy, the Creation. And with what Genius? God Almighty is represented, as leaping into Chaos and boxing it about with his Fists and kicking it about With his feet, till he tumbles it into Order.!!! Nothing is too impious or profane for this great Master who has painted So many inimitable Virgins and Childs.

To help me on in my career of improvement I have now read four Volumes of La Harps Correspondence with Paul and a Russian Minister.

Phylosophers! Never again think of annuling Superstition per Saltum. Festine lente.

JOHN ADAMS

RC (DLC); at foot of text: "President Jefferson"; endorsed by TJ. FC (Lb in MHi: Adams Papers). Recorded in SJL as received 30 Dec. 1816.

TJ's letter to Adams FROM POPLAR FORREST was dated 25 Nov. 1816, not 15 Nov. THE ANALYSIS: Destutt de Tracy, *Analyse Raisonnée*. Although Destutt de Tracy's *Commentary and Review of Montesquieu's Spirit of Laws* had already been published, TJ's revised TRANSLATION of his *Treatise on Political Economy* had not. URANOLOGIA: Johann Elert Bode, *Uranographia sive Astrorum Descriptio* (Berlin, 1801).

The Archangel Raphael's MODERATOR, or governor, was God. AYE! THERE'S THE RUB! is from William Shakespeare, *Hamlet*, act 3, scene 1. The phrase IS NOW AND EVER WILL BE TIME WITHOUT END is from the Christian doxology. The Italian painter Raphael's mosaic depicting THE CREATION is in the dome of the Chigi Chapel at the Santa Maria del Popolo Church in Rome. The Grand Duke PAUL later became Paul I, emperor of Russia. PER SALTUM: "at a single bound."

[1] Omitted closing quotation mark supplied from FC.

[2] RC: "deligted." FC: "delighted."

[3] Preceding two words interlined.

[4] RC: "respresenting." FC: "representing."

[5] RC and FC: "espcially."

[6] RC: "Coutry." FC: "Country."

[7] RC: "Rception." FC: "Reception."

[8] FC: "side."

[9] RC: "Governmen." FC: "Government."

[10] RC: "Convension, Congres." FC: "Convention, Congress."

[11] RC: "Candiate." FC: "Candidate."

[12] Omitted closing quotation mark editorially supplied.

[13] FC: "adorned."

[14] RC: "Noth-." FC: "Nothing."

From Nicolas G. Dufief

MONSIEUR A Philad^{e} ce 16th Dêcembre 1816

D'après la lettre que vous me fites l'honneur de m'adresser le 9 Juin dernier, vous donnâtes ordre à Messrs Gibson & Jefferson de Richmond de me faire passer trente-un dollars, montant de quelques livres que je vous avais envoyés. N'ayant point reçu cette petite somme, j'ai cru de mon devoir de vous en prévenir afin de détruire l'impression où vous êtes qu'elle a été payée.

Je profite de l'approche du renouvellement de l'année pour vous prier d'agréer mes souhaits pour tout ce qui peut contribuer à votre Satisfaction & à votre repos Je Suis avec tout le respect qui vous est du,

Votre très-dévoué serviteur N. G. DUFIEF

EDITORS' TRANSLATION

SIR Philadelphia 16 December 1816

According to the letter with which you honored me on June 9 last, you ordered Messrs Gibson & Jefferson of Richmond to send thirty-one dollars to me, the total for some books I had sent you. Not having received this small sum, I think it my duty to inform you so as to remove your impression that it has been paid.

As the New Year approaches I beg you to accept my wishes for everything that might contribute to your satisfaction and tranquility. I am with all due respect,

Your very devoted servant N. G. DUFIEF

RC (DLC); endorsed by TJ as received 30 Dec. 1816 and so recorded in SJL. Translation by Dr. Genevieve Moene.

From William D. Meriwether

DEAR SIR December 16th 1816

Understanding that you have returned from Bedford and being desirous to receive the rents due to Mr Hornsby and Mr Wood the representatives of the three younger legatees of Bennet Henderson D^{d} I request the favour of you to appoint a time and place wher the business can be done that will be mutually convenient to us baoth and if necesssary to appoint an umpire to deside any matter of controversy which may arise in the settlement of the accounts Accept assurance of my esteem &c W D. MERIWETHER

RC (MHi); at foot of text: "Thomas Jefferson Esqr."; endorsed by TJ as received 16 Dec. 1816 and so recorded in SJL.

The THREE YOUNGER LEGATEES OF BENNET HENDERSON D^{D} (deceased) were Frances Henderson Hornsby, Lucy Henderson Wood, and Nancy C. Henderson Nelson.

To William D. Meriwether

SIR Monticello Dec. 16.[1] 16

On my return from Bedford after an absence of 7. weeks I find here a great accumulation of letters and other business. as soon as I can dispatch the most pressing of these, I will take up the transactions with the representatives of mr Henderson and prepare a statement of the account for rents. this done I shall put the matter into the hands of my grandson to settle with you and to arbitrate if necessary. I will give you notice when I have got the account ready, and will lose no time in getting it ready. Accept the assurance of my respect.

TH: JEFFERSON

PoC (MHi); on verso of reused address cover of Elisha Ticknor to TJ, 16 Nov. 1816; at foot of text: "Capt Wm D. Meriwether"; endorsed by TJ.

The REPRESENTATIVES were Thomas Hornsby and John T. Wood. TJ's GRANDSON was Thomas Jefferson Randolph.

[1] Reworked from "17."

To Thomas H. Palmer

Monticello Dec. 16. 16.

Th: Jefferson, with his respectful salutations to mr Palmer, returns him the inclosed letter, which has not been called for as mr Palmer expected.

PoC (MHi); on verso of reused address cover of Joseph Dougherty to TJ, 25 Nov. 1816; dateline at foot of text; endorsed by TJ. Enclosure: enclosure to Palmer to TJ, 23 Oct. 1816.

To Thomas Mann Randolph (1792–1848)

DEAR SIR Monticello Dec. 16. 16.

The bearer of this, mr George Flower, is an English gentleman farmer, on a tour thro' the US. to look for a settlement fo[r] his family and friends. he wishes to see examples of the best farming as adapted to the circumstances of our country. on this ground I take the liberty of asking him to call on you, as he will see those examples in your own, and the neighboring farm of mr Wickham. in return for the information he may derive from you of this kind, he will give you that of Europe generally & of England most particularly, being well informed of the men and things of the day. he was the travelling companion of Birkbeck in his tour thro' France, which you have probably seen, and brings me letters of introduction from the Marquis de la Fayette & M. de Lasteyrie the agricultural writer who speak in the highest terms of his worth. I avail myself of the occasion he furnishes of assuring you of my high esteem and respect.

TH: JEFFERSON

PoC (MHi); on verso of reused address cover of James B. Pleasants to TJ, 28 Nov. 1816; one word faint; at foot of text: "Thomas M. Randolph jun^{r} esq."; endorsed by TJ.

To Richard Rush

DEAR SIR Monticello[1] Dec. 16. 16.

On my return after an absence of 7. weeks, I find here your favor of Nov. 13. and have examined the file of Dr Rushes letters to me, of which I send you the whole except two or three. these were merely medical on the subject of a visceral complaint which attacked me when I first went to live at Washington. the letters of advice which he wrote me as a friend & physician on that subject, I have retained, because a return of the complaint might happen and again render them useful to me. Accept, with this act of duty, the assurance of my great esteem and respect. TH: JEFFERSON

RC (NjP: Rush Family Papers); at foot of text: "Richard Rush esq."; endorsement by Rush reads, in part, "Enclosing certain letters from my father." PoC (MHi); on verso of reused address cover of Joseph Delaplaine to TJ, 20 Nov. 1816; endorsed by TJ.

Filed with the RC of this letter is an initialed note by Rush dated 19 June 1855 from Sydenham, his estate near Philadelphia: "The enclosed half dozen letters from my father to Mr Jefferson were found a few days ago in the course of searches I have lately been making and am continuing among old papers and manuscripts that had long remained unopened. How I came by these, which I had forgotten, will be seen by Mr Jefferson's letter to me of December 16. 1816, also enclosed; and be further explained by an earlier one from him, dated May 31, 1813, which I recently found in a different trunk, and now transfer to this packet" (NjP: Rush Family Papers). Rush appended a second initialed note, dated 8 Apr. 1856, indicating that "one of the six," which had subsequently been given away, was "a short one of a few lines—sending Mr Jefferson some muskmelon seed" (this letter was dated 2 Dec. 1800 [*PTJ*, 32:266]). The enclosed FILE evidently also included Benjamin Rush's letters to TJ of 11 June, 12 Dec. 1803, 28 May 1804, and 3 Dec. 1805 (all in NjP: Rush Family Papers), and an additional, unidentified text.

The letters from Benjamin Rush to TJ concerning a VISCERAL COMPLAINT of the bowels were dated 12 Mar. and 5 May 1803 (*PTJ*, 40:52–5, 320–1).

[1] Manuscript: "Montiello."

From Thomas T. Barr

[ca. 17 Dec. 1816]

On the 16th day of September 1816—Thomas Jefferson esq. of Monticello, Virginia was elected an Honorary member of the Kentucky Agricultural Society. The Society invites his co-operation and assistance in the advancement of their designs.

THO: T. BARR.
sec'y.

RC (DLC: TJ Papers, 208:37067); undated; addressed: "Thomas Jefferson, esq. Monticello Virginia"; stamp canceled; franked; postmarked Lexington, Ky., 17 Dec.; endorsed by TJ as a letter from Barr of 16 Sept. 1816 received 5 Jan. 1817. Recorded in SJL as an undated letter received 5 Jan. 1817 from Barr as "Secy Agricl soc. of Kentucky."

Thomas Tilton Barr (1779–1824), merchant, attorney, and public official, was the son of a merchant in Lexington, Kentucky. He helped to run the family business until 1811 and then became a lawyer. During the War of 1812 Barr served as a private and judge advocate general in the Kentucky volunteers. He withdrew his candidacy for the United States House of Representatives in 1816 in favor of Henry Clay. Barr was also a trustee of Transylvania University, 1808–13, and he represented Fayette County in the state House of Representatives, 1817–19 (June Lee Mefford Kinkead, *Our Kentucky Pioneer Ancestry* [1992], 141; Clay, *Papers*, 1:243n, 525, 2:182n; Robert Peter, *History of Fayette County, Kentucky* [1882], 65, 431; Robert B. McAfee, *History of the Late War in the Western Country* [Lexington, 1816], 353; Lexington *Western Monitor*, 7 June, 2 Aug. 1816; *Journal of the House of Representatives, of the Commonwealth of Kentucky* [Frankfort, 1815], 218; [Frankfort, 1817], 3; [Frankfort, 1818], 4, 12; Lexington *Kentucky Reporter*, 29 Nov. 1824).

Barr presumably enclosed in his letter a copy of the constitution of the recently established Kentucky Society for Promoting Agriculture, which listed the officers and their duties; allowed for the payment of premiums for "actual experiments and improvements," "the best essays written on proposed subjects," and "the best specimens of Stock" exhibited at society-sponsored fairs; and authorized the election of HONORARY members, who were asked to "attend our meetings, and assist in the deliberations and other purposes of the Society" (printed broadside in DLC: TJ Papers, 208:37067a; undated).

To Francis W. Gilmer

Dear Sir Monticello Dec. 17. 16

On my return from Bedford after an absence of seven weeks I find here your favor of Nov. 27. I have perused with care and satisfaction your translation of Quesnay's treatise on Natural right, and find not a word to alter. the sense thro the whole seems so consistent, that without having the original to collate with it, I have no doubt it has been truly preserved. the blank in the 5th page, if filled by the words 'obtained by surprise' and the word 'perceive' in the next line changed into 'recognise' will render truly the sense of the author as quoted at the foot of the page. I am in hopes it will be published, as nothing is less understood among us than the office of legislation and it's proper limits. hence the Augean stable of acts of the legislatures in all our states. I salute you with great friendship and respect.

Th: Jefferson

RC (CLU-C); at foot of text: "F. W. Gilmer esq." PoC (MHi); on verso of reused address cover of Horatio G. Spafford to TJ, 23 Nov. 1816; mutilated at seal; endorsed by TJ. Enclosure: enclosure to Gilmer to TJ, 27 Nov. 1816.

Gilmer entered TJ's emendations into his translation, which was published posthumously (Gilmer, *Sketches, Essays and Translations* [1828], 175–201, esp. 183).

From Thomas Law

Dear Sir— Washington Decr 19–1816—

Permit me to introduce to you Capn Hall a British officer of engaging manners, enlightened understanding & liberality of sentiment—He is travelling for amusement, & duly estimates the growing prosperity of this Country under a good Constitution.

That you may long enjoy otium cum dignitate, with the pleasing consciousness of having planned & aided to give success to this experimental Government is the earnest wish of Yrs

with sincere Esteem & regard Thos Law—

RC (DLC); dateline at foot of text; endorsed by TJ as received 7 Jan. 1817 and so recorded in SJL.

To Horatio G. Spafford

SIR Monticello Dec. 20. 16.

On my return from Bedford, after an absence of 7. weeks, I find here your favor of Nov. 23. with your magazine for Dec. 1815. for which be pleased to accept my thanks. you request permission to publish extracts from my letter of Mar. 17. 1814. on the anticivism of our professional crafts. on this subject I must observe that I have not now the buoyant spirits of youth which enabled me formerly to disregard hostile attacks, to assume to them a countenance of defence & defiance, and to enter the gladiatorial lists with them. writing, even a letter, is become my aversion. tranquility, reading and relaxation are the summa bona of my present moments, and I shrink from every thing which may disturb them. if the sentiments expressed in that letter are of any force or value, use them as your own, or as those of an anonymous correspondent. but do not, good Sir, make the least allusion to me or my name.

Whether the sale of a Gazeteer of this state would be extensive enough to make it worth your while to undertake it, I am less qualified to judge than almost any other person; because I rarely go from home but to another distant & more solitary one. I see therefore those only who visit me here. I should very much doubt the pecuniary success of such a work, and however desirable, it would be a serious wrong to encorage an undertaking which might very possibly lead to loss. our booksellers in Richmond could give you the safest advice on this subject. with my best wishes for your success & happiness, I salute you with assurances of esteem & respect. TH: JEFFERSON

RC (NjMoHP: Lloyd W. Smith Collection); at foot of text: "M[r] Spafford"; endorsed by Spafford as received 31 Dec. 1816; with his notation beneath endorsement concerning his reply of 20 (correctly 21) Jan. 1817 (one word editorially supplied): "Let. & sent [No.] 9 Am. Magazine. Requested his opinion of 'Franklin,' & the plan he proposes." PoC (DLC); on verso of reused address cover to TJ; torn at seal and damaged at fold, with some missing text rewritten by TJ; endorsed by TJ.

From Elizabeth Trist

Bird wood 20th Dec—16

My ever esteem'd friend I return you many thanks for your favor from Bedford, be assured it gives me great pleasure that your opinion coinsides with all I have consulted on the subject and be assured that it is very interesting to me, as it will give me an opportunity of seeing them every summer, the very Idea has renovated my health and sperits. Francis Gilmer mention'd to his Brother, that you were zealous for political Reformation, for conventions &c &c and indeed retain'd without diminution all the enthusiasm of your Youth—God grant that every blessing may be extended to you many many years, I have enclosed a letter for M[rs] Randolph which contains all the good wishes to the Family that we feel, and believe me ever and sincerely

Your much obliged friend E— Trist

RC (MHi); endorsed by TJ as received 12 Jan. 1817 and so recorded in SJL. Enclosure not found.

them: Nicholas P. Trist and Hore Browse Trist. The brother of Francis W. Gilmer mentioned above was probably Peachy R. Gilmer.

From Joseph E. McIlhenney

Honoured Sir charlottsville Dec[r] 21st

Taking every thing into consideration I think my return to Winchester will be to my advantage. This place as I have been informed by many will not afford sufficient employment for more than one in our buisness and of course I would run a risk which my circumstances will not admit of. If I should commence in opposition to this young man who perhaps may posess equal abilities to myself as respects our buisness it would take some time before we could assertain who should have the "palm"—. Another inducement for my not attemting an opposition is my remote distance from home and not having it in my power to furnish myself with goods. The young man I would be opposed to has a partner at Staunton with a capital to supply him with what good he may require. Taking these consideration into view I think you will excuse my abrupt departure after the repeated marks of friendship manifested by yourself and grandson. I shall remember your solisitude for my success with heart felt gratitude.

I remain respectfully yours &C. Jos E M[c]Ilheny

P.S. I shall leave this place for Winchester in the morning—

RC (MHi); partially dated; addressed: "The Honour[e] Thom[s] Jefferson Monticello"; endorsed by TJ as a letter of 21 Dec. 1816 received 24 Jan. 1817 and so recorded in SJL.

this young man was an employee or partner and likely a relative of a Staunton clockmaker named Logan. The latter was probably John Logan (TJ to Charles Willson Peale, 24 Dec. 1816; James Leitch to TJ, 17 Jan. 1817; Catherine B. Hollan, *Virginia Silversmiths, Jewelers, Watch- and Clockmakers, 1607–1860, Their Lives and Marks* [2010], 472–3). TJ's grandson was Thomas Jefferson Randolph.

To Joel Yancey

Dear Sir Monticello Dec. 21. 16.

I recieved 3 days ago your's of Dec. 14. and now inclose you an order on Richmond for 94.70 D the amount of my US. taxes in Bedford, which are exactly the half this year of what they were the last. I inclose you also a blank for the list of the stock, stating the heads under which they are to be stated. I am sorry to inform you that the completion of the waggon will be very much delayed by a very serious accident to my toll[1] mill during my late absence in Bedford. the shaft whose decayed state had been some time threatening, snapt suddenly in two at the mortises of the cogwheel. Goodman was of course taken off by this, and will still be a considerable time getting the mill to work again, our daily loss while she is idle being great in the article of bread. I think therefore you had better have the waggon there put into sufficient condition for bringing down the pork, as it will be no loss to have it in serviceable condition. our waggon here could not be spared till the 2^d^ week of January, and I think I had better put off her departure still longer, in order to give time for the repair of yours, and also in the hope that by the return of the 2^d^ trip with the pork the new one may be ready to accompany the old one back. in this I will be governed by what you will advise me by the return of Barnaby. I am anxious to hear that our flour is all gone down. I retain my confidence that from the great failure of crops in Europe generally and in America the price will be higher in the spring than ever was given before. I salute you with great friendship and respect

Th: Jefferson

PoC (MHi); on verso of a reused address cover from David Bailie Warden to TJ; at foot of text: "Mr Yancey"; endorsed by TJ.

Missing letters from Yancey to TJ of dec. 14. and 29 Dec. 1816 are recorded in SJL as received 18 Dec. 1816 from Poplar Forest and 2 Jan. 1817 from Bedford, respectively.

The enclosed order on richmond, not found, was drawn on Gibson & Jefferson "in favr. of US. Collector being my taxes due to US. for Bedford, to wit ante Mar. 15. 170.D. & Mar. 28. 19.40 ÷ 2 = 94.70" (*MB*, 2:1329). Other enclosure not found.

goodman: Rolin Goodman. A missing letter from his brother Jeremiah A. Goodman to TJ of 15 Dec. 1816 is inconsistently logged into SJL as received a day prior to its purported composition. On 17 Dec. 1816 TJ recorded a payment to the latter of "147.50 which reduces balance to 400.D." (*MB*, 2:1329).

[1] Word interlined.

From George Ticknor

Dear Sir, Göttingen Dec. 22. 1816.

Since I had the pleasure of writing you in April and July, I have not heard from you.—By a letter from Mr. Warden, however, I am extremely glad to hear he was able to purchase your Books in Paris for about the amount of your bill—and by a letter yesterday from Hamburg, that the vessel in which I forwarded you a few last August has safely arrived in Boston. I now write to you, to say definitively & certainly, that unless my health should prevent, I shall be in Paris in the first days of next May—& shall pass the summer there and the winter in Italy—and that if you or Colo. Randolph should have any commissions to execute, I can do them with great ease & will do them with great pleasure, as I shall send both from Italy & France many books home for myself.—In Geneva I shall not fail to inquire for Mr. Terril and will, if it should be in my power, return him some of the kindness you have extended to me—and there and everywhere else on my journey, I pray you to dispose of me without reserve.

I hope, at least, I may have the pleasure of hearing from you occasionally either on business or in continuation of your former kindness and any letters you may inclose to my father will come safely as I have already heard, during my absence, above forty times from him without a single miscarriage.

I pray you to present me respectfully to Colo. Randolph, Mrs. Randolph & their family—& to believe me

Your obliged & obedient Sert. Geo: Ticknor.

RC (MHi); at head of text: "No. VIII."; endorsed by TJ as a letter of 22 Dec. 1817 received 30 Apr. 1817 and so recorded (without year of composition) in SJL. RC (DLC); address cover only; with PoC of TJ to William Lee, 7 Aug. 1817, on verso; addressed: "Thos. Jefferson Esq—Monticello—Virginia—United States"; stamped "SHIP"; franked; postmarked New York, 23 Apr.

Ticknor had forwarded some books to TJ from Hamburg the previous August in the vessel *Cordelia*.

From John Barnes

Dear Sir— George Town Co^a^. 23^d^ Decr 1816.

Your Esteemd fav^r^ 15th on your Return from Bedford After 7. weeks Absence—Covered your 2 powers for my Receiving all divid^ds^ or profits due or may hereafter become due—&c^a^. Be pleased to Observe—Both these Stocks viz the $12,500. 6 pC^ts^ and the 46 share Colum^a^ Bank are in your Name.—and must first be transfer'd from you, to

the Gen[l]—As per Copy—I inclosed to you Oct[r] last.—Viz: Know all Men by these presents that I Thomas Jefferson of Monticello—in Virg[a] do hereby Constitute, and Appoint John Barnes of George Town Co[a] my true and Lawfull Att[y]—for me—and in my Name to transfer into the Name of Thaddeus Kosciusko of—
all the Stock of the United States standing to my Credit on the Books of— x as well, as all my shares in the Bank of Columbia.—
Witness my hand & seal (Seal)
the day of

x each separate

Note. it is also thought Necessary said powers be Acknowledged before a Magistrate—(the Public Officers) are so very particular—

at present I have only time to add, that my Accomodation with Mess[r] Smith & Riddle—has been mutual & satisfactory—for in lieu of the £200 Sterg Return'd, I have Recd as proposed—a good sett of ex—includ[g] damages £234—d[o1] 1[t] & 2[d] already on their passage thr[o] fav[r] M[r] Monroe—address[d] to B. B[rs] & C[o] for the sole Use & Benefit of Gen[l] K. which together with the £300 viz N York will I trust in Course of 2 a 3. m[os]—put his Acco[t] in London for Receipt of £534 Ster[g]. particulars of my Acco[t] therefor &: shall be handed you—when Compleated—waiting the Return of said powers—

I am, Dear Sir, most Respectfully Your Obed[t] servant.

JOHN BARNES.

P.S. I have to beg your forgiveness—my Negligence in not recollecting—I had lodged the Certificates in safe Custody in the Custom House iron Chest—where among Other particular[2] papers—as you truly observed—I should find them—I shall be sure to reserve & return you, Gen[l] K[s] Original power as well his private letter to you—

RC (ViU: TJP-ER); at foot of text: "Thomas Jefferson Esq[r] Monticello"; endorsed by TJ as received 30 Dec. 1816 and so recorded in SJL.

No draft power of attorney from OCT[R] LAST has been found. B. B[RS] & C[O]: Baring Brothers & Company. For Tadeusz Kosciuszko's ORIGINAL POWER and his PRIVATE LETTER to TJ, see the enclosures to TJ's first letter to Barnes of 12 Oct. 1816.

[1]In the manuscript this word appears beneath "Sterg" in the line above.

[2]Manuscript: "paticular."

To Nathaniel T. Eldredge

SIR Monticello near Milton Dec. 23. 16.

I have to ask your permission to become a subscriber to your 'New York public sale report' and inclose you a five dollar bill for the first year in advance. it is of the bank of Virginia which I understand is negociable with you at par. be pleased to direct the papers to me 'at Monticello near Milton.' and to accept the assurances of my respect.

TH: JEFFERSON

PoC (DLC); on verso of reused address cover to TJ; at foot of text: "Mr T. Eldredge"; endorsed by TJ, with his additional notation: "Newspapers. New York Sale report."

Nathaniel T. Eldredge (1793–1856), newspaper publisher and business agent, was a native of Connecticut who moved to New York City as a young man. He edited and printed the New York *Daily Express* in 1813, the *New-York Public Sale Report*, 1814–17, the *New York Times and Commercial Intelligencer*, 1838–40, and the *New York Times and Evening Star*, 1840–41. Eldredge also worked at various times as an auctioneer; a notary public; and a real-estate, legal, and commercial agent. He died in Eastchester, New York (Brigham, *American Newspapers*, 1:624–5, 683; *Longworth's New York Directory* [1817]: 191; [1835]: 237; [1837]: 227; Louis H. Fox, "New York City Newspapers, 1820–1850: A Bibliography," *Papers of The Bibliographical Society of America* 21 [1927]: 106; *New-Yorker*, 8 Feb., 16 May 1840; *Doggett's New-York City Directory* [1846/47]: 129; [1849/50]: 144; DNA: RG 29, CS, N.Y., New York, 1850; New York *Evening Post*, 21 July 1856).

TJ subscribed to the NEW YORK PUBLIC SALE REPORT for two years (*MB*, 2:1329, 1349).

From John Wayles Eppes

DEAR SIR, Mill Brook Decr 23. 1816.

I have directed Martin to remain at Monticello until he learns to Turn—He will be able to get the stocks necessary for the pieces 400 in number and I can send for them after his return—

My health is I hope gradually improving—I am able now to take exercise on horse back which I am in hopes in time with a rigid attention to diet will restore me—Martha unites with me in every wish of affection to yourself and family—I will write to you by Francis.

I am yours sincerely JNO W EPPES

RC (ViU: TJP-ER); addressed: "Thomas Jefferson Esqr Monticello By Martin"; endorsed by TJ as received 26 Dec. 1816.

To Nicholas H. Lewis

DEAR SIR Monticello Dec. 23. 16

Having occasion to look over my correspondence with mr Minor as Secretary of the Rivanna co. I find that I have either lost, mislaid or returned to him a draught of an Indenture prepared by him and inclosed to me in his letter of Nov. 10. 1810. by turning to that letter which is in my possession, but a copy of it, no doubt, retained by him, you will find a description of the Indenture. could you do me the favor to furnish me a copy of it it would oblige me much, for I take for granted there can be no impropriety in asking the copy of a paper the original of which had been sent to me. I pray you to accept the assurance of my great esteem & respect. TH: JEFFERSON

PoC (MHi); on verso of reused address cover to TJ; at foot of text: "M[r] Nicholas Lewis"; endorsed by TJ.

Peter Minor's LETTER OF NOV. 10. 1810. to TJ, which was accounted for as a missing document at TJ to Minor, 18 Nov. 1810, has since been located. It will be printed at 9 Feb. 1817 in a group of documents on Jefferson's Dispute with the Rivanna Company. For TJ's original proposition to which THE INDENTURE sent by Minor was a response, see enclosure to TJ to Minor, 31 Oct. 1810.

From Nicholas H. Lewis

SIR Dec[r] 23rd 1816

I rec[d] your[s] ℔ boy and am sorry I cannot this evening comply with y[r] request

Uncle W[m] Meriwether wished to paruse the correspondence between yourself and M[r] Minor the papers are now in his posession but as soon as I can possably get them I will examine and if the paper alluded to in your letter can be found a copy of it shall certainly be sent to you

I am respectfully[1] yours N, H, LEWIS

RC (MHi); at foot of text: "M[r] Tho[s] Jefferson"; endorsed by TJ as received 23 Dec. 1816 and so recorded in SJL.

[1] Manuscript: "resectfully."

From Hezekiah Niles

HONORED SIR, Baltimore, Dec 23, 1816

you may have observed a proposition of a correspondent, publĭshed in the Weekly Register of the 23rd ult. as to a collection of Speeches, &c. belonging to the period of our revolution. I have reason to believe it comes from one of the first men of our country, & it has excited no little attention. Be pleased to refer to it.

The collection being So loudly called for, I shall attempt to make it. May I ask your aid for this national work?

What I wish at present is—

A list of Such articles as you may have, not to be found in Any book or books accessible to me—shewing also such as you will be so good as to give me, & what you will permit me to have copied, at my expence.

A reference to books or collections where rare & almost forgotten things belonging to those times, may be found

I apprehend, I shall be able to make a very considerable collection. My friend C. A. Rodney, by the possession of his venerable uncle's [p]apers, will assist me much—his resources, I believe, are very ample. I also hope for aid from your predecessor in office Mr. Adams, & from the venerable Charles Thompson.

I mention this subject freely & frankly; for I think it is one that You also will feel an ïnterest in.

With great respect I Am sincerely your's H NILES

RC (DLC); torn at seal; endorsed by TJ as received 5 Jan. 1817 from "Niles Th." and so recorded in SJL.

"Your Well-Wisher," an anonymous CORRESPONDENT writing in August 1816 from Charleston, South Carolina, proposed that Niles "collect and print handsomely a volume of speeches and orations of our revolution"; supposed that TJ, John Adams, and Charles Thomson would "take delight in furnishing materials"; and suggested certain addresses for inclusion in the proposed work (Baltimore *Niles' Weekly Register*, 23 Nov. 1816).

Caesar A. RODNEY possessed the papers of his uncle Caesar Rodney, a signer of the Declaration of Independence.

To William H. Crawford

DEAR SIR Monticello Dec. 24. 16.

On my return after a long absence I learned that you had been so kind as to send the Collector's commission to mr Minor, and that he had declined it. it seems he had in the mean time engaged in a business from which he could not withdraw, a circumstance unknown to me when I troubled you on the subject. my thankfulness to you however is not the less. I mentioned at the same time mr Southall's claims. he is a young man of excellent character, correct and industrious, and from the kindness of his temper would be very acceptable I believe to every body. his experience in the office too as deputy gives him advantage over every other not possessing superior qualifications. I salute you with great esteem & consideration. TH: JEFFERSON

PoC (DLC); on verso of reused address cover of Fitzwhylsonn & Potter to TJ, 11 Dec. 1816; mutilated at seal, with one word and part of another rewritten by TJ; at foot of text: "The Secretary of the Treasury"; endorsed by TJ as a letter to "Crawford Wm H."

TJ had discussed the CLAIMS of Peter Minor and Valentine W. Southall in his 20 Oct. 1816 letter to Alexander J. Dallas, Crawford's predecessor at the Treasury Department.

From Destutt de Tracy

MONSIEUR à Paris ce 24 Decembre 1816.

Je viens de passer huit mois dans une campagne éloignée de près de cent lieux de la capitale. dans cette profonde Solitude, mes plaisirs habituels étaient les travaux de l'agriculture; mais mon plus grand bonheur a été d'y apprendre de vos nouvelles, & la continuation de la bonté extrême dont vous ne cessez de m'honorer. on m'y a envoyé la copie de votre lettre du 17 mai dernier à Mr de Lafayette, & celle d'un autre lettre de vous daté du 3 août à Mr Dupont de nemours; Je ne puis vous exprimer ma vive reconnaissance; mais Je Suis reellement confus de toutes les peines que vous avez prises pour moi. Je n'oserais Jamais reve que mon faible ouvrage en fut digne, Si je n'avais le bonheur de voir que vous en êtes content; ce Sera toujours Son plus beau titre à mes yeux, & ma plus grande consolation du triste état où me reduit la perte totale de la vue, & l'affaiblissement de mes autres facultés. Je ne forme plus qu'un vœu c'est que vous vouliez bien vous déclarer publiquement mon traducteur, & Je desire cette faveur encore plus pour le Succès de l'ouvrage que pour ma gloire. Si Je l'obtiens je dirai ensuite gaiement nunc dimittis. depuis mon retour ici J'ai eu l'honneur de voir une fois Mr Gallatin, qui a eu tant de bontés pour mon fils a Pétersbourg. J'ai eu bien du plaisir à causer avec lui de votre patrie, qui est l'exemple et l'espoir du genre humain. Je n'ai pas le courage de vous rien dire de la mienne, mais puisque Mr Gallatin veut bien permettre que mes lettres passent par lui, J'en profite, avec empressement, pour vous renouveller les assurances de mon admiration, de ma reconnaissance & de mon respect:

TRACY

P.S. vous avez tant de bontés pour moi, Monsieur, que je prends la liberté de joindre à cette lettre, un petit manuscrit intitulé principes logiques ou recueil de faits relatifs à l'intelligence humaine. Je ne puis pas juger de ce que cela vaut, mais il me parait que c'est un abrégé utile de mes trois premiers volumes, & fort propre à faire connaître en assez peu de pages tout ce que je Sais des opérations de notre intelligence, de la Source de nos idées, de la maniere dont nous les formons, les exprimons & les combinons, de la cause pour nous de toute certitude & de toute erreur & de nos veritables moyens darriver à la verité, c'est la, ce me semble, la Seule veritable logique; toute celle qu'on nous donne ne prescrivant que des formes, et ne remontant jamais jusqu'aux principes. comme je n'espère pas que dans votre pays heureusement essentiellement actif, on accorde beaucoup d'attention à des recherches purement Spéculatives; je ne me flatte pas que malgré votre importante protection, on prenne la peine de traduire ces trois premiers volumes qui forment mon traité de l'entendement, & encore moins qu'un libraire ose faire la speculation de les imprimer en français; je pense que ce petit écrit peut être un supplement utile, & même donner la curiosité de consulter l'ouvrage principal. d'ailleurs il renferme même quelques vues qui ne Sont pas dans celui là Je Soumets le tout à votre Jugement

Avec la permission de Mr Gallatin Je joins encore ici un exemplaire imprimé de ce même quatrième volume dont vous avez le manuscrit, & pour la traduction duquel vous daignez prendre tant de peine. je desire d'autant plus que ce volume ci vous parvienne, qu'il me parait que les exemplaires que je vous en avais déjà envoyé ont éte perdus, & qu'il y a dans l'imprimé un commencement de mon tome cinquieme traitant de la morale que je crains qui ne Soit pas dans le manuscrit

Je Serais bien curieux de Savoir Si jamais vous avez recu un petit écrit de moi Sur l'instruction publique, & un petit volume où mon nom n'est pas, contenant l'analyse du grand ouvrage de Mr Dupuis de l'académie des inscriptions Sur l'origine de tous les cultes. J'avoue que je tiens un peu à ces deux ouvrages; mais je n'ose pourtant vous les envoyer encore ci joint parce que je Sens que c'est aussi vous trop occuper de moi & de mes reveries. votre extrême bonté est ma Seule excuse.

EDITORS' TRANSLATION

Sir Paris 24 December 1816.

I have just spent eight months in the country nearly a hundred leagues from the capital. In this profound solitude, my habitual pleasures came from farming, but my greatest happiness was to receive news from you and hear of the great kindness with which you continue to honor me. The copies of your letter of 17 May to Mr. de Lafayette and that of 3 August from you to Mr. Du Pont de Nemours were sent to me. I cannot sufficiently express my deep gratitude, but I am really embarrassed by all the trouble you have taken for me. I would never have dreamed that my little book was worthy of it, if I did not have the pleasure of knowing that you approve of it. In my eyes, that will always be its greatest merit and my biggest consolation for the sad situation to which the total loss of eyesight and the weakening of my other faculties reduce me. My only wish now is that you would be willing to declare yourself as my translator publicly, and I desire this favor even more for the success of the book than for my own glory. If I obtain it I will then merrily say nunc dimittis. Since my return here I have had the honor of once seeing Mr. Gallatin, who was so kind to my son in Saint Petersburg. I really enjoyed talking with him about your country, which is the model and hope for mankind. I lack the courage to tell you about mine, but as Mr. Gallatin is so kind as to allow my letters to be sent through him, I eagerly take advantage of this opportunity to renew to you the assurances of my admiration, gratitude, and respect: TRACY

P.S. You are so kind to me, Sir, that I take the liberty of enclosing in this letter a short manuscript entitled *Principes Logiques, ou Recueil de Faits relatifs a l'Intelligence Humaine*. I cannot judge its worth, but, in my opinion, it is a useful summary of my first three volumes and particularly well-suited to convey in just a few pages everything I know about the operation of our intelligence, the origin of our ideas, the manner in which we form, express, and combine them, the reason for all our certainties and errors, and our real means of arriving at the truth. It seems to me that this is the only true logic, as all those given to us hitherto prescribe nothing but forms and never go all the way back to first principles. As I do not expect that in your country, which, fortunately, is essentially active, people pay much attention to purely speculative research, I do not flatter myself that, despite your important endorsement, anyone will take the trouble of translating these first three volumes, which constitute my treatise on the understanding. I flatter myself even less that a bookstore owner will risk having them printed in French. I think this little book can be a useful supplement and may even arouse the readers' curiosity to consult the main work. Besides, it even contains a few opinions that are not in it. I submit the whole to your judgment

With Mr. Gallatin's permission, I also enclose herein a printed copy of the same fourth volume of which you have the manuscript and for the translation of which you condescended to take so much trouble. I desire this volume to reach you all the more, because I suspect that the copies I had already sent you were lost and the printed version contains the beginning of my fifth volume dealing with morality, which I fear is not included in the manuscript

I would be very curious to know if you ever received a short piece written by me on public education and a small volume on which my name does not appear containing the analysis of the great work by Mr. Dupuis, of the Académie des Inscriptions, on the origin of all religions. I confess that I am a bit prejudiced in favor of these two works. I dare not send them to you with this letter, however, because I feel that that would be asking you to spend too much time on me and my daydreams. Your extreme kindness is my only excuse.

RC (DLC); in a clerk's hand, signed by Destutt de Tracy; endorsed by TJ as received 20 Mar. 1817 and so recorded in SJL. Translation by Dr. Genevieve Moene. Enclosures: (1) manuscript, not found, of Destutt de Tracy, *Principes Logiques, ou Recueil de Faits relatifs a l'Intelligence Humaine* (Paris, 1817; manuscript and printed volume listed in Poor, *Jefferson's Library*, 8 [no. 455]). (2) Destutt de Tracy, *Traité de la volonté et de ses effets* (1st ed. Paris, 1815; 2d ed. Paris, 1818; Poor, *Jefferson's Library*, 8 [no. 454]).

MON FAIBLE OUVRAGE was Destutt de Tracy, *Treatise on Political Economy*. His TRAITÉ was the *Élémens d'Idéologie*, and his examination of the work by Charles François DUPUIS was his *Analyse Raisonnée*.

From Hezekiah Niles

HON. SIR. Balt. Dec 24. 1816

Assured that it will afford you pleasure to notice any improvement in what, perhaps, may be called the household arts, I enclose a small piece of a preparation just offered for sale in our city for the purpose of clarifying coffee, as well as wines & other liquors. I have tried it for the former, And it completely answers the purpose—a piece an inch square is the quantity for a gallon, dropped into the boiler at the time of drawing it off the fire.

The inventor, as he claims himself to be, says "this menstruum may be compounded of all animal & vegitable mucilages"—but its nature will appear evident to you.

Very respectfully, H NILES

RC (DLC); endorsed by TJ as received 5 Jan. 1817 from "Niles Th." and so recorded in SJL; notation by TJ above endorsement: "Newspapers."

Niles soon published a similarly positive description of Daniel Bartling's IMPROVEMENT: "The mode of using this discovery, is simply to pour boiling water on its surface, and a pure and transparent mucilage is immediately produced: it instantly then expands to the dimensions of the vessel containing the liquor intended to be clarified, and will sink to the bottom carrying every mote, speck and particle in its descent" (Baltimore *Niles' Weekly Register*, 4 Jan. 1817).

To Charles Willson Peale

DEAR SIR Monticello Dec. 24. 16.

I recieved in October a letter from mr M[c]Ilhenny whom you were so kind as to recommend as a watchmaker, informing me he would come on to establish himself at Charlottesville as soon as he could hear from me. I was just about setting out on a journey to Bedford, and answered him therefore by advising him to postpone his coming till my return. he did so, and arrived in Charlottesville by the stage on Wednesday last. Thursday was rainy. on Friday he came here, I kept him all night, and on Saturday morning went with him to Charlottesville presented & recommended him to the principal persons there, procured him a shop in the very best and most public position, undertook to the landlord for his year's rent & board, and assuring him of all other necessary aid until he could stand on his own legs, I left him in charlottesville, on his promise to come to Monticello Monday mornin[g] to repair 3. or 4. clocks & as many watches which we had needing it, while his landlord would be fitting up the room for him. on Sunday morning without a word of explanation, as far as I have learnt, to any body, he got into the stage with all his baggage and went off. I can conjecture no cause for this. a watchmaker in Stanton (40. miles above this) who had recieved some work from this quarter, heard that I was procuring a person of that trade to come here. mr McIlhenny coming thro' Stanton called at that watchmaker's (Logan's) and Logan discovered th[at] he was the person. he instantly put one of his men into the same stage which brought McIlhenny, who on his arrival in Charlottesville engag[ed] a house. but the remoteness of this and the entire patronage of the place which I had ensured to McIlhenny, with his excellent stand left him nothing to fear from that competition. I have thought it best to state these things to you lest his friends might think I had not[1] fulfilled my proffers of aid to him, or discoragement be produced to any other real master of the business who might be disposed to come and relieve us from the bungler whom this incident has brought upon us. it is an excellent stand for a sober, correct & good workman. I am not the less thankful to you for the trouble you were so kind as to take in relieving our wants. something erratic & feeble in the texture of this young man's mind will I suspect prevent his becoming stationary & industrious any where. I salute you with affection and respect

Th: Jefferson

PoC (MHi); on reused address cover of Elizabeth Ticknor to TJ, 10 Sept. 1816; mutilated at seal, with one word rewritten by TJ; edge trimmed; at foot of first page: "Mr Peale"; endorsed by TJ.

[1] Word added in margin.

Josephus B. Stuart's Account of a Visit to Monticello

Tuesday 24th December 1816.

After breakfast proceeded to Mr Jeffersons—spent the day with him. Mrs Randolph & daughter[1] Helen (Granddaughter) The situation is delightfull—the prospect more extensive & diversified than any I ever saw—on the one hand you can see to Harpers ferry 110 miles—on the other the Pyramid (so called) 40 miles,

---

The day fine—the great man communicative, & the following is a summary of his observations on general subjects.—
This[2] country at present is governed by an aristocracy in which the great mass of the people have no voice.

In many of the states & also in the general goverment the constitutions should be so amended as that all offices should emenate directly from the people. Public officers at home & abroad should be well supported.—{He is in favor of Pickens amendment to the constitution}. This Country is most likely to have its Constitution undermined by a great national debt: which already is double to what he ever thought it would be.—He wishes the Constitution so amended that every age[3] (say 20 years) shall pay off their own debts, then ways & means would be provided at the same time—No State Banks, which by the by the General Goverment have the power to put down.

---

but have 2 national banks—one to receive specie & give drafts to facilitate exchange at par,[4] The other a more general Brokers establishment to advance money on bills or notes, deducting the Interest, & adding a reasonable per cent, by way of premium.

This of course would exclude every thing but specie from circulation, but in time of War to meet exigencies, the goverment could issue ten millions per ann— of Treasury notes, payable ten per cent annually & in this way carry on a war to any extent. England he thinks has expended the fee simple of her whole Island, & that no palliative will save her from a revolution, which he wishes for most ardently.

He rejoices[5] at the result of the Battle of Waterloo, as it saved France from a long reign of military despotism which Napoleon would have established if he had been victorious, now France suffers but her present sufferings are the prelude to her final emancipation—not that she will be a republic—but an elective monarchy which is all she is capable of[6]—& this will probably be the Duke of Orleans.—Germany also is nearly ripe for a revolution—
Napoleon he considers as a hard character.—The Emperor Alexander as one of the best of men.

---

he related circumstances relative to this goverment to prove this.—

He is a great friend to Gen[l] Wilkinson, & knows no one thing he ever did amiss.—Rather cast a censure on Madison, but spoke highly of Monroe Whose knowledge of human nature he thinks unequalled

---

Has a correct opinion of Tompkins—spoke well of Clinton—thinks old John Adams honest but had bad advisers—J Quincy a learned man, & reformed monarchist. would act for the best interests of his country.—

M[r] J. considers us as navy mad—we want in peace only the nest egg of a navy.—He fears it will yet dictate to the nation.[7] M[r] J. is opposed to a standing Army & military schools, only so far as may be necessary to teach the Rudiments of the science to a few who on an emergency should constitute our officers.—He thinks the late war has got up too much of a war spirit in this country, which may lead us into difficulties; we have nothing to do with wars but such as are offensive—[8]

Restrnt of Commerce to proper limits—let us be an agricultural, & so far as may be proper or necessary for our own purposes a manufactoring people—Extend good faith to all nations for never should have any other than a war of defence, which would seldom occur.—

We have made too much noise about our exploits, & turned molehills into mountains—the mania has pervaded the nation, & the worst consequences may follow—Let us have one or two more wars—continue our present strain of eulogy on ourselves, & bestow the same high marks of distinction on the officers, & it will be but a little time, 'till we must bid farewell to our Republic, & accept in return, a military despotism, or at best, an elective monarchy.—M[r] J says the Treasury depart[nt]—since Gallatin left it has been wretchedly managed.—That Marshall is destitute of principal.

M[r] J. Reads without glasses.[9]

---

as to commerce we want no more than to take away our produce & bring back what we really stand in need of from other countries.[10]—We ought to manufacture[11] all our own clothes.—& not be too proud to wear them.—He had on a blue quaker coat, blue cloth vest, olive cotton cordyroy breeches with horn buttons on the whole—all homemade.—Has his cloth manufactured at Wilmington N.C—He has the most despicable opinion of the Eastn Federalists—& particularly of Otis.—He thinks however that the great mass of the Federalists[12] are real friends[13] to their country—His House is a ⟊ & not yet compleated. I was disappointed in it.—His principal curiosities are of the Indian Kind.—He appears principally devoted to his estates, & spends 3 months of each year at Bedford where he has a plantation.

He is now 73.[14]—not much grey—his teeth apparently good—a great eater.—drinks French wines only.—
enjoys good health.

He commenced here in 1768—His father lived here before him.—Tobacco has gone by in this part of the country wheat is the principal crop which brings from 5 to 20 Bushels the acre, lands north about 20 the acre on an average.—He wishes to see the draw back act repealed.—I presented him with some Gypsum from New York, & a grapeshot from the field of Waterloo.—
He complains that he has outlived his generation—that go where he will he knows no one:—except now & then an old grey head tottering on the verge of the grave.—He is not as well informed of the improvements in the northern states, as to roads, Bridges—steam Boats—stages, & particularly manufactories as I had anticipated.—His Greatest solicitude is to see England revolutionized before his Death, We had a conversation on the subject of Louisiana, & the importance of that purchase:—He appears anxious to have me spend some time with him, & miss Randolph really insists upon it: but I shall depart tomorrow. T. M. Randolphs family reside constantly at M.

T.J.R. has lately married miss Nicholas & resides between his father & Grandfather.

The weather is as mild as the first of October at Albany Mr J. is extremely awkward & ungracefull in his manner—His house servants are all mulattoes.

Quere? His Venus is admirable.
Wednesday 25th Dec^{r}—wrote N. S. I. Lovett, & Frances Stuart & M. [...].

Charlottsville 2 m w of—m^{r} J. is the county town of Albemarle County—a mere village.—
Mr Jefferson considers this country as labouring under a great degree of Religious fanatacism. That freedom of conscience is less tolerated here than on the Continent of Europe, for tho we have no spanish inquisition, yet we have what is worse, an Inquisition of public opinion! That our Bible societies & foreign Missionary-Societies are not

only impolitick, but unjust; for they carry misery & wretchedness into every country where they are introduced, as the proselytes are rejected from all society as outcasts.—what said he, would we say if Mahometans, with their alcoran, or even Roman Catholicks with their Vaticcan Bibles were to inundate our Country?—& shall we arrogate to ourselves that we are right & all the world beside are wrong?—this surely does not look like allowing every man to worship God in his own way.—Further this fanatacism of the day, will have an injurious effect on this country as it will tend to extend the empire of Bigotry & superstition, which are hostile to a Republic, which is based[15] on liberality of sentiment, & a general diffusion of knowledge. In the evening took my departure, drove 22 miles one Horse died.—Very warm weather.—Bad roads.—

MS (MiU-C: Stuart Papers); in Stuart's hand; extracted from diaries 4–5; one word illegible.

Josephus Bradner Stuart (1787–1828), physician, businessman, and attorney, was a native of Blandford, Massachusetts. He received an M.D. degree from the University of Pennsylvania in 1810 and, after moving to New York, served as a medical officer in the state militia, 1811–12, and as a first lieutenant and regimental paymaster in the United States Army, 1813–15. Stuart was chancellor of the American consulate in London, 1815–16. Returning thereafter to the state of New York, he worked as a land speculator, farmer, miller, storekeeper, lawyer, and from 1818–21 as the proprietor of a steamboat on Lake Erie (MiU-C: Stuart Papers; Joel Munsell, *The Annals of Albany* [1850–59], 3:239; Stuart, *An Inaugural Essay, containing Experiments and Observations in defence of the Doctrine of Cutaneous Absorption* [Albany, 1810]; Hugh Hastings and Henry Harmon Noble, eds., *Military Minutes of the Council of Appointment of the State of New York, 1783–1821* [1901–02], 2:1246, 1398; Heitman, *U.S. Army*, 1:934; *ASP, Commerce and Navigation*, 2:51–2; Ogdensburgh, N.Y., *St. Lawrence Gazette*, 14 Apr. 1818; New York *National Advocate*, 10 May 1819; *New-York Spectator*, 9 Nov. 1821; gravestone inscription in Albany Rural Cemetery, Menands, N.Y.).

THE PYRAMID was Willis's Mountain in Buckingham County. North Carolina congressman Israel Pickens proposed an AMENDMENT TO THE CONSTITUTION in January 1813 that would require every state to be divided into districts with roughly the same population for the purpose of electing members of the United States House of Representatives and the electoral college (*Mr. Pickens' Motion to amend the Constitution of the U. States, on the Subject of the Election of Representatives and Electors* [Washington, 1813]). J QUINCY: John Quincy Adams. The most recent DRAW BACK ACT was "An Act to allow drawback of duties on spirits distilled and sugar refined within the United States, and for other purposes" (*U.S. Statutes at Large*, 3:338–40 [30 Apr. 1816]).

[1] Word interlined in place of "miss."

[2] An unmatched opening double quotation mark at the beginning of this word is editorially omitted.

[3] Word interlined in place of "century."

[4] Stuart here wrote "(See next book) Ended at Monticello in Albemarle County Virginia Decr 24th 1816." At the start of his next diary notebook, he added the words "Commenced at Monticello (the seat of Mr Thomas Jefferson) Decr 24th 1816—J. B, Stuart" and a brief note unrelated to his visit.

[5] Manuscript: "rejoics."

[6] Manuscript: "off."

[7] Stuart here interlined "{See Decr 27th}" to indicate the location of the remainder of the diary entry for 24 Dec. 1816. The continuation, which is headed "See 24th

Instant" and "Army," is editorially inserted here.

[8] Thus in manuscript, with "defensive" probably intended.

[9] The continuation of the 24 Dec. entry inserted at 27 Dec. 1816 ends here.

[10] Preceding three words interlined.

[11] Manuscript: "manufacre."

[12] Manuscript: "Federalilsts."

[13] Manuscript: "feinds."

[14] Reworked from "74."

[15] Manuscript: "basised."

To Joseph Delaplaine

Dear Sir Monticello Dec. 25. 16.

My general aversion from the presumption of intruding on the public an opinion of works offered to their notice has yielded in the present instance to the merit of your undertaking, and to your belief, well or ill founded, that my testimony in it's favor may be of advantage to it. I have written therefore, in a separate letter, which you are free to publish, what I can conscientiously[1] say on that subject. indulging a wish to render you a service, I have availed myself of the same occasion to obtain relief from a corvée which is become entirely intolerable. the first part of my other letter will have the effect of an indirect appeal to the mercy and commiseration of those who are torturing the remnant of my life by letters and applications, generally respectful, often kind, but always, increasing my exhaustless labors, and unintentionally prostrating all the ease and comfort of my life. if the expressions in that letter should have the effect of saving me from being thus killed with kindness, your book will become a blessing to me, as I hope it will be to yourself.

To the enquiries in your's of Nov. 23. I answer 'say nothing of my religion. it is known to my god and myself alone. it's evidence before the world is to be sought in my life. if that has been honest and dutiful to society the religion which has regulated it cannot be a bad one.'

I repeat the assurances of my esteem and respect.

Th: Jefferson

RC (LNT: George H. and Katherine M. Davis Collection); addressed: "Mr Joseph Delaplaine Philadelphia"; franked; postmarked Charlottesville, 30 Dec.; endorsed by Delaplaine. PoC (DLC); on verso of reused address cover of Francis Adrian Van der Kemp to TJ, 8 Sept. 1816; torn at seal, with missing year in dateline rewritten by TJ; endorsed by TJ.

[1] Manuscript: "conscientitiously."

To Joseph Delaplaine

Dear Sir Monticello Dec. 25. 16.

On my return from Bedford, after an absence of 7. weeks, I found here your favors of Oct. 28. Nov. 13. 20. & 23.[1] with a copy of the 1st N° of your Repository. but I found also an immense accumulation of letters recieved during my absence, some of which claimed my first attentions. you know my aversion to the drudgery of the writing table. the great affliction of my present life is a too oppressive correspondence. it is wearing me down in body and mind; and leaves me scarcely a moment to attend to my affairs or to indulge in the luxury of reading and reflection, which would soothe as a balm the decaying powers of life. yet I take up my pen with chearfulness to express the satisfaction with which I have read & examined this first number of your work. I think it well executed both in manner and matter. a judicious selection of facts, related[2] in an elevated style, and enlivened by a rich fancy carries the reader on with the ardor of his author, while the fine traces of the graver embody in his mind the figure with the facts of the relation. I have understood that the scale of the narrative has been censured, by some as too short, by others as too long. I think myself it is well proportioned to the object of the work. were I to indulge a criticism, it would be on the omission to quote authorities for the lives & portraits of Columbus & Vespucius. their age was so remote from ours in time and place that whatever can be learnt of them now must be from public sources with which the reader might wish to be acquainted. in recent histories authorities are not required, because their publication is itself an appeal, to living witnesses of their truth. with my wishes that you may recieve a just remuneration for the labors and expences of this interesting publication accept the assurance of my esteem and respect. Th: Jefferson

RC (LNT: George H. and Katherine M. Davis Collection); at foot of text: "Mr Delaplaine." PoC (DLC); endorsed by TJ. Printed in *New-York Evening Post*, 22 Jan. 1817, and elsewhere.

TJ's plea for respite from a too oppressive correspondence was paraphrased as follows in *Delaplaine's Repository*, 1:151–2: "Since his last retirement, in addition to the necessary attention to his agricultural and domestic affairs, at Monticello, where he chiefly resides, and occasional visits to his other estates, his great reputation has been productive of frequent calls upon portions of his time which ought to have been yielded only to ease and relaxation. The scientific and literary, throughout the union, have looked upon him as their adviser and patron; and have, indeed, seldom failed to gain considerable advantage by their applications. But the increase of his correspondence has, at length, become so enormously great, that although a strict economist of time, he has found it utterly impossible to allow himself a sufficient portion of rest, being obliged to devote five or six hours of every day of his life, merely to the business of answering letters, many of which are, of course, of the most uninteresting character. This kind of labour was justly complained of by general Washington, in a communication to a military friend, soon after the revolutionary war, as compelling him to neglect his private affairs, almost to the ruin of his fortune, and as depriving him of exercise, comfort, and health. Mr. Jefferson, therefore, at a much more advanced age, will be justified in the expression of his desire on this subject, contained in his letter recently published." The letter from George Washington voicing similar complaints was addressed from Mount Vernon, 7 Feb. 1785, to David Humphreys (Washington, *Papers, Confederation Ser.*, 3:487–9).

[1] *New-York Evening Post*: "your favour of the 23d of November."

[2] Word interlined in place of "clothed."

To Chapman Johnson

DEAR SIR Monticello Dec. 26. 16.

You have heretofore known something of jarrings between the Rivanna company and myself. certain claims of right, equal, & even paramount to my own, which they set up to my canal, a work which has cost me 30,000.D. and which would render it's value almost null to me, oblige me to bring a suit in chancery to quiet my title. I have prepared a bill, but cannot finish it until I can see an act of ass. of 1794. Dec. 22. no copy of which is to be found in this part of the country. as soon as ready, I will inclose you the bill, ask the favor of you to suggest any alterations in it, to inclose me a spa[1] in Chancery against the proper defendants and to be my counsel in the case.

I think I have on some former occasion asked the favor of you to be my counsel in any case in which I may be concerned in any court in which you practice. If I am mistaken in this, I now make that request that in such cases, and without waiting for a particular application[2] which accidents may retard, you will be so good as to appear & act for me as a thing of course. I pray you to accept assurances of my great esteem and high consideration TH: JEFFERSON

P.S. Jan. 1. 17. the above is a copy of a letter addressed to you at Staunton at it's date but recollecting that you may be at Richmond, I have thought it advisable to send a duplicate there. having found satisfactory evidence of the contents of the act of 1794. I have finished the bill. where shall I direct it to you, that after a perusal of it, you may decide as to the defs & the style of naming them.

PoC (MHi); on verso of reused address cover of Joseph E. McIlhenney to TJ, 17 Sept. 1816; adjacent to signature and above postscript: "Chapman Johnson esq."; endorsed by TJ as a letter of 26 Dec. 1816 with a "P.S. Jan. 1. 17."

TJ's bill of complaint against the RIVANNA COMPANY will be printed below at 9 Feb. 1817, the date on which TJ sent it to Johnson in its finished form. The Virginia statute OF 1794. DEC. 22. was "An Act concerning the clearing of the

North Fork of James River" (*Acts of Assembly* [1794 sess.], 30–1).

[1]Abbreviation for "subpoena."
[2]Manuscript: "applications."

From John Trumbull

SIR New York 26th December 1816

Twenty eight years have elapsed since, under the kind protection of your hospitable roof at Chaillot, I painted your portrait in my picture of the Declaration of Independance, the composition of which had been planned two years before in your library: the long succeeding period of War & Tumult palsied & Suspended my work, and threw me, as you know into other pursuits

Peace is at length restored, and we live to See our Country enjoying a State of public prosperity, & of individual Happiness[1] such as no enthusiast of our Revolution could have anticipated.

The Government of the U.S. are restoring to more than their original Splendor the Buildings devoted to national purposes at Washington, which were barbarously sacrificed to the Rage of War.—& I have thought this a proper opportunity to make my first application for public patronage, & to request to be employed in decorating the Walls of those Buildings with the paintings which have employed So many years of my Life.

The Declaration of Independance is finished—Trenton Princeton & York Town are far advanced, in addition to Bunker's Hill & Quebec which were long since finished & engraved—I shall take them all with me to the Seat of Government, in a few days that I may not merely talk of what I will do, but show what I have done: And I hope it will be thought that the declaration of Independance with portraits of those eminent Patriots & Statesmen who then laid the foundation of our Nation; and the military pictures with portraits of those Heroes who either cemented that foundation with their Blood, or lived to aid in the Superstructure, will be appropriate Ornaments for the Halls of the Senate & the House of Representatives.[2]

The work has been carried thus far by my own unaided exertion & can be finished only by me:[3] future Artists may possess superior talents, but time has already withdrawn almost all their models of that most interesting period:[4] and I who was one of the youngest Actors in the early Scenes of the War, have passd the age of Sixty: no time remains therefore for hesitation,[5] and I can scarcely hope for what is necessary to complete Such an undertaking.

The memory of your early kindness, and of the interest which you formerly took in the work is too strongly impressed on my mind to Suffer a doubt to intrude of your approbation & powerful protection at this time.

May I request that you will favor me with an Answer addressed to me at the Post Office in Washington.[6]

With grateful remembrance of your former friendship

I am Sir Your Obed^{t} Servt & friend JN^{O} TRUMBULL

RC (DLC: TJ Papers, 163:28630); endorsed by TJ as received 5 Jan. 1817 and so recorded in SJL. RC (DLC); address cover only; with PoC of TJ to James Madison, 8 Feb. 1817, on verso; addressed: "Thomas Jefferson &c &c &c Monticello Virginia"; franked; postmarked New York, 27 Dec. Dft (CtY: Trumbull Papers); endorsed by Trumbull. Tr (ICHi); entirely in Trumbull's hand; subjoined to Tr of a similar letter from Trumbull to John Adams of 26 Dec. 1816; endorsed by Trumbull: "Drafts of Letters to John Adams and Thomas Jefferson … on the Subject of paintings."

John Trumbull (1756–1843), artist and diplomat, was born in Lebanon, Connecticut, and graduated from Harvard College (later Harvard University) in 1773. During the American Revolution he served as an aide-de-camp to George Washington in 1775 and as deputy adjutant general of the Continental army's Northern Department, 1776–77. In 1780 Trumbull sailed to Europe, where he studied painting with Benjamin West in London. He was expelled from England later that year under suspicion of espionage, but he returned to the British capital following the peace and continued to hone his skills under West, 1784–89. Trumbull met TJ in Paris in 1786, was his guest for short periods of time, and executed his life portrait there, 1787–88. He returned in 1789 to the United States and continued his work as an artist. Trumbull accompanied the American diplomat John Jay to Great Britain as his private secretary in 1794, and he spent much of the following twenty years in the British Isles, during which time he served on a commission to settle claims under the Jay Treaty. Following the War of 1812 he returned to America and offered to paint a series of historical pictures for the fire-ravaged United States Capitol. On 6 Feb. 1817 Congress commissioned Trumbull to produce "four paintings commemorative of the most important events of the American Revolution." In 1824 he completed the twelve-by-eighteen-foot artworks: *The Declaration of Independence*, *The Surrender of General Burgoyne at Saratoga*, *The Surrender of Lord Cornwallis at Yorktown*, and *The Resignation of General Washington*. Trumbull was elected a member of the American Philosophical Society in 1792, served as president of the American Academy of the Fine Arts, 1817–36, and published his autobiography in 1841. He died in New York City (*ANB*; *DAB*; *Sibley's Harvard Graduates*, 18:331–48; Theodore Sizer, ed., *The Autobiography of Colonel John Trumbull, Patriot-Artist, 1756–1843* [1953]; Sizer and Caroline Rollins, *The Works of Colonel John Trumbull: Artist of the American Revolution* [rev. ed., 1967]; Heitman, *Continental Army*, 550; *PTJ*, esp. 9:456, 10:438–41; Bush, *Life Portraits*, 5–7; APS, Minutes, 20 July 1792 [MS in PPAmP]; *U.S. Statutes at Large*, 3:400; *New York Herald*, 11 Nov. 1843).

TJ's primary residence in Paris during the 1780s, the Hôtel de Langeac, was located next to one of the city gates, La Grille de CHAILLOT (Howard C. Rice Jr., *Thomas Jefferson's Paris* [1976], 51).

[1] Reworked in Dft from "of Prosperity & general Happiness."

[2] In Dft, next paragraph begins with "<*powerful*> Several considerations decide me to make my application at the present moment."

[3] Preceding seven words underscored in Dft.

[4] Preceding five words not in Dft.

[5] Remainder of sentence not in Dft.

[6] In Dft paragraph reads "May I Hope that my <*plan*> application will meet your approbation, & <*Such*> Support, & that you will honor me with an Answer addressed to me at Washington—poste restante."

To Patrick Gibson

DEAR SIR Monticello Dec. 28. 16.

A load of flour was sent off from hence a few days ago, and another will follow within two or three days. that from Bedford is of necessity later, it's distance from Lynchburg rendering it impracticable to be sent there until they have done all their fall seeding. mr Yancey informs me he will not be able to get his tobacco down till March.

My grandson is the bearer of an order for 220.D. and I shall have to draw on you about the middle of next month for somewhere between 500. & 750.D. to pay for a purchase of corn. I salute you with great esteem & respect TH: JEFFERSO[N]

PoC (DLC); on verso of reused address cover of James Freeman to TJ, 2 Oct. 1816; mutilated at seal; at foot of text: "Mr Gibson"; endorsed by TJ.

The order for $220 repaid TJ's GRANDSON Thomas Jefferson Randolph for loans to his grandfather of $155 and $50 on 17 and 18 Dec. 1816, respectively, reimbursed him $8 "for having had a gun of mine repaired" by Richard Garner, and left a balance of $7 in TJ's favor (*MB*, 2:1329, 1330).

To Fitzwhylsonn & Potter

MESS^RS FITZWHYLSON AND POTTER Monticello Dec. 29. 16.

Your's of the 11th is received, as also the 2^d vol. of Pleasan[ts'] edition of the laws. the bundle of Edinburg Reviews was sent from Milton at the time formerly mentioned, and are supposed to have been left at a place where the stages are changed. my grandson is now setting out for Richmond and will enquire for them. when you send them and the collection of laws, be so good as to add a copy of the English translation of Josephus, the 8vo edition as no other is desired. I am in great distress for the Sessions acts of 1794. if you can single out that volume and send it to me by mail, you will oblige me. Accept my respectful salutations TH: JEFFERSON

PoC (DLC); on verso of a reused address cover from Timothy Banger to TJ; edge trimmed; endorsed by TJ.

TJ's GRANDSON was Thomas Jefferson Randolph.

From Joseph Milligan

Dear Sir Georgetown December 29th 1816

Together with this you will receive the first proof of Political Economy

No doubt you have long since given me up as one of the most Carless men regardless of what I had Said and without intention to perform My promise to you Respecting the publication of the book. but truly this was not the case; I have for two or three years laboured under pecuniary Embarassments from malicious Reports that were circulated against me amongst my Creditors They have like the Prophet Jonah with the great City laboured hard and felt much grieved that their predictions have not as yet become true—but that they might not altogether be accounted false Prophets they have brought about ten Law-suits against me principally arrising out of Endorsements for others and that because the drawers of the Notes were out of town but in no instance will those Result in Loss to me, Indeed the whole that I Shall have to pay including Cost will not be more than fifteen hundred dollars and that I trust I shall be able to do without a Sacrafice but I am determined to pay them the last Cent

I have had the paper and type for the work past me more than a year but when I received the manuscript I was Engaged printing the Laws of the last Session of congress and that and Some other matters have delayed me thus long but now that I have commenced the work I must get it out as fast as it is possible to get the proofs to and from you I hope you will pardon me for troubling you with my difficulties but I thought it Necessary to tell you the true cause of the delay not with a view of asking assistance for that I trust is not necessary—

There is one thing which you could do for me that is to Say to the present Secretary of State (If you thought So) that I would Execute any printing binding or Stationary business that might be wanted for the public with Care and attention and on Equitable terms—

business is all that I want and that I will Execute on the best terms and If I get it I will in a few years be placed out of the grasp of those that used me in Such a manner as I trust I may never be tempted to treat them even If I should have them in my power

With respect yours Joseph Milligan

PS. by the next post you may Expect an other proof please Return the manuscript Copy with the proof sheet J.M.

RC (DLC); addressed: "Thomas Jefferson Esqr Monticello Milton via [i.e., Virginia]"; at foot of first page: "over"; endorsed by TJ as received 5 Jan. 1817 and so recorded in SJL. Enclosure: manuscript and proofs, not found, of a portion of Destutt de Tracy, *Treatise on Political Economy*.

The GREAT CITY in the biblical book of Jonah was Nineveh. James Monroe was the PRESENT SECRETARY OF STATE.

To Nicolas G. Dufief

Dec. 30.

wrote him a note for the best dict. not larger than 8vo Ital. & Eng. or Ital. & Fr. the former preferred caeteris paribus.

FC (DLC: TJ Papers, 208:37184); on recto of reused address cover of William Sampson to TJ, 30 Nov. 1816; abstract in TJ's hand; partially dated; subjoined to PoC of TJ to Dufief, 14 Dec. 1816. Not recorded in SJL.

Notes on the Rent Claims of the Heirs of Bennett Henderson

[by 30 Dec. 1816]

Some Notes on the claim of rents by Frances, Lucy & Nancy C. Henderson.

The loss I have sustained by this purchase amounts to the whole value of the lands. it is a fair object in me then to[1] save as much of that loss as I possibly can; it is justifiable to avail myself of every principle of law or equity, which can protect me, and a candid judge, either in law or equity, would give me the benefit of every such principle.[2] the other party, on the other hand, is struggling, not to avoid any loss, but, under colour of law, to catch a gain.[3] they have recieved the money once, have been raised and maintained on it, as I have been informed and believe, on better evidence than I have yet had to the contrary, which evidence will be produced, and they are now endeavoring to get payment a second time.

The questions are

1. Who has had possession of their lands?
2. for what rents am I responsible?[4]
3. have not these been paid?

1. Who has had possession of these lands? On the death of a parent the law casts the possession of his lands directly on his children; and they are from that moment seised and possessed of them.[5] the guardian has no possession of them other than that of an overseer or other

agent, in the name and right of his principal; he merely occupies or[6] employs them. during the time they are occupied or[7] employed, the rents or profits belong to his wards; while unoccupied or[8] unemployed, the loss is theirs.

Where there are opposite claims to lands, the law adjudges the possession to be in that party in which the right is found ultimately to be; unless the other has an actual occupation or possession, by enclosure, or culture or other actual and exclusive[9] use. while I occupied these lots I am, as any other tenant would have been, liable for reasonable rents, no specific rent having been settled by agreement. but while they were open and unoccupied, the claims I might have upon them, if I ever had[10] any, no more placed the possession of them in me, than their claims did in them: and the right being in them, the law adjudges the possession to have been in them also, while it was not held exclusively by another. how could I be liable for rents of what I had neither the possession or occupation?[11] the lands laid open to them to occupy or to lease. what hindered them? no act,[12] of mine either did oppose it, or would have opposed it. the Lower field has been constantly occupied by a tenant. with the rents of my own part, he has paid their parts also, for which I am accountable. if it be asked why I did not account for them from year to year? I answer that their guardian having recieved from me, for them, a sum of money equal to the value of the land, and having the benefit of the annual interest of that, I did expect that when they came of age they also would have preferred, as the other two did for whom he acted,[13] the money to the land; and altho' the legal possession had never been out of them, (for their guardian could not convey it out of them as it never was in him[14]) that they would have conveyed it themselves, as he had covenanted they should do,[15] with the right to the rents recieved.

The legal[16] possession of their lands then has been always in themselves; and they might have had the actual possession and occupation if they had chosen it.[17] if they let parts of them lie idle, it was their fault and loss. but while others actually cultivated them, these cultivators are liable to pay reasonable rents.

2. For what rents am I responsible?[18] for the rents of the lower field constantly, because it has been constantly occupied by a tenant; and that part of them which he has paid to me I am responsible for.

For the Upper field I am responsible where I have actually recieved rents; and for[19] the years during which I had it under inclosure, and culture; deducting the expence of inclosing & all other reasonable expences.[20] I think the rents of this field, my own as well as theirs, were lost for a year or two by bankruptcy. mr Peyton, who leased them, can state the facts. if we are considered as acting for these parceners, it was voluntarily and without reward, and if we took as good care of their concern as of our own, we are not responsible for their share of the loss.

Of the lots between the town and river I have never had any actual[21] occupation. the owners have permitted them to lie open, as I permitted my own which are intermixed with them.[22] there is no more reason why I should pay them rent for theirs, than they me for mine.[23] and it would be truly hard, if, after losing the fee simple value of these lands, I were to be made chargeable for the profits of theirs, of which I had neither possession, nor occupation, nor any legal power over them.

The Forest lots have also laid entirely open: theirs neglected, & mine little better.[24] knowing that the people of Milton would cut their firewood on those lots, with or without permission, I gave permission as to mine; but always on written leases, confining them expressly to my own lands,[25] which extended to my other lands on the same side of the road, as well as these, being upwards of 1000. acres of woodlands in addition to those bought of the Hendersons. with respect to these last the lessees had the same means of knowing the allotments which I had myself, to wit, the recorded plat, and as knowing the grounds better, were better able to shew me my lots, than I them. if therefore they cut on the lands of these parceners, it was as if they had cut on mr Watson or mr Alexander,[26] they committed a trespass for which they are answerable, not I. but so little could ever be got for what they cut on my own lands, that for some time past all attention to it has been abandoned.[27]

3. Have not all the rents for which I was responsible been paid?

I paid to John Henderson, the legal guardian 100.£ and to James Henderson the acting guardian[28] £390. making £490. or $1633\frac{1}{3}$ D.

Where there are several existing debts a payment may be placed, at the will of the parties to the credit of whichever they chuse. where there is but one debt it must go to that. if it be said that this payment was for the conveyance of the right in the land to me, has that right been conveyed to me? is the right in me? on the contrary, is not this very claim of rent founded on the right to the land being in them? and are they not in possession also? how else could they have sold them? the law forbidding the sale of a right to lands of which the party is not in possession. if they are now in possession, they must have been so always; for no act of mine at any time has put them into possession.[29] I have received then no consideration, either of right, or of possession, for these £490. consequently they have never had any money-claim against me but for rent, and the payment can be credited to no other account. James Henderson acted as their next friend,[30] their guardian in fact, their legal guardian being in this state, not in that. he furnished them with necessaries, and did all their business.[31] he maintained them, the mother being scarcely in circumstances to maintain herself. they had no property but this, no other resource but this, or charity,[32] for their food, cloathing or education,[33] as will be proved, and as indeed is substantially[34] proved by the conduct[35] of the two elder of the five parceners whose shares were the subjects of the same transaction, and who, conscious of the truth of these facts, confirmed the sales after they came of age. where infants possess nothing but lands, the rents of which will not maintain them, the Chancellor will order the lands themselves to be sold, and the money to be applied to their maintenance and education. it is equally presumable[36] then that he would approve, when done by their guardian,[37] or next friend, what he would have ordered himself to be done; & that were I disposed to take the trouble of carrying this case[38] into a court of equity,[39] and the fact should be proved that they had no other resource for subsistence but this, or charity, the sale would be confirmed. more certainly then the court of equity would apply this payment to the rents, and the rents to their maintenance. if James Henderson had advanced his own money for their subsistence, he had a right, out of this payment, to reimburse himself for the past and to anticipate for the future. I say then that, as they can have no claim on me but for rents, and this money was paid to their guardian for them, and he had[40] a right to recieve their rents, the payment I made is justly[41] applicable to the rents, and that there is no other ground of demand to which it can be applied.[42] consequently whatever rents I am responsible for to them have been paid.

MS (ViU: TJP); entirely in TJ's hand; undated. Dft (ViU: TJP); in TJ's hand; undated; with final page on verso of reused address cover of Ambrose Spencer to TJ, 2 Dec. 1816; heavily revised, with only the most significant corrections and emendations noted below; endorsed by TJ: "Rents in case of Henderson's lands."

TJ began composing these notes around 24 Dec. 1816, when he received the letter from Ambrose Spencer on the address cover of which he wrote the last page of the Dft, and finished them by 30 Dec. 1816, when he advised William D. Meriwether that he had left them and related papers with his grandson Thomas Jefferson Randolph, whom he authorized to act for him.

According to TJ, the Hendersons' LOWER FIELD HAS BEEN CONSTANTLY OCCUPIED by William Johnson, of Milton (see Lease Agreement with Johnson, 17 Jan. 1811; enclosure to TJ to Dabney

Minor and Peter Minor, 24 Jan. 1817). The OTHER TWO former Henderson minors, Bennett H. Henderson and Eliza Henderson Bullock, had already confirmed the sales made on their behalf in Kentucky by their brother James L. Henderson (Albemarle Co. Deed Book, 15:164–5, 207–8; Haggard, "Henderson Heirs," 7–8).

Although Thomas Eston Randolph rented the upper field in 1808–09, it remained unenclosed and unoccupied thereafter until 1813, perhaps due to his BANKRUPTCY (enclosure to TJ to Dabney Minor and Peter Minor, 24 Jan. 1817). For an example of the WRITTEN LEASES with which TJ provided Milton residents the right to cut firewood on his land, see his Lease of Firewood Rights to James Marr, 6 Feb. 1813.

[1] In Dft TJ here canceled "avoid."

[2] In Dft, remainder of paragraph is added in left margin.

[3] Dft: "at gain."

[4] Sentence reworked in Dft from "what rents have been received?"

[5] In Dft TJ here canceled "the kind of possession which the guardian has is merely."

[6] Preceding two words interlined in Dft.

[7] Preceding two words interlined in Dft.

[8] Preceding two words interlined in Dft.

[9] Preceding two words interlined in Dft.

[10] In Dft TJ here canceled "pretended."

[11] Sentence interlined in Dft.

[12] In Dft TJ here canceled "no pretension."

[13] Phrase interlined in Dft.

[14] Preceding six words not in Dft.

[15] Preceeding seven words interlined in Dft.

[16] Word interlined in both texts.

[17] In Dft phrase reads "and they might have occupied them by actual possession."

[18] Sentence reworked in Dft from "What rents are due?"

[19] Preceding eleven words interlined in Dft in place of "rents are due from me for," with "for" inadvertently repeated.

[20] Remainder of paragraph not in Dft.

[21] Word interlined in Dft.

[22] In Dft TJ here interlined "I no more occupied theirs than they did mine, and."

[23] Remainder of paragraph not in Dft.

[24] Preceding six words not in Dft.

[25] Remainder of sentence not in Dft.

[26] Phrase from "it" to this point not in Dft.

[27] Sentence in Dft reads "the real fact however is that few of the persons who took leases, ever paid any thing; and for some time past all <*have ceased*> attention to them has been abandoned."

[28] Reworked in Dft from "the guardian de facto."

[29] Section in Dft from "also? how else" to this point interlined in place of "of it?"

[30] Preceding three words not in Dft and interlined in MS.

[31] In Dft TJ here added "as will be proved to have been notorious."

[32] Preceding four words not in Dft.

[33] Remainder of sentence interlined in Dft.

[34] Dft reads "as is further."

[35] MS: "conducted." Dft: "conduct."

[36] Preceding three words interlined in Dft in place of "would be equally reasonable."

[37] Preceding three words interlined in Dft, which omits the following three words.

[38] Phrase in Dft reworked from "and that if this case were carried."

[39] Dft: "Chancery."

[40] Preceding thirteen words reworked in Dft from "and their guardian had."

[41] Dft: "just."

[42] Dft ends here.

To William D. Meriwether

SIR Monticello Dec. 30. 16.

I have put into the hands of my grandson the papers and notes relative to the rents due to the three younger representatives of the late mr Henderson, and have left to him entirely the settlement of them, and whatever he does I will confirm and execute. he sets out to Richmond this morning, will return on Saturday, & then be always ready to finish the business. I am Sir

Your humble serv[t] TH: JEFFERSON

PoC (MHi); on verso of left half of reused address cover of George Logan to TJ, 16 Oct. 1816; at foot of text: "Cap[t] W[m] D. Meriwether"; endorsed by TJ.

TJ's GRANDSON was Thomas Jefferson Randolph. The THREE YOUNGER REPRESENTATIVES of Bennett Henderson's estate were his daughters Frances Henderson Hornsby, Lucy Henderson Wood, and Nancy C. Henderson Nelson.

To Craven Peyton

DEAR SIR Monticello Dec. 30. 16.

I lent you some time ago the deed & receipt of John Henderson as to the property of the younger children of Bennet Henderson, which I must ask the favor of you now to send me as it is essential to fix the time when I begin to be accountable for rents, which matter is now immediately to be settled with Cap[t] Meriwether and mr Wood. have you been able to collect any testimony of the age of Bennet the younger. I salute you with esteem and respect.

TH: JEFFERSON

PoC (MHi); on verso of right half of reused address cover of George Logan to TJ, 16 Oct. 1816; at foot of text: "M[r] Peyton"; endorsed by TJ.

TJ had enclosed the DEED & RECEIPT OF JOHN HENDERSON, both dated 17 Nov. 1807, in his letter to Peyton of 7 May 1814.

Bennett Hillsborough Henderson (BENNET THE YOUNGER), the youngest son of Bennett Henderson, was born on 5 Sept. 1784. He had, therefore, been eighteen years old when his brother James sold his portion of his father's estate to TJ on 18 Sept. 1802 (Elizabeth Henderson's affidavit relating to the lands of Bennett Henderson, 22 Nov. 1815 [KyHi]; Haggard, "Henderson Heirs," 3, 7–8, 26).

From Craven Peyton

DEAR SIR Monteagle De[r] 30th

I am very sorry You have been put to the trouble of Sending for the Deed You lent me. it is in the Clerks office; I will call or send it thursday or frydar Next with othar papars—I have for You, with Sincere esteem C. PEYTON

RC (ViU: TJP-ER); partially dated; addressed: "Thomas Jefferson esqre Monticello"; endorsed by TJ as a letter of 30 Dec. 1816 received that day and so recorded in SJL.

To William Sampson

SIR Monticello Dec. 30. 16.

Your favor of Nov. 30. came to hand some time ago, and I delayed answering that I might acknolege at the same time the receipt of mr Ensors volumes which you had been so kind as to forward. that on National government with your letter of Nov. 26. were forwarded by mr Lovett by Doct^r Stuart and delivered me a few days ago. he informed me that that on the defects of the English law, had been forgotten somewhere, I believe at[1] lodgings in Washington. it will come probably by some other occasion. I have barely had time to run my eye over the volume on National government; yet I see in it proofs that the author is the scholar you represent him. it presents learned research thro' the whole, & is well calculated for Europe where the appeal to great opinions constitutes authority. here, you know, we shorten the process by appealing to our own opinions. be so good as to make my acknolegements to your friend the author for this mark of his attention, and to recieve my thanks for the trouble you have had with the assurance of my great esteem and respect.

TH: JEFFERSON

RC (Mrs. Livingston T. Dickason, Short Hills, N.J., 1944); addressed: "William Sampson esquire New York"; franked; postmarked Charlottesville, 3 Jan.; endorsed by Sampson. PoC (MHi); on verso of reused address cover of Robert Turner to TJ, 29 Nov. 1816; endorsed by TJ.

[1] TJ here canceled "his."

To John Barnes

DEAR SIR Monticello Dec. 31. 16.

Your favor of the 23^d came to hand last night, and I now inclose you two powers of Attorney, one to be used at each place, and copied verbatim from the form in your letter. I have not attested it before a magistrate, because it would cost me a ride of many miles to find one, which I am not able to take, but it is impossible that this can be requisite for a power of attorney to transfer a mere personal property. my hand fails me so much in writing that I can only add my affectionate and friendly salutations. TH: JEFFERSON

P.S. will you be so good as to jog mr Millegan's memory?

PoC (DLC); on verso of reused address cover of John D. Vaughan to TJ, 30 Nov. 1816; postscript adjacent to signature; at foot of text: "Mr Barnes"; endorsed by TJ.

For TJ's earlier request that Barnes JOG Joseph Milligan concerning Destutt de Tracy's *Treatise on Political Economy*, see his second letter to Barnes of 12 Oct. 1816.

ENCLOSURE

Power of Attorney to John Barnes for Transfer of Assets

Know all men by these presents that I Thomas Jefferson of Monticello in the county of Albemarle Virginia do hereby constitute and appoint John Barnes of George town Columbia my true and lawful Attorney for me and in my name to transfer into the name of Thaddeus Kosciuzko, heretofore a General in the service of the United States, and at present of Switzerland, all the stock of the United States standing to my credit on the books of[1]
as well as all my shares in the Bank of Columbia. Witness my hand and seal this 31st day of December 1816. TH JEFFERSON

Witness
TH M RANDOLPH
JAMES L. JEFFERSON

MS (OTU: Maher Family Papers); in TJ's hand, signed by TJ, Randolph, and Jefferson; sealed by TJ; endorsed in an unidentified hand: "Thomas Jefferson to John Barnes} Power of Attorney." FC (ICPRCU); in TJ's hand, signed by TJ and by Randolph as sole witness; sealed by TJ; with note by TJ at foot of text: "another copy signed Jan. 26. 1817. and acknoleged before a magistrate." Also enclosed in Barnes to TJ, 13 Jan. 1817, and TJ to Barnes, 28 Jan. 1817.

[1]In FC an unidentified hand here adds "the Treasury."

To John Melish

SIR Monticello Dec. 31. 16.

Your favor of Nov. 23. after a very long passage is recieved, and with it the Map which you have been so kind as to send me, for which I return you many thanks. it is handsomely executed and on a well chosen scale; giving a luminous view of the comparative possessions of different powers in our America. it is on account of the value I set on it that I will make some suggestions.[1] by the Charter of Louis XIV. all the country comprehending the waters which flow into the Missisipi was made a part of Louisiana. consequently it's northern boundary was the summit of the highlands in which it's Northern waters rise. but by the Xth art. of the treaty of Utrecht, France & England agreed to appoint Commissaries to settle the boundary between their possessions in that quarter; and those Commrs settled it at the 49th degree of Lat. see Hutchinson's topographical description of Louisiana. pa. 7. this it was which induced the British Commrs in settling the boundary with us, to follow the Northern waterline to the Lake of the woods at the latitude of 49° and then go off on that parallel. this then is the true Northern boundary of Louisiana.

The Western boundary of Louisiana is, rightfully, the Rio Bravo, (it's main stream) from it's mouth to it's source, and thence along the highlands & mountains dividing the waters of the Missipi from those of the Pacific. the usurpations of Spain on the East side of that river have induced geographers to suppose the Puerco or Salado to be the boundary. the line along the highlands stands on the Charter of Louis XIV. that of the Rio Bravo, on the circumstance that when La Sale took possession of the bay of St Bernard, Panuco was the nearest possession of Spain, & the Rio Bravo the natural halfway boundary between them.

On the waters of the Pacific we can found no claim in right of Louisiana. if we claim that country at all, it must be on Astor's settlement near the mouth of the Columbia, and the principle of the jus gentium of America that when a civilized nation takes possession of the mouth of a river in a new country, that possession is considered as including all it's waters. the line of latitude of the Southern source of the Multnomah might be claimed as appurtenant to Astoria. for it's Northern boundary, I believe an understanding has been come to between our government & Russia, which might be known from some of it's members. I do not know it.

Altho the irksomeness of writing, which you may percieve from the present letter, and it's labor, oblige me now to withdraw from letter writing yet the wish that your map should set to rights the ideas of our own countrymen as well as foreign nations as to our correct boundaries has induced me to make these suggestions that you may bestow on them whatever enquiry they may merit. I salute you with esteem & respect. TH: JEFFERSON

PoC (DLC); at foot of first page: "Mr Mellish"; endorsed by TJ. Extracted in Washington *Daily National Intelligencer*, 4 Mar. 1817, and elsewhere, with prefatory comment that "The following extracts of a letter from Mr. Jefferson, shew his opinion of this work."

HUTCHINSON'S TOPOGRAPHICAL DESCRIPTION OF LOUISIANA: Thomas Hutchins, *An Historical Narrative and Topographical Description of Louisiana, and West-Florida* (Philadelphia, 1784).

[1]The newspaper extract is composed of the preceding two sentences and the final sentence prior to the closing, with an editorial comment in square brackets in between: "Here follows a minute account of various treaties, relative to the boundary lines, which have been made use of on the map, after which the letter concludes."

To Jerman Baker and Archibald Thweatt

Dear Sir Monticello Jan. 1. 1817.

I lately addressed a letter to mr Thweatt, intended equally for you in a case of my own: I now address this to you equally intended for mr Thweatt, in the case of another. it is to sollicit your attention to the petition of Visc^{o} Philip S. Barziza one of the coheirs of Col^{o} Ludwell owner of the Green spring estate. the mother of the petitioner was sole daughter of mr & mrs Paradise, the latter a daughter of Col^{o} Ludwell born in Virginia, the former a naturalized citizen. miss Paradise married Count Barziza of Venice, & this petitioner is one of their two sons & heirs, who pray to be remitted to their maternal estate, which I hope will be done, for certainly [the ri]ghts of man do not depend on the geography of his birth. [...]ing your attention to the case either of myself or others I a[m] as incapable of asking you to do any more than what you think right as you would be to grant it. I only request that attention which in cases not immediately under your auspices you might not bestow. Accept my affectionate & respectful salutations for mr Thweatt as well as yourself.

Th: Jefferson

PoC (MHi); on verso of reused address cover of James Monroe to TJ, 22 Oct. 1816; mutilated at seal; at foot of text: "Mr Baker"; endorsed by TJ as a letter to Baker.

The two sons & heirs were Count Giovanni (John L.) Barziza and his brother, Philip I. Barziza.

To Philip I. Barziza

Dear Sir Monticello Jan. 1. 17.

Your favor of Dec. 14. is but just recieved, informing me of your petition to the legislature. I have outlived all my antient acquaintances in that body; but I have two or three young friends there to whom I write by this mail, and ask their attention to your case. these are mr Thweatt of Chesterfield & Baker of Cumberland in the house of Delegates, and mr Cabell of the Senate from this district, who I am sure will endeavor to have right done you.

I shall be very happy indeed to hear of the arrival of the books with respect to which I troubled you. if forwarded on their arrival to mr Gibson at Richmond they will come safely to me, and on recieving a note of the costs and charges from you, I will immediately remit it to you. I salute you with great respect & esteem.

Th: Jefferson

RC (IaU: Presidential Letters); edge frayed, with missing text supplied from PoC; addressed: "Viscount Philip S. Barziza Williamsburg Virga"; franked; postmarked Milton, 1 Jan. PoC (DLC); on verso of reused address cover of John Steele to TJ, 26 Oct. 1816; endorsed by TJ.

To Joseph C. Cabell

DEAR SIR Monticello Jan. 1. 17.

A member of a family to which I have been much attached by long intimacies sollicits my asking the attention[1] of some of my friends to his petition before the legislature. he is the Viscount Barziza, youngest of two sons of Count Barziza of Venice by the only daughter & heiress of the late mrs Paradise, who was the daughter of Col^o Philip Ludwell proprietor of Greenspring where she was born. mr Paradise her husband was a naturalised citizen. their grandchildren petition for the maternal estate, and as the rights of man do not depend on the geography of his birth, I hope they will obtain it. it is to this petition I sollicit your attention and that you will procure to be done in it what you think right.

There was a petition from Capt Meriwether & others for the establishment of a turnpike from Rockfish gap to Moore's ford, which they never meant to carry into execution, but merely to fix the passage of that road at Moore's ford to parry a process now in court to substitute a better ford & road. we counterpetitioned. should this matter come up to your house, the counterpetition will inform you accurately of the circumstances of the case, in which you will I am sure do what is right as well from a principle of justice as of regard for

Your's affectionately TH: JEFFERSON

RC (ViU: TJP); addressed: "Joseph C. Cabell of the Senate of Virginia now in Richmond"; franked; postmarked Milton, 1 Jan.; endorsed by Cabell as answered 12 Jan. 1817. PoC (DLC); on verso of reused address cover of Thomas H. Palmer to TJ, 23 Oct. 1816; final line and closing faint; endorsed by TJ.

As the younger brother of a count, Philip I. Barziza could use the courtesy title of VISCOUNT.

[1] Word interlined in place of "notice."

To Nicolas G. Dufief

DEAR SIR Monticello Jan. 1. 1817.

I recieved yesterday your favor of Dec. 16. and hasten by the first return of the mail, to express my mortification that the remittance of 31.D which I had desired Messrs Gibson & Jefferson to make you in June, and which I had taken for granted was done had however never been done. it must have been ac[c]identally overlooked by mr Gibson, as in a mass of business happens sometimes with the most attentive men. I hasten to repair the omission by inclosing you a fifty dollar note of the bank of Virginia which I am told are negociable with you. if to a loss, debit me with the loss. it will still I presume cover what I have lately requested as well as the former balance. the new year being now commenced I hope daily to recieve it's Nautical Almanac. accept my friendly & respectful salutations.

TH: JEFFERSON

PoC (DLC); on verso of reused address cover of William H. Crawford to TJ, 28 Oct. 1816; one word faint; at foot of text: "M. Dufief"; endorsed by TJ.

To Robert Patterson

DEAR SIR Monticello Jan. 1. 17.

Your favor of Dec. 13. came to hand but two days ago. nothing could be so desirable to me as to have settled in the neighboring village of Charlottesville such a family of artists as is described in mr Hassler's letter to you. yet I dare not advise it; because I do not believe they could find employment there. it would be a good stand for a single workman, a real proficient in the watchmaking business. it would consist in selling & repairing watches & clocks. I had therefore wished to get a young man, just out of his apprenticeship and not as yet fixed in position, and if he added the silversmith's business or brought an associate of that kind [it w]ould greatly enlarge the field of his business.

Altho it is long since I have visited Richmond, yet from whe[re I] am I believe it to be the best place in the US. for mr Montaudon to take his stand. it is large, growing, commercial and rich, & there is not at present a Watchmaker of the least eminence; not one with whom we trust a fine watch with any confidence. yet it is the only place to which all the upper country can send their watches. there would be full employment there for mr Montaudon's whole establishment, as I believe; but he would of course examine the place for himself before he would venture on a removal. until we can get such an artist in Charlottesville I could recommend to him the business of this quarter. Accept, dear Sir, the assurance of my constant friendship and respect. TH: JEFFERSON

PoC (MHi); on verso of reused address cover of Nicolas G. Dufief to TJ, 22 Oct. 1816; damaged at seal; at foot of text: "Doct[r] R. Patterson"; endorsed by TJ.

MR MONTAUDON: Pierre Henry Montandon.

From the Société Agricole et Manufacturière Française

Philadelphia January 5th 1817.[1]

A vous, thomas Jefferson, qui avez Signé la chartre de L'indépendance de votre pays; Vous qui, comme premier Magistrat de cette heureuse République, L'avez administrée durant les tems les plus périlleux, avec toute la prévoyance de la Sagesse et qui dans la retraitte avez emporté les vœux de tous Ceux qui Savent aimer la patrie!

A Vous qui dans les vississitudes d'une longue existence avez appris a connaître la Nature humaine, Ses faiblesses, Ses besoins, Surtout ceux les plus difficiles a Satisfaire, ceux qui Sont nés de L'Etat de L'homme en Société.

Nous, réfugiés Sur L'unique terre hospitalière qu'offrent les deux mondes, après avoir pendant vingt cinq ans lutté vainement Contre tous les obstacles pour établir dans la vieille Europe les principes politiques qui font la gloire et le bonheur des citoyens de L'Amerique du Nord. Nous dépouillés de tout, Excepté de L'honneur Seul bien que nos oppresseurs ne nous ont point envié.

Nous nous adressons à Vous pour que, dispensant un de ces rayons & philosophies par les quels les Minos les Solons ont Sçu régir leurs concitoyens; Vous veuilliez bien tracer les bases du Contract Social qu'il est indispensable d'établir entre nous pour L'administration intérieure de notre Société agricole et manufacturière.

Qui peut plus peut moins; Celui qui dans Sa jeunesse a été le Législateur de Son pays et qui n'a présenté que des lois que les tems n'ont fait que rendre plus respectables Ne refusera pas à des hommes échappés d'un Nauffrage qui a englouti une Nation tout-entière, de les faire Jouir du fruit de Ses pensées Muries par Quarente anneés d'expérience & de reflexions Sur L'art de rendre heureux Ses Semblables; Ces hommes respirent après un bonheur paisible, dans une vie agreste, à L'abri des inquiétudes que L'incertitude Sur les titres de propriété et une responsabilité retroactive ne manquent jamais de produire. Condessendez a notre demande et le ciel demeurera Serein pour nous. Cette faveur insigne, ne pouvant qu'affirmer celles que nous Sollicitons des representans de la Nation pour la concession d'un terrein Suffisant a Notre entreprise, vous assurera de notre part et de Celle de nos neveux une gratitude qui ne pourra être égalée que par le respect et L'admiration que nous professons pour vos inaltérables vertus.

Les Membres du Bureau de la Société agricole et manufacturière française.

JOSEPH MARTIN—
vice p^r & tresorier

L M: DIRAT
Censeur.

N S PARMANTIER
Secretaire redacteur

P.S. Notre vice président Mr Wm Lee, dont vous fîtes L'heureux choix pour representer les Etats Unis dans le poste important de Consul général à Bordeaux où il a fait Autant pour L'honneur de Sa Nation que pour les hommes proscrits de la Nôtre, est en ce moment à Washington city où il presentera notre demande au gouvernement: Nous vous prions de vouloir bien Correspondre avec lui pour les bases du monument législatif que nous Sollicitons de vous. N S P

EDITORS' TRANSLATION

Philadelphia, January 5th 1817.

To you, Thomas Jefferson, who signed your country's charter of independence; who, as chief magistrate of that happy republic, administered it during the most perilous times with all the foresight of wisdom; and who have carried into retirement the good wishes of all those who know how to love their native land!

To you, who, through the vicissitudes of a long life, have gotten to know human nature—its weaknesses and needs, especially the ones that are most difficult to satisfy, those born out of the condition of man in society.

We, who are refugees in the only hospitable land that the two worlds have to offer, after having struggled in vain for twenty-five years against all obstacles to establish in old Europe the political principles that are the glory and happiness of the citizens of North America; we, who are stripped of everything except honor, the only thing that our oppressors did not want from us.

We address ourselves to you so that, by dispensing one of those rays and philosophies through which the Minoses and Solons ruled their fellow citizens, you might outline the basis of the social contract that must be established among us for the internal administration of our agricultural and manufacturing society.

Those who can do great things can also grant small favors. The one who in his youth was the legislator of his country and who has introduced nothing but laws that time has made even more respectable will not refuse to men who have escaped from the shipwreck that engulfed a whole nation the benefit of the fruit of his thoughts, which have been matured by forty years of experience and reflection on the art of making his people happy. These men aspire to the peaceful happiness of a rustic life, sheltered from the worries that uncertainty over titles of ownership and retroactive responsibility never fail to produce. Condescend to our request and the sky will remain clear for us. This distinguished favor can only reinforce those we are soliciting from the representatives of the nation through the concession of a piece of land sufficient for our enterprise, and it will assure you, on our part and from our descendants, a gratitude that can only be equaled by the respect and admiration we profess for your unalterable virtues.

The members of the board of the Société Agricole et Manufacturière Française.

JOSEPH MARTIN—
vice president and treasurer

L M: DIRAT
censor.

N S PARMANTIER
corresponding secretary

P.S. Our vice president Mr. Wm Lee, whom you so happily chose to represent the United States in the important post of consul general at Bordeaux, where he did as much for the honor of his nation as for those banished from our country, is at this moment in Washington city, where he will present our request to the government. We beg you to be so kind as to correspond with him regarding the basis of the legislative monument we are soliciting from you.

N S P

RC (MHi); in Parmantier's hand, signed by Martin, Dirat, and Parmantier; dateline above postscript; at head of text: "a Thomas Jefferson"; endorsed by TJ as a letter from "Martin & Parmentier" received 12 Jan. 1817 and so recorded in SJL. Translation by Dr. Genevieve Moene.

The Société Agricole et Manufacturière Française was established in Philadelphia in the autumn of 1816 in order to promote the establishment of an agricultural colony of French expatriates somewhere in the western United States. Although it received a sizable CONCESSION of land in present-day Alabama from the national government early the following year, the resulting Vine and Olive Colony never prospered and had been largely abandoned by the 1830s (Rafe Blaufarb, *Bonapartists in the Borderlands: French Exiles and Refugees on the Gulf Coast, 1815–1835* [2005], 44–9, 159–74).

Joseph Martin du Colombier (1761–1846), merchant and physician, was born on the island of Saint Domingue. The youngest son of a wealthy planter, he was educated in France and took part in the American Revolution, during which he spent time on a British prison ship. Martin returned to the West Indies following the conflict. The subsequent Haitian revolution found him serving as a captain of dragoons in the government forces. In the winter of 1792–93 Martin immigrated to the United States. Settling in Wilmington, Delaware, he became a successful trader and pro bono medical practitioner. Martin moved to Philadelphia in 1805, and in 1827 he relocated to and lived thereafter in the nearby suburb of Nicetown (Townsend Ward, "Germantown Road and Its Associations," *PMHB* 5 [1881]: 122–5; Blaufarb, *Bonapartists in the Borderlands*, 45, 213; Philadelphia *Public Ledger*, 18 Nov. 1846; gravestone inscription in Laurel Hill Cemetery, Philadelphia; *Weekly Notes of Cases argued and determined in the Supreme Court of Pennsylvania, the County Courts of Philadelphia* . . . 28 [Apr.–Nov. 1891]: 193–8).

Louis Marie Dirat (b. ca. 1774), soldier, public official, and journalist, was a native of Nérac, France. Condemned to death during the French Revolution, he won release from captivity in 1794 and joined the army as an aide-de-camp to his relative, General Catherine Dominique, marquis de Pérignon. Dirat was appointed subprefect of his hometown late in 1799, and he retained that position until 1813. In the latter year he moved to Paris to work as an accountant and edit a leftist political journal. On Napoleon's return to power in March 1815, Dirat asked for and obtained his former office in Nérac. Perhaps in consequence, following the emperor's defeat at Waterloo, Dirat's name was added to the restored monarchy's 24 July 1815 proscription list. Exiled from France, he sailed to America and by September 1816 was in Philadelphia, where he established a lace and millinery shop with his wife. Dirat received permission to return to France in 1819 and arrived there early the following year. His former political associates avoided him, however, suspecting that he had become a police informant (*Galerie Historique des Contemporains, ou Nouvelle Biographie* [2d ed., Brussels, 1822–23], 4:206; *Petit Almanach de la Cour de France* [Paris, 1813], 197; *New-York Courier*, 2 Feb. 1816; Kingston, N.Y., *Ulster Plebeian*, 21 May 1816; New London *Connecticut Gazette*, 25 Sept. 1816; Washington *Daily National Intelligencer*, 12 Nov. 1816; Blaufarb, *Bonapartists in the Borderlands*, 12, 198; Boston *Repertory*, 20 July 1819; Philadelphia *Franklin Gazette*, 29 Oct. 1819; Philadelphia *Poulson's American Daily Advertiser*, 22 Mar. 1820; *Le Livre Noir de Messieurs Delavau et Franchet, ou Répertoire Alphabetique de la Police Politique sous le Ministère Déplorable* [1829], 2:265).

Nicholas Simon Parmantier (ca. 1776–1835), businessman and educator, was born in France and served in that nation's army prior to his immigration to the United States during TJ's second presidential administration. He had settled in Philadelphia by the time he obtained American citizenship in 1809, and he worked there as a distiller and as a manufacturer of spermaceti oil. A founder and early vice president of the Academy of Natural Sciences of Philadelphia, Parmantier fought on the American side during the War of 1812. Having moved with other settlers to the Vine and Olive Colony in 1817, he relocated four years later to Pensacola and served there as a notary public and justice of the peace. Parmantier migrated in about 1831 to Nashville, Tennessee, where he taught French language and literature at the local university from 1832 until his death (P. William Filby, ed., *Philadelphia Naturalization Records* [1982], 525; *List of Patents*, 70; J. Thomas Scharf and Thompson Westcott, *History of Philadelphia. 1609–1884* [1884], 3:2280; James Robinson, *The Philadelphia Directory, for 1811* [Philadelphia, 1811], 241; John A. Paxton, *The Philadelphia Directory and Register, for 1813* [Philadelphia, 1813]; William S. W. Ruschenberger, *A Notice of the Origin, Progress, and Present Condition of the Academy of Natural Sciences of Philadelphia* [1852], 51, 55, 77; *Pennsylvania Archives*, 6th ser. [1907], 9:142–3; Washington *Daily National Intelligencer*, 12 Nov. 1816; Blaufarb, *Bonapartists in the Borderlands*, 57, 216; *Terr. Papers*, 22:308–10, 23:469, 778, 24:330; Lucius Salisbury Merriam, *Higher Education in Tennessee* [1893], 35; *National Banner and Nashville Whig*, 17 July 1835; gravestone inscription in Nashville City Cemetery).

[1]Reworked from "1816."

ENCLOSURE

Minutes of a Meeting of the Société Agricole et Manufacturière Française

Société agricole et manufacturière française
Présidence de Mr Lee
Seance du 2e jour de janvier 1817

Après un profond examen Sur le choix important d'un terrein propre a Asseoir notre nombreuse Société—après avoir considéré les avantages qui doivent résulter d'un établissement Sous les 33^ie au 35^ie degres de latitude dans un pays elevé, Sain, jouissant d'un climat tempéré et de toute Sa vigueur Végétative naturelle, un pays Sur lequel on puisse Se rendre par terre et par mer a peu de frais—un pays Non loin des grands établissements du tenessée et de la Nouvelle Orleans Sur une rivière Navigable et dont lamélioration entre déjà dans les vues bienfaisantes des differentes branches de l'administration

La Société Arrête

Qu'en exécution des dispositions prises dans Sa Séance du 25 octobre dernier Son Vice président Mr Lee Sera invité, de Concert avec les autres membres du bureau Mess. Martin, Parmantier & Dirat, a présenter au Congres des Etats Unis La demande de la société en nom Collectif pour une Concession de 250,000 acres de terres a choisir entre les 32 & 35^ie degrés de latitude Sur l'une des rives de la riviere Tumbigbee, ou tout autre lieu non encore Sousmissionné, Aux conditions les plus avantageuses et que reclame La situation des Pétitionnaires; Ainsi qu'on prendre avec le gouvernement tous les arrangemens nécessaires pour mettre en pleine & prompte exécution les intentions du présent arrêté.

art 2^e

Que comme nulle Société ne peut prétendre a un bonheur permanent Si elle n'est régie par des reglemens Sages qui découlent du même esprit que celui qui a enfanté les loix bienfaisantes de cette grande Société républicaine dont nous faisons dès-à-présent parti Il Sera écrit au Sage de Monticello pour le frais de nous tracer les bases d'un pacte Social pour les reglemens locaux de notre réunion afin que nous présentions aux Siecles un monument de la félicité à la quelle peuvent atteindre de vrais amis de la liberté mettant en commun toute la partie de leurs facultés dont il est nécessaire de faire un faisseau pour[1] la protection et l'avancement de chacun deux en particulier Et tout-à-la fois vivant dans la plus parfaite indépendance l'un de l'autre quant à lexercise de leurs droits politiques, la disposition de leurs propriétés de leur industrie et lexpression la plus illimité de leurs opinions.

Signé au régistre
W^M LEE 1^r vice president
J. MARTIN 2e " & trésorier
DIRAT censeur
N. S. PARMANTIER Secretaire

Certifié Conforme à Loriginal
N S PARMANTIER S^re

EDITORS' TRANSLATION

Société Agricole et Manufacturière Française
Mr. Lee presiding
Meeting of 2 January 1817

After thoroughly examining the important choice of a suitable piece of land on which to settle our numerous society—after considering the advantages that must result from an establishment located between the 33d and 35th degrees of latitude in a region that is elevated, healthy, and enjoys a temperate climate and vigorous natural vegetation, an area accessible at little expense by either land or sea—a place not far from the large settlements of Tennessee and New Orleans and on a navigable river that the different branches of the administration, in their beneficence, have already considered improving

The Society decrees

That in execution of the steps taken at its 25 October meeting, its vice president Mr. Lee will be asked, together with the other members of the board, Messrs. Martin, Parmantier, and Dirat, to present to the Congress of the United States, on behalf of the whole society, the request for a concession of 250,000 acres of land between the 32d and 35th degrees of latitude on one of the banks of the Tombigbee River, or any other place not yet granted, under the most advantageous conditions, as demanded by the petitioners' situation, and make all the necessary arrangements with the government to execute fully and promptly the intentions of the present decree.

2d article

That inasmuch as no society can expect permanent happiness unless it is governed by wise regulations proceeding from the same spirit that gave rise to the beneficial laws of this great republican society to which we currently belong, we will write to the Sage of Monticello for the purpose of having him outline for us the basis of a social pact for our internal government, so that we may present posterity with a monument to the happiness that true friends of liberty can attain when they share all the faculties that must be combined for the protection and advancement of each individual while living in perfect independence of each other as regards the exercise of their political rights, the disposition of their property and industry, and the most unlimited expression of their opinions.

Signed at the register
W^M LEE first vice president
J. MARTIN second " and treasurer
DIRAT censor
N. S. PARMANTIER secretary

Certified as conforming to the original
N S PARMANTIER Secretary

Tr (MHi); entirely in Nicholas S. Parmantier's hand. Translation by Dr. Genevieve Moene.

The "petition of Joseph Martin and others, emigrants from France" was presented to the United States Senate on 31 Jan. 1817. On that date it was read and referred to the Public Lands Committee, which reported a bill in the petitioners' favor on 10 Feb. (*JS*, 6:172, 211–2). Under the resulting 3 Mar. 1817 statute, "An Act to set apart and dispose of certain public lands, for the encouragement of the cultivation of the vine and olive," the federal government agreed to sell the society 144 square miles of Mississippi Territory land, some 92,160 ACRES, for $2 an acre (*U.S. Statutes at Large*, 3:374).

[1]Manuscript: "pour pour."

From Fitzwhylsonn & Potter

SIR Richmond Jan: 6, 1817.

We were honored with your favor of the 29th Ultimo, by Mr Randolph, about thursday last, since which we have been making the most diligent enquiry for a copy of the sessions acts of 1794, but without success. The acts of the four sessions immediately preceding the last, formerly ordered, we should not have been able to have procured had it not been for the polite and effectual exertions of Mr Linah Mimms of the Council of State, who interested himself in searching for them in the offices attached to the Executive department. These acts are nearly bound and will be ready to be forwarded, by the return of Mr Randolph, or by some other early opportunity. We are Sorry to say, sir, that no information has been received relative to the bundle of Edinburg Reviews.

In the title pages of the different sets of Josephus no mention is made of the ordinal rank of the respective editions, except as to the date when the work was printed. The last we have seen is the New York Edition of 1815.[1] But which of the European editions it is copied from we are unable to say. Should it be desirable we shall take great pleasure in procuring and forwarding it to you.

We are sir Your respectful, humble Servants

FITZWHYLSONN & POTTER

RC (MHi); in William H. Fitzwhylsonn's hand; endorsed by TJ as received 12 Jan. 1817 and so recorded in SJL. RC (DLC); address cover only; with PoC of TJ to William Duane, 24 Jan. 1817, on verso; addressed: "His Excellency Thomas Jefferson Monticello"; franked; postmarked Richmond, 7 Jan.

The NEW YORK EDITION was *The Genuine Works of Flavius Josephus; The Learned and Authentic Jewish Historian, and Celebrated Warrior*, trans. William Whiston, 7 vols. (New York, 1815).

[1]Reworked from "1715."

To Joseph Milligan

DEAR SIR Monticello Jan. 6. 17.

Your favor of Dec. 29. came to hand last night, and I am very much relieved by it's reciept. your long silence had reduced me to despair, which would have been quieted had you sent me earlier the candid explanation you have now given, inasmuch as it would have let me understand the real ground of the delay. I am happy however that you have begun, and that it will be your interest to get it through without any intermission. your proof sheet shall never rest with me more than one day. this 1st proof sheet induces me to recommend more attention to the stopping, or pointing, and a more correct system for that. I am glad you are surmounting your difficulties and wish you every possible success. TH: JEFFERSON

PoC (DLC); on verso of reused address cover of Mathew Carey to TJ, 22 Oct. 1816; at foot of text: "Mr Millegan"; endorsed by TJ. Enclosure: manuscript and proofs, not found, of a portion of Destutt de Tracy, *Treatise on Political Economy*.

From John Barnes

DEAR SIR— George Town Coa 7th Jany 1817.

The inclosed particulars & general statemt of Genl Kosciusko's a/c with me up to 26 Novr last—together with my remarks—will I flatter my self, fully explain to you—(and thro you to the good Genl) the cause of the Balance being thus in my favor—$812. EE.— Owing to the perculiar Circumstances Attending the protested £200—as well the Accomodation¹ of the £234. remitted, in lieu thereof—with the £300—Remitted from New York—and be Assured, I feel my self, perfectly gratified—in having the Means whereby to Apply—so sovereign a Remedy—in so Critical a Case—

I also inclose you, the Genl private letter to you of date 16 April—

Most Respectfully Dear Sir, Your very Obed. servt

JOHN BARNES,

RC (ViU: TJP-ER); at foot of text: "Thomas Jefferson Esqr Monticello"; endorsed by TJ as received 12 Jan. 1817 and so recorded in SJL. Enclosure: Tadeusz Kosciuszko to TJ, Apr. 1816. Other enclosure printed below.

EE.: "errors excepted."

¹Manuscript: "Accomdation."

ENCLOSURE

John Barnes's Account with Tadeusz Kosciuszko

Genl. Thads Kosciusko in a/c. with John Barnes for Sale of Treasury notes bearing 5⅔ pr. ct. Int. and payable 21st April, 1816.

1816.	To C. Smith, Esqr.		4,500.	
March 21	For 11 month's int. @ 5⅔ per cent	222.75		
	advance on do. 7½ per cent	337.50	560.25	
			5,060.25	

Deduct ½ per cent. Brokerage	25.30	5,034	95
For purchase of 46 shares Columbia Bank stock of C. Smith, @ $110 per whole share	5,060		
add ½ per cent. Brokerage	25.30	5,085	30
To the debit of Genl. Kosciusko for this difference		$ 50	35

E. E. 21st March, 1816.
Georgetown, Cola

JOHN BARNES,[1]

Genl. Thads. Kosciusko, Dr

To John Barnes.

1816. July 25.	For purchase of a sett of exchange from Messrs. Smith & Riddle of Richmond, drawn by A. P. Heinrich[2] of Baltimore, at 30 days, on John Rapp, London, for £200 sterling, @ 20 per cent advance	888.88		
	Advance	177.78		
		1,066.66		
	Negn	21.33	$1,087	99

E. E. Georgetown, Cola.
25th. July, 1816.

JOHN BARNES,

Genl. Kosciusko Dr

To John Barnes.

1816. Novr. 26.	For the purchase of a sett of exchange, vice (Buckley & Abbott of New York) viz: L. N. & G. Griswold, No 3—at 60 days on Saml. Williams, Esq. London, £300 sterling, ex. rated on average, @ 12½ pr. ct. advance	1,333.33⅓		
	Advance	166.66⅔		
		1,500.00		
	Commission, including Buckley & Abbott's, charged J. B. 1 per cent exch	30.00	$1,530	00

E. E. Georgetown, Cola.
26th Novr. 1816.

JOHN BARNES,[3]

Genl. Thads Kosciusko in a/c with John Barnes, for proceeds of $10,000 as per scription to United States' Loan of 25 millions, at $88 for 100—Liquidated at 80 for 100—of 6 per cent Stock of the U. States, payable quarterly—on amt. Liquidated

$12.500

1815. Jany. 7.	By interest accruing on the above on average from the 10th July to 31st Decr. 1814, say	$358.32		
	Negotiation	8.95	349	37
April 8	By 3 months interest due 1st instant	187.50		

	Negotiation			4.68	182 82
July 1	By do	do same			182 82
Oct. 2	By do	do same			182 82
1816.					
Jany. 1	By do	do same			182 82
April 4	By do	do same			182 82
July 2	By do	do same			182 82
Octr. 2	By do	do same			182 82
			Nett		$1,629 11

E. E. Georgetown, Cola.
2[d] Octr. 1816.

JOHN BARNES,[4]

Genl. Thads. Kosciusko in a/c. with John Barnes, for proceeds of forty six shares of Bank of Columbia stock; for dividends payable thereon, half yearly, from 20th March to 20th September, on 46 shares of $100 each $4,600. 00

1816.			
Octr. 22	By Dividend due 20th September, 6 months, at 8 per cent	$184.00	
	Negotiation	4.60	$179 40

E. E. Georgetown, Cola.
22[d] Octr, 1816.

JOHN BARNES,[5]

Genl. Thad[s] Kosciusko in Several, & General, a/c. with John Barnes, as agent for Thomas Jefferson, Esq. from 26th April, 1815 to 26th Nov. 1816.

1815.				1815		
March 21	To the difference in sale of Treasury Notes & purchase of 46 shares Columbia Bank Stock, per a/c.	50	35	April 26.	By balance on settlement of a/c. rendered	50

		Dolls.	Cts.			Dolls.	Cts.
July 25. (£200. st'g.)	To purchase of sett of exchange from Smith & Riddle, Richmd. drawn by A. P. Heinrich[6] Balt° on John Rapp, of London, at 20 pr. ct. advance, as pr. a/c.	1,087	99	Jany. 7.	By interest accruing on $12,500 of U. States' stock, liquidated @ 6 pr. ct. on average, from 10th July to 31st Decr. 1814, & to 2d Octr. 1816, as pr. statement nett.	1,629	11
Nov. 26. £300 sterlg.	To purchase sett of exchange, via Buckley & Abbott, New York, L. N. & G. Griswold, on S. Williams of London, @ 12½ pr. ct. average advance, per a/c.	1,530		Octr. 22	By Dividend due 20th Sept. on 46 shares Bank of Columbia Stock, of $100 each, at 8 per cent nett.	179	40
	To sundry postages, foreign & inland. Duplicates	2	17	Novr. 26.	By Balance due this a/c. carried to new a/c. and to Genl. Kosciusko's debit.	812	
	Dolls.	2,670	51		Dolls.	2,670	51
Nov. 26.	To Balance carried to new a/c.	$812	00				

E. E. Georgetown, Cola.
26th. Nov. 1816.
JOHN BARNES,[7]

J. Barnes' Remarks on his general a/c. with Genl. Thads Kosciusko.

Be it remembered, That the sett of exchange for £200 sterling dated 25th. July, Purchased of Smith & Riddle, & therewith charged to his debit—

$1,087.99—was returned 20th Nov. protested for non payment with expenses thereon, by Messrs. Baring Brothers, & Co.—Amount £3.9.6. Sterling.

That an accommodation on said returned sett of £200. took place—and said Smith & Riddle transmitted J. Barnes—John Mutton & Co's sett of exchange dated Richmond, 29th. Nov. on Messrs. John & James Dunlop—London, including 15 per cent damages, &c as per estimate in sterling Amount for £234—which sett was, on the 12th Dec'r. through favor of J. Monroe, Esq. transmitted by J. Barnes to Messrs. Baring Brothers, & Co. London—for the sole use of Gen'l. Thads Kosciusko—exclusively—and in lieu of the above £200 sterling—sett returned—protested.

Under these circumstances, no alteration becomes necessary, with reference to John Barnes's statement of his a/c. with Gen'l. Kosciusko up to 26th Nov. 1816. which includes said £200 or $1,087.99—E.E.

for the difference on the renewed sett for	£234 St'g.	
in lieu of the one protested and returned	200 —say	£34.00.00. st'g.
will finally be adjusted by Messrs Baring & Co. & after deducting their expenditures thereon, protest. Comm's postage, &c as per their a/c.		3. 9. 6.
Leaves a balance of		£30.10. 6. st'g.[8]

in favor of the Genl which at the current exchange, say 12½ per cent. equal to 152\frac{61}{100}$—as some atonement for his disappointment—nor has J. Barnes made any charge, either on the returned sett for £200, or on the one of £234. transmitted in lieu thereof:—

Of course, no other reference need be applied to the general account current up to the present date.—apparent balance in favor of the subscriber,

Errors Excepted,

$812. as per a/c. Rendered.

Georgetown, Cola.
Nov. 26th 1816.
JOHN BARNES,

MS (ViU: TJP-ER); in a clerk's hand, with multiple signatures by Barnes.

[1] Page ends here.
[2] Manuscript: "Henrich."
[3] Page ends here.
[4] Page ends here.
[5] Page ends here.
[6] Manuscript: "Henrich."
[7] Page ends here.
[8] Page ends here.

From Nicolas G. Dufief

MONSIEUR, A Philade ce 7 de Janvier 1817

J'ai déjà eu l'honneur de vous adresser le nautical almanach pour 1817, la connaissance des temps pour 1817 & 18, 2 vols. & un petit dictionnaire Italien & anglais qui vous Sera passé a 2.50. Je n'ai pu vous procurer un format entre celui-ci & l'en 4to dont nous avons plusieurs exemplaires. Il m'a été impossible de trouver "Enfield's history of Philosophy" ni une bible du format que vous demandez. Le papier ci-Inclus vous donnera une idée d'une dont les dimensions approchent le plus de celui que vous m'avez envoyé, Je puis vous en adresser une autre mais Sans apocryphe & dont la grandeur correspond presque à votre mesure. Je vous ai crédité de 50[dls] 50[cts]. Les billets de Richmond gagnant un pour Cent Sur notre place. Aussitôt que j'aurai fini l'envoi des ouvrages que j'ai pu avoir, Je vous enverrai le compte & tiendrai à votre disposition la balance Qui vous Sera due.

Je Suis avec le plus profond respect votre très-dévoué Serviteur

N. G. DUFIEF

EDITORS' TRANSLATION

SIR, Philadelphia 7 January 1817

I have already had the honor of sending you the nautical almanac for 1817, the *Connaissance des Temps* for 1817 and 1818, 2 volumes, and a small Italian-English dictionary, which will be sent to you for $2.50. I was unable to procure for you a size between this one and a quarto, of which we have several copies. I could not find either "Enfield's history of Philosophy" or a Bible in the format you requested. The enclosed paper will give you an idea of one with dimensions most similar to that which you sent me. I can address another one to you, albeit without the apocrypha, whose size almost corresponds with what you want. I have credited you with $50.50. Richmond banknotes are valued one percent more here. As soon as I finish mailing the works I was able to obtain, I will dispatch the account to you and hold the balance due you at your disposal.

I am with the most profound respect your very devoted servant

N. G. DUFIEF

RC (DLC); endorsed by TJ as received 12 Jan. 1817 and so recorded in SJL. Translation by Dr. Genevieve Moene. Enclosure not found.

The NAUTICAL ALMANACH was by Edmund M. Blunt (TJ to Dufief, 24 Jan. 1817). Giuspanio Graglia's PETIT DICTIONNAIRE ITALIEN & ANGLAIS was printed regularly under different titles from the 1780s on. This copy cost TJ $2.50 (account enclosed in Dufief to TJ, 30 Jan. 1817).

Francis Hall's Account of a Visit to Monticello

[7–8 Jan. 1817]

MONTICELLO.

HAVING an introduction to Mr. Jefferson, I ascended his little mountain on a fine morning, which gave the situation its due effect. The whole of the sides and base are covered with forest, through which roads have been cut circularly, so that the winding may be shortened or prolonged at pleasure: the summit is an open lawn, near to the south side of which, the house is built, with its garden just descending the brow: the saloon, or central hall, is ornamented with several pieces of antique sculpture, Indian arms, Mammoth bones, and other curiosities collected from various parts of the Union. I found Mr. Jefferson tall in person, but stooping and lean with old age, thus exhibiting that fortunate mode of bodily decay, which strips the frame of its most cumbersome parts, leaving it still strength of muscle and activity of limb. His deportment was exactly such as the Marquis de Chastellux describes it, above thirty years ago: "At first serious, nay even cold," but in a very short time relaxing into a most agreeable amenity; with an unabated flow of conversation on the most interesting topics, discussed in the most gentlemanly, and philosophical manner. I walked with him round his grounds, to visit his pet trees, and improvements of various kinds: during the walk, he pointed out to my observation a conical mountain, rising singly at the edge of the southern horizon of the landscape: its distance he said, was 40 miles, and its dimensions those of the greater Egyptian pyramid; so that it accurately represents the appearance of the pyramid at the same distance; there is a small cleft visible on its summit, through which, the true meridian of Monticello exactly passes: its most singular property, however, is, that on different occasions it looms, or alters its appearance, becoming sometimes cylindrical, sometimes square, and sometimes assuming the form of an inverted cone. Mr. Jefferson had not been able to connect this phenomenon with any particular season, or state of the atmosphere, except, that it most commonly occurred in the forenoon. He observed, that it was not only wholly unaccounted for by the laws of vision, but that it had not as yet engaged the attention of philosophers so far as to acquire a name; that of looming, being in fact, a term applied by sailors, to appearances of a similar kind at sea. The Blue Mountains are also observed to loom, though not in so remarkable a degree.*

It must be interesting to recall and preserve the political sentiments of a man who has held so distinguished a station in public life as Mr. Jefferson. He seemed to consider much of the freedom and happiness of America, to arise from local circumstances. "Our population," he observed, "has an elasticity, by which it would fly off from oppressive taxation." He instanced the beneficial effects of a free government, in the case of New Orleans, where many proprietors who were in a state of indigence under the dominion of Spain, have risen to sudden wealth,

* Vide for a more detailed account of this phenomenon in Notes on Virginia, p. 122.

solely by the rise in the value of land, which followed a change of government. Their ingenuity in mechanical inventions, agricultural improvements, and that mass of general information to be found among Americans of all ranks and conditions, he ascribed to that ease of circumstances, which afforded them leisure to cultivate their minds, after the cultivation of their lands was completed.—In fact, I have frequently been surprised to find mathematical and other useful works in houses which seemed to have little pretension to the luxury of learning. Another cause, Mr. Jefferson observed, might be discovered in the many court and county meetings, which brought men frequently together on public business, and thus gave them habits, both of thinking and of expressing their thoughts on subjects, which in other countries are confined to the consideration of the privileged few. Mr. Jefferson has not the reputation of being very friendly to England: we should, however, be aware, that a partiality in this respect, is not absolutely the duty of an American citizen; neither is it to be expected that the policy of our government should be regarded in foreign countries, with the same complacency with which it is looked upon by ourselves: but whatever may be his sentiments in this respect, politeness naturally repressed any offensive expression of them: he talked of our affairs with candour, and apparent good-will, though leaning, perhaps, to the gloomier side of the picture. He did not perceive by what means we could be extricated from our present financial embarrassments, without some kind of revolution in our government: on my replying, that our habits were remarkably steady, and that great sacrifices would be made to prevent a violent catastrophe, he acceded to the observation, but demanded, if those who made the sacrifices, would not require some political reformation in return. His repugnance was strongly marked to the despotic principles of Bonaparte, and he seemed to consider France under Louis XVI. as scarcely capable of a republican form of government; but added, that the present generation of Frenchmen had grown up with sounder notions, which would probably lead to their emancipation. Relative to the light in which he views the conduct of the Allied Sovereigns, I cannot do better than insert a letter of his to Dr. Logan, dated 18th October, 1815, and published in the American Newspapers:

[*Here follows a faithful transcription of TJ's letter to George Logan of 15 (not 18) Oct. 1815, printed above at that date and accordingly omitted here.*]

The same anxiety for his country's independence seems to have led him to a change of opinion on the relative importance of manufactories in America. He thus expresses himself, in answer to an address from the American society for the encouragement of manufactories: "I have read with great satisfaction, the eloquent pamphlet you were so kind as to send me, and sympathise with every line of it. I was once a doubter, whether the labour of the cultivator, aided by the creative powers of the earth itself, would not produce more value than that of the manufacturer alone, and unassisted by the dead subject on which he acted; in other words, whether the more we could bring into action of the energies of our boundless territory, in addition to the labour of our citizens, the more would not be our gain. But the inventions of the latter times, by labour-saving machines, do as much now for the manufacturer, as the earth for the cultivator. Experience too, has proved that mine was but half the question; the other half is, whether dollars and cents are to be weighed in the scale against real independence. The question is then solved, at least so far as respects our own wants. I much fear the effect on our infant establishment, of the policy avowed by Mr. Brougham, and quoted in the pamphlet. Individual British merchants may lose by the late immense importations; but British commerce and manufactories, in the mass will gain, by beating down the competition of ours in our own markets, &c."

The conversation turning on American history, Mr. Jefferson related an anecdote of the Abbé Raynal, which serves to shew how history, even when it calls itself philosophical, is written. The Abbé was in company with Dr. Franklin, and several Americans at Paris, when mention chanced to be made of his anecdote of Polly Baker, related in his sixth volume, upon which one of the company observed, that no such law as that alluded to in the story, existed in New England: the Abbé stoutly maintained the authenticity of his tale, when Dr. Franklin, who had hitherto remained silent, said, "I can account for all this; you took the anecdote from a newspaper, of which I was at that time editor, and, happening to be very short of news, I composed and inserted the whole story." "Ah! Doctor," said the Abbé making a true French retreat, "I had rather have your stories, than other men's truths."

Mr. Jefferson preferred Botta's Italian History of the American Revolution, to any that had yet appeared, remarking, however, the inaccuracy of the speeches. Indeed, the true history of that period seems to be generally considered as lost: A remarkable letter on this point, lately appeared in print, from the venerable Mr. John Adams, to a Mr. Niles, who had solicited his aid to collect and publish a body of revolutionary speeches. He says, "of all the speeches made in Congress, from 1774 to 1777, inclusive, of both years, not one sentence remains, except a few periods of Dr. Witherspoon, printed in his works."

His concluding sentence is very strong. "In plain English, and in a few words, Mr. Niles, I consider the true history of the American revolution, and the establishment of our present constitutions, as lost for ever; and nothing but misrepresentations, or partial accounts of it, will ever be recovered."

I slept a night at Monticello, and left it in the morning, with such a feeling as the traveller quits the mouldering remains of a Grecian temple, or the pilgrim a fountain in the desert. It would indeed argue great torpor, both of understanding and heart, to have looked without veneration and interest, on the man who drew up the declaration of American independence; who shared in the councils by which her freedom was established; whom the unbought voice of his fellow-citizens called to the exercise of a dignity, from which his own moderation impelled him, when such example was most salutary, to withdraw; and who, while he dedicates the evening of his glorious days to the pursuits of science and literature, shuns none of the humbler duties of private life; but, having filled a seat higher than that of kings, succeeds with graceful dignity to that of the good neighbour, and becomes the friendly adviser, lawyer, physician, and even gardener of his vicinity. This is the "still small voice" of philosophy, deeper and holier than the lightnings and earthquakes which have preceded it. What monarch would venture thus to exhibit himself in the nakedness of his humanity? On what royal brow would the laurel replace the diadem? But they who are born and educated to be kings, are not expected to be philosophers. This is a just answer, though no great compliment either to the governors or the governed.

My travels had nearly terminated at the Rivannah, which flows at the foot of Monticello: in trying to ford it, my horse and waggon were carried down the stream: I escaped with my servant, and by the aid of Mr. Jefferson's domestics, we finally succeeded in extricating my equipage from a watery grave. The road to Richmond follows the James River, and has few features to attract notice. There are no towns, and very few villages.

Printed in Hall, *Travels in Canada, and the United States, in 1816 and 1817* (London, 1818), 374–86; date supplied from an itinerary on p. 340. Reprinted in Boston the same year.

Francis Hall (d. 1833), soldier and author, was educated at Winchester College, 1802–07, and Trinity College, Cambridge University, 1807–10. He joined the British army as a cornet in the 14th Light Dragoons in 1810 and was promoted to lieutenant the following year. After campaigning against the French in the Iberian Peninsula, 1811–12, Hall was invalided home and did not return to the service until after the Battle of Waterloo. Appointed a military secretary to General John Wilson in October 1815, he accompanied him to Canada a year later. Hall retired from active duty in the British army in September 1817 and subsequently published accounts of his travels through Canada, the United States, and France. In 1819 he joined Simon Bolívar's attempt to end Spanish rule in South America. Having attained the rank of colonel in the newly formed nation of Colombia, Hall settled there and made his living as a writer, journalist, hydrographer, and as the head of the government's topographical department. He was killed during a later revolutionary upheaval in Quito, Ecuador (*Chambers's Journal*, 7th ser. [1917–18], 8:303–4; *A List of the Officers of the Army and Royal Marines, on full and half-pay* [London, 1821], 508; Hall, *Travels in France, in 1818* [London, 1819]; London *Morning Chronicle*, 22 Aug. 1822; Hall, *Colombia: Its Present State* [London, 1824]; Mark J. Van Aken, *King of the Night: Juan José Flores and Ecuador, 1824–1864* [1989], 68–9, 78, 88–9; Washington *Daily National Intelligencer*, 1 Jan. 1834).

The Marquis de Chastellux described TJ as being AT FIRST SERIOUS, NAY EVEN COLD in his *Travels in North-America, in the years 1780, 1781, and 1782* (London, 1787; Sowerby, no. 4023), 2:44 (see also *PTJ*, 7:585–6n). The CONICAL MOUNTAIN was Willis's Mountain in Buckingham County, TJ's drawing of which is reproduced elsewhere in this volume. For TJ's ANSWER TO AN ADDRESS FROM THE AMERICAN SOCIETY FOR THE ENCOURAGEMENT OF MANUFACTORIES, of which Hall provides an accurate excerpt, see TJ to William Sampson, 26 Jan. 1817.

"The Speech of Miss POLLY BAKER, before a Court of Judicature, at Connecticut near Boston in New-England; where she was prosecuted the Fifth Time, for having a Bastard Child: Which influenced the Court to dispense with her Punishment, and induced one of her Judges to marry her the next Day," is printed in Leonard W. Labaree and others, eds., *The Papers of Benjamin Franklin* (1959–), 3:123–5. Guillaume Thomas François (Abbé) Raynal printed the story in book 17, section 42, of the sixth volume of his *Histoire Philosophique et Politique* (Amsterdam, 1770, and other eds.; Sowerby, no. 466), 330–6.

A lengthy extract from John Adams's letter to Hezekiah Niles of 3 Jan. 1817 on REVOLUTIONARY SPEECHES (MHi: Adams Papers) was printed in the Baltimore *Niles' Weekly Register* on 18 Jan. 1817. The biblical reference to a STILL SMALL VOICE is in 1 Kings 19.12.

Prior to his journey to Monticello, Hall visited Natural Bridge. He quoted from TJ's description in *Notes on the State of Virginia* and commented on Chastellux's and TJ's hypotheses about its origins. Hall also indicated that TJ owned the property and "commonly makes a visit once in the year, 'to look upon its beauty'" (Hall, *Travels in Canada and the United States*, 369–72).

From Chapman Johnson

DEAR SIR, Richmond 7. Jan^{y}[1] 1817.

I had the pleasure of receiving this morning, your letter, of the 26^{h} Decr addressed to me, at Staunton, and the duplicate thereof, addressed to this place—

In your suit in chancery, with the Rivanna company you may count on my Services as counsel, and so, according to your request, you may expect me to appear for You as counsel, in any cause, in which You may be concerned, within the range of my practice, whenever such appearance shall not be inconsistent with engagements heretofore made by me. I believe you had not heretofore, bespoken my services, in the general manner in which you now request them. As well as I recollect, your former request related only to a controversy which you anticipated respecting a Tract of land to which m^r Michie had some claim—

I shall remain in Richmond, during the Session of the Legislature,—till some time, in February, I expect,—and if you will forward your bill to me, at this place, within that time, I will give orders for issuing the proper process; and do what else you may desire.

Very respectfully Your most obedient se^t C JOHNSON

RC (MHi); endorsed by TJ as received 12 Jan. 1817 and so recorded in SJL.

For TJ's FORMER REQUEST for Johnson's legal services, see Johnson to TJ, 10 June 1813, and note.

[1] Reworked from "Dec^r."

From Joseph Milligan

DEAR SIR Georgetown Jany 7th 1817

Enclosed I send you the Second proof of Political Economy please return the Manuscript with the Corrections
I sent you the first proof on the 29th December I have not yet received it from you

Yours With respect JOSEPH MILLIGAN

RC (DLC); at foot of text: "Thomas Jefferson Esqr"; addressed (trimmed): "Thomas Jeff[...] M[...]"; endorsed by TJ as received 12 Jan. 1817 and so recorded in SJL. Enclosure: manuscript and proofs, not found, of a portion of Destutt de Tracy, *Treatise on Political Economy*.

From Charles Thomson

MY VERY DEAR, ANCIENT AND BELOVD FRIEND [by 7 Jan. 1817]

I received your[1] letter of January last when I was under a paralytic stroke but not Sensible of it. I felt no acute pain, and my Sight was as usual. I could read without spectacles but could not comprehend what I read, nor its connextion with what preceded or followed. I read your letter and was pleased. I made sundry attempts to answer it but in vain, and what at last I sent as an answer, I do not now recollect.

The powers of my mind were[2] weakened to such a degree that I forgot the names not only of my neighbours but even of my family and even of what I myself had said or done but a few minutes before.

After this stroke fell suddenly another[3] on the powers of the body (excepting the[4] eye which still continued as usual).[5] One night (at what distance of time from the first stroke I do not recollect) I went to bed in usual health and in the morning I found I was struck dumb. I could not utter a sound from my mouth. When I attempted to speak a strange rumbling sound seemed to come out at the ear, but not a word could I utter from the mouth. My Appetite for food now failed and all of my bodily powers (except the eye)[6] became weaker and weaker till the first or[7] second week[8] in November, at the end of the 87th and beginning of the 88 year of my Age. The beginning of my recovery was as Sudden as the strokes I had received. One morning being unusually refreshed with sleep I awoke as from a transe[9] and found a wonderful change in my whole System. From that time to this I have been gradually but slowly[10] recovering the due exercise of the powers both of mind and body except the hearing[11] which continues dull as it was.

I have been thus particular to apologize for my answer to your letter, and for an Answer which I gave on the 9th of Sept to what I deemed an impertinent question of Mr Delaplaine which has occasioned a very improper application to you. The case as far as I can now recollect was simply this—Among many other questions he asked me one which seemed to refer to the slanderous charges bandied about respecting your infidelity and disbelief[12] of Christianity this roused my resentment and I wished to answer it by a sentence of your letter which at the instant occurred to my mind. On looking for the letter I could not find it. But after several questions I recollected that passage of your letter in which you informed me that you had employed some time in composing "a wee little book which was a document in proof that you are a real Christian that is a disciple of the doctrines of Jesus Christ." With these words I answered his question. He put several questions touching the meaning, but I answered all, with a repetition of the same words at the same [time][13] trying to recollect when or where I had lost the letter. At last it occurred to me that I had been in Philadelphia and had shewn the letter to Doct Patterson, I thereupon desired Mr Delaplaine[14] to call on Doct.[15] Patterson & enquire if I had left it there. This happened to have been the case. I had laid it on the table[16] and forgot it; But Mr D. it seems construed the favour I asked into a grant of something to himself

After all this detail accept

My ever dear friend, an Assurance[17] of the sincere and uninterrupted esteem and regard with which I am Yours

Charles Thomson

RC (CSmH: JF-BA); undated; endorsed by TJ as received 12 Jan. 1817 and so recorded in SJL. RC (DLC); address cover only; with PoC of TJ to Joseph Milligan, 27 Jan. 1817, on verso; addressed: "Thomas Jefferson—at Montecello Virginia"; stamp canceled; franked; postmarked Philadelphia, 7 Jan. Dft (DLC: Thomson Papers); undated, unsigned, unaddressed, and incomplete; differs substantially from RC, with only the most significant variations noted below.

Joseph Delaplaine made what Thomson apparently considered A VERY IMPROPER APPLICATION for information about the former president's religious beliefs in his letter to TJ of 23 Nov. 1816.

1 Dft here adds "kind."
2 Dft here adds "soon."
3 Word, not in Dft, is interlined in RC.
4 RC: "they." Dft: "the."
5 Omitted closing parenthesis editorially supplied.
6 Parenthetical phrase not in Dft.
7 Preceding two words not in Dft.
8 RC: "woek." Dft: "week."
9 Remainder of sentence not in Dft. Preceding six words reworked in Dft from "I awoke repeating this sentence/ Thanks for merci[e]s past received/ Pardon of my sins renew/ Teach me henceforth how to live/ With eternity in view." These four lines (one word editorially corrected) were taken from the first hymn in the second book of John Newton, *Olney Hymns, in Three Books* (London, 1779), 182.
10 Preceding two words not in Dft.
11 Remainder of sentence not in Dft.
12 Preceding two words interlined. Dft: "and utter disbelief."
13 Omitted word supplied from Dft.
14 RC: "Delaplane."
15 Reworked from "Mr."
16 Dft ends here with partially canceled beginning of a new paragraph reading "I have been thus par."
17 RC: "Assurane."

From James Barbour

DEAR SIR Washington Jany 9th 17

Colonel Trumbul the celebrated painter is on a visit to this City—bringing with him Several specimens of historical paintings—The Subjects he has Selected are of a character which impart the highest interest to an American bosom—The wish of the Colo. is to be employed in his line in embellishing the Capitol with Some of those pieces executed on a Scale commensurate with the building—A direct application has been made to me to patronize the views of Colo Trumbul and as a recommendation it has been Stated that while you were abroad you became So well acquainted with this Gentleman and impressed So favorably with his character both as a man and as an artist as to dispense to him many acts of kindness—

The design of Colo Trumbul has my entire approbation—for I have ever thought that the Statuary and the Painter were the best depositories of illustrious incidents—when embodied by their art they impart an infinitely higher delight than when read in history—As it is my misfortune however to be without taste and without information upon the Subject I am diffident in Committing myself—Hence I take the liberty of addressing you—If it be not incompatible with propriety I Should feel you had added to the many obligations you have already placed me under by your kindness were you to give me your views on the Subject—Your reply may, if you prefer it, be confined to myself tho were it your pleasure to Suffer me to use it, it could not fail to have a general influence—

I tender you my best respects JAS BARBOUR

RC (DLC); endorsed by TJ as received 12 Jan. 1817 and so recorded in SJL.

From William Duane

RESPECTED SIR, Phil[a] 9th Jan. 1817

There is a small sum of 60$ money paid by me for the translating of the continuation of Tracy's ideology; the pressure of the present times alone could induce me to trespass upon you, as the young man the Bookseller at George Town to Whom you proposed giving the work to be printed, intimated something like dissatisfaction or disapprobation on your part towards me. As I was wholly ignorant of any just reason, I forbore as I have been accustomed to do all my life, to offer no apologies for any unconscious offence; I could not with propriety to myself address you now without stating the reason why I had not as customary in former times written to you. With unchangeable feelings of respect and affection, I am your friend & Ser[t]

W[M] DUANE.

RC (DLC); endorsed by TJ as received 19 Jan. 1817 and so recorded in SJL; notation by TJ beneath endorsement: "acc[t] signed John B. Smyth for
W[m] Duane
60.D. transln
5. paper to May 1st 16." (the paper in question being the triweekly "country" edition of the Philadelphia *Aurora*).

The BOOKSELLER AT GEORGE TOWN was Joseph Milligan.

From William Sampson

DEAR SIR New york Jany 9 1817

I have received your favor of the 30th Ult[o] And Am glad that the expression of "shortening the process by appealing to our own Opinions" came so apropos to sanction the part I had in the enclosed address to the people of the United States from the Society for promoting domestic manufactures

I should be proud and happy if our Sentiments objects and proceedings should meet your approbation in which Case I should sollicit your patronage. If it were not trespassing too rashly upon your time and goodness it would be infinitely agreeable to me to know your opinion upon the Subject and the view we have taken of it. It has already worked a revolution in Opinion here in So much that all parties except the very British, and those more british [than][1] the british themselves have Coalesced and Subscribed to the patriotic sentiments which I think it Contains.

I am of a Committee charged to draft a memorial to Congress upon the Subject, and as I have no motives but the love of this Country's good I should like to be assured by the wise and judicious that I was well employed

I am Sir With profound respect Your Obed[t] Servant

William Sampson

RC (MHi); endorsed by TJ as received 19 Jan. 1817 and so recorded in SJL. RC (ViU: TJP-ER); address cover only; with PoC of TJ to Thomas Mann Randolph, 5 Mar. 1817, on verso; addressed: "M[r] Jefferson Monticello"; franked; postmarked New York, 9 Jan. Enclosure: *Address of the American Society for the encouragement of Domestic Manufactures, to the People of the United States* (New York, 1817; Poor, *Jefferson's Library*, 6 [no. 223]; TJ's copy in DLC), which argues that "a nation's industry" should advance "hand in hand with her civilization, glory, and independence" (p. 5); contends that, although the War of 1812 has ended, the conflict against foreign manufactures, and especially those of British origin, still rages in full force; denies that domestic manufacturing damages American commerce and agriculture; maintains that it can be economical despite the high wages paid to American laborers; refutes the idea that it degrades and demoralizes the workforce; supports legislation to protect United States industry from foreign competition; and posits that there can be "no other way to independence than that of manufacturing for ourselves, at least for our own consumption" (p. 25).

Sampson was identified as the author of the ENCLOSED ADDRESS in the Boston *New-England Palladium & Commercial Advertiser*, 31 Jan. 1817.

The society's MEMORIAL TO CONGRESS of 18 Jan. 1817 included proposals that, in order to encourage manufacturing in the United States, the tariff passed the previous session be made permanent, the importation of cotton products from "beyond the Cape of Good Hope" be disallowed, the revenue laws be strengthened to prevent smuggling and fraud, a 10 percent duty be placed on the auction of foreign goods, and "public supplies" bought for the army and navy be "of American manufacture" (New York *Commercial Advertiser*, 18 Jan. 1817, and elsewhere).

[1] Omitted word editorially supplied.

To James Monroe

Dear Sir Monticello Jan. 10. 17.

It would seem mighty idle for me to inform you formally of the merits of Col[o] Trumbull as a painter or as a man. yet he asks my notice of him to my friends, as if his talents had not already distinguished him in their notice. on the continent of Europe his genius was placed much above West's. Baron Grimm, the arbiter of taste at Paris in my day, expressed to me often his decided & high preference. not so in London, where all follow suit to the taste of the king, good or bad. Col° Trumbull expects that as the legislature are with liberality rebuilding the public edifices, they will proceed in the same spirit to their decoration. if so, his paintings should certainly be their first object. they will be monuments of the taste & talents of our country, as well as of the scenes which gave it it's place among nations. I recommend him to your kind offices, and rejoice in seeing that you are to be in a place where they may have effect Th: Jefferson

RC (PHi: Gratz Collection); addressed: "Col° Monroe Secretary of State Washington favored by Col° Trumbull"; endorsed by Monroe. PoC (DLC); on verso of reused address cover of William Munford to TJ, 29 Sept. 1816 (letter, not found, accounted for at TJ to Benjamin W. Crowninshield, 9 Oct. 1816); endorsed by TJ. Mistakenly recorded in SJL as a letter of 6 Jan. 1817. Enclosed in TJ to John Trumbull, 10 Jan. 1817.

To John Trumbull

Dear Sir Monticello Jan. 10. 17.

Our last mail brought me your favor of Dec. 26. the lapse of 28. years which you count since our first intimacies, has diminished in nothing my affection for you. we learn, as we grow old, to value early friendships, because the new-made do not fit us so closely. it is an age since I have heard of mrs Church. yet her place, in my bosom, is as warm as ever; and so is Kitty's. I think I learned from some quarter that mrs Cosway was retired to a religious house somewhere. and M[de] de Corny, what is become of her? is she living or dead?—thus you see how your letter calls up recollections of our charming Coterie of Paris, now scattered & estranged but not so in either my memory or affections. it has made me forget too that the torpitude of age, with a stiffening wrist (the effect of it's Paris dislocation) warn me to write letters, seldom and short.—to the object of yours therefore. you think you need a borrowed patronage at Washington. No, my dear Sir, your own reputation, your talent known to all, is a patronage with all; to which any addition offered would be impertinent, if you did not ask it. and mine especially is now obsolete. the turns of the magic lanthern have shifted all the figures, and those it now presents are strangers to me. merely to shew you my willingness however, I inclose you a letter to Col° Monroe, who without it would do every thing he could for you, and with it not the less. his warm heart infuses zeal into all his good offices. I give it to him the rather also because he will be in place when you will need them. mr Madison will be away, and it would be useless to add to the labors of his letter-reading: and I know moreover his opinions and dispositions towards you to be as favorable as can be wished. I rejoice that the works you have so long contemplated are likely to come to light. if the legislature, to the reedification of the public buildings, will take up with spirit their decoration also, your's must be the first objects of their attentions.

I hope they will do it, and honor themselves, their country and yourself by preserving these monuments of our revolutionary atchievements.—my daughter, whom you knew an infant, has with her family, given me a dozen associates at our daily table. she is well and remembers all her friends affectionately. I am, as I ever have been, sincerely yours.

TH: JEFFERSON

RC (CtY: Franklin Collection); addressed: "Col° John Trumbull at the Post office Washington"; franked; postmarked Charlottesville, 13 Jan.; endorsed by Trumbull. PoC (DLC); on reused address cover of Noah Worcester to TJ, 31 Oct. 1816; endorsed by TJ. Mistakenly recorded in SJL as a letter of 6 Jan. 1817. Enclosure: TJ to James Monroe, 10 Jan. 1817.

Angelica Schuyler CHURCH died in New York City on 6 Mar. 1814 (*New-York Evening Post*, 7 Mar. 1814). TJ fondly recalled her and her daughter Catherine Church Cruger's (KITTY'S) acquaintance. TJ's DAUGHTER was Martha Jefferson Randolph.

To Abigail Adams

Monticello Jan. 11. 17.

I owe you, dear Madam, a thousand thanks for the letters communicated in your favor of Dec. 15. and now returned. they give me more information than I possessed before of the family of mr Tracy. but what is infinitely interesting is the scene of the exchange of Louis XVIII. for Bonaparte. what lessons of wisdom mr Adams must have read in that short space of time! more than fall to the lot of others in the course of a long life. Man, and the Man of Paris, under those circumstances, must have been a subject of profound speculation! it would be a singular addition to that spectacle to see the same beast in the cage of St Helena, like a lion in the tower. that is probably the closing verse of the chapter of his crimes. but not so with Louis. he has other vicissitudes to go through.

I communicated the letters, according to your permission, to my granddaughter Ellen Randolph, who read them with pleasure and edification. she is justly sensible of, and flattered by your kind notice of her; and additionally so by the favorable recollections of our Northern visiting friends. if Monticello has anything which has merited their remembrance, it gives it a value the more in our estimation: and could I, in the spirit of your wish, count backwards a score of years, it would not be long before Ellen and myself would pay our homage personally to Quincy. but those 20. years, alas! where are they? with those beyond the flood. our next meeting must then be in the country to which they have flown. a country, for us, not now very distant. for this journey we shall need neither gold nor silver in our purse, nor scrip, nor coats, nor staves. nor is the provision for it more easy than the preparation has been kind. nothing proves more than this that the being who presides over the world is essentially benevolent. stealing from us, one by one, the faculties of enjoyment, searing our sensibilities, leading us, like the horse in his mill, round and round the same beaten circle.

—to see what we have seen,
To taste the tasted, and at each return,
Less tasteful; o'er our palates to decant
Another vintage.— until satiated and fatigued with this leaden iteration, we ask our own Congé. I heard once a very old friend, who had troubled himself with neither poets nor philosophers, say the same thing in plain prose, that he was tired of pulling off his shoes & stockings at night, and putting them on again in the morning. the wish to stay here is thus gradually extinguished: but not so easily that of returning once in a while to see how things have gone on. perhaps however one of the elements of future felicity is to be a constant and unimpassioned view of what is passing here. if so, this may well supply the wish of occasional visits. Mercier has given us a vision of the year 2440. but prophecy is one thing, history another. on the whole however, perhaps it is wise and well to be contented with the good things which the master of the feast places before us, and to be thankful for what we have, rather than thoughtful about what we have not. you & I, dear Madam, have already had more than an ordinary portion of life, and more too of health than the general measure. on this score I owe boundless thankfulness. your health was, some time ago, not so good as it had been; and I percieve, in the letters communicated, some complaints still. I hope it is restored; and that life and health may be continued to you as many years as yourself shall wish is the sincere prayer of your affectionate & respectful friend

TH: JEFFERSON

RC (MHi: Adams Papers); addressed (upper corners of address cover torn away, with possible loss of frank and postmark): "M[rs] Adams Quincy"; endorsed by Adams: "Jan[ry] 21 1817." PoC (DLC). Enclosures: enclosures to Adams to TJ, 15 Dec. 1816.

Following his defeat at the Battle of Waterloo in June 1815, Napoleon abdicated and was imprisoned on the South Atlantic island of S^T HELENA. The phrase NEITHER GOLD NOR SILVER ... NOR STAVES is adapted from the Bible (Matthew 10.9–10). TO SEE WHAT WE HAVE SEEN ... DECANT ANOTHER VINTAGE is from the third part of Edward Young's poem, *The Complaint: or, Night-Thoughts on Life, Death, & Immortality* (London, 1742; see also Sowerby, no. 4548). Louis Sébastien Mercier had given a VISION OF THE YEAR 2440 in his *L'An Deux Mille Quatre Cent Quarante* (London, 1771; Sowerby, no. 1352).

To John Adams

Monticello Jan. 11. 17.

Forty three volumes read in one year, and 12. of them quartos! dear Sir, how I envy you! half a dozen 8^vos in that space of time are as much as I am allowed. I can read by candlelight only, and stealing long hours from my rest; nor would that time be indulged to me, could I, by that light, see to write. from sun-rise to one or two aclock, and often from dinner to dark, I am drudging at the writing table. and all this to answer letters into which neither interest nor inclination on my part enters; and often for persons whose names I have never before heard. yet, writing civilly, it is hard to refuse them civil answers. this is the burthen of my life, a very grievous one indeed, and one which I must get rid of. Delaplaine lately requested me to give him a line on the subject of his book; meaning, as I well knew, to publish it. this I constantly refuse; but in this instance yielded, that, in saying a word for him, I might say two for myself. I expressed in it freely my sufferings from this source; hoping it would have the effect of an indirect appeal to the discretion of those, strangers and others, who, in the most friendly dispositions, oppress me with their concerns, their pursuits, their projects, inventions and speculations, political, moral, religious, mechanical, mathematical, historical E^tc. E^tc. E^tc. I hope the appeal will bring me relief, and that I shall be left to exercise and enjoy correspondence with the friends I love, and on subjects which they, or my own inclinations present. in that case your letters should not be so long on my files unanswered, as sometimes they have been to my great mortification.—to advert now to the subjects of those of Dec. 12. & 16. Tracy's Commentaries on Montesquieu have never been published in the original. Duane printed a translation from the original MS. a few years ago. it sold I believe readily, and whether a copy can now be had, I doubt. if it can, you will recieve it from my bookseller in Philadelphia, to whom I now write for that purpose. Tracy comprehends, under the word 'Ideology,' all the subjects which the French term Morale, as the correlative to

Physique. his works on Logic, government, political economy, and morality, he considers as making up the circle of ideological subjects, or of those which are within the scope of the understanding, & not of the senses. his logic occupies exactly the ground of Locke's work on the understanding. the translation of that on Political economy is now printing; but it is no translation of mine. I have only had the correction of it; which was indeed very laborious. le premier jet having been by some one who understood neither French nor English, it was impossible to make it more than faithful. but it is a valuable work.

The result of your 50. or 60. years of religious reading in the four words 'be just and good' is that in which all our enquiries must end; as the riddles of all the priesthoods end in four more 'ubi panis, ibi deus.' what all agree in is probably right; what no two agree in most probably wrong. one of our fan-colouring biographers, who paints small men as very great, enquired of me lately, with real affection too, whether he might consider as authentic, the change in my religion much spoken of in some circles. now this supposed that they knew what had been my religion before, taking for it the word of their priests, whom I certainly never made the confidants of my creed. my answer was 'say nothing of my religion. it is known to my god and myself alone. it's evidence before the world is to be sought in my life. if that has been honest and dutiful to society, the religion which has regulated it cannot be a bad one.' affectionately Adieu.

TH: JEFFERSON

RC (MHi: Adams Papers); addressed: "President Adams Quincy. Mass."; endorsed by Adams as answered 2 Feb. 1817. PoC (DLC).

TJ's BOOKSELLER IN PHILADELPHIA was Nicolas G. Dufief. William T. Woodman made LE PREMIER JET ("the first attempt") to translate Destutt de Tracy, *Treatise on Political Economy*. UBI PANIS, IBI DEUS: "Where there is bread, there is God." ONE OF OUR FAN-COLOURING BIOGRAPHERS: Joseph Delaplaine. TJ quotes from the first of his two 25 Dec. 1816 letters to Delaplaine.

To Nicolas G. Dufief

Monticello Jan. 11. 1817.

Th: Jefferson asks the favor of mr Dufief to inclose a copy of the Commentary on Montesquieu published by Duane in 1811. to mr Adams at Quincy Mass. charging it to Th:J. he salutes him with friendship & respect.

PoC (DLC); on verso of a reused address cover from George Ticknor to TJ; dateline at foot of text; endorsed by TJ.

From Joseph C. Cabell

DEAR SIR, Richmond. 12th Jan: 1817.

Your favour of 1st inst is now before me. With the nature & object of the petition you allude to, I was already acquainted from having received an explanatory letter from your grandson, covering a copy of the remonstrance. I had also conversed as well with him as with mr maury. I advised mr maury without delay to have an interview with his colleague, and to endeavor to obtain his co-operation. He took this course & his colleague yielded a ready assent to the justice of the remonstrance. Very soon after this mr maury became ill & for some time has not left his room. During this interval his colleague has changed sides and prepared the select committee for[1] a report favorable to the petition. But at the date of my last enquiry, the subject was suspended till mr maury's return to the House: when I expect he will be able to procure the rejection of the petition, or at least the modification you desire. Should it come to the Senate, you may be assured of my endeavors to have the bill altered in the manner you wish, which appears to me entirely conformable to reason & justice.

Should Count Barziza's petition succeed in the House of Delegates, I will not fail to pay every attention in my power to it, when it comes to the Senate.

Doctor Smith has received information that Say's treatise on political economy has been translated into English. He shortly expects a copy from England. Under these circumstances I consider myself absolved from my promise to you.

I imagine you would be pleased to see a copy of the Bank bill which has recently passed the[2] House of Delegates: & I accordingly enclose one. This bill is now under the consideration of a committee of the Senate consisting of the four members from beyond the Ridge, and the Senator from Loudon. I think it will be much altered in the Senate, and perhaps it will fail entirely in the end. you will perceive that the part respecting the Literary fund merely gives banking powers to the present Literary fund, & in no other respects adds to the fund. The late Governor's original scheme of augmenting the fund to $2,000,000, by an addition of 6 pr Cent stock, to be created by the commonwealth, & of giving banking powers to the whole, has been defeated.[3] This Bill has engrossed nearly the whole attention of the Assembly since our meeting. It has not yet been accompanied in its progress by symptoms of great exasperation, but should it fail, as I think is probable, except as to a few western banks, there will be much heat & violence. The petition from Port Royal is written by Col: Taylor.

I never received, untill within the last few days, the late Governor's letter of 18th Oct: appointing me one of the visitors of the Central College. I shall at all times be ready to attend to any business to which the appointment may give rise. I[4] fear it will be difficult if not impracticable to procure money for that Institution. The prevailing opinion seems to be to establish schools first, and colleges afterwards. Besides, when I was at Staunton the very spot where the University was to be placed, was pointed out to me. And Should there be a bank at Staunton, you may expect to hear it called the Central Bank.

I am, dear sir, faithfully yours, JOSEPH C. CABELL

RC (ViU: TJP-PC); endorsed by TJ as received 19 Jan. 1817 and so recorded in SJL. RC (MHi); address cover only; with PoC of TJ to Hutchins G. Burton, 28 Feb. 1817, on verso; addressed: "Thomas Jefferson esq. Monticello"; franked; postmarked Richmond, 14 Jan. Enclosure: copy, not found, of "An Act to establish sundry new Banks within this Commonwealth" (Richmond, 1817; see *JSV* [1816–17 sess.], 28).

TJ's GRANDSON was Thomas Jefferson Randolph, while Thomas W. Maury's COLLEAGUE also representing Albemarle County in the Virginia House of Delegates was Charles Yancey. TJ hoped to secure a MODIFICATION in the route of a proposed turnpike between Rockfish Gap and Moore's Ford in Albemarle County.

Philip I. BARZIZA'S PETITION was reported as rejected by the House of Delegates' Committee for Courts of Justice on 8 Jan. 1817 on the grounds that "the question is purely a judicial one, and no escheat to the Commonwealth has accrued, and that, therefore, the Commonwealth has nothing to release" (*JHD* [1816–17 sess.], 140–1).

The first English edition of Jean Baptiste Say's TREATISE ON POLITICAL ECONOMY was published in London in 1821.

On 7 Jan. 1817 the BANK BILL enclosed to TJ was committed to state senators George J. Davisson, Alfred H. Powell, Chapman Johnson, and Francis Preston from beyond the Blue RIDGE and Cuthbert Powell, the SENATOR FROM LOUDON County. It passed into law on 5 Feb. 1817 as "An Act to establish two new banks within this Commonwealth," the Northwestern Bank of Virginia, at Wheeling, and the Bank of the Valley in Virginia, at Winchester (*JSV* [1816–17 sess.], 28; *Acts of Assembly* [1816–17 sess.], 55–70). An 11 Dec. 1816 PETITION FROM PORT ROYAL requested that a bank be established in that town (Vi: RG 78, Legislative Petitions, Caroline Co.).

For the LATE GOVERNOR'S LETTER, see notes to Wilson Cary Nicholas to TJ, 18 Oct. 1816, and its enclosure.

[1] Cabell here canceled "the rejection."
[2] Cabell here canceled "Sena."
[3] Preceding two words interlined in place of "been essentially defeated."
[4] Cabell here canceled "apprehend."

From Isaac H. Tiffany

MOST RESPECTABLE SIR— [received 12 Jan. 1817]

If a sense of error can attone for the length of my last, it is fully acknowledged. With intent to do some good in the little circle of my exertions, the enclosed scheme to awaken a spirit of enquiry & action, by enabling every man to become known & useful, is drawn up. And

I have ventured to invite your perusal & correction of it, if you may think it worthy of a moment's leisure. The society for the promotion of the useful arts, in this state, cannot produce much practical good under its present regulations. It is merely theoretical. The Berkshire society affects much more than the State Society of Massach[ts]

State societies imply besides[1] a good police, national funds & patronage; this humble contrivance requires neither & it only demands faculties to understand & to communicate facts, truly. From the Several counties a State Institute may arise. The Shift for the removement of incompetent officers seems required from the nature of the constitution of N. York which directs the Governor & 4 Senators, in council, to appoint militia officers, during pleasure. Inferiors dare not, others will not, attempt to remove Superiors. Hence the general bad State of militia discipline. Were the constitution amended agreeably to your wishes for popular election & control, it would Supercede this device & put us in a much more respectable posture.—This points, Sir, to one of the errors of my last letter, which Spoke too much of the judiciary—nothing of the military. I have referred the militia discipline to the rural committee, because, out of Cities, that duty is performed mostly by the agricultural class. The whole arrangements Are arbitrary & susceptible of accommodation to any numbers, condition or extent. This county contains 20.000 inhab[s] agricultural, with due proportion of mechanics & professional gentlemen—

Sir—Yours with very great esteem. I. H. Tiffany

RC (DLC: TJ Papers, 209:37213); undated; endorsed by TJ: "Tiffany I. H. (supposed) Schoharie." Recorded in SJL as received 12 Jan. 1817.

STATE SOCIETY OF MASSACH[TS]: the Massachusetts Society for Promoting Agriculture. Under the CONSTITUTION OF N. YORK of 1777, articles 23–4, a council composed of the governor and four state senators appointed militia officers, who served DURING PLEASURE (*The Constitution of the State of New-York* [Fishkill, N.Y., 1777], 24–5).

[1] Word interlined.

E N C L O S U R E

Isaac H. Tiffany's Plan for an Institute in Schoharie County, New York

[before 12 Jan. 1817]

The Institute of the County of Schoharie is composed of a President 2 Vice Presidents,[1] Senate and five Committees

Objects

Committee of Religion and Morality

Nº of Ministers, Churches, and Religious Meetings,
State of Social Intercourse—To promote Charity of Opinion—Obedience to Parents, reverence to Age and respect for the Laws,
to direct taste in sports & amusements,
To expose and censure crime and offence; particularly theft, fighting and drunkenness—Licentious fashions and expenditures

Literature

State of the Professions—To enquire and report the best Institutions in or out of the State, for acquiring any Art or Profession or elementary science; The expense and time in the acquirement—Names of the professors—[2]
Common Schools in the County—Nº of Scholars qualifications of Teachers—Books taught and system of education. To inform where good teachers may be had,
Fine arts—particularly Sacred and Martial music, & drawing
History and Geography of the County; and Biography of its distinguished Inhabitants
Notice of all new Inventions and Discoveries.—With the other Committee, to form annually, an Almanack, useful for the community,

Jurisprudence

Courts of Justice. Solemnity, promptness and impartiality of proceeding, Capacity of Magistrate and dignity of character,
Improvement of Laws, and their visible influence upon society, To form a catalogue or index of books and parts[3] of books, to be read to fit a citizen for a respectable magistrate, representative or elector, To state the size and prices of the books and where they may be had,—
Clearly to define the rights and powers of Jurors

Rural Concerns[4]

State of Militia—
State of Agriculture—
To preserve and multiply forest and fruit trees,
To improve flocks and herds—Grasses[5] and grains
Roads, Bridges, Fences.
Taxes, Public funds and public debt—;—that each may know and feel the interest he has in the Commonwealth,
To promote domestic economy—and particularly the employment of children in the lighter occupations of planting and gardening.[6]

Arts { Useful Arts and manufactures—Their products. Best materials—Machinery and utensils. how to be procured, or constructed. Books useful to the apprentice and each trade or calling Masters and proficients in the arts, native or foreign noticed Cost and merits of domestic or American and foreign manufactures compared[7]
Internal and foreign commerce
Practical economy and agency of heat and water-cookery—

The five Committees choose each[8] a chairman, & convene upon their own adjournment or[9] at the call of the chairman. There may be subcommittees or agents at pleasure, A person may enroll himself under which committee he pleases; may be a member of two committees at the same time and no more and must serve in them at least one year from enrolment, when he may enroll himself under another committee if he please; every member is to be industrious in collecting information and is to communicate it to the chairman in writing or by word,

If one has information appertaining to another, he is to communicate it to one member of that committee or its chairman,

the chairman with such aid as may be advised, must form a well revised, clear and concise report to be read before the Institute. From these reports the expose of the county is made by the President

The Institute meets at the court house on the 4th of July, anually. the President[10] two Vice Presidents and Treasurer of the Institute are elected by the chairman of the committees, and may be removed by them,

The President appoints, a secretary two chaplains, 2 Physicians, 2[11] Counsellors and Two Marshals. These together with the Supervisor, and two delegates[12] from each town, to be chosen by the people at the anual town meeting, compose the Senate and meet at the court house on the 4th of July; and the day preceeding the Febuary term of the common pleas. When it is wished to remove a military officer for incompetency or misconduct, information is lodged with the marshals, and the informant is not to be exposed. It is the duty of the marshals or either of them to accuse such officer before the Senate and furnish proof—The officer is to be removed with a notice or copy of the accusation to be made, or if he does not see proper to deny or explain before the Senate

the Senate will hear, deliberate, and resolve to acquit or recommend his removal; a copy of the resolution shall be signed by the President & the senators, or a majority of them, present & delivered to the Governer[13] of the state, and another copy thus signed to the representative of the county in assembly When a civil officer is to be accused, the counsellors (or one of them) are to conduct the proceeding in like manner—

The Judges of the common pleas and sheriff, are[14] member of the institute by virtue of their offices; The supervisors of the several towns are also members, and are particularly charged to collect touching common schools and are to furnish the same as soon as may be

Tr (DLC: TJ Papers, 208:37082–4); in an unidentified hand, with emendations and corrections by Tiffany, only the most significant of which are noted below; undated; at head of text in Tiffany's hand: "(copy)"; endorsed by Tiffany: "Schoharie Institute."

[1]Reworked from "a President, Vice President."

[2] Word added by Tiffany in place of an illegible deletion.

[3] Manuscript: "parts parts."

[4] Manuscript appears to read "Conceurns."

[5] Manuscript: "Gasses."

[6] Here is canceled, presumably by Tiffany, "to encourage attention to Cows and sheep, among the poor, and discourage the keeping of large dogs."

[7] Word added by Tiffany.

[8] Word interlined by Tiffany.

[9] Word added by Tiffany.

[10] Preceding two words interlined.

[11] This and preceding number added by Tiffany.

[12] Word interlined by Tiffany in place of "Supervisors."

[13] Manuscript: "Goverer."

[14] Manuscript: "one."

From Jerman Baker

DEAR SIR, Richmond 13 Jany 1817

I have postponed a reply to yours of 14 Ult^o addressed to Mr Thweatt & myself untill the select Com^ee to whom was refered the petition for a Turnpike Road from Rock fish Gap to Lewis's ferry should have come to a decision thereon, which they have not yet done in consequence of the continued indisposition of M^r T— Maury. however I think I may hazard the opinion that the Road will be Stoped at Charlotsville

Your favor of the 1 Ins^t has this moment come to hand requesting my attention to the petition of Visc^t Philip I Barziza which it shall most certainly recieve Having been confined to my Room for several days, past, I know not how this Case at present Stands, but as soon as I am able to resume my Legislative duties I will make myself fully acquainted with it.

Mr John Wood opened a School in this place on Monday last and requested me to inform you that he should be highly gratified at having Francis Eppes with him I have promised him to put my Son Wayles with him provided you agreed to send Francis, as I know the boys would like to be together; I have writen to Mr Eppes also on this subject at request of M^r W— & expect an answer in the course of eight or ten days. And would thank you for an answer as soon as convenient as my Son is at home, as I had not met with a School with which I was pleased. I have within a few days past ascertained that a Mr Ewing keeps a very good Latin & Greek School in this place but shall wait for your determination about Francis before I dispose of my Son, Be pleased Sir to present my affectionate regards to Mrs Randolph & family & to accept for yourself the assurance of my most sincere esteem & respect— JERMAN BAKER

RC (MHi); endorsed by TJ as a letter from "Baker German" received 19 Jan. 1817 and so recorded in SJL. RC (MHi); address cover only; with PoC of TJ to

Fernagus De Gelone, 6 Mar. 1817, on verso; addressed: "Thomas Jefferson Esquire Monticello Albemarl C[ty]"; stamp canceled; franked; postmarked Richmond, 14 Jan.

LEWIS'S FERRY: Moore's Ford.

From John Barnes

DEAR SIR— George Town 13th Jan[y] 1817.

Notwithstand[g] what has been said, & done, Respecting your several powers—they have [not][1] had an Accomodating effect with the Comptroller—for Answer—He knows[2] of None—but the Law—and cannot therefore be Admitted:—still in Order to save you the trouble—a Ride of many Miles to the Majestrate—M[r] Randolph[3]—your Witness—his Attest to it before me—will be Accepted Of[4]—

My first Attempt on the Cash[r] of Bank of Colum[a]—the same objection was made—at which I expressed my surprize—and begd a Reference to the Board of Directors—whose decision the Next day—was—in your fav[r]—of course[5] I made a 2[d] Attempt on the Comptroller—but without the desired Effect.

I therefore inclose you the two powers—to be Attested to—by the Witnesses and when Compleatly—transferred: transmit you the proper Certificates of both The Bank Stock & 6 ℔C[ts] of their being—in the Name of Thad[s] Kosciusko—with the greatest Respect,

I am D[r] Sir, Your most Obed[t] JOHN BARNES.

RC (ViU: TJP-ER); at foot of text: "Tho[s] Jefferson Esqr Monticello"; endorsed by TJ as received 19 Jan. 1817 and so recorded in SJL. Enclosures: enclosure to TJ to Barnes, 31 Dec. 1816, and possibly also first enclosure to TJ to Barnes, 15 Dec. 1816.

Joseph Anderson was COMPTROLLER of the United States Treasury, 1815–36 (*JEP*, 2:622, 625, 4:560 [27, 28 Feb. 1815, 15 June 1836]).

[1]Omitted word editorially supplied.
[2]Manuscript: "knowns."
[3]Manuscript: "Randolp."
[4]Manuscript: "Off."
[5]Manuscript: "couse."

To Lancelot Minor

DEAR SIR Monticello. Jan. 14. 17.

Your favor of Nov. 25. came during an absence of 2. months in Bedford; that of the 6th inst. was recieved on the 10th

In my letter of Jan. 17th of the last year I promised that in the spring of the present I would pay out of my own resources the debt to Col[o] Callis's estate. this shall assuredly be done as soon as my crop of flour is sold; which however I do not expect will take place till March or April. I hold it up till then, because the want of bread thro' all Europe as well as America must produce here by that time a higher than the highest price ever yet known here. the debt as heretofore agreed on was 69.D. principal, and interest: from 1795. at 5. per cent, the rate fixed by law on all debts preceding May. 1797. adding therefore 22. years interest it will be 144. D 90 C I am thus exact because it is a case of innocent loss on mr Marks as explained in my letters of October 29. 1812 and May 26. 13. and of an executor who must adhere rigorously to law. You have been so kind as to pay the State & Congressional taxes on mrs Marks's lands; and if you will inform me of the amount it shall be added to the order on Richmond which will be given for the 144.90 D. we wish exceedingly that those lands could be sold, and if a proper offer[1] should occur we hope you will have the goodness to avail us of it, and add that to the many obligations we owe you. I pray you to accept the assurance of my great esteem & respect. TH: JEFFERSON

PoC (MHi); on verso of a reused address cover from Thomas Appleton to TJ; at foot of text: "Col° Lancelot Minor"; endorsed by TJ.

TJ paid the debt due from the estate of his brother-in-law Hastings Marks to COL° CALLIS'S ESTATE on 3 June 1817 (*MB*, 2:1334). The maximum interest RATE FIXED BY LAW in Virginia increased from 5 to 6 percent under usury legislation that came into effect on 1 May 1797 (*Acts of Assembly* [1786–87 sess.], 36; [1796 sess.], 16–7). TJ was the EXECUTOR in question.

Missing letters from Minor to TJ of 1 July, 25 Nov. 1816, and 6 Jan. 1817 are recorded in SJL as received from Louisa on 10 July, 11 Dec. 1816, and 10 Jan. 1817, respectively. Letters from TJ to Minor of 17 Jan. and 14 July 1816, not found, are also recorded in SJL.

[1] Reworked from "an offer."

To Archibald Thweatt

DEAR SIR Monticello Jan. 14. 17.

Our last mail brought me your favor of the 5th and I hasten to answer by it's first return. Jefferson Randolph is not yet returned, so that I am without the benefit of any information thro' him I inclose you a survey of the roads in question made by the county surveyor for the use of the court on the question of these roads; so I must beseech you to return it to me safely, and as soon as done with it. that it may be understood I must inform you that from Charlottesville downwards there are two roads, one on each side of the river, both crossing the spurs of the mountain about $1\frac{1}{2}$ or 2. miles from the river. it is proposed to suppress both these roads, and to substitute one along the bank on each side of the river. but the river road on the South side (which has already cost me 1500.D.) being not quite finished nor ready for a view, is not now in question: the roads on the North side are our only subject at present. the red road in the plan is the North mountain road, which we propose to discontinue from the Orange fork to the Chapel branch. this road crosses the river at Moore's ford or Lewis's ferry. the olive coloured road along the North bank of the river, crossing at the Secretary's ford, is the one to be substituted. the Surveyor states the distances; which are nearly the same, the difference being only of 128½ yards in favor of the river road.—Col° Yancey is mistaken in calling the distance from Charlottesville to Moore's ford[1] only half a mile, & that to the Secretary's ford 2. miles. the Surveyor has not stated these partial distances on his plan; but by his field-notes, which I have, that to Moore's ford is a mile, wanting 15. poles, & to the Secretary's ford 2. miles wanting 31. poles. but this is of no consequence; because nobody proposes to suppress the road to Moore's ford. that must be kept open to the Orange fork on account of it's being one of the ways to Orange & Fredericksbg. consequently the depot of flour at the landing at Moore's ford will continue, entirely unaffected by this question. as to popular voice supposed by Col° Yancey against the change, of the people of the county having interest in a good road only 9. out of 10. will be in favor of it. he affirms the necessary funds will be readily raised. turnpikes, as far as my information goes, have cost from 1. to 7. thousand dollars a mile. this turnpike is of 24. miles generally thro a red, rich, deep loam. if we state it's cost at 2000.D. a mile, it will be below fact. and to judge of the probability of raising 48,000.D. for a road, we have the fact, that in 10. years that they have been endeavoring to raise funds for making the river navigable from Moore's ford to Milton, they have raised but between 3. & 4000.D. and the locks built with this being now nearly rotted down, the Directors despair of raising as much as will rebuild them. finally; I offer any one of 3. propositions. 1. Stop the turnpike at Charlottesville. 2. if insisted to go to the river, leave the court to decide whether to Moore's or the Secretary's ford. 3. let the question lie over to the next session, before which the court will have decided it. ever and affectionately Your's

Th: Jefferson

PoC (MHi); on reused address cover of Elisha Ticknor to TJ, 1 Nov. 1816; at foot of first page: "Archibald Thweatt esq."; endorsed by TJ. Enclosure not found.

Thweatt's letter of the 5th, not found, is recorded in SJL as received 12 Jan. 1817 from Richmond. The county surveyor was William Woods. the directors headed the Rivanna Company.

[1] Preceding three words interlined.

From James Eastburn

SIR New york. 15 Jany 1817.

Will you permit me to lay before you the plan of a course of publications which, if due encouragement is given I shall be proud to undertake?[1] It has met the decided approbation of a few literary Gentlemen here, but it requires the recommendation of all those who have filled, or are now filling, eminent stations in the country to make it successfull—If Sir on having perused the plan, you can recommend it to public attention you will I believe promote the interest of literature & confer[2] a lasting obligation on

Sir Your[3] mo: obed hb s^t JAMES EASTBURN

RC (MHi); at foot of text: "His Exy Thos Jefferson"; endorsed by TJ as received 23 Jan. 1817 and so recorded in SJL.

James Eastburn (d. 1829), merchant, bookseller, and printer, emigrated from England to New York City by 1803. He worked there as a wholesale merchant until 1812 and then became a bookseller and publisher. For a number of years prior to his retirement around 1824, Eastburn also operated a reading room on Broadway. He was an officer of the New-York Bible Society and the New-York Historical Society, and he helped found a savings bank in his adopted city in 1819 (Hettie A. Walton and Eastburn Reeder, *The Eastburn Family* [1903], 186; *Longworth's New York Directory* [1803]: 139; [1812]: 98; [1813]: 130; [1821]: 166; [1823]: 165; [1824]: 168; *New-York Commercial Advertiser*, 27 May 1806; DNA: RG 29, CS, N.Y., New York, 1810, 1820; New York *Commercial Advertiser*, 5 Feb. 1813; James Grant Wilson, ed., *The Poetical Writings of Fitz-Greene Halleck* [1869], 375; *Sixth Report of the Board of Managers of the New-York Bible Society* [New York, 1815]; New York *Columbian*, 12 Oct. 1816; *New-York Columbian*, 14 Jan. 1818; *Laws of the State of New-York, passed at the forty-second session of the legislature* [Albany, 1819], 66, 68; *New-York Spectator*, 30 Oct., 13 Nov. 1829).

The enclosed PLAN OF A COURSE OF PUBLICATIONS, not found, may have been an early version of Eastburn, *Prospectus for printing by subscription, by James Eastburn & Co.... Limited Editions of Scarce Books, in the various Branches of Literature, from the Sixteenth Century Down to the Present Time* (New York, 1817). On 10 Jan. 1817 Eastburn sent President James Madison a letter covering, presumably, the same "plan," which is there described as "the prospectus of a course of publications" (DLC: Madison Papers).

[1] Manuscript: "undetake."
[2] Manuscript: "confr."
[3] Manuscript: "Yur."

From Louis C. Le Breton Deschapelles

SIR, New orleans January 15th 1817

the kindeness you have Ever Shewn to the inhabitants of Louisiana during your administration induces me to inform you of the attempt made By Mr Livingston to Exact from us Damages for having been Dispossessed of the Bature pursuance to a mandat of the president of the U.S.

in Such Situation, We beg Leave to Claim your interference towards the Government for Supporting us in the Supreme Court of the u.S. on a Writ of Errors Which M[r] Livingston hath interposed from a final Judgment rendered against him in the District Court of Louisiana. We Need not to mention you that the fate of a Large family is involved in that Suit.

Permit us, Sir to Suggest you the heavy Expences to Which We have been Subject for defending the Suit here and for retaining a Counsel for the Supreme Court We have already Expended fifteen hundred dollars for the Counsels only independant of our trouble & of the Smaler Expenses. We hope that our Equitable Claim on the Government upon that Subject Will be Supported By you

I Remain With the Greatest Regard,

Sir,

Your most obedient serv[t]

L: C. Le Breton Deschapelles

RC (DLC); endorsed by TJ as received 16 Feb. 1817 and so recorded in SJL.

Louis Césaire Le Breton Deschapelles (1774–1839), planter and public official, was a native of New Orleans who sat for a number of terms on his hometown's city council between 1803 and 1812. Elected to the newly established state legislature in the latter year, he resigned before taking office. During the War of 1812, Le Breton Deschapelles pledged funds to the war effort and served as a lieutenant in the Louisiana militia. Toward the end of his life he lived on a farm a few miles outside of New Orleans (Maurice Bernard, "Famille Le Bretton des Chapelles," *Généalogie et Histoire de la Caraïbe* 64 [1994]: 1163; "Mayors of New Orleans, 1803–1936," Works Project Administration project 665-64-3-112 [1940 typescript at LN]; Dunbar Rowland, ed., *Official Letter Books of W. C. C. Claiborne, 1801–1816* [1917; repr. 1972], 6:198; Alcée Fortier, *A History of Louisiana* [1904], 3:87; Marion John Bennett Pierson, comp., *Louisiana Soldiers in the War of 1812* [1963; repr. 1999], 36; John Adems Paxton, *The New-Orleans Directory and Register* [New Orleans, 1823]; *New-Orleans Argus*, 2 Oct. 1828; DNA: RG 29, CS, La., New Orleans, 1830).

Le Breton Deschapelles seems to be referring to the case of *Livingston v. D'orgenoy*, which had come before the SUPREME COURT OF THE U.S. in February 1813 before being returned to and settled by the DISTRICT COURT OF LOUISIANA in Edward Livingston's favor later that same year (Thomas B. Robertson to TJ, 7 Dec. 1810; *U.S. Reports*, 11 [7 Cranch]: 577–88; William C. C. Claiborne to TJ, 14 Aug. 1813).

To James Ligon (for Patrick Gibson)

Sir Monticello Jan. 15. 17.

Understanding that mr Gibson is too unwell to attend to business, I take the liberty of addressing to yourself directly a request of my account from the last period to which it was rendered (Sep. 1st) to the end of the year, that I may make my arrangements accordingly.

in my letter of Dec. 28. I mentioned that a purchase of corn would require me to draw about this time for between 500. & 750.D. we now ascertain that it will be for 555.D. and not immediately. Accept the assurance of my respect. TH: JEFFERSON

PoC (DLC); on verso of reused address cover of Joseph Milligan to TJ, 28 Aug. 1815; at foot of text: "M[r] Ligan"; endorsed by TJ as a 15 Jan. 1817 letter to "Ligan mr for Gibson Patrick" and so recorded in SJL.

The $555 was not needed IMMEDIATELY because TJ had obtained a loan this day from Thomas Jefferson Randolph for that amount, covering the purchase of 111 barrels of corn from Daniel F. Carr (*MB*, 2:1330).

To William Lee

DEAR SIR Monticello Jan. 16. 1817.

I recieved three days ago a letter from M. Martin 2[d] Vice-president and M. Parmantier Secretary of 'the French agricultural & manufacturing society' dated at Philadelphia the 5th instant: it covered Resolutions proposing to apply to Congress for a grant of 250.~~M~~ acres of land on the Tombigbee, and stating some of the general principles on which the society was to be founded: and their letter requested me to trace for them the basis of a social pact for the local regulations of their society, and to address the answer to yourself, their 1st Vice President at Washington. no one can be more sensible than I am of the honor of their confidence in me, so flatteringly[1] manifested in this resolution; and certainly no one can feel stronger dispositions than myself to be useful to them, as well in return for this great mark of their respect, as from feelings for the situation of strangers, forced by the misfortunes of their native[2] country to seek another by adoption, so distant, and so different from that in all it's circumstances. I commiserate the hardships they have to encounter, and equally applaud the resolution with which they meet them, as well as the principles proposed for their government. that their emigration may be for the happiness of their descendants, I can believe; but from the knolege I have of the country they have left, & it's state of social intercourse and comfort, their own personal happiness will undergo severe trial here. the laws however which are to effect this must flow from their own habits, their own feelings, and the resources of their own minds. no stranger to these could possibly propose regulations adapted to them. every people have their own particular habits ways of thinking, manners E[t]c. which have grown up with them from their infancy, are become a part of their nature, and to which the regulations which are to make them happy must be accomodated. no member of a foreign country can have a sufficient sympathy with these. the institutions of Lycurgus, for example would not have suited Athens, nor those of Solon Lacedaemon. the organisations of Locke were impracticable for Carolina, and those of Rousseau and Mably for Poland. turning inwardly on myself from these eminent illustrations of the truth of my observation, I feel all the presumption it would manifest, should I undertake to do what this respectable society is alone qualified to do suitably for itself. there are some preliminary questions too which are particularly for their own consideration. is it proposed that this shall be a separate state? or a county of a state? or a mere voluntary association, as those of the quakers, Dunkars, Menonists? a separate state it cannot be, because from the tract it asks, it would not be of more than 20. miles square, & in establishing new states, regard is had to a certain degree of equality in size. if it is to be a county of a state, it cannot be governed by it's own laws, but must be subject to those of the state of which it is a part. if merely a voluntary association, the submission of it's members will be merely voluntary also; as no act of coercion would be permitted by the general law. these considerations must control the society, and themselves alone can modify their own intentions and wishes to them. with this apology for declining a task to which I am so unequal, I pray them to be assured of my sincere wishes for their success and happiness, and yourself particularly of my high consideration & esteem. TH: JEFFERSON

PoC (DLC); at foot of first page: "William Lee esq."

[1] TJ here canceled "expressed."

[2] Word added in margin.

From James Ligon (for Patrick Gibson)

SIR Richmond 16 Jany 1817

I hand you inclosed Acc^t Sales of 175 Bbls Flour nett proceeds $1571.75. with your Acc^t Current to the 1st In^st Shewing Balance in my favor of $942.57 which I trust you will find correct

I have this day disposed of the remainder of your Flour say 93 Bbls Superfine & 9 Bbls Fine to mr Jno Leslie the Superfine at 13¾$ & the Fine at 13¼$ on 60 days Credit—as I can readily get this paper discounted I thought it best to Sell it on Credit, as not more than 13¼$ Cash could be obtained for it

respectfully PATRICK GIBSON
p JA^S LIGON

your note in Bank is due the 31st

RC (MHi); in Ligon's hand; postscript adjacent to Ligon's signature; addressed by Ligon: "Thomas Jefferson Esqr Monticello"; franked; postmarked Richmond, 17 Jan.; endorsed by TJ as a letter from Gibson received 19 Jan. 1817 and so recorded in SJL. Enclosures not found.

From John Wayles Eppes

Dear Sir, Buckingham Jan: 17. 1817.

Francis has been detained in consequence of the severe indisposition of two of my children—They are now however nearly restored to health.

I received by the last Mail a letter from Mr Baker at Richmond in which he States that Mr Wood had Just opened a School in that place and was very anxious to have Francis as one of his pupils—He has declined returning to Lynchburg[.] Mr Baker proposes sending his Son Wayles—

Having Stated to you on a former occasion the pleasure I Should feel in yielding to your Superior Judgement the direction of Francis's education the proposition is submitted for your approbation or rejection. If he goes to Mr Wood he might perhaps derive advantage from commencing as nearly as possible with the School—Of the time necessary for his learning Spanish I can form no opinion. Francis understood you to say two months—whenever you think it best for him to leave Monticello I will send for him and put him with Mr Wood or in any other situation Which you may prefer—

Since your leaving us I have received an appointment which I should not have Sought but of which I feel myself compelled to accept—I was brought forward in consequence of a letter from one of my friends proposing to me the appointment of Governor—In reply to this I stated that my health would prevent my accepting any appointment which would require my personal attention during the present winter, but that if Mr Mason declined a reelection as Senator and my friends thought proper to bestow on me that appointment I would endeavour to merit their confidence by a faithful discharge of the duties—Many of those who Supported me the last year voted against me I understand from an idea that the State of my health would prevent my accepting the appointment—

Be so good as to present me affectionately to Mrs Randolph and the family at Monticello—I hope at some other time we shall have an opportunity of seeing yourself and family in your way to or from Bedford—I need not add that it will afford us the highest gratification. Mrs Eppes unites with me in friendly greetings to the family. I shall

Send in February for the grape Slips of which I will give you notice—I have written to Mr Burton for the wine—

Whenever you think Martin can return after the first of February be So good as to give him a pass—I shall want him about that time as he is my clover man—

accept for your health & happiness every wish from yours sincerely

JNO: W: EPPES

RC (MHi); edge chipped; endorsed by TJ as received 22 Jan. 1817 and so recorded in SJL.

TJ's grandson FRANCIS Eppes carried the above letter from his father to Monticello (see TJ to John Wayles Eppes, 24 Jan. 1817). MANY OF THOSE WHO SUPPORTED ME THE LAST YEAR VOTED AGAINST ME: although the Virginia General Assembly had elected Eppes in December 1815 to fill the United States Senate seat vacated by William B. Giles, he declined the post at that time because of poor health (*JSV* [1815–16 sess.], 8 [7 Dec. 1815]; *Alexandria Herald*, 20 Dec. 1815).

From James Leitch

SIR Charlottesville Jany. 17th 1817

The Bearer Mr Logan a Watch & Clock Maker from Staunton (Who from every information I have is a first rate Workman) having commenced Business at this place; & having known your wish for an establishment of that kind Induces me to take the liberty of introducing[1] him to You; thinking that at this time you might require Some of his Services which I have no doubt he would execute to your Satisfaction yours respectfully

JAS LEITCH

RC (MHi); dateline at foot of text; addressed: "Thos Jefferson Esqr Monticello" by "Mr Logan"; endorsed by TJ as received 17 Jan. 1817 and so recorded in SJL.

On 15 Feb. 1817 TJ paid Logan "for work on the clocks, to wit kitchen clock 4.D. black marble do. 4.D. white marble do. 5.D. great do. 19 D. = 32 D." (*MB*, 2:1331).

[1] Manuscript: "introduing."

From John L. Sullivan

SIR Boston January 17th 1817

At a period when the importance of internal improvements is peculiarly felt by the most respectable members of the community, it must be unnecessary to apologize for addressing to you a communication on the subject of canals and inland navigation. Having had some practice in this pursuit, my experience & improvements may possibly become of use in Virginia.—

my Father the late James Sullivan deceased originated the Middlesex Canal which connects Boston harbour with merrimack river; Having paid some attention in Europe to civil engineering, at his request I undertook to complete & put the Canal in operation, and construct some smaller works of the kind at the falls and in the rapids of the merrimack and have at length effectuated the object as far as Concord NH and made it useful especially by means of an Incorporated Company for the purpose of navigating the canal & river systematically, as on the Canals of Europe:—& altho in its infancy, this company carried fifteen hundred tons of merchandize into the country the last summer

While at work on the river, I tried many experiments with a Steam boat of twenty horse power, in towing loaded boats upstream, conceiving that this power might be applied so as to require but a small draft of water, and that some advantage was to be gained from the reaction of the broken water or wake behind the preceeding boats. I was not disappointed in this expectation finding that while the steam boat was going at the rate of three miles an hour, with two boats loaded in tow, a man could draw those in tow up to the steam boat, and hold them there, while it would have required two horses to have carried them as fast separately

Having been at considerable expense; & the laws of the United States, according patents for the application of a known power to a new and useful purpose, I took one out, tho' not till after the question of right thereto, between the late Mr Fulton & myself, had been settled by arbitration under the authority of the Secretary of State in my favour.— I have since made several improvements on the steam Engine, as I conceive, rendering it more simple for use on rivers.—

It is obvious that the perpendicular action of the steam engine in common use renders it necessary that the boat should be very strong, and of course heavy— To get rid of this, I place the Cylinder horizontally—and have devised a way to support the piston in its central situation, to prevent the packing from wearing unequally.—

By this position amongst other advantages, I gain especially that of a direct action of the engine on the bottom of the river where it is Shallow & rapid, by means of poles. I have also several modes of acting upon the water with effect, better adapted to small boats than paddle wheels are—of which I shall take the liberty of forwarding a description.—

The experience of the incorporated company here is in favour of the formation of similar companies for the navigation of the Southern rivers. The capital and intelligence thus brought into this branch of business produces confidence in it—while it enables the proprietors to manage to more advantage.—The use of Steam Engine power, will liberate many men and cattle from the unproductive labour of the roads, giving them back to agriculture. The facility of conveying produce to market of course[1] raises its value at the plantation.—Our experience has demonstrated the importance of forming companies for the use of canals & rivers simultaniously with the construction of them—for if the transportation be left to individual enterprize, it will be slow, uncertain & inadequate to the wants of the country. The Income will be Small, & the works meanwhile fall into decay: but if every preparation be made, it is found that they become at once good property and are kept up.—

The Patent granted to me for the Steam tow boat[2] was I conceive wanted as a kind of protection to the undertakers of this new-branch of business, requiring considerable capital, and in the outset incuring some risk.—& I shall be very happy if it prove useful to any part of our common country.—

Fully aware Sir how thoroughly occupied your time must be, I do not expect the honor of your attention to the subject of this letter any further than[3] it may in your hands subserve the general object—but I cannot be insensible[4] how solicitously you regard the internal improvement of the Country 'tho' declining an active part in the board of publick-works, created by Virginia for great & important purposes; nor to the eminent degree in which you are competent to judge of the probable utility of discoveries in the use of machinery.—I hope however it may not be incompatible with your active pursuits to bestow as much reflection on this subject as you may think it deserves; and to mention the result of your thought to those of your friends, with whom you may happen to converse on subjects of this nature.—

With the highest respect & consideration

I am Sir Your most Obed Ser[t] Jn[o] L Sullivan

RC (MHi); endorsed by TJ as received 5 Feb. 1817 and so recorded in SJL. RC (MHi); address cover only; with PoC of TJ to Patrick Gibson, 9 Feb. 1817, on verso; addressed: "Thomas Jefferson Esq late President of the United States Virginia." Enclosed in Hugh Nelson to TJ, 30 Jan. 1817.

John Langdon Sullivan (1777–1865), civil engineer, inventor, and physician, was born in Saco, Massachusetts (now Maine), and initially made his living as a merchant in Boston. During this period he traveled to England and France, where he studied modern canal-building techniques. Sullivan joined the Massachusetts

Historical Society in 1801 and the American Academy of Arts and Sciences in 1810, became an agent and engineer of the Middlesex Canal in 1804, and served as a lieutenant in the Boston militia during the War of 1812. Having patented a "steam tow-boat" in 1814 and other shipbuilding improvements in 1817–18, he worked as an engineer for the national board of internal improvements, 1824–25. During the 1830s, however, Sullivan changed careers. He received a medical degree from Yale University in 1837 and practiced homeopathic medicine for a quarter-century thereafter, mostly in New York City, where he had moved early in the 1840s. Sullivan's estate was estimated at $100,000 a few years prior to his death in Boston (James Grant Wilson and John Fiske, eds., *Appletons' Cyclopædia of American Biography* [1887–89], 5:741–2; *The Boston Directory* [1798]: 109; [1813]: 237; [1816]: 198; DNA: RG 29, CS, Mass., Roxbury, 1800, 1840, N.Y., New York, 1860; Massachusetts Historical Society, *Proceedings* 29 [1894/95]: 94, 95; American Academy of Arts and Sciences, *Memoirs*, new ser., 11 [1882]: 50; John Lathrop, *The Gentleman's Pocket Register, and Free-Mason's Annual Anthology, for the year of our Lord 1813* [Boston, 1813], 119; *List of Patents*, esp. 137, 177, 190, 192, 196–7; *Catalogue of the Officers and Graduates of Yale University in New Haven, Connecticut, 1701–1910* [1910], 257; *New York City Directory* [1842/43]: 308; [1844/45]: 336).

The Massachusetts legislature created AN INCORPORATED COMPANY on 21 June 1811 with its "Act to incorporate John L. Sullivan and others, by the name and style of The Merimack Boating Company" (*Laws of the Commonwealth of Massachusetts, passed at the several sessions of the General Court holden in Boston, begining 31st. May 1809* … [Boston, 1811], 408–10). In February 1816 TJ declined an appointment to the Virginia BOARD OF PUBLICK-WORKS (Wilson Cary Nicholas to TJ, 16 Feb. 1816; TJ to Nicholas, 29 Feb. 1816 [two letters]).

[1] Preceding two words interlined.

[2] Preceding five words interlined.

[3] Reworked from "expect any more of your attention to the subject of this letter than."

[4] Manuscript: "insensble."

From Nathaniel Cutting

SIR, Washington City, D.C. Jan[y] 18th 1817.

If the name of so obscure an Individual as now presumes to address you, may be permitted to salute your friendly glance in the philosophic shades of Monticello, I hope you will at the same time feel a conviction that the Person who bears it still retains for you that sincere Esteem and profound Veneration with which a near view of your Virtues and Talents inspired him at a period more remote than he now wishes to bring to your recollection.

I once had some reason to flatter myself, Sir, that absence from my Country, and the lapse of many years, did not entirely dislodge me from that Niche I so highly prize in your Memory:—that experiment emboldens me to ask a favor of you, to grant which, will require your recurrence to circumstances long past.

What painful vicissitudes I have experienced since the period when, through your amicable intervention, the late President Washington honored me by the appointment to join Col[o] Humphreys in a special

Mission to Algiers.—In your Instructions to me on that occasion, now before me, I was authorised to assume the style & character of Secretary of Legation;—and although I never took the name nor attached much importance to the quality, yet I flatter myself that I performed all the duties of it to the entire satisfaction of those who had an undoubted Right to direct and scrutinize my relative conduct.—

Since that tour of duty terminated, I have endeavoured to render public service by various exertions:—during a series of years last past, the paucity of my pecuniary resources induced me, at the instance of my late worthy Friend, Joel Barlow, to accept a humble employ that was offered to me by Dr. Eustis in the War Dep't. of the U.S.—I have there completed Seven &[1] an half years of ill-requited Servitude:—and have never been absent from the Post assigned me more than three Weeks, altogether, during the whole of that period.

The Tax which I would now impose upon your amity is that, so far as your recollection of the transactions of the time when I had the honor to be employed under your auspices will warrant it, you will take the trouble to write for me as a humble Servant of the Republic, some brief memorandum, similar to what the Laws of the U.S. require in favor of a disbanded Soldier to entitle him to Bounty-Land;—viz. "a Certificate of faithful Service."—On such a Credential, I, too, may, perhaps, obtain from the liberality of Congress, at its present Session, a gratuity in uncultivated Land upon which I may retire, at this late period of Life, and hide the chagrin naturally excited in my Breast by the pointed neglect I have experienced from many superior Servants of the Republic who appear to have conferred on favorites those rewards that my honest and assiduous exertion, in the public service could never obtain, nor my proud Republican spirit stoop to solicit by indirect means.

If you will have the goodness to address such a Writing to me, "Poste restant,["] in this City, I shall thankfully receive it.

In the interim, I hope you will condescend to accept my best wishes for your health and felicity, together with my most respectful salutations.

Nat. Cutting.—

RC (DLC); edge chipped; at foot of text: "Thomas Jefferson"; endorsed by TJ as received 23 Jan. 1817 and so recorded in SJL.

Nathaniel Cutting (d. 1824), merchant and public official, was a native of Cambridge, Massachusetts. During the Revolutionary War he was captured while commanding an American sailing vessel. Taken to England, he escaped from captivity, fled to France, and was still there a decade later. Cutting met TJ at Le Havre late in September 1789 and helped arrange his return passage to the United States. Having entered into a partnership as a commission merchant in Le Havre in 1792, he was appointed United States consul there by President George Washington the following year. Cutting also served as secretary to David Humphreys during the latter's 1793 mission to Algiers, and he was secretary to the American claims commissioners residing in Paris in 1803. On his return to the United States in 1806, he settled in the District of Columbia, took out patents for machines to spin rope yarn and manufacture cordage, and worked as a War Department clerk from 1809 until his death in Georgetown (*PTJ*, 15:373, 490–9, 24:200–2, 27:845; MHi: Cutting Journal and Letterbooks, 1786–98; *JEP*, 1:129, 130–1 [19, 20 Feb. 1793]; Boston *Columbian Centinel & Massachusetts Federalist*, 1 Oct. 1803; Cutting to TJ, 26 Jan. 1806 [DLC], 5 July 1806 [DNA: RG 59, MLR]; *List of Patents*, 57, 63; Sowerby, no. 1102; *Letter from the Secretary of War, transmitting a Report of the Names of the Clerks employed in that Department in the year 1809* [Washington, 1810]; *Letter from the Secretary of War, transmitting a list of the names of the Clerks in the War Department* [Washington, 1824]; Washington *Daily National Intelligencer*, 9 June 1821, 9 Mar. 1824).

TJ gave Cutting his INSTRUCTIONS in a 31 Mar. 1793 letter (*PTJ*, 25:470–1). Later in 1817 Cutting unsuccessfully petitioned Congress for a GRATUITY IN UNCULTIVATED LAND (*JS*, 6:304–5, 431 [25 Feb., 3 Mar. 1817]).

[1] Manuscript: "& and."

Appendix

Supplemental List of Documents Not Found

JEFFERSON'S epistolary record and other sources describe a number of documents for which no text is known to survive. The Editors generally account for such material at documents that mention them or at other relevant places. Exceptions are accounted for below.

From Charles Bizet, 18 May 1816. Recorded in SJL as received 18 May 1816 from Montpellier.

From William B. Giles, 10 Aug. 1816. Recorded in SJL as received 12 Aug. 1816 from Charlottesville.

From John Maddox, 11 Sept. 1816. Recorded in SJL as received 18 Sept. 1816 from Richmond.

From N. Wright, undated. Recorded in SJL as received 8 Oct. 1816.

From Charles Vest, 11 Oct. 1816. Recorded in SJL as received 11 Oct. 1816 from Milton.

To Manuel Torres, 17 Oct. 1816. Recorded in SJL.

From Daniel Mayo Railey, 14 Nov. 1816. Recorded in SJL as received 11 Dec. 1816.

To Daniel Mayo Railey, 17 Dec. 1816. Recorded in SJL.

INDEX

INDEX

INDEX

INDEX

INDEX

The Papers of Thomas Jefferson are composed in Monticello, a font based on the "Pica No. 1" created in the early 1800s by Binny & Ronaldson, the first successful typefounding company in America. The face is considered historically appropriate for The Papers of Thomas Jefferson because it was used extensively in American printing during the last quarter-century of Jefferson's life, and because Jefferson himself expressed cordial approval of Binny & Ronaldson types. It was revived and rechristened Monticello in the late 1940s by the Mergenthaler Linotype Company, under the direction of C. H. Griffith and in close consultation with P. J. Conkwright, specifically for the publication of the Jefferson Papers. The font suffered some losses in its first translation to digital format in the 1980s to accommodate computerized typesetting. Matthew Carter's reinterpretation in 2002 restores the spirit and style of Binny & Ronaldson's original design of two centuries earlier.

✧

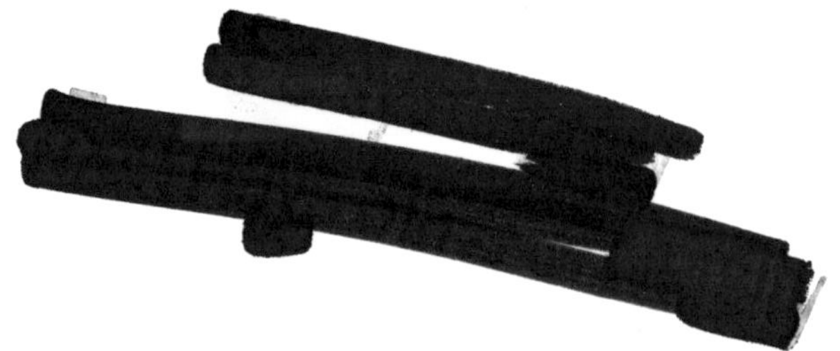